THE ELEMENT ENCYCLOPEDIA OF THE PSYCHIC WORLD

Theresa Cheung

THE ELEMENT ENCYCLOPEDIA OF THE PSYCHIC WORLD

the ultimate
a-z of spirits, mysteries
and the paranormal

HarperElement
An Imprint of HarperCollins*Publishers*
77–85 Fulham Palace Road,
Hammersmith, London W6 8JB

The website address is: www.thorsonselement.com

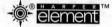

and *HarperElement* are trademarks of
HarperCollins*Publishers* Ltd

First published by HarperElement 2006
This edition 2006

1 3 5 7 9 10 8 6 4 2

ISBN 13: 978-0-00-778389-2
ISBN 10: 0-00-778389-2

Printed and bound in Thailand
by Imago

Contents

Acknowledgements

A project this huge simply couldn't have been completed alone. A big thank you to my team of researchers and all the paranormal experts, societies and organizations who provided help and information while we compiled the entries. I'm indebted to you all. I'd also like to thank my editor, Katy Carrington, for her vision and for encouraging me when the going got tough; Charlotte Ridings, for her very fine editing; and Wanda Whiteley, for her help, humour and support. Special thanks go to my husband, Ray, and my two children, Robert and Ruth, for their love and patience while I went into exile to complete this project. Last but by no means least, if any spirits were watching over us and subtly guiding our choice of entries and words as we worked, I'd like to thank them too.

Introduction

A mind that is stretched by a new experience can never go back to its old dimensions.

(Oliver Wendell Holmes)

In the last few decades interest in the psychic world has escalated. Beyond the basic Steven King novel, the idea of being psychic or having psychic abilities has penetrated deeply into mainstream culture.

The movie *Ghost* (1990), with Whoopie Goldberg as reluctant medium Oda May Brown, was the first blockbuster film to portray psychic phenomena in a positive light. Since then a steady stream of books, films and documentaries has followed. Organizations, seminars, workshops, websites, study programmes, chat rooms and courses in parapsychology (the study of the paranormal or unexplained) and psychic development have sprung up over night. Doctors and researchers in holistic health are assembling a startling body of evidence for the interconnectedness of mind, body and spirit. We can now speak 'openly' about alternative healings, meditative and psychic experiences without fear of ridicule.

Yet despite all the attention currently being given to psychic phenomena, their true nature still lies deeply shrouded in mystery. One of our favourite ways for dealing with the unknown is through language. We assign a word to an experience, to something we want to describe, and then we feel we have a handle on it. So let's try to get a grasp on this great unknown, the universe of psychic phenomena, by assigning words to it.

To begin with, what do we mean by 'psychic'? The word psychic describes anything in connection with the *psyche*. 'Psyche' dates back to ancient times when a goddess by the name of Psyche was thought to be in charge of the invisible but essential part of human existence. Over time the word and its meaning evolved, and today a Thesaurus offers the following synonyms: mind, soul, self, subconscious, spirit, subliminal self, inner self, awareness, ego and individuality.

Today we use the word psyche to refer generically to all kinds of phenomena, experiences or events that seem to be related to the invisible mind, internal body sensations and altered states of consciousness, which cannot be explained by established physical principles.

To qualify as psychic, an experience must therefore involve interactions that are qualitatively different from our normal, physical ways of exchanging with the world (e.g. verbal and nonverbal communication, sensations and bodily movements). A genuine psychic experience cannot be based even upon the most subtle, subliminal forms of perception or action.

As the experience is different for every person it is impossible to explain exactly what the psychic state is, but a large number of experiences are considered psychic. These include telepathy (mind reading), clairvoyance (psychic ability to see objects and visions), psychokinesis (mind-over-matter), psychic healing, out-of-body experiences, poltergeists, spirits and hauntings. Within the pages of this Encyclopedia you'll find a veritable compendium of all aspects of psychic phenomena – what they are, the evidence for them, the theories which have been proposed, the dynamics which favour or suppress them, and the techniques for discovering them in yourself. You will also find biographies of famous mediums and key figures in the psychic world as well as information about divination methods, well-known hauntings and paranormal beliefs from all over the world. The aim isn't to explain the unexplainable – as that is impossible – but to lift the veil and make the groping for words easier when it comes to researching, questioning and understanding the mysteries of the psychic world.

Introducing the psychic world [a very brief history]

Psychic traditions have existed since the beginning of recorded history and have been present in one way or another in ancient cultures all over the world. It seems that a belief in ghosts and communication with spirits of the dead has also always been with us from our earliest beginnings.

In the ancient Middle East, psychic powers were practised by prophets and are described in the Bible's Old Testament. The royalty of many ancient cultures used divination to seek guidance in times of war and to predict natural disasters such as drought. The Egyptians believed they could communicate with the dead and forecast future events using palmistry and dream divination. In Africa the ancient peoples used trance states to contact the spirits of their dead ancestors. The Greeks used oracles at sacred locations to give prophecies of the future and the Romans looked to the stars for messages from the invisible realm. Early American psychic practices have also been documented. The Aztecs in Mexico used astrology and oracles and Native Americans relied on advice given to them by shamans who entered deep trance-like states to contact spirits.

Although belief in ghosts was present from the very beginning of human history, the first extant report of a haunted house comes from a letter written by a Roman orator called Pliny the Younger (AD 61–112). He wrote to his patron, Lucias Sura, about a villa in Athens that nobody would rent because of a resident ghost.

The best-known psychic of the Middle Ages was a French physician called Nostradamus (1503–1566). He wrote about a thousand prophetic verses, which are still analysed today by scholars looking for references to the world's future.

After the Middle Ages and the Renaissance, during the Age of Reason, belief in psychic powers and the paranormal waned, but it was reborn again with the help of the Spiritualist movement. The foundations of spiritualism were laid by Emanuel Swedenborg (1688–1772), who allegedly went into trances and communicated with the dead. However, it was the Fox sisters, Kate (1841–1892) and Margaretta (1838–1893), who really brought psychic phenomena to the forefront. The sisters claimed they were able to manifest spirit communication through the rappings of a peddler who had been murdered and found in the Fox home. The public were fascinated as the sisters gave public demonstrations of this psychic manifestation throughout the United States.

Even though the sisters later confessed to fraud, the Spiritualist movement was by then well underway both in the United States and in Europe. Spirit rapping gave way to séances, table-tilting, trance writing and spirit communication through a medium. Many of these techniques are still practised today by Spiritualist churches.

Perhaps the biggest influence on the advancement of psychic knowledge was that of a man called Edgar Cayce (1877–1945), who is now considered the founder of the so-called New Age movement. Cayce had remarkable psychic powers. Allegedly he could see into the future and give predictions. He could look through objects and inside the human body. He was also able to enter another person's mind and know what that person was thinking, and sleep on a book and remember its contents.

The phenomena produced by mediums and psychics like Cayce during the height of spiritualism in the latter part of the nineteenth century quickly attracted the attention of eminent scientists and intellectuals, and the scientific investigation of alleged psychic powers, ghosts, apparitions, poltergeists and paranormal phenomena began in earnest. In 1882 the Society for Psychical Research was formed in London, and in 1885 the American Society for Psychical Research was founded in Boston. Clubs, organizations and societies dedicated to the paranormal sprung up all over the world, and as the twentieth century drew to a close the psychic world had successfully filtered into mainstream culture. It looks set to stay there.

Today we have televised séances and ghost investigations, celebrity mediums and psychics and bookshops, websites and university courses devoted to the paranormal. Over the years investigation of the paranormal has become increasingly sophisticated and precise. It isn't about superstition and eye-witness accounts any more, but about laboratory experiments, data, theories, statistical evaluation and high technology. There are those who are keen to offer theories to prove we live in a psychic world and those who are convinced it doesn't exist. There is a huge desire to unravel the mystery. The hotly debated question at the beginning of the twenty-first century is, are psychic phenomena real?

Fact or fiction?

Is the psychic world real? I'll give you the answer straight out: No one knows for certain.

There are, however, many theories to explain the thousands upon thousands of documented experiences that people around the world have had since the beginning of recorded history. Some believe psychic phenomena are real, whether or not science, fraud, misinterpretation, hallucination or natural phenomena can explain them. Others argue that if something is unexplainable by science, it cannot be real. These two sides – believers and sceptics – engage in heated debates over whether reports of paranormal experiences are misinterpretations, coincidences, the product of hallucinations or something more substantial.

Meanwhile, researchers into paranormal phenomena continue to seek explanations. It seems that the three hardest words for human beings to utter are 'I don't know'. We demand an accounting for every claim or experience, even if that experience seems unexplainable. Consequently, scientists, parapsychologists and psychologists have come up with a variety of theories for why paranormal phenomena exist, if they exist. For example:

Sceptic: 'Anecdotal evidence, characteristic of most psychic phenomena, is basically unreliable. Anecdotes may have natural, not mysterious explanations, such as random coincidence, fraud, imagination, or auto-suggestion.'

A believer responds: 'The hard evidence for psychic phenomena today is founded on repeatable experiments and not anecdotal evidence. Anecdotal evidence is considered valid in law and many other fields. The validity of anecdotal evidence does not depend upon the opinion of those listening to it.'

Sceptic: 'If an experiment is not controlled to prevent fraud, then the results may not be trusted. This is especially so given the fact that many people who claimed to possess psychic abilities were later proven to be frauds. Parapsychology experiments are usually poorly designed. They often lack proper controls, allowing paths of intentional or unintentional information leakage through normal means.'

A believer responds: 'There is no such thing as a completely foolproof experiment in any field of science, and it is unreasonable to hold parapsychology to a higher standard than the other sciences. Fraud and incompetence in parapsychology is addressed in the same way it is addressed in any other field of science: repeating experiments at multiple independent laboratories, and publishing methods and results in order to receive critical feedback and design better protocols, etc.'

Sceptic: 'Parapsychology experiments are rarely replicated with positive results at independent laboratories.'

A believer responds: 'The existence of certain psychic phenomena has been reasonably well established in recent times through repeatable experiments that have been replicated dozens of times at labs around the world.'

Sceptic: 'Positive results in psychic experiments are so statistically insignificant as to be negligible, i.e. indistinguishable from chance. For example, parapsychology may have a "file drawer" problem where a large percentage of negative results are never published, making positive results appear more significant than they actually are.'

A believer responds: 'Experimental protocols have been continually improved over time, sometimes with the direct assistance of noted sceptics. Meta-analyses show that the significance of the positive results has not declined over time, but instead has remained fairly constant. There are certain phenomena that have been replicated with odds against chance far beyond that required for acceptance in any other science.'

Sceptic: 'Currently unexplainable positive results of apparently sound experiments do not prove the existence of psychic phenomena, i.e. normal explanations may yet be found. In other words, psychic phenomena cannot be accepted as explanation of positive results until there is a widely acceptable theory of how they operate.'

A believer responds: 'Anomalous phenomena do not disappear for lack of a theory. There have been many instances in the history of science where the observation of an anomalous phenomenon came before an explanatory theory, and some commonly accepted non-psychic phenomena today still lack a perfectly satisfactory, undisputed theory. For instance, in the past, those who sighted meteors falling to the earth were dismissed as madmen or false prophets.'

The dialogue between sceptic and believer continues endlessly. It's a fascinating debate but as you can see from the brief snapshot above, each theory presented only fuels the arguments. While sceptics, scientists, parapsychologists, researchers and psychics debate the case for and/or against psychic phenomenon all we can do is decide on which side of the fence we wish to sit; and if we can't decide we just have to sit on the fence instead.

Perhaps some of the arguments and theories for and against will convince you; perhaps they won't. For the majority, though, the decision isn't going to be based on evidence or data or what the scientists say but on individual experience and belief.

Do *you* believe in the psychic world, or don't you?

Your psychic world

Those who believe in the psychic world suspect that most, if not all people have psychic ability to varying degrees. The ability is often likened to that of musical talent. Some people are naturally gifted with the ability to play and compose music, and practice makes them virtuosos. Others must learn and work and practise to be able to play an instrument even adequately or in the simplest way. But nearly everyone can learn to play to some degree. The same may hold true for psychic abilities.

This Encyclopedia is an intriguing reference tool but it has another use. If you're interested it can also be used to help develop your own psychic potential. The information boxes and advice sections within certain entries contain practical advice and exercises designed to help you access and make use of your psychic potential. Using them will make your psychic development interesting, easy and safe.

If you do decide to work through some of the psychic development exercises here, it's advisable to prepare yourself with the following three steps.

I. SELF-TALK

The first step is to believe that psychic potential exists and that it is present within you to develop. Although this might sound silly or trite, begin by telling yourself that you are psychic. Make it a mantra that you repeat to yourself daily and often. This kind of self-talk has a scientific basis. It is now known that when a person learns something, whether it is a physical skill like wood carving or a mental exercise like memorizing poetry, through repetition, his or her brain physically changes – 'rewires' itself, if you will – to accommodate that

task. This process of rewiring your brain for psychic ability begins with your belief in it.

It takes time for the subconscious to be able to communicate with the conscious mind, and the best way to do this is to simply start thinking about the psychic world. All these thoughts have a positive effect on developing your gift. Knowledge will help, as you need some understanding of how things work. Adopt the policy you would take with a new hobby. Get involved in it, buy books and magazines, read at least three or four entries from this Encyclopedia every day and look for more information on the Internet or, better still, from clubs, societies and organizations devoted to the study of the paranormal.

2. PRACTICE

The second step is to set aside a time every day for your psychic development. Find a place where you won't be disturbed and where you can read, study, calm your mind and have a go at the exercises. Like a difficult sport or musical instrument, psychic ability requires diligent practice. Unlike sports or music, however, your progress can be hard to measure because of the elusive nature of psychic phenomena (it's difficult to know how or when it's going to work). So the frustration level can be high, but the key to success is to not give up.

3. Patience

Finally, don't let frustration or failures make you stop. Be realistic. You can't expect to practise for a few days and then be able to see a ghost, predict when Uncle Joe is going to call or who is going to win the lottery. Psychic abilities, even for those who have developed them to a high degree, can be unpredictable and erratic. The trick is to learn to recognize when or if they are working – and that comes with time, practice and experience.

The mystery surrounds you

There are things that occur in the world – and which have occurred since the beginning of recorded time – for which there are no lasting explanations, and clearly psychic phenomena fall into this category of unexplained mysteries. Sceptics may argue their case, and theories may come and go, but all the while the psychic phenomena that these arguments and theories are supposed to debunk or explain carry on as mysteriously as ever.

Mysteries have always happened and will continue to happen. Belief in psychic phenomena has always been widespread all over the world and these beliefs have always had a very real influence on people's lives. Whether you believe in the psychic world, would like to believe in it but aren't sure, or think it's a lot of fascinating but ultimately unscientific nonsense, there is one thing that has to be accepted: we live in a mysterious world.

The universe is a puzzle, our consciousness is an enigma and even our existence in the world is an unexplained mystery. Mysteries are things we live with every day and simply have to accept, regardless of how irrational and incomprehensible they are.

If you are willing to accept that mysteries surround you, if you are willing to open your mind to new possibilities, the psychic world is out there waiting for you to discover it.

> The most beautiful thing we can experience is the mysterious. It is the source of all true art and science.
>
> (Albert Einstein)

THE ELEMENT ENCYCLOPEDIA OF THE PSYCHIC WORLD

A

A COURSE IN MIRACLES

A complete self-study spiritual thought system that was **channelled** through Helen Schucman between 1965 and 1972. It consists of a *Text*, *Manual for Teachers* and *Workbook for Students* and teaches that all humans share a capacity for love, forgiveness, compassion and peace. Rather than trying to change the world, it teaches, you must change yourself and your view of the world. Miracles are defined as a shift in perception from fear to love. It also emphasizes that it is but one version of the universal curriculum, of which there are 'many thousands'. Consequently, even though its language is that of traditional Christianity, the course expresses a non-sectarian, non-denominational spirituality.

A Course in Miracles was dictated by a clear inner voice to Helen Schucman, a psychologist at Presbyterian Hospital in New York and an assistant professor of psychology at Columbia University's College of Physicians and Surgeons. Schucman was born to a Jewish family in the early 1900s and was an atheist. For years she experienced mental images that came to her like photographs, and in the 1960s the images became so intense and meaningful that Schucman feared she was going mad.

In September 1965 a voice began dictating the course to Schucman with the opening words, 'This is a course in miracles. Please take notes.' Schucman was frightened and reluctant but felt compelled to write. She shared her experiences with her supervisor at work, William Thetford, who thought she might be having psychic visions.

In the days, weeks, months and years that followed, the voice, which never identified itself, dictated the course to Schucman, and by September 1972 the entire work was completed and arranged into chapters by Schucman and Thetford. The voice predicted that a woman would come along who would know what to do with it, and that woman turned out to be Judith Skutch, president of the Foundation for ParaSensory Investigation. Skutch and her husband, Robert, changed the name of their foundation to the Foundation of Inner Peace and dedicated it to publishing and distributing the course.

Information about the course spread quickly via word of mouth, and study groups independent of the foundation formed around the world and continue to flourish today. Schucman and Thetford chose to remain anonymous advisors to the foundation. The voice continued to speak to Schucman, who wrote down a collection of poems published by the foundation as *The Gifts of God*. As Schucman had wished, her identity was not revealed until after her death in 1981.

A Course in Miracles was first published in 1975. There are currently over one and a half million copies of the course in circulation worldwide.

ABACOMANCY

The art of foretelling the future by observing patterns of dust. The way the dust is blown, distributed or disturbed is read very much like tea leaves. The origins and precise method of this ancient type of **divination** are unknown. Sometimes the diviner uses the ashes of the recently deceased.

ABSENT HEALING

Healing that results from the sending of healing thoughts, **visualization, prayers** or energy towards some distant person or persons. It is based on the belief that all beings are interconnected by a **universal life force** or energy and that healing thoughts send out subtle energetic charges into this web of interconnection and out to the person being thought about.

Many **psychics, spiritual healers, reiki** practitioners and **medical intuitives** claim to be able to direct energy and perform absent healing. Typically healers will speak the name of the sick person or they will focus on a photograph of the person, or a candle or doll that represents the person. The healing energies are then directed to where they are needed.

How absent healing is accomplished, if it can be accomplished, remains an unproven mystery but there is compelling evidence to suggest that emotional and sometimes physical healing can take place from a distance. Aside from countless personal accounts from those who have benefited from absent healing, American doctor Larry Dossey conducted several double blind trials to test the effectiveness of absent healing in the early 1990s. At the end of the trials the groups that had been the object of prayer showed greater improvement in health than the control groups.

ACHERI

In Native American folklore Acheri is thought to be the **ghost** of a little girl who died of disease. Legend has it that Acheri is a frail and pale looking female **spirit** who lives on mountaintops and hills. At night she travels into the valleys to spread infection, disease and pain, usually to children, by casting her invisible shadow over innocent sleeping victims.

It is thought that the colour red affords protection against this entity and **amulets** of red thread worn as necklaces will protect children from the disease Acheri brings. Similarly, in European folklore, red **charms** are used to protect against harm from evil spirits.

ACUPRESSURE

An ancient Chinese healing method that involves applying pressure to selected points on the body to relieve pain and tension. It is based on the belief that the body has 14 'meridians' that flow through the major organs and carry energy, called chi, throughout the body. Acupressure is an **alternative medicine** technique that deals with all the aspects of a person – body, emotions, mind and spirit – as one whole rather than as separate parts.

Practitioners believe that acupressure can help relieve stress and tension, relax mind and body, increase blood circulation, aid in the removal of toxic wastes from the body, provide relief from head, neck and shoulder aches, promote the healing of injuries, increase energy levels and increase overall feelings of well-being. In a typical session the client lies fully clothed on a soft massage table while the practitioner presses gently on points on various parts of the client's body. The session is non-invasive and gentle and generally lasts for about one hour. However, most clients normally require a number of sessions to complete a treatment.

ACUPUNCTURE

An ancient Chinese healing system and **alternative medicine** technique that involves inserting and stimulating particular points on the body with fine needles. Acupuncture, like **acupressure**, is built on the theory that there are special 'meridian' points on the body connected to the body's internal organs and that 'vital life energy' (chi) flows along these meridian lines. According to this theory, disease is caused by interrupted energy flow; inserting the needles restores normal flow.

Acupuncture needles may be twirled, heated or stimulated with a weak electric current, with ultrasound and sometimes even with wavelengths of light. Acupuncture is used to treat pain, depression, allergies, asthma, arthritis, bladder problems, digestive upsets, colds, flu, smoking, fatigue, gynaecologic disorders, headaches, migraines, high blood pressure, low libido, stress, stroke, drug addiction, vision problems and even AIDS.

ADELPHI THEATRE, GHOST OF

The Adelphi Theatre in London is thought to be haunted by the **ghost** of a celebrated Victorian actor called William Terriss. Terriss was a stylish and popular actor highly regarded in his day and seldom seen without his trademark pale gloves.

On the night of 16 December 1897, during a run of *Secret Service*, a thriller staring Terriss and leading lady Jessie Milward, Terriss was murdered by an out-of-work actor, Richard Prince, who had been fired due to alcoholism and ever after bore a grudge against the profession. Prince especially resented the success and charisma of Terriss.

As night fell Prince ambushed Terriss as he unlocked the stage door in Maiden Lane and stabbed him. Terriss died in Jessie Milward's arms, whispering 'I'll be back'. Prince was tried and convicted of murder but declared insane. He spent the rest of his days at Broadmoor prison, where he passed the time writing his own plays and, of course, playing the heroic lead.

The first sighting of Terriss's ghost was in 1928. A stranger in London, who did not know about the murder, saw a male figure dressed in grey Victorian clothes suddenly vanish in Maiden Lane. Later he identified the figure as Terriss from a photograph.

Again in 1928 an actress who was using Jessie Milward's old dressing room, felt light blows on her arms, a sensation of being grabbed and the inexplicable shaking of her chaise longue. She also saw a green light above her mirror and heard tapping on the door. Later she discovered that Terriss used to tap Milward's door with his cane when he passed it. In 1962 there was another sighting: a greenish light that took the shape of a man was seen by a frightened workman. The light opened the stage curtains and then proceeded to the stalls and tipped down the seats.

Members of the station staff at Covent Garden tube station, which now occupies the site of a bakery where Terriss stopped daily, have several times reported hearing disembodied gasps and sighs after hours. One young porter, Victor Locker, immediately requested a transfer after encountering the **phantom**, an experience he described as being immobilized with an oppressive weight pushing down on him. In 1955 ticket collector Jack Hayden reported seeing on numerous occasions an elegant phantom with 'a very, very sad face and sunken cheeks', attired with opera cloak, cane and pale gloves walking the platform or ascending the spiral staircase. Hayden left Covent Garden in 1964 and the sightings have been less frequent, but Terriss still puts in the occasional cameo appearance, especially in the train tunnels between Covent Garden and Holborn.

ADEPT

One who has achieved the highest mastery of mystical and/or **occult** powers. An adept is particularly proficient or knowledgeable about the nature and laws of the universe.

Those who wish to become adepts may become apprentices, or 'chelas', to adepts, in which case the latter are known as masters. The activities of adepts are diverse. They can control forces both in the spiritual and physical worlds and prolong their lives for centuries. Adepts can use their wisdom both for good or for evil purposes. The term 'adept' was also employed by medieval alchemists to denote a master of their sciences.

AEROMANCY

One of the oldest forms of **divination**, practised by the priests of Babylonia, aeromancy is a method of divination by observing atmospheric – air or sky – phenomena, such as wind currents, cloud shapes and formations, comets and falling stars. Examples include the Bethlehem star heralding the birth of Christ and the appearance of Halley's comet around the time of the battle of Hastings, supposedly foretelling the victory of William the Conqueror. There are several different forms of aeromancy, including austromancy (wind divination); ceraunoscopy (observing thunder and lightning); chaomancy (aerial visions); and meteormancy (meteors, especially shooting stars).

AFFIRMATION

A positive phrase or sentence that through frequent repetition uses the power of your mind to create a truth or reality. Even though you may not be consciously aware that you are doing it, everyone uses affirmations (i.e., positive self-talk) to boost confidence and motivation at some time or other.

Affirmations are powerful verbal messages repeated over and over again, so that they become embedded in your brain and create new pathways of thought and action. In other words they provide your **intuition** with new avenues for insight and opportunity and prepare your mind for change. Once the mind is prepared for change and new opportunities it is thought to be far easier to create those opportunities.

Affirmations are typically used by men and women in sport and business but they can be useful for any career or life skill where goal setting and mental strength is crucial. Psychotherapists, motivational speakers and life coaches tend to use them

Using your will power

Affirmations are easy to do and can be beneficial if used correctly. It takes three to four weeks for the mind to absorb new information, so you need to be patient and persistent.

Think about what you want to improve in your life. Are you happy with your job? Do you want to stop smoking? Would you like to lose some weight? Choose your goal, but make sure it is achievable.

Let's say you want to lose weight. You now work out a statement suggesting that you are reaching your goal. Be careful how you word it though, because if you say something like 'I don't want to be fat anymore', your mind will focus on being fat, not on your goal, which is weight loss. But if you say something like 'I want to be thin', this is too vague for your mind to assess. However, something like 'I am going to lose six pounds this month' gets you in touch with the end result and is specific at the same time. It gives your mind something constructive to work with. Now write this affirmation down, and repeat it to yourself several times a day for at least three to four weeks.

Of course, besides affirming the statement, you also need to use your common sense and take the necessary steps to help you towards your goal, such as regular exercise and healthy eating if weight loss is your goal. Remember, the mind is a powerful tool, and affirmations can be a key factor in success because they help replace sabotaging negative self-talk with optimism, goal-setting and positive resolve.

as tools to help empower their clients and build self-esteem, and **alternative medicine** therapists tend to suggest the use of affirmations to encourage the body's self-healing process.

AFRIT

The Afrit comes from Arabian and Muslim folklore and is alleged to be a spirit **demon** who rises up like smoke from the spilt blood of murder victims. They are said to inspire unspeakable terror and, because of the unjust, brutal nature of their demise, they are ruthless towards their victims. Sometimes they are said to appear in the form of desert whirlwinds, and it has also been said that they can take on a form similar to the Christian Devil, with hooves for feet and horns on their head. Driving a new nail into the bloodstained ground is thought to prevent their formation.

AFTERLIFE

Afterlife (also known as life after death) is the continuation of existence beyond this world or after death. There are various sources for this belief, but the one most relied upon is the testimony of individuals who claim to have knowledge of the afterlife because they have:

❦. *Died and been sent back to life (**near-death experience**).*
❦. *Visited the afterlife when they were unconscious (**out-of-body experience**).*
❦. *Seen the afterlife in a **vision**.*
❦. *Remembered the afterlife from a previous existence (**reincarnation**).*
❦. *Been visited by a representative of the afterlife such as **angels** or **spirits**.*
❦. *Believe the testimonal of **shamans** or intermediaries between the living and the dead.*

Almost every society known has some belief in **survival after death**, although these conceptions vary enormously. Some common ones are: a continuation of life with little change in the nature of existence; spiritual improvement through a series of stages, planes or levels; a series of lives and deaths before ultimate extinction; or the afterlife as a place of reward or punishment based on faith or good deeds on earth and bodily resurrection at some future date.

Christian folk traditions suggest that the **souls** of good people are converted into **angels** upon death. However, a more orthodox reading of scripture suggests that the dead are not transformed until the **Last Judgement**, which is followed by a resurrection of the faithful.

Christian ideas heavily influenced nineteenth-century **spiritualist** authors like **Andrew Jackson Davis**, who dictated his lectures in a **trance**. Davis suggested that after their death, humans continue their spiritual progress through a series of spiritual spheres until they reach the seventh sphere and become one with the infinite vortex of love and wisdom.

Other cultures believe in a land of the dead and locate it in various places: for the Zulus, for example, it is under the earth, an underworld mirror of this world. For the ancient Egyptians, the afterlife was very important. The believer had to act well during his or her lifetime and know the rituals in the Egyptian **Book of the Dead** to gain entry into the underworld. If the corpse of the pharoah was properly embalmed and entombed, the deceased would accompany the sun god on his daily ride. Other societies believe in universalism, which holds that all will be rewarded regardless of what they have done or believed, while still others consider the afterlife less important compared to the here and now.

Another afterlife concept, found among Hindus and Buddhists, is reincarnation, either as animals or as humans. Followers of both traditions interpret events in our current life as consequences of actions taken in previous lives. Some traditions believe in personal reincarnation, whereas others believe that the energy of one's soul is recycled into other living things as they are born.

Those who practice **spiritualism** believe in the possibility of communication between the living and the dead. Some societies distinguish between the **ghost**, which travels to the land of the dead, and a different part of the **spirit**, which reincarnates. The ghost part of spirit is thought to be strong three or four days after death, and therefore various rituals are performed to discourage the ghost from returning to haunt the living.

AGE OF AQUARIUS

Term used to describe a new age of thinking in Western culture based on the astrological calculation of the Precession of the Equinoxes. According to Western astrologers, the Age of Aquarius is one of the 12 great ages, corresponding to the 12 signs of the **zodiac**, each lasting approximately 2,000 years.

Each of the 12 ages is thought to be characterized by particular cultural moves in society, thought and religion. Astrologers believe that for the past 2,000 years or so our world has been in the Age of Pisces, characterized by disillusionment and scepticism, and that we are now experiencing the dawn of a new age: the Age of Aquarius.

The shift to Aquarius is believed to herald revolutionary change, because Aquarius is the sign of knowledge, scientific breakthroughs and discoveries, but many think that there could be a price to pay for this overemphasis on intellect and science – the breakdown of old domestic structures. Although Aquarius can be tolerant and humanitarian, suggesting the possibility of a golden age, the Aquarian need for total freedom without interference may be uncompromising and dangerous.

No astrological organization or official body has agreed upon a specific date to begin the Aquarian Age: some say that it began as early as 1904, others that it begins around the year 2000, and still others say that it will not start until as late as 2160. The 2160 date was calculated by the Hermetic Order of the **Golden Dawn** and coincides with various predictions of cataclysms which are to be followed by 2,000 years of peace. The disagreement in dates is due to the backward movement of the vernal equniox through the zodiac. The vernal equniox takes around 26,000 years to make a complete cycle in the zodiac, but a gradual slipage creates a retrograde of one zodiac sign every 2,160 years – some astrologers take this into account, others do not.

Edgar Cayce, called by some the father of **New-Age** thinking, believed that the transition between the ages of Pisces and Aquarius overlap and the implications of this wouldn't be fully understood until the twenty-first century.

Theories about the Age of Aquarius vary as much as the date. Some believe it is a time of new beginnings while others associate it with times of ending such as Armageddon or Judgement Day. This disparity may be because Aquarius is ruled by two planets: Saturn, the symbol of time and endurance, and Uranus, the symbol of revolution. Generally, though, the Age of Aquarius is thought to be an era of enlightenment, joy, accomplishment, peace and spiritual empowerment.

The term 'Age of Aquarius' was popular in the 1960s, a period of great upheaval, social change and interest in spritual development and alternative lifestyles. The great conjunction of Sun, Moon, Venus, Mars, Mercury, Jupiter and Saturn on 5 February 1962 was said to be a sign of the dawning of a new age, and 'Age of Aquarius' has since been supplanted by the term New Age.

AGENT

A **ghost** or **spirit** that is seen by someone. It can also be used to describe the energy that is causing a **haunting**. For example, in a **poltergeist** situation it is often thought that a child at the age of puberty is somehow causing the disturbances through some form of **telekinetic** projection. In this case, the child is considered the agent.

AILUROMANCY

A form of **zoomancy** also known as 'feliomancy'. It is the art of predicting the future by observing the movements of cats, especially the way they jump and where they land. For example, a cat washing its face and ears could indicate rain; a cat washing one ear three times might suggest visitors from the direction in which the cat is looking; a cat following you could mean you will come into money, etc. Since ancient times cats have been associated with mystery and the occult, so it is hardly surprising that diviners used them to search for clues to the future.

AIR

One of the four natural **elements** harnessed in magical rites and associated with the **Zodiac** signs of Gemini, Libra and Aquarius. Air symbolizes communication and intellectual pursuits as well as new beginnings. In magical use, the element of air corresponds to the East and the colour yellow. It is one of the two elements that are associated with the masculine (the other being **fire**). Its ritual tool is the athame and/or sword, although in some traditions it is the **wand**. Its **symbol** is an equilateral triangle, with its point pointing upwards and a horizontal line passing through the centre. In **Wicca** an air **elemental** is one of the four **spirits** that energize a spell and help bring the spellcaster's wishes into being.

AKASHA

In Buddhism and Hinduism, akasha is the all-pervasive life force, a universal medium. It fits all space and penetrates all matter. It is everything, and everything is in it.

Hindu philosophy interprets the akasha as the ether, the fifth **element** that permeates the universe, acting as an agent through which electromagnetic forces operate. In the practice of **Yoga**, the akasha is one of the three universal principles, along with *prana* (breath of life) and creative mind; the three are all sources of psychic power. From akasha comes will, which makes anything possible.

In Buddhism the akasha is space, both space that is bound to the material world and space that is infinite. **Madame Blavatsky**, co-founder of the Theosophical Society, introduced this notion to the West and compared the akasha to other forms of the **universal life force**, such as the sidereal light of the **Rosicrucians**, the Hebrew *ruah* or moving spirit and the quintessance or luminous fifth element, invisible to humans, which binds the other four elements. Blavatsky suggested that the akasha forms the world soul, or *anima mundi*, and produces mesmeric operations of nature.

AKASHIC RECORDS

Akashic is a Sanskrit word meaning the fundamental etheric substance of the universe. According to **Theosophy**, the Akashic Records, or Book of Life, is extrasensory information that exists in another dimension, like the ultimate cosmic library. The records contain information on all world events and all thoughts and deeds that have taken place or will take place on earth. They may be read only by **adepts**. **Rudolf Steiner**, for example, claimed to have consulted the Akashic Records for his descriptions of Atlantis. **Edgar Cayce** also claimed to have seen the Book of Life. Some psychics say they consult the Akashic Records through **clairvoyance** or during **out-of-body experiences**.

The Akashic Records are also called the Universal Memory of Nature, and it is thought that everyone has an inherent ability to see his or her own book and all the things they have done or felt in life. It is simply a matter of developing the psychic ability.

The process of consulting the Records is described by psychics as like visiting an enormous library and looking up information in books. Some say they are greeted by doorkeepers or **spirit guides** who assist them in finding the correct information. The books are kept in rows, line upon line, stack upon stack, corridor upon corridor. Some books are charred, turned up at the edges and blackened, as if they have been pulled out of a fire, some are beautifully illuminated scrolls, and others are embossed in gold leaf with pages in rainbow colours. Yet others are bound in red leather with special emblems.

ALAMO

The Alamo in San Antonio, Texas, is a landmark that is believed to be truly haunted. Originally a chapel built in 1718 by monks, the Alamo was later expanded into a fortress for Texans to use as a stronghold against the Mexicans in the battle over land rights. In March 1836 the President of Mexico, General Antonio López de Santa Anna, and 4,000 troops laid siege to the Alamo. The 11-day battle led to the deaths of almost all the 188 defenders of the Alamo and 1,600 Mexicans. The victorious General López ordered the bodies of the dead Texans to be dumped in a large grave and the Alamo to be torn to the ground. Legend has it that when the Mexicans tried to tear down the walls, ghostly hands extended to stop them and they fled in terror.

Today the suffering of those who died has not been forgotten. There have been several sightings of grotesque **apparitions** coming from the walls of the Alamo, and screaming and yelling at night as if the terrible events of 1836 are replayed over and over again. There are other reports of a ghost on top of the Alamo, walking back and forth as if trying to escape.

See **Residual haunting**.

ALCATRAZ

Alcatraz, the harshest, loneliest and most haunted of America's federal prisons, is located on a dark and damp rock in San Francisco Bay. The story of Alcatraz does not begin or end with the use of the rock as a prison – the island was known to Native Americans as a place that contained evil **spirits**. Many believe that an evil energy still remains to this day. As parapsychologists suggest, where so much trauma and negative emotion has occurred there is bound to be residual energy, and Alcatraz has the feel of an immense haunted house, complete with fog and restless spirits, despite the fact that Alcatraz was closed as a prison in 1963, and today is maintained by the Golden Gate National Recreation Area as a tourist attraction.

Alcatraz, originally named La Isla de Los Altraces (The Island of the Pelicans), was first an army fort and prison. In 1934 it was turned into a maximum-security federal penitentiary where convicts were sent solely for punishment, not rehabilitation. Conditions were terrible and escape impossible. Many inmates were driven insane; others preferred to kill themselves rather than endure the brutal conditions.

Since the prison's closing no visual **apparitions** have been seen, but guards and tour guides have reported feelings of sudden intensity pervading the cells and corridors, the sound of men's voices, whistling, clanging metal doors, screams, the running of feet down corridors and anxious feelings of being watched. Some of the more haunted locations on Alcatraz appear to be the warden's house, the hospital, the laundry room, and Cell Block C utility door, where three convicts and three guards died in an attempted escape in 1946. The most haunted area, however, is the punishment block – D Block, or solitary, as it was called. Some guides refuse to go there alone. The cells reportedly remain intensely cold, even if it is a hot day.

To this day visitors continue to report feeling strange on their visit to Alcatraz, although some acknowledge their reaction might be influenced by their knowledge of the misery and suffering that went on there.

ALCHEMY

The term alchemy, commonly believed to refer to attempts to change base metals into gold, covers a wide range of topics – from the discovery of a single cure for all diseases to the quest for immortality, from the creation of artificial life to straightforward descriptions of scientific techniques. Broadly, one could describe alchemy as the art of converting that which is base, both in the material and spiritual world, into something more perfect. Symbolically, alchemy is the mystical art for human spiritual transformation into a higher form of being.

The spiritual teachings of alchemy were based on the idea that humans have a **spirit** or **soul** as well as a physical body, and it was thought that if the spirit could be compressed or concentrated, the secret of changing one aspect of nature into another could be discovered. The elusive catalyst that allowed this change to take place is known as the **philosopher's stone**, which is not a stone but a powder or liquid that turned base metal into gold and, when swallowed, gave everlasting life.

Alchemists are often pictured as stirring a bubbling concoction of base metal on a fire, hoping it will turn to gold. However, not all alchemists were like this, and some of the best minds of the last twenty or so centuries have studied alchemy as a way to unlock the secrets of nature.

Alchemy probably first emerged in ancient Egypt and China. In China it was purported to transmute base metals into gold, and the gold so produced was thought to have the ability to cure disease and prolong life. In Egypt the methods of transmutation were kept secret by temple priests. Western alchemy has its basis in the skills of those Egyptian priests, Eastern **mysticism** and the Aristotelian theory of the composition of matter. Aristotle, following the theory of Empedocles, taught that all matter was composed of four **elements**: **water**, **fire**, **earth** and **air**. Different materials found in nature contained different ratios of these four elements, and so by proper treatment a base metal could be turned to gold.

In the eighth and ninth centuries, Chinese, Greek, and Alexandrian alchemical lore entered the Arab world. Arabian alchemists postulated that all metals were composed not of four elements but of two: sulphur and mercury. They also adopted the Chinese alchemists' concept of a philosopher's stone – a medicine that could turn a sick (base) metal into gold and act as the El or elixir of life – and so begun a never-ending quest for this elusive catalyst.

Arab alchemical treatises were popular in the Middle Ages. Indirectly, through Arabic, Greek manuscripts were translated into Latin, and alchemical explanations of the nature of matter can be found in the treatises of such scholars as Albertus Magnus (c.1200–1280) and Roger Bacon (c.1214–1292).

Before the scientific revolution, alchemists were respected figures on the European scene, and kings and nobles often supported them in the hope of increasing their revenue. But among the sincere were charlatans and swindlers, and their fraudulent activities led to alchemy getting a bad name. Even as late as 1783 a chemist called John Price claimed he had turned mercury into gold. When he was asked by the Royal Society to perform the experiment in public, he reluctantly agreed. On the appointed day, however, he drank some poison and died in front of the invited audience.

In the sixteenth and seventeenth centuries, many practical alchemists, like Paracelsus, the first in Europe to mention zinc and use the word 'alcohol', turned from trying to make gold towards preparing medicine. The story is told of a seventeenth-century chemist who claimed he had found the elixir of life in the waters of a mineral spring. This substance has since been identified as the laxative sodium sulphate.

After the scientific revolution in the seventeenth century, alchemy became marginalized, and interest in transmutation became limited to astrologers and numerologists. Nevertheless, the scientific facts that had been accumulated by alchemists in their search for gold became the basis for modern chemistry. In the West, interest in the spiritual dimension of alchemy was rekindled in the mid-twentieth century through the work of psychiatrist **Carl Jung** on alchemical spirituality.

Today there are few practising alchemists. The fact is, scientists have discovered how to change base metals into gold, but the process is uneconomical and so alchemy today is a spiritual rather than a practical quest. Sincere seekers are people of great wisdom and morality. For them the search for spiritual perfection takes precedence over the quest for easy riches. Genuine alchemists see the universe as a unity and believe that by exploring the infinite workings of its parts they can better understand the whole. The symbolism of turning base metal into gold represents exactly what they are trying to do within themselves – refine themselves spiritually – and it could be said that alchemists are simply taking a more scientific approach to the age-old quest to 'know thyself'.

ALECTROMANCY

An ancient Roman method of **divination** using a cock or a hen placed in a circle of grain, round which are written the letters of the alphabet. The letters close to where the bird pecks are gathered and assembled to answer specific questions. If a simple yes or no is required, then only two piles of grain are used, and the most pecked grain pile provides the answer.

Alectromancy was also practised by listening to the crows of a cock and the periods at which they were heard. Another method was to recite the letters of the alphabet, noting those at which the cock crowed.

A well-known story involving alectromancy is that of the Roman emperor Valens, who used alectromancy to divine the name of his successor. He always got the name 'Theod', and so Valens ordered all those with the name Theodorus to be killed. Had he done his research properly, however, he might have been more successful: it was a man called Theodosius who actually succeeded him.

ALEUROMANCY

Divination through **sortilege** of fortunes written on slips of paper inserted into balls of dough and baked, mixed and distributed randomly. Used mainly by the ancient Greeks it is seldom practised today, although it is the origin of modern-day fortune cookies.

ALLHALLOWS EVE

See **Halloween**.

ALOMANCY

A method of **divination** that interprets random patterns of salt. Little is known of this ancient art of divination, but it accounts for some of the modern salt-related **superstitions**, including the saying that bad luck is likely when the salt cellar is overturned and the practice of throwing a pinch of salt over the shoulder for good fortune.

ALTERED STATE OF CONSCIOUSNESS [ASC]

The term 'altered state of consciousness' was coined by parapsychologist Charles Tart (b.1937), and it refers to a shift in the pattern of consciousness or normal waking state, for example during **hypnosis**, **trance** or **dream** state, when the conscious mind is subdued and the **unconscious** takes over. The operation of some psychic phenomena depends on being in an altered state of consciousness, but ASCs are difficult to study because of their subjective and internal nature, and because there is no universal state of **consciousness** from which to begin such a study.

States of consciousness take place in four levels of brain-wave activity: beta, alpha, theta and delta. Beta level is complete waking consciousness. Alpha level is where material from the subconscious is available to the mind, as in **meditation** or daydreaming. The theta level is equivalent to light sleep, a state of unconsciousness in which one is vaguely aware of what is going on around one. The delta level is deep sleep.

Many ASCs can be differentiated, ranging from dreaming to trance to mystical states of consciousness, such as that experienced during a **shamanic** state. ASCs can occur spontaneously or can be induced through disciplines such as **Yoga**, **Zen** and other forms of meditation, **prayer** and magical techniques. They can also be induced through chanting, dancing, fasting, sex, hypnosis, trauma and sleep deprivation.

Orthodox science largely rejects the experiences and knowledge gained from ASCs, many of which are intensely spiritual in nature, but scientific research has been effective in the areas of dreams, meditation, biofeedback and drug-induced states. Laboratory tests since the early 1950s on ASC-induced techniques such as **relaxation**, hypnosis and meditation have also been shown to enhance **psi** function, especially **extrasensory perception** (or **ESP**).

ALTERNATIVE MEDICINE

Medical or health practices based on unconventional principles, methods, theory, practice, treatments and knowledge – unconventional in that they are not in line with standard, traditional or orthodox medical practice and scientific beliefs. If the alternative therapy is offered alongside orthodox medicine it is called complementary medicine.

Alternative medicine is often (but not always) based upon metaphysical belief. Some of the most popular alternative techniques that incorporate metaphysical beliefs include **acupressure**, **acupuncture**, **aromatherapy**, **Ayurvedic medicine**, body cleansing, **bodywork**, chelation therapy, chiropractic, craniosacral therapy, **energy medicine**, electrodiagnosis, herbalism, **holistic** medicine, **homeopathy**, iridology, macrobiotics, naturopathy, osteopathy, **polarity therapy**, **psychic healing**, **reflexology**, **Reiki**, Rolfing, subliminal tapes, **therapeutic touch** and **traditional Chinese medicine**.

American Ghost Society [AGS]

A society of **ghost investigators** with members throughout the United States and Canada. The society was formed in 1995 by Troy and Amy Taylor, as the Ghost Society of Central Illinois. It expanded quickly and became the American Ghost Society in 1996. Within a few years it had nearly 500 members, including many prominent authors, law enforcement personnel and **paranormal** investigators.

The AGS maintains a network of area representatives and local research groups, and the Taylors organize annual conferences and meetings. The AGS publishes a magazine dedicated to ghosts and **hauntings**, the quarterly *Ghosts of the Prairie*, and also operates a website (www.prairieghosts.com), which includes the largest Internet bookstore dedicated to the subject.

Membership of the AGS is open to all, and the emphasis is on a high standard of investigation of hauntings using detective work – visiting and inspecting sites, interviewing witnesses and using high-tech ghost detection equipment. **Psychics** and **mediums** are not used because they are considered too subjective. All data, once analysed, is presented to the public. The following is an extract from the AGS mission statement:

The American Ghost Society is a national network of ghost hunters and researchers who conduct investigations into the paranormal in a non-metaphysical manner. One of our main goals is to seek out allegedly haunted locations and to assist those who are experiencing problems with the paranormal. The group members then look for authentic evidence of the paranormal and try to determine if the location is haunted. We are seeking genuine evidence and are careful about the presentation of this evidence … insuring that it is legitimate, researched, and analyzed before being presented to the general public … The credibility of the group is maintained above all else as we do not work with psychics or conduct investigations using metaphysical methods. We are not 'Ghost Busters,' but when a case does prove to be genuine, assistance through other channels may be provided at the location owner's request … In addition, we do not claim to be experts in the paranormal, as no experts exist when it comes to the supernatural, no matter what anyone may claim or who may claim to be one. We are instead working to present an image of competent researchers who are collecting the most authentic evidence possible. Investigations conducted under the auspices of the American Ghost Society are always held to the standards of the group and are conducted with integrity, honesty, and with discretion.

The Taylors opened the Haunted Museum in 2000 in Alton, Illinois. The museum houses a collection of books, articles, photographs and materials concerned with ghost research. Prior to the museum's opening, when the displays were being prepared, several strange phenomena were reported at night. Lights that were switched off were mysteriously turned on by the morning, books fell from shelves, items would vanish one night and reappear the next and displays were rearranged. Curiously, the building's alarm system was never activated to indicate the presence of human intruders.

American Society for Psychical Research [ASPR]

Founded in 1885, the American Society for Psychical Research is the oldest psychical research organization in the United States. It investigates psychic or **paranormal** phenomena through scientific means. Among its founders was the Harvard psychologist and professor of philosophy **William James** while among its benefactors was the inventor of the Xerox machine, physicist Chester Carlson. Its library and archive contain rare books, case reports, letters and manuscripts, which date back to the 1700s.

The ASPR serves as a global information network, providing publications and educational services which offer 'responsible information about relevant contemporary and historical research'. It has an exhaustive library of information on almost every experiment conducted on just about every type of paranormal phenomena. You can visit the society in New York City or look it up on the Internet: www.aspr.com.

See also **Society for Psychical Research**.

Amherst Haunting

The Amherst Haunting is a tale of **poltergeist** activity that took place in Amherst, Nova Scotia, in 1878 and centred on a 19-year-old woman, Esther Cox, recently threatened with rape. One night, soon after the traumatic event, Esther started to feel ill and went to bed early. Later she woke up screaming that she was dying. It is said that 'Her eyes went bloodshot, her hair stood on end, and her body puffed up to twice its normal size.'

Strange, violent movements filled the small, two-room cottage where Esther lived with her extended family. Thunderous bangs erupted from under the bed. Sheets were ripped off her and tossed into a corner. A doctor who came to examine her watched a bolster move of its own accord. Along the wall he watched words a foot high being scratched into the plaster: 'Esther Cox you are mine to kill!'

The disturbances in the house continued, including terrifying claps of sound and unexplained fires – lit matches materializing out of nowhere and dropping on to beds. After some time, the longsuffering landlord decided he'd had enough of his property being damaged and asked Esther's family to leave. She alone left instead, finding work at a nearby farm, but her job was cut short when the barn erupted into fire and the farmer had Esther charged with arson. She was sentenced to four months in jail, of which she served one month before being released. The story ended happily, for the disturbances subsided after Esther was freed from jail and eventually ended completely. Later she married, twice, and finally died in 1912 at the age of 53.

The case was never solved. Some at the time put forward the theory that electricity was responsible. Electricity was a new notion at the time, the latest wonder of the age, and people did not yet understand how it behaved. Some theorized that the unexplained fires were bolts of lightning and the noises were thunder.

In light of modern theories of the origin and nature of poltergeists, it is likely that Esther was the focus of **psychokinetic** energy, in which repressed emotions and sexuality burst forth, causing the phenomena. The case remains unusual in that Esther was beyond the age when poltergeist problems tend to occur, and that the disturbances also occurred in her absence.

AMITYVILLE HORROR

The Amityville Horror, although now considered a hoax, remains one of the most sensational and controversial cases of alleged **haunting** of all time. A small house in Amityville, New York, had been on the market for a year at a bargain price because it was the scene of a mass murder, by 23-year-old Ronnie DeFeo of his father, mother and younger siblings in November 1974. George and Kathleen Lutz bought the house a year later, in December 1975, and moved in with their three children.

A month later the Lutzes fled the house, never to return. They told the media of bizarre happenings – mysterious odours, doors slamming shut, gelatinous substances oozing out of nowhere. In 1977 *The Amityville Horror* by Jay Anson was published by Prentice-Hall as a non-fiction book. It sold six million copies and led to a top-grossing movie in 1979 and a host of other books and films.

The haunting was quickly dismissed as a hoax, and while it is possible haunting may have occurred, sceptics argue that there are too many discrepancies. The **American Society for Psychical Research** found the whole matter questionable and did not investigate, believing that the incidents were not **paranormal**. Also, when the Lutzes moved out the house became quiet. The next owners, Jim and Barbara Cromarty, said they experienced no unusual phenomena. However, they grew so annoyed by the tourists flocking to see their house that they sued the Lutzes, Anson and Prentice-Hall for $1.1 million. They won a settlement for an unspecified lesser amount, with the judge ruling that 'the evidence shows fairly clearly that the Lutzes during this entire period were considering and acting with the thought of getting a book published'.

AMNIOMANCY

From the Latin *amnion*, meaning membrane, amniomancy is an ancient method of **divination** by means of the membrane that sometimes envelops the head of a baby at birth. From inspecting the membrane, called a caul, the diviner predicted what sort of life the newborn would have.

AMULET

An object, drawing, inscription or **symbol** believed to have **supernatural** or magic power to ward off evil, the **evil eye**, disease, poor health and other misfortunes. Amulets are also worn to bring good luck as a kind of mascot or lucky **charm**.

Amulets are typically worn around the neck in the form of jewellery or a charm – a magical phrase, rhyme or **prayer** inscribed on paper. Amulets are also worn as rings. Some amulets are found as designs, symbols or inscriptions engraved on doors or posts.

Simple amulets have a colour or shape that catches the eye, but almost anything can become an amulet depending on a person's beliefs and resources. Among the most common are gems and precious stones fashioned into jewellery or statues of animals. Representations of eyes are also common and one of the best-known amulets is the ancient Egyptian Eye of Horus, which guarded health and protected against evil **spirits**. Organic amulets such as fruit, vegetables, berries, nuts and plants are common in some parts of the world. For example, the use of garlic as an amulet against evil may be traced back to the ancient Romans, while peach wood and stones are considered strong amulets against evil spirits in China. Certain metals are believed to have protective properties. Iron, for example, is universally thought to keep away **demons** and **witches**. Written amulets such as formulas, **spells**, words of power, secret symbols, religious phrases or signs have also been common since ancient times. See **Talisman**.

ANCESTOR WORSHIP

Ancestor worship involves paying respects to the **spirits** of dead relatives or ancestors in the hope this will ward off evil and bring good fortune to the community.

As the ancestors are not really thought of as gods, 'worship' may not be entirely the right term to use. Typically, offerings of food or drink or gifts for the spirits of the dead are made in the hope this will please the ancestors and make sure that they continue to look out for the community. In West Africa each family has its own ancestral shrine, inhabited, it is thought, by the founder of the lineage. These shrines are often carved in the likeness of the founder and must be tended and cared for.

See also **Day of the Dead**.

ANGEL

An immortal **supernatural** being which mediates between God and humanity. Angels are specific to Judaism, Christianity and Islam, but they occur as helping **spirits** in other traditions.

The word 'angel' comes from the Greek *angelos*, 'messenger', and the name refers to one of the angel's most important duties, which is to travel back and forth between the celestial and earthly realms, bringing human **prayers** to heaven and God's answers to earth. Angels are representatives of God on earth, delivering divine messages or helping humans according to God's will. Angels exist in a celestial realm but have the ability to assume a physical form and pass as human beings. They may bring fire or bright light; sometimes they are pictured with wings and sometimes without. Where appropriate, they appear to humans in visionary experiences or **dreams**.

Prior to the Western Enlightenment, angels were believed by many to play a magical role in daily life. However, after the scientific revolution angels were no longer taken seriously except by poets and the romantically inclined. The mystic **Emanuel Swedenborg**, among other **occult** figures, claimed to commune with angels. Swedenborg called the **souls** of the dead 'angels' and said he visited them in the **afterlife** during his **trances**.

Today angels have made a comeback in popularity, due in part to a widespread spiritual hunger for supernatural assurance and guidance. Some people consider the appearance of a spirit of the dead, such as a family member, to be an angel that comes to warn or comfort them. In **deathbed visions** the souls of dead friends and family members who come to help the dying person are often believed to be angels. Many people still claim to experience angelic visions, especially those who have gone through **near-death experiences**, and in many such accounts an angel greets them at the threshold of death. Angels are most often sensed through **clairaudience**. They sometimes manifest as balls of brilliant white light or appear as real persons in a mysterious encounter with a stranger. These encounters often occur when a person is in crisis and needs decisive action. A mysterious, calm but firm stranger who is knowledgeable about the crisis appears out of nowhere and offers a solution. Once the problem has been solved the person vanishes. It is the abrupt and strange disappearance that makes people wonder whether they have been helped by a human or an angel. Famous examples of reported angel encounters include those of George Washington, who suggested that angels helped him during the Delaware crossing of 1776, and the composer Handel, who believed angels helped him to compose the famous Hallelujah Chorus.

ANGELS OF MONS

See **Battlefield ghosts**.

ANIMAL PSI

Animal **psi** is the ability of animals to experience **clairvoyance**, **precognition**, **telepathy** and **psychokinesis**.

Are animals clairvoyant, and can they communicate telepathically? Do they possess special powers that enable them to sense danger? Although it is not known conclusively if this is the case, scientific evidence suggests that, if psi exists, it probably does so in both humans and animals.

Sceptics argue that animals thought to possess psi are simply responding to subtle changes in body language and physical cues from their owners, but many animal lovers are certain that psi exists in animals and that psi-gifted pets are those that are the most loved, as love nourishes psi. Many **psychics** like to have animals accompany them when they are investigating **hauntings** because animals are thought to be more sensitive to **ghosts** and **spirits**, and many cats and dogs have been known to react visibly in fear in places of suspected **paranormal** activity.

Evidence for animal psi is largely anecdotal, as animals do not respond well to scientific testing for psi. However, American parapsychologist **J B Rhine** at Duke University investigated around 500 reported cases of animal psi. Rhine concluded that there were five basic types of animal psi: the ability to sense death or injury to a loved one; the ability to sense the impending return of an owner; the ability to sense impending danger; the ability to find the way home; and the ability to 'psi trail' or to find an owner when separated by long distances.

There are also numerous reports of animal hauntings, in particular stories of much-loved pets who have appeared to their owners to offer comfort and love. The stories remain anecdotal, but animals have and always will be associated with the supernatural and paranormal. Strange and mysterious stories of dragons, snakes, cats, dogs, serpents and unicorns linger among **superstitions** and fairy tales today. Religion, folklore and **witchcraft** have borrowed heavily from the animal world, for they know that the qualities and energies of animals represent strength, power, devotion, **intuition**, intelligence and wisdom.

ANIMISM

Animism is rare today, but this very ancient way of perceiving the world may once have been universal. At the root of magic beliefs and practice, animism is the belief that every natural object, both living and non-living, has a spirit or life force and is endowed with reason and intelligence. The animist sees movement in trees, rocks, streams, wind and other objects and believes that everything is inhabited by its own spirit.

Animism is found among many tribal societies throughout the Americas, Asia, Australia and Africa. Having observed that during sleep and dreaming, **visions** and **trances** – what today we call **out-of-body experiences** – the spiritual part of a body could detach from the physical, animists deduced that it could also survive death. Instead of going to the land of the dead, the **soul** might take control of another person (**possession**) or send messages to the living through **mediums** or **shamans**. It might lodge in various features of the natural world such as trees or rocks, or in human objects such as spears or statues.

Beliefs that a person may have more than a single soul are not unusual. For instance, among many Eskimo groups, a name is one type of soul. In societies that lived close to nature not only people but also animals and plants were thought to have souls, and human spirits might be reborn in animals (**reincarnation**). In some cases people may have a special affinity with certain species of animal, and the animistic beliefs concerning this human relationship to animals are known as **totemism**.

For the animist, the world abounds with spirit entities. Water spirits and forest spirits are especially common, but animism is more than just a belief in soul and spirits; it has its own logic and consistency and in many respects can be called a religion.

ANKOU

Ankou is part of the fairy lore of the Celtic countries. He is thought to be the personification of death, who comes to collect the **souls** of humans when they die. Largely forgotten in Cornwall, Wales and Ireland, Ankou remains a part of the living folklore in Brittany. Every parish in Brittany has its own ankou.

An old Irish proverb says, 'When Ankou comes, he will not go away empty.' He is depicted as a tall, dark, haggard figure, wearing a black-robed costume pulled up high about his head and with a large hat that conceals his face. Legend has it that he is always preceded by a gust of wind and you cannot see his face, for if you do it means you have died. He is said to drive a small black coach drawn by four black horses and accompanied by two ghostly figures on foot. Many believe it is not really a coach at all but a hearse and that the job of the ghostly figures is to collect corpses and place them in the hearse.

One legend says that Ankou was once a cruel prince who met up with Death in the forest and challenged him to a contest. The prince loved to hunt and kill, and on this particular night he was chasing a white stag (a magical animal in Celtic stories). The prince set out a challenge before the enormous, black-robed rider: whoever could kill the stag would not only keep the meat but also determine the fate of the loser. The stranger readily agreed, and it is said that his voice was raspy, like leaves scraping castle walls.

They set off at a gallop, and the prince realized immediately that he was bested. No matter how hard he rode, the stranger rode faster. And when the prince was still stringing his bow, the stranger had already set loose his arrow and felled the stag.

As the winded prince approached the stranger said, 'You can have the stag – and all the dead of the world.' The stranger sentenced him to an eternity of hunting the souls of all who died around the world.

ANTIETAM

The American Civil War battle of Antietam took place near Sharpsburg, Maryland, on 17 September 1862. Twenty-three thousand men were killed or wounded – the bloodiest single day of battle in American history – and **ghosts** and strange phenomena still greet visitors to the site today.

George B McClellan, commander of the Federal Army of the Potomac, had not yet been victorious for the Union because of his cautious tactics. Robert E Lee of the Confederate army therefore determined to occupy Northern territory and marched his men into Maryland.

But Lee's luck was about to run out. A copy of Lee's field orders had been lost, just about the time Union soldiers spotted a small packet lying on the ground. Opening it, they found three cigars wrapped in paper. The cigars themselves were rare and valuable, but only later did they truly realize what they had: the paper wrapped around the cigars contained Lee's field orders. McClellan went on the march.

When the two sides came face to face at 5 am on the 17th, both generals were determined to make a stand and change the course of the war. The battle was fierce and frenzied. By late afternoon, thousands had died and, although both sides claimed a victory, in actuality it was a draw. It did change the course of the war, however, for Lee's failure to successfully invade the North led to Britain postponing its recognition of the Confederate state.

Today the battlefield looks much as it did all those years ago. Some woods have been cleared away and monuments erected, but you can stand on the site and perhaps experience what other visitors have reported – hearing the sound of gunfire and smelling the scent of gunpowder. One visitor to the park saw what he thought was a group of Confederate re-enactors, but realized his mistake when the company suddenly vanished from his sight.

A school field trip became quite an experience for some of the children one spring day. After the guided tour, they were invited to wander the area of the bloody battle for a short time before their departure. Later they reported to their teacher that they had heard what sounded like chanting – like fa-la-la-la-la of 'Deck the Halls'. The teacher, who was a Civil War buff, knew – but the children could not possibly have – that the war cry of the Irish Sixty-Ninth New York militia, which fought among the Union troops, was *Faugh A Ballach*, which in English is 'Clear the Way!' but in Gaelic is pronounced 'Fah-ah-bah-lah'.

The nearby Burnside Bridge, named after Major General Ambrose E Burnside, who held the bridge for the Union, also is said to be haunted, as is a local bed-and-breakfast.

APANTOMANCY

A method of **divination** by taking cues from chance meetings with animals, birds and other creatures. The superstition associated with a black cat crossing one's path is apantomancy.

APPARITION

The **supernatural** appearance of a person, animal or object too far away to be seen, felt or heard by normal senses. Contrary to popular belief, most apparitions are of the living not the dead, but apparitions of the dead are also called **ghosts**.

Only a small number of apparitions are visual; most apparition experiences feature noises, unusual smells, extreme cold or heat and the displacement of objects.

Every civilization throughout history and around the world has held beliefs about apparitions. Among Asian peoples belief in ancestral ghosts is strong, and rituals exist to honour and placate them, as the spirits of the dead are thought to interfere regularly in the affairs of the living and are credited for both good and bad fortune. The ancient Hebrews, Greeks and Romans believed that spirits of the dead could return to haunt the living.

During the Dark Ages people believed in all manner of apparitions: **demons**, **vampires** and devil dogs. Around this time the Christian Church taught that ghosts were souls trapped in **purgatory** until they expiated their sins. The only apparitions that were holy and permitted by God were apparitions of religious figures, such as **angels**, saints and Jesus. All other apparitions, including spirits of the dead, were delusions created by Satan to confuse the living.

In seventeenth-century Europe apparitions of the dead played an important role as advisors to the living. Belief in ghosts fell out of favour in the eighteenth century, returning in the nineteenth with **spiritualism**, which espouses **survival after death** and mediumistic contact with the dead. Many motifs of apparitions appear in the folklore of different cultures, such as the **Flying Dutchman** or the **ankou**.

According to a study of apparitions by American psychical researcher **Hornell Hart**, published in 1956, there is no significant difference between apparitions of the living and of the dead. Apparitions can move through solid matter and appear and disappear abruptly. They can cast shadows. Some are corporeal and lifelike in their movement and speech while others are luminous or limited in movement and speech. Apparitions are typically dressed in clothing of their time. The majority of apparitions are thought to manifest for a reason, for instance, to communicate a crisis or death, give a warning, offer comfort or convey important information. Some **haunting** apparitions appear in places where emotional traumas have taken place, such as murders or battles, but other hauntings seem to be aimless.

Systematic studies of apparitions began with the **Society for Psychical Research**, London, in the late nineteenth century. By the 1980s polls in the Unites States conducted by the University of Chicago's National Opinion Research Council showed a dramatic increase – around 78 per cent – in reported apparitions, perhaps due in part to changing public attitudes towards acknowledging **paranormal** experiences.

Although many ghost investigators have their own categories, the following are the most typical types:

- *Crisis apparitions: usually images that appear in moments of crisis to communicate death or danger. They typically appear to a person who has close emotional ties to the **agent** (the person who is the source of the apparition).*
- *Apparitions of the dead: manifestations of someone who has died, usually within a short time after death, to comfort a loved one or communicate important information.*
- *Collective apparitions: manifestations of the living or dead that occur to multiple witnesses. Approximately one-third of reported apparitions are witnessed collectively.*

☙. *Reciprocal apparitions: apparitions of the living in which both agent and the **percipient** (the person who experiences the apparition), separated by a distance, experience apparitions of each other simultaneously.*

☙. *Deathbed apparitions: visual images of divine beings, religious figures and dead loved ones that are reported by the dying in the last moments of life.*

☙. *Apparitions in cases suggestive of **reincarnation**: cases when the deceased appears in a **dream** to a member of the family into which it will be reborn. Such dreams occur frequently among Native American tribes of the Northwest and in Turkey, Burma and Thailand.*

A large number of theories have been put forward to explain apparitions, but none explain all the different types. Society for Psychical Research founders **Edmund Gurney** and **Frederick Myers** at first believed apparitions were mental hallucinations that had no physical reality, either produced by **telepathy** from the dead to the living or projected out of the percipient's mind in the form of an image. Gurney also believed that collective apparitions were a product of telepathy among the living, projected by the primary percipient to others around him or her. However, telepathy among the living does not explain why witnesses in collective sightings notice different details.

Myers, who believed strongly in survival after death, began to doubt the telepathic theory as early as 1885. In his landmark book *Human Personality and Its Survival after Death* (1903), he suggested that the apparitions consisted of a 'phantasmogenic centre', a locus of energies that could be perceived by the most psychically sensitive people. He conceived of a 'subliminal consciousness' as the basis from which the consciousness springs and which survives the body after death. He theorized that the subliminal **consciousness** was receptive to extrasensory input and that apparitions appeared to psychically receptive people.

Other theories that have been advanced subsequently about apparitions suggest they are:

☙. *Idea patterns or etheric images produced by the subconscious mind of the living.*

☙. *Astral or etheric bodies of the agents.*

☙. *An amalgam of personality patterns, which in the case of hauntings are trapped on a psychic or **psi** field.*

☙. *Projections of the human **unconscious**, a manifestation of an unacknowledged need or guilt.*

☙. *Vehicles through which the 'I', the thinking consciousness, takes on a personality as well as a visible form.*

☙. *Projections of will and concentration; see **Thought form**.*

☙. *True spirits of the dead.*

☙. *Localized physical phenomena directed by an intelligence or personality.*

☙. *Recordings or imprints of vibrations impressed upon some sort of psychic ether. In Eastern mystical philosophy, the cosmos is permeated by a substance called the **Akasha**. Oxford philosopher H H Price called this substance 'psychic ether', a term adopted by some psychical researchers to suggest that if all events are recorded on some invisible* *substance, then perhaps psychically tuned people can get glimpses of these records and get a playback. See **Akashic Records**.*

It is unlikely that any one theory can explain all apparitions, and it is conceivable that some apparitions are created by the living, that some have their own reality, that some are hallucinations and that some are psychic recordings.

Twentieth-century psychical researcher Andrew Mackenzie suggested that the ability to have hallucinations could be a function of personality. In his studies he found that one-third of cases occurred just before or after sleep, or when the percipient was woken in the night. Other experiences took place when the witness was in a state of **relaxation** or doing routine work such as housework, or concentrating on some activity such as reading a book. Only when the external world was shut out was the unconscious able to release impressions, which sometimes took the form of an apparition.

English psychical researcher G Tyrrell also made this link between dreamlike states and sightings of apparitions. Tyrrell theorized that there were two stages in an hallucinatory experience. In stage one the witness unconsciously experiences the apparition, and in stage two the information from stage one is processed from the unconscious in dreams or hallucinations with the required details added, such as clothing and objects.

APPLIED PSI

Also known as applied parapsychology and psionics, applied psi is a branch of **parapsychology** that assumes psychic ability exists and seeks ways to apply it in everyday life.

Applied psi is used today when anyone acts on his or her **intuition** to make a decision. Experimental studies of applied psi date back to the eighteenth century, but it wasn't until the twentieth century that the discipline was seriously explored. In 1963 the Newark College of Engineering in New Jersey became one of the first engineering centres in the US to explore **psi** ability in people. Researchers found that successful people use psi and **precognition** daily in their jobs in the form of intuition, **hunches** and **gut feelings**. In the early 1980s, American parapsychologist Jeffrey Mishlove urged parapsychologists to assume that psi existed and to focus on ways to use it in everyday life. By 1984 applied psi did become an informal part of a number of fields, including archaeology, agriculture, executive decision-making, scientific discovery, military intelligence, criminal investigations and weather prediction. However, over subsequent years the erratic nature of psi made it an unreliable tool.

Some experiments raised interesting questions as to how effective applied psi can be when it comes to making financial investments. It is not uncommon for people to place a bet or buy and sell stock on gut instinct. Experiments, such as one conducted by the *St Louis Business Journal* in 1982, compared the results of a group of experienced brokers with a **psychic**. The stocks picked by the brokers fell in value, but the ones picked by the psychic rose. Despite such successes, however, widespread use of applied psi in the stock market has never materialized – if it did it would probably spell the end of the stock market, thriving as it does on unpredictability and chance.

APPORT

In his *Encyclopedia of Psychic Science* (1933), Hungarian psychical researcher **Nandor Fodor** defined apports as the 'arrival of various objects through an apparent penetration of matter', one of the most baffling phenomena of **spiritualism**, he thought. Apports are objects that **mediums** claim to be able to produce from thin air or transport through solid matter, and to this day they remain as mysterious as ever.

The majority of apports are everyday small objects such as rings, sweets and pebbles, although some can be large and unusual such as books, garden tools, live animals and birds. When spiritualism was at its most popular apports were commonplace at **séances**. Sufis, mystical **adepts** of Islam, and Hindu swamis are also renowned for the apports they produce. Some mediums have been exposed as **frauds**, producing apports that were hidden under the table or on their person prior to the séance, which is held in the dark, making trickery easier. Some adepts also have been exposed as frauds, but there are adepts and mediums whose reputations

hold. **Sai Baba** of India, for example, seems to be able to produce apports, such as sweets, banquets of hot food, statues and many other objects, from his closed fist, while others are pulled from the sand.

Theories to explain apports that appear to be genuine include apports as gifts from the **spirits**, the pulling of objects from another dimension through some sort of psychic magnetism or the medium somehow taking objects from another location, making them disintegrate and then transporting and reassembling them.

ARCHANGELS

The name given to incorporeal beings that are said to guide the spiritual destiny of groups of people rather than of individuals, which is the role of **angels**. This explains why archangels are often pictured as carrying formalized models of cities in their hands. In Judaism and Christianity, the most important are the seven archangels, each of whom is assigned one of the seven spheres of heaven: Gabriel, Michael, Raphael, Uriel, Joophiel, Zadkiel and the fallen archangel, Samuel (Satan).

ARCHETYPES

Psychiatrist **Carl Jung** first used this term in 1919 to refer to apparently universal images that are inherited from our ancestors. Archetypes are unconscious instinctual patterns or mental images that are passed down to us all but are modified according to individual experience. Interpretations of archetype images have been applied to many fields, such as **past-life therapy**, psychotherapy, **Tarot**, women's studies, mythology, **astrology**, the healing professions and even sales and marketing.

According to Jung, archetypes are unlimited in number and created by the repetition of experiences that are imprinted on the psychic mind. When a situation occurs that corresponds to an archetype, the archetype is triggered and instinct takes over. God, death, birth, power, magic, the sun, the moon, the wind, animals and the elements are all archetypes, as are the figures of the hero, the lover, the judge, the child, the mother and the father. Archetypes develop and change as an individual grows and encounters new situations. Archetypes communicate with the conscious mind, and it is possible to gain insight into oneself by paying attention to the archetypal forces in one's life. Jung believed that archetypes were psychic forces that demand to be taken seriously: if neglected they could lead to compulsion, neurosis and illness.

Jung thought that the existence of archetypes could be proved through **dreams** and through **imagination**, and by understanding your dreams you learn what you need to move forward with your life.

ARITHMANCY

An ancient method of **divination** using numbers, arithmancy is an early form of **numerology**. The father of arithmancy was **Pythagoras**, who believed there were connections between gods, man and numbers that could be decoded and used to foretell the future of an individual and the outcome of certain events. Ancient Greeks would examine the numbers and values of letters between two combatants to predict who would be victorious. In the story of the Trojan wars, the victory of Achilles over Hector was predicted in this way.

AROMATHERAPY

Holistic caring for the body through the use of scents, usually pleasant-smelling botanical oils such as rose, lemon, lavender and peppermint. The essential oils of these botanicals are added to a bath or massaged into the skin, inhaled directly or diffused to scent an entire room. The oils are administered in small quantities to improve mood or promote health, and they are thought to contain hormones, antibiotics and antiseptics and to represent the 'life force', 'spirit' or 'soul' of the plant.

Some proponents claim that aromatherapy is a complete medical system that can strengthen immune systems and cure disease, and studies have shown aromatherapy is effective in relieving pain and in alleviating fatigue, reducing anxiety and promoting **relaxation**. When inhaled, scents work on the brain and nervous system by stimulating the olfactory nerves.

Botanical essential oils are aromatic essences extracted from plants, flowers, trees, fruits, bark, grasses and seeds which have distinctive therapeutic, psychological and physiological properties to improve and prevent illness. There are about 150 essential oils. Most of these oils have antiseptic properties; some are antiviral, anti-inflammatory, pain-relieving, antidepressant and expectorant. To get the maximum benefit from an essential oil, it should be made from natural, pure raw materials. Synthetically made oils do not work.

Aromatherapy is one of the fastest growing fields in **alternative medicine**. It is widely used at home, in clinics and in hospitals for a variety of applications such as pain relief for women in labour, relieving pain caused by the side effects of chemotherapy undergone by cancer patients, and rehabilitating cardiac patients.

In Japan, engineers are incorporating aroma systems into new buildings. In one bank, the scent of lavender and rosemary is pumped into the customer area to calm the waiting customers, while the perfumes from lemon and eucalyptus are used in the bank teller counters to keep the staff alert.

ARRIVAL CASES

The appearance of a person before their actual arrival. Frequently the arriving **phantom** appears in the same clothing the individual is wearing at the same time. The individual is usually not aware of appearing in a distant location until told about it.

Arrival cases were collected and studied by the founders of the **Society for Psychical Research** in the early twentieth century. They collected their evidence in their exhaustive survey *Phantasms of the Living* (1918).

Arrivals have been claimed to eat, sleep and seem so real that anyone could believe it was a double (**doppelgänger**) of the real person. The most likely explanation of arrival cases is that the individual somehow projects a double, which is perceived as real, perhaps as an out-of-body projection (**bilocation**) or as a psychic projection of intent or desire to be in that different place. Others think that arrival cases are a quirk of time duplicating itself.

In the Highlands of Scotland, the term for arrival cases is 'spirits of the living'. In Norway, the arrival case phenomenon is called *vardøger*, which means 'forerunner'.

One unusual *vardøger* case occurred in Oslo and concerned Erikson Gorique, an American importer. For years, Gorique had wanted to go to Norway but was forced to keep postponing the trip. In July 1955 he was finally able to go. On his arrival in Oslo, Gorique asked where he might stay. Much to his astonishment, when he arrived at the recommended hotel he was greeted by name by the hotel clerk. The clerk told him it was nice to see him again. When Gorique protested that he had never before travelled to Norway or been at the hotel, the puzzled clerk insisted that he could not mistake Gorique's unusual name and American appearance. He said Gorique stayed at the hotel several months earlier and had made reservations to return that month.

Gorique was even more surprised when he visited a wholesale dealer, who also greeted him like an old friend, saying it was terrific to have him back to conclude previous business. Gorique told the dealer that he hadn't been there before, whereupon the dealer nodded knowingly and explained the *vardøger* phenomenon: 'It is not uncommon in Norway', he said.

ART, PSYCHIC

Also known as automatic painting, psychic art occurs when individuals who often have little or no artistic training suddenly feel overcome by a desire to draw or paint in distinctive, professional styles. They feel guided by a **spirit** and may actually feel an invisible hand pushing theirs.

A psychic artist can produce amazing likenesses of deceased relatives of an enquirer, people unknown to the artist. Such an artist may also draw or paint **spirit guides**, **angels**, animals or figures who are subsequently discovered to be connected to the enquirer in some way.

In addition to artists who create images of guides and people in spirit, there are others who unconsciously collaborate on pieces of original artwork. Some psychic artists claim contact with great masters who have taught them a special skill or who use them as a vehicle to add new collections to works they produced while still alive. Some psychic art is also sacred art.

Many **shamanic** or healing traditions from around the world have used sacred art in ceremonies of healing and as a bridge between the physical and non-physical worlds. The Navajo people, who reside in the Southwestern region of the USA, have passed down the practices of hand painting from generation to generation. Tibetan monks, too, conduct healing ceremonies that involve the creation and destruction of detailed sand paintings.

One of the most famous psychic art cases is the **Thompson-Gifford case**, which occurred early in the twentieth century. In 1905 an engraver from New York, Frederic Thompson, was seized with the urge to draw and paint in the style of the recently dead artist Robert Gifford. Thompson had met Gifford when he was alive but was not well acquainted with him. When Thompson painted he felt he was Gifford, and he often heard Gifford's voice urging him to sketch. Thompson produced many works that reminded buyers of Gifford's style and sold at good prices.

See also **Automatic writing**; **Automatism**.

ARUNDEL CASTLE

This magnificent castle in the heart of West Sussex has been the home of the Dukes of Norfolk since 1580. It was severely damaged by fire in the seventeenth century but has now been restored to its former glory. Not only is Arundel Castle the home of countless priceless works of art, but it also is thought to house several **ghosts**.

The ghost of a young woman dressed in white has been seen wandering round Hiorne's Tower, particularly on moonlit nights. According to legend, she threw herself off the tower because of a tragic love affair. A ghost has also been encountered in the library and has become known as the 'Blue Man'. He has been seen on several occasions searching through books, and is thought to date back to the time of King Charles II (1660–1685).

A kitchen boy of 200 years ago or so is said to have been so badly treated that he died young. His ghost has been seen furiously polishing pots and pans. Another ghost is that of a small white bird, which reputedly flutters around the windows of the castle. It is said to signify the imminent death of someone connected to the castle and was reported to have appeared just before the death of the Duke of Norfolk in 1917.

ASH MANOR GHOST

Psychical researcher **Nandor Fodor** solved the mystery of the Ash Manor **ghost** in 1930s England. The case was one of his most famous and helped to establish his theory of the psychological underpinning of some **hauntings**. He recorded the case in detail in his book *The Haunted Mind* (1959).

Mr and Mrs Keel (a pseudonym assigned by Fodor) moved into Ash Manor House in Sussex, England, with their 16-year-old daughter and servants on 24 June 1934. They were aware that parts of the house dated back to the thirteenth century and that it had a reputation for being haunted. It wasn't long before the daughter and servants reported strange noises coming from the attic, and Mr and Mrs Keel heard strange bangs on their bedroom doors.

The Keels suspected something **supernatural** was afoot, and on 23 November Mr Keel woke to see 'a little oldish man, dressed in a green smock, very muddy breeches and gaiters, a slouch hat on his head and a handkerchief around his neck'. Keel tried to grab the man, thinking him a servant, but was astonished to see his hand go right through him. Keel ran to his wife, who also saw the man and tried to strike him, but her fist went through him too. The strange noises continued, and the green man, as the Keels called him, continued to appear. Once the phantom raised his head, and Mrs Keel could see that his neck had been cut all the way around. She concluded that he must have been murdered and that perhaps his skeleton was hidden in the house.

The manifestations were so frightening that the servants quit their jobs. The Keels were advised to get help in exorcizing the ghost by advertising in a newspaper. Several individuals tried to do the job but did not succeed.

In July 1936 Fodor was invited to investigate the case by a writer who was including the Ash Manor ghost in his book about hauntings. Fodor arrived and saw that the Keels were fearful of any harm being done to their reputations by the publicity. He stayed in the house for several nights, but no manifestations occurred.

At that time the medium **Eileen Garrett** was living in England, and Fodor asked her to visit Ash Manor. Garrett arrived on 25 July and immediately received the clairvoyant impression of a man who had been half brother to Edward IV or V and had started a rebellion. He had been tortured and left crippled as a result. That evening Garrett entered the haunted house and went into a **trance**, and her **control**, Uvani, spoke. Uvani explained that ghosts often manifest when an atmosphere of unhappiness enables a spirit to draw energy and revive its suffering. 'Haven't you discovered that these things only happen to you when you are in a bad emotional state, physically or mentally disturbed?' Uvani asked. The control went on to say that in the fifteenth century a jail had existed near the house, where many unhappy souls had lost their lives. Anyone living in the house who was 'nervously depleted' would give out energy that would attract a ghost, who would use that energy to build himself up, like a 'picture on the stage'.

Uvani permitted the ghost to possess Garrett, and the Keels said that her features looked like those of the green man. Speaking through Garrett, the ghost announced, in a medieval English accent, that he was called Charles Edward. He claimed to have been robbed of his lands by the Earl of Huntingdon and betrayed by a friend called Buckingham. He asked the witnesses to help him wreak revenge upon his enemies. Fodor informed the ghost that he was dead and begged him to give up his quest and join the spirits of his loved ones.

The ghost reluctantly agreed to do so, and Garrett returned to normal consciousness.

The hauntings, however, did not stop, and Fodor conducted another session with Garrett, this time without the Keels present. The ghost once again appeared and pleaded for help in getting vengeance. Uvani announced that the Keels had used this 'poor, unhappy creature' in order to embarrass each other and that they did not want the ghost to leave. The control also said that if the unhappiness in the house persisted, it would become truly haunted.

Fodor at last felt that he was close to solving the case. Mrs Keel confessed to him that her husband was homosexual and that a great deal of tension existed between them. Fodor suggested that the ghost provided a distraction that prevented that tension from breaking out into the open.

When the Keels admitted they were hanging on to the ghost, the ghost departed. A scholarly investigation of the statements made by Charles Edward deemed they were not authentic, and Fodor, in analysing the case, considered the ghost to be an invention of Mr Keel's subconscious mind, which Garrett had tapped into.

However, some of the haunting phenomena at Ash Manor could not be explained, for example, the independent sightings by servants and other witnesses. Fodor concluded that 'it may be that those who put themselves in an unguarded psychological position, in a place filled with historical memories and traditions, do, on rare occasions, come into contact with a force or an intelligence other than their own.'

ASPORT

The opposite of **apport**, asport refers to psychic phenomena involving the disappearance or transportation of objects, supposedly accomplished with the help of the **spirits** of the dead. During the height of **spiritualism** in the late nineteenth and early twentieth centuries, apports produced at **séances** would often become asports and mysteriously vanish from one room to be found in another room. Sometimes, though, asported valuables would vanish altogether and remain forever with the spirits, causing sceptics to question the integrity of the **mediums**.

Although trickery is undeniable, there are also reported cases of asports that appear genuine. Sai Baba of India, famous for his apports of holy ash, food, precious jewels and other items, has also been said to dematerialize apports if the recipients do not like them and change them into something else.

ASSOCIATION FOR RESEARCH AND ENLIGHTENMENT

See **Cayce, Edgar**.

ASTRAL BODY

Various **esoteric** traditions talk about the many bodies – the different levels of **consciousness** and existence – that each person has. Some people think of these different aspects as 'subtle bodies' or selves that exist in a parallel plane but are all part of a larger consciousness. This theory suggests that the body itself does not contain these aspects. Rather, this larger consciousness contains the body, as well as other levels of existence, and you can learn to create a closer connection to any of these aspects within yourself.

A commonly recognized 'extra' self is the astral body, also known as an energy body. The word 'astral' is derived from the Greek for 'star'. The astral body can also be called a **double** or **doppelgänger**, because it is a duplicate of the physical body. **Theosophists** refer to it as the 'etheric' or 'spiritual double' containing the **soul** and made from the vibrations that make up the physical body.

The astral body exists on the **astral plane**, also known as the astral realm, astral world or astral sphere, and in metaphysical terminology the astral plane is contiguous in space, if not in time, with the material world. The astral realm is the one that the spiritual part or astral body enters during periods of sleep, under the action of anaesthetics or drugs, by accident when a person is unconscious, or immediately after death. The astral realm is not normally visible to ordinary sight, yet it is regarded as the proper dwelling of people's higher spiritual bodies.

According to **shamans** and Theosophists the astral body or second self resembles the physical body but is made up of a subtle field of shining and flexible light that encases the body, visible only by a psychically sensitive person. It is thought that when you are sleeping the astral body can separate from the physical body, which results in flying dreams and the experience of disorientation experienced if you wake suddenly and the astral body hasn't had time to line up with the physical one. Driven by emotions, passions and desires, the astral body is believed to be a bridge between the physical brain and a higher level of mind.

ASTRAL DOORWAYS

Symbols and pictures that are used to help individuals in **astral projection** reach the **astral plane**. **Tarot** cards can be used as astral doorways but the definitive doorways, used by **psychics** and **magicians** for hundreds of years, are the Tattwas of the Eastern esoteric tradition. The five primary tattwa symbols are simple coloured shapes – a yellow square (earth), blue circle (air), red triangle (fire), silver crescent (moon) and black oblong (ether) – and each one can be used as a focal point to trigger astral projection and give access to a specific part of the astral plane.

ASTRAL PLANE

According to occultists the astral plane is an alternate and non-physical dimension of reality that can be visited during **astral projection** or **out-of-body experiences**. The word 'astral', from the Greek word

Using tattwas to trigger astral projection

Tattwa cards are easy to make. All you need is some white cardboard, a pair of scissors and some colouring pens or paint with strong brilliant shades of yellow, blue, red, silver and black. When you have cut out your shapes you only need to colour or paint one side; leave the back of the card plain and white.

Once you have made your cards, find a quiet place, get comfortable and relax. Choose a symbol and gaze intently at it for a minute, then turn it over and gaze at the blank side. As you do an optical reflex will cause the symbol to appear on the back of the card. Now close your eyes and visualize what you have seen, mentally enlarging the image until it is big enough for you to pass through. Imagine yourself steeping through this mass of colour as if it were an actual door to the astral plane.

meaning 'star', originally described the heavens of the Greek gods, but as time passed the concept expanded to refer to a spirit world inhabited by etheric entities, disembodied spirits and higher beings.

The astral world is believed to be invisible to the ordinary eye because it vibrates at a higher rate than the energy that comprises the material world. However, occultists believe that it can be perceived through astral projection and **clairvoyance** and it is a world just as real as ours. It has scenery, inhabitants, countries and seas and is subject to the laws of nature and constant change just as the physical world is.

Modern psychologists argue that accounts of trips to a strange and alien dimension spring from the imagination, but according to occult theory the astral plane is undeniably real. It is an intermediate and invisible level of reality between the physical plane and the divine realms where communication with higher beings can be established and where the individuals thought forms take on a reality.

This process of consciously leaving the body and travelling free of physical constraints is often referred to as astral projection or astral travel. Although the terms are often used interchangeably, experts define astral projection as becoming aware that your consciousness is separate from your physical body. For instance, people describe floating above themselves and viewing their bodies during astral projection. With astral travel an individual uses this conscious awareness to experience a sense of flying to new, non-physical or physical realms.

How the mind disconnects from its everyday type of **consciousness** and separates from the body remains a mystery. Experts agree that having a relaxed focus, such as in **meditation** or when you are just about to fall asleep, helps you to reach that state, as concentrating too hard on achieving the experience may interfere with the process.

See also **aura, bilocation, out-of-body experiences, lucid dreaming** and **near-death experiences.**

Astral projection/ Astral travel

The **astral body** is believed to be capable of a very special type of travel. While leaving the physical body at rest, it can get up, walk around and look at its physical body, explore its surroundings and journey to new places. What makes this experience unique is that you are fully conscious and in control throughout the experience.

Astrology

An ancient system of **divination** that uses the positions of the moon, stars and planets to interpret how their movements in relation to each other affect our lives. According to astrologers, celestial bodies exert forces and exhibit personalities that influence people and events on earth. These influences may be determined by mapping

Getting started on the astral traveller's path

Like any skill, astral travel takes time and practise, and it is difficult to prove what actually happens, but those experienced in astral travel tell fascinating stories of their experiences. Some travel to secret realms where they meet spirit guides and spend hours researching ancient texts. When they wake up, their clocks show that only a few minutes have passed. In all likelihood most of us won't be able to accomplish these feats. But here is an exercise that can help you get started on the astral traveller's path:

* *While relaxing, imagine your astral body positioned just in front or above you in the exact position of your physical body.*
* *Take note of how your astral body looks. Check out the back of your head and body and parts of your body you can't normally see.*
* *Allow your consciousness to move into your astral body and look at your surroundings from this new perspective.*
* *Ponder what you would like to do next and where you would like to go. You may want to visit a place or person who is normally far away, through a process called targeting. This can be done by focusing on the image of the location or the person's face, then seeing it at the end of a tunnel. Move forward through the tunnel until you arrive at the desired place or the intended person.*
* *When you are ready to return, think yourself back into your physical body, and move your body until you feel comfortable back in it.*

their positions in the sky at various points in time.

Astrology appears to be one of the most ancient of the surviving occult sciences, and evidence of highly sophisticated systems in Babylonian, Egyptian and Aztec cultures has survived. For centuries in the West, astrology was a revered method of divination supported by royal courts. **Nostradamus** used astrology to make predictions in the sixteenth century that are still being studied today. With the development of science in the seventeenth century, astrology was relegated to the realm of **superstition**, but it never fell completely out of favour. Today it is followed by celebrities and the rich and powerful as well as the general public.

Popular astrology is concerned with the reading of a **horoscope**, a chart of the positions of the planets, moon and stars at the moment of one's birth and interpreting the influence of the planets on human affairs. It is based on the belief that the movements of the celestial bodies affect human potential and other events on earth, such as the

True to your sign?

Aries: March 21–April 19

The symbol for this first sign of the Zodiac in Western astrology is the ram; the ruling planet is Mars. Aries is influenced by the **fire** element and assertive is a good way to describe people born under this sign. They tend to be enterprising, impulsive, warm hearted and confident free spirits who say what they mean and mean what they say, but they can also be impatient, rash, tactless, excitable and bossy.

Taurus: April 20–May 20

The symbol of Taurus is the bull and the ruling planet is Venus. Taureans are influenced by the **earth** element and a good word to describe them would be determined. Those born under the sign of Taurus are persistent, reliable, loyal and patient individuals with a discriminating taste for quality and the good things in life. The downside is that they can at times be lazy, materialistic and moody.

Gemini: May 21–June 20

The symbol for Gemini is the twins and the ruling planet is Mercury. Geminis are influenced by the **air** element with inquisitive being a good description of them. Those born under Gemini are intellectual and natural communicators but at times they can also be inconsistent and flighty. Their endearing zest for ideas and something new sometimes makes committing to anyone and anything problematic.

Cancer: June 21–July 22

The symbol for Cancer is the crab and the ruling planet is the moon. Cancerians are influenced by the **water** element, and sensitive would be a good word to describe their nature. Those born under Cancer tend to be emotional and empathetic with a good sense of humour, but they can at times be oversensitive and insecure.

Leo: July 23–August 22

The symbol for Leo is the lion and the ruling planet is the sun. Leo is influenced by the **fire** element and charismatic would be a good description of Leos. Those born under Leo tend to be courageous, vivacious, energetic and natural leaders but they can also be prone to arrogance and attention seeking.

Virgo: August 23–September 22

The symbol of Virgo is the virgin and the sign's ruling planet is Mercury. Virgos are influenced by the **earth** element, and a good word to describe them would be methodical. Those born under Virgo tend to be meticulous, disciplined and analytical. They can appear cool and reserved but great sensitivity tends to lie behind the detached exterior.

Libra: September 23—October 22

The symbol of Libra is the scales and the ruling planet is Venus. Libras are influenced by the **air** element with balance being a good word to describe them. Those born under Libra tend to be peace-loving, agreeable, harmonious people, but their natural ability to understand the viewpoint of everyone and fit in everywhere can be interpreted as insecurity and indecisiveness.

Scorpio: October 23—November 21

The symbol of Scorpio is the scorpion and the sign's ruling planets are Mars and Pluto. Scorpios are influenced by the **water** element and intense is a good word to describe them. Those born under Scorpio tend to be passionate, focused, sensitive and sensual, but they can also be secretive and destructive.

Sagittarius: November 22—December 21

The symbol for Sagittarius is the archer and Jupiter is the ruling planet. Sagittarians are influence by the **fire** element and open minded is a good description of them. Those born under Sagittarius tend to be unconventional, idealistic and visionary, with a need to seek spiritual enlightenment. They can also be reckless and ruthless.

Capricorn: December 22—January 19

The symbol of Capricorn is the goat and the ruling planet is Saturn. Capricorns are influenced by the **earth** element and steady is a good word to describe them. Those born under the sign of Capricorn are persistent, cautious, self-disciplined, warm-hearted and stable but they can also be mean and inflexible at times.

Aquarius: January 20—February 18

The symbol of Aquarius is the water carrier and the sign's ruling planets are Saturn and Uranus. Aquarius is influenced by the **air** element and a good word to define them would be independent. Those born under the sign of Aquarius tend to be idealistic, intellectual, generous, altruistic and unconventional, but they can also be unpredictable and emotionally detached.

Pisces: February 19—March 20

The symbol of Pisces is two fish and the ruling planets are Jupiter and Neptune. Pisceans are influenced by the **water** element, with imaginative being a good word to define them. Those born under Pisces tend to be intuitive, sensitive and spiritual, but they can also be dreamy, impractical and impressionable at times.

moon's influence on the oceans. From your horoscope your **zodiac** sign can be determined, and this allows an interpretation of what sort of person you are (or will be) as well as what is likely to happen in your future.

Over the years many elaborate systems have been developed to enable astrologers to predict the future through the movement of the planes. More than one system of astrology has developed. For example, Chinese astrology is based on signs, named after animals, which last a year rather than a month, as in Western astrology.

In popular Western astrology – the sort that appears in magazines and newspapers – the term 'horoscope' is based on the position of an individual's sun sign, or the portion of the zodiac that the sun was passing through when that individual was born. The sun travels through the 12 houses of the zodiac through the course of a year, and so when someone is said to have been born under Aries, he or she was born when the sun was passing through that portion of the zodiac named after the constellation Aries.

Each of the 12 signs has its own personality traits (see box), and the daily positions of the planets affect each sun sign. However, since this method of divination divides the population into 12 different categories many find it difficult to take astrology seriously for character analysis or predictions. That's why serious astrologers use more detailed horoscopes that chart the position of all the heavenly bodies, not just the sun, at the moment of birth.

Along with the signs and planets, planetary houses are the basic components of a birth chart. As previously mentioned the planets each have a meaning, as does the sign the sun was in at the time of your birth. The twelve divisions of the birth chart are called the astrological or planetary houses and indicate areas of life where the planetary energies become manifest.

The houses carry a theme based on the signs that are part of the natural order of the Zodiac, i.e. Aries equates with the first house, Taurus with the second, Gemini the third, Cancer the fourth, and so on. The planetary effects are interpreted not only in terms of the planets' positions in the zodiac (for instance, the moon in the sign of Cancer means something different from the moon in Aries) but also in terms of the angles that the planets describe in relation to one another. This branch of astrology is the study of planetary aspects.

When carried out using accurate birth information this planetary aspects approach creates an analysis unique to the individual concerned. For this reason it is taken more seriously by some academics and scientists, who believe that it can be useful for counselling and therapy. Psychiatrist **Carl Jung** began this process when he began to consult the horoscopes of his patients to search for insight. He believed that astrology sprang from the collective **unconscious** and that it was a symbolic language of inner psychological processes.

Sceptics argue that astrology's suggested link between planetary position and human destiny is unproven and perhaps even absurd. Several large-scale studies have shown no correlation whatsoever between personality characteristics and planetary positions. Despite this many people still believe that astrology can and does work, leading to the suggestion that it only works when there is an intuitive or psychic aspect involved in its interpretation. The astrologer uses the planetary positions as a rough starting point for the interpretation and thereafter intuition takes over.

Then, in the early 1970s, Professor Alan Smithers of Manchester University compiled data from the British population census showing clearly that architects tended to be born in the spring, secretaries in the summer, miners in the autumn and electricians in the winter. He also asked members of the British Astrological Association to indicate which signs were associated with the professions of nurse and trade union official. Without knowing what the BAA had predicted, Smithers conducted a massive survey of nurses and trade unionists and discovered that, just as the astrologers had indicated, there was a statistical bias of nurses being born under the signs of Taurus, Cancer, Virgo, Scorpio and Pisces, while trade union officials were born under one or other of the other six signs.

ATHENODORUS, THE HAUNTING OF

The story of Athenodorus may be the first written record of a **haunting**, and it dates back at least 2,000 years. The story was related by several ancient authors, the historian Tacitus among them, but the version below is by the Roman letter writer Pliny the Younger (AD 61–115). In it we see the classic chain-clanking **ghost**, the restless corpse and even the beckoning finger. The translation is that of William Melmoth (1746), slightly revised.

There was in Athens a house, spacious and open, but with an infamous reputation, as if filled with pestilence. For in the dead of night, a noise like the clashing of iron could be heard. And if one listened carefully, it sounded like the rattling of chains. At first the noise seemed to be at a distance, but then it would approach, nearer, nearer, nearer. Suddenly a phantom would appear, an old man, pale and emaciated, with a long beard, and hair that appeared driven by the wind. The fetters on his feet and hands rattled as he moved them.

Any dwellers in the house passed sleepless nights under the most dismal terrors imaginable. The nights without rest led them to a kind of madness, and as the horrors in their minds increased, onto a path toward death. Even in the daytime – when the phantom did not appear – the memory of the nightmare was so strong that it still passed before their eyes. The terror remained when the cause of it was gone.

Damned as uninhabitable, the house was at last deserted, left to the spectral monster. But in hope that some tenant might be found who was unaware of the malevolence within it, the house was posted for rent or sale. It happened that a philosopher named Athenodorus came to Athens at that time. Reading the posted bill, he discovered the dwelling's price. The extraordinary cheapness raised his suspicion, yet when he heard the whole story, he was not in the least put off. Indeed, he was eager to take the place. And did so immediately.

As evening drew near, Athenodorus had a couch prepared for him in the front section of the house. He asked for a light and his writing materials, then dismissed his retainers. To keep his mind from being distracted by vain terrors of imaginary noises and apparitions, he directed all his energy toward his writing.

For a time the night was silent. Then came the rattling of chains. Athenodorus neither lifted up his eyes nor laid down his pen. Instead he closed his ears by concentrating on his work. But the noise increased and advanced closer till it seemed to be at the door, and at last in the very chamber. Athenodorus looked round and saw the apparition exactly as it had been described to him. It stood before him, beckoning with one finger.

Athenodorus made a sign with his hand that the visitor should wait a little, and bent over his work. The ghost, however, shook the chains over the philosopher's head, beckoning as before. Athenodorus now took up his lamp and followed. The ghost moved slowly, as if held back by his chains. Once it reached the courtyard, it suddenly vanished.

Athenodorus, now deserted, carefully marked the spot with a handful of grass and leaves. The next day he asked the magistrate to have the spot dug up. There they found – intertwined with chains – the bones that were all that remained of a body that had long lain in the ground. Carefully, the skeletal relics were collected and given proper burial, at public expense. The tortured ancient was at rest. And the house in Athens was haunted no more.

ATLANTIS

The name of a vast island continent and the many civilizations that flourished upon it that sank under the sea in a cataclysm. At least fifty locations around the globe have been proposed as sites of the lost continent, but no proof has ever been found of its existence.

There are numerous legends about the Atlanteans and how their highly advanced civilization was destroyed by their misuse of power, but the story was first recorded by Plato in around 350 BC. Plato described the Atlanteans as a wealthy, successful, politically advanced and militarily powerful society that overran Europe with its armies before being defeated by the Greeks. Shortly afterwards an earthquake caused Atlantis to sink beneath the ocean.

The modern myth of Atlantis began in 1882 with the publication of *Atlantis: The Antediluvian World* by former American congressman Ignatius Donnelly. Donnelly proposed that Atlantis might be located in the middle of the Atlantic Ocean, to serve as a bridge and source of culture to other areas around the globe.

Numerous other theories have been put forth. The Atlanteans have been linked to the Titans of Greek mythology, the first race of beings on earth who came from the sea and possessed the power to create thunderbolts, earthquakes and terrestrial disturbances. **Madame Blavatsky**, mystic and co-founder of the Theosophical Society, believed that Atlantis was located in the North Atlantic Ocean and that the Atlanteans were psychically developed descendants from another legendary lost continent, **Lemuria**. The Lemurians migrated to Atlantis when their own continent was destroyed. In *The History of Atlantis* (1926), Lewis Spencer, who founded and edited *The Atlantis Quarterly*, a journal reporting on Atlantean and **occult** studies, concluded that Atlantis existed on both sides of the Atlantic and was the means of dissemination of culture from East to West.

American **medium Edgar Cayce** believed Atlantis was located at Bimini, one of the Bahama Islands off the coast of Florida. Cayce said that the Atlanteans had misused the forces of nature and destroyed their own continent and that in subsequent reincarnations Atlanteans exhibited the same potentially destructive traits.

Of all the world's unsolved mysteries, that of the lost continent of Atlantis is probably the biggest, exerting an influence over humankind for thousands of years. Even though centuries have passed, and scientists and scholars seem intent on banishing it to obscurity, interest in the fabled continent has not diminished and probably never will.

ATMOSPHERE

A term used by **psychics** to describe a feeling for the environment they are in or the people they meet. Walking into a house with an unhappy atmosphere may leave them with an unsettled feeling, whereas meeting someone who is genuinely kind and honest and friendly creates a positive feeling or atmosphere.

We all pick up information from the environment we are in and from any person we meet for the first time. On a visual level we are influenced by the way a person looks and dresses and by the colours, shapes and styles around us. Sounds and smells influence us too, even before we consciously decide if we like what we see. Operating alongside our other senses is a kinaesthetic awareness, which registers an emotional reaction to the atmosphere that exists in an environment or in a person. In some people this awareness is more developed than others, and for **clairsentients**, who can sense and respond to the atmospheres created by places and people, it is highly attuned, giving detailed information about the physical, emotional and energetic nature of people and places.

Few of us have not felt at some time that a place is spooky or unfriendly or that we feel irritable or afraid for no reason. When this happens we are psychically tuning in to an atmosphere, and a person who readily senses an atmosphere in a place usually has that same knack when summing up people.

Clairsentients who work with environmental energy believe that everything that happens within an environment affects the way it feels. For example, there is a discernable difference between the feeling of a room used by people who respect and love each other and the feeling of a room in which people have been in bitter competition. Practitioners of the art of **feng shui** know a great deal about the need to balance environmental energy, and in feng shui the placing of objects such as mirrors and ornaments can help to regulate energy that is out of balance and create a healthier, more harmonious atmosphere in which to live and work.

Some clairsentients may be able to channel a form of healing energy, which can harmonize the feeling of a room, or they may, like feng shui experts, suggest colours, shapes, objects or spiritual practices to help transform the feeling or atmosphere of an environment.

Aubrey, John [1626–1697]

One of the first known collectors of **ghost** stories, antiquarian and biographer John Aubrey's compilation, *Miscellanies*, was published in 1696 and is packed with eye-witness accounts of ghostly sightings gathered from all points of Great Britain. Aubrey's interest in the **supernatural** was reinforced by his own personal experiences. In *Miscellanies*, Aubrey writes about strange knocking sounds on the walls of his house a few days before his father died. 'Three or four days before my father died', he wrote, 'as I was in my bed about nine o'clock in the morning, perfectly awake, I did hear three distinct knocks over the bed's head, as if it had been with a ruler or ferula.' This mysterious incident, when combined with his interviews of others who had encountered ghosts, utterly convinced Aubrey that the spirit world existed.

Augury

A form of **divination** using the flight or song of birds. This was common practice in ancient Rome, where augurs foretold the future by observing and interpreting bird omens, which included noticing the type of bird seen as well as the direction of its flight and its singing. The Romans also used the term 'augur' to refer to divination by thunder and lightning, which was believed to be communication from the god Jupiter.

The term 'augury' also refers to the general art of divination, especially the interpretation of the future based on divinations and **omens**, mostly related to the appearance and behaviour of animals. These practices include:

- *Ailuromancy (cats).*
- *Alectromancy (chickens).*
- *Arachnomancy (spiders).*
- *Batrachomancy: (frogs).*
- *Entomancy (insects).*
- *Hippomancy (horses).*
- *Ichthyomancy (fish).*
- *Myomancy (mice).*
- *Ophiomancy (snakes).*
- *Zoomancy (any animal).*

A related practice was **Haruspicy**, or interpreting animal entrails.

Aumakua

A family of **guardian spirits** from Hawaiian mythology, the aumakua are worshipped to ensure the wellbeing of the family. The aumakua are thought to have laws that must be followed, and transgressions are sometimes punished for decades. Many believe it is of vital importance to be on good terms with your family's aumakua, or a **soul** may be abandoned before it reaches the land of the dead. Such abandoned souls haunt the living and remain in **limbo** until another aumakua takes pity on them and leads them to their new home.

Offspring of the aumakua can be born into families, and various legends tell of people born with **supernatural** powers, such as the ability to transform into animals.

According to lore the aumakua escort the souls of the dead to the **afterlife** in a ghostly procession, and if you have not rectified your sins against the aumakua before death, you have one chance to beg for pardon when the procession reaches its first stopping place. It is believed that the aumakua take the entire body to the next world, but if for any reason the body is not taken, the family must prepare the corpse for burial and its transformation into the aumakua form, which is that of a snake or shark.

Aura

The name given to a subtle envelope of vital energy that is thought to radiate round natural objects, including human beings, animals and plants. The colours and forms of each aura are believed to be characteristic of the person, animal or thing it surrounds and to fluctuate and shift according to mood and state of health.

The aura is normally invisible, but it can be seen by **clairvoyants** as a halo of light and colour. Two clairvoyants viewing the same aura might see different colours or interpret it in different ways. State of health and a person's emotions show up as differences in colours and energy patterns or breaks in an aura. Physical illness seems related to the part of the aura that is closest to the body, often called the **etheric body**. Some **psychics** see the aura as a psychic screen for the projection of information, past, present and future.

Although the body does have a magnetic field – a biofield – there is no scientific evidence that auras exist. However, the belief that the human body emits radiations of a kind that in certain circumstances becomes visible has been encountered for centuries, and was present in ancient Egypt, India, Greece and Rome. In the sixteenth century, discourses on the **astral body** and its 'fiery aura' abound, and in the eighteenth century the theory of animal magnetism was developed by **Anton Mesmer**, who promoted a variety of scientific experiments to try to identify the phenomenon.

Just before World War I, Dr Walter Kilner from St Thomas's Hospital in London developed a method to view auras, which he claimed appeared as a faint haze around the body, using an apparatus that rendered ultraviolet light visible. His theory of auric diagnosis of illness linked the appearance of an aura to a patient's health. Kilner's work was greeted with scepticism and interrupted by the outbreak of hostilities. In 1939, Semyon Davidovich Kirlian, a Russian electrician, developed a technique that he claimed recorded auras on film, but this technique remains to be verified. See **Kirlian photography**.

Auras, like parking places, are easy to find when you aren't looking for them. So if you want to see an aura, you need to feel as relaxed and calm as possible. Breathe slowly and deeply for a few minutes. Then, instead of looking directly at someone, look straight past them and casually glance in their direction, allowing your eyes to lose focus. The idea is to trick your rational brain by deliberately putting a lot of your concentration on something else, but to keep a vague focus on the person whose aura you want to read.

With practise you may see a dim haze of energy around someone. Keep breathing deeply, and the aura may brighten to a colour. Don't expect people to light up like Christmas trees and stay that way. Visions of auras tend to be lightning quick, but the more you practise the more natural it will feel and the more likely it is for colour to become noticeable. To find out what different auric colours could mean, see **Colour divination**.

AUTOMATIC WRITING

The most common form of **automatism**, automatic writing is writing that does not come from the conscious mind and is done in an **altered state of consciousness**. Some attribute it to spiritual beings who are somehow able to manipulate a writing utensil in order to communicate. Psychical researchers believe automatic writing emanates from material in the person's subconscious mind or is obtained through **ESP**.

Many people try automatic writing in an effort to make contact with spirits or to communicate with the dead. Typically the writer is unaware of what is being written and the writing is much faster, larger and expansive than their normal handwriting. Some people experience tingling in the arms or hands. Pens are a common tool, but slates and typewriters may also be used. Automatic writers have been known to produce mirror scripts, starting at the bottom right of the page and finishing at the top left. At the height of **spiritualism**, automatic writing was common in **séances**, and it replaced the much slower methods of spelling out messages from spirits with table **rappings** or pointers.

In some cases automatic writing occurs involuntarily, as in the case of Anna Windsor. In 1860 Windsor began automatic writing with her right hand, which she called Stump. Stump had a personality of its own, writing out verses and prose while the left hand did something else.

Through automatic writing, mediums have claimed to produce messages not just from deceased relatives or loved ones but from famous persons in history, such as

Exercise to practise automatic writing

Make sure you are in a calm and relaxed mood. If you feel stressed or anxious, leave it and try another day.

Find a good pen or pencil and a quiet place at a table. Sit there and let your hand move as it will. You may like to ask your hand if it has any messages for you. Hold your pen loosely in whichever hand you normally write with and let your mind roam freely. Write down whatever comes into your head for about five to ten minutes at the most.

If nothing happens, visualize a column of light made up of golden letters, forming and reforming words. Focus on one letter, and let the light flow down into your fingers and the pen. Wait until you feel your pen tremble, and let it move. At first it may scribble and make patterns, but words may follow. Don't try to read or make sense of them or you will lose the spontaneity.

When you feel you are losing concentration, stop. Lay your pen down and see the column of light fading. Read what you have written. It may seem to relate to you or to another person in your life, perhaps a persona that is deep within you. Don't be concerned if your first attempts appear nothing more than random scribbles or a jumble of disconnected words. It takes practise to establish a clear delivery of information.

Do something mundane or physical to bring you back to earth.

Francis Bacon, **Emanuel Swedenborg** and even Jesus Christ. **Frederick Myers**, one of the founders of the **Society for Psychical Research,** found little evidence that spirits communicated through automatic writing but, curiously, after his death several **mediums** claimed to receive automatic writing messages from him.

While psychical researchers continue to investigate automatic writing as evidence for the existence of the spirit world, the field of psychology has adopted automatic writing. Psychologists use it as a way for the unconscious mind to express thoughts and feelings that cannot be verbalized. Automatic writing continues to be used as a therapeutic tool to this day. Some critics warn of dangers in automatic writing – they claim that the writer is vulnerable to harassment from the evil-minded dead. However, psychologists maintain that the real danger is in exposing material from the unconscious that has been repressed.

AUTOMATISM

Automatism is divided into two categories: motor automatism and sensory automatism. Motor automatisms are **unconscious** movements of the muscles, which seem to be directed by **supernatural** guidance. The most common forms of motor automatism are **automatic writing** and automatic painting or **psychic art**, and other creative pursuits such as speaking, singing, composing and dancing. **Dowsing** is a type of motor automatism, an extrasensory guidance influenced by the movements of the rod held by a dowser. Other types of motor automatisms include impulsive behaviour, such as deciding to do or not do something at the last minute without knowing why, sudden inhibitions and sudden physical incapacities.

Sensory automatisms are thought to be produced by an inner voice or **vision** and can include **apparitions** of the living, inspirations, hallucinations and **dreams**. Hallucinations were once assumed to be caused by physical disorders, but **Edmund Gurney**, an early psychical researcher and a founder of the **Society for Psychical Research**, established that **paranormal** visions and sounds can occur without the presence of physical disorders.

After automatic writing and drawing, automatic music composition is perhaps the most common form of automatism. An unusual case was that of a London woman called Rosemary Brown, who, although she had limited musical ability, began in 1970 to compose music that she said was **channelled** to her from dead composers such as Chopin, Liszt and Beethoven. Recordings were made, and the works did indeed resemble the various styles of the composers, but critics declared them not as good as definitive compositions by these musical geniuses.

Problems associated with automatisms include compulsion, obsession and a feeling of **possession**. The practice may grow until a person feels taken over by it. Some people talk of possession by **demons**, but psychologists say that the effects are created by paranoia, not demons.

Since ancient times, inspired activity has always been attributed to the divine, the supernatural or the spirits, but today's view is that automatisms are products of **ESP** or secondary personalities who produce knowledge or information that has been repressed or forgotten.

AVALON

According to Celtic legend, a mystical land of immortal heroes where the enchanted sword Excalibur was forged and where a mortally wounded King Arthur was taken after a bloody battle.

The story of King Arthur may be based on a historical figure of a Celtic king of the sixth century, who defended his kingdom against Saxon invaders, but it is the legends of King Arthur that have had a timeless, mystical hold over people's imagination for centuries. According to legend Arthur came to power when he pulled a magical sword from a stone with the help of the wizard **Merlin**, an act that proclaimed his royal heritage. He started the Order of the Round Table, peopled by noble and virtuous knights, and married the beautiful but adulterous Guinevere who betrayed him for his best friend Lancelot. Arthur was mortally wounded by his treacherous nephew, Mordred, and is said to be buried on the mythical Isle of Avalon, from where he will rise again in Britain's hour of need.

There is a tradition that **Glastonbury** was the Isle of Avalon. In 1191 the monks of Glastonbury unearthed, from 16 feet under the ground, an oak coffin that they said was Arthur's. They showed an inscription: 'Here lies beneath the renowned King Arthur with his beloved Queen Guinevere his second wife in the Isle of Avalon' on a lead cross, which they said had been found in the coffin.

With its miraculous weapon of destiny, its goddess-like Lady of the Lake appearing by moonlight from the water and, most of all, the mysterious realm of Avalon, where Arthur journeys by water to be healed from death, the Arthurian world shimmers with a Celtic supernatural glow. Like a faraway, half-heard song, Avalon conveys a sense of something lost forever, never to be found – the mystical quest for the lost land, the lost world, the lost self and lost psychic powers.

AVATAR

Derived from the Sanskrit word *avatora*, which means 'descent', avatar is used in Hinduism to denote a god who has descended, by way of incarnation, to either human or animal form, coming into this world for the duration of one lifespan. An avatar is believed to be a mediator between people and the divine.

An avatar is similar to the Christian figure of an incarnated being but is different in two ways. First, a Hindu god can become incarnate in many places at the same time through partial avatars (*amshas*); second, the avatars do not fully participate in human activity or lose the knowledge and power of their divinity.

Exceptional holy men and women in India are called avatars. Hindus accept Gautama, Buddha, as an avatar. Vishnu, sky god and protector of the universe, is most famous for his numerous avatars, which include Krishna and Rama, but other gods, such as Shiva, also have avatars. Many charismatic leaders, such as the Indian mystic Chaitanya (c.1486–1533), have been regarded as avatars. In our own time, Ammachi – Mata Amritanandamayi – the South Indian woman who was given the Gandhi-King award at the United Nations in Geneva in 2002 for her promotion of non-violence, and who greets her long lines of followers by giving each person a warm hug, is considered an avatar of the Great Mother.

The *bhakti* (devotional) movements of Hinduism have often centred round avatars who are supposed to possess psychic abilities and **paranormal** powers, such as the ability to **levitate** or **bilocate**.

AVEBURY

A village in Wiltshire, England, eighty miles west of London, and site of the Avebury stone circle, one of the oldest prehistoric monuments in Britain. More extensive than **Stonehenge**, Avebury is large enough that it is said more than a quarter of a million people could stand within the boundaries of its circle. The circle was in active use in later Neolithic/early Bronze Age times, between 2600 BC and 1600 BC, so it pre-dates the **Druids**.

The Avebury circle was probably constructed by people from the Beaker culture. It is the largest stone circle in Europe; its 100 standing stones, reaching up to 14 feet high, mark a circle that is 1,100 feet in diameter. Another nearby landmark, Windmill Hill, bears an earthwork on top and may pre-date Avebury as a cattle market or ritual site. The purpose of Silbury Hill, yet another nearby landmark and Europe's tallest man-made mound, remains unknown.

No records survive attesting to the original purpose and uses of the Avebury stone circle, and excavations have yielded few insights. According to theories Avebury may have been used for religious festivals to honour the Goddess, or it may have had astronomical purposes, as the stones align to the May Day sunrise. It is believed by some that the Avebury stones are repositories of Earth and psychic energy, which can be detected by **clairvoyance** and **dowsing** and that tapping the stones can enable communication with other **megalithic** sites. Such psychic energy may be responsible for **paranormal** phenomena that have long been reported at this site, including strange lights drifting on the ground and eerie small figures and **apparitions** flitting around the stones. In the 1980s Avebury became a major site of mysterious **crop circles**, geometric patterns made in arable fields that defy explanation.

AXINOMANCY

A term derived from the Greek *axine* (axe) and *manteia* (divination) and applied to the art and practice of **divination** by an axe, hatchet or saw.

An obscure form of axinomancy recorded among ancient Greeks is that of placing an agate stone on a red-hot axe. Its motion is taken to indicate the identity of someone guilty of a crime. Another method is of reading the direction an axe, saw or hatchet handle quivers or points when driven into a tree or post. Yet another method involves observing the way an axe falls to the ground. This method is usually used by diviners to determine the direction a thief has taken, or the location of buried treasure.

AYURVEDIC MEDICINE

A traditional Indian approach to healing that includes **meditation**, purification procedures, rejuvenation therapies, herbal and mineral preparations, exercises and dietary advice. Ayurveda is a **holistic** medical system that claims wellbeing is only possible through a balance in the flow of life energy (*prana*) between body, mind and soul.

Ayurvedic medicine is the national health system of India and has been found to be extremely beneficial for many medical conditions, in particular chronic ailments and conditions associated with unhealthy lifestyles. To qualify as an ayurvedic physician candidates must complete a five-year training course and are strictly regulated by professional and governmental bodies.

Ayurveda's basic theory states that the body's functions are regulated by three 'physiological principles' called *doshas*, whose Sanskrit names are *vata*, *pitta* and *kapha*. Like astrological signs, these terms are used to designate individuals as well as traits and body types that typify them, and imbalances of the *doshas* are said to be the underlying cause of all disease. Ayurvedic treatment with diet, meditation and other therapies supposedly corrects these imbalances. Leading promoters claim that positive thoughts lead to healing but sad, angry and hostile thoughts depress the immune system and increase the risk of poor health. The aim is to harness **consciousness** as a healing force.

See **Behavioural medicine**.

B

Ba

In ancient Egyptian mythology the Ba is what we would call '**soul**', but there are differences. According to the **Book of the Dead**, after death the Ba rises up out of the body in the shape of a falcon, with a human head, that can fly between the tomb and the **underworld**. It was also believed that the Ba could take on any form it chose but that it had to reunite itself with the deceased every night in order for the deceased person to live forever. So the Ba remains very much attached to the physical body, contrary to the concept of the soul or **spirit** separating from the body at death. It was thought that the Ba had the same physical needs as the person, like food and water, so offerings of cake and water were left at tombs for the Ba.

Bachelor's Grove Cemetery

A small, abandoned cemetery that is overgrown, unkempt and subject to vandalism, Bachelor's Grove Cemetery is one of Chicago's most haunted sites. It is located on the edge of the Rubio Woods Forest Preserve, near the suburb of Midlothian, Illinois. There have been over a hundred **paranormal** incidents reported here, including inexplicable lights and voices, **apparitions**, strange photos, anomalous recordings and even sightings of magical creatures.

The first burial took place in 1844, but it wasn't until 1864 that the cemetery became known as Bachelor's Grove. This may have been because around this time a group of German immigrants, hired to help build the Illinois–Michigan Canal, settled on small farms nearby, and most of these settlers were unmarried men. Burials became less frequent in the 1960s, and the last recorded burial was in 1989.

It was in the 1960s that stories of **hauntings** began. Unfortunately, this was also when the vandalism and desecration began, and today the cemetery is in a terrible condition. Vandals have left few of the graves still standing, and many tombstones have been stolen or dumped elsewhere, giving rise to legends that the gravestones sometimes move by themselves.

The reporting of strange phenomena peaked in the 1970s and 1980s, but hauntings continue to be reported to this day, including flashing lights and **phantom** vehicles. The strange lights are said to be red or blue in colour, dancing just out of reach of those who chase them, as if the lights had an intelligence of their own. Phantom cars appear and disappear on the cemetery path. One couple even had a car crash with a vehicle that vanished before their eyes, leaving their own untouched despite the sounds of bending metal and breaking glass.

The most-often reported apparition at Bachelor's Grove is a vanishing house or floating house. Access to the cemetery is gained by way of a narrow gravel trail that was once a main road through the area. Along this trail, many visitors have reported seeing a phantom farmhouse that seems to appear and disappear at random. The house is always seen from a distance and described in the same way, as a white house with porch pillars, a swing and a soft light burning in the window, but it is never reported in the same place. As witnesses approach the house, it shrinks and disappears. According to legend, anyone who succeeds in entering the house will never return.

Just past the fence surrounding the cemetery is a small lagoon that borders the nearby turnpike road. This pond was a favourite corpse dumping ground for Chicago gangsters during the years of Prohibition, so it isn't surprising that the pond is thought to be haunted. One ghost linked to the lagoon is said to be a two-headed man, reported on many occasions. Others report seeing a ghostly farmer who was pulled into the water by his plough and horse in the 1870s. The horse was drowned by the weight of the plough, taking the farmer with it.

Still others report seeing people dressed in monks' robes, and in 1984 the vision of a glowing yellow man was reported. In the 1990s several people reported seeing a large black dog near the entrance, which would vanish as people appeared, perhaps as a warning to go no further. The most famous ghost is the 'White Lady' or the 'Madonna of Bachelor's Grove', who has been seen on nights of the full moon, wandering the cemetery with a baby in her arms. She is said to be the ghost of a woman buried there, next to her young son.

Paranormal investigators have reported **electronic voice phenomena** at Bachelor's Grove, with the names of those buried there being called out repeatedly. There have been many attempts to capture Bachelor's Grove phenomena on film, and plenty of photographs exist with images resembling **ectoplasm**. Perhaps the most famous photograph of Bachelor's Grove was taken in 1991 by Mari Huff, a member of the **Ghost Research Society**. It shows a waif-like transparent young woman dressed in old-fashioned clothes sitting on a crumbling tombstone. According to Huff, this woman was not visible when the picture was taken. Sceptics argue that the photo is a double exposure, but a number of professional photographers do believe it to be genuine.

BAKECHOCHIN

Translated as 'haunted lantern', in Japanese folklore a bakechochin is a lantern inhabited by **ghosts**. According to lore the lantern has a long tongue and wild eyes and is home for the ghosts of people who died with hate in their hearts; for this reason, they are doomed to haunt the earth for all time. If someone should light one of these haunted lanterns, it is thought that a hateful ghost may leap out of it and attack.

BALANCE

Achieving the harmonious interaction of light and dark, masculine and feminine, **Yin** and **Yang**, and creative and receptive energies in mind, body and emotions is an integral part of **meditation**, dreamwork, **psychic** development or any creative work on personal growth.

Many situations in life can prevent balance in mind, body and emotions. You may be thrown off balance by the people around you, by your environment, by feelings of fear or anger or by psychic information you receive. It is easy to be overwhelmed by these stimuli, both external and internal, and psychics believe that one of the most important aspects of psychic growth is the ability to keep oneself balanced, to stay rooted within yourself whatever is going on around or inside you.

Visualizing a golden light or bubble around you to protect yourself from distraction, self-doubt or misfortune is a technique often used by psychics to encourage inner balance, as is reconnecting with the earth after psychic work by going for a walk or taking a drink of water to ground yourself again in everyday reality.

BALLECHIN HOUSE

Hauntings at Ballechin House in Tayside, Scotland, came to public attention in the late 1890s, but they had been reported there for several decades before.

In 1806 Ballechin House was built by the Stuart family, and in 1834 Robert Stuart inherited the house from his father and rented it out to tenants while he was posted to India with the army. He returned in 1850 after achieving the rank of Major.

From his years in India, the Major had come to believe in **reincarnation** and **transmigration**, the ability of the **soul** to inhabit a non-human body. He vowed that when he died he would return to Ballechin in the body of his favourite black spaniel – he preferred the company of dogs to humans. Although he never married, he did enjoy the company of a young housekeeper called Sarah, who died mysteriously – it was said in his bed – at the age of 27, in 1873. Major Stuart died a few years later and was buried beside her at Logierait churchyard.

In his 1853 will the Major left Ballechin House to his nephew, John Stuart, who, fearful that the Major might be reincarnated as one of his dogs, cruelly shot all the Major's hounds, starting with the black spaniel. This later would lead to the theory that the Major was forced to remain a **disembodied spirit**, haunting the house in protest. John Stuart was a devout Roman Catholic; his aunt, the Major's sister Isabella, had become a nun and, after her death in 1880, was said to make ghostly appearances to visitors.

Almost immediately after the Major's death in 1876 strange happenings were reported. One day in the Major's study, Mrs Stuart noticed a strong smell of dogs in the room. She opened the window to let some air in and felt a nudge on her leg, as if an invisible dog had rubbed itself against her. This was followed a few days later by knocking sounds and the sound of gunfire and voices quarrelling. There were also sounds of someone limping around the master bedroom. Soon Ballechin House got a reputation for being haunted, and governesses and servants would flee the house in fear.

The Stuarts managed to live in the house for more than twenty years, but the children were so frightened that John Stuart was forced to build a new wing for the children to live in outside the haunted area. A Jesuit priest and family friend, Father Hayden, who often stayed at Ballechin, heard the haunted sounds, including screams, on many occasions. In January 1895, John Stuart was in the Major's old study talking to his agent when three loud knocks were heard. This may have been an **omen** because a few hours later John Stuart died in London after being run over by a cab.

After John's death the house was rented to a family for a year, but they left after a few weeks complaining of being terrorized by **poltergeist** activity, such as thumps and bumps, strange noises, **apparitions** and unseen hands moving objects.

In 1896 the Marquis of Bute, an avid ghost researcher, rented Ballechin House and asked two psychic researchers to help him carry out investigations. Almost immediately after moving in the researchers reported hearing loud clanging noises, muffled voices and gunfire.

Other guests invited to stay at the house reported supernatural activity. Several of the group conducted sessions with a **Ouija board**. During one session a person with the name of Ishbel came through and asked the investigators to go to a nearby pond. On doing so, the investigators clearly saw the figure of a nun, thought to be the Major's sister, Isabella, wearing a black habit and walking through a snowy wood before suddenly vanishing.

From 1932 the house remained empty, and it was demolished in the 1960s. An account of the investigations that took place there at the turn of the century was published in 1899 with the title *The Alleged Haunting of B House.* The Stuart family disliked publicity so much that they asked for all names to be changed or excluded from the story. As a result the hauntings had to be reported as alleged and could never be credited as genuine.

BALTIMORE POLTERGEIST

Between 14 January and 8 February 1960, alleged **poltergeist** activity caused havoc in the Baltimore household of a couple called Jones, their daughter and son-in-law, and their 17-year-old grandson, Ted Pauls.

The first incident occurred on 14 January when the family sat down for dinner. A miniature pottery pitcher, one of Mrs Jones's favourite pieces in her china collection, inexplicably exploded, showering Mr Jones with tiny pieces of china. Upset by the loss, Mrs Jones immediately went into the kitchen for a dustpan and brush, but before she reached the kitchen another pitcher shattered, followed by another and another and another, until fifteen of her precious ornaments had been shattered. The Jones family jumped away from the table in fear and panic.

In the month of misery that followed, objects flew off shelves and crashed through windows, pictures fell from the wall, plants leapt out of their holders, a sugar bowl floated up to the overhead ceiling light and dumped its contents all over the table, chairs and tables moved about and overturned, soda bottles exploded, books tumbled over and a brass incense holder was seen flying across a room. When the dining room light began to swing about violently during meal-times the Joneses took to eating in their bedrooms, but this did not stop knives and forks vanishing from beside their plates.

Surprisingly, the only injury to occur was on the night of 17 January, when Mr Jones tried to pick up a can of corn that had fallen off a shelf and a tin of sauerkraut smacked him on the back of the head. There was an occasional day of respite, but more often than not the family spent their time running from room to room to tidy up and repair the damage. Then suddenly, on 9 February the incidents stopped as myste-riously as they had begun.

Not surprisingly, word spread during the month of terror, and reporters and investigators were regular visitors to the house. Several theories were put forward. Some thought Ted was playing tricks on his family, but this was denied by his par-ents. Others suggested radio signals, sound waves and earth tremors, but no proof was found. The police could find no evidence of explosives. A local plumber suggested that the hot air furnace might be the culprit. He urged the family to equalize pressure by opening the dining room windows. The Joneses followed his instructions, and the incidents stopped, causing the family to credit the plumber with solving the mystery.

Before the phenomena ceased, however, the respected psychoanalyst and researcher of **paranormal** phenomena **Nandor Fodor** suggested that poltergeists were not 'ghosts' but were bundles of 'projected repressions' that quickly wore themselves out.

Fodor theorized that so-called polter-geist activity was usually associated with a teenaged member of the family. When he investigated the case, he concentrated on Ted Pauls, the 17-year-old grandson. According to Fodor, Ted was a shy but tal-ented and intelligent boy who was uncon-sciously using his mental power to create the disturbances. Fodor believed that the human body and mind could release energy 'similar to atomic bombardments', and could project this force into objects such as soda bottles, which would then burst from within.

Fodor thought that Ted felt misunder-stood and longed to be esteemed for his writing talent. He theorized that Ted was unconsciously venting his frustrations by projecting them into aggressive poltergeist activity. Fodor explained this to Ted and suggested that if a way could be found to help him feel appreciated and valued as a person, he would have no need to express himself in such a destructive way. Fodor then took a risk by announcing that Ted was a gifted writer and that if his talent could be recognized the poltergeist activity would stop. He suggested that Ted should write his own account of what had hap-pened, and, as expected, this had a thera-peutic effect on Ted. His family gave Ted a newfound respect, and his self-esteem was boosted. Although a few more incidents happened (the psychological working-out process, as Fodor explained), they gradually stopped.

The Joneses, however, remained convinced that the plumber had solved the mystery.

BANSHEE

In the words of the Irish playwright and poet, and expert in Irish folklore, **William Butler Yeats**:

The banshee (from *ban* [*bean*], a woman, and *shee* [*sidhe*, a fairie]) is an attendant fairy that follows the old families, and none but them, and wails before a death. Many have seen her as she goes wailing and clapping her hands. The keen (*caoine*), the funeral cry of the peasantry, is said to be an imitation of her cry. When more than one banshee is present, and they wail and sing in chorus, it is for the death of some holy or great one. An omen that sometimes accompanies the banshee is the *coach-a-bower* (*cóiste-bodhar*) – an immense black coach, mounted by a coffin, and drawn by headless horses driven by a *Dullahan*. It will go rumbling to your door, and if you open it ... a basin of blood will be thrown in your face. These headless phantoms are found elsewhere than in Ireland. In 1807 two of the sentries stationed outside St. James's Park died of fright. A headless woman, the upper part of her body naked, used to pass at midnight and scale the railings. After a time the sentries were stationed no longer at the haunted spot. In Norway the heads of corpses were cut off to make their ghosts feeble. Thus came into existence the *Dullahans*, perhaps; unless, indeed, they are descended from that Irish giant who swam across the Channel with his head in his teeth. (From *A Treasury of Irish Myth, Legend, and Folklore*, ed. W B Yeats.)

In Irish and Scottish folklore the banshee is believed to be a **death omen** who attaches herself to families, usually those whose surnames begin with *Mac*. Thought to be the spirit of a young woman who died in childbirth, she strikes terror into the hearts of those who encounter her as she only manifests when there is to be a death in the family.

There are variations in the way she appears. According to Irish lore the banshee is known as *Bean Si* and is a beautiful young woman with long, flowing hair, wearing a grey cloak over a white, red or green dress. Her eyes are always red and sore from crying. In both Scottish and Irish lore she is also known as *Bean Nighe* or 'little washer by the ford'. The *Bean Nighe* is thought to signal an imminent death by washing bloodstained clothes in a stream but, unlike the *Bean Si*, who is beautiful, the *Bean Nighe* is evil and ugly, with just one nostril, buck teeth, pendulous breasts and red webbed feet.

A few banshee stories entered into American folklore with the arrival of immigrants. One of them comes from the American South, where a crying banshee with long flowing yellow hair is thought to haunt the Tar River in Edgecomb County, North Carolina.

Barrett, Sir William Fletcher [1844–1925]

A professor of physics at the Royal College of Science in Dublin, Sir William Barrett was one of the founders of both the **Society for Psychical Research** and the **American Society for Psychical Research**. His published works included *On the Threshold of the Unseen* (1917) and *Psychical Research* (1920).

Barrett was fascinated by all things **paranormal**, and along with investigating **ghosts** and **hauntings** and **ESP** he also explored subjects such as **altered states of consciousness** induced through hypnotism and hallucination phenomena. Barrett's study on **apparitions** remains a classic read for students of the paranormal.

Battle Abbey

Battle Abbey was constructed by William the Conqueror on the site of his triumph over King Harold at the Battle of Hastings in 1066. Legend has it that a mysterious fountain of blood appears after rain on the ground, representing the Christian blood that was spilled there, although sceptics argue that the presence of iron in the soil accounts for reddish puddles of water.

A **phantom** is also thought to haunt Battle Abbey. Some believe it to be the Duchess of Cleveland, who lived at the abbey for a time. Others believe it to be the **ghost** of a monk who cursed Sir Anthony Brown for taking church property, after Sir Anthony

was given Battle Abbey by Henry VIII in 1538. In 1932, two men holding a vigil in the crypt reported hearing strange noises in the room above, even though it was paved with asphalt, and a man's voice singing 'Gloria in excelsis'.

Battlefield hauntings

Places identified with violence, trauma and intense emotion are typically thought to be subject to **hauntings**. There are few places more violent and traumatic than battlefields, and it isn't surprising that many battlefield locations have hauntings associated with them. It is thought that most battlefield hauntings are **residual hauntings**, in which fragments of the battle are imprinted upon the **psychic** space of a place and picked up by sensitive individuals. Other hauntings are from **spirits** who can't find peace due to the violent and abrupt nature of their deaths. Those who specialize in **spirit releasement** try to find ways to help these confused and traumatized **souls** move on. Some believe **retrocognition** is also an element in battlefield hauntings. Re-enactors, people who recreate battle scenes in history, often report hauntings during their recreations.

In the USA there are numerous haunted battlefields from the American Civil War (1861–1865) and other violent struggles in American history. For example, **Antietam** and the Old Baylor's Massacre site in River Vale, New Jersey, where members of the local militia (known as Baylor's Dragoons) were brutally slaughtered by German Hessians in 1778, abound with reports of hauntings and strange happenings. In the UK both medieval warrior phantoms and ghostly soldiers from the English Civil War have been reported, and numerous battlefields from the world wars have ghost stories linked to them.

One of the most well-known cases in World War I actually occurred in the midst of the conflict itself. The so-called Angels of Mons were thought to have saved retreating French and British soldiers during the battle of Mons, Belgium. According to reports of survivors, the retreating soldiers saw **phantom** figures on horseback preventing the Germans from slaughtering them all, but sceptics argue that they may have had **visions** due to intense stress, fear and pain. In World War II, one-seventh of Britain's casualties came from losses due to bombing raids, and not surprisingly countless hauntings and phantom sounds of aeroplanes and sirens have been reported where bomber pilots made their runs.

Paranormal investigators who believe that hauntings can be caused by the **consciousness** of the living often use battlefield hauntings to support their case. They argue that the anguish war causes imprints itself on a nation's collective memory, and that phantoms are a way of keeping the memory of such a tragic and vast loss of life alive.

BEALINGS HOUSE BELL RINGER

Between February and March 1834, Bealings House, a Georgian house at Great Bealings, Suffolk was the scene of mysterious bell ringing, where the pulley bells in various rooms used to summon servants began to jingle without anyone pulling them. Major Edward Moore, a retired officer from the Indian Army, the owner of the house at the time, was fascinated and recorded the phenomena later; thanks to him we have a day-by-day record of what happened.

On Sunday, 2 February 1834, Major Moore came home from church and was told that between 2 and 5 pm the dining room bell had been rung. The following day the same bell rang three times, the last time being just before five o'clock in the evening, and was heard for the first time by Major Moore personally. The next day the Major was out, and when he returned he was told the same thing had happened. There were a total of nine bells in the kitchen, and the Major discovered that the right-hand five bells, connected with the dining room, drawing room, a first-floor bedroom and two rooms in the attic, were the ones doing most of the ringing.

On 5 February at 11 am the bells were heard ringing again while the Major was in the breakfast room with his son and grandson. Immediately he went to the kitchen and saw the same five bells ringing. A few minutes later they started to ring again; one of the bells rang so violently that it almost touched the ceiling.

From that time onwards the bells rang many times, and the Major and his servants became convinced that no living person was responsible, as they always seemed to ring when there was no one in the rooms concerned. During the time that the bells were ringing, Major Moore was careful to ensure that this wasn't the work of a prankster. On numerous occasions the bells rang when all the members of the household were in the kitchen and the rest of the house was empty.

The phenomena lasted until 27 March when the ringing stopped as mysteriously as it had started. Then, in July 1836, the bells started ringing again. This time a bell-hanger was sent for. He examined all the wires but could not find any rational explanation. After about an hour the ringing stopped and was never heard again, except when the bells were being used by a member of the family.

The mystery was never solved, and Moore and his family concluded that **paranormal** activity must have occurred. Despite the most vigorous investigation, there has never been any explanation for the mysterious bell ringing at Bealings House.

Beans

Beans have a long tradition of association with **ghosts** and the dead. American Indian traditions include elaborate rituals and dances involving beans. Ancient Greeks believed beans were associated with the **souls** of the dead, and the ancient Romans considered beans to be sacred and used them in rituals connected with the dead. They threw beans behind their backs as food offerings for ghosts, and they also spat beans at ghosts as a protection against them.

The connection of the bean to the realm of ghosts seems to be that it grows in a spiral and that its white flowers are symbolic of the purity of the bleached bones of death. Because breath is the evidence of life, as bizarre as it may seem to us today, the eating of beans and the flatulence it causes were thought by ancient Romans to be proof that the living souls of the dead resided inside the lowly bean.

Behavioural medicine

Behavioural medicine is an approach to healing that acknowledges the effects of behaviour on health, and takes into account not just the interaction between a human and the environment but the interaction between body, mind and spirit.

Non-Western healing systems, such as **traditional Chinese medicine** and **Ayurvedic medicine**, for centuries have based their approach on the interaction between mind and body but it wasn't until the 1960s that Western medicine began to acknowledge that mind and body may not be as separate as it had previously been thought. Psychiatrist George Solomon observed that feeling unhappy and depressed increased arthritis symptoms, and in his experiments he found that rats put under stress died more quickly than those who were not. But the real breakthrough came in the 1970s with psychoanalyst Robert Ader, who suspected from experiments with rats that the nervous system played a part in a body's immune system. He coined the term 'psychoneuroimmunology' (PNI). Later research confirmed that the nervous system does indeed produce reactions that influence brain function and that there is a collaboration between the mind, the brain and the immune system.

PNI suggests that emotions have a part to play in physical health, and over the years research has shown that **relaxation** and positive thinking techniques can produce changes in wellbeing and can be used in the treatment of illness. Relaxation, **visualization** and **imagery** have been used with success to treat a whole range of conditions, from headaches and indigestion to serious conditions such as depression, heart disease and cancer. Studies also show that unhappy feelings, in particular suppressed anger, fear and guilt, low self-esteem and a lack of loving relationships, can also increase a person's chances of developing heart disease, cancer and infertility.

Many medical experts now acknowledge the important role relaxation, loving relationships and positive outlook play in mental and physical health and wellbeing. **Psychic healers** have always used the power of the mind to heal physical and emotional problems, believing that if people feel better mentally and emotionally they will improve physically.

BELL WITCH

The Bell Witch is one of the most unsavoury **poltergeist** cases on record, even though it has since been described as perhaps the 'greatest American ghost story'. According to legend, it caused the death of a man.

The haunting took place in Robertson, Tennessee, in 1817 and intrigued many people, including future US President General Andrew Jackson. There are several versions of the story so it is hard to know what is fact and what is fiction, but the version generally relied upon is that based on the diary of Richard William Bell, one of the Bells' sons.

John and Lucy Bell lived with their nine children on a farm. The phenomena started with noises and scraping and progressed to clothes being pulled off and furniture and stones being thrown about. Two of the children, Elizabeth and Richard, had their hair pulled one night, and Elizabeth was slapped and punched and pinched. Under investigation by the family and a neighbour, James Johnson, the poltergeist stepped up its activity, tormenting the family, especially Elizabeth, even more. Elizabeth was sent to stay with a neighbour, and the disturbances went with her, indicating that she was the focus of the activity.

The strange events continued over the next few years. Later activity included strange lights outside the house, stones thrown at Elizabeth's brothers and sisters and visitors receiving slaps similar to Elizabeth's. The entity also began to speak using foul language. According to reports a voice would appear from nowhere and with no identifiable source. The voice claimed to be various different people but eventually settled on the name of Kate Bates, a woman who had been dissatisfied with business dealings with the Bells. From then on the voice was called Kate.

Johnson advised forming a committee to investigate, and with that the Bell family became the object of much curiosity: General Jackson even paid a visit with a 'witch layer', a professional exorcist. According to legend, just outside Bell Lane their carriage got stuck. Kate's voice could be heard promising to appear that night, and the carriage became unstuck. Later in the evening the witch layer tried to shoot Kate with a silver bullet but was slapped and chased out of the house.

On one occasion it was said Elizabeth was given an emetic to make her sick, and she threw up brass pins and needles. The poltergeist, who had a sick sense of humour, suggested that if she did it again Elizabeth would have enough to set up a shop.

Elizabeth's father, John Bell, began to suffer from repeated bouts of illness, and Kate claimed she was the cause. He couldn't eat, his tongue was swollen and Kate declared that she would torment him for the rest of his life. Unfortunately, this is exactly what she did. Finally the ordeals and cursing wore John down, and on the morning of 19 December 1820, he fell into a stupor, dying a day later. A bottle was found in the medicine cabinet, and when the contents were given to an animal the animal died. Kate declared with delight in her voice that she had poisoned John with the liquid while he was asleep.

After John Bell's death the poltergeist activity diminished. Some time later Elizabeth got engaged to a Joshua Gardener, who apparently did not meet the poltergeist's approval. The entity told Elizabeth not to marry Joshua and the couple could not go anywhere without the entity following them and persistently taunting them. In 1821 their patience finally snapped and they broke off their engagement.

Elizabeth eventually married a man called Dick Powell, and Kate finally disappeared with the words 'I will be gone for seven years'. John's widow, Lucy Bell, and two of her sons who stayed at the farmhouse, did hear manifestations seven years later, but they kept quiet about it this time and the torment stopped after two weeks. Apparently the poltergeist promised to return in 1935 but failed to do so, or wasn't noticed by anybody.

The Bells never understood why they were 'attacked' in this way, and Kate Bates never made any statements. The most commonly accepted theory is that the poltergeist activity focused on Elizabeth, who was the right age, around puberty, for sexual guilt and tension. It has been suggested that there was some kind of incestuous relationship between Elizabeth and her father, which would have distressed the young girl. This theory, however, does not account for poltergeist activity that took place when she was not around, such as that with General Jackson.

The legend of the Bell Witch continues to haunt the Bell farm to this day. Thankfully, the violent and terrible manifestations are a thing of the past, but she is believed to haunt a cave, called the Bell

Witch Cave, where unearthly screams, knocks and noises have been reported.

BENTHAM, JEREMY [1748–1832]

The bizarre sight of the body of Jeremy Bentham, law reformer, scientist and philosopher, can be seen to this day mounted on display in University College London. Bentham was fascinated by mummification and believed that corpses, put on permanent display as memorials to the dead, or 'auto icons' as he called them, would become commonplace items in the houses of family and friends.

Prior to his death Bentham gave detailed instructions in his will about how his body should be preserved. He requested that his body be dissected, his bones be wired in a sitting position and his mummified corpse be dressed in his favourite black suit and straw hat, with his hand on his favourite walking stick, 'Dapple'. Bentham's preserved form is on display today in a case with glass sides. Apparently the mummification of his head was not successful, so it was removed and replaced by a wax head modelled in his likeness.

Over the years there have been various sightings of Bentham's **ghost** walking the university corridors, tapping the floor with his cane or cradling his head in his arms.

BERMUDA TRIANGLE

Reports indicate that dozens of ships, twenty or so aeroplanes and a thousand people have mysteriously vanished in this restricted wedge of the ocean just east of Florida in the United States. The ocean region was named the Bermuda Triangle in 1945, after six airforce planes and their crews disappeared on a calm day in good flying conditions.

Although accidents and mysterious disappearances are to be expected at sea, the ones in this area are unusual because they often occur in good weather and no traces of wreckage or survivors are found. Just before disappearing, crews often report that nothing is amiss, and in rare instances ships have been found days later with their entire crews missing. The area is policed by the US government, but despite this the number of disappearances far exceeds the law of chance for such a relatively small area. This had led many investigators to believe that the 'vanishments' in this area are caused by some sort of **paranormal** force.

The mysterious history of the Bermuda Triangle reaches as far back as its first recorded traveller, Christopher Columbus. While sailing into the area, Columbus and his men were unnerved by bolts of lightning, strange lights and the erratic action of the compass spinning wildly.

Over the years the area became notorious for strange occurrences. Until World War II only ships were thought to be affected, but since then aeroplanes have also disappeared. All the most obvious causes – human error, weather and so forth

– have been investigated, and by the mid-1970s logical explanations for virtually all the reported mysterious incidents had been uncovered. Despite this, the Bermuda Triangle – also known as the Devil's Triangle and the Limbo of the Lost – continues to intrigue and defy rational explanation. Various incredible theories have been put forward to explain the disappearances, such as time warps, black holes, atmospheric aberrations, magnetic anomalies, alignments of the planets, tidal waves, earthquakes, hidden sea beings, death rays from outer space, forces emanating from **Atlantis** and alien abduction.

BERRY POMEROY CASTLE

This ruined castle, located at Berry Pomeroy, Devon has been the scene of ghostly sightings and strange phenomena for hundreds of years. Even today, visitors to the castle remark upon its strange atmosphere and the feelings of foreboding and terror it inspires.

The great majority of the **hauntings** can be traced to the castle's original owners, the Pomeroy family, who occupied it from about 1086 to 1550. The most terrifying apparitions are those of a white and a blue lady. The White Lady is believed to haunt the dark dungeons. According to the legend, she is the spirit of Margaret Pomeroy, who was imprisoned in the dungeons by her sister Eleanor. Eleanor was jealous of both Margaret's beauty and her success with men, and Margaret slowly starved in the dungeons, a long drawn-out and painful death. Perhaps Margaret's agony is the source of the feeling of unease and horror some people experience at the castle.

The Blue Lady roams around the castle as she pleases and has been seen trying to lure people into parts of the ruin. According to some stories she is the **ghost** of the daughter of one of the Norman lords of the castle. She was raped by her father, who then strangled the resulting baby in one of the upper rooms. In other tales it is she who smothers the child, haunting the castle in anguish. When she is seen, her face is said to portray this suffering. She is regarded as a death portent to those who see her. The well-known nineteenth-century physician Sir Walter Farquar is said to have seen the **spirit** while he was attending to the wife of one of the castle stewards. The wife died soon afterwards, although she seemed to be making a full recovery.

Other **apparitions** reported include a woman in a grey dress, the ubiquitous cavalier and strange shadows that appear to have no earthly presence to cast them.

BHUT

In Hindu mythology a bhut is believed to be the restless **ghost** of someone who has died a violent death or committed suicide. According to legend, the bhut has no shadow and can be detected by the smell of burning turmeric. It is thought that lying on the ground offers protection against it, as the bhut never rests on the earth.

BIBLIOMANCY

A method of **divination** still popular today. Originally bibliomancy was used to discover if a person was innocent or guilty of a crime. The suspect was weighted against the great Bible in the local church. If the suspect weighed less, he or she was declared innocent. Later bibliomancy came to mean any divinatory use of the Bible, from resting it on a child's head to calm him or her down to picking a verse at random to offer comfort and support. Finally, the term was used for divination from books in general, not just the Bible. Today we understand it as a method of divination that involves taking any book, usually a collection of prose or poetry or wise thoughts, closing one's eyes, thinking about a particular problem or question, opening the book at random and interpreting the first words or sentences read in a prophetic or advisory way.

BILOCATION

The appearance of a person or animal in two places at the same time. What exactly occurs in the phenomenon of bilocation is uncertain, but one theory is that a person's double or **doppelgänger** is somehow projected elsewhere and becomes visible to others either in solid physical form or ghostly form. Generally the double remains silent or acts strangely. In folklore, bilocation sometimes presages or heralds the death of the individual seen.

Bilocation allegedly has been experienced and practised at will by mystics, ecstatics, saints, monks, holy persons and magical **adepts**. Several Christian saints and monks were skilled at bilocation, including St Antony of Padua, St Ambrose of Milan, St Severus of Ravenna, and Padre Pio of Italy. In 1774, St Alphonsus Liguori was seen at the bedside of the dying Pope Clement XIV, when in fact the saint was confined to his monastic cell in a location that was a four-day journey away.

Reports of bilocation were collected in the nineteenth century by pioneering psychical researcher **Frederick Myers**, one of the founders of the **Society for Psychical Research** in England. Myers published his reports in 1903 in *Human Personality and Its Survival after Bodily Death*, but the phenomenon has received little interest in modern times.

Among the most remarkable of the documented cases of bilocation was the appearance of Friar Padre Pio in the air over San Giovanni Rotondo during World War II. While southern Italy remained in Nazi hands, American bombers were given the job of attacking the city of San Giovanni Rotondo. However, when they appeared over the city and prepared to unload their munitions, a brown-robed friar appeared before their aircraft. All attempts to release the bombs failed. In this way Padre Pio kept his earlier promise to the citizens that their town would be spared. Later on, when an American airbase was established at Foggia, a few miles away, one of the pilots of this incident visited the friary and found, to his great surprise, the little friar he had seen in the air that day over San Giovanni.

As to how Padre Pio accomplished such a feat, the closest he ever came to an explanation of bilocation was to say that it occurred 'by an extension of his personality'.

BINDELOF SOCIETY

In spring of 1932 a group of American teenage boys began to experiment with **table tilting**. One of the boys had been associated with **poltergeist** activity a few years previously, and both he and his mother were fascinated by **psychic** phenomena. To their delight, the boys were able to get the table to tilt, then to lift off the floor and then to rise high into the air.

New York psychiatrist and **dream** researcher Montague Ullman visited the group in September 1932, and a regular schedule of meetings was drawn up. All regular sitters were aged between 15 and 17 years old. The teenagers would sit around a table in a dark room, their hands resting on the table and their feet underneath, for a period of 15 to 20 minutes, then there would be a break followed by another 15 to 20 minutes. After several sessions the group began to produce table tiltings and **raps** on a regular basis, and they decided to attempt psychic photography. When this became routine they turned their hand to another way to induce psychic phenomena. A pen and pencil were simply placed on a table and communication invited. It wasn't long before writing could be heard and lengthy written messages appeared. The communicator identified himself as the deceased Dr Bindelof, who found himself able to use the psychic force the teenagers were generating to communicate with them. From that point on a dialogue was set up, and Dr Bindelof answered questions about the psychic world and the nature of the **soul**. By 1933 the Bindelof Society was formed.

Not all the boys were convinced that Dr Bindelof was who or what he said he was, and some thought they themselves were creating this entity through thought alone. None, however, doubted that the experience was real, and it was one they would never forget. The group split up around 1934, but in 1949 the core members met again to recreate the phenomena, this time without success. Attention now turned to making a permanent record of what had occurred, and the eventual product of this was a series of articles published by Montague Ullman in *Exceptional Human Experience* in 1993 and 1994.

BIOENERGETICS

Bioenergetics, like **acupuncture** and **acupressure**, assumes the existence of a **universal life force** that affects health and wellbeing, and a capacity for self-healing within everyone. It is a form of psychotherapy that involves a high degree of intuitive awareness on the part of the therapist, and patients have been known to report **psychic** experiences, such as episodes of **clairvoyance**, as a result.

Bioenergetics works with the physical, emotional and mental patterns of men and women to reduce emotional stress and help with the challenges of living. It is a way of understanding personality in terms of the body and its energetic processes.

According to bioenergetic theory, repressed emotions and desires affect the body by creating chronic muscle tension and a loss of wellbeing and energy. The theory is based on the premise that there is no fundamental separation between the mind and the body: that psychological stress reflects and creates what is happening physically, and physical or somatic events both reflect and create mental and emotional states. Emotional stress from many areas – relationships, family crises, jobs, health – produce tension in the body. Contractions in the muscular system are often the result of carrying unresolved emotional tension. These contractions can have a direct effect on the energy level of the individual, on the capacity for spontaneous and creative self-expression, and on feelings of wellbeing.

Bioenergetic analysis seeks to bring about the conscious integration of mind and body. Therefore, the focus is on both the psychological issues presented and the manifestation of these issues as shown in the individual's body, energy and movement. **Bodywork** is combined with psychoanalysis of **dreams** and childhood experiences.

BIOFEEDBACK

Biofeedback is the measuring of vital bodily functions that are normally unconscious, such as breathing, brain-wave rhythms, heart rate and blood pressure, through information provided by electronic devices. This information is then used to help control these processes. Biofeedback is a relatively new field, emerging only during the 1960s. Since that time biofeedback has been used in **parapsychology** for **psi** testing.

Originally biofeedback was applied to **brain waves**. Brain waves were first discovered in 1924 by Hans Berger, but it wasn't until the 1950s that it was thought possible to control them at will – in 1958, researcher Joe Kamilya was able to help college students control their alpha brain waves. By the early 1970s the attention of researchers turned to how biofeedback could help one achieve **altered states of consciousness**, such as those achieved in **meditation**, and how in meditation bodily processes could be changed. Other experiments concentrated on training subjects to alter involuntary processes, such as blood pressure.

To monitor physiological processes, biofeedback electrodes, which look like stickers with wires attached to them, are placed on the client's skin. The client is then instructed to use **relaxation**, meditation or **visualization** to bring about the desired response, whether it is muscle relaxation, a lowered heart rate or lower skin temperature. The biofeedback device reports progress by a change in the speed of beeps or flashes, or pitch or quality of the tone. The results of biofeedback are measured in the following ways:

- 🖐. *Skin temperature.*
- 🖐. *Electrical conductivity of the skin, called the glavanic skin response.*
- 🖐. *Muscle tension, with an electromyograph (EMG).*
- 🖐. *Heart rate, with an electrocardiograph (ECG).*
- 🖐. *Brain-wave activity, with an electroencephalograph (EEG).*

Biofeedback demonstrates the connection between mind and body by teaching subjects to use thoughts and relaxation to control bodily process, and as a result it is typically used as an **alternative medicine** technique to treat health problems ranging from stress-related disorders to raised blood pressure, chronic pain, addiction and asthma. Biofeedback can also teach people how to increase their alpha brain waves. The alpha state is not necessary for psychic experience, but studies have shown it is conducive to it, since subjects who can slip easily into alpha states tend to score high in psi testing.

BIRDS

Birds appearing in **dreams** are thought to represent **spirits**, **angels**, transcendence and the **supernatural**. In mythology birds are messengers from the **spirit** world, **souls** of the dead or carriers of souls of the dead. In European folklore black birds, such as crows and ravens, that cross your path or gather near your house are thought to be **death omens**.

BLACK ELK, NICHOLAS [1863–1950]

Black Elk was an Oglala Sioux mystic born in December 1863 on the Little Powder River, South Dakota. He was the son of the elder Black Elk and White Cow Sees Woman, and he devoted his life to helping his people find unity and strength.

From an early age Black Elk knew he was destined for great things. Around the age of four he began to hear voices, and a year later he had his first **psychic** vision. Aged nine he had his great **vision**, in which he was empowered by the Grandfathers, who represented the powers of the world. For two days he fell ill, and during this time he went in an **out-of-body experience** to the clouds, where he was greeted by the Grandfathers. They took him to the centre of the universe and gave him **supernatural** power to heal. The Grandfathers showed him the sacred hoop of his people, which represented their **soul**, and in the centre was a crossroads: one path, the red one, was sacred, while the other, black path was the path of materialism. A voice told Black Elk that he had been given his nation's hoop and it was up to him to set them on the right path.

From the day of his vision Black Elk changed. He found he had prophetic visions and he could understand the songs of birds and animals. He used his great powers of healing and wisdom to help his people rediscover their traditions.

During Black Elk's young adulthood, missionaries tried to convert the Oglala Sioux to Christianity, often by force. Black Elk himself was baptized Nicholas Black Elk on 6 December 1904, near present-day Pine Ridge, South Dakota, but his Lakota spirituality remained strong throughout his life. He took part in the underground movement supporting traditional religion, which became necessary after the US government outlawed native rituals. Throughout his life, he took part in both secret traditional practices and public Catholic rites.

Black Elk feared that US policies would destroy the Lakota Nation's identity, so during the summer of 1930 he dictated his life story to John Neihardt. The resulting book, *Black Elk Speaks*, was published in 1932 and has been reprinted many times. In it Black Elk described the history of the Lakota Nation and provided a sense of hope for the future. His vision eventually became a message to the Lakota people – a warning not to assimilate completely and thereby lose their unique heritage.

Although Black Elk died in 1950, long before the passage of the Indian Religious Freedom Act in 1978, his teachings, combined with this legislation, created a new respect for and interest in Lakota spirituality.

BLACK MAGIC

The use of **supernatural** and **psychic** power for evil ends, the opposite of **white magic**, which is concerned with healing and promoting what is good.

The term 'black magic' has been used with a wide variety of meanings and evokes such a variety of reactions that it has become vague and almost meaningless. It is often synonymous with three other multivocal terms: **witchcraft**, the **occult** and **sorcery**. The only similarity among its various uses is that it refers to human efforts to manipulate the supernatural with negative intent and the selfish use of psychic power for personal gain. Workers of black magic are thought to have but one goal: to satisfy their own desires at whatever cost to others.

Magic, good or evil, is universal, with no ethnic or racial association, and it is unfortunate that not just in Western civilization but many cultures around the world, good and evil have for centuries been denoted as white and black. White often designates healing, truth, purity, light and positive energy, while black is darkness, falsehood, evil and negative energy.

In modern times probably the most popular synonym for black magic is the occult. Originally the term meant hidden, hence mysterious, and was routinely used by classical and medieval scholars to refer to 'sciences' such as **astrology**, **alchemy** and **kabbalah**, but from the late nineteenth century, when magical sects such as the Order of the **Golden Dawn** emerged, the term began to take on the meaning of evil or satanic. Perhaps the best-known occultist and black magic practitioner was **Aleister Crowley** (1875–1947), who dubbed himself the Antichrist. More than any other person Crowley gave the occult an evil connotation.

See also **Magic**, **Occult**, **Witchcraft**, **Satanism**, **Sorcery**.

BLACK SHUCK

Spectral dogs in general play a role in many **haunting** legends and it is reported that **Sir Arthur Conan Doyle** based his story *The Hound of the Baskervilles* on accounts of the Black Shuck legends.

Black Shuck is alleged to be a **phantom** dog in British folklore that has frequently been sighted in Norfolk, Suffolk, Essex and Devon. The common name of this ghostly animal varies according to locality: 'Old Shuck' (Norfolk), 'Old Shock' (Suffolk), 'Yeth' (Devon), 'Pooka' (Ireland), 'Barguest' (Yorkshire), to name but a few. His appearance is often considered a **death omen**.

The origins of Black Shuck remain shrouded in mystery, but the stories probably originated from the hound of the Viking raiders' god Odin and from the Celtic legends of Arawn, whose hounds of hell searched for human **souls**. The name Black Shuck may have originated from a local word, *shucky*, meaning 'shaggy', or an Anglo-Saxon term *scucca*, meaning 'satan' or 'demon'. Other local names have been 'Galley Trot', 'Old Snarleyow' and 'Old Scarfe'.

Black Shuck is described as being black, and the size of a very large dog or even a small calf. It is reported to have large, saucer-shaped eyes of red or yellow. In some instances it has been reported as being headless or having just one large Cyclops-type eye and to wear a collar or chain, which rattles as it moves.

The hound is said to roam graveyards and lonely country roads, and on stormy nights its howling can be heard. It is believed to leave no footprints, but its icy breath can be felt. To see or even hear the phantom animal is thought to be a foreboding of misfortune, madness or death. In parts of Devon even speaking its name is thought to bring misfortune. In Suffolk, though, it is thought that Black Shuck is harmless as long as it is not bothered. In Cambridgeshire, Black Shuck is said to have favourite haunts along the banks of the river Ouse and in the flat landscape of the fens.

There is little evidence of Black Shuck causing anyone any harm on contact, but there is a curious account of an attack back in 1577 in the parish of Bungay, Suffolk. The parishioners were at church when the church darkened and a violent storm broke out. Black Shuck appeared from nowhere in the middle of the congregation. It charged through the church, causing mass panic, and killing two men who were kneeling in prayer. A third man is thought to have died from severe burns. At the same time, a few miles away in Blythburgh, another black dog reputedly appeared out of nowhere in the local church, killed three men and left burn marks on the church door.

BLAKE, WILLIAM [1757–1827]

William Blake was a mystic, poet, artist and engraver whose visionary art was much misunderstood by his contemporaries. He published his first set of poems when he was 26, and six years later, in 1789, he printed the *Songs of Innocence*, which he also engraved and illustrated. In his forties he wrote his more symbolic epic poems, *Milton* and *Jerusalem*, and his best-known illustrations of the Book of Job and Dante's *Divine Comedy* were created in the last few years of his life.

Blake lived and died in relative poverty. He received little formal schooling, which makes his visionary interpretations of the Bible and the classics all the more remarkable. From a young age he experienced **visions**; when he was ten he told his father he had seen hosts of **angels** in a tree, and when his brother, Robert, died at the age of 20, he saw his **soul** 'ascend heavenward clapping its hands for joy'. Throughout his life Blake drew his strength from the **spirit** world. He believed deeply in the human imagination – indeed, that it was the only reality – and he often spoke with the **apparitions**, angels, devils and spirits that he drew and engraved in his work. His interest in the spirit world brought him into contact with many of the visionaries and writers of his time, such as **Emanuel Swedenborg**.

BLAVATSKY, MADAME [1831–1891]

Helena Petrovna Blavatsky, daughter of Russian aristocrats, was a key figure in the nineteenth-century revival of **occult** and **esoteric** knowledge. A highly intelligent and energetic woman, she helped to spread Eastern philosophies and mystical ideas to the West and tried to give the study of the occult a scientific and public face.

Blavatsky became aware of her **psychic** abilities at an early age. She travelled through the Middle East and Asia learning psychic and spiritual techniques from various teachers, and she said that it was in Tibet that she met the secret masters or **adepts** who sent her to carry their message to the world.

In 1873 Helena immigrated to New York, where she impressed everyone with her psychic feats of **astral projection**, **telepathy**, **clairvoyance**, **clairsentience** and **clairaudience**. Her powers were never tested scientifically, but her interests were always more in the laws and principles of the psychic world than psychic power itself. In 1874 Helena met and began a life-long friendship with Colonel Henry Steel Olcott, a lawyer and journalist who covered spiritual phenomena, and a year later they founded a society 'to collect and diffuse a knowledge of the laws which govern the Universe'. They called this society the Theosophical Society, from *theosophy*, a Greek term meaning 'divine wisdom' or 'wisdom of the gods'.

Travelling to India, Blavatsky and Olcott established themselves at Adyar, near Madras, and a property they bought there eventually became the world head-quarters of the society. They established the nucleus of the movement in Britain and founded no fewer than three Theosophical Societies in Paris.

Throughout her life Blavatsky's powers were dismissed as fraud and trickery, but this did not stop the Theosophical Society from finding a home among intellectuals and progressive thinkers of her day. The society was born at a time when **spiritualism** was popular and Darwin's theory of evolution was undermining the Church's teachings, so the Society's new thinking flourished. Many people appreciated the alternative it provided both to church dogma and to a materialistic view of the world.

Blavatsky's two most important books are *Isis Unveiled* and her magnum opus, *The Secret Doctrine*, published in 1888. She drew her teachings from many religious traditions: Hinduism, Tibetan Buddhism, Platonic thought, Jewish **Kabbalah** and the occult and scientific knowledge of her time. Although they influenced many people, her books are extremely difficult to read. Nevertheless, her teachings were absorbed by many people and then simplified into a worldview that was taken up by many later **New Age** groups. This worldview includes a belief in seven planes of existence; the gradual evolution and perfecting of spiritual principles; the existence of nature spirits ('**devas**'); and belief in secret spiritual masters or adepts from the Himalayas, or from the spiritual planes, who guide the evolution of humanity. All of these beliefs are derived from Blavatsky's **Theosophy**.

BLOCKED ENERGY

Energy is believed to be the basis of all matter, and psychics and **alternative medicine** practitioners believe that a field of energy, called an **aura**, surrounds your body and a flow of energy ('chi') exists within it. If these energy forces are interrupted for some reason the energy becomes blocked and will not flow freely. **Chakras** are an essential part of this energy flow. If one or more of them is closed, then the energy is blocked at these points.

It is thought that blocked energy which is not cleared can lead to serious consequences, affecting your mental, physical and spiritual health, and impeding your spiritual and **psychic** development.

See **Energy balancing**.

BODHISATTVA

In Buddhism, the bodhisattva is an enlightened being who instead of going straight to **nirvana** – and not being reborn – decides to delay eternal bliss in order to help others on the path.

The concept of a bodhisattva can be used to describe anyone who is dedicated to compassion and the greater good. In many ways it could be said there is a bodhisattva nature in every one of us.

BODY SCANNING

The ability to look psychically into and around a human body in order to determine the person's heath and state of mind. Body scanning can be experienced through any of the five senses.

A **medical intuitive** can psychically read a body and come up with a diagnosis in actual medical terms. Each intuitive works differently, for example, some read **auras** while others read energetically the insides (organs, blood, glands) of our insides. Intuited information can then be provided to the client's medical doctor and/or health care professional for further evaluation and discussion of possible treatments. Many medical intuitives work with, or are, medical doctors themselves.

BODYWORK

Alternative medicine therapies that take into account the role of the mind and emotions in physical health and look especially at how the body interacts with the environment and universal life energies.

There are many types of bodywork therapies, involving manipulation, **massage**, movement, breathing, **energy balancing** and energy transfer. All these therapies assume the existence of a **universal life force** and the ability of the body to self-heal when therapy stimulates that life force.

See: **Acupuncture, Acupressure, Bioenergetics, Energy balancing, Massage, Reflexology, Reiki, Shiatsu, Therapeutic touch.**

BOGEY

Also referred to as the bogeyman in British folklore, this is said to be an evil **spirit** who loves to cause trouble. The bogey is believed to travel alone or in groups, and in some instances they are synonymous with the devil. Usually the bogey is described as big and nasty and for years the threat of calling upon the bogeyman was used by parents to frighten children into good behaviour.

The precise origins of the bogeyman legend are unknown but it is possible that it came from the old Central European gods. The Slavic for god is 'bog' and after Christianity came to Central Europe and made its way to the British Isles, many of the deities in the old religions became transformed into evil spirits. It is possible that the gods of pre-Christian Britain became known as these horrible, frightening beings – bogs, bogeys, boggles or boggarts.

The boggart is a type of bogey hobgoblin in British folklore with **poltergeist** characteristics. A boggart is said to be helpful, but most of the time it is devious and frightening, never appearing but playing tricks on people, such as knocking books off shelves or tripping people up. It is also thought to punch, scratch and kick. In parts of Yorkshire the threat of being thrown into the 'baggart hole' is still used today by parents if their children aren't behaving.

BOLEYN, ANNE [1501–1536]

Anne Boleyn was the second wife of Henry VIII, and their marriage changed the course of English history. Her larger-than-life story is matched by the many sightings of her **ghost** since her death.

Besotted with the beautiful Anne, Henry asked the Catholic Church for a divorce from Catherine of Aragon. The Church refused, so in order to marry Anne, Henry created a reformed version of the church, making himself the head – a direct challenge to the authority of the Pope. Having obtained his divorce and married Anne, Henry was determined to have a son, but Anne gave birth to a girl, Elizabeth, in 1533, and from then on the relationship between Anne and Henry deteriorated. Henry found a new love interest in Jane Seymour. Anne became pregnant again, but the child was stillborn. Henry, determined to rid himself of Anne, fabricated a charge of treason and confined her to the Tower of London. Her execution took place on 19 May 1536.

Anne Boleyn is reputed to haunt **Hampton Court** – along with many of Henry's other five wives – and the **Tower of London** where she was executed. Predictably, she has been seen there as a headless female figure near the Queen's House, where she was confined prior to her execution. At Blickling Hall in Norfolk, Anne's family home, there have been sightings of a headless young woman riding a horse and carrying a severed head on her lap, typically on the anniversary of her death. Anne has also been sighted in the Hall's corridors. An administrator reported seeing a woman walking down towards the lake wearing an old grey gown with a white lace collar and cap. He thought she was either lost or trespassing and went out to ask if she was looking for someone. The woman replied, 'That for which I seek has long since gone.' Then, in a moment, she disappeared.

BOND, FREDERICK BLIGH [1864–1945]

Born in Wiltshire, England, in 1864, Frederick Bligh Bond became a well-known author, editor, architect and archaeologist. Considered to be the pioneer of 'psychic questing', he was regarded as exceptionally talented but 'irascible, eccentric, difficult to work with, moody and confrontational' by his colleagues. He had a deep interest in all things **psychic**, **occult** and **esoteric**, and his work involved analysing medieval woodwork and construction techniques.

In 1908 Bond was commissioned to excavate the ruins of **Glastonbury** Abbey, burial place of three kings of England and reputed to have connections to the legendary King Arthur and the Holy Grail. It was while working on this project that Bond claimed to have been in communication with spirit monks, called the Watchers, who once had lived at Glastonbury. The Watchers established regular communications with Bond and allegedly penned messages to Bond in a curious mixture of Old English and rudimentary Latin, giving clues to the hidden history of Glastonbury

Abbey and insights into the building's original design and architecture. In all, these communications gave a startling insight into everyday life within the abbey and a glimpse back into the medieval world.

Bond's claim to have psychic guidance from **spirits** drew sharp criticism from his conventional colleagues in both the fields of archaeology and architecture. But his communications with the ghostly monks won him the support of members of the British **Society for Psychical Research**. In 1918 he published *The Gate of Remembrance*, a collection of transcripts and reports from his **automatic writing** sessions, and it sealed his fate by firmly undermining his reputation as a professional once and for all. However, Bond's enthusiasm for his interaction with the ghosts of Glastonbury Abbey prompted him to follow up his book with *The Hill of Vision*, in which he revealed allegedly prophetic warnings given to him by the spectral monks, including a prediction of World War I.

Despite great success in locating unknown and little-known structures, Bond was gradually pushed out of his work at Glastonbury. It would be easy to say that this was due to his psychic work, but it may simply have had to do with the fact that he was vain and arrogant and made a lot of enemies along the way. He was an amateur archaeologist at a time when the field was professionalized, and his refusal to follow a systematic plan of excavations laid down by professionals was bound to create tension. By 1921 he was reduced to cleaning the artefacts he had found, and by 1922 he was asked to leave Glastonbury.

In 1926 Bond took up an offer from a wealthy American to pay for his passage to the US. He found work as an architect and began a successful lecture tour organized by the **American Society for Psychical Research**. In 1935, again at his patron's expense, he returned to England jobless, penniless and homeless. He died in a cottage in Wales in 1945 at the age of 82. Throughout his life Bond never lost his love for Glastonbury or his fascination for the **paranormal**, but many of the suggestions given by the Watchers have never been followed up, and to this day his books are banned from the Glastonbury Abbey bookstore.

BONES, READING

An ancient Chinese method of **divination** that used bones from the shoulders of oxen, sheep, deer or pigs, or the shells of turtles, to predict the future. A petitioner would approach a diviner with a question that could usually be answered by yes or no. The diviner would write the petitioner's question on a bone or a turtle shell from a sacrifice, and would then heat the bone by inserting into it a hot bronze poker. The heat would cause the bone to crack. The patterns of the resulting cracks were then interpreted according to mystical techniques, providing an answer to the petitioner's question. Answers and results were recorded after the divination had been completed.

Rulers seem to have consulted the oracle bone diviners on even the most trivial aspects of life. Questions were asked about auspicious days for sacrifice and **ancestor worship**, births, illness, marriage, weather, agriculture, hunting, court appointments, government policy and warfare. A sample divination record reads:

On day 49 the king, making cracks, divined: 'Hunting at Chi, going and coming will there be disaster?' The king, reading the cracks, said, 'Extremely auspicious.' At this point we drove off in our chariots. We caught 41 foxes and 8 hornless deer.

The first oracle bones known to modern researchers were discovered by late-nineteenth-century Chinese peasants digging in their fields, and since then nearly 155,000 oracular inscriptions have been recovered. Most date to the period of the Shang Dynasty in the twelfth and eleventh centuries BC, or, in other words, to shortly after the time of Moses, and they are an invaluable source of historical insight. Although the use of oracle bones eventually died out, divination continued to play an important role in Chinese life. By the ninth century BC, bones were replaced by divination through the oracular book known as the **I Ching**, which continues to be used in China today, and around the world.

BOOK OF CHANGES

See **I Ching**.

BOOK OF THE DEAD

The Book of the Dead refers to the funeral literature of ancient Egypt. The texts consist of **charms**, hymns, **spells** and formulas designed to help the **soul** pass through the dangerous parts of the **underworld**. By knowing these formulas, it was thought that the soul could ward off evil **spirits** and pass safely into the realm of Osiris, god of the underworld. At first carved on to stone sarcophagi, the texts were later written on papyrus and placed inside the mummy case, and therefore came to be known as Coffin Texts.

BOOK OF SHADOWS

A book that contains rituals, laws, healing lore, **chants**, **spells**, divinatory methods and other topics to guide **witches** in practising their craft. There is no single definitive Book of Shadows for **witchcraft**; each tradition may have its own book, and local covens and individual witches can adapt books for their own use. In past centuries Books of Shadows were held secret; however, some witches in recent years have made their books public.

Traditionally a coven kept only one Book of Shadows, kept safe by the high priestess or priest. But today individual witches have their personal Books of Shadows in the form of diaries or notebooks, often now on hard drive and disk.

See also **Spells**, **Witchcraft**.

BOOK TEST

The book test is a way for the deceased to communicate with the living and provide evidence of their **survival after death**. It was developed in the early twentieth century by English **medium Gladys Osborne Leonard** and her spirit **control**, Freda.

In the book test the deceased communicates through a medium and provides the title of a book not known to the medium. The deceased gives the book's exact location and then specifies a page number, which is supposed to contain a message from the deceased. Leonard's book tests were very successful, and almost always the passage selected contained personal messages.

Book tests were very popular around the time of World War I, when interest in communicating with the dead was strong, but not all book tests were as successful as Leonard's. A study published in 1921 suggested that only around 17 per cent were successful.

Paranormal factors may well figure in some book tests, but this does not necessarily imply that there is life after death, as book tests can be easily explained by the idea that the medium him or herself is picking up **psychic** information. Another problem with book tests as proof of life after death is that on almost any page of a given book some passage may be interpreted as a message.

BORLEY RECTORY

Borley Rectory has been called 'the most haunted house in England'. It was investigated between 1929 and 1938 by **Harry Price**, founder of the National Laboratory of Psychical Research in London. Price, a celebrated ghost hunter, claimed the house to be 'the best authenticated case in the annals of psychical research'.

The rectory, a gloomy and unattractive red building located in the county of Essex, was built in 1863 by the Reverend Henry Dawson Ellis Bull. He later expanded the original building to accommodate his large family of 14 children.

The first reported ghostly incident occurred in the afternoon of 28 July 1900, when one of the Reverend's daughters, Ethel, thought she saw a **ghost** that looked like a nun dressed in dark clothes. Local legend had it that the rectory was built on the site of a thirteenth-century monastery, where a monk and a nun had fallen in love but had been killed before eloping. Sightings of the nun's ghost, and the ghost of a dark man wearing a tall hat, were reported frequently by Ethel Bull and her sisters. Ethel lived a long life, dying at the age of 93 in 1963. She maintained her story until the end, saying, 'What would be the use of an old lady like me waiting to meet her Maker, telling a lot of fairy stories?'

In 1929 Harry Price invited himself to the rectory to investigate. According to his book, *The Most Haunted House in England*, published in 1940, the occupants at the time, the Reverend G E Smith and his wife, both professed sceptics of the **paranormal**, told him that strange occurrences began almost immediately after they moved in. They heard strange whispers, saw odd black shapes and magic lights, heard **phantom** footsteps, smelled strange odours and, in general, witnessed odd occurrences such as objects smashed, doors banged, spontaneous combustions of portions of the house, wall writings, paranormal bell ringing, the sounds of galloping horses, mysterious smoke in the garden, **rapping** in response to questions and appearances by the **phantom nun**. Price said he investigated the matter thoroughly and actually witnessed the phenomena for himself while he was there. He held a **séance**, and he and others present heard a faint tapping in response to questions. The **spirit** claimed to be the Reverend Bull.

In 1929 the Smiths moved out and the Reverend Lionel Algeron Foyster and his wife, Marianne, moved in. The **poltergeist** activity increased, and Price returned to continue his investigations. He found the phenomena to be much more violent than before, terrifying Marianne and their three-year-old daughter in particular. In 1935 the Foysters moved out, and in 1937 Price leased the property himself for a year. During his stay he witnessed many paranormal incidents and compiled a book of procedures using camera equipment and other methods of documenting spirit activity. He enrolled 40 assistants to help him.

Many of his assistants were **mediums**, and they produced some fabulous theories, suggesting that the monk and nun were strangled and buried in the garden and that they longed for mass and a proper burial. Other assistants began the project with great enthusiasm but dropped out after getting no results.

Price left the rectory in 1938, convinced that paranormal activity was taking place and that there was a medieval monastery on the site, even though it had already been proved that the only building ever to have existed on that site was a twelfth-century church, not a monastery. His book publishing his findings was well received for its meticulous psychical research but also criticized for being sensational. After Price's death in 1948 his allegations were re-examined by psychical researchers Trevor Hall, Kathleen Goldney and Eric Dingwell. Charles Sutton, a *Daily Mail* reporter, suspected Price of faking phenomena. During a visit to the rectory with Price he had been hit on the head by a pebble – and subsequently found Price's pockets to be full of pebbles.

Perhaps the most damning condemnation, however, came from a previous inhabitant of the rectory, Mrs Smith, who in 1949 signed a statement saying that nothing unusual had happened in the house until Price arrived. The Smiths suspected him of being the perpetrator.

Hall, Dingwell and Goldney, in their book *The Haunting of Borley Rectory*, concluded that nothing out of the ordinary had happened there during Price's stay and that everything could be explained rationally. They accused Price of concocting hocus-pocus to serve his own need for publicity. They suggested that Borley Rectory lent itself well to the influence of suggestion, since 'In every ordinary house sounds are heard and trivial incidents occur which are unexplained or treated as of no importance. But once the suggestion of the abnormal is put forward – and tentatively accepted – then these incidents become imbued with sinister significance: in fact they become part of the haunt.'

Borley Rectory is an old, gloomy-looking building, and a psychological explanation is plausible. However, it may not explain everything, and the possibility that something paranormal did occur or that certain individuals who lived there, including Price himself, were sympathetic and sensitive enough to become a focus of **psychic attack** cannot be dismissed totally.

not actively seek members and always favoured quality over quantity in research and publication. Among its most important bulletins was a report in the 1920s on **ESP** experiments conducted at Harvard University, and a paper entitled 'Toward a Method of Evaluating Mediumistic Material', published in 1936. The society also published a number of groundbreaking books on **mediumship**, including *Beyond Normal Cognition* by John Thomas (1937). The Boston Society also published **J B Rhine**'s work *Extra Sensory Perception* (1934), which described laboratory experiments carried out at Duke University.

BOSTON SOCIETY FOR PSYCHICAL RESEARCH

A psychical research organization that was well regarded in its day, publishing a series of books and pamphlets between 1925 and 1941.

The society was created as a result of internal strife within the **American Society for Psychical Research**. When **spiritualist** Frederick Edwards became president in 1923 and introduced more popularist policies, Walter Franklin Prince, the ASPR's well-respected research officer, left to start a rival society in Boston with an academic focus. The Boston Society was officially set up in 1925 'in order to conduct psychic research according to strictly scientific principles.'

Prince was the backbone of the society, and it faded away after his death in 1934. During its brief existence the society did

BOTANOMANCY

An ancient practice that can be traced all the way back to the Druidic tree worship, botanomancy is a method of **divination** by burning branches of trees, typically vervain and briar, upon which questions have been carved. The fire and smoke indicate the course of future action to be pursued.

BRAIN/BRAIN WAVES

Although it's possible that **psychic** power is a bridge that connects your brain to a higher mind or spiritual force, some experts believe that psychic ability should be treated as another aspect of brain function. They regard **psi** as an additional sense that is somehow located in our brains, and believe that understanding psi can help explain how we perceive and process information.

One of the most amazing discoveries in medicine was made by Roger Sperry in the 1960s, when he revealed that the right hemisphere of the brain, responsible for **intuition** and creativity, makes an equally valuable contribution as the left hemisphere of the brain, responsible for reason and logic and previously thought to reign supreme. Opinions differ on what part of the brain psi function exists in, but many believe that the ability to connect to intuitive information is housed in the right side of the brain and that for optimal brain function both the right and left sides of the brain need to work together.

Some scientists suggest as well that brain waves need to work together. Brain waves are electrical impulses our brains constantly release, and they are measured in hertz, or cycles per second. There are four major stages of brain-wave activity, beginning with beta, the shortest and fastest waves, and moving through to delta, the strongest and slowest.

When the brain is emitting beta waves, the individual is active, awake and conscious, with his or her eyes open. Alpha brain waves operate just below waking **consciousness**, a state that is attained in **meditation** and **relaxation**. The average person can maintain awareness in this state. Typically, eyes are closed and the body is relaxed, but alpha waves are also produced during daydreaming with eyes open. The alpha state is not essential to achieve success in psi testing results, but

studies show that it is conducive to psi. Theta brain waves are achieved during deep relaxation. The average person cannot maintain awareness in this state, but some meditators claim that they can. The final state, delta, is one of sleep or unconsciousness.

Some scientists maintain that the blending of all four brain waves creates a brand-new brain wave. Some followers of Eastern philosophy propose that the awakened mind, which occurs when a person is more aware of their spiritual existence, is a state that combines all four brain waves at once.

BREATH

The first and last thing you do in life is to breathe. Breathing is the essence of life. And so it is not surprising that breathing and breath are often identified with the **soul**. In Roman times a close relative would inhale the last breath of someone who was dying, because it was thought that the soul had to enter into another body or it would be lost. In Hinduism the breath or life energy is seen as the force that controls the mind; healthy breathing is healthy thinking and healthy being, which is why **yoga** always teaches breathing exercises.

In the past half century or so many Westerners have tried to learn the techniques for breathing, **meditation** and mind control that Eastern yogis have studied for millennia. In recent years psychiatrist Stanislav Grof developed a method that

Breathing exercises

Simple breathing exercises are thought to help give you quick access to psychic states of mind. One Eastern technique is to visualize, with each in-breath, drawing in coloured light – pink light for harmony and quiet contemplation and white or gold light for spiritual energy – and slowly breathing out black mist or smoke as all the negative energies leave the body.

A yoga breathing exercise that is thought to be wonderfully effective for saturating your aura and your body with energy is alternate nostril breathing.

Using your right thumb, close your right nostril and inhale slowly through your left nostril for a count of four. Then keeping the right nostril closed, use your fingers to close the left nostril, so both nostrils are closed for a count of eight. Then, keeping your left nostril closed, remove your thumb from your right nostril and exhale for a slow count of four. Switch nostrils, closing the left nostril and inhaling through the right nostril for a count of four. Close both nostrils again for a count of eight, and exhale slowly for a count of four through the left nostril. Repeat the whole exercise four or five times.

combines breathing and meditation and called it Holotropic Breathwork; it helps individuals enter an unordinary state of consciousness for **psychic healing** by using evocative music, accelerated breathing, energy work and **mantra** drawing. Aspects of this meditation involve exploration of the inner self and spiritual opening.

BRIDGE OF SOULS

The Bridge of Souls in mythology and folklore is the heavenly road **souls** of the dead must travel in order to get to the **afterlife**. The most common motif used for the Bridge of Souls is that of the rainbow.

In Hawaii, Polynesia, Austria, Japan and among some Native American tribes, the rainbow is thought to be the path souls take on their way to heaven, and has been called a bridge or ladder to higher or other worlds. The Russians call the rainbow the 'Gate to Heaven'. In New Zealand dead Maori chiefs are believed to travel up the rainbow to their new home. In parts of Germany and Austria, folklore suggests that children's souls are led up the rainbow to heaven, and in some parts of England it is considered unlucky to point at a rainbow.

People all over the world have different ways of looking at and understanding rainbows. For some they suggest magical possibilities, for others a rainbow indicates that a project is going to fail – 'building rainbows in the sky' – but whenever a rainbow appears, and however rationally it can be explained as a natural phenomenon, even the most hardened sceptic cannot help but be struck by its magic and its beauty.

BROOM

The broom is intimately connected with **witches** and **witchcraft**. It was commonly believed that witches anointed their bodies with a salve given to them by the devil that enabled them to fly through the air upon a variety of sticks or stems, including broomsticks. The choice of the broom or besom as a likely means of transport is probably due to the association between brooms and female domesticity, though male witches were thought to ride in this way as well as women.

In Eastern European folklore a broom may be used in **exorcism** ceremonies to sweep evil **spirits** out the door. It is also thought that stepping over a broomstick, placing it under your pillow or putting a broom across a threshold will offer protection against evil spirits and **ghosts** at night.

BROWN LADY

An English manor house in Norfolk has been haunted for nearly 300 years by the so-called 'Brown Lady', who is believed to have been captured once on film in one of the most famous **spirit photographs** ever taken.

Raynham Hall is the seat of the Marquesses of Townshend. The Brown Lady is believed to be the **ghost** of Lady Dorothy Townshend, wife of the second Marquess of Townshend and sister to Sir Robert Walpole, the first prime minister of England. At the age of 26 Dorothy married Lord Charles Townshend. According to lore when Townshend discovered that Dorothy had been the mistress of Lord Wharton he locked her in her apartment until her death from either a broken heart or chicken pox or a fall down the stairs.

Until 1904 a portrait identified as Lady Dorothy hung in the hall. In the portrait the woman is dressed in brown and has large shining eyes. It was said that the portrait looked normal by day but at night the face became evil looking.

Over the centuries there have been a number of reports of encounters with the Brown Lady at Raynham Hall. In the early nineteenth century George IV allegedly woke in the middle of the night to see a woman dressed in brown. He was said to be so terrified that he refused to stay another hour in the house. In 1835 she was witnessed several times by a Colonel Loftus, a guest staying in the castle. Not long after, novelist Captain Frederick Marryat was invited to a ball at the house. He allegedly encountered the ghost in the corridor and when it grinned diabolically at him he shot at it. The bullet was said to have gone right through the ghost and was later discovered lodged in a door behind where the ghost appeared.

In 1926 the ghost was seen again by the young Lord Townshend. In 1936 Lady Townshend hired a photographer called Indra Shira to take photographs of the house. While taking the photographs Shira noticed what looked like a shadowy figure dressed in white moving down the stairs. He asked his assistant to take a photograph and although the assistant could not see anything he aimed his camera in the direction indicated by Shira. When the photograph was developed the Brown Lady appeared as an outline wearing what looked like a wedding gown and veil. The photograph was published in *Country Life* magazine on 1 December 1936 and became an overnight sensation. Experts past and present have examined it and no evidence of **fraud** has ever been found.

BROWNIE

In Scottish folklore brownies are kindly **spirits**, also known as the *bwca* in Wales and the pixies in Cornwall. When they appear they are believed to look like small men – about three feet high – and are unkempt and wild in appearance. They are said to become attached to particular families and are happy to do chores for the family at night.

According to lore brownies don't like to be offered payment for their work, either because they are too proud or because they are compassionate by nature, but they do enjoy and expect gifts of cream and good food. If gifts aren't left out, or their work is criticized, brownies are said to become mischievous and cause trouble.

There are different stories about the origin of the name. One of the most plausible is that in the early seventeenth century, when the Covenanters in Scotland were being persecuted for their beliefs, many of them were forced to hides in caves and secret places, and food was carried to them by friends. They dressed themselves in a fantastic manner, and if seen in the night they would be taken for fairies. One band of Covenanters was led by a hunchback named Brown who, being small and active would slip out at night with some of the others and bring back the provisions left by their friends. Those who knew the truth named Brown and his band the 'Brownies'.

BROWNING CIRCLE

The Browning circle was organized by nineteenth-century **medium D D Home** for poets Robert and Elizabeth Browning. The activities of the circle converted Elizabeth to **spiritualism**, but her husband condemned and ridiculed Home, calling him a toady, a fraud and a leech in a poem entitled 'Mr Sludge, the Medium' (1864).

The Brownings met Home in 1855 when they attended a **séance** he held for a wealthy couple who wanted to establish contact with their son, who had died three years previously. At the séance they witnessed **table tilting**, ghostly hands and **rapping**. Elizabeth was amazed, but Robert was unimpressed and expressed publicly his loathing for Home, suggesting that the whole thing could easily have been faked, as Home always wore loose clothing that could conceal tubes and strings to produce the phenomena. No one knows what caused Robert's hatred, although some believe it may have been his low opinion of what he called Home's 'effeminacy'. Homosexuality was illegal in 1855, and there were many rumours of Home's affairs with young men.

The Brownings' disagreement over spiritualism was the only public quarrel the couple had; Robert loathed Home so much that Elizabeth stopped talking about it. *Punch* magazine took Robert's side, using rich imagery to suggest Elizabeth's gullibility.

Buguet, Edouard [1841–1901]

Edouard Buguet was a famous **spirit photographer** during the 1860s and 1870s until he was exposed as a **fraud** in 1875. Buguet's photographs were remarkably clear, unlike the misty pictures from other contemporary spirit photos of the era. The French photographer went to extraordinary lengths to impose ghostly images upon his photos, using live models at first but later switching to sculpted heads when he began to fear being exposed.

In 1875 Buguet's studio was raided after a tip-off from a dissatisfied customer. His tricks were exposed, and he was convicted of fraud and sent to prison for a year. Buguet never again worked as a photographer, but his photographs have become collectors' items, with some believing that he did actually succeed in photographing **ghosts**.

Bull, Titus [1871–1946]

Titus Bull was an American physician and neurologist who believed that **spirit possession** was at the root of many illnesses. In the 1920s and 1930s he worked in New York City and treated many of his patients with spiritualist therapy. With the help of **medium** Carolyn Duke, he claimed to treat and cure manic depressives, schizophrenics and alcoholics.

Bull believed that possessing spirits entered their victims through the base of the brain, the solar plexus or the reproductive organs. He thought that these spirits were not evil, just confused, and that they needed help to pass to their proper plane and leave the victim in peace. In 1932 he published a pamphlet entitled *Analysis of Unusual Experiences in Healing Relative to Deceased Minds and Results of Materialism Foreshadowed*. In it he suggests that spirit possession, although not a cause of mental illness, is a complicating factor and that trauma and stress can attract spirits to a person.

Bull practised general medicine in a time when little attention was paid to the mind-body connection in health, but as he was not systematic in his explanations, his work is often ignored by medical and psychical research societies.

BURIAL RITES

The idea of a journey to the **afterlife** is evident in every culture and every age, and it has always been considered a duty of the living to set the dead on their path to the other world. In primitive times **symbols** were carved on rocks and implements and weapons buried with the dead to help them in the next life. In Greece a gold coin was buried with the dead to pay the ferryman to take them across the River of Death. The Egyptians had the most elaborate burial rituals, which lasted for days. Today the idea of a journey can still be said to exist when we lay flowers on graves to provide beauty and peace in the hope the **spirit** will find it on the other side.

As well as preparations for the journey to the afterlife, the other important part of ancient burial rites was to make sure the spirit found peace and did not return to haunt the living. Some ancient cultures maintained contact with the dead, keeping artefacts of the deceased so that communication could take place with the help of a go-between. In many places in the world ancestral spirits and **ancestor worship** still play an important role, and burial rites create a doorway from this world to the next.

Gradually burial rites in the West have taken on the idea of paying respect to the person and his or her family, and the ritual has become a way to say goodbye. It is an important time because, according to psychics, the bereaved need to let go of the spirit so it can go on its way, and the spirit needs to let go of the bereaved. Burial rites therefore still represent a bridge between physical life and spiritual life.

BURUBURU

Buruburu, meaning the sound of shivering, is a terrible **ghost** from Japanese folklore that for reasons unknown is said to lurk in forests and graveyards in the form on an old person, who is sometimes one-eyed. According to legend it attaches itself to its victim's spine and causes a chill to run down them, or in the worst case causes them to die of fright.

BYRD, EVELYN [1707–1737]

The **ghost** of Evelyn Byrd, daughter of William Byrd II, an early American colonial settler and founder of the city of Richmond, Virginia, is reputed to haunt the grounds of her childhood home, Westover, on the James River.

Born in 1707, Evelyn was sent to England at the age of 10 to be educated, and at the age of 16 she fell in love with a man her family considered unsuitable, possibly because they thought him too old for her. At 19 Evelyn returned to Westover depressed and heartbroken. She withdrew from all company except for that of her friend and neighbour, Anne Harrison, whom she met almost daily in a grove in the plantations. For ten years Evelyn wasted away, until her death in 1737.

Before her death Evelyn made a pact with Anne that if one of them was to die the other would return as a friendly ghost, and, true to her promise, Evelyn's ghost is alleged to have been seen by Anne smiling in the grove where they used to meet. Over the years Evelyn's ghost has been seen dressed in white or green lace many times at Westover. She is never frightening, and when she appears she always smiles.

BYRON, LORD GEORGE GORDON [1788–1824]

One of the greatest poets of English literature, Lord Byron was deeply fascinated by the **supernatural** and would investigate tales of **hauntings** himself. As a young man Byron reported seeing a **phantom monk** in the family home of Newstead Abbey, who may or may not have died at the hands of one of Byron's ancestors.

The phantom's appearance was thought to herald misfortune for the family, and Byron claimed to see the 'goblin friar' again shortly before his ill-fated marriage to heiress Anne Milbanke in 1815. He described it as:

> ... *monk arrayed*
> *In cowl, and beads, and dusky garb appeared*
> *Now in the moonlight, and now lapsed in*
>   *shade,*
> *With steps that trod as heavy, yet unheard.*

C

Cabinet

A box or confined space thought to attract, store and release spiritual forces, enabling a **medium** to produce phenomena. The use of cabinets to manifest **paranormal** activity began in the mid-1800s with the **Davenport brothers**. The brothers had themselves bound and locked in a wooden cabinet, where they were supposedly incapable of moving, but somehow musical instruments would play as if guided by **spirit** hands. Their act was a huge success, and until the early twentieth century cabinets or black curtains for the medium to retire behind were all the rage. Cabinets are rarely used by modern mediums.

Cagliostro, Count Alessandro [1743–1795]

A charismatic figure in the courts of eighteenth-century Europe, Cagliostro was a **magician**, **alchemist** and **psychic healer**. Born in 1743 in Palermo, Sicily, to a poor family, Cagliostro turned his natural psychic talent into a lucrative fortune-telling business. He travelled to Malta at the age of 23 to study the **occult** and later in London joined the **Freemasons**. Using the name 'The Divine Cagliostro', he spent most of his adult life among the royal courts of Europe, performing various occult arts, such as healing by the **laying on of hands**, conjuring spirits and producing an 'elixir of immortal life' with the aid of his beautiful wife, Lorenza.

Cagliostro's success created resentment, and in 1785 in France he and his wife fell out of favour with the Queen over the 'Affair of the Diamond Necklace'. The Comtesse de La Motte set him up by swindling 1.6 million francs for a diamond necklace and then accused Cagliostro of stealing it. Alessandro and Lorenza were sent to the Bastille and tried for fraud.

Following his release, Cagliostro travelled to Rome, where he tried to set up an 'Egyptian Freemasonry' order. He was questioned by the Inquisition and sentenced to death in 1791. His sentence was later reduced to life imprisonment by Pope Pius VI. Cagliostro died of apoplexy on 6 March 1795, but for years after there were rumours that he was alive and had miraculously escaped.

Calvados Castle

From October 1875 to October 1876 Calvados Castle – more a chateau than a castle – was the focus of **poltergeist** activity that forced the owners to leave. In the written accounts of the **haunting**, the people involved are identified only by their initials. The case has never been explained and remains a mystery to this day.

Calvados Castle was built on top of the foundations of an earlier Norman castle that had fallen into disrepair and apparently had been haunted ever since. In 1875 the castle was occupied by M. and Mme X, their son and his tutor, Abbe Y. Almost immediately they began hearing noises, thumps and sighs and other unusual occurrences. M. X began to keep a journal of the strange phenomena. The following are excerpts:

This is October 1875. I propose to note down and record every day what happened during the night before. I must point out that the noises occurred while the ground was covered with snow, there was no trace of footsteps around the chateau. I drew threads across all the openings, secretly. They were never broken …

A very disturbed night … It sounded as if someone went up the stairs from the ground floor at superhuman speed, stamping his feet. Arriving at the landing he gave five heavy blows to the walls, so strong that the objects suspended on the walls rattled in their places …

Some being rushed at top speed up the stairs from the entrance hall to the first floor … with a noise of tread that had nothing human about it. Everybody heard it … It was like two legs deprived of their feet and walking on their stumps.

The family also heard what sounded like a body rolling down the stairs and saw chairs move around the room with no human hands to guide them.

Everybody heard a long shriek, and then another, as if a woman outside were calling for help. At 1.40 [am] we suddenly heard four cries in the hall, and then on the staircase …

It is no longer the cry of a weeping woman, but shrill, furious despairing cries, the cries of demons or the damned.

In addition to the shrieks and the moving objects, doors and windows flew open, the Bible was desecrated and the house itself was 'shaken twenty times'. The person who was affected the most seems to have been the Abbe, who had ice-cold water thrown over him from nowhere on a sunny day and his locked room ransacked.

At first M. and Mme X believed humans to be responsible, and they bought two guard dogs, but when something invisible terrified the dogs as well they were forced to conclude that **supernatural** activity must be at work. Believing the house to be haunted, perhaps by its previous owner (a woman who had died unrepentant), M. X had an **exorcism** performed by church officials, who believed the house to be 'diabolically supernatural'. The exorcism didn't solve the problem, and M. and Mme X finally decided to sell the castle and leave. There have been no reports of hauntings at Calvados Castle since.

CAMPBELL, DONALD [1921–1967]

Donald Campbell was one of the more colourful ghost hunters in recent times. In the 1960s he became the only person ever to hold both the world land speed record (403.1 mph, Lake Eyre, Australia) and the world water speed record (276.33 mph, Lake Dumbleyung, Australia).

Campbell had grown up with stories of Scottish **ghosts** that allegedly haunted his family line, and he developed a deep interest in the **psychic** world, becoming an active member of the **Ghost Club** in

London and taking part in many investigations. On the evening of 3 January 1967, Campbell was playing cards when he pulled what was known as a 'bad luck hand'. If the hand was meant as a warning, Campbell chose to ignore it. The next day, while trying to break his water speed record on Lake Coniston in England, he lost control of his boat at speeds in excess of 300 mph. His body was finally located and recovered in May 2001.

CANDLES

Candles have cast a light on human progress for centuries, but little is known about their origin. We do know that they were used as early as 3000 BC in Egypt, but it is the Romans who are credited with developing the wick candle to light homes and places of worship at night.

For thousands of years candles have been used in burial ceremonies to dispel evil **spirits**, and **superstitions** about candles abound – from ancient Egyptians using candles to interpret **dreams** to all of us asking for a wish to be granted when we blow out our birthday cake candles.

It is said that the seventeenth-century treasure hunter Captain Kidd believed that carrying lanterns containing consecrated candles would conjure up the **ghosts** of the dead to help him in his quests. In American folklore, a candle left burning in an empty room will bring death to a family. In British folklore candle wax that drips around and not down the candle is a **death omen**,

Candle magic

Candle magic is the use of candles in performing spells and rituals for granting wishes and desires. Different types and colours of candles are thought to have different magical meanings. For example, for new beginnings and energy it is suggested that white should be used; for change and courage use red; for happiness and health use orange; for communication and travel use yellow; for love and healing use green; for power and work use blue; for psychic development use blue or indigo; for love use pink; for house and home use brown; for secret desires use silver; for wealth use gold; and for banishing guilt use black.

To activate the magic of candles you should write your wish on a piece of paper and burn it in the candle, or engrave your wishes on the candle with a pin. You can also light the candle and focus your intention on your wish as you gaze into the flame.

while in Germany a candle wick that splits in two spells misfortune. Typically the death omen is allegedly minimized by extinguishing the candle under running water or by blowing it out. Lastly, a candle that burns blue or dimly is thought to suggest a ghost is nearby.

CAPNOMANCY

An ancient method of **divination** believed to have originated in Babylon but also used by the **Druids**. In capnomancy, people interpreted the movements of smoke rising from a fire, especially from sacrificial offerings. If the smoke rose straight to the clouds it was a good sign, but if the smoke hung about and did not disperse it was an unfavourable sign.

CARD GUESSING

A **psi** clinical testing procedure for **ESP** in which the test subject guesses the identity of cards randomly selected from a pack of playing cards. Typically the subject is blindfolded so that it is impossible to see the pack of cards.

CARROLL, LEWIS [1832–1898]

Lewis Carroll (real name Charles Dodgson), best remembered as the author of *Alice's Adventures in Wonderland* and *Through the Looking-Glass and What Alice Found There*, was a celebrated poet, mathematician, logician, photographer and **paranormal** investigator. As one of the original members of the **Society for Psychical Research**, Carroll was interested in ghostly phenomenon. He was also fascinated by **psi** abilities such as **telepathy** and convinced that they would one day become accepted and valued by the scientific community. In a letter dated 4 December 1882, Carroll wrote on this subject to his friend James Langton Clark:

I have just read a small pamphlet, the first report of the Psychical Society on 'thought reading'. The evidence, which seems to have been most carefully taken, excludes the possibility that unconscious guidance by pressure will account for all the phenomena. All seems to point to the existence of a natural force, allied to electricity and nerve-force, by which brain can act on brain. I think we are close on the day when this shall be classed among the known natural forces, and its laws tabulated, and when the scientific sceptics, who always shut their eyes till the last moment to any evidence that seems to point beyond materialism, will have to accept it as a proved fact in nature.

CARTOMANCY

A form of **divination** using cards. The practice of cartomancy is ancient and is often associated with gypsies. It is used to predict the future and interpret the past and present.

Tarot cards are the most popular form of cartomancy, but a set of ordinary playing cards can be used in much the same way: they are in fact said to be derived from the Tarot, and indeed there is a great deal of similarity between them. Both have four suits: the swords of the Tarot are the clubs of an ordinary playing pack, the pentacles diamonds, the cups hearts and the wands spades.

If you have a reading with cards, you will be asked to shuffle the pack, cut it and think of a question as the cards are dealt out. Common methods of laying out the cards are the star formation, the wheel of fortune or the quick seven. Each card has a meaning and a significance, and having laid out the cards the reader will use intuition to answer the question. There is an overall pattern for each of the suits, typically interpreted as follows: a dominance of hearts shows happiness and strong relationships. Hearts can suggest sensitivity (both sorrow and joy) and also strong emotions and ambitions realized. Spades are the cards of obstacles and challenges and can show where you might need to be creative in your approach to life. Diamonds are more concerned with everyday matters, particularly finances and hard work. Clubs are the cards of loyal and trustworthy friends or people, but can also mean disappointment and betrayal depending on where they are placed.

CATTABOMANCY

A practice of **divination** using bowls of brass – a metal thought to protect against evil **spirits** – which were filled with water or ink and used as focal points in **scrying** or capturing glimpses of the future in scenes and images appearing in the bowl. The diviner would stare at the liquid without blinking until a trancelike state was entered and visions experienced. Said to have been the practice by which **Nostradamus** came about his knowledge of the future.

CAUL

A thin membrane of amniotic fluid that sometimes covers the head of a baby at birth. Since the time of the ancient Romans those born with a caul are considered to be blessed with good luck and **supernatural** powers, such as the ability to see into the future and to communicate with **ghosts** and **spirits**.

See also **Amniomancy**.

CAULD LAD OF HILTON

In English folklore the Cauld Lad of Hilton is a **spirit** who is half **brownie** and half **ghost** and who is alleged to have haunted Hilton Castle in Northumbria. Hilton Castle is now in ruins.

According to legend the spirit was supposed to have been that of a stable boy killed by a past Lord of Hilton in a rage because the boy didn't immediately obey his order to fetch a horse. The boy was killed with a hayfork and his body was tossed into the pond. The spirit, a young naked boy, was supposedly heard working about the kitchen at nights. Usually he would tidy up and do chores, but sometimes he would toss things about and disarrange whatever had been left tidy.

He was an unhappy spirit who could be heard singing sadly. The servants eventually banished the spirit one night by laying out a green cloak and hood for him. At midnight he put them on and frisked about 'til cock-crow singing,

Here's a cloak and here's a hood,
The Cauld Lad of Hilton will do nae mair
good!

And with the coming of the dawn it is said he vanished forever.

CAUSINOMANCY

A form of **divination** that involved placing objects on a fire. If the object burned slowly or failed to ignite, it was taken to be a bad **omen**. If the object ignited and burned quickly, it was considered a good omen.

CAYCE, EDGAR [1877–1945]

A psychic reader and **ESP** researcher who arguably did the most in the twentieth century to advance **psychic** knowledge. Born in rural Kentucky, Cayce was close to his grandfather, Thomas Jefferson Cayce, who was said to be psychic. One day tragedy struck; Cayce witnessed the horrific death of his grandfather in an accident with a horse. After this incident, and encouraged by his mother and grandmother, the young Cayce claimed to visit his grandfather's spirit in the barns.

Cayce experienced other traumas in his youth. At 15 he was hit from behind by a baseball and began to feel dizzy. His father sent him to bed, and he entered into a hypnotic trance, telling his father exactly what needed to be done to make him better. His father followed these instructions, and Cayce recovered within a day. When he was in his early twenties he lost his voice. Helped by a travelling hypnotist, Cayce again entered into a **trance**. While in the trance he was once again able to diagnose a cure. He coughed up some blood, and his voice returned.

In 1901, Cayce started to give psychic readings to clients, and over the next 40 years he gave and recorded in writing over 12,000 readings on health, past lives, ancient mysteries and predictions of the future. These readings are still being studied today.

In 1933 Cayce and his supporters formed in Virginia Beach (where it still remains today) the Association for Research and Enlightenment for the purpose of studying, researching and providing information about ESP, as well as life after death, **dreams** and **holistic** health. Three other programmes or organizations were also established around Cayce's work: a master's degree in transpersonal studies at Atlantic University, Virginia Beach, was set up in 1930; the Edgar Cayce Foundation, also at Virginia Beach, was set up in 1948 to provide custodial ownership of the Cayce readings and documents; and a diploma in preventive health care based on Cayce's readings was set up in 1986 at the Harold Reilly School of Massotherapy.

Cayce was a remarkably gifted psychic with an incredible intellect. It is said that he could sleep on any book, paper or document and remember its contents when he awoke. He was able to use his psychic abilities in four ways: **precognition, retrocognition, clairvoyance** and **telepathy**. That is, he could see into the future and predict events to come; he could look into a person's past to find the origins of an existing health problem; he could see inside the human body and see through objects; and he was able to enter another person's mind to discover what they were thinking.

Called the 'Sleeping Prophet', Cayce practised **absent healing** for several years, helping to cure people all over the world, even though he had no formal education and never went to medical school. Receiving a name and address, Cayce would enter a trance state and then read the person's condition and prescribe cures and treatments, which were, reportedly, 90 per cent accurate. His success was so great that thousands sought his help. Cayce's ability to diagnose accurately and name body parts astonished some medical experts, although others dismissed his readings on account of his lack of formal training.

In August 1944, with three to four years' backlog of mail, Cayce collapsed with exhaustion. He was aware that doing more than two readings a day was too much for his body and mind, but over the years he had been so moved by the suffering of others that he was doing far in excess of this number. He retired to the mountains to recuperate, returning home in November 1944. On 1 January he told his friends he would find healing on the 5th, and they prepared for the worst. On 5 January, Cayce died peacefully at the age of 67.

Cayce spent much of his life trying to understand what he did when he entered a trance. He spoke about unknown civilizations where the soul could travel without the restriction of gravity and communicate through thought. He attributed poor health to harmful deeds in a past life, and many of his readings concerned **karma** and **reincarnation**. The chief difference between Cayce's suggested treatments and conventional medicine was that Cayce sought to heal the whole body by treating the causes rather than the symptoms of a patient's problem. The patient, however, needed to have faith and hope in the reading for it to work. Mind is the builder, Cayce would always say, and he firmly believed that the body responded to commands from the mind.

Cayce maintained that we all have psychic ability and that experiences such as dreams and **intuition** are proof of that. He also believed that if a person had good intentions and love in their heart they would always have a steady supply of psychic power to tap into.

CELESTIAL LIGHT

Known within the **New Age** movement as 'the pure white light of the universe', the celestial light is believed to be energy transmitted from a more spiritually advanced realm to protect and heal those who invoke it.

CELLULAR MEMORY

The concept that every single cell in our body contains a blueprint of our personalities and every experience we have had in our lives because all matter, including cellular, is held together by energy. Whatever is stored in one cell – love, hate, happiness, unhappiness – is passed on by **psychic** osmosis to the next cell.

The concept of cellular memory has gained popularity from accounts of organ donor recipients who take on the persona of the original donor. It can also explain why universal shared **archetypes** of the **collective unconscious** pass down through the generations.

CEREBRAL ANOXIA

The medical term for a lack of oxygen flowing to the brain, which sometimes triggers sensory distortions and hallucinations. Some believe it to be the physical means by which phenomena such as near-death experiences and out-of-body episodes might be rationally explained.

CEROMANCY

A form of **divination** in which wax is heated in a brass bowl until it is liquid. The melted wax is then slowly poured into a container of cold water in order to read the discs or patterns and shapes of wax that form.

CHAFFIN WILL CASE

An unusual case in which a father who had died appeared to one of his sons to tell him about an unknown will. Many believe that this case provides proof of **survival after death**, but others believe it can be explained by **clairvoyance**.

James L Chaffin was a farmer from Davie County, North Carolina, who had four sons. In 1905 he made a will, formally witnessed and signed, in which he left his farm to his third son, Marshall. No provision was made for the other members of his family. In 1921 he suffered a fatal fall.

In June 1925 Chaffin's second son, James P Chaffin, started to have vivid **dreams**. In these he saw his father standing at his bedside. What he saw is best described in his own words, as given in a sworn statement that was taken down by a Mr Johnson, a lawyer and a member of the **American Society for Psychical Research**, who visited the family in 1927 to interview them about their unusual experience.

In all my life I never heard my father mention having made a later will than the one dated in 1905. I think it was in June of 1925 that I began to have very vivid dreams that my father appeared to me at my bedside but made no verbal communication. Some time later, I think it was the latter part of June 1925, he appeared at my bedside again, dressed as I had often seen him dressed in life, wearing a black overcoat which I knew to be his own coat. This time my father's spirit spoke to me, he took hold of his overcoat this way and pulled it back and said, 'You will find my will in my overcoat pocket', and then disappeared.

The next morning I arose fully convinced that my father's spirit had visited me for the purpose of explaining some mistake. I went to mother's and sought for the overcoat but found that it was gone. Mother stated that she had given the overcoat to my brother John who lives in Yadkin County about twenty miles northwest of my home. I think it was on the 6th of July, which was on Monday following the events stated in the last paragraph, I went to my brother's home in Yadkin County and found the coat. On examination of the inside pocket I found that the lining had been sewed together. I immediately cut the stitches and found a little roll of paper tied with a string which was in my father's handwriting and contained only the following words: 'Read the 27th chapter of Genesis in my daddie's old Bible.'

At this point I was so convinced that the mystery was to be cleared up I was unwilling to go to mother's home to examine the old Bible without the presence of a witness and I induced a neighbor, Mr Thos. Blackwelder, to accompany me, also my daughter and Mr Blackwelder's daughter were present. Arriving at mother's home we had a considerable search before we found the old Bible. At last we did find it in the top drawer in an upstairs room. The book was so dilapidated that when we took it out it fell into three pieces. Mr Blackwelder picked up the portion containing the Book of Genesis and turned the leaves until he came to the 27th chapter of Genesis and there we found two leaves folded together, the left hand page folded to the right and the right hand page folded to the left forming a pocket and in this pocket Mr Blackwelder found the will.

The 27th chapter of Genesis tells how Jacob, the younger brother, supplanted Esau in winning his birthright. The paper that they found was in the father's handwriting and it read as follows:

After reading the 27th chapter of Genesis, I, James L Chaffin, do make my last will and testament, and here it is. I want, after giving my body a decent burial, my little property to be equally divided between my four children, if they are living at my death, both personal and real estate divided equal if not living, give share to their children. And if she is living, you all must take care of your mammy. Now this is my last will and testament. Witness my hand and seal. James L Chaffin, This January 16, 1919.

The will, although unwitnessed, was legally valid under the laws of the state of North Carolina, but by the time the second will was discovered the son who had inherited the farm had died and the property had passed to his widow and son. In December 1925 the three remaining sons brought a suit against them to recover their share of the estate. On the day of the trial, after the selection and swearing in of the jury, the widow and her son were shown the second will for the first time. They immediately admitted that the document was genuine, and withdrew their objections to having it certified by the court as his valid will.

There have been many explanations for this extraordinary case. Some think that James, upset at being excluded, forged a will and concocted a ghost story to back it up, but this does not explain why he waited four years, why so many people believed the second will to be genuine or why he created a ghost story. He could simply have said that he had found the will and this would have been just as plausible.

Other explanations put forward include the suggestion that James did know about the will but forgot about it until the memory was dramatized in dream form and brought back into his consciousness. It is also possible that this is an excellent example of **ESP** on the part of James. Finally it must be considered that a genuine **apparition** of the dead did appear to James and deliver information to him telepathically. As none of these explanations can be proved, the case remains inconclusive.

CHAKRAS

Chakra is Sanskrit for 'wheel', and in Hindu and Buddhist yogic literature the chakras are thought to be energy vortices, shaped like petals or spoked wheels, that whirl at various speeds. They penetrate the body and the body's **aura**, and it is thought that through them various energies, including the **universal life force**, are received and distributed throughout the person. You cannot see chakras physically, only psychically.

There are seven major charkas, which are most directly concerned with physical health, and hundreds of minor ones. The universal life force is thought to enter the aura through the chakra at the top of the head and filter down along the spinal column to the other chakras. The higher the position on the spinal column the more complex the chakra.

Each chakra has its own colour and speed of rotation, and each is associated with a major endocrine gland, a major nerve system, a major physiological function and a **psychic** function. The chakras are connected to each other through thousands of channels of energy called *nadis*. Three of the most important *nadis* include the *sushuma*, which processes energy coming in, and the *ida* and *pingala*, which are concerned with the outflow of energy.

There isn't any accepted scientific and medical evidence that chakras exist, but recently they have begun to be acknowledged in the West in **alternative medicine**. **Clairvoyants** say that they can diagnose the health of chakras by energy scans with the hands and that health problems often show up in chakras months or

The seven major chakras

Each chakra involves a different part of the body and also different concerns, so you can focus directly on one specific chakra. The seven chakra centres are the following:

1. The base or root chakra (*muladara*). The lowest of the seven chakras, the root chakra is located at the base of the spine and is the simplest of the seven. Orange-red in colour, it relates to physical strength as well as the senses of taste and smell. You can summon this chakra when you need courage and physical strength. It is in the base chakra that kundalini energy is stored in a coiled state of readiness.

2. The sacral or belly chakra (*svadishana*) is red or pink in colour and is located just below the navel. It controls sexual energy and reproduction. It influences the release of adrenaline in your body and can keep it on a high state of alert. You can summon this chakra not only when you need to invoke fertility but also when you need projects and relationships to be successful. In some psychic systems the sacral chakra is overseen by the spleen chakra, which governs digestion.

3. The solar plexus chakra (*manipura*). Located below the breastbone and above the navel, the solar plexus chakra is where mediums get their psychic information. Green or light red in colour, it controls the adrenal glands, and when it is out of balance it can affect the stomach, liver and pancreas. You can use this chakra when you want to achieve an ambition or when you are planning a career move.

4. The heart chakra (*anahata*). Located in the centre of the chest and in the middle of your shoulder blades, the heart chakra is golden in colour and relates to emotions such as love and compassion. If it becomes blocked it can affect the lungs, the heart and breathing and immunity in general. You can use this chakra for matters of love and friendship and for understanding others.

5. The throat chakra (*visudda*). Located at the top of the throat, the throat chakra is silvery blue in colour and relates to creativity and self-expression. It is prominent in musicians, singers and public speakers. When it becomes blocked, your throat, ears, eyes, nose and mouth may be affected. You can use this chakra when truth and principles are at stake.

6. The forehead or third eye chakra (*ajna*). Located between your eyebrows in the centre of your forehead, the third eye chakra is blue and purple in colour and relates to your pituitary

gland. It influences intelligence, intuition and psychic ability. When it becomes blocked it can affect your head, eyes and brain. You can use this chakra for psychic awareness and harmony.

7. The crown chakra (*sahasrara*). Located at the top of your head, the crown chakra is a glowing purple colour and will not open until all other chakras are balanced. When it is open you experience the highest connection to the universal mind by your mental, physical and spiritual self. You can use this chakra when striving for wisdom and perfection.

even years before they manifest in the body. When the chakras are balanced and healthy, their colours are clear and their rotation smooth, but in poor health they become cloudy and irregular in rotation. Blocked chakras are thought to cause health problems, and in alternative healing therapies there are various techniques for clearing chakra blockages, including **visualization**, **colour therapy**, **acupuncture** and **energy healing**.

CHANNELLING

The process through which a **medium** communicates information from **spirits** and other non-physical beings, such as **angels**, deities or **guardian spirits**, by entering into a **trance** or some other **altered state of consciousness**.

The urge to communicate with the spirit world is as old as humankind itself. In primitive cultures certain individuals – priests, **shamans** or medicine people – would seek out the wisdom of the spirit world. The ancient Egyptians and Romans, as well as the early Chinese, Babylonians, Tibetans, Assyrians and Celts, all channelled spirits and entities, and holy men and women of Judaism, Christianity and Islam received divine guidance.

Divination and **healing** are forms of channelling, as is **possession**, when an entity seizes control of an individual. In the Middle Ages possession was seen as demonic rather than divine. In the nineteenth and twentieth centuries, when **spiritualism** was at its height, channelling grew in popularity. The **Fox sisters**, three young women from New York, first brought public attention to channelling in 1848 when they announced the arrival of spirits in their **séances**.

One famous medium of the mid-nineteenth century was Nettie Colburn, a trance channeller whose **spirit guides** advised President Lincoln. Between 1861 and 1863 Mrs Lincoln called her to the White House to use her skills to advise the

President on a wide variety of subjects — advice he was known to have followed. For example, Colburn channelled advice about how Lincoln could raise morale among the Yankee troops, and her advice worked.

After spiritualism declined in the early twentieth century, channelling did not receive widespread attention again until the early 1970s, when **Jane Roberts** published the Seth books, which were allegedly channelled to her by a non-physical entity called Seth. Channelling is no longer a hot topic, but popular interest remains to this day.

Different mediums have different ways of channelling. Sometimes it happens when the channeller falls into a sudden trance-like state, or it can be induced. Methods to induce channelling include **meditation**, **prayer**, **hypnosis**, fasting, **chanting**, dancing, **breath** exercises, sleep deprivation and taking hallucinogenic drugs.

Direct voice channelling occurs when another entity or personality takes temporary possession of the channeller's body, often using voices and mannerisms different from those of the channeller. The channeller may be unaware of what is being said or done and may not recall anything afterwards. Mental channelling, the mediation of thoughts, words, images and feelings, is also done in a state of light trance, but this time the channeller is aware of the process. The channeller's voice may or may not change, and he or she may communicate through **automatic writing**, a **Ouija board** or similar device, or even sleep or **dreams**. Physical channelling involves physical effects such as **psychic healing**, **apports** and **levitation**. In the wider sense of the term, channelling could also include

intuition, **inspiration** and **imagination**, and as such it becomes a way for everyone to connect to a higher source of wisdom.

A number of theories have been put forward to explain channelling. The simplest is that channellers do actually get in touch with the spirit world. Others believe that channellers engage in deliberate **fraud** or that it is symptomatic of multiple personality disorder. The trouble with the latter argument is that mentally ill people do not tend to have control over their communicators, but channellers typically do. The view advanced by some psychologists is that channelled entities are not separate entities but part of the channeller's subconscious that takes on the personality of an entity in order to express itself.

Many psychics believe that channelling is a skill anyone can learn and that it shouldn't just be the preserve of professional mediums. It's important to remember that everyone will have a different experience of channelling, and the insights received may come in any number of different forms. It is up to the individual to translate and interpret.

CHANTING

The frequent repetition of a word, phrase, or **mantra** as part of **meditation** or a religious or magical rite. Some believe that chanting is a way to achieve an **altered state of consciousness** so that **psychic** power or energy can be raised for the purposes of **healing** or magic. Others believe that chanting helps them commune with the divine.

Chanting can be done alone or in a group. It can be accompanied by hand clapping, drumbeats, musical instruments or dancing. Sometimes chanting is melodious; sometimes it is monotone.

In all major religions the most powerful chants are the names of God. In Vedic scriptures the name of God awakens spiritual **consciousness**. The Hare Krishnas incorporate the name of God in their group chanting believing it can help liberate them from **reincarnation**. Various Hindu and Buddhist chants use the word *Om*, a sound that is believed to encompass the whole universe. Followers of Islam chant the 99 names of Allah, called the beautiful names, and the name of Jesus figures strongly in Christian chants.

In primitive tribal societies chanting was used to raise psychic energy, appease **supernatural** powers and bring blessings. The practice occurred in ancient Greece, where female **sorcerers** would howl their chants, believing that strong vibrations enhanced the power of their words. Medieval sorcerers and **magicians** also sang their chants in very forceful voices, and the practice was continued into the twentieth century by men like **Aleister Crowley**, who believed that the sound of chanting could profoundly affect both humankind and the universe. Native Americans also observe chanting in preparation for activities and ceremonies such as healing, hunting, fighting, rites of initiation and funerals.

In magic, the belief that the success of a **spell** can depend on the sound vibrations created by chanting dates back thousands of years. It is thought that rhythmic chanting sends out waves of energy that help the magician or **witch** summon their inner power. Modern **pagans** and witches still combine chanting and circle dancing to raise a group psychic energy field called a cone of power. When the energy peaks, the group releases it towards their goal, such as a spell or healing.

CHAOS THEORY

A principle from **quantam physics** that suggests that chaos or lack of order does in fact obey particular laws or rules and only appears to be random. The theory was first brought to public attention with the butterfly effect discovered by Edward Lorenz in 1961 (a theory whereby the flapping of a butterfly's wings might, through a series of events involving climate and location, cause a storm on the other side of the globe). The idea contradicts the traditional Newtonian principles of physics, which states that unseen effects can be predicted through precise measurements, as according to chaos theory even tiny errors can result in enormous unpredictability, far out of proportion to what would be expected mathematically. In a nutshell, what chaos theory means is that anything is capable of affecting anything else – a principle belief of **New Age** and **holistic** thinking.

CHARISMATIC

Coming from the Greek *charisma* meaning a gift of grace, charismatic is a term often used to describe someone with psychic and/or spiritual gifts, which can include **channelling**, **healing** and the ability to perform miracles.

CHARLTON HOUSE

Now a municipal building but formerly a stately home, Charlton House in Greenwich, London, has been the focus of many **paranormal** investigations by ghost researchers.

Charlton House was built in the early seventeenth century and sold in 1680 to William Langhorne, a wealthy East India merchant, who, desperate for an heir to his wealth, married for the second time, at 85, to a woman of 17. He died two months later, in 1715, before his new wife conceived. His restless **ghost** is said to haunt the house to this day, still looking for a woman who will bear him a child. There have also been sightings of a servant girl from the Jacobean period carrying a dead baby in her arms, and of **phantom** rabbits.

During World War I the house was turned into a hospital, and in World War II it suffered much damage from bombing raids. Workers found the body of a child walled up in one of the house's chimneys. Today Charlton House is a public library, and employees and visitors have reported **hauntings**, especially in two rooms on the third floor: the Grand Salon and the Long Gallery, where a rabbit hutch used to be kept.

The house has been investigated by the **Society for Psychical Research**, the Association for the Scientific Study of Anomalous Phenomena and the **Ghost Club**. Some unusual phenomena have been recorded, including cold spots, unexplained sounds of explosions, objects moving and mysterious voices. In late 1995 an **apport** is thought to have manifested during a taping for a BBC show on the paranormal. Prior to the vigil, when the lights were turned off, the room was searched. Around 11 pm an explosion was heard in the room. The lights were turned on, and in the centre of the floor was a blue and white teacup, broken neatly and arranged into a circle of seven pieces, as though laid out by someone rather than having fallen to the floor. No one could identify the cup as belonging to Charlton House. The BBC team investigated, and no evidence of a hoax was found.

Vigils continue to be held to this day, with some investigators saying they make contact with spirits. One of the most dramatic contacts took place on 30 July 1999, with members of the Ghost Club. A loud noise was heard and a test object placed in the room by the investigators, a carved wooden mushroom, flew about ten feet into the air. Again, no evidence of a hoax was found.

Charms

The word charm comes from a Latin word for a song or chant, but today it is associated with magic and can mean much the same thing as a **spell**. It is sometimes said that someone leads a charmed life, meaning a lucky or happy one. Many people also wear what they call good luck charms – **talismans** and **amulets**. Most people think particular objects are lucky, such as a four-leafed clover, a rabbit's foot or horseshoe. Whether or not these can bring luck is controversial, but one thing is sure: if the belief is there, the chances for good luck are increased, for the power of the mind actually does the work.

In folklore the world over there are also various charms against **ghosts** and **spirits**. Crossing oneself is a simple charm to ward off evil. Various gems, stones and metals like iron are thought to possess special powers to protect against ghosts. Salt scattered across the threshold or carried in a pocket and silver amulets, jewellery and crucifixes are also considered to be protective charms.

When a person dies various rituals are thought to act as charms against ghosts. For example, some say that all doors and windows should be left open so that the soul doesn't feel trapped. The corpse should be carried out of the house feet first, otherwise the dead person may return; and during the funeral, furniture in the house should be rearranged so that if the ghost tries to come back it will not recognize anything. Finally, it is regarded as unwise to speak ill of the dead, in case they return to haunt the living.

Chase Vault

On the island of Barbados there is a burial vault in Christ Church cemetery known simply as the Chase Vault. In 1807 a Mrs Goddard was buried there, followed in 1812 by Dorcas Chase, a possible suicide. When the vault was opened a month or so later to bury Dorcas's father, Thomas Chase, all the coffins had been moved from their original places. At first it was thought that the only explanation was grave robbers, but curiously, the seal of the tomb had not been tampered with.

In 1816 there were two more burials, and in both cases, when the vault was opened, the coffins already there had been moved into different places. Most peculiar of all was the fact that the casket of Thomas Chase, made of lead, weighing 240 pounds, and virtually impossible to move by a single individual, had also been relocated. Each time the coffins were put back in their proper places and the vault sealed with cement, but again in 1819 the vault was opened and the coffins had been rearranged.

This time the governor sprinkled sand on the floor to see if any footprints would be left and pressed his personal seal into the fresh cement. In 1820 when the vault was opened again, the coffins had been rearranged; some were even flipped upside down, even though the concrete seal was undisturbed and no footprints showed. The governor eventually ordered the coffins to be removed and buried elsewhere and for the vault to be left open. On investigation no water was discovered in the vault that could have shifted the coffins, and the possibility of earthquake movement was also ruled out. The mystery of the Chase Vault has never been solved.

CHELTENHAM HAUNTING

See **Morton case**.

CHI

See **Universal life force**.

CHIANG-SHIH

In Chinese folklore Chiang-shih, or 'hopping ghost', is a combination of **spirit** monster and unburied corpse, which vaguely resembles a Western **vampire**; it comes to life and wreaks death and misfortune. The Chinese believed that an unburied corpse was a great danger because it could easily be inhabited by evil spirits.

Traditionally the Chinese would bury their dead in garments that bound their legs together, so the spirit was thought to hop instead of walk. The Chiang-shih are blind but intensely powerful, with great supernatural powers, including gale-force breath, swordlike fingernails, incredibly long eyebrows that can be used to lasso or bind an enemy, **shape-shifting** powers and the ability to fly.

The Chiang-shih is created when a person dies a violent or painful death or when the **soul** has been angered because of an improper burial or improper preparation for burial, or when improper respects are paid to the dead. Something even being buried in the wrong location can cause a person to become a Chiang-shih.

Traditionally the Chiang-shih were believed to suck the breath out of their victims. The main items used in defence against Chiang-shih are death blessings, written on yellow paper and stuck to the forehead of the deceased, garlic, **mirrors**, straw and chicken blood.

CHICKAMAUGA

One of the bloodiest battles of the American Civil War was fought in Tennessee on the morning of 19 September 1863. Nearly 125,000 men fought at Chickamauga, and the combined casualties numbered 37,129. They compare with the 23,582 suffered at **Antietam**, known as the 'bloodiest day of American history'.

The name Chickamauga is derived from an ancient Cherokee word meaning 'River of Death'. Not surprisingly, there are several legends about **hauntings** there, but one of most bizarre concerns Old Green Eyes, a soldier who died in the battle. According to legend he is the ghost of a Confederate soldier whose head was severed from his body by a cannonball. Only his head was found, and his ghost is thought to roam the battlefield, moaning mournfully, searching for his body. There have been many sightings, some as recent as the 1970s, of two big, glowing eyes moving in the dark and reports of groaning sounds that send shivers up and down the spine.

CHILDREN

It is generally thought that **psychic** ability, often referred to as **intuition** or **gut feeling**, is natural in childhood, but as children get older they tend to lose that instinct and are taught to regard psychic experiences as **imagination** and **superstition**. Children's minds can easily accept the existence of the non-physical, but don't yet have boundaries of space and time and other models of perception that develop when they become adults. Their imagination is a reality to them, and they can see and comprehend things that adults no longer can do. They can cross the line into a fantasy world that adults have long since forgotten and exist in an altered state of reality that **Edgar Cayce** called unmanifest reality.

Anyone wanting to develop their psychic ability must start by returning to that childlike, dreamy state of mind where imaginary friends, gut instinct, make-believe, fantasy, awe of the amazing world we live in and the endless possibilities of our inner world are natural and real to us.

There are those who believe children are our real teachers and that their first task on earth is to teach adults about aspects of life they are neglecting. It may be something as simple as unconditional love or as com-plicated as resolving complex situations from the past. Unfortunately, many adults ignore the demands and idle chatter of children and don't grasp this opportunity to get back in tune with themselves, missing a fabulous opportunity to learn and grow up again.

See **Indigo children**.

CHINESE HERBAL MEDICINE

See **Traditional Chinese medicine**.

CHUREL

In India, the ghost of a low-caste woman who cannot find peace as she died in childbirth or during ritual impurity, i.e. during menstruation. Churels are thought to haunt graveyards or squalid places and take the form of a young woman with reversed feet and no mouth. They entice young men to them and hold them captive until they are old. Burying the corpse of a potential churel is said to prevent the ghost from escaping. If this fails, the area needs to be **exorcised**.

CIA, STAR GATE PROGRAMME

In 1972 the CIA, concerned by reports that the Soviet Union was dedicating substantial resources to what it called **psychotronics** – research into potential military applications of **psychic** and fringe science phenomena – began Project STAR GATE, a programme of psychic spying, or **remote viewing**. The project cost $20 million (£12 million) and lasted 23 years until the US military shut it down in September 1995.

The aim of the programme was to close the Cold War 'psychic warfare gap' and discover how serious a threat there was from Soviet psychotronics. Parapsychologists Hal Puthoff and Russell Targ of the Stanford Research Institute were asked to look for repeatable psychic phenomena that might be useful to military intelligence. Working with psychic Ingo Swann, the duo developed what they called 'a perceptual channel across kilometer distances', in other words, the ability to witness objects, people and events at a distance: remote viewing.

Initially called SCANATE, meaning 'scan by co-ordinate', the project required the viewer to describe what they could see at map grid references provided by the CIA. Early signs were encouraging, and the programme expanded. Also known as SUN STREAK, GRILL FLAME and, finally, STAR GATE, the programme was used to help many US military and intelligence-gathering operations over its 23 years. There were a few successes, but more than a few failures.

The team is said to have located Soviet weapons and technologies, such as a nuclear submarine in 1979, identified spies, helped find lost SCUD missiles in the first Gulf War and located plutonium in North Korea in 1994. All in all, more than 20 psychics were employed. With lives at stake, many of them found the work traumatic, some ending up in psychiatric hospitals.

The project was closed down in 1995, probably because the Defense Department lost confidence in it, but even today some psychics continue with police and government work; one assisted the FBI – clearly unsuccessfully – during the hunt for Osama bin Laden in late 2001.

CIPHER TEST

See **Survival tests**.

CIRCLE

A symbol of oneness, completion and protection, the circle is believed to represent a sphere of personal power or **psychic** energy. It is often used for **séances**, where participants hold hands around a circular table. Ceremonial magic rites are also often performed within the sphere of a magic circle, which functions to concentrate the user's power and protect against psychic entities. In ritual, a circle represents a holy space that protects from negative forces on the outside and facilitates communication with **spirits** and deities on the inside.

CLAIRAUDIENCE

The word clairaudience comes from the French and means 'clear hearing'; it is the ability to receive **psychic** impressions of sounds, music and voices that are not audible to normal hearing.

Humans have been guided by their **inner voices** since the beginning of time. The Bible refers to the Voice of God speaking to the prophets and kings. The ancient Greeks received guidance through *daimons* or divine **spirits** that offered guidance by whispering it into the ears of men and women. The **shamans** of many cultures use the voices in their heads for divine guidance. In **Yoga** the energy centre for clairaudience is the throat area, and it is thought that when it is clear you can open yourself up to inner hearing. Great men and women in history have experienced clairaudience. For example, **Joan of Arc** claimed to hear the voices of her **angel** spirit guides St Catherine, St Margaret and St Michael. In the eighteenth and nineteenth centuries messages from the spirits received clairaudiently were an established part of many **séances**. Today clairaudience often occurs in psychic readings.

Tuning in: an exercise to help develop clairaudient ability

If you're a good listener, if you find certain sounds and noises unbearable and if you are good at noticing changes in tone, pitch and frequency of noise, chances are you're more likely to receive psychic information through clairaudience. We all have some degree of clairaudient ability; we all experience those words or thoughts or ideas that seem to come from nowhere, but we tend not to recognize them or we take them for granted. You may wonder how you can tell if the voices you hear are psychic information or your own daily thoughts. One way to figure this out is to listen carefully. Your intuition tends to speak to you in a kind, loving and positive way. Self-talk tends to be harsher.

Find a place where you feel comfortable and won't be disturbed. Sit down, relax and breathe deeply. Imagine a shield of golden light around your ears for hearing and protection. Next, imagine a tuning knob such as on a radio in front of you. With this knob you can tune your hearing to a new frequency – that of your higher awareness – where you can receive clairaudient guidance. Sense a subtle sound change as you adjust the frequency. Note whatever information you receive. You may receive very little at first, but keep trying, and after a while you may find that your ears automatically tune to receive clairaudient information whenever you focus.

Clairaudience differs from the disembodied voices heard at séances and **poltergeist** cases, which are considered to be collective apparitional phenomena. It also differs from **telepathy**, which is the ability to read the thoughts of another person. Clairaudience can be identified in many different ways. You may hear sounds or voices that you know aren't happening in the real world and that you know aren't the same as your own inner voice. These voices may come when you are awake or in your **dreams**. They may be the voices of dead relatives or the voices of **spirit guides**. Besides voices, certain sounds may provide you with psychic insight. Some people hear ringing in one or both of their ears and believe this to be a message from the universe. Others hear music, whispers, laughter, crying, bells ringing or other sounds.

CLAIRFRAGRANCE

Often considered a form of **clairsentience**, clairfragrance occurs when a person smells the fragrances of those who are no longer alive, for example, the perfume of a deceased loved one when no one close to them is wearing or using that perfume, or from which the source is unidentifiable, for example whiffs of flowers or plants when none are around.

CLAIRGUSTUS

Experiencing sweet or sour tastes in the mouth that are not associated with eating or belching. Often classed as a form of **clairsentience**.

CLAIRSENTIENCE

The word clairsentience comes from the French and means 'clear feeling or sensing'. It involves the ability to pick up information through smell, taste, touch, **gut feeling** or **intuition**.

One of the most important experiments to test clairsentience took place in 1922 at the University of Groningen, Netherlands, where a psychic by the name of van Dam was tested in **psi** guessing games. The experimenters tried to transmit telepathically colours, tastes, feelings and moods, and the results were impressive.

Feeling what is around you is the most common way to receive **psychic** information. All people experience clairsentience through fleeting impressions but just aren't aware of it. For example, we all feel drawn to some people more than others for no apparent reason. But if a person is emotional, empathetic and compassionate by nature, and often affected by the moods of those around them, then chances are that psychic impressions typically come to them through clairsentience rather than through **clairvoyance** or **clairaudience**.

Investigate your clairsentience

Are you an emotional person? If so, what moods do you feel? Can you feel the moods of other people and animals? Can you feel the moods of specific locations or from objects? Can you feel the moods of spirits who have died with unresolved issues? Do you feel emotions about certain events in history and don't know why? Do you feel the emotions of friends or family or people close to you? Do you ever get a gut feeling that you should contact someone immediately? When you touch something or someone, do you get a rush of feelings? Do you sometimes experience physical sensations such as warmth or cold for which there is no external cause? Do you often have gut instincts about people or places you know nothing about? The following exercise is a fantasy meditation that is designed to stimulate clairsentience – your awareness to sense, read and respond to the feelings and atmospheres around you.

Find a quiet place and sit down in a comfortable position. Breathe deeply, and imagine you are a beautiful fish in the ocean. Enjoy the feeling of freedom as you glide through the water. Now imagine yourself to be one fish in a school of brightly coloured fish. You swim in rhythm with your group, sense its mood and shift your direction in perfect time and rhythm with the others. Now take this one step further and imagine yourself to be able to feel the mood of an entire oceanic world. You automatically sense and locate where to feed, play and swim and where you will be safe. You feel in total harmony with your ocean world.

CLAIRVOYANCE

Parapsychologists consider clairvoyance to be one of the three classes of **psychic** perception or **extrasensory perception** (**ESP**), along with **telepathy** and **precognition**, although there is overlap among the three. The word clairvoyance comes from the French, meaning 'clear seeing', and refers to the power to see an event or an image in the past, present or future. This type of sight does not happen with your physical eyes, but with your inner eyes. A person with clairvoyant ability can receive information in the form of visual **symbols** or images. Some clairvoyants describe it as a bit like having a movie screen in your head with images moving across it. Other clairvoyants may see symbols that they learn to interpret, or perhaps people and animals in their **spirit** form.

Psychic **visions** typically appear internally, through the mind's eye, and this is called subjective clairvoyance, but in rare cases they can also appear externally, in the environment around them as if they were real, and this is called objective clairvoyance. Many people think of the term 'inner eye' as a figure of speech, but the yogic tradition also uses the term. According to Eastern tradition, the **third eye** or sixth **chakra** is the seat of clairvoyance. Located in the centre of the forehead, it is the screen that receives clairvoyance, whether in the form of visions or **imagery**. In mediumship, clairvoyance may account for the ability of **mediums** to provide unknown information at **séances**.

There are several different types of clairvoyance, including the ability to see **auras** (auric sight), to see into the past (**retrocognition**) or into the future (**pre-cognition**). Different states of clairvoyance also include the ability to see through objects (**X-ray vision**), the ability to see health conditions in other people or animals (**body scanning**), the ability to see things from far away (travelling clairvoyance), the ability to experience visions in dreams (dream clairvoyance), the ability to see things that transcend time and space (spatial clairvoyance), and the ability to see astral, etheric and spiritual or divine planes (astral and spiritual clairvoyance).

Throughout history clairvoyance has been used and cultivated by prophets, fortune-tellers, **witches**, and seers of all kinds. Some were gifted naturally with clairvoyance while others learned how to develop it through training. In the 1830s

Under your eyelids

People who have strong visual skills tend to be particularly attuned to clairvoyance. If you think in pictures and notice how things look or appear first, rather than how they sound, feel, taste or smell, you may have clairvoyant abilities just waiting to be developed. Perhaps images that you can't relate to anything currently taking place just pop into your head. The following exercise will help you identify and work with your clairvoyant ability.

Find a quiet place where you won't be disturbed, and sit comfortably. Take a deep breath, and feel a protective bubble of light surround you. Let your eyes go out of focus as you concentrate on your third eye chakra. When you are ready, focus your mind's eye on the images that are behind your eyelids. What do you see? It's possible you will not see anything at all, and if so, that's OK. Clairvoyance may not be your strength or you may need to practise some creative visualization exercises. If you do see images, can their meanings be understood? When you are ready, take a deep breath, exhale and return to consciousness in a positive, relaxed mood.

the first scientific experiment to study clairvoyance was conducted on psychic Adele Maginot, and impressive results were achieved. Tests for clairvoyance of concealed cards began in the 1870s with French physiologist Charles Richet, and Richet's work was taken further in the 1930s by American parapsychologist **J B Rhine**. Rhine developed a special deck of symbol cards to conduct tests (see **ESP cards**). In the years since considerable evidence has been accumulated to suggest that clairvoyance exists in both humans and animals, although sceptics disagree.

CLEDONOMANCY

A method of **divination** in which significance is ascribed to chance remarks. It dates back to ancient Greece and Rome, where **omens** of good and evil were established from chance remarks spoken without premeditation.

CLOUD BUSTING

Also known as cloud dissolving, this is the psychokinetic ability to make clouds disappear by thought or will. Sceptics argue that clouds naturally appear and disappear every 15 to 20 minutes on their own, and tests on cloud busting have never been conclusive. However, various cultures around the world perform weather control ceremonies in the firm belief that humans, being connected to all things living, can influence the weather. Whether or not this is possible remains unknown.

CLOUD READING

Cloud reading is one of the oldest forms of **divination** and was commonly practised by the **Druids** and the Celts. By looking at cloud formations and how the clouds moved, fortunes could be determined.

Odd-looking clouds, and clouds that take on the distinct shape of something or someone, have intrigued and fascinated people through the ages. Clouds, mist and vapour are basic elements in human mystery, and many reports of **apparitions** begin and end with curiously shaped clouds.

COCK LANE GHOST

From 1762 to 1764 in Cock Lane, London, so-called **poltergeist** activity both terrified and fascinated onlookers. The story was written down by Andrew Lang and published in 1894 with the title *Cock Lane and Common Sense*.

It all began in 1760 when a stockbroker, Mr Kent, rented a house in Cock Lane from Mr Parsons, a parish clerk. At the time, a Miss Fanny was Kent's housekeeper; the two fell in love and decided to make wills naming each other as beneficiaries. Not long after, Kent and Parsons had a disagreement over money. Mr Kent moved out of the house and began legal proceedings against Parsons. In the meantime, Fanny died of smallpox, and Parsons seized upon the chance to get his revenge on Kent. He concocted a story whereby Mr Kent had murdered Fanny for the inheritance, and in 1762 Parsons began to claim that Fanny was haunting the house. He alleged that Fanny had told his 12-year-old daughter, Elizabeth, that she had been poisoned by Kent. Parsons invited a committee of 20 or more men to his house to witness Fanny's ghost possessing his young daughter. Elizabeth, apparently under the influence of Fanny, declared once again that she had been poisoned and that the only way she could rest would be if Kent were hanged.

Before long Cock Lane was full of the curious – Parsons even took to charging a fee for people to enter the house and listen to the ghost knocking. There were, however, many who were suspicious of the ghost tale, and their suspicions were confirmed when the ghost failed to appear as promised when Kent was brought to Fanny's vault. Parsons tried to argue that the ghost did not appear because Kent had moved Fanny's coffin, but Mr Kent countered this by taking several witnesses to the coffin, which he had opened to reveal Fanny's body. Afterwards, Kent indicted Parsons and his daughter for fraud. Parsons was found guilty and sentenced to two years in prison.

COINCIDENCE

See **Synchronicity**.

COLD READING

A cold reading is a **psychic** reading made for someone the psychic has never met. This type of reading is different from one in which there may have been previous contact or one in which the psychic has a certain amount of information already about the person being read. Typically, people visit their favourite psychics on a regular basis, and when this happens the readings are no longer cold, as the psychic becomes familiar with aspects of a client's personality and life.

COLLECTIVE UNCONSCIOUS

The collective or universal unconscious was a concept developed by psychiatrist **Carl Jung** (1875–1961) and later supported by Joseph Campbell in his study of world mythology. It refers to the part of the mind that is 'inborn' or determined by heredity and that shares memories, mental patterns and images with all humans. Prior to Jung, the prevailing view of the unconscious had been that of **Sigmund Freud**, who believed that it was the product of repressed childhood traumas.

Jung affirmed that a personal **unconscious** of repressed or forgotten material

Psychic or fraud?

A cold reading can be a good way to see if a psychic really can pick up relevant information that can help you. Be aware, though, that some psychics are very skilled at getting information about you without you even knowing it. They may be experts in observation, using every movement of your body and every expression on your face to verify information they give you; even a slight hesitation on your part can speak volumes. They may repeat information that you unconsciously already gave. Another technique is to make general statements or questions that could apply to anyone and to watch your reaction to pick up clues about what you are looking for in the reading. Be sure to recognize this approach – it is not how genuine psychics work.

existed but that the collective unconscious consisted of patterns of instinctual behaviour, called **archetypes**. The word archetype comes from the Greek *arche*, meaning 'first', and *type*, meaning 'imprint' or 'pattern'. Psychological archetypes are thus patterns that form the basic blueprint for human personality. For Jung archetypes pre-exist in the collective unconscious of humanity and determine how we both perceive and behave. These patterns are inborn – part of our inheritance and psychological life as human beings. They are both inside us and outside us. We can meet them by turning inwards to our **dreams** or **imagination**, and by turning outwards to our myths, legends, literature and religions.

COLLEGE OF PSYCHIC STUDIES

Founded in 1884 as the London Spiritualist Alliance, the college changed its name in 1955 to the College of Psychic Science, and in 1970 it became the College of Psychic Studies. The college is now a non-profit organization, based in South Kensington, London, which explores **psychic** phenomena and other spiritual matters such as **healing**. The college seeks 'to promote spiritual values and a greater understanding of the wider areas of human consciousness, welcoming the truths of all spiritual traditions and, equally, each and every individual.' An extensive library, materials and courses in psychic development, spiritual healing and **mediumship** are offered to the general public and to psychical researchers. The college also has a website where useful information can be accessed: www.college-ofpsychicstudies.co.uk.

Colour divination

Because colours are a dynamic part of our lives, affecting us in many ways (see **Colours**), some believe that colour can be used as a tool for **divination** and guidance.

Each colour has its own unique qualities. Some are uplifting and exciting, and some are soothing. Some stimulate healing, and some are depressing. We all have colours we like and dislike. Many believe we subconsciously pick colours we know will help

All about colours

The following provides some typically accepted attributes of colour that can help us gain insight into people no matter how they present themselves.

* **Red:** *Colour of strength and power, linked to sexual energy; can indicate an active person with lots of energy; darker shades can reflect strong emotions, even anger; can also indicate a creative person.*
* **Orange:** *The colour of fun, creativity and generosity (they may be too generous); a bright and optimistic person.*
* **Yellow:** *Intelligence, happiness, curious by nature; a person who prefers to take the lead.*
* **Green:** *Colour of healing; peaceful, emotional balance and compassion; a person who is honest and helpful.*
* **Blue:** *Spiritual understanding; a person who is usually perceptive, has a need for calm and is deeply involved in their work, sometimes to the point of neglecting other things; someone who*

is dedicated and talented and can be critical of others.
* **Indigo:** *Vision, intuition, psychic ability.*
* **Purple and Violet:** *Seekers, impatient with others, including themselves; have high ideals but can become depressed if ideals not met; someone who needs and seeks spiritual experiences.*
* **Black:** *Colour of protection and groundedness, psychic ability; when worn with another colour strengthens that colour; secretive, a quiet strength.*
* **White:** *Colour of spirit and of balance, could also indicate detachment; a person who is hopeful and spiritual; when worn with other colours amplifies those colours.*
* **Brown:** *Strength and nobility; someone who is down to earth, practical and helpful; someone who has strong friendships, is a devoted worker but can be overly critical.*
* **Pink:** *Love, warmth, tenderness, innocence, the impulse to nurture.*

us through the day and that it is possible to divine the mood of others by the colours they choose to wear or the colours they are most drawn to.

Energy healers who read **auras** believe that auras are made up of colours and that the colour of a person's aura can tell an enormous amount about a person and how she or he is feeling at that moment. For example, a person with a happy disposition might have a bright yellow aura, but it could change to red if they are angry. Someone else might have a red aura, suggesting they are often angry. If someone's aura has dark spots it could suggest ill health or disturbing emotions.

COLOURS

Every colour is believed to vibrate with its own energy and to have specific effects on individuals. Seven colours in particular – red, orange, yellow, green, blue, indigo and violet, the colours of the rainbow – have carried religious, occult, mystical and healing meanings since ancient times.

Red, which has the longest wavelength, typically represents the physical and material, while violet, the shortest wavelength, represents spirituality and enlightenment. White, the combination of all colours, is usually associated with divinity and purity, while black, the absence of all colour, is associated by some people with evil but by others with protection and comfort, like the warm darkness of a summer night. Traditionally, the body is associated with

red, the mind with yellow and the spirit with blue.

Healing with colour has a long tradition dating back to ancient times. The Pythagoreans believed that white light, the Godhead, contains all sound and colour and that the seven colours of the spectrum correspond to the seven planets and the eight notes of the musical scale (both the first and the eighth notes are red).

Despite the fact that colour healing has been in use for centuries, it wasn't until the late nineteenth century that it began to receive attention in the West. In 1878 Edwin Babbitt published *The Principles of Light and Colour*, reaffirming the Pythagorean correspondences of music, colour and sound, and by so doing drew attention to the potential of colour healing. In the 1930s Dinshah Ghadiali proposed that imbalances are created by too much or too little of particular colours, and that balance can be restored with the use of coloured lights. Today modern colour therapy or healing is a controversial but popular **alternative medicine** technique involving the use of coloured lamps as well as coloured foods and drinks in coloured containers.

Modern science is able to provide evidence for some of the ancient claims about colour. In the 1970s and 1980s it was shown that coloured light triggers biochemical reactions in the body. Later research confirmed that blues and greens have a soothing effect and help lower stress, **brain-wave** activity and blood pressure. Warm colours such as orange and red have been shown to have a stimulating effect. Pink has been shown to have a relaxing effect in the short term, although in the longer term it can trigger irritability.

Each colour is associated with a specific vibrational frequency, so when there is a predominance of one or two colours in the environment that vibrational frequency – and the characteristics or qualities associated with that frequency – will tend to influence the activities conducted in that environment and the attitude of those in it. It is small wonder, then, that many psychologists use colour to produce beneficial effects in the home, workplace and in hospitals, and in **visualization** techniques patients are asked to imagine themselves bathed in a particular colour to encourage healing in mind, body and spirit.

COMMITTEE FOR THE SCIENTIFIC INVESTIGATION OF CLAIMS OF THE PARANORMAL

A non-profit scientific and educational organization, started in 1976 and based in Buffalo, New York, to 'encourage the critical investigation of paranormal and fringe-science claims from a responsible, scientific point of view and disseminate factual information about the results of such inquiries to the scientific community and the public'. It also aims to promote science and scientific enquiry, critical thinking, science education and the use of reason in examining important issues. The organization maintains a network of people who critically examine **paranormal** claims and sponsors research into such claims.

The group originated as an offshoot of the American Humanist Association following a disagreement over the claims made by astrologers. It soon gathered a following of committed sceptics, including scientists, academics and science writers such as Isaac Asimov, Philip Klass, Ray Hyman, Sidney Hook, and others. *The Skeptical Inquirer* is the society's official journal, and its aim is to explore and expose public gullibility about the paranormal.

Many local branches of the group are scattered across the US. Members include academics and scientists as well as magicians, many holding religious views, such as atheism, that are not in accord with belief in the paranormal. Although the group has debunked many claims of the paranormal, from **hauntings** to **ESP** to faith **healing**, there are some who believe it goes too far in its attempt to debunk from a scientific point of view. Nonetheless, it does provide a valuable counterbalance to paranormal claims.

CONE OF POWER

See **Circle**.

CONSCIOUSNESS

A funtion of the mind, generally thought to incorporate qualities such as subjectivity, self-awareness and the ability to perceive the relationship between oneself and one's environment.

In popular language the term 'consciousness' denotes being awake and responsive to one's environment; this contrasts with being asleep or being in a coma. The term 'level of consciousness' denotes how consciousness seems to vary during anaesthesia and during various states of mind such as daydreaming, **lucid dreaming**, imagining, etc. **Esoteric** techniques such as **meditation** and **pathworking** and shamanic techniques such as **chanting**, rhythmic drumming or dancing, as well as experimental techniques such as sensory deprivation and narcotics to induce hallucination all involve **altered states of conciousness**. Non-consciousness exists when consciousness is not present. There is speculation, especially among religious groups as well as occultists, **psychics** and **spiritualists**, that consciousness may exist after death or before birth.

Consciousness is notoriously difficult to define or locate. Many cultures and religious traditions place the seat of consciousness in a **soul**, separate from the body. Conversely, many scientists and philosophers consider consciousness to be intimately linked to the neural functioning of the brain.

CONSTELLATION, USS

The USS *Constellation*, floating in the harbour of Baltimore, is perhaps one of the most haunted ships in America.

The ship was commissioned by the US navy and first launched as a 36-gun frigate in 1797. Commodore Thomas Truxton was the first captain, and he set a bloody precedent. In 1799, after the Americans had won a battle against the French, the captain learned that seaman Neil Harvey had fallen asleep while on watch. The captain ordered another sailor to run a sword through the sleeping man and then had Harvey's body tied to a cannon and blown to pieces in order to warn the other sailors. Many visitors to the ship report seeing Neil Harvey's **ghost** wandering on deck, and it is said that some people even mistake him for a costumed tour guide.

During the nineteenth century the warship was damaged in battles, and the original ship was broken up in 1853. The *Constellation* reborn in 1855 as a sloop, and served the US navy until 1933, when it was decommissioned and sat quietly in harbour. In 1955 it was brought home to Baltimore to await repairs, and this is when stories of ghosts began to be told. Sailors standing night watch on nearby ships said they heard odd noises and reported seeing ghosts walking on its deck.

To this day reports of sightings of spirits continue to occur. Captain Truxton has been seen, and cries and moans have been heard in the hold. An anonymous seaman has been spotted sadly wandering around the gun deck. He is believed to be a sailor who became overwhelmed by the harsh life at sea and hung himself.

The USS *Constellation* is docked at Pier 1 in Baltimore's Inner Harbor and is open to the public for tours.

CONTROL

A **discarnate entity** or **spirit** of the dead that is thought to communicate through a trance **medium**. The term is derived from the notion that a control is the entity that generally controls the **trance** state and decides which spirits will communicate and how they will communicate to the living through the medium. The term control would have been a familiar one during the height of **spiritualism**, but today it isn't widely used and mediums prefer to use terms such as spirit helpers, gatekeepers or friends instead.

A control manifests during a trance state and generally takes over a medium's body and **consciousness**, communicating through the medium. According to various controls that have been questioned, controls are separate entities from the medium, and during trance, when the control takes over, the medium's consciousness is displaced out of body or transported to the spirit world. In some case a medium may not be aware of the control until told by others who have witnessed the manifestation. A medium typically has one control, as was the case with **Mina Crandon** and her spirit control, Walter, but some may have more than one.

There are many who believe that controls are secondary personalities of the medium rather than spirits of the dead. Even prominent mediums like **Eileen Garrett** concluded that her control might have been a construct drawn from her own **unconscious**. Most controls do reflect aspects of the medium's personality, and it is logical to conclude that they are second-

ary personalities of the medium. However, if controls are secondary personalities, they are unusual in that they do not interrupt and intrude during waking life, as secondary personalities do in multiple personality disorders.

COOK, FLORENCE [1856–1904]

Florence Cook is best remembered as the **medium** who was able to produce the full spirit **materialization** of her **controls**. She said she first noticed her **psychic** powers as a child when she heard **angel** voices and experienced her first **trance** state at the age of 14. At the age of 15 she lost her job as a teacher due to **poltergeist** phenomena and from then on devoted herself to her development as a medium.

Cook's most prominent control **spirit** was called **Katie King**. Cook would retire into a **cabinet** and be tied to a chair with rope, the knots sealed with wax. After a few minutes King, who could not speak but only nod and smile, would emerge in front of the cabinet. After the spirit disappeared, the sitters waited for Cook's instructions to release her, and they always found her in the cabinet still clothed and tied and exhausted from the experience.

Cook was not reluctant to allow the press in, and a reporter from the *Daily Telegraph* attended several of her **séances**. On the first occasion, he saw faces, and the following year he witnessed the materialization of Katie King and took photographs of her. In view of the precautions taken, such as Cook being bound with seals, 'he was baffled'.

Cook's abilities led to various prominent persons attending her séances, and in 1872 she begun to receive financial support from the businessman and **spiritualist** Charles Blackburn. She also attracted the attention of spiritualist investigators, including the British scientist **Sir William Crookes**.

The appearances of Katie King were investigated many times, with sitters regularly reporting that they were able to see Katie and Cook at the same time, for the cabinet would be opened and Cook would be visible in the back while Katie appeared out front. Many sitters also reported that Katie King and Florence Cook were very similar in appearance, and some charged that Cook and Katie were, in fact, the same person.

Cook was caught at least twice in **fraud**. On one occasion a sitter grabbed a spirit hand and found he had grabbed Cook. On another occasion in 1880, Sir George Sitwell noticed that King was wearing corsets. He seized her and pulled aside the curtain to reveal an empty chair and the ropes untied.

Sir William Crookes vigorously investigated the case, taking photographs, witnessing both Cook and Katie at the same time and even attaching Cook to a galvanometer to record Cook's movements while Katie appeared. Despite allegations of fraud, Sir William and other supporters remained convinced that Florence Cook was a genuine medium.

In 1874 Katie King departed. Afterwards first Leila, and then a French girl calling herself Marie became Cook's controls.

Marie remained her control until shortly before Florence Cook's death in 1904. A photograph was taken of her at a séance in about 1902, which later appeared in *Psychic Science* (January 1927); one of the sitters made the important observation that those present 'saw the form of the tall slim young woman that appears in the picture; Mrs Corner [Florence Cook] being short, rather stout, and of darker complexion'.

COOKE, GRACE [1892–1979]

Grace Cooke, born in London in 1892, became a **spiritualist** medium in 1913. Unlike most **mediums** of the day, intent on communicating with the dead, Cooke focused on spiritual development, which she felt the world badly needed.

From an early age Cooke experienced psychic visions of a Native American **spirit guide** called White Eagle, who told her they would accomplish great spiritual work together. In 1936 White Eagle instructed Cooke to form a church for people ready to be light bearers and to practise brotherhood and sisterhood. After several false starts, the **White Eagle Lodge** was established in Hampshire in 1945. It soon grew into an international organization publishing tracts and books.

Until her death in 1979 Cooke emphasized living by the light of love and healing. In her later years she experienced vivid memories of previous lives, and the stories of these past lives are recorded in her book *The Illuminated Ones*.

Corpse candles

According to British folklore, corpse candles are mysterious candles that float through the air by night and hover near locations where death is imminent. They are said to vanish when approached and warn of death to those who see them or of the death of a loved one. In Welsh folklore a pale bluish corpse candle is said to presage the death of a child, a bigger candle the death of an adult and multiple candles a multiple loss.

Although corpse candles have been witnessed all over the British Isles, their origin is supposed to date back to fifth-century Wales. Legend says that St David, the patron saint of Wales, was concerned that the people he served were always unprepared for death, so he prayed that they might have some kind of warning. He received a vision in which he was told that the Welsh people would always be forewarned of a death by the dim light of mysterious candles.

Corpse lights

Corpse lights are similar to corpse candles in that they are seen at night and are believed to be **death omens**. They are believed to be phosphorescent lights in white, red, or blue that can appear almost anywhere, inside or outside a house, on the ground, on the roof or over a person's chest. They are also known as **jack-o'-lanterns**, **ignis fatuus**, corposant, fetch-candles and **fetch** lights. It is possible they are produced by atmospheric gas, but in folklore there are many reports of their seemingly mysterious and **supernatural** appearance.

Cottage City poltergeist

A fascinating and curious case that was the inspiration behind the 1971 best-selling book by William Peter Blatty, *The Exorcist*. In the book, later made into a film, a young girl is possessed by the devil and subject to **exorcism** by a Roman Catholic priest, but in the original 1949 case that inspired the book, the subject was a 13-year-old boy.

The case began in Cottage City, Maryland. The family of a young boy, called in some newspaper reports 'Roland Doe', began to experience **poltergeist** activity. It started with scratching noises from the house walls, and then the boy's bed began shaking and moving on its own, with similar events occurring at school.

A psychiatrist was called in to examine the boy but could find nothing wrong with him. The family called in a minister who believed that a **ghost**, perhaps the spirit of the dead aunt, might be involved. Some reports say that a Lutheran minister performed an **exorcism** or a series of exorcisms, while other reports say exorcisms were performed by a pair of Jesuit priests.

After the movie appeared, new reports surfaced of a detailed diary kept by one of the Jesuit priests of the entire exorcism process. The diary says that the exorcism took place in a hospital, the boy's reactions to the exorcism were violent and that it took four months for the 'demon' to be expelled. Afterwards the boy remembered nothing and the case was quietly buried. The room at the hospital where the exorcism took place was rumoured to be haunted in the years following. Many people who worked near the room continued to report cold waves of air and unusual noises coming from inside the room.

What truly happened in the case remains a mystery. Were there natural or psychological explanations for what occurred in the case? Or was this simply the story of an attention-starved boy tricking the adults around him into believing he was possessed by the devil?

COTTINGLEY FAIRIES

In July 1917, 16-year-old Elsie Wright and her 10-year-old cousin Frances Griffiths claimed they could see **fairies** in the small wooded creek behind Elsie's house in Cottingley, West Yorkshire. Elsie's father dismissed their claims, and so one day the girls borrowed his camera to take a picture of them.

The picture, when developed, showed Elsie with a group of fairies dancing in front of her. A month later the girls took a picture of Elsie with a gnome. Elsie's parents were startled by the photographs, but her father remained unconvinced. Her mother, however, took the pictures to a Theosophist meeting one evening, and

soon the photos were published. The girls' most famous supporter became **Sir Arthur Conan Doyle**, the creator of Sherlock Holmes. Conan Doyle printed the first two pictures in *Strand Magazine* in 1920 and three more photos a couple of years later. He then expanded his articles into a book, *The Coming of the Fairies*. Shortly after, Frances's family moved away from Elsie's, and the girls stopped seeing fairies.

In the decades that followed, the photographs were widely circulated and deemed false, and even Conan Doyle himself finally admitted that he may have been the victim of a hoax. It wasn't until the 1980s, though, that Frances and Elsie admitted that they had faked the photographs to get back at the adults who had told them off for believing in fairies. They said that when Conan Doyle had got involved they didn't want to embarrass him by admitting that the photos were faked. They also said that as young girls they had actually seen fairies, but that the fairies didn't like to be photographed.

CRANDON, MINA STINSON [1888–1941]

This Boston **medium**, also known as Margery, left a controversial legacy behind her. Opinion is divided as to whether she was one of the greatest mediums of her day or a complete **fraud**.

Unusually for mediums, Crandon's early life did not offer any hints of her future psychic power. It wasn't until her divorce in 1918 and second marriage to prominent surgeon Le Roi Goddard Crandon, who had an interest in the **paranormal** and set up a psychic **home circle**, that her abilities began to surface. Soon she was demonstrating remarkable abilities as a medium managed by her **control**, Walter. Walter was in fact Mina's brother who had died five years earlier, with whom she had been very close.

Several investigations of Crandon's power were put together by prominent academics and psychical investigators, including **Harry Houdini** the magician, who was utterly convinced that she was a fraud. Despite causing bitter controversy, Crandon had many supporters at the **American Society for Psychical Research**, and a book published in 1925, *Margery the Medium* by Malcolm Bird, editor of the *Scientific American*, was very favourable to her.

Mina Crandon appeared to enjoy all the attention she received from press and public alike. By all accounts it wasn't just her psychic powers that her supporters admired. She was a vivacious and charismatic person who was not adverse to holding **séances** in the nude and to having extramarital affairs with more than one of her investigators.

When asked on her deathbed if fraud had taken place, she refused to set the record straight. With the hint of a smile and a twinkle in her eye, she is said to have replied, 'Why don't you guess? You'll all be guessing for the rest of your lives.'

CREATIVE VISUALIZATION

Creative visualization is the process by which the creation of a visual image is believed to promote the desired outcome.

Creative visualization is built on the ancient belief in the power of the mind to create what you want in your life. If you think about what you'd like to achieve in your life, you can do just that, as positive images and thoughts attract positive energy. Creative visualization is widely used in business, sport, art, psychotherapy, **psychic** development, mystical and **occult** arts and personal self-development.

Imagination has a powerful influence on self-image, and a poor self-image can often mean the difference between success and failure in life. Creative visualization, which seems to be most effective when practised in a relaxed state, can be used to feed your mind positive images to create a better self-image and improve your personal experiences. For example, if you want to develop your psychic awareness, you need to imagine being psychic. If you want to pass an exam, you imagine yourself passing it. Those who practise visualization say it's important to fill in all the details of your experience so that the image is as real to the mind as possible.

CREWE CIRCLE

The Crewe Circle was a group of **spirit photographers** based in Crewe, England, in the latter half of the nineteenth century.

Led by William Hope, the circle claimed to be able to photograph the souls of the dead. Many psychical research organizations investigated the claims, but the most documented are those sponsored by the Royal Photographic Society and **Sir Arthur Conan Doyle**, the author of the Sherlock Holmes novels. Conan Doyle was so intrigued by the Crewe Circle that he wrote a book about it entitled *The Case for Spirit Photography* (1922).

Over the years the spirit photographs taken by the members of the Crewe Circle have come under detailed examination, and have been dismissed as fraudulent by many, but so far none has been proven conclusively to be a hoax. It is possible that the photos could be spontaneous images of **spirits** captured on the film plates.

Willem Tenhaef from the University of Utrecht. Tenhaef was so impressed by Croiset's ability that he began to mentor him, and introduced him to police work. In the years that followed Croiset became famous for his help in solving crimes all over the world. His passion was finding missing children.

Croiset never accepted payment for his psychic readings, but he did accept donations for his healing clinic where he treated thousands of clients. He was able to diagnose a person instantly on seeing them. Perhaps his most famous contribution to the field of **parapsychology** was to popularize the chair test. In this test, chairs in a room would be numbered, and Croiset was able to predict successfully who would sit in a selected chair a month or so before a meeting took place.

CROISET, GERARD [1909–1980]

Born in the Netherlands, Croiset grew up to become an internationally renowned clairvoyant, highly regarded as a **police psychic** for his ability to find missing people, animals and objects.

Croiset was raised in foster homes and orphanages and began to experience **clairvoyance** at the age of six. He dropped out of school at 13 and drifted into unskilled work. The turning point in his life came in 1935 when he was introduced to a group of local **spiritualists**, and over the next few years his reputation as a psychic and healer grew. In 1945 Croiset volunteered to be a test subject for the parapsychologist

CROOKES, SIR WILLIAM [1832–1919]

Sir William Crookes is perhaps best known as a ground-breaking chemist and physicist who discovered X rays and explored the existence of subatomic particles such as the electron. For much of his life he was also deeply committed to **spiritualism**. He served as president of the **Ghost Club** of London for a while and took a great interest in the cases investigated by this organization. During his own investigations Crookes believed that many times he did in fact witness the **materialization** of human forms, and he also studied and photographed teleplasm and **ectoplasm**.

Published posthumously in 1926, Crookes's work, *Researches in the Phenomena of Spiritualism*, is still considered required reading for any serious student of the subject.

CROP CIRCLES

Patterns, typically circle shaped, that appear mysteriously in the middle of grain fields in the middle of the night. The grain inside the circles is usually crushed as if knocked down by force. No tracks have been found leading to these circles, resulting in the belief that some **paranormal** force must have been involved in their creation. Some crop circles have been exposed as hoaxes, but others remain unexplained.

Crop circles have been reported all over the world, including in the USA, but they began appearing in southern England in the 1970s. They vary in size from about 10 feet to 200 or even 300 feet in diameter. They aren't always circles but can also appear in elaborate formations and patterns. They are always immaculate and cleanly made.

Natural forces, such as violent or freak weather patterns, stationary **whirlwinds** or the effects of irrigation have been put forward as theories, but all these fail to explain the more complex patterns, which often resemble pictograms. There are those who believe some intelligent life force is trying to communicate with humankind, while others believe extraterrestrial forces must be at work. The mystery remains unsolved.

CROSS CORRESPONDENCES

A method used extensively in the early twentieth century to test the powers of **mediums**. The correspondences were made up of the same or similar information allegedly from **discarnate entities** delivered to mediums while they were in a **trance** or through **automatic writing**.

It is difficult to explain how these messages occur, and many psychical researchers believe they provide good evidence to support the case for life after death. Others believe that the mediums draw the information from their own **unconscious** or from others using **telepathy** or **clairvoyance**.

Between 1900 and 1932, cross correspondences were studied intensively by the **Society for Psychical Research**, in particular, by **Frederick Myers**. Myers believed that human life might continue after death and that finding evidence for it required the help of the dead – in fact, the dead would have the best idea for how the living could discover this evidence. He stated that producing this evidence would require a group effort on the part of several **spirits** rather than just contact with one spirit.

Cross correspondences were produced during Myers' lifetime by several mediums. Words spoken under trance and written during automatic writing sessions by mediums sitting at the same time but in different locations showed similarities to one another. But it was after Myers' death in 1901 that cross correspondences became more frequent; a message delivered to one medium would be undecipherable until combined with a message from another.

By 1918 the Society for Psychical Research concluded that cross correspondences did form large, interlinked groups and were evidence for **survival after death**. However others, such as another of the Society's founding members, **Frank Podmore**, believed they were the result of telepathic communication among the living.

Interest in cross correspondences faded in the 1930s, and although they do appear now and again in psychical research, today they are not studied with great interest.

CROSSROAD GHOSTS

Crossroads – the meeting and parting of ways – have long been regarded as likely places for **ghosts** or other spirit activity to take place. Crossroad **superstitions** can be found in Europe, India, Japan and among Native Americans, perhaps because in some parts of the world murderers, **sorcerers** and suicides were buried at crossroads with a stake or nail driven through the corpse, an act known as 'nailing down the ghost' to prevent the ghost's return. Or perhaps the cross shape of the intersection mimicked the consecrated ground of a churchyard, a burial place denied to murderers and suicides. Or perhaps crossroads were places where territories, routes or villages collided, and they therefore became regarded as meeting places between the spirit realm and earth.

Crossroads are believed to be haunted by **spirits** who take delight in leading travellers astray. In German folklore a ghostly rider is believed to haunt a crossroads in Schleswig; the neck of his horse stretches across the path and prevents people passing. In European lore the dead are said to appear at crossroads, and in Welsh legend every crossroad is thought to be inhabited by spirits of the dead on Allhallows Eve. In modern evolutions of the tradition, crossroads in the rural Mississippi Delta area are reportedly frequented by either Lucifer or his minions; wandering musicians and minstrels seeking to bargain their immortal souls for success in their musical endeavours know to go to crossroads to meet with the Devil.

The cross shape of crossroads is in some traditions protection against the spirits that are said to haunt it. For example, in Irish folklore humans who have been kidnapped by **fairies** are thought to be able to gain their freedom at crossroads. One German **superstition** holds that if you are chased by a ghost or **demon**, you should head to a crossroads for protection. On reaching the crossroads the spirits will vanish with an unearthly shriek.

CROWE, CATHERINE [c.1800–c.1870]

The author of *The Night Side of Nature*, which is one of the earliest and most important studies of **apparitions**, Catherine Crowe used a scientific approach to study **ghosts**. Some contend that her fascination with apparitions may have been brought about by a brief period of insanity, but this does not take away from the fact that her work has often been cited as the model for subsequent investigations of the **paranormal**.

CROWLEY, ALEISTER [1875–1947]

Called by the media 'the wickedest man in the world', Aleister Crowley courted controversy all his life with his fascination for sex, magic and blood. Despite his excesses, there are some who think this English occultist was a truly great magician.

Born Edward Alexander Crowley on 12 October 1875, in Leamington Spa, Warwickshire, Crowley was raised by parents who were members of a fundamentalist Christian sect called the Plymouth Brethren. Crowley was drawn to blood and torture from a young age and was branded 'the beast' or Antichrist by his mother when he rebelled against the Brethren.

After leaving Trinity College, Cambridge without a degree but fluent in occultism, Crowley joined the London Chapter of the Hermetic Order of the **Golden Dawn** and quickly advanced up the ranks. He renamed himself Count Vladimir and began to pursue his **occult** activities full-time in London. Stories began to circulate about his alleged **supernatural** powers, including **psychic attacks** on his enemies with **demons** and **vampires**. Whether this is true or not is uncertain, but one thing is clear: he had incredible charisma and presence. A dis-

agreement with another Golden Dawn member forced him to leave London and live in Scotland for a time.

Crowley's sexual appetite was huge. He married twice but had a number of mistresses, and a seemingly unending stream of willing women were attracted to him. He also had a homosexual relationship with the poet Victor Neuburg, who became his assistant in magic.

In 1912 Crowley became involved in the Oro Templi Orientis occult order, becoming its leader in 1922. From 1915 to 1919 Crowley lived in the US before visiting Italy, where he set up his hillside villa called the Sacred Abbey of the Thelemic Mysteries. The villa became the site for his sexual orgies and magical rites, and the behaviour led him to be expelled from Italy in 1923 by Benito Mussolini.

In his later years Crowley was a victim of poor health, drug addiction and financial trouble. He earned a meagre living from his writing, since much of it is incoherent and rambling, but many continue to read his work today. His most important work, *The Book of Law*, was allegedly communicated from the Egyptian god Horus's spirit messenger Aiwass. Central to this book is the Law of Thelma: 'Do what thou wilt shall be the whole of the law', which Crowley maintained meant doing what you must do and nothing else. His other important work is *Magick in Theory and Practise* (1929), which many practitioners consider to be a fine work on ceremonial magic. (He spelled 'magic' as 'magick' to distinguish it from stage magic.)

Crowley's other published works include *The Diary of a Drug Fiend* (1922), *The*

Equinox of the Gods (1937), and the *Book of Thoth* (1944), which is his interpretation of the **Tarot**. Two volumes of his autobiography were also published. In 1934 he tried to sue Nina Hammett for her biography of him, *Laughing Torso*, in which she stated that he practised **black magic** and human sacrifice, but the jury found in favour of Hammett.

Crowley died on 1 December 1947, in a boarding house in Hastings. His final years were spent practising ritual magic with Gerald B Gardner, whom some call the father of modern **Wicca**. Even though Crowley has been dead for decades, his influence is still very much felt today. One of the many attractions of Crowley's type of magic was his advice to follow your own way, become your own self and create your own lifestyle – you don't need a priest or a judge to tell you how to act; you work it out for yourself. It is easy to see how, in the hands of the young, impressionable or immature, this advice can be misinterpreted and become not only misguided but dangerous.

CRYPTOMNESIA

Information that is forgotten or repressed but which comes to the surface in **mediumship** or contact with **spirits** of the dead.

Forgetting information and storing it in the subconscious mind are essential if the conscious mind is to function efficiently and stay uncluttered. However, during **trance** or **altered states of consciousness**, forgotten or repressed information may break free from the subconscious and surface again, where it appears as new information to the **medium**. Psychical researchers always consider the possibility of cryptomnesia when investigating mediums and cases of **past-life recall**.

The earliest recorded case of cryptomnesia was in 1874 when English medium **William Moses** was said to have contacted the spirits of two young brothers who had died in India. The deaths were verified; however, six days before the **séance** it was discovered that an obituary to the brothers had appeared in the newspaper. Moses's information about the brothers was similar to that in the obituary, and psychical researchers concluded that Moses must have read the obituary and had forgotten that he had done so.

It is not known how long the brain can store information and how much information it can store without taking conscious note of it, so it is difficult to rule out cryptomnesia in cases of memories of **afterlife** and **reincarnation**. In one famous cryptomnesia case, a woman identified as Ms C communicated under **hypnosis** with a woman called Blanche from the court of Richard II. The period details were uncannily accurate, but when asked under trance what books she had read about Richard II, Ms C acknowledged that when she was 12 she had read an Emily Holt novel, *Countess Maud*, which contained the same material as Blanche had given.

The only time cyrptomnesia may possibly be ruled out is when the information received by the medium goes beyond accessible records to facts that can only be verified by other persons or in personal accounts. However, even then other explanations such as **ESP** and **telepathy** can't be entirely ruled out.

CRYSTAL BALL

A tool used to help diviners go into a psychic **trance**, the crystal ball is perhaps the classic and best-known method of **divination**. Most people assume it is the ball that has the power, but it is not. The secret is not the ball but the technique of **scrying**, which involves keeping your eyes open while staring into a shiny, reflective surface to induce a form of **meditation** or self-hypnosis – the prime state for opening awareness to **clairvoyance** and psychic insight.

Scrying and crystal gazing practitioners were found in ancient times throughout Mesopotamia, among the **Druids** and other peoples of Europe and in China. Modern scryers most commonly use crystal balls that are usually three to six inches in diameter. The ideal crystal ball is made of quartz, not glass, because quartz crystal is thought to increase psychic energy.

Crystal gazing exercise

Find a quiet place where you won't be disturbed and, holding your crystal in your hand, begin slow rhythmic breathing. Focus on what the problem is or on what you want to know about. As you hold the crystal, feel it coming to life. Imagine the electrical energy within it growing stronger, helping to stimulate your psychic vision. Hold the crystal so you can look into it easily. Don't stare intently into it, just look at it with a soft gaze – the kind of stare you have when daydreaming. Stay relaxed, and as you look into the crystal pay attention to its formation.

Turn your crystal slowly in your hand so you can see how the light plays through it in different ways. As images begin to form, ask yourself what they mean to you. Pay attention to the emotions you feel, and trust them. When you are ready, close your eyes, take some deep breaths and come back to the here and now.

Crystal gazing takes time and practice, but in time you will probably see clouds appearing and disappearing and images becoming clearer. Eventually detailed scenarios may even start to appear in your crystal, leading to great psychic vision.

CRYSTALS

Crystals have been used for centuries for their alleged protective and healing powers. Ancient peoples typically wore crystals as **amulets** in jewellery and on their clothing, and the practice continued through the Middle Ages, when they were worn to guard against the plague. Today crystals continue to be worn in pendants and rings and other jewellery, or carried around in small pouches, or placed about workplaces and houses.

Because of the ability crystals have to retain and focus electromagnetic energy they are believed to be ideal tools for repelling bad energies or for attracting good ones, and for stimulating and balancing the body's energy flow, also known as its life force or chi. They are used in **meditation**, **divination** and **alternative healing** techniques and are thought to help alleviate stress, stimulate creativity, enhance **dreams**, energize, promote healing, enhance luck and happiness and awaken psychic powers. In some healing techniques they are laid upon the body's **chakra** points and energy meridians to enhance the energies of the ailing chakra.

There is no scientific evidence that crystals have magical or **paranormal** powers, but crystal enthusiasts are convinced that the stones emit silent and unseen vibrations. Some even believe that crystals can be programmed for certain functions using techniques such as exposure to sunlight and moonlight or through meditation.

Crystal healing in some form has been practised by almost every society on earth, many of which held deeply rooted **holistic** beliefs. However, without this cultural foundation, crystal healing has largely become a matter of faith. You either believe or not, as there is little or no rational explanations of *how* it might work, if it does.

Crystals are often fashioned as **wands** or magical tools, but they come in all shapes

Crystal power

Below is a list of commonly known crystals and their reputed benefits. Please note that this information is not intended to replace any licensed medical or psychological treatment, and no guarantee is made towards their validity.

* *Amethyst: This purple and white stone is the most valuable form of quartz crystal and it is thought to have wonderful healing and cleansing abilities. It is used to reduce anger and impatience and to ease insomnia and headaches. It is also used to cleanse other crystals before their use in healing and*

divination, and is sometimes called the psychic crystal for use in enhancing intuition and ESP. In magic, wearing an amethyst or using one in a spell will ward off evil.

* **Aquamarine:** Known as the 'water stone', it is thought to prevent seasickness, ease water retention and help purify drinking water. Aquamarine is also used for its calming, uplifting properties and its ability to help release anxiety, fear and restlessness.

* **Bloodstone:** As the name suggests, this crystal is thought to cleanse the blood. It is also believed to promote courage and help people face difficulties calmly.

* **Carnelian:** Thought to be good for the circulatory, reproductive and digestive systems and to help stimulate libido, energy and fertility, as well as to boost confidence and drive.

* **Coral:** Thought to be a good aid to digestion and to encourage self-esteem and positive thinking.

* **Diamond:** Believed to stimulate a powerful sense of direction in life and help strengthen one's courage.

* **Emerald:** The stone of true love, emerald is thought to generate insight into a relationship – which may or may not be welcome. It is also thought to bestow psychic ability, heal inflammation and promote a feeling of inner peace and relaxation.

* **Garnet:** This stone is said to be good for balancing out sexual problems. Both overactive sexuality and repressed urges are thought to benefit from the power of garnet. It is also thought to encourage assertiveness and to help regularize blood pressure.

* **Jade:** Said to be good for the heart, thymus, immune system and kidneys and for cleansing the blood and the nervous system. Jade is thought to help promote courage, knowledge, justice, compassion, emotional balance, humility, generosity, harmony, wealth and longevity. It remains the crystal most revered by the Chinese, where it is believed by some to be of divine origin. In magic, jade is used to help remember dreams and to use them to solve problems.

* **Kunzite:** Discovered in 1902, this stunning pink stone is thought to be superb for women with gynaecological problems, and for women seeking to come to terms with all aspects of their sexuality. It is believed to be a reassuring, healing, calming stone.

* **Lapis lazuli:** Honoured as a royal stone by the ancients, this blue and gold stone has always been used to help create a link between reality and the realm of intuition. Egyptian high priests used to wear it ground up as eye makeup and in jewellery during rituals. It is thought to be good for anyone undergoing spiritual awakening or instruction in a particular religion.

* **Malachite:** Said to be good for the stomach, liver, kidney stones, respiratory

system, immune system, vision and the circulatory system. It is often used to help ease pain, inflammation, depression and anger, and to stimulate psychic vision and concentration.

* **Opal:** The common misconception that opal is unlucky is due to Sir Walter Scott's fictional story *Anne of Gererstein, but opal is in fact* considered to have profound magical, spiritual and healing powers. Opals are said to enhance intuition and positive beliefs as well as bring luck and money to business leaders. They are also thought to reveal the state of your physical and emotional energy, being dull when energy is low and brilliant when it is high.

* **Pearl:** Thought to be a gem of hope and inner strength. If a pearl loses its lustre, it is unlikely to regain it or attract good energy; crystal enthusiasts believe when it has lost its life force a pearl becomes dull.

* **Quartz:** Generally a term for a number of crystals, including amethyst and topaz, but clear quartz is the substance used to make crystal balls. Rose quartz is thought to have special powers to attract affection and is used in love spells or at times of high emotion, like the break-up of a relationship or a bereavement. Along with amethyst, no person serious about crystals would be without this versatile, powerful stone, believed to emit a form of electrical energy that helps to stimulate psychic powers. Many

people believe that wearing quartz crystals benefits a person's health and spiritual wellbeing. Quartz is typically used to rid an environment of unhealthy vibrations and electromagnetic toxins. In magic quartz is used as a protective amulet against evil and for spells, and for centuries quartz has been used to enhance a person's ability to foretell the future.

* **Ruby:** Thought to boost blood circulation and to attract love, courage, confidence, vitality, stamina and strength, and to help one triumph over adversity.

* **Sapphire:** Thought to be a stone of control that can help you overcome temptation and guide your thoughts to higher things. Also thought to be good for reducing fever.

* **Tourmaline:** Thought to be a stone of transition, both physical and emotional, and to help people through the processes of birth, menopause and death, as well as other rites of passage. It is believed to be good for people who feel the world is against them and for those who have a great need to forgive – especially themselves.

* **Turquoise:** An ancient symbol of the sky, this stone is thought to benefit lungs and throat, and because it contains a good deal of copper it is believed to be a superb conductor for the healing force. It is also good for those terrified of speaking in public or of appearing physically or emotionally weak.

and sizes. It is claimed that an odd number of facets on the stone aid in healing, while an even number of facets create the best energizers. Red, yellow and orange stones are said to produce energy; clear and aquamarine stones are healers; and lavender and blue-violet stones create calming effects.

Practitioners of modern-day crystal therapy believe that the stones' ability to work as conductors allow them to focus energy by way of a person's thoughts to stimulate healing – both physical and non-physical – and thousands of people worldwide swear by the use of crystals to help a variety of mental, emotional and physical problems.

Many people who work with crystals believe that the stones choose whom to work with, not the other way round. But whatever you believe you need to be selective with the stones you use. Once selected it is suggested that you should never let anyone touch your crystals, and should 'programme' it to attune to your particular energy. Each crystal should be cleansed before use to clear any stored energy, by either soaking it in salted water or by wrapping it in silk and burying it in the ground for 24 hours.

CURSES

Associated with **black magic** and intended to cause someone harm, curses are deliberately malevolent or vengeful oaths, **spells** or **invocations** of **spirits** directed against another person by psychic means.

See also **Psychic attack**.

D

Dactylomancy

An ancient form of **divination** involving rings. A ring was tied to a string, or dropped into a bowl of water, with the position of the ring at the end of the string, or at the bottom of the bowl, determining the answer or response to the question asked. Dactylomancy is thought to be one of the earliest forms of divination involving the use of **pendulums**.

Dagg poltergeist

Poltergeist activity that eventually manifested itself as a speaking entity in 1889 on a farm in Quebec owned by George Dagg.

According to records the activity began with streaks of animal faeces or manure appearing on the floor of the house. A young boy, Dean, was blamed; however, when the boy was out of the house the stains continued to appear, proving that he was not the cause. Soon the activity increased: windows were smashed, objects were thrown and fires broke out. This time the focus was identified as 11-year-old Dinah McLean, an adopted child of the family.

In November 1889 an investigator named Percy Woodstock asked Dinah to take him to the woodshed where she had reported seeing a strange man. To Woodstock's amazement, from the middle of the empty shed a few feet away came the clearly audible voice of an old man. It cursed them both in a deep, gruff voice, using language Woodstock would not record. It said, 'I am the devil, I'll have you in my clutches, I'll break your neck.' Woodstock talked to the voice for several hours, during which it admitted causing the fires, spreading the manure, smashing the windows and moving objects. Eventually it calmed down and admitted it was only doing the **hauntings** for fun.

A crowd soon heard about the phenomena and gathered around the house and woodshed, where the entity allegedly performed incredible feats for the audience. Woodstock organized a statement signed by 17 witnesses acknowledging that they had seen the phenomena of flying stones and a mouth organ playing by itself:

To whom it may concern:
We, the undersigned, solemnly declare that the following curious proceedings, which began on the 15th day of September, 1889, and are still going on, on the 17th day of November, 1889, in the home of Mr George Dagg, a farmer living seven miles from Shawville, Clarendon Township, Pontiac County, Province of Quebec, actually occurred as below described.

1st, That fires have broken out spontaneously through the house, as many as eight occurring on one day, six being in the house and two outside; that the window curtains were burned whilst on the windows, this happening in broad daylight whilst the family and neighbors were in the house.

2nd, That stones were thrown by invisible hands through the windows, as many as eight panes of glass being broken; that articles such as waterjug, milk pitcher, a wash basin, cream jug, butter tub and other articles were thrown about the house by the same invisible agency; a jar of water being thrown in the face of Mrs John Dagg, also in the face of Mrs George Dagg, whilst they were busy about their household duties, Mrs George Dagg being alone in the house at the time it was thrown in her *face*; that a large shelf [mouth organ] was heard distinctly to be played and was seen to move across the room on to the floor; immediately after, a rocking chair began rocking furiously. That a washboard was sent flying down the stairs from the garret, no one being in the garret at the time. That when the child Dinah is present, a deep gruff voice like that of an aged man has been heard at various times, both in the house and outdoors, and when asked questions answered so as to be distinctly heard, showing that he is cognizant of all that has taken place, not only in Mr Dagg's family but also in the families of the surrounding neighborhood. That he claims to be a discarnated being who died twenty years ago, aged eighty years; that he gave his name to Mr George Dagg and to Mr Willie Dagg, forbidding them to tell it. That this intelligence is able to make himself visible to Dinah, little Mary and Johnnie, who have seen him under different forms at different times, at one time as a tall thin man with a cow's head, horns and cloven foot, at another time as a big black dog, and finally as a man with a beautiful face and long white hair, dressed in white, wearing a crown with stars in it.

What is of particular interest is that the entity made itself visible in a variety of guises to Dinah and the two younger children of the house – as a devil, a black dog and a man in white robes. Finally, when the entity had got the attention it craved, it was said to have departed from the farm singing beautiful music in the sky.

Sceptics argue that Dinah and the children may have been responsible for the whole phenomena, tricking their parents into believing an entity existed, but this does not explain how they could convince a whole crowd of adults. The case has never been resolved but some experts believe that the poltergeist, having finally got some attention, calmed down and went away. According to this theory, poltergeists can act like humans at times, perhaps behaving badly out of boredom or a need to attract attention. Once they get the attention they want their disruptive behaviour ceases.

DAPHNOMANCY

A form of **divination** that predicted the future through burning a branch of laurel in an open fire. If the laurel burned with a good crackling sound this was a good **omen**, but if the laurel burned slowly and quietly this was a bad sign.

The practice dates back to ancient Rome where a sacred grove of laurel trees was planted by each emperor when they ascended to the throne. In the year AD 68 the laurel grove withered and died. This was the same year Emperor Nero died and the long line of Caesars came to an end.

Davenport brothers

The Davenport brothers conducted one of the most popular and successful **séance** acts of the nineteenth century. Ira Erastas and William Henry Davenport added the spirit **cabinet** to the **medium**'s repertoire and their sophisticated performances amazed and mystified audiences all over America and Europe.

Ira Davenport was born in Buffalo, New York on 17 September 1839, and his brother William two years later, on 1 February 1841. Their father, a New York policeman, was interested in stories of **rappings** reported in nearby Rochester and decided to try a sitting at home with his family. Almost immediately they got results and Mr Davenport would later tell friends that the boys and their younger sister Elizabeth levitated about the room.

The family began to hold regular séances and at one in 1850 the family made contact with their **spirit guide**, an entity named **John King**. It was King who allegedly told the family to rent a hall and give public performances, and in 1855, the boys went on stage for the first time, aged 16 and 14. At first their act consisted of **table tilting** and rapping but soon the Davenport brothers began to introduce new phenomena, such as floating musical instruments playing under their own power and playful spirit hands that touched and pulled at audience members. By the end of the year the brothers had introduced escapes from complicated rope bindings and knots into their séances and, what would eventually become the signature for their act, the spirit cabinet.

The cabinet was a box, similar to a closet, which would be erected on stage. A sceptical member of the audience would be asked to bind and tie the brothers inside the cabinet, making it seemingly impossible for them to escape. However, as soon as the cabinet doors were closed, and the lights turned off, spirit music would play and disembodied hands would appear through apertures that had been left open on the exterior walls.

On occasion, a volunteer from the audience would be placed between the brothers in the cabinet. A few moments after the doors were closed the volunteer would be tossed out of the box with a tambourine on his head. When the doors were opened the Davenports would be found tied up, in exactly the same way they were before.

The act was billed as a séance and created a sensation. Although the brothers never admitted to being mediums – leaving that to the audience to decide – and critics labelled them mere stage magicians, **spiritualists** hailed their act as genuine proof of spirit phenomena.

In 1864 Southern preacher Jesse Babcock Ferguson joined the brothers to act as master of ceremonies. He travelled with them on their controversial but successful four-year tour of Europe, and claimed to know of no occasion when their phenomena were not genuinely **paranormal**.

William died suddenly in July 1877 on a trip to Australia and Ira, lost without his brother, retired from performing. During his retirement he was interviewed and befriended by the magician and anti-spiritualist **Harry Houdini**. According to Houdini, Ira confessed that the brothers were expert conjurers, not spiritualists, but had got carried away with the public's enthusiasm for all things supernatural. Ira explained many of the brothers' escape tricks, such as rubbing their hands with oil so that they could slip out of the ropes more easily, and employing as many as ten hidden accomplices at a time. The most important part of their escapes took place during the binding, when they managed to get plenty of slack into the ropes by twisting, flexing and contorting their limbs. Once they relaxed, the ropes could be easily slipped off.

Despite their natural ability many people remained convinced that they were spirit mediums and that Houdini's testimony contradicted the signed statements of distinguished believers and reporters. Newspaper accounts, such as the one below, which appeared in the conservative *London Post*, gave them credit for producing miracles.

The musical instruments, bells, etc., were placed on the table; the Davenport Brothers were then manacled, hands and feet, and securely bound to the chairs by ropes. A chain of communication (though not a circular one) was formed, and the instant the lights were extinguished the musical instruments appeared to be carried about the room. The current of air, which they occasioned in their rapid transit, was felt upon the faces of all present.

The bells were loudly rung; the trumpets made knocks upon the floor, and the tambourine appeared running around the room, jingling with all its might. At the same time sparks were observed as if passing from south to west. Several persons exclaimed that they

were touched by the instruments, which on occasion became so demonstrative that one gentleman received a knock on the nasal organ which broke the skin and caused a few drops of blood to flow.

With the media in awe of the brothers and convinced of their powers, it is hardly surprising that spectators were equally amazed and that the Davenports – who were never caught cheating once in their performing career – created a sensation.

DAVIS, ANDREW JACKSON [1826–1910]

A nineteenth-century **medium** who was able to detail the creation and spiritual evolution of the world through **trance** revelations, Andrew Jackson Davis was born in Blooming Grove, Orange County, New York on 11 August 1826. Davis's family was poor and he had little formal schooling, drifting from job to job. In 1843 he began work as a **clairvoyant** after discovering that under trance he could see through the body as if it were transparent and make astonishing medical diagnosis.

In March 1844 Davis went into a trance and wandered about 40 miles from his home into the Catskill Mountains, where he had a series of mystical visions of Galen, the Greek physician, and **Emanuel Swedenborg**. Repeated visions convinced Davis that he was to serve as an oracle of divine truth, and he moved to New York City with S Silas Lyon, a botanic doctor who was to act as his mesmerist. Within a few months Davis selected Rev William Fishbough, a Universalist minister, to be his scribe and in November 1845 the three men began their work.

In their New York apartment Lyon would hypnotize Davis. After a few minutes Davis would go into shock and become rigid and cold, hardly breathing. Then Davis would begin talking and Fishbough would write everything down. Typically there would be three witnesses watching the dictation. Edgar Allan Poe was frequently present. The most influential visitor was a professor of Hebrew at New York University, George Bush, and he endorsed the accuracy of Davis's trance pronouncements, calling Davis the greatest prodigy since Swedenborg.

It took around 157 sessions for *The Principles of Nature, Her Divine Revelations, and a Voice to Mankind, By and Through Andrew Jackson Davis, the Poughkeepsie Seer and Clairvoyant* to be written down and published in 1847. It was an overnight success and the 21-year-old Davis became an instant celebrity. He did not get instantly wealthy though, as he assigned all copyright of the book in trance to Lyon and Fishbough.

The book seems rambling and dense to the modern reader but in the mid-nineteenth century people were fascinated by complicated creation, philosophy and religious theories. Covering a huge range of topics, from the evolution of the solar system and the biological history of earth to the life of Jesus and the precepts of Swedenborg, Davis defined God as the great positive mind that is by its nature progres-

sive. According to Davis, after death man progresses through the celestial spheres to the seventh sphere, where he becomes one with God's infinite mind, wisdom and love; throughout the book he gives hope to readers for future regeneration, both in the secular and the spiritual world:

It is a truth that spirits commune with one another while one is in the body, and the other in the higher spheres, and this, to when the person in the body is unconscious of the influx, and hence cannot be convinced of the fact: and this truth will ere long present itself in the form of a living demonstration. And the world will hail with delight the ushering in of that era when the interiors of men will be opened, and the spiritual communion will be established.

Davis claimed to have had little or no formal schooling and critics, recognizing creation theories and spiritual concepts of the likes of Robert Chambers and Swedenborg, accused him of fraud. It is unlikely that Davis could have recited from all these texts under trance but some believe that Davis simply had a remarkable memory.

On 31 March 1848, Davis predicted the birth of **spiritualism** when he wrote in his diary that he felt a warm breath on his face and a voice telling him that the good work had been done and a living demonstration was born. It was on that day – 31 March 1848 – that the **Fox sisters** allegedly first made contact with a **spirit** from the **afterlife**.

Davis continued to lecture and write about divine philosophy and healing for the next 30 years, until he became a legitimate physician at the age of 60 with a medical degree. In addition to healing, another subject that interested him was the discovery of electrical vibrations, as early evidence of **psi**. Despite being hailed by the **spiritualist** movement as their John the Baptist, Davis faded into obscurity in his later years. He ran a bookshop in Boston until his death in 1910, where he sold **occult** literature and prescribed herbal cures to patients.

DAY OF THE DEAD

A festival held every year that brings the living and the dead together for a great feast and celebration, to remember the dead and placate them for another year. It often involves parties, songs, parades and special foods.

Ceremonies for the dead are part of Chinese and Japanese culture but perhaps the most elaborate ceremonies occur in Mexico on 2 November, All Souls' Day. A few days before, offerings of food and toys for children who have died are placed on clay altars. Around midnight the **spirits** of the dead children are thought to come and enjoy their presents. On All Souls' Day itself children enjoy special food and adults prepare an even bigger feast; altars are decorated with skulls and bones made from bread for the spirits. Later in the day neighbours go from house to house sharing memories of the deceased, who are thought to gather to listen to what is said about them. No dead soul is neglected for fear it

may become sad or angry. These visitations last all night and are followed by a mass early the next morning, at which time the dead return to their graves. After a day of rest everyone goes to the cemetery to enjoy a picnic with the departed so that they can rest happily until they rise again to mingle with the living next year.

DEATH

The opposite of life, ceasing to exist. Also a personification of the destroyer of life, typically represented as a skeleton holding a scythe. Dying, when all bodily functions cease, is the great unknown that neither religion nor science has been able to fully explain or understand. Because it is unknown and inevitable, death has always both fascinated and terrified the living. Some cultures, such as the Egyptians and the Christians of the Dark Age, have been absolutely obsessed by it. All cultures have had their own myths about it.

Most people see death as a time of sorrow and regret but some religions, such as Hinduism and Buddhism, see it as a blessed release for the **soul** that has gone. Funerals are a time for great rejoicing as to cry and mourn will literally hold the soul to the earth.

For psychics and **mediums**, who say they can communicate with the dead, and those who have had **near-death experiences** (i.e. they have technically died and have been revived to tell their story), death is almost always described as a beautiful process. However much pain the physical body is experiencing the moment the soul gets into the **astral body** this disappears and there is a feeling of lightness and peace. Typically a loving soul appears to tell them that their work on earth has not been completed and they need to go back. That marvellous feeling of peace and oneness, however, stays with them and the person is left with an understanding that death is not the end but simply the end of a cycle, for the soul goes on eternally learning lessons and seeking perfection.

DEATHBED VISIONS

Visions experienced by the dying. Most are visions of the **afterlife**, glowing entities of light and **apparitions** of the dead known to the person dying, or great religious or mythical figures such as the Virgin Mary. Deathbed visions are extremely significant because they provide evidence in support of life after death. Although most religions and cultures believe in an afterlife, Western science believes that **consciousness** cannot exist separately from the body and death is the destruction of the personality.

Deathbed visions have been recorded in the literature of all ages and have been researched scientifically since the late nineteenth century. In the early twentieth century **Sir William Barrett**, professor of physics and a psychical researcher, conducted the first systematic study of such visions. Barrett's interest in the subject was fuelled by his wife, an obstetric physician, who told him about a woman who spoke of seeing a vision of great beauty and seeing her dead father and sister before she died. What impressed Barrett was the fact that although the woman's sister had died a few weeks earlier there was no way she could have known that.

The next systematic study of deathbed visions took place in 1960, when **American Society for Psychical Research** investigator **Karlis Osis** collected information from doctors and nurses on thousands of deathbed visions in the US and India. Other studies followed, including an Indian survey in 1972. The findings and observations found in these studies confirmed those made by Barrett.

Typically deathbed visions occur to those who die gradually from a terminal illness or injury rather than those who die suddenly. Many of the visions are of apparitions of dead loved ones or family members known to the dying person, such as parents, siblings and spouses, or beings of light perceived as mythical or religious figures. The purpose of these apparitions – called take away apparitions – appears to be to command the dying to come with them and thus assist them in the transition to death. The response of most of the people dying to these visions is one of happiness, peace and a willingness to go. Their mood changes from one of suffering to one of radiance and joy.

Approximately a third of deathbed visions involve a vision of the afterlife, which is typically described as a beautiful garden. Some see apparitions there, others see streams, bridges and boats and other symbols of transition. Again the emotional response is one of great happiness and peace. The great majority of visions appear just before death with the patient dying shortly afterwards.

There are various natural explanations given for deathbed visions. Drugs, fever, disease, the brain suffering oxygen deprivation, hallucinations and wish fulfilment have all been given as possible causes. Although they are plausible explanations, Osis's research showed clearly that deathbed visions are most likely to occur in the fully conscious and that medical factors do not trigger visions. Wish fulfilment is not a likely explanation either because visions appear both to those who believe and to those who do not believe in an afterlife, and also appear to those who want to recover and live. Finally there have also been reports by the living who are in attendance to the dying of clouds of silvery energy floating over the body, as well as take away apparitions and **angels**.

Deathbed visions are significant not just because they suggest the possibility of **survival after death**, but because they also demonstrate that the moment of transition to death should not be feared. If reports of deathbed visions are to be believed, for the person who is dying death can be a wonderful and beautiful experience.

DEATH CHART

Used with the birth chart of **astrology** this is a means of forecasting the date or time of death.

DEATH OMENS

In folklore a death omen is a sign of an impending death. Every culture has its own unique death omens.

Death is frequently foretold by the appearance or behaviour of certain animals, insects or birds associated with the **afterlife**. Black birds – crows, owls, ravens, rooks – are often though to be death omens when they appear in a village or cluster around a house. The howling of a dog or a black cat crossing the path are also thought to be signs that portend the death of someone nearby. Spiders are often associated with death, and according to American, British and European lore the deathwatch beetle, which makes a ticking or tapping sound during the summer months as it bores into wood, is considered the harbinger of a death in the family.

Death omens can be natural occurrences, for example the way wax drips from a candle, or accidents, such as a chair falling over backwards as a person gets up, or signs of nature, such as cloud shapes or star formations. They can also be **supernatural** occurrences, such as candles and lights that flicker in the night – see **corpse candles** and **corpse lights** – or the appearance of an **apparition**, such as the **banshee**, or a **phantom coach** with a headless coachman, or spectral black dogs, or other animals.

DECATUR HOUSE

The haunted house of one of America's most celebrated naval captains in the war of 1812, Stephen Decatur. Located in Lafayette Square, Washington, DC Decatur House is said to be haunted by the ghosts of both Stephen and his wife, Susan.

Stephen Decatur moved to Washington with his wife in 1818 after the war ended. He was admired and even considered a presidential hopeful, but unfortunately for him, in 1807 he had served on the court-martial board of his friend, Commodore James Barron. Decatur had agreed with the rest of the board that Barron should be court-martialled, starting a feud that ended in Decatur's death at Barron's hands during a duel 13 years later in Bladensburg, Maryland (duelling being illegal in Washington). On 14 March 1820, the morning of the duel, Decatur was mortally wounded and taken home to die. His wife was so broken-hearted she could not bring herself to look at him or to live in the house after he had died.

A year after his death his **apparition** was allegedly seen looking sadly from the window where he had stood on the eve of his death. The window was walled up but this did not stop the ghost returning. Later sounds of a woman weeping – said to be Susan Decatur – were also heard.

Residents of Washington still report seeing Decatur's spirit peering out of the second-storey window or slipping out the back door of his house with a black box under his arm, just as he had done on that fateful day of the duel.

DECLINE/INCLINE EFFECTS

Terms used to describe phenomena witnessed in **psi** testing. The decline effect is a term used to describe the diminishing of **psychic** ability when tested. The incline effect refers to an increase in ability.

Experiments to test psychic ability tend to show that the decline effect occurs more often than the incline effect. Some gifted individuals score highly consistently but many gifted test subjects, who have scored highly in the initial tests, report a loss of spontaneity and enthusiasm during a run of tests. This may be due to the fact that the perception of psi is a very subtle process and without feedback a subject has no way of judging his or her success. Another major factor is boredom as many tests involve repetitive tasks such as guessing numbers or cards.

DEDUCTIVE PSYCHIC INTUITION

Psychic images that come from the **unconscious** mind's ability to take in external sensory stimuli. The unconscious mind is a kind of storage facility, absorbing and storing all the stimuli, such as pictures, sounds, noises and so on, we are constantly being bombarded with but can't process all at once, as this would lead to information overload.

When the conscious mind – the part of the mind that is objective and in charge of reasoning and making decisions – has a question about something that it just cannot answer, the question will go to the unconscious mind, which will mull over the problem and rely on its stored data to come up with a response. In the meantime the conscious mind goes on to another subject and forgets what it was looking for, but the unconscious keeps hard at work until, out of nowhere, an insight appears. This is deductive psychic intuition at work.

See also **Random psychic intuition**, **Goal-focused intuition**.

Dee, John [1527–1608]

Official court astrologer to Queen Elizabeth I, admiralty spy – with the code name 007 – and transcriber of the angelic **Enochain** alphabet of **alchemy** and **magic**, John Dee was one of the most learned and remarkable occultists of his day. It is thought that **Shakespeare** used him for his model of the magician Prospero in *The Tempest*.

Dee was responsible for setting the date of Elizabeth's coronation by casting a **horoscope** to find the most auspicious day, but he is perhaps best known for his relationship with **medium** Edward Kelley. Dee was greatly interested in communicating with **spirits** and employed Kelley for the sum of £50 a year. The two men believed themselves to be in contact with a number of entities, including an impatient **angel** called Ave. It was Ave who dictated to Kelley, with Dee recording, the text of an entirely new system of magic in a language called Enochain. Dee and Kelley were also associated with the divinatory art of **scrying** (crystal gazing). Their experiments in crystal gazing, using a shewstone that is now in the British Museum, began in 1582 and continued to 1587.

Kelley may have had some **psychic** ability but he was undoubtedly a scoundrel as well. On one occasion he managed to persuade Dee that the spirits had instructed them to 'hold their wives in common', an arrangement that broke down within a matter of weeks when the less gullible wives began to get suspicious.

Kelley also persuaded Dee to leave his position at court and concentrate on producing gold alchemically. When this failed the Queen took pity on Dee and reinstated him as a rector of a small college, but he was never to regain his earlier prestige.

Déjà vu

An expression of familiarity that is unexpected, déjà vu is the sensation of having been to a place or experienced a situation before. The French term for 'already seen' can apply to feelings, thoughts, places, **dreams**, meetings and living in general – whenever something familiar seemingly happens for the first time. The idea was first introduced to science in 1896 by F L Arnaud.

Studies conducted on déjà vu suggest that it is a common experience, with more than half of those polled reporting instances of déjà vu. It also seems more common in children and women than men.

The phenomenon is thought to be a psychological process where the **unconscious** mind is stimulated to recall past events of a similar nature that somehow get mixed up with the present event. Some feel that it is evidence for **reincarnation**, memories of past lives being pushed to the surface of the mind by familiar surroundings or people in the present. Some say it happens when one draws on the collective memories of mankind – see **collective unconscious** – while others believe it to be the result of **out-of-body experiences** during sleep, or other extra-sensory phenomena.

DEMON/DAEMON

To the ancient Greeks daemons, from the Greek word *daimon* meaning 'divine power', 'fate' or 'god', were intermediary **spirits** between the gods and humankind, rather like **guardian spirits**. They could be either good or evil. Good daemons were supportive and encouraging but evil daemons could lead people astray with bad counsel.

The Christian Church labelled all such **pagan** spirits as evil, which is why daemons, better known to us today as demons, are traditionally associated with evil. For centuries demons have been blamed for a host of ills and misfortunes including demonic sexual molestation, where a demon masquerades as a man or woman to molest its victim. Many **possession** cases in the Middle Ages involved sexual molestation by demons, although this may have been more to do with repressed humans than **supernatural** activity. In many cultures and religions demons have been exorcised. In Catholicism cases of demonic possession – in which demons battle for a person's **soul** – are dealt with by formal **exorcism** rites that date back to 1614.

DEMONANCY

Also called necyomancy. A form of **divination** that calls on **demons** to reveal the truth of a matter or of future events. This is done by summoning **spirits** via an **oracle** or **occult** magic. Demons, however, are reputedly perverse, so the accuracy of any predictions made is thought to be unreliable. Moreover, some demons are believed to be hard to control and, if they are able to free themselves from the constraints put on them, they can take over the body and **soul** of the summoner.

DEMONOLOGY

The study of **demons** or malevolent **spirits** and their powers, attributes and derivations. Demons were thought to be extremely evil and extremely clever, masters in the art of persuasion. Humans had to be constantly on their guard against them. In 1580 philosopher Jean Bodin claimed that:

It is certain that the devils have a profound knowledge of all things. No theologian can interpret the Holy Scriptures better than they can; no lawyer has a more detailed knowledge of testaments, contracts and actions; no physician or philosopher can better understand the composition of the human body, and the virtues of the heavens, the stars, birds and fishes, trees and herbs, metals and stones.

The hierarchy of demons was much discussed among theological experts in the last centuries. According to Alphonse de Spina (1467) there were ten types of demon:

- *Fates that can change destiny.*
- ***Poltergeists*** *that cause mischief.*
- *Incubi and succubi – demons who stimulate lust and perversion.*
- *Hordes – demons that bring conflict.*
- ***Familiars*** *that assist* ***witches.***
- *Nightmares that disturb sleep.*
- *Demons formed from human semen.*
- *Disguised demons.*
- *Demons that trouble the saintly.*
- *Demons that instigate* ***witchcraft.***

DEPOSSESSION

Also known as **spirit releasement**. Depossession is practised all over the world and is the **exorcism** of human and non-human **spirits**, such as elemental spirits and **demons** thought to be attached to an individual and causing physical, mental and emotional distress.

American psychologist Edith Fiore used depossession in her **past-life therapy**, believing that in regressing patients to past lives interference from attached spirits could be observed. According to Fiore, amongst about 70,000 cases 70 per cent were unaware that they were showing signs of **spirit attachment**, such as mood swings, chronic pains, illnesses and addictions.

Most spirits are thought to be those of humans who have died but not left the earthly plane. They are believed to attach themselves to humans during moments of poor health and emotional weakness. Depossession is typically accomplished by persuading the spirits that they need to leave, and patients subsequently say they feel much better afterwards. Depossession was common practice at the height of the popularity of **spiritualism**, but the first medically trained person to approach mental illness as caused by spirit possession was the American physician and psychologist **Carl Wickland**.

Wickland and his wife, Anna, a **medium**, attributed all sorts of mental illness to confused spirits trapped in the **auras** of living people. In the late nineteenth and early twentieth centuries the Wicklands depossessed a large number of their patients. They used a static electricity machine that transmitted low voltage electric shocks to the patient, causing the possessing spirit distress and forcing it into Anna's body and then to leave. If the spirit resisted, Wickland called on spirit helpers to keep the spirit in a 'dungeon', out of the aura of Anna or the victim, until it stopped its selfish quest and departed.

DERMOGRAPHY

Skin writing. Although dermography is similar to **stigmata** it has one very essential difference: stigmata last for years or an entire lifetime, skin writing usually lasts only for a few minutes. Some cases appear to be genuine, such as that of Charles H Foster cited by **Nandor Fodor** in his *Encyclopaedia of Psychic Science* (1934):

Charles H Foster, the 'Salem Seer', gave abundant demonstrations of the phenomenon. Before the Dialectical Society Edward Laman Blanchard told the story of how the name of his father appeared in red letters on the arm of the medium and immediately afterwards, in answer to a question, the numbers 24 on the palm of his hand, indicating the number of years since his death. The phenomenon was very rapid, the letters and numbers disappearing in the sight of those present without the arm of the medium being withdrawn. Dr Ashburner examined Foster's skin-letters under a powerful magnifying glass. He observed clearly that they were in relief and that the colouring matter was under the skin. Foster's biographer, George C Bartlett, describes an amusing incident. A certain Mr Adams came to consult Foster. He saw the room filled with spirits in his presence. About two o'clock the next morning he woke up, complained to Bartlett that he could not sleep as the room was still filled with the Adams family. They were writing their names all over him. To his astonishment Bartlett counted eleven distinct names, one written across Foster's forehead, others on his arms, and several on his back.

Fraud in skin writing is thought to be widespread. Given the sensitive skin of neuropsychopaths writing may appear in a few minutes after the letters are directly traced on to the skin by any blunt instrument or the nails. Many 'mediums' of skin writing burn up a pellet on which a question or name is written. They then rub their forehead or arm with the ash, which gives the opportunity for covertly tracing the message.

DEVAS

From the Sanskrit meaning 'shining', in Hinduism and Buddhism devas are believed to be exalted beings with great powers. In **Theosophy** and **occult** traditions they are a class of beings midway between **angels** and elemental spirits, having special authority over the world of nature. In modern times devas are popularly thought to be nature spirits, in charge of the elemental spirits of **air**, **water**, **fire** and **earth**. They are invisible and etheric in nature, inhabiting the **astral plane**. They communicate with people by **psychic** means, such as **channelling** and **ESP**. It is thought that the channelled wisdom of devas was responsible for the location of the **Findhorn** community in Scotland.

DEVIL

An evil **spirit** or **demon** and the supreme personification of evil. The word devil is derived from the Hebriac *Satan* via the Greek *diabolos*, but over the centuries the devil has collected a number of other names, including Beelzebub, Lucifer, Belial, Abaddon and Asmodius. In modern times the theologically conceived supreme embodiment of evil that the devil represents accommodates in one **supernatural** being all that is evil, ugly, perverse and unjust in the world.

DEVIL'S MARK

A name given by **demonologists** and medieval witch-hunters to a scar, blemish or mark on the skin said to be imprinted by the devil as a seal or sign of his **possession** of the person.

The finding of such marks became an important business of the expert pricking that took place at many witch persecutions. Devil's marks were said to be insensitive to pain and pricking pins into such areas was supposed to draw no blood.

DICE TEST

Experimental technique used in **psi** testing for investigating **psychokinesis**, the psychic power of the mind to influence objects,

DIY psychokinetic test: dice

Concentrate your mind upon the throwing of a six. You can speak or shout at the dice but you may not in any other way influence it. If you score a six write this down. Do this 30 times. How many sixes did you score?

* *8+: There is less than 1 per cent chance of attaining this score. Good evidence for psychokinetic ability.*

* *7: Psychokinetic potential high – there is less than 8 per cent chance of attaining this score.*
* *6: Psychokinetic potential still likely as this is above chance.*
* *3–5: Within the area of chance.*
* *2: Less than 3 per cent chance of attaining this score.*
* *1: High psychokinetic potential but working backwards – less than 1 per cent chance of attaining this score.*

in which a subject attempts to influence the fall of dice, for example, by trying to throw more sixes than any other number (chance would give a success rate of 1 in 6 correct throws).

DICKENS, CHARLES [1812–1870]

The author of perhaps the most famous of all ghost stories, *A Christmas Carol*, Dickens also wrote a number of less-well-known ghost stories, including *The Haunted Man* and *The Haunted House*. As well as writing about the **paranormal** Dickens held a tremendous interest in the study of **ghosts** and **spirits**. He went to extraordinary lengths to gain access to some of Britain's **haunting** hotspots to experience the unknown for himself.

DICTIOMANCY

A form of **divination** where a question is asked and a dictionary opened at random. The first word seen is interpreted as an answer or comment to the question asked.

See also **Bibliomancy**.

DIEPPE RAID CASE

Reports by two Englishwomen on a seaside holiday at Puys, Dieppe in France of ghostly sounds from the World War II air and sea battle fought at Dieppe. The case was widely documented in the 1950s by **paranormal** investigators and is thought to be an example of collective auditory hallucinations.

On the morning of 4 August 1951 both women were awakened by loud noises of gunfire, shellfire and men shouting and crying out. The women could find nothing to account for the noises and later, when they asked if other people had heard anything, they got negative replies.

The accounts they gave of the sounds and noises showed strong consistencies with a fierce battle that took place in Dieppe on 19 August 1942. Although the women knew a battle had taken place there, they knew none of the details and the information in the guidebook was not enough to match their description to the real event. When interviewed by psychical researchers the women came across as well balanced and with no desire to court publicity. Sceptics proposed other explanations for the experience, such as noise from the surf or aeroplanes flying above, but none of these could explain the remarkable accuracy of the accounts the women gave.

Direct voice mediumship

The independent speaking of a **spirit** voice that does not seem to emanate from any living person in a given environment and without using the **medium**'s vocal cords. Commonly associated with the **séances** of the early **Spiritualist** movement, direct voices seem to come from out of thin air or through a medium's **trumpet**, which was specifically used for this purpose. Most early spiritualists used direct voice communication, although some, like Ohio farmer Jonathan Koons, whose spirit room was famous in the 1850s for voices that sang 'unearthly songs', were more proficient at it than others. According to some spiritualists the voices were made possible by an artificial voice box, constructed by spirits and activated by **ectoplasm**.

Nineteenth-century records of direct voices talking at the same time as the medium or from different locations attest to their authenticity, but direct voice mediumship was always at risk of being exposed as ventriloquist **fraud**. In the twentieth century the practice became very rare indeed, with most mediums receiving information from spirits and relaying in their own voices. However from the 1940s to the 1970s medium **Leslie Flint** of England became famous for giving what appeared to be genuine direct voice readings. Flint was investigated and tested by several psychical researchers but the possibility of fraud was ruled out. The most dramatic test took place in 1970 in New York, when Flint's mouth was sealed with plaster and a microphone placed down his throat. No evidence of vocal activity could be found while direct voices seemed to speak from above and slightly to the left of his head.

Discarnate entity / Disembodied spirit

Terms used to describe a **spirit**, **ghost**, or other non-physical or non-material entity contacted during a **séance** or other sitting by a **medium**. Discarnate entities once had an earthly body (incarnate existence) but now they are dead they have become discarnate – from the Latin *dis* 'without' and *caro*, 'flesh'. This is in contrast to other entities, which have just existed in the spirit realm. They are called 'disembodied spirits'.

Disneyland's haunted mansion

In the early 1960s Walt Disney began developing plans for a mansion using secrets of the magic trade to create illusions of **ghosts** and **spirits**. In 1966 when Disney died, building work halted, but the attraction finally opened in 1969. There have been several sightings of ghosts over the years and many believe that real ghosts haunt the place.

One of these ghosts is thought to be that of a man who died when his plane crashed in a nearby lake. Referred to by employees as 'the man with the cane', he is often seen late at night, especially after closing.

Another spirit is the so-called 'Man in a tuxedo', who is said to occasionally appear as a reflection in the mirror used by attendants to see visitors in the area where they disembark. One female employee resigned immediately after seeing the figure of a man wearing a tuxedo in the mirror when there was no one present to create a reflection. She also reported feeling a chill and a hand placed on her shoulder.

Another ghost sometimes seen is said to be a crying boy near the exit. According to legend his mother scattered his ashes secretly inside the Mansion when Disney officials forbade it, and it seems this isn't what the little boy wanted.

Sceptics argue that the artificially created haunted atmosphere of the place triggers the imagination and creates illusions that seem real. It's also possible that Disney and his design team threw in a few secrets and surprises to baffle tourists, but most people who visit the haunted mansion find the experience unusually chilling and eerie.

DISPLACEMENT

First documented in 1939 by Cambridge University psychical researcher Whitely Carrington, and now observed as a common occurrence, displacement is lack of synchronization in **psi** testing. For example, a person asked to give the order of a pack of playing cards or **ESP cards** may be one or two cards ahead or behind in sequence. Displacement also occurs in precognitive **dreams** and **psychic** readings, when difficult or challenging information is placed out of context or buried in non-threatening information or **symbols**.

Parapsychologists call displacement 'psychic noise' and believe it to be caused by the absence of earth time in the higher planes where psychic insight functions and the psychic association of a group of potential targets that are difficult to tell apart.

DIVINATION

The art or practice of foretelling the future to discover hidden knowledge, find the lost or identify the guilty by the interpretation of **omens** or by **supernatural** powers. All divination is an attempt to communcate with the divine, higher spirit realm or supernatual or to learn the will of the gods. If a distinction is to be made with fortune telling, divination has a formal or ritual or social character, while fortune telling is a more everyday practice for personal purposes. Sceptics often dismiss divination as mere **superstition** but there is plenty of anecdotal evidence for the efficacy of divination. Others believe that divination is the process by which messages from the **unconscious** mind are decoded and that these messages have a supernatural source.

Divination is a universal phenomenon that has served a social function in most religions and cultures throughout history as a means of solving problems and resolving conflicts. The responsibility for divination typically falls to a prophet, priest, medicine man, **shaman**, **witch** or other person with **psychic** powers.

In ancient civilizations divination was often a royal or holy function, used for guidance in matters of war or state and to forecast natural disasters. Many courts employed astrologers. In ancient Greece a special caste of priests, called augers, interpreted natural phenomena such as cloud and smoke paterns. The Greeks consulted **horoscopes**, **dreams** and **oracles** for divination purposes, the most famous oracle being the one at Delphi, near Mount Parnasus. In tribal and shamanic cultures divination is a sacred function performed by shamans who go into a **trance** to consult spirit helpers. In the East divination is more an accepted part of daily life than it is in the West where it has been criticized strongly by the Church and by the scientific community. Despite condemnation, however, divination has not been eradicted in the West and the majority of people remain open minded and curious about the possibility of seeing into the future.

There are hundreds of different types of divination, but they can be classified as belonging to one of two categories: direct communication with gods and **spirits** through **visions**, **trance**, dreams and **possession**, or the interpretation of natural or artificial signs, lots or omens via a system. The most common example of the latter involves the sorting or casting of bones, stones, beans or other objects, with conclusions drawn from the patterns of their fall. Two well-known divination methods – the **I Ching** and the **Tarot** – are of this type.

When a card, coin or stick is selected the randomness of the action allows the spirits or gods to affect the outcome and give a message.

Scientific research has shown that it is possible to predict future events, e.g. weather forecasts, but this is not divination. Unlike science, divination assumes the influence of some supernatural force.

Divination methods range from the accepted and well known, such as **astrology**, **palmistry** and Tarot, to the forgotten, such as **entomancy** (divination interpreting the appearance and behaviour of insects), to the bizzarre, such as **uromancy** – divination by reading the appearance of urine in a pot. Most terms associated with divination end in 'mancy', from the Greek *manteia* (divination), or 'scopy' from the Greek *skopein* (to look into or behold). A diviner is someone who foretells future events based on the practice of divination.

DIXON, JEANNE [1918–1997]

A modern-day psychic who claimed to be able to predict the future. Information came to her in the form of dramatic **visions**. According to her supporters Dixon accurately foretold the assassinations of Mahatma Gandhi, Martin Luther King, John F Kennedy and Bobby Kennedy. She also predicted the launch of Sputnik and the sinking of the submarines USS *Thresher* and USS *Scorpion*, as well as the unexpected presidential defeat of Thomas Dewey by Harry Truman, the landslide election of Dwight Eisenhower, the demise of Nikita Khrushchev, and the plane crash that killed UN Secretary-General Dag Hammarskjöld.

Jeanne Dixon, who was told by a gypsy when she was eight years old that she would become a great psychic, also made hundreds of trivial predictions about celebrities and insignificant events and earned the dubious nickname of 'gossip prophet'. As she explained it, 'When a psychic vision is not fulfilled as expected, it is not because what has been shown is not correct; it is because I have not interpreted it correctly.'

Like **Nostradamus** (C. 1:60) and St John (in the Book of Revelation 8: 10–12), she prophesized that Earth will be struck by a comet. Her timing, however, was premature:

I have seen a comet strike our Earth around the middle of the 1980s. Earthquakes and tidal waves will befall us as a result of the tremendous impact of this heavenly body in one of our great oceans.

And like several other prophets, Dixon also has foreseen the advent of the Antichrist and the False Prophet:

Satan is now coming into the open to seduce the world and we should be prepared for the inevitable events that are to follow. I have seen that the United States is to play a major role in this development.

Ms Dixon believed her powers were a gift from God. She made little financial profit from them, making it a policy not to charge fees and to donate income to a children's charity. Sceptics argue that her predictions were vague, wide open to interpretation and often completely inaccurate or wrong. They also believe that the media played a part in the cult surrounding her.

The term 'Jeanne Dixon effect' is used to refer to a common ploy used by 'psychics' to make dozens of predictions knowing that the more that are made, the better the odds that one will prove accurate. When one comes true, the psychic counts on people conveniently forgetting the 99 per cent that were wrong. The term also refers to the tendency of the mass media to hype or exaggerate a few correct predictions by a psychic, guaranteeing that they will be remembered, while ignoring the much more numerous incorrect predictions.

DOLPHINS

In classical mythology dolphins are associated with the **soul**'s journey to the **underworld**, and in Christian myth the dolphin represents salvation through Christ. To many alternative therapists dolphins are a symbol of healing and emotional release. This may have something to do with the fact that dolphins live in water. Water in many traditions (including that of **astrology**) is related to feeling and emotion. Dolphins invite us to enjoy water in its physical form and also to swim freely and flow with our feelings. We can also learn from their breathing patterns. The dolphin breathes deeply, holds its breath while underwater, and then exhales explosively. This is an excellent breathing pattern for releasing tension.

Dolphins and humans have had a special bond for centuries. Swimming with dolphins is thought to have remarkable healing benefits, especially for those suffering from learning difficulties. In the words of the Greek essayist Plutarch: 'The dolphin is the only creature that loves man for his own sake.' Indeed, dolphins are highly intelligent animals that appear to enjoy human company for its own sake, perhaps enjoying the observation of our antics and as much as we do theirs.

DOMOVIK

In Russian folklore the domovik is a **spirit** with a grey beard that typically lives behind the stove in every home. He is always referred to as the grandfather or he – never by his personal name. Traditionally it is the spirit of the ancestor that founded the family and it moves with the family from house to house. The domovik is believed to watch over the family, keep evil spirits away and occasionally help out around the house. If, however, family members do something that displeases the domovik it is said to resort to **poltergeist** activity, and that can include burning down the house!

DOORS

As a universal **symbol** of opening and new possibilities it's not surprising that there are many **superstitions** concerning doors and **spirits**. Most of these superstitions are concerned with keeping **ghosts** from entering homes or letting ghosts escape to the **afterlife**. For example, it is widely thought unlucky to enter a house via the back door, as traditionally corpses are carried out the back door. Opening doors and windows when there has been a death in the house is thought to help the spirit leave the corpse. A circle chalked on a door is believed to prevent evil spirits from entering, and slamming a door several times during a row is believed to trap a ghost between the frame and the door and force it to leave.

DOPPELGÄNGER/DOUBLE

The appearance of a double of a living person, thought to be a **death omen**, or **bilocation** – the **astral body** of someone having an **out-of-body experience**. 'Doppelgänger' comes from the German, meaning 'double walker'.

The belief in the spirit or **soul** existing in a double is ancient and widespread. The ancient Egyptians said the soul had a double or **Ka**, and a special kind of tomb, called the house of Ka, was reserved for the double. Doubles are said to be exact copies of the living person and are usually seen at a location distant from them.

As a death omen there are reports of seeing doubles just as the individual in question is about to die. The double usually appears real but has a ghostly, filmy look about them and can sometimes act mechanically. In some rare cases, such as that of the poet Shelley who saw his own double before drowning, the double appears to the dying individual him or herself. As well as being a death omen, many psychical researchers who have examined cases of doppelgängers believe they are projections of **consciousness** that somehow take on a form resembling reality. This can happen involuntarily or it can be accomplished at will. English **medium Eileen Garrett** suggested that the double is a **clairvoyant** projection that can be manipulated to develop **supernatural** powers.

DOWDING, AIR CHIEF MARSHALL LORD HUGH [1882–1970]

The hero of the Battle of Britain Air Chief Marshall Lord Hugh Dowding claimed on numerous occasions to be in contact with the **spirits** of the dead, especially airmen who had served with him or under him in both world wars. Dowding was a prominent member of the London **Ghost Club** and took an active part in many investigations of allegedly haunted locations with the organization.

DOWSING

Also known as divining, rhabdomancy and water witching dowsing is a form of **divination** performed using a forked stick, **pendulum** or rods to find hidden things, in particular underground water, minerals and oil. Today it is used to locate lost objects, buried treasure, mineral deposits and water wells, and to diagnose illness.

Dowsing is an ancient practice with unknown origins, however it is thought to date back at least 8,000 years. Wall paintings, estimated to be about 8,000 years old, discovered in the Tassili Caves of North Africa show tribesmen surrounding a man with a forked stick, possibly dowsing for water.

Ancient Chinese and Egyptian artwork depicts people using forked tools in possible dowsing activities. Dowsing may have been mentioned in the Bible, although not by name, when Moses and Aaron used a 'rod' to locate water. It was in the Middle Ages, however, that the first unambiguous written accounts of dowsing come, when it was used to find coal deposits. In seventeenth-century France, there are records of a man called Jacques Vernay, a stonemason by trade, who used his dowsing talents to successfully track criminals. However, during the fifteenth and sixteenth centuries, dowsers were often thought to be practitioners of evil. Martin Luther described dowsing as 'the work of devil' – hence the term 'water witching'.

How the dowsing technique was first discovered and how dowsing works is unknown, yet those who practise it are convinced that it does work. Dowsing is

How you can dowse

Dowsers say that anyone can have a go at dowsing because, like psychic ability, it is a hidden power that all humans possess. And, like any other ability, such as learning a musical instrument, the more you practise and learn your strengths the more you will define your abilities. Here are some steps for a do-it-yourself dowsing test.

1. Decide which dowsing tool you want to use:

   Forked stick: This is a Y-shaped tree branch (most often from a willow). The dowser holds the branch parallel to the ground at the top of the Y shape, and then starts to walk. If he or she passes over the hidden object the end of the branch is pulled down, pointing to the correct spot.

   L-shaped metal rods: For this method two L-shaped metal rods (easily made from a pair of coat hangers) are held in each hand parallel to the floor, and if the dowser passes over the hidden object the rods swing apart or cross each other.

   Pendulum: Some dowsers believe it is sufficient to hold a pendulum over a map is sufficient. If the pendulum begins to move in a circle or back and forth they know they have located the hidden object. Pendulums are also used for diagnosing illness.

   Your bare hands: Some exceptionally skilled dowers seem to be able to dowse without a tool, claiming that they feel a resisting force when they locate the hidden object.

2. Ask someone to bury a metal object or bottle of water in the garden just a few inches below the surface.

3. Before starting, mentally ask your dowsing tool to indicate to you when you are passing over the hidden object.

4. Walk slowly in any direction you like, concentrating on the object and trying to remain open and sensitive to the movements of the dowsing tool.

5. If your dowsing tool reacts or you simply 'get a feeling' that helps you make a decision about the location of the object, stop and see if the spot indicated is correct. If not, keep trying at different times of the day to see if you have ability for dowsing.

still very much in use today in archaeological digs, searching for minerals and missing persons and in alternative healing, when the dowser swings a pendulum over the patient's body to determine the location and cause of illness. It is not widely known but petrochemical companies employ dowsers to confirm underground sources of oil and gas, and dowsers have also made a contribution towards the understanding of mysterious earth energies, such as those represented by **ley lines**. The American Society of Dowsers estimates there may be as many as 30,000 dowsers in the United States, but despite this, dowsing still struggles to be regarded as a legitimate field.

Dowsing has attracted some well-known names from history, including Leonardo de Vinci, Robert Boyle (considered the father of modern chemistry) and Charles Richet (a Nobel Prize winner). Albert Einstein was also convinced of the authenticity of dowsing:

I know very well that many scientists consider dowsing as they do astrology, as a type of ancient superstition. According to my conviction this is, however, unjustified. The dowsing rod is a simple instrument which shows the reaction of the human nervous system to certain factors which are unknown to us at this time.

Some believe there may be a psychic connection between the dowser and the hidden object. According to this theory all things – living and inanimate – have an energy force and the dowser, by concentrating on the hidden object, is somehow able to tune in to the energy force field or 'vibration' of the object, which, in turn, forces the dowsing rod or stick to move. In other words, the dowsing tool may act as a kind of amplifier or antenna for tuning into the energy and it is common for the dowser to find a tingling sensation, chills or shivering when the object is located.

Recent experiments in Russia have shown that dowsing rods can be sensitive to electromagnetic fields and that almost anyone can learn to dowse – although women tend to be more successful at it than men. Scientists believe this may be because unknown force fields respond better to the polarity in women's bodies. Sceptics argue that dowsing is a matter of luck and that those with a high rate of success just have good instincts for where objects or water may be found. For both believer and sceptic there is no definitive evidence either way.

DOYLE, SIR ARTHUR CONAN [1859–1930]

Renowned for his Sherlock Holmes detective stories, Sir Authur Conan Doyle is also regarded by many as one of the founders of **spiritualism**.

During the years 1885 to 1888 when Conan Doyle was a physician in Southsea, he was invited to participate in table-turning sittings at the home of one of his patients. He wasn't convinced of the amazing phenomena produced – or the **medium**'s integrity – but it aroused his interest in the subject, and shortly after he joined the **Society for Psychical Research**.

Almost immediately Conan Doyle participated in a series of experiments that convinced him that **telepathy** was genuine. He continued to investigate **paranormal** phenomena for the next 30-odd years, until finally, at the peak of his literary career in his late fifties, he took the bold step of publishing two books that firmly associated him with spiritualism: *The New Revelation* and *The Vital Message*.

His critics suggested he was merely grief-stricken over the loss of his son, Kingsley, who had died of pneumonia, but Conan Doyle denied this. He said instead that a year after his son's death, he attended a sitting held by a Welsh medium who he believed truly had made contact with his son. 'It was his voice and he spoke of concerns unknown to the medium', he said.

Sir Arthur Conan Doyle's most impressive book on spiritualism is the two-volume set *The History of Spiritualism*, and it is essential reading for all serious students of the subject.

Conan Doyle was involved in a number of public controversies over spiritualism. In the late 1920s, while he was president of the London Spiritualist Alliance, a medium sanctioned by the Alliance was charged with fortune-telling (it was illegal at the time), and the Alliance was fined £800. Conan Doyle wrote a public protest in *The Times*, suggesting that this was persecution of **spiritualists**. He also urged that the Fortune Telling Act be modified, and only six days before his death in July 1930, he led a petition to this effect.

A week after his death, a large spiritualist reunion was held in London, where a chair was left empty in his honour. A respected medium of the day said she saw him in the chair and offered a personal message from the great writer to his family. Since then dozens of mediums have claimed to receive messages from the author.

DRAGSHOLM CASTLE

Dragsholm Castle is one of Denmark's best-known haunted castles and many investigations there by psychical researchers have yielded positive results.

Located in Zeeland, Dragsholm was built in the twelfth century and became the residence for kings and several noble families. It is thought that the castle has three **ghosts**: a grey lady, a white lady and the ghost of the Earl of Bothwell.

The grey lady is seldom seen but is thought to be the ghost of a woman who served in the castle and who had terrible toothache. She was cured and is said to return now and again to see if everything is in order, and as a thank you for her cure.

The other two ghosts are believed to be considerably less happy and thankful than the grey lady as both met their deaths in the castle in particularly unpleasant manners. The white lady is said to be the daughter of one of the many owners of the castle. She fell in love with a commoner and when her father found out he was so angry that he imprisoned her inside the thick wall of the castle. It is said that every night she returns to the castle and walks around the corridors, and there have been plenty of reported sightings of her. There is factual evidence to back this story up; in the 1930s, when the old walls of the castle were torn down, workers found a hole in the wall and a skeleton with a white dress in it.

The castle also has old cellars for prisoners. In the 1500s the Earl of Bothwell, the third husband of Mary, Queen of Scots, was incarcerated there for five years and died mad in the cellar in 1578. It is said that every night he comes riding into the courtyard of the castle with his horse and carriage.

DREAMCATCHER

Considered to be a **talisman** to ensure restful sleep and productive dreaming, the dreamcatcher is a North American device hung above the bed to dispel nightmares and retain the essence of good dreams.

Use of the dreamcatcher by Native American cultures is based on an old Lakota folktale about a spiritual leader to whom the god Iktomi, the great teacher of wisdom, appeared in the form of a spider. As he gave advice about the cycles of life, the importance of working with nature and of taking good advice when it was offered, rejecting bad advice, Iktomi began to spin a web. When the web was completed it had a hole in the centre. Iktomi gave it to the elder saying: 'Use the web to help yourself and your people to reach your goals and make good use of people's ideas, dreams and visions. If you believe in the great spirit, the web will catch your great ideas, and the bad ones will go through the hole.'

DREAMS

Everyone dreams. It is estimated that in an average lifetime a person will spend approximately 25 years asleep and experience at least 300,000 dreams, regardless of whether these dreams are recalled on awakening. Researchers believe that babies dream the most, children dream for four or five hours a night and adults for one or two hours. Animals also appear to dream.

Research from the University of Chicago has shown that dreams occur during the rapid eye movement (REM) period of sleep, which occurs for between five and forty minutes every sixty to ninety minutes of sleep. Most people only remember the last dream prior to waking but if they are woken up during earlier dream periods they will recall other dreams.

Unless written down immediately on waking most dreams fade within a few minutes. Dreams usually occur in colour but seldom have smells or taste, and this may be due to the fact that only visual brain neurons fire during REM. Almost all dreams use metaphors to deal with issues in the life of the dreamer, and every event in the dream is believed to have some kind of significance for the person dreaming it.

A brief history of dreams

People have always been fascinated by dreams and what they mean. All primitive religions viewed dreams as ways for the **spirits** or deities to speak to humans. The earliest known dream dictionary dates back around 4,000 years. Now called the Chester Beatty Papyrus it came from Thebes in Upper Egypt and is kept in the British Museum. In the Chester Beatty Papyrus dreams are interpreted and translated as **omens** or prophecies. For example, dreaming that your teeth fall out is interpreted as a loved one trying to kill you.

In ancient Greece dreams were also thought to be unlucky or lucky predictions. Around AD 200, Artemidorus, a dream interpreter who lived in Asia Minor, wrote a book about dream interpretation that suggested that dreams were continuations of the dreamer's day. The Old Testament makes countless references to dream interpretation.

The importance of dreams and their meanings were prominent in the writings of the Early Church Fathers, including St Augustine, up until the time of St Thomas Aquinas (1225–1274) who regarded dreams as insignificant; for several hundred years afterwards, dreams were no longer considered important. Even **Shakespeare** called them 'children of the idle brain'. Although dream interpretation did continue to be an important part of the service of magicians and astrologers, this dreams-should-be-ignored school of thought persisted until the nineteenth century. Then along came psychiatrists **Sigmund Freud** and **Carl Jung**, the two men who have had the greatest impact on the way we look at dreams today.

Sigmund Freud (1856–1939) opened the door to the scientific study of dreams with his book *The Interpretation of Dreams*; he considered dreams to be the 'royal road to the unconscious' and believed them to be wish fulfilment of repressed sexual desires from childhood. To interpret dreams Freud used a method called free association in which the dreamer says whatever comes to mind in relation to events in the dream.

Freud's work paved the way for the work of Carl Jung (1875–1961). Jung considered dreams to be expressions of the contents of the **collective unconscious**, a source of shared knowledge that exists within us all. Jung believed the purpose of dreams was to offer guidance and information about the self. They were the language of the **unconscious** and they could tell us about the state of our inner lives; to ignore dreams was to court disaster. Even though dream **symbols** from the collective unconscious have universal or archetypal meanings, according to Jung, only the dreamer could interpret the dream's true meaning, not an outsider.

There have been other theories since Freud and Jung but for the most part dreams are regarded as tools for change, growth and wellbeing. No one knows how, but dreams seem to be able to link the conscious (waking) mind with the hidden part of the mind called the unconscious or **intuition** and by so doing they provide a rich and powerful inner resource that can enhance life considerably. Today dream interpretation is extremely popular, with people from all walks of life using dreams as unique and very personal sources of comfort, guidance and inspiration.

Dreams, health and creativity

Scientists tell us that dreaming is essential to our mental, emotional and physical health and wellbeing, because dreams can help us relax, release frustrations, sort out information, solve problems or alert us to them, play out fantasies, offer inspiration and restore balance.

There are numerous famous examples of dreams offering inspiration. Solutions to problems, ideas for inventions and artistic endeavours have all found their way to the conscious mind via dreams. Mary Shelley dreamed of the creature that was to become Frankenstein. Other famous literary dreamers include Edgar Allan Poe, Samuel Taylor Coleridge, Charlotte Brontë, Robert Louis Stevenson and J R R Tolkien. Paul McCartney heard a haunting melody in one of his dreams and wrote it down. It became the song 'Yesterday'. Inventions and ideas that have sprung from dreams include the model of the atom, the M9 analogue computer, the isolation of insulin in the treatment of diabetes and the sewing machine.

Dreams and the paranormal

Dreams of the dead are viewed in the West from a psychological perspective and not as actual encounters with **ghosts**, but many believe that the dead appear in dreams because they have a purpose: usually to offer advice and instruction, as happened in the **Chaffin Will case**. Some dreams involving the dead are also thought to be **death omens**. In the eighteenth century **Lord Lyttelton** dreamt of a fluttering bird and a woman in white who told him he would die in three days' time. Despite his best efforts to prove her wrong, Lyttleton died as predicted.

Although dreams that focus on communication between the living and the dead have been accepted in many cultures since ancient times as proof that the dead have the ability to interfere with the lives of the living, dreams have also always shared a strong link with supernatural powers, in particular with **precognition** and **telepathy**.

Although rare, precognitive dreams are ones in which you see the future before it happens. The ancient Chaldeans, Chinese, Egyptians, Greeks, Romans and Native Americans all believed dreams were a method of foretelling the future, and even today there are instances when people claim to have dreamt of things before they happen. Many people, for example, claim to have had dreams of the 9/11 World Trade Center disaster before it happened. There are also stories of people who cancel trips or flights because of a foreboding dream or people who dreamt the winning lottery numbers.

There is strong evidence that some precognitive dreams warn about future health problems. Jung noticed that if his patients dreamt of injury to a horse – the archetypal symbol of animal life within the human body – they were often in the early stages of serious illness. A 1987 study at Michigan State University showed that cardiac patients who dreamt of destruction were far more likely to have worse heart disease than those who did not. Dreams also serve as a preparation for death, with terminally ill patients sometimes reporting transitional dreams of crossing bridges or walking through doors just before death. These dreams often bring peace of mind.

Dream telepathy has interested psychical researchers since the late nineteenth century. The founders of the **Society for Psychical Research** in London collected numerous dream telepathy cases in their study of **paranormal** experiences published in *Phantasms of the Living* (1886).

Interpreting your dreams

Have you ever wondered why dreams are often hard to make sense of? It's because the information they contain is presented in the language of images and the number of images your brain can present is endless. Dream experts believe that the images are your own thoughts, feelings and ideas turned into a series of pictures or scenes and it's up to the individual to translate and interpret them.

Your unconscious mind is working all the time using images, feelings and pictures from your past and present and linking them in with the issues currently concerning you. For example, if you feel stressed you may have a dream where you are swimming and can't keep your head above water. If you feel confused you may have a dream where you are lost in a dark wood. Some of these images can be universally recognized – a boat, for example, is typically is a symbol of transition – but most of the images in your dreams can only really be interpreted by you. That's why a dream dictionary isn't always help-ful as the interpretations in there will be universal and not unique to you.

A good way to uncover the meanings of your dreams is by free association. You simply go with the first thing that pops into your mind when recalling an image you had in a dream. For example, if you dream of a dog what are the first thoughts that come into your mind when you think about dogs? Forget about universal asso-ciations; what are your personal associa-tions with dogs? What a dog means to you and what a dog means to someone else may be entirely different. Perhaps you had an unpleasant encounter with a dog once and rather than being symbols of love, loyalty and devotion dogs repre-sent fear and trauma for you?

The more you work with your dreams the more familiar you will become with your personal images. Always bear in mind that your dream symbols and images will be unique to you. What do you think your dream is trying to tell you?

A number of other telepathic dream studies have been conducted since, the most famous of which is perhaps the one con-ducted at the dream laboratory of the Mai-monides Medical Center in Brooklyn, New York from 1963–1974. When subjects were in REM stages of sleep, a person in another room attempted to transmit images to the sleeping subject and the cor-relation of dream images was significantly above average.

Some dreams are interpreted as having past-life content. Recurring dreams which involve the same action, people and scenery are thought to be memories from past lives that have lingered for some reason and the dreamer needs to work out why. Others are thought to be **out-of-body experiences** when the **astral body** travels – seven out of ten people experience the sensation of flying in their dreams at some point in their life. Another type of dream is the **lucid dream**, in which the dreamer is aware that they are dreaming and is able to influence the content of the dream and, in some instances, its outcome.

Many believe that dreams are a powerful way to connect with and harness psychic power. Studies of **ESP** experiences show that dreams are involved in between 33 and 69 per cent of all cases. In precognitive cases dreams are involved around 60 per cent of the time and in telepathic cases dreams are involved around 25 per cent of the time.

Most of us forget our dreams immediately on waking. There is so much to do when the new day starts and the wonderful world of meaning dreams can reveal to us is neglected. According to a Jewish proverb, 'An unremembered dream is like an unopened letter from God.'

To work with your dreams you do need to remember them. Keeping a dream journal and recording your dreams as soon as you wake will help your dream recall. If dreams are not written down they will fade away. The technique of dream recording is simple. You leave a notepad and pencil within reach of your bed and immediately on waking you write down whatever you can remember about your dream – the people, the colours, the places, the events – every detail, however small, is significant.

DREAMTIME

Similar to **Carl Jung**'s concept of the **collective unconscious**, dreamtime is an Australian Aboriginal belief of a psychic realm that is shared by everyone. Dreamtime is not separate from the real world; it inhabits the part of our **consciousness** that can be accessed in **meditation**, **trance** or in **dreams**.

Aborigines typically believe that all life is spiritually interconnected and that the human race originated in dreamtime before taking human form. Dreamtime is the 'land' to which the **spirits** of the Aboriginal dead must return, and it is the dimension from which **shamans** draw their psychic power.

DROP IN COMMUNICATOR

A mysterious entity, entirely unknown to **medium**, sitter or anyone present, who appears without warning and without an invitation at a **séance**. Sceptics argue that drop ins are constructs of the medium's **unconscious** but many psychical researchers who have investigated drop in cases believe them to be genuine. They are seen as possible evidence to support the belief that mediums do actually contact the **spirits** of the dead and are not simply manifesting secondary personalities or demonstrating their powers of **clairvoyance** or **telepathy**.

On rare occasions drops ins are accompanied by phenomena such as **table tilting**, mysterious lights, **apports** and strange sounds and smells, and occasionally they speak in a language the medium is not fluent in. Many cases are inconclusive but in the best cases the information a drop in communicator brings is personal and has never been made public, but can be verified by a small group of friends or family members.

Some drop ins are said to be very talkative, revealing personal information that can be verified upon research. One of these was 'Harry Stockbridge', who dropped in on a **Ouija board** séance of a group meeting in Cambridge, England between 1950 and 1952. Stockbridge claimed to be a second lieutenant in the Northumberland Fusiliers who had died on 14 July 1916. The information he gave was verified through old military records.

Other drop ins have a motive or task they are intent on accomplishing. One of these was the case of **Runolfur Runolfsson** who, according to reports, dropped in on medium Hafsteinn Björnsson in 1937. Runolfsson was a rough, hard drinking Icelander who had drowned in 1879; his corpse was picked apart by birds. After several sittings Runolfsson revealed that he wanted to find his missing thighbone. Runolfsson's identity was verified and his thighbone discovered and buried.

DRUGS

The use of drugs and the visions they induce in religious ceremonies is an age-old practice. Opinions vary greatly as to whether certain drugs can stimulate genuine **psychic** experiences or not. Some believe that drugs can duplicate mystical experiences and heighten the emotions, and are of value to psychotherapy. Others believe that drug-related experiences are simply illusions.

There have been a number of tests on drugs and their effects on **psi** ability since the 1920s. Both caffeine and alcohol have been shown to both improve and depress test results. Marijuana and other strong psychedelic drugs, such as LSD and mescaline, which loosen the boundaries of ego generally, trigger too much instability to yield meaningful conclusions. In general results have been largely inconclusive as drugs affect each person differently.

Most psychics would discourage the use of mind-altering drugs, believing that true insight and power can only be created or raised from within, not from without.

DRUIDS, DRUIDRY

A Celtic priestly class in Britain and Europe during the first centuries BC and AD, the Druids were widely known as visionaries and prophets. They were also thought to preach a doctrine of **reincarnation** believing in the immortality of the **soul**, which, after death, travelled to the underworld, entered a new body and lived again on earth.

The Druids followed **pagan** traditions of nature and goddess worship and possessed knowledge of magic, healing, astronomy and **sacred geometry**. Druid means 'knowing the oak tree' in Gaelic and the robust oak tree was sacred to the Druids. Their reverence for tree wisdom is expressed in their alphabet, the Ogham, which consists of different tree symbols each embodying the elemental wisdom of the particular plant.

The Romans feared the Celts and found their rituals – some of which may have included human sacrifice – ignorant and barbaric. In AD 43 Druidism was banned and the sacred oak demolished, plunging the European Celts into decline (although those at the margins of the Roman Empire, for example in Ireland and Scotland, survived). Interest in the Druids was not renewed until the sixteenth and seventeenth centuries, when they were romanticized in literature. The Ancient Order of Druids was formed by British carpenter Henry Hurle in 1781 and other groups followed. There are modern Druids in the UK and US today.

Becoming a Druid means a lifetime of study through three levels to reach spiritual awareness. The first level is that of the Bard. Bards learn to understand the creative and magical power of sound. The second level is that of Ovate, where the student learns to alter their consciousness using methods such as **astral travel**. The third level is that of the Druid, and when this level is achieved the student is considered a master of his or her craft with the power to divine the future and access the power of nature.

DRUMMER OF CORTACHY

Ghostly drumming said to portend the death of a member of the Ogilvy family, the earls of Airlie and owners of Cortachy Castle, Scotland.

According to lore, which dates back to medieval times, it is said that a messenger who arrived one day at the castle with unpleasant news was stuffed into a drum and tossed over the castle walls. Just before he died he vowed to haunt the family forever, and for hundreds of years after it was said that whenever ghostly drumming was heard a member of the family died.

One of the most famous drumming cases happened during Christmas in 1844, when a guest staying at the castle triggered a panic when she heard the drumming and asked the Earl and his wife where the sound was coming from. Lady Airlie died six months later, leaving a note saying that she knew the drumming was for her. Some believe that panic and fear about the **curse** brought about her death.

The drumming stopped in 1900 when the then Earl died in the Boer War and nobody heard the drumming – or admitted that they had heard it.

DRUMMER OF TEDWORTH

In 1661 in Ludgarshall, Wiltshire, an anonymous drummer annoyed residents with his constant drumming. Eventually the drummer was arrested and his drum confiscated.

The drum eventually ended up in the house of John Mompesson who lived in the neighbouring village of Tedworth and was responsible for the arrest of the drummer. During Mompesson's absence on a business trip in London violent **poltergeist** activity erupted in his house terrifying his family and servants. For days on end drumming was heard both inside and outside the house, objects were moved about, voices spoke and the younger children were levitated in their bed.

The disturbances went on for two years and drew widespread interest from curious visitors. Aside from the constant beating drum other phenomena included the sound of footsteps, floating candles, disembodied voices, animal noises, chamber pots emptied on to beds, knives found in a bed and money turned mysteriously black.

Meanwhile the drummer turned up in custody again and was put into Gloucester gaol charged with theft. During this time he claimed to be responsible for the activity at Mompesson's house, as revenge for taking away his drum, and this lead to his trial for **witchcraft**. He was condemned to transportation and forced to leave the area.

Many years later the drummer returned to Tedworth from time to time, and whenever he did the disturbances began again. The house was only quiet when he was gone.

DRURY LANE THEATRE

The Theatre Royal, Drury Lane, is the oldest theatre site in London (save the rebuilt Globe), the original theatre having been built in 1663. It has a long history packed with intrigue, romance and murder, and there have been numerous sightings of **ghosts**.

King Charles II, who gave the theatre its Royal Charter, is said to visit now and again, but the theatre's most famous ghost is the Man in Grey, so named for his eighteenth-century long grey coat, tricorn hat, powdered wig and sword. He is said to come and watch the play from the balcony, where he slowly walks from one end to the other only to disappear into the wall. He is often seen at rehearsals and his presence is considered very lucky – when he appears during rehearsal the play tends to be successful. Another ghost is thought to be that of twentieth-century comedian Dan Leno. Leno's ghost has allegedly been spotted in the dressing room he used last before his death.

DUDLEY TOWN, CONNECTICUT

Dudley town is an abandoned eighteenth-century village in the woods of Cornwall, Connecticut and one of the most curious haunted locations in America.

Members of the Dudley family were among the first to settle into the area in the mid-1740s, earning their living by cutting lumber to fuel iron production in a nearby town. It wasn't long before there were reports of strange beasts and **apparitions** and a host of strange, unusual and violent deaths, suicides and corpse mutilations. Over the years many people, believing that the Dudley family were cursed, left Dudley town, and by 1900 it was mostly deserted.

During the 1920s a man called Dr William C Clark set up a summer home in the abandoned town. One evening he came back from a business trip to find his wife talking hysterically about the apparitions and **demons** that had visited. She killed herself soon after.

Even today some visitors to Dudley still report disembodied voices whispering and laughing. A woman on a white horse has been spotted, among other apparitions. People also hear wagon wheels and other sounds of the past. Curiously few living sounds are heard, as birds and animals never seem to settle in the area. This may be due to lack of sunshine as, being in the shadow of three mountains, the town receives little natural light, but others believe that Dudley is an area of negative energy that attracts evil **spirits** and entities.

Duppy

A **ghost** of West Indian tradition and unknown origin, regarded as the personification of evil, i.e. the **Devil**. The duppy allegedly operates only at night and is required to return to the grave before dawn; if it is prevented from doing so for any reason, the **spirit** forfeits its power to do harm to any living person. West Indians believe that the breath of a duppy will make a victim violently ill, while the mere touch of the spirit will induce epileptic fits and seizures. The duppy can allegedly be summoned by a secret ritual to do the conjurer's bidding, and the traditional method to keep the duppy at bay is to place tobacco seeds around the doors and windows of the home it comes to plague.

See **Voodoo**.

Dybbuk

The Hebrew word dybbuk comes from a word meaning 'cleaving' or 'clinging', and according to Jewish lore a dybbuk is a wandering, disembodied, evil **spirit** which enters a person's body and holds fast. The **kabbalah** contains many instructions for exorcising a dybbuk, some of which are still performed today. When exorcised the dybbuk is thought to leave the body via the small toe and leave a bloody mark there on departure.

In early folklore dybbuk were thought to only inhabit the bodies of sick people and possessive evil spirits and **exorcisms** to banish them appear in the Old Testament. However, by the early sixteenth century many Jews believed that a dybbuk could not enter an innocent body, because of its past sins, and could only inhabit the body of a sinner. It was also thought that dybbuk were the souls of people not buried properly and they therefore became **demons**. **Transmigration** of souls and **reincarnation** are not parts of mainstream Judaism but the dybbuk offers a revealing glimpse of the **supernatural** in the Jewish tradition.

E

EAR OF DIONYSIUS

A famous example of mediumistic **cross correspondences**. In this case, a series of communications that needed to be brought together before they made sense.

A **medium** by the name of Mrs Willet first communicated the phrase 'Ear of Dionysius' when she went into a trance in August 1910. At the time the phrase meant nothing to the sitter, a Mrs Verrall, but her husband, the classical scholar A W Verrall, explained that the name was given to a huge abandoned quarry at Syracuse, which was roughly shaped like a donkey's ear. In this place unhappy Athenian captives were confined from 405 to 367 BC and the peculiar acoustic properties of the cave were said to have enabled Dionysius the Tyrant to overhear his victims speaking.

There was no more talk of the Ear of Dionysius for several years until, in January 1914, Mrs Willet produced, during an **automatic writing** session, a script for Mrs Verrall that contained a passage referring to the Ear of Dionysius. The script was allegedly sent by Dr Verrall, who had died a year or so before. The Verralls were supporters of the **Society for Psychical Research**, which stressed the importance of private communications as evidence for life after death, so it seemed likely that Verrall would try to communicate his **survival after death** to his wife in this way.

For the next year Verrall, along with another communicator, S H Butcher, another dead classical scholar and a close friend of Verrall when they were both alive, reportedly began a series of communications to Mrs Willet that made allusions to Ulysses and Polyphemus. It wasn't until August 1915, however, when a communication referred to a man called Philoxenus, who had been imprisoned for seducing Dionysius's wife, that all the references eventually began to make sense. It seemed that a satirical poem of the passionate and tragic life of Philoxenus was being communicated, in which Philoxenus was portrayed as Ulysses and Dionysius as Polyphemus.

The Ear of Dionysius case is often held up as an example of cooperation between two dead communicators and proof of survival after death. Sceptics, however, argue that only one medium was involved, not several as is more usual in cross correspondence cases, and Mrs Willet could have discovered the knowledge for herself from university research libraries. It's also possible she managed to learn the key points through **ESP** when Verrall was alive and unconsciously wove them into her **trance** communications.

EARTH

In magical symbolism one of the four (or five) **elements**, corresponding to matter that is solid and to cold and dry qualities.

Earth typically symbolizes order, both in nature and in society. It also represents the female principle, the nurturing and mothering aspect of Mother Nature and the material realm of money and business. The magical tool associated with earth is the bell. Earth colours are green or brown and earth is associated with the **zodiac** signs of Taurus, Virgo and Capricorn. In Chinese philosophy earth is associated with the season of late summer and represents stability and practicality, but it is also the element involved in personal transformation. Dampness, the colour yellow, worrying and the sound of singing are also related to the earth element.

EARTH LIGHTS

Also known as **ghost lights**, earth lights are mysterious patches of light reported to have been seen at more than a hundred or so sites in remote locations, such as isolated buildings and mountain peaks, in the United States, Britain, Japan and elsewhere. The lights appear at random or regularly at some sites. They often bounce up and down, almost in a playful fashion, and are said to be red, orange, blue, yellow or white in colour.

Earth lights have been linked to locations where sacred shrines have been erected by ancient peoples, and according to some Native Americans they are doorways to the world beyond. Others believe that earth lights are **extraterrestrial** in origin and convincing evidence of **UFO**s or some as yet unidentified electromagnetic energy.

Research in the phenomenon of earth lights suggests that that they might be produced by seismic stresses beneath the earth which generate ionized gas that is released into the air near a fault line. Several locations where earth lights have been reported, such as the Brown Mountains in

North Carolina and eight of the lochs in Scotland, are near major fault lines.

Some lights have been shown to have natural explanations, such as car headlights, radioactivity from ore in the ground or the shifting of geological plates, but some, such as the **Marfa lights** seen southwest of the Chinati Mountains, Marfa, Texas, along with those seen in Joplin, Missouri, appear to be true mysteries that defy attempts to explain them.

EARTHQUAKE EFFECT

A phenomenon involving the room shaking as if there was an earthquake. The phenomenon is usually associated with the **medium D D Home**.

ECKANKAR

A patented form of **astral travel** devised by American guru Paul Twitchell (1908–1971). In a series of **out-of-body experiences** Twitchell claimed to have made contact with superior beings in the **astral plane** called the Eck Masters, who showed him this special technique for astral travel and taught him a series of complex, universal and comprehensive spiritual truths. It was on the basis of these truths that Twitchell founded the Eckankar organization in 1965: an international organization where followers can learn the truths and practise **astral projection** or 'soul travel' according to the methods and techniques revealed to Twitchell by the Eck Masters.

Twitchell lectured all over the world, establishing 284 Eckankar centres in 23 countries. He claimed to use soul travel to heal, exorcise **ghosts** from haunted places, find missing persons and help others in their spiritual self-discovery. Twitchell was adored by his followers who called him *Mahanta*, the living embodiment of the God consciousness on earth. He died in 1971 and in 1986 the Eckankar headquarters moved to their current location in Minneapolis, Minnesota: www.eckankar.org/.

ECTOPLASM

From the Greek words *ektos* and *plasma* and meaning 'exteriorized substance', ectoplasm a whitish substance that allegedly extrudes from the mouth, nose, ears or other orifices of the **medium** during a **séance**.

The phrase was coined in the late nineteenth century by French psychologist Charles Richet, who recorded the phenomenon in his own research with the ectoplasm-producing medium Madame d'Esperance. It is said to smell like ozone (a sweet, clover-like smell), to be either warm or cold to the touch and to appear either light and airy or sticky and jelly-like, with a structure that varies from amorphous clouds to a net-like membrane that can transform into limbs, faces or bodies of ghosts or **spirits**. If exposed to light the ectoplasm is said to snap back into the medium's body, sometimes causing discomfort, pain and injury. Many believe this substance to be the matter that composes one's **astral body** and is the basis of all **psychic** phenomena.

In experiments in the early 1900s, medium Marthe Béraud was said to produce masses of white or grey material during a sitting. She was thoroughly examined beforehand by a German doctor, **Baron Albert von Schrenck-Notzing**, to confirm that she wasn't hiding anything. The Baron described Béraud's ectoplasm as sticky icicles that ran down her face and onto the front of her body where they assumed faces or shapes.

Perhaps the most well-known ectoplasm-producing medium was **Mina Crandon**. Famous photographs from the 1920s show Mina with long strings of ectoplasm streaming out of her mouth, ears, nose and even from between her legs.

Research into ectoplasm was conducted well into the twentieth century and analyses of small pieces of ectoplasm did in some cases, although not all, reveal fraud, with the use of substances such as muslin, toothpaste, soap, gelatine and egg white. Magician **Harry Houdini** once said that he couldn't believe superior beings would allow the production of such disgusting substances from the human body. Interest in ectoplasm has declined but some modern mediums are still said to produce the phenomenon.

EDGAR ALLAN POE HOUSE

This tiny home on 203 N. Amity Street in Baltimore was once occupied by Edgar Allan Poe from 1832–1835. It is believed to be haunted – but surprisingly not by the famous author who had a fascination for all things **paranormal**.

Poe only lived in the house for three years and it had several other occupants, including his grandmother, his aunt and his cousin, Virginia Clemm, who later became his wife. The house was taken over by the Edgar Allan Poe Society of Baltimore in 1941 and is now open to the public. There is a picture of Poe's wife painted from her corpse on permanent display.

Since the 1960s **psychic** phenomena, mostly centring around Poe's attic room and Virginia's bedroom, have been reported there, including lights turning mysteriously on and off, strange voices and noises, and windows and doors closing by themselves. There have also been sightings of the **ghost** of an old lady with grey hair, dressed in period clothes. None of the phenomena seems to be hostile but many residents of Baltimore, including street gangs, to this day report an irrational fear and anxiety about the place and prefer to stay away from it.

EDGEHILL, BATTLE OF

A famous case of phantom battle re-enactment. The battle of Edgehill was the first major, intense and bloody conflict of the English Civil War between the royalist forces of Charles I and the parliamentary forces of the Earl of Essex. It took place on 23 October 1642 about two miles south-west of Kineton and is said by some to be still witnessed today.

The first account of **phantom armies** fighting was reported on 24 December 1642 by shepherds herding their sheep on the former battleground. They reported hearing voices and the screams of horses and then experienced a huge **apparition** of the battle in the sky. The shepherds reported the apparition to the local priest who went the following night and witnessed the phenomenon for himself. In the days that followed Charles I sent a group of investigators and they all witnessed the re-enactment too, with some even recognizing fallen colleagues. Their incredible experience is reported in a leaflet: *The Prodigious Noises of War and Battle at Edge Hill. Near Keinton in Northamptonshire and its truth is certified by William Wood, Esq and the Justice of the Peace for the same County and Samuel Marshell, Preacher of God's word in Keinton and other persons of quality.*

Psychical investigators believe that the re-enactment, which is still said to appear periodically to this day – although not typically as the full re-enactment but as phantom battle sounds – is caused by the restless, traumatized **spirits** of those who died that day. Sceptics argue that certain individuals may be influenced by the history associated with the place and mistake imaginative conjecture for reality.

EEG [Electro-encephalography]

A test that measures and records the electrical activity of the brain by using sensors (electrodes) attached to the head and connected by wires to a computer. The computer records the brain's electrical activity on the screen or on paper as wavy lines. Certain conditions, such as seizures, can be detected by observing changes in the normal pattern of this electrical activity.

Measurements of electrical activity in the brain have been instrumental in measuring stress, determining sleep patterns and monitoring body metabolism. They have also been used to detect what happens in the brain during **psychic** experiences, such as **meditation** and episodes of **clairvoyance**.

Electrokinesis

A form of **psychokinesis**, electrokinesis is the ability to create and control electricity using only the powers of the mind. So far there have been no conclusive studies on or cases of factual electrokinesis.

Electrokinetic ability allegedly causes the psychic to act as a human conductor, able to receive, store and transmit large to small quantities of electricity. There is also the act of draining electricity from electronically based devices and in return recharging them. Those who practise electrokinesis claim to be able to actually explode, start up or switch off electronic devices either via intense **meditation** and visualization or through overwhelming emotional response.

Electrokinesis is mostly used by stage magicians as a part of their narrative when performing tricks that involve some form of electricity, such as lighting a lightbulb simply held in the palm.

Electronic Voice Phenomena [EVP]

Communication from a voice recorded on a tape recorder from which there is no known source. EVP researchers believe the voices captured on tape are those of **spirits** of the dead, but sceptics argue that they are simply voices from radio or TV transmissions being picked up by the recording device.

Interest in EVP began in the late 1920s when the famous inventor Thomas Edison predicted that one day there would be a machine to allow communication with the spirits. In 1959 EVP was said to have been discovered by accident by the Swedish filmmaker Friedrich Jürgenson. Jürgenson was recording birdsong when he discovered an unknown voice on his tape. On replaying the recording later he believed that he had recorded a message from his mother, who had died four years previously.

EVP was further reported in the 1970s by Latvian psychologist **Konstantin Raudive**, who picked up unexplained voices in the background while recording something else. He began to record in empty rooms and still picked up voices, which were later thought to be messages from spirits of the dead. Raudive published his research, in German, in *The Inaudible Made Audible*, which was translated into English in 1971 with a new title *Breakthrough*. EVP voices are also called Raudive Voices in recognition of the extensive work he did recording over 100,000 voices.

In the 1980s and 1990s there were thousands of EVP researchers at work devising machines and recording the phenomenon. Several organizations, including the American Electronic Voice Phenomenon in the United States, sprang into existence. Perhaps the most well-known and best-funded device was the 'spiricom', invented by George Meek, a retired engineer, with the alleged help of a discarnate scientist who communicated to him during a **séance**. Unfortunately the success rate of the spiricom was poor but this did not stop Meek pursuing increasingly sophisticated ways to reach **astral planes**.

Allegedly EVP voices are never heard during recording, only on playback. They are said to be either faint or clear and can speak or sing in a variety of languages. They are identifiable as men, women and children and according to reports the voices suggest that they can communicate through central transmitting agencies in the spirit plane.

EVP has many enthusiastic supporters who believe the phenomenon is evidence of **paranormal** activity, but there are also many critics who doubt the recordings are genuine. Between 1970 and 1972 the **Society for Psychical Research** commissioned psychical researcher D J Ellis to investigate EVP voices, and he concluded that the sounds were susceptible to imagination and most likely a natural phenomenon. Other sceptics believe that the voices are caused by **psychokinesis**, when sounds are imprinted on the tape by the experimenter.

Despite poor experimental records EVP researchers continue to devote time and energy to finding a way to capture something on tape that proves life after death. In the last decade or so EVP has moved into

DIY EVP

There are many ways to attempt to record EVP voices, and enthusiasts tend to use highly sophisticated recording equipment, but perhaps the quickest and simplest way is to turn a recorder on and leave it running. Night-time seems to be the best time to reduce the risk of interference. Often headphones must be used to hear the voices. It is said that the attitude in which the experiment is approached is important and that an open minded, relaxed and positive attitude is best. Doubt has a negative impact on results.

other media, including TV, video and film cameras and computers. Researchers all over the world have reported images and voices appearing or coming from their TVs for which there is no known cause, as well as spontaneous printouts from computers.

ELEMENT

A natural or spiritual substance thought to be one of the fundamental energies of the universe with inherent power. Many belief systems have rituals and techniques to harness these energies and powers for boosting health or creating magic. Each culture has slight variations in the type and number or elements consulted. In Western traditions there are four elements: **air**, **water**, **fire** and **earth**. In Hinduism there are five elements: air, water, earth, fire and **ether**. In **Taoism** there are also five elements: earth, **metal**, water, **wood** and fire.

ELEMENTAL DIVINATION

Divination by means of the four elements: **air** (aromancy), **fire** (see **pyromancy**), water (see **hydromancy**) and earth (see **geomancy**).

ELEMENTALS

Indo-European nature spirits or **angels** believed to be manifestations of the four elements – **water** (**undines**), **air** (sylphs), **fire** (salamanders) and **earth** (gnomes). In addition, there are two other groups of nature spirits inhabiting magical elements – dryads (vegetation) and fauns or satyrs (animal life).

In modern magical philosophy elementals are seen as conscious elements inhabiting the physical world. They have extensive powers over the elements they indwell and their powers are at the disposal of the **magician** who has mastered the elemental force within. Elementals are thought to be able to help bring desires or wishes into being and they are important in the practice of many magical traditions, such as **druidry**, **alchemy** and **Wicca**. In the latter they are called down during rituals to charge **spells** with the power of nature. In an **occult** sense it is thought that they can be created by an emotional thought form, and if suffused with enough energy by their creator they can cause problems through **possession** or as **poltergeists**. This is because as creatures of a single element they can have an unbalancing effect on the human **psyche** and too much contact with them can be upsetting and even dangerous.

ELONGATION

Term used to describe the elongation of a **medium**'s body while under **spirit** control. Historically, elongations were attributed to **possession** by gods or **demons** but by the third century AD similar experiences are reported with mediums. Elongations often feature in the data collected for canonization proceedings and some of El Greco's paintings appear to illustrate saints that are 'stretched'.

Elongations were a common occurrence in Victorian **spiritualist séances**, the most well-known and reported being those of the famous Scottish medium **D D Home**, who allowed witnesses to measure him. At one of the test séances which Home undertook with Lord Adare and the Master of Lindsay, a journalist who was present, H T Humphries, wrote that Home 'was seen by all of us to increase in height to the extent of some eight or ten inches.'

Elongations are still occasionally reported in séances, but no other medium has even been tested in the detailed way Home allowed. Sceptics argue that elongations are illusions and made possible with simple tricks such as slipping feet out of shoes and standing on tiptoe. Although trickery might have been the case in many instances, throughout his career as a medium, Home was never exposed as a **fraud**.

EMPATHY

The ability to tune in intuitively or psychically to the moods and characteristics of a person, animal or place. Empathy is a vital skill for **clairsentients** and may involve **telepathy**, but it can also simply be derived from an **unconscious** or conscious reaction to the body language of another person.

Empaths are people with highly developed feelings of empathy to others and the world around them. They are particularly sensitive to feelings of pain and distress and in some cases physical and emotional pain may manifest in the empath's own body as a result of sensing the pain of others, sometimes resulting in depression and fatigue. In some cases, empaths can sense illness before a person is aware of it, and a person's death before it occurs. Empaths can also pick up information from places as well. For example, an empath may visit a house and sense particular suffering that has happened there in the past.

Empathy from a distance is most likely to occur when there are strong emotional links between people. For example, twins and long-term partners often have empathetic links with each other and mothers are empathetic for their children. There is also evidence to suggest that animals exhibit empathetic links for each other and for their owners. See **animal psi**.

Are you empathetic?

Empathy occurs when we feel for others, both their joy and their pain. It is possible to develop empathy so strongly that just by touching someone you can feel or experience what that person does. We are all empathetic to some degree but some are more empathetic than others. If you answer yes to two or more of the questions below you should consider yourself somewhat empathetic:

* *Are you easily persuaded by others?*
* *Do your moods change according to the people you are with?*
* *Do you find large groups of people overwhelming?*
* *Do you feel drained after being around people?*
* *Do you seem to know what others are feeling?*
* *Are you a 'touchy-feely' kind of person?*
* *Are you overly emotional at times?*
* *Do you have a tendency to take on the problems and worries of others?*
* *Do you have a hard time telling how you truly feel at times?*
* *Do children and/or animals take to you?*

For psychic development and clairsentient awareness empathy can be a valuable asset but it does, however, have a downside. If we are strongly empathetic, someone else's feelings, emotions and attitudes can register so strongly upon us that we assume these are our feelings. We may not realize that what we are feeling may actually be tied to someone else we have encountered or the location we are in. It is very easy to link with the problems and issues of others and carry them with us as if they are our own. If you are not aware you are doing this you can begin to think you are going crazy.

If you find that you have a strong tendency to be empathetic and to experience what others are experiencing it is vital to find ways to deliberately disconnect yourself from others and to have time to be alone every day. Some suggest using visualization techniques to disconnect yourself, such as visualizing cutting threads or pulling out cords from the other person. Others suggest visualizing a protective bubble of light around yourself during the day. Gardenia and eucalyptus essential oils are also thought to help you remain objective while dealing with others. Just a tiny drop diluted in water and worn like perfume or a few drops in a bowl of water in your bedroom when you sleep at night is all that is necessary.

ENCOUNTER PHENOMENON

Encounters with alternate realities and non-physical beings. Encounter phenomenon covers a wide range of experiences including **visions** of **angels**, **fairies** or **spirits**, **near-death experiences**, **UFO** abductions, **channelling** and **possession**. Despite great variety in individual cases, historical records show similar characteristics, such as some or all of the following: **psi** in various forms; feelings of love, wonder or awe; being anointed as a teacher or leader to humanity; instruction or initiation; the presence of light; transportation to a non-physical realm; revelations and **ESP**. Encounters with alternate realities seem accidental but more often than not they have intention. For instance, many come to give guidance or help to humans at times of crisis, and some encounters are so powerful that a person's life is permanently changed.

Research shows that some people are more likely than others to have encounters with alternate realities. It seems that childhood tendencies towards fantasy, role-play and **imagination** are contributory factors. Childhood trauma is another significant factor. Such trauma can result in dissociation, in which part of the **psyche** splits off from itself as a means of self-defence.

There are those who believe that encounters with alternate realities are genuine interactions with external non-physical reality, but others hold that encounters are exteriorizations of the **unconscious**. The encounter is said to happen when the unconscious creates an escape from reality to relieve stress. In extreme cases this can lead to mental illness, such as schizophrenia. Another theory is that encounters are interactions with a higher realm of consciousness or the divine power that permeates the universe and are intended to further spiritual development. Sceptics argue that encounters with alternate realities are simply the result of over-active and highly suggestible imaginations.

ENERGY BALANCING/MEDICINE

Any type of complementary **or alternative medicine** whose methods involve working with the body's natural energy field – the **universal life force** – in the hope of stimulating the body's own healing mechanism. For example, **traditional Chinese medicine**, **Ayurvedic medicine**, **acupuncture**, **reiki** and **spiritual healing**.

ENFIELD POLTERGEIST

A **poltergeist** case that took place in the late 1970s in an ordinary suburban house in Enfield, North London.

On the night of 30 August 1977, Janet Harper, aged 11, and her brother Pete, aged 10, went to their bedroom. According to reports later compiled their beds began to jolt up and down. When the children ran to get their mother, Peggy Harper, the movements stopped. The following night the children called their mother to their room again, claiming to hear shuffling sounds like a chair or table moving. Peggy took the chair downstairs and turned out the light. As soon as she did she herself heard the sound of shuffling. On turning on the light the children were both in bed with their hands under the covers. All three of them then heard loud knocks on the wall and witnessed a chest of drawers moving towards the centre of the room. Terrified, the entire Harper family went to their next-door neighbours.

When the neighbours walked into the Harper house they too heard the knocking and could not explain what was causing it. The police were called and on arrival they witnessed the phenomena of unexplained knocking and moving chairs. The next day, when marbles and Lego began to fly across the room, the Harpers contacted the local press. A reporter from the *Daily Mirror* was sent out and he took a picture of a piece of Lego flying at him from out of nowhere. The paper called the **Society for Psychical Research**, who sent North London resident and psychical researcher Maurice Grosse to investigate.

Grosse arrived at the house on 5 September, a week after the disturbances had begun. After a few days he heard a crash in Janet's bedroom. Investigation showed that her bedside chair had been thrown across the room while she was asleep. It happened again a few hours later and this time a photographer was able to capture the event. Grosse was to spend the next two years investigating the house and there were many more strange occurrences.

Children in puberty or about to reach puberty tend to be the focal point of many poltergeist cases and the Harper case is no exception: Peggy had two young children. The case also had another typical feature: internal family tension. Peggy was having problems getting over her divorce from the children's father and the children were having problems adjusting to the new situation, and it is possible that the emotional trauma played a part in the disturbances.

Two other investigators sent by the Society for Psychical Research, Anita Gregory and John Beldoff, were convinced that the phenomena were caused by trickery, and video cameras set up in the house did show Janet and Pete producing muffled voices – with their faces covered by sheets – and bouncing up and down on their beds. It seems that this remarkable case may have begun with genuine phenomena, but over time developed into fraud when the children began to enjoy the attention they were getting from the investigators and media.

ENNEAGRAM

See **Gurdjieff, Georgei Ivanovitch**.

ENOCHIAN MAGIC

A system of **magic** that uses the numeric symbols and letters of the Enochian alphabet, said to have been received from the angel Enoch by the Elizabethan court astrologer **John Dee** and his **medium** Edward Kelley. In many ways the magical tradition is similar to that used in the **kabbalah** to understand the **Tree of Life**.

According to Dee's detailed journals **angels** who appeared to Kelley communicated hundreds of pages of complex material known as Calls or Evocations to the watchtowers of the universe. These calls, which later formed the raw material for Enochian magic, were dictated letter by letter and backwards because, according to Dee and Kelley, the material was so powerful that even writing it down in the normal way might stir up unwanted magical powers.

The Calls were not in English but in a language Dee referred to as angelic or Enochian. It was supposed to have been the language spoken by inhabitants of **Atlantis**. The Enochian language has its own alphabet, grammar, script and syntax, similar to Hebrew but not identical to it. The following passage from the *Second Key* will give a sense of the language's flavour:

Enochain spelling: *torzu ghohe L zacar eca c noquod zamran micalzo od ozazum vrelp lap zir lo-lad.*

Pronunciation according to Golden Dawn: *Torzodu gohe El; zodacare, eca, ca noqoda. Zodameranu micaelzodo oda ozadazodme vurelpe lape zodire Io-Iada.*

Translated: *Arise, saith the first: move, therefore, unto my servants. Show yourselves in power and make me a strong seer of things, for I am of Him that liveth forever.*

Doubt has been cast over Kelley's mediumistic abilities but on analysis the language does appear to be genuine, and linguistic scholars claim it is not possible to create an entire pseudo-language without the help of language experts and years of work. It is hard to imagine how Kelley could have faked Enochian and how he managed the amazing feat of memory to dictate it backwards.

Dee's diaries recording the language of the Enochian Calls are now in the British Museum but the Enochian language lives on. In Victorian times **Golden Dawn** initiates used the material to create their vast and complex system of Enochian magic, which, along with Dee's original material, is still being studied today by **occult** enthusiasts.

ENTITY

See **Discarnate entity**.

ENTOMANCY

A form of **divination**, interpreting the appearance and behaviour of insects.

To this may be referred the various **omens** and **superstitions** of popular folklore, such as crickets bringing good luck, deathwatch beetles bringing bad luck and ladybirds indicating visitors. The ancient Greeks had many beliefs about insects. For instance, the great wealth of Midas was allegedly foretold by ants coming to him as a boy while he slept; and bees were thought to indicate future eloquence, as illustrated by the story of Plato who, as a baby in the cradle, was supposedly visited by a swarm of bees which alighted on his lips.

EPWORTH RECTORY

Epworth Rectory in Lincolnshire was the scene of one of the earliest reputed **poltergeist hauntings**. For about two months from December 1716, although some accounts say 1719, the household of the Reverend Samuel Wesley experienced poltergeist activity, such as **rappings** and the movement of furniture.

Epworth Rectory was a gift to Rev Wesley from Queen Mary. His wife bore him 19 children in 20 years, 14 of whom died in infancy. The only year she didn't bear children was in 1701 when Wesley, a Hanoverian, left his wife because of her sympathy for the Jacobites. Rev Wesley did return but the conflict between the two was never resolved and some think that Mrs Wesley's repressed anger over her husband's desertion may have played a part in the disturbances.

According to records the servants were the first to hear strange groaning and the sounds of stamping feet even though no one was present, on 1 December 1716. The children were the next to hear unusual knocking, footsteps, chains clanking and door latches being rattled. Finally the knocks sounded in the bedroom of Rev and Mrs Wesley.

A routine began to develop, with the raps and knockings and strange noises starting at around 9.45 every night. Sometimes the house itself would shake or there would be the sounds of bottles smashing; on inspection nothing would be out of place.

At first Mrs Wesley thought that rats were the cause and she requested a horn be sounded through the house to scare them. After that the noises, almost as an act of revenge for the horn, sounded during the day as well as the night. Other manifestations included a bed levitating with one of the children in it and the spectres of what looked like a rabbit and a badger.

The children called the spirit by the nickname 'old Jeffrey' and it was suggested that either **witchcraft** or the **spirit** of someone who had died in the house was to blame. Attempts to establish contact with the spirit failed and it was particularly active during **prayers** – although curiously if the prayers omitted mention of the King it remained silent. Although Wesley was advised to leave the rectory by his friends, he refused to be intimidated by what he called 'the devil'. Then mysteriously, at the end of January the disturbances stopped.

The most likely explanation for this case is **psychokinetic energy** unleashed by a member of the Wesley family. Mrs Wesley harboured deep resentment against her husband because of his desertion of her and his family. It's also possible that one of the children was the prime **agent** of the activity. One daughter, Hetty, was around the age of 15 at the time and according to reports she intensely disliked Epworth Rectory and the surrounding villages. She was also probably deeply hurt by the tension that existed between her parents.

Equinox

Term used to refer to the two days each year, one in spring (usually around 20 to 23 March) and one in autumn (usually around 20 to 23 September) in which day and night are of equal length. At the moment of the Equinox the Sun crosses the celestial equator – the projection of the earth's equator into space.

In the **Golden Dawn** magical system the equinoxes are two of the most important days of the year because it is thought that on these days the spiritual energies of the Sun come to Earth directly. Rituals are held to draw on these energies. Equinoxes are also significant in the **pagan** calendar of the year as festival days called Sabbats. The spring celebration is called Ostara and the autumn celebration Mabon.

Esoteric

From the Greek *esoteros* meaning 'inner', esoteric is a term usually applied to mysterious or **occult** teachings. It is used to describe ideas and concepts that are to be understood only by a select few with specialized training and/or knowledge.

ESP [Extrasensory perception]

Term used to describe the ability of some people to perceive things beyond which their five senses of sight, hearing, touch, smell and taste can tell them. ESP is often described as a **sixth sense**, but it does not function like a sense and is not dependent on the other senses, age, location, time or intelligence. It seems to originate in an alternate reality and to bring people information about the past, present and future that they couldn't be aware of under normal circumstances.

Information that comes through ESP is not always significant or accurate, possibly because it is affected by the thoughts of the waking consciousness, but in some cases it is. For example, in one case recorded by the **Society for Psychical Research**, a woman driving on the M62 motorway near Irlam in Lancashire claimed to hear an **inner voice** crying 'Get out!' She swerved dangerously into the fast lane and at exactly the same moment avoided a collision with a lorry. Another case was that of Maureen Blyth, wife of yachtsman Chay Blyth, who was suddenly overcome with unexplained nausea in restaurant. Later she found out that at the exact moment of her nausea her husband's yacht had overturned in the freezing cold Atlantic Ocean; he was trapped underneath for hours before being rescued.

The term 'ESP' was first used as early as 1870 but it was American parapsychologist **J B Rhine** who popularized the term in 1934, when he was one of the first to test for **GESP**, or general extrasensory perception, in the laboratory. ESP is often applied to any **psychic** or **paranormal** experience but strictly speaking it is divided into two main categories: **telepathy** and **clairvoyance**, which can be perceived forward (**precognition**) and backwards (**retrocognition**); if a person possesses these powers they are known as **psychics**. ESP should not be used to describe **out-of-body experiences** or **psychokinesis**. The term **psi** is also sometimes used to cover ESP, and some Russian scientists call ESP bioinformation.

Since Rhine's experiments in the 1930s ESP has become the subject of investigation in its own right as scientists discovered that information can enter the brain/mind in other ways apart from the five senses. Research shows that ESP does exist but how it happens remains a mystery. With **quantum theory** pointing to the existence of a second, non-material universe, more and more scientists are coming round to the idea that an extrasensory force exists in another reality and from time to time this force may interact with the physical world.

Theories to explain ESP

There have been several theories to explain ESP. Psychiatrist **Carl Jung** suggested that the conscious mind has psychic access to the **collective unconscious**, where all accumulated wisdom and experience of the human race is collected. Researcher **Louisa B Rhine**, the wife of J B Rhine, suggested that **dreams** might be the most efficient messengers of ESP because in sleep the barriers to the conscious mind appear to be at their weakest. An interesting theory first suggested in the 1960s proposed that macrophages, cells present in connective tissue and bone marrow and tied to nerve endings, are the body's ESP organs. These cells are more active in childhood and deteriorate when diet is poor. The most recent theories tend to centre on the existence of a second **consciousness** (which can also be called 'soul', 'super consciousness', 'dream self' or a number of other names) that somehow integrates physical and alternate realities. Subliminal barriers separate the second consciousness from the waking consciousness, otherwise the waking consciousness would be overwhelmed with data.

Who has ESP?

It seems that ESP is in many cases an inherited skill, but this does not mean that only a selected few are psychic and the rest of the population isn't. There are theories that ESP is a super sense developing in the nervous system but by far the most popular theory is that ESP is a primitive sense everyone has, but with the advance of technology (where we need to rely less and less on our **intuition**) it has become less accessible. With training, however, or techniques such as **yoga** or **meditation**, ESP ability can be developed and strengthened.

Research confirms that all people have ESP but that some, such as **mediums**, are more gifted than others. It seems that people who are relaxed, believe in ESP and are intuitive by nature tend to be more sensitive to ESP and perform better at ESP tests. This may explain why some people are more affected by haunted sites and others are not affected at all. And it's not only people who possess ESP: animals, in particular dogs, cats and horses, have been known to display it. See **animal psi**.

According to surveys most people believe they have had at least one ESP experience in their life, for example thinking of a person and a few moments later receiving a phone call from that individual, or looking at a person from a distance only for that person to turn around as if they sense they are being looked at.

ESP CARDS

Also known as **Zener cards**, ESP cards are a deck of 25 cards of 5 symbols: star, cross, circle, square and wavy lines. They were once a standard laboratory testing-tool for ESP but have now been replaced by the computer.

ESP cards were first used in the 1930s by **J B Rhine** and Karl Zener, faculty members of Duke University in North Carolina, and soon replaced the playing cards that had been used previously to test for ESP. Rhine used the cards in thousands of tests and found eight subjects with consistently high scores. He published the results in 1934 in a controversial pamphlet called *Extra Sensory Perception*. Critics argued that the results were invalid as there was too much potential for **fraud** and for picking up of sensory clues such as body language.

To avoid the accusation of fraud Rhine changed his test procedures and the tester

and the subject are now typically placed in separate rooms. To test for **telepathy** the tester goes through the deck, concentrating on one symbol at a time, and the subject writes down the symbols that come to his or her mind. In **clairvoyance** testing the tester selects some cards and places them face down while the subject attempts to record the hidden symbols. In **precognition** testing the subject attempts to name the cards in the right sequence before they are picked by the tester.

ESSENTIAL OILS

Oils or essences extracted from parts of plants, including the leaves, bark, flowers, root, stems and fruit. These oils, which may have been developed by plants to attract pollinating insects and birds, are used in perfumes, **massage** and **aromatherapy**.

Each essential oil is thought to have a wide variety of different chemical substances and, when used in aromatherapy, to have pharmaceutical effects. When absorbed into the bloodstream via massage or inhalation (ingesting most essential oils is not a good idea) they are believed to have physiological effects on the body and psychological effects on the mind. Essential oils also carry the bioenergetic qualities of their individual plants and many believe that this can affect a person's spirit as well as their body.

Certain essential oils are thought to help clear the mind to receive **psychic** insight,

Using essential oils

Usually a drop or two of an oil is used by placing it in a burner in a room. You could also place a few drops on a handkerchief and place it under your pillow at night or carry it around during the day. As well as an aromatherapy massage perhaps the most relaxing way to use essential oils is in the bath, using about ten drops of essential oils that encourage psychic awareness. Place the oils in the bath after it has filled so that they float on the surface. Either mix three drops each of oils such as geranium, neroili or ylang-ylang or use ten drops of one oil.

especially jasmine and rose oil. Others that are typically used to stimulate psychic awareness include frankincense, lavender, neroili, lemongrass, jasmine, peppermint, magnolia, eucalyptus, gardenia, honeysuckle, ylang-ylang, yarrow root and sage. Sandalwood, pine, lavender, gardenia, anise, clove and eucalyptus are often used for **psychic protection**. In some instances, healers use a small amount of essential oil to activate the body's **chakras** with their hands and fingers. The theory is that these oils increase the healer's psychic awareness of energy in the patient.

ETHER

From the Greek *aither*, meaning 'upper air', ether is the term used to describe the substance that makes up all matter, according to mystical and magical belief. In Hinduism it is considered to be one of the five natural elements, along with **air, fire, earth** and **water**.

Also known as **akasha**, ether can be thought of as space: space as in outer space, space between all living matter, space as in the substance that sound and thought waves travel through, and space as the place the **astral body** inhabits. In **Ayurvedic medicine** ether has the elemental qualities of light, sound and purity.

ETHERIC BODY

Also described as an **aura**, the etheric body is thought to be a second, subtle body which is typically a mirror image of the physical body and which can, under certain circumstances, be projected and travel great distances in a short space of time. It is often said to be the same as the **astral body** but some traditions believe that the **astral plane** is one step closer to higher consciousness. In magical traditions the etheric body is said to be composed of fine energy. Recent research not only suggests that the etheric body may exist but that its substance may be electrical energy.

EVIL EYE

The ancient and greatly feared belief that certain people can inflict bad luck, misfortune or death simply with a glance or intense stare. Negative energy is transmitted to another person with a glance or lingering look from a malevolent person.

The **superstition** was known as far back as 3000 BC, appearing in the cuneiform texts of the Sumerians and Assyrians. There is also evidence that the Babylonians and ancient Greeks believed in it. Women in ancient Egypt would paint their eyes and lips with makeup to keep the evil eye out. Most tribal cultures are aware of it and it is mentioned in both the Bible and the Koran. Even today in Mexico and Central America superstitions about the evil eye still exist.

The evil eye is said to most likely strike when an individual is at the height of his or her happiness and success and for some unknown reason children and cows seem to be special targets of the evil eye. **Witches**, **sorcerers**, **magicians**, medicine men and **witch doctors** are said to cast the evil eye. Native America **shamans** often combine the menacing look with a pointing stick, finger or **wand**. A person may also be cursed with the evil eye at birth and not

know it. Pope Leo XIII was said to possess the evil eye. Because of this those who believe in the evil eye must constantly be on their guard as a malevolent stare could come from anyone, even a stranger in the street.

If a person is hit by the evil eye various superstitions offer protection against disaster striking. If a witch or sorcerer is not available to offer a counter-spell, the fig hand – a clenched fist with the thumb stuck through the middle and fourth fingers – and a curved horn are said to offer protection. Other protective **amulets** include bells, brass, red ribbons, blue beads, garlic, horseshoes or hanging **charms** in windows to confuse a witch's gaze. Denying success and good fortune could also deflect it, and admired infants would be smeared with dirt before being taken out. Touching wood was also thought to offer protection against the **curse** of the evil eye.

EVOCATION

From the Latin for 'calling forth' an evocation is the summoning in magic or ritual of a **spirit** into a manifestation that is external to the **medium** or **magician**. It is distinguished from **invocation**, which is the process of summoning a spirit into the medium or magician.

EXORCISM

The process by which an evil **spirit** or possessing entity is driven out of a human host, object or place. From the Greek *exorkizein* meaning 'to bind by oath' (invoking a higher power to make a spirit act in a certain way), rituals of exorcism exist universally in societies where spirits are thought to interfere with earthly affairs and cause misfortune.

Typically exorcisms are performed by trained individuals, usually religious officials or magical or **occult adepts**. Rites vary from simple requests to leave to complex rituals involving **trance** and techniques including fasting, **prayer**, sacred herbs and blessed water.

In Hinduism, Buddhism and Islam possessing spirits are blamed for a number of misfortunes and are cast out of people and places, but unlike in Christianity, such conflicts are not considered battles for the person's **soul**. Typical Hindu exorcism techniques include offering copper coins, candy or other gifts and pressing rock salt between the fingers. In some shamanic traditions it is thought that possessing spirits can steal souls, and the **shaman** enters a trance to search for the soul and force the evil spirit out. Jewish rabbinic literature refers to exorcisms. The best-known rite concerns that of the **dybbuk**.

Christianity associates exorcism with demonic **possession**. The Roman Catholic Church offers a formal rite of exorcism, the *Rituale Romanum*, dating back to 1614. In order to 'qualify' for an exorcism the victim must display certain symptoms including superhuman strength, **levitation** and speaking in tongues (**glossolalia**). Some Protestants also perform exorcism. Pentecostalists practise 'deliverance ministry', where healers drive out evil spirits by the **laying on of hands**.

A more moderate view on exorcism and possession was put forward by American psychologist **Carl Wickland**, who believed that spirits were not evil but simply confused and trying to finish their worldly business in a living person. This could cause any number of mental problems. Wickland recommended using mild electric shock to help the spirits leave in his controversial book *Thirty Years Among the Dead* (1924). This view still has a number of supporters, among them psychiatrist Dr Ralph Allison, who wrote in his book, *Minds in Many Pieces* (1980), that various of his patients exhibited signs of demonic possession and required exorcism as well as conventional treatment.

In Christianity there are no formal exorcism rites for banishing **ghosts** from places. There are, however, plenty of **superstitions** and magical rites, and these include entering a house at midnight with a candle, compass, crucifix and Bible and drawing magic circles and crosses. In China ghosts are exorcised from houses by **Taoist** priests in a complex ritual, involving a mystic scroll placed on an altar, a cup and a sword and mystical signs, repeated to all four corners of the room.

EXPERIMENTER EFFECT

A term used in laboratory tests for **psi** to describe the unconscious **psychic** influence or bias of the experimenter on the subject. The effect may show up as **unconscious** telepathic communication or use of body language or attitude communicated to the subject.

The experimenter effect was noticed first in psychology in the tendency of patients and therapists to establish a rapport, and then in psychical research in the 1930s when it became apparent that in some cases the experimenter became the determining factor for the outcome of a test. It was shown that experimenters who seemed negative and unsupportive yielded poorer results than experimenters who were positive and encouraging. Subjects also seemed to be influenced by how much they thought their experimenter believed in psi and whether or not the experimenter liked them. In 1949 American psychologist and psychical researcher **Gardner Murphy** suggested that certain brilliant test results were due to the intense feelings of the experimenters.

Some experimenters do appear to get more positive and more conclusive results than others. According to some psi researchers this doesn't necessarily invalidate their test results. It is argued that it is important for the experimenter to believe in psychic ability and to have a positive, encouraging attitude towards the subject, as this creates the kind of relaxed and positive atmosphere conducive to psychic development.

EXTRASENSORY PERCEPTION

See **ESP**.

EXTRATERRESTRIALS

Beings that are not of this earth and whose existence has not been proven. The term applies to alien visitors from another planet or world. Various **psychic, paranormal** and strange occurrences have been reported in conjunction with alleged sightings of extraterrestrials and their spacecrafts.

Thousands upon thousands of sightings of extraterrestrials have been reported since interest in the phenomenon began in earnest with the famous Roswell incident in 1947. Three **UFOs** reportedly crashed near Roswell in New Mexico and although the US government claimed they were weather balloons, eyewitness reports years later suggested that they had seen the bodies of aliens in the wreckage. The great majority of ET encounters have been explained as natural phenomena, aircraft or hoaxes but a tiny majority can't be explained away, leading many to believe in the extraterrestrial hypothesis (ETH): that extraterrestrial encounters and UFOs are a reality. ETH is a dominant belief in America, but European ET experts are more inclined to support what is called the 'encounter theories' view.

This encounter theories view of ET occurrences holds that there are encounter-prone personalities and that encounters are psychological projections in response to the mass yearning of mankind to raise **consciousness**. As yet there are no real answers to the question whether ET encounters are objective or subjective.

There are various types of extraterrestrial encounters: hovering nocturnal lights, discs or saucer-shapes seen in daylight, radar-visual sightings and sightings of aliens – typically as small humanoid beings with large heads and grey or green skin. There have also been reports of so-called alien abductions: when mysterious events left individuals with unaccounted missing time, when the details can only be uncovered under **hypnosis**, and when there are inconspicuous scars.

Some eyewitnesses state that prior to an extraterrestrial encounter they acquired psychic powers that helped bring about the encounter or helped them communicate telepathically with the aliens. Others say that psychic abilities developed as a result of the encounter. Many witnesses feel transformed after an encounter and make major changes in their lifestyles, such as becoming active in environmental concerns, moving to a new area or becoming actively involved in psychic development and paranormal research.

EYE OF HORUS

Also known as the 'all seeing eye', the stylized eye of the falcon-headed sky god, Horus, was one of the most common **amulets** of ancient Egypt. Egyptians used the amulet as protection from evil and it was typically associated with health and prosperity. However, according to some myths it was also associated with terror and anger and as result has since become associated with **magic** and the **occult**. A variation of the eye of Horus is the open eye symbol in the Great Seal of the United States. According to **esoteric** teaching an open eye symbolizes the flowering of intellect and **psychic** awareness.

EYELESS VISION

Also known as skin reading and dermo-optics, this quite literally means seeing images and colours through the skin. Eyeless vision is said to work best in daylight rather than in darkness.

In 1937, *Life* magazine ran a three-page story on a 13-year-old Californian boy named Pat Marquis, who convinced his doctor that he could see after his eyes had been taped shut. Professors and reporters who tested him later to satisfy themselves of this claim found no trickery. Rosa Kuleshova also impressed scientists in the former USSR by identifying colours and reading print with her finger tips while her eyes were covered, *Time* magazine printing her remarkable story in 1963.

In 1920, French psychologist Jules Romains studied the phenomenon and concluded that all skin has the capacity for eyeless sight, in particular the hands. In the early 1960s eyeless vision was extensively researched in the Soviet Union, where researchers attempted to train individuals to read colours, words and images through their skin while blindfolded.

Various theories have been put forward to explain eyeless vision. Some believe that skin readers have special unknown cells in their bodies, others suspect fraud, suggesting that when a person loses their sight, nature compensates by heightening another of the senses – usually the tactile and/or auditory sense – and it is possible with diligent practice to develop the senses to achieve extraordinary feats. Another theory suggests that electromagnetic energy and the meridian energy points on the body may be the cause.

F

FACELESS GRAY MAN OF PAWLEYS ISLAND

The **ghost** of a grey-looking man with no face who is said to warn residents of Pawleys Island, off the coast of South Carolina, of an impending natural disaster, for example a hurricane. The faceless **apparition** has only been sighted when dangerous storms are approaching and he is thought to have saved countless lives, appearing before the hurricanes of 1822, 1893, 1916, 1954 and 1955. Locals believe that if you see him, your residence will be spared.

Some say the Gray Man is the ghost of Percival Pawley, the first man to settle on the Island and to give the Island its name. Others say it is the ghost of the lover and cousin of a beautiful eighteenth-century Charleston belle. The belle could have married anyone, but she disappointed her family by falling in love with her cousin, who had a reputation for being a lady's man. Her family succeeded in breaking up their relationship by sending the cousin to France and telling her that her lover had died in a dual. The woman was devastated but eventually married someone else.

One night when her husband was away on business a hurricane arose and sank a brigantine off the Island's shore. There was only one survivor from the ship – her cousin – who came to the woman's house for shelter. She was horrified to discover that he had not died in a dual, and the cousin was horrified to see a ring on her finger. He ran away and a few weeks later died of fever and, some say, a broken heart. The woman stayed with her husband but remained troubled for the rest of her life by the ghost of a grey man with no face.

FACELESS WOMAN

A beautiful female **ghost** who is said to terrify all who see her because she has no face. Typically she is young and slender and is first seen from behind.

The faceless woman is often thought to be an **urban myth**, but she appears in **haunting** legends all over the world. Her origins are unknown but may be Japanese. In his book *Kwaidan* (*Weird Tales*) published in 1904, **Lafcadio Hearn**, one of the first Westerners to study the folklore of Japan in depth, documented ancient stories of the *Mujina*, faceless ghosts of either sex.

The most recent sightings of the faceless woman have been in Hawaii. In 1959 the faceless woman was said to have appeared at the Waialee Drive-In and a few years later in Oahu. There are also rumours of her being spotted in a Waikiki hotel, shopping mall and college.

FAIRIES

Fairies are thought to be non-human, immortal earth **spirits** with **supernatural** powers who occupy a limbo between earth and heaven.

From the latin *fata* meaning fate, the term comes from the Fates of Greek and

Roman mythology – three sisters who spun the thread of life and determined the fate of all human lives. In archaic English fairies were also known as *fays*, a term which means enchanted or bewitched, and is in recognition of the skill fairies were thought to have in predicting and even controlling human destiny. Fairies are thought to bring good or bad luck on a person and to possess magical power and the ability to cast **spells**. They are sometimes said to be **witches** or their **familiars**.

Fairy legends are universal and show many similarities. There are numerous ideas about how they originated. One is that they are descendants of the children of Eve, another is that they are fallen **angels**, not evil enough to be dismissed from heaven but not good enough to stay in heaven. A third idea is that stories about fairies arose to explain misfortunes and disasters, another suggests they are **spirits** of the restless dead, and yet another that they are simply small human beings.

Regardless of how they originated, getting involved with fairies is never considered to be straightforward. They can be good but numerous **superstitions** also suggest a darker side. For example, it is thought that fairies may steal away babies and turn them into changelings, or they might curse a person to ill health or a household to poverty. If they fall in love with a human that person may be blessed with immortality, but this also brings the curse of living forever and watching loved ones die. In order to stay in favour with the fairies some superstitions suggest that humans should leave out food, drink and gifts for the fairies. In return the fairies will bestow wealth and health on a family.

Fairies, also known as the good people, the little people, elves or good neighbours, come in all shapes and sizes but traditionally they are tiny, resemble humans and have wings. It is said that they are only visible to those with **clairvoyant** sight but if they wish they can make themselves visible to anyone. Some are said to be fearsome creatures with awesome powers, while others, like leprechauns or **brownies**, are almost cute and loveable by nature. Whatever their shape or appearance, fairies are thought to have great affinity for nature. They are said to live in the Land of Fairy or Elf Land, which is believed to exist in a timeless underground world. At night they allegedly step out from Elf Land to dance, sing, travel and have fun or make mischief.

Fairies are mainly associated with Northern European cultures, especially the Celtic folklore of Ireland, Wales, Brittany and Cornwall. In Ireland they are known as *Tuatha de Danaan*, or people of the goddess *Danu*, a divine race that once ruled Ireland. The Tuatha are thought to be strong and beautiful and skilled in **magic**. Celtic folklore was also transported to American colonies and to Asia. Native Americans have their own 'little people' fairy lore. The little people live in the Pryor Mountains of Montana and are said to have powerful medicine and strong teeth.

From the eighteenth century onwards stories report that the fairies have departed or are fading away. Some people believe that they are disappearing because humans have stopped believing in them. Others say pollution, urbanization and technological advances are the main cause of their decline. Yet, however often they are reported as gone, belief in fairies still lingers, reports of sightings still occur and the traditions continue.

Around the beginning of the nineteenth century, a man called Hugh Miller recorded what was supposed to be the final departure of the fairies from Scotland at Burn of Eathie.

On a Sabbath morning ... the inmates of this little hamlet had all gone to church, all except a herd-boy, and a little girl, his sister, who were lounging beside one of the cottages; when, just as the shadow of the garden-dial had fallen on the line of noon, they saw a long cavalcade ascending out of the ravine through the wooded hollow. It winded among the knolls and bushes; and, turning round the northern gable of the cottage beside which the sole spectators of the scene were stationed, began to ascend the eminence toward the south. The horses were shaggy, diminutive things, speckled dun and grey; the riders, stunted, misgrown, ugly creatures, attired in antique jerkins of plaid, long grey cloaks, and little red caps, from under which their wild uncombed locks shot out over their cheeks and foreheads. The boy and his sister stood gazing in utter dismay and astonishment, as rider after rider, each one more uncouth and dwarfish than the one that had preceded it, passed the cottage, and disappeared among the brushwood which at that period covered the hill, until at length the entire route, except the last rider, who lingered a few yards behind the others, had gone by.

'What are ye, little mannie? and where are ye going?', inquired the boy, his curiosity getting the better of his fears and his prudence.

'Not of the race of Adam,' said the creature, turning for a moment in his saddle: 'The People of Peace shall never more be seen in Scotland.'

(Hugh Miller, *The Old Red Sandstone*)

FAIRY RING

According to folklore, fairy rings are circles of inedible mushrooms or differently coloured grass, thought to be magical **circles** where **witches** and **fairies** meet to sing and dance at night. It is said that if you run around the outside of a fairy ring nine times on a full moon to see the fairies your wish will come true. It is unwise, however, to interfere with the fairy ring ritual because if a human is lured inside he or she can't escape unless pulled out of the circle by a human chain. Inside the ring time is thought to be different, and what seems like a couple of minutes could actually be several days, months or even years.

FAKIR

From the Arabic word *faqir*, meaning 'poor person', a fakir was an initiate in a mendicant Sufi order who renounced his ties to family life to live as a beggar so that he could develop his **psychic** powers. Today the word is used to refer to holy men of India who can allegedly perform magical, mystical or **paranormal** feats, such as lying on a bed of nails or walking on hot coals.

FALSE AWAKENING

A vivid or lucid **dream** experience in which the subject believes that he or she has woken up from sleep; the person is in fact still dreaming. See **Lucid dreaming**.

FAMILIAL APPARITIONS

Ghostly **apparitions** thought to be associated with a particular family. They are most often described as an ancient ancestor who lingers in **spirit** form on the earth to ensure the continuation and prosperity of the family line. In other cases, the spirit of an ancestor allegedly follows the family line and only appears when misfortune is about to strike, such as in the case of the Black Friar who haunted the family of the poet **Byron**.

FAMILIAR

The name given to a **spirit** companion, usually in animal form, who aids or attends the needs of **witches**. Familiars are also said to be given to witches by the Devil as their companions and helpers. The word is derived from the Latin *familiaris*, meaning 'belonging to a household'.

A familiar is thought to have magical power and to offer protection from danger to their master or mistress. The most common familiars are cats, followed by dogs, birds, hares, snakes and frogs or toads. At the height of the seventeenth-century witch paranoia a lone woman owning a black cat was enough ground to convict her of witchcraft.

FENG SHUI

Sometimes associated with **geomancy**, a Western practice that works with the magnetic and life force energies of the earth, Feng Shui is the ancient and complex Chinese art of placement to enhance the flow of 'chi' or **universal life force** in an environment. It is the belief that how items are placed in living and work areas affect the health, wellbeing and success of those who live and work there. Making changes to a room's layout can assist or block the flow of chi and the goal of Feng Shui is to determine what changes need to be made to an environment so that positive energy and good fortune are attracted to it.

Feng Shui translates as 'wind and water' and a fundamental concept is that in order to be healthy and happy you must be in harmony with the earth and the flow of chi. It is extremely important that the **yin** (female) and **yang** (male) aspects of chi are in balance and it is thought that the yin–yang balance is affected by landscape, the presence or absence of water, green trees and plants, the shapes of buildings, the placement of doors and furniture and so on.

In Feng Shui advice for improving the flow of chi is given by a feng shui master who typically combines keen observation with intuitive and/or **psychic** skills. By visiting a location the master determines the existing state of chi and makes recommendations for changes that will maximize it or, if problems exist, he or she will suggest ways to overcome them.

Straight roads are considered particularly unfortunate and to live at the end of one is to invite problems. Ideally houses should face south and be located near yang and yin energies of strength and protection. The five **elements** – **water**, **fire**, **earth**, **metal** and **wood** – are also thought to suit different types and functions of buildings. Common remedies to solve problems and enhance chi or repel negative energy include lights, wind chimes, plants, fish tanks, moving items of furniture to face another direction, painting rooms a different colour and, in extreme cases, moving house.

The Chinese believe that the best chi is one that doesn't flow too fast and isn't too straight but one that flows along natural contours. **Mirrors** are a common remedy for stagnant chi as, strategically placed, they are thought to block negative energy. Particular types of chi are associated with the different directional points: north is associated with success and business, east with family life, south with fame and west with children's fame.

Feng Shui dates back to around the second century BC. Its roots come from nature **divination** practices, **Taoism**, a system of belief that is based on patterns in nature, **numerology**, **astrology** and other ancient Chinese divination methods to determine the correct location for things. Many of the early Feng Shui masters were priests and holy men who gave counsel and advice and prescribed Feng Shui cures. Around AD 890 Feng Shui split into two different schools – the form school and the compass school. The form school is based on landscape contours and is an intuitive method of assessing visually the environment, instead of measuring it precisely using a compass to chart astrological factors, **I Ching** hexagrams and other elements, as used in the compass school.

Feng Shui is practised all over the world today. It has spread to the West and is growing in popularity but it is most actively practised in China, and other pacific countries – Japan, Hong Kong, Korea, Singapore, Malaysia and Thailand. Feng Shui experts believe it's no coincidence that in Hong Kong and Taiwan many of the buildings have Feng Shui-inspired features, and that these two states have two of the highest per-capita incomes in the world, followed by Singapore and Malaysia. Businessmen and women in these countries take Feng Shui very seriously and regularly consult Feng Shui masters in the course of their business, especially when it comes to property.

Some Feng Shui tips for health and wellbeing

Remove clutter

Clutter is thought to stagnate chi energy in your home or office, blocking positive energy from coming into your life. If your house is full of clutter Feng Shui experts would probably urge you to dispose of at least half or more of what's there in order to allow new things to enter your life.

Personal space

Feng Shui suggests that it is vital for your health and wellbeing that you surround yourself with souvenirs, artwork, books, images and mementos that nourish your spirit. Remember, less is always more as far as Feng Shui is concerned, so don't go overboard. The space doesn't have to be big, it can be as small as a favourite corner of the room. The important thing is that it is all yours, a place where you can dream and find peace.

A good night's rest

Have a look around your bedroom to see if anything is preventing you from getting a good night's rest. Get rid of as much electronic equipment out of your room as you can because, according to Feng Shui, electrical equipment emanate waves that disturb chi. Close the bathroom door leading to your room, as well as the toilet lid, as bathrooms are associated with draining energy. Cover up mirrors that activate yang energy, as the bedroom should be a yin environment of rest and peace. It is probably best in the bedroom to stay away from bright, bold colours like red and gold, and use yin colours such as blues, greens and pastels instead.

Room for love

If you're looking to renew or find companionship, love, romance and commitment, Feng Shui stresses the importance of the southwest area. You'll probably be advised to examine the southwest aspect of your house. Is it filled with clutter or is it barren? Ideally there should be symbols of romance, such as a pair of doves or a heart shape, as well as pink quartz crystals, anything made of earth materials such as china, clay, stone or terracotta and fire elements such as lights and candles to add some sparkle. Anything green or made of wood is considered unlucky here.

Create an environment that promotes health and wellbeing

In Feng Shui fresh, clean, moving water, good air quality, a balance of dark and light and soft and hard surfaces all facilitate the flow of beneficial chi. If you often suffer from illness or accidents a Feng Shui expert would perhaps recommend that you walk around the outside of your house and notice if there are any corners of buildings pointing directly towards your front entrance or bedroom. If there are, block the view with plants or place a small mirror so it faces the sharp corner and sends the negative energy away.

Let nature back in

Feng shui is all about harnessing the power of nature to bring health and good fortune so you are advised to let the natural world back into your home and office. In all rooms except for the bedroom bring in vital energy with mirrors, lighting, bright colours and water features such as fountains or fish tanks. In all rooms including the bedroom bring in lots of indoor plants and flowers, placed in the east, southeast and south areas of your home. Replace silk plants with live plants, and remove all dried flowers to bring in fresh, moving energy. Throw open the blinds and curtains and let the sun shine in.

FETCH

In English folklore the term for a ghostly double of a living person. The fetch is remarkably similar to a double or **doppelgänger** but witnessing your own fetch, also called a co-walker, is believed to be a sure sign of your own death, which isn't typically the case for the doppelgänger. If the fetch isn't you it is taken to be a sign that someone close to you will die. In Irish folklore, however, the fetch is only a **death omen** if it is seen at night; if it is seen in the morning it is thought to suggest a long life.

Legend has it that Elizabeth I of England was shocked to see a corpse lying on her bed. On closer inspection she saw that it was her. Shortly afterwards she died.

John Donne, the sixteenth-century English poet, was allegedly visited by an **apparition** of his wife while he was in Paris. She appeared to him holding a newborn baby. Donne's wife was pregnant at the time, but the apparition was a portent of great sadness because at the moment it appeared, his wife had given birth to a stillborn child.

FETISH

From the Latin *facticius* meaning 'made by art', via the Portuguese *feitiço*, meaning 'charm', a fetish is an object that is thought to represent **spirits** and exert magical powers. Fetishes are widely used in **animism** traditions to create or symbolize a union between the **supernatural** and the human. Fetishes are often worn as **amulets** or **talismans** to impart magical powers such as luck, protection, health or to ward off evil, but should not to be confused with these; amulets and talismans are not thought to embody spirits. Fetishes come in all shapes and sizes but are often dolls, carved images, stones or animal body parts, such as a tooth or bone.

See also **Gris-gris**.

50 Berkeley Square

In the late nineteenth century, 50 Berkeley Square became known as London's most haunted house, with reports emerging of **paranormal** activity, evil entities and even deaths.

Years before, in 1859, the house was rented by a man called Myers who allowed the property to deteriorate. Mr Myers became an eccentric recluse after his bride-to-be called their wedding off. He would lock himself away in a small garret room by day and by night he would wander unhappily around the house with a lighted candle. By 1879, 50 Berkeley Square was in such a state of disrepair and ruin that it soon gained a reputation for being haunted in the press.

According to the magazine *Mayfair*, a maid who lived in the house after Myers, and who slept in the attic room Myers used to lock himself in, was said to have gone mad with fright when something malevolent appeared to her, 'rigid as a corpse, with hideously glaring eyes.' However, *Mayfair* refused to jump to conclusions, observing dryly that 'this, of itself, did not mean much – women may go mad now and then without any ghostly dealings.'

A sceptical guest agreed to stay in the room overnight and he promised to ring the servant's bell twice if he needed assistance. That night the bell rang frantically and when the owners rushed up to the room they found the guest dead on the bed. *Mayfair* urged the owners of the house to come forward and discuss the matter but no response was made.

Many other occupants of 50 Berkeley Square have allegedly gone mad or died suddenly. Others have talked about a 'shapeless, slithering, horrible mass', which has left them both terrified and repulsed. Neighbours in the 1880s complained of loud noises, cries and moans and objects being moved about or thrown. In 1939 the house was leased to antiquarian book-sellers, and there have been no further reports of phenomena since.

There are some who believe that the house was genuinely haunted by the **ghost** of Myers, or by the ghost of a woman who lived there and committed suicide by throwing herself out of the garret window to escape being abused by her uncle. A natural and quite plausible explanation put forward by Charles Harper in *Haunted Place* (1924) is that the house was owned by a Mr Du Pre of Wilton Park, who imprisoned his mad and violent brother in the garret. Other explanations are that natural noises came from the house or near-by but were exaggerated because of the associations with the house.

FINDHORN

A community in the north of Scotland that was established in 1962 by Eileen and Peter Caddy and Dorothy Maclean under alleged **spirit** guidance.

The Findhorn community believes that a spiritual reality underlies the material world and unites all life and all people; through collaboration with nature spirits or **devas** they grow vegetables – sometimes of incredible size – in soil so tough that even weeds struggle to grow. As the community developed in the 1960s the media reported 40-pound cabbages growing in the sand and the garden did appear to have special powers. Today the Findhorn experiment is regarded as a demonstration of the potential power of human beings and the natural world living in harmony, and the remarkable story is told in Paul Hawken's book, *The Magic of Findhorn.*

Today, with a new generation of Findhorn members, the plants, fruits and vegetables are no longer supersize but normal size. Nonetheless the community preserves the spirit and ideas of its founders and it is one of the most successful of **New Age** communities, specializing in educational seminars on personal transformation and **spiritualism**. It also has many New Age businesses on its site, including a publishing house.

There have been several attempts to imitate Findhorn. Perhaps the most successful is a place called Perelandra, a garden and woodland area southwest of Washington DC. Perelandra was founded in the mid-1970s by Machaelle Small Wright, who,

like the Caddys and Maclean, claimed to be in contact with devas and nature spirits. Today the area remains remarkably abundant, regardless of season, compared to surrounding gardens and woodlands.

FIRE

In magical symbolism one of the four natural **elements**. Fire symbolizes masculine energy, light, sun, joy, ambitions and worldly achievements. The magical tool associated with fire is the **wand**. Fire colours are red, gold and orange, and fire is associated with the **zodiac** signs of Aries, Leo and Sagittarius. In Chinese philosophy fire is one of the building blocks of the universe. It is associated with the season of summer and represents emotions, in particular joy, passion, love and the sound of laughter.

FIRE WALKING

Walking through a bed of hot coals or fire without harm or burn marks to the feet or body. Fire walking is a universal and centuries old rite that formed part of religious practice in India and some Polynesian countries. It also was a phenomenon of **spiritualism** in the late nineteenth century. The practice has been revived somewhat in recent years as part of business and self-development seminars, and thousands of ordinary people claim to have walked unharmed over hot coals after attending seminars that teach them how to overcome fear and demonstrate the power of mind over matter.

Despite temperatures of 1,200 to 1,400°F or more, firewalkers seem to be able to walk across 30–60 feet-long beds of glowing coals, white-hot stones or through pits of fire without suffering any pain or showing any signs of burns.

How this happens is not entirely understood as doctors say that human flesh exposed to such intense heat should suffer terrible burns. Dr Myrne Reid Coe, Jr, an American scholar and a firewalker himself, suggested that vaporized moisture from sweat or saliva forms a protective air cushion that prevents flesh from burning. This is called the 'Ledenfrost effect' – levitating on a protective layer of vapour – the same thing that keeps water droplets glistening on the top of a hot stove. Dr Bernard Leikind, an American plasma physicist, maintains that fire walking is not **paranormal** and that the coals, like air in an oven, do not contain enough heat to burn the soles of a walker's feet. However, neither of these theories explain why many people get burned the instant they set foot on the hot coals.

Firewalkers claim that fire walking is the ultimate demonstration of the power of mind over body. Californian teacher Tolly Burkan, who introduced fire walking as a personal development tool to the United States in the 1980s, suggests that intense belief in your own ability to cross hot coals causes the brain to secrete chemicals that alter the body's chemistry so that it is not affected by the heat. Others suggest that a psychoneurological mechanism is responsible and when a firewalker is free of fear and in a state of deep **relaxation** the body's nervous system absorbs physical energy and transmutes it to the brain, creating an intense high.

Firewalkers themselves compare the experience to one of **hypnosis**, a state of total concentration to the exclusion of all else. Others compare the fire walking state of mind to being in some sort of **trance** (either self-induced or brought on by hypnosis). Both trance and hypnotic states have been shown to reduce pain and provide immunity to injury.

FISCHER, DORIS

A famous example of alleged spirit **possession** investigated by the President of the **American Society for Psychical Research, James A Hyslop**. Hyslop's experiences with Doris Fischer are recorded in his book, *Life After Death* (1918).

Doris Fischer was born in 1889 and early on experienced a traumatic incident at the hands of her abusive father. From the age of three she demonstrated multiple personality disorder and **psychic** ability, for instance, she successfully predicted her own mother's illness and death. When she was eventually adopted by an Episcopalian minister and psychologist, Walter Prince, who was familiar with multiple personality disorder, she had completely retreated into the personalities of 'sick Doris' and 'wicked

Margaret'. Prince and his wife dedicated themselves to helping Fischer lead as normal a life as possible.

Hyslop, who believed that the existence of **discarnate entities** had been proved scientifically and that some cases of mental illness were caused or aggravated by **spirit** influence, got involved with the case between 1914 and 1919. He took Fischer to sit with a **medium, Minnie Soule**, in the hope of eliminating the possessive spirits he believed were destroying the girl's quality of life. During her **séances** Soule was able to communicate messages to Fischer from her mother. Soule also communicated with the spirit of **Count Cagliostro** and the spirit of a young Indian, called 'Laughing Water', but as far as Hyslop was concerned, the most convincing spirit communication was the one from Richard Hodgson, a former member of the American Society for Psychical Research. Hodgson's communication with Soule to Fischer convinced Hyslop that this was not a case of multiple personality but a case of spirit possession.

According to Hyslop, Soule's communicators told him that the spirits wanted to hurt Doris because they were evil and that the case of Doris was no different from thousands of other people diagnosed with mental illness who could easily be cured by psychic **exorcism**. Hyslop performed an exorcism to remove what he believed to be the leader of the possessing spirits, the entity known as Count Cagliostro. Doris returned to live with the Princes and enjoyed a normal life for a while, prompting Hyslop to quit the case believing she had been cured. Unfortunately Doris wasn't cured and she spent the rest of her life dealing with her multiple personalities – eventually dying in a mental home.

FLAMMARION, NICOLAS CAMILLE [1842–1925]

French astronomer and pioneer of science fiction writing, Flammarion was fascinated by the **paranormal** and the possibility of life after death. His book *Inhabitants of the Other World* (1862) consists primarily of **spirit** communications allegedly given to him by a **medium** called Mlle Huer. Flammarion was also an avid **ghost** hunter and throughout his life investigated personally around a thousand cases of suspected **hauntings**. In his book *Haunted Houses* he claimed to have visited 180 houses that were actively and genuinely haunted. He also quoted the Italian-born father of criminology, **Cesare Lombroso** (1836–1909), as his reference in suggesting that there were around 150 homes in England that were unoccupied or uninhabitable because of paranormal activity.

FLIGHT 401

On the night of Friday, 29 December 1972, Eastern Airlines Flight 401, an L-1011 jumbo, was carrying 176 people as it prepared to land at Miami Airport. Captain Bob Loft and Second Officer and flight engineer Don Repo were engaged in routine landing procedures when a warning light flashed indicating a problem with the landing gear. What they didn't realize was that the plane was actually descending much faster than it should have and seconds later it crashed into the Florida Everglades, killing 101 people on impact. Captain Loft survived the crash but died before he could be pulled from the wreck, and Officer Repo died a day later. Eastern Airlines salvaged much of the aeroplane and redistributed parts among similar aircraft in their fleet.

Soon after this redistribution there were reported sightings of the **ghosts** of Repo and Loft in the planes that had received spare parts from Flight 401. Repo's ghost was said to appear frequently, in the cockpit and in the galley. According to accounts from crew members he seemed to be very concerned about safety, pointing out fire hazards and hydraulic leaks. Loft's ghost was also seen sitting either in first class or in the crew's cabin. On one occasion a stewardess who saw him aboard and could not identify him from her passenger list reported him to her flight captain. The flight captain recognized Loft, who vanished before the eyes of a dozen or so witnesses present. Other strange happenings attributed to the ghosts of Repo and Loft were a tool mysteriously appearing in the hand of a flight engineer, a plane's power suddenly coming on, and messages and warnings on the public address system.

Eastern Airlines were sceptical of the reports of sightings and suggested counselling for those involved at the company's expense. Despite their scepticism, however, they did eventually remove all of the salvaged parts of Flight 401 from the aircraft they had been put into. Almost immediately after the 401 parts were removed from the planes the sightings ended.

The alleged **hauntings** remain a mystery. Eastern Airlines no longer functions but the story of Flight 401 was published in a best-selling book, *The Ghost of Flight 401* (1976) by John Fuller.

FLINT, LESLIE [1911–1994]

English **medium**, considered by some to be the greatest medium of the twentieth century, who was noted for **direct voice mediumship**. Purportedly **spirits** of the dead spoke from a point just above and to the left of Flint's head. His powers were tested vigorously by psychical researchers but no evidence of **fraud** was ever found.

Flint was unusual in that for the majority of the time when voices communicated he did not go into **trance** but remained aware of what they were saying. The voices also did not use his vocal cords. Sometimes the voices were clear, at other times they sounded muffled. Sometimes they were from spirits of the dead, sometimes they were from living people who were asleep or in a coma.

Flint was born in a Salvation Army home in Hackney, London and had his first **psychic** experience at the age of seven in the summer of 1918, when he recognized the **ghost** of his uncle following his aunt around the house trying to get her attention. His aunt had just learned that her husband had been killed in France. After this experience Flint began to hear the voices of the dead on a regular basis, but his family doubted and disapproved so he kept the experiences to himself.

Flint attended his first **séance** at the age of 17 where a medium urged him to develop his mediumistic ability, but he chose not to do this and became a teacher of ballroom dancing instead. He finally decided to become a medium when he got a letter from a Munich woman who told him the spirit of Rudolph Valentino (who had died in 1926) was trying to get in touch with him. Flint attended a séance and Valentino allegedly manifested with spirit writing and **table tilting**.

It didn't take long after Flint decided to develop his psychic powers for spirit voices to manifest, and he held his first public séance in 1955. Besides Valentino, other famous spirits, such as those of **Sir Arthur Conan Doyle** and Thomas Edison came through. Flint formed an association called the Temple of Light and moved to Henley, a London suburb. In order for the voices to manifest Flint insisted on total darkness and as his reputation and popularity grew he would sit on a chair enclosed in a small **cabinet** in front of as a many as 2,000 people at a time.

Flint's public success attracted the interest of psychical researchers and he was tested so many times that he once referred to himself as 'the most tested medium in the country … I have been boxed up, tied up, sealed up, gagged, bound and held, and still the voices have come to speak their message of life eternal.'

A test administered by the **Society for Psychical Research** involved Flint's lips being sealed with adhesive tape, his mouth tied with a scarf and his hands bound behind a chair. Voices still manifested, but one of the researchers believed that Flint could speak from his stomach. Another researcher suggested that the voices were auditory hallucinations produced by Flint using **hypnosis**. The latter theory was disapproved as the voices were recorded on tape.

The most convincing tests performed on Flint took place in 1970 in both London and New York. William Bennett, professor of engineering of Columbia University, sealed Flint's lips with plaster and placed a small microphone down his throat along with an infrared telescope to pick up any movement of Flint's voice box. Bennett came to the conclusion that Flint's vocal cords were not used in the manifestation of voices and the only possible explanation was mediumship.

When Flint was observed through an infrared view he appeared to have mist over his left shoulder. His spirit **controls** said that it was **ectoplasm** – the substance they used to communicate through Flint. The process is described in detail in Leslie Flint's autobiography, *Voices in the Dark: My Life as a Medium*, where Flint writes:

Every living being has a substance known as ectoplasm, which is life force, and a physical medium like myself has a great deal more of it than most people. During a séance, this substance, which is sometimes also referred to as 'the power', is drawn from the medium and fashioned by spirits into a replica of the physical vocal organs, which is known as the voice-box or sometimes the mask. The communicating spirit then concentrates his or her thoughts into this voice-box, creating a frequency of vibration which reaches the sitter on earth as objective sound.

According to Flint, the ectoplasm voice box could only exist outside the medium's body in total darkness. If the lights were turned on suddenly, the ectoplasm would rush back into the medium's body, causing injury and possibly death.

In 1956 Sidney George Woods and Betty Greene began to make recordings of Flint's spirit voices, after the spirit of actress Ellen Terry told them, through Flint, that it was their task to help spread the message:

You are going to have some remarkable communications. And I suggest you keep these contacts going regularly to build up the power, and to make possible this link which has been deliberately arranged for your tapes. The tapes you record give us the opportunity to reach many people in all parts of the world … We shall bring various souls from various spheres to give talks and lectures. We need willing helpers on your side.

For the next 17 years Woods and Greene built up an impressive collection of recordings, which has been called 'the most complete account of life in the hereafter ever received.' Samples of the Wood/Green collection and transcripts of the tapes are available on the Internet: www.xs4all.nl/~wichm/deathnoe.html.

FLOROMANCY

From the Latin *flos* or meaning 'flower' and the Greek *manteia* meaning 'divination', floromancy is a form of **divination** first practised by the ancient Greeks but still in use today. Many **omens** concerning the gathering of flowers at Midsummer's Eve have survived to modern times, and the 'good luck' commonly attributed to the finding of a four-leafed clover falls into this category.

Floromancy is based on the belief that flowers radiate vibrations, have curative properties and respond to sympathetic and hostile environments. Professor Jagadish Chandra Bose of Calcutta's Presidency College experimented with the effects of electrical currents on plants around the beginning of the last century and was convinced that plants possess a life force or **soul**. Because of this sensitivity the appearance, smell and shape of flowers can be interpreted to predict the future or understand the present.

FLOWER REMEDIES

Flower remedies are specially prepared flower essences, created by soaking a flower in water and exposing it to sunlight or heat. It is thought that doing this imparts the healing energies of the plant to the water and the essences thus created have been shown to have beneficial effects on a person's emotional health.

Emotional healing: The 38 Bach Remedies

Bach Flower Remedies consist of 38 remedies, each for a different disposition. The basic theory is that if the remedy for the correct disposition is chosen, the physical illness resulting from the present emotional state can then be cured. Traditionally, flower essences are taken orally by putting two or three drops of the essence under the tongue. Usually, this is done three or four times per day for a period of one month.

* *Agrimony: puts on a cheerful front, hides true feelings, worries or problems.*
* *Aspen: feelings of apprehension, dark foreboding, premonitions.*
* *Beech: critical, intolerant, picky.*
* *Centaury: easily comes under the influence of others, weak willed.*
* *Cerato: unsure, no confidence in own judgement and intuition, seeks approval from others.*
* *Cherry plum: phobic, fear of being out of control, tension.*
* *Chestnut bud: repeats mistakes, does not learn from experience.*
* *Chicory: self-centered, possessive, clingy, demanding, self-pitying.*
* *Clematis: absent-minded, dreamy, apathetic, lack of connection with reality.*
* *Crab apple: a 'cleanser' for prudishness, self-disgust, feeling unclean.*

* *Elm: a sense of being temporarily overwhelmed in people who are usually capable and in control.*
* *Gentian: discouraged, doubting, despondent.*
* *Gorse: feelings of pessimism, accepting defeat.*
* *Heather: need for company, talks about self, concentrates on own problems.*
* *Holly: jealousy, envy, suspicion, anger, hatred.*
* *Honeysuckle: reluctance to enter the present and let the past go.*
* *Hornbeam: reluctant to face a new day, weary, can't cope (mental fatigue).*
* *Impatiens: impatience, always in a hurry, resentful of constraints.*
* *Larch: feelings of inadequacy and apprehension, lack of confidence and will to succeed.*
* *Mimulus: fearful of specific things, shy, timid.*
* *Mustard: beset by 'dark clouds' and gloom for no apparent reason.*
* *Oak: courageous, persevering, naturally strong but temporarily overcome by difficulties.*
* *Olive: for physical and mental renewal, to overcome exhaustion from long-standing problems.*
* *Pine: for self-reproach, always apologizing, assuming guilt.*
* *Red chestnut: constant worry and concern for others.*

- **Rock rose:** *panic, intense alarm, dread, horror.*
- **Rock water:** *rigid-minded, self-denial, restriction.*
- **Scleranthus:** *indecision, uncertainty, fluctuating moods.*
- **Star of Bethlehem:** *consoling, following shock or grief or serious news.*
- **Sweet chestnut:** *desolation, despair, bleak outlook.*
- **Vervain:** *insistent, fanatical, over-enthusiastic.*
- **Vine:** *dominating, overbearing, autocratic, tyrannical.*
- **Walnut:** *protects during a period of adjustment or vulnerability.*
- **Water violet:** *proud, aloof, reserved, enjoys being alone.*

- **White chestnut:** *preoccupation with worry, unwanted thoughts.*
- **Wild oat:** *drifting, lack of direction in life.*
- **Wild rose:** *apathy, resignation, no point in life.*
- **Willow:** *bitter, resentful, dissatisfied, feeling life is unfair.*

There is also a Rescue Remedy made up of five of the essences – cherry plum, clematis, impatiens, rock star and Star of Bethlehem – that is recommended for the treatment of any kind of physical or emotional shock. Therapists often recommended that Rescue Remedy be kept on hand to help with all emergencies.

Perhaps the most famous and widely used system is the Bach flower remedies system, originated in the 1920s by British physician and bacteriologist, Dr Edward Bach (1886–1936). However, since the 1930s the field has grown to include flower essence remedies from India, the United States, Asia, South America and Australia.

Flower remedies are more **homeopathic** than herbal in the way they work, affecting energy levels rather than chemical balances. They have been described as 'liquid energy'. The theory is that they impart the flowers' healing energy, and are said to deal with and overcome negative emotions, and so relieve blockages in the flow of human energy that can cause illness.

FLYING DUTCHMAN

According to legend, the *Flying Dutchman* is a **phantom ship** doomed to sail the seas forever as punishment for evil or rash behaviour. The ship is typically spotted from afar, sometimes glowing with ghostly light and is believed to be an **omen** of disaster.

The *Flying Dutchman* legend has many versions. In the Dutch version the captain, a man named van Straaten, was an arrogant man who claimed he could sail around the Cape of Good Hope and would not retreat even in the face of a storm. The ship was lost and its dead crew condemned to sail forever. In the German version the captain is called von Flakenberg. Von

Flakenberg engages with the devil in a game of dice, loses the game and is condemned to a living death. According to other versions, some horrible crime took place on board, or the crew was infected with the plague and not allowed to sail into any port for this reason. Since then, the ship and its crew were doomed to sail forever, never putting in to shore.

An **apparition** of a phantom ship believed to be the *Flying Dutchman* was seen in 1923 at the Cape of Good Hope. An account of the sighting is recorded by **Society for Psychical Research** member Sir Ernest Bennett, in his book *Apparitions and Haunted Houses: A Survey of the Evidence* (1934). Bennett attempted to explain the apparition with a theory, now discounted, that some form of **consciousness** survives death and is capable of telepathically projecting images to the living, which are perceived as apparitions.

Sceptics suggest that the ghost ship is nothing more than an optical illusion and hazy-looking ships appearing over the horizon are simply mirages caused by the refraction of light rays. Although the existence of the ill-fated *Flying Dutchman* is known and eyewitness accounts of sightings appear genuine, it is plausible that stories of a phantom ship were started by superstitious sailors who saw this kind of mirage.

FLYING SAUCER

See **UFO**.

FOCAL PERSON

Person or **agent** who is at the centre of **poltergeist** activity. This person may or may not be aware that **paranormal** phenomena centre around them. Typically, but by no means in all cases, the focal person is a female approaching or in puberty.

FODOR, NANDOR [1895–1964]

A member of both the American and British **Society for Psychical Research**, and best recalled for his ground-breaking work in the study of **poltergeist** phenomena and the psychological aspects of **mediumship**, Nandor Fodor was a psychoanalyst and psychical researcher with ideas way ahead of his time.

Fodor was born in Hungary in May 1895 and later went on to work as a lawyer and journalist, first in New York and then in London. His fascination for psychical research began when he read Hereward Carrington's book *Modern Psychic* (1919), and, after an interview with **Sigmund Freud** in 1926, approaching psychical phenomena from the viewpoint of a psychoanalyst became Fodor's primary focus in life.

In 1936 Fodor became London correspondent for the American Society for Psychical Research and this position gave him the opportunity to conduct numerous investigations of **paranormal** phenomena and apply his interest in psychoanalysis to his research. Prior to this, very little attention had been paid to emotional causes and repressed desires as contributory factors to some paranormal activity and his work came under severe attack. **Spiritualists**, in particular, disliked the implication that a worldly explanation was possible, and eventually he was dismissed from his post as research officer. Despite this, Fodor's work was very influential, especially in two investigations, the **Ash Manor ghost** and the **Thornton Heath poltergeist**. In both these instances personal and emotional problems appeared to be at the root of the activity.

In another of his celebrated investigations, Fodor was called to Baltimore, Maryland, to investigate a well-publicized case involving the Jones family (the **Baltimore poltergeist**). For several weeks the family had endured a number of terrifying incidents, including furniture purportedly moving of its own accord and curious knocking sounds within the wall. In his study of the case, Fodor concluded that the activity centred around 17-year-old Ted Pauls. He attributed the activity to **recurrent spontaneous psychokinesis**, random outbursts of psychokinetic energy from the subject's **unconscious** mind. Fodor's use of the term and his conclusion that this was causing the poltergeist outbreaks opened new ground in the field of **parapsychology**, and many of the terms and definitions coined by Fodor to explain elements of the cases he investigated are still in use today.

In addition to numerous papers on the subject of poltergeist activity, Fodor wrote a number of influential and thought-provoking books, including: *Mind Over Space*; *New Approaches to Dream Interpretations*;

and *Freud, Jung and Occultism*. Perhaps his most important work, however, was *The Encyclopaedia of Psychic Science* (1934) – a detailed study of psychical research from the late nineteenth century to the early 1930s. The *Encyclopaedia* is still regarded as a classic and one of the most important reference studies in the field of psychical research.

FORCE, THE

In the *Star Wars* films, the Force is filmmaker George Lucas's stylized take on the concept of the **universal life force**.

FORD, ARTHUR [1896–1971]

American **spiritualist medium** and founder of the International General Assembly of Spiritualists who became internationally famous for his ability to communicate with the dead through a **control** named Fletcher.

Ford was born on 8 January 1896 at Titusville, Florida. Although he had no profound **psychic** experiences as a child he was drawn to religion and he liked to pray for the dead because he thought this helped them. He attended Transylvania College, a Disciples of Christ school in Lexington, Kentucky and later was ordained as a Disciples minister, serving a church in Barbourville, Kentucky.

The Element Encyclopedia of the Psychic World

It was during World War I that Ford first realized his psychic abilities. While in the army he would often 'hear' the names of people he served with, and those names would, several days later, appear on the casualty lists. At first he thought he was going mad but when he returned to Transylvania College, a psychology professor convinced him he was psychic rather than insane.

In the years after the war Ford investigated psychic phenomena and joined the Spiritualists. It wasn't until 1924, however, that he began to communicate with the **spirits** of the dead and a spirit named Fletcher announced he would be Ford's control. Fletcher had been a friend of Ford in his youth but had been killed in action during the war.

Ford's psychic abilities grew more impressive and he developed a popular following, travelling all over the world. The press called him 'the international ambassador of spiritualism'. He was accused of **fraud** many times but always managed to produce compelling evidence that his communications with the dead were genuine. In 1927 Ford travelled to Great Britain and one of his lectures was attended by spiritualist **Sir Arthur Conan Doyle**, who thought Ford was incredible, saying to friends the next day: 'One of the most amazing things I have ever seen in 41 years of psychic experience was the demonstration of Arthur Ford.'

In 1928 Ford allegedly broke a secret code between the late **Harry Houdini** and his wife Bess. Houdini had told his wife that if he died before her he would try to communicate from the grave with a coded phrase 'Rosabelle, believe' to prove there was life after death. No other medium had been able to produce the secret phrase, but Ford did.

Ford founded the first Spiritualist Church in New York City in the late 1920s and this was the first of many. His belief in **reincarnation**, however, led to conflict with the **National Spiritualist Association**, who did not accept the concept. After many years of disagreements Ford founded the International General Assembly of Spiritualists in 1936, which had a more open-minded approach to reincarnation.

Ford suffered a traumatic car accident in 1931, in which he lost his sister and was severely injured. The crash was the beginning of his addiction to morphine and then to alcohol. In his autobiography *Nothing So Strange* (1958) he writes about his struggle to deal with the problem of alcoholism.

When Ford was 71 he conducted his most famous **séance** on television: he went into a trance and delivered several messages to Episcopal bishop **James Pike**. One claimed to be from Pike's son and another from the prominent theologian Paul Tillich. The televised séance revived public interest in psychic phenomena and Ford was inundated with mail and requests for help.

Ford died in Miami, Florida, on 4 January 1971. Shortly after his death, mediums all around the world claimed to receive communications from him. Ruth Montgomery, one of Ford's close friends, said in her book *A World Beyond* (1971) that he communicated to her via **automatic writing**.

Ford was a complex and unpredictable man, at times bright and charming and witty but at other times moody, lonely and tormented. He denounced fraud but after his death researchers Allen Spraggett and William Rauscher, while compiling material for his biography, discovered that he might have cheated from time to time by researching the backgrounds of famous people who came to his sittings. He was said to have a photographic memory and to keep huge files of newspaper clippings and notes. Nonetheless many were convinced of his genuine psychic ability and Ford himself was honest enough to admit that no psychic, however gifted, can perform accurately 100 per cent of the time.

FORT MONROE

This moated heptagonal stone fort in Virginia, USA, faces the Chesapeake Bay on three sides. It is a lonely, isolated spot and there have been a number of reported sightings of **ghosts**.

Perhaps the most illustrious ghost that has allegedly been sighted is that of the President of the Confederate States, Jefferson Davis. Brought here in shackles after the end of the Civil War, Davis slowly grew weak within its walls. His wife, Varina, followed him here and pleaded to have him removed from his cell to a private apartment to die in peace. It is said that both of their ghosts can be found at Fort Monroe still, Davis in his cell and Varina, gazing from a bedroom window towards her husband's cell.

Another ghost said to put in an appearance is that of Edgar Allan Poe, who in

1829 served for four months at Monroe. While there he wrote *The Cask of Amontillado*, a story based on the tale of a Virginian military man walled up inside an empty stone building. Poe's ghost has reportedly been seen in his former barracks, now located at Building no. 5.

There have also been reports of a ghost called the 'Light Lady'. It is thought that she is the ghost of Camille Kirtz, who was murdered by her husband when he discovered her with her French lover on Matthew Lane within the fort. The Frenchman managed to escape but Camille was fatally shot and is said to wander a nearby copse of oak trees searching for her lover in vain.

The ghosts of two children have also been spotted at the fort, one in the upstairs of an old house next to the moat wall and the other in the basement of an enlisted man's home. It is thought they are the **spirits** of two small boys who died from disease or poverty within the isolated walls of Fort Monroe. Some believe that these spirit children try to seek out living children to play with when they visit the fort.

FORTEAN PHENOMENA [FORTEANA]

Term used to describe any type of phenomena that defies natural explanation, such as rains of fish, stones and frogs, floating balls of light in the night sky, **ghosts**, **spirits** and **poltergeists**, inexplicable events such as spontaneous human combustion, monstrous creatures and religious experiences such as **stigmata**.

American journalist Charles Fort (1874–1932) is the inspiration behind the term. Fort, who has been called 'the father of modern phenomenalism', left his job when he came into an inheritance at the age of 42 to devote himself not to explaining but to collecting and cataloguing phenomena that had no explanation, to highlight the limits of scientific knowledge. He challenged the scientific belief that a phenomenon was only genuine if it could be explained and proved. To Fort the fact that it had occurred was proof enough. His research, gathered from the British Museum and the New York Public Library, was compiled into four books: *The Book of the Damned* (1919), *New Lands* (1923), *Lo!* (1931) and *Wild Talents* (1932).

Fortean research has continued since Fort's death and some enthusiasts pursue it on a scholarly basis. The International Fortean Organization in Arlington, Virginia was founded in 1965 and it provides research and educational programmes. The Society for the Investigation of the Unexplained, based in Little Silver, New Jersey is another organization devoted to Fortean research. Charles Fort himself discovered reports of unusual objects in the sky dating back to 1779, and the phenomena of **UFO**s, missing time and close encounters are of particular interest to modern Forteans. Forteans are also very interested in sightings of monstrous creatures such as the Loch Ness Monster, the Yeti, the abominable Snowman and Big Foot.

FORTUNE, DION [1890–1946]

The magical name of a woman called Violet Mary Firth, considered by some to be one of the most important occultists of the twentieth century. Fortune's work remains popular among modern **witches** but Fortune herself never considered herself to be a witch or her work to be **witchcraft**.

Fortune was born in Llandudno, Wales, on 6 December 1890. Her mother was a Christian Scientist and her father a solicitor, and the family motto, which Fortune later used as her magical motto and the inspiration for her magical name, was *Deo, non Fortuna*, meaning 'By God, not by chance'.

Fortune was an independent child and showed early signs of the **psychic** abilities that were to shape the rest of her life. Her interest in **magic** and the **occult**, however, was not sparked until the age of 20, when she went to work in an educational institution and was under the supervision of a woman who had studied occultism in India. According to Fortune this woman was a bully with a foul temper, who used **hypnosis** and the projection of negative thoughts, called **psychic attack**, to get her own way and destroy Fortune's self-confidence. Fortune managed to survive these attacks but experienced a three-year-long nervous breakdown.

The experience stimulated Fortune's interest in the human mind and, while she was recovering, she began to study psychology and Freudian analysis, even though she never totally believed his theories. By the age of 23 she became a lay psychoanalyst and was convinced that many of her patients were not mentally ill but victims of psychic attack. At the same time she also began to experience **visions** and memories of past lives, and in one extremely powerful vision she was accepted as a follower of Jesus Christ.

At the end of the Great War, after serving in the Women's Land Army, Fortune met Theodore Moriarty, an Irishman, occultist and freemason, who gave her training in the occult. Her learning experiences with Moriarty are featured in her occult autobiography, *Psychic Self-Defence* (1930).

In 1919 Fortune was initiated into the greatest magical order of its day, the Order of the **Golden Dawn**. Fortune progressed rapidly through the ranks of the order, but she did not get along with Moina Mathers, the wife of one of the Golden Dawn founders. Fortune believed that Moina was subjecting her to psychic attack so she established her own independent order, called the Fraternity of the Inner Light. (The Fraternity, now called The Society of the Inner Light, is still based in London offering teachings in Western occultism, and over the years it has profoundly influenced the development of the **esoteric** tradition in the West.) In addition, Fortune also founded the Belfry, a temple in West London dedicated to the Mysteries of Isis.

In the winter of 1923/4 Fortune travelled to **Glastonbury** where she allegedly made spirit contact with three great masters: the Greek philosopher Socrates, Lord Erskine, Lord Chancellor of England and a World War I officer, David Carstairs. According to Fortune these masters dictated her magical writings to her and Socrates was responsible for her essential work, *The Cosmic Doctrine*. Throughout the rest of her life Fortune was to return periodically to Glastonbury to resume her writing and make contact with another master, **Merlin**, the great magician of English myth. She founded the Chalice Orchard Club there, a pilgrim centre. Her experiences are recorded in *Glastonbury: Avalon of the Heart*, and the house she lived and worked in while at Glastonbury is thought to be haunted.

Dion Fortune was well known in her day and attracted a large following of devoted followers. In 1927 she married Welsh physician and occultist Penry Evans, who became one of her priests and brought a new **pagan** element to her work. The marriage was stormy but not passionate, as Fortune apparently had little interest in sex, and in 1939 Evans divorced her and married again.

Fortune was a prolific author. Her most famous works are *Psychic Self-Defence*, considered by many to be the definitive text on the subject, and *The Mystical Qabalah*, in which she outlines how the **kabbalah** can be used by Western students. She also wrote a number of novels and her last two – *The Sea Priestess* and *Moon Magic* – are considered by many to be fine examples of magical fiction.

Fortune never fully recovered physically or spiritually from her divorce and she died of leukaemia on 8 January 1946. For several years after her death she was said to still run the Fraternity through **mediums**, but eventually it was thought that her presence was no longer needed and a magical banishing ceremony was performed.

Fortune-telling

A phrase particularly associated with the Romany people (or Gypsies), who have a special word for it – *dukkerin*, fortune-telling is the art of predicting the future and understanding the present using a vast number of different forms of **divination**, such as **Tarot, scrying** and **runes**, to name but a few.

Fox sisters

Three New York sisters, Maggie, Kate and Leah Fox, who are credited historically with the birth of **Spiritualism** in the late nineteenth century, when they discovered they could communicate with **spirits** by **rappings**.

On the night of 31 March 1848, Maggie, aged 15, and Kate, 12, who were living with their parents in Hydesville, first discovered that if they clapped their hands raps would answer back. Neighbours were invited around to witness the phenomenon. According to accounts, by rapping for the letters of the alphabet the spirit communicating with the sisters claimed to be a peddler, Charles Rosa, who had been murdered by a previous owner of the house, John Bell, and buried in the cellar. On later investigation some human teeth and bones were discovered in the cellar.

The media went into a frenzy about the story and the girls' older sister, Leah, who was living in Rochester in poverty after her husband had deserted her, seized the opportunity to manage her younger sisters and their special powers. Fee-charging public demonstrations were arranged and the press coverage was intense. The Fox sisters became a sensation and their demonstration grew to include objects moving, tables levitating and communications with the spirit of Benjamin Franklin. Suddenly other **mediums** began to discover their own powers and within a few years **séances** became all the rage.

Despite accusations of **fraud** and attempts to uncover deception, no trickery was ever found and the sisters impressed a number of serious reporters and journalists, in particular Horace Greeley, editor of the *New York Tribune* who allowed them to stay at his mansion.

The pressure of fame and success proved too much a burden for both Maggie and Kate and by the late 1850s they were both drinking heavily. Maggie was disillusioned and wanted to opt out of the act but family pressure forced her to stay. Leah abandoned her sisters in 1857 when she married a wealthy businessman. Kate continued performing and in 1861 allegedly manifested spirits of the dead. However, she withdrew from the stage act in 1872 when she married Englishman, Henry Jencken. Her first son, Ferdinand, born in 1873, was hailed as a medium from the age of three and was allegedly practising **automatic writing** by the age of five.

In 1888, with interest in spiritualism beginning to wane, Maggie and Kate made a shocking public confession in New York: they denounced spiritualism as fraud. Maggie confessed that she and her sister had created the rappings by cracking their toes to play a trick on their mother. They had learned to use muscles below their knees and Maggie demonstrated on stage how this had been done. She also said that Kate had given them body cues for the rapping. Some spiritualists denounced Maggie's statement as the rantings of an alcoholic and in 1891 she recounted her confession: the reason why is unclear.

The three sisters died within a short time of each other, in 1890, 1892 and 1893. In 1904 school children discovered a skeleton behind the cellar door in the Hydesville house where the Fox phenomenon had first begun. Spiritualists hailed it as proof that the sisters were genuine mediums but sceptics were convinced that the skeleton had been deliberately put there. Unfortunately the truth can't be revealed by modern forensic analysis as the house burnt down in 1955 and was rebuilt a decade later as a tourist attraction.

FRAUD

The deliberate practice of simulating **paranormal** phenomena for the purpose of financial gain, psychological manipulation or to attract publicity. Faking such phenomena for the purpose of entertainment or education, such as in the case of stage magicians, is not normally considered fraud.

FREEMASONRY

An international fraternal movement believed to have evolved from medieval guilds of stonemasons. Freemasons, also referred to as the Masonic Order or the Masons, originally started as an **esoteric** society with secret **initiation** rites, rituals and codes and a possible link to the religious order of the **Knights Templars**.

There are many legends concerning the origins of Freemasonry but it is generally believed to be linked to small groups of stonemasons who would travel from town to town to build churches commissioned by the clergy. To protect their knowledge they organized themselves into trade guilds. It is unclear how the guilds changed to lodges and why unskilled members were included, but Freemasonry's present form dates from 24 June 1717, when a Grand Lodge opened in London. Since then lodges grew throughout England and spread to North America. There are now approximately five million Freemasons in regular lodges scattered throughout the world. Many noted men in history have been members, including Benjamin Franklin, Mozart, Christopher Wren, Rudyard Kipling, Winston Churchill, George Washington and Henry Ford.

The society has met religious and political opposition at various times because of its secret and exclusive anti-Catholic reputation, and is now banded in several countries, including Germany, China and Italy. Freemasons will never stop anyone applying for membership, but they do exercise the right of refusal to those who do not fit into their 'quality of membership'.

Members tend to be wealthy, educated, white men from Protestant backgrounds, however in recent years there has been a conscious effort to become a more open-minded organization.

Devotion to a single religion is not essential, although belief in God is required. All members are sworn to secrecy and are forbidden to talk about the organization even to their friends and loved ones. The ethos of the order is for members to meet in harmony and to help each other by providing an international network for business, professional and social advancement.

FREUD, SIGMUND [1856–1939]

Physician and writer who is often referred to as the father of psychoanalysis and universally acknowledged to be one of the most influential thinkers of all time. He coined many of the phrases we still use today to describe human behaviour and his ideas about the mind and the personality have become the foundation for nearly all schools of psychology.

Born in 1856 in Moravia, Freud spent most of his life in Vienna but died in London in 1939. His career began in Vienna General Hospital where he first became interested in psychology and began to treat patients using **hypnosis**. By researching into his patients' thoughts and behaviour he developed psychoanalysis.

Central to Freud's work is the idea that most of our behaviours can be explained as motivations we are unaware of. We are driven by basic desires – sex, power, anger, pleasure (which actually means avoiding pain) – by the *id* or primitive part of our mind. The part of our mind we call the *ego* is the part that attempts to control these primitive forces, but when it comes to making decisions about what is good or bad, right or wrong our *superego* takes over. All three parts of our mind – the id, the ego and the superego – are constantly at war and which part of our personality dominates depends on our childhood experiences.

According to Freud there are five stages of psychosexual development: oral (birth to age one), where the mouth is the source of pleasure; anal (one to three years), when the act of eliminating is our main focus; phallic (three to five years), when the focus switches to the genitals; latency (five to puberty), a period of rest; and genital (puberty onwards). Getting developmentally stuck in any of these stages when growing up can explain any neurosis you have as an adult.

Freud was convinced that through psychoanalysis, i.e. analysing a person's behaviour, investigating their **dreams** and current problems, you could discover what the cause of any neurosis was and help them heal wounds from the past. In 1900 Freud's seminal work *The Interpretation of Dreams* was published, followed by *The Psychopathology of Everyday Life* in 1904 and *The Theory of Sex* in 1905.

During his life Freud's theories dominated psychotherapy and psychiatric treatment and he influenced several generations of great psychologists, in particular

Carl Jung. However, his emphasis on sexual repression and infantile sexual trauma as the cause of all neuroses created conflict and some of his key supporters, including Alfred Adler and Jung, eventually broke with him. Today his theories have fallen into disfavour for the same reason.

Even though he had a sceptical view of **occult** phenomena throughout his career, Freud was deeply interested in the **paranormal**. He visited a psychic on at least one occasion, and although he was amazed at the psychic's ability to pick up personal information he attributed it to **telepathy**. In his casework with clients he often confronted occult phenomena such as telepathy, **premonitions** and the **evil eye** and this may have prompted his membership of both the American and British **Society for Psychical Research**. He was a frequent guest at lectures sponsored by the Society for Psychical Research in London and was known to visit allegedly haunted locations in search of greater understanding of the **supernatural**.

Freud wrote a number of papers and books on psychoanalysis and the occult, including *Dreams and Telepathy* (1922), *The Occult Significance of Dreams* (1925) and *Premonitions and Chance* (1904). In his writings he equated the occult with **superstition**, which he believed originated from repressed urges, and suggested alterative explanations for many paranormal phenomena. Telepathy, however, was one phenomenon he found impossible to explain, even though he did believe it to be a psychological and not a **psychic** occurrence. Later he confessed that it was a mystery to him.

Freud and Jung met in Vienna for the first time in 1907. Jung was greatly impressed by Freud's theories but found he could not agree with Freud's belief that psychical research should be abandoned because it made psychoanalysis appear ridiculous to scientists. The two men drifted apart when Jung began to investigate what **mysticism**, religion, the paranormal and philosophy could reveal about human behaviour and psychology.

In 1921 Freud turned down an invitation to join the Advisory Council of the American Psychical Institute. In a letter to the director of the Advisory Council dated 24 July 1924, Freud said he did not dismiss completely the study of occult phenomena as 'unscientific, discreditable or dangerous' – and if he was at the beginning of his career rather than at the end he might have chosen it as a field of research – but as far as he was concerned psychoanalysis had nothing to do with the occult. He went on to say that he had certain prejudices against the occult and rejected completely the idea of life after death.

FREUDIAN SLIP

A popular way of referring to 'paraplexis', a term coined by **Sigmund Freud** to describe the way he believed the **unconscious** worked. Freud suggested that the following behavioural tendencies were examples of paraplexis: forgetting something you intended to do, forgetting the names of people, a slip of the tongue or pen, misunderstanding something, losing things, remembering things incorrectly, and making a mistake or causing an accident. According to Freud these were the subconscious's way of coping with painful or difficult thoughts and the mistakes were made because the person was doing or saying something and thinking or feeling something else. In short, the Freudian slip reveals the *real* thoughts of the person.

Fyvie Castle

Situated just outside Turriff in Aberdeenshire, Fyvie Castle is one of Scotland's finest castles. Royal connections can be traced to 1211 and Charles I spent much time there as a child. Although **Glamis Castle** is considered by many to be the most haunted castle in Scotland, Fyvie Castle comes a close second.

During building work in the early 1900s, a secret room was uncovered with a skeleton in it. Nobody knows who the skeleton is, but from that day onward, stories of 'The Grey Lady' prevailed; allegedly there was a large amount of **paranormal** activity until the bones were returned to the secret room in which they had been found.

The most famous ghost of Fyvie Castle is, however, that of a woman whose name was Dame Lillias Drummond, now known as The Green Lady. Dame Drummond died tragically on 8 May 1601. Some say she was starved to death by her husband, Sir Alexander Seton. Six months after her death Lord Seton married Lady Grizel Leslie and on the night of 27 October, while the newly weds were waiting for new bedrooms to be made in the castle, they slept in a tiny, unused room. Allegedly when they woke up in the morning, the name 'Lillias D Drummond' was carved deeply and with great skill and precision into the stone windowsill right outside their room. The most peculiar thing about the carving was that it was upside down and could only be read if someone hovered outside and faced inside the room, several hundred feet in the air. The only possible way for a human hand to do this was to erect a scaffold, but Lord Seton and his new wife are said to have slept peacefully that night, hearing only the sound of soft sighing. Today the name can still be read and continues to mystify all who see it.

G

GAIA

In Greek mythology Gaia is Mother Earth, the creator goddess who mated with her son, Uranus, to create the first race of gods and goddesses, the Titans. As one of the most important goddess **archetypes**, whose function was to draw life from chaos, Gaia became the inspiration for the 'living earth' theory of British scientist James Lovelock in his book *Gaia: A New Life on Earth*.

The 'living earth' theory (also known as 'Gaia theory') postulated by Lovelock in 1979 suggests that the earth is not simply a planet of dead rock but a living, constantly changing and evolving organism. Lovelock made a number of discoveries in the 1970s that suggested the earth was a self-regulating entity, and that homeostasis seemed to be at work. For example, the oceans contain approximately 3.4 per cent salt even though a much higher concentration should have been achieved by now, and the atmosphere does not contain nearly as much carbon dioxide as it should for a planet the age of the earth – in fact, computer calculations based on the law of thermodynamics indicate that after five million years there should be nothing much left oxygen-wise in the air we breathe now.

Although scientists had noticed these discrepancies before, it was Lovelock who brought the idea to the public's attention. He came up with the theory almost by accident when NASA asked for his help in designing life-detecting probes for their unmanned Viking Mars missions. While researching he came across what he called the 'Goldilocks phenomenon'. In other words, because Venus was too hot for life to exist, Mars was too cold and earth was just right, the earth must have transformed into a self-evolving and self-regulating system over the centuries. According to Lovelock's theory Earth is therefore a living being in its own right. Many proponents of the Gaia theory see it as confirmation of the insights of generations of mystics: life created the planet Earth and not the other way round.

The Gaia hypothesis does seem to support the idea that the earth has one shared mind and that all minds are connected, even without people being aware of it. According to this theory the earth as a living organism will do whatever is necessary to ensure its survival. The idea that it consciously controls people's thoughts sounds absurd, but it is conceivable that people's minds may respond to the earth's needs in a unified way, just as the human body's nervous system responds to stimuli without the brain being aware of it. In other words, human minds may respond and follow trends or thought patterns without making a conscious decision to do so. And some people believe this could help explain **intuition** or **psychic** awareness.

See also **Planetary consciousnesses**, **Raising consciousness**.

GALLEY BEGGAR

Old English **ghost** often reported in the country roads and deserted lanes of the North of England and first mentioned way back in 1584 in Reginald Scot's *The Discovery of Witchcraft*. The galley beggar is often described as a skeletal thin, fearsome ghost with a deathly scream who sometimes carries its head under his arm. The origin of the legend is uncertain but the name could be derived from the Old English word *gaestlic*, meaning 'to terrify'.

GANZFELD

Well-known technique used to research **psychic** ability in people. *Ganzfeld* is German for 'entire field' and refers to the blank field of vision stared at by a test subject. During these experiments, the subject, or person being tested for **GESP** or **ESP**, is placed in an environment without light, sound or other sensory input. Typically the subject's eyes are covered and they are given microphones to describe their impressions to the tester, although they would not be given any feedback at that time.

Once external distractions have been removed, the mind is thought to be more susceptible to picking up psychic signals and the subject is sent information psychically. In most cases, a person (called the sender) telepathically sends the subject a picture of an image and the subject describes the images and feelings he or she picks up. The sender transmits information for one minute and then rests for four minutes and this on/off sequence typically continues for half an hour. Once the sending is completed the subject is shown four images, including what the sender had been focusing on. The subject chooses the image closest to what he or she saw or picked up during the sending process. If the correct image is picked the experiment is regarded as a success.

The first scientific use of Ganzfeld stimulation in ESP research took place in 1973 when Charles Homerton was researching ESP in **dreams** at the Maimonides Medical School in New York. Of the thirty people being tested almost half showed signs of ESP. From 1979 to 1988 Homerton became director of the Psychophysical Research Laboratories in Princetown, New Jersey, the largest facility in the world to use Ganzfeld stimulation. Other research centres around the world have also studied and used Ganzfeld. Overall success rates tend to be good. Pure chance would suggest a success rate of 25 per cent, but the cumulative result of thousands of experiments over the years suggests an average success rate of 34 per cent. This increase is not dramatic but it does indicate that some sort of **telepathy** must be occurring between sender and subject.

GARRETT, EILEEN [1893–1970]

One of the most respected **mediums** of the twentieth century, who encouraged the scientific and open-minded investigation of **paranormal** phenomena. As an author, lecturer, psychic researcher and publisher Garrett devoted her life to sharing her **psychic** powers and her ideas with psychical researchers and the public. She defined psychical research as 'the scientific study of the human consciousness beyond the threshold of what man calls the human mind', and was convinced that it could help heal the rift between science and religion.

Garrett was born in 1893 in County Meath, Ireland in a culture steeped in Celtic myth and magic. Tragically her parents both committed suicide soon after her birth and she was adopted by her aunt and uncle. From an early age Garrett had psychic experiences that included sensing various forms of light and energy around people, animals and even plants, which she initially termed 'surrounds'. She also claimed to have imaginary playmates called 'the children' and to see **visions** of the dead.

Garrett's younger years were marked by tragedy and illness. Her first marriage to Clive Barry, whom she met while staying in England with relatives, ended in divorce. She had three sons, all of whom died young, and a daughter. During World War I she ran a hostel for wounded soldiers and **clairvoyantly** saw the deaths of many of her patients. She married one of her charges but he perished a month later in the war. In 1918 Garrett married again, but that marriage, too, ended in divorce.

It was after the war that Garrett's mediumship began to manifest. One day she joined in a table **rapping** session and unexpectedly became drowsy and fell asleep. When she woke up she learned that dead relatives of others in the room had communicated through her. Garrett sought the advice of a **hypnotist** who was able to communicate with a so-called **control**, called Uvani, who said that Garrett was to become a vehicle to prove **survival after death**.

Garrett sought help from the **College of Psychic Studies** in London and from 1924 to 1929 worked with James McKenzie there, who helped her develop her psychic and mediumistic powers. Over the years Garrett was to work with many leading psychical researchers, including **Nandor Fodor**.

Perhaps her most famous **premonition** was that of the loss of the British dirigible **R-101** that crashed in France on its way to India in 1930. For several years beforehand Garrett had experienced premonitions of disaster involving a dirigible and she allegedly knew about the crash before the media did. Here is what Nandor Fodor says about this in his *Encyclopaedia of Psychic Science*:

In a sitting at the National Laboratory of Psychical Research on October 7, 1930, two days after the explosion of the R101, Flight Lieutenant H C Irwin, Captain of the airship, suddenly entranced Mrs Garrett, announced his presence and gave the listeners a highly technical account of how the airship crashed. The narrative was taken down in shorthand and a copy was submitted to the Air Ministry. According to the opinion of experts, a number of observations in the message tallied in every detail with what was afterwards found in the course of the official inquiry. E F Spanner, the well-known naval architect and marine engineer, came to exactly the same conclusions in his book, *The Tragedy of the R101*.

In 1931 Garrett was invited to the States by the **American Society for Psychical Research**. During her time in the United States she made astounding connections with many noted scientists and parapsychologists, and subjected herself to intense physiological and psychological experimentation, in the hope that such testing might shed some light upon the processes of mediumship and psychism. She became an American citizen in 1947 and launched her own publishing house and magazine, both of which no longer function. In 1951 she helped establish the **Parapsychology Foundation** to encourage scientific research of the **paranormal** throughout the world and in 1953 organized the first International Parapsychology Congress at the University of Utrecht. Her common sense approach and business acumen helped make the Parapsychology Foundation one of the most respected foundations of its type.

During the 1960s Garrett worked with American psychologist Lawrence LeShan in his studies of 'clairvoyant reality', a state of **consciousness**, or shift in awareness where psychic, **healing** or mediumistic ability functions. LeShan believed that there were four central aspects of this clairvoyant reality: first, a central unity to all things which form part of the bigger picture; second, the timeless now; third, the harmonious whole of the universe which is above good or evil; and fourth, the existence of a superior way of getting information than through the senses alone.

Garrett came to the conclusion that her psychic experiences were the result of a shift of awareness to a different reality, which she could reach by choice or through a change in breathing. She eventually learned how to control her powers so she was not exhausted by what she called the 'climax of clairvoyance', a state of perception in which past, present and future become fused and a unity of vision is presented.

Garrett remained uncertain about her controls (Uvani was the most dominant, followed by the seventeenth-century Doctor Latif) and as early as 1938 suggested that they were not **supernatural** but sprang from her own inner nature and her spiritual needs. In the preface to her autobiography, she wrote a statement that sums up well her point of view concerning her work:

I have a gift, a capacity – a delusion, if you will – which is called 'psychic'. I do not care what it may be called, for living with and utilizing this psychic capacity long ago inured me to a variety of epithets – ranging from expressions almost of reverence, through doubt and pity, to open vituperation. In short, I have been called many things, from a charlatan to a miracle woman. I am, at least, neither of these.

In addition to her remarkable contribution to the field of psychical research Garrett was also a prolific writer and during her career wrote seven non-fiction books on the paranormal, and numerous novels under the pseudonym Jean Lyttle. She died in France in 1970. After her death her daughter Eileen became president of the Parapsychology Foundation.

GASHADOKURO

In Japanese folklore a giant skeleton many times taller than a human. It is thought to be made of the bones of people who have starved to death. After midnight the **ghost** roams the streets making a ringing noise that sounds in the ears. If people do not run away when the gashadokuro approaches it will bite off their heads with its giant teeth.

GASTROMANCY

An ancient method of **divination** that interprets the sounds and signs of the stomach. Gastromancy is reported as a low, hollow-sounding voice that seems to be coming from the stomach. It is often dismissed as a form of ventriloquism. One ancient description of a gastromancy technique described placing a person in front of a glass filled with water and illuminating the glass with a candle; divination was done by interpreting the images on the glass.

GELEY, GUSTAVE [1868–1924]

French physician, distinguished psychical researcher and the first director of the **Institut Metapsychique International** from 1919 to 1924.

Unlike most psychical investigators of his day Geley was a **spiritualist** who accepted the possibility of both **reincarnation** and communication with the dead through **mediums**. His first book was concerned with the origin of the species but in his second book, *l'Etre Subconscient*, published in 1899 in Paris, he expounded a theory of dynamo-psychism, a sort of soul energy that is able to affect atoms of matter. In his third book, *From the Unconscious to the Conscious* (1919), he developed his idea of mind/body interaction further. Shortly before publication of this third book Geley gave up his medical practice and accepted the post of director of the Institut Metapsychique International founded by Jean Meyer, a wealthy French industrialist.

Geley was a skilled and tireless investigator of the **paranormal** who produced supernormal results from his laboratory under **fraud**-proof circumstances. Although careful not to alienate the scientific community with his work he did have to defend himself from accusations by medical colleagues that he was a fraud and an accomplice of mediums. The most successful evidence he produced for mediumistic phenomena were the wax casts of limbs materialized by Polish medium Franek Kluski. The Kluski plaster casts are still on view in the Institut. In his last book, *Clairvoyance and Materialisation*, Geley recorded his work with Kluski, and **Jan Guzyk**, another Polish **materialization** medium. He also reports on the case of French materialization medium Marthe Béraud ('Eva C').

A few days after a last experiment with Kluski in Warsaw Geley died in an aeroplane accident on 15 July 1924.

Twenty-five years after his death an article by R Lambert accusing Geley of fraud appeared in the *Journal of the Society for Psychical Research*. Geley's reputation has been damaged ever since, but despite this his work is considered by many to mark a milestone in psychical research.

GELLER, URI

Israeli psychic noted for his apparent ability to bend metal objects by stroking or staring at them and to stop watches or make them run faster. Some call psychokinetic ability of this kind the 'Geller effect'. Geller was born in Tel Aviv on 20 December 1946. He says that **psychic** powers were bestowed on him at the age of five when he received an electric shock from a sewing machine, and by the age of seven he claimed to be able to read minds, speed up watches and, shortly afterwards, bend spoons merely by using the power of his mind.

In 1969 Geller's performing career began and during the 1970s he performed his **metal-bending** and mind-reading techniques for audiences all over the world. His appearance on a British TV show on in November 1973 turned him into a household name and started a controversy that continues to this day. After his appearance the studio switchboard was jammed with reports of cutlery bending and clocks stopping at home, particularly when children were watching the programme. The whole affair became an international sensation with journalists even questioning whether it was safe to let Geller fly on commercial aeroplanes because of possible interference with machinery.

Scientists sought permission to test Geller and, much to the surprise of those who refused to take him seriously, he agreed. He participated in a number of laboratory tests that suggested that he could produce phenomena, but no one could find out how. Geller gave impressive demonstrations of **clairvoyance** at the Stanford Institute in California and in 1974 British mathematician John Taylor conducted experiments that seemed to validate Geller's metal-bending powers. Geller's powers were also tested extensively by a neurologist and medical electronics expert, Andrija Puharich, who observed such phenomena as a compass needle spinning under the power of Geller's gaze. Puharich came away convinced that Geller was genuine.

Geller's international fame grew, but the more famous he became the more he was accused of trickery by detractors who attempted to demonstrate how metal bending could be achieved using stage magic. Puharich's claim in his book *Uri* (1974) that Geller had told him under **hypnosis** that his powers were the result of a meeting with aliens from outer space who had landed on earth in a **UFO** did nothing to increase Geller's credibility. The alien story was widely criticized and was later disavowed by Geller in his autobiography *My Story* (1975).

In the late 1970s Geller dropped out of the limelight to concentrate his efforts on private consulting work, including dowsing for minerals and oil. He re-emerged several years later as a millionaire. In his book *The Geller Effect* (1986), Geller relates how he learned to dowse using his hands. He says that others can learn similar powers using a combination of willpower, faith and concentration.

GEMATRIA

A branch of **kabbalah** that derives hidden meanings from words or phrases by translating them into their numerical equivalents and interpreting the results.

In Hebrew, each letter possesses a numerical value and gematria is the calculation of the numerical equivalence of letters, words or phrases, and, on that basis, gaining, insight into the mystical connection between different concepts and the interrelationship between words and ideas.

Early kabbalists employed gematria to discover the secret and indescribably powerful names of God, and these secret names were incorporated into rituals and incantations of ceremonial **magic** used to conjure **demons**. Not all kabbalists endorse the use of gematria, believing it can be manipulated into providing false proof of connections and theories.

Perhaps the famous example of gematria is neither Jewish nor Hebraic. It can be found in the Book of Revelation, where St John mentions the number of the Beast as 666. Early Christians thought this referred to the Roman Emperor Nero, who violently persecuted Christians. The number equivalent of his name in Greek, Nero Caesar, comes to 666.

See **Numerology**.

GEOMANCY

A term that is applied to any practice or belief, such as **Feng Shui, dowsing**, **sacred geometry** and **ley lines**, to suggest working with the natural magnetic and life force energies of the earth. Although geomancy is now used to describe most forms of 'earth magic', originally it referred to a system of **divination** in which a pebble, nut or seed would be thrown several times on to a grid composed of 12 squares that had been drawn on the ground. An interpretation of the pattern made would then take place.

Modern theories of geomancy suggest that our ancestors probably knew a lot more about the energies of the earth than we do today. The earth is seen as something equivalent to the human body that is criss-crossed by the planetary equivalent of **acupuncture** meridians or energy centres. Many believe that prehistoric people built great monuments or **megaliths**, like **Stonehenge**, to manipulate these cosmic currents.

GEOPATHIC STRESS

From the Greek *ge*, 'earth' and *pathos*, 'suffering', the term refers to naturally occurring radiation from the earth that gets disturbed by man-made structures, such as power lines and buildings and underground water and mineral concentrations. It is thought that the negative effects of these energies can be detrimental both to structures and people's health. For example, geopathic stress may explain events like 'sick building syndrome', which is thought to be caused by electromagnetic fields surrounding office equipment, sealed buildings with inadequate or non-existent fresh air supplies and radiation from blocked underground streams.

There are thought to be certain things that can be done to relieve geopathic stress. **Feng Shui** is one method. Increasing the amount of outside light and ventilation in an office and improving electromagnetic fields by bringing in plants and certain **crystals** are others. Relocation away from the toxic location and new systems of ventilation are other options in extreme cases.

GESP [GENERAL EXTRASENSORY PERCEPTION]

A form of **ESP** in which it is unclear whether the results are due to **clairvoyance, precognition, retrocognition** or **telepathy**.

In the laboratory, many parapsychologists prefer to use the term general ESP (or GESP) to avoid having to label a particular experimental result as being caused by telepathy or clairvoyance, as in some cases it cannot be said for certain which of the two caused the result. For example, in some remote viewing tests for clairvoyance, the subject could be obtaining information telepathically. Or in other tests, such as **ganzfeld** in which a person tries to send an image telepathically to another person, the receiver may be using clairvoyance to view the image.

GETTY, J PAUL [1892–1976]

Billionaire oil magnate John Paul Getty is said to have personally investigated an alleged ghostly encounter while staying at England's **Woburn Abbey**. From an early age Getty had an interest in **ghosts** and is known to have travelled extensively and stayed in several locations exclusively for the purpose of experiencing **paranormal** phenomenon, often in the company of noted paranormal investigators associated with either the British or American **Society for Psychical Research**.

GETTYSBURG

Decisive battle of the American Civil War that was fought in Gettysburg, Pennsylvania, between the 1st and 3rd of July, 1863. Today the battlefield attracts over a million tourists a year, many of whom still report experiencing the sights, sounds and smells of the battle.

The battle of Gettysburg was relentless, intense and bloody. It lasted for three days and resulted in 50,000 casualties. Ghostly phenomena such as the sound of gunfire, screams and shouts and **apparitions** of wounded solders have been reported all over the huge battlefield, in the town of Gettysburg itself and in the surrounding areas. According to one account by a park ranger a group of foreign tourists witnessed what they thought was a re-enactment at the summit of Little Round Top, a strategic hill secured by Union forces during the battle where intense fighting took place, but were later astonished to learn that no such re-enactment had been performed at that time.

There are a particularly large number of reported phenomena at Devil's Den, where Confederate snipers hid to fire upon Little Round Top. After the battle bodies were strewn everywhere in the rocks of Devil's Den and sightings of soldiers were reported soon after the battle stopped and continue to this day. Other haunted locations include Pennsylvania Hall, which became a makeshift hospital during the battle, and Rose Farm, which served as a burial ground. An apparition of a Confederate soldier has also been reported at Cashmere Inn, about 8 miles from Gettysburg, which was visited by the Confederates prior to battle. In the 1890s the apparition of a soldier standing near the porch was allegedly caught on film.

Hummelbaugh House is also thought to be haunted. Brigadier General William Barksdale of the Confederate army was mortally wounded and brought there to die. His anguished cries are still said to be heard, along with the howling of a dog. The Brigadier's loyal hunting dog refused to budge from his grave, refusing all food and water and mournfully howling. It died soon after its master and many believe its **ghost** still haunts the area.

See **Battlefield ghosts**.

GHOST

Popular term for supposed **apparition** of the dead. (Psychical researchers tend to use the term apparition.) Ghosts are often depicted as resembling human form and described as fog-like, misty, silver, transparent and the like. They can be visible but they can also make their presence felt with strange noises, smells, cold air, the switching of lights on and off and by movement of objects.

The ancient meaning of the term ghost typically refers to the disembodied **soul**, which after death is thought to travel to the **underworld** or **afterlife**. Beliefs vary as to what happens to the soul after death but virtually every culture has believed at some point that the ghost can return to the world of the living and when they return they can have either good or bad intent.

In the West, those who believe in ghosts sometimes hold that they are the souls of those who cannot find peace in death or realize they are dead, and so they linger on earth. Their inability to find peace is often explained as a need to deal with unfinished business, to deliver advice or information, to protect or stay close to loved ones or simply to re-enact death (see **Grateful dead**). In some cases the unfinished business involves a victim seeking justice or revenge after death. The ghosts of criminals are sometimes thought to linger to avoid **purgatory**, **hell** or **limbo**.

In Asian cultures (such as China) many people believe in **reincarnation** and ghosts are thought to be souls that refuse to be reborn because they have unfinished business, similar to those in Western belief. In Chinese belief ghosts can also become immortal, or they can go to hell and suffer forever, or they can die again and become a 'ghost of ghost'.

Every culture has **superstitions** and beliefs about ghosts but both the West and the East share some fundamental ideas. There are often procedures and rituals for dealing with troublesome ghosts, such as **exorcism**. Ghosts may wander around places they frequented when alive, or where they died. Contrary to popular belief most ghosts are not reported at graveyards where the body may be buried but in houses and buildings where a person may have died, suffered or lived for many years.

Many ghosts are reported when conditions are foggy and could well be explained as tricks of the light, just as those reported during thunderstorms may be caused by electrical charges in the atmosphere. Although there are reports of appearances during the day, the majority seem to appear at night. It's possible that a person is more sensitive to **clairvoyance** when relaxed or asleep at night – many ghosts also appear during **dreams**. However, some believe that ghosts reported to have been seen at night when a person is wide awake may actually be hallucinations that occur when they are drifting off to sleep.

While some believe ghosts to be an objective reality, sceptics argue that there is always a simple explanation. First of all the the sincerity and motive of the person reporting the **haunting** will be called into question – there have been instances when reputed sightings of ghosts has been fabricated as a scare tactic to seek justice or revenge. The possibility of a hoax or con is considered, and then explanations grounded in knowledge about human physiology are offered. For instance, the appearance of ghosts is often associated with a chilling sensation and pale, semi-transparent apparitions. But a natural response to fear is hair-raising, which can be mistaken for chill, and the peripheral vision is very sensitive in detecting motion but does not contain much colour or provide focused shapes; therefore, movement outside the focused view, such as a moth darting towards a light or a curtain moving, can create a strong illusion of an eerie figure. And certain infrasonic frequencies are known to create unexplained feelings of anxiety or dread, which are so often associated with sightings of ghosts. Finally, psychological factors are often cited as natural explanations for ghost sightings: susceptible people tend to be prone to exaggerated interpretations of sensations or feelings they experience when visited a reputed site of haunting.

Frederick Myers, one of the founders of the **Society for Psychical Research** in

London, believed that ghosts were 'manifestations of persistent personal energy, or an indication that some kind of force is being exercised after death which is in some way connected with a person previously known on earth.' Myers believed that ghosts were projections of **consciousness** without a conscious identity, but more recent research has argued that ghosts may possess some kind of awareness.

Ghost investigators have found that in the majority of cases there are natural explanations for sightings, but this still leaves a tiny number – perhaps as small as 2 per cent – that just can't be explained naturally, however sceptical or unconvinced the investigator. There is as yet no definitive answer as to whether ghosts are genuine or figments of the **imagination**, or if they have personality or are flashbacks of the past.

See also **Ghost investigation**.

GHOST BUSTER

Based on the popular 1984 and 1989 *Ghostbusters* movies, the term is sometimes used to describe those within the ghost hunting community who use either spiritual or technological means to bring an end to a **haunting** activity.

GHOST CLUB

One of the oldest existing organizations associated with the **paranormal**. The Ghost Club of London traces its origins to the year 1855, when a group of Cambridge University fellows began to discuss and speculate upon the nature of **ghosts** and **haunting** phenomena. The club was formally established in 1862.

Little is known of the club's earliest members except that they were a select group of London gentlemen who decided to form a group dedicated to unmasking fraudulent **mediums** and investigating **psychic** phenomena. One of their first investigations was into the claims of the **Davenport brothers**, who came to London in 1862 and maintained that they could contact the **spirits** of the dead. Over time the club became less and less active until it was revived in 1886 by medium and **spiritualist William Stainton Moses**.

Membership was considered eternal and attendance mandatory. The club's motto was *Nasci, laborare, mori, nasci*, which means 'Be born, work, die, be born'. Between 1888 and 1936 the Ghost Club annually celebrated All Souls' Day on 2 November, and on this date the names of Ghost Club members, both living and dead, were read out. Until 1936 the club was a private club of 82 men – it was not customary for women to join such organizations – and members included noted psychical researchers such as **Nandor Fodor**. The first woman to join was a Mrs Mallow, but her membership only lasted five months before the club wound itself up on 2 November 1936.

In 1938 the Ghost Club was revived again under the leadership of **Harry Price**. He limited membership to 500 people, including women, and stressed that the club was not a **spiritualist** organization, but a 'body of extremely sceptical men and women who get together every few weeks to hear the latest news of the psychic world and to discuss every facet of the paranormal.' Members included such notables as the biologist **Sir Julian Huxley**, Earl Mountbatten and novelist Osbert Sitwell. The club continued until Price's death in 1948.

In 1953 ghost investigator Philip Paul managed to revive the club yet again, and **Peter Underwood** took over as president in 1960, serving until 1993 when he left to form another organization – the **Ghost Club Society**.

After 1993 membership of the Ghost Club was no longer by invitation and applications for membership from those seriously interested in the paranormal were accepted, subject to screening. Members are mainly based in London but come from all parts of the world and include scientists, lay investigators, authors, spiritualists and others. The *New York Times* described the club as 'the place where skeptics and spiritualists, mediums and materialists meet on neutral ground.'

The Ghost Club is still in existence today (www.ghostclub.org.uk) and continues to explore the vast realm of the paranormal. The club does not subscribe to any creed or belief about the paranormal and has investigated a large number of hauntings and paranormal phenomena, as well as sponsoring investigations into **UFOs**, **crop circles** and all manner of psychic phenomena. A quarterly magazine is published, and regular meetings and discussions held on a wide variety of aspects of psychic investigation.

GHOST CLUB SOCIETY

Society formed in 1994 by British ghost investigator **Peter Underwood** after his departure from the **Ghost Club** of London, and still active (see www.theghostclubsociety.co.uk).

Membership is by invitation only although interested persons may contact the Society. It meets regularly in London and conducts investigations all over Britain and abroad. A quarterly newsletter, *Society News*, is also published for members.

GHOST DANCE RELIGION

Named after the ghost dance – a shuffling circle dance accompanied by **chanting**, during which dancers experienced mystical **visions** of the dead – the ghost dance religion was a Native American religious movement which preached the return of the dead and a new world inhabited by Native Americans, both dead and living.

In the latter part of the nineteenth century the ghost dance religion spread quickly through the Western, Southwestern and Plains tribes, giving hope to Native

Americans, and in particular the Sioux people, suffering under White oppression. In some instances the dance would last four or five days with dancers experiencing visions of the Native American dead returning to help the living and bringing back the old ways to the world. Whites perceived the ghost dance religion to be hostile and in November 1890 banned it in all Sioux reservations. The religion continued despite the ban but finally ended on 29 December 1890, with the massacre of ghost dance advocates at Wounded Knee, South Dakota.

GHOST INVESTIGATION/ GHOST HUNTING

Techniques and methods used to investigate reports of **ghosts**, **poltergeists**, **hauntings** and **spirits** to determine if the phenomena are genuinely **paranormal** or can be explained naturally. Modern ghost investigators prefer not to be called ghost hunters or **ghost busters** because the terms are associated with popular sensationalism.

With the surge of interest in **spiritualism** in the late nineteenth century scientific investigations of alleged paranormal activity became the norm. Early investigators had to rely on eye-witness accounts, photographs, their observation skills and research but in the last few decades increasingly high tech and expensive equipment has been used to help investigators with their research. Psychical researcher **Harry Price** was among the first to use modern technology in ghost investigations, the most famous being that of **Borley Rectory**. Between 1929 and 1938 Price created a high-tech laboratory in the Rectory, complete with telescope, portable phone, felt overshoes, steel tape measures, cameras and fingerprinting equipment.

Contrary to popular opinion ghost investigators are not biased by belief in the paranormal or **afterlife**. The very best investigators are those that approach an investigation with an open mind. The majority estimate that up to 98 per cent of reported hauntings are false or have natural explanations, such as animal noises, tricks of the light or geological stresses. Some cases are thought to be **fraud** or caused by a human **agent**, in particular poltergeist attacks, which are often explained as examples of unconscious **psychokinesis**. As for the estimated 2 per cent of cases that investigators claim cannot be explained, despite a century or more of impressive research, ghost investigators know very little about how and why they occur.

The good investigator is obliged to look for all possible natural causes of alleged paranormal events, and these tend to fall into three categories: mechanical, personal and natural. Mechanical causes include machines, lights, cars, computers, etc. Personal causes are those attributable to human mistake or deliberate error, and natural causes include freak weather conditions, tricks of the light, underground geological activity, etc. Eliminating these potential causes requires a detailed and

Ghost investigation pointers

If you wish to investigate a haunting yourself there are some important things to remember:

* *If possible, contact a local ghost investigation organization for advice, information and ideas.*
* *If a particular location intrigues you learn more about it by visiting your local library or meeting the current owners.*
* *Obtain permission from property or landowners before conducting an investigation.*
* *Prior to your first investigation visit the location to note all obstacles for safety – this is especially important if you are investigating at night.*
* *Never go alone on an investigation. This isn't just for safety reasons but because it is important to have someone else's perspective.*
* *Clean camera lenses and equipment before you start.*
* *Do not wear perfumes or cologne on your hunt.*
* *Do not photograph in difficult weather such as rain or snow.*
* *Hold your breath if photographing in cold weather to avoid false photographs.*
* *Be mindful of hair, camera cords and other loose objects when taking photographs.*
* *Avoid smoking and drinking alcohol during an investigation and take something to eat and drink.*
* *Keep a thorough and accurate record of your investigation, noting dates and times, weather conditions and special circumstances.*
* *Always keep an open mind.*

The Society for Psychical Research publishes guidelines for investigators, and effects to look out for are divided into five categories: 1) unaccountable movement of objects; 2) unaccountable noises, voices and music; 3) mysterious lights, shadows and apparitions; 4) unaccountable touches, pushes and feelings of hot and cold; 5) feelings of fear, horror, disgust and unseen presences.

In photos look out for ghostly mist, balls or bright streams of lights and dark shadows, although bear in mind that they may be caused by bad film processing, steam, slow shutter speed and other camera mistakes.

Both the American Ghost Society and Ghost Research Society offer guidelines to potential ghost investigators, suggesting equipment to use, things to look out for and investigation techniques.

thorough investigation of the alleged event both during the day and the night to determine natural lights and noises and any possible patterns. Maps are consulted to see if the cause may be underground such as a tunnel, stream or fault line. Historical research of a particular location must also be done, again to eliminate any possible cause.

In addition to the above, three other investigation techniques are used by the serious ghost hunter: description, experimentation and detection. Description is a matter of recording accurately eyewitness accounts. Witnesses must not only record their experience but also inform the investigator of their previous knowledge, encounters with the paranormal and their current circumstances, health and state of mind.

Experimentation involves bringing in **mediums** or psychics to see if their impressions match those of the eyewitnesses and to locate areas where the hauntings allegedly occur. Some believe that the use of psychics is not constructive as they may pick up information telepathically or clairvoyantly, but if psychics are given no information but are sent alone to a building and come up with similar reports, their evidence is considered valuable. The detection technique involves testing rooms for disturbance by securing them, spreading dust, sand, flour, etc. on the floor to pick up footprints and setting up cameras, tape recorders, temperature sensors and the like.

Some ghost investigators are worried about relying too much on high-tech equipment as they can simply detect environmental changes and detract from important eyewitness observations. The equipment is also extremely expensive and finance is often a problem for most ghost investigators. Critics, however, argue that ghost investigation relies too heavily on eye-witness accounts. It is also virtually impossible to rule out **telepathy** and **clairvoyance** as factors influencing a haunting. The use of high technology and computer programs to investigate hauntings is controversial but it enables researchers to record phenomena and witnesses it in real time without being present at a site. One day, however, they could prove crucial if there is ever to be any conclusive proof of ghosts and the afterlife.

GHOST LIGHTS

Typically this phenomenon is described as a glowing ball or balls of light that defy natural explanation. The lights are widely reported in remote locations in the United States, Britain, Japan and other countries and are said to come in every colour of the rainbow, although at some sites the balls emit only one or two colours of light. The lights can sparkle, be stationary or in motion, high in the air or low to the ground. They can also be accompanied by humming or buzzing. Sometimes the lights are said to behave bizarrely, for example, vanishing or displaying evasive action when one moves too close to them. In some cases ghost lights are associated with **haunting** folklore due to a tragedy that took place at the location they are reported.

The **Ghost Research Society** and the **American Ghost Society** house impressive collections of research on ghost lights. A number of natural explanations have been proposed, ranging from car headlights and phosphorescences (see **Ignis fatuus**) to shifting geological plates and radioactivity from, ore but some sightings of lights, such as the **Marfa Lights** in Texas, the Brown Mountain lights in North Carolina and the Hornet Spook Light in Missouri, remain unexplained.

See also **Earth lights**.

GHOST RESEARCH SOCIETY

Founded in the late 1970s by hypnotherapist Martin V Riccardo, the Ghost Research Society is a Chicago-based organization with an international membership dedicated to the investigation of **paranormal** phenomena related to **ghosts**, **poltergeists**, **hauntings** and **survival after death**. The society was originally called the Ghost Tracker's Club but changed its name in 1981. In 1982 Dale Kaczmarek became president of the Ghost Research Society and editor of the *Ghost Tracker's Newsletter*, the society's journal. It's website is www.ghostresearch.org.

Society members undertake investigations all over the USA and since the early 1990s they have relied more and more upon high-tech equipment and computer programs. The society, like most paranormal organizations, states that in most cases – 90 to 98 per cent – there is a natural

explanation for an apparent haunting. However, the majority of members remain convinced that the 10 or so per cent of unexplained phenomena is enough to conclude that ghosts do exist and there is life after death.

The Ghost Research Society maintains an impressive collection of data that defy natural explanation, such as the presence of **orbs** and unmistakable audio disturbances. It also houses a large database on **ghost lights** and **electronic voice phenomena** as well as one of the largest collections of **spirit photographs** in the world. One of the society's most famous, and controversial, photos is that of the girl on a gravestone at **Bachelor's Grove Cemetery**.

GHOST SEERS

The universal belief that certain people born on certain days or certain times of the day have the **clairvoyant** ability to see **ghosts** and things other people cannot see. A person born on a Sunday is thought to have clairvoyant power in some parts of Europe, and in some parts of England children born during twilight are thought to be able to tell which relative will die next. In Scotland people born on Christmas Day or Good Friday are said to be able to see **spirits**. In other parts of the world it is believed that only **shamans** and seers can see ghosts and others can see them only in **dreams**.

GHOST SICKNESS

A belief that **ghosts** of the recently deceased can cause disease and even death to the living. The **spirit** of the dead person is thought to linger near its body in the first few days after death before journeying to the place of the dead, and during this time it is thought to be lonely and likely to seek the company of humans. Children are thought to be particularly vulnerable as their **souls** are less firmly attached to their bodies.

This belief is rooted in many tribal societies around the world, where preparations are made to ensure that the dead cannot find their way back to the house they lived in. Some American Indians believed that ghost sickness can be caught from either the dead, the sight of the corpse or their possessions. The Apaches, for example, buried their dead on the same day as they died and reduced to an absolute minimum the time the living spent with them. The relatives would typically move to a new house and to mention the name of the dead was strictly forbidden.

Fear of ghost sickness could explain some funeral rites and customs, such as carrying a corpse out through a window, rather than the door, to make it difficult for the ghost to find its way back home. Even though a ghost is feared most in the first few days after death, in many cultures seeing any ghost is also thought to be a **death omen**.

GHOUL

From the Arabic words *ghul* (meaning 'male') and *ghula* (meaning 'female'). In Islamic legend a ghoul is a **demon** who feeds on the flesh of humans, in particular corpses stolen from graves, travellers and children.

Ghouls are thought to travel at night around graveyards, deserts and lonely, deserted spots. Sometimes they are said to be dead humans who rest in secret graves and then awake to feast on human flesh, living and dead. In Islamic tradition there are many kinds of ghoul, both male and female, but perhaps the most terrible is the female variety who has the power to transform into a real woman that can entrap and feast on an unsuspecting admirer.

GLADSTONE, WILLIAM [1809–1898]

One of England's most prominent politicians, Prime Minister William Gladstone was also a keen investigator of the **paranormal**. His fascination for the unexplained was so great that in 1882, after having read Ignatius Donnelly's book, *Atlantis: The Antediluvian World*, he made a request to the British Cabinet for an expedition to be funded to find and map **Atlantis** somewhere in the Atlantic Ocean. His application was unsuccessful.

It is known that Gladstone attended numerous **séances** and was a noted member of the **Society for Psychical**

Research. On 29 October 1884, Gladstone visited William Eglinton, an English **medium**, and discussed confidential questions with him in three languages: Spanish, Greek and French. Eglinton was able to respond correctly to all the questions in the same three languages. The experience impressed Gladstone so much that he joined the Society for Psychical Research to learn more about the **spirit** world.

GLAMIS CASTLE

Built in the fourteenth century, Glamis Castle is the oldest inhabited castle in Scotland. It is also considered the most haunted castle in Scotland and perhaps the United Kingdom. Legend has it that Glamis is home to numerous **ghosts**, a **vampire** and a **witch**.

According to the earliest records Glamis Castle was originally a hunting lodge owned by lords of Glamis, who are thought to have lost their fortune through drinking and gambling. By the middle of the seventeenth century the castle was in a state of ruin. The family fortune was rebuilt by Patrick Lyon, who was made the Earl of Strathmore, but by the eighteenth century the family had fallen back into its bad ways.

According to legend, in the early 1820s the first son of the 11th Earl of Strathmore was born a deformed monster, with an egg-like body, no neck and tiny arms and legs. The child was not expected to live so he was locked away in a secret room, but to everyone's amazement he lived an incredibly long life, and didn't die until 1920 or, according to some accounts, 1940. The estate of Glamis Castle passed unlawfully to the second son and over the years each successive earl was informed of the existence of the monster of Glamis, as he became known, on his 21st birthday. Allegedly the earls were profoundly influenced by the experience of meeting the true heir, becoming moody and withdrawn; some refused to acknowledge the room for fear they would lose their sanity.

There are no records to prove that the monster existed but in 1880 there is a record of a workman accidentally knocking down a wall and finding the secret chamber. The workman disappeared soon after and it was rumoured that he was given a large sum of money to relocate to Australia.

Over the years there have been numerous sightings of ghosts at Glamis Castle. One most frequently seen is that of Janet Douglas, wife of James Douglas, the sixth Lord of Glamis. James died one morning after eating his breakfast and Janet was suspected of killing him, even though no evidence could be found. Six years later, in 1537, she was convicted of **witchcraft** and burned at the stake at Castle Hill, Edinburgh. Her ghost is said to appear above the clock tower, wrapped in fire or an orange glow.

Another ghost frequently sighted is that of the seventeenth-century 4th Earl of Strathmore, better known as Earl Beardie. Legend has it that Earl Beardie gambled with some chieftains one night in the tower. They argued and cursed. The Devil appeared and condemned them to dice there until Judgement Day. Others say that Earl Beardie could find no one to gamble with him that night and got so vexed that he said he would play cards with the Devil. The Devil appeared and Beardie lost all his money, and his **soul**. Sounds of arguing, swearing and stamping are said to waft from the tower and Beardie's ghost has also been reported wandering around the castle.

The number of ghosts associated with the castle is staggering. They include the ghost of a madman who walks along the roof on stormy nights on a spot called 'the Mad Earl's Walk', a woman without a tongue who runs across the gardens tearing at her mouth – her tongue may have been cut out because she learned the secrets of Glamis castle, mysterious **grey ladies**, 'Jack the Runner' – a thin boy who races up to the castle, a black boy who sits by the door of the royal sitting room, a tall figure dressed in a long cloak and a woman with sad eyes who clutches at windows as if imprisoned.

Glamis' vampire is said to be a servant girl who was discovered sucking blood from her victim. According to lore she was walled up alive in a secret chamber, where she sleeps the sleep of the undead and waits for someone to set her free. The castle is also thought to have been the site of two legendary murders – Macbeth's murder of King Duncan, because Shakespeare mentions Glamis Castle in *Macbeth*, and the murder of eleventh-century King Malcolm II. Historical fact demonstrates that neither of these murders took place at Glamis, nonetheless Macbeth's ghost is believed to haunt the castle and an entire floor was boarded over because a mysterious bloodstain from Malcolm's murder was said to be impossible to remove.

Poltergeist phenomena continue to be reported to this day and include screams, banging noises, sheets being ripped off beds in the middle of the night and doors that mysteriously open even though they are locked and bolted. Guests staying in the castle claim to have seen faces appearing and disappearing at windows and hovering over beds.

GLANVILL, JOSEPH [1636–80]

Celebrated by many as 'the father of modern psychical research', Glanvill was a conservative and highly educated Englishman who approached tales and legends associated with both **witchcraft** and **ghosts** with an open mind. Published in 1681, after his death, Glanvill's book *Sadducismus Triumphatus* claimed to explore the 'full and plain evidence concerning witches and apparitions'. Today it is regarded as one of the pioneer pieces of **paranormal** research.

Glanvill personally involved himself in a number of investigations, the most famous being the so-called **Drummer of Tedworth**. He also attended **séances**, interviewed **mediums** and people who claimed to have seen ghosts or experienced unnatural phenomena, and attended a large number of witch trials, often attempting to inject some common sense into the hysteria.

It is clear that many incidents reported in *Sadducismus Triumphatus* were hoaxes and that many of the conclusions drawn by Glanvill are naive because of the limited knowledge of science in his day, but Glanvill's pioneering contribution to psychical research and **ghost hunting** was immense. Many of his techniques are still being practised to this day, for instance interviewing witnesses and visiting the site where the alleged incident took place. In 1945, **Harry Price**, a celebrated ghost hunter himself, wrote: 'He it was who first stimulated those persons fortunate enough to possess a ghost to investigate the affair in a proper manner, to record the case systematically, and to have the phenomenon attested by responsible witnesses.'

GLASTONBURY

Long regarded as the magical capital of Britain, Glastonbury is a small market town in Somerset that is steeped in legend, religion, magic and mystery. Not only is Glastonbury the cradle of Christianity in England but it is also reputed to be the burial place of King Arthur. Many visitors claim to feel the powerful atmosphere of this town.

It is thought that Glastonbury was a site for pre-Christian worship, perhaps because of its location near what is now known as Glastonbury Tor, a terraced volcanic rock 522 feet high with the remains of a ruined medieval church at the top. Several thousand years ago, at the foot of the Tor there

was a lake called Ynys-witrin, the Island of Glass, and this is perhaps the reason for the association of Glastonbury with legendary **Avalon**. In Celtic folklore Avalon was an island of enchantment, the meeting place of the dead.

Glastonbury Abbey was founded in the fifth century, reputedly by St Patrick, who is said to have lived and died there. According to legend King Arthur and his wife Guinevere are buried in the grounds of Glastonbury Abbey, south of the Lady Chapel, between two pillars. The monks of the Abbey, having heard the rumours, decided to excavate the site and unearthed some bones and hair and a stone slab, under which was found a lead cross inscribed in Latin: 'Here lies beneath the renowned King Arthur with his beloved Queen Guinevere his second wife in the Isle of Avalon.' Glastonbury lore unites Christianity, King Arthur and the Holy Grail. After the crucifixion, it is said that Joseph of Arimathea travelled to Britain with the **Grail**, the cup used by Christ at the Last Supper and later by Joseph to catch His blood at the crucifixion. Upon arriving on the isle of Avalon, Joseph thrust his staff into the ground. In the morning, his staff had taken root and grown into a strange thorn bush, the sacred Glastonbury Thorn in the ruins of Glastonbury Abbey. Joseph is said to have buried the Grail just below the Tor, where a spring, now known as Chalice Well, began to flow; the water is reputed to have healing qualities. Many years later it is said that one of the quests of King Arthur and the Knights of the Round Table was the search for the Holy Grail.

Glastonbury is also believed to rest at the intersection of powerful **ley lines**. In 1907 the ruins of Glastonbury were excavated under the supervision of **Frederick Bligh Bond**. Bond believed that Glastonbury was connected to **Stonehenge** and **Avebury** by ley lines. He was successful in locating unknown parts of the abbey but his controversial method of excavation, in which he claimed to be guided by **spirits**, created scandal in the Church and he was dismissed.

In 1929 sculptor Katherine Maltwood discovered that natural landscape formations over a 10-mile area in the Glastonbury area recreated the 12 signs of the **Zodiac**. The origins of the patterns are unknown. The occultist **Dion Fortune** also spent a great deal of time at Glastonbury living in a house at the foot of the Tor, where she worked, wrote and practised her magic rituals in an adjacent chalet. The chalet is said to be haunted by a **ghost** who opens and closes doors.

Today the High Street is packed with shops selling mystical objects and artefacts. With its myths, legends, mystery and ley lines the town has become a centre for Christian pilgrimages as well as for **spiritual healing** and seasonal **New Age** rituals practised by **witches**, **magicians** and **pagans**.

GLOSSOLALIA

Unintelligible speech or speech in an unknown tongue generally uttered in a **trance** state, also known as 'speaking in tongues'. The gift of tongues has been divided into three categories: pure glossolalia, or speaking in a language unknown to the speaker or listener; **xenoglossy**, speaking in a language unknown to the speaker but recognized by the hearer; and heterglossolalia, speaking in a language known by the speaker but heard by the hearer in his or her native tongue.

From the Greek *glossa* meaning 'tongue' and *lalia* meaning 'a talk', in Christianity glossolalia is said to have first come to the apostles at Pentecost when they were filled with the Holy Spirit and began to speak in unknown tongues. Those listening were also said to be able to hear and understand what was spoken in their own language.

Glossolalia was used by the early Christians of Corinth in their services, although few knew what was being said or what the tongues meant. St Paul postulated that unless the words were understood and could be interpreted they served no purpose and, as a result, glossolalia became less prominent in worship. By medieval times the Church deemed glossolalia a miracle that was no longer possible and those who tried to revive interest in the practice were branded as heretics. It wasn't long before speaking in tongues became a sign of demonic **possession**, a position still held by the Catholic Church today.

During the nineteenth century some Methodists and some Presbyterians spoke in tongues and today Pentocostal Christians see glossolalia as a sign of baptism by the Holy Spirit. Other groups that accept speaking in tongues are the Quakers, the Shakers and the Mormons. Glossolalia has also been observed in **shamanism** and **Voodoo**. Sceptics dismiss these cases as simply being in a state of **trance**, self-hypnosis, heightened emotion or religious ecstasy. Modern advocates of glossolalia believe that speaking in tongues is a **psychic** gift a select few are born with.

GLYPH

Carved or painted **symbol** used in magic and thought to represent graphically a person's name and birth date and the heart of who that person is. It is constructed in a similar way to a **sigil**, with a sequence of letters and numbers fashioned into one picture. It can be worn as an **amulet** or **talisman** and is thought to have protective powers against illness and misfortune.

GNOSTICISM

From the Greek *gnostos* meaning 'known', Gnosticism was a school of **mysticism** that flourished in the early years of Christianity. It was based on the idea that it was the search for hidden spiritual knowledge rather than faith or conduct that could save a person.

Gnostic sects varied in their approach to **esoteric** truth; some focused on techniques like **astrology** or **numerology**, while others concentrated on the secret teachings of Jesus. All seem to have been influenced by the controversial belief that God has a dual nature – that he is both masculine and feminine – and his feminine counterpart takes the form of Sophia, the divine wisdom.

Gnostic practice was forbidden by orthodox Christianity but the movement never lost its influence and survived in followers of the **Kabbalah**, and in secret societies such as the **Rosicrucians** and **Freemasonry**. Then, in 1945 the 'Gnostic Gospels' were discovered in Nag Hammadi, Egypt. The discovery confirmed that Gnosticism was a part of early Christian practice and that many gospels had been suppressed by later Church factions. As a result there has been a revival of interest in Gnostic Christian traditions.

Another significant influence on the revival of Gnosticism was the work of pro-Gnostic writers and thinkers such as existentialist Hans Jonas and historian Kurt Rudolph. Perhaps the most influential was psychiatrist **Carl Jung** who found in early Gnostic thought a prototype for depth psychology. He believed that Christianity had suffered as a result of the suppression of Gnostic ideas and that **alchemy** might be a way to reintroduce them to a modern public.

GOAL-FOCUSED INTUITION

A combination of **deductive psychic intuition** and **random psychic intuition**, goal-focused intuition involves making a conscious effort to gain insights using **psychic** ability. In other words **intuition** or psychic ability is used for a specific goal or aim. A good example of this is the work done by **psychic criminologists**. Some of their information would be drawn from deductive intuition and some may be generated at random but all clues gathered relate to the specific goal of locating a missing person or solving a crime.

GOAT

The name for a subject in a clinical test for **psi** who does not believe in **psychic** phenomena. See also **sheep/goat effect**.

GOBLIN

A goblin is an evil or mischievous creature of French folklore, often described as hideously disfigured or an elf-like phantom. They are similar in many ways to household **spirits** in other countries, for instance, **brownies** in England and Scotland, **domoviks** in Russia and **kobolds** in Germany.

Goblins are believed to live in grottos but may also attach themselves to house-holds, especially those that have lots of wine and children. They may help with household chores but on some nights they show their mischievous nature and instead of doing chores will create choas by moving furniture and banging pots and pans. They are also said to count the dead among their companions and to be able to weave nightmares out of gossamer and insert them into the ear of a sleeping human.

Legend also has it that goblins borrow horses from stables and ride them all night, leaving the horses exhausted by the morning. It is also said that they sometimes steal women and children and hide them away underground. If a goblin woman takes a liking to a human baby she may steal it away and replace it with a goblin baby, or changeling.

GODDESS

Term used for the divine feminine force. The Goddess appears universally as the **symbol** for fertility but she is also the ruler of truth, wisdom, nature, earth, the home, justice, healing, love, birth, death and those aspects of life that cannot be explained using logic or science, namely emotion, **intuition** and **psychic** power. She has many facets to her nature, indicating a multiplicity that is natural to women, and is often said to be She of a Thousand Names.

This rediscovery of female divinity in the West was triggered by archaeological discoveries in the 1960s and 1970s indicating a peaceful, ordered and mainly vegetarian Bronze Age society with a dominant goddess cult. These discoveries coincided with the women's movement and encouraged women not only to challenge the subordinate role assigned to them by the major religions but also to celebrate female strength and power within themselves.

Many modern advocates of the Goddess hold that the worship of the Goddess has been handed down since prehistoric times. The actual history of the Goddess, however, is more complex, and it can be argued that the Goddess is essentially a modern figure – her emergence an example of the birth of a new divinity.

The so-called Venus figurine, a carving of a female with exaggerated belly and breasts, is one of the most common archaeological finds throughout Europe. It is said to be a clear sign that goddess worship in prehistory may have been universal and as old as the Stone Age of 30,000 years ago. However, some experts say it is difficult to prove the role of these artefacts conclusively as evidence surrounding their place in their society is scanty. Despite an enormous amount of speculation we know very little about the religious traditions of prehistory. The fact that people in the carved female figures tells nothing about what these figures symbolized. Were they goddesses, magical **talismans**, works or art, erotica, or something else? It's impossible to know. What is known, however, is that even though the rise of male-centred religions from around 4000 BC lead to a subordination of the Goddess cult, her influence lingered and remains an important part of many belief systems today, in particular **paganism**, Hinduism, and the cult of the Virgin Mary in Christianity.

In recent years there has been a trend for a 'return' to Goddess worship as a way to reconnect with the earth and to intuitive ways of living. This revival of interest is most visibly seen in paganism and nature religions, where the Goddess is given primacy. In many **neo-pagan** traditions the Goddess has three forms – Maiden, Mother and Crone – corresponding to the story of a woman's life cycle and the waxing, full and waning phases of the moon. As Mother Nature, the Moon, Creator, Destroyer, the Queen of the Heavens, and the primary source of magic and inner power, the Goddess embodies, for all those who believe in Her, the very essence of modern **witchcraft**.

GOLDEN DAWN, HERMETIC ORDER OF THE

The most famous **occult** society of modern times.

The two main founders of the order, William Wynn Westcott (1848–1925) and Samuel Liddell MacGregor Mathers (1854–1918), were **Freemasons** with connections to the English occult scene. One day in 1886, Westcott was browsing through a bookstall in Farringdon Street, London when he came across a set of documents in cipher. Suspecting they were magical he bought them immediately. Other versions of the story state that

Westcott found the documents in the library of British **clairvoyant** Frederick Hockley or that they reached Westcott from Hockley's library via a freemason and clergyman named Woodman. Wherever the manuscripts came from Westcott needed help decoding them and he selected Mathers for this task.

When decoded the documents turned out to be outlines for the rituals and teachings of an eighteenth-century German magical order, the *Orden des Gold-und Rosenkreuz*. There was also the address of a **Rosicrucian adept**, Anna Sprengler, of Nuremberg in Germany. Westcott wrote to her and over the course of their correspondence, although it has been suggested that Westcott himself wrote the letters, Sprengler revealed many secrets of practical magic and in 1888 granted him permission to establish his own magical lodge in London. This he did with the help of Mathers and Woodman and they called the new lodge the Hermetic Order of the Golden Dawn.

Initial membership was drawn from friends of the founders but gradually the society expanded to embrace more than a hundred members, including some of the best minds of its day. **W B Yeats**, the Irish poet, became a member. So did writers Bram Stoker and Algernon Blackwood and actress Florence Farr. The Golden Dawn attracted people of this calibre because the system Westcott and his colleagues put together was intellectually challenging, and aimed at developing human **consciousness** and mystical experience. Although based on the Jewish **Kabbalah** it had considerable Christian and oriental

influences and its hierarchical structure, study courses and **initiation** rituals set a new standard for magical ritual societies.

Structurally the Golden Dawn was a hierarchy led by Mathers under the guidance of mysterious and unseen secret chiefs. There were inner and outer orders, which were in turn subdivided into ten grades, each linked to a sphere in the Kabbalistic **Tree of Life**. Entry to each grade involved a course of study, an exam and a ritual initiation.

Temples of the Golden Dawn included Isis-Urania No. 3, which was the first founded temple (temples nos. 2 and 3 seem to have been fictions created by Westcott), Osiris No. 4 in Weston-super-Mare, Horus No. 5 in Bradford, Amen-Ra No. 6 in Edinburgh and Ahathoor No. 7 in Paris. There were also two temples founded in the United States – Them No. 8 in Chicago and Thoth-Hermes No. 9 in New York.

In 1897 the Order broke apart as a result of internal conflict and disagreements over leadership when Westcott resigned in 1896. The survival of the Golden Dawn tradition into twentieth century was largely due to the influence of three members who broke the vows of secrecy they took on initiation. The first was **Aleister Crowley**, who joined the Golden Dawn in 1898 and later published information about its rituals and knowledge in his magazine *The Equinox*. The second was **Dion Fortune**, who included Golden Dawn teaching in her masterwork *The Mystical Qabalah*. The third was American **Israel Regardie**, who was convinced that the only way the order could survive would be if it were made public. He gathered as much material as he could find and published it in four large volumes between 1937 and 1940.

Even though they had been made public Golden Dawn teachings were not picked up to any significant extent until the 1980s, when a number of new Golden Dawn orders were formed by people who simply took the published material and created their own groups. The Golden Dawn revival has had mixed results, due to the same troubles with internal politics as the original founders, but the order is still very much alive today. In fact there are probably more people practising Golden Dawn magic today than there have ever been, and the quality and quantity of published material available has significantly improved in the last few decades.

GRAIL, HOLY

The Holy Grail is thought to be the cup used by Christ at the Last Supper and for that reason it is considered a symbol of perfection and virtue by Christians. As a **pagan** motif, the Grail is the cup of healing and new life, which symbolizes the body of the **Goddess**. In **esoteric** traditions the Grail is believed to be a point of contact with both the spiritual and the **supernatural** realm. It is said to possess magical powers of healing and communion with the divine force. In **alchemy** the grail is likened to gold, the **philosopher's stone** which represents apprehension of the divine. According to tradition the grail can only be seen by those who have reached a cer-

tain level of spiritual awareness. It is not known whether such an object ever existed or still exists.

There are various versions of the Grail legends. One of the most well-known suggests that one of Jesus' followers, Joseph of Arimathea, supposedly brought the Grail to Britain and hid it somewhere in the vicinity of **Glastonbury** Tor. In another Joseph passes the Grail to Bron, his sister's husband, and it is eventually housed in a temple on Munsalvaesche, the mountain of salvation, where it is guarded by an order of Grail knights. The Grail keeper, who is known as the Fisher King, is wounded and as a result the kingdom becomes a wasteland that can only be restored when the King's health is restored. This sets the scene for the legendary quests for the Holy Grail by King Arthur and his Knights of the Round Table. Early origins of the Grail legends can also be found in the ancient and universal feminine image of a cup as a symbol of power, rebirth and inspiration, but this is complicated by the fact that the Grail sometimes appears as a dish, a womb, a cauldron and a stone.

Whatever the source of the legend, the real importance of the Holy Grail lies in its mysterious power to fascinate the human mind. Psychiatrist **Carl Jung** said that the story of the Holy Grail represents a search for meaning and the inner self. Seen in this light there can be no doubt that the quest for the Holy Grail is psychically very much alive today.

GRAPHOLOGY

From the Greek *grapho* meaning 'to write' and *logos* meaning 'theory' graphology is the study of a person's handwriting in order to analyse their character. Graphology is an ancient method of **divination** and character analysis first developed by the Chinese approximately 3,000 years ago. The Romans experimented with graphology and since then various civilizations and cultures have analysed handwriting, although more to identify the essence of the person who produced it than to predict the future.

Theories that attempt to explain graphology date back to the seventeenth century but the modern approach to handwriting analysis owes much to a group of French clerics led by a man called Abbé Michon, who outlined key theories and evidence for graphology in the 1870s, after decades of study.

A graphologist will typically take a sample page of handwriting, together with a signature, analyse it in detail and then make deductions about a person's personality from the writing's style, size, shape and appearance. There are hundreds of features that can be examined and they include the slant of the letters, letter hoops, dotted Is, crossed Ts, letter spacing, end strokes, joined-up letters, separated letters, readable or illegible script, upper and lower case and so on.

According to graphologists handwriting analysis is an extremely powerful tool that can be used to highlight an individual's talents and potential, particularly in career guidance and improving relationships. Like other behavioural or intuitive models, it is not easy to explain how and why graphology works, but graphologists believe that certain handwriting features express unique impulses of the individual because the brain sends signals to the hand holding the pen or pencil being used to write.

Today graphology is still being used and researched but there is great debate about its value, as sceptics argue that many external factors, from the kind of pen and paper used to poor health, can affect the quality and consistency of handwriting. In Britain and North America graphology isn't considered a science and is generally not taken seriously, but in countries like Germany, Switzerland and Austria graphology is considered a branch of psychology and submitting a handwriting sample in a job application is not considered unusual.

GRATEFUL DEAD

Motif in folklore where **ghosts** return from the world of the dead to help the living. Typically the ghost helps those who have been kind, generous and deserving. For example, a man on his travels comes across a group of people who refuse to bury a corpse, so he decides to pay for the corpse to be buried. Later he meets a stranger who helps him towards fame and fortune and only at the very end of the story does the man discover that the stranger who became his friend and helper was the ghost of the corpse.

In Chinese folklore the grateful dead often take on a didactic role, returning to

Brief introduction to handwriting features

Professional graphologists can recognize several hundred handwriting features and all these features need to be considered together when a number of them appear in a handwriting sample, but here are some basic features that can be readily understood by the beginner and which may give interesting information.

Size

Large size handwriting can mean a friendly and sociable personality, or it can mean that the writer puts on an act of confidence, although this behaviour might not be exhibited to strangers. Small size is generally an indicator of a detailed, academic and technical personality.

Line slope

Writing which rises to the right shows optimism and cheerfulness. Sagging downwards shows physical and mental weariness.

Slant

A right slant indicates the more extrovert kind of person. If the handwriting is generally upright, this indicates independence, and a left slant tendency shows emotion and reserve.

Spacing between words

This indicates social attitudes towards others. Words that are close together are a sign of sociability. Large spaces indicate a person who is most comfortable alone.

The three cases – divisions of personality

Graphologists believe that the three cases or registers of letters represent the three aspects of our personality: the upper case represents our higher self or thinking about spirituality; the middle case our mental and social approach to life; and the lower case our physical aptitudes and attitudes.

The upper case is the area in which the extended up-strokes are found in tall letters like b, d, h, t, etc. The middle case is the central region occupied by letters with neither long up-strokes nor down-strokes, such as a, c, e, m, n, o, etc. The lower case is the area occupied by down-stroke letters such as g, j, p, etc.

Look where the emphasis of the writing is, as according to graphologists this is where the emphasis of the personality is too.

Some other simple indicators:

* *Large upper loops are a sign of emotion.*
* *Uneven upper loops show mood swings.*
* *Closed 'e's show secrecy.*
* *Stand alone or properly formed 's's at word ends show independence.*

honour the brave, and reward those who have given corpses a proper burial and the **spirits** of their dead ancestors respect.

GREEN LADIES

Phantom **apparitions** of courtly ladies dressed in green gowns that often act as heralds of misfortune or death. Green ladies have been reported all over the world and the following account is but one example.

Stirling Castle in Scotland is thought to be haunted by a Green Lady who appears at unexpected times and places in the castle. The castle used to house an officers' mess and it is said that one night dinner was served late in the officers' mess because the cook fainted after seeing a misty-green figure watching what he was doing.

In life some believe that the Green Lady may have an attendant to Mary, Queen of Scots who saved the Queen's life one night when she awoke with a start from a **dream** warning her that the Queen's life was in danger. She ran to the Queen's bedchamber and discovered that the curtains of royal four-poster bed were aflame with the Queen herself asleep inside. It has also been suggested that the Green Lady may have been the daughter of a governor of the castle who was betrothed to an officer garrisoned there. The officer was killed accidentally by the girl's father and she, in despair and torment, is said to have thrown herself from the battlements to her death on the rocks 250 feet below.

Even today any appearance of the Green Lady is taken very seriously by those who believe in her. It is said that many of her appearances have been followed by a disaster of some kind, and indeed, several fires at the castle have followed alleged sightings of the silent figure.

Greenbriar ghost

The only known case in the United States where the **ghost** of a victim is thought to have helped expose and convict the murderer. Testimony relating to the ghost's appearance was even added to the records of the trial.

Elva Zona Heaster Shue was born near Greenbriar, West Virginia in 1873. On 26 October 1886, a year or so after giving birth to an illegitimate child, she met and married blacksmith and newcomer to the district Erasmus Trout Shue (also given as Edward). Zona's mother, Mary Heaster, was opposed to the marriage because she did not like Erasmus and thought him to be a stranger.

On 23 January 1897, an 11-year-old boy called Andy Jones was sent by Shue to his house with instructions to ask Zona if she needed anything, Jones found Zona lying on the floor with her feet stretched out straight in front of her, one hand at her side, one lying across her body and her head tilted to one side. The local physician, Dr George W Knapp, was called. When he arrived Shue had dressed his wife in her Sunday best and was cradling her corpse in his arms. Knapp found it hard to conduct any investigation into the cause of death properly because of Shue's overwhelming display of grief, and announced that Zona had died of an everlasting faint, then officially decreed the cause as 'childbirth'.

At the funeral mourners noticed some unusual behaviour on the part of Shue, in particular his insistence that she wear her 'favourite' red scarf around her neck at all times. They also noticed that when the body moved the head seem to be strangely loose. The local rumour mill began to grind.

Mary Heaster was convinced that her daughter had been murdered and prayed for her ghost to return from the dead to reveal the truth. Within a week or so her prayers came true when Zona's ghost reportedly woke her mother in the middle of the night and described in detail how her husband had been violent and abusive and had killed her in a fit of rage because there was no meat to cook for supper. To illustrate the ghost turned its head completely round.

Mrs Heaster urged the prosecutor, John Alfred Preston, to investigate and, intrigued by local gossip as well as Heaster's story, he agreed to have Zona's body exhumed on 22 February 1897. An autopsy revealed a broken neck. Shue was arrested and charged with murder.

While Shue was in jail awaiting trial details about his past began to emerge. He had abused his first wife and his second wife had died under mysterious circumstances from a head injury or fall. Shue vigorously denied murdering Zona and attempted to shift the blame to Andy Jones, the boy who had discovered her body.

Even though all the evidence against Shue was circumstantial and the defence raised the matter of Mary Heaster's ghost story as evidence that she may be unstable, Shue was found guilty and imprisoned for life. He died on 13 March 1900, in Moundsville State Penitentiary, West Virginia.

Near Greenbriar a highway marker commemorates the case. It reads:

Interred in nearby cemetery is Zona Heaster Shue. Her death in 1897 was presumed natural until her spirit appeared to her mother to describe how she was killed by her husband Edward. Autopsy on the exhumed body verified the apparition's account. Edward, found guilty of murder, was sentenced to the state prison. Only known case in which testimony from a ghost helped convict a murderer.

It's extremely likely that Shue was guilty but afterwards some speculated that Zona may have died a natural death and her mother had broken her neck to frame Shue. Even though the autopsy mentioned nothing about pregnancy, some also thought Zona may have been pregnant with another illegitimate child, and that Dr Knapp had killed her while trying to abort it and had broken her neck to cover this up.

Serious doubt has also been cast over Mrs Heaster's ghost story. At the trial Mrs Heaster stated that Zona's ghost had said her neck had been 'squeezed off at the first vertebrae'. This seems an unlikely assertion from a simple countrywoman and it is possible that she had read the autopsy. Historians have also discovered that in the 28 January 1897 issue of *Greenbriar Independent*, which announced Zona's death, there was a story about a case in Australia where a murder victim had been discovered because of reports of the ghost of a murdered man sitting near a pond where his body had been thrown. Years later a dying man confessed to spreading rumours of a ghost, in an attempt to get the body discovered, because he had witnessed the murder but was afraid to reveal details, in case the murderer came after him.

It's impossible to know if Mrs Heaster read the story and decided to avenge her daughter's death by making up a ghost story, or if she really believed her daughter's ghost appeared to her to reveal details of her untimely death.

GREMLIN

A mythological, mischievous **spirit** that is often depicted as mechanically orientated and devious. The word 'gremlin' comes from Old English *grëmian*, meaning 'to vex' or 'to anger' and from *grim*, meaning 'severe' and is related to the German *grämen*, 'to grieve'.

Gremlins have been described as around six inches tall with horns and black leather boots, while others say they are a cross between a rabbit, a fish and a dog. They have also been described as little people around one foot tall who wear red jackets and green trousers. Typically gremlins appear in connection with aircraft but they also can appear in factories and offices. They could be described as modern, technologically aware versions of **brownies**, **domoviks** and other such spirits who like to play games with humans to keep them alert.

The concept of gremlins being responsible for sabotaging aircraft is said to have originated in reports of misty, **goblin**-like spirits told by Royal Flying Corps pilots sent on dangerous missions during World War I. The term didn't enter public usage, however, until 1939 during World War II, when British pilots in India suffered numerous incidents of seeming sabotage and blamed gremlins. Since then gremlins have been reported in relation to problems with both military and civilian aircraft all over the world.

Gremlins are thought to have a great knowledge of technology, engineering, meteorology and aerodynamics. It has been said that they can bore holes into aircraft, sever fuel lines, bite cables, slash the wings of aircraft and terrify pilots by suddenly appearing at the windscreen. The reason for their enmity is not clear, but it has been suggested that gremlins were once friendly towards humans, showing them how to use technology wisely but when humans started to take the credit for their work their relationship broke down.

Despite their fondness for playing pranks and causing accidents not all gremlins are thought to be dangerous. Some have been credited with helping pilots fly damaged aircraft to safety, and incidents have been recorded where gremlin voices have allegedly spoken to pilots and given them instructions to land, change course or turn to avoid disaster.

One of the most famous pilots who claimed he had been helped by gremlins was Charles Lindbergh when he made his historic solo flight across the Atlantic Ocean in 1927. In his book *The Spirit of St Louis* (1953), Lindbergh says that around the ninth hour of his 33½-hour journey, when he became tired and run down, gremlins appeared to give him instructions and reassure him of his safety.

GREY LADIES

The **ghosts** of women who are said to have died violently for the sake of love or through the heartless actions of a family member or loved one. They frequently appear in grey, but they can also appear in white, black and brown. Grey ladies appear all over the world, often in connection with **poltergeist** activity, and the following is but one example of numerous reported sightings.

Chambercombe Manor at Ilfracombe, North Devon, has reportedly been haunted since the seventeenth century by a grey lady. Legend has it that one night a William Oatway deliberately lured a ship ashore on a stormy night so it would crash on the rocks and he could plunder it. A female survivor was washed ashore, her face so badly beaten she could not be recognized. William took her home but she died in the night. Her death didn't stop him taking her jewellery and money belt.

A few days later, the Admiralty called round to William's dwelling to inform him that his daughter, Kate, had gone missing when a ship was washed ashore. William was devastated that he had unwittingly caused the death of his own daughter and walled up her body in a secret room. A century or so later the room was discovered and the bones buried in a pauper's grave, but Kate's ghost still lingers in the house where she grew up with her father, and murderer, William Oatway.

Stories of ghosts described as 'ladies in grey' are also associated with the Tudor period when the destruction of abbeys and monasteries in England caused the death of many nuns who then dressed in grey. There are famous grey ladies to be found at **Newstead Abbey** and Rufford Abbey as well as Holy Trinity Church in Micklegate, York.

GRIMOIRES

Books of magical knowledge written between the late-medieval period and the eighteenth century. Grimoires contain astrological correspondences, lists of **angels**, instructions on casting **charms** and **spells**, as well as information on how to mix medicines and make **talismans,** but they are perhaps best known as texts that set out the names of **demons** as well as instructions on how to summon them.

The word grimoire is from the Old French *gramaire* or 'grammar' and indicated to both educated and illiterate alike a book of basic instruction. Noted historical grimoires include:

- *The Book of the Sacred Magic of Abra-Melin the Mage.*
- *Liber Juratis, or, the Sworn Book of Honorius.*
- *The Black Pullet.*
- *The Greater Key of Solomon.*
- *The Lemegeton, or, the Lesser Key of Solomon.*

Many of the above texts were reclaimed in the late nineteenth century by neo-Masonic magical organizations such as the **Golden Dawn**. Typically the texts of grimoires were in French, German or Latin and were quite rare. Although accurate editions were available a cottage industry developed selling false or poorly translated grimories.

A modern grimoire is the *Necronomicon*, named after a fictional book of magic in the stories of author H P Lovecraft, and inspired by Sumerian mythology and the *Ars Goetia*, a section in the *Lesser Key of Solomon* which concerns the summoning of demons.

GRIS-GRIS

In **Voodoo**, gris-gris are small cloth bags containing herbs, oils, stones, bones, hair, nails, tiny pieces of cloth soaked with perspiration and/or other personal items gathered for the protection of the owner. They are kept as **talismans** to ward off evil.

The origin of the word isn't known, but some experts trace it to *juju*, the West African name for **fetish** or sacred object, or to the French word *joujou*, doll or plaything. Many African fetishes were shaped like dolls, and early Europeans travelling to the African West Coast may have mistaken religious objects for dolls or toys.

The gris-gris became commonplace in New Orleans, the American Voodoo capital, where they were used for attracting good luck, stopping gossip, protecting the home, maintaining good health and numerous other things. At one time, almost everyone would carry a gris-gris for protection. A gris-gris is traditionally made at an altar with incense and a candle burning. One, three, five, seven, nine or thirteen ingredients are used. Ingredients are never an even number or more than 13 (see **numerology**). Stones and other objects are chosen for their **occult** and astrological meanings depending on the purpose for which the gris-gris is to be used.

GROTTENDIECK STONE-THROWER

Unexplained **poltergeist** activity that occurred in September 1903 on the island of Sumatra, formerly a part of the Dutch East Indies and now a part of Indonesia.

One night Dutch engineer W D Grottendieck of Dordrecht, Holland returned from a trip into the Sumatran jungle when he found that his regular quarters had been taken by another member of the Dutch oil company he worked for. Exhausted he decided to stay in a new house that had been erected on bamboo poles with a roof made of large, dried leaves, known as kadjang or awning leaves.

At about one o'clock in the morning Grottendieck was woken by something falling on the floor beside him. In the darkness he saw that small black stones were falling through the roof even though the roof had no holes. He went to the next room to wake up his servant boy, Malay, and told him to go outside with his torch to see if he could see anyone. The boy found nothing.

Inside the hut Grottendieck tried to catch the stones but they seemed to change direction mid-air, preventing him from catching any. Frustrated he went outside and fired his rifle to scare off pranksters but the stones continued to fall. The terrified servant boy fled into the jungle; as soon as he had gone the stones stopped falling. The next morning Grottendieck found a number of the stones still on his floor. He observed that they had fallen within a radius of three feet and had all come through one single kadjang leaf.

The theory that the boy was the focus of the activity was discounted by Grottendieck when he corresponded with the **Society for Psychical Research** and explained that the stones were falling while the boy was asleep. Before the incident Grottendieck had been a sceptic, but he was now convinced that there was a link between the death of his sister three months previously and the falling stones. He believed she was trying to communicate with him. His story was published in the *British Journal of the Society for Psychical Research* in 1906.

There have been a number or suggestions as to what caused the incident. Perhaps Grottendieck's experience was genuine. Perhaps he was hallucinating. Perhaps the boy was throwing the stones or perhaps the stones were fruit seeds dropped by bats that fly into houses at night. The case remains unsolved.

GROUNDING

Term used to describe reconnecting with one's sense of self and the physical world after **psychic** development work.

Grounding is a way to get rid of the disconnected or spaced-out feelings that sometimes occurs with **meditation** or **visualization** work. Experts in psychic development believe it is vitally important after any meditation or visualization exercise to return to daily life and reconnect with the physical world. This can be done with simple activities, such as yawning and stretching, making a cup of tea, eating a light snack, writing in a journal or anything that helps body and mind focus on the physical rather than the spiritual or mystical.

GUARDIAN SPIRIT

In tribal cultures a personal protective **spirit**, that typically takes animal form. The major function of the guardian spirit is look after its possessor and protect him or her from harm. If misfortune strikes this is often attributed to a failure on the part of the guardian spirit but if things run smoothly the guardian spirit is thanked.

In some societies guardian spirits are thought to be the spirits of ancestors, but in others they are free and independent spirits. They are not to be confused with spirit helpers, who are summoned by **shamans** when specialized help is needed, for example, for healing disease. They should also not be confused with **familiars**, who are also spirits in animal form. Guardian spirits are believed to be present from birth. However, they can also be discovered in **dreams** or acquired by undertaking a **vision quest** in the wilderness.

Although guardian spirits are strongly associated with tribal and shamanic cultures, they do figure in the Christian concept of guardian **angels**. In **Spiritualism** a person is believed to have a guardian spirit or spirits from birth, although most people aren't aware of them, thus depriving themselves of a source of inner strength and power.

GUIDE

Term used to refer to inner guidance (see **intuition, gut feeling, sixth sense, inner guide, higher self**) that can help a person discover wisdom and/or **psychic** guidance and assistance from inside him or herself.

The term also refers to **spirit guides**. Spirits guides are thought to be **angels, fairies, ghosts** or **spirits** whose function is to help and guide people on their spiritual path. In contrast to intuitive guidance, help from a spirit guide is thought to come from an outside source, although some people think that their spirit guide is somehow connected to their intuition.

GUIDED IMAGERY

The idea that a person can improve their health and their life by imagining it in more positive terms. Guided imagery is a term used to refer to a kind of directed daydreaming, **creative visualization**, **hypnosis** or **meditation** which allows a person to enter a state in which they can picture and experience images that help to heal or motivate them. For example, a cancer patient may picture army tanks shooting down cancer cells, while a sprinter may imagine the speed and grace of a cheetah. In other words, the **imagination** is used in a directed way to help achieve goals.

Imagery has long been considered a healing tool in virtually all of the world's cultures. For example, Navajo Indians practise an elaborate form of imagery that encourages a sick person to 'see' himself as healthy. The Egyptians and ancient Greeks believed that images released **spirits** in the brain that aroused the heart and other parts of the body.

In the late 1960s guided imagery came to public attention with encouraging reports from oncologist O Carl Simonton of unexpected longevity in cancer patients following the use of imagery and **visualization** to stimulate immune response. Although Simonton's work created controversy in medicine, it wasn't until the late 1980s, with the development of psychoneuroimmunology as a field of study, that researchers began to research the effects of the mind on physiology and healing in earnest.

While this research is just beginning, Simonton's early hypothesis that people can stimulate their immune response through imagery has been validated. Study after study shows that when performed correctly guided imagery can help lower blood pressure, reduce anxiety and depression, boost the immune system, ease physical pain and nausea during chemotherapy, reduce stress, balance hormones, speed recovery from cuts, burns, fractures and surgery and lower allergic responses. It also improves performance in sport and business, as well as learning.

Today guided imagery is a term variously used to describe a range of techniques from simple visualization and direct imagery-based suggestion through metaphor and storytelling. In medicine guided imagery is used to help teach psychophysiologic relaxation to relieve symptoms, to stimulate healing responses in the body and to help people tolerate procedures and treatments more easily.

In addition to using thoughts and images, guided imagery also involves imagining how things sound, feel, taste and smell. It is thought that because sensory input is how the mind takes in information, guided imagery goes straight to the **unconscious** mind. It is particularly powerful when it involves emotions, because emotions also by-pass words and logic and go straight to the unconscious. In addition, emotions carry a history with them that interacts with the image. For example, if you imagine you are on a happy holiday with people you love, your body re-experiences the same joyful physical responses.

Some people prefer to use imagery created by someone else, and a person (or a tape recording of the person) talks them

Sample guided imagery exercise to reduce stress

To begin, sit or lie down in a comfortable position and close your eyes. Once you feel relaxed enough, begin to imagine a scene, object or place that is beautiful and relaxing to you. Imagine every aspect of the scene, involving all of your senses. For example, if you visualize a waterfall on a mountain, imagine first what this looks like: the rushing water, the stream flowing from it, the size and height of the trees all around, the sky above and the sun filtering through the branches, and so on. Then imagine how this place would smell – damp and musty or fragrant pine. Next listen for the sounds you would hear if you were there: the water rushing over rocks, the wind rising and then quieting down, birds singing. How does the ground feel beneath your feet? Is it rocky and rough, or soft and smooth from pine needles or moss? Imagine chewing on a blade of grass, or taking a long, cool drink from the waterfall. How do they taste?

As you become fully involved in your imagery, your body will relax and problems and worries will begin to melt away. To encourage this relaxation to occur, you can punctuate the images with positive affirmations, such as 'I am letting go of tension' or 'I feel calm and relaxed'.

through the visualization, while others prefer to make up their own. Whatever method is used, the most important thing is to relax and let your imagination work. Imagery, whether guided or not, is most effective when it encourages someone to imagine with all their senses.

See also **Pathworking**.

GUPPY, AGNES [1838–1917]

In the mid-1860s to early 1870s Agnes Nichol Guppy, also known as Mrs Samuel Guppy, became the first **medium** in Great Britain to perform full-form **materializations**.

Agnes was orphaned by her first birthday and raised by her grandfather. She began to have **visions** around the age of nine, despite her grandfather's disbelief and disapproval. In her teens she became a photographer and a painter to Mr and Mrs Sims, a couple who encouraged her to develop her mediumistic talents, which included **levitation** and **telepathy**. On 14 December 1866 Agnes allegedly made her first **apport**, a bunch of fresh flowers, at a **séance** attended by the naturalist Alfred Russel Wallace.

Agnes was a heavily built woman and in the darkness, while holding the sitters' hands, it was said she would float on top of the table in her chair. On numerous occasions flowers and fruits would appear on the séance table from an unknown source. The request of the sitters was often honoured. When a friend of Wallace asked for a sunflower, a six-foot high sunflower with a mass of earth around the roots fell upon the table. In Naples Princess Marguerite desired specimens of a prickly cactus. More than twenty dropped on the table and had to be removed with tongs. The most amazing apport she produced, however, was herself. In June 1871 Agnes was allegedly teleported from her house at Highbury to a séance being held at 61 Lamb's Conduit Street, a distance of three miles.

In December 1867 Agnes married the wealthy but elderly **Spiritualist** Samuel Guppy, and for the next few years they resided on the Continent, holding séances and dazzling audiences. More marvels were witnessed on their return and in 1872 Agnes produced the first full-form materialization using a **cabinet**.

Mr Guppy was wealthy and the complete absence of any financial motive on the part of Agnes greatly puzzled psychical researcher **Frank Podmore**, who believed that every medium was a **fraud** out for financial gain. He writes:

But Mrs Guppy, even during the few months in which, as Miss Nichol, she practised as a professional Mesmerist, can scarcely have found her main incentive in the hope of gain. On the assumption of fraud, the mere cost of the flowers lavished on her sitters must have swallowed up any probable profit from her increased mesmeric clientele. And even such a motive would have ceased with her marriage.

At the height of Agnes's fame a new medium called **Florence Cook** appeared on the scene, but Cook's full-form materializations of **Katie King** did not get Mrs Guppy's support. Agnes was a rather large woman and Florence's youthful beauty attracted many of her former sitters. Allegedly she conspired to have acid thrown in Florence's face but her plans backfired and ended her reign as London's top medium.

After Samuel Guppy's death Agnes married William Volckman, who had tried to grab Katie King during one of Cook's séances. His actions were condemned but Florence's reputation was ruined and Agnes got her revenge. For the rest of her life she was known as Mrs Guppy-Volckman.

GURDJIEFF, GEORGEI IVANOVITCH [c.1865–1949]

Considered by some to be the greatest **occult** and mystical teacher of all time, and by others as a complete **fraud**, Georgei Ivanovitch Gurdjieff founded the Gurdjieff system, a series of physical and psychospiritual exercises designed to jolt people out of their **somnambulist** state.

Russian-born Gurdjieff's early years are shrouded in mystery but from his youth he was fascinated by the occult sciences and **spiritualism**. He was probably familiar with **Madame Blavatsky's** Theosophical Society but after years of travel and investigation of various sects and cults, such as the Sufi dervishes of Central Asia, instead of following an established occult philosophy he created his own and attracted a large number of followers. He postulated that people were similar to machines and controlled by forces they could not influence. In such a state humans were asleep, and in order to wake up they needed to work hard to overcome their normal state of unconsciousness and reach for true **consciousness**.

Gurdjieff taught that people could only learn how to 'wake up' by studying under those who had escaped their robotic existence – a teacher or 'person who knows'. People should form schools and obey their teacher in all things. Self-realization could only be achieved by a technique called self-remembering – a conscious awareness of surroundings and self in a situation.

The first Gurdjieff school opened just before the start of World War I. It attracted pupils at once, among them the mathematician Pyotr Demianovitch Ouspensky, who believed in endless **reincarnation** and saw Gurdjieff's work as a way to break the cycle and attain perfection. In the years that followed the movement grew stronger and more schools were opened. Gurdjieff established his procedures, called 'shocks', designed to further the process of self-awareness. These shocks consisted of hard, physical labour, intense emotional experience, and complicated and energetic dance moves. The idea was that while experiencing 'shocks' a student lost preconceived notions about themselves and began to

unify all the different aspects of themselves – which was called the 'Is' in harmony. By working on oneself in this way, one can allegedly rise above a robotic existence and attain immortality.

Students of the Gurjieff schools took part in strenuous activity and dance movements. They attended lectures in hypnotism, music, language and science, and learned Sufi breathing techniques. To help them stay 'alert', techniques such as being asked to stand like statues for minutes at a time or being woken up in the middle of the night were used.

The cosmology Gurdjieff propounded is complex and detailed. It talks of rings within rings and **souls** sucked up to feed the moon and is so symbolic that even his most devoted followers are forced to rely on the work of his disciples, like Ouspensky, to understand it. Despite the complexity, however, at the root of all his teachings is the belief that the great majority of human beings live in a state analogous to sleep. Although we think we are awake and in control, the opposite is true.

Gurdjieff also postulated that the Universe is governed by the 'law of three' and the 'law of seven'. The law of three states that humans have three bodies – carnal, emotional and spiritual – and by working on themselves they can rise from the carnal to the spiritual. The law of seven refers to Gurdjieff's belief that life's processes are governed by seven stages of development, and one only progresses from one to the next if a 'shock' is given.

The enneagram, a circle whose circumference is divided by nine points, creating an uneven six-sided figure and a triangle, was Gurdjieff's **symbol** for his worldview. It shows the law of three and the law of seven and how people cross phases of development in life by 'shocks'.

Gurdjieff called his system the Fourth Way or the Way of the Cunning Man. He explained that traditionally there were three paths to immortality: those of the **fakir**, who had to undergo physical torture; the monk, who is emotionally committed to God; and the yogi, who is a spiritual seeker. All three of these paths, Gurdjieff argued, were incomplete, but the Fourth Way – his way – was complete. In the Fourth Way people started with their own experiences and attempted to unite all the paths to immortality, using every cunning trick to stay 'awake'.

Gurdjieff left Russia in 1922 and eventually settled in France. Despite his following he was a difficult and intense man to be around and most of his supporters eventually rejected him. After 1924 he stopped teaching and spent the rest of his life writing down his theories and worldview.

Gurdjieff is probably best known through Ouspensky's *In Search of the Miraculous* – perhaps the best explanation of Gurdjieff theories – and his own works, the most accessible of which is *Meetings with a Remarkable Man*, which was made into a film by director Peter Brooke. Gurdjieff foundations, dedicated to teaching and promoting the Gurdjieff philosophy in practical ways suited to a modern lifestyle, enjoy a moderate following today and can still be found all over the world.

GURNEY, EDMUND [1847–1888]

A graduate of Trinity College, Cambridge, Gurney became a musician, a physician and an attorney before finally devoting his life to psychical research in 1883. Over the next few years, Gurney became one of the founding members of the **Society for Psychical Research** as well as one of the foremost authorities of his day on **hypnosis**. He also gathered together a huge collection of papers and reports exploring **psychic** phenomena. In 1886 he published his research on the evidence for **telepathy**, particularly from crisis **apparitions**, in the classic work *Phantasms of the Living*, a book that broke new ground by setting forth for the first time a scientific approach to ghost hunting and methods of investigation appropriate to psychic phenomena.

GURU

According to Hindu philosophy a guru (from the Sanskritt *gu* meaning 'darkness' and *ru* meaning 'light') is a spiritual teacher who helps dispels darkness and bring pupils to the light. The guru leads and inspires by example, in order to help followers reach enlightenment or self-knowledge. In the West the term is used to describe many kinds of spiritual teachers or leaders.

GUT FEELINGS

Gut feeling is the term used to describe an intuitive reaction or feeling about people, places or situations. For example, you walk into a room and feel uneasy, or you meet someone new and feel a warm glow.

The term 'gut feeling' isn't accidental. The area around the stomach has always been considered important in the Eastern system of **chakras**. Now in the West it has gained new-found importance as scientists have discovered that the body has a second primitive 'brain' in the layers of tissue lining the stomach, small intestine and colon. It is actually a network of neurons, neurotransmitters and proteins called the enteric nervous system.

The enteric nervous system and its interaction with the brain in the head are so complex that it is a field of study in its own right, called *gastroenterology*. Experts in the field have suggested that once animals had a primitive brain in their gut because their efforts for survival were based around food. As these animals developed, neural pathways out of the gut extended to a newer brain in the head, used for other needs such as memory and sex. Eventually the connection between the two brains shrunk to a single nerve, called the vagus nerve.

This primitive brain is deeply connected to our survival instincts and may explain why we sometimes get unexplained, intense feelings about people, places and situations – even when it may pertain to areas of our lives that are not life-or-death situations, such as jobs and relationships with other people.

Psychics believe that when we talk about instinct, gut feelings, **intuition**, **hunches**, vibes and so on what we are really referring to is one distinct area of psychic awareness, the skill of **clairsentience**. Clairsentience is the ability to get intuitive insight and information through your sense of touch or feeling what is around you. It's possibly the most common of psychic abilities, yet it is the least recognized and acknowledged.

GUZYK, JAN [1875–1928]

Polish **materialization medium**. Guzyk displayed **psychic** ability from an early age and by the age of 15 he became a professional medium. In 1921 he was investigated by the **Insitut Metapsychique International** and researchers reported witnessing a number of materializations, including that of a head and a face that seemed to be alive and able to speak. More investigations followed in 1922 and 1923. The psychical researchers assigned to the project were so convinced by the full form materialization of an 'ape man', whom Guzyk nicknamed Pithecanthropus, that they all signed a document declaring that trickery had been ruled out and that what they had witnessed were genuine phenomena.

In November 1923 Guzyk's impressive track record collapsed when a committee of four professors from the Sorbourne in Paris held a series of ten **séances** with him. They found that Guzyk would sometimes use his hands and knees to produce spirit touches or move objects. Even though they could not explain all the séance phenomena they declared him a **fraud**. Despite the damage to his reputation Guzyk continued to hold séances, and the investigators who had worked closely with him remained convinced that his powers were genuine.

GYPSY MAGIC

Also known as Romany magic, gypsy magic refers to methods of **divination** and **magic** used by the Romany people. Gypsies were once thought to have been of Egyptian descent, but recent archaeological findings suggest they may have originated from Northern India. Today there are thought to be around three million Romany people, living mainly in Russia, Eastern Europe, Turkey and Greece.

The Romany people have been travellers from as far back as the eleventh or twelfth centuries AD. Their religious beliefs are a mix of nature worship, folk magic and Christianity and to treat them unfairly or disrespectfully is thought to bring bad luck – the origin of the gypsy **curse**. They believe strongly in the **afterlife** and the **spirit** world and are renowned for their skills in the divinatory arts of **palmistry**, **tarot** and **scrying**.

GYROMANCY

From the Greek *guros* ('round') gyromancy is an ancient **divination** method where the diviner walks or whirls around a circle marked with letters of the alphabet until too dizzy to continue; the letters against which they stumble or the direction of the fall are interpreted, thus 'spelling out the prophecy'.

Another method of gyromancy consisted of interpretations of prophetic utterances from people exhausted from dancing in an enchanted circle. In yet another method it is a divination procedure where a clipped coin is whirled on a circle of letters.

H

Hag

An **apparition** reported to resemble an ugly old woman with tangled hair, rotting teeth, a hooked nose, mad eyes and claw-like fingers. The Hag is also related to the *mara* (from which the word 'nightmare' is derived), a **demon** that likes to attack humans at night and abuse them.

Victims of hag attacks (known as Old Hag Syndrome) claim that they awake abruptly to find that they cannot move, even though they can see, hear, feel and smell. There is sometimes the feeling of a great weight on the chest and the sense that there is a sinister or evil presence in the room. Old Hag Syndrome has been documented since ancient times and modern research suggests that around 15 per cent of people experience at least one Old Hag attack in their lives. The name of the phenomenon comes from the superstitious belief that a **witch** – i.e. an old hag – sits or 'rides' the chest of the victims, rendering them immobile.

Sceptics argue that rather than witches or demons there is probably a medical or scientific explanation for Old Hag Syndrome, such as indigestion, sleep disorders or repressed tension. Some researchers believe that tales of encounters with the hag might be attached to the phenomenon known as **sleep paralysis**. Medical explanations, emotional tension and sleep paralysis can explain the great majority of cases, but not all.

Halcyon House, 3400 Prospect Street, Georgetown

Located in the Georgetown district of Washington, DC Halcyon House, built by Benjamin Stoddert, the first secretary of the US Navy, is said to be haunted.

Following Stoddert's death in 1813 the house passed to a number of owners. During the Civil War its basement was connected to an underground railway road and was used by runaway slaves. It is said that some runaways died in the basement and began **haunting** it with ghostly cries. In the early twentieth century the tunnel was walled up, but the cries continue to be heard.

In the 1930s Halcyon House passed to an eccentric called Albert Adsit Clemons. Clemons was passionate about building extensions on to the house, believing that as long as he worked on the house he wouldn't die. He worked like crazy, adding rooms, doors that opened to walls and a staircase that led nowhere. After he died in 1938, hauntings in the house began to increase. On two separate occasions, occupants awoke at night to find themselves floating above their beds. A **phantom** woman, odd sounds, movements of objects and a **ghost** matching the description of Stoddert have all been reported.

Halloween

Observed annually on the night of 31 October and originally a **pagan** festival of the dead, Halloween (also known as Allhallows Eve) is celebrated today as a night of fancy dress, trick or treating and superstitious fun and games.

The festival traces its origins back to the ancient Celts who celebrated the start of the New Year and the end of the summer around 1 November. The Celts believed that on this night the veil between the dead and the living was at its thinnest and the dead could rise out of their graves to wander freely on earth. The living dressed themselves in disguise so **spirits** would not recognize them, and huge bonfires would be lit in an attempt to rekindle the diminishing energy of the sun god in the winter.

The ancient Romans also celebrated festivals that influenced the development of the Halloween tradition. The festival of Pomona, the goddess of orchards and the harvest, was celebrated around the same time. Apples and nuts still have their place in Halloween traditions observed today.

As time went on **fairies**, **witches**, **goblins** and spirits, as well as the dead, were said to come out in force on Halloween night. In England Guy Fawkes Night, celebrated on 5 November absorbed many of the traditions of Allhallows Eve but currently the tradition of Halloween is enjoying new-found popularity. This isn't just in America – where Halloween has been an established part of American folklore since the 1840s, when poverty stricken Irish fled to the United States – but in Europe and England too.

Wiccans and Pagans observe Allhallows Eve (also known as Samhain) as one of their most important sacred days. For them it is a time for fun but also a time to honour the dead, communicate with spirits and observe rituals. It is also thought to be a particularly good time to make a fresh start and commence new projects.

Hallucinogens

See **Drugs**.

Halo

In art, a circle of bright light that crowns the head of holy people or people with special powers. In ancient Greece and Egypt the halo was used in art to suggest **supernatural** power and great intellect. In Christian art it signifies grace and piety. In **clairvoyance** the halo can appear as an **aura**, which is often visible around the head. It can also represent the crown **chakra**, which is said to be pronounced in people who are spiritually developed.

HALOMANCY

Ancient form of **divination** using salt. The diviner throws salt up into the air or into a fire and the way in which the salt falls, or the random patterns it makes when it is poured or spread over a surface, are interpreted as good or bad **omens**. Ridges typically indicate problems and obstacles while valleys show delays and frustrations. Halomancy may be the inspiration for many **superstitions** concerning salt, such as to spill salt brings misfortune, and throwing a pinch of salt over your left shoulder wards off bad luck. The idea of spilled salt as a sign of good or bad luck may come from the association of salt with life. Salt symbolizes semen, so to spill it is to upset the balance of life.

HAMILTON, THOMAS [1873–1935]

Canadian physician and founder of the Winnipeg Society for Psychical Research. For 15 years Hamilton conducted important research on mediumship in a laboratory constructed in his own house.

Hamilton graduated from Manitoba Medical College in Winnipeg in 1903 and after a year's internship at Winnipeg General Hospital established his own private medical practice. He was first attracted to psychical phenomena as an undergraduate when an article by the **spiritualist W T Stead** prompted him to read and research in psychical research and to devise his own experiments to test **telepathy** and mediumship.

Hamilton's early experiments with a non-professional **medium** called Elizabeth Poole greatly impressed him but, aware that his research might affect his standing in the medical community, he decided to give up psychical research. This was a decision he found impossible to carry through and less than a year later a special **séance** room had been fitted out in the Hamiltons' house, complete with a **cabinet**, round table and chairs facing the cabinet and carefully positioned cameras. The room, together with Hamilton's medical credentials and standing in the community, made an impressive contribution to psychical research in his day.

In April 1923 the new sittings began, with a group of sitters which included four doctors, a lawyer and two engineers. The phenomena recorded and photographed in the room included partial **levitation** and communications through a medium from the writer Robert Louis Stevenson and the explorer David Livingstone. These communications convinced Hamilton that mediumship and life after death were genuine. In 1928 **materializations** began to occur. Photographs showed **ectoplasm** emerging from the head of medium Mary Marshall. It ranged in size from a few inches to three or four feet high, some showing faces.

As his research developed and the evidence stacked up Hamilton broke his silence and began to speak about it in public and publish articles in Spiritualist publications. His only book, *Intention and Survival*, was published after his death and the title expresses his belief that communications via séances provided evidence of **survival after death**.

Hamilton died in 1935 at the age of 61. The sittings were continued by his wife and in February 1939 ectoplasm with Hamilton's likeness allegedly emerged, proving to his followers that Hamilton had successfully communicated his continued existence after death.

HAMPTON COURT

Some say that Hampton Court, the palace given to King Henry VIII in 1525 by Cardinal Thomas Wolsey, is the most haunted place in England.

Once home to a long line of royals, Hampton Court has provided the magnificent setting for jealous husbands, affairs, intrigue, treachery and scandal for hundreds of years. Its enormous structure and grounds are said to be haunted by as many as 30 **ghosts**.

The ghost of Jane Seymour, Henry's third wife who died in childbirth, has been reported on numerous occasions. She is said to appear with a lighted taper on the Silverstick Stairs on the anniversary of her son's birth.

Cardinal Wolsey's ghost has been reported under one of the archways by a member of an audience viewing a light and sound show in 1966. Strange happenings and mysterious noises have also been reported on the anniversary of the death of Christopher Wren. Wren redesigned the

Palace for Queen Anne from 1702 to 1714 and died there while supervising a renovation on 26 February 1723.

Catherine Howard, Henry VIII's fifth wife, who was beheaded in 1542, is another famous ghost. The young queen was accused of infidelity in 1541, and arrested and charged with treason. Knowing that she would be executed, Catherine broke away from her guards and ran toward her husband's rooms, hoping to plead for mercy. But before she could reach the king, guards dragged her, kicking and screaming, through what is now called the Haunted Gallery. Terrifying shrieks are still heard occasionally today, and it is said that her **apparition** appears along the gallery every November.

Also reported are the ghosts of officers who fought under Charles I, the ghost of **Anne Boleyn**, Henry's second wife, and the ghost of Sibell Penn, nurse to Edward VI. The White Lady of Hampton Court, the headless Archbishop Laud, a hooded figure that lurks in the kitchens, a dog, a girl, a cat, unexplained balls of light and an odd shape nicknamed 'Mr Blobby' also appear on Hampton Court's impressive roll call of ghosts.

HANDFASTING

Handfasting comes from an old Celtic ceremony in which a couple's hands are ritualistically tied together, hence the phrase 'tying the knot'. The ceremony can either symbolize the beginning of a trial marriage, typically lasting a year and a day, or, with proper legal procedures, handfasting can be a legal marriage ceremony.

There is no universal procedure for the ceremony, but typically it involves **chanting** and **spells** and the raising of magical energies within a sacred space. Although a **pagan** priest or priestess will preside the couple devise their own ceremony and perform their own ritual. They get themselves married as opposed to being married by someone else. For some the marriage is for a year and a day, renewable 'so long as love shall last', while for others it is a commitment to be together through many lives.

HANUSSEN, ERIK JAN [1889–1933]

Conjurer who earned the dubious honour of being Adolf Hitler's favourite clairvoyant.

Born Herschel (or Herman – accounts vary) Steinschneider in Vienna the son of a travelling comedian, Hanussen's upbringing was far from conventional. After a brief stint as a newspaper reporter he joined a small circus and began publishing books that denounced skills such as **telepathy** and **clairvoyance** as fraudulent hoaxes. Then he did an about-turn and claimed he had clairvoyant and telepathic powers. Despite being labelled a swindler by the Austrian and Czech police he moved into the cabaret scene and began giving public shows at major theatres.

Hanussen soon became a well-known public figure, though from the descriptions given, the tricks he was performing were clearly derived from extant conjuring sources. His skills came to the attention of Hitler and he served the Nazis as one of their most vehement and savage anti-Semitic propagandists. By the end of 1932 he was living a life of luxury and excess in his huge mansion outside Berlin, which was referred to as 'The Palace of Occultism'. Success, however, went to Hanussen's head. In a **séance** in February 1933 he made the fatal error of revealing information obtained from his close association with top Nazis about a fire that would take place at the Reichstag as proof to the German people that the Communists were trying to disrupt the government. Hanussen knew that the fire would be set by the Nazis themselves within less than 12 hours, and he couldn't resist using that inside knowledge to demonstrate his psychic powers.

The Reichstag fire took place the next morning in accordance with the Nazi plan and although there was huge public excitement about the accuracy of Hanussen's clairvoyance, he had now become a danger to the Nazi cause. He had outlived his function of charming the dilettantes that the Nazis needed to finance their cause and his mutilated body was discovered in a shallow grave in the woods outside Berlin on 7 April 1933. Hanussen's 'Palace of Occultism' closed and never re-opened.

Harmonic Convergence

On 16 and 17 August 1987 thousands of people from all over the world gathered at sacred locations such as **Glastonbury** and **Stonehenge** in England and Mount Shasta in California believing the world was about to end. The event was called the Harmonic Convergence.

The Harmonic Convergence was largely the idea of an American art historian, Dr Jose Arguelles, who believed the date was set long ago by the 'galactically informed' ancient Mayans. Arguelles calculated that the Earth was entering a new phase where minds would unite in harmony and create a special energy or human power grid that could not only promote world peace but also make possible contact with beings from other planets. According to Arguelles, the fall of the world's stock markets in October 1987 and increased sightings of **extraterrestrials** in the years that followed were fulfilments of the prophecy.

Harpers Ferry

Many **ghosts** are thought to haunt this small town in West Virginia where pre-Civil War fighting and the arrest and execution of slavery abolitionist John Brown took place.

John Brown of Kansas was a radical revolutionary violently opposed to slavery. In 1859 he hatched a scheme whereby he and his followers would seize control of the strategically important town of Harpers Ferry and arm slaves with weapons. The siege ended in blood and chaos. Brown was convicted of conspiracy to incite insurrection and executed on 2 December 1859. According to reports Brown left a note saying he was 'certain that the crimes of the guilty would never be purged away but with blood' and he died with a wild delight in his eyes that terrified onlookers so much wax had to be poured over them. Harpers Ferry changed hands between Confederate and Union forces several times during the Civil War.

Most of the ghosts reported at Harpers Ferry relate to the Civil War era but perhaps the most well known is the tall thin ghost of John Brown himself. He is reportedly seen at the site of the siege accompanied by a large black dog. Dangerfield Newby, a former slave and one of Brown's men who died in the siege, has also been reported walking along Hog Alley displaying a gashed throat and the same baggy trousers he wore the day he died.

Other ghosts reported at Harpers Ferry include ghostly Civil War soldiers lighting campfires, and the ghost of priest Father Costello, who saved St Peter's Church, located above the town on a hill, when fighting broke out by raising the British flag. Both armies avoided shelling the church in case it would create problems internationally. Father Costello's ghostly figure has been spotted walking towards the church, where he disappears through the walls.

HART, HORNELL NORRIS [1888–1967]

Psychical researcher and sociologist with a special interest in **out-of-body experiences** and **survival after death**.

Hornell Hart was born in St Paul, Minnesota on 2 August 1888. He received a PhD from the State University of Iowa in 1921 and later became professor of Sociology at Duke University, where **J B Rhine** had his **parapsychology** laboratory. Throughout his life Hart was fascinated by psychical research, particularly the question of survival after death, and managed to retain this interest alongside his religious convictions. As one of the first sociologists to employ statistics in psychical research he was well equipped to work with Rhine.

Hart contributed a number of important writings to the field of psychical research. He published several papers in the journal of the **American Society for Psychical Research** and in 1953 suggested the idea of a 'psychic fifth dimension'. His 1956 paper, *Six theories about apparitions*, has become a classic read for students of parapsychology. He also wrote a number of books on the subject including *The Science of Social Relations* (1927) and *The Enigma of Survival: The Case For and Against an Afterlife* (1959).

In *The Enigma of Survival* Hart introduced the term 'super ESP' to describe hypothetical **ESP** ability that extends beyond the boundaries set by laboratory experiments. He also introduced his 'persona theory'. According to this theory, **apparitions** and communications through **mediums** are not from the spirit world but rather are projected 'personas' that can somehow interact with the **unconscious** of individuals to produce psychic phenomena.

HARUSPICY

Ancient form of **divination** where the entrails, especially the liver, of sacrificed animals, typically sheep, goat and oxen, would be examined and then burned in a sacrificial fire. The overall shape of a liver was examined, as were any discolorations or deformities. A swollen gallbladder indicated an increase in power. A depression in the liver-gate was seen as a lessening of power. Vein markings and colourings would be inspected for signs of resemblance to **symbols**, tools and weapons.

Clay models of livers dating from around 2000 BC have been found. They are divided into sections and bear markings and inscriptions. The practice evolved from Babylonian ritual and was handed down to the Greeks and Romans, who employed an official called the *haruspex* to oversee the ritual. The idea behind the practice was that when an animal, and in some cases a human, was sacrificed to a deity, the god or goddess would absorb the essence of the animal and a link was created back to the priest or priestess. When the animal was opened up they were looking into a god's mind and could therefore interpret the future or answer a question based on the size, shape and appearance of the entrails. Haruspicy is still practised today in areas of Africa, Borneo and Southeast Asia and forms part of some **black magic** rituals.

HARVARD EXIT CINEMA

Formerly a meeting hall for a women's organization, the Harvard Exit cinema opened in Seattle, Washington in 1968. There have been numerous reports of **hauntings** since the original hall was built in 1925. The cinema has been the topic of many newspapers stories and TV shows, and many **psychics** and psychical researchers have investigated the building using equipment, **medium** contacts and personal experiences. The third floor is where most of the alleged phenomena are said to occur. At least three or four female **spirits**, one or two male spirits, footsteps, laughter and a **thought form** have allegedly been identified by witnesses and researchers. The phenomena ceased around 1987.

It has been suggested that the theatre was haunted by the ghost of Seattle's first and only woman mayor – the feminist and reformer Bertha Landes. Around the time the phenomena ceased at the cinema a museum opened in downtown Seattle with objects and photographs concerning Landes on display. Newspaper accounts mention a workman at the museum reporting strange incidents and objects being moved. Some believe that Landes relocated to the museum to be close to her things, however museum officials claim no knowledge of **paranormal** or strange happenings during or after building work took place.

HAUNTING

The manifestation of strange and inexplicable phenomena said to be caused by **ghosts** and **spirits**. The phenomena include **apparitions**, unusual changes in temperature, the movement of objects, noises, smells and so on.

Only a small number of hauntings involve seeing ghosts. When they are reported they vary in appearance, sometimes resembling real people, often in period costume, while at other times appearing filmy and transparent or terrifying with body parts missing. Some ghosts always appear in the same guise while others are said to change their appearance and their age. Most hauntings involve noises such as mysterious sighs and whispers, smells such as perfume or burning wood, or sensations such as the pricking of skin, cold breezes or being touched. Some hauntings involve **poltergeist** activity, such as objects moving, or glasses smashed. Those who experience hauntings typically report receiving negative emotions such as fear, anger and hatred, but friendly ghosts have also been reported.

The term 'haunt' is believed to come from the same word root as 'home' and implies an occupation of a home or dwelling place by spirits of dead people or animals who once lived there. However, some hauntings occur at places the deceased person merely visited or liked or places where violence or death involving the deceased person occurred. In some cases there may be no association with the place at all and no apparent motivation or purpose for the haunting. Some hauntings are said to last for centuries, or to occur at roughly the same time each year, whereas others only last for a brief period of time and never manifest again. Objects as well as sites may also be haunted. For example, there are tales of haunted skulls or stones or statues that seem to cause mayhem wherever they are placed.

Not every person who visits a haunted site will experience **paranormal** phenomena. It is suggested that only those who are psychically or emotionally receptive at the time of visiting can pick up paranormal sensations.

Despite a hundred years of research and investigation from scientists and psychical researchers still very little is known about hauntings and why they occur. Several theories have been suggested but none has proved to be entirely satisfactory.

Eleanor Sidgwick, former secretary for the **Society for Psychical Research** suggested that hauntings were a form of **psychometry** – vibrations of events and emotions imprinted into a house or object. For example, a house could incorporate the feelings of its former occupants, which could then manifest as a haunting. Those who have developed her theory believe that hauntings are impressions on a psychic **ether** or **psi** force field, which can be accessed by receptive people under certain conditions. Often these hauntings seem to be 'psychic recordings' or endless re-enactments of events.

Another **spiritualist** theory suggests that hauntings happen when the spirit of a dead person or animal is trapped on earth and doesn't know how to leave. **Exorcisms** or other remedies such as **prayers** for the dead may be required to send the spirit on its way.

Psychical researcher **Frederick Myers** defined haunting as a 'manifestation of persistent personal energy', in other words, proof that some kind of energy was being transmitted after death, which was somehow connected to the dead person. Myers believed that ghosts had no intelligence or **consciousness** and were merely fragments of energy left behind by the dead person.

A popular explanation among ghost investigators is the so-called 'portal' theory. Haunting occurs at sites where there is an opening to another dimension that permits spirits to travel to the physical world. Belief in portals is age-old and numerous sacred places around the world have been thought to be gateways or entry points for spirits. Portals are also thought to open at places where there has been intense violence or trauma, such as battlefields or hospitals, as well as in lonely, deserted places or spots such as lighthouses or graveyards.

See also **Ghost investigation**.

HAWTHORNE, NATHANIEL [1804–1864]

Acclaimed American author whose preoccupation with **psychic** phenomena can be identified in his work *The House of the Seven Gables* (1851) and his short stories 'The White Old Maid' and 'Young Goodman Brown'.

Nathaniel Hawthorne was born and raised in Salem, Massachussetts, and was directly descended from John Hathorne, who had been one of the judges presiding over the infamous Salem Witch Trials. He added a 'w' to his name to disassociate himself from his family's dark past. *The House of the Seven Gables* is loosely based upon the legend of a **curse** placed on Hawthorne's family by a woman who was executed for **witchcraft** during the Salem trials and is often recommended as a classic American ghost story.

In 1840 while he was living in Boston Hawthorne reported seeing an **apparition** and told his story in 'The Ghost of Dr. Harris', which was published after his death by *Nineteenth Century* magazine. The story concerns the ghost of an old clergyman that Hawthorne believed he saw reading a newspaper in his usual seat at the Athenaeum Club a few weeks after the clergyman's death.

Hawthorne devoted a great amount of time in the later years of his life investigating the **paranormal**, questioning those who believed they had seen **ghosts** and seeking out haunted locations in the hope of witnessing a **haunting** himself. Given his devotion to the subject it seems only fitting that after his own death Hawthorne was reported to have returned from the grave to haunt his son, Julian. Julian Hawthorne, a writer himself, reported the incident, along with other supernatural stories, in his book *The Spectre of the Camera* (1915).

HEALING, FAITH AND PSYCHIC

Treatment of illness that involves the **channelling** of healing, psychic or spiritual power through the healer into another person, often involving touch or the **laying on of hands** and/or **prayer**. Some healing is instant but other patients require numerous treatment.

Religious belief is not an essential part in healing although many healers do have strong religious or spiritual beliefs. True healers believe that they themselves do not heal but simply transform, restore and balance the **universal life force**, thought to permeate and sustain all living things. An imbalance or depletion in this life force can be caused by poor diet, lifestyle habits or negative thinking and this can lead to illness and unhappiness.

Many healers are said to be born with special healing powers but it is also thought that anyone can tap into this power to some extent. Typically healing power develops at a young age, along with psychic ability such as **clairvoyance**. The healer is often drawn to healing and begins to develop his or her power through practice. Healing powers are also said to come with high spiritual attainment, through visionary experiences or through the tutelage of another healer.

In *faith healing* the healing is thought to come from God. The healer usually lays hands on the patient and becomes a kind of conduit for divine energy to transfer to the patient. Belief in faith healing has been central to all kinds of societies throughout history. It is fundamental to Christianity and despite opposition from the medical establishment remains universal among Christian prayer groups and healing circles today.

In *psychic* or *spiritual healing* there are various forms of healing. One is the sucking of disease out of the patient. **Shamans** sometimes produce objects purportedly sucked out of the body and which are said to be the cause of the illness. **Psychic surgery** also involves the removal of objects from the body. **Exorcism** is also used in healing. Perhaps the most common form of psychic healing, however, is one that involves the transfer of the universal life force through touch or the sending of healing energy through intense thought projection. The healer again becomes a kind of conduit for healing energies and may even feel something similar to heavy air leaving their body. The patient typically reports feeling a burst of new energy or tingling sensations or warmth.

There is plenty of anecdotal evidence to suggest that spiritual or psychic healing works, but how it does is unknown. It's very likely that **consciousness** plays a part. **Quantum physics** has demonstrated that matter is not static but energy, and the invisibility of this matter forms the basis of Taoist, Buddhist and Hindu healing practices. Traditional Western science holds that the universe is inert but healers reflect the non-Western view that the universe is a living entity and all things are interconnected by energy. The will of the healer may also play a part; laboratory experiments have shown that healers can speed up or slow down the growth of cancerous cells in mice through prayer or intense thought projection.

Several factors have been identified as influential – but by no means a guarantee of success – when it comes to healing. First, the presence of large amounts of universal life force; certain places, such as Lourdes in France, are thought to be bursting with healing energy. Next, an open and trusting attitude on the part of the patient is considered important as fear, distrust and guilt can act as barriers to the healing. A positive attitude on the part of the patient is also believed to make it easier for the healer to transmit energy. Thirdly, **relaxation** on the part of both healer and patient is thought to be helpful as again this helps the healer tune in and transmit energy. Fourthly, the healer must be filled with loving, positive and compassionate thoughts, and finally the healer must ask for help from a higher source and give recognition to and thanks for it.

Some healers slip into an **altered state of consciousness** or **trance** when they are healing. Psychologist Lawrence LeShan, who conducted numerous experiments in the 1960s on psychic healers, called this state of consciousness 'clairvoyant reality' – a shift in metaphysical understanding of the world. LeShan experimented with various **meditation** techniques himself to reach this level of consciousness and found that with practice clairvoyant reality could be attained and controlled to some extent. He came to the conclusion that others could be taught how to awaken their clairvoyant and healing powers.

The majority of medical and scientific opinion is sceptical of psychic healing, suggesting that the reported benefits are often psychological. However in the United

Harness the power of healing energy

Below is an exercise designed to help you bring the universal life force through you as a healing energy. Remember as you work on yourself or someone else with healing energy that you are *not* offering a substitute for medical care. It is also important to remember that you are not the healer – the universal life force is. You are simply a conduit for it.

Take a deep breath and exhale slowly. Breathe in and out until you feel yourself relax deeply. When you are ready focus on your third eye chakra and let yourself feel the universal force of peace and healing flow in through you. Let the healthy feeling of peace and healing flow through to your throat chakra and continue on until all your energy centres are open and filled with the healing universal force. Thank the universal healing force and ask that it flow through you to be passed on to the proper area of your or someone else's physical, mental or spiritual body. Ask this loving healing energy to allow the person for whom it is intended to find balance and become tuned into this universal energy. Allow the energy to flow through you in the way that works best for you. You may see it, hear it, feel it, taste or smell it. Use your senses to help you connect to the healing energy of love and peace.

Kingdom a doctor is allowed to prescribe this sort of healing, as long as a strict code of practice drawn up by the Royal College of Medicine, the General Medical Council and the Confederation of Healing Organisations (www.confederation-of-healing-organisations.org/) is adhered to. The code prevents healers from promising or claiming cures.

See also **Body scanning**, **Magnetic healing**, **Medical intuitive**, **Reiki**.

HEARN, LAFCADIO [1850–1904]

Lafcadio Hearn played a vital role in bringing the **supernatural** mysteries from China, Japan and the Far East to public attention in the West. His research on Eastern **paranormal** phenomena is recorded in two important texts: *Some Chinese Ghosts* (1897) and *In Ghostly Japan* (1899).

As well as travelling extensively in the Orient and investigating hundreds of haunted locations, Greek-born Lafcadio also spent a number of years exploring Ireland, England and the United States in search of mysteries of the paranormal, which were posthumously published in the collection titled *Fantastics* (1914).

within us all when negative thinking gets the upper hand.

See also **Purgatory** and **Limbo**.

HEAVEN

Traditionally the place where the **spirits** of good people are thought to go after death. Depending on your belief system heaven can be found within in peaceful, loving thoughts or it can be a place where the righteous, **angels** and God dwell. The ancient Greeks thought that heaven was Mount Olympus, where their deities resided, although the dead were thought to go to the **Underworld** – Olympus was only for the gods. Buddhists do not believe in a supreme being but they do believe in **nirvana**, a state of divine detachment that can be reached after enlightenment.

HELL

The opposite of **heaven**, hell is traditionally a place where wicked or evil people go in **spirit** form after death. Depending again on your belief system, hell can be a fiery pit of eternal damnation, as it is for the Christian and Islamic traditions, or a grey **underworld** as it was for the ancient Greeks, or eternal fire as it is in Jewish traditions. Jean-Paul Sartre felt that hell was other people, while some think hell exists

HELPIDIUS, DEACON [SIXTH CENTURY AD]

Possibly the first investigator on record to have been attacked by a **poltergeist** as a result of his psychical research. According to an ancient manuscript titled *Monumenta Germaniae Historica*, during the year 530 the deacon, who served as a spiritual and medical advisor to the Ostrogoth King Theodoric, was troubled by a 'diabolic infestation' after being ordered to investigate an alleged **haunting** in a local village. The deacon claimed to have been showered with small, sharp stones by a ghostly spirit on numerous occasions. A priest was summoned from Gaul to offer a blessing to relieve the activity and, according to the report in the *Monumenta Germaniae Historica*, it seems that the **exorcism** worked. The deacon was troubled no more by **ghosts** and went on to live a peaceful life.

HERMETICA/HERMETICISM

One of the foundation stones of the Western **occult** tradition. Hermeticism has its roots in the fusion of Greek philosophy and Egyptian magic that took place in Egypt

Sample extract from *The Corpus Hermeticum*

'Poemandres, the Shepherd Man', translated by G R S Mead

Note: Not all the Hermetic texts have survived and those that remain have been the subject of several translations. Mead's 1906 translation, although awkward in places, is still considered to be one of the best. Below is Mead's translation of part of the most famous of the Hermetic documents, 'Poemandres, the Shepherd Man', a revelation account describing a vision of the creation of the universe and the nature and fate of humanity.

1. It chanced once on a time my mind was meditating on the things that are, my thought was raised to a great height, the senses of my body being held back – just as men who are weighed down with sleep after a fill of food, or from fatigue of body.

Methought a Being more than vast, in size beyond all bounds, called out my name and saith: What wouldst thou hear and see, and what hast thou in mind to learn and know?

2. And I do say: Who art thou?

He saith: I am Man-Shepherd (Poemandres), Mind of all-masterhood; I know what thou desirest and I'm with thee everywhere.

3. [And] I reply: I long to learn the things that are, and comprehend their nature, and know God. This is, I said, what I desire to hear.

He answered back to me: Hold in thy mind all thou wouldst know, and I will teach thee.

4. E'en with these words His aspect changed, and straightway, in the twinkling of an eye, all things were opened to me, and I see a Vision limitless, all things turned into Light – sweet, joyous [Light]. And I became transported as I gazed.

But in a little while Darkness came settling down on part [of it], awesome and gloomy, coiling in sinuous folds, so that methought it like unto a snake.

And then the Darkness changed into some sort of a Moist Nature, tossed about beyond all power of words, belching out smoke as from a fire, and groaning forth a wailing sound that beggars all description.

[And] after that an outcry inarticulate came forth from it, as though it were a Voice of Fire.

5. [Thereon] out of the Light [...] a Holy Word (Logos) descended on that Nature. And upwards to the height from the Moist Nature leaped forth pure Fire; light was it, swift and active too.

The Air, too, being light, followed after the Fire; from out of the Earth-and-Water rising up to Fire so that it seemed to hang therefrom.

But Earth-and-Water stayed so mingled with each other, that Earth from Water no one could discern. Yet were they moved to hear by reason of the Spirit-Word (Logos) pervading them.

6. Then saith to me Man-Shepherd: Didst understand this Vision what it means?

Nay; that shall I know, said I.

That Light, He said, am I, thy God, Mind, prior to Moist Nature which appeared from Darkness; the Light-Word (Logos) [that appeared] from Mind is Son of God.

What then? – say I.

Know that what sees in thee and hears is the Lord's Word (Logos); but Mind is Father-God. Not separate are they the one from other; just in their union [rather] is it Life consists.

Thanks be to Thee, I said.

So, understand the Light [He answered], and make friends with it.

after its conquest by Alexander the Great in 332 BC.

Very little has survived of the original Hermetic schools and their teachings but mystical philosophy, ceremonial **magic**, **astrology** and **alchemy** were all part of the courses of study. The cornerstone of the Hermetic tradition is the maxim 'As above, so below', and the aim was to lead students to an experience of wisdom and rebirth in which the individual soul realized its connection with the divine power of the universe.

According to legend the wisdom is contained in 42 books, known as the Hermetica, allegedly written by Hermes Trismegistus, a philosopher-priest-king and metaphysical equivalent of the Egyptian and Greek gods Thoth and Hermes. The books were written on papyrus and stored in the great library of Alexandria. After fire destroyed the library most of the books were lost but surviving fragments,

The Corpus Hermeticum, were supposedly buried in a secret location.

In most of the texts Trismegistus's revelations are presented as a dialogue with his pupils. Surviving texts include *The Vision* and *The Divine Pymander*. *The Vision* describes Egyptian **esoteric** wisdom and the development of the **soul**. *The Divine Pymander* tells how divine wisdom was revealed to Hermes, the personification of universal wisdom and patron of magic. The legendary *Emerald Tablet*, on which Hermes is said to have recorded all of Egyptian philosophy including the magical secrets of the universe, supposedly dates back to 1200 BC but no two versions are the same.

Controversy over the age and authenticity of the Hermetica has raged for centuries. French scholar Isaac Casaubon (1559–1614) suggested that the books were not of Egyptian origin but were written by early Christians. Although occultists continued to study Hermeticism Casaubon's work, published in 1614, lead to books to be cast aside as forgeries. Modern opinions differ but most experts today believe that the writings are probably the work of a number of anonymous authors combining **Neo-Platonic**, **Kabbalistic** and Christian elements and passed off as Egyptian wisdom.

The nineteenth-century occult revival saw the reprinting of several Hermetic documents but for the most part Hermetic teachings were reinterpreted through the filters of **theosophy** and occult societies. This began to change in the 1960s, when a new generation of occultists, seeking to reclaim Western occultism's historical roots, sparked renewed interest in the Hermetica for all students of the occult mysteries. **Carl Jung** also found much of value in Hermetic writings and drew on them in his work.

HERMITAGE CASTLE

One of the most haunted castles in Scotland, located near Newcastleton, Roxburghshire.

The castle was built under the guidance of the master mason John Lewin of Durham sometime in the thirteenth century. Despite the beauty of the land surrounding it, the castle itself is isolated, dark and oppressive with only a few windows. In 1560 Mary, Queen of Scots, visited the castle and nearly died of a fever there, but the castle's most famous **ghost** is said to be that of Redcap Sly, the spirit **familiar** of evil Baron de Soulis, an early owner of the castle.

De Soulis is said to have practised **black magic** and performed sacrificial rituals using kidnapped children as victims. According to lore it was Redcap Sly, a horrible old man with long fangs, who told de Soulis that he could not be harmed unless someone used a three-stranded rope of sand. There are several versions of the Baron's demise. Some say that the villagers pleaded with wise **wizard** Thomas of Ercildoune for help and the wizard created a belt of lead, which could hold sand. The belt was put on the Baron while he was sleeping and he was imprisoned and boiled to death. Another story has de Soulis abducting the Laird of Branxholm, a crime that led to his being bound in a sheet of lead and then boiled to death. Others say his victims' enraged parents stormed the castle and attacked de Soulis.

Many psychical researchers believe that tragic deaths can leave a residue of feeling or **psychic** imprint in which the acts are forever replayed as if burned into the atmosphere of the place. The castle is now a tourist attraction and visitors continue to report hearing screams of the young murder victims coming from inside the building.

HERNE THE HUNTER

Ghostly huntsmen appear in German and French folklore but perhaps the most well known in Europe is Herne the Hunter, who allegedly haunts the forest of Windsor Great Park near Windsor Castle in England. He is said to appear riding a spectral black horse and to have stag's antlers growing from his head.

According to legend Herne was once a royal huntsman of King Richard II who saved the King by throwing himself in front of him when a wounded stag lunged towards the King. As he lay dying a **wizard** appeared and told the King that if the stag's horns were cut off and tied on to Herne he would be saved. The King did as instructed and Herne recovered. He became the King's favourite for many years and was lavished with gifts, until other jealous huntsmen persuaded the King to cast him aside. Unable to cope without the King's support the devastated Herne hanged himself from the branch of an oak tree in the park. He is said to have haunted the forest ever since.

The story of Herne the Hunter may have much older **Pagan** roots and his horns give him the appearance of Cernunnos the Celtic horned god of fertility, the hunt and the dead. Herne is also one of the deities worshipped in **Wicca** and is the archetypal nature god who appears as a stag or bull and is sacrificed each year to symbolize the cycle of life, death and rebirth.

It is said that Herne the Hunter appears in times of crisis, and there were alleged sightings of him prior to the Great Depression, and again before World War II.

HEX

From the German *hexe* meaning 'witch', a hex is a **spell** or bewitchment. It is typically used to describe a spell or **curse** that is negative or evil and can also mean to practise **black magic** or **sorcery**.

HIDDEN MASTERS

According to **Madame Blavatsky**, in her classic book *Isis Unveiled* (1887), the hidden masters were an **esoteric** brotherhood of superhuman beings hidden in the Himalayan fastness of Tibet who watched over the welfare of humanity.

Blavatsky claimed to have met the hidden masters face to face and to have been chosen to bring the news of their existence to the West. With the assistance of newspaper editor Mr A P Sinnett, letters of two members of the brotherhood were published outlining their worldview.

Blavatsky's hidden masters were a part of the Eastern esoteric tradition. There is, however, a western esoteric tradition that propounds a similar doctrine. This tradition first came to light in the Renaissance with a pamphlet entitled *Fama fraternitatis* outlining the existence of a secret **Rosicrucian** brotherhood of masters who were watching over the welfare of Europe. The concept came to the fore again in the nineteenth century, with members of the Hermetic Order of the **Golden Dawn** claiming that secret chiefs adept in the **occult** arts and interested in the welfare of humanity were overseeing the running of the order and the doctrines it preached. These secret chiefs spent most of their time in **spirit** form but would incarnate in physical form for special missions.

Dion Fortune insisted on the existence of hidden masters – she called them Inner Plane Adepti – running her own society. She felt, however, that they existed chiefly on the **astral plane** and rarely took on physical form. Her society used trance **mediums** to communicate instructions from them.

Numerous other occult and mystical societies claim to be guided by one or more hidden masters.

HIGHER SELF

A concept that is common in **esoteric** thought, particularly in connection with **intuition** and **psychic** development. In religion it is often thought of as the conscience or the spark of divinity within. The concept of the higher self is frequently linked with the theory of **reincarnation** and the belief that there is a part of us that has been alive before: personalities that are incarnated are facets of but one individual.

The term 'higher self' or 'higher consciousness' refers to the concept that each of us has a part of ourselves that is thought to act as a bridge between the spiritual and the mental and physical dimensions of our awareness. Simply put, there is a part of us that is a reservoir of higher wisdom that can help guide us through our lives. This part of us is better able to see the bigger picture of the daily dramas we get tangled up in and can help bring us perspective. Acting with the guidance of our higher self can lead us in the direction of our greatest fulfilment.

Psychics believe that the higher self communicates by sending messages through the psychic senses. Developing your psychic potential will help strengthen your connection to your higher self and allow you to communicate with it more efficiently.

There is growing evidence from psychology for the existence of a higher self. When patients with multiple personality disorder are researched it's often the case that one personality is more mature, intelligent and developed than the others, and some psychologists believe there are elements of multiple personality in all of us. Dr Eric Berne's Transactional Analysis, for example, arranges the personality into three different types of self. Occultist Colin Wilson developed the theory of a hierarchy of selves presided over by a mature and developed self that can take charge with 'an act of will'.

HILDEGARD OF BINGEN [1098–1179]

Christian abbess who experienced religious **visions** after years of contemplation in a Benedictine convent. In spite of poor health Hildegard was an incredibly strong woman, founding two convents, getting involved in ecclesiastical politics, travelling extensively and writing nine books as well as numerous poems, songs and plays.

The first major mystic to emerge from Germany Hildegard became known as 'the Sibyl of the Rhine'. She is best known for her mystical illuminations, which she chronicled in detail from 1140 to 1157. Her work survives to this day and is considered remarkable for its understanding of and empathy for the natural world. Hildegard believed that every part of nature was divine and that plants, animals, trees and stones had healing powers. Central to her work is the idea in her first book, entitled *Scivias*, that God is the living light: 'All Living creatures are, so to speak, sparks from the radiance of God's brilliance, and these sparks emerge from God like rays in the sun.'

HIPPOMANCY

An ancient form of **divination** using horses that was especially popular among the Dark Age Celts of England and Ireland, who would keep white horses in a consecrated, sacred circle of trees for this purpose. The horses would be hitched to a sacred cart and made to walk straight. The toss of the horse's head, the spontaneous prancing, the leading with left or right foreleg, the neighing and movement of the horse as it pulled the cart would then be interpreted to predict the most likely outcome of events in the future. When the horse was released back to the sacred circle

it was noted whether a horse crossed the line of the circle with left or right leg. The right leg was regarded as propitious, the left leg as foretelling inauspicious events.

HOFDI POLTERGEIST

In early October 1986 Hofdi House, located on the outskirts of Reykjavik, Iceland, was thought to be the most haunted house in the world. The house was the designated meeting place for US President Ronald Regan and Soviet President Mikhail Gorbachev, and with its history of alleged **poltergeist** activity press and TV networks anticipated possible disturbances. When none took place the media lost interest and investigation showed that, apart from stories of objects moving and strange noises, the so-called poltergeist had never been very active.

There are various stories concerning the haunted reputation of Hofdi House. One tells of poet and government employee Einar Benedictsson, who was called upon to investigate the murder of a baby produced by brother-sister incest. On the day of her investigation the sister killed herself, dying an agonizing death by poison in the presence of Benedictsson. After that Benedictsson claimed to be haunted by her **spirit**, who followed him as he moved around the country. In 1914 he bought Hofdi House and reported unusual happenings to his friends.

The British ambassador to Iceland reported disturbances as his reason for selling Hofdi House in the 1940s. The house was subsequently bought by the city of Reykjavik for use in official receptions; members of staff did report incidents such as a bottle of wine flying out of the fridge and pictures falling off walls. The disturbances ceased when a member of staff reported that a spirit had appeared to her in a **dream** and told her the disturbances would stop.

HOLISM/HOLISTIC MEDICINE/ HOLISTIC THERAPY

From the Greek word *holos* meaning 'whole', the holistic approach refers to a philosophy or therapy that aims to treat the whole person – mind, body and spirit – rather than just the symptoms or problems they are manifesting. To holistic therapists the underlying cause of the illness may not be physical but emotional, mental or spiritual, so it is pointless just treating the physical symptoms.

A holistic practitioner will encourage patients to take an active part in their recovery with lifestyle and diet changes, and/or a change in thinking patterns or patterns of belief. Body treatments such as **massage, reflexology** or **acupuncture** or remedies from herbalism or **homeopathy** may also be administered. When it comes to non-critical illnesses holistic therapies can have a higher rate of success in some instances than orthodox remedies.

HOME CIRCLE

Also known as home sitting. This is a **séance** that is held in a private home, typically with a **medium** present but not always. The main purpose of a home circle is to communicate with **spirits**. Participants usually sit around a circular table holding hands or linking fingers, or place their hands flat on the tabletop. A table is not always necessary as some just sit in a circle.

HOME, DANIEL DUNGLAS [1833–1886]

Considered by some to be one of the greatest **mediums** in the history of modern **spiritualism**, Daniel Home was renowned for his incredible feats of **physical mediumship**.

Home was born in Edinburgh on 20 March 1833. His mother was a clairvoyant and claimed to be descended from the seventeenth-century Brahan Seer, Kenneth MacKenzie. Home's remarkable powers were said to be present almost from birth when his aunt reported that his cradle rocked by itself as if pushed by a **spirit**. He had his first **vision** at the age of 13, when he saw his boyhood friend at the moment the friend died far away. His second vision came four years later in 1850 when he predicted accurately the death of his mother.

From that time onwards Home's thoughts turned more and more to the spirit world. He went to live with an aunt,

Mary Cook, in Norwich, Connecticut. **Rappings** began in her home and Cook blamed Home for bringing the devil into her house. She appealed in turn to a Congregationalist, a Baptist and a Wesleyan minister for **exorcism**. The ministers, however, backed Home and were convinced that he had a God-given gift. This support marked the turning point in his life. He had a vision of his dead mother – as he would do many times in his life – and she told him not to be afraid and to use his gift for the good of others.

Mary Cook threw Home out of her house, and from then on he lived on the hospitality of friends attracted by his curious gift. Avoiding contact with other mediums, because he felt he had nothing to learn from them, Home held **séances** in lighted rooms, which was the opposite of the usual custom of holding them in rooms that were darkened. He allegedly produced rapping, spectral lights and ghost hands which shook hands with the people present. He also moved objects and produced visions of ghostly guitars playing music. He was seen to stretch his body by 11 inches to 6½ feet tall while his feet were on the floor, or shrink to 5-foot tall, with his shoes disappearing into his trousers. Guests were often asked to hold him to prove that he was not a **fraud**.

Home was 19 when he experienced his first **levitation** in a Connecticut home. He reportedly rose a foot or so off the ground and bobbed up and down before hitting the ceiling. Later he would be able to control his levitations better, with some witnesses reporting that he could fly. Home claimed to be able to perform his feats with the help of friendly spirits who came and went as they pleased. The most reliable spirit was called Bryan.

In 1855 Home travelled to Europe and England and began associating with royalty and the rich and famous. He became a popular but controversial figure in the media and his supporters included **Sir Arthur Conan Doyle** and Elizabeth Barrett Browning. In France he had an audience with Napoleon III and the Empress Eugenie. The Emperor had serious doubts about Home but these were dispelled when Home produced the spirit of Napoleon Bonaparte. In addition to his many admirers there were also many who despised and doubted Home, which may have had more to do with his mood swings and alleged homosexual leanings than his **psychic** abilities. His detractors included the noted scientist David Brewster and the poet Robert Browning, who so disliked him that he wrote a poem about him called 'Mr Sludge, The Medium'.

In 1867 Home reached a low point in his career when a wealthy widow, Mrs Lyon, aged 75 years old, filed a suit against him. In the previous year Home had taken the Lyon family name and had received £60,000 pounds in cash and securities on the alleged instructions of the dead Mr Lyon to Mrs Lyon in a series of séances held by Home. The trial was a tawdry affair with Mrs Lyon implying that she and Home had been more than affectionate friends, but when Home made advances she was so repulsed she decided she wanted her money back. The court found in Mrs Lyon's favour and denounced spiritualism as 'mischievous nonsense, well calculated on the one hand to delude the vain, the weak, the foolish and the superstitious.'

After the trial Home's supporters deserted him. He responded by producing some of his most remarkable psychic feats while in a state of **trance**, including levitation, carrying red-hot coals and putting the top of his head into a fire without being burned. To support himself financially Home toured England and Scotland reading poetry, and in 1871 he married a wealthy Russian widow, Julie de Gloumeline.

From 1871 to 1873 Home began a series of experiments with **Sir William Crookes**, a scientist and psychical researcher. To see if Home's abilities were genuine the scientist wrapped an accordion with copper wire and placed it in a wire cage. He also ran an electric current through the wire to block any electromagnetic force from Home. Somehow Home was still able to make the accordion play without touching it. Despite criticism from his scientific peers, Crookes came to the conclusion that Home possessed independent psychic powers. The scientist summed up his opinion as follows:

During the whole of my knowledge of D D Home, extending for several years, I never once saw the slightest occurrence that would make me suspicious that he was attempting to play tricks. He was scrupulously sensitive on this point, and never felt hurt at anyone taking precautions against deception. To those who knew him Home was one of the most lovable of men and his perfect genuineness and uprightness were beyond suspicion.

Home announced his retirement as a medium soon after the experiments with Sir William Crookes concluded. Suffering from poor health he spent the rest of his life travelling and died of tuberculosis on 21 June 1886 in Auteuil, France. Home's published works include an exposé of fraudulent mediumistic techniques, *Light and Shadows of Spiritualism* (1877), and two autobiographies – *Incidents in my Life* (1862) and *Incidents in my Life – 2nd Series* (1872).

Lord Adare, Earl of Dunraven, describes Home's character thus, in the 1925 edition of *Experiences in Spiritualism with D D Home*:

He had the defects of an emotional character, with vanity highly developed (perhaps wisely to enable him to hold his own against the ridicule and obloquy that was then poured out upon spiritualism and everyone connected with it). He was liable to fits of great depression and to nervous crises difficult at first to understand; but he was withal of a simple, kindly, humorous, lovable disposition that appealed to me. He never took money for séances failed as often as not. He was proud of his gift but not happy in it. He could not control it and it placed him sometimes in very unpleasant positions. I think he would have been pleased to have been relieved of it, but I believe he was subject to these manifestations as long as he lived.

There is little doubt that Home was charismatic and clever, but was his psychic ability genuine? The jury is still out. Rumours abounded that Home produced his **paranormal** feats through trickery though none was ever proved and nobody, not even the great **Harry Houdini** himself, was able to duplicate them.

Frank Podmore, a most sceptical psychical researcher, says of Home in his *Modern Spiritualism*:

A remarkable testimony to Home's ability whether as medium or simply as conjurer, is the position which he succeeded in maintaining in society at this time (1861) and indeed throughout his later life, and the respectful treatment accorded to him by many leading organs of the Press. No money was ever taken by him as the price of a sitting; and he seemed to have had the entrée to some of the most aristocratic circles in Europe. He was welcomed in the houses of our own and of foreign nobility, was a frequent guest at the Tuilleries, and had been received by the King of Prussia and the Czar. So strong, indeed, was his position that he was able to compel an ample apology from a gentleman who had publicly expressed doubts of his mediumistic performance (Capt. Noble in the *Sussex Advertiser* of March 23, 1864) and to publish a violent and spiteful attack upon Browning on the occasion of the publication of Sludge (*Spiritual Magazine*, 1864, p. 315). His expulsion from Rome in 1864 on the charge of sorcery gave to Home for the time an international importance.

He further stated: 'Home was never publicly exposed as an impostor; there is no evidence of any weight that he was even privately detected in trickery.'

Between the publication of his *Modern Spiritualism* and *The Newer Spiritualism* in 1910, Podmore did manage to discover one piece of evidence against Home. A letter sent to Podmore from a witness at a séance claimed to have noticed Home's shoulder sink or rise in concordance with the movements of a spirit hand. Podmore seized on this flimsy testimony as evidence of trickery, but even though he finally came to the conclusion that Home was more conjuror than medium, Podmore was at a loss to explain how some of the things were done and, in his own words, he left the subject, 'with an almost painful sense of bewilderment'.

HOMEOPATHY

One of the most well known and widely practised systems of **alternative medicine** in the modern world, homeopathy has been heavily influenced by **occult** traditions at numerous times during its history.

Originally founded by German physician Samuel Hahnemann (1755–1843), who discovered that substances that caused disease symptoms in large doses could cure diseases with similar symptoms when given in small doses. Thus the basic principle of homeopathy, 'like is cured by like', was born. Hahnemann claimed to have discovered homeopathy from his own experimentation, but footnotes in his research show that he was familiar with the writings of certain alchemists.

There are four basic principles to classic homeopathy:

1. The law of similars, or like cures like.
2. Minimum dose – the right dilution of the right substance. The more diluted

the solution the more potent it is thought to be.

3. The single remedy – the one substance that most closely models the disease's symptoms is the right remedy. (Modern homeopaths have supplanted this with a more accurate mix of several remedies.)

4. The whole person is treated, not just the symptoms.

The reason for the **holistic** approach is that homeopaths believe a vital force (similar to the **universal life force**) is alive in each person, and that their remedies work because the correct potions vibrate at the same resonance as the individual, which stimulates the immune system.

The idea of sympathetic energy explains why homeopaths ask so many questions of their patients: in order to prescribe the right remedy they need to determine which one of the 15 constitutional types is predominant in a personality. Even though homeopathy defies orthodox medical conventions several controlled, double-blind experiments have verified its effectiveness.

Hahnemann's work was carried on and developed by a number of other practitioners, most notably Dr Constantine Herring (1849–1916) who gave practitioners a framework to match remedies to personality types. In the late nineteenth and early twentieth centuries homeopathy became closely associated with the followers of **Emanuel Swedenborg**. With the decline of orthodox dominance over medicine, homeopathy has become commonplace in the Western world, but its occult connections remain largely unrecognized in the alternative medicine and magical communities.

HOMER [APPROX 1200 BC]

Celebrated Greek poet best remembered for *The Illiad* and *The Odyssey*. Little is known for sure about Homer's life but it is thought he was born and raised a Greek citizen in Asia Minor sometime around 1200 BC, although historians disagree as to the exact date, not to mention whether there was ever one particular poet called Homer at all. There is no doubt, however, that 'Homer' frequently wrote about **ghosts** and **spirits**, particularly in his epic *The Odyssey*, where he describes 'thin airy shoals of visionary ghosts', and had a strong belief in them. Stories suggest that he would often go to extraordinary lengths to investigate reports of haunted sites during his travels.

HOPE, WILLIAM [1863–1933]

Famous **spirit photographer** thought to be genuine by some but a **fraud** by others.

Born in Crewe, England in 1863, Hope first discovered his talent for spirit photography in 1905 when he took a photograph of a friend and an image of his friend's dead sister emerged on the photograph. Soon after this Hope formed a spirit photography group in the local Spiritualist Hall called the **Crewe Circle**. The group was given significant credence when Archdeacon Thomas Colley became a member.

Hope's reputation grew and he moved to London. The **Society for Psychical Research** sent researcher **Harry Price** to investigate him. Price claimed he found evidence of trickery but his accusations backfired when questions arose as to whether it was Price, not Hope, who had doctored the photographic plates of alleged spirit photographs under investigation.

Hope had his supporters and his detractors. He was often accused of fraud but was never caught openly in trickery. There was, however, reason to suspect trickery in the case of one of his supporters, **Sir William Crookes**. Crookes's assistant, J H Gardner, told Crookes's biographer that a photograph Hope produced with an image of Crookes's recently deceased wife showed clear signs of double exposure, but the grieving Crookes chose to ignore these signs.

HOPKINS, ROBERT THURSTON [1884–1958]

A professional photographer by trade, British-born Robert Thurston Hopkins was a dedicated psychical researcher and ghost hunter. He claimed to have seen many **ghosts** himself and recorded his experiences, alongside fictional short stories, in his books *War and the Weird* (1916), *Adventures with Phantoms* (1947), *Ghosts Over England* (1953), *The World's Strangest Ghost Stories* (1955) and *Cavalcade of Ghosts* (1956).

HOROSCOPE

In **astrology** a map of the heavens at a specific point in time which displays the positions of the planets in the signs of the **zodiac**. Where a person was born is thought to be just as significant as the time they were born at, as the date and time determine the sun sign, but the place determines where the other planets lie on the horoscope. Astrologers interpret the positions of the various planets and their relationship to a person's sun sign to determine personality characteristics and to make predictions for the future.

The most common horoscope is the birth chart, which determines what a person's sun sign is, but horoscopes can be drawn to determine the most favourable conditions and date for any event.

HORSE

Sacred and revered around the world, horses have been associated with the mystical, spiritual and **paranormal** for centuries. The Celts believed horses carried souls to the underworld. In the Hindu *Brihadaranyaka* the horse is the symbol for the cosmos. The Greek goddesses Aphrodite, Artemis and Demeter were associated with horses. In various shamanic cultures the horse is a mystical **symbol** and in **witchcraft** lore horses are vulnerable to bewitchment. According to psychiatrist **Carl Jung** the horse represents the intuitive part of humanity and in **dreams** the horse is often thought to be an archetypal symbol of the human body.

Along with cats and dogs, horses are believed to be the most **psychic** of animals. There are many stories of horses sensing danger and saving their riders. In the late 1920s an American horse named Lady mystified psychical researchers with her reputed ability to tap out **precognitive** messages that allegedly predicted the entry of the United States and the Soviet Union into World War II and the presidential victory of Harry Truman.

Hot reading

A reading in which the **medium** or **psychic** has been given prior knowledge of the person they are doing the reading for, often employed for devious or fraudulent means. Compare **Cold reading**.

Hotel del Coronado

Resort hotel off the coast of San Diego, California that is said to be haunted by the **ghost** of a woman who died there in November 1893.

There are many versions of the story but the ghost is thought to be that of Kate Morgan, who checked into the hotel on 24 November under the name of Lottie A Bernard. She was given room 3312. Her husband, Tom, a card shark, did not arrive

as expected. Apparently the couple had quarrelled on the way to the hotel, when Tom was surprised by news of Kate's pregnancy, and he had got off the train agreeing to meet her there.

Kate waited for two days. She then took a ferry to San Diego where she bought a .44 calibre gun. The next day she was found dead on the steps of the hotel's north entrance. In her hand was the gun with one bullet missing and suicide was assumed, even though the bullet that killed her was from a .40 calibre gun. The mystery of her death remained unsolved, and a maid in room 3502 who had taken care of Kate disappeared the day after the funeral. Even though Tom was never seen at the hotel, the most likely explanation is that Tom killed his wife and perhaps the maid too as she may have been a witness.

Another version of the story has Kate married to a different man – a womanizing gambler called Lou. The couple checked into room 3502 and when Kate went to the gaming room to surprise her husband with news of her pregnancy she found him with another woman. In shock she killed herself.

Whether Kate was murdered or committed suicide, the **apparition** of Kate has been reported on numerous times moving through corridors or standing by windows waiting for someone. Guests that stay overnight in rooms 3312 and 3502 (especially 3502) report voices whispering and feel cold chills and a presence in their room. Other guests in the hotel report problems with their telephones and strange images on their television screens.

Houdini, Harry [1874–1926]

History's greatest escape artist, **magician** and master illusionist, Houdini (who was born Erich Weiss in Budapest, Hungary), became fascinated with the **supernatural** very early on in life. He was particularly interested in **spiritualism** and gained a reputation in the **paranormal** community for his work in exposing fraudulent **mediums** who used trickery and technology to hoax fee-paying spectators.

In a career that spanned 26 years Houdini performed the most spectacular feats ever witnessed: escaping from ropes in ice-cold water, emerging from seemingly impossible confines, hanging from ropes off tall buildings and then freeing himself, even escaping from being buried alive. There seemed to be no contraption or device that could hold him.

Throughout his life Houdini wanted to believe in spiritualism but was never convinced that it was genuine. This was particularly the case when his mother died. Houdini had been exceptionally close to his mother and after her death searched desperately for a way to contact her in the spirit world. In 1920 he met and struck up a friendship with **Sir Arthur Conan Doyle**, who was convinced that Houdini had **psychic** powers himself, but the friendship broke down a few years later because Doyle was upset by Houdini's refusal to believe. After attending countless **séances** and exposing numerous mediums as **frauds**, Houdini published *A Magician Among the Spirits* (1924), in which he stated that he could not find any genuine evidence of spirit **materialization**.

Despite his work in exposing charlatans preying upon those willing to put their trust in mediums, Houdini always maintained that he had an open mind. Before his death Houdini and his devoted wife, Bess, worked out a code using their mind-reading secrets that would convince her that he had succeeded in coming back.

After Houdini's death in 1926 mediums claiming communications from Houdini besieged Bess and in 1929 she attended a séance with **Arthur Ford**, pastor of the first Spiritualist Church of New York. Fletcher, Ford's **control**, produced the communication, 'Rosabelle, believe.' Bess immediately confirmed that this was the password she had worked out with her husband prior to his death and **spiritualists** rejoiced that Houdini the sceptic had joined forces with them in death.

A few years later Bess retracted her statement when she discovered that radio mentalist, Joseph Dunninger, had read Houdini's code word in a 1927 biography. She condemned Ford and mediums in general. Despite this condemnation she continued to hold séances in an attempt to reach Houdini. He remained silent and Bess, like her husband, was never successful in conveying the message that there really is a life beyond this one.

Hull House

In 1913, Hull House, now a museum, was thought to be the home of a 'devil baby'. Even today visitors still report feeling uncomfortable when touring the museum and the story of Hull House was the inspiration for Ira Levin's 1967 novel *Rosemary's Baby*, in which a young woman gives birth to the devil's child.

Hull House was built in 1856 in the south-western suburbs of Chicago. By the late 1880s it had became a settlement house for immigrants and later a refuge for the poor, abused and homeless established by social workers Jane Addams and Ellen Gates Starr. In 1913 crowds of women descended on Hull House demanding to see a so-called devil baby. The perplexed and surprised Addams explained over and over again that there was no such baby in the house, but still the visitors came.

On interviewing the women Addams discovered that the rumours were based on the superstitious fears of the immigrant women. There were numerous ethnic versions of the story. For instance, in one Jewish version a husband and father of several daughters tells his wife that he would rather his wife gave birth to the devil than another daughter. In an Italian version a woman marries an atheist who tells her he would rather have the devil in the house than a picture of the Virgin Mary.

Eventually the rumour mill stopped turning and the exhausted Addams wrote about her experience in her book *The Second Twenty Years at Hull House*. In it she suggests that the story appealed to immigrant women who felt outsiders in America and the devil baby story was something they could relate to.

The devil baby legend has refused to go away. Sightings continue to this day of a devil baby glimpsed in an attic window at Hull House. Addams's **ghost** and the ghost of a woman who allegedly committed suicide in an upstairs bedroom are also thought to haunt the house.

HUNA

An ancient system of healing magic of the Hawaiian Islands that can be summarized by seven principles: the world is what you think it is; there are no limits; energy flows where your attention is; now is your moment of power; to love is to be happy with; all power comes from within; and effectiveness is the measure of truth.

Huna means 'that which is hidden or not obvious'. The tradition nearly died out as a result of Christianization by Westerners in the eighteenth century but it was revived in the last century. Initiated practitioners are known as kahunas, the 'Keepers of the Secret', and there is evidence to show that they exhibit unusual **psychic** powers: they are able to cure or curse, develop immunity to fire, see into the future and even raise the **spirits** of the dead. Like all psychic **healers**, kahuna are thought to be conduits of *mana*, the Huna concept similar to the **universal life force**. Kahunas consider psychic ability natural to all people and cultivate **psi** abilities, including **telepathy**, **clairvoyance**, **precognition** and **psychokinesis**. Magical skills are gained from mental disciplines and use of *mana*.

In the early twentieth century, Max Freedom Long devoted 36 years to the study of Huna and published six classic books on the subject. Long came to the conclusion that Huna contained a system of ancient magic based on a sophisticated model of the human **psyche**.

HUNCH

A sense or feeling based more on **intuition** than on logic or hard facts. People with **psychic** ability often say they make decisions based on hunches rather than on facts or evidence available to them.

HURKOS, PETER [1911–1988]

Professional **psychic** who became famous for his work with the police during the 1960s. He is perhaps best known for his involvement with the Charles Manson murders in 1969.

Hurkos was born in Dordrecht in the Netherlands on 21 May 1911. He didn't exhibit psychic talent until July 1941 when a brain operation saved his life after he fell from a ladder and slipped into a coma. When he awoke from the coma he claimed he was psychic and could hear noises in his head. He discovered an ability to play the piano, having never played before, and was able to tell others personal information and predict deaths. Later Hurkos stated that he had had a **near-death experience** while in his coma. He found himself sucked up into a great

pyramid of light where a jury of bearded men told him he had not finished his work on earth and that he now had great power in him and must use it for good. He was also told that he would hear music from the otherworld and would be able to play it on the piano.

In 1946 Hurkos attended a psychic demonstration and performed better than the psychic on stage. The theatre immediately offered him a contract and his fame spread. In 1947 he took on his first detective case. The method he used for solving crimes was **psychometry**. He claimed to get the strongest energy vibrations from clothing but he also worked with locks of hair, nail clippings and from photographs. He said that he could hear voices speaking to him when he touched the items. He would often sleep with the items and awake with information.

In 1956 Dr Andrija Puharich, a neurologist and parapsychologist, brought Hurkos to the United States to test his powers. He was also tested by **parapsychology** researchers Charles T Tart and Jeffrey Smith, who found no evidence of **ESP** in his readings of hair samples. Despite this, and the fact that his career had more lows than highs, Hurkos stayed in America and gained celebrity status. William Belk, who financed Puharich's experiments, lost money in uranium searches based on Hurkos's advice, and in the Boston Strangler case Hurkos failed to identify Albert DeSalvo, who confessed to the killings. In the Charles Manson case Hurkos did get the name Charlie and was able to describe ritualistic killings by a gang preoccupied with sex and drugs, but after two weeks of working on the case he was dismissed for unknown reasons.

Hurkos predicted he would die on 17 November 1961, but in fact he died of a heart attack in Los Angeles on 25 May 1988.

HUXLEY, ALDOUS [1894–1963]

Internationally respected English novelist and essayist, noted for his social and political insights and interest in Eastern philosophy and **mysticism**. His experimentation with **drugs** had an impact on the psychedelic drug movement in the 1960s.

Huxley had a keen interest in the **psychic** and **paranormal** and in 1952 wrote *The Devils of Loudun* – the definitive study of the diabolic possession of Ursuline Convent nuns in seventeenth-century France, which formed the basis of Ken Russell's film, *The Devils*. His thoughts on the use of psychedelic drugs and mysticism can be found in two essays: *The Doors of Perception* (1954) and *Heaven and Hell* (1956). He naively believed that drugs, such as mescalin and LSD, could reduce the efficiency of the brain as a filter and allow an escape from selfhood and a wider perception of reality to flow through.

HUXLEY, SIR JULIAN [1887–1975]

British biologist noted for his ability to make complex scientific concepts accessible to the general public through his writings and public lectures. Brother of noted author **Aldous Huxley**, Julian's intellectual gifts and scientific credentials led to his appointment as the first director-general of UNESCO. A staunch atheist who embraced humanism, Huxley nonetheless joined the London **Ghost Club** and contributed his incredible scientific expertise and credentials to the Club's quest for better understanding of the world of **ghosts** and **spirits**.

HYDROMANCY

From the Greek *hudro*, 'water', and *manteia*, 'divination', hydromancy is an ancient form of **divination** by means of water or rain. Most cultures considered water to be pure and sacred and because of this quality it was thought to have the ability to reveal the truth about a person or situation.

Several methods were used to draw conclusions. Typically the speed of the water, the ripples and the colour would all be studied and interpreted. A stone might be dropped into water and the number of circles formed counted. A ring might be suspended by a string and dropped into a container of water. The number of times the ring struck the side of the container and the number of ripples it created when it hit the water would all be counted and interpreted.

Another method of hydromancy was to study the actions of the sea and interpret it by its movement and colour. There was also divination using rivers and fountains; for example, the fountains of Palicorus in Sicily were some of the most famous for consultation.

Hydromancy is probably the cruel inspiration behind the gruesome seventeenth-century practice of throwing suspected **witches** or criminals into water to prove or disprove themselves guilty of a crime or **witchcraft**. It was a lose-lose situation for the victims: if they sank and drowned they were declared innocent because the water would only claim those with a pure heart; if they floated they were declared guilty and condemned to death.

HYDROTHERAPY

The use of water to ease stress and heal illness. The healing powers of water have been known throughout history and every culture has tales of sacred fountains and pools with healing powers. Bathing, for example, was an important therapy for the ancient Greeks, Egyptians, Native Americans and Indians.

Medical research has shown that nerves stimulated at the surface of the body by blasts of hot or cold water can boost the immune system, decrease the production of stress hormones, relieve pain and invigorate circulation. Spiritually **water** is consid-

ered to be one of the most important substances in life with positive energetic qualities and is often used by healers to help balance the flow of **universal life energy** in those who are sick or ailing.

HYPNAGOGIC STATE

The hypnagogic state is that state between being awake and falling asleep, where the mind is most receptive to ideas, images, sounds, feelings, impressions and **intuition**. It should not be confused with the *hypnopompic* state, which is the corresponding transition state of semi-consciousness between sleeping and waking, i.e. when a person is waking up.

Some believe that the sketchy **imagery** that occurs in these states can be helpful to the individual in terms of self-understanding. Images are often presented through the individual's own set of **symbols** and once interpreted, symbols can provide answers to problems and even alert one to future events. Some believe that taking the time to record these images, feelings and sounds can be as helpful as recording **dream** imagery.

HYPNOSIS

A state of intense concentration or **altered state of consciousness** when a person can be more receptive to new ideas and suggestion and display heightened **psychic** awareness.

The technique of hypnosis has been known and used for centuries – it was practised in ancient Greece and Egypt and even earlier in ancient India. The term itself comes from Hypnos, the Greek God of Sleep, and was first used in 1842 by James Braid, an English surgeon.

The eighteenth century's **Franz Anton Mesmer** is often referred to as an early exponent of hypnosis. Mesmer believed he was using a mysterious force he called 'animal magnetism' to heal his patients. His techniques included the **laying on of hands** and staring fixedly in the eyes. Animal magnetism became popular in Europe with magnetized patients, or 'somnambules' as they were referred to, reporting that they felt no pain during surgery. In 1818 D Valenski, a surgeon and professor of physiology at the Imperial Academy of St Petersburg, described Mesmer's animal magnetism as the most important physical discovery in several centuries.

Side effects of Mesmer's techniques often included 'higher phenomena' such as **clairvoyance**, **telepathy** and other **psi** phenomena. Mesmer had little interest in these higher phenomena, preferring to focus on the healing. However, other 'mesmerists' began to investigate them and to exhibit them in public.

In the 1840s medical practitioner James Braid set out to expose animal magnetism as fraud. However, when he used the technique on his own patients with great success he was forced to revise his opinions. Braid noticed how similar the **trance** state and sleep were, and coined the term 'hypnotism' to describe it. The name has remained even though hypnosis is actually a very natural state of mind that never involves sleep. Individuals do not even lose consciousness. Braid also discovered that Mesmer's techniques of fixed stares and waving or laying on of hands were not needed. Patients could enter a state of hypnosis by staring at a light or by suggestion alone.

Until chloroform was developed in 1848 hypnosis was frequently used to relieve the pain and discomfort of illness and surgery. Interest revived in the later nineteenth century when American and English psychical research societies began investigating the psi phenomena associated with it, and when its potential as a therapeutic tool in medicine was once again recognized.

From the 1940s onwards research has shown that hypnosis can enhance performance in psi games, especially if positive suggestions are made that it can. It has also been shown that hypnosis can help enhance memory and learning and form part of a treatment plan for psychological disorders and behaviour modification (see **hypnotherapy**). Hypnosis is often used by **mediums** to communicate with **spirits** and is the preferred method for **past-life recall**.

Individual response to hypnosis can vary enormously. It is thought that the majority of the population – around 85 per cent – can be hypnotized, although only a small percentage can achieve deep trance. Several steps seem essential to achieving an altered state. These include deep **relaxation**, concentration, turning inwards, focusing on specific sounds, words or

Self-hypnosis exercise

Self-hypnosis is a useful tool you can use to help you achieve your goals in any area of your life:

1. Find a place where you can get some peace and quiet for five or ten minutes. Take off your watch and turn off your mobile.
2. When you are ready, get comfortable and close your eyes. Take a few deep breaths and tell yourself that you are relaxed and are going to go into a light trance.
3. Begin to imagine yourself at the top of a set of stairs. There are 20 steps in front of you and each time you step down you feel yourself becoming more and more relaxed.
4. When you reach the bottom of the stairs you are in a deep state of relaxation. Say to yourself the following: 'I listen to and act on my intuition and/or inner guidance.'
5. Spend a minute or so in your trance. Then tell yourself, 'At the count of 20, I will be fully awake, open to my intuition and feel terrific.' Count from 1 to 20 and when you reach 20, say 'My eyes are open' and open your eyes.

You may prefer to read this exercise into a tape recorder. Then you can listen to your self-hypnosis tape whenever you want. If you practise this exercise every day, not only are you more likely to get better at self-hypnosis but you're also likely to find yourself more in tune with your intuition.

images and choosing to change one's conscious state. There also appear to be three major stages of hypnosis: light, in which the individual feels lethargic but aware of what is going on around them; cataleptic, in which the muscles become tense; and somnambulistic, which is a state of deep trance where the subject can be manipulated by the suggestions of the hypnotist and experience psi phenomena.

Contrary to popular belief hypnosis cannot be used to force people to do things against their will. In a sense hypnosis is like a guided **meditation**. The individual passes through a series of steps to go deeper into the **unconscious**, but actually hears every word during the process. Hypnosis is achieved when the **brain waves** slow down and the individual reaches such an intense level of concentration that he or she blocks out any interference or distraction to his or her focus. During this state of intense concentration certain innate abilities are heightened, including imagination, memory and suggestibility. All these abilities are linked to the intuitive part of the brain, which explains why hypnosis is considered a powerful tool by psychics and those seeking intuitive insight.

HYPNOTHERAPY

Therapy that uses **hypnosis** to treat physical, mental and emotional ailments. Hypnosis is the induction of a state of mind where a person is more receptive to suggestions made to them. The conscious mind, with all its ingrained thoughts and habits is bypassed, allowing the hypnotherapist to directly contact the **unconscious** and implant healthy ideas. Hypnotherapy has proved to be particularly useful in treating stress-related conditions, phobias, bedwetting in children, eating disorders, weight problems, low self-esteem, stopping smoking and digestive complaints.

Even though hypnotherapy has a high success rate when it comes to helping people make positive changes in their lives, it has earned an unfortunate reputation from hypnosis stage shows using conjuring tricks. The best way to avoid this is to seek out a practitioner with a proven track record of success or a psychologist or therapist who practises hypnotherapy.

Typically a hypnotherapist will discuss with a client the reason why they want to undergo hypnosis as well as what they hope to achieve and take a full mental and physical health history. The first step would be to induce a **trance**-like state with a series of **relaxation** techniques. The client would then be asked to visualize a particular place they find relaxing and calm. Once in a state of deep relaxation the hypnotherapist will address the client's subconscious mind, with suggestions like, 'When you smoke you will find the taste of every cigarette in your mouth unpleasant', or 'When you go for your job interview you will feel relaxed and confidant about yourself and your ability to do the job'. Before the client is brought back to total awareness they may be given a post-hypnotic suggestion (called self-hypnosis) that will enable them to induce a state of relaxation and suggestion whenever they want.

HYSLOP, JAMES HERVEY [1854–1920]

Psychical researcher and author with a special interest in **mediumship** and **survival after death**.

James Hyslop was born on 18 August 1854 to Presbyterian parents and grew up on a farm in Ohio. When he was ten his brother and sister died of scarlet fever, leaving him with a life-long preoccupation with death. His family expected him to enter the ministry but he had a crisis of faith and went to study philosophy instead. He received a PhD in psychology from Johns Hopkins University and then taught ethics and logic at Columbia.

Hyslop first became interested in the **psychic** world when he read an article about **telepathy**, and in 1889 he joined both the **Society for Psychical Research** and the **American Society for Psychical Research**. He soon got involved in investigating cases, and after studying the work of a number of **mediums** he converted to a belief in survival after death. In 1905, the first of many books on psychical research, *Science and a Future Life*, was published.

In 1906 Hyslop became secretary and treasurer for the American Society for Psychical Research and is best known for his work with the society, the massive contribution he made to its publications and to psychical research in America. His most famous investigations are the **Doris Fischer** and **Thompson-Gifford** cases. He also worked with a number of mediums, most notably **Minnie Meserve Soule**, to investigate spirit **possession**.

I

I CHING

An ancient Chinese system of **divination**, also known as the *Book of Changes*. The I Ching consists of 64 interrelated hexagrams along with commentaries. The hexagram formations to be used in the divination are decided by the results of throwing three coins three times or by tossing yarrow sticks. Each hexagram has a meaning and when lines of hexagrams are taken into account the oracle is capable of delivering more than 4,000 answers without repetition.

The I Ching embodies Taoist philosophy by describing all nature and human endeavour in terms of the interaction of **yin** and **yang**. The universe operates according to fixed laws and there is no such thing as coincidence or chance, only cause and effect and meaningful association. If a person is in harmony with the flow of yin and yang energy the possibilities for fulfilment and harmony are endless.

I Ching doesn't exactly tell the future; it is intended to guide the searcher to find his or her own answers. It is the sage that is aware of all possibilities and suggests probable outcomes if various approaches to life are taken. The aim is to show how a wise person in tune with yin and yang energy would respond to particular situations. The onus of effecting the changes needed is on the enquirer accepting the advice and acting upon it.

According to tradition the I Ching dates back thousands of years. It was first devised from observing the natural world, the ebb and flow of is cycles. As it developed sages began to see it as a blueprint for understanding the universe. The two trigrams which form the hexagrams were allegedly developed by Emperor Fu-his around 2852 BC. The solid lines represent yang – the male, creative, active energy; the broken lines represent yin – the female, passive, receptive energy. In c.1143 BC the trigrams were developed into 64 hexagrams by King Wen, founder of the Chou dynasty, and his son, the Duke of Chou, added commentary on the meaning of the symbols. In later years Lao-tzu (604–531 BC) drew upon the I Ching for inspiration when writing the Taoist text the **Tao Te Ching**. Confucius (551–479 BC) was also inspired by it and added ten commentaries, named the 'Ten Wing' appendices.

The I Ching first reached the West in the nineteenth century when it was translated by James Legge and Richard Wilhelm. The language of the I Ching can often seem obscure and ambiguous for Western readers and it requires much patience and reverence towards the oracle itself to be fully understood.

Consulting the I Ching may be a simple or a complicated ritual. The simple way is to toss stones or coins. The yarrow stick method is more complicated. Typically the enquirer faces south and passes 50 sticks through incense while meditating on the question. One stick is cast aside leaving 49 remaining ones to toss into hexagrams and interpret accordingly. Whatever method is used the most important thing needed is a reflective state of mind.

The counsel the I Ching offers is based upon adopting a more harmonious approach to life and having an awareness and respect for the influences acting upon every part of the universe, including humanity. While time consuming and often difficult to understand and interpret, the I Ching is considered an infallible source of inspiration and divination, respected by figures such and **Carl Jung** and the Dalai Lama for its accuracy and insight.

ICTHYOMANCY

The ancient art of examining the heads and the entrails of fish and interpreting them for **divination** purposes; a branch of **haruspicy**. This was an important method of divination practised by many ancient nations in the Near East. Early Christians used the fish as a symbol for Christ.

ID

According to **Sigmund Freud,** the id represents instincts, the **unconscious** part of the mind that is concerned only with the gratification of biological needs such as sex and hunger. It is also the seat of primitive emotions, like anger and fear, and expresses itself through **dreams**, which is why Freud believed dream interpretation to be a crucial part of psychoanalysis. Freud maintained that when a child is born the id is dominant but as he or she grows older the ego and **superego** try to control the id to make it behave in socially acceptable ways.

IDEOMOTOR EFFECT

Term used to describe the influence of suggestion on involuntary and unconscious movement. It is often thought to be the psychological phenomenon that underlies **dowsing**, **automatic writing** and **Ouija** board messages. Quite unconsciously, the participant moves his or her hand or other body part to make the movement of the particular tool occur, though he or she may attribute the motion to divine or **supernatural** forces. The effect is very powerful with some personalities, while no amount of evidence will disabuse believers in the magical nature of the phenomenon.

William B Carpenter first used the term 'ideomotor action' in 1852 in his explanation for the movements of rods and **pendulums** by dowsers. Carpenter suggested that muscular movement could be initiated by the mind independently of volition or emotions. Suggestions may be made to the mind by others or by observation and these suggestions can influence the mind and affect motor behaviour.

Scientific tests by French chemist Michel Chevreul, English scientist Michael Faraday, and American psychologist Ray Hyman have suggested that many (but certainly not all) phenomena attributed to spiritual or **paranormal** forces, or to mysterious forces, such as chi or the **universal life force**, are due to ideomotor action. Furthermore, according to Hyman in a 1999 paper entitled 'The Mischief Making of Ideomotor Action' these tests demonstrate that 'honest, intelligent people can unconsciously engage in muscular activity that is consistent with their expectations'.

Ignis fatuus

Spectral lights that appear as bluish or yellow flames or candle lights in the countryside at night. Translated literally *ignis fatuus* means 'foolish fire'. It is considered foolish to follow these spectral lights because they are thought to be **death omens**, often playing tricks on those travelling alone at night by luring them away from their path until they lose their way. Ignis fatuus lights appear in folklore all over the world. They are also known as **corpse candles, jack-o-lanterns** and by a host of other names.

There are various legends to explain the lights. Typically they are believed to be the **ghosts** of souls who cannot rest, either because they were sinners on earth who did not repent or because some wrong done to them while they were alive stands uncorrected. In German lore the light is an *Irrlicht* or wandering spirit who accompanies an invisible funeral possession. In Sweden the light is that of an unbaptized soul trying to lead travellers to water in the hope of being baptized. In parts of Africa, the lights are called witch lights and are believed to be sent by **witches** to scare wrongdoers. Natural explanations for the phenomenon include: unknown energy from the earth; electrical and magnetic vibrations; and marsh gas. See also **Ghost lights**.

Ikiryoh

In Japanese folklore the ikiryoh is the name used to describe an entity that is thought to be created by the evil thoughts and feelings of a person. When it is energized by hatred the ikiryoh becomes so powerful it can leave the person harbouring hateful thoughts and enter and possess the person who is the object of the hatred. Once inside it can kill the victim slowly by draining away the person's energy. The ikiryoh is thought to be extremely difficult to exorcise and there are numerous rites to drive it away, including the reading of Buddhist scriptures.

Illuminati

Secret brotherhood of magical practitioners. The brotherhood is rumoured to have existed in ancient Egypt but the term was first used in the fifteenth century to describe **adepts**, especially those who possessed 'light' or 'illumination' (i.e. wisdom) from a higher source. The term was associated with a number of secret societies and **occult** groups, such as the **Rosicrucians** and **Freemasons**.

One of the best-organized illuminati sects, called the Order of Perfectibilists, was established on 1 May 1776 by a 28-year-old professor of Law called Adam Weishaupt. In 1780 Baron von Knigge, a high level Freemason, joined and the group began to incorporate Masonic elements into its organization and rites.

Illuminati members tended to be anti-monarchists and its republican tendencies gained it many members in Germany. Noted illuminati members included Goethe, **Count Cagliostro** and **Franz Anton Mesmer**. In 1784 the Bavarian government banned illuminati organizations as politically subversive and attempted to suppress all secret orders, including illuminati and the Masons.

After its suppression in Bavaria the order revived in 1880 and in 1895 was renamed the Ordo Templi Orientis (Order of the Temple of the Orient) by Dr Karl Kellner. **Aleister Crowley** was a particularly high-profile member. Upon Kellner's death in 1947 the order broke into two organizations, one based in England and the other in Berkeley, California.

In 1995, Gabriel López de Rojas founded the Illuminati Order in Barcelona, after consulting two members of The Illuminati of the United States (Grand Lodge Rockefeller), and he helped establish the Operative Rite of The Illuminati of Bavaria. The Bavarian Illuminati Order was slow to grow initially, but by 1999 it had expanded to include members and chapters (lodges) all over the whole world.

In Western ritual **magic**, the term 'illuminati' also refers to secret masters called upon by **magicians** and **psychics** to assist them in their work. These secret masters include holy figures such as archangel Gabriel, mythical figures such as the magician **Merlin,** and historical figures such as **Joan of Arc**. Typically the secret masters exist on the **astral plane** but **Madame Blavatsky**, co-founder of the Theosophical Society, gave them a physical dimension.

Although the concept of illuminati has been known to mystic occult societies for centuries, it has been popularized in recent years by the fictional writings of Robert Anton Wilson and Dan Brown.

IMAGERY

Mental images, thoughts, feelings and sensations that plays an important role in **psi** activity, **meditation**, spiritual and psychic **healing**, mystical experiences and **magic**. Since ancient times imagery has been seen as a way to tap into the **unconscious** and harness its power.

Imagery is subjective, with studies showing that some people are better at imagery than others. It occurs spontaneously in **dreams** and daydreams but, with training, research has shown it can be used for goal-orientated tasks. It is generally thought that imagery training benefits psi ability, and since the nineteenth century parapsychologists have explored the link between psi and imagery.

Imagery is a right-brain function, which synthesizes images, sounds and emotions. Experiments with psi imagery have shown that there are five mental processing stages involved:

1. The image is presented unchanged to the conscious awareness.
2. The image is reorganized into recognizable patterns, but which are different to the original.

3. The imagination and memory fill in missing elements.
4. The image is transformed into a different, but similar, image.
5. The image stimulates associations; for example, a person may associate an image of a half-eaten apple with cancer. The association could have been formed because the night before a beloved relative died of cancer she had left a half-eaten apple by her bedside.

It is thought that gifted psychics can receive their psi information in all five ways, or in one or two dominant ways, as the five mental processing stages are not necessarily sequential.

Process-orientated imagery (visualizing carrying out the task) and goal-orientated imagery (visualizing the task as already completed) are used in **creative visualization** techniques designed to improve health, relationships, career prospects, personal growth and fulfilment. Imagery is an absolutely essential part of **martial arts** training and individuals in sport and business use imagery to boost their chances of success. Studies of sportsmen and women show that physiological changes occur during creative visualization and that their internal imagery is a highly effective way to boost performance.

Imagery has also played an important role in many kinds of healing since the ancient Greeks recognized how important the mind–body link was to physical and emotional health. If disease is present both patient and healer imagine the relevant parts of the body in perfect health as a way of combating the disease.

The Renaissance physician Paracelsus said that the imagination has the power to cure or cause illness, but it is only in the last 40 years that Western medicine has begun to recognize the true healing potential of mental imagery. Since the 1970s imagery has been used as an alternative or supplemental treatment for a large number of illnesses, especially cancer. In Eastern medicine, **meditation** and **yoga** imagery is employed to reach illumination – a state where there is no thought and no imagery. In magic, imagery is used to imbue **symbols** with power and to effect **spells**. By visualizing the symbol a **magician** or **witch** believes that he or she can access its power.

IMAGINATION

Imagination is the ability to visualize and make sense of the universe in pictures and **symbols** not words. It is something that comes from within a person's own mind and involves images and sensations that do not demonstrate any basis in reality, yet. Imagination is sometimes confused with **psychic** skills such as **telepathy** and **precognition** but it is not the same. Psychics believe that imagination is the first stage in reawakening latent psychic potential because imagination involves mental images and pictures, and these images can have great power and meaning. See **Creative visualization, Imagery, Intuition, Visualization**.

Exercises to stimulate your imagination

We often dismiss insights by telling ourselves that we're imagining things, but a vivid imagination is believed to be the bridge between intuition and psychic development. To develop psychically you need to think in pictures and sensations, not words, and to allow yourself to dream, fantasize and play.

Here are some simple suggestions to develop your imagination as a path to psychic awakening. Let your imagination run free.

1. Draw two shapes on a piece of paper. One is simply a straight vertical line no more than a few inches long. The second is shaped like a capital Y – again no more than a few inches long. Look at both these shapes for a few mintures. Now cover up the Y shape and look at the vertical line. In your mind's eye let the vertical line transform into the Y shape. See the line dividing and splitting into the Y. Try it again, only this time see one arm of the Y growing faster than the other. Do it again, and see one arm waiting for the other to complete before it moves. See in your mind's eye one of the arms moving and, when it stops, see the other moving.

2. Choose a picture you like. It can be a photo or a painting or a drawing. You want this to be an uplifting experience, so try to pick something simple and calm rather than something crowded with detail. Find a place where you won't be disturbed and where you can relax. Take the picture with you. Get comfortable and take some deep breaths to help you relax. Tune out everything else and look at the picture for a few minutes. Try to remember every detail in your picture. When you are ready, close your eyes and slowly melt into the picture. Stand in your imagined picture, look at everything and see it all in your head. Take a walk around in your picture. Enjoy the mood of the picture. If there are people there talk to them. Take a good look around. When you feel ready, slowly walk out of the picture and come back to reality.

3. When the phone rings see if you can imagine who is on the other end before you pick up. Do the same with your post. Imagine who has sent you a letter before you tear it open. And if you're feeling confident, see if you can imagine what will be in the next day's newspaper headlines.

Don't worry if you have more misses than hits with these exercises; the important thing is to get your imagination muscles working, because it's your imagination that will take you on your first psychic adventure.

INCANTATION

Words used in **magic** to infuse power into **spells** or **charms** or summon help from the spirit world. Incantations, from the Latin *incantare*, meaning 'to consecrate with charms', are believed to work because of their alleged ability to invoke sacred vibrations that can reach a deity or the **universal life force** or a source of power. They can be used for good, as in **white magic**, or for bad, as in **black magic**.

Names of supposedly powerful **spirits** are often chanted by **shamans** who may also beat a drum as they do so. The most likely explanation for using an incantation is that the constant repetition of the chant induces an **altered state of consciousness** or semi-**trance**. The actual choice of word or phrase is less important than the chanting and repetitive tone itself.

INCORRUPTIBILITY

Inexplicable lack of decay in a corpse, particularly in the Catholic tradition where the bodies of saints and martyrs do not show signs of decay or decomposition, sometimes decades or centuries after the death of the person. When no logical explanation, such as preservative methods or extreme temperatures, can be found to explain the phenomenon some believe that **supernatural** or **paranormal** forces are at work.

Incorruptibility is by no means confined to saints. After his death the body of **yoga** teacher Paramahansa Yogananda was said to manifest a phenomenal 'state of immutability'. The story below, reported in the 4 August 1952 edition of *Time*, appeared in *Self-Realization* magazine (Los Angeles) in the May 1952 issue.

The great world teacher demonstrated the value of yoga (scientific techniques for God-realization) not only in life but in death. Weeks after his departure his unchanged face shone with the divine light luster of incorruptibility.

Mr Harry Rowe, Los Angeles Mortuary Director, Forest Lawn Memorial-Park (in which the great master is temporarily placed) sent Self-Realization Fellowship a notarized letter from which the following extracts are taken:

'The absence of any visual signs of decay in the dead body of Paramahansa Yogananda offers the most extraordinary case in our experience ... No physical disintegration was visible even twenty days after death ... No indication of mold was visible on his skin, and no visible desiccation (drying up) took place in the bodily tissues. This state of perfect preservation of a body is, so far as we know from mortuary annals, an unparalleled one ... At the time of receiving Yogananda's body, the mortuary personnel expected to observe, through the glass lid of the casket, the usual progressive signs of bodily decay. Our astonishment increased day after day without bringing any visible change in the body under observation. Yogananda's body was apparently in a phenomenal state of immutability ... No odor of decay emanated from his body at any time ... The physical appearance of Yogananda on March 27th, just before the bronze cover of the casket was put into position, was the same as it had been on March 7th.'

INCUBATION

In Greek **Pagan** tradition, a process of **divination** and spiritual **healing** typically used by people suffering from chronic illness. The patient would go to a temple of a god or goddess with healing powers and, after making a sacrifice and performing certain ceremonies, he or she would sleep through the night in the temple in the hope of receiving a **dream** from the deity with a message. Records show that miraculous healings did occur at incubation shrines. The emphasis placed on the importance of dream work by psychiatrist **Carl Jung** has inspired some modern pagan and **occult** groups to revive the practice of incubation.

INCUBUS

In Western **demonology**, a male **spirit** or **demon** that disturbs the sleep of women, often subjecting them to nightmares or unwanted sexual intercourse. Incubi (from the Latin, 'one who lies upon') were thought to be particularly fond of seducing nuns and other women committed to the celibate life. Sexual repression is thought to be the most likely explanation. The female equivalent of the incubus is the **succubus**.

INDIAN HEAD MASSAGE

Holistic massage technique based on principles found in **Ayurvedic medicine**, which aims to encourage the body to heal and rebalance itself. It involves working along specific points on the head to stimulate the flow of 'prana' (the body's energetic life force).

Practised in India for over a thousand years, head massage has a number of health benefits: it stimulates blood and lymph circulation; it releases tension and stress and can help with the pain of migraines. Last but by no means least, it is incredibly relaxing and most people report feeling calmer and more energized after a head massage.

INDIGO CHILDREN

During the later part of the 1970s Nancy Ann Tappe, a **psychic** and lecturer at the University of San Diego, noticed a change taking place in the colour of children's **auras**. Nancy believed that her ability to see auras was due to the fact that she had been diagnosed with synesthesia, a condition where two neurological systems become crossed so that the senses get reversed. As part of her research and study Nancy published a book in 1982 called *Understanding Your Life Through Color*, and in this book she first mentioned the term indigo. A few years later, Lee Carol, a channeller for an **entity** he calls Kryon, and his wife, Jan Tober, presented Tappe's research on varying colours of

How to recognize the Indigo Child

The Indigo Child is recognizable by his or her aura and by certain other traits, according to The Indigo Children website (owned by Kryon Writings), www.indigochild.com:

* *They come into the world with a feeling of royalty (and often act like it). They have a feeling of 'deserving to be here', and are surprised when others don't share it.*
* *Self-worth is not a big issue. They often tell the parents 'who they are'.*
* *They have difficulty with authority without explanation or choice.*
* *They simply will not do certain things; for example, waiting in line is difficult for them.*
* *They get frustrated with systems that are rule oriented and don't require creative thought.*
* *They often see better ways of doing things, both at home and in school, which makes them seem like nonconformists.*
* *They seem anti-social unless they are with their own kind. If there are no others of like consciousness around them they often turn inward. School is often extremely difficult for them socially.*
* *They will not respond to 'guilt' discipline.*
* *They are not shy in letting you know what they need.*

The Indigo Children website advises that if you recognize the characteristics of an Indigo Child in someone you know, it is important you give this child respect, support and love. They need attention and stimulation and an outlet for their creativity. They need things explained to them, because 'I told you so' isn't an adequate reason for an Indigo. Give them a sense of direction, but above all empower them by giving them choices, responsibility and a sense of independence. If psychic ability manifests itself allow them to nurture and develop it.

---

the aura in *The Indigo Children* and *Indigo Celebration*.

According to Tappe, from 1980 about 80 per cent of the babies being born had an indigo aura around them that she equated to their life mission and their life colour. From 1990 she suggested that there were about 90 per cent being born, and as many as 99 per cent by the year 2000. Prior to 1980 babies with indigo colour were born – so there are indigo adults – but it was after 1980 that a significant increase occurred.

Indigo is the colour of the third eye **chakra**, which is an energy centre inside the head located between the eyebrows. This chakra stimulates **clairvoyance**, or the ability to see energy, **visions** and **spirits**, so, according to Tappe, many of the Indigo Children are classed as clairvoyant.

Tappe believed that Indigo Children have a warrior nature, a 'rebel with a cause' personality with absolutely no sense of guilt. They are often labelled as hyperactive or aggressive but this is their purpose. They are here to break down old and outmoded systems – legal, educational, medical and so on – and to force honesty and integrity on a global level.

According to Tappe and her followers, the Indigos are often mis-diagnosed with Attention Deficit Disorder (ADD) or Attention Deficit Hyperactivity Disorder (ADHD). This is because of their warrior nature. Adults find it hard to handle their intense energy and think that the only way to calm them down is with powerful pharmaceutical drugs, like Ritalin. Tappe suggested that these children actually have right- and left-brain alignment, something people on the spiritual path strive for throughout their lifetime. They are highly sensitive, have psychic abilities and possess incredible wisdom. According to Tappe being an Indigo isn't easy, but it foretells a mission. The Indigo Children are the ones who have come to raise the vibration of our planet and bring to humanity the age of enlightenment.

The National Institute of Mental Health says that ADHD is the most commonly diagnosed childhood disorder. It affects some 3 to 5 per cent, possibly more, of all school-age children. The hype and near-hysteria surrounding the use of Ritalin and its potential side effects (although none has so far been confirmed) have contributed to an atmosphere that makes it possible for the Indigo Children theory to be taken seriously. Given the choice, what parent wouldn't rather believe their child is highly intuitive and chosen for a high mission rather than a victim of a brain or personality disorder?

INDIRECT VOICE MEDIUMSHIP

Form of **spirit** communication where the **entity** speaks using the vocal apparatus of the **medium**, often sounding very different from the medium's natural voice. This is in contrast to **direct voice mediumship** where the entity speaks independently of the medium.

INDRIDASON, INDRIDI [1883–1912]

Icelandic **medium** who became one of the country's biggest celebrities. He exhibited remarkable phenomena but was never caught in trickery or **fraud**.

Indridason attended his first **home circle** in 1905. As soon as he sat down the table allegedly jerked and moved and this was the start of his career as a medium. At first he communicated with **spirits** through **trance** and **automatic writing** but soon he moved on to **levitation**, apports, **direct voice mediumship**, remote playing of musical instruments and full-form **materializations**.

Indridason's powers were considered so remarkable that an Icelandic Psychical Research Society was set up to study and support him. The society included a number of distinguished academics, such as Gudmundur Hannesson, professor of Medicine at the University of Iceland, and in 1907 it built a small house to better conduct its work. The society invited people to attend **séances** and before audiences of sometimes 60 or 70 people, Indridason was able to produce phenomena. Even sceptics, like Hannesson, were convinced that Indridason's powers were genuine.

Phenomena allegedly occurred at every sitting Indridason gave. He never had a 'blank sitting'. Sometimes dozens of spirit voices would speak directly; with witnesses claiming that the voices sounded exactly like people they knew who had died. Indridason claimed to have a number of **controls** but his primary control was his great-uncle, who had once been a university professor.

In June 1909, when Indridason was at the height of his power, he succumbed to a bout of typhoid fever and stopped giving sittings. He never fully recovered and died in a sanatorium on 31 August 1912. After his death the Psychical Research Society shut down, but in 1918 the research it had gathered was passed on to a newly formed Icelandic Society for Psychical Research.

INITIATION

Initiation is essentially an individual transformation that involves a transition from one level of awareness to the next. Ritual and ceremony to mark this transformation generally feature, but most occultists believe that the only really worthwhile initiations are inward, often occurring in visionary or revelatory experiences that trigger a change in outlook or in the abilities of the individual.

Initiation rituals (from the Latin word *initium* meaning 'beginning') designed to stimulate transformation have existed since ancient times, ranging from initiations at puberty to the elaborate ceremonies of **Freemasonry** by which members advance to the next grade or degree, receiving the teaching, rights and formal title of that level of membership.

Details vary widely but most initiations in magical lodges start by secluding the initiate to create a space physically and magically for the ceremony. The candidate usually blindfolded before being brought to the sacred space and left to wander around in circles, sometimes bumping into things, to create a heightened state of awareness. While in this state the candidate is taken through teachings, with the blindfold raised at significant moments to reveal important images. At some point during this process the candidate takes an oath binding him or herself to abide by the rules of the order. The candidate also receives at some point the secrets of the order – typically passwords, **symbols** or other signs. The ritual often closes with a lecture or talk on the teachings of the order to ground the student from his or her heightened state, and to communicate more useful information. Many initiation rituals have been published, including those of the Hermetic Order of the **Golden Dawn**.

Inner Light, Society of

English magical order founded in the mid- to late 1920s by **Dion Fortune** as the Fraternity of the Inner Light. In 1946, after Fortune's death, the name was changed to Society of the Inner Light.

According to its website (www.inner light.org.uk/intro.htm) it is a: 'Society for the study of Occultism, mysticism and Esoteric Psychology and the development of their practice. Its aims are Christian and its methods are Western.' The Society's teachings derive from material from **astral plane** contacts brought through in **trance** by Dion Fortune in 1922. The Society has a grade structure of three degrees of lesser mystery and two degrees of greater mystery. Fortune's books, *The Cosmic Doctrine* and *The Mystical Qabalah* are central texts.

While Fortune was alive the Society served as a vehicle for her work and teaching but after her death the Society expanded on her work under the guidance of Arthur Chichester and principal trance **medium** Margaret Lumley Brown. In 1961 the Society stopped working all but the first degree of lesser mysteries and focused more on Christian mysticism. A large number of members left to join other magical lodges. In 1990 the society re-established the full degree structure and brought out many of Fortune's previously unpublished works.

Inner voice/Inner guide

Term used to describe the so-called mystical or divine spark that exists within a person. Because of the way individual divinity is expressed in modern culture, the idea of connecting to an inner divine aspect, an internal guide, can be more appealing to some individuals than the belief in spirits. They talk to the god within, rather than god somewhere out there.

Many people never work with **spirits** but follow their own inner knowing, their **intuition** or **higher self**. The spirits or guides encountered are not thought of as spirits as such but as parts of a person's **consciousness** and aspects of their own personality.

The inner voice is not to be confused with the concept of the Inner Child, which is the popular term for the part of the consciousness that is childlike and innocent. Working with the Inner Child is a way to heal pain by giving the Inner Child the love and parenting it needed but perhaps did not get when a person was growing up.

Connecting with your inner guide

Psychics believe that within each one of us is an inner voice, sometimes called your higher self, inner guide or creative spark. The following exercise will help you connect to your higher awareness, listen to your inner voice and meet your inner guide.

Find a place where you can relax and get comfortable without being disturbed. Close your eyes and imagine a beautiful place of light and sound. As you breathe slowly and deeply, imagine a bridge leading to this place and see yourself walking on it. As you reach the end of this bridge you are surrounded by light and colour and sound. Take time to explore the feeling of the place and to listen to the sounds. You come to a full-length mirror. As you look into the mirror you realize that the image you see is the real you, the ideal you, the magical you – your inner guide. To your amazement your inner guide steps out of the mirror and stands in front of you saying in a kind, gentle voice, 'I am the most creative part of you. I see what you do not. How can I help you?'

You sit down with your guide. You may request some insight or discuss a problem or ask what lies ahead for you. You listen and remember what your guide has to say. Your guide tells you that he or she will always be with you and that as you spend time together he or she will become stronger and of more help to you. Then your guide melts into you and you feel your true essence awakening. You heart is filled with hope. You feel greater than you imagine. When you leave, see yourself taking some of the sounds, images and sensations back with you to inspire you in your day-to-day life. Gradually open your eyes and make note of any ideas or insights that have come to you.

In time, all you will need to do is close your eyes and see, feel or hear your inner guide and notice how your guide responds to situation. This will give you the clues you need as to what you should do and how you should respond to people and events around you. And the more you work with your inner guide the more you will know that your psychic powers are coming to life within you.

INNOCENCE GHOST

Traditionally, the **spirit** of a woman who is seduced and then deserted by her lover, only to die in a consequence of the act (e.g. in childbirth or by suicide in grief over the illicit love affair). The **ghost** will haunt the woman's seducer and perhaps even generations of his family to come.

See **La Llorona**.

INSPIRATION

A right-brain function in which insight, information and **intuition** enable a person to make great leaps in thought and creativity. Everyone experiences inspiration at some time or other in their lives. Some believe it comes from a divine source, while others believe it to come from **supernatural** sources. This is because when inspiration occurs it often feels as if the ideas come from outside of oneself, as if one has become the instrument not the instigator of ideas and creativity.

According to musical genius Beethoven,

Inspiration is for me that mysterious state in which the entire world seems to form a vast harmony, when every sentiment, every thought re-echoes within me, when all the forces of nature become instruments for me, when my whole body shivers and my hair stands on end.

Literary artist W M Thackeray wrote in one of his 'Roundabout' papers (*Cornhill Magazine*, August, 1862): 'I have been surprised at the observations made by some of my characters. It seems as if an occult power was moving the pen. The personage does or says something and I ask: "How did he come to think of that?"'

Research by the **American Society for Psychical Research** on the relationship between creativity and **ESP** demonstrates three factors in common: shared principles; positive motivation (the need to make contact with distant material); **relaxation** and dissociation (the mind is most passive and receptive in these states).

Typically inspiration occurs suddenly and with great intensity, but it is thought to be the product of a long period of incubation where the **unconscious** integrates and collates information into new patterns, which are then pushed forward into consciousness. This was certainly the case, for instance, with Thomas Edison's discovery of the light bulb. The flash of inspiration came after years of research and experimentation. Sometimes chills, burning, tingling and fuzzy feelings are said to accompany moments of inspiration – Beethoven said his body shivered when inspiration occurred and his hair would stand on end. Inspiration only lasts for a few moments and if the insights are not written down or acted upon, the memory of them will fade.

Inspiration can be triggered by **meditation**, **prayer**, relaxation and fasting and tends to occur most when a person is in a relaxed, contented state. However, it can occur at any time and at any place. Many artists, writers, inventors and scientists have found that inspiration can fuel long periods of creativity or insights of great significance. For instance, Mozart found inspiration would come to him when he was alone or in 'good cheer' or during sleepless nights. The music allegedly poured into his mind in finished form. Albert Einstein described the inspiration that lead to his breakthrough on the theory of relativity as the 'happiest thought of his life'. He was inspired by the thought of a man falling of a roof and the realization that both rest and motion were occurring simultaneously.

INSTITUT METAPSYCHIQUE INTERNATIONAL

Psychical research organization based in Paris. The Institute Metapsychique International (IMI) was founded in 1918 with backing from Jean Meyer, a French industrialist and **Spiritualist**. The first director was **Gustave Geley**; under Geley's directorship **mediums** such as **Jan Guzyk** were investigated. The second director, after Geley died in in 1924, was **Eugene Osty**, who continued Geley's research but brought his own emphasis to it. With Meyer's help Osty built a laboratory and fitted it with advanced equipment. His experiments with the **Schneider brothers** in 1930 are thought to be some of the most important in psychical research.

In 1940 the war forced the IMI to close, and although it reopened after the war it never regained its former prestige and popularity. It is still in business today (www.metapsychique.org/) but will only accept visitors if a prior appointment has been made, and is not as well supported by the French public as its American and British counterparts, the **American Society for Psychical Research** and the **Society for Psychical Research**, are by their respective countrymen.

INSTRUMENTAL TRANSCOMMUNICATION

Instrumental transcommunication (ITC) is the use of tape recorders, TVs, radios, computers, telephones and other technical devices to get meaningful information from the **spirit** plane in such forms as voices, images and text.

Electronic voice phenomena (EVP) experimentation produced the first ITC contacts using a tape recorder and a simple microphone. Later on there occurred ITC contacts via telephone, computer, fax, special devices and so on. Transmission involves the energy of **consciousness**; receivers try to tune themselves to resonate with entities in the spirit world.

Since 1980 ITC has attempted to establish communication with the spirit world with varying degrees of success. Results include images and messages on telephones, radios and television screens, text and picture files appearing in computers or on disks or other recordable media and text and pictures via fax machines. **Apports** have also materialized with explanations from the spirits delivered via technical equipment.

In 1985 Klaus Schreiber began to receive spirit images on his TV set, including the faces of scientist Albert Einstein, Austrian actress Romy Schneider and various departed family members, especially his two deceased wives and daughter Karin, with whom he was particularly close. Schreiber's technique, set up by his colleague Martin Wenzel, involved aiming a video camera at the television and feeding the output of the camera back into the TV, in order to achieve a feedback loop. The result was a churning mist on the screen out of which the spirit faces would slowly form over a period of many frames. In 1994 the first 24-second colour picture transmission of the face of EVP researcher Friedrich Jürgenson, was allegedly received on a TV set belonging to Adolf Holmes in Germany.

In 1995 the International Network for Instrumental Transcommunciation (INIT) was founded in Luxembourg by a group of scientists and researchers from eight different countries. The aim was to establish reliable communication with the spirit world and enable people to receive messages from dead loved ones. They claimed to be assisted in their work by the Timestream spirit group and the People of the Rainbow, who live on the **astral plane**. 'The Seven' is a council of Rainbow people who provide direction for information sent to Earth and its most active member is 'Technician' who has been assigned to help the development of ITC. The Seven has communicated that it does not wish to see a widespread use of ITC but prefers to concentrate its efforts on a select group of researchers united by an ethical and moral duty to ITC.

According to the INIT website (www.worlditc.org/):

The ethereal beings said they had accompanied our world for many thousands of years and had come close six times when the Earth had reached a crossroads leading either to a dark age or to a period of enlightenment. This, they said, was the seventh time, and they wished to establish a lasting bridge between Earth and their formless realm of wise, loving consciousness. ITC research would be the means by which to establish that bridge. Through the work of INIT, it became evident that the more miraculous forms of ITC contacts were made possible by such ethereal beings, who provided protection and guidance for ITC researchers and their spirit colleagues.

In its first few years INIT's membership doubled, but it then began to suffer internal problems and questions were asked about research results. One area of concern was that images received from the spirit realm looked similar to places on Earth. The People of the Rainbow explained that material things could exist simultaneously on a higher plane.

INIT researchers continue to attempt to establish a reliable form of communication with otherworldly realms and to develop new technology to assist them in this quest.

INTELLIGENCE

In magical tradition, a **discarnate entity** that appears to humans as a pattern or ideas or states of consciousness. Sometimes described as 'thoughts that think themselves' or '**thought forms**', intelligences are thought to reside on the **astral plane**. **Aleister Crowley** believed that information received in **divination** comes from intelligences, and that each system of divination has its own group of intelligences.

International Spiritualist Federation [ISF]

Organisation based in London for **Spiritualist** and **Spiritist** associations, churches and members all over the world. The aim of the ISF is to promote dialogue between spiritualists and spiritists and provide a network of support for people in countries not yet ready to accept spiritualist societies. It recognizes the existence of a creative life force, the survival of the human personality after death and communication with the **spirit** world. According to its website (www.isfederation.org/aim.htm) it aims to 'reveal that Spiritual nature of mankind which harmonises with natural law'.

The ISF was founded in 1923 in Liège, Belgium, but its origins date back to 1888 when the first international conference of spiritualists took place in Barcelona. It was closed down during World War II but re-established itself soon afterwards and has remained ever since. Every year the ISF sponsors a week of lectures, experiments, classes and seminars. It also runs a scientific forum for research into spiritual philosophy and sends teaching and research teams to visit countries all over the world to raise standards in spiritual healing, **mediumship** and the presentation of spiritualistic philosophy.

Internet

There are countless Internet sites that offer information and advice about the psychic world. From well-established research centres and **spiritualist** groups to websites set up by individuals who share an interest in the **paranormal**, the World Wide Web can be a fascinating resource of useful information and a meeting ground for like-minded individuals. It is important to point out, though, that a large portion of the sites is not regulated by any codes or standard to monitor the information they present. A round up of some of the better known and well-established paranormal and **psychic** sites are listed in the Resources section at the end of this book.

There are also numerous sites on the Web that offer to tell fortunes. Internet **divination** has become big business, with people paying – typically by credit card – to have their fortunes told. By going to a search engine and entering in a method of divination a number of sites will be found. There are **astrology** sites, **palmistry** sites, **I Ching** and **Tarot** and even those that delve into the lesser-known methods of divination. There are far too many to include in this book, but some of the more long-standing ones can be picked up in the rersources at the back of this encyclopedia.

INTUITION

Intuition is the state of knowing something without being aware that you know it. It is a knowledge that seems to come from nowhere, a sudden revelation or insight without any logical evidence.

Intuition is commonly believed to be a **sixth sense**, a form of **ESP** or an indication of potential **psychic** ability. Many psychologists, however, believe that intuition does not rely on a sixth sense; it is simply a case of knowing without being aware of how you know. Present understanding of how the brain works provides a logical explanation of this phenomenon. There is an overwhelming sea of awareness we all possess that never reaches conscious awareness. This is subliminal knowledge gleaned by the senses that completely bypasses **consciousness**. When some aspect of this awareness surfaces into the consciousness, it is called intuition.

It is thought that we have two systems of awareness: conscious and intuitive. The conscious or logical mind (left-brain function) is able to verbalize what it experiences. It records information received by the five senses – seeing, hearing, smelling, feeling and tasting. The intuitive system (right-brain function) is non-verbal. It picks up the same information from the five senses. It organizes, processes, records and stores the information for later use.

The mind's intuitive awareness system is believed to be so efficient that it picks up millions of bits of information that the conscious mind misses, and it stores this information continually throughout all the years of a person's life. As a result a vast storehouse of knowledge is stored in our subconscious without any conscious awareness of it. The intuitive mind never lies dormant and is always trying, through **symbols**, **dreams** and feelings, to bring its information to conscious awareness. So when an intuitive insight occurs, it is not a sign of ESP but rather information that has being gathered and stored on a subliminal level.

Some people seem naturally able to extract and use intuitive information from the world around them. They seem to reach conclusions, solve problems and sense reality easily and in a mysterious way that others cannot. It is often said that these people are sensitive, talented, inspired, intelligent, creative and even psychic, but often these gifts are just the benefit of intuitive awareness – and there is growing evidence that this is an ability everyone possesses and can develop to some degree.

INVISIBILITY

Attempts to disappear are a fairly common goal in magical practice. Methods of ritual **magic** aimed at invisibility are common in medieval and modern sources.

According to the teachings of the Hermetic Order of the **Golden Dawn**, invisibility is a state attained by establishing an astral and etheric shell – called the 'Shroud of Concealment' – around the body of the **magician**. The shroud works by distorting the consciousness of those within sight of the

Exercises to develop your intuition

Intuition tends to come to us when we are in a relaxed state of mind. Ever remember thinking 'It's right on the tip of my tongue' but you can't remember what it is? Later, seemingly from nowhere, the information comes to mind. This is a classic example of your intuition working. When you are struggling with a problem try this:

Gather all the information you can about a problem. Then concentrate on all the possible issues. Turn the matter over and over in your mind. Then let it go. Stop thinking about it completely. The problem will slip into your subconscious mind where it will be filed and processed. It is now that your intuition gets to work, scanning all the information you have stored and making new connections. Then, out of the blue, a solution will present itself, hours, days or weeks later. It may also present itself after a good night's sleep.

The most favourable conditions for receiving intuitive messages are during quiet and serenity, when your logical mind is subdued or shut down. A good way to entice your intuition is to gaze at the sky and slow moving clouds. This can create a restful atmosphere that helps intuition surface. A warm bath, a long walk, yoga, meditation, tai chi, listening to your favourite music or any activity that calms the mind and takes you away from distractions and gives you time to think, dream and imagine can all help your intuition take centre stage.

Do be aware that intuition speaks in a different language from the one we use in daily life. Feelings and moods are the basic language of intuition. Have you ever felt angry for no reason? Have you ever felt alone in a group of people? Perhaps your intuitive mind is trying to reach you. Dreams are another important voice of the intuitive system, when the non-verbal mind dominates. You may also physically manifest a message from your intuition. Headaches when you feel stressed are a classic example. If you aren't sure how your intuition comes to you carry a pen and paper around and jot down random thoughts that could be your intuition talking. At the end of the day review what you have written and in the days and weeks ahead see if a pattern emerges.

You may find it hard to distinguish between intuition and anxiety. When you know something intuitively, you just know it quietly. The feeling is much different from the noisiness of fear with its explanations that clatter around your head. Intuition is not only quieter it is much gentler than fear. If the thoughts in your mind are full of guilt, anxiety and judgement they are likely to originate from your conscious mind. Intuition tends to be gentler, warmer, kinder and non-judgemental. For instance, if something inside your head is saying you are a loser and you haven't got what it takes because you always give up, it probably isn't your intuition talking to you. You intuition might tell you that something doesn't feel right, that it isn't right for you and that it's time to change direction. There may be no words or thoughts, just a gut feeling that it is time to make a change.

magician; while their eyes see an image of his or her presence; their minds are unable to process it and so the magician is not seen.

The ninja-assassin-mystics of feudal Japan used this technique to evade discovery and a number of modern magicians have also found it to be partly effective.

INVISIBLE ASSAILANTS

Term used to describe **spirits** who inflict painful and mysterious physical attacks upon the living. See also **Incubus**, **Succubus**.

INVISIBLE FRIENDS/INVISIBLES

Term generally used to describe the invisible playmates of many young children that only they can see. Although it is widely accepted that such figures are figments of the **imagination**, it has also been often suggested that children are inherently more apt to see **ghosts**, an ability that gradually disappears through age and social conditioning.

Young children often have imaginary friends. Sometimes they're human, other times they're animals. Sometimes the imaginary friend is an occasional visitor, stopping by only once every few days. But at other times it may be a child's constant companion. Children may talk to their imaginary friends, draw with them, or even read books to them.

Child development experts believe that imaginary friends are a normal part of growing up – especially during the toddler years. They can be wonderful companions for pretend play, which is an important way to stimulate creativity and imagination, and can help children understand right and wrong. For instance, blaming the imaginary friend for eating sweets before dinner is often a sign that the child understands what is right and what is wrong but isn't yet ready to assume responsibility for his or her actions.

Imaginary friends should only be a cause for concern if they are a child's only friend – children need to socialize with others their own age – and if the child shifts responsibility for everything bad to the friend. Most children lose their imaginary friends between their third and fifth birthdays.

Psychics believe that all children are naturally more in tune with their **intuition** than adults because they accept the world around them without the boundaries they develop when they grow up. There are no limitations as far as a child is concerned. Their imagination is a reality to them and the subject of imaginary friends needs to be handled with great deal of sensitivity and respect. See **Children**, **Indigo Children**.

INVOCATION

Invocation, from the Latin *advoco*, 'summon', is the act of calling a deity or other spiritual power into a **medium**, **magician** or **witch**. It is not the same as **evocation**, which is the process of summoning a spirit into some form of manifestation external to the medium.

IRON

In folklore iron has played a curious role in **witchcraft**, **sorcery** and the **supernatural**. It is thought to protect against **witches**, **sorcerers**, **demons** and other evil entities, but at the same time witches and sorcerers use iron quite happily.

Iron has been a popular metal for making **amulets** with which to ward off danger, bad luck and the **evil eye**. Iron amulets were worn by ancient Babylonian and Assyrian men in the belief that it would enhance their virility, while women rubbed themselves with iron powder in order to attract men. The ancient Egyptians inserted iron amulets in the linen of mummy wrappings in order to invoke the protection of the **Eye of Horus**. In certain areas of Burma, the river men still wear iron pyrite amulets for protection against crocodiles.

In European folklore it is believed that no witch can pass over cold iron, nor enter any house which has a knife buried under its doorstep. Ancient Saxons would not put iron **rune** wands in cemeteries for fear that the iron would scare away the departed **spirits**. In India iron is believed to repel the Djinn and other evil spirits; in America and the UK iron is thought to keep away **ghosts** and evil spirits. Iron amulets as a deterrent for evil include knives buried under doorsteps or gates, horseshoes hung over doorways, iron hoops, hooks and shears kept in the bedroom to ward against nightmares and nails in the pocket to serve as protection when travelling.

Despite all this iron has been used by witches and sorcerers for such items as cauldrons and utensils used in magic. Ghosts and **vampires** also don't seem to suffer any evil effects from iron, if reports about iron-chain clanking ghosts are to be considered. Vampires must be warded off with silver, garlic or wolfbane, not iron.

In the eighteenth century **Franz Anton Mesmer** used iron in his healing treatment. He believed iron conducted animal magnetism, a vital energy that everybody had and needed.

IRVING, WASHINGTON [1783–1859]

Author of the well-known short story 'The Legend of Sleepy Hollow' with its infamous Headless Horseman character, Irving was fascinated by the **paranormal** and travelled all over America and Europe in search of ghosts and haunted spots. He was a close friend of **Sir Walter Scott**, who shared with Irving a passion for the **supernatural**. The two writers would sometimes explore the English countryside in search of **spirits** and both left behind an enduring legacy of ghost literature.

JABUTICABAL POLTERGEIST

The alleged **poltergeist** attacks that took place in Jabuticabal (about 200 miles north of São Paulo, Brazil) are among the most vicious ever recorded.

In December 1965 a Catholic family was disturbed by bricks falling inside their house. At first the family assumed the bricks had been thrown into the house by someone outside, but when this was ruled out (and the bricks continued to fall) a local priest was called and an **exorcism** performed. Unfortunately, the exorcism made the attacks worse.

The family turned to a neighbouring **spiritist** called Joao Volpe for help. Volpe decided that Maria Jose Ferreira, an 11-year-old girl who was living in the house, was a **medium** and unwittingly causing the phenomena. He offered to take Maria home to his house to see if he could investigate the problem. Maria moved in with the Volpes and there were a few days of peace, but then stones began to fly about the Volpe home whenever Maria was present. Volpe counted over three hundred. Eggs also began to disappear and reappear mysteriously. On one occasion a stone appeared, tapped three people on the head and hit the floor. Maria Jose also had a host of **invisible friends** who would tend to her every need. If she wanted sweets they would materialize at her feet. The attacks even continued when Maria was asleep, with cups and glass appearing over her mouth.

Around 40 days after the first brick-throwing incident Maria was attacked with needles, which appeared deeply embedded in her left heel. On 14 March 1966, Maria's clothes caught fire while she was at school, and on the same day the Volpes' bedroom caught fire, badly burning Volpe.

After a year Volpe took Maria to the **Spiritist** centre in Uberaba to see Chico Xavier, Brazil's best-known medium. Through Xavier the **spirits** announced that Maria was a **witch** and that many people had suffered and died because of her. Presumably this implied that she had been a witch in a previous life and was now being repaid by her angry victims. Maria was treated with **prayer** by Volpe's **home circle** and the worst of the phenomena subsided, although fruit and vegetables continued to be thrown about from time to time.

At the age of 13 Maria returned to live with her mother. Tragically she was found dead after consuming a soft drink laced with pesticide. Perhaps it had all got too much for Maria and she took her own life, or perhaps her **invisible assailants** had forced her to drink pesticide. The mystery remains unsolved. Volpe compiled a report, which was signed by numerous witnesses.

JACK IN IRONS

A tall and terrible **entity** that is said to terrify travellers at night on lonely paths and roads in Yorkshire, England. Jack in Irons is so called because he is covered in chains. Folklore has it that Jack was a criminal who died in prison during a time when prisoners were kept chained.

Jack-o'-Lantern

A spectral light that is said to float around at night, beckoning travellers to follow it until they become lost. According to British lore a jack-o'-lantern is a **soul** denied access to both **heaven** and **hell** and destined to wonder the earth carrying a lighted wisp of straw. It is thought that carrying an object made of iron can protect against them. Irish lore urges children outside after dark to wear their jackets inside out so they are disguised and the jack-o'-lantern will pass them by. These remedies travelled to America, along with the practice of flinging oneself to the ground, shutting your eyes and holding your breath until the jack-o'-lantern passes.

There are numerous stories to explain the origin of the jack-o'-lantern legend but the most well known is the Irish tale of a man named Jack who was infamous for his drinking and his mean spirit. As the story goes Jack was a miserable old drunk who liked to play tricks on his friends, family and even the Devil. One day he tricked the Devil into climbing up an apple tree and then placed crosses around the trunk of the tree so the Devil could not get down. Jack made the Devil promise not to take his soul when he died, and only let the Devil down when the Devil had made this promise.

When Jack finally died, several years later, he went to the pearly gates of Heaven but was told by St Peter that he had led a miserable and worthless life on earth and was not allowed to enter. He then went to Hell but the Devil, keeping his promise, wouldn't allow him in either. Jack now had nowhere to go and could only wander in the darkness between heaven and hell. The Devil tossed Jack an ember from the flames of Hell to help him light his way. Jack placed the ember inside a turnip and it has supposedly been Jack's light on his eternal wanderings on earth ever since.

On Allhallows Eve the Irish hollowed out turnips, swedes, potatoes and beet and placed a light in them to ward off evil **spirits**. In the 1800s Irish immigrants to America quickly discovered that pumpkins were bigger and easier to carve out, so they used pumpkins for jack-o'-lanterns instead.

See also **Corpse lights, Ignis fatuus**.

Jade

Crystal gem thought to have special powers of **healing** and protection. Jade was sacred to the ancient Egyptians who associated it with Maat, the goddess of truth. Revered most by the Chinese, jade is considered one of the most important symbols of purity, love and serenity.

The ancient Chinese believed that jade could help inspire the mind to make quick and precise decisions. The ancient trader would often hold this gem in the palm of his right hand while he engaged in business transactions. Carved into a **scarab**, jade is also said to bring its owner a long and prosperous life. In **magic** jade is used for protection and to help remember **dreams** and solve problems. In healing it is used to enhance fertility, strengthen the cardiovascular system, cleanse the blood and dispel negative emotions.

James, William [1842–1910]

American psychologist and founder member of the **American Society for Psychical Research** and President of the **Society for Psychical Research** in London, who made significant contributions to psychical research.

James was born the oldest of four children to a wealthy family in New York City. His father was a renowned philosopher and his brother was the novelist Henry James. William graduated from Harvard at the age of 27 with a medical degree and two years later he began a distinguished career at Harvard teaching psychology and philosophy.

His first book, *The Principles of Psychology*, was published in 1890 and established his reputation as one of America's foremost thinkers. In this work he documented his belief that the human mind and body were inseparable, and mentions 'changes in the nutrition of the tissues which may be produced by the power of suggestion.' He also attacked discrimination against **spiritualism**.

At the age of 57 James had a visionary experience while on a climbing trip to the Adirondack Mountains, which he described as a meeting between the gods of nature and the moral gods of the inner life. In 1886 he began his Gifford Lectures on Natural Religion at the University of Edinburgh and these were published in book form in 1902, as *The Varieties of Religious Experience: A study in Human Nature*. In these lectures James suggests that personal religious faith need not be in conflict with science.

In all his work James envisaged a universe created by a person's own experience and a never-ending evolutionary process. He described his philosophy as 'pragmatism', which he believed concerned the concrete and the practical: if a choice had to be made he preferred the concrete. His writings on the subject include *Pragmatism: New Name for Some Old Ways of Thinking* (1907) and *The Meaning of Truth* (1909).

From 1869 onwards James became fascinated by the **paranormal** and regularly attended sittings with **mediums** – in particular, Boston **trance** medium **Leonora Piper**. Her ability so impressed him that he continued to research **mental mediums** for the rest of his life. Throughout his life James was concerned with enlarging the scope of science to include phenomena that could not be explained by known physical laws and was far ahead of his peers in not separating mind and body into different spheres. His approach to the subject was cautious and logical, and he had a keen interest in facts and evidence. **Physical mediumship** with its table **rapping** and **slate writing** did not appeal to him as he believed it offered too much possibility for **fraud**. As well as being a key member of the British and American societies for psychical research, James also established the Lawrence Scientific School for psychical research at Harvard.

Psychical research convinced James that **telepathy** was genuine. Although he wanted to believe in **survival after death** his sittings with mediums never offered adequate proof. Around 1899 James investigated an incidence of **clairvoyance**. A Mrs Titus of Lebanon, New Hampshire, said that she had had a **dream** detailing where the body of a missing girl could be found. He was sceptical at first, but in a 1907 article for the American Society for Psychical Research he came to the conclusion that the case offered solid evidence 'in favour of the admission of a supernormal faculty of seership'.

James admired fellow psychical researcher **Frederick Myers**'s concept of the subliminal self, or **psychic** region where higher mental processes occur, but his own theory of the 'hidden self' was developed years before. He described the subliminal self as 'the most important step forward that has occurred in psychology.'

James died on 26 August 1910 in New Hampshire. There are numerous reports of communications with him through mediumship.

Jimmy Squarefoot

Ghost of a half-man and half-beast creature that is said to haunt the Grenaby district of the Isle of Man. Originally tales implied that this creature was a large ghostly pig, which was ridden about like a horse by a cruel stone-throwing giant. More contemporary reports state that the ghost has the body of a man but the head of a tusked wild boar. Jimmy Squarefoot is the name of the man who became the phantom. As a mortal it is said he was a stone-thrower himself, and his favourite target was his wife.

Joad, Dr C E M [1891–1953]

Distinguished philosopher and former head of philosophy at London's Birkbeck College, Cyril Joad penned numerous works which are still regarded as essential reading for some university level studies. His writings include *Modern Philosophy* (1924), *Matter, Life and Value* (1929), *Guide to Philosophy* (1936) and *Guide to the Philosophy of Morals and Politics* (1938). Joad also took a keen interest in the possible existence of **ghosts** and played a key part, alongside renowned ghost hunter **Harry Price**, in many investigations into allegedly haunted locations, the most famous of which was **Borley Rectory**.

Joan of Arc

Joan of Arc was born in Domrémy, near Vancouleurs in 1412 to a humble and pious family. She never learned to read or write, as this would have been considered unnecessary for someone of her station in life.

Joan began to hear voices, or what psychologists might call 'auditory hallucinations' around the age of 13. In other words she heard voices when no visible person was there. At first she was alarmed, but in time she grew to trust the voices as they seemed to have her best interests at heart, telling her often that she 'must be a good girl and go often to church'. Then she began to have **visions** of St Michael, St Catherine and St Margaret and was told about her divine mission to help the

Dauphin, the future Charles VII, regain the throne of France from the English.

Joan eventually went to the Dauphin and was put in charge of 6,000 men. Her army advanced to the relief of Orleans, which was surrounded by the English. After two weeks, with Joan's army showing great bravery and tactical skill, the French were victorious and the British retreated in 1429. A few months later Charles was crowned king at Reims.

Joan felt that her mission was accomplished and expressed her wish to return to her family, but this was overruled by the King and she was ordered to fight again against the allied English and Burgundian forces. In November 1430 she fell into enemy hands and was thrown into a dungeon at Rouen. After a year in prison she was tried for heresy and **sorcery**. She showed remarkable courage and avoided making any heretical statements, but the trial was a sham and her fate had already been decided. She was condemned to the stake. To the last she affirmed the reality of her voices and died with such dignity that many began to believe she must have been a saint. Inspired by her example the French found new courage and the English were eventually swept out of the country. In 1456 Joan was declared innocent by the Pope and she was canonized in 1920.

Joan's importance in history is great but were her powers and her voices genuine? Many believe that they were merely hallucinations induced by her patriotic upbringing and the plight of her people. An ignorant and superstitious army would readily believe the **supernatural** nature of her mission and find great energy and courage from it.

This explanation, although plausible, is not fully satisfactory, as it does not explain how an ignorant peasant girl could persuade the Dauphin to give her such responsibility and power. And there is strong evidence that Joan gave the Dauphin proof that she was on a divine mission by demonstrating skills of **mind reading** and **clairvoyance**. It is thought that she was able to repeat a prayer that the Dauphin had made mentally, and find a sword hidden behind the altar of Fierbois Church.

JOHNSON, DR SAMUEL [1709–1784]

Renowned as a lexicographer, literary critic and poet, Dr Samuel Johnson also devoted a great deal of his time to the study of **ghosts** and the **paranormal**. His friend and biographer James Boswell (1740–95) detailed Johnson's passion for psychical research and quotes him as saying, 'It is wonderful that six thousand years have now elapsed since the creation of the world, and still it is undecided whether or not there has been an instance of the spirit of any person appearing after death. All argument is against it, but all belief is for it.'

JOTT

Acronym for 'just one of those things', JOTT is used by modern psychical researchers to describe **paranormal** phenomena that defy rational explanation.

Psychical researcher and vice president of the **Society for Psychical Research** Mary Rose Barrington coined the acronym when she collected and classified numerous cases of paranormal phenomena. According to Barrington there are two groups of JOTTs: *oddjotts*, which concern happenings that have no explanation, and *jottles*, which concerned the displacement of objects. *Jottles* are broken down into smaller categories: *walkabout*, where an article disappears and is found somewhere else later without explanation as to how it got there; *comeback*, where an article disappears from a location and minutes or years later reappears in the same location; *flyaway*, where an article disappears and never reappears; *turn-up*, where an article known to the observer turns up in a place where it is not expected to be; *windfall*, in which an article turns up that isn't known to the observer; and *trade-in*, when a *flyaway* is followed by a *windfall* that is similar but not the same as the object that disappeared.

JOURNALS, PARAPSYCHOLOGY

For much of its history **parapsychology** research has had for its only outlet the journals of a few societies for psychical research. In 1937, however, **J B Rhine** established the *Journal of Parapsychology* and this remains one of the major channels for disseminating research in the field. More recently some other major English-language journals have been established, including the *European Journal of Parapsychology* (from 1975) and the *Journal of Scientific Exploration* (from 1987). All these journals adhere to the strict code of acceptance for papers that characterizes orthodox scientific journals.

There are also a number of specialized publications. For example, *Theta* (published since 1963) provides a forum for research relevant to **survival after death** theories, the *Journal of Near Death Studies* (formerly *Anabiosis* and published since 1981) features research on **near-death experiences** and related phenomena, and *Exceptional Human Experience* (formerly *Parapsychology Abstracts International* and published from 1983) includes reports of various experiences and commentaries on their investigations. Journals in languages other than English include *Psi Comunicacion, Quaderni di Parapsicologia, Revista Argentina de Psicologia Paranormal, Revista Brasileira de Parapsicologia, Revue de Parapsychologie, Revue Français de Psychotronique, Tijdschrift voor Parapsychologie* and *Zeitschrift für Parapsychologie und Grenzgebiet der Psychologie*.

Over the years parapsychologists have demonstrated that their journals and the research published in them are subject to the same rigorous codes of conduct applied to orthodox science. This is well illustrated by a statement published by Rhine in a 1974 edition of the *Journal of Parapsychology*. The statement gave details of an incident where a respected psychical researcher, Dr Levy, had been caught tinkering with recording apparatus being used in one of the laboratory's **psi** experiments. It advised that all of Levy's publications should now be regarded as unacceptable.

The perseverance of academic parapsychologists publishing their work in the above mentioned journals has contributed to the growing acceptance of parapsychology as an orthodox discipline. It has also seen the establishment of parapsychology courses in many universities and colleges in America, Britain, Europe, Australia, India and other countries.

For a full list of parapsychology journals and accredited courses see the Resources section.

JUNG, CARL [1875–1961]

Swiss psychologist whose impact on twentieth-century **New Age** thought has been enormous. Jungian principles have been adapted to nearly all academic disciplines from psychology to mythology to religion to **quantum physics**. He was the founder of the analytical school of psychology, known as Jungian psychology, and, along with **Sigmund Freud**, the most influential author of psychoanalytical theory. Jung coined phrases such as introvert, extrovert, repression, projection and complexes, which have become part of our language, and added a spiritual element to psychology. Prior to that people's thoughts, feelings and behaviours were analysed scientifically

on the basis of what could be observed and experienced. Jung suggested that there were parts of the human personality that could not be explained logically and that mystic aspects had to be considered if a person was to deal with their psychological issues.

Jung was born on 26 July 1875, in Kesswil, Switzerland. His mystical experiences began early and from childhood and throughout his life he experienced visionary **dreams**, **precognition**, **clairvoyance**, **psychokinesis** and **hauntings**. His **psychic** ability may have been a hereditary gift as his mother and maternal grandmother both described themselves as **ghost seers**.

It wasn't until around 1897, while an undergraduate, that Jung took a serious interest in the **paranormal**. During his medical training at Basel, he discovered that his 16-year-old cousin had become a practising **medium**. He invited her to perform experiments for his doctoral thesis and first published work: *On the Psychology and Pathology of So-Called Occult Phenomena* (1902). Jung studied the medium for over two years and later said this investigation changed his mind about the reality of **spirits** and **spiritualism** and made it possible for him to observe psychic phenomena from a psychological point of view.

In December 1900 Jung took a position at Burghölzli Mental Hospital in Zurich and found in psychiatry a way of combining his two main interests, medicine and spirituality. He began to correspond with Sigmund Freud and soon became a devoted follower. In 1905 he gave a key lecture at the University of Basil entitled 'On Spiritualistic Phenomena', in which he discussed the history of spiritualism and referred to numerous cases he had investigated in Zurich. Although he insisted it was important to keep an open mind, in general he was not impressed and in the majority of cases he diagnosed hysteria.

In 1909 Jung wrote to Freud about his interest in paranormal phenomena and the two later met to discuss **parapsychology** in Vienna. Much to Jung's disappointment, Freud, a confirmed sceptic (although later he would change his mind about **ESP**), dismissed the subject. During the meeting Jung began to experience a curious sensation in his stomach. Suddenly there was a small but loud explosion from the bookcase. Jung explained to Freud that this was a classic example of psychokinesis. Freud replied that this was 'sheer bosh'. The two argued and another explosion followed.

For the next few years Freud's dogmatism and emphasis on sexuality as the root cause of all crises increasingly clashed with Jung's interest in spiritual and psychic phenomena. In 1913 Jung broke openly with Freud and resigned from his professorship at the University of Zurich. The change of direction prompted scorn from his peers and a six-year nervous breakdown, during which Jung experienced numerous paranormal phenomena. He became obsessed with the world of the dead, publishing *Seven Sermons to the Dead* in 1916, under the name of the second-century Gnostic Basilidies.

When he had recovered from his breakdown Jung began work on his important theory of psychological types, first published in 1921. In this he suggests there are two psychological types – extroverts and introverts – who could be classified by four basic functions: feeling, sensation, thinking and **intuition**. Other important theories include the anima (feminine principle of the personality) and animus (the masculine principle), the **collective unconscious** and **archetypes**. He defined the 'self' as the **psyche** – the mind, **soul** or spirit. The psyche was divided into the ego, which Jung identifies with the conscious mind, the personal **unconscious**, which includes anything that is not presently conscious, and the collective unconscious, which is a reservoir of our experiences as a species, a kind of knowledge we are all born with and yet are not directly conscious of.

Some parts of our unconscious the ego will recognize but other parts, especially taboo beliefs, the ego will repress. That hidden element of the psyche is the **shadow,** and the persona (the aspect of the ego we present to the world for its approval) and shadow are constantly struggling with each other to find a balance. If the struggle becomes too great a crisis occurs and the collective unconscious enters our awareness. Jung suggested that this was a psychic realm, common to everyone, in which all elements of experience, which express themselves in the form of mythical archetypes, were stored.

In 1919 Jung gave a lecture to the **Society for Psychical Research** called 'The Psychological Foundations of Belief in Spirits'. In it he outlined his belief that there were three sources of belief in spirits: **apparitions**, dreams and 'pathological disturbances of psychic life'. He suggested that spirits are created psychologically when someone dies – images and thoughts

Jung's dream

It is interesting to note that the fundamental infrastructure of Jungian psychology, which underpins almost all the ideas we have today about the human mind, was revealed to Jung in a dream. In this dream he was in a two-storey house. The upper storey was a pleasant-enough salon furnished in rococo style but Jung realized he did not know what the other floor looked like. He went downstairs and discovered a much older and darker room with medieval furnishings. As he continued to explore he found a heavy door and a descending staircase. This took him to a chamber with a Roman architectural style. From this chamber he found another staircase leading down to the depths and a low cave cut into rock with remains of primitive culture and two human skulls.

In his autobiography, *Memories, Dreams, Reflections*, Jung wrote:

It was plain to me that the house represented a kind of image of the psyche – that is to say the state of consciousness, with hitherto unconscious additions. Consciousness was represented by the salon. It had an inhabited atmosphere, in spite of its antiquated style. The ground floor stood for the level of the unconscious. The deeper I went in the more alien and darker the scene became. In the cave I discovered remains of a primitive culture – a world which can be scarcely reached or illuminated by my consciousness. The primitive psyche of man borders on the life of the animal soul, just as the caves of prehistoric times were usually inhabited by animals before men laid claim to them.

In this primitive bottom floor Jung created his most famous theory – the collective unconscious – patterns and images that are common to us all. And out of the collective unconscious came his ideas about archetypes and his enduring insights into the human mind, heart and soul.

remain attached to loved ones left behind and are activated by the intensity of grief to form spirits.

An experience that occurred to him in 1920 confirmed this view to him. He spent several nights in an allegedly haunted house while on a visit to London to give lectures. Over the course of his stay he heard strange noises and smelled odd smells. On the final night of his stay he heard rustling, cracking and banging, and while trying to fall asleep he saw the image of an old woman with half her face missing on the pillow beside him. Jung interpreted his experience as being prompted by the smells in the room, which reminded him of a patient he had once had who was similar to the old lady he had seen in his vision. He believed that the sounds he heard were sounds in his ear exaggerated by his **hypnogogic state**.

Jung had a **near-death experience** in 1944, following a heart attack. As he lay in bed a nurse saw a **halo** of light around his head, and later, when he had recovered, Jung recounted what had happened to him during that time. He said that he felt he was floating high above the earth and could see all the way from the Himalayas across the Middle East to the Mediterranean. He saw a huge block of stone that had been hollowed out from a temple. As he drew closer to the temple he felt his earthly desires fall away from him and he knew that once inside he would understand the meaning of life. Suddenly his earthly doctor appeared in the form of a mythical healer to the gods and told him he must return to earth. Jung did so but with great resentment. He also knew that the doctor would die as he had manifested in what Jung interpreted as his primal form. The doctor did die soon after.

In the last years of his life Jung developed his ideas further on a number of topics, including mythology, symbolism, the **I Ching**, **alchemy**, **mandalas** (which he believed pictorially represented the wholeness of the self), **reincarnation** and the phenomenology of the self, the later culminating in the significant work *Aion* in 1951. Perhaps his most important work of this period was *Synchronicity* (1952), where he applied the theory of meaningful coincidences to **psi** phenomena and other phenomena including alchemy, the I Ching and **astrology**.

Although Jung proposed a psychological explanation for spirits of the dead he did believe in paranormal concepts like precognition and psychokinesis, and the language of dreams, visions and fantasies. He believed that God existed in everyone and that the way to salvation was to become more self-aware. He believed in reincarnation but thought that his own incarnation was not due to **karma** but to a 'passionate drive for understanding in order to piece together mystic conceptions from the slender hints of the unknowable' (Nandor Fodor, *Freud, Jung and the Occult*, 1971).

After his wife of 52 years died in 1955 Jung began work on building a stone castle in his newly acquired property in Bollingen. He carved a number of alchemical and mysterious **symbols** into the stone and the on-going building and alterations to the tower represented to him an extension of consciousness achieved in old age.

The last of Jung's visionary experiences occurred a few days before his death and was to be a portent. In his dream he saw a tree laced with gold – the alchemical symbol of wholeness. Curiously when he died on 6 June 1961, a storm arose on Lake Geneva and lightning struck his favourite tree.

Jung left behind him an impressive legacy of written work and founded the analytical approach to psychology – also known as Jungian psychology – which is still influential today. Analytical psychology interprets mental and emotional problems as an attempt to discover spiritual and personal wholeness. Jung believed that everyone has a story to tell and that some of this story is hidden in the unconscious. In telling this story the archetypes of the collective unconscious reveal wisdom and knowledge to help a person heal their psyche and come to terms with their shadow to find a healthy psychological balance. Other important aspects of Jungian psychology are the interpretation of dreams and visions, and exploring a person's creative and spiritual drives.

K

KA

To the ancient Egyptians ka was the vital force that infused everything – people, animals and plants. It was also part of the **soul**.

The precise meaning of ka is no longer clear to us, as ancient Egyptian ideas concerning soul and spirit refuse to fit into any traditional Western categories, but ka is generally portrayed in Egyptian art as a double or **doppelgänger** that lingered on in the tomb inhabiting the body or even statues of the deceased. It was thought to be independent of the body and able to move, eat and drink at will. There was both a higher, guardian angel-like ka and lower ka that came from knowledge learned on earth.

The tomb was considered to be a home for the ka and it was important to leave offerings of food and drink and pay respects so the dead would send benevolent ka energy to the living. A priest would be appointed to see that the needs of the ka were met. If inadequate offerings were made the ka would be forced to leave the tomb and wander the earth in **ghost** form looking for food and drink.

KABBALAH

Also Cabala, Kabala, Qabalah.

Ancient Jewish mystical tradition that refers to secret teachings handed down from teacher to pupil and promises spiritual enlightenment to those who follow its precepts. The Kabbalah is a doctrine of esoteric knowledge concerning God and the universe. It is largely mathematical in nature and concentrates on the configuration of magical words, anagrams, **angel** and **demon** names and the most holy, the secret name of God.

According to Jewish tradition the Kabbalah was first taught to Adam by the Archangel Gabriel and passed on from 'mouth to ear' through a long chain of secret initiates. Whatever the truth of the origins of the Kabbalah there is no doubt that it is very old indeed. It remained an oral tradition until AD 1980, when Moses ben Shemtob de Leon produced a lengthy commentary on the first five books of the Old Testament – the books of Moses – known as the *Sefer ha-Zohar* (Book of Splendour).

The *Zohar* allegedly represented the work of another rabbi, the mystic visionary Simeon bar Yohai. It departed dramatically from Orthodox Judaism and is the primary work from which classical Kabbalah developed. The *Zohar* teaches that the ultimate godhead was *Ein Sof* ('without end'), a limitless being beyond all description. The *Ein Sof* created the world from itself and the aim of humankind is to realize union with the divine. The *Ein Sof* 'condensed' a somewhat lesser being, the Yahweh or Jehovah of the Hebrews, who nonetheless had the prime characteristics of the ultimate. Since the name of Yahweh was considered too holy to be spoken aloud, Kabbalists prefer to use the term *Tetragrammaton*, which means 'Name of Four Letters' and refers to the fact that Yahweh is spelled YHVH.

In attempting to describe the attributes and essence of this god, Kabbalists conceived of their manifestation as 10 interlinking states of activity, called *sephiroth*, that humanity must achieve to attain wisdom. The *sephiroth* form the central image of Kabbalah **meditation**, the **Tree of Life**, and show the descent of the divine into the material world, and the path by which people can reach up to the divine while in their physical bodies. The first *sephiroth*, *Kether*, is the state of unity encompassing all the rest and is most closely associated with Yahweh; the remaining nine culminate in *Malkuth*, the physical world.

The Kabbalist ascends the Tree of Life through contemplation, study and meditation. The *sephiroth* are contemplated by visualizing them vibrating with **colours** that correspond to their level of attainment in knowledge, along with images of the names of God, angels, planets and energy centres.

Also key is the idea that the 22 letters of the Hebrew alphabet are sacred **symbols** of the universe (known as arcana) and to understand them is to understand life. A way to access the arcana's energy is to chant the sounds of each letter, and to meditate on the letters is to meditate on all of creation and to achieve oneness with the whole. The arcana are also linked to the ten *sephiroth* on the Tree of Life, forming branches or pathways. This means there are 32 ways to reach understanding or enlightenment. All of them involve years of long and intense study.

The teachings of the *Zohar* spread into Europe in the fourteenth and fifteen centuries and by the sixteenth century Kabbalah had become more accessible to the masses. Over the centuries it has not only had a profound impact on the development of Judaism but has also left an indelible impression on the Western **magical** tradition.

Since the establishment of the **Golden Dawn** in the Victorian era, the Kabbalah has played a key role in the development of Western **mysticism**. **Dion Fortune** called Kabbalah the 'Yoga of the West', but it is a Kabbalah the ancient Hebrews might have had difficulties recognizing – over the years the ancient tradition has been heavily influenced by elements from Christianity, Eastern and **occult** traditions such as **Tarot**, **alchemy**, **Wicca**, **Paganism**, **Theosophy**, **Witchcraft** and **astrology**. In recent times emphasis has shifted almost entirely back on to the Tree of Life and practices such as **pathworking**.

The study of the Kabbalah is considered a life-long occupation, and because of its emphasis on revealing secrets by **initiation** it is hard to simplify and clarify. Typically students of the Kabbalah spend a great deal of time and effort on building in their minds traditional associations with the *sephiroth* and the paths of the Tree of Life, and then go on to formulate their own personal associations. In this way the Tree can be applied to almost any mystical system and can be used as a basis for ritual magic.

Today, Kabbalah is enjoying a revival of interest. Thousands of people around the world are turning to the Kabbalah and finding in it a rich, meaningful spiritual practice, whose roots reach deep into the past, and whose path can help them find fulfilment and understanding in the here and now.

Kachina

Native American **spirit** of the ancestral dead who is believed to be a messenger from the gods. Most kachinas are thought to be benevolent, and in addition to bringing rain they will also entertain and discipline children.

According to myth, kachinas live in the sacred San Francisco Mountains. At first they would visit the villages to dance and take the **souls** of the newly dead back with them to the mountains, where they transform into rain-giving clouds; but the visitations became such hard work that they decided others should go in their place. The kachina cult was born. At appointed times men would dress in costumes and masks and perform the kachina dance.

The Zuni tribe call their kachinas *koko*: spirits of men who take the form of ducks to bring rain and visit the living as clouds. The *koko* live happily in a great village at the bottom of the mythical Lake of the Dead, which is thought to be located at the junction of the Zuni and Little Colorado rivers. In Zuni myth the original *koko* were children who drowned after the emergence of people from the underworld. *Koko* also include the recently deceased and **spirits** of ancestors long dead who can bestow health, rain and good corn crops.

Kant, Immanuel [1724–1804]

Perhaps the greatest philosopher to hail from Germany, Immanuel Kant made a significant contribution to **paranormal** research with his much-admired *Traüme eines Geistersehers* (Dreams of a Ghost-Seer) (1766). While researching for this work Kant visited a number of haunted locations and interviewed numerous witnesses who claimed to have encountered unusual phenomena. Although Kant never realized his hope of actually seeing a **ghost** for himself, in his intriguing treatise on the **supernatural** he writes, 'I do not care wholly to deny all truth to the various ghost stories, but with the curious reservation that I doubt each one of them singly, yet have some belief in them all taken together.'

Kardec, Allan [1804–1869]

Pseudonym used by French physician and founder of **spiritism**, Hippolyte Leon Denizard Rivail.

During sessions with **medium** Celina Japhet, **spirits** allegedly revealed to Rivail his past lives, in which he was known as Allan and Kardec. **Automatic writing** spirits, produced while Japhet was in a **trance**, discussed the importance of **reincarnation** and urged Rivail to publish these revelations in *Le livre des esprits* (The Spirits Book) in 1856. The book later became the handbook of spiritist philosophy. In 1864 *Le livre des mediums* (The Mediums Book) was published and was soon followed by *The Gospel as Explained by Spirits, Heaven and Hell, Genesis* and *Experimental Spiritism and Spiritualist Philosophy*.

Drawing on the communications with spirits through Japhet, Rivail (now Kardec) expanded spiritism beyond a basic belief in **survival after death** to claim that reincarnation was essential for spiritual progress and to understand and heal suffering – in particular epilepsy and multiple personality disorder (the latter being thought to be caused by interference from past incarnations). Kardec accepted spirit communication on faith alone and through his monthly magazine *La Revue Spirite*, which he founded, and the Society of Psychologic Studies, of which he was President, he actively discouraged the need for psychical research.

European Spiritism faded away after Kardec's death in 1869, to be replaced by **spiritualism** and interest in **psi** phenomena. It does, however, remain alive in Brazil where a number of Kardecist healing centres work alongside conventional medicine.

KARMA

In Hinduism and Buddhism, karma is the sum of a person's thoughts and actions, which are regarded as determining that person's future states of existence. The law of karma originated in the Vedic system of religion. As a term, it can be traced right back to the early **Upanishads**, around 1500 BC.

In Hinduism karma literally means 'deed' or 'act', and describes the universal principle of cause and effect, action and reaction that governs all life. Karma is not fate, for man acts with free will and creates his own destiny. There are three types of karma: *sanchita* karma, the sum total of past karmas yet to be resolved; *prarabdha* karma, that portion of *sanchita* karma that is to be experienced in this life; and *kriyamana* karma, the karma that humans are currently creating that will bear fruit in the future. The playing out of karma can take place over many lifetimes.

According to the **Vedas**, if we sow goodness, we will reap goodness; if we sow evil, we will reap evil. Karma refers to the totality of our actions and their concomitant reactions in this and previous lives, all of which determines our future. All karma, good or bad, creates more karma and only the attainment of enlightenment eliminates karma and the need to be reborn.

In Buddhism, karma is the universal and inescapable law of cause and effect that may be played out over many incarnations. Karma is created by acts, words, thoughts and intent, even if that intent is not carried out. Karma can only be overcome by adherence to the Three Pure Concepts: cease evil; do good for others; and keep a pure mind. Only when a person is free of hate, delusion and desire is he or she free of the cause and effect of karma.

The idea of karma was popularized in the West through the work of the Theosophical Society. Karma is featured in the **trance** readings of American **medium Edgar Cayce**. Cayce said that the effects of karma could be mitigated by the law of grace, which was both a state of mind and a gift from God and involved forgiveness.

Cayce also attributed many of the problems and illnesses his patients suffered to karma from past lives.

People who undergo **past-life recall** therapy often feel that their present circumstances are the result of actions taken in past lives. Although there are cases of anxieties and birthmarks corresponding to wounds from alleged previous lives, scientific investigation of such cases shows no evidence in support of karma. It has been suggested that feelings related to karma could be a result of cultural expectation concerning reward and punishment for good and bad deeds.

Western **New Age** reinterpretations of karma use the concept to help explain the reason for misfortunes encountered in life. Karma is frequently cast as a sort of luck that is associated with virtue: if one does good or spiritually valuable acts, one deserves and can expect good luck; conversely, if one does harmful things, one can expect bad luck or unfortunate happenings.

KELPIE

Treacherous water **spirits** from Scottish folklore that are thought to inhabit every lake and stream. According to myth kelpie are a **death omen** when seen in the shape of a horse or a shaggy-looking man. In the shape of a horse it is said that they appear grazing peacefully on riverbanks. They lure travellers to mount them and then plunge their victims into the water, where they drown them and eat them save for the livers, which float to the surface.

Fairy horses are known throughout the British Isles and Ireland by many names including the Irish phooka and Scottish kelpie. These beings are believed to be fairy **shape-shifters** with the ability to take on both a human and equine countenance. Even when they are in the guise of an animal they possess full command of the human language and can therefore speak.

It has been suggested that these fairy steeds are all that remains of a pre-Christian equestrian cult but it is likely that these or similar creatures, such as the Loch Ness monster, that inhabit the lakes, lochs, rivers and seas of the world are perhaps the mechanism peoples have used for centuries to keep children away from the dangers of the water's edge.

KEPHALONOMANCY

An ancient and unusual form of **divination** that was used by the ancient southern Germanic clan of Lombards to determine the guilt or innocence of those accused of crime. The head of a goat or ass would be baked and burning charcoal would be poured onto it while reciting the names of suspected criminals; if a crackling sound was heard when a person's name was mentioned this was taken as proof of his or her guilt.

KERE

A **spirit** of the dead. In ancient Greece it was thought that keres were spirits that escaped from the jars used to contain dead bodies. Once free they would devote their energy to upsetting the living and inflicting disease and illness. Rituals and **incantations** were methods used to exorcise them, along with the paining of sticky tar on doorframes to catch them and prevent them from causing harm.

KHU

An ancient Egyptian belief referring to a number of **souls** that together constituted the individual. According to the Pyramid texts, humans are composed of a mortal body, kha, and at least three immortal (or at least able to survive bodily death) elements: the **ka**, **ba** and khu. These are sometimes translated as 'double', 'soul' or 'spirit' but these Western terms do not really give the full nuances of the concepts implied.

Often mentioned in connection with the ba, the khu cannot die and dwells in the sahu (spiritual body). It is the radiant shining one; the transfigured dead that ascends to heaven and dwells among the gods, or among the immortal pole stars which never set. As spirit, the khu is the opposite of the perishable body, kha.

KIDD, JAMES [1879–1949]

Mysterious American prospector who disappeared in 1949 leaving a will stating that that his estate of approx $174,000 should be used to investigate and prove the survival of the human **soul** after death. A controversial court case, in which the will was contested by relatives, followed lasting nearly 20 years.

Little is known about Kidd. He arrived in Arizona in 1920 and worked at a copper mine and prospected. He never married and throughout his life gave no indication of his interest in **spiritualism**. On 9 November 1949, he went to prospect a claim and never returned. It was speculated that he died when falling into a canyon in the Superstition Mountains. He was declared dead seven years later, and the authorities gathered together a large amount of assets in cash and stocks. A safety deposit box was found. It contained his will written in his own hand on lined notebook paper. It read:

this is my first and only will and is dated the second of January 1946. I have no heirs and have not married in my life and after all my funeral expenses have been paid and $100 given to some preacher of the gospel to say fare well at my grave sell all my property which is all in cash and stocks with E F Hutton Co Phoenix some in safety deposit box, and have this balance money go in a research or some scientific proof of a soul of the human body which leaves at death I think in time their can be a photograph of soul leaving the human at death.

James Kidd.

Even though the will was declared legal relatives of Kidd attempted to have it declared invalid. In 1964 the University of Life Church filed a suit against the relatives and a lengthy court battle over the money by a number of interested parties began. In 1967 in Phoenix, Judge L Myers heard 133 petitions from a number of organizations claiming to be the ideal candidates to carry out Kidd's intent. The media dubbed it the 'Soul Trial' and 'The ghost trial of the century'. Judge Myers eventually awarded the estate to the Burrow Neurological Institute in Phoenix, as he thought their combined fields of science, psychiatry and psychology would be best able to utilize the money, but the ruling was overturned. A higher court intervened, and awarded the majority of the estate to the **American Society for Psychical Research**, which used it to investigate **deathbed visions**.

James Kidd, prospector, miner and eccentric, left a small fortune behind to anyone who could prove the existence of a visual soul. The fact that a poorly educated and reclusive man gave such a generous contribution to psychical research has created a mystery that remains unsolved. His body has never been found and science has been unable (so far) to prove the existence of life after death. Some say that his restless and unsatisfied **spirit** still roams the Superstition wilderness.

KIKIMORA

Ancient Slavic term for an invisible female **ghost** that is said to attach herself to certain households. If treated with respect the kikimora will protect the family from misfortune and occasionally assist in housework by tidying up and cleaning. It is sometimes said that the kikimora is the ghost of an ugly woman who died in a swamp but, because the Slavs lived all over Eastern Europe with lots of different languages and beliefs, the origins of this legend remain a mystery.

KINAESTHETIC SENSE

The human body has eight senses (nine if you count psychic sense): sight, hearing, taste, smell, touch, balance (vesibular), organic (internal organs) and kinaesthetic, which is the ability to sense body position and movement of muscles, tendons and joints. For instance, if a person walks through a car park and there are a lot of cars parked together they have to turn and adjust their body in order to get through the tight spaces. The reason they are able to sense whether they can fit, what type of movements they need to make and how to adjust their body position is because they have kinaesthetic sense.

Psychics who receive their information primarily though the sense of touch are thought to have an expanded kinaesthetic awareness. These individuals typically display **clairsentient** ability and often

Kinaesthetic evocation

Awakening the senses is an important part of **visualization** techniques to awaken clairsentient ability. To help awaken your kinaesthetic sense, the sense through which we are aware of the body and its movements, imagine that you are:

1. walking and then running along a beach: feel every movement of your muscles, the feel of the sand on your feet and the wind in your hair.
2. driving a car: sense with precision each movement you make in turning the steering wheel, pressing the pedals, and so on.
3. swimming, playing tennis, football or basketball, or practising any other sport you enjoy.

practise **psychometry**, which is the ability to sense information by touching people, objects and energy fields.

KINESIOLOGY, APPLIED

Developed by the American chiropractor Dr George Goodheart, applied kinesiology is a method of diagnosis and treatment that combines muscle-testing with the principles of **traditional Chinese medicine** to assess energy function and bodily health. It claims to induce proper structural and chemical-nutritional organization in the body, as well as left- and right-brain balance. It also claims to evaluate and correct problems of the nervous, circulatory, lymphatic and skeletal-musculature systems, thereby maintaining health. Its practices are believed to permit the even flow of cosmic energy (see **universal life force**) throughout the body, thus nurturing individual organs and systems with the proper supply of chi energy.

Kinesiology assumes that illness is caused by improperly balanced energy fields in the body. Problems are diagnosed by testing the muscles, each of which is presumed to be connected to a different organ, to determine what is wrong. The proposed solution is to apply particular types of muscle massages that are supposed to release blockages and stimulate energy flow, thus returning the patient to good health.

Applied kinesiology is not a scientific but a philosophy-based medicine, starting from the idea of mystical energy in the body and creating treatments based upon that alone. One outgrowth of applied kinesiology is behavioural kinesiology, developed in the later part of the twentieth century by John Diamond. Diamond follows the same basic philosophy, in that he believes that each muscle relates to some particular organ, but he adds to this the central role of the thymus gland in regulating a person's **psychic** energy.

It should be noted that applied and behavioural kinesiology have nothing to do with the science of kinesiology, which is the legitimate study of muscular movement and tension as it relates to joints, tendons and skeletal structure.

KING HOUSE, MAYPORT, FLORIDA

King House was originally built on an old Spanish graveyard and was used as a boarding house for sailors. It was destroyed by fire and rebuilt sometime after 25 April 1881. King House still stands in Ocean Street, Mayport to this day.

Before his death in the late 1970s the house was owned and occupied by a John King and it was during these years that it became known as the most haunted house in the area. A master storyteller, Mr King would tell ghost stories to visitors from all over the county and a number of mysterious incidents were reported at the house. Psychical researchers investigating the house have concluded that the atmosphere in it is perfect for **hauntings** and that there may be some kind of evil presence there.

A distant aunt of Mr King who was pitch-forked to death as she sat in a green rocking chair by her jealous sailor ex-boyfriend is said to roam the halls of the house, and many people, including Mr King, have claimed the chair rocked with no one sitting in it. A little man in red who liked to play tricks on guests in the house has also been reported, as has a lady in white who is thought to be the **ghost** of a young woman killed on her wedding night in a car crash near the King House. There have also been reports of ghosts pulling the covers from Mr King and guests while they slept in their beds at night, and of doors opening when the handles were reached for.

KING, JOHN

Famous spirit **control** for a number of major nineteenth-century **mediums**. John King served as a control for the **Davenport brothers**, **Agnes Guppy** and **Madame Blavatsky**, to name but a few. According to his own account John King claimed to have been Henry Owen Morgan, the pirate who was knighted by Charles II and appointed Governor of Jamaica. He first appeared in the flash of a pistol fired by Ira Davenport in 1850, and remained as spirit manager with the Davenports throughout their career. His activity was multifarious. While faithfully serving the Davenports he also appeared during **séances** to Jonathan Koons in Ohio. King introduced himself as the head of a band of 160 **spirits** that, he claimed, descended from a race of men known by the generic title Adam, and having as leaders 'the most ancient angels.

They signed their communications as King No. 1, No. 2., etc., and sometimes: Servant and Scholar of God.'

In the early years of British **spiritualism** it was the aspiration of many mediums to secure his influence. A Mrs Marshall was the first, Mrs Guppy, Miss Georgina Houghton, Charles Williams and William Eglinton Husk followed, whilst in America he was claimed by Madame Blavatsky in her early career as a **spiritualist**. Typically King communicated by **direct voice mediumship** and **trumpet** – a conduit he is crediting with inventing. He was described by **Sir Arthur Conan Doyle** as tall and swarthy with a full black beard. He had a deep voice and spoke many languages.

On 20 March 1873, during a daylight séance, John King manifested so successfully that a sketch was made of him by an artist. A week later he appeared again in solid and material form. He was usually seen in the light of a peculiar lamp which he carried and which illuminated his face and sometimes the room. In Paris, on 14 May 1874, a young man tried to seize him. John King eluded his grasp and left a piece of drapery behind. The medium was found entranced. On being searched no paraphernalia or evidence of **fraud** was discovered.

In the early 1870s King began a memorable association with Italian medium **Eusapia Palladino**. Scientists who investigated Palladino throughout her career described King as anxious to produce good and convincing phenomena. He said in many messages that Eusapia was his reincarnated daughter, but in most spiritualist circles John's daughter was **Katie King**.

KING, KATIE

Spirit **control** for **Florence Cook**, among others. Katie King was a colourful character. She claimed to be Annie Owen Morgan, the daughter of **John King**, but, like her so-called father, of her identity there is very little proof available. It was said that she had died at the age of 23 after allegedly murdering her children, and had returned to try to expiate her sins, attaching herself to Florence Cook mainly for that end. It seems she achieved that purpose because on her farewell appearance, after three years of constant manifestations, she declared that her years of suffering were over. She allegedly said that she would ascend to a higher sphere from where she could only correspond with her **medium** through **automatic writing** at long intervals, though Florence would be able to see her **clairvoyantly**.

Katie began to manifest in the Cook house when Florence was a girl of 15. She was seen almost daily, the first time in April 1872, showing a death-like face between the curtains. Later her **materializations** became more perfect, but it was only after a year of experimental work that she could walk out of the **cabinet** and show herself full figure to the sitters. According to reports she was a nearly permanent inhabitant of the Cook household, walking about the house, appearing at unexpected moments, and even going to bed with Florence, much to her annoyance. When Florence married, complications arose and it was said that her husband used to feel at first as if he had married two women, and was not quite sure which of the two his wife was!

According to all accounts Katie King was a beautiful woman. **Sir William Crookes** had forty flashlight photographs of Katie. In most of them she noticeably resembles Miss Cook, but Crookes had no doubt of her independent identity. He wrote in *Researches into the Phenomena of Modern Spiritualism,*

Photography is inadequate to depict the perfect beauty of Katie's face, as words are powerless to describe her charm of manner. Photography may, indeed, give a map of her countenance; but how can it reproduce the brilliant purity of her complexion, or the ever varying expression of her most mobile features, now overshadowed with sadness when relating some of the bitter experiences of her past life, now smiling with all the innocence of happy girlhood when she had collected my children round her, and was amusing them by recounting anecdotes of her adventures in India?

In her early manifestations in the **Davenport brothers'** **séances** Katie King was apparently far less spiritual than at the time of the Crookes records. Psychical researcher Robert Cooper, describing a direct voice consultation of the **spirits** by the Davenports, wrote:

The next minute a shrill female voice was heard immediately in front of us. It was like that of a person of the lower walks of life and talked away, like many persons do, for the mere sake of talking. It was intimated that it was 'Kate' who was speaking. There was a great attempt on her part at being witty, but according to my ideas on such matters, most of what

was said would come under the category of small – very very small – wit.

In another passage he wrote:

Unlike John [King], Kate will talk any length of time, as long in fact as she can find anything to talk about, even if it be the most frivolous nonsense; but I must do her the justice to say that she talks sensibly enough at times, and I have heard great wisdom in her utterances, and satisfactory answers given to profound philosophical questions.

In October 1930, Katie King unexpectedly manifested in Dr Glen Hamilton's **home circle** in Winnipeg. Photographs were taken. According to Dr Hamilton:

Obviously it is wholly impossible to say whether or not this Mary M-Mercedes-Katie King is the same being as the entity appearing in the experiments of Crookes and others. We have the word of the controls in this case that it is so and we have seen how, so far, these controls have repeatedly established the fact that they know whereof they speak ... While there are, I may say, some points of similarity to be traced between Katie as photographed by Crookes and Katie as photographed in the Winnipeg experiments, both faces for instance being rather long in formation, the eyes in both being large and luminous, the angle of the jaw in both being rather pronounced, the later Katie is so much younger in appearance, her beauty so much more apparent that it is evident that we cannot use the earlier record of her presence in any way as conclusive proof that there is any connection between the two.

Both Katie King and John King appeared for the final time in February 1930 at a séance conducted by **Thomas Hamilton** in Winnipeg. Just why a seventeenth-century pirate and his daughter became the ones chosen to promote the cause of **spiritualism** in the nineteenth century remains a mystery. In his book *Mind Over Space*, **Nandor Fodor** speculated that the Kings were **archetypes** of **psychic** manifestation, able to appear at any séance and produce phenomena under the leadership of a medium.

KIRLIAN PHOTOGRAPHY

Controversial technique for photographing people, animals or objects in the presence of a high frequency, high voltage, low-amperage electrical field to produce photographs that show glowing, multicoloured emanations, said to be **auras** or biofields. The technique is named after its inventor, Russian Professor of Engineering, Semyan Kirlian.

When Kirlian visited Krasnodar hospital in 1939 he saw a patient receiving treatment from a high frequency generator. As the electrodes came close to the patient's skin there was a small flash. Kirlian recognized this as a type of flash which occurs when a gas is charged with electricity and wondered what gas was being charged here.

With the help of his wife, Valentina, Kirlian set up two metal plates to act as electrodes and placed a photographic film on one of them. Then he put his hand between the plates and switched a high frequency current on. When the film was developed it showed Kirlian's hand surrounded by an aura. The Kirlians began experimenting with living and dead objects and discovered that if the subject was dead – say in the case of a dead leaf – the photograph showed none of the sparks of energy that were shown when an object was living. What was even more fascinating was that when a part of a leaf was torn or cut away the photograph showed a ghostly image of the missing part.

For over forty years the Kirlians and a number of other Russian scientists tried to discover what all this meant. Then two American travel writers, Sheila Ostrander and Lyn Schroeder, published a best-selling book, *Psychic Discoveries within the Iron Curtain*, which described Kirlian photography and the subject was forced into the spotlight.

Response in the scientific community was mixed, with some scientists pointing out that similar effects had been recognized for years. For instance, if a roll of film is connected to electricity it will show distinctive tree-like patterns in the voltage changes, and if the voltage changes this will show up in strange flares on a photograph. This, however, didn't explain how research projects using volunteers showed the aura changing in relation to a person's mood and how auras were influenced by personality reactions and, according to one study, by drinking a shot of vodka.

Other studies revealed that Kirlian photographs of the human body showed flares at the same points used for centuries in acupuncture. It wasn't long before a relationship between the strength of the Kirlian field and health was discovered: illnesses would show up in the aura, sometimes before they manifested. In the 1970s, at the Neuropsychiatric Institute of UCLA, California, a scientific team led by Thelma Moss and Kendall Johnson used Kirlian photographs to show energy flares coming from the fingertips of faith healers as they worked.

Some researchers believe that Kirlian photography reveals a physical form of **psychic** energy. Others think it reveals the **etheric body**, one of the layers of the aura that is thought to permeate all things, and that understanding this etheric body will lead to great insights into healing, life after death and **psi**.

Work with Kirlian photography continues with indications that it may have diagnostic potential. Experiments using Kirlian photographs to detect cancer and other forms of disease have been sporadically successful.

KITSUNE

In Japanese tradition kitsune are regarded as fox spirits. They can also transform into a beautiful female **apparition** dressed in white, flowing robes. Occasionally they will use this appearance to seduce men and, **vampire**-like, drain them of their life force.

Like their counterparts in the West, Japanese foxes are believed to possess great intelligence, long life and magical powers.

Foremost among these is the ability to take the shape of a human; a fox is said to learn to do this when it attains a certain age (usually a hundred years, though some tales say fifty). Kitsune usually appear in the shape of a beautiful woman, a pretty young girl, or an old man. Foxes figure in all kinds of Japanese folk tales and are prominent at various **Shinto** shrines throughout the country. A pair of foxes guard the entrance to these shrines, lean and bright-eyed with vigilance.

The word kitsune is often translated as 'fox spirit'. However, one should not take this to mean that a kitsune is not a living creature, nor that a kitsune is a different creature than a fox. The word 'spirit' can also be used in its Eastern sense, reflecting a state of knowledge or enlightenment. In Japanese lore, any fox that lives sufficiently long, therefore, can be a fox spirit.

The kitsune are often presented as tricksters – sometimes very malevolent ones. Capable of possessing the **souls** of the unwary, they have been known to turn their victims into **zombies** or drive them permanently insane. However, there is a second common portrayal: as a lover. These love stories usually involve a young human male and a kitsune who takes the form of a woman. Such a story typically centres around a young man (unknowingly) marrying the fox, and emphasizes the devotion of the fox-wife. Many of these stories also possess a tragic element – they usually end with the discovery of the fox-wife, who then must leave her husband.

The oldest known story of a fox-wife, which provides a folk etymology of the word kitsune, is an exception. In this story, the fox takes the shape of a woman and marries a human, and the two, in the course of spending many happy years together, have several children. She is ultimately revealed as a fox when, terrified by a dog, she returns to her fox shape to hide, in the presence of many witnesses. She prepares to depart her home, but her husband prevails upon her, saying, 'Now that we have spent so many years together, and I have had several children by you, I cannot simply forget you. Please come and sleep with me.' The fox agrees, and from then on returns to her husband each night in the shape of a woman, leaving again each morning in the shape of a fox. Therefore, she comes to be called Kitsune, because, in the classical Japanese, *kitsu-ne* means 'come and sleep', while *ki-tsune* means 'always comes'.

The children of human–kitsune marriages are generally held to possess special physical and/or **supernatural** qualities. The specific nature of these qualities, however, varies widely from one source to another.

KNIGHTS TEMPLARS

The largest and most powerful of the medieval Christian military orders, and one of the most powerful monastic societies in Europe.

The Order of the Knights Templars was founded in 1118, in the aftermath of the First Crusade, to ensure the safety of the large numbers of European pilgrims who flowed towards Jerusalem after its conquest. A group of noblemen and crusaders travelled to the Holy Land and encamped next to the alleged site of King Solomon's temple. The knights vowed to protect Christians in the area and made a pledge of chastity, poverty and obedience. They called themselves the Order of the Knights Templars and the name alludes to their first encampment at the Temple Mount in Jerusalem, which they renamed *Templum Domini*. The name is also an indication of their interest in building. The real power behind the order was St Bernard of Clairvaux, head of the Cistercian Order of monks, and it was his greatest wish to build cathedrals that would esoterically teach the secrets he carried from early church fathers.

In 1128 the Pope officially recognized the Templars as a separate order, giving it unheard-of sovereignty. The order was exempt from taxes and answered only to the Pope. Membership was restricted to men of noble birth who had to undergo vigorous probations and **initiation** rituals before acceptance. The head of the order was the Grand Master, followed by his deputy the Seneschal, the Marshal and the Commander. The Templar battle cry was *Vive Dieu Saint Amour* (Long Live God's Holy Love) and their motto was *Non Nobis Domine, Non Nobis, Sed Nomini Tuo Da Gloiam* (Not for us Lord, not for us, but to thy name give glory). The Templar seal displayed two knights sharing a horse: a sign of poverty and service.

By the beginning of the fourteenth century the Templars had become enormously wealthy and enormously powerful in

Europe and the Middle East, with branches in Scotland, England, Aragon, Castile, Portugal, Germany and Naples. As their influence grew stories circulated about the Knights Templars' secret rituals and possible links with Sufis (a mystical sect of Muslims): sharing their **esoteric** interest in the **Kabbalah** and **alchemy**. Others believed the Templars were devil worshippers and that their rituals included bestiality, sodomy, idol worship and intercourse with **demons**. These rumours proved particularly useful for King Philip IV of France who was in debt to the Templars and irritated by their immunity from secular jurisdiction.

On 13 October 1307, Philip seized the Templars' property in Paris and arrested the Grand Master Jacques de Molay and 140 Templars, charging them with heresy. He bullied the weak Pope Clement V into signing a papal bull authorizing the Templars' trials and seizure of their property. For the next seven years the Templars were persecuted for heresy and **witchcraft** while the King and Pope argued over jurisdiction and disbursement of the property.

In 1312 Pope Clement officially abolished the Order and all its branches. The great majority of its assets were seized by King Philip and King Edward II of England. However, the kings of Spain and Portugal resisted papal pressure and transferred the assets into new orders, allowing Templars to become members. In 1314 Grand Master de Molay was promised life imprisonment and not death if he confessed to his crimes in public, but when he was led out in front of a packed crowd of nobility, clergy and commoners he loudly proclaimed his innocence and that of all the Templars. King Philip, who had once been a friend of Moley and had asked him to be his daughter's godfather, was furious and sentenced Molay to be burned alive. As Molay died he allegedly cursed Philip's family to the thirteenth generation and said that Philip and Pope Clement would join him before God's throne within a year. Clement died within a month and Philip's Capetian dynasty dwindled after just one generation to be replaced by the Valois.

Templar legend insists that the truth did not die with Molay and that some of the persecuted survivors of the Order fled to Scotland disguised as stonemasons. As a cover the Templars borrowed Masonic **symbols** and called themselves **Freemasons**. Another theory says that a Templar called Geoffrey de Gonneville was given a message from Molay to deliver to a group of Templars meeting in Dalmatia, telling them that their order would revive again in six hundred years. After this meeting the Supreme Council of the order remained in Corfu for three years, before supposedly launching the Order of the Rose-Crux or **Rosicrucians**. Other theories suggest that the eighteenth-century **adept**, the Comte de St Germain, who participated in Freemason and Rosicrucian rituals, was a Templar and attempted to introduce Templar secrets into these two organizations. It has also been suggested that another eighteenth-century occultist and student of St Germain, **Count Cagliostro**, was a Templar agent.

Many researchers of the esoteric have claimed that the order stored secret knowledge, linking them to the Rosicrucians, the

Freemasons, Hermetics, Gnostics, Essenes, and even to relics such as the **Shroud of Turin**. Whether of not the Knights Templars did found such organizations may forever remain a mystery, but their spiritual power most definitely lives on in all secret societies and esoteric organizations.

The mythos of the Knights Templars as keepers and defenders of the Holy **Grail** is a central plot point in the box office smash hits *Indiana Jones and the Last Crusade* (1989) and Umberto Eco's novel *Foucault's Pendulum* (1988). However, recent interest in Templar mythology has been sparked by its prominent role in Dan Brown's international bestseller, *The Da Vinci Code* (2003), and by its similar role in the 2004 movie, *National Treasure*.

KNISSOMANCY

From the ancient Greek *knisa*, meaning the fatty smoke of a burnt sacrifice, knissomancy is an ancient form of **divination** by the burning of incense. There was an old belief that the smoke of incense carried prayers up to the gods. The Etruscans used incense on burning coals to ascertain if anyone had bewitched them.

It would seem that the incense smoke was interpreted according to its volume and density, the way in which it ascended and the shapes it made in the air. The direction it moved in and the consistency would have probably been considered important – whether it was sporadic or flowing, for instance. Thick, swirling

smoke might have indicated troubles and problems, while thin, wispy smoke could indicate activity that was inconsequential.

KNOCKERS

Spirits that haunt mines, especially tin mines. They were thought to frequent the tin mines that formed much of the local economy in eighteenth and nineteenth-century Cornwall. Knockers are also called Buccas, Gathorns, Knackers, Nickers, Nuggies, Spriggans, Blue Caps and Cutty Soams. In American folklore they are known as Tommyknockers. As well as mines, the knockers were thought to haunt some **wells** and other natural features, which, along with the other names for them suggests there may have been a wider use of the term to describe **supernatural** creatures.

According to folklore, knockers are friendly and willing to help miners in trouble, but they can also be mischievous if food and offerings are not left for them in payment and respect not given them. It has been suggested that they are the **ghosts** of Jews who worked the mines, or the ghosts of Jews who crucified Christ and were punished by being sent to work under ground. They are so named because of the knocking sound they make as they work – according to lore they are extremely hard workers. They are often linked with rich lodes of ore so miners always listen closely when they hear the supernatural knocking. From time to time knocker laughter and footsteps can be heard and if they manifest they do so in doll-sized form. Strange tricks were often played on those who offended them by whistling or making the sign of a cross, and a miner could find himself led to potentially dangerous places in the mine.

Belief and sightings of knockers have died with the tin-mining industry, although they are still thought to haunt unused and un-worked tunnels in some quarters.

KOBOLD

In German folklore a kobold is an ugly, mischievous and occasionally evil **spirit**. The name comes from the German word meaning 'evil spirit' and is often translated in English as **goblin**. In the sixteenth and seventeenth centuries they were usually depicted in paintings as little devils with a conical hat, pointy shoes, a hairy tail and bald feet in place of hands.

There are two types of kobold: a house kobold that is similar to a **brownie**, and a mine kobold that is similar to the Cornish **knocker** and the American tommyknocker. The mine kobold is evil and will try to cause accidents and rock falls while miners are working, but the house kobold will help with chores and sing to the children. If, however, food is not left out for him the kobold will become vindictive, hiding household objects or tripping people up.

KOESTLER, ARTHUR [1905–1983]

Hungarian-born British journalist and novelist, Koestler, who did not consider himself **psychic**, experienced a wide range of inexplicable phenomena, including encounters with **ghosts**. He took an active part in investigations of **hauntings** and was often in the company of some of the more noted ghost hunters of the day. In his will, Koestler left his entire estate to establish the Koestler Foundation at Edinburgh University to promote the study of **parapsychology** and found the Chair of Parapsychology there.

KONAKIJIJII

In Japanese folklore the **spirit** of a baby who has been left to die in the woods. The konakijijii lures people out to the woods with the sound of its crying, but when people get close they see that the baby has the face of an old man. If they pick the baby up it is impossible to put down and suddenly becomes so heavy that it crushes unsuspecting victims to death.

KOSHAS

Yoga says that each person has five distinct energy bodies, states of mind called koshas, vibrating at different speeds. These interacting and overlapping layers of energy form the complete spiritual, mental and physical nature of the human personality.

Kosha is a Sanskrit word meaning 'sheath'. Moving from the gross physical body to the subtle spiritual body, each kosha signifies a more refined dimension of consciousness. The koshas are known as *annamaya, pranamaya, manomaya, vijnanamaya* and *anandamaya. Maya* means 'composed of', so these sheaths are composed of food, energy, intellect, **intuition** and bliss. The basic premise of this magnificent body-science is that while aspiring towards intuitive awareness and inner, lasting bliss, physical health and existence in the here and now cannot be ignored.

KUBIKAJIRI

Head-eating **ghost** from Japanese folklore. The kubikajiri has a distinctive smell – that of fresh blood – and is said to lurk around graveyards at night searching for its head. If it can't find its own head it will try to eat the heads of anything – living or dead – that crosses its path.

KUMALAK

Kumalak has been practised in Kazakhstan, Central Asia, for thousands of years. The word means 'sheep droppings' and it was a method of **divination** practised by the local shaman of the area. In modern times it is carried out using such items as coffee beans rather than sheep droppings.

The method is to use 41 broad beans, coffee beans or any other types of beans from a bag. The beans are sorted by the soothsayer and separated into a pre-ordained order on a grid on a cloth so that there are three rows of three groups of beans, with each group of beans containing one, two, three or four beans. Each combination is codified and refers to the enquirer's past, present and future. The actual interpretation is based on **numerology**, numbers being of great importance in the Kazakh tradition.

KUNDALINI

'Kundalini' is derived from a Sanskrit word meaning either 'coiled up' or 'coiling like a snake', and refers to a psycho-spiritual energy said to be sleeping within the body, which can be awakened through spiritual illumination. There are a number of other translations of the term, usually emphasizing a more serpent nature to the word, e.g. 'serpent power'. The caduceus **symbol** of coiling snakes is thought to be an ancient symbolic representation of kundalini physiology. According to the Yogic tradition Kundalini is curled up in the back part of the root **chakra** in three and one-half turns. The awakening of this serpent and the manifestation of its powers is a primary aim of the practice of Kundalini **Yoga**.

The power of kundalini awakening is said to be incredible and associated with bizzare physical sensations, pain, **clairaudience**, visions, psychical powers, ecstacy, bliss and transcendence of the self. The concept of kundalini is also associated with religious experiences of an **altered state of consciousness** brought about either spontaneously, or through spiritual practice or through a **near-death experience**. Sometimes it is regarded by yogis as a sort of deity, hence the occasional capitalization of the term.

According to Yogic phenomenology kundalini awakening is associated with the appearance of bio-energetic phenomena referred to as pranic awakening. Prana is interpreted as the vital, life-sustaining force in the body. Uplifted, or intensified life-energy is called *pranotthana* and is supposed to originate from an apparent reservoir of subtle bio-energy at the base of the spine. This energy is also interpreted as a vibrational phenomenon that initiates a period or a process of vibrational spiritual development. Some Western translators interpret the energetic phenomenon as a form of **psychic** energy.

Since the 1970s kundalini awakening has been reported with increasing frequency in the West. It is typically regarded as a rich source of psychic- or libido-enchancing energy in our **unconscious**. Not all kundalini awakenings follow the classic yoga model but seem to vary in application and intensity. The yogi mediates to arouse kundalini energy and bring it up through his or her body, activating the chakras in succession until the crown chakra is reached. The duration of kundalini can be fleeting or several minutes long.

The results of kundalini awakening can defy description, or may be described in many different ways, using the language and inflections of the individual person. One of the most sensational cases of kundalini awakening was experienced by Gopi Krishna (1903–1984) of India, who meditated every morning for three hours for 17 years. On 25 December 1937 he experienced an explosive, roaring kundalini awakening of liquid light. He described the experience in his book, entitled *Kundalini: Path to Higher Consciousness*:

Suddenly, with a roar like that of a waterfall, I felt a stream of liquid light entering my brain through the spinal cord. Entirely unprepared for such a development, I was completely taken by surprise; but regaining my self-control, keeping my mind on the point of concentration. The illumination grew brighter and brighter, the roaring louder, I experienced a rocking sensation and then felt myself slipping out of my body, entirely enveloped in a halo of light. It is impossible to describe the experience accurately. I felt the point of consciousness that was myself growing wider surrounded by waves of light. It grew wider and wider, spreading outward while the body, normally the immediate object of its perception, appeared to have receded into the distance until I became entirely unconscious of it. I was now all consciousness without any outline, without any idea of corporeal appendage, without any feeling or sensation coming from the senses, immersed in a sea of light simultaneously conscious and aware at every point, spread out, as it were, in all directions without any barrier or material obstruction. I was no longer myself, or to be more accurate, no longer as I knew myself to be, a small point of awareness confined to a body, but instead was a vast circle of consciousness in which the body was but a point, bathed in light and in a state of exultation and happiness impossible to describe.

Kundalini meditation exercise

Kundalini release can be triggered by unguided meditation, such as the one below, but it is important to point out that Yogis stress the importance of proper mental, physical and spiritual preparation, sometimes including several years of instruction and guided meditation, before attempting to awaken Kundalini by yourself.

Find a quiet place free of distractions. Sit or lie down and find a position that is comfortable for you. Quieten your mind. Still your thoughts. Relax your body, starting with your face, your jaw and forehead and working down your shoulders, arms, hips, legs and feet. Now focus on your breathing. Inhale slowly and deeply through your nose. Hold your breath as long as is comfortable. Exhale through the mouth slowly and completely. Repeat for two more breaths or as is comfortable.

Now focus your attention on your chakras. Starting from the top of your head visualize your crown chakra opening. Watch as pure white light enters your crown chakra and slowly spirals down through your spine. The white light opens your third eye chakra. You may experience vibrant colours, especially blue and violet. The white light moves down to your throat chakra, releasing your energy blockages. You may feel like chanting or singing. Allow the tones to resonant from your throat. The white light now enters your heart chakra. You experience a feeling of unconditional love and compassion. The white light enters your solar plexus. Gently your fears, anger, tensions are released. See the white light enter your sacral chakra, releasing any pain and guilt linked to that chakra. The white light now enters your root chakra, the seat of your kundalini energy. As it does, it begins to activate the energy of this chakra. Feel the energy suddenly emerge from your root chakra, spiralling up through the base of your spine as if it were a coiled snake of liquid gold energy bringing you to higher levels of consciousness. Allow the energy to flow through your chakras. See the energy wheels of your chakras rotating.

When you are ready, come back into your physical body. Relax and balance your energies. You might want to stretch and drink some water to ground yourself.

Kundalini is believed to open new pathways to the nervous system. The pain and extreme physical sensations associated with kundalini awakening is said to be due to the inability of the nervous system to cope with it all at once. Yogis stress that the body must be properly prepared for the shock through yoga, as an explosive awakening to someone unprepared for it can cause insanity or even prove fatal.

Western psychologists have determined that people can experience minor kundalini states. Symptoms may not occur all at once but build up gradually over a period of time, creating cycles of kundalini states when the individual thinks, feels and acts differently to normal. Symptoms include involuntary movements, pain, unusual breathing patterns, itching, vibrating sensations, insomnia, hypersensitivity to environment, intensifed sex drive, inability to think clearly, detachment, dissociation and **out-of-body experiences**. Symptoms can generally be alleviated through the introduction of a higher calorie diet and the cessation of **meditation**.

Scientific research has come to no definite conclusions concerning the nature of kundalini, due in part to its unpredictability and to the fact that many of its symptoms are hard to distinguish from those caused by mental illness and stress.

L

LABIOMANCY

From the Latin *labium*, or 'lip', labiomancy is a form of **divination** involving lip reading. Even if the exact words are not heard or understood, it is the movement of the lips that is significant and the suggestion of words leads the diviner towards his or her interpretation.

LABYRINTH

A complicated, **maze**-like path or building with twists and turns. The aim is to find the centre of the maze without getting lost.

The term comes from the Greek myth of Theseus who battled the half-man, half-bull Minotaur of Knossos on the Island of Crete. According to legend the only way to safely confine the Minotaur was to put him at the centre of a complicated maze. People would be sent into the maze as sacrificial victims. The hero, Theseus, successfully navigated the maze, killed the monster and found his way out.

Labyrinths are known as universal symbols of transformation, created to help people find spiritual meaning. They can often be located on sacred land (for example in churches or cathedrals) where they can be walked in a spirit of contemplation. They can also be drawn or made by an individual for the purposes of **meditation** and contemplation: focusing on getting to the heart of the maze will help you focus on getting to the heart of your concerns.

Labyrinths once played a part in **pagan** fertility rites. They also were thought to represent the map to the **underworld**, which the **spirit** of the dead used to find its way to the **afterlife**. If a spirit got lost in the labyrinth it was doomed to eternal **limbo**.

LA LLORONA

Also called The Weeping Woman (Llorona is Spanish for 'weeper'). In Mexican folklore La Llorona is a ghostly weeping woman who floats around at night searching for her murdered children.

There are several versions of the La Llorona story. In one La Llorona is looking for her lost child. In another she killed her own child and now drifts the earth in eternal torment. In yet another she had many children but fell in love with a man who didn't want any. To please her lover she drowned her children but was overcome by grief and guilt and drowned herself.

Folklorists believe that the story may have drawn its inspiration from Aztec mythology. The goddess Chihuacohuatl dressed in white and carried an empty cradle. It was said she walked among Aztec women screaming and crying for her lost child. It's also possible that the story has a historical basis. Around 1550 an Indian princess fell in love with an Italian nobleman and bore him twins. The nobleman, despite promising to marry the princess, married someone else. Consumed with rage the princess killed her children with a dagger and wandered the streets in torn and bloody clothes wailing for her children. She was found guilty of murder and executed. It is said that her **ghost** is cursed and must forever wander the earth looking for her children.

Typically La Lorena is described as shapely and dressed in white or black. She has long hair and long fingernails but no face. She is usually seen by riverbanks and deserted places at midnight, with her back turned, but sometimes she appears during daylight asking for her missing child. She is also said to wait by the roadside and if unsuspecting motorists pick her up they are told her sad story. Sometimes she will appear in a car and disappear a few minutes later. Some say she will entice and kill men if they are drunk and stumble across her in lonely areas.

Seeing La Llorena is thought to be a bad **omen**. Bad luck or death are said to follow within a year.

LAMBERTINI, PROSPERO [1675–1758]

As Archbishop of Bologna (he later became Pope Benedict XIV) Lambertini penned *De Canonisatione*, a study of miracles that marked 'a watershed in the Catholic Church's attitude to the miraculous. It proposed that the divine will could manifest itself through **supernatural** agencies. Lambertini also warned that it was easy to mistake natural manifestations as supernatural events and that there were phenomena,

such as 'the knowledge of things to come, things past,' that might occur without God or the devil being directly involved.

Some of the guidelines Lambertini laid down in *De Canonisatione* for assessing what could and could not be regarded as divine are still broadly adhered to by the Vatican today.

LAMPADOMANCY

Lampadomancy is **divination** from the form, colour and movements of a candle or flame of a lamp. It was a popular form of divination in ancient Egypt where diviners would perform it a midday in a darkened room illuminated by a single lamp.

Depending on the type of fuel used a lamp or candle may burn clearly, with little flicker, or it may burn with much spluttering and smoke. It was considered good fortune if the flame had a single point. However, two points was regarded as a sign of bad luck. A flame that bent was thought to indicate illness and sparks indicated news. Sudden extinction of a flame was considered a very bad **omen**. Other interpretations depended upon the individual seer.

An alternative method involved the interpretation of spots of carbon deposited on paper sheets held over the flame. In another method the diviner used the lamp to attract **spirits** to the flame in the hope of consulting them.

LANG ANDREW [1844–1912]

Novelist, historian, anthropologist and expert on folklore, Lang is best known for his series of fairy-tale anthologies. However, he was also a serious student of the **occult**, a devoted ghost hunter and psychical researcher.

Lang gained enough acclaim as a ghost hunter and sufficient respect for his knowledge of the field that he was contracted to write a number of entries related to **ghosts** and the occult for the ninth edition of the *Encyclopaedia Britannica*, published in 1875. In the 'Apparitions' entry he argued that **apparitions** were not satisfactorily explained as coincidental and suggested that crisis apparitions, which were seen around the time of the **agent**'s death, were telepathically induced hallucinations. In particular, Lang emphasized the similarity between testimony reported from tribal communities and those being reported from **Spiritualist séances** – **mediumship, levitation, rappings, poltergeists** and so on. Although Lang did not mention his own experience in the apparition article his views may have been influenced by an apparition he himself had seen a few years before in 1869. He believed he saw an Oxford professor standing by a streetlight in front of the college he taught at; at the same time this man lay dying elsewhere.

In 1911, Lang again contributed to the prestigious reference book with an essay on poltergeists, which displays his critical but sympathetic approach, and it is still regarded as one of the best statements in print regarding the phenomenon.

Among Lang's other works on the subject were *Cock Lane and Common Sense* (1894), *The Book of Dreams and Ghosts* (1897) and *The Making of Religion* (1898). In *Cock Lane* (the title drew its inspiration from the famous London poltergeist case: see **Cock Lane ghost**), Lang attempted to heal the rift between anthropologists and members of the **Society for Psychical Research**. In *The Book of Dreams* he aimed at a more general audience and brought together a number of real-life ghost stories around the world arranged in chapters that progress from **dreams** to hallucinations to apparitions and **hauntings**. Again he did not mention his own experience in the book but he did see an entity himself once: a young female relative dressed in blue crossing a well-lit hall. In *The Making of Religion* Lang discussed **crystal** gazing experiments and once again tried to unite psychical research and anthropology. He never quite succeeded but he did raise public awareness of the issues and many believe it is thanks to his impressive work that the field of psychical research was no longer regarded as disreputable.

Lang became President of the Society for Psychical Research in 1911, a year before his death which he himself predicted by what he described as an 'hereditary hallucination' – a **phantom** cat which traditionally appeared to members of his family who were a few months from death.

LA PIERRE, JOSEPH [FL. FIFTEENTH CENTURY]

Perhaps the most extreme of all known historical ghost hunters, La Pierre was a French occultist who convinced himself that it was possible to actually create a **ghost** from the blood of those who had recently died.

The theory suggested by La Pierre was that when a corpse was buried, the release of salts and other minerals from the body during the heating process of fermentation and bodily decay could create an ethereal form. 'The saline particles then resumed the same relative positions that they had occupied in the living body, and a complete, complex, but ethereal human form would result.' This, La Pierre states, explains why ghosts habitually linger around haunted graveyards and cemeteries.

La Pierre was so taken with his theory that he began experiments designed to create his own ghost. These included applying varying degrees of heat to blood specimens to show that that this was the medium by which the saline particles comprising the ethereal body of a ghost were carried.

In 1482, a contemporary of La Pierre made this report:

About midnight, he [La Pierre] heard a terrible noise like the roaring of a lion. And continuing quiet after the sound had ceased, the moon being at full, suddenly between himself and the window he saw a thick little cloud, condensed into an oval form which after, little by little, did seem completely to put on the shape of a woman and making another and sharp clamour, did suddenly vanish.

LARES

Ancient Roman **spirits** of the dead. Lares acted as protectors and were said to live in households, cities or regions. Household lares were regarded as part of the family and offerings of food and drink would be left out for them at every meal. They are usually depicted as dancing youths, with a horn cup in one hand and a bowl in the other.

The cult of the Lares may have originated from the worship of Lar, the household god. It was believed that Lar blessed the house and crops in the fields. He would be worshipped in small sanctuaries or shrines, called Lararium, which could be found in every Roman house, typically in the atrium (the main room) or in the peristylium (a small open court) of the house.

There were many different types of lar **guardian spirits**. The most important are the Lares Familiares (guardians of the family), Lares Domestici (guardians of the house), Lares Patrii and Lares Privati. Other spirits were the Lares Permarini (guardians of the sea), Lares Rurales (guardians of the land), Lares Compitales (guardians of crossroads), Lares Viales (guardians of travellers) and Lares Praestitis (guardians of the state).

LAST JUDGEMENT

Central **supernatural** event of early Christian, Jewish and Islamic eschatology, sometimes called the Day of the Lord, Judgement Day or Doomsday.

References to the Last Judgement are numerous in the Bible. The Christian belief in the Last Judgement asserts that this world will one day end, the dead will be raised up in the general resurrection, and God, or Christ, will gloriously come to judge the living and the dead according to their earthly lives. The sinners shall be cast into **hell**, and the righteous shall be raised to **heaven**. These concepts are also common themes in early Jewish apocalyptic literature and the Last Judgement also figures in the Koran.

No generally accepted Christian teaching pronounces when Judgement Day shall occur, but many individuals have attempted to divine its date. Doomsday believers are called chiliasts, millenarians, or, specifically, Adventists.

LAVATER, LUDWIG [1527–1586]

In 1570, Ludwig Lavater published *De Spectris* in Geneva, Switzerland, a work dealing primarily with **poltergeist** phenomena, and established his reputation as an influential ghost hunter. Based entirely on Lavater's own extensive research and investigations of **supernatural** phenomena, during the Elizabethan era the work became the principal reference book for all those who were interested in the study of **ghosts**. It is thought that **William Shakespeare** may have used it as a reference for scenes in several of his plays, particularly *Hamlet*. The book described in detail numerous types of supernatural phenomena

and catalogued various **spirits** and ghosts for the first time in a glossary. Lavater's approach throughout is objective but often sceptical and to this day it remains a classic text for all those interested in psychical research.

LAVEAU, MARIE [1794–1881] AND GLAPION, MARIE LAVEAU [1827–1897]

Mother and daughter with the same name who became famous **Voodoo** queens in late nineteenth-century New Orleans. In death they are believed to haunt the city still.

Everything that is known about the elder Marie Laveau comes from local legend, hearsay and oral tradition. It is thought that she was born in New Orleans in 1794. Her father, Charles Laveau, is said to have been a wealthy white planter and her mother, Darcantel Marguerite, a mulatto with a strain of Indian blood. Marie herself is described as being tall and statuesque with curling black hair, fierce black eyes and good features, which at the time meant she was more white than black. She married Jacques Paris, a free man of colour, on 4 August 1819 and because the ceremony was performed in St Louis Cathedral, her contract of marriage can still be found in the files there. At the time of her marriage, there is no evidence that either she or Jacques were practising Voodoo. A short while after the wedding, Jacques disappeared and Marie began calling herself the Widow Paris. A record of his death did not appear until several years after he had gone missing.

It was after the strange disappearance of Jacques that Marie supported herself by becoming a professional hairdresser. Her clients would confide to her the most intimate secrets and this is perhaps how Marie got her start in Voodoo. Being a shrewd woman she took careful note of these secrets and later used them to strengthen her reputation as a voodoo queen.

Around 1826 Marie became the lover of Louis Christopher Duminy de Glapion. A few years after the record of Paris's death appears de Glapion moved into Marie's home and lived there until he died in June 1855. They didn't marry but they had 15 children. After establishing her relationship with de Glapion Marie devoted her energies to becoming the most famous and most powerful Voodoo queen in New Orleans.

During the 1830s Marie achieved her ambition of becoming the supreme Voodoo queen. At the time there were numerous other Voodoo queens but Marie saw off the competition with her sensational ceremonies. A devout Catholic, she added elements of the Catholic service, such as holy water, incense and prayer, and turned her rites at Lake Ponchartrain into vast spectacles. Everyone was invited to attend, provided they paid a fee. Marie created a carnival atmosphere with dancing, spectacular rituals, secret orgies and animal sacrifices; she even performed herself with a 20-foot long snake. It wasn't long before her knowledge of **spells**, her style and flair and the intimate knowledge she had gleaned from her hairdressing clients made

Marie the most powerful woman in New Orleans, with both whites and blacks seeking her advice and magical potions. She charged whites high fees but few blacks paid for her services.

Numerous stories of Marie abound but there is no evidence in most cases to support them, except hearsay. There are several small articles that mention Marie appearing in the New Orleans newspapers. These mostly deal with small legal battles she had with various Voodoo practitioners. One of the most well-known of Marie Laveau's exploits involved the murder trial of a young Creole gentleman, a trial which was almost certain to end in a guilty verdict for the young man. His powerful father approached Marie and promised her anything if she could rescue his son. Marie agreed, asking for the man's New Orleans house on St Ann Street, in the French Quarter near Congo Square, in return. He agreed, and Marie secretly placed several **charms** throughout the courtroom. When his son was declared not guilty, the gentleman gave her his house as promised, and Marie Laveau lived there until her death in 1881.

The story doesn't end there: the freed young man later sought Marie's help again when a girl refused to marry him. Marie made the man a **gris-gris** bag containing 'love powder' to wear around his waist and took some hair from the young man and spread it on the woman's footsteps. She promised him that the girl would marry him within a month, and her prophecy turned out to be true. When the lady sprained her ankle attempting to run away from her admirer, he picked her up tenderly and took her home. The man's act of kindness impressed the woman so much she agreed to marry him the next day.

Marie allegedly played a role in another high-profile love match. A wealthy old bachelor fell madly in love with a girl young enough to be his granddaughter, but the girl had already given her heart to a dashing young adventurer who was expected to return soon from his travels. The girl's father was heavily in debt and begged his daughter to marry the wealthy old man. When she refused he locked her away in a cabin and sought the advice of Marie. Marie promised that the wedding would take place. She gave the old man a gris-gris bag containing the testicles of a black cat that he was to wear around his genitals, and the father a love powder to put into the girl's food.

After two weeks the girl emerged from the cabin she had been locked in and, looking very pale and weak, agreed to the wedding. Overjoyed both men planned the wedding and it took place in a crowded St Louis Cathedral where everyone was invited to a huge reception. It seems, however, that the excitement of the celebrations and dancing were too much for the wealthy gentleman and he crumpled to the floor – probably from a heart attack. The girl inherited his fortune and a year after the wedding married her first and only love – the dashing young adventurer. When questioned about her role, Marie would reply that she had only promised the wedding would take place, nothing more.

Marie was known to have regularly performed Christian acts of charity, helping with yellow fever victims and the wounded during the Battle of New Orleans (1814). By the 1850s she had such influence with the local authorities that she could even enter prisons and take food and solace to convicted prisoners in their cells.

In 1852 Marie spent a great deal of time with two convicted prisoners, Jean Adam and Anthony Deslisle. On the morning of their execution she stayed with them until the last minute before joining the crowds waiting to watch the execution. Just as the executioner was about to hang them rain began to fall in torrents and lightning filled the sky. A terrified crowd saw the ropes holding the men snap. Police were called in to calm the situation and a few minutes later the execution was completed successfully. Everyone believed that Marie Laveau had caused the storm and nearly saved the prisoners' lives. The whole affair caused such an uproar that the Louisiana State legislature was forced to outlaw public executions.

On 16 June 1881, the newspapers announced that Marie Laveau was dead. She would have been around 87 years old. Her obituaries praised her for her being a pious Catholic woman with compassion towards the sick, and said that she had been a great beauty. Her role as alleged Voodoo queen was taken by her 50-year-old daughter, also named Marie Laveau, who bore a striking resemblance to her mother, which caused many people to mistakenly believe that Marie had defied death.

Marie Laveau remains a figure shrouded in mystery. She was a Voodoo priestess and a devoted Catholic. She weaved **spells** and charms but wielded even more influence through her earthly network of spies and informants. She ruthlessly wielded her power yet went to great pains to help the injured, sick and downtrodden. Though her true personality may never be known there is no doubt she was a fascinating and complex woman and her life has become a legend.

The younger Marie lacked the charisma and compassion of her mother but she took up her mother's mantle of supreme Voodoo queen, presiding over sensational rituals, secret Voodoo meetings and liaisons between white men and black women at 'Maison Blanche', the house built by her mother for that purpose. The police would turn a blind eye because they were afraid of being cursed. According to legend Marie died during a big storm in the 1890s but there are reports of her still alive as late as 1918.

Marie the elder is supposedly buried in a crypt at St Louis Cemetery. Faithful followers and the curious still visit the tomb, offering food, money and flowers in return for Marie's help after turning round three times and marking a cross with a red brick on the stone. Marie the younger is also believed to be buried in St Louis Cemetery, where another crypt marked Marie Laveau serves as a wishing vault for young women seeking husbands.

Both Maries are thought to haunt New Orleans in human and animal form and tour operators certainly play their part in keeping the Laveau legend alive. The elder Marie is said to haunt the cemetery where she is buried in the shape of a big, black crow, whose stand-up head fathers bear a resemblance to the way Marie used to pin her hair. The Maries have also been sighted as young women in long white and blue dresses, as snakes and as dogs on St Ann Street and on St John's Bayou, Lake Pontchartrain, where they allegedly conducted their secret Voodoo rituals.

LAYING ON OF HANDS

A **healing** practice, in which the psychic's or healer's hands are placed on or near the body of the sick person.

See also **Healing**, **Reiki** and **Therapeutic touch**.

LECANOMANCY

Ancient method of **divination** by the inspection of fluids, either in a cup or basin or other container. It was performed by dropping precious stones into water. The fact that the water was in a basin seems to have been important but it is unclear how interpretation was to take place. Perhaps the action of adding precious and colourful jewels to the water might have been triggers and the diviner was supposed to read answers represented by patterns on the water's shimmering surface or the sound the stones made when being dropped into the water. Sometimes oil was used instead of a rock. In this case the diviner interpreted the shapes of the oil floating on the water.

There is a reference to lecanomancy in the Old Testament. The Hebrew patriarch,

Joseph, may have practised this ancient magic: 'Isn't this the cup my master drinks from and also uses for divination?' (Genesis 44: 5).

Leek, Sybil [1923–1982]

One of the first to declare herself publicly to be a **witch** in Britain in the 1960s, a time when **witchcraft** was considered socially unacceptable because the law against witchcraft had been repealed a few years previously. With the publication of her autobiography, *Diary of a Witch* (1968), Leek announced that witchcraft was not dead and never had been. From then on she attracted public attention for almost everything that she did.

At the beginning of Sybil's public life as a witch, her openness about and adherence to the craft changed her life, as her landlord refused to renew her antique shop's lease until she renounced witchcraft. She refused, closed up shop and began a new career as a professional witch.

She moved to the United States and established herself as a high profile, media friendly witch, master astrologer and gifted **psychic** with numerous books and features on witchcraft, **astrology**, **numerology** and **reincarnation** to her credit. In *Diary of a Witch* she claimed to have been born to a family of hereditary witches of Irish and Russian descent. A colourful character in her time, her trademarks were a cape, loose gowns and a pet jackdaw named Mr Hotfoot Jackson, who perched on her shoulders. Her whole family was involved in witchcraft and astrology and some of the noted guests who allegedly visited her home included H G Wells, Lawrence of Arabia and **Aleister Crowley**.

LEFT-HAND PATH

Phrase used to describe the path of **black magic** where there is intention to harm a person, property or living being, or use force against a person's free will. The left earned these negative associations because the Latin word for left – *sinister* – has become associated with evil.

The phrase '**right-hand path**' is typically associated with healing magic and goodness, while 'left-hand path' is popularly associated with selfishness, cursing and evil. The distinction between left- and right-hand paths may have been handed down to modern times from Hindu and Buddhist traditions, where **yoga** involving sexual acts is left-hand tantra and right-hand tantra is breath work and celibacy.

Obviously left-hand paths include **Satanism** and cursing, but it is important to note that, like most dualities, this system of classification has its contradictions and left-hand methods may be found in traditionally right-hand groups and vice versa. For example, right-hand paths tend to place divinity outside of the self, while left-hand paths place it within. Right-hand practitioners usually seek to serve the divine and left-hand practitioners seek to realize the divine within themselves. Right-hand paths emphasize service, cooperation, humility and charity; left-hand paths emphasize self-development, self-reliance, mastery and pride.

Today, there are varying opinions of the two Paths; some see them as equally valid approaches to truth, whose relationship is akin to the balance between **yin** and **yang**, while others criticize the right-hand path for being too restrictive. According to the latter view, the right-hand path's imposition of formal dogmas and codes of behaviour can take away a person's ability to be truly responsible for his or her own life, thereby destroying a part of a person's identity. According to some, this is the main difference between the two paths: the left-hand path preserves individuality, while the right-hand path destroys it. Conversely, some accuse the left-hand path approach of narcissism while praising the right-hand path for its altruism.

LEMP MANSION

Lemp Mansion, located in St Louis, Missouri, is considered to be one of the most haunted places in America. It was built in the early 1860s and stands four storeys tall with 34 rooms.

William J Lemp, the son of the founder of Lemp Brewery, John Adam Lemp, was the first member of the Lemp family to live there. The Lemps were one of the richest families in St Louis due to the enormous success of their brewery, and the mansion overlooked the brewery. William Lemp and his wife had seven children and lived a life of luxury and excess. Their troubles began in 1901 when eldest son, Frederick, died of a heart attack at the age of 28. He was the heir apparent to the Lemp legacy, and his father was crushed. In 1904, still despondent over his loss, William went into the mansion's marble office and shot himself through the heart with a small calibre pistol.

The family business went to William Lemp Jr, who was not as well versed in the brewing trade as his father or brother had been. He and his wife, Lillian, lived a glamorous lifestyle, spending freely on clothes, entertainment, furnishings and art. Three vaults were built in the mansion to house their vast collection. Lillian, who delighted in wearing lilac-coloured dresses and coats, was known as 'The Lavender Lady'.

In 1919 Prohibition began and the brewery was forced to close. The Lemps weren't able to adapt to this change and the family fortune dwindled. William Jr's older sister, Elsa, committed suicide in 1920 by shooting herself with a small calibre gun, although not in the mansion. In 1922, William sold the brewery at a huge loss. Six months after the sale he went into the same marble office that his father had nearly two decades before and shot himself with a small calibre gun.

Despite all the tragic events that transpired in the mansion, another Lemp sibling, Charles, remained there. He was an eccentric man who had an extreme fear of germs and wore gloves virtually all the time. In 1949 at the age of 77, he went into the mansion's basement one morning with his dog. Using the trade-mark small calibre gun, he shot the dog and then himself.

Brother Edwin sold the mansion, having moved out of it in 1917 to escape its oppressive atmosphere. He never married and had no heirs but perhaps out of fear he kept a companion with him at all times. He died in 1970 at the age of 90 of natural causes.

Once sold the mansion became a boarding house until 1977. It was then purchased by Mr Dick Pointer and his father, who intended to renovate it and turn it into a restaurant. This is when reports of **hauntings** began.

During the renovations workers were disturbed by inexplicable banging noises and objects moving about on their own. One night Pointer heard a door slam shut even though no one else was in the house at the time. Another time a workman heard the sounds of footsteps on cobblestones outside the window, even though no cobblestones were there. A few months later, when grass was being dug up beneath the window, some cobblestones were discovered. What was most distressing, though, to the point where several workmen quit, was the strange sensation of being watched. Some of the men claimed that the unseen stares practically burned through them. There were also sightings of a strange and sad face staring from the attic window. It has been speculated that the Lemps had an eighth child who was retarded and hidden from sight, who might be responsible for the hauntings, although no record of an eighth child exists.

Unusual phenomena continued when the restaurant opened. There were reports of glasses flying through the air, mysterious voices were heard, **apparitions** glimpsed, doors opened and closed on their own and an oppressive and intense atmosphere in the marble office where so many suicides took place. Guests have claimed to feel cold spots and see strange lights. Both guests and employees have been frightened by a 'Lady in Lavender' on the third-floor stairwell. She has also been seen in the first-floor bathroom. Inexplicable noises still abound, the most notable being piano music and the barking of a **phantom** dog.

LEMURE

One of two types of **ghost** in Roman belief, lemures were thought to be the ghosts of people who died without leaving any relatives behind. They were associated with evil **spirits**.

According to Roman belief it was considered a curse to die without any surviving family. Lemures also included victims of murder, drowning and violent death, executed criminals and those who had died prematurely and were trapped on earth until their allotted life span expired. Black beans would be laid around the tomb of a body to prevent a lemure rising up from the grave, and if a lemure did haunt the living the standard method of **exorcism** was the banging of drums.

See also **Lares**.

Lemuria

According to some **occult** traditions, Lemuria was believed to be a lost continent from 25,000 years ago – variously located in the Indian Ocean, the eastern Pacific, or portions of both – which sank before the heyday of **Atlantis**.

Said to be the cradle of the human race, the concept of a lost continent of Lemuria was created in the 1860s by geologists who noticed strong similarities in rocks and fossils from southern Africa and central India. The modern theory of continental drift had not been proposed at that point and the geologists suggested that the similarities could indicate a land bridge crossing the Indian Ocean. Nineteenth-century biologists noted that such a bridge would explain the distribution of lemurs – primitive primates now found mostly on the Island of Madagascar – and the British zoologist Philip Sclater gave the theory its permanent name by suggesting that the land bridge be called Lemuria after them.

The discovery of continental drift and lemur fossils over a much wider range made the theory of Lemuria implausible to modern scientists, however in the meantime it was been picked up by **Helena Blavatsky**, the founder of **Theosophy**, who included Lemuria in her Theosophical vision of cosmic history. According to Theosophy Lemuria once reached from the Indian to the Pacific Oceans, and included parts of what are now south-east Asia, Australia and New Zealand. Its inhabitants were members of the so-called third root race: hermaphrodite, egg-laying ape men with four arms and an eye in the back of their heads. It was less culturally advanced than Atlantis but the hermaphrodites had highly developed **psychic** powers and communicated telepathically.

Accounts of the destruction of Lemuria differ. Theosophists believe it was destroyed in the biblical flood, but philosopher **Rudolf Steiner** (who had described the Lemurians as the telepathic third root race, and who credited them with the goal of developing clairvoyant powers of **imagination** to control the forces of nature) suggested volcanic activity. Theoretically all that is left of Lemuria's land mass are the peaks of Kauai, Hawaii to the north and Easter Island in the South. People living in this community were known as the **Mu**, according to the nineteenth-century author and amateur archaeologist, Colonel James Churchward.

Lemuria doesn't just appear in Theosophical versions of occult history but in the cosmic histories of many other occult groups over the last century or so. It's worth noting, however, that Lemuria traditions only date from the Blavatsky era and there is no concrete evidence whatsoever that Lemuria actually ever existed.

Leonard, Gladys Osborne [1882–1968]

Considered by many to be one of the world's greatest trance **mediums**, Gladys Osborne Leonard worked closely with the **Society for Psychical Research** to produce evidence for **survival after death**.

Gladys was born in Lancashire, England on 28 May 1882. Her parents tried to keep death a secret but at the age of eight a maid informed her that a family friend had died and been buried. This awareness shocked Gladys deeply but it also prompted **visions** of a happy valley with radiantly happy people. On one occasion when her father was with her she talked about another vision she was seeing on the wall.

Later Gladys spoke of her visions in *My Life in Two Worlds* (1931):

In whatever direction I happened to be looking the physical view of the wall, door, ceiling, or whatever it was, would disappear, and in its place would gradually come valleys, gentle slopes, lovely trees and banks covered with flowers, of every shape and hue. The scene seemed to extend for many miles, and I was conscious that I could see much farther than was possible with the ordinary physical scenery around me.

Gladys' father did not approve of her visions and forbade her to look upon her happy valley again. His disapproval was a recurring theme during her teens, when Gladys found herself drawn to **spiritualist** meetings.

Although Gladys trained to be a singer her career was short lived as she contacted diphtheria, which ruined her voice. So she joined a touring theatrical company instead. One morning, while on tour Gladys awoke at 2 am to see her mother standing in her room surrounded by a **halo** of bright light. The next day a telegram arrived, informing her that her mother had died at 2 am, leaving Gladys in no doubt that her mother had visited her in her room. She decided to experiment with her mediumistic talent and began **table-tilting** exercises with friends after shows. After numerous attempts, in 1913 she finally made contact with a **control** named Feda, who was to remain Gladys's main control throughout her career.

Feda sounded and behaved in a childish manner and claimed to be the spirit of one of Gladys's great-great-grandmothers, an Indian woman who had died in childbirth at the age of 14, around 1800. It was Feda who urged Gladys to take her mediumship into the public arena with presentations. Feda insisted that something terrible was going to happen to the world and Gladys needed to be there to provide comfort.

By this time Gladys had married a fellow actor named Frederick Leonard, who was also interested in the psychic world. She did all she could to make herself open and pure enough for discarnate communicators. She stopped smoking and drinking and gave up meat. At first her **séances** involved small groups of people but after World War I broke out she was besieged by people wanting sittings.

A significant turning point came when Gladys gave a sitting to a widow who had lost two sons in the war. The woman was so stunned by the accuracy of Gladys's descriptions that she mentioned them to her friend, Lady Lodge, the wife of physicist **Sir Oliver Lodge**. When Lady Lodge's son, Raymond, died in 1915 she booked an appointment with Gladys and was so impressed that she urged her husband to attend. During her sittings with the Lodges Gladys mentioned a photograph taken just before Raymond's death that the Lodges were not aware of. When it finally turned up they were amazed at how accurately Gladys had described it. Lodge wrote about his sittings with Gladys in *Raymond: A Life* (1916). This brought Gladys even more publicity and a much-needed increase in income enabled the Leonards to step out of the poverty they had been living in previously.

Lodge arranged for Gladys to train two of his friends, Una, Lady Troubridge and Radclyffe Hall in séance proceedings in the hope of contacting Hall's dead friend Mabel Batten. Their training lasted eight years and during that time a communicator showed a good knowledge of events in Hall's life and commented on things unknown to Hall or Troubridge. What was unusual about the Batten communicator (called A.V.B in the reports) was the unique way Batten's personality came through Gladys's mediumship with characteristic gestures and words.

In 1918 Gladys, mindful of the importance of strict séance procedures for the evidence of survival after death, agreed to give exclusive sittings arranged by the Society for Psychical Research for three months. As a condition of employment she agreed not to read any of its publications and after this three-month stint she continued to work for the society on an ad hoc basis.

Records of these sittings were published by Mrs W H Salter. In speaking of the evidence obtained by new sitters, Mrs Salter writes:

In justice to Mrs Leonard, it should be pointed out that the phenomena obtained in these circumstances are not likely to be as interesting or remarkable as those obtained by sitters who have sat regularly with Mrs Leonard during some months or even years. First sittings, even when they are on the whole successful, are apt to be of a rather tentative nature, and they usually follow certain conventional lines. Moreover, they afford little scope for evidence concerning the character and personality of the supposed communicator. For one thing, such evidence is largely cumulative in its effect, and for another, whether it is obtained by telepathy between Mrs Leonard and the communicator, or between Mrs Leonard and the sitter, or by some combined interaction of all three minds together, it is likely that a well-established rapport between Mrs Leonard and her sitter will facilitate matters. I think there is a general agreement among those who have sat repeatedly with Mrs Leonard – among whom I may include myself – that good evidence of surviving personality is sometimes obtained.

Many of the successful sittings with Gladys arranged by the Society for Psychical Research were not attended by grieving friends or relatives hoping to contact a loved one but by proxies who knew nothing about the people or subjects involved in the communication. This made the likelihood of the medium obtaining information directly from the sitter via **ESP** or **fraud** much less likely.

On occasions when Gladys's control Feda had trouble understanding a communication, sitters claimed to hear a voice from somewhere else in the room – a phenomenon called **direct voice mediumship**.

Sometimes Feda and the direct voice would talk to each other.

Psychical researcher Charles Drayton Thomas had more than 500 sittings with Gladys and it was with Thomas that Feda first suggested the **book test** (see **Survival tests**). In this test a communicator would tell a sitter to go to a certain room, take a book from a certain shelf and on a specific page there would be something of interest to the sitter. Later tests included the newspaper test, where the sitter would predict what would appear in the newspapers before they appeared on sale.

The mediumship of Gladys Leonard was so superior to that of other mediums that it was investigated a number of times. The philosopher C D Braud did a major study on the subject in his *Lectures on Psychical Research* (1962), and concluded that Feda was not an independent entity but an aspect of Gladys's personality. In the great majority of cases, though, like her American counterpart **Leonora Piper**, Gladys's mediumistic ability defied explanation and impressed her investigators.

Towards the end of the 1950s Feda instructed Gladys to take on no more new work and to cut back on the amount of work she did. She died at her home in Kent on 10 March 1968 at the age of 85.

LESLIE, BARONET SHANE [1885–1971]

A colourful figure in psychical research Irish-born Sir Shane Leslie spent his early years in Russia, where he befriended author Leo Tolstoy, before travelling through Europe as a vagabond. Leslie became fascinated by the **paranormal** while on his travels and laboriously researched and investigated a vast number of cases firsthand before publishing his collection in *Shane Leslie's Ghost Book* (1955). According to family tradition, Leslie's lineage had a **banshee** that would appear to predict the death of a family member. Leslie is reported to have encountered this banshee before his own death in 1971.

LETHBRIDGE, T C [1901–1971]

English psychical researcher, archaeologist and explorer, T C Lethbridge was noted for his ideas about **ghosts**, **dreams**, **dowsing** and the nature of time.

After graduating from Cambridge, Lethbridge became an archaeologist. He supported the theory – popular at the time but eventually discounted – of historian Margaret A Murray, that **witchcraft** was a pre-Christian religion of fertility worship. His interest in the Murray theory made him unpopular in Cambridge but led him towards the major discovery in the turf at Wandlebury Camp, an Iron Age fort near Cambridge, of the figure of a woman on horseback, with the symbol of the moon behind her, a sun god on one side and a sword-wielding warrior on the other. Lethbridge came to the conclusion that this was evidence that prehistoric England worshipped a moon goddess, Magog, and the sun god her husband, Gog. He published his theory in *Gogmagog, The Buried Gods* (1957).

Lethbridge's interest in the **supernatural** began in earnest around 1957 when he moved into Hole House, near Branscombe in Devon. A neighbour of his claimed to be able to project herself astrally out of her body and this triggered his interest in dowsing and the supernatural. In the course of his fieldwork, Lethbridge had become aware that he himself was prone to experiencing unusual happenings and that an investigation of these incidents was merited. He believed that a 'scientific' explanation lay behind what could be termed the 'odd'. History had proved to him that the supernatural of one generation often become the natural of the next and this notion fired his investigations. For the rest of his life Lethbridge explored other dimensions of reality.

He regarded the natural world as full of energy that could be picked up by the human brain or a **pendulum**. As a young man he had experienced a chilling presence while at school that he called the ghoul and at this stage of his life he explained it as a projection or picture from the subconscious mind of a person afraid of **ghosts**. He also believed that primitive human kind had greater powers of awareness than modern humanity.

Lethbridge experimented with his own dreams and suggested that there are two types: those that come from within the dreamer and those that come from beyond the control of the 'earth mind'. It was the latter type of dream that he believed contained memories of the future. He suggested that ideas about the nature of time were confused and that when the future is dreamt about, the dreamer is beyond the point of sleep and death.

As far as ghosts were concerned, Lethbridge said he felt 'reasonably convinced'. He believed that some people were transmitters and others were receivers and this created the dynamics of **hauntings**.

In addition to *Gogmagog* Lethbridge wrote eight other remarkable books about the **paranormal**: *Ghost and Ghoul* (1961), *Witches: Investigating an Ancient Religion* (1962), *Ghosts and Divining Rod* (1963), *ESP: Beyond Time and Existence* (1965), *A Step in the Dark* (1967), *The Monkey's Tail: A study in Evolution and Parapsychology* (1969), *Legends of the Sons of God* (1976) and *The Power of the Pendulum* (1976).

Lethbridge was a controversial figure, ridiculed in his day, but he left behind him an impressive body of work rich in bold and revolutionary ideas that were way ahead of their time.

LEVELS OF EXISTENCE

Many **esoteric** teachings propound the idea of a series of worlds or gradations of being; for example, the so-called theosophical 'planes' is one particular version of this. Another is the tantric theme of chakras, which is associated with an ascending series of states of consciousness, culminating in the Absolute Reality located either at or above the crown chakra.

Various numbers of planes are referred to in esoteric literature, often up to seven, but it is perhaps simplest to refer to three: physical, astral and spiritual. The physical plane is physical, visible and solid manifestation. The **astral plane** is non-physical. It is sometimes thought of as a template for what is manifested in the physical plane, but it can also be a realm in itself. The spiritual plane is the level of existence where there are no boundaries of tangibility, time or space. It is beyond a need for form and looks much less like the physical world than the astral does. Each of these major planes can again be divided up and various traditions use different names for the different sub-divisions.

The physical body is thought to have counterparts existing in different planes. Manifestations in the higher planes are often referred to as **subtle bodies**. In various traditions one might refer to an etheric, an emotional and a mental body as part of the physical plane, and other subtle bodies as part of the higher planes. The ones closest to the physical are roughly in the shape of the physical body and intimately connected to the physical body. As to the astral bodies, they are usually also in the shape of the physical body but they can under certain circumstances move away from the physical body, which partially accounts for **astral travel**, or **out-of-body experiences**.

Levi, Eliphas [1810–1875]

Considered one of the most influential and fascinating **magicians** of the nineteenth century Eliphas Levi's book, *The History of Magic* (1913), is still regarded as essential reading for students of the **occult**. Born Alphonse Louis Constant, the French occultist was a controversial figure, having served briefly as a priest before being defrocked for his involvement with the occult. It was said that Levi possessed an impressive array of **supernatural** powers and abilities and was able to summon **ghosts** at will.

Towards the end of his life Levi befriended English author Edward Bulwer Lytton who encouraged Levi to visit sites of **hauntings** so that **spirits** of the dead could be documented. It was in this capacity that Levi became the inspiration for the character of the magician in Lytton's short story, 'The Haunted and the Haunters' (1859).

Levitation

The act of raising a person or an object off the ground by **supernatural** means. This may be through **psychokinesis**, or through **magic** or by **spirits**. Most cases of levitation seem to be spontaneous, lasting only a few seconds or minutes, but some **psychic** or spiritual **adepts** are said to practise levitation as a demonstration of the mental control they have over themselves and other matter.

There is a vast body of anecdotal evidence for the levitation of a person, also known as self-levitation, reaching far back into history, but it remains a controversial subject. Levitation of objects, however, has been the subject of intense investigations since the Victorian era, with some evidence attesting to its reality. In the 1970s researchers reported success in levitating tables, and Soviet **medium** Nina Kulagina was photographed levitating small objects in her hands.

Christianity, Islam, Hinduism and Buddhism have recorded many cases of self-levitation. Saints and mystics reportedly levitate as proof of the power of God. St Teresa of Avila was said to levitate during states of rapture and, according to one eye-witness account by Sister Anne of the Incarnation, she levitated a foot or so off the ground for about half an hour. In Eastern mysticism self-levitation is a feat made possible by mastery of breathing and concentration that invokes the **universal life force**.

Louis Jacolliot, a nineteenth-century French judge, travelled the East and wrote of his **occult** experiences. In *Occult Sciences in India and Among the Ancients* (1884, 1971) he describes the levitation of a **fakir**:

Taking an ironwood cane which I had brought from Ceylon, he leaned heavily upon it, resting his right hand upon the handle with his eyes fixed upon the ground. He then proceeded to utter the appropriate incantations ... [and] rose gradually about two feet from the ground. His legs were crossed beneath him, and he made no change in his position, which was very like that of those bronze statues of Buddha ...

For more than twenty minutes I tried to see how [he] could thus fly in the face and eyes of all known laws of gravity ... the stick gave him no visible support, and there was no apparent contact between that and his body, except through his right hand.

Jacolliot was further told by the Brahmans that the 'supreme cause' of all phenomena was the 'agasa' (**akasha**), the vital fluid, 'the moving thought of the universal soul, directing all souls', the force that the adepts learn to control.

The **Transcendental meditation** movement claims to be able to train its adepts in the art of levitation and photographs have been taken of meditators seemingly floating about a foot or so above the floor. Sceptics remain unconvinced, arguing that the technique is more hopping than levitation.

In the West self-levitation has been regarded as a sign of evil if the person levitating was not a saint or holy man or woman. During the Middle Ages it was thought to be a sure sign of the diabolical, according to the Catholic Church's requirements for demonic **possession**. In 1906 Clara Germana Cele, a 16-year-old schoolgirl from South Africa, was said to be possessed by **demons**. She rose up five feet in the air, sometimes vertically and sometimes horizontally. When sprinkled with holy water she came out of these states of possession. This was taken as proof of the demonic nature of her possession.

Poltergeist cases and **hauntings** sometimes feature self-levitation and flying objects. Some investigators believe that in certain cases a human focal point with intense repressed emotion may unwittingly create enough psychokinetic energy to generate the phenomenon. Levitation reached the height of its popularity in the early days of **spiritualism**. It was fairly commonplace for **spirits** to allegedly cause **mediums** to rise out of their chairs and for objects to float around the room. One of the most fascinating cases of self-levitation was that of **D D Home**, who allegedly floated out of one window and in through another in front of a startled audience. Even more incredible was that Home was not in a **trance** during this levitation but was fully aware of what was happening. He said an unseen power lifted him up and he had an 'electrical fullness' in his feet.

Descriptions of what it feels like to levitate are hard to come by, but in addition to Home's account, the sixteenth-century saint Philip Neri was reported as saying that it was as if he had been caught hold of by somebody and 'wonderfully lifted'. Teresa of Avila's account reports that it was a 'very sore distress' to her, for fear it would cause scandal, which is why she forbade nuns who saw her floating to speak of it; it was also frightening: 'I confess that it threw me into great fear', but there could also be 'great sweetness if unresisted', and she was sure that it was not a **dream** or an illusion. 'The senses are not lost; at least I was so much myself as to be able to see that I was being lifted up.'

Sceptics explain reports of levitation by hallucination, **hypnosis** or simple **fraud**. Home was accused of using hypnosis techniques to trick his audience into thinking he levitated. Stage magicians often fake levitation in the dark by removing their shoes and placing them on the top of their hands, convincing audience members who see the hazy shape of the boots rising in the air that the magician is actually levitating.

LEY LINES

Patterns of powerful, invisible earth energy running through, along and beneath the earth that are thought to possess great spiritual, astrological and healing qualities and to connect various sacred sites, such as churches, stone circles, **megaliths**, holy places and other locations of spiritual or magical importance. The study of ley lines forms part of the so-called 'earth mysteries', a field of holistic investigation into ancient sites and their surrounding landscapes.

The phrase was first coined by English beer salesman and amateur antiquarian researcher, Alfred Watkins, in 1921 when he was out riding one day. As he approached a crest in the Bredwardine hills of Herefordshire he suddenly noticed that the ancient mounds, burial sites and churches were all built in straight lines. It occurred to him that these sites must have been deliberately placed along a worldwide power network of lines, criss-crossed and interconnected.

Four years later, in 1925, he described his vision in a book he titled *The Old Straight Track*:

Imagine a fairy chain stretched from mountain peak to mountain peak, as far as the eye could reach, and paid out until it reached the 'high places' of the earth at a number of ridges, banks, and knowls. Then visualise a mound, circular earthwork, or clump of trees, planted on these high points, and in low points in the valley other mounds ringed around with water to be seen from a distance. Then great standing stones brought to mark the way at intervals, and on a bank leading up to a mountain ridge or down to a ford the track cut deep so as to form a guiding notch on the skyline as you come up … Here and there, at two ends of the way, a beacon fire used to lay out the track. With ponds dug on the line, or streams banked up into 'flashes' to form reflecting points on the beacon track so that it might be checked when at least once a year the beacon was fired on the traditional day. All these works exactly on the sighting line.

Watkins called these lines leys, a word derived from the Anglo-Saxon *lea* or *leigh*, meaning 'grassy track'. He surmised that these straight tracks were probably the remnants of prehistoric trading routes. He went on to associate ley lines with the Greek god Hermes (Roman Mercury, Norse Woden) who was the god of communication and of boundaries, the winged messenger and the guide to travellers on unknown paths. Watkins identified Hermes with the chief god of the **Druids** and argued that

A Celtic god, Tout, or in its Romanised form Toutates, is supposed to be what Caesar referred to, and this name has been found on a Romano-British altar. It is a fact that sighting mounds called Tot, Toot, Tout, Tute and Twt abound all over the Kingdom, and the root is probably Celtic … The fact that such mounds

are mark-points on track ways strengthen the link.

After Watkins published his suggestions in *The Old Straight Track* public interest grew, as did controversy within the archaeological community. (The magazine *Antiquity* refused to advertise the book, describing it as a rank work.) Despite the fuss the popularity of his theory grew steadily and a 'Straight Track Club' was formed to which members could report their own observations of leys.

Watkins's observations were initially confirmed when straight line alignments were found throughout the UK but his theory about their nature was seriously doubted almost from the start. By the late 1930s Major F C Taylor noticed that leys often consisted of parallel tracks. If they marked prehistoric sites, why would travellers have needed two, both going in the same direction? Later larger-scale maps revealed that certain British ley lines carried across into Europe. Whatever leys were it was unlikely they were roads.

But if not roads, what were they? Some insist they are nothing but a random collection of points that happen to be in a straight line. Even ley supporters have differing opinions. Some assert that the prehistoric alignments can be validated while others suggest that leys mark paths of some sort of earth energy that can be detected by **dowsing** and may have been sensed by early humans. The energy is similar to the flow of the **universal life force**, found in **feng shui**. Points where key energy paths intersect are said to be prone to **paranormal** phenomena such as **UFO** sightings, **earth lights** and **hauntings**.

A brief guide to ley hunting

In his books Alfred Watkins laid down meticulous rules for ley hunters and gave advice that incorporates reference research, mapwork and fieldwork. Points to look for on the map are of the following types, listed in order of importance:

1. Ancient mounds, whether called tumulus, tump, barrow, cairn or any other name.
2. Ancient unworked stones – not those marked as boundary stones.
3. Moats and islands in ponds and small lakes.
4. Traditional or holy wells.
5. Beacon points.
6. Crossroads with place names and ancient wayside crosses.
7. Churches of ancient foundation and hermitages.
8. Ancient castles and old castle place names.

Watkins suggests ringing each of these features on the map so that they are clearly visible. Next, stick a pin into the exact location of a grade 1 or 2 marker point and place a straight edge against it, swinging it around to see if three other ringed points (or two and a stretch of straight road or track) can be found to align. Draw a thin pencil line through the points and then check for further confirmation points along its course. To conform to the Watkins's prototype, the ley should consist of at least four marker points and terminate at both ends in a natural hill or mountain peak.

If successful in this first stage, the next thing is to walk the ley on the ground. Watkins says that this is detective rather than surveying work, as much evidence has been lost to ploughing and modern development. An important aspect of field observation that Watkins does not mention is the intervisibility of sites. In short distance leys, such as those between standing stones, the ability to see the next marker stone from your point of observation is a good indication that the alignment was deliberate.

Modern ley hunters are more likely these days to start their search for ancient straight tracks in the local reference library. The local studies collection is a good starting point, and these days there are many fine studies of local village histories that often contain obscure references to old funeral paths and church paths. Armed with this information, it is time to consult the Ordnance Survey map. If you can get hold of the older versions of these so much the better. They often contain a wealth of detail missing from the modern maps and will show areas of the countryside which are now developed and old footpaths that have disappeared.

The Society of Ley Hunters (www.ley-hunter.com/index.html) is a good source of information on ley lines and hunting ley lines.

The issue of evidence – how many alignments over what distance – to validate a ley remains a hot topic among ley enthusiasts. Author John Michell gathered seductive evidence when he identified 22 alignments between 53 megalithic sites over 7-mile distances. Michell also pointed out similarities between the ley lines of Europe and the 'dragon paths' of China, which were thought to carry energy to the Emperor.

Other investigators have discovered evidence that suggests an energy aspect associated with certain ancient sites. Dowser Guy Underwood, for example, confirmed that underground streams ran under the length of some long burrows. Physicists Professor John Taylor and Dr Eduardo Balinovski of London University used a gaussmeter on a South Wales megalith and found it surrounded by a magnetic field phenomenon. Theories of magnetic interaction at ley line points suggest to some observers that these points were used to induct energy but current data remains inconclusive.

Although Britain has been the principal site of ley investigation there is also interest in Europe and the United States. Straight line systems also exist in Bolivia, where holy tracks have been shown to merge towards Indian shrines at the tops of holy hills, and Peru, where 41 lines called *ceques* spread out from the Sun Temple in Cuzco into the country, marked by various shrines and other sites.

LIEKKO

In Finnish folklore, Liekko, which means 'the flaming one', is thought to be a small flame-like **apparition** that bobs at eye level and presages death or mishap for all who see it, often being mistaken for the light of a welcoming farmhouse.

The Liekko is reported to be the **spirit** of a child who was secretly buried in a forest, but another version of the story explains that a long-ago New Year festival had children sing while marching through the village holding candles above their heads. The custom ended when a **witch** kidnapped the children who were never heard of again, save in the form of their lost **souls** wandering the marshes, still holding their candles – the flames of liekko. Since they can only return to earth by replacing one of their number with a living child, mothers warn their children never to follow the lights.

LIFE AFTER DEATH

See **Survival after death**.

LIFE FORCE

See **Universal life force**.

LIFE REVIEW

A popular folk belief is that when a person is close to death or confronted with death they will see their life flash before their eyes. A number of **near-death experience** stories do report this.

Typically the life review consists of unusually vivid, instantaneous images of either the person's whole life or fragments of it. In some instances the images may appear in an orderly sequence, from the present to childhood but sometimes the images seem to appear all at once. There may also be glimpses of an imagined future or identification with the feelings of other people. It seems that the life review occurs without any conscious effort on the part of the person and many report feeling like passive witnesses.

LIMBO

Modern-day use of the word limbo to refer to states of oblivion, confinement or transition is derived from the theological sense of Limbo as a place where souls that cannot enter **heaven** or **hell** remain, for example, unbaptized infants. The traditional view of **ghosts** is that they exist in a kind of limbo because they are **spirits** of dead people who for some reason are stuck between this plane of existence and the next, often as a result of some tragedy or trauma.

LINCOLN, ABRAHAM [1809–1865]

Sixteenth President of the United States, Abraham Lincoln had a strong interest in **Spiritualism**. He was assassinated while in office and his body was moved numerous times to different graves. In death it is thought he has not found peace as his **ghost** has been said to haunt many locations.

Early in his political career Lincoln develop a fascination for Spiritualism that would remain with him all his life. In a letter to his friend Joshua F Speed in 1842 he observed that he had 'always had a strong tendency to mysticism' and had often felt compelled 'by some other power than my own will' which he felt came 'from above'.

Throughout his presidency Lincoln may have had intuitive or **psychic** insights that prompted him to take or not take action. **Mediums** were frequent visitors to the White House and although it is unlikely he made his decisions solely based on advice from the **spirit** world, he may have heard things from mediums that reinforced his own convictions to take action. For example, mediums may have had an influence on his issuing of the decree in 1863 to free all slaves in the rebellious states.

Lincoln's beloved son Willie died in 1862 from scarlet fever and both Lincoln and his wife, Mary Todd (who was also committed to the spiritualist cause) suffered deep grief. Lincoln once told his secretary Salmon P Chase that he often felt Willie near him and spoke to him.

A week or so before his assassination by actor John Wilkes Booth on 14 April 1865,

Lincoln had a dramatic and prophetic **dream** of his own death.

About ten days ago, I retired very late. I soon began to dream. There seemed to be a death-like stillness about me. Then I heard subdued sobs, as if a number of people were weeping. I thought I left my bed and wandered downstairs. There the silence was broken by the same pitiful sobbing, but the mourners were invisible. I went from room to room. No living person was in sight, but the same mournful sounds met me as I passed alone. I was puzzled and alarmed. Determined to find the cause of a state of things so mysterious and shocking, I kept on until I arrived at the East Room. Before me was a catafalque on which rested a corpse wrapped in funeral vestments. Around it were stationed soldiers who were acting as guards; and there was a throng of people, some gazing mournfully upon the corpse, whose face was covered, others weeping pitifully. 'Who is dead in the White House?' I demanded of one of the soldiers. 'The president,' was his answer. 'He was killed by an assassin.' Then came a loud burst of grief from the crowd, which awoke me from my dream. I slept no more that night; and although it was only a dream, I have been strangely annoyed by it ever since.

There was a big demand to see Lincoln's body and a special funeral train carried his him from Washington through New York State and west to Illinois to his hometown of Springfield. The trip took over two weeks and the train stopped in numerous cities with about 2 million mourners filing past the open coffin. Since then every April a **phantom** funeral train is said to travel along the route taken by the official funeral train.

Lincoln's body was moved several times before it was placed in a marble sarcophagus in the family catacomb on 9 October 1874. In November 1876 there was an attempt to rob the grave and Lincoln's body was moved to a secret grave deeper in the catacomb to prevent such attempts. There was another move in 1886 when a new crypt was built for him, followed by yet another in 1889 when his body was placed in a white marble sarcophagus. In 1901 the casket was opened again for the purposes of identification and reburied in an underground vault. There have been many reports by visitors to the tomb over the years of weeping, footsteps and hushed voices.

Mary Todd never fully recovered from her husband's death. She became increasingly dependent on opium and advice from mediums. She claimed to be able to talk to her husband every day. Under an assumed name she sat for **spirit photographer** William Mumler and a hazy likeness of the dead president was produced. In 1875 her son, Robert Lincoln, had his mother institutionalized and after her release she went into self-imposed isolation in France. After her death in 1882 she was buried in the Lincoln catacomb in Springfield.

The Lincoln family home, now owned and maintained as a historical site, has long been associated with reports of unusual phenomena and **hauntings**. **Apparitions** of a tall thin man, sometimes accompanied by a small boy, believed to be Lincoln and his son, Willie, have been reported on numerous occasions. Visitors have said they noticed cold spots and have been touched by what feels like invisible hands. There have also been reports of objects moving, voices muttering and phantom music playing.

Ford's Theatre, Washington, where Lincoln was assassinated, has also been associated with haunting phenomena. Visitors have claimed to hear assassin John Wilkes Booth's footsteps running up the back staircase towards the presidential box. Actors to this day report icy sensations centre stage, strange noises, weeping and laughter, lights turning on and of and a tendency to forget their lines. The Lincoln box is permanently closed, but singers have reported being distracted by a light mysteriously flashing and off from the box during performances.

Lincoln's ghost is also thought to haunt the White House. His silhouette has frequently been seen, or sensed, standing near a window in the Oval Office. The haunting replays a real-life scene observed late in Lincoln's presidency by army chaplain E C Bolles. When Bolles arrived in the Oval Office he saw the President gazing sadly out of the window. Later Bolles wrote, 'I think I have never seen so sad a face in my life and I have looked into many a mourner's face.'

President Harry Truman (1945–53) thought he heard Lincoln walking about the White House and during the administration of Ronald Reagan (1981–89) the President's daughter, Maureen, reported seeing Lincoln's ghost in the Lincoln room.

LITHOMANCY

Ancient method of **divination** – popular in the British Isles and Europe – by stones or by studying light reflected by precious or coloured stones or even glass beads. Photius (c. AD 820–891) the Patriarch of Constantinople, spoke of an oracular stone called the baetulum, and referred to it as a tool for lithomancy.

There are different methods of lithomancy. In the reflection method a ceremonial candle is used and the gemstones are cast on a black cloth for reading. A blue reflection typically suggests good luck and peace. Red reflections indicate sex, love or marriage; yellow reflections are said to indicate betrayal; dark or grey reflections are said to foretell calamities or the presence of evil; green reflections indicate success and money; and purple reflections are said to signify sorrow in the near future.

In another method each stone supposedly has a significance of its own, and the divination is accomplished by tossing the stones and interpreting the arrangement in which they fall. Thirteen stones are used. They are selected from their natural environment during favourable astrological configurations, and with the aid of intuitional guidance. Ideally, the stones should be smooth and nearly uniform in size and shape. They may range from pebbles found on a beach to semi-precious stones such as agates or various **crystals**. Seven stones represent astrological signs: the sun, moon, Mars, Venus, Mercury, Jupiter and Saturn. The remaining six stones represent the home, love, life, magic, luck and news.

LITTLE BASTARD, CURSE OF

One of the most persistent Hollywood **curse** stories is that of American movie star James Dean's death car, on which the *Rebel Without a Cause* icon bestowed the name Little Bastard.

James Dean lived a short, dangerous and thrill-seeking life. He loved fast cars and motorcycles and his favourite hobby was racing. He was a skilled driver with top honours in numerous races but his racing prowess couldn't save him from a fatal collision at high speed in the Diablo Mountains in September 1955. The rare Silver Porsche Spyder that carried him to his grave was bought after the accident for $2,500 by Dean's former racing car designer, George Barris.

The car fell while being unloaded, breaking a mechanic's leg, and so began a string of weird accidents – including two more deaths – among those who had anything to do with the Little Bastard or its parts. Wherever the Little Bastard went injury, death and misfortune seemed to follow. For instance, fans were injured when they attempted to steal souvenir parts from the car, and when the car was on display at a Sacramento high school it fell off its stand breaking a student's hip. When the car was sent by truck to Salinas the driver lost control of the truck and crashed. He was thrown free, only to have the Little Bastard fall off the truck on top of him and crush him to death. The final mishap took place in 1960 when the car disappeared while being transported across country. To this day, its whereabouts are unknown.

There is a superstitious belief that not just places but objects can become cursed when associated with violence and tragedy. Was the Little Bastard really cursed when Dean bought it brand new? Were those who came into contact with it simply victims of bad luck? Or did it become cursed as a result of Dean's violent death?

According to **psychometry**, objects absorb the emotions of their owners and remain a permanent focus of these emotions. Although the mystery may never be solved, there may be a possibility that in the final seconds of Dean's life he experienced such intense terror and fear that their negative energy was literally imprinted on the car.

LITTLECOTE HOUSE

Once the setting of the great romance between King Henry VIII and Jane Seymour, Littlecote House on the Berkshire–Wiltshire border is allegedly haunted by numerous **ghosts**.

The Littlecote estate dates back at least as far as the thirteenth century but the mansion standing today (now a hotel) was built in the late fifteenth century by the Darrell family. Henry was the first recorded royal visitor to Littlecote in 1520 and it is here that he later courted the beautiful Jane Seymour, a relative of the Darrells.

In 1575 Littlecote became the scene of a despicable crime. The owner at the time was William Darrell, known as Wild Darrell because of his outrageous behaviour.

According to lore, one night a nobleman sent for a midwife from another village, had her blindfolded and taken to the house where she was instructed to help deliver the baby of a woman in labour. As soon as the child was born the nobleman threw it on the fire. The midwife was given a purse of money and taken home blindfolded. She did, however, snip a piece of curtain before she left and count the stairs on the way out. She reported the crime to the local magistrate the next day. Littlecote was suspected as the scene of the crime as the piece of fabric matched that of a hole in the curtains and the number of stairs matched those the midwife had counted. In another version of the story the midwife was so frightened that she didn't say anything until she was on her deathbed.

Whatever happened Darrell was arrested but somehow acquitted. It was said that the judge had been bribed. Fourteen years later in 1589, when out hunting in Littlcote Park, Darrell was thrown from his horse and died. It was said that the ghost of the dead baby had startled the horse and ever since the site where Darrell died is thought to be haunted by the infant's ghost, named the Burning Babe, Darrell himself and his **phantom** hounds.

Darrell is also said to appear at Littlecote as a **death omen**, appearing with **phantom coach** and horses when a death in the family is about to occur.

There are other ghosts at Littlecote apart from Darrell and the infant, including a woman who carries a rush light, a woman who appears in the garden, a woman in a pink nightdress who appears on the stairs carrying a lamp and a silent woman holding a baby – thought to be Darrell's wife's maid, or his sister, in the room where the murder occurred. Gerald Lee Bevin, a one-time tenant of Littlecote House who was convicted of fraud, is also said to put in a ghostly appearance from time to time. Phantom footsteps have been heard on the stairs and a terrifying scream from the murder room.

LITTLEDEAN HALL

Stately home located in Gloucestershire and thought to be haunted by as many as 16 **ghosts**. The Hall was originally Saxon and it has been occupied since the eleventh century.

Many of the ghost stories associated with Littledean are concerned with the English Civil War when the house was garrisoned by both Roundheads and Royalists. The ghost of John Brayne, believed to be a Roundhead captain who spied on the Royalists by disguising himself as a gardener, is said to appear now and again in a long cloak. Two Royalist officers were murdered in the dining hall and a **phantom** stain that looks like a pool of blood is said to appear on the same spot that they fell.

There have also been sightings of the ghost of a black manservant who murdered his master, the owner of Littledean, in 1741 because the man had raped his sister is seen near the stain. Another story tells of a pistol duel that ended in the death of a man in 1740 and his ghost is said to linger.

Ever since Littledean Hall opened to the public in 1983 visitors have reported feeling uneasy, with some encountering **apparitions** on the drive and in the courtyard.

LIZZIE BORDEN'S HOUSE

Now a bed and breakfast hotel located at No. 92 Second Street, Fall River, Massachusetts, the former home of suspected murderer Lizzie Borden is said to be haunted.

Although Lizzie was never convicted of murder it is very likely that on the morning of 4 August 1892 she killed her stepmother, Abby Durfee Gray, with an axe, in the Borden's family house and an hour or so later she killed her father, Andrew Borden, in the same way. Abby's body was found between the bed and bureau, in the guest room. Mr Borden's body was found lying with his head on the sofa arm, next to the door, in the downstairs sitting room.

The Borden household was not a happy one and there is little doubt Lizzie was guilty, but due to lack of evidence she was acquitted at her trial. Despite being ostracized by the community she continued to live in the house until her death on 1 June 1927.

After her death, the house remained a private residence for several decades before being converted into a bed and breakfast. Guests that stay there can, if they so wish, view the murder scene and sleep in Lizzie's bedroom, Abby and Andrew's bedrooms or the guest room where Abby was killed.

With such violence taking place in the house it is hardly surprising that the house is reportedly haunted by the **spirits** of the Bordens. Guests report feeling cold spots in certain rooms and people who work in the house report hearing voices, unexplained footsteps and doors opening and closing. Abby has been seen pulling the covers of the bed from guests and dusting and making beds in the guest room. Some have seen what looks like a body lying down appear and disappear on the beds.

LODGE, FRATERNAL

A form of social and community organization that was once universal but is all but forgotten today, the fraternal lodges came into being around 1600 when the medieval guild system was reshaped to meet the needs of a new mercantile society. **Freemasonry**, which evolved out of the Scottish stonemasons' craft guild, is one of the few orders to have survived from this early period. Between 1800 and 1920 a vast number of fraternal orders sprang up, many of which are no longer in existence.

A fraternal lodge is made up of a number of initiated members who receive a charter from the order's grand lodge that lays down rules and regulations for the lodge's business. There are standard patterns for ceremonies that open and close lodge meetings but titles for officials within lodges vary enormously. **Initiation** rituals, which form the core of the fraternal lodge system, illustrate the same combination of similar patterns but wildly diverse symbolism and terminology.

Many fraternal lodge organizations are open only to men but there are exceptions, such as the Independent Order of Odd Fellows. One branch of Freemasonry, Co-Masonry, also admits women as well as men to membership, but a number of Masonic organizations refuse to accept the validity of Co-Masonic initiation.

During the golden era of the fraternal lodge – between 1750 and 1950 – a large percentage of male occultists belonged to fraternal lodges and a lot of **occult** material found its way into lodge systems, for example **hermetic** traditions, found its way into various Masonic lodges. Magical societies such as the Hermetic Order of the **Golden Dawn** draw heavily on fraternal lodge practices in their ceremonies.

LODGE, MAGICAL

The standard social structure for Western occultism, the magical lodge was derived from the structure of the fraternal lodge. **Occult** writers between 1780 and 1950 claimed that that the lodge system dated back centuries, however, although older lore may have played a part, it is generally thought that the earliest magical lodges were formed in the middle of the eighteenth century. While there may have been occult secret societies before that time the standard set up of magical lodges – **initiations**, an ascending ladder of degrees, passwords, secret handshakes and so on –

were an eighteenth-century fraternal lodge-inspired addition.

Like the fraternal lodges from which they borrowed so much, most magical lodges went into a steep decline during the second half of the twentieth century. The reasons are not entirely known but it's possible that the ritual and hierarchical male-dominated structure of many lodges did not appeal to the radical, experimental and freedom-loving people who were attracted to occultism in the 1960s. The magical lodge system has not completely faded away though, and some magical lodges remain active today.

See also **Lodge, fraternal**.

LODGE, SIR OLIVER [1851–1940]

Physicist, psychical researcher and prominent member of the **Society for Psychical Research** Lodge is best known today for his book *Raymond: A Life* (1916), which records communications through a **medium** with his son, who was killed in World War I.

Oliver Joseph Lodge was born on 12 June 1851, in Staffordshire, England. In 1874 he enrolled in University College London and upon earning his doctorate was appointed assistant professor of physics there. In 1881 he was appointed Professor of Physics at Liverpool University and began conducting his first experiments on **ESP** subjects with surprisingly positive results. He joined the Society for Psychical Research and began to attend meetings regularly. When the society invited medium **Leonora Piper** to England, Lodge had his first sitting with her and was extremely impressed by messages given to him from his beloved Aunt Anne who had recently died. He invited Piper to Liverpool so he could study her mediumship further, and during these **séances**, where Piper told Lodge things that were later verified, he concluded that the idea of **telepathy** – which he believed to operate among the living – needed to be extended to include the possibility of communication with the dead.

In 1900 Lodge was appointed Principal of the University of Birmingham and his psychical research continued there. In 1901 he was elected president of the Society for Psychical Research and soon became a major figure in research on **cross corre-spondences**. It wasn't until August 1915, however, that Lodge became a dedicated believer in the possibility of **survival after death**. Leonora Piper delivered a message to Lodge warning him of a great blow and a few days later he learned that his son Raymond had been killed in France.

Lodge and his wife began to attend séances with other sitters and at one of these he was told that his son had appeared in a photograph with a walking stick. Another medium, **Gladys Leonard**, described the picture in detail. At the time the Lodges know nothing about the photograph but when a friend – who knew nothing about the séances – sent them the photograph it proved to exactly match Leonard's description.

Lodge recorded this and other sittings he had with his dead son in *Raymond: A Life*. The book was an overnight sensation, earning Lodge praise from **spiritualists** and ridicule from scientists. Undaunted Lodge wrote a number of other books on psychical research and **spiritualism**, including: *Survival of Man* (1909), *Science and Religion* (1914), *Ether and Reality* (1925), *Evolution and Creation* (1926), *Phantom Walls* (1929) and *My Philosophy* (1933). In addition to his contribution towards psychical research Lodge was also a highly honoured physicist responsible for many advances in that subject. In his later books he tried to relate the **paranormal** to physics by drawing on the popular nineteenth-century concept of **ether**, which was said to pervade the entire universe as the common basis between the physical and psychical world.

Lodge died on 22 August 1940 at his Wiltshire home. He left a sealed envelope the contents of which he intended to try to communicate after death; but no convincing messages seem to have been received from him. Lodge's autobiography, *Past Years*, was published in 1931.

LOGOMANCY

Logos is Greek for 'word', 'speech' and 'discourse' and logomancy is the term used to describe **divination** by words. The exact method does not seem to be have been recorded and it appears to cover a number of different forms of fortune telling. Considering the written word it could cover such methods as **bibliomancy**. Considering the spoken word it could cover **cledonomancy**. It could also cover **psychography** (spontaneous writing of a divine nature) and **onomancy** (using the letters of a name).

LOMBROSO, CESARE [1836–1909]

Italian criminologist with an interest in **spiritualism**, Lombroso is perhaps best known for his studies and theories on the relation between mental and physical characteristics. Lombroso tried to relate certain physical characteristics, such as jaw size, to criminal psychopathology. His theory has been scientifically discredited, but Lombroso had the merit of introducing the importance of the scientific study of the criminal mind, a field which became known as criminal anthropology.

During a distinguished career Lombroso studied at the universities of Padua, Vienna and Paris and was later (1862–76) a professor of psychiatry at the University of Pavia and of forensic medicine and hygiene (1876), psychiatry (1896) and criminal anthropology (1906) at the University of Turin. During the last years of his life Lombroso became passionately interested in **paranormal** and mediumistic phenomena, spiritualism and **hypnosis** in an incompatible attempt to explain these phenomena by resorting to positivist science

Early in his career Lombroso was a staunch materialist and stated in his 1909 work *After Death – What?*, 'If ever there was an individual in the world opposed to spiritism by virtue of scientific education, and I may say, by instinct, I was that person. I had made it the indefatigable pursuit of a lifetime to defend the thesis that every force is a property of matter and the soul an emanation of the brain.' He was forced, however, to significantly alter his sceptic viewpoint after extensive study of the **medium Eusapia Palladino** and later wrote, 'I am ashamed and grieved at having opposed with so much tenacity the possibility of the so-called spiritistic facts.'

LONGLEAT

Stately home in Wiltshire, England, that has been surrounded by superstition and ghost lore for centuries. Longleat is said to be haunted by several **ghosts**, the most famous of which is Lady Louisa Carteret, the Green Lady, whose portrait hangs in the lower dining room.

The story goes back to the early eighteenth century when Lady Louisa married the second Viscount Weymouth. Their marriage was a disaster, her husband being vicious and unpleasant. Lady Louisa fell in love with another man and they were found together in Longleat House by her husband. A duel was fought which resulted in the death of the lover who, it is said, was buried beneath the cellar flagstones. (Four generations later a body was unearthed there when central heating was installed.) Lady Louisa died in childbirth on Christmas Day 1736 and allegedly roams the corridors looking for her long dead lover.

LOURDES

The shrine at Lourdes, France, where the Virgin Mary is said to have appeared to Bernadette Soubirous in 1858, has become synonymous with miraculous healings. Although there are only a handful of documented and verified healings attributed to the waters of Lourdes, the case of Pierre de Rudder is a remarkable one.

In 1867, Pierre de Rudder suffered an injury when a falling tree smashed his left leg. The doctors who examined the wound felt that the leg should be amputated but de Rudder refused, preferring to keep his leg even if it caused him agony every day. For eight years he lived in pain, hobbling about on crutches, hoping that somehow he would someday be cured.

In 1875, de Rudder's employer generously arranged for de Rudder and his wife to make a pilgrimage to Lourdes, where, they had heard, many miraculous cures had taken place. Before his pilgrimage de Rudder visited a Dr Van Hoestenberghe, for one final diagnosis on his leg. In his notes Van Hoestenberghe confirmed that de Rudder had 'an open wound at the top of the leg. In this wound one could see the two bones separated by a distance of three centimetres. There was no sign of healing.'

De Rudder and his wife set off from their home in Jabbeke, Belgium, and arrived at the crowded shrine in Lourdes on 7 April. Although de Rudder wanted to walk around the shrine, his leg was too painful so he sat and prayed. Suddenly, overcome by emotion and without thinking what he was doing, he stood and walked over to the statue of Our Lady of Lourdes and knelt down. He then realized what had happened and screamed joyfully to his wife, who promptly fainted.

Doctors' examinations at Lourdes and in Belgium confirmed what the de Rudders already knew – his leg had been healed. The open wound was gone. The bone had completely mended.

LUCIAN [C. AD 117–180]

Greek satirist Lucian is credited with one of the first known stories involving a group of ghost hunters in his dialogue *Philpseude*. Written nearly 2,000 years ago this piece contains elementary descriptions and ideas about psychical research, suggesting that Lucian was himself familiar with the work of ghost hunters. This is backed up by contemporary reports that state that Lucian enjoyed discussions concerning the **paranormal** and would frequently travel through Greece in search of **ghosts**. He also wrote pieces that exposed fraudulent **mediums**, and debunked allegedly paranormal events with logical explanations.

LUCID DREAMING

Lucid dreaming, a phrase coined by Celia Green of the Institute of Psychophysical Research in Oxford (in her 1968 book *Lucid Dreams*), is the state of knowing you are dreaming while you are dreaming. This may sound like a contradiction but many people report lucid dreaming, including subjects in sleep research laboratories.

In AD 415 St Augustine made what was perhaps the first written mention of lucid dreaming. Then in the eighth century, *The Tibetan Book of the Dead* described a form of **yoga** that maintains full waking consciousness while in a dream state. This ancient art reveals an understanding of

Steps towards having a lucid dream

Everyone can learn how to have lucid dreams. According to dream experts the likelihood of lucid dreaming increases dramatically when the dreamer holds tight to the intent to have them, and to remember them afterwards.

You are most likely to experience a lucid dream when you are in a light sleep – for example, when you have dozed off after your alarm clock has gone off or when you nap in the day.

1. Be aware while you are asleep that you are in fact dreaming. To do this you need to prepare during the day. Pick a common object that might appear in your dreams – a flower, book, apple, cat, etc. Tell yourself several times during the day that when you see your chosen object it will serve as a signal that you are dreaming. In addition prime yourself to go into lucid dreaming mode. Tell yourself at regular periods during the day and just before you sleep that you want to go into lucid dreaming mode.

2. Before you go to sleep have a pen and pad nearly and be prepared to record your dream immediately on waking. Don't kid yourself that you'll remember in the morning because it was so vivid. The chances are you won't.

3. When you are in the in-between stages of waking and sleeping your conscious mind is most open to suggestion and lucid dreaming, so restate your intent and remind yourself that seeing your chosen object will let you know that you are dreaming. Let the image of your object rest in your mind.

4. What may happen is that you start to dream and then think you have woken up. You haven't – you are still in a dream state because your chosen object has appeared. It's now that you can take control. Try to set the scene, talk to people you need to or ask for help to find solutions.

5. When you do finally wake up immediately write down your dream. Then give yourself time to ponder what your dreaming self has discovered.

dreams as advanced as those proposed by modern sleep researchers, such as Stephen Laberge – an accomplished lucid dreamer himself – at Stanford University, which has a famous sleep lab.

Lucid dreaming can happen without trying to make it happen, but most of the time people who practise lucid dreaming do so deliberately, often for the purpose of controlling the dream. The idea is that once a person is aware they are dreaming they can alter their dreams and dictate what happens: they can do anything they have ever wanted and go anywhere they have ever desired.

The lucid dream state allows the dreamer unbelievable freedom of choice and action, as the laws that govern daily life do not apply in dreams – for example, why walk when you can fly? But this is only half the picture. There are also some serious practical and therapeutic uses for lucid dreams. The dreamer can try out new behaviours and test themselves in different scenarios, discovering more about their individual strengths and weaknesses. Dream experts believe that if dreamers see themselves resolving problems or overcoming difficulties in dreams this gives them the ammunition to solve them in daily life.

Lucid dreaming can be an important tool for achieving goals, relieving stress, rehearsing new behaviours, solving problems, finding artistic or creative inspiration or coming to terms with emotional problems. It can also be directed to help the dreamer access their **intuition**. Once dreamers are able to control their dreams they can direct them to offer intuitive insights in certain areas.

LUCIDITY

A faculty by which supernormal knowledge may be obtained. It is a collective term for the phenomena of **clairvoyance**, **clairaudience**, **psychometry**, **premonitions**, etc.

LUCK

According to *Webster's Dictionary* luck is described as a force that brings good or bad fortune.

That which happens to a person; an event, good or ill, affecting one's interests or happiness, and which is deemed causal; a course or series of such events regarded as occurring by chance; chance; hap; fate; fortune; often, one's habitual or characteristic fortune; as good, bad, ill or hard luck.

It is commonly held that the observance of certain **superstitions** will bring good luck. For example, some believe that touching wood, searching for a four-leaved clover or carrying a rabbit's foot will in some way attract good luck.

In recent years the whole question of luck has been investigated and the conclusion drawn by modern psychologists is that there is in fact no such thing as luck, only chance. Good or bad luck is created by the way a person responds to chance – i.e. random events. In other words what truly sets lucky people apart isn't superstition or **supernatural** power but the way they

How to get lucky

- *Listen to your intuition – it's often right.*
- *Be willing to experiment and explore new possibilities.*
- *Define your mission and goals in life and turn setbacks into opportunities.*
- *Develop a positive mindset. Imagine yourself being lucky. Luck is very often a* *self-fulfilling prophecy. That's how good luck charms and superstitions work according to psychologists. If you truly believe something can bring good luck, you do in a way endow it with a magical power.*

behave and react to the environment they find themselves in. This has been backed up by research. In general studies have shown that so-called lucky people tend to be more open-minded, adventurous, intuitive and optimistic than people who consider themselves less fortunate.

LUCKS

Objects, such as cups, dishes or ornaments, kept by families for generations as tokens of good luck. According to tradition lucks cannot be bought; they must be given to a family, typically by royalty or magical individuals such as **witches** or **fairies** and as long as they remain intact the family line will thrive. Lucks were once commonplace in the British Isles among the gentry and nobility, and it is conceivable that in the days when reading and writing were not common some lucks were tokens of tenures

One of the most well known lucks is the luck of Edenhall in Cumberland – a cup made of yellow and brown glass, decorated with colourful enamel and kept in a leather case, belonging to the Musgrove family since the fifteenth century. There are a number of stories of how the luck came to be the family's prized possession. The popular version is that one day the butler came to draw water from a fairy well. He interrupted a group of fairies dancing and they left behind their drinking cup, which the butler picked up. As he left with the cup in his hands the fairies called after him:

If this cup should ever break or fall,
Farewell the luck of Edenhall.

There are a number of theories as to the origins of the Edenhall cup. The letters IHS inscribed on the leather case has lead to speculation that it is Spanish in origin, but these letters may have been added to the case later. Other theories suggest that it is of Damascene, French or English origin from the thirteenth or fourteenth century.

The first written reference to the luck of Edenhall is in 1689 but it didn't become really famous until the eighteenth century when the Duke of Wharton nearly broke the luck during a drinking bout when visiting Edenhall in 1721. Fortunately the butler caught the cup before it fell. Wharton later immortalized the luck in a ballad: 'The Drinking Match'.

The Edenhall luck is now on display in the Victoria and Albert Museum, London.

LUCRETIUS [c. 99–55 BC]

Historical records clearly demonstrate that the Roman poet Lucretius was a passionate believer in **ghosts** who devoted a great deal of time to investigating and researching claims of **apparitions**. He eventually gathered enough material together to propose the theory, commonly known as Lucretius's shell, that ghosts were a kind of shell which diffused or splintered from the body of a dying person and lingered in the atmosphere after death, moving at will. This theory is considered the forerunner of theories regarding the possible existence of the **astral body**, which may separate from the body of a living being under **altered states of consciousness**, such as a **trance** or deep sleep.

Lucretius is thought to have died raving mad from the effects of a love potion administered to him by his wife.

LUMINOUS PHENOMENA

The **paranormal** production of light phenomena, often around objects and people. The phenomena generally occur in the presence of certain physical **mediums**, but can also appear independently.

See also **Aura**, **Ghost lights**.

LUNOMANCY

Divination by the shadows created by moonlight on a person's face after silver dust has been rubbed on the diviner's hands and subject's face. The shadows must be observed randomly, without the seer trying to position the person for special emphasis. The depth of the shadow, length and observed shape are all taken into consideration. Lunomancy is a form of **selenomancy**.

LYCANTHROPY

The magical belief, common in European folklore, that it is consciously possible through **witchcraft** or **sorcery** to transform into the form of an animal, typically a wolf. Lycanthropy is responsible for many **werewolf** legends and is similar in practice to the **shaman**'s ability to **shape-shift** into a totemic animal.

The oldest known records of lycanthropy date from classical times when people or whole tribes turned into wolves appeared in various works. The lore of lycanthropy is deeply intertwined with **magic** and a number of magical methods of talking on wolf form or **spells** for managing the transformation have survived in Russian, Norse and Slavic sources.

A feature of lycanthropy common in medieval and Renaissance literature and later magical works, although neglected in modern horror-movie imagery, is the nature of the wolf body created. In contrast to popular legend the lycanthrope does not transform physically into a wolf but the wolf form is constructed of **ether**. The human body of the lycanthrope is typically left behind in a **trance** state and it could be said that lycanthropy represents a form of etheric projection.

LYTTELTON, LORD THOMAS [1744–1779]

The story of Lord Thomas Lyttelton, known as the 'Wicked Lord' and 'Bad Lord Lyttelton' because of his wicked reputation, involves both a **death omen** and a crisis **apparition**.

In 1779, Lyttelton returned from a trip to Ireland to his house in Hill Street, near Berkeley Square in London. A number of guests visited him, including Lord Fortescue, Lady Flood, the Amphlett sisters and a friend who was later to record the strange circumstances surrounding Lyttelton's death.

According to the friend's account Lyttelton was not a well man and had suffered suffocating fits in the preceding month. Three days before his death Lyttelton dreamt that he saw a fluttering bird and afterwards a woman dressed in white, who appeared to him and said, 'Prepare to die; you will not exist three days.' The **dream** upset Lyttelton so much that the following morning he told all his friends, but he could not get it out of his mind. During the following days he suffered bouts of depression as the fatal hour neared. On the third evening, he invited some guests to dinner in an attempt to forget about the dream, retiring to his bed at eleven. When he noticed his manservant was using a toothpick to stir his dose of rhubarb and mint water he called him a 'slovenly dog' and told him to fetch a teaspoon. When the servant returned he found his master in a fit, but instead of helping immediately, the servant ran away in fright. When he returned he found his master dead and the apparitional dream was proved true.

Premonitory death dreams are not unusual and Lyttelton's is a very direct example. The appearance of a bird and a woman in white are both symbols of **spirit** and associated with **heaven**. As was typical of the day, it was suggested that revenge might have been the motive. A rumour started that Lyttelton's dream and death were somehow connected with Mrs Amphlett, who was said to have died broken hearted when both her daughters were seduced and cast aside by Lyttelton.

There was another apparition connected to the death of Lyttelton. On the day of his death Lyttelton had been scheduled to visit his friend Miles Peter Andrews, who lived at Dartmoor but at the last moment

Lyttelton decided not to go, forgetting to send his apologies to Andrews. Later that night Andrews was startled when the curtains of his four-poster bed were drawn aside and Lyttelton appeared dressed in his nightgown. Andrews assumed Lyttelton had decided to visit him after all and was playing a trick on him. Andrews threw a slipper at Lyttelton, who before disappearing responded by saying, 'It's all over for me Andrews.' The next day, Andrews, still suspecting mischief on Lyttelton's part, nearly fainted when he heard the news of Lyttelton's death.

Accounts of Lyttelton's death and apparitional appearance to Andrews do not mention timing but, as is the case in most crisis apparitions, it is most probable that Lyttelton appeared to his friend at the moment of death.

M

McDougall, William [1871–1938]

Considered to be one of the greatest psychologists of his day, William McDougall was a strong proponent of psychical research and co-founder, with **J B Rhine**, of the **parapsychology** laboratory at Duke University.

McDougall's interest in psychical research began while he was a psychology student at Cambridge University. He joined the **Society for Psychical Research** and was elected its president in 1920, the same year that he was offered the position of Professor of Psychology at Harvard. When he arrived in the United States to take up his position he was also elected president of the **American Society for Psychical Research**, making him the first (and probably last) person to have held presidencies in both psychical research societies simultaneously.

At Harvard, McDougall ran a series of experiments on white rats to support the theory, known as the Lamarckian theory of inheritance, that acquired characteristics could be inherited. Of his numerous academic studies the one of most interest to psychical researchers is *Body and Mind: A history and defence of Animism*, published in 1911, where McDougall uses **cross correspondences** and other **psychic** phenomena to support his mind–body dualism argument.

At the ASPR, McDougall attempted to strengthen the society's academic credentials by setting up an academic board of advisors, but this was an unpopular strategy with board members and in 1923 he was replaced as president by **spiritualist** Frederick Edwards. Shortly after McDougall became the first of several psychical researchers to investigate the Boston **medium Mina Crandon**. They witnessed a number of phenomena including the movement of objects, but when a piece of string was discovered that could have been used to move a stool the investigation stopped. McDougall tried, without success, to get Crandon, who had gained considerable support from the ASPR, to confess to **fraud**. Disillusioned with the ASPR's reluctance to apply academic criteria to psychical research, he gave his support to a rival society that was setting itself up, the **Boston Society for Psychical Research**.

Although McDougall helped draft the constitution for the Boston society, his focus changed from psychical research societies to championing parapsychology as a field for university study. His chance came in 1927 when he was hired by Duke University in Durham, North Carolina, to head its psychology department. He accepted **John Thomas** as a graduate student studying **trance** mediumship, and in 1933 Thomas received the first PhD degree in parapsychology awarded by an American university. It was also through Thomas that McDougall came into contact with J B Rhine, who was working as Thomas's research assistant.

With McDougall's help, Rhine was hired as a Professor of Psychology and began developing **ESP card** tests. By 1935 Rhine's research was so large that it moved out of the psychology department into its own separate unit, which later became known as the parapsychology laboratory at Duke University (see **Rhine Research Center**).

McLoughlin House

House located in Oregon City, a community in the Willamette valley, Portland, near Oregon that is thought to be haunted. Once owned by pioneer Dr John McLoughlin (1784–1857) – a colourful character in pioneer history who founded Oregon City in 1839 – phenomena reported at the house include mysterious footsteps and **voices**, **poltergeist** activity and a shadowy figure thought to be McLoughlin's **ghost**.

In 1821, McLoughlin, a physician for the Hudson Bay Company, was sent to Oregon to preside over the company's new headquarters. Despite incredible generosity to the Oregon City community he founded, McLoughlin was resented because he was British, wealthy and a Catholic in a Protestant town who was married to a Chippewa woman. When the US government disputed his claim to the land he had few supporters. In a desperate bid to save his title he became an American citizen but this still wasn't enough and Congress stripped him of ownership. McLoughlin died bitter and disillusioned in 1857. His house became a bordello before being abandoned. In 1908 it was moved to its present location overlooking the city and in 1930 was restored and opened to the public. In 1970 McLoughlin's grave was moved to the new grounds.

Haunting phenomena were not reported at the house until the mid-1970s when Nancy Wilson, who had no belief in ghosts prior to working at the house, became its curator. One of the earliest experiences Wilson reported was a tap on the shoulder when the house was closed to the public and she was cleaning upstairs. On turning around no one was in sight and the only other employee was downstairs. As the days passed the phenomena increased. Wilson and other staff members began to report seeing a shadowy figure that resembled a painting of McLoughlin in the upstairs hall. Footsteps on the upstairs hall were also heard when no one was there. A child's bed mysteriously appeared to have been slept in when staff arrived in the morning to open up. Rocking chairs rocked by themselves and objects were moved with no logical explanation. The phenomena continued until the late 1980s when the house became quiet again, although McLoughlin's non-threatening presence continued to be felt by Wilson and her staff.

After the hauntings began Wilson began to research her past to see if there was any link between her and McLoughlin that might have activated the haunting. She discovered that her ancestors included the Wells, a family of pioneers who arrived in Oregon City in 1842. When Mr Wells died leaving behind a wife and family, McLoughlin had loaned them money, which they were never able to fully repay. Wilson speculated that McLoughlin may have been attempting to collect his debt, or perhaps he wanted to express his satisfaction with the quality of her work in preserving and promoting the house and his reputation.

McRaven House

Considered to be one the most haunted places in Vicksburg, Mississippi, McRaven House was used as the Union headquarters during the American Civil War.

The occupation of Vicksburg delivered a severe blow to the Confederate cause, for now control of the Mississippi lay in the hands of General Grant. A Colonel Wilson and his aide, Captain McPherson, of the occupying forces decided to headquarter at 1445 Harrison Street. McPherson served as the liaison between the occupying troops and the residents of the town. One night, McPherson failed to return from his usual rounds and was declared missing. A search was started, but he wasn't found. The following night McPherson returned although not in the flesh. His mutilated-looking **apparition** dripping with blood allegedly appeared to Colonel Wilson in McRaven House to inform his commander that he had been murdered by Confederate sympathizers and thrown into the river.

Since that time, reports of Captain McPherson's **ghost** continue, delivering the same message to other occupants of the house. There have also been sightings of civil war soldiers and a woman with long brown hair and a plain dress in the middle bedroom of the house. In 1991, the house, which is currently a private residence open daily for tours, was blessed by an Episcopal priest, but reports of **hauntings** from startled tourists and tour guides continue.

Macro PK

Parapsychologists usually make a distinction between 'macroscopic PK' (large-scale effects observable by the naked eye or by a single measurement) and microscopic PK (small-scale effects only observable by statistical analysis of multiple measurements); both types are still studied today, although with more attention paid to the micro variety.

Accounts of macro PK include the so-called physical phenomena observed during **séances** with **mediums** of the **spiritualist** era in the late nineteenth and early twentieth centuries. Such phenomena included **table tilting**, **rapping** and **levitation**, and the playing of musical instruments with minimal or no contact. In more modern times, claimed macro PK phenomena include **metal bending** and the production of images on unexposed photographic film by **Uri Geller** and other **psychics**.

See also **Micro PK**.

Macromancy

Derived from the ancient Greek *macros*, meaning 'large', macromancy is the word used to describe **divination** by studying the largest object in the area. Whether a rock, a tree or a house the object is studied and the **seer** interprets. Size, general shape and colour, and the closeness of objects to others or the distance from them all have their place in the interpretation.

MAD ANTHONY

The **ghost** of American Revolutionary Major General and hero Anthony Wayne is said to haunt several states in the United States.

Impetuous and hot-headed and admired for his daring exploits, Wayne was sometimes known as 'Mad Anthony', but he was an able general. He died on 15 December 1796, in Erie, Pennsylvania and was buried at St David's Church in Chester County.

One of Wayne's best-known **hauntings** is along Route 1 near the revolutionary battlefield of Brandywine at Chadd's Ford, Pennsylvania. During the battle of Brandywine (1777) the ferocious fighting of Wayne and his men enabled Washington to escape inevitable slaughter by the British. There have been several sightings of Wayne's ghost in full army dress astride a galloping white stallion.

Wayne's ghost is said to appear at Lake Memphremagog where he once found a bald eagle's nest and while attempting to steal it received a scar from one of the chicks that stayed with him all his life. Wayne kept the eagles and trained them to be his hunting companions and his **apparition** was reportedly seen on the lakeside with an eagle on each of his shoulders.

His ghost also appears at Fort Ticonderoga where he was commandant in 1771 and had an affair with a lady called Nancy Coates. Nancy set her heart on marrying Wayne, but when he refused the devastated Nancy drowned herself in a nearby lake. The apparition of a sobbing woman thought to be Nancy has been seen in various parts of the fort, and Wayne's ghost is said to appear in the dining room of the commandant's quarters smoking a pipe and drinking from a pewter mug.

There have been other sightings of Wayne astride his beloved horse Nab at Storm King Pass on the Hudson River and at a house he chanced upon while riding to join General Lafayette in Virginia. The house was in a half-finished state, and according to lore Wayne dreamed of buying it after a transient life spent in barracks. More than two centuries later the house remains inexplicably unfinished and it is thought by those who believe in the ghost of Mad Anthony that he visits the house and wonders why it is still only half built!

MAGI

Magi were Zoroastrian astrologer priests from ancient Persia. The word *magi* is plural; the singular is *magus*. It is derived from the Old Persian word, *Magupati*, in modern Persian *Mobed*. Magus is also a word for a **shaman**, **magician**, **wizard**, **sorcerer** or wise man, especially one of experience and accomplishment. According to the New Testament, the three Kings who visited the baby Jesus in Bethlehem were magi.

MAGIC

Magic is about power and control – the ability to create change in accordance with **Magical Will**. The change is effected through ritual acts in which **supernatural** forces are invoked and made subservient to the will of the **witch** or **magician**. Will is understood by magical practitioners as the focusing of desire to achieve goals. Will is not the same as desire; will is something that must be created and trained. Belief in one's ability to perform magic involves coming to accept a belief that one is capable of creating change (that one is powerful) and that the change will occur according to one's will (that one is in control).

Aleister Crowley, one of the **Golden Dawn**'s most famous and most controversial magicians, suggested that every intentional act is in essence an act of will. He believed that if more people practised magic they would learn more about their true selves and purpose in life and this would reduce conflict and confusion in humanity.

Magic has existed in all cultures since ancient times. The word is derived from the Greek *megas*, which means 'great'. Magic is often sub-divided into **white magic** or **black magic**, or even grey magic, but magic itself is neither good or bad – it is the magician's will that determines whether the magic serves good or evil. Every culture has different names for practitioners of the magical arts, for instance **witch doctor**, **wizard**, wise woman, witch, magician, **sorcerer**, **shaman** and so on. In some cases magic is the speciality of a priest or religious leader. The ability to practise the magical arts is typically considered to be hereditary, passed down through family lines. Practitioners are also considered likely to possess **psychic** ability.

The earliest form of magic was probably mechanical **sorcery**, in which an act is performed to achieve a particular result. Palaeolithic cave paintings at the Trois Frères caves in France, for instance, reveal images of magical rituals for a successful hunt. It is thought that the systems of low and high magic were first developed by the ancient Greeks. High magic – which involved working with spirits – was considered to be akin to religion, but low magic – providing **spells** and potions for a fee – developed an unsavoury reputation by the beginning of the sixth century BC.

In the centuries that followed, as Christianity spread throughout Europe, low magic became the folk magic and **witchcraft** of rural peoples, while high magic became intellectual, spiritual and ceremonial. High magic (which drew its inspiration from **Hermetica**, the **Kabbalah**, **Neo-Platonism** and Oriental law) thrived in the Renaissance as a reaction to the Church's denial of all magic outside that of religious miracles. It was nurtured by secret societies and **lodges**, such as **Freemasonry**, the Order of the **Knights Templars** and the **Rosicrucians**.

During the scientific revolution of the seventeenth and eighteenth centuries magic fell out of favour, but interest was revived in the nineteenth century by the Hermetic Order of the Golden Dawn and occultists such as **Eliphas Levi**, whose *Dogma and Ritual of High Magic* (1856) was very influential.

The foundation of high or ceremonial magic is the Hermetic Kabbalah, an amalgam of the Hermetica and Jewish Kabbalah used by the Golden Dawn. Ceremonial magic rituals have three elements:

1. Love and devotion.
2. **Invocation**.
3. Drama, which involve the magician identifying with the deity.

Ritual clothes and tools and symbols are crucial as they are thought to attract magical forces. The ritual itself serves as a means of uniting the microcosm with the macrocosm, i.e. as a way to join the human **consciousness** with God or a god.

It is a path of self-realization. The initiate first learns how to achieve **samadhi**, a state of concentration where forces akin to primal archetypal forces, are personified as astral beings or **elementals**. It is through these forces and the invoking of gods and goddesses, or communication with or entry into alternative states of reality, that the magician begins to understand him or herself and discover his or her strengths and weaknesses.

Magic in the modern religion of **neo-pagan** witchcraft includes both high and low magic. There are prescriptions advising against the use of magic for anything other than good, and against blood sacrifice. Effectiveness at magic is believed to be the result of study and practice. Often magic is presented as an on-going discipline, the cornerstone of which is self-knowledge. Neo-pagan magical training begins with knowing oneself and training one's will. 'Knowing oneself' is a complex, introspective process and a number of exercises designed to raise awareness of one's thoughts, feelings and **intuition** are suggested to facilitate it. Neo-pagan witches and magicians believe that through increasing self-knowledge, one increases the effectiveness of one's magical will.

All of these activities have their counterparts in secular equivalents such as psychotherapy and the modern self-help movement. Where neo-pagan magical activities appear to be alien to outside observers is in their use of material elements in spell work, such as **candles**, oils, herbs, coloured robes and so on. Magical practitioners tend to explain the use of physical elements in spell work as aids to concentration, **meditation** and **visualization**. They also believe that objects do not just suggest moods and energies; they embody them or are attuned to them in some way. Manipulation of objects therefore is a microcosmic way of manipulating the broader energies to which they are connected.

In essence, neo-pagan magic is more about changing the internal landscape than the external and in this way it is closer to religion than to science, which seeks only to explain the material world. This is not to say that spells are not expected to work in the material world. They are, but according to neo-pagan magic, changing the external landscape is not all that magic does – even though many people think that that is all it is meant to do. Magic changes the internal landscape as well and is an elaborate, dramatic metaphor for the individual's relationship with him or herself and the universe.

Transforming yourself

Most people associate magic with outer change and spell work. There are many books and techniques designed to help you harness the power of nature, through the use of herbs, stones, colours, candles and symbols. These are powerful ways to do magic, but magic is essentially about creating *inner* change. Props may be useful but it is the mind that works magic, and success at spell work is believed to rest upon the mastery of meditation and visualization exercises.

You may want to begin a meditative visualization by lighting a candle, asking for inner guidance, breathing deeply and closing your eyes. You can use body relaxation, incense, guided countdowns and soothing imagery to get into an altered state of mind where you can access your inner energy patterns – your conscious and unconscious thoughts, emotions, dreams, hopes and fears. Most importantly, you can connect with your inner guidance, awaken your psychic abilities and connect with healing spirits and gods.

Now in your inner vision, imagine yourself the way you want to be. Use images of coloured light and simple symbols to work with the energy. If you need courage, think about what colour feels most like courage to you. Then imagine yourself surrounded in that colour. You could also create an affirmation to give you more courage

Other techniques for magical change include creating an inner sacred space that you can go to anytime and anywhere, regardless of where your altar or ritual tools are. In your imagination build an inner temple of learning and healing. Create a gateway to your spirit guides. Look into an inner mirror or crystal for glimpses of your past lives. All of this takes place on the inside, but creates a powerful and lasting change. Listen to your inner guide and let it take you on your own incredible healing journey. It can help you look through magical eyes and see the spirit of all things.

MAGICAL PERSONALITY

In modern **Hermetic** magical tradition, the magical personality is an artificial personality created for use in magical practice to prevent the inflation of the ego that can occur in magical training. The practitioner's ordinary personality is thought to be insufficiently stable to handle the stresses of sustained magical training. The apprentice **magician** or **witch** therefore creates an alternate personality based on concepts such as courage, love, wisdom and power, and practises moving into and out of this personality at will, often using as a cue some action such as putting or taking off a bracelet.

MAGICAL WILL

Confidence in one's ability to perform magic involves accepting two beliefs: first, that one is capable of causing change (that one is powerful) and second, that change will occur according to one's will (that one is in control).

Magical Will is that ability of the individual to perform **magic** with success. It is similar to, but not the same as, desire and the individual's everyday determination to get things done. Will is thought to be something that must be trained into being. It also represents one's magical integrity. If one treats people well and acts with integrity, Magical Will is strengthened. If one acts selfishly and causes harm to others, Magical Will is weakened.

MAGICIAN

A person who practises **magic** and is skilled in **spell** casting and the magical arts. A magician studies supernormal scientific knowledge and masters **psychic** skills in the quest to understand humankind's purpose on earth. The popular image of a magician is characterized by the figure of **Merlin** – a wise old man in flowing robes and a pointed hat covered with stars. This image is rather outdated today.

Someone who practises magic for the good of mankind is thought of as a white magician, whereas one who practises magic with evil intent may be considered a black magician or **sorcerer**. The term magician is also used to describe someone who practises magical tricks and illusions in front of an audience.

MAGICK

Obsolete spelling of the word **magic** used by **Aleister Crowley** to 'distinguish the science of the magi from its counterfeits' – in other words to distinguish it from the 'magic' of **magicians** who entertain audiences with tricks and illusions. Since Crowley's time the term has been used by numerous magicians, writers and groups, some with connections to Crowley's magical beliefs, and some without. The adjective *magickal* and the noun *magickan* have also been in use in recent years. There have been other attempted respellings of the word magic, including *magik*, *majick* and *majik*, but none of these has caught on.

MAGNETIC ENERGY FIELDS

The earth is surrounded by a magnetic field, referred to as the geomagnetic field. For decades, experts believed that this magnetic force was too minimal to have any effect on human behaviour or physiology. However, recent research shows that when the right mix of frequencies or patterns occurs, this geomagnetic energy field may affect us in a variety of ways. For example, on days when there are high levels of geomagnetic energy, traffic accidents tend to occur more often. As the magnetic force levels decrease, telepathic ability appears to improve. This supports the theory suggested by many **ganzfeld** practitioners that a decrease in external influences, whether from a subject's physical senses or the earth's unseen forces, improves receptivity to **psi**.

MAGNETIC HEALING/THERAPY

The therapeutic use of magnets to improve health and ease pain. It is based on the theory first proposed by **Franz Anton Mesmer** that invisible fluid in the body could be rearranged to bring about **healing** and that magnets can be used to help rebalance the electromagnetic energy field that surrounds the body. It is also thought that magnets are able to electrically charge iron atoms in red blood cells so they work more efficiently. This circulatory speed up helps remove toxins faster and stimulates natural healing processes. As magnets contain a positive and negative charge they are also thought to aid the flow of the **universal life force** or energy (chi) through the body.

Magnets come in a range of sizes and are used in a variety of ways. They can be inserted into mattresses, shoe insoles or cushions or worn as jewellery like bracelets. Although there is plenty of anecdotal evidence to suggest their effectiveness for relieving pain associated with back and neck problems, arthritis, injuries, headaches and fibromyalgia, magnet therapy is not currently accepted by conventional medicine.

MAH-JONG

Four-handed game of Chinese origin, popular in Europe and the United States. In 1920, Joseph P Babcock, an American traveller in China, devised a set of rules for Western play and invented a complete terminology. He patented the game under the trademark Mah Jongg. The game enjoyed a remarkable popularity. The goal of the game, which is similar in principle to rummy, is to accumulate sets. The equipment for the currently popular mah-jong set consists of 152 tiles – small rectangular blocks of wood with ivory or bone faces. There are 108 suit tiles, 16 wind tiles, 12 dragon tiles, 8 flower tiles and 8 jokers. The three suits are bamboo, or sticks; circles, or dots; and characters, or cracks.

In addition to being a game mah-jong tiles have been used for **divination** purposes for centuries. The **symbols** on them come from ancient Chinese systems of mystical knowledge, and they were used for obtaining answers from the gods long before they were used in games.

MAIMONEDES EXPERIMENTS

Researchers at the Maimonedes Dream Laboratory in Brooklyn, New York, Montague Ullman and Stanley Krippner, devised methods for testing **ESP** during dreaming and conducted some fascinating studies with high success rates. Their results published in the 1970s and 80s showed that **telepathy** while dreaming is not that unusual or hard to do.

In various experiments the Maimonedes team had a 'sender' look at a picture that contained a striking scene and then send this image telepathically to the dreamer. When awakened during REM sleep and questioned about their **dreams**, the dreamers frequently reported the image or aspects of it that the sender had relayed to them psychically. Subjects had 102 hits versus 48 misses. The hit rate according to chance would be 50 per cent, but these statistics showed a much higher success rate of 68 per cent.

The Maimonedes experiments inspired other researchers to explore dream telepathy. For example, recent experiments in the late 1990s by Kathy Dalton at the University of Edinburgh showed significant results in a **clairvoyance** dream experiment that did not involve high-tech equipment. The research team recorded the dreams they had each night in their own homes. The next morning they found their dreams matched up with video clips randomly selected by a lab computer and projected overnight in a locked room. This research, like the Maimonedes experiments appears simple but it does suggest that dreams can access a level of information that extends beyond the dreamer's own mind.

MANDALAS

From a Sanskrit word meaning 'magic circle' or 'disc', a mandala is a circular visual representation that is used as a focus point for the practice of **meditation**. When creating a mandala the artist attempts to coordinate his or her personal circle with the universal circle, reflecting how his or her life fits into the larger whole.

The mandala art form is widely used in the East and often associated with Tibetan monk artists and Navaho Indians who create them out of multicoloured sand as a formal geometrical expression of sacred vibrations; however mandalas transcend culture and religion, time and place. When a person concentrates on a mandala they are attempting to approach a higher plane of **consciousness** and, according to psychologist **Carl Jung**, they are the ultimate symbols for uniting our inner and outer selves. Jung found that the integrative properties of the mandala had benefits in psychotherapy; by drawing mandalas patients could make order out of inner confusion.

MANDRAKE

The plant *Mandragora officinarum*, whose roots are used in **magic** and **supernatural** traditions. Despite being a popular ingredient for folk magic love potions in medieval European culture the mandrake gained a sinister reputation that it still hasn't managed to shake off, due to the fact that its roots resemble the form of a human being.

Creating your own mandala

You do not need to be an artist to create a mandala. You can make one in any way that you want and with any material. There are no right or wrong mandalas. It can be drawn, shaped of clay, cloth or flowers or any material that you like. It can even be created in your mind's eye. Here is one way to go about creating a mandala.

Gather your materials and go to a quiet, private space. Light a candle or burn incense to establish a reflective mood. You may find it helpful to sit quietly for a few moments of prayer or meditation before beginning your mandala. This helps focus your attention on messages from the unconscious. Perhaps an image, a colour, or even a movement will come to you as the beginning point for your mandala.

Next draw a circle freehand, with a compass, or traced around a plate or other template. The circular shape represents a natural and ultimate wholeness and appears in symbols dating back to the Palaeolithic Age. Then fill in the circle with the colour and content of your choice. Typically the circle is orientated to four points. Sometimes this is done by squaring, in which a square is drawn outside the circle; other times it is drawn by geometric designs such as interpenetrating triangles or other designs drawn inside the circle. Allow your mandala to unfold with as little thought as possible. Let go of all your notions about how a mandala should look. Virtually anything round can be viewed as a mandala: the sun, the moon, a clock, the earth, a wheel. Octagons also have mandala shapes. Squares and triangles suggest mandalas too, since circles and triangles may be drawn within squares and vica versa.

When you have completed your mandala, write the day's date on it, and then put it somewhere in your living space where you can walk by and see it often. Let it be part of your life for a few days. Be open to receive any messages it has for you. The colours, shapes and numbers of a mandala can show us our inner picture. Like the symbols in dreams it is thought they hold a specific message and by meditating on it we can reach a higher awareness of self.

Mandrakes were commonly found under the bodies of hanged men at crossroads and they were said to thrive on the agony of death. According to lore when mandrakes are harvested they shriek, leaving the harvester insane. All these negative associations are probably due to the high levels of psychotropic compounds found in the plant, which, if taken in high amounts, can cause delirious fantasies and **visions**.

MANES

Ancient Roman **spirits** of the dead. In general the manes were considered 'good' or 'benevolent' spirits and the *Di Manes* were divine spirits. The term 'manes' was also used to refer to an individual spirit of the dead, to underworld spirits and to the **underworld**. The Romans placated manes with offerings.

MANTRA

A word or phrase or set of words which, when repeated over and over again is thought to influence the human mind. The term is generally used to describe **chants** used in Buddhism, Hinduism and **Transcendental Meditation** in order to induce a **trance**-like state, but in recent years it has also come to mean one's personal life philosophy and/or goal which, if repeated often enough, might just become a reality.

Since the time of the ancient Egyptians and Assyrians, **magicians** have used mantras, or names of power, for conjuring **spirits** and casting **spells**. Hindus and Buddhists also use mantras as **amulets** for protection against evil, illness and bad luck. Twentieth century-magician **Aleister Crowley** created the mantra AUMGN, an expansion of the most sacred Hindu mantra **Om**, the supreme reality, the sound from which the universe was created. According to Crowley the sound vibrations of AUMGN were so powerful that a magician using them could control the forces of the universe.

MAORI MAGIC

Magic practised by the Maoris of New Zealand. The priests, known as Tohungas, are similar to **spiritualist mediums** in that they claim to be able to act as a bridge between this world and the world of the dead. The Tohungas are usually trained from childhood, being presented by their parents for this training. Through years of **prayer**, fasting, **chanting** and **meditating** they acquire the powers of **spirit** communication, **healing** and **prophecy**.

MAP DOWSING

The following explanation of map dowsing is given by the American Society of Dowsers (www.dowsers.org):

With a map or a sample sketch of the terrain, an individual property, whether a house lot less than an acre in size or a ranch of several hundred square miles, can be dowsed by one proficient in this method. Map dowsing is best performed not with Y or L rods but with a pendulum. One way is to overlay the map with a grid dividing it into rectangles (though this grid can be mentally pictured or imagined). The dowser then asks which rectangle(s) on the grid will contain the best site(s) for drilling a water well. The pendulum will supply the answer.

Common **dowsing** could be partially explained by magnetic field theories but this isn't the case with map dowsing. Here

Experimenting with mantras

Perhaps the most widely known Buddhist mantra is *Aum mani padme hum*, translated as 'hail to the jewel in the Lotus'. However, the meaning is of little importance; what matters is the way this mantra is thought to help create a change in consciousness.

Try chanting it aloud first. Make it flowing and run the final *hum* into the beginning of *aum* to create a mantric circle. Rhythm and pronunciation are as follows:

Aw-um mah-nee padmeh hummmmm um mah-nee padmeh hummm …

After you have spoken it aloud a few times lower the volume until you with-draw the sound into your mind and hear it mentally. Experiment with speed until you find a rhythm which grips your attention, so that all other thoughts are cast aside by the spinning mantra and there is no room for anything else. Once the spinning mantra is established it will continue with no conscious effort, leaving you free to relax with an untroubled mind. When you wish to return to your normal mode of consciousness, slow the spin rate of the mantra; then externalize it by speaking it aloud several times, before stopping altogether.

the dowser will take a map of the search area, run a **pendulum** across it and find the location of what he or she is looking for on the map. Map dowsers believe that what appears to be happening in the case of map dowsing is a kind of **psychic** reading, where the map is a focusing device and the pendulum becomes a psychic amplifier.

MARA

A mara, or mare, is believed to be a kind of malignant **supernatural** entity in Scandinavian folklore. She appears as early as in the Old Norse sagas, but the belief itself is probably of even older date.

The mara was thought of as a **discarnate entity** that would seat herself on the chest of a sleeping person and 'ride' him or her, thus causing terrible nightmares. In Norwegian, the word for nightmare is *mareritt* or *mareridt*, meaning 'mare dream' or 'mare ride'. The weight of the mara could also result in the victim suffering breathing difficulties or a feeling of suffocation.

The mara was also believed to 'ride' horses, which left them exhausted and covered in sweat by the morning. Even trees could be ridden by the mara, resulting in branches being entangled. The undersized, twisted pine-trees growing on costal rocks and on wet grounds are known in Sweden as *martallar* (mare pines).

According to a common belief, the free-roaming **spirits** of sleeping women could become maras, either out of wickedness or as a form of **curse**. In the latter case, finding out who the cursed person was and repeating 'You are a mara' three times was thought to be enough to release her from this condition.

The English word *nightmare* stems from the Anglo-Saxon and Old English belief in this creature. In English folklore, **hags** and **witches** later took on many of the roles of the mara. In Germany the activities of the mara were shifted to the elves ('nightmare' in German is *Albtraum* or 'elf dream'). Similar mythical creatures are the **succubus/incubus**, although the belief in the mara lacks the fundamental sexual element of these beings.

MARCHERS OF THE NIGHT

In Hawaiian folklore the marchers of the night are thought to be a procession of gods and **spirits** who march on nights considered sacred to certain deities to welcome the dying to the land of ancestral **guardian spirits**. They are symbols of the Hawaiian belief in the unbroken connection between the living and the dead and the ability of the dead to revisit sites they were familiar with while they were alive. Each of the Hawaiian Islands still has paths believed to be used by the night marchers.

It is thought to be very dangerous to encounter such a procession and a spirit is said to warn away the living by shouting '*kapu*'. According to lore, if a person is unlucky enough to get in the procession's way, the procession leader will shout out '*O-ia*', or 'let him be pierced', and unless there is a dead relative of the living person in the procession to protect him or her, the person will be struck with a ghostly spear. The only way to protect against this happening is to remove all clothing and lie down pretending to be asleep.

See also **Wild Hunt**.

MARFA LIGHTS

Multicoloured balls of light reportedly to be seen nightly, just after sunset, in the skies south of Marfa, Texas (see **Earth lights**). The phenomenon, which has generated much debate over the origin of the lights, has been documented since 1880.

MARIAN APPARITIONS

Over the centuries there have been numerous reports of appearances by the Blessed Virgin Mary. Most Marian apparitions consist of the appearance of an otherworldly woman who is identified as Mary. She may or may not be accompanied by lights, spinning crosses, sweet music and smells. If she speaks she typically urges people to live a more devout life or for churches to be built for her. Sometimes miraculous **healings** occur.

The Catholic Church, which has investigated at length a number of Marian apparitions, has decreed only a few of them to be genuine, including those that occurred at **Lourdes** in France (11 February–16 July 1858), Guadalupe in Mexico (1531) and Fatima in Portugal (13 May–13 October 1917). Sites of authenticated apparitions are visited by pilgrimages in search of miraculous cures, but unauthenticated sites, such as at Zeitoun in Egypt and Medjugorje in Bosnia, also draw pilgrims.

According to Catholic dogma Marian apparitions are not **ghosts** but mystical phenomena that God permits. To those who believe in her, Mary's authority cannot be denied and she brings about a transformation in all who see her. Psychologists explain the apparitions as **archetypal** projections from the human **unconscious** to answer a need for spiritual direction.

Marriott, William [1854–1938]

English stage **magician** and illusionist who devoted a great deal of his time to the study of ghostly phenomena, Marriott is best recalled for his exposure of fraudulent **mediums** and debunking of the **Spiritualist** movement.

Marriott's special interests were **spirit photography** and the alleged **materializations** of **spirits** during **séances**. Like his contemporary **Harry Houdini**, Marriott was able to reproduce many of the tricks and illusions used by **frauds** and as a skilled photographer he reproduced accurately a number of **paranormal** photographic effects. His uncompromising search for truth led to the exposure of numerous unscrupulous mediums and he also played a significant part in bringing an end to the popularity of and sensation surrounding ghostly photographs of the Victorian era. His photographic work was so convincing that even committed **spiritualist Sir Arthur Conan Doyle** was forced to admit that Marriott's assessments of photographic forgery were accurate.

Martial arts

Various types of Oriental combat, either with empty hands or with weapons, that were originally developed to achieve victory in battle but over the centuries have become philosophical, moral and spiritual disciplines. Regardless of style the key to all martial arts is the skilful use of the **universal life force** (chi in Chinese, ki in Japanese), which is thought to permeate all things. The force is controlled by uniting it with mind and body through breathing techniques, movement and **meditation**.

The father of martial arts in China is Kung Fu, Chinese boxing, which dates back to around AD 520 in Northern China. Kung Fu practitioners widely believe in the art of *dim mak*, a traditional death touch possessed by a rare number of ancient masters. If a body is struck in a certain place at a certain time of day in a certain way, a delayed death follows; the victim falls unharmed at the time, but later falls ill and dies. A softer version of Kung Fu, **Tai Chi**, was developed in the thirteenth century by a Taoist monk, Chang Sang-fen. Instead of meeting force with force, the soft school emphasizes avoidance of blows rather than strikes and counter-strikes. Karate, which means 'empty hand', originated in Okinawa and is based on blows delivered to the hands, head, feet and knees. It was used against the Japanese when they invaded the island in 1609.

In Japan the father of martial arts is Ju-jitsu, which according to legend is about two thousand years old. It was heavily influenced by **Zen** philosophy and empha-sized the striking of vital points, kicking, strangling and joint locking. It has evolved into Judo, a sports version, and is also the precursor of Aikido, a modern Japanese martial art founded in 1922 by Morihei Ueshiba after a mystical experience. The main goal of Aikido is the unification of mind, body and self through discipline and the manifestation of harmony in all actions.

Most martial arts can demonstrate feats of immense power, such as the breaking of thick pieces of wood, layers of bricks and so on with the hand, foot, elbow, head or even fingertips. Other incredible feats include immunity to fire and pain. The goal of these actions is to increase awareness of the power within. The life force or chi is directed to various parts of the body and when the body is full of chi it is strong.

Chi cannot be acquired quickly, but must be built up slowly with regular training and practice. Fun, laughter and patience are important parts of the discipline. Chi is regulated with breathing techniques. The goal is to learn to anticipate hostile moves and avoid or pre-empt them. This requires a state of 'no mind' when the body going with the flow of chi energy reacts instantly. In Japanese this state is called *nen*, and when proper connection is made it be-comes a **supernatural** power that sees all things clearly. Ueshiba said this supernatu-ral power enabled him to intuitively sense from which direction bullets or sword thrusts would come.

There are a number of less well-known Oriental martial arts that have gained a fol-lowing in the West. Kyudo, 'the way of the bow', and Kendo, 'the way of the sword', are Japanese martial art forms that place an emphasis not on the weapons used but on spiritual development and moral conduct. Tae Kwon-Do is a 1,300-year-old empty hand style of combat from Korea. Hwarang-Do, also from Korea, arrived in the States in the early 1970s. It focuses on external power, internal power, weapon power and mental power, and training includes controlling the mind with medita-tion and developing **psychic** powers, in particular **clairvoyance** and **telepathy**.

MARY CELESTE

The fate of the crew who mysteriously 'van-ished' while aboard the *Mary Celeste* has led to much speculation over the years as to whether **supernatural** activity played a part.

On 3 December 1872, the crew of the *Dei Gratia*, sailing from New York to Gibraltar, found the *Mary Celeste* floating about 600 miles west of Portugal. The ship was in perfect condition but its captain, Benjamin S Briggs, his wife, his daughter, and the ship's crew of seven were gone. The sails were set and the ship's cargo of 1,700 barrels of alcohol were untouched (except for one barrel, which had been opened); a half-eaten breakfast meal remained on the table and all of the crew's belongings remained onboard.

All that seemed to be missing was the ship's chronometer, the sextant and the cargo documents. There was no sign of a struggle, violence, storm, or any other kind of disturbance, which ruled out the theory of pirate attack. The last entry in the ship's log was made on 24 November, and gave no indication of any trouble. If the ship had been abandoned soon after this entry, the *Mary Celeste* would have been adrift for a week and a half, but according to the *Dei Gratia* crew this was unlikely considering the ship's position and the way its sails had been set. Someone – or something – must have worked the ship for at least several days after the final log entry. The fate of the crew of the *Mary Celeste* remains a mystery.

The mysterious abandonment of the *Mary Celeste* might have remained a minor footnote in nautical history had it not been for **Sir Arthur Conan Doyle**, who penned a fictional story based on the incident, changing the name of the ship and entitling his work the *Marie Celeste*. Many of the details attributed to the real incident actually come from Conan Doyle's fictional story or from the two movies made based on that story. Although there are numerous rational explanations for the abandonment, the *Mary Celeste*, like the **Flying Dutchman**, will always be prized sightings among of the world's **phantom ships**.

MARY WORTH/BLOODY MARY

According to lore, Mary Worth, also known as Bloody Mary, is an evil **ghost** who cannot find peace. She is said to appear in a mirror when summoned.

The origins of the Mary Worth story may point back to seventeenth-century Massachusetts. Mary Worth was a young girl whose face was covered in hideous dark-red scars that were either an accident of birth or caused by an injury. The village children teased her and followed her in the streets calling out 'Bloody Mary' over and over again.

During a **witch** scare, Mary was accused of **witchcraft** and hanged. According to lore, one night, not long after Mary's execution, a group of children decided to play a game of conjuring. They set up a mirror against the wall and began to chant, 'Bloody Mary, Bloody Mary'. Suddenly Mary appeared in the mirror. Her face was even more hideous and her hands had turned into claws. She reached through the looking glass to tear the children's faces. Shrieking and screaming, the terrified children ran out of the room.

Although Bloody Mary disappeared that day, it is said that her **spirit** remains, waiting for someone to stand in front of a mirror and chant her name.

In some versions of the legend, the summoner must say 'Bloody Mary, I killed your baby.' In these variants, Bloody Mary is believed to be the **spirit** of a mother who murdered her children, or a woman who was murdered shortly before or after her wedding. On the other hand, it has been suggested that the story about taunting Bloody Mary about her baby may relate tenuously to folklore about Mary I, Queen of England from 1553–58, who became known as Bloody Mary for her persecution of Protestants. The Queen's life was marked by a number of miscarriages or false pregnancies; if she had succeeded in having a child, this would have established a Roman Catholic succession and the continuance of religious persecution after her death.

The mirror ritual by which Bloody Mary is summoned may also relate to a form of **divination** involving mirrors and darkness that was once performed on **Halloween**. Young women were encouraged to walk up a flight of stairs backwards, holding a candle and a hand mirror, in a darkened house. As they gazed into the mirror, they were supposed to be able to catch a glimpse of their future husband's face. There was, however, a chance that they would see a skull-face instead, indicating that they were destined to die before they married.

MASSAGE

The kneading, pressing, rubbing or stroking of muscles and the soft tissues of the body for therapeutic purposes. Massage therapy is an ancient **healing** art practised by all cultures that was first documented in Chinese writings around 3000 BC. Today it is a popular, non-invasive and safe alternative therapy known for its physical, psychological and even mystical benefits. There are different schools of massage based on these three effects.

The physical school of massage concentrates on producing physical benefits, such as pain relief, relaxation for tense muscles, increasing blood circulation, and stimulation of lymphatic drainage, which promotes the removal of toxins from the body. It is perhaps best represented by 'Swedish massage', so named because it was developed by Swede, Per Henrik Ling in the early nineteenth century. Most masseurs today are taught six classical massage movements as defined by Ling: effleurage, petrissage, kneading, hacking, cupping and tapotement.

The primary focus of **holistic** massage is physical *and* psychological benefit. This school works on the whole person and incorporates theories of **energy medicine** into its practice. The masseur works to balance the flow of **universal life force** through the body while also providing physical benefits. Psychological benefits include the reduction of stress and promotion of feelings of well being because of the release of endorphins into the body after a massage treatment. **Shiatsu**, Rolfing, **reflexology** and **aromatherapy** are examples of holistic massage.

The 'spiritual' school of massage may or may not involve physical massage and its primary aim is to align energies in the body. Examples of this type of massage school are **therapeutic touch**, **reiki**, **zero balancing** and **polarity therapy**.

MATERIALIZATION

This is the appearance of seemingly solid objects or **spirit** forms out of thin air. Eastern **adepts** are said to be able to materialize objects such as food, precious stones and so on, but materialization is typically a phenomenon of **physical mediumship**.

At the height of **spiritualism** materialization manifestations usually followed the same pattern. A **medium** would enter a **cabinet** to concentrate and collect enough psychic energy for **ectoplasm**. Gradually a spot or white light that spread into a vapour-like cloud would appear, followed by a face or in some cases a full body. The spirit would circulate around the room and then return to the cabinet or melt away. The medium would then be found in the cabinet, typically exhausted and weak and, in some cases, a few pounds lighter.

The first recorded full-form materialization appeared to John Dale Owen in 1860 through the **Fox sisters**. According to Owen a veiled transparent figure materialized, walked about the room and then disappeared. According to reports Kate Fox was later to produce a number of other full-form materializations, including the spirit of Benjamin Franklin. The first British medium to claim to be able to materialize spirits was **Agnes Guppy** who allegedly brought **John King**'s **ghost** into her circle, but she was soon to be outdone by the **Katie King** materializations of **Florence Cook**.

Cook's speciality was materialization and by the mid-1870s the white-veiled barefoot figure of Katie King who walked around the **séance** room touching and caressing sitters had became a much-talked about sensation. Katie resembled Cook and in December 1873, during a séance for the Earl of Caithness, William Volckman, who claimed that Katie was not a ghost but Cook in costume, grabbed Katie and a fight broke out between the two. They were separated by the other sitters and Katie was returned to the cabinet to rejoin Cook, who was found a few minutes later still bound as she had been at the start. Although Cook had her doubters she also had strong supporters, among them the scientist **Sir William Crookes**, who investigated her after the Volckman incident and pronounced her materializations completely genuine.

French materialization medium Marthe Béraud (1886–?), better known by her pseudonym Eva C, allegedly materialized the Indian Brahman Bien Boa. Photographs reveal Boa to be a tall, bearded man who wore a monk's habit and bore no resemblance at all to Béraud. Unfortunately doubt was cast over Boa's authenticity when a family friend came forward suggesting that Béraud herself had confessed to **fraud** by smuggling in an impersonator via a trap door beneath her cabinet. Investigation, however, showed no evidence of a trap door.

Psychical researcher Charles Richet held sittings with Béraud where he claimed to have seen a gooey substance, for which he coined the term ectoplasm, emerge from various parts of Béraud's body. The ectoplasm would quickly organize itself into a face or the shape of a hand or head, sometimes in miniature. It would solidify to the touch into a sort of paste before retracting into the medium's body or disappearing. Later Béraud was also said to materialize the faces and forms of several government and historical figures. Critics found the materializations flat and two-dimensional, accusing Béraud of using cut outs from magazines draped with muslin.

There were numerous reported cases of fraudulent materializations. Instructions for preparing the best effects circulated among mediums. One method suggested that 21 yards of fine white silk veiling be washed seven times and while still damp the fabric was to be dipped into paint, varnish, odourless benzene and lavender oil. The fabric would then need to be dried for three days and washed with naphtha soap to remove all odours.

The fact that séances often occurred in darkened rooms made it easy to fake materializations using sleight of hand or various ingenious stage props and stunts. Rosina Showers, a friend of Florence Cook, gave a description of a method for fraudulent materialization: the medium should wear a dress she could take off easily, with two or three shifts underneath. A filmy muslin veil and a handkerchief were to be concealed in her underwear, the veil to be worn over the shifts and the handkerchief to cover her hair. The fraud relied on the sitters' gullibility and a belief that few investigators would be so bold as to break with Victorian etiquette and search a medium's underwear.

Despite the seedy reputation it gained from numerous incidents of fraud and trickery some materialization mediums, such as **D D Home** and **Madame Blavatsky**, although suspected of being fraudulent were never proven guilty.

MAZE

Mazes typically represent a path to the **underworld** or otherworld that **spirits** of the dead must navigate. They exist universally all over the world and the oldest is believed to have been built in Egypt 5,000 years ago. During the Middle Ages mazes were built into churches and cathedrals. Today they are created primarily as designs for gardens.

In myth and legend mazes are often complex, challenging, dangerous **labyrinths**. To navigate a maze successfully is to gain access to the mysteries of life and death. Mazes come in a variety of sizes but one of the most common is the spiral, a symbol of the Goddess, which was the shape of the mythical labyrinth of Crete. According to legend the maze at **Glastonbury** Tor is said to lead to a point of entry to the Celtic underworld and the Holy **Grail**.

Mazomancy

Ancient method of **divination** by observation of a nursing baby – which breast is chosen, for example. Mazomancy is derived from the ancient Greek *mazos* or *mastos*, meaning 'breast'.

Meconomancy

Meconomancy is **divination** by drug-induced sleep. The word is derived from the ancient Greek *mekon* or 'poppy'. (Meconium is the thickened juice of the poppy; meconic acid is the crystallized, white acid obtained from the opium.) It's highly likely then that this is a divination from **dreams**/hallucinations induced by opium and should not be confused with **oneironmany**, which is divination from dreams obtained in natural sleep.

Medical intuition/ intuitive

A person with specific spiritual **healing** ability who has learned to hone and apply skills of **intuition** to the field of medical diagnosis. A medical intuitive can visualize the anatomy of the human body and its energy field, the **aura**, and correctly diagnose the root causes of disease and poor health. They can then direct their healing energies to the afflicted area.

A gifted medical intuitive uses their intuitive powers to 'see' and pinpoint specific illnesses, imbalances, weaknesses and pre-clinical disease states in the organs of the human body, as well as fields of force or auras around the human body. This work is done by intuitively scanning the body for areas or imbalance that may need alignment or treatment. Often the medical intuitive will be able to explain the connection of the energy to an emotion or an event causing the illness.

There are three ways a medical intuitive can access information: clairvoyantly, clairsentiently, clairaudiently. **Clairvoyant** medical intuitives claim to be able to see the inner workings of the body. They are able to see **universal life force** energy, or chi, as it flows through the body and around the body, and are able to detect where this energy has stagnated or become blocked. **Clairsentient** intuitives claim to be able to feel energy or emotions in the body. Medical intuitives who use this ability will typically scan the body using their hands, seeking out changes in temperature, energy vibrations or fluctuations in the density of the aura or body. **Clairaudient** medical intuitives claim to be able to hear health information intuitively from a **spirit**, their **higher self**, the universe or God.

Put simply, medical intuitives claim to be able to 'see' or sense things that even the most sophisticated medical diagnostic tests cannot reveal. Sceptics argue that such abilities are impossible, and that auras and energy fields in the body do not exist.

There is evidence throughout history that medical intuition was used for diagnosing illness, right back to the Pythagoreans in 500 BC. They held that there was a luminous body of light around a person that could produce certain effects in the human body. In the sixteenth century, alchemist and physician Paracelsus diagnosed illness using intuition and an ability to read energy. It was not, however, until the nineteenth century that the first formal study of intuitive diagnosis appeared. The study was conducted by Dr John Elliotson, a British physician who used the technique of **mesmerism** to entrance his subjects. While in this state, he found that they could use their intuition to access information for the purpose of identifying illnesses. Elliotson would take his mesmerized subjects to hospitals and ask them to use their intuition to identify illnesses. Even though the accuracy of their diagnoses was said to be astonishing, Elliotson's research did not meet with approval from his medical peers.

In 1911, physician Dr William Kilner put forward the theory that auras differed considerably from patient to patient depending on sex, mental ability and health. His research suggested that there was an association between disease and what could be seen in the energy system. He found that certain illnesses showed up as blockages, patches or as irregular patterns of energy within the energy field.

The most widely known medical intuitive diagnostician was **Edgar Cayce** (1877–1945). Cayce claimed to be able to read many aspects of a person's health intuitively and his focus centred on the health of the energy body and the physical body. Cayce proposed that stress, attitudes and emotions affect one's health and that negative emotions released toxins that could create energy depleting imbalances. He believed that all illness is the result of overloads and blockages in these three main aspects of energy – physical, mental and spiritual. In one of his readings, Cayce said, 'Healing of the physical without change in the mental and spiritual aspects bring little real help to the individuals in the end.'

A noted medical intuitive of today is Caroline Myss. Since 1982 Myss has gained an international reputation for intuitive medical diagnosis – even at long distance. Given a person's name and age she claims to be able to scan an individual's electromagnetic field and diagnose the nature of the illness. Her philosophy is rooted in the interconnection of the mind, body and spirit in disease and her work with Dr Norman Shealy, a Harvard-trained neurosurgeon and founder of the American Holistic Medical Association, has helped define how stress and emotion contribute to the formation of disease.

MEDICINE MAN

Mostly found in Native American cultures (and also known as a **witch doctor** among indigenous tribes of Africa and South America and in parts of Australia and Polynesia), the medicine man is a magical practitioner who uses **spells** and potions to cure the sick, protect his community from evil and to contact **spirit guides** for guidance and **divination**.

MEDITATION

A contemplative technique of focusing your concentration on a specific object or thought for self-improvement or spiritual growth.

The supreme goal of meditation, typically practised by the non-secular world, is union with the absolute. Secular meditators use meditation in their daily lives to create feelings of calm or peace in body and soul and to improve health, creativity, self-esteem, success and relationships, to cultivate **psychic** powers and gain self knowledge. Meditation by itself cannot achieve these goals but it can help develop the power and ability to do so.

There are a number or documented physical and psychological benefits to meditation. In the 1970s Harvard medical school professor Herbert Benson discovered the relaxation response in **transcendental meditation** practitioners. Just twenty minutes of meditation reduced blood pressure, heart and breathing rates and reduced muscle tension. Other studies have shown that meditation can help relieve anxiety, stress, fatigue, migraine, insomnia and boost feelings of energy and confidence.

Meditation is an age-old universal practice and an important part of many religions including Sufism, Judaism and Christian mystical tradition, but it is most closely associated with Hinduism, Buddhism and the practice of **Yoga**. Although meditation can be done walking, sitting, standing or lying down the most popular method is sitting mediation, called *zazen*. There are a number of types of meditation, which can be grouped in two categories: contemplation and concentration.

Contemplation, credited to Buddha for its development and found more in the West, includes practices that require passive examination of the changing content of individual awareness, taking care not to select the content or cling to any aspect of it. The aim of this meditation is increased awareness, but it also presents a very effective way for the **unconscious** mind to present itself to the conscious mind.

Concentration meditation, found more in Sufi, Yoga and Christian meditation techniques, involves attempts to transform **consciousness** by mental control, to go beyond thought to a place where there is no thought. The practitioner gives his or her undivided attention to a single idea or perception, seeking the total absorption that leads to understanding. If successful a **trance**-like state occurs when external stimuli die away. Experts believe this is the oldest form of meditation and for advanced practitioners it can lead to ecstatic states.

MEDIUM/MEDIUMSHIP

Mediumship is the receipt of information that is not available through the normal senses, typically from **spirits** of the dead. Mediums serve as a channel for communication between the living and the dead. They may also heal and produce physical phenomena, such as the movement of objects. A medium's communication with spirits is often governed by entities known

Simple meditation exercise

If you are interested in more complex methods and visualizations, many websites, books and audio tapes are available: see the Resources section.

Focusing inward

Close your eyes, breathe deeply and regularly, and observe your breath as it flows in and out of your body. (Focusing on the breath is one of the most common and fundamental techniques for accessing the meditative state. Breath is a deep rhythm of the body that connects us intimately with ourselves and the world around us.)

Give your full attention to the breath as it comes into your body, and full attention to the breath as it goes out again. Whenever you find your attention wandering away from your breath, gently pull it back to the rising and falling of the breath. Inhale through your nose slowly and deeply, feeling the lower chest and abdomen inflate like a balloon. Hold for five seconds. Exhale deeply, deflating the lower chest and abdomen like a balloon. Hold for five seconds. Do this as many times as you like, then allow your breathing to return to a normal rhythm. Gradually you will become less aware of your breathing, but not captured in your stream of thoughts. You will become more inwardly centred. You will just 'be there'.

As you breathe separate yourself from the chatter of the stream of thoughts which flow through your mind. Become aware of the variety of sounds that surround you. There is no need to do anything but listen. Let your focus gently float among the sounds of the world and as you do you will find that you gradually begin to focus inwards.

Imagine that you are going deep, deep into a well within your centre. Visualize that this beautiful, deep well goes infinitely down and down. Breathe in as you descend, and absorb all the cool, soothing, healing energy that is buried deep in this bountiful well. Breathe out as you descend, and expel all the negative thoughts and energy that you have accumulated during your day.

Your deep inner world has its own essence, its own reality, and its own light. Feel the silence, peace and calm; no noise can reach you here, no words and no sound. Breathe deeply and slowly, experiencing your deepest, most serene essence in the silence of your deep well.

When you are ready, gradually allow the sounds of the external world to return to your awareness. Imagine yourself coming out of the well towards the light. Open your eyes, stretch and return to your daily life with a renewed sense of peace and optimism.

as **controls**. Some psychical researchers believe that so-called controls are not spirits but are secondary personalities of the medium instead.

A number of other words are used to describe mediums, such as channeller, fortune-teller, **witch, medicine man**, mystic, priest, prophet and wise woman, but important distinctions can also be made. According to experts the role of the medium may have developed historically out of the role of the **shaman** who communicated with the spirit world by becoming poooocooed by spirit deities and animal spirits. Mediums serve as a conduit between the physical world and the spiritual realm. During a self-induced **trance**-like state they allow spirit **entities** to take possession of them and this can manifest itself in physical ways, like a change of voice, or using gestures and mannerisms unique to the dead person. In the majority of cases a medium will have no memory of what has taken place during their trance-like state.

Some mediums practise what they call 'soul rescue': they contact a spirit or **ghost** to persuade them to move on to the **afterlife**. These spirits are thought to be trapped souls, who do not know they have died, or who cannot bear to leave the physical world behind.

Typically mediumship manifests in adulthood, but early in life there may have been indications – a child hearing or seeing things others do not, for example. Often a medium will resist the gift but gradually begin to accept it as unavoidable. If the mediumship is to develop into a real skill it often requires training. There are some who believe mediumship is an inherited characteristic but this is not generally the truth. Many mediums have no family history of mediumship. In contrast to shamans, who are typically male, mediums are often women from ordinary working-class or middle-class backgrounds.

Modern mediumship began in the nineteenth century when research on **mesmerism** showed that certain subjects who were hypnotized fell into trances under spirit control and delivered messages from the dead. As **spiritualism** grew in popularity, mesmeric mediums began to demonstrate their abilities at private and public **séances**. In the mid- to late nineteenth century, during the height of spiritualism, a large number of mediums were housewives who, frustrated by the limited range of opportunities open to them, found in séances an outlet for their boredom and frustration.

The huge popularity of mediumship prompted hundreds of women to hold tea party séances with their friends. For the majority the diversion was all they sought but some became professional mediums charging fees for private séances or performing in public. Cora Richmond became an international sensation with her instant trance lectures on a random topic selected by a jury. Despite the fame and notoriety, however, mediumship seldom led to riches, unless, as was the case with **D D Home**, a medium attracted wealthy patronage. Female mediums frequently complained about low incomes. In America the typical medium earned $5 for a séance away from home and $1 per hour at home. There was also the issue of becoming social outcasts. Even though mediums enjoyed the admiration of their clients, many women who practised mediumship were cast out by friends and family.

Social and sexual revolt against Victorian oppression certainly played a part in the immense popularity of late-nineteenth-century spiritualism. Some mediums revelled in their possession by male spirits, who 'forced' them to swear, drink whisky from a bottle and fistfight. Mediums and their clients took great pleasure in holding hands and in other forms of physical contact during séances. Some mediums would have affairs on the so-called advice of spirits, and the illegitimate babies born were called 'spirit babies'; others would leave their husbands or urge other women to leave their husbands.

Psychical researchers categorize mediumship as either physical or mental. **Physical mediumship** was popular at the height of spiritualism towards the end of the nineteenth century. It involves activity attributed to spirits, such as **rapping**, **table-tilting**, **levitation**, **materialization**, **apports** and **spirit lights** and sounds. Physical mediumship, although sensational, actually offers very little evidence for life after death because of the huge possibility of **fraud**. During the height of spiritualism mediums frequently resorted to **magic** tricks to create the necessary special effects. Numerous mediums were caught impersonating themselves or indulging in trickery. Eminent British physicist and psychical researcher, **Sir William Crookes**, believed that all mediums, even those he vouched for, like **Florence Cook** and **Eusapia Palladino**, resorted to trickery from time to time. Some however, such

as celebrated physical medium D D Home, were never exposed as frauds.

Mental mediumship involves the communication of messages from the other side through **clairvoyance**, **clairaudience**, **clairsentience** and through **automatic writing**/speech and offers one of the strongest lines of evidence for **survival after death**. Although **cryptomnesia** and **telepathy** may play a part in sittings, mental mediums often mirror mannerisms and characteristics of alleged spirit communicators, who may in turn offer previously undisclosed information or offer some purpose for the communication, such as warning sitters of danger. However, although early proofs of **survival tests** have yielded the occasional success, more recent ones have been disappointing.

As is the case with physical mediumship, **fraud** has often existed in mental mediumship, especially when spiritualism was at its peak. Medium **Arthur Ford**, who was often accused of fraud but never exposed, said that no medium could perform every time and rather than admit defeat on an off-day might be inclined to cheat. There have however been a number of noted mental mediums, such as **Leonora Piper** and **Eileen Garrett**, who have never been suspected of cheating.

Sceptics argue that much of the phenomena associated with mediumship, such as **visions, altered states of consciousness, possession** by spirits, and so on also occur in mental disorders such as schizophrenia and multiple personality disorders. Some psychiatrists and psychologists that have investigated prominent mediums have concluded that mediumship is a form of mental disorder and that the so-called 'spirits' are merely secondary personalities of the medium that emerge from the **unconscious** to find expression.

Spiritualists, however, argue that the similarities between mediumship and schizophrenia and multiple personality disorder are not strong enough. Schizophrenics and people afflicted with multiple personality disorder, for instance, typically have little control over the **voices**, visions and personalities, which appear at random and without any warning. They also find the experience disorientating and unproductive and in some cases find themselves unable to carry on with their day-to-day lives. Mediumship, on the other hand, is a **psychic** gift that mediums learn to have control over so that they can carry on with their daily lives. Mediums also use mediumship for spiritual growth and to help others.

The study of mediumship falls within the parameters of **psychical research**. Early investigators found much evidence of fraud in physical mediumship and began to investigate **telepathy** and **apparitions**. In 1882 the **Society for Psychical Research** was founded in London, soon followed in 1885 by the **American Society for Psychical Research** (ASPR) in Boston. There psychical researcher **William James** came into contact with trance medium Leonora Piper and attention was directed to mental mediumship. Piper was approached with a sceptical mindset and investigated thoroughly and when it became obvious that her performances were genuine, other explanations of spirit communication, such as **ESP** and **super ESP** became focal points

for investigation. To remove the possibility that Piper was reading people's minds, precautionary measures such as absent sittings and **proxy sitters** attending in place of persons for whom the sitting was intended were taken. Later research focused on **drop in communicators**, those unknown to the medium, and **cross correspondences** in communications through several mediums in different parts of the world.

The first scientific assessment of séance communications began in earnest in 1930 when psychical researchers Henry Saltmarsh and S G Soal devised a statistical procedure for estimating the **paranormal**. Their method involved weighing statements as to the likelihood they could have been correct simply by chance. In 1933 **John F Thomas** took this one step further in a doctrinal dissertation, in which he had a number of people judge records as right or wrong for themselves. **J G Pratt** later introduced more statistical procedures.

Physical mediumship, now generally classed as **macro PK**, was investigated less than mental mediumship in the twentieth century but prominent physical mediums were still subjected to stringent controls and test procedures. From the mid-twentieth century onwards the psychical research establishment has had little interest in either physical or mental mediumship, preferring instead to focus on **psi**. The **Psychical Research Foundation** and **Survival Research Foundation**, however, continue to investigate and research all forms of mediumship.

See also **Channelling, Séance, Spiritualism**.

MEGALITHS

From the Greek *megas*, 'great' and *lithos*, 'stone', megaliths are large prehistoric structures typically built as rows of single standing rocks or circular arrangements in a table-like format. Megalithic monuments have been found all over the world from Easter Island in the Pacific Ocean to **Stonehenge** in England to Carnac in France. When arranged in post or tomb-style they are known as 'dolmens' and when found as sole standing stones they are known as 'menhirs'.

Research has shown that megaliths tend to be placed on **ley lines** (the earth's energy network) and appear to have spiritual, astronomical, astrological and therapeutic associations. **Ghost lights** are often reported at megalith sites and many sites are said to possess **healing** and magical powers or to be the focus for electromagnetic energy. They are also thought to be gathering places for **fairies**, **spirits** and **witches**. Individuals have reported discomfort near some megaliths at night, saying that the stones radiate energy forces that produce electric shock sensations.

In 1934, engineer Professor Alexander Thorn took meticulous measurements at megalithic sites throughout Britain and Europe. He found that every circle examined was based on a single standard measurement, which he called the 'megalithic yard' of 2.72 feet. The circles were automatically aligned, the majority of them huge markers for predicting the eclipse of the moon. Thorn's theory has passed accuracy checks but there is considerable con-troversy as to what the findings suggest. Eclipses of the moon have no known effect on crops or human fertility cycles so why did prehistoric humanity spend so much time and energy building huge monuments to predict them?

In 1977 the Dragon Project Trust conducted extensive research on the energies associated with megalith sites throughout Britain. Sites have not been fully checked since early 1990 but many have been **dowsed** and measured for radioactivity, magnetism and light phenomena. The Dragon Project Trust has also set up a **dreams** project, in which volunteers sleep at various sites. The results indicate intriguing dream patterns.

MENEHUNE

Race of small people who once lived on the Hawaiian Islands and are often described as **fairies**. According to lore they lived there for centuries before the Hawaiian settlers arrived and the places where they lived are thought to be haunted. Historians believe that menehune comes from the Tahitian *menahune*, or 'commoner', and refers to a race of people who were small in social rather than physical stature.

Whatever their past the menehune have emerged as playful elves – pot bellied, naked, hairy and muscular with bushy eyebrows and hair over large eyes and a short nose with a trace of the mischievousness of their European counterparts. According to lore they are between four inches and two feet high. They enjoy singing, dancing and archery and are strong workers who prefer to work at night to avoid people. Legend has it that they are engineers who build walls, ponds and temples, but they lose interest in a project quickly and if a job is not completed in one night they are unlikely to return to finish it. If the menehune approve of a project they are said to help the construction process at night, but if they disapprove or if offerings of food are not left out for them, they will attempt to disrupt work with mysterious breakdowns and happenings.

Mental mediumship/ phenomena

Mental phenomena that make use of a person's psychical senses of **clairvoyance**, **clairaudience** and **clairsentience**.

See also **Medium/mediumship**.

Mental plane/body/energy

In **occult** philosophy the mental plane is the level of existence above the **astral plane** but below the **spiritual plane**. It is the part of the self that allows awareness of meaning. It exists outside space and time and is thought to be the lowest part of the self to survive the body after death.

As with all the planes of occult theory the mental is above or below other planes only in a metaphorical sense; in reality all the planes interpenetrate one another. The mental plane is the plane of pure meaning, pattern, and the laws of nature and mathematics, number, geometric form and music. It is outside space and time and most methods of occult **meditation** aim to raise the mind up towards the pure meaning of the mental level.

Mentalism

Mentalism is a kind of mystery entertainment. It is a performing art in which the mentalist uses his five senses to create the *illusion* of a sixth. Amazing experiments in the performance include such **supernatural** abilities as **telepathy**, **clairvoyance**, **precognition**, and **telekinesis**. Mentalists are primarily different from stage **magicians** because they insist that their abilities are real, as opposed to stage magicians who use props and sleight of hand to perform tricks.

Arguably, mentalism is a branch of modern stage magic, featuring many of the same basic tools and skills in its performance. Styles of presentation vary greatly. Some use techniques to give the impression that they actually possess supernatural powers. Other contemporary performers misdirect their audience by attributing their results to other skills – the ability to read body language or manipulate the subject through psychological means. Some mentalists make it known to their audiences that they are performing illusions, while others claim to be able genuinely to read minds or see into the future.

One constant is that mentalism typically requires the magician to display an authoritative, charismatic stage presence.

MERLIN

Archetypal British magician, once thought to be a **Druid**, who is largely a fictional creation but with some basis in fact. In some traditions Merlin is a **wizard**, enchanter and prophet, who used his magical powers to enable the legendary ruler of England, King Arthur, to gain and retain his power. He is best known for his role in ensuring that Arthur took the throne through magical means and in all traditions he is pictured as a scholar and genius advisor to the King. His name is Latin for the Welsh Myraddin, a sixth-century bard who reportedly had the gift of **precognition**. At the end of his long life, it is said that Merlin was captured by the evil **witch** Viviane, with whom he fell in love, who stole his magic and imprisoned him in a cave where, immortal, he languishes to this day.

MERMAIDS

Tales of mermaids – mythological half-fish, half-human creatures, with the upper torso, head and arms of a woman and the bottom half of a fish – are known throughout many cultures. Her male counterpart is called a merman.

Mermaids are thought to be **elementals**, nature spirits of the water, who have the ability to change their fish tails into human legs and venture on to dry land. According to lore if a mermaid falls in love with a human the only way for the human to keep the mermaid on land is to hide the mermaid's tailskin.

From the navel upward, her back and breast were like a woman's … her body as big as one of us; her skin very white; and long hair hanging down behind, of colour black; in her going down they saw her tail, which was like the tail of a porpoise, and speckled like a mackerel.

This remarkable account of a mermaid sighting was taken from the journal of English navigator Henry Hudson. He was describing what two of his crew claimed to have seen on 15 June 1608, when looking overboard from Hudson's ship off the coast of Novaya Zemlya, a group of North Russian islands. There have been numerous other sightings throughout history, including one that took place in 1830 on the island of Benbecula off northwest Scotland. The story goes that a woman washing her feet in the sea saw a mermaid and hit her on the back with a stone. A few days later the woman's dead body was washed up on the shore.

Mermaids were considered by lonely sailors to be bewitching temptresses who liked to sit topless on rocks combing their hair. Sightings were considered unlucky **omens**, no doubt linking back to the tale of Odysseus and the deadly sirens.

The mermaid legend almost certainly goes back to the fishtail gods of early civilization but it probably owes more to the creatures of the sea that seem almost human. It is now thought that sightings of mermaids were actually sightings of large marine animals such as manatees or dugongs.

MESMER, FRANZ ANTON [1734–1815]/MESMERISM

Austrian healer and physician who postulated that an all-pervading force of magnetic fluid linked all beings. He called this force 'animal magnetism', because he believed that it shot through his fingertips and eyes and induced a **trance** state. In many ways 'animal magnetism' is similar to the Hindu *prana* and Chinese **universal life force** or chi. Even though Mesmer was branded a charlatan his technique of **laying on of hands** and giving suggestions to patients led to the research and development of therapeutic **hypnotism**.

Franz Anton Mesmer was born in Switzerland and later studied medicine at the University of Vienna. He was especially interested in the influence doctors exerted over their patients. According to folklore there was a belief that certain divinely inspired individuals had the power to cure the sick by touch, with the 'laying on of hands', and some of these healers used magnets to strengthen the healing force that allegedly emanated from them. Mesmer believed that a similar kind of energy was involved in the ability of physicians to encourage the return to health of their patients. Through experiments he discovered that he could influence the rate of blood flow by movements of a magnet. Later he found that a magnet was not necessary and the same effect could be achieved with any object that he passed over his hands. Mesmer concluded that there was a healing force or fluid he called animal magnetism.

Mesmer moved to Paris in 1778, where his method of treatment became highly fashionable despite criticism from the medical community. Mesmer's technique involved making magnetic passes over his patients so that they fell into a trance-like sleep. In this state the magnetized individuals would be extremely compliant with Mesmer's suggestions, reporting, for instance, complete freedom from pain. Other reported effects of magnetic induction were so-called 'higher phenomena', such as the ability to 'see' events that were sensorially inaccessible; for example, gestures made by the magnetizer in another room might be described accurately. Following this initial observation, followers of Mesmer tried to use the magnetic trance as a means of evoking **telepathy, clairvoyance** and other **psi** phenomena.

Even though Mesmer was regarded as a charlatan by the medical community the populace continued to patronize him and his clinic became so full that he started to treat patients on masse. He maintained his clinic until 1789 when the French revolution forced him to flee the country.

Although mesmerism had no direct effect on psychical research it raised the possibility that parapsychological phenomena could be tested, experimented and examined outside occultist and quasi-religious contexts.

MESSING, WOLF GRIGORIEVICH [1899–1974]

Famous Russian psychic who predicted the end of World War II and impressed audiences all over the Soviet Union with his **clairvoyant** powers.

Messing was born near Warsaw on 10 September 1899. His **psychic** ability emerged early in life and by the time he was a teenager he was performing in public. In 1915 Albert Einstein invited him to his apartment, where tests with **Sigmund Freud** produced impressive results. In 1937 Hitler put a 200,000-mark price tag on his head when Messing predicted that Hitler would die if he 'turned towards the east'. Messing fled to Russia where, under the oppressive rule of Stalin, Russian psychics were forced to go underground or risk being shot; however, Messing managed to impress Stalin. On one occasion Stalin told Messing to rob a bank psychically. Messing took an empty attaché case into a Moscow bank and, using telepathic **hypnosis**, handed a clerk a blank piece of paper and ordered him to fill the case with 100,000 roubles – which the clerk promptly did. Messing claimed to use telepathic hypnosis to influence others in this fashion.

On 7 March 1944 Messing predicted the exact dates of Hitler's death and the Nazi surrender. After the war he worked as an entertainer and became very successful and popular. In explaining his secrets of clairvoyance Messing said the thoughts of others became colourful images in his mind; he saw pictures rather than heard words. He always tried to touch his subjects by the hand, which he said helped clear his mind of distractions.

Russian scientists tried to find a physiological reason for his clairvoyance but Messing rarely let himself be examined. A neurologist did discover that portions of Messing's head generated large amounts of heat, but never discovered why. Other scientists believe that when Messing took a person's hand he subconsciously received muscle movements that helped his reading.

METAGNOMY

A term used by French psychical researchers to indicate knowledge acquired in a **trance** without the use of the five senses. Metagnomy or meganome is **divination** by **visions** obtained when in a trance. In other words, the divination of **mediums**, **seers** and **shamans** and all those who go into trance-like states to receive their knowledge in some **psychic** manner. All such would be termed metagnomes.

The term was derived from the Greek words *meta* ('after' or 'beyond') and *gnomon* ('one who knows'), and although it was employed by the French psychical researcher Dr Eugene Osty, it seems to have been originally coined by the researcher Emile Boirac (1851–1917) in his book *L' Avenir des sciences psychiques* (Paris, 1917).

METAL

In Chinese philosophy and medicine metal is one of the five **elements** that make up the building blocks of the universe, along with **fire, earth, wood** and **water**. Metal represents grief and sadness but it also is said to protect the body during times of stress and emotional intensity. The sound of weeping and the elimination of body wastes are also associated with this element.

METAL BENDING

A psychokinetic effect, most often associated with well-known **psychic Uri Geller**, in which metallic objects such as keys, cutlery and so on are subjected to more or less permanent deformation or other structural change when stroked or touched.

Paranormal metal bending is a controversial subject in **parapsychology**. One source of difficulty is that very few people are actively involved in this area of research and therefore the standing of the research relies heavily on a small number of individuals. Despite the controversy, metal-bending research is important as it could provide insight into the physical

characteristics of **psychokinesis,** an issue in which other research areas have not been particularly enlightening.

METAPHYSICS

Metaphysics is a branch of philosophy concerned with the study of first principles and being. Its central doctrine is that all things are part of one main source (intelligence and energy) and that each thing, animate or inanimate, should be respected for its particular form of this one main source; therefore each thing has an independent function and is dependent upon every other thing, and all are contributing to the main source.

In recent times, the meaning of the word metaphysics has become confused by popular signifiers that are actually unrelated to metaphysics. **Magic** and the **occult**, for example, are not so much concerned with the metaphysical enquiry into first principles or the nature of being, though they do tend to proceed on the metaphysical assumption that all being is 'one'.

METEORS

In many cultures shooting stars that light up the night sky are associated with the **spirits** of the dead. According to the ancient Romans every person had a star and when he or she died, it fell to earth in the form of a meteor. From this is evolved the folklore belief in Europe and America that a meteor shooting across the sky is the **soul** of a person who has recently died. Similar beliefs are held in tribal societies and in some places meteors are said to be the souls of murdered men. Some Native American tribes believe that stars are the souls of the dead and when they fall a soul is about to be reborn.

and broken lines had other interpretations. Cardan also noted various combinations of facial spots, moles and other blemishes and equated them with the twelve signs of the **Zodiac**. Taurus, Aries and Gemini were on the upper part of the forehead; Cancer, Leo and Virgo lower down; Libra was at the top of the nose; Scorpio near the ear; Sagittarius at the top of the cheek; Capricorn below it; Aquarius below that; and Pisces at the bottom of the cheek on the chin.

METOPOMANCY

Mathematician and astrologer Jerome Cardan (1501–1576) is thought to be the first to suggest that the wrinkles on a person's forehead might represent a collection of indicators as to a person's character and that no two people would have the same wrinkles. In 1658 his work *Metoposcopia* was published in Latin by Thomas Jolly in Paris and later the same year a French translation appeared.

Cardan suggested that the lines of a person's forehead could be used for **divination** purposes, in a similar way to the lines of the hand in **palmistry**. According to Cardan there could be up to seven lines on a forehead and these could be equated with the seven planets of **astrology** from the bottom to the top of the forehead: Moon, Mercury, Venus, Sun, Mars, Jupiter and Saturn. No one was likely to have all seven lines.

Long and perfectly straight lines were said to indicate simplicity of soul and a sense of justice. Wavy lines, crossing lines

MIAMI POLTERGEIST

Poltergeist case that occurred in a Miami warehouse in early 1967. It stands out as being the first case in which scientifically controlled experiments were conducted.

On 14 January 1967, Miami police were called by warehouse manager Alvin Laubheim, who stated that a ghost was in his warehouse breaking things. Officers arrived and witnessed objects falling off shelves on their own accord.

Parapsychologists **William Roll** and **J G Pratt** were called in to investigate. Almost immediately a 19-year-old shipping clerk called Julio was identified as the focal point, because the breakages and movement of objects always took place when he was in the vicinity and the activity increased when he was agitated or upset.

Roll and Pratt investigated thoroughly and found no evidence of trickery to stage the effects. Roll used the case to test his 'psi field' theory, which suggested that phenomena reduce with distance from the agent due to a weakening **psi** energy field. Activity did appear to reduce with distance from Julio but objects furthest from him travelled the longest distance and objects nearest to him travelled the shortest distance. Roll explained this by proposing controversially that the psi field rotates in a circular motion.

Julio agreed to have a number of personality and psychological tests. Results that would indicate unconscious **psychokinesis** included anger, guilt, fear, rebellion, dissociation and anxiety. Julio did acknowledge that he disliked his boss and a few weeks prior to the start of the phenomena he had started to have nightmares and suicidal feelings when his stepmother attempted to get him to move out from home. On 30 January a break-in occurred; the police were called and Julio confessed to the crime. Police officers suspected that Julio had used trickery with threads to instigate the poltergeist activity but Roll and Pratt doubted this claim. A few days later Julio stole a ring from a jeweller and this time was sent to jail for six months. The phenomena ceased after his departure from the warehouse.

When Julio came out of jail, Roll attempted to arrange financial support for him so that he could undergo laboratory testing for **ESP** and psychokinesis. He eventually underwent tests that showed significant results for psychokinesis but not for ESP. His case provides evidence that some cases of poltergeist activity may unwittingly be caused by individuals due to repressed anger and fear.

Micro PK

Psychokinetic effects that cannot be directly observed or recorded, but can only be inferred from the statistical analysis of data. Parapsychologists usually make a distinction between macroscopic PK (large-scale effects observable by the naked eye or by a single measurement) and microscopic PK (small-scale effects only observable by statistical analysis of multiple measurements). Both types are studied today, however with more attention paid to the micro variety.

By its nature, the study of micro PK phenomena requires an experimental approach. The first recorded experiments of this type were conducted by **J B Rhine** and his associates in 1934, investigating whether subjects could affect the throws of dice. Similar experiments have since been conducted by many other parapsychologists.

See also **Macro PK**.

Micromancy

The opposite of **macromancy**, micromancy is **divination** by studying the smallest object in the area. The object is studied and the **seer** interprets what he or she sees. Size, general shape and colour are all taken into account, as is the closeness of the object to others or the distance from them.

MIND READING

See **Telepathy**.

MINI GELLER

A child or young person who, after having seen **Uri Geller** perform, can duplicate by **paranormal** means his **metal-bending** feats. It is as if the ability were transferred and released. Many mini Gellers have reported to parapsychologists with claims of spoon bending abilities. The majority of these children have been unable to demonstrate their alleged talents under laboratory conditions and when given an opportunity to cheat many do so. Despite this John Hasted, a professor of physics in London, carried out a large number of successful experiments on mini Gellers and published the results in *The Metal-Benders* (1981). The book has photographs of paper clips being put into a glass sphere, one by one, and these being bent by the teenagers into a tangle, allegedly by mental power alone.

MIRACLE

A miracle is something that happens beyond the scope of reality and it typically occurs within a religious context. Miracles are usually attributed to a divine and/or **supernatural** power that intervenes in the normal course of events and changes their

expected or predicted outcome. Examples include miraculous **healing** and changes in weather that the weather forecaster had failed to identify.

Modern scientific views of nature, and therefore the definition of miracle, fall roughly into two schools of thought. The rational materialist view, dominant in the nineteenth century, attempted to explain everything in terms of matter and energy, governed by rigid laws that determine all events. In this view the supernatural is an illusion. In the twentieth century, however, a less rigidly deterministic scientific model of the universe began to emerge, thanks mainly to Einstein's theory of relativity, Heisenberg's **quantum theory** and growing acceptance of the mind's control of the body. Many scientists therefore have been more willing than before to admit that there are 'more things in heaven and earth' than nineteenth-century scientists realized. This is not so much an acknowledgement of the supernatural as it is a willingness to include in nature what may seem supernatural according to our present knowledge.

MIRROR

For centuries mirrors and reflective surfaces have been used for **divination, magic** and repelling evil. In recent years they have been used as tools for psychic development to increase **clairvoyant** ability and gain insight into past lives.

Glass mirrors were introduced in the thirteenth century in Venice. Prior to that mirrors were made of polished metal surfaces and gold and silver. The ancient Romans believed they originated from Persia, where they were used by the **magi** for divination. Mirror divination is called crystallomancy, catoptromancy and **scrying**.

In the West magic mirrors were popular among **magicians**, **witches** and **sorcerers** from the Middle Ages to the nineteenth century. In more recent times mirrors as magic tools have fallen out of favour but they are still used by some **psychics** and diviners. In the East mirrors are more commonly used for divination purposes. In Tibet mirrors are used for *tra*, divination by the reading of signs and **visions**.

Mirrors are traditionally associated with fear and evil. In some tribal societies the reflection is thought to be the **soul** and exposing the soul in a mirror makes it vulnerable to misfortune or death. This is echoed in many other cultures in the common belief that if a person sees their own reflection they will soon die. A worldwide folklore custom is the removal of mirrors from sick rooms in case the mirror draws out the soul, and the turning of mirrors when there is a death in the house. According to lore whoever looks into a

Mirror gazing

Mirror gazing is one of the many forms of scrying: divination by looking into a reflective surface. The mirror is used in much the same way as a crystal ball, with the diviner seeing images from the past, present and future. All types of mirrors have been used, including those with polished metal faces, glass, crystal and obsidian. The mirror may or may not be enclosed in a frame and if it is it is usually engraved or marked in some way with sigils to help amplify the images given.

Many diviners say a black or concave mirror is far superior to any other. One way to make a mirror that follows both suggestions is to obtain one of the old framed pictures from around the turn of the twentieth century, which has an oval, convex glass. Reversing the glass and painting what then becomes the back of it with black paint produces a convex black mirror that is perfect for mirror gazing. Old magic books suggest that the glass should be painted three times with asphaltum. To make the asphaltum stick to the glass, it first needs to be cleaned with turpentine. The asphalt should be laid on with a camel-hair brush. However, using black enamel paint from a spray can seems to work just as well. As with all magical practices and rituals, while making the object it is recommended that you concentrate on its purpose – scrying for projecting scenes of the past, present and future.

mirror after a death will also die. In other superstitions, if one looks long enough into a mirror at night or by candlelight one will see the devil (hence it is advised to cover up mirrors at night). Witches and **vampires** are said to cast no reflection in a mirror. Curiously mirrors can also be used to protect against evil, reflecting it away.

There are a number of mirror superstitions. Breaking one is thought to bring bad luck for seven years and perhaps a death in the family. A mirror that falls of its own accord is a **death omen**. A girl who gazes at the moon's reflection in a mirror will learn the date of her wedding day, and if she does this at **Halloween** she will see a reflection of her future husband.

Mirrors painted black on the convex side are thought to be excellent tools for the development of clairvoyance. Gazing into one is thought to reveal visions of **spirit** guides and help one gain auric sight. Some believe that the face changes that occur when staring in a mirror are images of past lives.

MOLEOSOPHY

Divination and character analysis according to the size, shape, colour and location of moles on the human body. Mole divination

Position of moles and how they are typically interpreted in molesophy

* *Arms: Moles on the arms indicate that the person is polite, diligent and will lead a happy married life.*
* *Armpits: A mole under the left arm is indicative of great struggle early in life, which is, however, well rewarded. A mole under the right arm shows that one needs to be alert and cautious in matters of security.*
* *Back: People with moles on their backs are generous but occasionally arrogant.*
* *Breast: A mole on the right breast is indicative of laziness, which may affect family life. A mole on the left breast belongs to active and energetic people,*

who generally get what they want in life.
* *Buttocks: People who have a mole on their buttocks are un-ambitious, and like to go with the flow.*
* *Cheek: A mole on either cheek indicates a serious and studious person who has no interest in material pleasures.*
* *Chin: A mole on either side of the chin is indicative of people who are affectionate and caring. These people adapt easily to any situation. They love travelling and respect the law of the land. They are also dedicated and conscientious workers and willingly accept responsibilities.*

- **Ear:** People who are born with a mole on their ear are generally considered lucky.
- **Elbow:** People who have moles on their elbow love to travel. They are adventurous and spirited.
- **Eye:** If the mole is located on the outer corner of the eye, this indicates that the person is honest, reliable and forthright.
- **Eyebrow:** If a mole is located on the right eyebrow, it signifies that these people will have a highly active life and will be successful in all ventures. A mole on the left eyebrow is considered less fortunate, and in some cases can indicate misfortune.
- **Finger:** People who have a mole on any finger turn out to be dishonest and tend to grossly exaggerate.
- **Foot:** People with a mole on their foot are easy going and laid back.
- **Forehead:** People who have a mole on their forehead are often prosperous and well settled in life.
- **Hand:** Those people who have a mole on their hand are often talented and make a success of their lives.
- **Heel:** People who possess a mole on their heel can make enemies easily and are prone to losing friends.
- **Hip:** A mole on any part of the hip except the buttocks signifies that these people are contented, resilient and spirited.
- **Knee:** If a mole is on the right knee, it implies a friendly person. A mole on the left knee signifies an extravagant lifestyle.
- **Lips:** People with a mole on or near their lips always aspire to get ahead in life.
- **Neck:** If the mole is on the front of the neck, it signifies unexpected good fortune. If it is on either side of the neck, it indicates an unreasonable temperament. A mole on the back of the neck indicates a desire to lead a simple life.
- **Nose:** A mole on the nose belongs to a person who will be a sincere friend and a hard-working individual.
- **Shoulder:** A mole on the right shoulder indicates a sensible, industrious individual. One on the left shoulder, however, is regarded as unlucky.
- **Wrist:** A mole on the wrist indicates that the person is frugal, ingenious and dependable.

When there are twin moles, irrespective of their location, the person possesses a dual nature. The presence of two moles, side by side, is indicative of a person being in love with two people.

The shape of the mole is significant: a round mole signifies the goodness in people; an oblong mole depicts a modest share of acquired wealth; while an angular mole suggests that the individual has both positive and negative characteristics.

Those who have light coloured moles are considered lucky, but black or red moles denote a person who will have to surmount challenges in life.

was not a major feature of Greco-Roman culture, and references to the practice are rare. Birthmarks enjoyed a somewhat higher status, and are mentioned. A short Greek manual of mole interpretation survives from antiquity, appended to the end of a much longer work on divination by twitches ascribed to the legendary Greek **seer** Melampus. Although the treatise on moles lacks an author, and differs in style from the work on twitches, in general it relies on fairly straightforward and logical reasoning – for instance, a mark on the back of the throat portends beheading; one on the lips portends overeating.

MONONOKE

In Japanese lore the mononoke is a **ghost** that resides in inanimate objects. It is found in temples, shrines and graveyards and likes to scare or even kill people. Priests are thought to be able to drive it away by reciting Buddhist sutras. According to Shinto belief, all things, including inanimate objects, have their own unique spirit (*kami*), which gives them life.

MONROE, MARILYN [1926–1962]

The Hollywood Roosevelt Hotel on Hollywood Boulevard is said to be the current residence of several **ghosts** of popular film stars, including Marilyn Monroe, the glamorous and funny star of such pictures as *Some Like It Hot* and *Gentlemen Prefer Blondes*, who was a frequent guest of the Roosevelt at the height of her popularity. Although she died in her Brentwood home, her image has allegedly been seen on several occasions in a full-length mirror that once hung in her poolside suite.

Marilyn Monroe lived a dramatic, sensational but tragic life and died of a drug overdose on 8 August 1962. There has been much speculation about her death and the events surrounding it. Most believe that suicide was likely, although it has been suggested that her drug overdose was administered by someone other than Marilyn herself. There are some who believe that this uncertainty explains why her ghost lingers behind and why her sad image has impressed itself on the mirror.

MOON

Age-old **symbol** of the feminine, the **psychic**, **intuition**, emotion, inspiration, **imagination** and the deep layers of the **unconscious**.

The moon's phases correspond to the seasons of nature and primitive man came to believe that it regulated life cycles, fertility and the tides. In the first century AD Pliny the Elder catalogued the moon's influence over life and put forth numerous prescriptions for regulating daily life according to the moon's phases, in a 37-volume work entitled *Natural History*. Because the moon

Moon-infused waters

The ancient Greeks called this technique drawing down the moon or the Thessalian Trick. They believed that the Thessalian witches held great power and magical knowledge. The following formula for moon-infused water was considered to be one of their most important:

1. Fill a jar or dish to the brim with pure spring water.

2. Bring this container inside and position it so that the full moon is reflected within. Maintain this position for as long as you can.

3. The moon-charged water may now be used as a potent ingredient in potion and spells, substituted whenever a spell demands water.

waxes, wanes and reappears in fullness each month it also became associated with life, death and rebirth. In mythology the moon is the destination for **souls** after death and deities of the **underworld** are often lunar deities. The ancient Greeks believed the moon to be a midway point for souls making their transition to or from earth.

The predominance of the moon at night, a time considered mysterious and dangerous overall, created a logical link with the night-time activity of **witches** and over the centuries the moon became associated with **witchcraft**, **magic** and **sorcery**. Today it remains a major symbol for modern witchcraft and **paganism**. Moon power is mind power and nights of the full moon are still regarded as the most potent for magic and the world of **spirits**. Coven activities are often set around the cycles and phases of the moon and witches work their magic in accordance with lunar phases: the waxing moon is said to be positive for growth, achievement, good fortune and healing **spells**; the waning moon is said to be positive for banishing spells and the undoing of harm and negative influences.

In general, although not always, magic worked with the moon is considered women's magic. This is because the moon is recognized as having a profound effect upon menstrual cycles and the tides. (In ancient times women would often withdraw to huts during menstruation to contemplate and absorb the power of the dark moon.) In many (but not all) cases lunar deities are female and the moon is most often personified by the Triple Goddess – virgin, mother and crone – represented by the classical goddesses Artemis/Diana, Selene and Hecate.

The ancient witches of Thessaly were thought to have the power to draw down the moon from the sky on command and a symbolic ritual of drawing down the moon is still performed in modern witchcraft, although it is likely that this very ancient term predates **Wicca** and may refer to other rites and practices, in particular the process of creating moon-infused waters.

MORTON CASE

Also known as the 'Cheltenham Haunting', this case is unique in that an **apparition** of a woman was seen for several years by a number of independent witnesses.

The house in Cheltenham, England, was built in 1866. Its first owner was one of its builders, Henry Swinhoe. Swinhoe's first wife died and three years later he married a woman called Imogen Hutchins. The marriage was unhappy and shortly before Swinhoe died in 1876 Hutchins left him. She died in 1878. After Swinhoe's death the house was briefly owned by an elderly man who died six months after moving in. The house remained vacant for four years before being taken by Captain Despard, his wife, their two sons and three daughters. A fourth married daughter visited occasionally with her husband.

It was during the Despard's occupation of the house that the apparition was most often seen. The Despard's 19-year-old daughter, Rosina, was the most frequent **percipient** and it was she who later wrote an account of her experiences for the *Proceedings of the Society for Psychical Research.*

Rosina claimed to have seen a crying woman dressed in a black dress that made a swishing sound as it moved a number of times at the house. Typically she would descend the stairs and go into the living room, generally standing awhile to the right-hand side of the bay window. Then she would leave the living room and walk along the hall to the door to the garden, before which she disappeared. Rosina tried to speak to the woman but she never spoke. She did, however, seem aware of her surroundings and would move around objects in her way. When cornered she would disappear.

Rosina was not the only one to see the lady in black. One night her sister Edith was playing the piano in the living room when the apparition appeared. Rosina's two other sisters and one of her brothers, along with the Despard's cook and the housemaid also saw this woman from time to time. The Despard's dog also behaved oddly – wagging its tail happily as if expecting to be stroked and then shrinking away in fear.

In early 1885 psychical researcher **Frederick Myers**, from the **Society for Psychical Research**, visited the Despards and urged Rosina to take a photograph. She tried but got no results. Sightings continued until 1887, and in some cases the figure appeared so genuine it was mistaken for a real person. It was suggested that the apparition was that of Imogen Hutchins, on the basis that she wore mourning clothes and when she was alive she often used the living room.

In 1893 the Despards left the house and it remained vacant until 1898 when it became a preparatory school for boys. During this time the apparition of a woman was frequently encountered on stairs, always leaving the house in daylight from the garden door and walking down the short drive. The school closed soon after opening and for a number of decades after the house remained empty for long periods of time, occupants only staying there a few years. In 1958 and in 1961 the same **ghost** was allegedly seen again. In 1974 the building was converted into apartments and since then there have been no reported sightings. Some believe that modernization disturbed the phenomenon.

Moses, Rev. William Stainton [1839–1892]

Prominent university-educated British **spiritualist** and **medium**. William Stainton Moses was born on 5 November 1839 and in 1852 he won a scholarship to Oxford University where he proved to be a highly ambitious and hard-working student. He was ordained as a minister of the Church of England in 1863 and was sent to Kirk Maughold on the Isle of Man.

In 1871, Moses accepted a mastership at University College London and was persuaded in 1872 by the wife of his close friend Dr Speer to attend a **séance**. It was the first of a number of séances he attended, including some with **D D Home**, and as time wore on Moses found himself converted to **spiritualism**, showing signs of mediumistic talent himself.

Moses established a **home circle** with his friends the Speers, and revealed powerful **paranormal** physical abilities, including self-**levitation**, **apports**, **table-tilting**, **materializations** and movement of objects. Also in 1872 Moses began **automatic writing** and recorded his scripts in a series of notebooks that were serialized in a widely read newspaper called *The Spiritualist* under the false name, M A Oxon. They later formed the basis of his books *Higher Aspects of Spiritualism* and *Spirit Teachings*.

Moses' writings and experiences were sufficiently sensational to attract the interest of leading psychical researchers **Sir William Crookes** and **Frederick Myers** and it was after attending a séance with Moses in 1874 that Myers persuaded **Henry Sidgwick** to join in organizing a group to investigate mediumship. This group was the beginnings of the Society for Psychical Research. When the Society for Psychical Research eventually formed, Moses sat on the first council as vice president. He resigned shortly after, however, disappointed with the critical approach displayed by the researchers.

In 1884 Moses formed his own organization, the London Spiritual Alliance (LSA). This was intended to replace the British National Alliance of Spiritualists (BNAS), which had been in existence from 1872–84. The new LSA issued a spiritualist journal, *Light*, edited by Moses, and the journal continues to be published today by the LSA's successor the **College of Psychic Studies**.

Sceptics argue that Moses' notebooks are not substantial enough as evidence because most of the séances were private and the records, even though they are

The spirit teachings of William Stainton Moses

The following is a sample of spirit teaching claimed to have been either written or spoken through the English medium Rev. Stainton Moses by a band of 49 spirits led by their chief, 'Imperator'.

On the state after death

(From *More Spirit Teachings*, Part 2)

S M asks about a friend, now in spirit.

She is being gradually roused from the torpor into which she fell. She will continue long in a state of weakness and development, and gradually gain spiritual strength before being removed from her present state. She is tended by spirits in the place set apart for those who need fostering care. Many who are withdrawn prematurely or roughly, are tended by those spirits who devote themselves to the work in a special sphere set apart for them near the earth on which they have been incarnated.

This is the intermediate sphere of rest, in which spiritual functions are developed, and that which is lacking is supplied. Such a sphere there is near to each world, and into it the weary and suffering, the spiritually famished, the prematurely cut off, are gathered, that they may be nourished and tended by ministering angels. There they must need remain till they are fit to progress. Then they go to their sphere, take up their progress, and are developed by degrees. A harbour of rest after a stormy passage. None from that sphere can be permitted to manifest on your earth. They are housed in the garden of the Lord, and may not be exposed to the rude blasts of your air. Cease to wish. The effect of your wish is but to disturb. Pray, rather, that your friend may fare well in the charge of her guardians.

detailed, were kept either by Moses or the Speers. Despite this Moses, along with Home, remains one of the mediums that was never caught, or suspected of, **fraud**.

MOUNT, THE

Allegedly haunted country retreat in Lenox, Massachusetts, called the Mount, that was once owned by author Edith Wharton (1862–1937).

Wharton did some of her writing at the Mount and enjoyed the company of famous literary guests, such as Henry James. She sold the house in 1912 and it passed through a succession of owners. In 1980 it was purchased by Shakespeare and Company, a troupe of actors that live and perform there.

A number of **apparitions** have been reported by members of the acting troupe, including a figure of a woman, thought to be Wharton, and a figure of a man thought to be James. There have also been reports of strange noises and laughter and a hooded figure that manifests at bedsides and presses down on individuals. One of the best-documented occurrences took place in 1979 and is recorded in Arthur Myers's *Ghostly Register* (1986). Actress and voice teacher Andrea Haring was sleeping in what was formerly Wharton's writing room. She awoke at 4 am to see three figures − a woman whom Haring recognized as Wharton, and a man, whom she recognized as Edith's husband, Teddy Wharton. She didn't recognize the third man. Wharton seemed to be dictating to this third man, who was sitting at a desk. Haring got up to leave and the ghosts turned to her, acknowledging her presence. She returned a few minutes later to find the room empty. Later when Haring was looking through the photographs she recognized the man at the desk as Wharton's secretary, who may also have been her lover.

MOVEMENT OF OBJECTS

See **Psychokinesis**.

MOVING COFFINS

Disturbances of coffins inside sealed crypts have been recorded in places all over the world. Mysteriously heavy lead coffins are found in disarray. They are put back in the correct position only to be found disturbed or moved again when the vault is next opened for a burial.

So far there has been no completely convincing explanation for this phenomenon. Some researchers believe that the movement is caused when crypts are flooded with water. Although this may be possible in some cases it is unlikely in locations above sea level. Others believe that the movement is caused by restless **spirits**, especially those who have been murdered or committed suicide.

In the nineteenth century disturbances were recorded in the Getford family vault near Stamford, Lincolnshire and in the Boxhowden crypt on the Island of Oesel (now called Sarmea) located in the Baltic Sea. Perhaps the most famous moving coffin case, however, is that of the **Chase Vault**.

MU

Supposedly the inhabitants of **Lemuria**, according to **Madame Blavatsky**, but there is also a theory proposed in 1870 by Colonel James Churchward that Mu itself was a lost continent. The former Bengal Lancer believed that the island of Mu was six thousand miles long and three thousand miles wide and was once located in the Pacific Ocean, with its centre just south of the Equator. Churchward claimed to have discovered this from secret clay stone tablets hidden in India and revealed to him by a Hindu priest.

According to Churchward, human beings appeared on Mu some 200,000 years ago, evolving into an advanced race of about 60 million people. Their civilization was destroyed 12,000 years ago by a massive volcanic eruption and tidal wave. Churchward believed evidence of Mu could be found in many of the ancient Greek, Egyptian, Mayan and Chinese legends, rocky roads and artefacts. He never produced the tablets to prove his theory and said his research also included **trance**-like visions of former lives. Although Churchward had his supporters, his books are no longer taken seriously by researchers and historians.

MURPHY, GARDNER [1895–1979]

Respected psychologist and academic whose passionate interest in psychical research gave the field increased status and prominence.

Gardner Murphy was born on 8 July 1895 in Chillicothe, Ohio, but he grew up in Concord, Massachusetts. His life-long interest in psychical research began at the age of 16 when he discovered a copy of **Sir William Barrett**'s *Psychical Research* (1911) in his grandfather's library. In 1917

Murphy graduated from Harvard with a master's degree in psychology and in 1919 he visited and joined the **Society for Psychical Research**. In 1922 Murphy was granted money, via Harvard's Hodgson Memorial Fund, to support psychical research and for the next three years he devoted himself to psychical research. It was during this time that he had numerous sittings with **Leonora Piper**.

From around 1926 Murphy came to the realization that he could help psychical research more by establishing himself in psychology than by committing himself entirely to the former field. Although he directed his energies towards mainstream psychology and achieved great stature and success (in 1944 he was elected president of the American Psychological Association) he remained in close contact with the field of psychical research. When **J B Rhine** approached him about supervising **J G Pratt**, a Duke graduate who had been working at the Parapsychology Laboratory at Duke University, Murphy agreed. In the early 1940s Murphy began to spend more and more time at the **American Society for Psychical Research** (ASPR) where he became vice president. Under his direction the society began to conduct research and to collect and analyse reports of psychic experiences. In 1949 Murphy was elected president of the Society for Psychical Research, and from 1962 to 1971 he served as president of the ASPR.

Throughout his distinguished career Murphy's intellect was unequalled. He contributed more than 100 articles to psychical research journals and even more to mainstream psychology publications, and was the author of numerous books, many of which attempted to show the association between psychical research and psychology. Murphy's experimental psychical research yielded disappointing results, but despite this he remained convinced that research on **survival after death** was an important area of study.

MUSCLE READING

Also known as contact mind reading, muscle reading is a technique simulating **telepathy**, in which the 'mind reader' (who generally holds a hand or arm) responds to and interprets slight muscle movements produced unconsciously by the person whose mind is apparently being read.

MUSIC

The ability of musical sounds to influence positively or negatively health, mood, morality and consciousness has been known for centuries. Music as form of therapy has been used in almost all cultures for **healing**, **meditation** and expanding **consciousness**.

In Eastern traditions sound vibration has long been used for healing and spiritual development, combined with chants, musical instruments and movement. The ancient Chinese believed music to be the basis of all things and Confucius stated that

if the music of a civilization changed, then its society would change too. The ancient Greeks believed in the healing power of music for insomnia and anxiety. Aristotle believed that music affected character. Pythagoras found that all music can be reduced to numbers and concluded that the universe could be similarly explained.

According to modern research the elements of music that have been shown to have physical and psychological effects are rhythm, tone and pitch, interval (the distance between notes) and timbre (the nature of the music which creates associations in the listener's mind). It is thought that music's beneficial effects are due to the principle of entrainment, a physics principle in which stronger vibrations cause weaker vibrations to begin pulsing in the same harmony. Therefore music is able to entrain the body, mind and spirit by affecting physiological rhythms, and studies have indeed shown that music can alter pulse rate, **brain waves** and blood pressure. It can also help release emotion, ease physical pain, induce relaxation and encourage the release of the body's feel-good hormones – called endorphins.

Music therapy, which focuses on the areas of pain relief and stress reduction, enjoyed a revival in the late twentieth century largely due to the work of violinist Helen L Bonny, whose book *Music and Your Health* (1973) was the first in a series of books and features on the health effects of music.

Music can also have a toxic effect on the body. Some forms of music, such as heavy metal, have been shown to negatively affect the health of plants and animals and have been associated with depression and aggressive behaviour.

New Age music, which came to the fore in the 1970s, has been criticized as bland and tuneless, but supporters believe that it can expand consciousness and foster physical and psychological wellbeing. **Clairvoyants** claim to be able to see colours or shapes when listening to music and also report an awareness of music **thought forms** created by the sound vibrations. Others claim that music helps them induce **altered states of consciousness, out-of-body experiences** and **peak experiences** similar to those achieved by **meditation**.

MYERS, FREDERICK WILLIAM HENRY [1843–1901]

Scholar, psychologist, psychical researcher, prominent member of the **Society for Psychical Research** and author of a seminal book that summarized and systemized the findings of psychical research: *Human Personality and Its Survival of Bodily Death* (1903).

In the summer of 1871, two years after Myers had resigned his position as Fellow of Trinity College, Cambridge to become a school inspector, he was out walking with his friend **Henry Sidgwick**. Myers asked Sidgwick 'almost with trembling, whether he thought that when Tradition, Intuition, Metaphysic had failed to solve the riddle of the universe, there was still a chance that from any actual observable phenomena – ghosts, spirits, whatever they might be –

some valid knowledge might be drawn as to the World Unseen.' Sidgwick replied that there might be and this was to be the beginning of the organization later known as the Society for Psychical Research.

In 1872 Myers and Sidgwick formed a group to study **mediums**, such as **William Stainton Moses**, and ten years later the Society for Psychical Research was born, with Sidgwick as president and Myers on the governing council. Myers also assisted in the investigations of, among others, **Leonora Piper** and **Eusapia Palladino** and became a key member of a literary committee assigned the task of collecting cases for publication in the Society's journal and proceedings.

In 1890 Myers became president of the Society. Apart from *Human Personality and Its Survival of Bodily Death*, his contribution to the landmark book published by the Society for Psychical Research in 1886, *Phantasms of the Living* and his investigation of **cross correspondences**, perhaps the most significant contribution made by Myers to psychical research was his concept of the 'subliminal consciousness'. His theory had similarities to **Freud**'s theory of the '**unconscious**' of several years later, but differed in that Myers conceived it not as repressed energy but as the root from which conscious thought sprang. According to Myers the subliminal consciousness was receptive to extrasensory input and, because it was somehow separate from the body, it could survive life after death.

Myomancy

Ancient form of **divination** by the movements, cries, noises and gnawing that rats make. All these signs were thought to foretell evil. Ephraim Chambers's *Cyclopaedia, or Universal Dictionary of Arts and Sciences* (1728) states 'Some authors hold myomancy to be one of the most ancient forms of divination; and think that it is on this account that Isaiah lxvl, 17, reckons mice among the abominable things of the idolater.' The Roman commander Quintus Fabius Maximus was said to have resigned his dictatorship because of the warnings of rats and mice and, according to Marcus Varro (116–27 BC) cavalry commander Cassius Flaminus also retired for the same reason.

Myrtles Plantation

According to the US Tourist Bureau, the Myrtles Plantation, located 70 miles north of New Orleans, is one of the most haunted places of America.

Numerous **spirits** are thought to roam both the beautiful landscape of the plantation and inside the manor. The most famous **ghost** is that of Chloe, a governess who was hanged around 1820 for the murder of the wife and children of her lover who was also her employer. It is said that Chloe roams the mansion at night and likes to disturb guests by lifting the mosquito netting that surrounds the beds. Another spirit that is said to appear is that of William Winter who owned the plantation between 1860–71, his spirit is said to linger because of the tragic nature of his death. One night while out on the porch Winter was shot in the chest. He managed to stagger back into the house and climb 17 of the 20 stairs, where he died in his wife's arms. Allegedly he is heard climbing the stairs, but he only makes it to the seventeenth one.

Other sightings at the Myrtles Plantation, often called 'the house of spirits' include two little blonde girls peering through the windows, a Confederate soldier marching across the porch and a **Voodoo** priestess who, according to lore, was unable to use her powers to save a young girl from a fatal disease.

The Myrtles attracts an almost endless stream of visitors each year and many of them come in search of ghosts. Psychical researchers believe that the most important key to discovering why it might be haunted in the first place is the unusual and violent history of the house, which has left ghosts behind. Since the Myrtles Plantation was built by David Bradford in 1794, it has allegedly been the scene of 10 murders. In truth, only one person was probably murdered there but this does not take away from the fact that previous owners of Myrtles did experience more than their fair share of unhappiness, violence and tragedy.

MYSTERY CULTS

In a strict sense, secret religious cults that flourished in the Hellenistic period. In a broader sense, it also refers to **esoteric** teachings and the rites of secret societies outside the classical word. During the Hellenistic period many cults flourished, the Dionysian mysteries and Eleusinian mysteries being perhaps the most well known. As well as the Greek mysteries, the mystery tradition can also be traced back to the Egyptian mysteries of Isis and Osiris and the Mithraic mystery cults from Persia. Centuries later there were the **Gnostics**, the **Kabbalists**, the **Neo-Platonists**, the **Rosicrucians** and the **Freemasons**. At the heart of the mystery schools is the concept of salvation, life after death and secret, or hidden, knowledge.

'Mystery' derives from the Greek *musterion*, which means 'sacred secret'. The preservation of the secrets of the cult was required by members or initiates. There were also elements of **magic** and ecstasy in mystery school rites.

MYSTICAL EXPERIENCE

An experience in which a person transcends the bounds of ordinary consciousness to awareness beyond time, space and the physical.

Mystical experiences are typically spiritual but not necessarily religious; a person need not be a monk or a nun to have one. According to a 1987 survey by the National Opinion Center in Chicago, over 40 per cent of American adults claimed to have had some type of mystical experience.

Psychologist **William James** believed there were four characteristics of mystical experiences:

1. They are difficult to describe or convey to others.
2. Time and space are transcended.
3. Although they seem eternal in real time they are fleeting, lasting only a few seconds.
4. The individual feels swept up and held by a separate power and this may be accompanied by a feeling of separation from the body, as is the case with **out-of-body experiences**.

James believed the simplest type of mystical experience was that 'ah ha' moment that bursts upon a person when a new insight occurs or when something is seen in a new light. He also believed **déjà vu** was a simple mystical experience. Higher up the mystical experience ladder he placed sudden awareness of the absolute and a feeling of unity with it.

Typically mystical experiences occur when a person is alone and feeling relaxed. A number of things can trigger a mystical experience including **dreams**, music, art, day-dreaming, light and words. Although it can occur spontaneously most mystical experiences are induced by techniques such as **hypnosis**, fasting, **chanting**, **prayer**, dancing, breath control and **meditation**.

Mystical experiences are said to flood an individual with immense joy and a sense of gratitude, wellbeing and, in some instances, ecstasy. Awareness of the body seems to be lost and bodily functions slow right down. The rise of powerful **kundalini** energy and the physical sensations associated with that are also reported, as are **paranormal** powers such as **levitation**, **clairvoyance**, **materialization** and so on. Mystical states are also frequently characterized by light and heat, but in the very highest of states all physical, mental and emotional sensations fall away. A dramatic change in life circumstances typically follows a mystical experience.

According to Freudian psychology mystical experiences are illusions, and psychologist **Carl Jung** regarded them as liberations of the **unconscious**. Humanist psychologist Abraham Maslow described certain mystical experiences as 'peak experiences', which were therapeutic and essential to health, wellbeing and the development of potential.

Some scientists think that mystical experience is a brain function that can be induced with the stimulation of the temporal lobes, which lie beneath the brain's hemisphere. At the turn of the twentieth century British doctor John Hughlings noticed that epileptics have different temporal lobes from others, and in 1933 American doctor Wilder Penfield was able to induce mystical experience phenomena in epileptics by stimulating their brains with electrical currents. Although the lobe theory remains controversial, in the 1970s and 80s the relationship between

paranormal experiences and the temporal lobes was established further with electromagnetic stimulation.

MYSTICISM

From the Greek *mustes*, meaning 'initiated person', mysticism is the belief that absorption or union into an ecstatic experience through contemplation, **meditation**, **trance**, music or **chanting** will allow a person to become one with the Absolute. It is a system of behaviour, belief and practice that derives from personal experience of universal unity. Secret knowledge, inaccessible by ordinary means, is given if the experience of surrender to universal unity is total and the individual is absorbed into a greater whole.

Mysticism is often accompanied by phenomena such as **visions**, **voices** and **dreams**, paranormal powers such as **clairvoyance**, **levitation** and **telepathy** and feelings of intense joy and intense pain. The experience is universal and interpreted in different ways by different belief systems. Thus the Christian might see it as union with the Godhead; the Buddhist might regard it as achievement of **nirvana**; the atheist might regard it as recognition of the essential nature of reality, and the **spiritualist** might see it as possession by **spirits**.

N

Names

Throughout the world and throughout history names and naming have been of great importance in religion, **magic**, the **occult**, **psychic** phenomena and mythology. In ancient Egypt not to have a name was thought to be a terrible curse – the worst possible thing that could happen to a person. The Egyptians believed that not to have a name meant that when you died you couldn't move forward to the **afterlife** but would fall backwards into the void. Criminals had their name taken away when charged with a crime; it was as if the person with no name did not exist and all hope for eternity was gone.

Psychics believe that names carry a certain energy vibration and changing a person's name changes that vibration (see **numerology**). Certain religions often give converts a new name when they join, and it is also common to have a spiritual name as well as a given one. In ancient China names were often kept secret to prevent their use by enemies. A person's real name might only ever be revealed to the local astrologer and priest and another name was used for daily use.

Nasby, Battle of

According to accounts reported in English Civil War studies, while Charles I was staying at the Wheatsheaf Hotel in Daventry he was visited by the **ghost** of a former supporter, the Earl of Strafford.

For two nights in a row the ghost allegedly urged him to continue marching north and not to confront the Parliamentarian forces encamped at Northampton. However, uncertain as to whether he should follow the ghost's advice, Charles allowed Prince Rupert and the other leaders of his cause to convince him that the time was right to attack, and the disastrous battle at Nasby, which ruined Charles's chances of defeating the Parliamentary forces, took place on 14 June 1645. It's conceivable that if Charles had listened to the so called ghost's advice and marched northwards he might have gathered more supporters and met the superior Parliamentarian forces on more equal terms.

As a point of interest, the headless ghost of Charles I is said to haunt Marple Hall in Cheshire, the family seat of John Bradshaw who presided over the council which condemned the King to death.

National Spiritualist Association of Churches of the USA

Founded in 1893 and based in Cassadaga, Florida, the National Spiritualist Association of Churches of the United States of America (NSAC) is the oldest and largest **spiritualist** organization in the United States. It has eight affiliated state organizations and affiliated churches in 27 states, the District of Columbia and Canada. Ten states have **spiritualist camps**, including the famous Lily Dale Camp in New York.

The NSAC defines canonical spiritualist beliefs in the US, certifies spiritualist teachers and ministers and publishes a monthly magazine, *National Spiritualist*. The definition of **spiritualism** adopted by the NSAC in 1919 states that 'Spiritualism is the Science, Philosophy and Religion of Continuous life, based upon the demonstrated fact of communication by means of mediumship with those who live in the spirit world.' According to the society's website (www.nasc.org/):

Life is continuous, the consciousness never dies for it is part of God and the Infinite is forever. Upon the cessation of the physical housing the spirit graduates to the next plane of existence. This plane is similar to our earthly plane but at a higher rate of vibration and luminosity. One method of service in spirit is to communicate, assist and help illuminate those that are living on the earth plane. Mediums in the Spirit World and mediums in the physical world adjust their vibrations to enable communications between the two planes of existence. It has been demonstrated in our Churches, home circles and in scientific investigations that 'there is no death, there are no dead.'

In 1950 the NSAC recognized spiritualist phenomena as consisting of 'prophecy, clairvoyance, clairaudience, gift of tongue, laying on of hands, healing, visions, trances, apports, levitation, raps, automatic and independent writing and painting, voice, materialization, photography, psychometry and other manifestation proving the continuity of life as demonstrated through the physical and spiritual senses.'

The NASC offers bachelor and associate degrees in religious studies and diploma courses in ministry, **healing**, **mediumship** and teaching through the College of Spiritual Science. With the help of the Morris Pratt Institute – which was established in 1901 in Milwaukee, Wisconsin and has an excellent research library open to the public – it also offers a correspondence course in spiritualism, two-week residential courses in pastoral skills and special seminars on various aspects of spiritualism.

NATIVE AMERICAN SPIRIT TRADITIONS

As the indigenous peoples of North America, Native Americans have always honoured what they believe to be the **spirit** energy of the world around them. Rather than controlling, using and destroying the environment, the Native American belief is that humanity needs to take care of the environment, the earth and the riches it supplies to make life possible. It is the duty of every creature to look after its daily business in a responsible fashion. Failure to do so destroys the balance and results in disease, illness and misfortune, not only to the offending creature but to the Whole. Native Americans feel a strong connection with animals and in many respects regard them as superior beings, because they were placed on the earth before humankind.

Within most Native American belief systems is the idea that life is unending and unbroken, existing across time and space.

Those who have passed to spirit simply exist in a different form than those who have physical bodies. Rituals and ceremonies stress the connection between the earth plane and the spirit world and communication between the two.

For Native Americans the sacred is part of everyday life, accessible by everyone not just a select few. At an early age most Native Americans will be exposed to the **supernatural** through experience of **dreams** and **visions**; and what a Westerner might term **paranormal**, a Native American would consider part of ordinary reality. Therefore it is not considered unusual to communicate with animals or supernatural beings and have precognitive dreams. **Medicine men**, endowed with greater than normal powers, are able to use these powers to serve, help and heal others. See **Shamanism**.

NATURE SPIRITS

Spirits with **supernatural** powers that are said to dwell in the natural kingdom. Belief in the existence of nature spirits, which are typically invisible to humans, except those with **clairvoyant** ability, is ancient and universal. The ancient Greeks and Romans worshipped nature spirits believing them to inhabit every tree, rock, stream and even the air.

Nature spirits come in all shapes, sizes and dispositions. Some are said to be half human, others assume the shape of plants, animals or flowers. Some are thought to be benevolent and enjoy the company of humans, while others are evil and intend on causing harm. Typically nature spirits are attached to places, plants or things such as mountains, trees or minerals.

Elementals are perhaps the most well-known type of nature spirit. They function as a harmonious life energy force in all things natural: minerals; plants; animals; the four **elements** of **earth** (called gnomes by third-century **Neo-Platonic** Greeks), **air** (sylphs), **fire** (salamander) and **water** (**undines**); the planets; the stars; and the hours of the day and night.

According to British **spiritualist Grace Cooke**, elementals understand human speech, enjoy human company and can respond to music. They also have their own spiritual evolution and their aim is to progress towards higher forms of life. Despite this some elementals are said to be hateful of humans. These evil entities are typically associated with ritual magic and can be natural and artificial. Practitioners of **black magic** purportedly command elementals on missions of **psychic attack**. Artificially created elementals are called 'thought forms' and when summoned they are said to attach themselves to the human **aura**. Unless they are properly exorcised they can drain energy from the aura and cause great harm.

NEAR-DEATH EXPERIENCE

A phenomenon reported by people who have been declared clinically dead by medical experts, or passed close to death through accident or illness, but who are later revived. They report an **altered state of consciousness** where they feel they are travelling through a tunnel towards a warm and bright light, or that they are floating above their body watching medical effects to revive them.

Intriguingly near-death reports from different cultures around the world are typically consistent and in many instances agree well with the essential features of the post mortem state that is described in *The Tibetan Book of the Dead*. There is also a marked similarity to reported inner journeys of **shamanism** and **astral travel**.

The term 'near-death experience' (NDE) was coined by an American doctor, Raymond Moody, in the 1970s to describe the above phenomenon. Prior to the publication of Moody's book *Life After Life* in 1975, NDE was not openly talked about, but afterwards it became more acceptable, and by 1982 a Gallup poll suggested that as many as eight million Americans had had some kind of NDE.

Moody and a number of other NDE researchers like Kenneth Ring, a psychologist and founding member of the International Association of Near Death Studies at the University of Connecticut, were able to identify a number of traits in common to NDE, even thought the experience was always unique to each individual. They concluded that in a NDE people typically experience one or more of the following phenomena in this sequence: a sense of leaving the material world behind (being dead), or an **out-of-body experience** in which they feel they are floating above their bodies looking down; cessation of pain and a feeling of great calm and peace; travelling down a dark tunnel towards a light at the end; meeting **spirit** beings, many of whom are dead friends and relatives; meeting a **spirit guide** who takes them through their life story (see **life review**) and puts their life into perspective without any negative judgement; and finally an abrupt, and sometimes reluctant, return to life.

The great majority of NDEs are described as positive and uplifting; around 3 per cent are described as negative or frightening. Almost anyone can have the experience and it is not limited to the religious, although many people who have experienced an NDE do become more spiritual or develop a belief system afterwards. Almost all say they lose their fear of death and it is replaced by a strong belief in an **afterlife**. Many discover a new meaning and purpose to their lives that they may have previously lacked. In some cases the NDE leaves a person with heightened **intuition** or **psychic** powers.

On the negative side some people find adjusting back to life difficult after an NDE. Feelings of anger, guilt, depression and disappointment because they have to return to life are common. However, many people are thrilled by the wonder of their unique experience and intensely grateful and empowered by it, as well as humbled.

Research by Ring and his colleagues indicated that people with a difficult or traumatic childhood could be more prone to NDE than others due to their personality and psychological make-up. Ring also suggested that an NDE may be a form of enlightenment and can have a

Typical near-death experience

NDE researcher Raymond Moody found a striking similarity in the accounts of 150 people who claimed to have had an NDE – so much so that he was able to identify 15 different elements that recur again and again in these reports. He constructed a typical experience that contains all of these elements:

A man is dying and, as he reaches the point of greatest physical distress, he hears himself pronounced dead by his doctor. He begins to hear an uncomfortable noise, a loud ringing or buzzing, and at the same time feels himself moving very rapidly through a long dark tunnel. After this he finds himself outside of his own physical body, but still in the immediate physical environment, and he sees his own body from a distance, as though he is a spectator. He watches the resuscitation attempt from this unusual vantage point and is in a state of emotional upheaval.

After a while he collects himself and becomes more accustomed to his odd condition. He notices that he still has a 'body', but one of a very different nature and with very different powers from the physical body he has left behind. Soon other things begin to happen. Others come to meet and help him.

He glimpses the spirits of relatives and friends who have already died, and a loving, warm spirit of a kind he has never encountered before – a being of light – appears before him. This being asks him a question, nonverbal, to make him evaluate his life and helps him along by showing him a panoramic instantaneous playback of the major events of his life. At some point he finds himself approaching some sort of barrier or border, apparently representing the limit between earthly life and the next life. Yet, he finds that he must go back to the earth, that the time for his death has not yet come. At this point he resists, for by now he is taken up with his experiences in the afterlife and does not want to return. He is overwhelmed by intense feelings of joy, love, and peace. Despite his attitude, though, he somehow reunites with his physical body and lives.

Later he tries to tell others, but he has trouble doing so. In the first place, he can find no human words adequate to describe these unearthly experiences. He also finds that others scoff, so he stops telling other people. Still the experience affects his life profoundly, especially his view about death and its relationship to life. (Raymond Moody, *Life After Life*) tremendously positive effect on the world if enough people experience it or assimilate the lessons that can be learned from it.

Even though millions of people claim to have had an NDE it is impossible for researchers to scientifically prove that the experience is genuine. Evidence therefore is entirely based on anecdotal reports.

According to sceptics the NDE is a **dream** or hallucination caused by lack of oxygen, the release of the body's natural painkillers (endorphins) or increased levels of carbon dioxide in the bloodstream as the brain dies. NDEs were reportedly reproduced by Ronald Siegel, a researcher at the University of California, Los Angeles school of medicine, when LSD and other drugs were administered to subjects. NDE supporters stress that drug-induced hallucinations and NDEs are totally different things. Such explanations do not take into account the fact that may people brought back to life can give accurate accounts of their resuscitations, or procedures carried out, or report conversations they overheard at the time they were allegedly dead. This suggests that some part of **consciousness** can separate from the body at death.

There is also the argument that people are simply making the whole experience up. A Dr Sabom, a Georgia cardiologist, interviewed 100 hospital patients who had narrowly escaped death. Of these, 61 per cent reported experiencing classical NDEs of the type closely resembling those described in 1975 by Moody. By the end of his investigation Dr Sabom admitted that before he started to investigate he felt sure that NDEs must be 'conscious fabrications' either on the part of those reporting them or those writing about them. However, once he began to investigate he was surprised by the genuineness of the phenomenon.

Another respected cardiologist who was initially sceptical was Maurice Rawlings, who states in his book *Beyond Death's Door* (1978) that he had always believed in death as extinction until one day a 48-year-old postman died in his surgery. As he began to resuscitate him the patient began screaming: 'I'm in Hell! Keep me out of hell!' At first Rawlings told him: 'Keep your hell to yourself – I'm busy trying to save your life', but gradually he became convinced by the sheer terror of the man. So absolutely traumatic and convincing was the experience that Dr Rawlings went on to write books about it.

Elizabeth Fenwick, co-writer of the book *The Truth in the Light – An Investigation of Over 300 Near-Death Experiences* (1996) also started her research convinced that NDEs could be explained scientifically. However, after much investigation she came to the following conclusion:

While you may be able to find scientific reasons for bits of the Near-Death Experience, I can't find any explanation which covers the whole thing. You have to account for it as a package and sceptics … simply don't do that. None of the purely physical explanations will do. [Sceptics] vastly underestimate the extent to which Near-Death Experiences are not just a set of random things happening, but a highly organized and detailed affair.

Fenwick's viewpoint is supported by a study of NDEs in Holland by cardiologist Dr William van Lommel and his team, who studied 345 cases of people who would have died without resuscitation. Just fewer than 20 per cent recalled some form of NDE. The patients who claimed to have an NDE were compared to another group of patients with similar health conditions but who did not have an NDE. According to Dr van Lommel:

Our most striking finding was that Near-Death Experiences do not have a physical or medical root. After all, 100 per cent of the patients suffered a shortage of oxygen, 100 per cent were given morphine-like medications, 100 per cent were victims of severe stress, so those are plainly not the reasons why 18 per cent had Near-Death Experiences and 82 per cent didn't. If they had been triggered by any one of those things, everyone would have had Near-Death Experiences.

There is no doubt that the near-death experience is supported by impressive credentials, and for believers it constitutes a very powerful, objective argument for the afterlife.

NECROMANCY

The conjuring or summoning of **spirits** of the dead for magical purposes. Often considered dangerous and unwholesome, necromancy (from the Greek *nekros*, 'corpse' and *manteia*, 'divination') is a universal and ancient practice based on the belief that the dead, unrestricted by human limitations, are able to see into the past, present and future and, if conjured and questioned, can tell what lies ahead.

A classic case of necromancy is that of the Old Testament **Witch of Endor**. The **witch** was hired by King Saul to conjure the dead prophet Samuel, who foretold Saul's downfall (1 Samuel, 28). The practice dates back to Persia, Greece and Rome, and in the Middle Ages was widely practised by **magicians**, **sorcerers** and **witches**. The Church condemned necromancy as the work of 'evil spirits' and in England it was outlawed by the Witchcraft Act of 1604. Necromancy was also supposedly employed in Haiti by **Voodoo** magicians who, according to belief, become the incarnation of the god of death. The rites aimed to raise corpses from the dead in order to create a **zombie**.

Necromantic rituals aim to raise a corpse back to life or, more typically, to summon the spirit of the corpse. There are many different techniques recorded but rites usually take place in cemeteries or graveyards. For example, one medieval ritual involved going to a graveyard and, as the hour of midnight struck, scattering graveyard earth about and loudly proclaiming. *'Ego sum te peto et videre queto'* ('I seek you and demand to see you'). Elaborate preparations lasting days required fasting, **meditation** and dressing in clothes taken from the corpse. Some felt it necessary to eat dog's flesh and black bread and drink unfermented grape juice – items all associated with the **underworld** and the dead – and in some cases necromancers may have eaten the flesh of the corpse itself.

If the corpse had been a long time dead the necromancer would attempt to summon an **apparition** of the soul. If the corpse was only a few days old, however, the necromancer might attempt to force the soul back into the body to reanimate it to speak. After the ritual it was usual to burn or rebury the corpse to avert trouble from a disorientated spirit.

Necromancy has been compared by some to modern mediumship or **spiritualism** but many consider it to be a dangerous and repugnant practice – dangerous because it is thought that when some spirits are summoned they may take control of the **medium** and are reluctant to release that control.

NECYOMANCY

In the words of Henry Cockeram in *The English Dictionarie, or an interpreter of hard English words* (1623), necyomancy is 'divination by calling up damned spirits'. It is therefore very similar to **necromancy** but in necromancy, although **spirits** are called up, they are not necessarily damned. In necyomancy, however, the spirits summoned are of dubious origin and many not even have had a previous life on earth. In ceremonial **magic** these spirits are therefore **demons**, **devils** or similar evil **entities**. These spirits often do not want to be summoned and may harm the summoner if possible. It is therefore crucial that the necyomancer works within a consecrated **circle**.

NEGATIVE ENERGY

According to **psychics** it is through energy that **spirits** are able to communicate across the boundaries between the earth and spirit planes. Positive energy, created by good deeds, love, harmony, spirituality and respect is uplifting and enlightening, whereas negative energy is dangerous, unsettling and draining.

Albert Einstein (1879–1955) in his watershed publication, *Relativity: the Special and the General Theory* (1918), described all existence as energy, although it takes many forms. According to the theory of relativity all matter, from people and plants to tables and chairs, is comprised of energy structures – atoms, molecules and electrons – that vibrate at different frequencies. The energy of matter that forms an object we consider solid, such as this book, vibrates so slowly that we are able to physically perceive its matter. The energy of matter we cannot see, such as the air we breathe, vibrates very fast. Einstein's theory is in fact a very **New Age** concept.

Psychics and energy healers believe that the physical body vibrates slowly enough to be tangible, while energy on the spirit plane vibrates so fast that it doesn't seem to have an appearance or presence at all, unless a spirit chooses to represent itself in a tangible form. So when it comes to spirit contact the spirit needs to lower its energy vibration and the **medium** needs to raise his or her vibration so communication can be made.

According to psychics, negative energy can be disastrous to a person's life and can cause bad luck and poor health. There are a number of ways to cause or generate negative energy. For example, a person's thoughts can create negative energy. On a physical level, constant pessimism can lead to low self-esteem and the unhappiness such negativity attracts, and on a magical level pessimism can also be damaging as **magical will** responds best to optimism and good intention. In some cases (see **psychic attack**) enough concentrated negative thought about oneself or another person is believed to cause negative things to happen to oneself and/or others. Illness can also generate negative energy, as can negative thoughts about others, arguments, criminal acts, injustice, tragedy and violence.

Many mediums believe that spirits often come through because they want to make amends for negative energy that they once spread in their lives. They may also come through because the negative energy generated by intense emotion or acts of violence, trauma or injustice (see **battlefield hauntings**) has somehow trapped them and they can't break free.

Neo-Paganism

General term used to describe the **Pagan** movements that came to the fore in the second half of the twentieth century. Neo-Paganism is a loosely organized religion, philosophy and way of life that is interpreted on an individualistic basis and concerned with revived and reconstructed pre-Christian Nature religions and mystery traditions.

It is sometimes said that the term neo-Pagan was invented in the 1970s but the term was already in use by the 1890s when it was used to describe writers who rejected Christianity in favour of imagery and ideas drawn from ancient Greek and Celtic source. By 1908 a group of Cambridge scholars claimed the term for themselves, but they were not strictly the first European intellectuals to admire ancient and classical culture. The first known examples actually date back to the Renaissance, and the emergence of revived **Druidry** in England and Wales in the eighteenth century was a significant movement. **Freemasonry**, with its claimed connection to ancient mysteries, also contributed to the later revival. It was the great English Platonist Thomas Tyler (1758–1835), however, whose open rejection of Christianity in favour of a revival of Pagan spirituality who seems to have launched the nineteenth-century neo-Pagan movement in Europe.

The nineteenth-century neo-Pagan subculture, which enjoyed a significant revival in the Victorian era, consisted of largely urban, college-educated individuals who were familiar with recent trends in mythology, Eastern religions, **occult** and alternative thought. A number of organizations, such as the Theosophical Society and the Hermetic Order of the **Golden Dawn** also played a significant part in the spread of occult philosophy and practice in the last quarter of the nineteenth century.

By the end of the nineteenth century Christianity was no longer the only religion in the West, and a variety of people and small groups – most of them associated with occult traditions in some way – raised interest in Paganism. A major shift in the neo-Pagan scene occurred in 1951 with the repeal of the antiquated Witchcraft Act in Britain. The media started to present **witchcraft** in a more positive light and a number of individuals such as Gerald Gardner, who presented himself as the inheritor of an ancient tradition called **Wicca**, came forward claiming to have inherited their own traditions of witchcraft.

The cultural revolution of the 1960s developed the Pagan revival into a religious movement on an international scale. Wicca enjoyed a surge in popularity and the emergence of feminism also helped foster the spread of a religious movement that gave reverence to female images of the divine.

The first neo-Pagan organization in the United States was Feraferia, a goddess and nature system, established in 1957, that preached an abandonment of technology and a return to a peaceful, loosely organized vegetarian society. Two other organizations that influenced the spread of neo-Paganism in the United States were the Church of All Worlds (CAW) and Pagan Way. The Church of All Worlds was formally chartered on 4 March 1968, and became the first neo-Pagan church to be federally recognized. CAW's dogma was that it had no dogma and its goal was for each member to achieve self-actualization and union with all consciousness. Pagan Way was established in 1970 and was involved in the reconstruction of witchcraft as a religion.

In Britain the Pagan movement was established in 1971 when the Pagan Feder-ation was formed. It is still active today (www.paganfed.org/) and espouses three main principles: love and kinship with nature; adherence to the Pagan ethic, 'Do what you will but harm no thing'; and a belief in **reincarnation**. Today neo-Pagan networking is controlled mainly by the Circle Sanctuary (www.circlesanctuary. org/), established in 1974 with the aim of offering counselling, training and networking to neo-Pagans and Wiccans all over the world.

In the last few decades of the twentieth century Wicca was joined in the neo-Pagan community by groups and individuals worshipping other Pagan traditions and approaches, such as Celtic, Hawaiian, Greek, Egyptian and so on. Quasi-pagan systems, which drew their inspiration from fantasy fiction and the media, sprang up as well. A powerful shift from the group-centred approach of Pagan practice to a more individual approach based on self-initiation and solitary practice also began to emerge – the publication of Scott Cunningham's *Wicca; A Guide for the Solitary Practitioner* (1988) marked an important phase in this shift. Another powerful trend was the emergence of Pagan festivals as a major meeting ground for the growing Pagan subculture. Various surveys suggested that by 2000 there were around a million and a half people in the Western world who regarded themselves as Pagans, raising neo-Paganism to the level of a significant social force.

Generally neo-Pagans view creation as a whole and view all life as equally sacred. The divine force has a number of personifications as gods and goddesses, but the most revered is the **Goddess** in all her many aspects. Contrary to belief, neo-Pagans do not worship the devil in any shape or form. For most neo-Pagans the development of psychic and magical skills is central to their religion and many believe in reincarnation.

Neo-Pagan rituals are patterned on pre-Christian fertility and mystical traditions and are individualistic, but some neo-Pagans have also integrated into their faith elements of Native American religions, Eastern religions, **shamanic** practices and African religions. Whenever possible rites are conducted outdoors and involve dancing, **chanting** and drumming. Many Wiccans prefer to conduct their rituals in the nude ('**sky clad**') in order to feel more connected to nature. Because of neo-Paganism's focus on the cycles of nature there is generally a liberal attitude towards sex, suggesting that it should be celebrated and not repressed. However, sexual rites involving the Goddess and the Horned God (not to be confused with the devil) are less common today than in the earlier days of neo-Paganism, and are typically performed symbolically.

Religious holidays/festivals, called 'sabbats' by Wiccans, punctuate the neo-Pagan calendar. These festivals celebrate the wheel of birth-death-rebirth made possible by the union of the Goddess and the Horned God. Great outdoor festivals are organized around sabbats. They include the winter and summer solstices and spring and fall equinoxes, as well as pastoral festivals of Imbolc (1 February), Beltane (1 May), Lammas (1 August) and Samhain (1 November).

NEO-PLATONISM

Philosophy developed out of Platonic thought (see **Plato**) from the third century AD onwards by the philosopher Plotinus and later under Iamblichus and Porphyry. Neo-Platonism placed more emphasis on mystical vision. The goal of humankind is the vision and union with God and this can only be achieved by withdrawing from everything that is material. A combination of Platonic philosophy and Eastern **mysticism**, there are echoes of Neo-Platonism in the **Kabbalah** and other **esoteric** systems. Neo-Platonism was at its peak from about 250 to 550. It was banned in 529 by Emperor Justinian but was revived by Renaissance mystics.

NEW AGE

Umbrella term used to describe a movement that encompasses a broad range of Eastern and Western interests in **mysticism**, spirituality, religion, health, **parapsychology**, ecology, philosophy, self-development and the **occult**. It is impossible to define exactly as opinions differ greatly and a great deal of what is considered New Age is not new, but a rediscovery of ancient or earlier ways of thinking, being and living.

The term New Age replaced the **Age of Aquarius** label used in the 1960s to describe the astrologically predicted dawning of a new age characterized by **spiritualism**, **intuition** and revolutionary new ways of thinking. Although it has its roots deep in pre-history, New Age teaching became popular in the United States (and the rest of the Western world) in the 1960s and 1970s when New Age networks, periodicals and publications emerged. The 1960s saw much experimentation with mind-expanding **drugs** and **meditation** and the 70s saw the growth of humanistic psychology. The actress Shirley MacLaine was also influential in bringing New Age into the mainstream with her best-selling books about her own spiritual awakening. For many MacLaine's convincing account of her belief in **reincarnation** made acceptable the open exploration of many topics.

The movement grew partly as a reaction against the failure of the Christian Church to provide comfort and guidance in such fast-changing times, partly because a number of Eastern texts, such as the **I Ching** and the teachings of Buddha, became widely available in English translation, and partly because capitalist cultures, increasingly weary of materialism and dogma, were looking for gentler and more spiritually rewarding alternatives.

New Age beliefs and activities are highly individual and eclectic but there are certain key themes, such as self-understanding and transforming the world through a spiritual awareness that unifies all religion and environmental consciousness, i.e taking care of the planet. Other key concepts that stand out in New Age thought include the idea that one creates one's own reality, that divinity exists within and that there is a need for renewed recognition of the feminine principle and utilization of so-called feminine traits such as **intuition**. Those

who subscribe to the New Age philosophy share an understanding that science, technology and a higher standard of living in the material world do not necessarily make happier human beings or make the world a better place. They believe that there is a different way of being which is life-affirming and liberating, that everyone has far more potential than they realize, and that the only way to change the world for the better is to change oneself first.

Proponents of New Age thinking describe it as a 'revolution in consciousness'. Critics call it superficial, exploitative, vague, narcissistic, fraudulent, anti-Christian and cultish. Some of the criticisms are justified, however since the 1990s the need for a label has begun to disappear, as New Age thinking has slowly but surely penetrated mainstream culture – most notably in physics, psychology, behavioural medicine, environmental concerns and with an increasing acceptance of **psi** as a normal human function.

NEW LONDON LEDGE LIGHTHOUSE

Lighthouse near New London, Connecticut, said to be haunted by the tormented **spirit** of one of its early keepers, known only as Ernie.

The lighthouse, which was established in 1910, is three storeys high above a square pier. According to local legend its lonely keeper Ernie, on discovering that his wife had run off with the captain of the

Block Island ferry, threw himself to his death from the building's roof. Although Ernie's suicide is not in any of the lighthouse logbooks, staff working at there reported Ernie's ghostly presence. **Phantom** footsteps, cold spots and the movement of objects and doors of their own accord were reported right up to the day that the lighthouse became automated on 1 May 1987.

Sceptics believe that the **haunting** can be explained by strong belief in Ernie's story creating hallucinations. Contributing factors would have been mental strain caused by long periods of isolation. Others believe that haunting cannot completely be ruled out, as lighthouses are renowned for their ghostly reputation and it is possible that over the years the events and emotions associated with Ernie's suicide took on a **ghost**-like form.

NEWSPAPER TEST

Mediumistic test in which a **spirit** communicating through a **medium** predicts items in yet-to-be published newspapers. Feda, the spirit **control** of **Gladys Osborne Leonard** created the test in 1919 as a way of offering proof for **survival after death**.

Most of the tests were conducted through Leonard with Charles Drayton Thomas as the sitter, some with Thomas's father as the communicator. Thomas's father claimed, through Feda, that higher spirits took him to the newspaper office where he could see what was going to be published the next day in *The Times* of London before it went to press.

In 73 out of 104 of the tests Thomas's father (or Feda) correctly gave page numbers and the location on a page of specific words, names and numbers. By chance one would expect to find only 18 correct answers. Despite the success of the newspaper tests no evidence is yet considered conclusive scientific proof of survival after death. Sceptics argue that the words, names and numbers used were commonly used and likely to appear in virtually every issue of *The Times*.

NEWSTEAD ABBEY

Former priory and home of the poet Lord Byron, located in Nottinghamshire, England, that is said to be haunted by several **ghosts**. The priory was built around 1170 for the Order of St Augustine and was bought in 1540 by Sir John Byron who turned it into a mansion. It remained the Byron family home for three centuries. According to **superstition**, turning a religious house into a house for secular use is a recipe for misfortune and over the years the Byron family experienced more than its fair share of bad luck and declining fortune.

The romantic poet Lord Byron (1788–1824) was the last of his family to own the house and when he inherited the estate it was in a state of disrepair. His father, known as 'the wicked lord', lived and died alone in the scullery, the only room that was intact against water. In 1817

Byron went to live in Venice and sold the priory. The bad luck stayed with successive owners who were plagued by misfortune after misfortune.

The Black Friar ghost is the most famous ghost to allegedly appear at Newstead Abbey. The appearance of this **phantom** was thought to be a bad **omen** for the Byron family. Byron claimed to see the Black Friar on the eve of his wedding in 1815, which he was later to describe as the most unhappy event of his life. The marriage ended after a year.

A white lady is also said to haunt the property. It is said that she is the ghost of Sophia Hyett, a bookseller's daughter, who was infatuated and obsessed with the dashing poet.

Although Byron is not said to haunt the house, his beloved dog 'Bosun' is. Byron had his dog buried alongside site of the priory's high altar, and wished to be buried next to Bosun when he himself died. But his wishes were ignored. Some say that this is why the ghost of Bosun wanders the priory looking for his master.

NIGHTMARES/TERRORS

Psychics believe that **dreams** are a way to gain access to the higher realms and often one of the quickest and easiest ways to begin communicating with your **spirit guides**, **angels** and **higher self**.

Nightmares are a distinct type of dream distinguished from other dreams by their vividness and their frightening images and/or emotional content. Dream therapists believe that one reason for nightmares may be as a way for the **unconscious** to draw attention to a situation or problem that is being avoided or to show a person what is troubling them from within deeper levels. Discussing, analysing and understanding nightmares can often lead to a solution for some problem, internal conflict or personal difficulty.

There is another school of thought that believes that nightmares, especially those that recur over and over again, may stem from unresolved past life issues. If the details of the nightmare reveal the dreamer as being the opposite sex or dressed in odd clothes or speaking some other language, and is not recognized as a situation within the dreamer's experience, it may be a past-life memory that is begging to be remembered, healed and resolved. See **Past-life therapy**.

NIRVANA

State of ultimate bliss and enlightenment in Hinduism, Buddhism and the practice of **Yoga** which means the end of suffering and liberation from endless rebirth. The term comes from the Sanskrit word for 'blowing out', denoting the extinguishing of a fire and carrying the connotations of stilling, cooling and rest. When a **soul** has achieved nirvana, ego and self and the need for **reincarnation** have been obliterated; total peace has been found.

NIXIES

German water **spirits** that can haunt any large stretch of water. Legend states that nixies can change their appearance at will and can even become invisible. Their normal appearance is said to be a human body with a fish's tail, not unlike mythological **mermaids** and mermen. According to tradition they are not interested in humans and do not generally bother them, but they do require one human sacrifice a year and if this is not given they will lure some unsuspecting soul into the water to be drowned. A common **superstition** attributed to this spirit classification was that any child born with an abnormally large head was the result of a nixie disguising itself as a human being to copulate with a human female.

The origin of the belief in nixies is lost in the mists of time but may have evolved as a way to warn children away from the dangers of the water's edge.

NOSTRADAMUS [1503–1566]

Famous French **clairvoyant** whose prophecies have created controversy for centuries. Nostradamus made approximately one thousand predictions to the year 3797, which is the year he predicted the world would supposedly end. Among those predictions said to have come true are the French Revolution, the great fire of London, the rise of Hitler and the moon landing.

Michel de Notredame was born on 14 December 1503 in St Rémy, France, the son of Jewish parents who had converted to Catholicism. This exposed him to the mysteries of the **Kabbalah** and the prophecies of the Old Testament. From an early age he began to experience **visions**, which he believed were a gift from God.

Growing up he spent much of his time learning languages, mathematics, astronomy and **astrology**. In 1522 he was sent to the university at Montpellier to study medicine and become a physician. Later he began a private practice where he succeeded in treating plague victims in Montpellier and the surrounding areas. He possessed remarkable healing abilities and, despite criticism from his peers for not bleeding his patients (standard treatment at the time) and for using unorthodox methods, he soon became famous.

In around 1534 Nostradamus married and began a family. Tragically, his life collapsed around him a few years later when the plague took the lives of his wife and two children and the Inquisition sought him for questioning. Nostradamus packed his bags and drifted through Italy and France for the next six years. According to legend his prophetic visions began to develop at this time.

In 1554 Nostradamus eventually settled down in the town of Salon, France when he married his second wife, Anne Ponsart Gemelle, with whom he raised six children – three boys and three girls. It was during this time that he began his career as a prophet.

Nostradamus described his prophetic visions as coming to him by 'the subtle

Famous fulfilled prophecies

The death of Henry II of France in a jousting accident:

> *The young lion will overcome the older*
> *one,*
> *On the field of combat in a single battle;*
> *He will pierce his eyes through a golden*
> *cage,*
> *Two wounds made one, then he dies a*
> *cruel death.*
>
> *(Century 1, Quatrain 35)*

In June 1559, Henry participated in a joust against the Comte de Montgomery. Both men used shields embossed with lions. Montgomery was six years younger than Henry. During the final bout, Montgomery's lance shattered and sent large splinters through the king's gilded visor (golden cage) injuring his eye and temple. Henry lingered for ten agonizing days before dying.

The French Revolution:

> *From the enslaved people, songs, chants*
> *and demands,*
> *The princes and lords are held captive in*
> *prisons:*
> *In the future by such headless idiots*
> *These will be taken as divine utterances.*
>
> *(Century 1, Quatrain 14)*

The French Revolution, which began when the Bastille was attacked on 14 July 1789, was defined by violence and the imprisonment and beheading of members of the aristocracy.

Kennedy assassination(s):

> *The ancient work will be accomplished,*
> *And from the roof evil ruin will fall on*
> *the great man:*
> *They will accuse an innocent, being*
> *dead, of the deed:*
> *The guilty one is hidden in the misty copse.*
>
> *(Century 6, Quatrain 37)*

> *The great man will be struck down in*
> *the day by a thunderbolt,*
> *The evil deed predicted by the bearer of*
> *a petition:*
> *According to the prediction another falls*
> *at night,*
> *Conflict in Reims, London, and*
> *pestilence in Tuscany.*
>
> *(Century 1, Quatrain 27)*

The Hister (Hitler) Quatrains – often regarded as the Holy Grail of Nostradamus prophecies:

> *Beasts ferocious with hunger will cross*
> *the rivers,*
> *The greater part of the battlefield will*
> *be against Hister.*
> *Into a cage of iron will the great one be*
> *drawn,*
> *When the child of Germany observes*
> *nothing.*
>
> *(Century 2, Quatrain 24)*

In the year very not far from Venus,
The two greatest ones of Asia and of
    Africa:
They are said to have come from the
    Rhine and from Hister
Cries, tears at Malta and the Ligurian
    sea-coast.

(Century 4, Quatrain 68)

Liberty will not be regained,
It will be occupied by a black, proud,
    villainous and unjust man:
When the matter of the Pontiff is
    opened,
The republic of Venice will be vexed by
    Hister.

(Century 5, Quatrain 29)

The shocking and infamous armed one
    will fear the great furnace,
First the chosen one, the captives not
    returning:
The world's lowest crime, the Angry
    Female Irale [Israel?] not at ease,
Barb, Hister, Malta, and the Empty One
    does not return.

(From Nostradamus's Almanac of 1557)

spirit of fire'. They were delivered in fragments by a disembodied voice, which he believed to be the divine presence. The method of **divination** he used was **scrying**, which he did alone every night in his study, gazing into a bowl of water set in a brass tripod. He began his divination by touching the tripod with a **wand**, dipping the wand into the water and then touching the tip to his robe. Although he did not understand all he heard, saw and felt he recorded everything.

Aware of Inquisition disapproval, Nostradamus recorded the prophecies in an order that was not chronological and in rhymed quatrains written in a mixture of French, Greek, Provençal and Latin. He also disguised some words further with anagrams. The quatrains were arranged in groups of hundreds or centuries. In 1555, at the age of 52, his first collection of 100 quatrains was published as *Les Prophéties de M. Michel Nostradamus*. The book was a huge success in aristocratic circles and for the next few years he wrote a further ten centuries and enjoyed great fame and success.

In 1564 Nostradamus was appointed Royal Physician to King Charles IX but his health began to decline with gout and dropsy. On 1 July 1566 he is said to have offered his final prediction to his priest. In response to the priest's farewell of 'Until tomorrow', Nostradamus is said to have answered: 'You will not find me alive at sunrise.' Nostradamus died that night. His body was buried in a wall of the Church of the Cordeliers in Salon. In 1791 his grave was opened by superstitious French soldiers and his bones were reburied in the Church of St Laurent, Salon.

Altogether there are over a thousand predictions. Only a very small number mention any specific date. Nostradamus claimed that he could have put dates to all of them but feared to do so lest he be accused of **witchcraft** and heresy. Scholars have puzzled over the predictions for centuries. Some are clear but the majority have a variety of interpretations. Not all the predictions have come true but among the events Nostradamus is thought to have foreseen are the Napoleonic Wars, the succession of British monarchs from Elizabeth I to Elizabeth II, the American Civil War, the rise and fall of Hitler, and the assassination of John F Kennedy. He also allegedly predicted air and space travel and the development of the atomic bomb. Some believe Nostradamus predicted the attack on the World Trade Center in 2001, although many scholars are now convinced that these particular verses were manipulated to fit the context of 9/11.

Nostradamus did predict three reigns of terror, created by what he described as the three Antichrists. Napoleon and Hitler are thought to be the first two. Interestingly, he predicted that the third King of Terror would be a Middle Eastern despot who, with the aid of the Soviet Union, would destroy New York City. This Antichrist was scheduled to appear in July 1990 heralding famines, drought, earthquakes and volcanic eruptions for 27 years, after

which he would be defeated and killed. Following that a 1,000-year golden age of peace would follow.

Sceptics argue that Nostradamus's predictions are so ambiguous that they can be twisted around to mean just about anything, as was demonstrated by the so-called 9/11 predictions. To this day hot debate continues as to whether Nostradamus was a fraud or one of the world's greatest visionaries. It's worth pointing out that, although Nostradamus claimed to be able to predict the future, he also believed that it was possible to alter the course of the future through awareness and positive action. And if his prophecies concerning war and disaster have been interpreted accurately it is evident that humanity still has a long way to go before it can claim to be thinking in terms of the greater good.

NUGGLE

A relative of the **kelpie**, the nuggle is found in the Shetland Isles where it appears as a little **phantom** horse similar in size and appearance to a Shetland pony. The **spirit** is said to be very quick and a little mischievous. It enjoys luring unsuspecting humans into stretches of water, not to drown them but to play tricks on them. When the nuggle has had enough fun it is said to disappear in a flash of blue light.

It has been suggested that these phantom horses are all that remains of a pre-Christian equestrian cult, but it's likely that these or similar creatures, such as **Nixies**, that are said to inhabit the lakes, lochs, rivers, streams and seas of the world, are perhaps the mechanism peoples have used for centuries to keep their children away from the dangers of the water's edge.

NUMEROLOGY

The use of numbers in **magic** and **divination**. Numerology is based on the concept that the universe is mathematically constructed and the vibrational energy of people, places and things can be expressed through numbers. By reducing names, birth dates and birthplaces to numbers a person's personality and destiny can, allegedly, be determined.

Although numerology probably has its origins in ancient Babylonia and among the early Hebrews, and many different numerology systems have been used in different parts of the world, numerology is often associated with the fifth-century BC Greek mathematician and philosopher, Pythagoras. Pythagoras believed there were mathematical connections between gods, men and numbers that could be codified, and if certain number patterns appeared they could be used to predict the fate of a person or future event. According to Pythagoras, numbers were the source of energy in the world and the numbers 1 to 9 represented the nine stages of life. He is quoted as saying, 'The world is built upon the power of numbers.'

In numerological divination all numbers are reduced to a number between 1 and 9 and each number is also associated with a letter of the alphabet. Any number larger than 9 can be reduced to a single number by adding all the digits together; for example, the number 821 becomes $8 + 2 + 1 = 11$; this can then be reduced to $1 + 1 = 2$. The qualities of 821 are, therefore, equivalent to the symbolic number 2. Using the single digit as a guide, the patterns of different dates and a person's name can then be analysed to define character and to predict the future. Briefly the numbers 1 to 9 represent:

1. Independent, creative, ambitious, extrovert.
   Downside: Can be selfish and have tunnel vision.
2. Sensitive, domestic, imaginative, musical.
   Downside: can be timid and gullible.
3. Scientific, powerful, seeker of knowledge, multitalented.
   Downside: Can be superficial and hedonistic.
4. Practical, stable, dependable, honest, trustworthy.
   Downside: Can be stubborn and overly serious.
5. Energetic, sensual, daring.
   Downside: Can find it hard to commit.
6. Perfectionist, creative, compassionate.
   Downside: Can be supersensitive and over-emotional.
7. Intellectual, philosophical, imaginative (psychic).
   Downside: Can be impractical, secretive and unapproachable.

Divination by numbers

In numerological divination all numbers correspond to the letters of the alphabet, as follows:

1 = A, J, S
2 = B, K, T
3 = C, L, U
4 = D, M, V
5 = E, N, W
6 = F, O, X
7 = G, P, Y
8 = H, Q, Z
9 = I, R

Your name number describes your purpose in life – your mission and what you must do and how you must act to feel fulfilled. Your name carries an energy pattern and spells out to the universe your direction in life. In other words the numbers of your name indicate what you are destined for and the direction in which you will find happiness. Various formulas exist for name analysis. Adding up consonants reveals aspects of the personality. Adding up vowels reveals the heart's desire. The number of times a letter is repeated indicates what karmic lessons need to be learned.

Strictly all names should be used, including middle names, but most numerologists suggest using the names most often used, even nicknames, as these are the most influential. To find your name number refer to the letter and number table above. All the numbers are added together and reduced to a single digit; for example Ann Smith (1 + 5 + 5 + 1 + 4 + 9 + 2 + 8 = 35, 3 + 5 = 8) has a name number of 8.

One's full name given at birth is the expression of the vibrational energy of the universe, which determines one's character and destiny. Changing one's name can alter this somewhat, and many celebrities have done so with remarkable results but it may take several years for the vibrational patterns to readjust.

Your life path number

The sum of the day, month and year of birth tells the birth path or the general direction of one's life. Write down the date of your birthday. For example if you were born on 6 April 1970 you write down each number and then simply add all the single digits together: 6 + 4 + 1 + 9 + 7 + 0 = 27. Reduce the total: 2 + 7 = 9. You now know that a person born on that date has a life path number of 9.

Your power number

The sum of one's full name and birth date equals a power number, which, numerologists believe, acts like a light guiding one through life.

8. Materially successful, just, trustworthy.
   Downside: Can be opinionated, impatient and intolerant.
9. Spiritual, humanitarian, healer.
   Downside: Can be self-serving, possessive and volatile.

Numerologists believe no number is better or worse than another. All the numbers have potential as well as a downside. The downside simply suggests challenges associated with a particular number and if these challenges are faced and overcome they can be a source of incredible strength.

In numerology all numbers and words that figure in a person's life can be added up and converted into numbers to reveal how they complement or challenge one's life. It is thought that a person can improve their chances of happiness and success by understanding the numbers influencing different areas of their life. For example, the energy created by the number of a house will influence the experience of all those living and working there; a telephone number will attract certain situations; and the number of a person's name and/or birthday will bring certain strengths and challenges. The start date of a new job, or business venture, the date set for a wedding – all can give crucial clues about possible pitfalls and potential outcomes.

According to numerologists, numerology is a vital tool that can not only be used to predict future outcomes but, more importantly, can also be used to increase a person's understanding of themselves, their purpose in life and the people they live and work with.

NURIKABE

In Japanese folklore on the Island of Kyushu, the nurikabe is said to be a 'wall poltergeist'. It appears as a large, white wall, with pairs of small arms and legs, in front of people out walking late at night. If a person attempts to pass the wall it may fall and crush them and if attempts are made to run away or turn around the wall reappears in front. According to lore the only way to escape the **phantom** wall is to hit the bottom of it with a stick and it will vanish. The origin of the nurikabe legend is uncertain but it may have developed as a way to explaining delays caused when people got lost or went out walking for a long time without reaching their destination.

Oakland poltergeist

Poltergeist case that took place in Oakland, California in 1964 and involved the malfunctioning of an office telephone system and other equipment.

The phenomena began in January 1964 when the telephone system at an Oakland court transcription firm started to experience unexplained problems. Phones would ring with no one on the other end and calls did not connect properly. The number of problems increased and by March business was being affected. Telephone repairmen could find nothing to explain the problem and eventually the firm had the phone system replaced.

The office electric typewriters were next, with keys on several machines failing to work. The typewriter suppliers replaced the machines but the new machines also failed to work. It was only when the typewriters were relocated to another floor in the office that they worked fine.

Just prior to the typewriters being moved other strange things happened. Telephones and ashtrays inexplicably fell on to the floor. Objects fell off shelves in cupboards. The firm notified the building manager, who witnessed several of the phenomena. Reporter James Hazelwood visited the office and kept a diary of events. Every few minutes in the hour he was there he would hear a sound and, on investigation, find something lying, usually broken, on the floor.

Suspicion immediately fell on a 19-year-old employee, John O, who always seemed to be around when the disturbances occurred. However, even though he was closely watched he was never caught doing anything.

Psychical researcher John Hastings believed that John was somehow connected with the phenomena through unconscious **psychokinesis**. Hastings discovered that John was under considerable stress because he was the newest and youngest employee at the firm. He suggested that John be allowed to work from home and, just as he predicted, the phenomena stopped.

As soon as John returned to the office the phenomena started up again. The police, who were also investigating the case, took him in for questioning and he confessed to being responsible for everything. John admitted that he had pushed filing cabinets and telephones on to the floor and interfered with the phone system. His confession brought an end to the activity.

Neither Hazelwood nor the firm's employees believed John to be responsible for the phenomena by natural means and later he admitted to Hazelwood that he had felt pressured by the police to confess. But all, including John himself, believed he was in someway connected to the strange events that had occurred.

Object reading

See **Psychometry**.

Occult/Occultism

The word 'occult' means 'secret' or 'hidden', and is used to describe practices involving secret or hidden magical or mystical knowledge followed by initiates through the ages. It is also applied to mystical societies like the **Rosicrucians** and **Freemasons**. It is similar to the term 'esotericism', but esotericism suggests a theoretical knowledge, whereas occultism implies the idea of practice as well as study.

Ocean-born Mary

Ocean-born Mary is alleged to be a six-foot tall **ghost** who dresses in white and has red hair and green eyes. She is said to appear in a house near Henniker, New Hampshire and is believed to be the ghost of a woman who once lived there.

Mary Wilson was born at sea on 17 July 1720, soon after her parents had set sail from Ireland aboard a ship called the *Wolf*. As the ship approached Boston harbour, it was attacked by pirates, led by the ruthless Captain Don Pedro. Just as Captain Pedro was about to order his men to kill everyone on board a baby's crying was heard. When he discovered that the baby had been born that very morning to Mrs James Wilson, the young wife of the captain, and was yet unnamed Captain Pedro promised to spare the life of everyone if he could name the baby Mary, after his mother. The Wilsons eagerly agreed, and Don Pedro honoured his promise.

However, before his ship of sailed away, Don Pedro returned to the *Wolf* with a length of Chinese silk. He told the Wilsons that the fabric should one day be used for Mary's wedding gown. And so it was, when Mary and Scotsman Thomas Wallace married, in Londonderry, New Hampshire, just before Christmas in 1742. Within 10 years Mary was the mother of four sons but became a widow soon after the birth of the last child.

Don Pedro heard about the tragedy and began to visit Mary on a regular basis. He would often take her to watch his new house being built near Henniker in New Hampshire. When the house was completed he asked Mary to become his housekeeper; in turn he would support her and the boys. For the next ten years Mary and her children lived in a grand style.

One night, Mary heard a curse from outside her window, and then a groan. Recognizing the voice of Don Pedro, she rushed to the garden and found him alone, dying with a pirate's cutlass in his chest. Before he died, he told Mary where he'd hidden his gold, and asked her to bury him beneath the hearth in the home they'd shared so happily.

Mary honoured Don Pedro's wishes and lived a long and comfortable life, never leaving the Henniker home. After her death in 1814 at the age of 94 the house remained in the Wallace family's hands for a hundred years. In 1916 it was bought by the Roy family.

The Roys soon noticed that when the house or its occupants seemed in some kind of danger something would always happen to avert it. For example, a passer-by once stopped a group of boys from burning the house to the ground. And Louis Roy, the son of the first Roy family occupants, survived 17 near-fatal accidents while living in the house. In 1938 when a hurricane struck New England Louis attempted to drive out in the storm but found the road washed away. On returning home he saw the garage swaying and worked to prop it up. When he finally found shelter in the house his mother told him she had seen a tall lady in white helping him. Roy had, of course, seen nothing.

Later on, the house was opened to the public, and visitors have often reported seeing Mary's old rocking chair mysteriously sway backwards and forwards. She has also been seen walking down the staircase. **Psychics** have claimed to sense Mary's presence near the hearth she tended carefully after it became the final resting spot of Don Pedro. Some believe the body of Pedro – who – allegedly may have been an English Lord who didn't want his family to know about his pirate ways – is buried there. Two state troopers claimed to see Mary one night, crossing the road in front of her house. It is also said that every October she makes an appearance at midnight in a **phantom coach**.

Even though he never saw her for himself, Louis Roy cherished the belief that Mary's ghost visited the house and protected him from harm because he cared about the house as much as she had done. Subsequent owners have also reported feeling as if a power was watching over them and the house. In 1963, there were claims that a potentially damaging fire was suddenly and inexplicably put out.

OCTAGON

House in Washington DC that is now a museum. It is said to be haunted by numerous **ghosts**.

The Octagon was built in the early 1800s for a Virginian plantation owner, Colonel John Tayloe. Designer Dr William Thornton, who also was the architect of the Capitol Building, gave the house three storeys, six sides and an unusual shape. Even though it has six sides it was still called the Octagon by the Tayloes.

The Tayloes had 15 children and lived in the house until 1855. The first ghost alleged to haunt the house was the ghost of one of the Tayloes' eight daughters. According to lore the Tayloe girls had a number of stormy love affairs that met with their father's disapproval. One daughter is said to have fallen in love with a British officer and after an argument with her father about the affair took a candle and went upstairs. A cry was heard and the girl tumbled over the railing and down the stairwell to her death. It is not known if this was suicide or a terrible accident. Nonetheless some believe her restless **spirit** can still be seen carrying a candle upstairs.

Another Tayloe daughter is also said to have met her doom on the staircase. She had run away with her lover and returned to ask her father's forgiveness. When the two met on the stairs the angry Tayloe tried to move the girl aside to pass by her but she lost her footing and, like her sister, fell to her death. Her ghost is also said to haunt the staircase of the house.

After Mrs Tayloe died in 1855 the house was sold and there were a number of different owners. Just before the Civil War a gambler was killed on the upper floor during a dispute over cheating. As he was shot it is said he reached for the bell pull. There have been reports of his ghost re-enacting his final moments.

Towards the end of the nineteenth century a number of people reported seeing the ghost of First Lady Dolley Madison. The Madisons had moved into the house for a few years in 1814 when the presidential house was being reconstructed. Dolley was a sociable woman who loved the smell of lilac and hosting large parties. Her lilac-scented ghost has been seen dancing and smiling in the house.

During the early to mid-twentieth century a number of other phenomena have been reported at the house, including **phantom** footsteps, moans, smells of phantom food cooking in the kitchen, ghostly shapes flitting through the garden and walking up and down the staircase and thumping within the walls. The wall thumping is attributed to a legend that during the war of 1812 a soldier killed his slave-girl lover and interred her body in a wall. Another legend says that during the Civil War the rear tunnels of the house (said at one time to have led to the White House which is nearby) formed part of an Underground Railroad for runaway slaves and housed wounded and dying Union Army soldiers.

OCULOMANCY

From Latin *oculus*, an eye, oculomancy is **divination** from a person's eye. It was once said that a thief could be identified by 'the turn of his eye', when this was accompanied by a certain ritual, and that the 'eyes are the window of the soul'. Generally, however, oculomancy is the act of gazing deep into someone's eye and 'seeing' the future there. It could be said that the reflective surface of the eye is being used for **scrying** purposes.

O'DONNELL, ELLIOTT [1872–1965]

English ghost hunter and one of the most prolific authors on the subject of **ghosts** and **hauntings** of the early twentieth century.

Although born in Bristol, England, O'Donnell was descended from an old Irish family and claimed that they were haunted by their own family **banshee**, which prompted his interest in the **supernatural**. He went on to become the author of more than 50 books on ghosts and related lore and also investigated numerous hauntings, claiming to have witnessed hundreds of ghosts and other **paranormal** phenomena. He often lectured and made radio and television appearances in Britain and the United States.

An enthusiastic collector of **spirit photographs**, O'Donnell became one of the first authors to include photographs of an allegedly paranormal nature in his works, which included countless stories and articles submitted to a wide variety of magazines and newspapers. His books include such titles as *Some Haunted Houses in England and Wales* (1908), *Twenty Years Experiences of a Ghost Hunter* (1917), *The Banshee* (1928), *Haunted Britain* (1948), *Dangerous Ghosts* (1954) and many more.

ODONTOMANCY

From the ancient Greek *odontos*, 'tooth', odontomancy is **divination** by inspecting a person's teeth. The **seer** will be guided by the colour, size, regularity and spacing, and whether or not any teeth are missing and, if so, which ones.

ODOURS

Psychics believe that unexplained odours are rare, but possible, manifestations of **ghost** or **spirit** energy. Sceptics claim they can be explained naturally but, according to psychics, unexplained odours may belong to a spirit who wants to make an individual aware of their presence in a subtle way. The kinds of odours detected are typically one of the following:

- *Light or strong scents or odours without source.*
- *Smell of perfume.*
- *Smell of cooking.*
- *Smell of tobacco.*
- *Unidentified foul odours.*
- *Unidentified pleasant odours.*
- *Smell of familiar scents connected with a deceased family member or friend.*
- *Acrid smells or smells of decay.*
- *Smells associated with sickness.*
- *Scents associated with a person's childhood.*

Some ghost hunters are convinced that ghosts can make their presence known by an odour. Certain **haunting** cases that have involved violent **poltergeist** activity have often included reports of foul odours or the smell of rotten flesh. Many hotels and inns associated with hauntings also tell of stories where guests have detected a certain perfume or cologne, and attributed it to the ghost of some long dead guest.

Strange unaccountable odours are by no means proof positive of **paranormal** activity, but they could be an indication.

OLD HAG

See **Hag**.

OLD SHUCK

Phantom dog that is well known in the area of Norfolk and in other parts of East Anglia. The beast's name derives from the Anglo-Saxon *sceocca*, meaning 'Satan'. The shuck is said to be as large as a year-old calf, black in colour (hence the alternative name, **Black Shuck**), with enormous yellow eyes that glow eerily in the darkness. It is said that anyone who is unfortunate enough to meet this phantom canine is destined to die within a year of the encounter.

OLOLYGMANCY

Ancient method of **divination** by the interpreting the howling of dogs. Divination is by the pitch, length of howl and the distance from the observer. The Greek poet Theocritus (310–250 BC) wrote of a dog howling near a house, which foretold the death to come in the house: 'Hark! The dogs are barking through the town. Hecate is at the crossways. Haste, clash the brazen cymbals.' It is said that the clashing of the cymbals was to drown out the sound of the dog howling and by so doing rob the **omen** of its deadly power.

OM

A Sanskrit term, pronounced 'aum', which is the most well-known **mantra** in Hinduism and Tibetan Buddhism. Om is considered a mystical and powerful **symbol** because it is believed to be the origin of every sound in the universe. It is a symbol for absolute spiritual power and represents supreme consciousness. In **Yoga**, to meditate upon Om is to connect with the self.

OMEN

A sign, typically of a **supernatural** or **psychic** nature, that is thought to foretell future events. It can be interpreted in a positive or a negative way. Omens are often revealed through various forms of **divination**.

Many omens are found in the natural world. The ancients would observe the behaviour of animals, the movements of the clouds during the day and the positions of the stars at night and draw conclusions. Natural disasters such as earthquakes, floods and hurricanes were thought to be omens of divine discontent with humanity. The ancient Babylonians, Sumerians and Assyrians were especially interested in omens and almost everything that happened was taken as a sign of good or bad fortune.

Omens could also be precognitive **dreams** and the appearance of **banshees**, **spirits, ghosts**, spectral animals, **phantom ships** and **visions**. The English Civil War, for example, was predicted by numerous people who claimed to have seen visions of armies battling in the sky.

Oneiromancy

Term used for the ability to see the future in **dreams**. The ancient Mesopotomians, Egyptians, Sumerians and Babylonians all believed in oneiromancy. In Egypt there was a ritual practice called **incubation**, where a priest or priestess would sleep in a temple for the purpose of receiving instruction through a dream. In ancient Greece and Rome dreams were thought to be tools by which the gods revealed the future, and to interpret these 'sleep thoughts' there were interpreters known as the *oneirokritai*. One of the books used in which the oneirokritai recorded their interpretations is the *Oneirokritika of Artemidorus*, produced sometime in the second century BC and still in existence today.

Ancient Hebrew literature has a number of example of portentous dreams but perhaps the best known example of oneiromancy is found in Genesis 41: 14–36, when Joseph foretold of seven years of plenty coming to Egypt followed by seven years of famine. This interpretation was based on Pharaoh's dream of seven fat cows being devoured by seven thin ones.

In his *Summa Theologiae* (1266–73) St Thomas Aquinas stated that 'divination by dreams is not unlawful [in the eyes of the church]. It is the experience of all men that a dream contains some indication of the future. Therefore it is vain to deny that dreams have efficacy in divination.'

There are plenty of well-documented examples throughout history of foreknowledge through dreams. Napoleon is said to have dreamed of his defeat at Waterloo before it occurred and **Abraham Lincoln** had many prophetic dreams, including one of his own death. Perhaps one of the most startling and more recent example of oneiromancy is the tragic case of Eryl Mai Jones from the Welsh Village of Aberfan, who had a dream on the night of 20 October 1966 that there would be no school the next day because 'something black came down all over it'. But she went to school anyway, and shortly after nine o'clock that morning a half-million-ton mountain of coal waste, saturated by rain, slid down over the village burying houses and the entire school; 150 people, mostly school children died, including Eryl. Many other people all over the United Kingdom also reported similar dreams to Eryl. There were so many that a survey was done and at least 36 prophetic dreams were confirmed. As a result of this the British Premonitions Bureau and the New York Central Premonitions Registry (http://mainportals.com/precog.shtml) were formed.

Another incredible example of oneiromany occurred in Ohio in May 1979. David Booth, a 23-year-old office manager from Cincinnati, had a series of vivid recurring dreams about an aeroplane crash. In his dream he saw a three-engine American Airline jet roll over in the air and fall to the ground in an explosion. He became so concerned that he telephoned American Airlines and the Federal Aviation Authority. His concerns were noted but there was nothing they could do on the basis of a precognitive dream. Four days later on 26 May an American Airline DC 10, taking off from Chicago's O'Hare International Airport, turned on its back and smashed to the ground killing 273 people. The previously contacted authorities were amazed at how accurate Booth's prediction had been but admitted that under the circumstances there was nothing they could have done to prevent the accident.

Shortly after the chilling attacks on the World Trade Center Twin Towers in New York in 2001, a number of people came forward claiming to have had precognitive dreams about the tragedy. The number of people that came forward was so large that the **American Society for Psychical Research** launched a massive survey of dreams and premonitions about the 9/11 attacks (www.aspr.com/911survey.html).

OPHIOMANCY

Ophiomancy is **divination** by snakes and other reptiles. According to the ancient Egyptians to **dream** of a snake was considered lucky and suggested that a dispute would soon be resolved. However to the Greeks dreaming of a snake was a warning of impending sickness or enemies. To actually see a snake in Greece is to know that good fortune is coming, because the snake is thought to be a **guardian spirit** that looks after its own. The Etruscans would paint a serpent on the wall to keep away the **evil eye** and to bring good luck.

ORACLE

Oracles are thought to act as an intermediary between deities and **supernatural** beings and those seeking guidance or prophetic **visions**. Typically the priest or priestess who served as a mouthpiece of the deity would fall into a **trance-**like state and channel the wisdom of the gods, rather like a **medium** channels spirit communication.

Throughout history cultures all over the world have referred to oracles for advice on the best course of action. In ancient Greece and Rome the mediums were **sibyls** or women priestesses, and one of the most famous oracles was at Delphi, where a priestess called the Pythia was the oracular medium.

Today various state oracles can be found in monasteries throughout Tibet, and African **witch doctors** continue to use oracles to determine the cause of bad luck and poor health. Oracular practices were banned by the Christian Church and in the modern West the term oracle is not in common use. It could, however, be said that a modern-day priest is treated as an oracle when he or she is thought to have a superior line of communication to God. It could also be said that mediums who consult **spirits**, and certain **divination** methods, such as the **I Ching** and **runes**, which attempt to provide inspired answers to questions, also perform an oracular function.

ORBS

Form of energy of unknown origin that can't be seen by the naked eye but which can be seen through infrared monitors and recorded on photographic film. They aren't the same as **ghost lights**, which are visible. Orbs are not dust particles, static discharge, moisture or stray lights, and they are not strong enough to set off motion detectors. They seem to float and change direction at lightning speed. They react to people around them and appear both indoors and outdoors, and are particularly strong at haunted sites.

According to modern ghost investigators orbs offer the strongest evidence for **spirit** activity. The **Ghost Research Society** has pioneered the investigation of orbs with high-tech night vision equipment and has recorded numerous cases.

Orbs are not to be confused with arcs of light on the camera lens that often appear in photographs, especially those from a digital camera. These are caused by light bouncing back from reflective surfaces and light sources not visible to the eye. False orbs are typically pale blue or white, whereas genuine orbs appear dense and bright on film.

For those who believe that at least some orbs are **paranormal**, there are many beliefs regarding their purpose and how they came to be:

✋ *Orbs are a method for spirits to show people that they are there.*

How can you tell if an orb is paranormal?

The word orb has been assigned by popular usage to the circular anomalies that are present on some photographs or videos. Orbs are typically spherical and of varying intensity and colour, although they are often white. Some orbs give the appearance of having been in rapid motion when caught by the camera, illustrated by a blurry effect travelling away from the orb.

If you think you may have photographed or videoed an orb the first thing to do is to eliminate all natural possibilities.

The appearance of orbs can be caused by dust, moisture and light reflection and refraction. If your photographs were taken in a clean, dust-free, moisture-free clean room, which also has all known causes of light reflection removed, it is impossible to eliminate completely the possibility of an orb having a supernatural explanation. If this is the case analyse the time before and after the orb was taken – were there any unusual circumstances? Did you or anyone else sense anything in the atmosphere?

✋. They are energy emitted by people and objects, which the spirit uses for its own energy.

✋. They are viewing instruments for spirits not in the atmosphere.

✋. Orbs are the souls of spirits manifesting on earth as a ball of energy.

✋. Orbs are energy from past events that has been held within the atmosphere of a place. The idea here is that the atmosphere records events and the more energy dispersed in a place – such as a violent murder – the more energy is absorbed and held in the form of an orb.

An alternative explanation for the existence of orbs, apart from the **supernatural**, has also been put forward and can be examined in more detail at www.orbstudy.com. The theory goes along the lines of orbs being natural energy structures that are a normal part of the physical world but have gone undetected until recently. The orb is an electrical object – a plasma – which for some reason holds together in a spherical shape, so is considered a stable plasma; something which physics cannot reproduce or explain.

ORDER OF THE KNIGHTS TEMPLARS

See **Knights Templars**.

ORGONE ENERGY

A term used by **Wilhelm Reich** to refer to a **universal life force** associated with sexuality.

Orgone energy is psychiatrist Wilhelm Reich's name for the substratum from which all nature is created. It is the creative force in nature. As a psychoanalyst and student of **Freud**, Reich's point of departure was Freud's concept of libido. Libido is life energy, desire, the source of human striving. Reich developed the libido concept in his psychiatric work, concentrating on its physical expression and simultaneous psychological content, until he was able to show the relation of bodily attitude and emotion.

In the 1930s, Reich claimed to have discovered a physical energy, which he called orgone, and which he said was contained in the atmosphere and in all living matter. He developed instruments – orgone accumulators and cloud busters – to detect and harness the energy, which, he said, could be used to treat illnesses like cancer. Reich was convinced that orgone was type of primordial cosmic energy, blue in colour, which he claimed was omnipresent and responsible for such things as weather, the colour of the sky, gravity, the formation of galaxies, and the biological expressions of emotion and sexuality.

According to his theory, illness was primarily caused by depletion or blockages of the orgone energy within the body. He conducted clinical tests using the orgone accumulator on people suffering from a variety of illnesses. The patient would sit within the accumulator and absorb the 'concentrated orgone energy'. The effects were claimed to boost the immune system and Reich was convinced that he had developed a groundbreaking theory of physical and mental health.

Reich's views were not accepted by the mainstream scientific community, and that remains the same today, but his influence continues to be strongly felt in body-oriented, emotion-based psychotherapy.

ORINTHOMANCY

Interpreting the flight, song and cries of birds was a common form of **divination** in ancient Greece and Rome. It was also practised in India, Africa, South America and New Guinea.

Omens were inferred from the behaviour, appearance and song of birds. The Greek biographer Plutarch (AD 46–120) said that

birds, by their quickness and intelligence and their alertness in acting upon every thought, are a ready instrument for the use of God, who can prompt their movements, their cries, their pauses and wind like flights, thus bidding some men check and others purse to the end, their course of action or ambitions.

In Greece bird divination was based mainly on observing the actions of large, strong, solitary birds with an individual character, such as eagles, vultures, ravens, crows, hawks, herons, owls and woodpeckers. Of these the raven was the preferred choice of bird for many diviners.

For successful divination it was important to know the correct species of bird. For example, if a raven cried out from behind you it meant difficulties lay ahead, but with a crow the same meaning came from hearing the bird in front of you. Along with knowing the correct species the actions of the bird had to be carefully observed. There were meanings given to the bird's flight, its cry, its movements and so on. Numbers were also significant, as in the number of cries it made or the number of times it circled in the air.

In all cultures special meanings have been associated with certain birds. For example, a dove was a favourable sign for lovers; an owl was considered unlucky in Rome, although in Greece it signified wisdom. In English folklore crows and single magpies were considered unlucky, although you could reverse this bad luck by saluting the auspicious bird. Sailors still believe an albatross to foretell storms and that harming an albatross brings bad luck. Modern-day ornithomancy is concerned more with the behaviour of birds before natural disasters like hurricanes and earthquakes.

OSIS, KARLIS [1917–1997]

Latvian-born parapsychologist who had a strong interest in **survival after death** at a time when it was a neglected area of research. Born in 1917 Osis emigrated to the United States in 1950. He settled in Tacoma, Washington and, because of his poor English, he began to try an **ESP** experiment with hens where he would will hens to go in a certain direction. The results were so successful that he sent them to **J B Rhine** at Duke University's parapsychology laboratory and was soon invited to join the staff there studying ESP in animals.

In 1957 Osis became the director of the **Parapsychology Foundation** in New York and elected its president in 1961. It was in New York, inspired by his own experience at the age of 15 of a **deathbed vision**, that he began the first of three famous surveys on deathbed **apparitions**. In 1962 he worked with the **American Society for Psychical Research** and broadened his survey to include cases from Northern India. Later he was to publish the international bestseller *At the Hour of Death*, which is based on more than 1,000 cases reports of deathbed apparitions. The book comes to the conclusion that the best possible explanation for the phenomena is the theory that something survives death.

As well as survival after death, throughout his life Osis was also involved in the study of **mediums, poltergeist** cases and ESP. Despite his often controversial choice of subject matter, he was highly regarded and honoured by his fellow parapsychologists.

OSTY, EUGENE [1874–1938]

French psychical researcher and physician and director for many years of the **Institut Metapsychique International** in Paris.

Osty's interest in the **psychic** world began in 1909 when a palmist impressed him greatly with the accuracy of her reading. His research on the subject led him to the conclusion that the palm served as a focal point for the clairvoyant mind. In 1919 Osty published *The Meaning of Life* and linked the mental evolution of human beings with their psychic abilities. In 1923 he published a book describing his theories concerning **clairvoyance** and human nature, called *Supernormal Faculties in Man*.

While he was director at the Institut Osty began to study physical **mediumship**. He developed a technique of photography for use in **séances** using ultraviolet light and devised an infrared beam which if crossed would cause automatic cameras to take pictures. The aim was to catch any **fraud** in the act. When experiments with the **medium Rudi Schneider** showed that every time the beam was crossed the medium was hunched in his chair in deep **trance**, Osty came to the conclusion that some invisible emanation from the medium was causing the movement of objects from a distance. These 1930 experiments with Schneider, reported in Osty's book *Unknown Powers of Mind over Matter* (1932), are still considered among the most important in psychical research.

OTHERSIDE/OTHERWORLD

Popular terms used to describe the concept of an **afterlife** or a place where **spirits** of the dead reside. See **Survival after death**.

OUIJA BOARD

A device used to seek out answers to questions about the past, present and future and messages from **ghosts**, **spirits** and other **entities** in **spiritualism**. The name is taken from the French (*oui*) and the German (*ja*) words for 'yes' and it is often thought to be one of the most controversial methods of spirit communication because in untrained hands it is believed to attract evil spirits.

Various forms of this method of **divination** have been used for centuries. In ancient Greece and Rome a small table on wheels was used to point out answers to questions, while in China in 550 BC similar devices were used to communicate with the dead. In 1853 the **planchette** came into use in Europe. It consisted of a heart-shaped platform on three legs, one of which was a pencil, and the **medium** would move the device over the paper to spell out messages.

The modern Ouija board, which is now marketed as a game, was invented by an American called Elijah J Bond, who sold it to William Fuld in 1892. Fuld founded the Southern Novelty Company in Maryland, which later became the Baltimore Talking Board Company. They called the Ouija board 'Ouija, the Mystifying Oracle'. In 1966 Parker Brothers, the big toy manufacturers, bought the rights to the board and marketed it so effectively as a game that it sold more than their famous Monopoly game.

The Ouija board itself is a flat smooth-surface board with the letters of the alphabet marked on it, the numbers one to ten and the words yes and no. During a **séance** or other session each participant places a finger on the pointer, called a planchette, and asks a question or for a message to be communicated. Although the fingers of the participants are on the planchette there is no conscious control of it and the planchette spells out the answer allegedly under the control of a **spirit**.

In **parapsychology** the ouija board is believed to be a form of **automatism**: an unconscious activity that picks up information from the subconscious mind. Critics say that not only is the Ouija dangerous because it can attract evil entities but also because users have no control over repressed material that might be released during a session. **Edgar Cayce** described it as a 'dangerous toy' and Ouiju boards have been known to fly out of control as though being directed by some unseen force. Advocates of the Ouija believe it to be a powerful and effective way to make contact with the spirit world, to divine the future and obtain daily guidance.

The Ouija has figured in many cases of mediumship. For example, on 8 July 1913 Pearl Curran, a St Louis homemaker, was persuaded by her friend Emily Hutchinson to try the Ouija board. She did so and the name **Patience Worth** came through. This turned out to be the beginning of an

The talking board

The Parker Brothers' recommended way of using the board is for two people to sit opposite each other with the board resting on their knees between them. The planchette should be in the centre of the board and both people should have their fingers lightly resting on it. One person should act as spokesperson and ask, 'Is anybody there?' This should be repeated until the planchette begins to move, hopefully to the yes, and then back to the centre. It is also possible to work with the board with a number of people sitting around a table, as the more people there are the more energy is thought to be available to move the planchette. Also just one person can have success working alone with the Ouija board.

Those who have used the Ouija board say that when the planchette moves it feels as it someone is pushing it. This can soon be discounted if the information given out is not known to anyone present and needs to be researched to prove authenticity, but if the information is known by one of the participants it is possible that someone may have been pushing the planchette consciously or unconsciously.

Advocates claim that the spirits are making use of the participants' muscles to produce the physical movement. Thought should be given to the phrasing of questions asked to make sure they are clear, and it is important that all letters that are pointed at by the planchette are recorded immediately. It is often difficult to make sense of the communication at first and words may run into one another or anagrams or codes may be used. In other words although some messages come through loud and clear it is often necessary to study any messages carefully to make sense of them.

There are certain precautions that beginners must take. If you get a lot of negative messages – especially messages that ask you do things that harm yourself and/or others – then don't do it and stop using the board. Don't think the board is a supreme authority and has all the answers. It hasn't. In other words use your head. The board is not an oracle and you shouldn't go running to it to solve every single problem. However if you use it with common sense and with a relaxed and positive mind set you may find that some interesting insights can be obtained through it.

avalanche of information over a period of five years. Mrs Curran produced 2,500 poems, short stories and plays, and six full-length novels, all allegedly authored by Patience Worth, who claimed to be a seventeenth-century Englishwoman.

OUT-OF-BODY EXPERIENCE

A phenomenon in which a person feels that they have stepped out of or have separated from their physical body and have the ability to travel to another location on earth or to non-worldly realms.

Approximately one in four adults believe they have had an out-of-body experience (OBE) but despite this scientific evidence for OBEs remains inconclusive, prompting sceptics to argue that OBEs are nothing more than an **altered state of consciousness**.

Descriptions of out-of-body experiences or the separation of the consciousness from the body (also known as **astral travel** or **astral projection** or exteriorization) have been recorded since ancient times and often show remarkable similarities. The ancient Egyptians described a **ka**. Plato believed the **soul** could leave the body and travel. Socrates and Pliny gave many descriptions of experiences that closely resemble OBEs. The ancient Chinese believed that an OBE could be achieved through **meditation**. *The Tibetan Book of the Dead* described a 'Bardo body', which is an etherical double of the physical body. Tribal **shamans** claim to be able to project

themselves out of body and belief in **doubles** or **doppelgängers,** ghostly duplicates, is widespread.

Common to most OBE experiences is the existence of a second body that is described as ghostly double of the physical body. It is usually invisible to the eyes of others, though it may be sensed or witnessed as an **apparition**. In some cases a silvery cord connecting the **astral body** to the physical body is reported and it is said that if this cord is severed death will occur. In this astral form OBE travellers report floating around the earth or to an **astral plane** and they say they travel as fast as the speed of thought and feel no pain or anxiety. Individuals claim that they leave their body through their head or that they simply rise up and float away. Return occurs by simply re-entering the head or melting into the body.

It's worth pointing out that even those who describe the experience as something fantastic that occurs during sleep are very specific in describing the experience as one which was clearly not a **dream**. Many stress a sense of feeling more awake than they did when they were normally awake.

An OBE can occur when a person is awake or before, during and after sleep. It can also occur during times of stress, illness, trauma and fear and can be induced by **hypnosis** and meditation. The **near-death experience** typically involves some form of OBE when subjects report that they watched efforts to restore them to life while they lay close to death or were unconscious.

Early research into OBE was conducted by Frenchman Yram (Louis Fohan,

1884–1917), who believed that everyone was capable of astral travel in a variety of guises and he recorded his observations in *Practical Astral Travel*. Fohan claimed to have made astral visits to a woman he later married, and to have experienced astral sex. American Sylvan Muldoon was another early researcher who investigated OBEs from 1915 to 1950. Muldoon, like Fohan, claimed to have experienced astral travel himself and collected his research in *The Projection of the Astral Body* (1929).

Between 1902 and 1938 Englishman Oliver Fox took research into OBEs one step further, when he claimed to have succeeded in inducing OBEs with **lucid dreaming**. He published his discoveries in 1920 in *English Occult Review* and later in a book, *Astral Projection*. Fellow Britain and OBE investigator, J H M Whiteman, claimed to have had thousands of OBEs, sometimes in the form of a woman or a child, between 1931 and 1953, which he described as mystical experiences and reported in *The Mystical Life* (1961).

Robert A Monroe (1915–1995), former television executive of Westchester County New York, attracted widespread interest in OBEs from both the public and the scientific community when he published his account of OBEs in *Journeys out of the Body* (1971). His interest in OBEs had been triggered in 1958 when he began having spontaneous OBEs in his sleep. In his book he described the experience as follows:

In 1958, without any apparent cause, I began to float out of my physical body. It was not voluntary; I was not attempting any mental feats. It was not during sleep, so I couldn't dismiss it as simply a dream. I had full, conscious awareness of what was happening, which of course only made it worse. I assumed it was some sort of hallucination caused by something dangerous – a brain tumour, or impending mental illness. Or imminent death. It occurred usually when I would lie down or relax for rest or preparatory to sleep – not every time but several times weekly. I would float up a few feet above my body before I became aware of what was happening. Terrified, I would struggle through the air and back into my physical body. Try as I might, I could not prevent it from recurring.

In *Journeys out of the Body* Monroe sets out an astonishing range of experiences, some of which were unpleasant and involved meeting **entities** or **thought forms** that attacked him. He also described an overwhelmingly powerful energy, meeting the astral forms of other humans and sexual experiences on the astral level. He outlines his belief that there are various levels of existence in the OBE state. Locale I is earth, the here and now. Locale II is the infinite astral plane, where everyone goes to sleep and where countless entities exist. Locale III transcends space and time and is a parallel universe. After that even higher realms, beyond our comprehension, may exist.

Following the success of *Journeys* Monroe conducted research at his own laboratory in Richmond, Virginia – the Monroe Institute for Applied Sciences. He attempted to induce OBEs through sound by creating brain waves similar to the OBE state and in 1975 obtained a patent for Hemi-Sync, sound that harmonizes the left

Triggering the out-of-body state

In his book *Journeys out of the Body* Robert Monroe described a technique for triggering out-of-body states. Here is a brief description of this technique:

1. Lie down in a darkened room in a relaxing position.
2. Loosen your clothing and remove all jewellery.
3. Enter into a very relaxing state and consciously tell yourself that you will remember everything that happens to you.
4. Begin breathing through your half-open mouth.
5. Concentrate on an object.
6. When other images start to enter your mind, just passively watch them.
7. Try to clear your mind and observe your field of vision through your closed eyes.
8. Do nothing more for a while; simply look through your closed eyelids at the blackness in front of you.
9. After a while, you may notice patterns of light.
10. When these cease, a state of such relaxation will happen that you lose all awareness of the body.
11. You are almost in the state where your only source of stimulation will be your own thoughts.
12. It is this relaxed and refreshed condition where out-of-body journeys are triggered.
13. To leave your body, think of yourself getting lighter and of how nice it would be to float upwards.

With sufficient practice Monroe claims that a wide variety of experiences can occur.

and right brain and encourages sleep while allowing the mind to stay alert and active. Using the Hemi-Sync he devised a programme called 'Gateway Voyage', which allegedly took people to Locale I and II levels of consciousness, where they would meet spirits of the dead and other entities. No one, apart from Monroe, could apparently reach Locale III.

Recent research on OBEs has been inconclusive due to the fact that experiences of OBEs do vary from individual to individual; surveys have speculated that a quarter of the population has had an OBE. Laboratory tests have been equally inconclusive, even with individuals who claim to be able to project themselves out of body at will. Tests with animals have been a little more promising with kittens showing a change in behaviour during out-of-body efforts to comfort them, but it is possible this was achieved through **telepathy** or **clairvoyance**.

Those who believe that something leaves the body offer three explanations: a physical double leaves the body and travels the physical world; a non-physical double travels in the physical world; and a non-physical double travels in the astral world. All these explanations are problematic as they require the existence of unknown matter, energy or realms. Those who think nothing leaves the body suggest that OBEs are a combination of **imagination** and **psi** or a hallucinatory experience. These explanations are equally problematic as they assume that nothing survives death, a concept many people refuse to accept.

Out-of-body experiences cannot be disproved, but there is no solid evidence that anyone has actually left their body. Many of those who have had the experience have given detailed observations they reportedly could not have made by any other means, but these have not yet been studied to the satisfaction of the scientific community. Strong advocates for the authenticity of OBEs say that attempts to prove anything are simply not necessary, because OBEs must simply be accepted for what they are: the departure of consciousness from the physical body, allowing a person to observe the world from a point of view that transcends the physical body and the physical sense.

OVOMANCY

Ovomancy is **divination** by eggs. It was a popular method of divination in ancient Greece and Rome. Also known as oomancy the word comes from the Latin for egg, *ovum*.

A typical method was to break and egg and allow the inside to fall slowly into a glass of water. The shapes formed by the white of the egg were then interpreted. This was also a popular Victorian method of divination that was done at full moon, **Halloween** or New Year's Eve.

Divining was also done on the number of eggs laid by a chicken, how many were found and how many of them were together. According to the Roman biographer Suetonius, when Livia Drusilla (c.55 BC–AD 29), the mother of the future Emperor Tiberius, was pregnant she was anxious to divine the sex of the baby. She did this by taking a freshly laid chicken's egg and carrying it in her bosom, to keep the temperature appropriate. When it hatched a chick with a beautiful cockscomb emerged; sure enough, a few months later Livia gave birth to a boy.

P

PAGAN, PAGANISM

From the Latin *paganus* meaning 'villager' or 'rustic dweller', Pagan was once a derogatory term applied to those who did not profess Christian, Jewish or Islamic faith. The label has, however, since been voluntarily adopted by groups who hold the natural world, magical ritual and, particularly, the divine feminine principle through **goddess** traditions in reverence. Typically Pagans are pantheistic, which means they find divinity in everything. In many ways it could be said that Pagans worship nature as their magical practices are closely tied to the seasons and they share a belief that a **universal life force** resides in all things, be it mineral, vegetable, or animal. Sexuality and fertility are also celebrated in pagan rituals and way of life.

There are numerous pagan traditions, but the six of the most common are **witchcraft** and **Wicca**, **Druidry**, **shamanism**, Celtic Spirituality (umbrella term for nature and goddess worship using the deities and practices of ancient Ireland, Scotland, Cornwall and Wales), Northern Paganism (pagan traditions based on the mythology of ancient Norse and Anglo-Saxon gods and goddess) and eco-paganism, also known as green spirituality. Each of these traditions places an emphasis on one or more elements over others but all pagan traditions hold in common the two key elements of paganism: 'As above, so below', and 'An it harm none, do what you will'.

See also **Neo-Paganism**.

PALATINE LIGHT

Phantom ship that has often been reported off Block Island, near the east coast of America.

According to one version of the story, the *Palatine* was a Dutch ship that left Holland in 1752 with a host of immigrants. The ship was travelling to Philadelphia but off the coast of New England it was damaged in a storm. The crew killed the captain, robbed the passengers and abandoned them, taking off in the lifeboats. The unmanned ship drifted towards Block Island, a place so dangerous for passing ships that a band of land pirates called the Block Island Wreckers made their fortune from salvaging wrecks. Curiously in the case of the *Palatine*, the pirates saved the lives of the passengers before plundering the ship. One woman, who had been driven insane by the trauma of the mutiny, refused to leave the ship even when it was set alight by the pirates. According to lore her screams could be heard as the flaming wreck drifted out to sea. In other versions of the story the pirates were not so merciful, but plundered the ship and set it alight with the living still on board. Yet another version claims that the captain and crew deliberately wrecked the ship so they could plunder it and rob the passengers.

Whatever the fate of the *Palatine*, the Palatine light, as the phantom is called, was frequently reported in the late-eighteenth and nineteenth centuries by inhabitants of Block Island. Many believed that the light had been sent by God to punish the wicked pirates who had murdered the passengers and that when the last of the pirates was dead the light would go out and be seen no more. The light has, however, refused to disappear and to this day Palatine light sightings continue to be reported.

PALLADINO, EUSAPIA [1854–1918]

Famous, but controversial **physical medium** who was investigated by a large number of European, English and American scientists and researchers. Although she was found guilty of trickery on a number of occasions, she was also able to produce phenomena such as **levitations** and **materializations**.

Eusapia Palladino was born in southern Italy on 21 January 1854. Her birth cost her mother's life and soon after her father died. Thus orphaned, she was taken into the family of friends at Naples who had an interest in **spiritualism**. They soon detected that Eusapia was not an ordinary peasant girl when the table began to levitate at a **séance** with her present. Soon Eusapia began to sit as a medium demonstrating a range of powers, although she often said she was afraid of them and never knew what would happen next.

A curious incident led to the identification of the dead pirate **John King** as Eusapia's alleged **control**. One day an unknown woman came to visit Palladino at the house she was staying at, claiming to have received a message from King that there was a powerful medium living at that address, through whom he wished to communicate phenomena. After that King was a constant throughout Palladino's career, announcing himself through raps as soon as she sat at a séance table.

The first scientist who was impressed by Eusapia's extraordinary ability was Neapolitan Professor Dr Ercole Chiaia. On 9 August 1888 Chiaia addressed an open letter to renowned psychiatrist **Cesare Lombroso** and challenged him to observe a special case, saying:

The case I allude to is that of an invalid woman who belongs to the humblest class of society. She is nearly thirty years old and very ignorant; her appearance is neither fascinating nor endowed with the power which modern criminologists call irresistible; but when she wishes, be it by day or by night, she can divert a curious group for an hour or so with the most surprising phenomena. Either bound to a seat, or firmly held by the hands of the curious, she attracts to her the articles of furniture which surround her, lifts them up, holds them suspended in the air like Mahomet's coffin, and makes them come down again with undulatory movements, as if they were obeying her will. She increases their height or lessens it according to her pleasure. She raps or taps upon the walls, the ceiling, the floor, with fine rhythm and cadence. In response to the requests of the spectators something like flashes of electricity shoot forth from her body, and envelop her or enwrap the spectators of these marvellous scenes. She draws upon cards that you hold out, everything that you want – figures, signatures, numbers, and sentences – by just stretching out her hand towards the indicated place …

This woman rises in the air, no matter what bands tie her down. She seems to lie upon the empty air, as on a couch, contrary to all the laws of gravity; she plays on musical instruments – organs, bells, tambourines – as if they had been touched by her hands or moved by the breath of invisible gnomes. This woman at times can increase her stature by more than four inches …

Her shoes are too small to fit these witch-feet of hers, and this particular circumstance gives rise to the suspicion of the intervention of mysterious power.

It was not until two years later that Lombroso found time enough to visit Naples and attend a sitting with Eusapia. His first report states:

Eusapia's feet and hands were held by Professor Tamburini and by Lombroso. A handbell placed on a small table more than a yard distant from Eusapia sounded in the air above the heads of the sitters and then descended on the table, thence going two yards to a bed. While the bell was ringing we struck a match and saw the bell up in the air.

A detailed account of Lombroso observations and reflections appeared in the *Annales des Sciences Psychiques* in 1892. He was so convinced of the reality of the physical phenomena produced by Eusapia that he arranged more tests by scientists in Milan, Naples and Rome. Although the scientists were impressed by the phenomena produced by Eusapia they and Lombroso could also not fail to notice her tendency to indulge in trickery if given the chance. Lombroso writes:

Many are the crafty tricks she plays, both in the state of trance (unconsciously) and out of it – for example, freeing one of her two hands, held by the controllers, for the sake of moving objects near her; making touches; slowly lifting the legs of the table by means of one of her knees and one of her feet, and feigning to adjust her hair and then slyly pulling out one hair and putting it over the little balance tray of a letter-weigher in order to lower it. She was seen by Faifofer, before her séances, furtively gathering flowers in a garden, that she might feign them to be 'apports' by availing herself of the shrouding dark of the room

Similar observations were made by other investigators, and her penchant to cheat caused Eusapia no end of trouble in her later years.

The sittings in Naples, which started Lombroso on his career as a psychical researcher, were followed by an investigation in Milan in 1892.

Another investigation in 1894 was significant because it involved for the first time investigators from the **Society for Psychical Research**. The Society's **Sir Frederick Myers** and **Henry** and **Eleanor Sidgwick** were present. The group was impressed and prepared a report for the Society's proceedings. When the report was published it was criticized as leaving room for trickery, and as a result a series of sittings were arranged in Cambridge. The sittings proved to be a disaster when Eusapia was found to be adept at cheating.

Palladino's advocates fought against the Society for Psychical Research's pronouncement of **fraud**. They claimed to have known all along that if given the chance Eusapia would cheat, and that if properly controlled she could still produce incredible effects. More studies followed and eventually in 1908 the Society commissioned three sceptical investigators to sit with Palladino in Naples: Mr W W Baggally, a practical conjurer, Dr Hereward Carrington, an amateur conjurer whose book, *The Physical Phenomena of Spiritualism*, was considered the standard authority on fraudulent performances, and the Hon. Everard Fielding, who had also brought many a fraudulent medium to grief.

Much to the surprise of the investigators, at the end of the sittings the three admitted that the phenomena were genuine and inexplicable by fraud. Their report was published in the Society's *Proceedings* in November 1909 and is thought to be among the most important documents in the literature of psychical research, compelling even a hardened sceptic like **Frank Podmore**, to say:

Here, for the first time perhaps in the history of modern spiritualism, we seem to find the issue put fairly and squarely before us. It is difficult for any man who reads the Committee's report to dismiss the whole business as mere vulgar cheating.

In 1918, Eusapia Palladino, the overweight, almost illiterate and vulgar peasant from Naples, who thrilled, confounded and disappointed so many investigators, died. She was without doubt the medium who was more investigated than any other during this period, and whose feats continue to provoke controversy and heated debate. She helped establish the reality of what is today called **macro PK** and it is only fitting that the final words on the matter should be those of Everard Fielding, a sceptic until his encounter with Eusapia. After commenting on having to abandon his initial scepticism, Fielding declared:

I have seen hands and heads come forth, that from behind the curtain of an empty cabinet. I have been seized by living fingers ... I have seen this extraordinary woman sitting visible outside the curtain, held hand and foot by my colleagues, immobile.

PALM SUNDAY CASE

English case involving **cross correspondences**, **mental mediumship** and **automatic writing** that is important in the history of psychical research for its impressive evidence for **survival after death**.

The Palm Sunday Case spanned more than thirty years and involved numerous **mediums**, spirit 'communicators' and psychical researchers. There seemed to be two motives for the phenomena. The first was an apparent effort on the part of one spirit communicator to make contact with a renowned English statesman and former lover. The second appeared to be a collective effort on the part of all the communicators to provide evidence of life after death. Although the case is impossible to prove scientifically, it is held up by psychical investigators as compelling evidence to support survival after death.

The case is named from the death date of one of its communicators, Mary Catherine Lyttleton, who was born in 1850. In 1870 the young and beautiful Mary met Arthur James Balfour, first Earl of Balfour. Arthur fell in love with Mary instantly. It took a while for Mary to return his ardour but eventually she did and in 1875 Balfour announced his intention to marry Mary. Unfortunately, a few weeks after, Mary fell ill with typhus and died on Palm Sunday, 21 March 1875.

Balfour was broken hearted and lost much of his joy in living. He never married and remained devoted to Mary's memory until his own death in 1930. He became a firm believer in survival after death.

The first communications came in 1901 when Margaret Verrall, a friend of **Society for Psychical Research** founding member, **Frederick Myers**, started to receive communications from Myers through automatic writing, full of obscure classical references. In 1903 automatic writing scripts allegedly from Myers also began to come through to Verrall's daughter, Helen, and Alice Fleming, the sister of famous author Rudyard Kipling. In 1908 Winifred Tennant (later Willett) also began to receive scripts. All the scripts were, like those received by Verrall, laced with classical references. None of these mediums knew the story of Balfour and Lyttleton.

The scripts were investigated by the Society for Psychical Research, who came to the conclusion that a group of **discarnate entities** must be producing the scripts. It seemed that the purpose of the messages was to reveal the post death identities of Lyttleton and Francis M Balfour, one of Arthur Balfour's brothers who had been killed in the Alps in 1882. All the messages seemed to be directed at Arthur Balfour and it was only when he became involved in the investigation that the case began to change. In addition to Myers, Balfour and Lyttleton, other communicators allegedly included other Society founders, **Henry Sidgwick** and **Edmund Gurney**.

In 1912 Mary Lyttleton began to communicate through Mrs Willett, whose mediumship had developed dramatically. It became obvious that the purpose of her communication was to reach Balfour and let him know that she had survived death and loved him in death as much as she had done in life.

When told about the communication Balfour was unable to accept it at first but eventually he agreed to have sittings with Mrs Willett. During sessions with Mrs Willet in **trance**, the cryptic messages that had been delivered in the automatic scripts since 1901 started to make more sense and clearly relate to the Palm Sunday case. Over the years Balfour seemed to accept that his brother and former fiancée were communicating with him, and in the final years of his life the communications became a great source of comfort and inspiration to him. He died on 19 March 1930 and with his death the case closed.

All those involved in the case firmly believed that they were communicating with spirits, as they claimed no knowledge of the material they received. However, since the material revealed was known to someone living somewhere the possibility of **telepathy** and **clairvoyance** should not be ruled out. Some of the material may have arisen from the minds of the mediums but the same cannot really be said about the similarities of the symbolisms and cryptic messages used by the communicators to deliver messages to a number of different mediums. Small wonder many psychical researchers believe that the scripts do offer possible evidence that discarnate entities were working together to gain the attention of the living.

After the conclusion of the Palm Sunday case, interest waned in cross correspondences, and by the late 1930s they were no longer a major talking point among psychical researchers. They have not been the subject of much study since. The details of the Palm Sunday case were not released until 1960, long after the deaths of all of the participants.

PALMISTRY

Method of **divination** by the shape of the hands and fingers and the lines and mounds on the palms.

Palmistry is one of the oldest forms of divination. The earliest palm prints come from the Stone Age, so from very early on people have considered hands to be of great importance. At some point in time people began to notice that every hand was different and from that discovery, palmistry – also known as cheiromancy or choromancy – was born.

Palmistry is thought to have originated in ancient China around 3000 BC but evidence of the practice can also be found in ancient Indian scriptures. The ancient Egyptians were probably also students of the art and they may have passed it on to the Greeks. The famous Greek philosopher Aristotle wrote a book on palmistry for Alexander the Great and the basic principles outlined there have not altered much over the years. Palmistry spread to Europe in the early fourteenth century, but it wasn't until the nineteenth century that it became one of the most popular fortune-telling methods.

A palmist first looks at the shape of a person's hand, as the shape is thought to reveal artistic or physical talents. The left hand is said to reveal destiny at birth; the right hand is a map of how to carry out that destiny successfully. If a person is left-handed the roles of the hands are reversed. The palmist then observes the lines and fleshy mounds, which are thought to have correspondences with the signs of the **zodiac** and indicate such things as health, life span, emotions, intelligence, love, luck, money, **intuition**, and so on.

According to palmists life choices made can, to an extent, physically change the hands and the markings on the hands. Age and experience are recorded on the hands as the memory of life is written in them. The lines, mounds and other markings found on the palm of the hand all tell a story about a person's life experiences. Taking the time to study the hands will help a person discover the quality of that journey, advantageous routes to take and warning signs for possible danger spots.

Well-defined lines that are strong and clear signify positive qualities associated with that line, whereas broken weak lines

Fingers and thumbs

According to palmists fingers tell you how to use your talents and energies to their best advantage. For example, long-fingered people are thought to be creative and talented, whereas short-fingered people are thought to have initiative and discipline. In palmistry each finger is linked to the energy of a celestial body – Jupiter, Saturn, the Sun, Mercury.

* *The first (Jupiter) finger: The index finger suggests to palmists your leadership qualities. A long Jupiter finger, in comparison to the third finger, represents a person who is independent and strong willed with good leadership ability. A short Jupiter finger, in comparison to the third finger, indicates a person's lack of confidence in his or her own judgement.*

* *The second (Saturn) finger: This finger represents the logical, practical, materialistic things in life. It is often the longest on a person's hand but if it is very long it may suggest a serious nature with great ability to concentrate and absorb study. If it is short you may lack responsible judgement at times. The finger should be straight, but if it leans towards the left or right a lack of confidence may manifest itself.*

* *The third (Sun or Apollo) finger: The third finger represents the sun – growth, expansion, luck, fame and fortune. It should be about the same length as the first finger but if it is longer it indicates someone who is energetic, sociable and creative. A short Apollo finger indicates a nature that is self-motivated but sometimes selfish and insecure.*

* *The fourth (Mercury) finger: This finger relates to communication and the longer this finger is (typically it reaches to the first joint from the tip of the third finger) the better you are at communication. A straight Mercury finger is also a sign of honesty. When it is bent or twisted it could show a potential for dishonesty.*

* *Thumb: Many palmists believe that the thumb reveals most clearly a person's personality. Thumbs contain a radial nerve that runs through the spinal column and is found in our brains and it is this radial nerve that gives us our reasoning abilities. In short, the larger the thumb the greater degree of success a person may enjoy in life.*

indicate setbacks. As a person ages more lines will appear on a person's hand, indicating whether potential has been fulfilled and what experiences a person has had. These lines can be read like a road map of a person's life journey. The main horizontal lines in a person's hand – the life line, the heart line, the head line – are the major highways, whereas the minor lines – marriage lines, health lines, travel lines and so on – are accessible only to those who wish to travel them. The thumb is thought to be like a set of traffic lights indicating which route a person is likely to follow, and fingers also signify a person's ability or inability to cope with their destiny.

Well-developed mounds on the hand signify positive energy that comes from the planetary influences associated with the mound, while under-developed mounds seem to indicate a lack of opportunity to use these resources. Markings on the palm of the hand, such as crosses, stars, chains and dots, are all significant signs of good or bad fortune. If the lines and mounds on both hands appear identical a palmist would interpret this as the person not being able to change the course mapped out for them, but if the hands vary greatly this is a sign that a person has used their free will to change their destiny.

Palmistry differs from a number of other forms of divination because it focuses both on predicting the future and on interpreting personality and character traits. Although often associated with the fairground there are indications that palmistry is starting to be taken seriously by scientists. Palmistry's best-known twentieth century exponent, Count Louis Hamon,

better known as Cheiro, was noted for the accuracy of his predictions.

PARANORMAL

From the Greek *para* meaning 'next to' or 'beyond' and *nomos* meaning 'rule', paranormal is the term used to describe events or phenomena that cannot be explained by rational and/or scientific means, or by the laws of nature, as currently understood by science. As a noun it is loosely interchangeable with the term psychical phenomena.

PARAPSYCHOLOGICAL ASSOCIATION

A professional association of parapsychologists that is affiliated with the American Association for the Advancement of Science. The Parapsychological Association is an international professional organization of scientists and scholars engaged in the study of **psi** (psychic) experiences, such as **telepathy**, **clairvoyance**, **psychokinesis**, psychic **healing**, and **precognition**. According to the Association's website (www.parapsych.org):

Such experiences seem to challenge contemporary conceptions of human nature and of the physical world. They appear to involve the transfer of information and the influence of physical systems independently of time and space, via mechanisms we cannot currently explain. The primary objective of the Parapsychological Association is to achieve a scientific understanding of these experiences.

The Association was officially created in Durham, North Carolina, on 19 June 1957. Its formation was proposed by **J B Rhine** (Director of the Duke Parapyschology Laboratory) at a workshop in **parapsychology** that was held at Duke University. Rhine proposed that the group present form itself into the nucleus of an international professional society in parapsychology.

PARAPSYCHOLOGY

The scientific study of **psi** experiences relating specifically to the human mind, and normally encompassing the study of unusual mental phenomena such as **telepathy**, **astral projection**, **out-of-body experiences** and **ESP**.

Para means 'beyond' in Greek, and parapsychological phenomena indicate the operation of factors currently unknown or unrecognized by orthodox science, popularly referred to as **paranormal** factors. Proponents of the existence of these phenomena usually consider them to be a product of unexplained mental abilities.

Throughout its history parapsychology has met with a lot of resistance and scepticism by the scientific community. As a science it could be said to date back to the late nineteenth century with the formation of the **Society for Psychical Research** in London.

Before the beginnings of parapsychology, paranormal phenomena in Western culture were typically associated with divine or malevolent forces. The ancient Greeks, for example, believed that precognitive **dreams** were messages from the gods. The Old Testament contains many references to paranormal phenomena including **levitation**, prophetic **visions** and **apparitions** but in the Middle Ages the Catholic Church declared all such phenomena diabolical unless associated with a holy person.

In the eighteenth century Pope Benedict XIV investigated alleged miraculous and paranormal phenomena, and his conclusion that paranormal experiences are neither divine nor demonic but are linked to the capabilities of the person having the experience could be said to make him a very early parapsychological researcher (see **Prospero Lambertini**). Two other key figures in the eighteenth century were **Emanuel Swedenborg**, with his incredible **clairvoyant** visions, and **Franz Anton Mesmer** and his theory of mesmerism.

The nineteenth century saw the rise of **spiritualism** and interest in **mediumship** and communication with the dead. In 1872 physicist **Sir William Crookes** conducted experiments on the famous **medium D D Home** and came to the conclusion that he had without doubt witnessed paranormal phenomena. Another physicist, **Sir William Barrett**, was not convinced and in 1876 started to experiment with hypnotized subjects and mediums. Barrett was devoted to the idea of forming an organization to study the paranormal and he realized this goal in 1882 with the founding of the Society for Psychical Research.

The Society's early years were spent investigating psychic phenomena, mediumship and **survival after death**. Members included highly educated researchers such as **Sir Frederick Myers, Frank Podmore** and **Henry Sidgwick**, who gathered an impressive amount of research that laid the foundation stone for future investigations of the paranormal. Their work also led to the foundation of the **American Society for Psychical Research** (ASPR).

Prior to 1930 psychical research was typically carried out outside the science laboratory. Mediums would be investigated under controlled conditions and evidence of spontaneous phenomena, such as **ghosts**, would revolve around eye-witness accounts and interviews. Then along came pioneer researcher **J B Rhine** and the era of controlled laboratory experiments and statistical evaluation began. Rhine's objective while conducting ESP experiments at Duke University in North Carolina was to demonstrate scientifically that psychic ability was a natural faculty. Test subjects were not mediums but ordinary people, and experiments involved ESP tests such as guessing cards. The results were then evaluated statistically.

In 1934 Rhine released the first of a series of impressive but controversial test results and interest in parapsychology was well and truly sparked. Rhine's era lasted until 1965 and he is credited with adopting the term parapsychology from the German *parapsychologie*. (Prior to that parapsychology was referred to as **psychical research**.) He also coined the term 'extrasensory perception' (ESP) and much of the terminology still used in the field today dates back to Rhine's research at Duke University.

During the 1960s parapsychological interest shifted to the psychological processes involved in psi, and how psi is affected by factors such as **altered states of consciousness**, mood, personality, time and so on. Free response ESP tests were designed where individuals described whatever came to mind. One of the best examples of this is the **dream** work conducted at Maimonides Hospital in Brooklyn, New York, during the 1960s and 1970s under the direction of Montague Ullman and Stanley Krippner. Other significant research was carried out in **remote viewing, clairvoyance** and out-of-body experiences at the Stanford Research Institute in California. Interest in **psychokinesis** also revived with experiments on **Uri Geller**. In the 1970s some parapsychologists focused on applying psi to other fields, such as archaeology and criminology.

As far as European parapsychological research is concerned, statistical research in the style of Rhine was conducted but never to the same extent as it was in the United States or Britain; most research was carried out on individual cases. In 1918 the **Institut Metapsychique International** was formed in Paris, and after World War II the first Chair of Parapsychology was founded at Utrecht University in the Netherlands. In 1953 the university hosted the first international conference on parapsychological studies. In recent years experimental research on psi has finally gained a foothold in Europe and some impressive research has been produced and published in the *European Journal of Psychology*.

Psychical research societies have been established in Latin America, Japan and South America. Investigation of psi in Eastern Europe developed independently of the West with its own terminology, such as 'bio communication' or 'psychotronics' instead of parapsychology. Russian interest was sparked in 1871 when D D Home paid a visit, and by the late 1870s research was already being conducted into **hypnosis** and telepathy. During the Stalinist regime, however, psychical research was repressed, and little has been heard about it since. There were, however, unconfirmed reports before the death of the Soviet Union that the Soviets were more advanced compared to the West and were focusing their efforts on harnessing psychic power for military purposes. Today the veil of secrecy has lifted and films of Russian psychics at work can be seen on Western TV shows and documentaries.

Despite Rhine's remarkable efforts to gain academic acceptance for parapsychology, progress has been slow. Few universities have courses in parapsychology, although a select number do (see the Resources section). In 1969 the **Parapsychological Association** was finally admitted to the American Association for the Advancement of Science and in 1985 the Koestler Chair of Parapsychology was founded at the University of Edinburgh.

Some researchers feel that psi has been proven scientifically but the great majority feel that evidence remains inadequate. The lack of progress can be attributed to a number of factors, including lack of research funds, lack of serious support from the scientific and academic communities and the frequent exposure of fraudulent practices, which has strained credibility and increased scepticism among scientists.

Despite the lack of significant progress so far, a significant number of researchers believe that the twenty-first century will witness an explosion of interest in parapsychology and the science of unusual experience. They believe that one day it will be commonplace for individuals to develop and use their psychic abilities to enrich their lives. They also predict that advances in physics will prove that psi is, without doubt, a unique physical phenomenon common to everyone.

PARAPSYCHOLOGY FOUNDATION

Non-profit, educational organization that was founded in New York in 1951 by **medium Eileen Garrett** to support 'scientific and academic research about the psychical aspects of human nature' (www.parapsychology.org). Claiming to be a worldwide forum supporting the scientific exploration of psychical phenomena, the Foundation awards research grants, sponsors **parapsychology** conferences and publishes the *International Journal of Parapsychology* and a series of informative and educational pamphlets. The Foundation also has an impressive collection of documents, photographs and videos and a library that is open to the public. When Garrett died in 1970 her daughter, Eileen Coly, and then her granddaughter, Lisette Coly, took over responsibility for the Foundation.

PARSLEY

Since ancient times parsley has been associated with death and **ghosts**. The ancient Greeks and Romans believed parsley to be a herb that was sacred to the dead and it was placed on graves or made into funeral wreaths, and this association with death earned it a reputation for bad luck that it hasn't been able to shake off. Even in fairly recent times it was considered unlucky to give parsley and there was a **superstition** that to transplant parsley would cause a death in the family.

PAST-LIFE RECALL

The remembering of alleged previous lives on earth. It is not known if the memories are actually of past lives or if they spring from the subconscious. Even though scientific investigation of past-life recall has been impressive enough to support a belief in the possibility of **reincarnation**, to date the evidence is insufficient to prove it conclusively. Other explanations of past-life recall suggest that the memories are not images of past lives but are produced by **telepathy**, spirit **possession,** inherited memory or **cryptomnesia**.

Past-life recall can be induced by a number of methods such as **hypnosis**, **meditation** or rhythmic activity such as **chanting**, dancing or long distance running. **Bodywork**, such as **acupuncture**, has also been known to stimulate memories. According to ancient Eastern **mysticism** details of past lives can be awakened through **yoga** meditation.

Past-life memories are also said to occur spontaneously, especially in young children. It is argued that children remember past lives more easily because the more mature a person is, the less open they become and the harder it is for past-life memories to emerge.

The majority of scientific research on past-life recall has focused on children, and one of the leading investigators in the field was Professor of Psychiatry at the University of Virginia, Ian Stevenson. Stevenson began collecting cases in the 1960s and by the 1980s had a collection of over 2,000. He considered a case to be genuine when the details the child revealed accurately fitted a deceased person. Most of these cases came from the East where cultural acceptance of past-life recall is strong. The reason for the reduced number of Western cases could perhaps be that parents tend to dismiss possible cases as fantasies.

A contemporary American parapsychologist and anthropologist, James Matlock, has identified four types of spontaneous past-life recall:

- *Verbal – the recall of names.*
- *Imaged – when children recognize people and places.*
- *Behavioural – personality traits and talents.*
- *Physical – similarities in appearance to the deceased, such as birthmarks.*

These memories vary in intensity but certain common features do exist. In almost all documented cases the child was between two and five years old when he or she began talking about a past life. There is often unfinished business and a large number involve violent or sudden death. Birthmarks may exist where a death wound was inflicted or an unexplained phobia may relate to the manner of death. Some children talk about their experiences all the time, while others talk about it now and then. In some cases children say they can remember their past life because they did not eat the fruit of forgetfulness given to them by their **spirit guides**.

Some people say they experience past-life recall through **dreams**, flashes of insight or a sense of **déjà vu** but the memories are often sketchy. Traumas of some kind – typically physical – have been known to stimulate alleged past-life memories. Hypnosis is perhaps the most common means of inducing past-life regression. In hypnotic regression an individual is placed in a **trance** and told to go back in time and describe what they see, hear, sense and feel. In numerous instances hypnotic recall has been proved unreliable but in some cases, such as the famous case of Bridey Murphy, regressions have defied rational explanation. In 1952 Morey Bernstein, an amateur hypnotist in Pueblo, California, regressed a 27-year-old housewife to the life of Bridey Murphy, who lived in County Cork, Ireland between 1798 and 1864.

While under hypnosis in 1952, Virginia Tighe told Bernstein that over 100 years ago she was an Irish woman named Bridget Murphy, who was known as Bridey. During their sessions together, Bernstein was impressed with his conversations with Bridey, who spoke with a pronounced Irish accent and discussed details of her life in nineteenth-century Ireland. When Bernstein published his book about the case, *The Search for Bridey Murphy*, in 1956, it became famous around the world and sparked an excited interest in the possibility of reincarnation.

Over six sessions, Virginia revealed many details about Bridey's life, including her birth date in 1798, her childhood amid a Protestant family in the city of Cork, her marriage to Sean Brian Joseph McCarthy, and even her own death at the age of 60. As Bridey, she provided numerous details such as names, dates, places, events, shops and songs, but could these details be verified? Although Professor Stevenson could find no evidence of fraud the results of many investigations were mixed. Much of what Bridey said was consistent with the time and place, and it seemed inconceivable that someone who had never been to Ireland could provide so many details with such confidence. However, researchers could find no historical record of Bridey Murphy – not her birth, her family, her marriage, nor even her death – leaving the case an intriguing mystery.

From the late 1960s to the late 1970s, American psychologist Helen Wambach conducted a 10-year investigation of 1,088 past lives recalled under hypnosis. She collected data on them all and concluded that genetic memory and an overactive imagination could not account for the patterns and correspondences that emerged in her data. For example, she found that 49.4 per cent of past lives were female and 50.6 per cent were male, which matched true biological balance. In the great majority of cases all descriptions of clothing, objects and attitudes were consistent with the time frame regressed to. Of those who reported experiencing death, around half claimed to have experienced calm and acceptance, 10 per cent said the experience was distressing and 20 per cent claimed to have watched their own past life death while floating above the body.

PAST-LIFE THERAPY

A technique often used by psychotherapists in which the causes of current psychological problems are linked to alleged past-life experiences. Past-life therapy (PLT) has allegedly been helpful for treating phobias, fears, aversions, cravings, guilt, sexual dysfunction, depression, insomnia, fatigue, headaches and other weaknesses of the body. Deep-rooted fears, such as fears of falling or burning, that psychotherapy alone can't treat, can sometimes be successfully treated by PLT. It is said that the relief is achieved by the release of pent-up energy trapped in the past life.

PLT is based on a belief in **reincarnation** and most therapists believe the memories reported are genuine, citing as evidence the fact that most memories reported are dreary and humdrum rather than glamorous and exiting. However some therapists acknowledge that reincarnation may not be the only explanation, and hold that fantasizing events can have the same therapeutic effect as real memories.

PLT came to the fore in the 1960s following the acceptance of **hypnosis** as a clinical treatment by the American and British Medical Associations. Thanks to the pioneering theories of **Freud** and **Jung** hypnosis was being used to uncover deep-rooted pain and trauma from childhood, buried deep in the **unconscious**. Psychoanalyst Otto Rank (1884–1939) suggested going back further, to the time spent in the womb, and with the increasing use of hypnosis therapists began to discover that their patients regressed to what seemed like previous lives to address the source of a problem.

The use of PLT as an alternative therapy led to the formation of the Association of Past Life Research and Therapy (APRT) in Riverside, California in 1980. In 1982 psychologist and past-life therapist Helen Wambach conducted a massive investigation of APRT therapists and their patients. According to her research almost all patients regressed to one or more past lives and many claimed to address past-life karmic ties with individuals and were able to release pent-up emotions, resulting in an improvement in present relationships. Twenty-five therapists reported regressing their patients to a past-life death: 72 per cent observed their death while floating over their bodies and 54 per cent saw a white light and moved towards it. Sixty per cent of patients who were experiencing physical problems before their regression reported relief of symptoms after it.

Since the 1980s research on PLT has been patchy and in most cases the material produced during a session often cannot be proved. Despite this, most people who practise PLT today do not seem to require proof to notice an improvement in their mental, physical and emotional wellbeing. They say it can shed light on present-life personal issues and relationships and can help to heal the wounds suffered in a past life. It can also change a person's view of life, seeing it as part of a greater whole in which the soul is forever learning and striving for perfection. Perhaps the most beneficial aspect of PLT, however, is its apparent ability to take away the fear of death. PLT is sometimes used with terminally ill patients or people with an extreme fear of death to help them overcome their fears. Many clients claim that even though a past death may have been traumatic, death itself brings a feeling of freedom and relief.

PAST LIVES

See **Reincarnation**.

PATHWORKING

A type of **visualization** designed to expand consciousness for personal and spiritual development. The term pathworking derived from Kabbalistic practice and is very similar to **guided imagery** except that it has magical connotations. Through the use of a guide an individual is led into a semi-**trance** state during which they are asked to paint pictures in their mind using **occult** or archetypal symbols, typically from **Tarot** cards or the **Kabbal-**

ah's **Tree of Life**. At the end of the visualization the things experienced can be used to reject negative habits and replace them with positive habits.

Pathworkings are not new. They were used in ancient Egypt and are believed to have formed an important part of Chaldean star magic. For centuries they remained in the hands of initiate occultists until the 1980s when a modern exponent of the practice, Dolores Ashcroft Nowicki, created a furore among occultists by bringing the method to a wider audience. Despite extreme disapproval from her peers she went into print and reached a wide audience with her book *The Shining Paths*, later reprinted as *Highways of the Mind*.

PEAK EXPERIENCE

A moment of intense and ecstatic feeling when body and mind are lost in bliss. Psychologist Abraham Maslow (1908–1970) coined the phrase to describe getting so totally absorbed in an experience or moment that an individual is 'lost in the present', and experiences 'detachment from time and space'. It often occurs in response to intense emotions such as love, or intense life experiences such as childbirth, and also occurs when communing with nature, listening to music or viewing great art or theatre. Physical exercise, **meditation,** religious experiences, **mediumship** or magical rituals and selfless behaviour can also trigger peak experiences. Maslow believed that peak experiences were within the reach

Pathworking exercise

Pathworking is generally more effective if it is led by a person or by a tape recording. (You can always make your own tape of a Pathworking you wish to follow, and then play it to yourself.) The following sample Pathworking is designed to reveal your inner self. It's a simple but powerful exercise that should not be repeated more than twice a year.

Make yourself comfortable and let go of any thoughts and preconceived notions you may have about pathworking. Let your mind drift until you find yourself in front of a large stately mansion. A wise old gardener tending the flowerbeds nods at you as you pass him on your way into the grand entrance hall. The hall is very large and every wall is full of doors of different shapes, colours and sizes. One of the doors appeals to you, so you go to it, open it and step inside a room. The room is dimly lit and you look around at its furnishing and decoration. You see a full-length mirror, and walk towards it, knowing it is magical. The surface of the mirror is misty and unclear. As you stand in front of it the mist slowly disappears and you examine the reflection before you, which is your true inner self revealed. After a few moments the mirror becomes misty again and you calmly leave the room, and the house. The sun is shining and the flowers in the garden are beautiful. As you pass the gardener he stops you and speaks to you. Listen to what he has to say as he has an important message for you. Thank him and say goodbye, then calmly, and in your own time, return back to our reality. Take your time to ponder the insights you gained.

of everyone and people who experienced them felt an increased sense of connection, confidence and happiness with the universe.

PEARLIN JEAN

In the words of Scottish antiquarian, Charles Kirkpatrick Sharpe (1781–1851), 'Pearlin Jean was the most remarkable ghost in Scotland and my terror as a child.'

According to lore Pearlin Jean is a female **ghost** with head and shoulders covered in blood, which haunted the mansion of Allanbank at Edrom in Berwickshire. She was said to be the **spirit** of a beautiful seventeenth-century French girl named Jeanne who was scorned by her lover, Sir Robert Stuart of Allanbank and knocked over and killed by his carriage when he drove away from her pleading cries. As a result of her tragic death she returned to haunt Allanbank. Those who saw her would know it was Jean as she was dressed in the same pearlin lace she had always worn in life.

PENDULUM

A suspended weighted object, usually a crystal, used in **dowsing** and **divination** to locate lost people or items and answer questions. The pendulum is suspended from a fixed point and allowed to swing freely to and fro. In dowsing it acts like a pointer and in divination it is used to answer yes or no questions.

The archaeologist **T C Lethbridge** believed that different lengths of string produced pendulums specifically tuned to various substances and emotional states. **Map dowsing** demonstrates one of the most curious uses of the pendulum. A pendulum is held over a map and its behaviour is thought to indicate the location of water sources, minerals and even ancient treasures. During World War II a Pendulum Institute was established in Berlin to determine the location of Allied shipping convoys by pendulum dowsing sea charts.

A pendulum is also used in **radiesthesia** diagnosis to locate the source of illness in a person's body. A pendulum is held above a chart on which is placed a patient's blood sample and the movements of the pendulum are thought to determine the nature of the illness.

Dowsing has its roots in ancient civilization. Its revival in the twentieth century has led to a refinement of the art, and while willow branches and metal rods are still popular tools for detecting underground water and mineral sources – sometimes even buried treasure – the pendulum is often the tool of choice for modern dowsers, because it is attractive, portable and easy to use.

Like the dowsing rod the pendulum is thought to work on the principle that every organism is encased in positive or negative energy and, just as radios pick up information from unseen radio waves, pendulum dowsers believe that pendulums are powerful antennae that receive information from the vibrations and energy waves emitted by people, places, thoughts and things. The process by which this takes place is unknown but users claim to be able to 'tune in', perhaps using **psi**, to the energy of what is being sought or requested.

As far as pendulum divination is concerned, some say that the pendulum connects them with a higher power. A few pendulum users also claim the ability to communicate with astral entities by way of the pendulum. In this process, the pendulum user questions the **spirits** present in much the same way as one might question an **Ouija board**. Yes and no answers are indicated by the swing of the pendulum, and other patterns of communication can seemingly be established with individual entities.

Others believe that the pendulum creates a bridge between the logical and intuitive parts of the mind and the basis of using a pendulum for divination purposes can be explained by **ideomotor effect**. This is when thoughts or ideas are

Pendulum power

Pendulums can be particularly helpful if you have a question that requires a simple yes or no answer. You may want to buy a pendulum but you can also make your own.

Tie a thin white or red natural string to a golden ring, a needle, a crystal tip, acorn, hazel nut or herb bundle. Hazel nuts make particularly good pendulums, as they are associated with wisdom, occult knowledge and dowsing. To make a herbal pendulum, tie a string tightly around one end of a herb bundle. In all pendulums made with string, leave enough string so that, when held at one end, the pendulum can dangle freely from the other.

Before using your pendulum you must charge it. Hold the string in your hand between the thumb and first finger with your elbow slightly bent at your side and let the string hang down. It is important to let the natural vibrations of your body move the pendulum. The pendulum works like muscle-testing or kinesiology: your unconscious knows what you need to know. The pendulum will show you the answer by picking up and amplifying the subtle vibrations from your subconscious, causing the pendulum to swing.

Tell your pendulum which direction will indicate Yes. It can be clockwise or counter-clockwise or a straight line – either horizontal or vertical. You decide. Then tell the pendulum to indicate No. This time tell it to move in another direc-tion. After you've charged it, ask it to show you Yes and see if it moves as you had directed it. Do the same for No.

The pendulum can provide a good second opinion. Remember, it draws its strength from your energy so it should not be touched by others who might impart their vibrations into the pendulum and thereby reduce its reliability. Keep the pendulum with you as much as possible during the first few weeks to have it absorb your own ener-gies. Ask the pendulum simple questions that will help build your trust in the answers. The pendulum will learn to resonate with you, within your own energy field.

Your pendulum will answer any ques-tion with either a 'yes' or 'no', so it is important to ask your questions correctly. For example, 'Will I pass my driving test?' is a good question as the answer will either be a yes or a no. A poor question is 'Will I pass or fail my driving test?' This does not give the choice of a yes or no answer.

You can hold your pendulum over any object to determine a range of answers. For example, hold the pendulum over food to determine if it is suitable for you to eat. If you need to determine a date to do some-thing, you can use your pendulum over a calendar. Hold the pendulum over each date of the month, waiting until the pendu-lum registers an answer. The more you use your pendulum the more likely it is that the answers will become almost instant.

automatically translated into specific patterns of muscular activity. The pendulum works by measuring ideomotor response when a question is asked. In many ways it could be said to work on the same principle as a lie detector. The involuntary muscular response is translated as answers by the direction of pendulum movement. This process bypasses the conscious mind or ego and allows direct access to intuitive information from the **unconscious**. The pendulum therefore has no power of its own, as it is a person's thoughts and muscle responses that bring about the pendulum's motions.

It's not precisely known how pendulum dowsing and/or divination works, and scientists remain sceptical; but despite this pendulums continue to be universally popular and, according to those who use them, uncannily accurate.

PENTACLE/PENTAGRAM

The five pointed star, and an important **symbol** in **magic**. In **white magic** it represents the five **elements** of **earth**, **air**, **fire**, **water** and **ether**. The pentagram or star is a symbol of power and protection; when it is placed on a disc or a circle is drawn on the outside it is called a pentacle. If the pentagram is inverted it suggests the practitioner is involved in **black magic**.

Upright pentacles and pentagrams have been used throughout history by many cultures and religions of the world: by ancient Pagans, ancient Israelites, Christians, magicians, **Wiccans** and others. This symbol apparently originated as the symbol of a goddess called Kore, the divine maiden, who was worshiped in ancient Egypt and Greece. Kore's sacred fruit was the apple. When an apple is cut through its equator, both halves will reveal a near-perfect pentagram shape at the core, with each point on the star containing a seed. Many Wiccans continue to cut apples in this way.

In ancient Greece, **Pythagoras** (c.580–500 BC) established a school to pursue knowledge in mathematics, music, religion and other specialties. Driven underground, his followers used the pentagram as a secret sign to identify themselves to each other. Today many religious and spiritual groups continue to use the pentacle or pentagram as a symbol of unity, community, power and protection.

PERCIPIENT

A person who receives impressions in an extrasensory perception **ESP** test.

PERFUME GHOSTS

Some researchers hold that certain ghosts are sensed only as 'phantom scents', i.e. they often appear in the form of a **phantom** scent in the air.

There have been numerous reports of people who have suddenly become conscious of a smell they can instantly identify with people who have died. Perhaps the most famous historical instance of a ghostly scent was given by **John Aubrey**, in his *Miscellanies* (1696): 'Anno 1670, not far from Cirencester, was an apparition. Being demanded whether a good spirit or bad, it returned no answer, but disappeared with a curious Perfume and most melodious Twang.'

PERIWINKLE

In folklore, this trailing evergreen plant, which blooms in five-petaled purple or white flowers, is thought to have powers associated with **ghosts** and **witches**. It was traditionally grown on graves or used in garlands for the dead. In France it is called *violette des sorciers* ('violet of the sorcerers') and if hung over doorways is believed to ward off evil **spirits**. In Welsh folklore if a periwinkle is plucked off a grave it is said that one will be haunted by the dead for a year.

In magical tradition, periwinkle is considered a powerful herb that should be gathered according to strict procedures before it is of any efficacy in **magic**. It should be gathered when one is 'clean of every uncleanness', and when the moon is one night old, nine nights old, eleven nights old or thirteen nights old. After gathering the plant can be carried to obtain grace, to attract money, and to protect against snakes, poison, wild beasts, terror, the **evil eye** and spirits. Periwinkle is also thought to increase passion when carried or sprinkled under the bed.

PERKS, THOMAS [1680–1703]

The story of Thomas Perks, who attempted to raise **spirits** from the dead and in the process drove himself mad, has been repeatedly cited as a warning to all those who attempt to control the spirits of the dead.

Perks, a gunsmith who lived in Mangotsfield, near Bristol, became fascinated by the **supernatural**. He acquired an old book of magic **spells** and discovered a spell that gave instructions for raising **ghosts**. One night in 1703 he drew a ritual **circle** at a crossroads and, according to Lionel A Weatherby in *The Supernatural* (1891), 'the spirits appeared faster than he desired, and in most dismal shapes, hissing at him and attempting to throw spears and balls of fire, which did very much affright him and the more so that he found it was not in his power to lay them, insomuch that his hair stood upright and he expected every minute to be torn to pieces.' According to Weatherby these spirits trapped Perks in his circle until daybreak and 'he never recovered from the shock and pined away and died.'

PETERHOUSE COLLEGE

The oldest college in Cambridge, England, dating back to the thirteenth century, which was the site of a much publicized haunting.

One night in April 1997 a white hooded figure floating outside the combination (or common) room was allegedly seen by two members of pantry staff who were fetching food for an official dinner upstairs. The college dean was informed and other staff members came forward reporting strange knockings and sudden drops in temperature.

In November 1997 the **apparition** appeared again to members of staff. The college dean was present and although he did not see a **ghost** he heard the strange knocking. It was noticed that the ghost disappeared through a window that had originally been a door until 1870.

A month later the apparition put in another appearance in the combination room, this time to the college bursar. The bursar described hearing a knocking sound and feeling a cold presence behind him, before seeing a small man in a wide-brimmed hat wearing a jacket. The haunting attracted media interest and in April 1999 an **exorcism** was performed, despite opposition from those who said the ghost was doing no harm.

The ghost was not seen again and was never identified, although it was suggested that it could have been the ghost of former college bursar Frederick Dawes, who committed suicide in 1789 by hanging himself in the stair turret next to the combination room.

cy have been practised for centuries in China, India and other cultures. In Tibetan and Hindu tradition it is considered unlucky for a man to be over-endowed and a large penis brings problems in all areas of life. The ideal husband should have a penis no longer than the width of six fingers.

Divining by the penis starts with the flaccid, not erect, penis. Taking its natural length first, if less than three inches it is classed as short; longer than three inches is long. A long penis is considered to be the mark of an extrovert and innovator. (According to the Hindu tradition, a very long penis means the man will be poor and have no sons.) A short penis denotes a romantic and a dreamer. (Hindus believe that a small penis foretells of riches to come.) A thick penis is considered a sign of energy and determination. A thin penis indicates a sensitive, poetic lover. If the penis curves to the left, in matters of love and sex the man is a taker, not a giver. If, however, it curves to the right he is a giver in love and sex. Thick bushy pubic hair indicates a strong and physical lover. Thin sparse pubic hair indicates someone with refined sexual tastes and a libido that fluctuates according to the level of self-confidence.

PHALLOMANCY

The science and divinatory art of judging a man's character and lovemaking style by the shape of his penis. Forms of phalloman-

PHANTASM

Archaic term for an **apparition**.

PHANTASMAGORIA

A **ghost**-making machine that was a popular form of entertainment in the closing years of the eighteenth century and through into much of the nineteenth. Since the fifteenth century the principle of using an apparatus like a magic lantern to project ghostly figures before an audience had been known, but it was Belgian optician in the 1790s, E G Robertson, who is credited with developing ghost illusions that were both convincing and popular. As one reporter wrote in 1798, 'Go to Robertson's exhibition and you will see the dead returning to life in the crowds. Robertson calls forth phantoms and commands legions of spectres.'

The phantasmagorias were so convincing that once the techniques were understood by fraudulent **mediums** they were put to use all over Europe to raise the 'spirits of the dead'. It took a concerted effort by the authorities and psychical researchers to prove trickery and to wean a gullible public away from them.

PHANTOM

Something apparently seen, heard or sensed but having no physical reality. Alternative term for an **apparition, ghost** or **spectre**.

PHANTOM ARMIES

Places of violence, trauma and tragedy are often associated with **haunting** phenomena and because of the terrible carnage that typically occurs during battle it is no surprise that phantom armies have been reported throughout history in many different cultures. The earliest reports of phantom soldiers date back to the ancient Assyrians, when ghostly warriors were said to have made attacks on desert cities, and it is said that on certain nights of the year armoured knights from the time of King Arthur can be heard at **Glastonbury**. There have been continuing reports of men in Civil War uniform (both English and American) and that both World Wars have produced a large number of phantom army stories. Perhaps the most recent sighting occurred in 1971 when a group of American soldiers in Vietnam were mystified by the footsteps of a ghostly platoon close behind them.

See also **Battlefield hauntings**.

PHANTOM BELLS

The ringing of phantom bells that once tolled in churches now submerged in the sea is a commonly recorded phenomenon all over the world. For example, many people living near Dunwich, a city that was once prosperous but is now submerged off the Suffolk coast in England, report hearing bells when stormy weather is due and at Christmas time. The people always check after hearing the bells to make sure no church bell is ringing on land, and they say that the real proof that the tolling comes from a phantom bell is that there is always a note missing.

There have also been instances when families have claimed to be haunted by phantom bells ringing shortly before a person in the family is about to die. These sounds cannot be traced to any source in the house or from church bells nearby. One of the most famous instances of a family haunted by a bell sound whose source could not be traced is the appropriately named Pine-Coffin family from Portledge in North Devon, whose story is related in *Apparitions: A Narrative of Facts* by Revd B W Saville (1905).

PHANTOM BIRDS

There are a number of examples of phantom birds appearing at a person's bedside when they are close to death. A good description of this appears in a seventeenth-century pamphlet entitled: *A True Relation of an Apparition in the likeness of bird with a white breast that appeared hovering over the death bed of the some of the children of Mr James Oxenham of Orehampton in Devon.* The pamphlet goes on to describe the phantom bird, which had been reported as appearing for over a hundred years whenever a member of the Oxenham family was close to death.

PHANTOM COACH

A phantom coach that, according to lore, comes to collect the dying and is also used by the dead as a means of late night transport. It is either a coach or a hearse but it is always black and the driver and horses are typically headless. The coach never makes a sound and travels at lightning speed. If anyone sees the coach it is thought to be a **death omen**.

According to an anonymous writer in 1847 in the *Athenaeum*:

The spectral appearance often presents itself in the shape of a great black coach, on which sit hundreds of spirits singing a wonderfully sweet song. Before it goes a man who loudly warns everybody to get out of the way. All who hear him must instantly drop down with their faces to the ground as at the coming of the wild hunt, an hold fast by something, were it only a blade of grass; for the furious host have been known to force many a man into its coach [and] can carry him hundreds of miles away through the air.

Although the motor car has long since replaced the coach and horses, phantom coaches are still being reported in parts of rural England, France and Germany. A famous example is the phantom coach of Francis Drake, which from time to time is allegedly seen driving across Dartmoor, on starless nights, followed by a pack of baying hounds.

PHANTOM HEADS

There are many cases of **hauntings** of floating heads in both Europe and America. One of the best accounts was reported in 1891 and comes from Oakville near San Francisco. According to the *San Francisco Examiner* a family with the name of Washington was haunted by a phantom head that first appeared as a phantom light and gradually developed into a head with long, grey, matted hair and bloodstains on its forehead. The head is said to have floated about six inches above the floor and if anyone came close to it they felt the sensation of icy fingers choking their throat. Such was the terror the head caused that the Washingtons moved out and requested that the house be destroyed. Remarkably a headless skeleton was discovered when the house was being pulled down, and according to local rumour the mystery was solved.

PHANTOM HITCHHIKER

Also known as the vanishing hitchhiker, the legend of the phantom hitchhiker is popular and widespread all over the world. It appears in Europe and in Asia but is especially popular in the United States, perhaps due to the accessibility of automobile travel and the romance of the open road. There are literally hundreds of different versions of the legend, many with sexual undertones and a woman-in-distress motif, and the story continues to be reported to this day.

Typically the phantom hitchhiker is a girl in a distressed state. She often stands by the side of a stretch of lonely road in the middle of the night, or she suddenly looms up in the headlights. She is often dressed in white. The driver, who is usually a man, stops and asks her where she is going and it is always in the same direction as him. He offers to give her a lift and when she gets inside he notices how beautiful she is. As they drive on she rarely says a word. When the driver reaches the address she has given him he turns around and she has vanished, although the seat she sat on may be wet and she may have left something – an object like a scarf, a pin or a book – behind.

The man knocks at the door of the house and is usually answered by a woman. The driver explains what has happened and is told it has happened before – the girl or woman is her daughter who was killed some time ago and the night is the anniversary of her death. The girl was either murdered or killed in an accident at the spot where the driver picked her up. The driver is shown a photo of the girl and it is the same girl he picked up, wearing the same clothes. Later the driver may visit her grave, and if he gave her his coat to keep her warm it may be draped across the grave.

In some cases the phantom hitchhiker may pick up travelling companions at other locations such as a nightclub. Again she is driven home or walked home but this time the man sees the woman step inside the house. When he decides to visit her later he is shocked to hear that the young woman died several years ago.

PHANTOM MONKS AND NUNS

The **ghosts** of monks and nuns and other religious persons that haunt religious sites and locations, such as churches and cathedrals or buildings built on the site of former religious institutions. They can appear alone or in groups and are often heard chanting and singing. Some of these ghosts are thought to have suffered violent deaths for their religion while others are said to simply want to remain at places they love in **spirit**.

The ghost of an abbess is said to haunt Holy Trinity Church in York. According to lore the abbess was killed when she defied soldiers who came to destroy the priory during the Reformation by saying they could enter only over her dead body. They killed her, and as she lay dying she promised to haunt the site.

Perhaps the most famous location for reports of phantom monks is St James Sag Church in Chicago. The church was built in 1833 and a church, a rectory and a cemetery can be found in its grounds. Even though no monastery existed there phantom monks are still said to appear. One of the most recent sightings took place in November 1977. A Cook County policeman was driving by the church's cemetery at around 2.30 am when he saw a group of hooded figures walking inside the gate. He called out to them that they were trespassing but they paid no attention to him. The officer tried to follow them but when he reached the top of the hill the monks had vanished.

Numerous phantom monk **hauntings** have been reported in Britain. For instance, the ghost known as the Black Canon, because he is always dressed in a black cassock, cloak and hat, is said to haunt Bolton Priory near Skipton in Yorkshire. The cathedral at Canterbury is said to be haunted by a mysterious hooded monk who appears in the cloisters at night. Two phantom monks have been reported at Chingle Hall, a thirteenth-century house near Preston. Mowbreck House, near Kirkham, is believed to be haunted by a priest who was arrested for his faith in London in 1583 and later hanged, drawn and quartered. At Smithills Hall near Bolton, the Revd George Marsh, Protestant vicar of Deane was accused of heresy in the reign of Catholic Queen Mary. According to lore, during the investigation Marsh stamped his foot on the flagstone floor. He was later burned at the stake but his footprint can still be seen and is said to become wet and red once a year. Sometimes phantom monks allegedly speak to visitors. At Bury St Edmunds in Suffolk, a local rector who was writing a book about St Edmund was told by a phantom monk that the saint's body had been removed from its tomb and safely buried elsewhere in the church.

PHANTOM SHIPS

Legends and stories of ghostly ships appear in the folklore of France, Germany, Demark, Ireland, England, Scotland, Canada, America and even China, while earlier tales appear in Hindu, Norse and

Russian legends. **Ghost** ships continue to be reported to this day, especially off the Atlantic coast. They often appear at the scene of the disaster and re-enact their final moments.

The **Flying Dutchman** and the **Mary Celeste** are perhaps the best-known examples of phantom ships that are said to sail the oceans of the world and haunt the coasts of many nations, but there are numerous other less well-known stories.

The SS *Violet*, a paddle steamer that ran aground crossing the English Channel in a snowstorm over 100 years ago, was witnessed at the start of World War II by a lookout at the East Goodwin lighthouse. A lifeboat was sent out to investigate but nothing was found. In American lore the ghost ship of the notorious pirate Captain Kidd is said to sail up and down the New England coast looking for treasure, but the Great Lakes are believed to be the most haunted waters of America.

The Great Lakes are dangerous to navigate and have claimed many lives during violent storms. One of the most famous phantom ships of the Great Lakes is the *Griffon*. On 7 August 1679 the *Griffon*, one of the largest ships to sail the lakes in her day, commenced her maiden voyage. At Detroit Harbor at Washington Island the *Griffon* was loaded with a fur cargo before setting out to return to Niagara on 18 September. After that no one knows what happened to the ship. According to lore it 'sailed through a crack of ice' and vanished. A wreck was discovered in 1900 but its identity remains unconfirmed. The ghost of the *Griffon* is reportedly still seen drifting about Lake Huron when the nights are foggy.

Nearly every town and seaside village has its tales of shipwrecks and ghost ships – those phantoms of the sea breaking through the fog and the mist on dark, stormy nights. Most of these stories are just legends, but some of them are based on truth and may even have a natural explanation. For example, in some cases the sailors may have abandoned ship thinking it was about to sink in a storm, but the ship sailed on without them. In other cases the sailors may have died one-by-one of disease or starvation, leaving a perfectly good ship to sail for months, or even years on the high seas with no hand at her helm. In other cases people may have mistaken mirages and false images for phantom ships. Despite this, belief in ghostly ships that sail for all eternity with their phantom crews remains strong, and reports of sightings continue to this day.

PHANTOM TRAVELLERS

Ghosts of humans and animals that haunt travel routes and vehicles have been documented as early as the 1600s in Europe and Russia. They are associated with tragedies that have occurred while travelling, the excitement of travel and the joy of reunion and the pain of parting.

Some phantom travellers seemed doomed to eternal wandering, as is the case with the **Flying Dutchman**. Another such traveller is the ghost of Peter Rugg, a man who lived in Boston around 1730. According to lore Rugg set off in an open carriage with his daughter one day to drive to Concord. He was warned on the return trip that a storm was brewing but chose to ignore the warnings and was never seen again. Their ghosts are said to be still trying to find their way home.

In some cases the phantom traveller appears very real to a fellow traveller. The ghost of the black lady who is said to haunt the train from Carlisle to London is said to sit silently in a carriage staring in her lap and rocking gently backwards and forwards. According to lore she and her bridegroom were travelling on the train when tragedy struck. Her husband stuck his head out of the window and was decapitated.

The headless body fell into the woman's lap and she was found singing a lullaby to it. She never regained her sanity.

Phantom travellers as well as the sound of footsteps and screams are frequently reported at railway and underground stations that have been the scenes of suicides and fatal accidents. London's Aldgate station on the Underground Circle line is one of several haunted stations that have had so many sightings they are entered into the station log.

Airports also have their fair share of ghosts. It is said that the ghost of a gentleman in a dark suit and bowler hat has haunted runway 2 at Heathrow airport since 1948. It was in 1948 that a DC3 Dakota of Sabean Belgian Airways crashed while landing in heavy fog, killing everyone on board. Other Heathrow **apparitions** include a ghost in a light grey suit that is said to haunt the VIP lounges.

Phantom travellers typically appear in the travel mode they used in their day.

They use trains and planes and ships, ride bicycles or motorcycles or drive carriages, cars, buses and vans. Sometimes they walk and if this is the case they can suddenly appear in the middle of the road. Drivers of vehicles may swerve to avoid hitting them but when they stop to see if the person is hurt there is no sign of anyone.

PHANTOM VEHICLES

Ghostly cars, buses, carriages and trains travelling at high speed along the same piece of road or highway are a common form of **haunting**. In many cases drivers of other vehicles will swerve to avoid them; in some cases they swerve too late and injury and death result. Sometimes the scene of the haunting is associated with tragedy or murder but in some cases the origins of the haunting are unknown.

The Midlothian Turnpike, which runs along **Bachelors Grove Cemetery** in Chicago, is an area where numerous phantom cars and trucks have been reported at dusk and at night by witnesses. The phantom cars and trucks are said to appear out of nowhere and in some cases they will hit the witness's car and sounds of splintering glass and crashing metal are heard. When the witness gets out to take a look at the damage there is never any sign of impact or the other car.

An apparition of a bright red double-decker bus has allegedly made hundreds of appearances in London. One night on 15 June 1934, a young man was driving his car in North Kensington when he found himself heading on a collision course with a driverless bus at the intersection of St Mark's Road and Cambridge Gardens. The man tried to swerve but was killed. The bus was allegedly a phantom vehicle. Over the years the phantom double-decker continues to cause accidents and is reported to this day.

PHASMOPHOBIA

An abnormal and persistent fear of **ghosts** and the unknown.

This surprisingly common phobia causes countless people needless distress. Known by a number of names – spectrophobia, phasmophobia, fear of spectres and fear of ghosts being the most common – the problem can significantly affect quality of life. It can cause panic attacks and keep people apart from loved ones and business associates. Symptoms typically include shortness of breath, rapid breathing, irregular heartbeat, sweating, nausea and overall feelings of dread, although everyone experiences fear of ghosts in their own way and may have different symptoms.

The condition is typically caused by the trauma experienced while watching Hollywood films of ghost and/or horror stories, such as the *Exorcist*. Treatment options are similar to those for any phobia and may involve counselling, therapy, alternative therapies such as hypnotherapy or, in severe cases, medication.

PHENOMENA

In general, apart from its specialized use as a term in philosophy, phenomenon stands for any observable event. Phenomena make up the raw data of science. The phenomena considered relevant for the field of **parapsychology** are called anomalous phenomena, which means they are observed phenomena for which there is no suitable explanation in the context of current scientific knowledge.

Often used as a synonym, but actually a subclass of anomalous phenomena, are the **paranormal** phenomena studied by parapsychology. Paranormal phenomena can be divided into three main classes:

1. Mental phenomena: unusual mental states or abilities, such as **telepathy**, **clairvoyance** and **precognition.**
2. Physical phenomena: unusual physical occurrences that may be controlled by a consciousness, such as **psychokinesis**, **poltergeists**, stigmata or **materializations.**
3. **Out-of-body experiences** and **near-death experiences.**

PHILADELPHIA EXPERIMENT

Allegedly, in the fall of 1943 a US Navy destroyer was made invisible to enemy detection and teleported from Philadelphia, Pennsylvania to Norfolk, Virginia, in an incident known as the Philadelphia Experiment. Records in the Operational

Archives Branch of the Naval Historical Center have been repeatedly searched, but no documents have been located which confirm the event, or any interest by the Navy in attempting such a thing.

PHILIP

Artificial **poltergeist** created by Canadian parapsychologists in the 1970s. The aim of the experiment was to create, through intense concentration, a collective **thought form** and demonstrate how **spirits** can be the products of human desire, will and **imagination**.

The research was carried out by eight members of the Toronto Society for Psychical Research, under the direction of A R G Owen and Iris Owen. First the group, none of whom were gifted psychically, created a fictitious personality and personal history. They fabricated a 'Philip Aylesford' who was born in 1624 England. At the age of 16 he was knighted and played a leading role in the Civil War, fighting for the royalists. He was a personal friend of Charles II and worked for him as a secret agent, but he brought about his own undoing by having an affair with a Gypsy girl. When his wife found out she accused the girl of **witchcraft** and the girl was burned at the stake. Philip committed suicide as a result in 1654.

In September 1972 the Owen group began to hold sittings to conjure Philip. They meditated and visualized him but no **apparition** appeared. After several months

of no communication the group decided to try **table-tilting**, an activity where spirits allegedly move or tilt a table, although sceptics argue the effects are created by the expectations of the sitters. After a few sessions the table-top began to move and Philip began to communicate to the group by **rapping** in response to questions.

Philip gave information consistent with his fictitious character as well as other accurate information, and the group theorized that this came from their **collective unconscious**. Sessions with Philip continued for a few years and in 1974 table movement was recorded on camera.

The success of the 'PK by committee experiment', as it was called by the group, prompted other groups in Toronto and Quebec to try the same. A World War II French-Canadian spy, Lilith, Sebastian, a medieval alchemist and Axel, a man from the future, were all created and all eventually communicated to the groups with rappings.

In 1977 the original Toronto group, buoyed by their success, attempted to progress beyond raps and create an apparition. This proved to be impossible and after numerous time-consuming, frustrating attempts interest in the project waned and the experiment was discontinued.

PHILOSOPHER'S STONE

In **alchemy** the philosopher's stone was the original metal from which all metals derived, and consequently could be used in the transformation of lead and other base metals into gold. It was also thought that the philosopher's stone was held together by all the elements of the universe, that it had remarkable healing powers and was the key to eternal life.

The philosopher's stone was not actually believed to be a stone but a power or elixir, and attempting to discover its formula was one of the main goals of alchemy. Many alchemists devoted years of study to searching for physical examples of the substance, but when it proved impossible the theory arose that it was non-physical, spiritual in essence, and could only be recognized by initiates.

PHONE CALLS FROM THE DEAD

It seems that the dead are willing to make use of whatever means or whatever technology is available to them to make contact with the living, and there have been numerous reports of communication with **spirits** via the telephone.

Phone calls from the dead appear to occur randomly and the great majority are exchanges with loved ones or people who shared close bonds with the deceased when they were alive. Sometimes the communicator wishes to impart a message but at other times there is no other purpose but to make contact. Those who claim to have received phone calls from the dead say that the voices sound the same as when a person was alive but the connection is often bad. The phone rings normally, although some

say it sounds odd or flat. In most cases the voice starts strongly and then begins to fade away, leaving the line open. In other cases the line simply goes dead.

The **phantom** phone call usually occurs when the person is in a relaxed state of mind and within 24 hours of the death of the caller, although sometimes it can be weeks or months after death. The longest interval recorded is two years. Some calls are made on special occasions such as birthdays or anniversaries. If the recipient is shocked and knows the caller is dead the phone call is very brief and lasts only a few seconds, but if the person does not know the caller is dead it can go on for up to half an hour. Later checks with the telephone company show no evidence of a call being placed.

In some cases a person may make a call to someone and have a conversation with them only to find out later that they were already dead at the time of the call. In other cases the caller is a stranger who says they are calling on behalf of a third party, and the recipients later find out that the third party is dead.

Researchers of such cases have also found that deceased callers sometimes make reference to a mysterious 'they', who have allowed the call to take place. The implication is that communication between the dead and the living is not just difficult but undesirable.

Intention phone calls are similar to phantom phone calls but are far rarer and not quite the same, as they occur between two living people. In an intention phone call the caller thinks about making a call but for some reason never makes it; the recipient nevertheless receives a call.

Two main theories have been put forward to explain phone calls from the dead: they are created subconsciously by the recipient, whose intense desire to communicate with a lost loved one creates a psychokinetic hallucination; or they are indeed communications with dead spirits who have found a way to manipulate the phone system. Although interest in phone calls from the dead was strong in the early to mid-twentieth century, in general modern parapsychologists don't take phantom phone calls seriously as evidence for **survival after death**.

PHYLLOMANCY

Ancient method of **divination** by studying the shapes, patterns, veins, colours and movements of leaves. Methods differ from area to area. For some the sound of leaves rustling in the wind was significant. For others the falling of leaves in the autumn – the way they fell and how many fell – was significant. If a leaf fell face up it was considered a positive sign. If it landed face down this was considered unfortunate.

PHYSICAL MEDIUMSHIP

Mediumship, the ability to communicate with **spirits**, takes two forms: **mental mediumship** and physical mediumship. In contrast to mental mediumship (when the phenomenon is demonstrated through the mind of the **medium**), the physical medium is able to produce for the benefit of those taking part in a **séance** physical phenomena such as lights, sounds, **materializations**, **levitations**, etc. Physical mediumship often (but not always) involves a state of **trance**.

PHYSIOGNOMANCY

Divination by facial features – judging mental and moral characteristics and future success in life by the features of a face. Physiognomy was a popular divinatory art in ancient Greece. Aristotleis thought to have written the first systematic treatise on the subject (*History of Animals and a Treatise on Phsyiognomy*) and many Greeks studied and practised the art.

The principles of physiognomy are a little vague, but in general faces are divided into seven planetary types. The solar face is round and joyful and framed in fair hair. The Venus face has perfect features, fair hair and a lovely smile. The Mars face is rugged and square cut. The Mercurial face is beautiful with black hair. The lunar face tends to be pale, cold and melancholy. The Jupiter face is beautiful and noble with bold features. The Saturn face is mournful and may have black hair.

The forehead is considered especially important. In his *Traite de Metoposcopie et Physiognomonie* (1635), physiognomist David L'Agneau writes:

Those with a high forehead are lazy and igno-rant and if it is fleshy and sleek they are wrath-ful, and if with this they have prick ears they are still more wrathful, according to Aristotle. Those who have little foreheads are bustling and foolish, as are they likewise who have them great and narrow. Those with long foreheads are docile and gentle with good sense; those who have them as it were square and pleasant are magnanimous and strong.

PICKENS COUNTY COURTHOUSE

The ghostly face of a hanged man that is said to appear at about 4 pm every day on a windowpane of Pickens County Court-house in Carrollton, Alabama.

Numerous versions of the story exist but the face is said to be the **ghost** of a black man called Burkhalter who, in the early 1800s, was accused of burning down the courthouse. Even though he protested his innocence he was convicted of the crime. On route to the state penitentiary in Montgomery the unfortunate Burkhalter was seized by a lynch mob and hanged from the branch of an oak tree. According to lore just as he was hoisted in the air, lightning struck and illuminated his terri-fied face.

The next day a member of the lynch mob passed the newly built courthouse and saw in the window the clear outline of Burkhalter's face as it had looked when he was being murdered. Over the years numerous panes have been replaced, and the glass has been scrubbed and cleaned

countless times, but all to no avail. The face of Burkhalter allegedly remains in the window.

PICTURE TEST

Mediumistic test, similar to the **book test** and the **newspaper test**, in which a com-municator predicts what picture the sitter will soon come into contact with or see. The picture test, like the book and news-paper test, was invented by Feda, the **spirit control** of **Gladys Osborne Leonard** as a means of proving **survival after death**. However, like the other tests, the picture test could be said to represent no more than the **medium**'s own psychic abilities.

PIKE, BISHOP JAMES [1913–1969]

Former official of the Episcopal Church in America who became a **spiritualist** after communication with his dead son. When the bishop died, messages were allegedly sent from him to **mediums** to support the case for life after death.

James A Pike was born in Oklahoma City on 14 February 1913. He was raised a Catholic and planned to become a priest but left the church when he disagreed with the Pope's stance on birth control. He went on to practise law in Washington DC, joined the Episcopal Church in 1944 and was ordained a priest in 1946. In 1953 Pike became Dean of the Cathedral of St John Divine in New York.

Although Pike came from a family with **psychic** ability and had had experience of **poltergeist** activity in at least two of his homes, he did not become seriously interested in **spiritualism** until the suicide of his eldest son, James Jr, in New York on 6 February 1966. Beginning on 20 February, strange things began to happen at Pike's apartment in Cambridge, England, where James Jr had recently spent several months living with his father. Postcards and books would be rearranged, fresh milk turned sour, the heart would turn up with no explanation, and cigarette butts appeared from nowhere.

Bishop Pike arranged the first of numerous **séances** with the medium **Ena Twigg** on 2 March 1966. After examining a passport belonging to James Jr, Twigg became very agitated and reported that James was desperate to communicate with his father and ask forgiveness for his suicide, saying it was an accident.

By the summer Pike had resigned his post as Episcopal bishop of California. He sat with other mediums and they too made contact with his son. James Jr urged his father to protest against the charges of doctrinal heresy made against him, charges which Pike addressed in his book *If This Be Heresy*, and encouraged Pike to establish the New Focus Foundation as a channel for his unorthodox views on church reform.

On 3 September 1967, Pike sat for a Canadian television **séance** with medium **Arthur Ford** and once again James Jr came through with information. By publicly revealing his connections to the spiritualist cause Pike became an even more controversial figure within the church, and in December 1968 the new bishop of California requested that Pike be kept from performing any priestly function in a church or elsewhere. Pike left the Episcopal Church and formed the Foundation for Religious Transition in April 1969.

On 1 September Pike and his wife, Diane Kennedy, took a trip to the Holy Land and got lost in the desert. Diane had to leave her husband behind to find help, and when she returned he was missing. Almost immediately efforts were made to contact James Jr in spirit to help with the search, but on 4 September a message came through from Pike himself indicating that he had died and was struggling with his transition to the other side. On the 7th his body was found.

Pike's wife Diane strongly believed in life after death, and she went on to publish an account of her husband's life and spiritual journey in the book *Search* (1970).

PIPER, LEONORA [1859–1950]

One of the foremost **trance mediums** in the history of **spiritualism**, Mrs Piper was investigated by psychical researchers on both sides of the Atlantic and is thought to have produced some of the best evidence for **survival after death**.

Born in New Hampshire on 27 June 1859, the first sign of Leonora's future career came at the age of eight when she felt a blow to the head while playing in the garden and heard a long sibilant 'S' in her ear. This sound melted into the word 'Sara' and then the words, 'Aunt Sara is not dead but with you still.' She told her mother who made a note of the day and time, and several days later it was found that Leonora's Aunt Sara had indeed died at that time. Leonora had several other psychic experiences as she grew up.

At the age of 18 Leonora married William Piper of Boston. Shortly after this she consulted Dr J R Cocke, a blind, professional **clairvoyant** who had a reputation for psychic diagnosis and cures. While there, Leonora fell into a spontaneous trance, and at a later trance, when Cocke put his hand on Leonora's head, she saw a 'flood of light in which many strange faces appeared.' Then, while entranced, she began writing some notes on a piece of paper and handed it to Judge Frost of Cambridge, a member of the circle. It was regarded as one of the most remarkable messages the judge had ever received from his dead son.

Soon after Piper began to give private sittings in her home and before long she was besieged by prospective clients. She withdrew from public and saw only close friends and relatives. Then she agreed to see a Mrs Gibbons, who happened to be the mother-in-law of Professor **William James**, a founding member of the **American Society for Psychical Research**. Mrs Gibbons was so impressed with Leonora Piper that Professor James spent the next eighteen months in deep investigation of her **séances**.

In this early period of her mediumship Piper's trance **control** was called 'Phinuit', who claimed to be a French doctor but actually knew very little medicine and very little French. Even though Phinuit was probably not who he said he was, and many regarded him as a secondary personality, through Phinuit Piper was able to tell things about other people she had no other way of knowing.

In 1889 and again in 1906 Piper visited England, and was investigated by the **Society for Psychical Research** with remarkable success. In 1901 the *New York Herald* led with 'Mrs Piper's plain statement', and although it is often said she confessed to **fraud** she in fact wrote only that she could not be sure the **spirits** were always controlling her and that she may have got her results through **ESP**. This was to be the key issue when questions were asked about her mediumship, with researchers finding themselves on both sides of the divide.

From 1908 to 1911 Piper's mediumship lapsed and when it resumed it returned in the form of **automatic writing** rather than trance. Some of the automatic writing she produced formed part of what is known as **cross correspondences**. All of the material produced appears to have come from the deceased psychical researcher, **Sir Frederick Myers**.

Piper died on 3 July 1950 at the age of 91. As a result of her work, many people, including Frederick Myers and **James H Hyslop**, were convinced that life after death was possible. She may even have convinced the hardened sceptic William James. In the *Psychological Review* of 1898 James wrote:

Dr Hodgson considers the hypothesis of fraud cannot be seriously maintained. I agree with him absolutely. The medium has been under observation, much of the time under close observation, as to most of the conditions of her life, by a large number of persons, eager, many of them to pounce upon any suspicious circumstance, for nearly fifteen years. During that time not only has there not been one single suspicious circumstance remarked, but not one suggestion has ever been made from any quarter which might tend positively to explain how the medium, living the apparent life she leads, could possibly collect information about so many sitters by natural means.

PK

See **Psychokinesis**.

PK PARTY

A gathering of between 15 and 40 people for the purpose of psychokinetic **metal bending**. A party leader will teach the others how to create a 'peak emotional experience' by focusing the group's unified mental energy on willing the metal objects to bend. Interest in metal bending was inspired by the media attention given to **Uri Geller** in the 1970s for his alleged ability to bend keys and spoons.

The idea behind psychokinetic metal bending is to create an intense point of concentration in the mind and bring that concentration down through the arm and hand to the metal, where energy is released and the metal bends. Participants say they feel the metal become warm and sticky and then soft enough to bend. Participant may also try other versions of metal bending, the most advanced of which is to bend metal without touching it. According to experts, silverware works best.

Experiments with Geller did yield some positive results, but whether or not psychokinetic metal bending is actually possible has yet to be proved conclusively.

PLANCHETTE

An early variation of the **Ouija board**, the planchette is an instrument used to communicate with **spirits** in **spiritualism**. It is typically about three inches wide and four inches long and rests on four legs. In use, one or more people lightly rest their fingers on the top edge of the device to channel into it the power to make it move. The planchette slides about the surface of a smooth board pointing at letters to spell out messages, allegedly from spirits guiding the movements of the planchette.

The legs are usually covered in felt to make it easier to slide on a polished surface, or they can have small wheels on them. If **automatic writing** is to be done one of the legs may be replaced with a pencil, the point writing letters on to a sheet of paper over which the planchette moves.

A very simple and effective planchette can be made by writing the letters of the alphabet on pieces of paper and laying them down in a circle around the edge of a table. A wine glass is turned upside down and the participants rest their fingers on the now top edge of the glass. The glass acts like a planchette and slides over the table surface to stop in front of the appropriate letters.

The term *planchette* comes from the French meaning 'little board'. It was named after M Planchette, who invented it in 1853, but it probably has much older origins. The Greek philosopher **Pythagoras** was said to hold **séances** at a mystic table mounted on wheels that moved to signs on stone slabs. Although rarely in use today, during the nineteenth century the planchette became a popular tool for **mediums**. In 1868 it was discovered by American toymakers, who produced and sold it through bookshops.

PLANETARY CONSCIOUSNESS

Concept of the earth as a living, self-regulating organism. Planetary consciousness involves a growing awareness of the interconnectedness between all living and non-living things on the planet. However, no such leap in awareness can take place if the human race continues to abuse and pollute the planet.

The **Gaia** hypothesis – that the earth is a self-regulating, living organism – was put forward by a British scientist, James Lovelock, in the 1970s. Lovelock believed that an evolutionary leap into unified human consciousness with no national boundaries was possible. This theory was developed a few years later by British physicist Peter Russell, in *The Global Brain: Speculations on the evolutionary leap to planetary consciousness* (1983). Russell hypothesized the evolution of a completely new and planetary level of consciousness called Gaiafield – a kind of super mind that would emerge from the interaction of all minds, working in harmony with the planet. In other words, if an increasing number of people meditate the beneficial effects may be felt on the human race as a whole.

PLANTS

Many cultures around the world believe that plants have consciousness and that it is possible to communicate with them psychically, a gift called 'biopsychokinesis'. Even in the West there are those who talk regularly to their plants, and many studies have shown that an empathetic understanding and emotional connection to plants by a gardener tends to produce larger and healthier plants. Other studies found evidence for a plant memory. Russian scientists attached electrodes to a geranium and it reacted negatively to a person who had pinched and burned it but positively to someone who had cared for it. Experiments with music have demonstrated that the type of music played to plants affects their growth. Disjointed and inharmonious sounds do not help them, but harmonious tunes do. While experiments with prayer have indicated that praying over seeds and plants seems to make them grow faster than control seeds that are not prayed over.

The **Findhorn** community in Scotland has demonstrated that by talking to plants, encouraging them and loving them they grow better and provide a bumper harvest. Sceptics argue that the evidence from **psi** experiments on plants is unconvincing because the fact that plants are healthier when a psychic connection has been established has nothing to do with communicating messages of love and encouragement but everything to do with the regular tending, care and feeding they receive while being talked to.

PLATO [c. 428–c. 347 BC]

Greek philosopher, and one of the most creative and influential thinkers in Western philosophical, religious and mystical thought.

Born in Athens in around 428 BC, Plato dropped his political ambitions after the trial and death of his friend Socrates in 399. He began to travel through Greece, Italy and Egypt and write dialogues in defence of Socrates. In c. 387 he returned to Athens and founded the Academy, the first university, to explore all fields of knowledge and their interrelation. His greatest pupil was Aristotle.

Plato is best remembered for his dialogues, among them *Meno, Phaedo, Sympo-sium, Phaedrus* and *Republic*, which outline his philosophy. Central to the dialogues is the theory of forms or ideas and a belief in the immortality of the soul as surviving the body and the mind after death. According to his theory of forms, the material world is an imperfect copy of the real and perfect world. Forms are the ideas or blueprints behind the material world. When an object is seen, it is seen for what it is, but the object's essence is the idea of the object or form, which is sublimely beautiful, good and perfect.

Plato believed the world of forms to be the ultimate highest reality, which he also named the Higher Self. In *Republic* Plato suggested the idea that most people go through life asleep and in a dream and it is the job of the philosopher to awaken them. He illustrated this with his famous metaphor of people living in caves preferring the shadows to the light because that is all they have known.

Plato died in Athens at about the age of 80 and his disciples divided into two camps. In the first century AD **Neo-Platonism** developed out of his ideas. In one way or another Platonic thought has had a huge impact on philosophy, science, religion and mysticism throughout history, enjoying several revivals.

PODMORE, FRANK [1856–1910]

Well-known psychical investigator and distinguished author who is best known for his critical approach to the phenomenon of **spiritualism**.

Podmore rapidly and enthusiastically became a convert to survival and communication with the deceased during his student days at Oxford, but his youthful enthusiasm turned sour when a number of the **mediums** he believed in were exposed as **frauds**. From beginning as a 'believer', over the years he developed into an extremely sceptical and cautious critic.

Despite his scepticism Podmore remained fascinated by the **paranormal** and was elected to the Council of the **Society for Psychical Research** and served for an unbroken period of 27 years. For eight or nine years he held, jointly with **Sir Frederick Myers**, the office of honorary secretary. He was a collaborator with Myers and **Edmund Gurney** in *Phantasms of the Living*. In *Phantasms* Podmore reviewed the evidence for **telepathy** and **apparitions** and argued that they could be explained as hallucinations by the **percipient** in response to information received via telepathy from the **agents**.

Podmore wrote a number of books, including *Apparitions and Thought-Transference* (1892); *Studies in Psychical Research* (1897); *Modern Spiritualism* (1902); *Spiritualism* (Pro and Con Series, against Wake Cook) (1903); *Biography of Robert Owen* (1906); *The Naturalisation of the Supernatural* (1908); *Mesmerism and Christian Science* (1909); *Telepathic Hallucination; The New View of Ghosts* (1909); and *The Newer Spiritualism* (1910). He is perhaps best known for *Modern Spiritualism* (1902), where he discusses and discredits numerous mediums of his day. The only medium to significantly impress Podmore was **Leonora Piper**, although he did attribute her success to telepathy rather than communication with **spirits**.

PODOMANCY

Also known as solistry, podomancy is **divination** from signs derived from examination of the feet. At one time very popular in China and Persia, podomancy is similar to **palmistry**. It was once believed that a person's feet were the 'symbol of the soul', and would reveal their personality and future characteristics when certain signs – size, shape, lines, etc. – were properly interpreted by a skilled diviner.

With feet, high arches are an indication of a high intellect, but also of being a dreamer. Low arches or flat feet are a sign that the person is a practical realist and should perhaps dream a little more. Swollen feet suggest someone who is introverted.

POLARITY THERAPY

A **bodywork** touch therapy that is based on energy principles found in **Ayurvedic medicine**. Dr Randolph Stone (1890–1981) developed this method of **healing** after decades of study of alternative therapies. He believed that the key to health was to balance out the body's subtle energies or **universal life force**. Stone mapped out what he called 'The Energy

Anatomy of Man', which showed the electromagnetic fields around the body and how the life force should appear in balance.

Polarity therapy works with the Human Energy Field, electromagnetic patterns expressed in mental, emotional and physical experience. Health is viewed as a reflection of the condition of the energy field, and therapeutic methods are designed to balance the field for the benefit of health. Like any energy field, energy can become positive or negative and polarity therapy seeks to balance this through an exchange between giver and receiver during a session. There are four ways to balance body energy: triggering **chakra** points on the body with a light touch; stretching exercises; dietary changes; and mental/emotional balancing exercises.

POLICE PSYCHICS

See **Psychic Criminology**.

POLTERGEIST

From the German words *poltern*, 'to knock', and *geist*, 'spirit', poltergeist is the term used to describe a **ghost** or energy which specializes in making sounds and moving things about a house or building, often resulting in breakages. These **spirits** can be malevolent but on the whole are thought to be mischievous nuisances. Some believe poltergeists to be manifestations of **telekinesis** due to the frequency of their occurrence in households with disturbed adolescents experiencing frustration and emotional tension.

The earliest reports of poltergeist activity date back to ancient Rome, and they continue to be reported to this day. Since the late nineteenth century poltergeists have been the subject of serious study by psychical researchers and a number of theories have been put forward to explain them.

Characteristics of a poltergeist attack typically include flying objects, especially dirt and rock throwing, extremely loud noises, terrible smells, raps, strange lights and **apparitions** and the opening and shutting of doors and windows. Up-to-date characteristics include light bulbs exploding or spinning in their sockets and telephone malfunctions. In a tiny percentage of cases physical assaults, such as scratching, biting, spitting and sexual molestation, are reported.

In most cases poltergeist activity starts and stops suddenly and lasts from a few hours to a few years, although most often it is a few months. Activity usually occurs when a particular individual is present and that individual is most often female and under 20 years of age.

Until the nineteenth century poltergeist activity was blamed on **demons**, **witches** or the devil. Such cases resembled **possession** and clergy were often called in for **exorcisms**. In the 1800s, however, poltergeists became associated with the **physical mediumship** of **spiritualism**. In the 1930s **Nandor Fodor** came to the conclusion that is still widely held today – that poltergeists are a type of unconscious **psychokinesis** on the part of the living, the so-called **agent**. In other words unconscious thought processes produce the phenomena. At first attention focused on repressed sexual tension as a cause or factor but later researchers theorized that poltergeists were projections of repressed anger and hostility.

In 1947 the **Cottage City Poltergeist** case came to the attention of **J B Rhine** at Duke University's Parapsychology Laboratory. A few years later the **Seaford Poltergeist** case came up and Rhine sent **J G Pratt** and **William G Roll** to investigate. Roll went on to specialize in poltergeist investigation and described his work in his 1972 book, *The Poltergeist*.

According to Roll poltergeist activity involved 'recurrent spontaneous psychokinesis', in other words, psychokinesis that occurs repeatedly in a natural setting as opposed to the laboratory. Since the poltergeist phenomena tend to occur when one particular person is present, Roll believed that they were expressions of unconscious psychokinesis on the part of that person.

Roll created a typical scenario or set of conditions for poltergeist activity. It typically involved a child or teenager who harboured internal anger from some sort of stress within the family. Psychokinesis was an unconscious way of expressing that anger without the fear of punishment, and in most cases the child had no idea they were causing the disturbances. Roll also noticed that agents are often in a poor state of health physically or mentally, and in some cases psychotherapy eliminates the problem.

Despite Roll's convincing model of a typical poltergeist attack, other poltergeist investigators have been at pains to point out that in numerous cases the agent is emotionally stable. Some believe that the theory that poltergeists are **spirits** of the dead has been too often overlooked. Others suggest that the poltergeist activity is activated by a stressful situation but the activity is not psychokinesis from the agent but a projection of some element of the agent's personality into an apparition-like form. The form could then separate from the agent's body and be the cause of the disturbances.

POSITIVE THINKING

According to **psychics** and occultists, thoughts (also known as the **magical will**) are the key elements in helping us create and manifest our reality. Negative thoughts are said to create obstacles whereas positive thoughts create a path with hardly any obstacles. Positive thinking is believed to literally raise a person's energy, making it easier to open up intuitive ability.

POSSESSION

Condition in which a person feels they have been taken over, or 'possessed', mentally, physically and emotionally, by an outside **spirit** entity or separate personality. This

The power of positive thinking

In order to create your reality, psychics and occultists say you must start with your thoughts. You cannot desire or pray for something but at the same time believe you are never going to get it or do not deserve it. This is how powerful your thoughts are: negative attracts negative, whereas positive attracts positive.

If you think negative or bad thoughts, you literally create more negative or bad energy. If, however, you think joy, you create more joy. It works like this: if you walk into a room and assume you are going to have a problem with those in the room, you literally put yourself on guard, and the other party is subconsciously going to pick up on this attitude. Hence you will get exactly what you expect because negative draws negative. But walk into a room with a smile, believing you are surrounded by light and love, and people will respond positively to this because positive draws positive. This does not mean everything will go your way all the time but you will be clear enough in your mind to not take everything personally, respond appropriately and see the bigger picture.

---

entity then controls all aspects of their personality. Temporary possessions that take place during a **séance** are considered benign, as are voluntary possessions by gods or spirits that take place during religious and healing rituals; but more often it is a malevolent spirit or **demon** that attempts to take over the personality and life of an unwilling subject permanently.

Unwanted possessions have been recognized since ancient times and have been blamed for a number of problems and ills. The cure for unwanted possession is **exorcism**, performed according to a specific ritual. Except for possession by the Holy Spirit, Christianity regards possession as the work of the devil, and cases of demonic possession with formal exorcisms to remove them continue to be reported to this day.

Possession is not always viewed as demonic, even in the West. It is sometimes held that possessing spirits are souls of the dead who do not realize they are dead and try to return to a body, or that they are spirits who have a message they want to communicate to someone. In either case the victim experiences mood disorders, strange noises and lights, voices, **poltergeist** phenomena and, possibly, temporary insanity.

The belief that mental illness may be caused by possessing spirits is also an ancient one. A European offshoot of **spiritualism**, **spiritism**, founded by **Allan Kardec** in the nineteenth century, holds that certain mental illnesses have a spiritual cause and can be treated through communication with spirit guides. Kardec's theories caught on in France but not the rest of Europe. They have, however, found an enthusiastic response in Latin America, particularly in Brazil, where Brazilians still practise spiritist healing. In the early part of the twentieth century **James Hyslop**, president of the **American Society for Psychical Research**, put forward the theory that many people suffering from mental problems such as multiple personality disorder could be showing signs of possession. This view has the support of some psychiatrists, but it is not endorsed by the wider medical or scientific community.

POSTCOGNITION

See **Retrocognition**.

POWER SPOTS

There are certain areas of the earth that are regarded as power spots or places where subtle earth energies collect. It is thought that these places possess magical or **supernatural** energies and are the dwelling place for **spirits**.

The power at these power spots is thought to come from a spiritual force generated by **ley lines**. Ley lines are straight lines that connect these natural power points and where one or two ley lines cross, a power spot is created that is thought to naturally draw people to assemble or build structures, such as temples, churches and standing stones or **megaliths**, as is the case at **Stonehenge**. Today many people use **dowsing** rods to map out ley lines and the power spots for themselves. Many man-made structures at these power spots are also believed to have been constructed according to principles of sacred geometry, or sacred architecture.

There are thousands of power spots all over the earth. Mountains and water sources are particularly venerated for their healing powers. Many of the greatest power spots have some structure erected over them, such as the pyramids in Egypt, megalithic sites, burial grounds, temples and so on. **Paranormal** phenomena are often reported at power spots, including **apparitions**, **earth lights** and **poltergeist** activity. In addition individuals have also reported **psi** ability such as **clairvoyance** and **out-of-body experiences** when visiting such sites. Some believe that there is a link between geomagnetic field activity and psi activity in humans.

In 1977 the Dragon Project Trust was founded in Britain to research paranormal phenomena at ancient sites. It was hoped that understanding these phenomena might lead to an understanding of and perhaps communication with some form of planetary intelligence or **spirit**.

Prana

See **Universal life force**.

Pratt, Joseph Gaither [1910–1979]

American parapsychologist and associate of **J B Rhine** at Duke University, who is best known for his work with **mediums** and **poltergeists** and his contributions to experimental **parapsychology**.

In 1934 and 1935, while a graduate student working in Duke University's Parapsychology Laboratory, Pratt was put in charge of studying mediumistic communications with **Eileen Garrett**. When he analysed his data Pratt found that it supported a **paranormal** interpretation. Later he refined his methods of evaluating verbal material delivered in **trance** by devising a procedure called the Greville method, where sitters score items as right or wrong for them and then all items are judged against each other. In 1958 Pratt was sent by Rhine to investigate the **Seaford Poltergeist**: the first poltergeist case to be studied by the parapsychology laboratory. Along with **William Roll**, Pratt invented the term 'recurrent spontaneous psychokinesis' to describe poltergeist cases.

From 1962 until his death Pratt served as president of the **Psychical Research Foundation** and in the 1970s he became a trustee of the **American Society for Psychical Research**. He died in November 1979. A few years earlier he had set a com-bination lock; he'd refrained from writing down the combination, lest anyone discover it, but every year he opened the lock using a mnemonic phrase. If he survived death his aim was to communicate this phrase through a medium, but to date the lock remains closed.

Prayer

A form of communication, distant healing or thought projection with the divine or **supernatural**. The simplest forms of prayer are requests for oneself or others or thanksgivings. These are directions of psychic energy towards a goal and involve words, **symbols** and images.

Today more scientists are prepared to acknowledge the power of the mind to affect the material world, and although the scientific community isn't sure what to call this force, the spiritual community calls it God, the **universal life force**, **magical will** or **chi**. Many religions call efforts to direct this force prayer.

Numerous studies have explored the relationship between healing and prayer. In 1988, at San Francisco General Hospital, Dr Randolph Byrd conducted one of the most frequently cited studies. For 10 months he studied 193 patients with heart disease, assigning people to pray for half the patients and leaving the other half with no assigned prayer helpers. The patients who received prayers showed improvement rates up to 7 per cent higher than those who were not prayed for. This group also required less medication and suffered fewer deaths.

Recently **psi** researchers have investigated the distinction between directed and non-directed prayer. When you pray in a directed manner you have a specific goal and outcome in mind, as in 'I want to win the lottery.' In non-directed prayer you ask God for the highest good for all concerned. Spindrift, an organization based in Salem, Oregon concentrating on prayer research, conducted studies on plants to see which technique was more effective. They discovered that both forms of prayer were beneficial to plant growth, but that the non-directed technique was the more effective.

The results of the Spindrift studies suggest that a prayer healer is most helpful if the individual keeps his or her mind free of specific goals. In other words to simply pray for what is best for the person seems to be the most effective form of prayer. It is important to point out that although this approach worked best in the Spindrift studies it has not been widely tested on humans, and the jury is still out on the best way for a person to pray for their own or someone else's healing and growth.

Although a person doesn't need to believe in a specific God to pray, love, faith and **positive thinking** are considered important ingredients to increase the chances of success. This is because research has shown that the body–mind connection can exert a powerful influence over almost every aspect of life and the first step towards creating positive change is adopting a positive outlook. If a person doesn't choose to pray they can still achieve an optimistic attitude that increases their chances of success and happiness, by using their mind to direct their thoughts.

Psychic phenomena and power are associated with prayer and **meditation** in the literature of Western mystics, who often describe **clairvoyance**, **levitation**, **precognition** and so on as by-products of prayer. Early in the history of **parapsychology** attention was focused on the link between psi and prayer. Frank Laubach's best selling book, *Prayer: The Mightiest Force in the World* (1946), suggested that prayer had the power to change the world.

In the late 1960s **Karlis Osis** from the **American Society for Psychical Research** conducted experiments which showed that prayer done in a group was more powerful than prayer done by an individual, for a synergy of **brain waves**, as demonstrated by his research on meditators, often takes place in group dynamics.

PRECOGNITION

The ability to know impending events before they happen through **extrasensory perception** (**ESP**).

Precognition is the most frequently reported of all ESP experiences, occurring most often in **dreams**. It can be induced through **meditation** and **trance** but also occurs spontaneously in waking **visions**, hallucinations, thoughts that flash from nowhere into the mind and through a sense of somehow just knowing.

Most cases of spontaneous precognition occur within two days of the future event but some occur months or even years before. The majority concern unhappy events such as death and disaster, and psychical researchers estimate that about half of all precognitive experiences may prove helpful in averting disaster. In a number of cases intimacy is a key factor, with over 80 per cent of experiences involving a family member or loved one. The remainder involve strangers or casual acquaintances.

Since ancient times precognition has been known and valued. The difficulty with precognition as far as researchers are concerned is the individual's apparent ability to alter the future. If a precognitive experience reveals a flash of the future then the effects are seen before the causes, which, according to **quantum theory**, is impossible. The most widely held belief is that precognition offers a glimpse of a *possible* future that is based on current conditions and information and which can be altered depending upon acts of free choice.

A few researchers have attempted to explain precognition by proposing more complex theories of time. Our common sense impression of time is purely linear; at a given moment we are at one point on a continuum linking past, present and future. It has been proposed that it is possible to move above this linear dimension to another temporal plane where points in the past and future may be observed.

Another theory is that precognitive experiences somehow unleash powerful psychokinetic energy that helps create the future. In other words, the premonition becomes a self-fulfilling prophecy. In his book *Scared to Death*, written in the 1960s, London psychiatrist J A Barker revealed that people who died in the manner predicted by fortune tellers contributed to their own demise with their fear. Barker went on to establish the London Premonitions Bureau, which collected precognitive data with the aim of averting disaster.

Precognition may be difficult to understand but it is one of the easiest phenomena to test in the laboratory. In 1927 J W Dunne published the first serious study of precognition in the classic *An Experiment with Time*, and came to the conclusion that precognition is common, so common that many people fail to observe it, perhaps because they fail to remember their dreams or to interpret their dreams accurately. **J B Rhine** was the first researcher to establish precognition via tests. His experiments with **ESP cards** initially aimed to prove **telepathy** but also revealed strong evidence for precognition and **psychokinesis**.

PREDESTINATION

Ancient Greek belief that a person's fate has been established before birth, that he or she has no choice or free will but can only follow his or her destiny.

PREDICTION

A form of **prophecy** in which insight into the future is gained through the use of psychic ability, divine inspiration or the reading of signs. Prophecies tend to concern large groups of people, whereas predictions concern the individual or a small group of people. Predictions are based on knowledge gained via **intuition**, **dreams**, **precognition**, **visions**, **scrying** or reading signs such as is the case in **divination** methods like **numerology** or **astrology**. Predictions will be coloured by the perceptions of the individual.

PRE-EXISTENCE

Belief that the intact personality or soul exists prior to physical birth. See **Survival after death** and **Reincarnation**.

PREMONITION

A sense or feeling of foreboding concerning a possible event in the future. Premonition is similar to **precognition** but differs in that it conveys a sense or **gut feeling** of unease rather than specific knowledge, which is the case with precognition. Premonitions can occur in both the waking state and **dreams** and are regarded as an intuitive early warning system. Some cause people to change their plans or act in a different way than planned without knowing why.

In the 1960s researcher W E Cox did a survey of rail passenger loads on trains that had had accidents between 1950 and 1955 and compared them with passenger loads on days when no accident occurred. He discovered an incredible drop off in passenger counts on some of the days. Cox concluded that some people who had intended to travel on the days the accidents occurred had unconsciously altered their plans or missed the train by being late. Why some people did this is and some did not is unknown but it has been speculated that it may have something to do with an individual's overall psychic and/or intuitive openness.

On 21 October 1966, 29 adults and 116 children were killed in a landslide of coal waste that tumbled down a mountain in Aberfan, Wales and buried a school. Up to two weeks beforehand at least 200 people claimed to have experienced both premonitions and precognitions about the disaster. Premonitions included a feeling that something bad was about to happen, as well as sensations of choking and gasping for breath. Following the disaster the British Premonitions Bureau was established to collect warnings to potentially avert disaster. A year later, in 1968, the Central Premonitions Bureau was established in New York for the same reason. Unfortunately most of the tips these bureaux received did not come to pass or were too vague to be interpreted meaningfully.

PRESENCE

A subjective feeling that a person, animal, or **discarnate entity** is present.

Premonitions of disaster

The sinking of the *Titanic* remains the single most famous shipwreck of all times. Not surprisingly, it also represents the strongest case for the veracity of premonitions of disaster.

The story of the *Titanic* is well known. On 14 April 1912, the ship struck an iceberg and sunk in the North Atlantic, taking with her more than 1,500 lives. The lack of sufficient lifeboats has often been blamed as the leading cause of fatalities; however, what is significant here is the large number of premonitions that foretold this disaster.

Probably the first premonition came from author Morgan Robertson, who published a novel about a shipwreck in 1898, which reveals remarkable similarities to the circumstances surrounding the sinking of the *Titanic*. Another author, W T Stead, wrote numerous stories and articles predicting that a large ocean liner would sink with the loss of over half on board, due to the lack of sufficient lifeboats. Stead was also interested in psychic mediums, and allegedly received three separate warnings that can be easily linked to the *Titanic* disaster. Despite all these warnings, Stead booked a passage on the *Titanic*, and died in the disaster.

Several people went as far as to act on their premonitions and cancelled their passage. Second Engineer Colin MacDonald declined his position on the *Titanic* because of a 'hunch' that disaster lay ahead.

One of the most dramatic premonitions occurred as the *Titanic* was steaming past the Isle of Wight. Hundreds of people lined the coast to watch the largest ship in the world. Among them was a Miss Marshall who suddenly began to scream in horror: 'It's going to sink! That ship is going to sink! Do something! Are you so blind that you are going to let them drown? Save them! Save them!'

Later, after the disaster, investigators were amazed by the huge number of premonitions about the sinking, numbering (according to some accounts) to over 50. More sceptical investigators, after discarding 'vague forebodings' and 'after the fact claims of prescience', came up with the still impressive figure of 19 cases of premonition that occurred during the two weeks prior to the *Titanic's* sailing date of 10 April.

PRESLEY, ELVIS [1935–1977]

Sightings of Elvis, the King of Rock 'n' Roll, have been reported all over the world, even though he died on 16 August 1977.

Graceland, Presley's ranch located at 3734 Elvis Presley Boulevard in Memphis, is one of Tennessee's greatest tourist attractions. Every year, millions of Elvis fans and non-fans make the trip to Memphis to see the home of Elvis Presley. Ignoring the official reports of his death a number of fanatics are convinced Elvis is still alive and he has been spotted all over the world, from sporting events to the local corner store. The problem is that almost all these sightings describe Elvis as wearing his trademark white cloak and looking the same as he did when he died, nearly 30 years ago. This has led some to believe that perhaps it's not Elvis in life they are seeing, but instead his **ghost**.

Graceland is, not surprisingly, the place where the most sightings of his ghost appear. Since Elvis's living quarters are closed to the public, some believe his ghost still resides there.

PRETA

A type of **ghost** in Buddhist and Hindu lore.

In Hindu belief the preta is a tiny ghost of the dead, no bigger than a thumbnail, that resides in the corpse or lingers near the home of the dead person for one year after the funeral. When the year is ended rituals are performed to send the soul to heaven, where it will be rewarded for good deeds performed while on earth.

In Buddhist belief the preta or hungry ghost is the lowest segment of the wheel of life. Their task is to work off, in a state of constant hunger, the bad **karma** accumulated by anger, greed, envy, etc. Their hunger is only relieved when their karma

has been balanced. Pretas are said to have tiny throats and huge bellies. They are thought to live at crossroads, which are well-known hiding places for **witches**, **spirits** and ghosts of the **underworld**.

PRICE, HARRY [1881–1948]

One of the most influential and colourful figures in the history of ghost research, Price was instrumental in bringing ghost research to the general public and was the author of numerous popular books on the subject. He was heavily criticized by contemporaries within the psychical research field because of his flamboyant manner, his frequent use of trickery to keep an audience entertained and, most of all, his lack of scientific training.

Harry Price was born in London in 1881 and had his first encounter with the **supernatural** at the age of 15, when he locked himself and a friend overnight in a reportedly haunted house and allegedly saw a **ghost**. By the time he joined the **Society for Psychical Research** in 1920 he was already an expert on conjuring and fraudulent mediumship.

One of Price's first efforts exposed the work of **spirit** photographer **William Hope**, who was making a fortune taking portraits of people which always seemed to include the sitter's dead relatives. In May 1922 Price visited Munich to investigate the famous **medium** brothers, Willi and Rudi **Schneider**, at the laboratory of **Baron Albert von Schrenck-Notzing**, a flamboyant investigator. Price was impressed with what he saw there and later said that the experience had made him realize that not all physical phenomena could be explained in terms of deception.

Price now began to measure aspects of **séances** in a scientific manner. He managed to record strange temperature drops and other phenomena and from this time on devoted his time to pursuing genuine phenomena rather than debunking mediums, which did not sit well with the Society for Psychical Research.

The relationship between Price and the Society grew more and more strained. In 1923 he established his own National Laboratory for Psychical Research. It would take three additional years for the laboratory to get up and running but the fact that it was housed in the quarters of the London Spiritualist Alliance did not endear him to the conservative psychical researchers, and in 1927 the Society returned Price's donation of a massive book collection.

From 1925 to 1931 Price was foreign research officer for the **American Society for Psychical Research**. He was also one of the British delegates to the second International Congress on Psychical Research in Warsaw in 1923, where he investigated the Polish medium **Jan Guzyk**. Guzyk did not impress Price but a Romanian girl, Eleanore Zugan, did.

In 1929 Price invited the Schneider brothers to his laboratory for tests and a series of experiments was conducted. All were initially successful, but then in 1933 Price claimed to have photographic proof that the brothers were using trickery. This accusation earned him points with the academic community and finally, after years of rejection, the University of London accepted his book collection and a University Council for Psychical Investigation was set up in 1934. Three years later the University gave office space for the council and made room for Price's books and equipment. His library remains housed at the University of London today, as the Harry Price Library of Magical Literature.

Price was a prolific author and his books include *Confessions of a Ghost Hunter* (1936), *Fifty Years of Psychical Research* (1939) and *Poltergeist Over England* (1945). Also to his credit are contributions on Faith and Fire Walking in the 1936 edition of the *Encyclopaedia Britannica* and a film, *Psychical Research* (1941).

Outside of psychical research Price is perhaps best known for his investigation of **Borley Rectory** and for his popular books on the subject, *The Most Haunted House In England: Ten years investigation of Borley Rectory* (1940) and *The End of Borley Rectory* (1946). During his life suspicions that the phenomena Price reported were not entirely genuine were harboured, but they were not made public until after his death, in *The Haunting of Borley Rectory* written by Trevor Hall, Eric Dingwall and K M Goldney (1956).

PROPHECY

A divinely inspired **vision** which is a form of **precognition** or knowledge of the future. Throughout history prophecies have been made through **oracles**, prophets, prophetesses and psychically gifted lay-people. The Old Testament has a large number of prophecies and the New Testament has the Book of Revelation in which St John gives an account of his vision of the end of the world. In Islam, Muhammad is chosen to be last of all the prophets. **Nostradamus** also discusses future history in verse and **Joan of Arc** was said to have visions of the future for France. The most famous prophet of the twentieth century was **Edgar Cayce**, while American psychic **Jeanne Dixon** prophesied the death of John F Kennedy.

Proxy sitting

A **séance** in which another person sits in on behalf of the person receiving communication from the **spirit** world.

Proxy sitting is an attempt by psychical researchers to eliminate the possibility of **telepathy** during a séance. Typically a third party goes to the sitting in place of the person who desires evidence of spirit communication. This proxy sitter knows nothing about the person he or she represents, nor about the deceased who will be requested to communicate. Thus, although **clairvoyance** or other **ESP** phenomena may be in operation, telepathy from the sitter is ruled out as the explanation of any information the **medium** may give.

Pseudopod

Term used for the **ectoplasmic** material that emerges from a **medium** and develops into a false hand or arm.

The first recorded pseudopods were attributed to **Eusapia Palladino** in 1894. In sittings with Professor Charles Richet and **Frederick Myers** she allegedly produced a third arm and hand, which had the ability to lift and push objects, but her emanations were soon to be spectacularly outdone by the ectoplasmic emanations of French medium Marthe Béraud. From 1909 to 1913 investigators witnessed writhing tentacles extruding from Béraud's mouth, ears, eyes and nose. Sometimes the tentacles would assume the faces or shapes resembling popular government or historical figures. Critics noticed that some of the faces were identical to magazine photographs. In 1911 Béraud allegedly produced a pseudopod that resembled an unformed baby. She was totally naked at the time. Sceptics argued that such occurrences were sexual rather than **paranormal** manifestations.

Medium **Mina Crandon** claimed that many of the phenomena produced at her **séances** were the work of a pseudopod that also emanated from between her legs. The pseudopod formed hands, rang bells and threw objects. Photographs taken at the time show a poorly formed hand that resembles a filled glove.

Psi

An acronym derived from 'paranormal sensory information' and used to describe **ESP**, **psychokinesis** and other related powers. Psi is also the 23rd letter of the Greek alphabet and was traditionally associated with psychic phenomena because it was the first letter of the word *psyche*, meaning 'breath', 'spirit', 'life' and 'soul'. Occultists believe psi to be a vibration that manifests in the universe but scientists are unwilling to accept this explanation due to lack of evidence.

In 1946 English psychologist Dr Robert Thouless and his colleague, Dr W P Weisner, started to use the term psi to describe ESP and psychokinesis because they were so closely linked. The term has since expanded to include almost any **paranormal** phenomena or experience.

Decades of research on psi have bought researchers no closer to understanding how it functions; all that is known is that it operates outside the boundaries of space and time. It has been suggested that psi is some kind of wave, force or particle but all these theories have been discarded as psi is not affected by the laws of physics. Neither is it subject to the laws of thermodynamics or the law of gravity. It does not require any exchange of energy and is not governed by the laws of relativity, which holds that nothing can move faster than the speed of light. The inability of researchers to explain psi scientifically has forced some to look for alternative explanations.

One way researchers have attempted to identify psi is through measurements of involuntary physiological processes in the automatic nervous system. The Galvanic test response (GSR), which measures sweat gland activity, the plethysmograph, which measures changes in blood volume, and the electroencephalograph (EEG), which measures brain wave activity are the most common measures used. The measures monitor emotional arousal and show that automatic nervous system activity increases when information that is emotionally charged for the subject appears to be conveyed psychically.

Ganzfeld stimulation experiments have revealed that an alpha state of **brain wave** activity is most conducive to psi. Psi performance also seems to improve with **positive thinking** and expectation and a friendly atmosphere. It decreases with anxiety, negative thinking, boredom and a hostile atmosphere.

Psi hitting and psi missing

In laboratory guessing games tests for **psi**, a correct response is called a psi hit and an incorrect response is called a psi miss. The results of hits and misses are calculated against chance. The performance of a test subject in psi tests can be affected by his or her mood and overall attitude towards psi. It can also be affected by the environment created by the experimenter, the mood and attitude towards psi of the experimenter and by boredom.

PSYCHE

According to psychiatrist **Carl Jung** the psyche is the mind or spirit of a person, consisting of the conscious part of the brain, the ego, the **unconscious** and the **shadow**. If the ego and the shadow are in harmonious balance a person will enjoy physical and mental wellbeing, but if either the ego or the shadow dominated the personality, anxiety and neurosis can occur.

PSYCHIC

Used as a noun the term psychic describes someone with ability to acquire information through **extrasensory perception** (**ESP**) and a host of other **paranormal** abilities such as **telepathy**, **precognition**, **clairvoyance**, etc. Used as an adjective it is an umbrella term used to describe the essence of these paranormal powers.

The word psychic comes from the Greek word *psyche* meaning 'spirit' or 'soul'. Throughout history psychics have appeared. They have taken many roles, from priests and priestesses to prophets, healers, **shamans** and **witches**. In recent times there have been efforts to integrate psychics into professional fields such as archaeology and criminology. Psychics are not necessarily the same as **mediums**, who obtain their information from **spirits** of the dead, but a psychic may possess mediumistic abilities. Occultists believe that everyone is born with psychic ability and tapping into it is just a matter of training and practice. A large number of people do claim to be psychic but few reach the level of exceptional psychics, and even the latter are not accurate or able to perform on demand 100 per cent of the time. Psychics are either born with their talents, or some emotional or physical stress triggers that ability later in life, or their psychic ability is developed by study and practice. Typically psychics find their ability unsettling,

Stimulating your psychic senses

The exercises below are classic psychic development exercises for beginners. They are all designed to stimulate your mind and help you become more open to psychic impressions. They will help you cross a very special line – the line between your non-psychic self (your physical self and five senses) and your psychic self (your mind, thoughts and spirit).

Walking backwards
For this exercise you don't have to walk backwards, you have to remember backwards. It sounds simple but it's harder

than you think and is an extremely powerful way to stimulate your mind.

Choose a quiet, comfortable place where you can pay attention to your thoughts and not be interrupted. Take a deep breath to relax your body and prepare your mind. Start from this moment and remember the events of the day backward to the moment you got up.

If you get stuck go back for just a chunk and then work forwards to untangle yourself. As you think backwards don't push yourself. You may only manage five- to ten-second bursts at first, but a mere ten or fifteen seconds now and then is sufficient for psychic purposes.

Different levels

Choose something familiar that you see or use every day – your coat, for example. Now you are going to think about your coat on four different levels:

* *Level one: Think about your particular coat. What colour is it? Where did you buy it? Have you had good or bad times wearing it? In short just think about your coat and your associations with it.*
* *Level two: Think about coats in general – think of all coats everywhere. Coats you like. Coats you dislike. How coats are made.*
* *Level three: Think of the purpose of coats. What do they do? Why do people wear them?*

* *Level four: Think about the quality coats have in the abstract, universal sense. For example, protection and warmth are the main features of coats. So let your mind focus on the image of warmth in the broadest sense. You might think of fire, or the taste of warm comforting soup.*

Scanning

Scanning is about seeing the energy of others. The next time you meet someone new take a moment to imagine that person as a ball of light or pure energy. Now scan that person from top to bottom, bottom to top, noticing any words, images, colours, thoughts and sensations that you feel.

If you can, write these impressions down. Once you get to know the person better, look back at your notes. Do your first impressions make sense?

Tomorrow is another day

Choose a comfortable place where you can concentrate on your thoughts. Close your eyes and breathe deeply, then project yourself into the next day. See yourself following through your plans for tomorrow. See, hear, feel and taste what your day will be like. What will you be wearing? Who will you meet?

When you are through, write down your impressions and read over them tomorrow night to find out if you were able to make any predictions.

confusing and in some cases terrifying at first, but in time the majority learn to live with their gifts and use them.

PSYCHIC ARCHAEOLOGY

The use of **psychic** skills in the field of archaeology, in particular to locate sites and identify artefacts. Psychic skills employed include **psychometry**, **dowsing**, **retrocognition**, **clairvoyance** and **automatic writing**. Also known as intuitive archaeology, psychic archaeology has had some good results but it remains a controversial technique.

A dramatic example of psychic archaeology in practice happened in 1893 when Herman V Hilprecht was able to decipher a cuneiform inscription following a dream in which an ancient Temple priest gave him vital information. But perhaps the most famous case was that of **Frederick Bligh Bond's** use of automatic writing while excavating the ruins of **Glastonbury** Abbey in England. Bond was asked by the Church of England in 1907 to find the remains of two chapels. He employed the services of his friend, John Bartlett, who was an automatic writer and with him requested the help of **spirits** to help him locate the ruins. According to Bond, entities that collectively called themselves the 'watchers of the other side' gave him the details of the chapels' locations, and when excavation began he found everything exactly as the spirits had allegedly told him.

Psychic archaeology has been used since the 1960s to find dig sites all over the world. Canadian archaeologist J Norman Emerson worked with psychic George McMullen and in the 1970s the two men went to Egypt to test the viability of psychic archaeology. McMullen was able to provide information that helped locate the ruins of Mark Antony's palace and the probable sites of the library of Alexandria and Cleopatra's palace.

Sceptics point to experiments that show that psychic archaeology is not reliable, and argue that archaeologists naturally use knowledge and instinct to guide them. Despite this psychic archaeology is still considered by some to be a valuable aid when attempting to locate sites and uncover information about the past.

PSYCHIC ATTACK

An alleged **supernatural** attack that causes physical and/or emotional distress to a human or animal. It is typically caused by non-physical agents, such as **thought forms**, **spirits** and **demons**, which attack a person, mentally and/or physically. In most, but not all, cases these agents are sent by one person to another.

Occultists believe that psychic attacks are the manipulation of supernatural energies and forces. They occur when dark and negative energetic vibrations are sent from one individual to another or to a place, creating disturbances in the energetic and physical bodies of that person or place.

This negative energy can be called a spirit, an **entity**, a thought form or a dark negative energy. Each of these energies can create harmful effects within the person receiving them. Some of these dark energies are sent unconsciously, for example, when a person thinks negative things about someone else. Others are sent intentionally to create harm and damage, often to control, manipulate or punish the individual. They can involve the psychic powers of the mind and/or ritualistic techniques or ceremonies, typically when the moon is either new or waning, as the moon is said to govern psychic forces and these phases rule the so-called left hand or evil path of magic.

Almost every culture has its techniques of psychic attack, from the **Huna** death prayer, to the **Voodoo** dolls of Haiti. In **sorcery** the equivalent of psychic attack is the **curse**. One of the most well-known examples of psychic attack is **hag** syndrome, in which a victim awakes from their sleep to feel a crushing weight on their chest.

In her classic text, *Psychic Self-Defence* (1930), occultist **Dion Fortune** said that psychic attack was much more common than believed. She gave an account of her own experience of psychic attack. When she was 20 she believed she was psychically attacked by her employer, which depleted her **aura** to such an extent that she suffered a nervous breakdown.

According to Fortune symptoms of psychic attack include overwhelming feelings of dread and fear, nervous exhaustion, mental breakdown, poor health, bruises on the body and **poltergeist** phenomena. The prescribed defences against psychic attack are to sever all contact with the suspected people and places; to avoid going to the sea, for water is the **element** of psychic forces; to keep the stomach full as this shuts down the psychic points of entry; to get plenty of sunshine; to avoid being alone; and to undertake certain protective and banishing rituals. See **Psychic protection**.

Most psychical researchers assume that if psychic attack works it is through suggestion, and that superstitious, poorly educated people are likely to be the most gullible and therefore the most vulnerable. It seems, however, that well educated, non-superstitious people are not immune to psychic attack, and that even domestic animals, not normally expected to react to suggestion, are affected. Occultists believe that psychic attack is real and, although they admit that in certain circumstances suggestion plays a part, they believe that the real technique operates via the **astral plane**.

PSYCHIC COLD

A situation in which a person feels unnaturally cold. There are thought to be two types of psychic cold. In the first a **spirit** materializes and draws energy from the environment, resulting in a lowering of temperature. In the second the materializing spirit will draw energy from people that are present in a **séance**. The people will feel cold but the thermometer will not register a lowering of the ambient temperature.

PSYCHIC CRIMINOLOGY

The use of **psychics** and/or psychic ability in the investigation of criminal cases and the location of missing persons.

From ancient times **seers** and dowsers have been petitioned to help solve crimes and mysteries, but it wasn't until the mid-nineteenth century that the field of psychic criminology really developed, when American physiologist Joseph R Buchanan coined the term **psychometry**. According to Buchanan objects retain imprints of the past and their owners that can be picked up by psychics, and psychics who handled objects belonging to crime victims could provide important information to the police.

Psychic detection was used during the world wars, and by the latter part of the twentieth century hundreds of psychics were working regularly with the police all over the world, although their success was variable. Today some law enforcement agencies maintain close links with psychics whereas others will have nothing to do with them. If a psychic does come up with helpful information, more often than not the news is kept from the public. When headline-grabbing cases occur the police often find themselves swamped with calls from psychics, the great majority of which are of no help whatsoever.

Police psychics often prefer to call themselves intuitives, **sensitives** or viewers in an attempt to have their efforts taken more seriously. Most of their detection work involves psychometry of items belonging to the missing person or, if a murder has taken place, from items at the crime scene. Allegedly by handling these items they are able to see images or receive information relevant to the crime. Some also receive information through **channelling, dreams, automatic writing**, flashes of **intuition** and **dowsing**. In some cases psychics will visit the scene of the crime to pick up useful information.

Lawyers also sometimes use psychics in selecting jurors and witnesses that will be beneficial to their case. Psychics may advise lawyers as to whether or not clients are lying. Results are variable but many lawyers remain open to the possibility of psychic help. It has been argued in America that psychics who read a suspect's mind are violating constitutional rights but as long as psychics are not called to the witness stand this is unlikely to be contested in court.

PSYCHIC HEALING

Therapeutic technique which is said to involve the **channelling** or transfer of psychic power or **universal life force** through the healer to the patient. It often involves the **laying on of hands** and/or **prayer** and healers claim to use psychic powers to cure illness.

PSYCHIC PHOTOGRAPHY

General term used to designate the documentation of the **paranormal** through photographic images. See also **Kirlian** photography, **Spirit photography** and **Thoughtography**.

PSYCHIC PROTECTION

Phrase used to define practices and routines designed to protect a person's energy from **psychic attack** and **curses**. These routines can be complex and detailed, such as conjuring up certain **spells** and **charms**, or they can be extremely simple, such as imagining oneself surrounded by a spinning wall of light that protects against negative energies. Psychic protection routines can also be performed by healers prior to treating someone so that they don't pick up the ill energy of a patient. They can also be used as a guard against everyday energy drains, like pollution or angry and depressed people.

Occultists believe that most forms of psychic attack take place through the **astral plane** by making contact with the victim and manifesting in his or her subconscious mind. Because of this astral association psychic protection will normally involve the visualization of defence structures

Psychic protection

Here are some simple psychic protection/self-defence exercises that only take a few minutes to do and can be done as many times a day as you feel a need.

* *Shield of light: When sensing a negative atmosphere it is easy to imagine yourself wrapped or surrounded in brilliant light of whatever colour most appeals to you. Once this is done, imagine yourself and those you love being covered in this protective light, which acts like a reflective shield, to bounce negative energy away from you and yours.*
* *Orb of light: This can easily be combined with the method above. Image an orb of white (or blue if this seems more effective) light hovering and sending out rays of light about 9 inches to a foot above the crown of the head.*
* *Colour defences: Imagine strong colours of white, silver or gold light around you. Let these cling to your body and then move out to about a foot away from the body.*
* *Mirrors: Another way to protect yourself if you feel threatened is to envision a circle of mirrors around you that face outwards. Do not visualize these mirrors reflecting the negativity back to whomever or whatever it came from but rather upwards towards the heavens to be dissipated.*

on the astral plane to stop external influences coming in. Methods of psychic protection vary but most involve the use of **visualizations** where a person imagines him or herself surrounded and protected by a shield of healing light. **Amulets** can also be worn for protection. The theory behind all these techniques is to activate and strengthen the **aura**, the energy field that surrounds everyone. A strong aura is thought to protect against psychic attack.

PSYCHIC READING

A sitting with a **psychic** or **medium** in which the psychic uses their psychic ability to answer questions, predict the future, give advice or speak with the dead. In most but not all cases the psychic will charge a fee for the reading.

Throughout history psychics have offered their services to people. Methods vary according to the individual psychic. Some will simply rely on their powers whereas others will use methods such as **astrology**, **tarot**, **palmistry** and so on to tap into their powers. Most psychics prefer to work in comfortable, pleasant environments and in low light, as they say it enhances their attunement to the sitter; some psychics give readings over the phone.

Reputable and responsible psychics do not believe their clients should seek frequent readings or become dependent on them for making decisions, as they believe that readings are simply one of many tools

a person can use for personal growth and self-knowledge.

PSYCHIC SELF-DEFENCE

See **Psychic protection**.

PSYCHIC SURGERY

Healing technique when a psychic allegedly performs surgery with his or her bare hands without administering anaesthetics to the patient who remains fully conscious throughout the procedure and allegedly experiences no pain. Simple knives or bare hands instead of surgical instruments are used to remove tumours and diseased organs and repair damaged tissue. The psychic surgeon claims that the power to cure comes from **paranormal** powers or the guidance of **spirit** helpers.

Some psychic surgeons say they operate only on the **etheric body** of the patient; they do not touch the flesh but make hand passes and signs in the air above the body. Others claim to cut into the body with hands, kitchen knives or scissors to remove growths. The operations are often accompanied by spurting blood and the production of lumpy masses said to be tumours. The patient is left with little or no scar if an incision was made and walks out to resume their daily lives. If patients complain of pain, surgeons often blame it on spirits, past life **karma** or lack of healing vibrations between the patient and surgeon. Some psychic surgeons also give spiritual injections, in which the surgeon points his finger and allegedly injects the patient with spiritual medicine. In some cases patients who have been 'injected' report feeling tingling or jabbing sensations.

This controversial healing method is practised mainly in Brazil and the Philippines and while a few observed surgeries remain unexplained many have been exposed as fraud. 'Tumours' removed have been found to be animal organs or balls of cotton or pebbles. Animal blood has been concealed in little bags and then squirted out on to the patient. Using diversion techniques, such as sheets and wads of cotton, the appearance of surgical penetration has been created by folding the knuckles against the skin.

The high level of fraudulent practice that has been exposed over the years prevents the serious study of psychic surgery by parapsychologists, but it is possible that some psychic surgeons have the ability to stimulate the body's natural healing processes.

The most well-known psychic surgeon to emerge in the twentieth century was Jose Pedro de Feitas of Brazil, known by his nickname Arigo, who allegedly treated several hundred patients for two decades, correctly diagnosing their illnesses and writing out correct prescriptions. In operations his trademark was a rusty knife and it was said that he could stop blood flow with verbal commands. He claimed to be guided by a Dr Fritz, the spirit of a dead German doctor. Between 1958 and 1964 Arigo was jailed by the Brazilian Medical Association for illegal medical practices. In 1968 he was investigated by an American doctor, Andrija Puharich, who came to the conclusion that Arigo controlled some form of life energy.

PSYCHIC VAMPIRE

Term used by occultists for someone who is believed to suck mental energy out of another person. This can be done unconsciously through the presence of a needy and/or gloomy person or it can be done through a concerted spiritual attack, such as **curses** or **voodoo**.

According to **Dion Fortune**, author of the classic *Psychic Self-Defence* (1930), psychic vampirism is rare. She defines a psychic vampire as someone with sharp teeth who travels astrally at night to bite victims and suck the life blood out of them. The term has since been used by occultists to mean any person whose presence is draining or depressing.

Everyone has experiences with people who seem to lower their energy level rather than raise it. They are the kind of person who has low self-esteem, is never satisfied with anyone or anything and always wants constant reassurance from other people to make them feel better. They are not, however, interested in getting better but only in feeding off the optimism, energy and care of others, which is why they are always attracted to caring people.

There are numerous methods of **psychic protection** to use, from spells and rituals to simple psychic self-defence routines, such as visualizing a great shield of protective light.

See also **Psychic attack**.

PSYCHICAL RESEARCH

Archaic term, with its origins in the late nineteenth century, to designate the scientific study of the **paranormal**. Now largely superseded by the term **Parapsychology**.

PSYCHICAL RESEARCH FOUNDATION

Non-profit organization devoted to research and education on **survival after death** and other **paranormal** phenomena, such as **near-death experiences, out-of-body experiences** and **poltergeists**.

The Psychical Research Foundation (PRF) was founded in 1960 by Charles E Ozanne, a benefactor of the parapsychology laboratory at Duke University, who became dissatisfied with progress made there. **J G Pratt** was named president and **William Roll** was named as administrator and project director. The PRF was initially based at Duke University but in 1962 Roll took the headquarters to Durham, North Carolina and then to Georgia College in California when he was offered a teaching position there.

The best-known research conducted by the PRF is Roll's investigation of poltergeists, described in his book *The Poltergeist* (1972). The PRF also hosted an important out-of-body experiment involving **psychic** Keith Harray and one of his kittens. When the kitten was placed in an enclosure by itself it got distressed, but when Harray allegedly visited the kitten out-of-body the kitten calmed down.

PSYCHOGRAPH

Supernatural curiosity much in evidence at the beginning of the twentieth century. Allegedly psychographs were photographs on which appeared ghostly messages or scripts from people who had died. The blurred and often illegible words appeared on photographs of relatives who posed in the hope of being contacted. Virtually all psychographs were exposed as **frauds** and the subject was discussed and the methods of perpetrating the fraud explained in *Ghost Photographs* (1923) by psychical researcher Fred Barlow.

PSYCHOKINESIS [PK]

General term for using the mind to control matter – without using any outside physical force. The term psychokinesis comes from the Greek words *psyche*, meaning 'breath', 'life' or 'soul', and *kinein*, meaning 'to move'. It is thought to occur spontaneously and therefore unconsciously, as may be the case in **hauntings**, **apparitions** and **poltergeists**, but it is also thought to occur deliberately and through conscious effort.

Psychokinesis could be said to be a form of **psi** where the mind influences matter through invisible means, but what psychokinesis is and how it actually operates remains a mystery. Psychokinesis can include activities such as **prayer** and healing to influence the outcome of events or amazing feats like **table-tilting**, **fire walking**, **metal bending** and the movement of objects. An individual who is psychokinetic can influence an object from a great distance or in a close proximity to their selves. Some psychokinetics can also manipulate their own bodies and mind.

Psychokinesis has been observed and recorded throughout history. **Levitations**, healings and movement of objects have been attributed to holy people all over the world. Magic **spells**, **curses** and rituals may all involve psychokinesis. For example, the **evil eye** is the universal belief that certain individuals have the power to harm with a look. Psychokinesis has been frequently observed in mediumship in alleged **materializations**, **apports**, levitations, and table tipping. **Rudi Schneider** and **D D Home** were two **mediums** renowned for their psychokinetic abilities.

Since the 1930s psychokinesis has been a major interest for parapsychologists and researchers, particularly in the United States and the former Soviet Union. Statistical results from laboratory experiments have so far produced inconclusive reports.

The conclusion frequently drawn is that psychokinesis does occur but it is not known how or under what circumstances, although there are indications that it is affected by anxiety and boredom.

A significant contribution to psychokinetic research was made by **J B Rhine** at Duke University, North Carolina. He began studying the subject in 1934 and experiments with a gambler who claimed to be able to influence the way dice fell yielded positive results beyond the possibilities of chance. Unfortunately follow-up research yielded uneven results but it was found that subjects tended to score better early in the experimental sequence, before boredom set in. Rhine noticed that psychokinesis did not seem to be connected to any physical processes of the brain or the laws of psychics. It seemed to be a non-physical force of the mind that could act on matter, even if that matter was far away. Rhine also found that psychokinesis is affected by the mental state of the subject and is similar to **extrasensory perception** (**ESP**). In fact he concluded that ESP is a necessary part of the psychokinetic process and one is unlikely to occur without the other.

Thanks to Rhine's pioneering work, from the 1940s onwards psychokinesis was no longer limited to **physical mediumship** but fell into two classes: **macro PK** (observable effects) and **micro PK** (weaker effects, requiring statistical analysis to evaluate), with emphasis placed on the latter.

In the late 1960s, American physicist Helmut Schmidt devised an apparatus called the 'electronic coin flipper', which operated on the random delay of radioactive particles. Subjects were asked to exert mental energy to flip a coin to tails or heads so that bulbs on the device would light up in one direction or another. Some were successful. The electronic coin flipper was the precursor for random event generators, computerized methods that have played a significant role in recent tests for both ESP and psychokinesis. Schmidt also conducted experiments on animal psychokinesis, but it proved difficult to tell if it were the animals or the researchers that were using psychokinesis ability.

During the 1970s and 80s a number of psychokinetic experiments were conducted on humans, animals, plants and microorganisms and enzymes. In many of these experiments a so-called 'linger effect' has been noticed. For example, temperatures that have been influenced by psychokinesis continue to rise and fall for a period of time after the experiment has finished. Although results have been less than impressive there have been some successes and researchers continue to believe that the area has potential, particularly for healing purposes.

In recent years, the term 'remote influencing' has become popular to describe the application of psychokinesis to biological systems. This may be to impact either positively or negatively upon health, mood or to influence decision making.

PSYCHOKINETIC ENERGY

The hypothetical energy source which fuels **psychokinesis** and other similar **psi** phenomena.

PSYCHOMANTEUM

Term used to refer to a place where communication with the dead can take place, such as the **oracles** that were commonplace in ancient Greece.

Modern interest in the concept of the psychomanteum was triggered by Dr Raymond Moody, who coined the term **near-death experience**. Moody first became interested in mirror gazing in the late 1980s and began to investigate ancient oracular practices and folklore about **mirrors** as portals to other dimensions. He eventually came to the conclusion that a mirror could be of benefit to those grieving the loss of loved ones, as the mirror, as a portal to the **otherworld**, could help bring closure. As he continued to research he considered the **visions** in a mirror to be more than **imagery** as they could take a person into the middle realm – another dimension, similar to **dreams**, which mediates between the physical realm and other realms.

In order to experiment further Moody constructed his own walk-in psychomanteum from a closet at home. The idea behind the psychomanteum is to eliminate as much outside distraction as possible so that the inner eye can see in the mirror. He covered the floor, walls and ceiling of his cupboard with black carpet and constructed it in such a way that a person could sit in the psychomanteum and not see his or her own reflection. In this way, if the person relaxed and gazed steadily into the mirror, the mirror could become the gateway through which the inner eye – or psychic vision – could see the unseen.

Moody spent many years researching and experimenting with the psychomanteum as a way to resolve grief. Numerous people reported a wide variety of experiences in it, from holding conversations with the dead to catching glimpses of the **afterlife**. Moody published his research in his book, *Reunions: Visionary Encounters with Departed Loved Ones* (1993).

Psychometry

The ability to gain intuitive impressions of an object's past history and associations simply by touching or handling it.

An American professor of physiology, Joseph R Buchanan (1814–1899), coined the term psychometry in the 1840s after observing experiments in which students were able to identify drugs held in tubes simply by holding the tubes. He saw psychometry as a way of measuring the 'soul' of things. The term is derived from the Greek word *psyche*, meaning 'soul' and *metron*, meaning 'to measure'. The concept of measuring soul refers to the idea that every object possesses certain vibrations that reflect its inner essence, and that these vibrations can be read by people open to them.

In 1854 American geology professor William Denton took Buchanan's ideas a stage further when he found that his sister was able to record vivid mental images of the appearance of geological specimens wrapped around her head. He recorded his experiments in his book, *The Soul of Things*.

During the height of **spiritualism** psychometry was popular at **séances**. Typically a **medium** would handle a sealed envelope and reveal the contents inside. They might also take a ring, watch or similar object that had been in close contact with a person and read the past and present of the object and those who have been in close contact with it for any length of time.

From 1919 to 1922 psychical researcher Gustav Pagenstecher conducted over a hundred psychometry experiments with a medium called Maria Reyes de Zierold. If given an object Maria would fall into a **trance** and provide information about its past and present. Pagenstecher came to the conclusion that this was not **telepathy** but the ability to pick up vibrations imprinted on the object by the thoughts of the object's owner.

Psychics and **sensitives** have traced lost and stolen property and even found missing people through the use of psychometry (see **Psychic criminology**). Metal is thought to be the best psychically conductive material and if an object has been owned by several people a psychometrist may pick up information about all of them.

The theory is that everything that has ever existed has left its mark, and this applies to people and places too. People can be psychometrized. The **percipient** focuses on a person and tries to pick up impressions and information. Places can also be psychometrized and a psychometrist can tune into past events when they are receptive to the vibrations of a place. It has been suggested that haunted houses demonstrate this on a large scale – events have taken place and left their impressions in the rooms to be picked up by psychics.

Psychometry exercise

It is thought that everyone has the ability to psychometrize, although regular practice is needed to tap into it. The steps are easy and the following exercise will help develop the ability.

Take five samples of different substances – cloth, cotton, leather, fur, wood, metal or stone. Sit in a comfortable position and close your eyes. Take a few deep, relaxing breaths. Choose an object and hold it in your hand. Concentrate fully on that object; feel its texture; think about its origins. Don't rush. Pay attention to images that come to your mind. You may receive fragments of information. They may come in words, feelings, symbols or a physical sensation. Some people just hold the object in their hands, others hold it over their forehead or their heart. Experiment till you find what comes naturally to you. If you pick up a strong impression that is upsetting try to shift your perspective to being an observer of the information and not an absorber of it.

Go through each of the five objects several times, ideally for five to ten minutes, and then place the samples in individual envelopes. The envelopes should all look the same from the outside so you have no idea what is inside.

Go through the concentration exercise again, but this time try to pick up a clue regarding what is in the envelope. You may find that you get a clear impression of the object inside or an impression of its origin – tree, animal, mountain, etc. When you are finished you may want to shake or wash your hands to release any of the vibrational impressions that came to you from the objects you were handling.

Move on to actual objects to see how you do with them. Take a friend's ring, watch or brooch. As you hold the object first think of the thing itself. Then ask yourself who has handled it the most? Where has it come from? How was it made? See if you can get a picture of a previous owner. Practise as much as you can with a wide variety of objects from a number of different people. Initially concentrate on personal objects and avoid coins, as they have been handled by too many people. You can also do this with letters; hold a sealed letter in your hands and try to pick up what is in the letter and who wrote it. Check your results and keep a record of them.

Many psychics regard psychometry as a form of **clairsentience**, which is perhaps the most common form of psychic ability. For this reason it is often recommended that beginners focus on psychometry as a first step to awakening their psychic powers. It is said that the ability can be mastered in a few months and lends itself to a natural progression towards more challenging skills.

PSYCHOPOMP

In mythology and folklore all over the world psychopomps are soul conductors: mythical beings with the ability to search for lost **souls**, find them and guide them to the **afterlife**. According to lore, in some cases when a death occurs the soul is caught unprepared and may not know where it is or where it should go. It is the job of the psychopomp to find that soul and conduct it safely to the **underworld**. Animals, such as **dolphins**, can be psychopomps, as well as deities and **spirits**. In shamanistic tradition **shamams** use mythical horses as psychopomps to conduct them to the underworld where they can commune with spirits.

PSYCHOTRONICS

Psychotronics is an interdisciplinary study of the relationship between matter, energy and consciousness. It was developed in Eastern Europe but has gained a following in the West and in the United States.

The term psychotronics was coined by Czechoslovakian researchers in the 1960s as a replacement for the term **parapsychology**, and the first international congress on the subject was held in Prague in 1973. In 1975 the United States Psychotronics Association was founded. Psychotronics is based on the theory that everything is comprised of humanity, universe and psychotronic energy, which is the **universal life force** in all living things.

Psychotronics focuses its research on applying psychotronic energy to other fields such as medicine, physics and psychology. Its particular interest is in harnessing cosmic energy in devices. The idea that psychic energy can be transmitted from humans to objects dates back to the eighteenth century, when German chemist Baron Karl von Reichenback suggested that energy could be stored. In the 1920s devices were designed that seemed to show movement when gazed upon by a human. In the late 1960s Czech inventor Robert Pavlia produced psychotronic generators which allegedly collected energy from any bological source and then used it to enhance plant growth. In the United States a device called a psionic generator was designed by Woodrow Ward in the 1970s. The device was allegedly activated by energy from the eyes.

In general the field of psychotronics is not recognized by mainstream science. Credibility has been further strained by its association with ideas that governments may be secretly developing psychotronic weapons for mass mind control.

Puca

A **spirit** in Irish folklore that is said to be both helpful and mischievous. According to lore the puca (also known as the pooka) can change shape and is often seen in the guise of a black animal. He may favour humans and protect them from evil, and even perform household chores such as cleaning and tidying, but people who are not grateful will incur his anger. In English folklore puca is known as Puck, a household spirit who in medieval times was thought to be particularly malicious. Puck is also known as Robin Goodfellow and is said to be the child of a human girl and a **fairy** who has the ability to change into animals and play tricks on humans.

Purgatory

A state of transition where it is said the soul goes to await judgement following the death of the physical body. Within the Roman Catholic belief system a soul in purgatory may atone for sins committed during its physical life and then qualify for eternal life in heaven.

Purposeful Ghost

A term used to describe a **ghost** that returns with a purpose for its **haunting** activity, such as to direct the living to the location of a hidden body or treasure, or to pass along a message that was left uncommunicated in life. Once the purpose has been fulfilled, these types of ghosts are normally never reported again.

Pyramid power

The geometry of the four-sided conical shape of the pyramid is alleged to generate **supernatural** powers. Pyramids are ancient structures found throughout the world, and are thought to have been built for ceremonial purposes or as burial chambers. Various **occult** theories suggest they were used for **initiation** into sacred mysteries or were the focus for cosmic forces.

According to the Egyptian **Book of the Dead** the power of the pyramid awakens the god who sleeps in the person's **soul**, and pyramid power is the belief that pyramids or sitting beneath a pyramid shape can enrich a person's psychic and healing power. It is thought by some that pyramids act as repositories or transformers of the earth's magnetic energies and atmosphere. The unique shape of the pyramid sucks vibrational energy from the earth up to the peak of the pyramid and at the same time cosmic or solar radiation is attracted to the peak, in an effect described as 'lightning rod'. The energy produced supercharges the atmosphere within and around the pyramid.

Experiments with pyramid power have yielded intriguing results. In 1959 Karl Drbal, a Czech engineer, claimed that razor blades placed in the cavity of a pyramid would be sharpened by some sort of energy within 24 hours. In another experiment plants grown in a pyramid-shaped greenhouse increased in growth by over 150 per cent when compared to plants raised in the same growing conditions, including soil and location, in a greenhouse that was a normal shape.

Pyramid power is best known for focusing psychic power and for demonstrating therapeutic properties. If a pyramid is placed under a bed or chair on which a person is sitting, or pointed towards the source of pain, some people claim that relief is almost immediate. Other people say that **meditation** under a pyramid helps open their psychic faculties.

PYROMANCY

Term used to describe a number of ancient **divination** methods using fire for predicting the future and uncovering knowledge. These methods ranged from interpreting the movements and sounds of flame to throwing sacrifices into flames and interpreting how they burned.

This type of divination was widely practised in ancient Greece and Rome. For example, the Vestal Virgins in Rome were in charge of divining by the observation of the perpetually burning fire. Fire was considered one of the primary **elements** of the universe and intrinsically pure, so anything sacrificed in fire, from plants to animals to people, was considered purified and acceptable to the gods.

The colour of the flames during a sacrifice would have been taken into account, as would the way flames flickered, the height they attained, their rise and fall and all other aspects of them. The presage was good if the flames quickly consumed a sacrifice, but bad if the fire refused to start or was disturbed by wind and took a long time to burn the sacrifice. If there was little smoke, if the flames burned with no sound or if they were bright and orange the interpretation was favourable. Not so if there was a lot of smoke, the fire crackled and the flames were deep red in colour.

The ancients divined not only by observing the flames of sacrificial fires but also by the flames of a torch. If the flame divided into two it was a bad **omen**, but a single point or three points was a good sign. If the flame bent it was a sign of sickness or even death to come. If the flame suddenly went out it was a sign of great disaster.

PYTHAGORAS [c. 580–500 BC]

Greek philosopher and mathematician, best known for the geometric theorem named after him, which states that the square of the hypotenuse of a right angled triangle is equal to the sum of the squares of the other two sides, but he was also the father of many mystical and divinatory practices, including **numerology**. His teachings influenced Socrates, Plato, Aristotle and other philosophers down the centuries, and continue to influence thinkers in numerous disciplines to the present day.

Pythagoras conceived of the universe as a living being animated by a great and intelligent soul. He called this soul God the Monad, the Supreme Mind. Humans were separate from the supreme mind apart from the soul, which was an immortal spark of the supreme mind imprisoned in the body until death released it.

Furthermore Pythagoras believed there were associations between the supreme mind, humanity and numbers that could be codified to predict the fate of a person or future events, when certain number patterns appeared. He described numbers as an intrinsic virtue of the supreme mind and ascribed to each a principle and an active force in the universe. The first four numbers – 1 to 4 – contain the basic principles of the universe, since adding or multiplying them produce all other numbers. Special meanings were given to the numbers 3, 7 and 10. Number 7 is comprised of the numbers 3 and 4: the union of humanity and divinity. It is the number of intuitives. Ten is the perfect number $(1 + 2 + 3 + 4)$ and represents all the principles of the supreme mind.

According to Pythagoras the whole universe, including the heavens, could be interpreted using numbers, and centuries before the telescope was invented he attempted to record and analyse the orbits of the sun, moon and stars. He also formulated the 'music of the spheres' theory, describing it as a 'divine symphony beyond perception by most humans played by the planets as they spin along in their orbits'. He believed in the healing power of music, thinking it could inspire and purify the **soul**.

QABALAH

See **Kabbalah**.

QI GONG

Ancient Chinese art and science of breath, motion, sound and **visualization** to cultivate *Qi*, the vital force throughout the body (see **universal life force**).

Translated *Qi gong* literally means to 'work on qi' (chi), and involves the expelling of toxins by forceful breathing; a kind of ultimate physical and spiritual detox. It typically involves the coordination of sound with breath, movement, vibration, visualization and intention to purify the major organs of the body.

Medical qi gong is often referred to as 'acupuncture without the needles', and qi gong doctors allegedly possess remarkable abilities, such as the ability to heal from a distance by projecting intention on **acupuncture** points. Buddhist and Taoist qi gong combine mental and spiritual development with **martial art** practices and **meditation**.

QUACKERY

Integrating metaphysics with sympathetic magic, or **spiritualism** with **healing**. The term is generally used to describe **frauds** that dispense useless or harmful treatments to vulnerable people.

QUANTUM HEALING

A variation of self-healing and mind/body medicine advanced by physician and writer Dr Deepak Chopra. Quantum healing draws its inspiration from the interconnectedness or wholeness of universe, mind and matter suggested by **quantum theory**.

Deepak Chopra, a respected New England endocrinologist, began his search for explanations when he saw patients in his own practice who had completely recovered after being given only a few months to live. In the mid-1980s he returned to his native India to explore **Ayurvedic medicine** and immediately began to see connections between Western medicine, neuroscience, physics and Ayurvedic theory. He put forward the theory that the human body is controlled by a network of intelligence grounded in quantum reality, and that this intelligence can change basic physiological patterns and has the potential to defeat cancer, heart disease and even ageing itself.

According to Chopra, quantum healing is

an alleged process of peacemaking wherein one mode of consciousness – the mind – corrects mistakes in another mode of consciousness – the body. Quantum healing is healing the body and the mind from a quantum level. That means from a level which is not manifest at a sensory level. Our bodies ultimately are fields of information, intelligence and energy. Quantum healing involves a shift in the fields of energy information, so as to bring about a correction in an idea that has gone wrong. So quantum healing involves healing one mode of consciousness, mind, to bring about changes in another mode of consciousness, body.

QUANTUM THEORY

The theoretical basis of modern physics that explains the nature and behaviour of matter and energy on the atomic and sub-atomic level and, by so doing, opens up the possibility of interconnection between mind and matter.

In 1900, physicist Max Planck presented his quantum theory to the German Physical Society. While attempting to discover why radiation from a glowing body changes in colour as its temperature rises, he made the assumption that energy exists in individual units in the same way that matter does, rather than just as a constant electromagnetic wave (as had been formerly assumed), and was therefore quantifiable. The existence of these energy units became the first assumption of quantum theory. Planck called these individual units of energy 'quanta' and so began a completely new and fundamental understanding of the laws of nature.

Over the next thirty years or so a number of scientists made their own significant contributions to our modern understanding of quantum theory. In 1905, Albert Einstein suggested that not just energy but radiation itself was quantized in the same manner. In 1924, Louis de Broglie proposed that there was no fundamental difference in the makeup and behaviour of energy and matter; on the atomic and sub-atomic level either may behave as if made of either particles or waves. This theory became known as the principle of wave-particle duality. In 1927, Werner Heisenberg proposed that precise, simultaneous measurement of two complementary values, such as the position and momentum of a subatomic particle, is impossible. This theory became known as the uncertainty principle.

The two major interpretations of quantum theory's implications for the nature of reality are the 'Copenhagen interpretation' and the 'many-worlds theory'. The Copenhagen interpretation of quantum theory suggests that a particle is whatever it is measured to be (for example, a wave or a particle), but that it cannot be assumed to have specific properties, or even to exist, until it is measured. The emphasis here is placed on the act of observation, which alters that which is being measured. The second interpretation of quantum theory is the many-worlds theory. This holds that as soon as a potential exists for any object to be in any state, the universe of that object transmutes into a series of parallel universes equal to the number of possible states in which that object can exist, with each universe containing a unique single possible state of that object. Furthermore, there is a mechanism for interaction between these universes that somehow permits all states to be accessible in some way and for all possible states to be affected in some manner.

Quantum physics revolutionized scientific and philosophical thinking by challenging the fundamental principle of cause preceding effect, and assigning as much importance to the observer as to his observations. It gave reasons to suppose that life is more than just a complex arrangement of physical matter brought about by chance and provides a more optimistic view of things. It opened up many possibilities by suggesting an interconnectedness or wholeness to the universe reminiscent of the teachings of many mystics. In itself it does not postulate the existence of soul or spirit, but it does provide a mechanism in which mind can affect matter, as is the case with **ESP** and **psychokinesis**, and a mechanism in which non-physical entities such as **ghosts**, **spirits** and other **paranormal** phenomena could exert their influence upon the physical universe by slightly shifting the probability distribution associated with individual quantum events.

QUARTZ

General term for a number of different **crystals** used for **divination** and magical and **healing** purposes. These crystals include citrine, amethyst, jasper, agate and topaz, but clear quartz is most often used to make crystal balls and **scrying** mirrors. Quartz is also used to rid the environment of unhealthy toxins and is believed to have

Some quartz crystal spells/remedies

* *Transformation spell: Rose quartz is thought to transform anger into love or at least into mild affection. Wear it. Give it as a gift to those who have problems with you.*
* *Talisman of love: Rose quartz also allegedly draws lovers to you. Wear it as jewellery or carry it with you. Should it draw too many, too fast, overwhelming you, add an amethyst for a stabilizing effect.*
* *Heart spell: Sew a rose quartz within a thin muslin sachet. Add healing herbs if desired and wear this sachet next to your heart for healing and vitality.*
* *Clear quartz crystal spells: Store tarot cards, runes and other divination devices with a quartz crystal to empower them and make them easier to read. You may also want to wear a clear quartz crystal around your neck or sleep with it*

under your pillow to enhance access to your psychic powers.
* *Amethyst headache remedy: Immerse an amethyst in moderately hot water for seven minutes. Gently pat it dry. Carefully rub the amethyst over the affected areas plus the back of the neck.*
* *Cleaning spell: Place large amethyst or clear quartz crystals in room and office corners to serve as spiritual vacuum cleaners and to boost mental powers and concentration.*
* *Talisman of protection: Wearing an amethyst allegedly protects against pickpockets and thieves.*
* *Topaz burn-healing spell: Gently place a topaz over the burned or bandaged area. Let your open palm rest several inches above the topaz and the burn, transmitting healing energy. This allegedly speeds up healing.*

a vacuum-cleaner effect on negative energy, helping to maintain a fresh atmosphere. It is thought to be especially good for cleansing an area full of electromagnetic toxins, such as an office with computers. In **magic**, quartz is used as a protective **amulet** against evil and for enchantments and **spells**. Rose quartz is believed to have special powers to attract attention, so it is often used for love spells. Quartz is also believed to help boost **psychic** powers and has been used for this purpose for centuries by cultures all over the world.

QUEEN ANNE'S COUNTY GHOST

The **ghost** which allegedly appeared in Queen Anne's County is the subject of a famous American ghost story first related in a rare early nineteenth-century pamphlet that bears the following title: 'Authentic account of the appearance of a ghost in Queen Anne's County, Maryland. Proved in said County Court in the remarkable trial, State of Maryland, use of James, Fanny, Robert and Thomas Harris versus Mary Harris, Administratrix of James Harris. From attested notes taken in court at the time by one of the council, Baltimore, 1807.'

The lengthy account that follows reports how the ghost of James Harris allegedly returned to torment his eldest daughter, Mary, who was attempting to deprive his other children of their rightful share of his estate. It was apparently as a result of Harris's appearances in **spirit**

form, telling them of the deception, that the four other heirs took their elder sister to court and established their claim. Unfortunately the pamphlet does not state the outcome of the claim but it is rumoured that so vividly and convincingly were the ghost's actions described in court that the judge ruled in favour of the four children. The ghost of James Harris was never seen again.

QUEEN MARY

Historic ocean liner that is believed to be haunted by numerous **ghosts**.

Considered the most luxurious ocean liner ever to sail the Atlantic, the *Queen Mary* first set sail in 1934, carrying 3,000 passengers and crew. Refitted during World War II, the ship carried as many as 16,000 troops at a time. After over a thousand voyages across the ocean, in 1967 the *Queen Mary* was permanently docked in Long Beach, California, where it is now an art deco hotel and interactive museum.

The First Class Swimming Pool is reportedly haunted by the ghosts of two women who drowned there, one in the 1930s and the other in the 1960s. The changing rooms near the pool are the source of negative feelings allegedly detected by numerous **psychics**.

Other haunted areas of the ship include the Queen's Salon (with the ghost of a young woman in a white dress), the First Class Suites (a man in a 1930s suit), the Forward Storage Room (children playing) and the Tourist Class Swimming Pool (a drowned woman). Cabin B340 is believed to be so full of psychic disturbance that it is rarely rented out.

Bosun's Locker is the site where the *Queen Mary* once sliced through her escort ship to evade German U-boats. Because of wartime sailing orders, the ship was not permitted to stop for survivors, so over 300 men drowned. It is said that pounding on the walls can still be heard in that area of the ship.

The kitchen is another haunted area. During the war a cook was murdered by troops aboard the ship who didn't like his cooking. He was stuffed into an oven and burned to death; his screams are said to still be heard.

About 50 people have died aboard the *Queen Mary*, and it's no surprise that the ship's morgue is thought to be haunted too. The most well-known ghost to appear in the morgue is believed to be that of 18-year-old John Pedder, a crewman who was crushed by door number 13 during a watertight drill. He is sometimes spotted wearing the blue overalls in which he died.

QUEEN'S BANK GHOST

Alleged **haunting** of Coutts & Co., one of the most prestigious banks in England, which gained international media attention.

Coutts & Co., called the Queen's bank because of its wealthy clientele and royal connections, was founded in 1692. Its headquarters have been at 440 Strand since the late 1970s. In 1992 a number of female employees began to complain of unusual phenomena, including light and computer malfunctions, plummeting temperatures and a terrifying shadowy black figure, sometimes without a head, darting around the building. When some employees became too frightened to work the bank contacted the **College of Psychic Studies** for help. The college sent **medium** Eddie Burks to help.

Burks visited the bank and interviewed the employees. He also allegedly made contact with the **ghost** and described him as a wealthy gentleman lawyer from the Elizabethan era. Sadly he had refused to cooperate with the Queen and was charge with treason and beheaded on a summer's day in a location not far from the bank. His execution had left him angry and bitter and unwilling to depart. The ghost knew that this anger and bitterness was holding him back in the **afterlife** and asked Burks to help him let go of it. Burks agreed and held his contact with the ghost until the man's daughter, dressed in Elizabethan clothing too, arrived in white and radiating light. According to Burks she took her father's hand and the two melted into the light.

When the media got hold of the story a search began for the identity of the ghost. It was suggested by Father Francis Edwards, a Jesuit priest and member of the Royal Historical Society, that it might have been Thomas Howard, the fourth Duke of Norfolk. During his lifetime Howard had been involved with plots to overthrow Queen Elizabeth in favour of Mary Queen of Scots. When Elizabeth found out about Howard's disloyalty he was arrested, sent to the Tower of London and beheaded on 2 June 1572, at the age of 37. The description of Howard matched that given by Burks and many of the details about his life also matched.

This wasn't the end of the story. On 12 January 1993 Howard allegedly told Burks that he was grateful for his release and was now in a peaceful place with his daughter. He returned again on 2 June 1993, the anniversary of his death, to acknowledge that he had let go of his bitterness. In the meantime, Howard's descendants, the seventeenth Duke of Norfolk and his family, had decided to organize a memorial service for him on 15 November 1993; the next day Burks informed them that the spirit of Howard had once again come to him to express his thanks for the service. The final communication came on 23 December 1993, when Howard expressed his thanks to Father Edwards for identifying him correctly.

Queen's House

The Queen's House at the National Maritime Museum in Greenwich, London, was built in the seventeenth century and in 1966 it provided the setting for one of the most famous **spirit photographs** ever taken.

The photograph was taken by R W Hardy, a retired clergyman from Canada, and his wife. The couple were visiting the house as tourists and had no interest in **ghosts**. They took numerous photographs, including one of the beautiful Tulip Staircase. When the photograph was developed the staircase, which had seemed empty at the time the photograph was taken, appeared to be occupied by two shadowy figures in the process of climbing the stairs.

Experts examined the film and could find no evidence of **fraud** or technical interference and no explanation could be found. Subsequent investigation of the area has yielded reports of ghostly footsteps and strange muttering noises.

Quinn's light

Strange ghostly phenomenon reported in Australia, similar to the **corpse candles** of the British Isles. Quinn's light is said to appear as a phosphorescent light that goes round and round in circles before disappearing as mysteriously as it appeared. It is often reported in bush areas and there are a number of reports from people who have followed the light and even fired at it – but to no effect. The Australians also have the Min-Min lights, which are said to appear in cemeteries and seem to dance around the gravestones.

Explanations for Quinn's lights, Min-Min lights and other similar **ghost lights** are as numerous and varied as the sightings themselves. They typically fall into the following five categories:

1. Misidentifications of natural phenomena such as wind-blown mists, escaping marsh gas (considered by many to be the most likely explanation as ghost lights typically appear in marshy areas), light refraction effects, ball lightning or other electric discharge and so on.
2. An unknown natural phenomenon involving low-level air oscillations, or ionisation in geophysically generated electrical fields.
3. **Psychokinetic** or **poltergeist** effects unconsciously produced by an individual.
4. Small **UFO**s acting as remote-control probes.
5. Non-physical **apparitions/ghosts**. Numerous accounts exist in folklore of the **supernatural** origin and appearance of ghost lights.

R

R-101 CASE

Case involving the Irish **medium Eileen Garrett**, who allegedly solved the mystery of the crash of the British dirigible R-101 using information communicated to her from the spirit world.

Garrett claimed to have had a series of **premonitions** of the disaster, which killed 48 passengers and crew. She sent a warning to the director of civil aviation, Sir Sefton Brancker, but he refused to take it seriously and declared the R-101 to be as 'safe as a house, except for the millionth chance'. She received a message during a **séance** from a deceased Captain Hinchcliffe, warning his friend, Ernest Johnston, the navigator of the R-101, not to go on the ship's flight because it would crash, but Johnston also did not take the message seriously.

The R-101 lifted off on 4 October 1930 and crashed the next day near Paris. Garrett allegedly knew about the crash before news reached the media. Brancker was one of the victims. A few days after the crash Garrett conducted a séance and, through her **control**, Uvani, began to receive messages from the dead captain of the R-101, Flight Lieutenant H Carmichael Irwin. The information that was received about the airship was of such a confidential nature that **Harry Price**, one of the sitters who was investigating Garrett's mediumship, worried about espionage. He sent a copy of the séance transcript to Sir John Simon, chairman of the Court of Inquiry investigating the disaster. The press got involved, as did a number of military officials, including Major Oliver Villiers, a close friend of Brancker.

Lieutenant Irwin allegedly communicated again and was joined by other members of the crew. The **spirits** claimed that the R-101 had had a gas leak and a number of other problems, which had been ignored by officials who wanted to launch the vessel on time. Major Villiers was convinced Garrett had been communicating with the spirits of the dead crew but Sir John Simon ruled that nothing could be done with the testimony as it would not be accepted in a court of law. Villiers, however, remained convinced that the dead crew wanted the world to know what had really happened, and 25 years later he gave a copy of the séance records to author James Leasor, who went on to write *The Millionth Chance: the Story of the R-101*.

RADIANT BOYS

Ghosts of boys who have been murdered by their mothers. They appear in glowing or misty light and are believed to be an **omen** of bad luck or death. Radiant boys feature in the folklore of England and Europe and may trace their origin to the *kindermörderinnen* (child murderesses) of Germanic lore.

Impressive Corby Castle in Cumberland is said to be haunted by a small, glimmering **spirit** known as the radiant boy. His origins are uncertain but he has been reported for over 200 years in a room in part of the old house adjoining the tower. His most famous appearance took place on 8 September 1803. The Rector of

Greystoke and his wife were among a number of guests who planned to stay several days, but after just one night they announced that they would be leaving. Some time later the Rector confessed to the owner of the house his reason for leaving:

Soon after we went to bed, we fell asleep: it might have been between one and two in the morning when I awoke. I observed that the fire was totally extinguished; but although that was the case, and we had no light, I saw a glimmer in the centre of the room, which suddenly increased to a bright flame. I looked out, apprehending that something had caught fire, when, to my amazement, I beheld a beautiful boy, clothed in white, with bright locks, resembling gold, standing by my bedside, in which position he remained for some minutes, fixing his eyes upon me with a mild and benevolent expression. He then glided gently away toward the side of the chimney, where it is obvious there is no possible egress, and entirely disappeared. I found myself again in total darkness, and all remained quiet until the usual hour of rising. I declare this to be a true account of what I saw at Corby Castle, upon my word as a clergyman.

Another famous encounter with a radiant boy occurred in the last years of the eighteenth century to a man called Captain Robert Stewart.

There are different versions of the story but according to one, Captain Stewart was out hunting while stationed in Ireland when he was caught in a terrible storm. He sought shelter at a country gentleman's house and was given a makeshift bed to sleep in beside a roaring fire. He awoke abruptly in the night and saw, gradually disclosing itself, the form of a beautiful naked boy, surrounded by a dazzling radiance. The boy looked at him earnestly, and then the vision faded, and all was dark again.

When Stewart told the owner of the house what he had seen the gentleman explained that the room was haunted by the radiant boy, and that anyone who saw him would obtain great power, but would die a violent death at the height of his fame and influence.

Robert Stewart later became Viscount Castlereagh, second Marquis of Londonderry, and entered the British House of Commons, becoming Secretary of State and Foreign Secretary. In 1822, depressed by overwork and responsibilities he cut his throat with a penknife.

Castlereagh's rise and fall is often cited as an example of the curse of the radiant boy, even though it took three decades to come to fruition.

RADIESTHESIA

A method of medical **dowsing** that uses a **pendulum** to determine if someone is ill or potentially ill. Typically a pendulum is held over the body and the direction in which it rotates or swings indicates the nature and location of the illness. Measures are then taken to rebalance the flow of energy (see **universal life force**) throughout the body and restore health.

Radionics

Medicine system developed by Dr Albert Abrams in the early twentieth century. It is based on **radiesthesia** (medical **dowsing**) but instead of a **pendulum** uses a 'black box' to detect and rebalance energy patterns in the body. All bodies radiate an electromagnetic field, and according to Abrams the 'black box' he created could distinguish which tissue was healthy and which was diseased, based on the vibrations of a person's electromagnetic field as they were scanned. Radionic instruments could then be retuned to emit 'healing vibrations' which could cure disease. Abrams's theories enjoyed a couple of years of popularity, and a few enthusiasts still practise radionics today, but it has yet to gain scientific backing.

Raising consciousness

The theory that change in the world can be created when large numbers of people concentrate, meditate or pray for that change. Modern physics supports the idea that everything exists as waves rather than specific points in time and space, and these waves or fields include time, space and gravity. Some scientists have also recently suggested that **consciousness** itself is a field.

Research in the area of field consciousness is new but scientists have been researching the theory that if many minds focus on a single topic they can have a measurable impact or effect on that topic. Experiments have attempted to show that normally random results can change when people focus their minds on a single event. Results have been measured by the use of random number generators – computerized machines that indicate when there is a definite change from randomness to order during such moments of intense mental focus.

In recent years many scientists have studied the phenomena of group mental focus. Random number generators have been used to measure the public's focused attention at events. Although the events vary in their topic of focus, location and the number of people involved they all show surprising evidence that something *does* occur when large numbers of people focus on the same event. In other words, experiments with random number generators show that thought alone, without any physical action, can somehow create an enormous amount of synchronization or order out of randomness.

The potential power of unity of thought adds a scientific basis to the idea of creating change by raising consciousness in large numbers of people. It also suggests that concentration, **meditation** and **prayer** may indeed be potent sources of healing.

Rakshasa

Demon spirit that appears in Hindu folklore as a black figure with yellow hair wearing a wreath of entrails. The name literally means 'destroyer', and rakshasa are believed to be evil, destructive and dim-witted creatures.

According to lore rakshasa are **shape-shifters** that can take on the shape of animals and humans, but generally they are hideous in appearance with huge bellies and slits for eyes. Some are believed to be particularly wicked and they are notorious for disturbing sacrifices, desecrating graves, harassing priests, possessing human beings and so on. Their fingernails are poisonous, and they feed on human flesh and spoiled food in a futile attempt to satisfy their insatiable hunger. They can reanimate corpses and can take **possession** of a human through his or her food, causing illness or madness. It is believed to be easy to banish them however – all a person needs to say is 'uncle'.

RANDOM PSYCHIC INTUITION

Random psychic intuition differs from **deductive psychic intuition** in that it is thought to be totally unrelated to anything that is known consciously or unconsciously. It can be about anything that has taken place, is taking place or will take place in the future. It can be induced during a light **trance** or **meditation** but typically comes at the most unexpected or unwanted times, when the conscious mind is open to images sent to it from the **unconscious**. It can create a powerful impression and may leave a person feeling confused and dazed. Sudden **premonitions** of disaster that appear for no reason are typical examples of random psychic intuition at work.

RAPPING

Means of alleged **spirit** communication during a **séance** that involves any knocking, thumping, bumping or tapping. It is also a characteristic of numerous **poltergeist** cases and **hauntings**.

Rappings associated with spirit messages appear in the ninth-century chronicle *Rudulf of Fulda* and rapping spirits were conjured away at the benediction of the medieval Catholic Church. Rappers also appeared in 1521 in Lyons, France and in 1610 in Ayr, Scotland. In 1661 **Revd Joseph Glanvill** mentioned rappings at Tedworth, England (see **Drummer of Tedworth**), and in 1716 Revd Samuel Wesley heard rapping at **Epworth Rectory**. It wasn't until 1848, however, when the **Fox sisters** asked 'Mr Splitfoot' to answer questions via rapping, that large number of people began to believe in it as a form of spirit communication. At first Spitfoot rapped twice for yes and not at all for no, but in time an alphabet code was worked out to communicate messages. From then on **mediums** all over America and Europe were communicating with spirits via rapping and the phenomenon remains an important part of spirit communication today.

Clearly much of the rapping was produced fraudulently and a number of mediums, including the Fox sisters, admitted that the raps were made by their toes cracking against the floorboards. The famous magician **Harry Houdini** offered a number of techniques and explanations for rapping, including the clicking of thumbnails together, slipping a shoe against a table leg and sliding moistened fingers across a table top. Others made use of trick magnets and devices operated by wires and hidden in their clothes and shoes to create the raps. Despite this many people were convinced that rappings were genuine proof of **survival after death**. The medium **D D Home** believed that spirits had to rap to obtain relief: by remaining in the earth's atmosphere they get so charged with electricity that the only way to release energy is to rap.

Rasputin, Grigori Efimovich [1871–1916]

Russian prophet, healer and mystic who predicted not just his own death but the downfall of Tsar Nicholas II and the Russian nobility.

Rasputin was born in Pokrovskoye to Siberian peasants. He had his first **vision** of the Virgin Mary in his early twenties, which prompted him to set out on a two-year pilgrimage to Athens. When he returned home he allegedly possessed the ability to heal and cure by **prayer** alone. Despite his odd ways, womanizing and unkempt appearance, Rasputin's healing abilities soon attracted the interest of Tsar Nicholas and his family. The Tsar's son,

Alexis, had haemophilia and Rasputin was able to ease the boy's condition.

Rasputin soon became a favourite in the royal court but the more his popularity grew the more he attracted jealously from the nobility, who plotted to kill him. In a letter Rasputin predicted his own death by 1 January 1917. He also wrote that if peasants killed him the monarchy would prosper but if he was killed by the nobility the royal family would collapse within two years and after 25 years of unrest the nobility would be erased from the country.

On the night of 30 December 1916, Rasputin was poisoned. Allegedly, when the poison failed to take effect, he was then shot and beaten with a bar. When this didn't work either he was bound and thrown into the Neva River. This did kill him but when his body was recovered no trace of poison was found. True to his prediction the royal family was murdered within the next two years. Twenty-five years later the nobility finally came to an end under Stalin's regime.

Raudive, Konstantin [1909–1974]

The pioneering force in exploring **electronic voice phenomena** (EVP), German psychologist Dr Konstantin Raudive discovered his life's work when a tape recording he had made of bird song produced anomalous voices speaking in long extinct dialects. This prompted him to set up equipment that he believed could record communications from the **spirits** of the dead. The results of his experiments yielded a huge range of responses, sometimes in foreign languages, at times quite audible, and at other times almost imperceptible, but the overall results were generally regarded as impressive.

Raudive went on to publish what is still regarded today as the major work in the field of EVP – *Breakthrough – An Amazing Experiment in Electronic Communication with the Dead* (1971) – and his methods and theories have become almost standard references in the field of **paranormal** investigations.

RAVENS

Considered to be the most intelligent birds with a long life span, corvids – ravens, crows and magpies – have been surrounded by **superstition** and myth for centuries.

The ancient Greeks and Romans considered the crow to be a weather prophet and the raven is still regarded by the Greeks as a 'thunderbird' because of its alleged ability to predict a storm. In Britain to find a dead crow on the road is considered to be a sign of good luck, while to find one in a churchyard is considered bad luck. In Wales, if one crow crosses your path it is good luck but if two cross it is a bad **omen**. In Scotland, a raven circling a house is thought to predict a death for someone in the house, while in England it is said that as long as ravens remain in the Tower of London the country will never fall to enemies. An old

Irish saying is 'to have raven's knowledge', meaning to have the ability to see and know all things. In Tibet, the raven is the messenger of the Supreme Being.

Counting crows has been a popular method of foretelling the future in many countries for hundreds of years:

- *One crow – signifies bad luck, possible death.*
- *Two crows – good luck, change for the better.*
- *Three crows – a celebration, a possible marriage or birth of a girl.*
- *Four crows – birth of a boy or significant event to do with a son.*
- *Five crows – a positive transaction.*
- *Six crows – gold, wealth.*
- *Seven crows – a secret.*
- *Eight crows – something profound, or a life-altering experience.*
- *Nine crows – denotes passion, or something sensual.*
- *Ten crows – denotes something overwhelming.*
- *Eleven crows – uncertainty.*
- *Twelve crows – fulfilment.*

RAYLEIGH, LORD [1842–1919]

Celebrated physicist with an interest in the **paranormal**, Lord Rayleigh is often recalled as one of the pioneers in the science of acoustics who received the Nobel Prize for Physics in 1904 for his part in the discovery of argon. Apart from his *Theory of Sound*, his other extensive and groundbreaking studies are reported in his

Scientific Papers – six volumes issued during the period 1889 to 1920. It is often argued that Lord Rayleigh was among the first British scientists to speculate on the connection between electromagnetic field fluctuations and paranormal activity, although this remains highly speculative. What is positively known, however, of Rayleigh's involvement with the paranormal is that he was an illustrious member of the British **Society for Psychical Research** and was involved in numerous investigations of allegedly haunted locations.

REBIRTHING

A technique of breath control that aims to release physical and emotional tension through relaxation, concentration exercises and the release of breath. Rebirthing involves a series of breathing sessions that are designed to re-establish the natural breathing patterns of birth. These breathing patterns have the effect of building up energy that has a vitalizing effect on the body. The increased physical and psychological relaxation can trigger the release of memories from the subconscious, which often date back to birth, life in the womb or even previous lives.

The technique was discovered in America by Leonard Orr in 1975 and has many similarities to Eastern breathing exercises, such as **yoga** breathing. Orr found that it helped his clients resolve repressions, negative attitudes and low self-esteem that supposedly originated with experiences before and during birth. Rebirthing practitioners instruct their clients in various breathing exercises that trigger hyperventilation and during the ensuing physiological response encourage clients to re-enact their birth. According to theory this leads to a cathartic rush of emotions and a renewed sense of physical and **psychic** energy.

There is no formal code of practice or formal training for rebirthing practitioners and it remains a controversial technique. During the 1990s it attracted a lot of negative publicity when a young girl died during a rebirthing ritual designed to 'help' her bond with her foster parents.

RECURRENT SPONTANEOUS PSYCHOKINESIS

Expression coined by **William G Roll** to refer to **paranormal** physical effects which occur repeatedly over a period of time, especially used as a neutral description of **poltergeist** disturbances.

REFLEXOLOGY

Alternative therapy in which pain relief and the alleviation of certain ailments is achieved by applying pressure and massage to different areas of the feet. Reflexology has been known for centuries with references found in ancient Chinese, Egyptian and Indian texts, but it was first used in the West in 1915 by Dr William Fitzgerald, an ear, nose and throat specialist with an interest in **acupuncture**. Fitzgerald noticed that applying pressure to one part of the body had a numbing effect on another and he mapped out ten body zones of energy (called chi) similar to the meridians in **traditional Chinese medicine**. In the 1930s physiotherapist Eunice Ingham took this one stage further when she suggested that all parts of the body could be treated by pressing certain areas of the foot. She coined the phrase 'reflexology', and mapped out many of the foot reflex points that are used today.

According to reflexology theory, specific foot zones are linked to every important organ, gland and muscle in the body. When a physical response occurs this is reflected in the relevant foot zone, which carries crystalline deposits beneath the skin. Reflexology breaks down these crystalline deposits so they can be taken away by the lymphatic system. This helps to detoxify the body. Most of the body's nerves also end in a reflex point on the feet and when these reflexes are pressed they stimulate the nerve and increase the flow of positive neurotransmitters, like endorphins, to the brain. Finally, like any therapy that aims to balance chi, reflexology helps break up blockages and regulate the flow of energy so that the body's self-healing mechanism can be stimulated.

Whether crystalline deposits are present or not there is plenty of evidence to suggest that reflexology works. There are no known side effects and it is thought to be particularly therapeutic for stress-related conditions such as insomnia and headaches, as well as for back pain, constipation, emotional distress and pain relief in general.

REGARDIE, F ISRAEL [1907–1985]

Israel Regardie was an occultist, author and one-time secretary to the legendary **Aleister Crowley**. As an **adept** of the secret order known as the Hermetic Order of the **Golden Dawn**, he became infamous among the occultists of his day for breaking his oath of secrecy and publishing the Order's complete rituals in his book *The Golden Dawn*. Today this book is a classic bestseller and has been revised and re-issued several times.

Regardie's decision to go public earned him the contempt of his fellow occultists but by the time of his death in 1985 he was regarded as the world's acknowledged authority on ceremonial **magic**. Born in England in 1907 Regardie spent much of his life in the United States where he worked as a body therapist. He was strongly influenced by Aleister Crowley and became his secretary for a number of years. He joined Crowley's magical order but managed to steer clear of the excesses associated with Crowley. In addition to his popular and best-selling four-volume *Golden Dawn*, Regardie also published other books, including *The Art of True Healing* and *The Middle Pillar* – both of which remain classics for serious students of the **occult**.

REGRESSION

See **Past-life therapy**.

REICH, WILHELM [1897–1957]

Psychoanalyst who is best known for taking Freudian doctrines to the extreme by suggesting that orgasm is the ultimate key to physical and psychological health. Reich claimed to have discovered the concept of **orgone energy**, which has similarities with prana or the **universal life force** (chi), and which he believed to be the specific basis for love and orgasm. He insisted that there was a physical bioelectric flow of energy through the body and this was not a metaphysical concept as there were biological entities in the body, called *bions*, which carried the energy.

According to Reich, when emotions and sexuality are repressed this energy flow becomes blocked and poor physical and emotional health are the result. The body holds these repressions as sexual armour but this shield can be dissolved using a series of approaches, such as deep breathing, **massage** and physical movement; a system called **bioenergetics**.

Despite his dubious claims, Reich's **bodywork** concepts and psychoanalytic theories have had glowing testimonials from those undergoing Reichian therapy. They have also heavily influenced other bodywork schools of thought, like Rolfing, that believe there is a correlation between muscular tension and repressed emotions and/or sexuality.

REIKI

Reiki is a holistic alternative therapy based on Eastern concepts of energy flow and the seven **chakras** (energy centres) in the human body. Reiki was formulated by a Japanese teacher, Mikao Usui, around 1890, but incorporates **meditation** techniques, beliefs, and **symbols** that are considerably older.

Reiki (pronounced 'ray-key') is a Japanese word representing **universal life force** energy, the energy that is all around us. It is derived from *rei*, meaning 'free passage' or 'transcendental spirit', and *ki*, meaning 'vital life force energy' or 'universal life energy'. Reiki masters, called 'initiates', are trained to act as channels for universal life energy. They use their hands to direct healing power down to a patient where it can promote healing and well-being, reduce stress and alleviate the symptoms of serious illness. In a similar way to **therapeutic touch** the Reiki master moves his or her hands above the body with hardly any physical contact, or they are placed on the body using specific movements and massage to direct the healing energy.

Reiki is believed to have originated thousands of years ago in Tibet. It had fallen out of use until it was rediscovered in Japan by Buddhist monk Mikao Usui, during the mid-1800s. After a three-week meditation on a mountain top Usui claimed to have been knocked down by a beam of light from heaven filled with bubbles of light containing symbols. He took this to mean that the symbols had healing power and started to use them in his healing practice with good rates of success. Usui kept these symbols secret and only passed them on to a chosen few followers. Reiki finally arrived in the West via Hawayo Takata, a Japanese woman who learned it from one of Usui's pupils.

The theory behind Reiki is similar to the concept of body energy in **traditional Chinese medicine, Ayurvedic medicine** and **spiritual healing**. Everyone has an energy field that, in good health, runs around and through their bodies in flow or vibration. When illness occurs the energy flow becomes unbalanced and the aim is to rebalance these energies and stimulate the body's self-healing mechanism. Reiki practitioners can also perform **absent healing** on a patient who is not physically present. When this is the case practitioners are believed to act as passive channels for the life energy that comes from a universal source. Practitioners do not direct the energy, which guides itself solely to where it is needed.

Training to become a Reiki master is a challenging process that is both expensive and exhausting. There are three levels of training and only the highest and most accomplished pupils are shown Usui's healing symbols. In a typical Reiki session the client would be asked to focus on their own 'healing intention', while the initiate goes into his or ritual to channel beneficial vibrations into the patient's energy centres, the chakras. Clients report feeling tingling and warmth in these areas and many say they feel relaxed and energized after a session.

Reiki is believed to be particularly beneficial for emotional and spiritual crises as well as health problems. According to a vast body of primary anecdotal evidence

and uncontrolled trials it has a high rate of success. Its popularity as an alternative therapy mushroomed in the 1990s and continues to grow today. Reiki is reported to be growing in popularity among clinicians too, but because of the lack of supporting evidence, and the secrecy and controversy surrounding its spiritual roots, orthodox medicine remains understandably cautious about embracing it fully.

REINCARNATION

The doctrine that the **soul** returns after death to a new physical body to live another life. Reincarnation is a central belief in Buddhism and Hinduism but it is not limited to the East and is also common in the West. For many people the idea that a person can be reincarnated is substantiated by stories of **past-life recall** that can be backed up with corroborating evidence. Accounts of people who claim to remember events between lives are often similar to accounts of **out-of-body experiences** and **near-death experiences**.

According to a 1981 Gallup poll, one in four Americans said they believed in reincarnation. Most people's ideas about reincarnation derive from Hinduism or Buddhism. These religions grew out of a set of animistic soul beliefs characteristic to the indigenous tribal peoples of India. One common characteristic of animistic beliefs about reincarnation is that the spirit of the dead person divides after death: one part travels to the land of the dead where it becomes a **spirit**, while the other part returns to earth to be reborn. Various methods were and still are employed in tribal societies to determine the past-life identity of a child. The parent may have an announcing **dream**, which predicts that a certain person will be born to them. Babies are checked for birthmarks or birth defects, which might indicate who they are. Reincarnation is facilitated or impeded through burial custom; for example, dead infants are sometimes buried beneath the floor of the home to make it easier for their souls to return to their mothers. Human beings may not always be reborn as human children; in many societies they may be reborn as animals.

Of the several ways animistic reincarnation beliefs differ from those typical of Hinduism and Buddhism, the most important is the concept of **karma** – the idea that the circumstances of a person's present life are moulded by their actions, good or bad, in previous lives. The theory of karma is absent from animistic beliefs about reincarnation. This is significant because scientific investigations of reincarnation support the animistic idea of reincarnation better than the Hindu and Buddhist view. Scientific studies of reincarnation have also shown how important beliefs about reincarnation are to the alleged recall of past lives. For example, children who claim memories of past lives, sometimes in the opposite sex, are common in cultures where this belief is considered acceptable, but less common in cultures when this belief is not taken seriously by parents.

The jury is still out as to whether reincarnation is a genuine phenomenon.

Efforts have been made to investigate reincarnation scientifically and validate claims of past lives. Most notable is the research conducted by Ian Stevenson, professor of psychiatry at the University of Virginia, who began investigating reincarnational memories of children all over the world in the 1960s with impressive results. The main problem, however, is that science does not recognize the existence of an essence that survives the brain after bodily death, and reincarnation by its very nature implies **survival after death**.

RELAXATION

A state of deep rest – not sleep, but rest – in which the metabolism of the body slows and **brain waves** slow to an alpha state. Relaxation of body and mind is stressed in all Eastern religions as a prerequisite for **meditation** and is believed to be vital for the development of **psychic** powers.

In 1952 the first scientific study of relaxation in relation to **psi** was conducted, by the American parapsychologist Gertrude Schmeidler. Schmeidler found that patients who had been hospitalised with concussion scored much better in psi guessing tasks than those suffering from other disorders, and came to the conclusion that it was due to their greater relaxation. Subsequent studies have confirmed Schmeidler's conclusion.

Relaxation can be achieved through **yoga** and meditation techniques as well as through muscular relaxation of every part

A basic relaxation exercise

Choose a quiet place where you won't be interrupted. Before you start, do a few gentle stretching exercises to relieve muscular tension.

Make yourself comfortable, either sitting or lying down. Start to breathe slowly and deeply, in a calm and effortless way. Gently tense, and then relax, each part of your body, starting with your feet and working your way up to your face and head.

As you focus on each area, think of warmth, heaviness and relaxation. Push any distracting thoughts to the back of your mind; imagine them floating away. Don't try to relax; simply let go of the tension in your muscles and allow them to become relaxed. Let your mind go empty. Some people find it helpful to visualize a calm, beautiful place such as a garden or meadow.

Stay like this for about 20 minutes, then take some deep breaths and open your eyes, but stay sitting or lying down for a few moments before you get up.

of the body from top to toe. Some people use other techniques, such as **visualization**, deep breathing, self-hypnosis and calming music tapes.

REMOTE VIEWING

The ability to see distant or hidden objects, events and locations beyond the range of the physical eye. For example, a viewer might be asked to describe a location on the other side of the world, which he or she has never visited; or a viewer might describe an event that happened long ago; or describe an object sealed in a container or locked in a room; or perhaps even describe a person or an activity – all without being told anything about the target, not even its name or designation.

The term 'remote viewing' was coined in the 1970s by American physicists Russell Targ and Harold Puthoff. Used extensively by so-called 'psychic spies' during the Cold War for classified military projects, it has a long history both as an intelligence-gathering tool and as the subject of research and applications in the civilian world. It is believed to be one of the oldest forms of **psi** and has been used for centuries in Tibet, Africa, India and the Americas. In the latter part of the nineteenth century, the founder of the **Society for Psychical Research**, **Frederick Myers**, suggested that remote viewing – or 'travelling clairvoyance' as it was called then – was a combination of **telepathy**, **precognition**, **retrocognition** and **clairvoyance**.

Sometimes the events 'seen' were taking place simultaneously but sometimes they were displaced in time. In the early twentieth century, American writer Upton Sinclair recorded data relating to remote viewing. This data was used in 1972 by Targ and Puthoff, who set up a remote viewing research project at Stanford Research Institute in California.

Targ and Puthoff researched remote viewing for 10 years. They conducted hundreds of experiments and collected some impressive results. They came to the conclusion that remote viewing is a **psychic** experience that occurs naturally in people but can also be learned. They found that they could train people to remote view regardless of psychic ability. For example, people could be taught to 'see' into a container to describe the contents inside.

Other major research in remote viewing has been done at Princeton University by the Princeton Engineering Anomalies Research group (PEAR) established in 1979. PEAR is the first research group to apply modern engineering science techniques to the study of psi. In studies of precognitive remote perception PEAR came to the conclusion that it is possible to obtain information by means that cannot be explained by 'known physical phenomena'. Other researchers in America and Canada have found that remote viewing is affected by geomagnetic activity; the higher the incidence of geomagnetic activity before a viewing test the less successful the results.

In 1972, during the height of the Cold War, the American CIA launched a classified project to train and utilize psychic spies. The 'remote viewing' project, based at the Stanford Research Institute, was a direct response to the USSR's similar training of military personnel for long-distance spying. The project, which purported to develop a systematic strategy for accessing latent clairvoyance, operated surreptitiously for 24 years, under such evocative code names as STARGATE, SUN STREAK and CENTER LANE, before it was finally declassified and terminated in 1995.

Due to the secrecy intrinsic to espionage, it is unknown whether remote viewing is still in use or still being researched within the intelligence community. Many private individuals, companies and non-profit organizations claim to be conducting continued research on remote viewing, although not all of these independent remote viewing projects approach the subject from the perspective of performing controlled studies.

Research operations in remote viewing continue today for such purposes as locating missing persons and equipment, in solving crimes and in commercial information gathering. Both scientists and occultists alike remained intrigued by the possibilities remote viewing can offer. According to the International Remote Viewing Association (www.irva.org) remote viewing is not really a 'psychic phenomenon' as such, but actually an imposed discipline or skill that helps the viewer to facilitate or harness his or her own innate, underlying intuitive abilities.

RESIDUAL HAUNTING

Term applied to **hauntings** in which the **ghost** characteristically goes about the exact same routines of behaviour without deviation, often re-enacting historical events or some great tragedy. As opposed to the traditional form of a haunting, the residual haunting is believed to be the result of **psi** energies being imprinted upon the environment and replayed time and again in a seemingly endless cycle.

RESURRECTION MARY

One of Chicago's most famous and often reported **ghosts**. Resurrection Mary is said to be a beautiful, blonde, blue-eyed young girl who wears a white dress, dancing shoes and a thin shawl. She is named after Resurrection Cemetery, a large burial ground on Archer Avenue in Justice, Illinois, where she is said to be buried.

According to the legend, a young woman was killed by a car in the early 1930s when she was walking home after an evening of dancing at the former Oh Henry Ballroom, now the Willowbrook Ballroom. The driver took off and was never seen again. The woman was buried by her parents, in her dancing dress and shoes, in Resurrection Cemetery.

Since 1936 when she made her first appearance several people have reported picking Mary up as a hitchhiker, taking her to or from the ballroom; as the car passes Resurrection Cemetery she usually vanishes or gets out of the car and disappears through the locked gates. She has also been seen inside the cemetery, staring through the bars of the gate. In some cases motorists have reported hitting a girl who runs out into the road in front of them. The car either passes through her or she vanishes. She is described as looking like a living person, speaking very little and wearing a 1930s' ball gown. Sometimes her flesh is cool to the touch.

In a 1976 incident, a passer-by saw a woman locked inside the fence of the cemetery after dark. Rather than stopping, he called the police, who came to let her out. When the police arrived, she was nowhere to be seen, but they discovered that two bars of the main gate had been bent outwards, and the bars bore the imprint of human hands. Officials quickly removed the bars but, embarrassed, later reinstalled them, using a blowtorch to obscure the handprints. The two burned areas can still be seen.

Mary's true identity has never been established although plenty of candidates have been put forward, including a young Polish girl who crashed her parent's car near Resurrection and was buried there, and a 12-year-old Lithuanian blonde girl called Anna Mary, who was killed in car crash following an evening of dancing at the Oh Henry.

Mary's story follows the **phantom hitchhiker** legend. She also has similarities to the so-called 'spectral jaywalker' – a person, typically a woman, who appears in front of cars and is struck. She usually vanishes immediately or lies down without moving until help arrives, whereupon she vanishes.

RETROCOGNITION

Retrocognition is the alleged ability to know, see into, or sense the past through **psychic** means. **Psychometry** and **past-life recall** can both be considered kinds of retrocognition.

Retrocognition is used in **applied psi** fields where past events need to be reconstructed, such as **psychic criminology** and **psychic archaeology**. The retrocognition is typically done by using psychometry on an object. Results have been impressive but it is difficult to test retrocognition scientifically because of the possibility of **clairvoyance** by obtaining access to historical records and/or information.

Retrocognition can occur spontaneously in daily life, **dreams** and **parapsychology** experiments. It typically manifests with a **vision**, sometimes featuring sounds, smells and movements, that replaces the present with scenes from the past. Retrocognition is a key feature of some **hauntings** and cases of **apparitions** that seem to be replays of past events, particularly violent and tragic ones such as murders and suicides. It has been suggested that reports of **ghosts** can be explained by retrocognition: an individual becomes displaced in time momentarily and witnesses scenes from the past.

One of the most famous cases of retrocognition occurred in the summer of 1901 in Versailles, when two Englishwomen believed they saw apparitions from the 1770s (see **Versailles ghosts**). Another retrocognitive experience consisting only of sound occurred in 1951 in Dieppe, France, when two Englishwomen believed they heard sounds of the famous air raid that took place there in World War II (see **Dieppe Raid case**).

In the 1960s a woman called Coleen Buterbaugh entered an office in the music building at Nebraska Wesleyan University. Almost immediately she said she saw a tall woman with old-fashioned clothes. Looking out of the window she witnessed the campus as it had appeared 50 years before. Buterbaugh realized that she had somehow slipped back in time. Another famous retrocognition took place on 2 January 1950 when a woman in her fifties, E F Smith, allegedly witnessed the aftermath of the battle of Nechtansmere, which took place in 685 in Scotland, while walking to the village of Letham, near Nechtansmere.

REVENANT

Term used to describe the undead. In earlier times it was used as a synonym for **ghost** (i.e. the returning dead).

The revenant is in fact quite different to the traditional ghost for it may wait years or even centuries to appear. In actuality, a revenant is any type of undead and that loose definition can include ghosts and **vampires** as well as mythical creatures we currently think of as **zombies, ghouls** and animated skeletons.

The legends of revenants are widespread over many countries throughout history, but occur most notably in the areas of Albania, Bulgaria, Germany, Greece, Hungary, Poland, Romania, Russia, Serbia,

Silesia, Transylvania and the Ukraine. Revenants can take many forms, from filmy beings to solid forms that appear living. If they appear in human form they typically appear fully dressed in the garments they wore when alive.

RHAPSODOMANCY

According to Ephraim Chambers' *Cyclopaedia, or Universal Dictionary of Arts and Sciences* of 1728, 'Rhapsodomancy is an ancient kind of divination performed by pitching on a passage of a poem at hazard and reckoning it as a prediction of what was to come to pass.' The typical method was to close one's eyes, say a brief **prayer** and then open a book of poetry at random, placing a finger on the page before opening the eyes. The verse touched by the finger would supposedly relate to the question being asked and give some indication of what the future held or what was the best course of action to take. Some diviners would use a pin or the tip of a dagger instead of a finger.

Rhapsodomancy is therefore similar to **bibliomancy** but instead of any book being chosen, a book of poetry must be used. The ancient Greeks tended to use **Homer**'s work, while the Romans favoured Virgil.

RHINE, J B [1895–1980]

Considered by many to be the father of **parapsychology**, the scientific study of **psi** and **paranormal** abilities such as **clairvoyance** and **telepathy**, Rhine was co-founder of the revolutionary Parapsychology Laboratory at Duke University in Durham, North Carolina.

Rhine was born on 29 September 1895 in a log house in the Pennsylvania Mountains. In 1920 he married Louisa Ella Weckesser and in 1925 he received his PhD in botany from the University of Chicago. But Rhine did not find botany fulfilling and more and more his interest turned towards the paranormal. He joined the **American Society for Psychical Research** and began to work for the Society's *Journal*.

In 1926 Rhine moved to Boston, where he investigated **spiritualist** mediumship with **William McDougall** and Walter Franklin Prince, two prominent figures in psychical research. Initial investigation proved disappointing when a sitting with **Mina Crandon** turned out to be a **fraud**, but later sittings with **Minnie Meserve Soule** proved to be more encouraging. When it came to interpreting the Soule sittings there was disagreement as to whether the **séance** communications were genuine messages from the dead or whether they could be explained on the basis of the **medium's extrasensory perception** (**ESP**); Rhine favoured the later interpretation.

In the fall of 1927 Rhine went to Duke University to assist McDougall in his data analysis. Encouraged by McDougall he set up a programme of statistical validation of

ESP, with emphasis initially on clairvoyance and telepathy using **Zener cards** as test cards. The ESP experiments that followed would make the Parapsychology Laboratory at Duke University world famous.

Even though Rhine believed that ESP played a key part in mediumistic communications he never lost interest in the question of **survival after death**. He did, however, place an emphasis on his conviction that until the limits of ESP were established the question of survival after death could not be investigated scientifically.

The parapsychology unit continued to operate at Duke University until Rhine retired in 1965 and moved it off campus to the new Foundation for Research on the Nature of Man (later the **Rhine Research Center**), where it is still in existence. Rhine died on 20 February 1980. His best-selling books include *New Frontiers of the Mind* (1937), *The Reach of the Mind* (1947) and *New World of the Mind* (1953).

RHINE, LOUISA ELLA WECKESSER [1891–1983]

American parapsychologist and wife of **J B Rhine**, Louisa Rhine is best known for her analysis of spontaneous case accounts, including **apparitions**.

Like her husband, Louisa studied at the University of Chicago and changed direction from botany to psychical research. In 1948 she took up the study of spontaneous cases at the Parapsychology Laboratory set up by her husband at Duke University. Her aim during the investigation was not to determine the truth of individual cases but to see if patterns existed. She came to the conclusion that the **percipient**, not the **agent**, was the key figure in **ESP** and apparition cases. (The terms percipient and agent were in use during the early days of psychical research; the agent was responsible for sending the communication of ESP experience to the percipient.)

Rhine's theories were controversial because they undermined one of the main lines of evidence for **survival after death**. If the percipient alone was responsible for spontaneous cases then there was no need for agent or **spirit** involvement. For example, falling objects in **poltergeist** cases could have been a result of the percipient's **psychokinesis**.

In 1981 Rhine became president of the **Society for Psychical Research**, one of the few Americans to have held the position and only the third woman to do so. Besides publishing numerous papers in **parapsychology** journals, her books include *Hidden Channels of the Mind* (1961), *ESP in Life and Lab* (1967), *Mind over Matter* (1970), *Psi: What is it?* (1975) and *The Invisible Picture* (1981).

RHINE RESEARCH CENTER

Parapsychological research and education centre, formerly the Foundation for Research on the Nature of Man that developed out of the Parapsychology

Laboratory at Duke University in Durham, North Carolina.

The Rhine Research Center dates back to the 1930s when **ESP card** tests conducted by **J B Rhine** were created within the Parapsychology Laboratory at Duke University, an offshoot of the psychology department. In 1965 Rhine retired from Duke University and moved the parapsychology unit off campus to form the Foundation for Research on the Nature of Man. In 1995 the Foundation was renamed the Rhine Research Center in his honour.

The Rhine Research Center has published the quarterly *Journal of Parapsychology* since 1937. The Center maintains a library and summer study programme for training in **parapsychology**. It is committed to the scientific exploration of:

- *Telepathy (mind to mind communication).*
- *Clairvoyance or remote viewing (extrasensory awareness of a physical object or contemporaneous physical event).*
- *Precognition (extrasensory awareness of a future event).*
- *Psychokinesis (mind over matter effect on physical or living systems).*
- *Survival of consciousness (including studies of mediumship, near-death experiences, out-of-body experiences and hauntings).*

According to its website (www.rhine.org) the Center strongly believes that:

Scientific knowledge gathered thus far strongly suggests that these capacities are real, but there is a critical need for more understanding of these anomalous mental phenomena. Very few scientists or scholars are committed to a critical and serious study of them. The Rhine Research Center (and the Duke Parapsychology Laboratory before it) has long stood in the forefront of gathering such scientific knowledge.

RIGHT-HAND PATH

Phrase often used to describe the path of **white magic**, where the magical practitioner's intention is to heal and cause no harm to anyone. In other words it is a path of light and spiritual awareness and contrasts with the **left-hand path** where there is an intention to harm a person, object or other living being, or to use force against a person's free will.

RITUAL MAGIC

The term 'ritual' really describes any sequence, action or habit that is frequently repeated, for example buying the same newspaper each day, but it has developed into a description of religious and magical ceremonies characterized by a particular set of actions and, typically, special clothing and equipment.

Although the inner nature of ritual magic was kept secret for centuries it is now known that magical ritual has an inner as well as an outer aspect – in other words practitioners typically engage in a series of

visualizations, intentions and **affirmations** in tandem with actions that are visible.

ROBERTS, JANE [1929–1984]

Twentieth-century author and poet who is best known for **channelling** an **entity** called Seth.

Jane Roberts was born in Saratoga Springs, New York and was the author of numerous short stories and poems. One day in September 1963, while she sat writing poetry, her mind was suddenly flooded with astonishing and new ideas and her consciousness allegedly lifted out of her body. When it returned she discovered that through **automatic writing** she had recorded the ideas that had come into her mind. The notes even bore the title *The Physical Universe as Idea Construction*.

Thereafter Roberts began to experiment with an **Ouija board** despite being warned that it could invite negative **spirits**. Roberts ignored the warning, maintaining that it was not the Ouija board but a person's superstitious fears that produced unpleasant results. Initial communications with the board were supposedly from Roberts's grandfather but then, on 2 December 1963, a communication came from a dead English teacher, whom Roberts identified as Frank Withers. Checks of local records indicated that he had indeed existed.

After several sessions with Withers the entity indicated that he wanted to be called Seth, to express 'the whole self I am, or am trying to be'. Withers, the entity said, was part of a much larger personality and on occasions he even called Withers a 'fat head'. Seth described himself as an energy personality essence that no longer had physical form. He told Jane and her husband, Robert Butt, that he had known them in a previous life in seventeenth-century Denmark. Seth also claimed to have had numerous lives as both a man and as a woman. He had been a cave man, a Roman, a spice merchant in the seventeenth century, when he met Roberts and Butt, an Ethiopian black man, a courtesan during the time of David, a Dutch spinister and several incarnations as a humble wife and mother.

Seth suggested communications should take place twice a week, and so began Roberts's incredible career as a channel for Seth. Over time she discarded the Ouija board for **clairaudient** channelling and it was noticed that in deep **trance** her voice would deepen and her features would change. Seth explained that speaking through Roberts involved a 'psychological extension, a projection of characteristics on both of our parts.'

Seth claimed to be a personality with a message and said that he had lived many lives, in various forms. His central message was that human beings create their lives with their thoughts, actions and beliefs. He also stated that each person has multiple personalities and there are no limits to the growth of the self. Humans reincarnate many times and the past, present and future exist in a simultaneous now. According to Seth there is no **karma** that punishes or rewards a person for actions in past

Famous Seth quotes

The following quotations are from Seth as channelled by Jane Roberts and recorded by Rob Butts.

'You get what you concentrate upon … there is no other main rule.'

'Therefore, as always, make of this voice what you choose to make of it. Make of me what you choose to make of me, but recognize within yourselves the vitality of your being. And look to no man or no idea or no woman or no dogma, but the vitality of your own being, and trust it. And that which offends your soul, turn away from, but trust yourself.'

'I come here because it is fun. I have fun when I come here. I do not come here because I feel that I have any great responsibility for your beings or welfare. Who am I to set myself against the innate wisdom of your own individual being, or to take upon my invisible shoulders the great privilege or joyful responsibility for your behaviour and destiny?'

'The self has no boundaries except those it accepts out of ignorance.'

'If you are in poor health, you can remedy it. If your personal relationships are unsatisfactory, you can change them for the better. If you are in poverty, you can find yourself surrounded by abundance … Each of you, regardless of position, status, circumstances, or physical condition, is in control of your own experience.'

'In the most basic sense, the purpose of life is being – as opposed to not being.'

'Using your free will, you have made physical reality into something quite different than what was intended. You have allowed the ego to become overly developed and specialized. You were here to work out problems and challenges, but you were always to be aware of your own inner reality, and of your non-physical existence. To a large extent you have lost contact with this. You have focused so strongly upon physical reality that it become the only reality that you know.'

'You create your reality according to your beliefs and expectations; therefore you should examine these carefully. If you do not like some aspect of your world, then examine your own expectations.'

lives; rather progress of the **soul** depends on its **psychic** and spiritual development.

Seth maintained that God is neither male nor female but the sum of everything that exists within each one of us. The drama played out by Christ was a manifestation of God in a way that humans can understand. Seth also predicted the 'second coming' in 2075, when an individual would emerge as a great psychic destined to teach others how to use their inner senses to make true spirituality possible.

Roberts was unique in that she never sought large audiences or fees when she channelled Seth. All her sessions were done at home before a small group of family and friends. Her husband took most of the notes during the channelling and in this way Seth dictated several books. Roberts also wrote other books herself about her contact with Seth and other channelled sources, which included the American philosopher **William James** and the French painter Paul Cezanne.

Roll, William [1926–]

American parapsychologist and professor who specialized in the study of **poltergeists** and **survival after death** phenomena.

William Roll was born on 3 July 1926 in Bremen, Germany. He enrolled at the University of California, Berkeley in 1947 and majored in philosophy and psychology. After a year of graduate work in sociology, Roll went to Oxford University to do research in **parapsychology** under Professor H H Rice until 1957. His thesis was entitled 'Theory and Experiment in Psychical Research' and he was president of the Oxford University Society for Psychical Research.

In 1957, Roll joined the staff of the Parapsychology Laboratory at Duke University, working under **J B Rhine** until 1964. During this period he investigated the **Seaford poltergeist** and came to the conclusion that the disturbances were most likely caused by unconscious **psychokinesis** on the part of a teenage boy in the family. Along with fellow parapsychologist **J G Pratt** he coined the term '**recurrent spontaneous psychokinesis**' to describe cases of recurring psychokinetic activity. The term continues to be used today as a synonym for poltergeist activity.

In 1959 Roll was named director of the **Psychical Research Foundation** and began to devote himself full time to the investigation of poltergeist cases and survival research. In 1986, when he was appointed Professor of Psychical Research and Psychology at West Georgia College (now the State University of West Georgia), he took the Psychical Research Foundation with him.

Roll has authored more than a hundred scientific papers and several articles for anthologies, has edited 11 volumes of *Research in Parapsychology* and has written five books: *The Poltergeist* (1972), *Theory and Experiment in Psychical Research* (1975, his M.Litt. thesis), *This World or That: An Examination of Parapsychological Findings Suggestive of the Survival of the Human Personality After Death* (1989), *Psychic Connections* (1995, with Lois Duncan) and

Unleashed (2004, with Valerie Storey). In 1996 he received the **Parapsychological Association**'s award for a Distinguished Career in Parapsychology, and in 2002 he was awarded the Dinsdale Memorial Award by the Society for Scientific Investigation for his recurrent spontaneous psychokinesis studies.

Throughout his research Roll remained sceptical of evidence for personal survival. He outlined a model of survival that holds that although the body disintegrates at death memory impressions may be connected to one another in a **psi** field, through which they are accessible to psychically gifted living persons. Roll also held fast to his theory that poltergeists should be viewed almost entirely in terms of recurrent spontaneous psychokinesis caused by repressed tensions on the part of subjects, typically young children or teenagers.

ROSE HALL

Rose Hall Great House in Montego Bay, Jamaica, was formerly the home of Annie Palmer, the so-called White Witch of Rose Hall.

Raised by a **Voodoo** nanny, Annie was in her late teens when she came to Rose Hall. Schooled in **black magic** and voodoo **curses**, Annie would often ride her white horse throughout the plantation, terrorizing her 2,000 slaves. While she lived there it is said that she murdered three husbands and was eventually murdered herself in 1831 at the age of 29 by one of her slave lovers.

Rose Hall was left in ruins for many years. Local residents were afraid to go near it, remembering Annie's declaration that it was her house, and no one else would ever have possession of it. Eventually a couple bought it and began to restore it themselves. When work began on the house a servant woman fell to her death from the observation balcony Annie allegedly used when she witnessed whippings. The fall was considered mysterious due to the waist-high railing that encircles the balcony, and it was rumoured that the woman was somehow lured there by Annie's **spirit**, and pushed over the railing.

Several years later, the house was restored and given to the Jamaican people as a historical landmark. It is open for guided tours but many Jamaicans still believe it is haunted. Tours of the house typically end early so that all of the employees can leave before Annie's spirit comes out to wander.

Many visitors have reported strange images in photographs taken at the house. Some report the appearance of woman's face in the mirror in Annie's bedroom. Others report lights and glowing areas on the bed in Annie's room. It has also been noted that film used in certain rooms of the house will not develop, while the rest of the roll in other parts of the house is fine. Some of these mysterious photographs are on display at the gift shop belonging to Rose Hall.

ROSENHEIM POLTERGEIST

Poltergeist case that took place in 1967 in the Bavarian town of Rosenheim.

The case began in a law office in Rosenheim with sharp banging noises and a series of electrical problems: fuses blew without any apparent cause, numerous problems erupted with the telephones, neon lights went out and photocopying machines went crazy.

Investigators were called in and it seemed that the human focal point was a 19-year-old employee called Anna S. Whenever she walked down the hall light bulbs would explode and light fixtures would swing from side to side.

Soon after the investigation began pictures began to rotate and move. Test apparatus seemed to indicate that telephone numbers were being dialled by invisible means. The investigators concluded that the phenomena defied explanation in terms of theoretical physics and the movements, in particular the telephone dialling, seemed to be performed by 'intelligently controlled forces that have a tendency to evade investigation'.

The case of the Rosenheim poltergeist remains unsolved.

ROSICRUCIANS

Umbrella term for a number of **esoteric** and **occult** sects which claim to be the oldest secret societies in the world. Many of them base their teachings on those of 'Christian Rosenkreutz', who was allegedly a medieval monk who travelled the Middle East studying mystic traditions. On his return he founded the Order of the Rosy Cross, where he and his fellow monks applied the lore of magic and healing Rosenkreutz had learned on his travels.

Rosenkreutz's writings may have remained in obscurity had it not been for the publication in Germany in 1615 of a pamphlet entitled *Fama Fraternitatis*, supposedly written by Rosenkreutz but probably the work of Johann Valentin Andreas, a Wittenberg theologian. The pamphlet told the story of the founding of the Rosicrucian order and attempted to fuse the Reformation with advances in scientific knowledge. Although obscure and difficult to read the publication sparked immediate interest and was reprinted four times within the space of two years and translated into Dutch and English a few years later.

The *Fama* was followed in 1615 by another pamphlet on the subject, the *Confessio Fraternitatis R.C.*, spelling out the order's aims, which included bringing an end to sectarianism and expressing the fraternity's opposition to the papacy, Islam and fraudulent alchemists. In 1616 the final book in the series was published, the *Chymische Hochzeit Christian Rosenkreutz*, which was translated into English as *The Hermetick Romance*. It was a lively story full of esoteric symbolism and **alchemy**.

These writings inspired the formation of a secret brotherhood of Rosicrucians with roots in occult mystic philosophy. By 1620 interest began to wane however, only to revive again in 1710 with the formation, by

Sigmund Richter, of the Order of the Gold and Rosy Cross, an alchemical fraternity. Later the terms 'Rose cross' and 'Rosicrucian' found their way into **Freemasonry** and the legend of Christain Rosenkreutz was taught to members of the Victorian Order of the **Golden Dawn**.

Today there are numerous organizations claiming links to this secret society and the answers to life's mysteries. Perhaps the best known is the American Ancient and Mystic Order Rosae Crucis (AMORC), founded by H Spencer Lewis (1883–1939), which teaches a wide body of esoteric doctrine and technique.

Rosicrucian symbols and beliefs have changed little from those early pamphlets published in the seventeenth century. Through study and practice members must strive for the perfection embodied by the Master of the Great White Lodge, with the ultimate goal being admittance into the Lodge and the attainment of true knowledge. Students must progress through 12 degrees of mastery, with the final three attained psychically, usually in the Order's temples in the East. Worthy members who have mastered the first nine degrees may enter the Illuminati, a higher organization of the Order.

Rosicrucians place an emphasis on **reincarnation** but they have most often been associated with alchemy. Members stress healthy living and abstain from meat, alcohol and tobacco. All Rosicrucian organizations employ the symbol of the rose – to represent love and secrecy – and the cross – to represent death, suffering and resurrection – although the combinations they appear in differ from organization to organization. The symbol of AMORC shows one red rose centred on a gold cross, with looped ends. AMORC also uses an equilateral triangle, point down, inscribed on the cross and has had both these symbols registered with the United States Patent Office as the only true Rosicrucian symbols.

RUNES

Ancient Norse and Teutonic alphabet **sigils** that are believed to have magical and divinatory properties. The term rune comes from the Indo European root *ru*, which means secret mystery.

Rune **divination** consists of a set of 24 or 25 small tablets or stones with Norse symbols inscribed on them. Typically the runes are kept in a small drawstring bag. One popular method of using them is simply to concentrate on a question, reach into the rune bag, pull out one rune out at random and interpret the symbol to fit the situation. This is called 'Odin's Rune' and is an indication of where your path lies. Another method is to spread all the runes on a table or the ground, face down, and then to pass the hands lightly over the backs of them until one rune in particular draws the person to it. This one is then turned over as 'Odin's Rune'. Yet another method is the Three Rune spread, when three runes are drawn from the bag to be interpreted as past, present and future, or as present situation, suggested course of action and new situation evolving and so on. Other variations are a five-rune spread, a seven-rune spread, etc.

Each rune character is made up of a combination of vertical and diagonal lines each with symbolic meaning. If the runes are cast down on the ground and the character appears upside down, it reverses the meaning of that rune. No one knows exactly what each rune meant originally; over the centuries meanings have been given by various authors. It is often suggested to those who wish to work with runes that they take each individual rune in turn and spend some time meditating on it in order to find what it means to them personally.

Archaeological finds show that runes were created by the Germanic peoples, the Saxons and Scandinavians, sometime between 1300 and 1200 BC. Typically they were made of wood, metal or stone and the act of inscribing the name of a natural element was thought to endow the rune with sacred power. This made runes popular for divination and as protective **amulets**. They were also used in weather rites, fertility, birth and death rights and to seal contracts, and in the writing of poetry. Each rune was also associated with a different Norse deity who was thought to serve as a guiding spirit to the person using them.

Runes began to disappear from use around the fourteenth century when the Christian Church started to persecute rune casters and Northern **Pagans**, who were burned at the stake until the seventeenth century. In the late nineteenth century German occultists revived interest in runes, which then became associated with Teutonic racial supremacy. In World War II the Nazi use of the swastika, originally Thor's hammer and the symbol of the Earth Mother and the sun, and the S sigil, used by the SS, threatened to condemn these symbols forever.

Only recently have runes begun to cast off their negative associations and their use in divination and guidance has started to rise again. Today rune tiles are typically drawn from bags and meditated upon, or cast in lots or laid out like **tarot** cards. In much the same way as tarot cards, runes do not give answers but provide the means to create an answer; they are considered keys to personal growth.

RUNNING WATER

Universal, age-old **superstition** that no **ghost** can cross over running water because streams are thought to be holy places — especially those that run in a southerly direction. In **exorcisms** holy water is used to rid the haunted place or the possessed person of troublesome **entities** and it is thought to be most effective if it is drawn from a clear, fast running brook.

RUNOLFUR RUNOLFSSON CASE

Case of a **drop in communicator** who claimed he was searching for a missing part of his body.

This unusual case took place between 1937 and 1940 and involved Icelandic trance **medium** Hafsteinn Björnsson. During a **séance** in the autumn of 1937 an unknown **entity** dropped in asking for his missing leg. Asked where the leg was he said, 'It's in the sea.' For the next year the entity continued to drop in on Björnsson asking for his leg. The entity was rude and would often brush other **spirits** aside.

Progress wasn't made until a fish merchant called Ludvik Gudmunsson joined the sittings. The entity said Gudmunsson would know about the leg, which was at his house in Sandgerdi. Gudmunsson got confused and professed to know nothing. The entity then revealed his real name, which was Runolfur Runolfson, or Runki for short, and he had died in October 1879 at the age of 52. One night after drinking at a friend's house he had tried to walk home but had passed out on the seashore and the tide had carried him out. His body washed ashore a few months later and birds and animals had picked at his bones. His corpse was buried but a thighbone was missing. The entity wanted the bone back.

An investigation was carried out and the life and death of Runki was verified. In 1940 a room in Gudmunsson's house was torn down and a thighbone that looked like it was human was discovered. A year later the bone was given a proper religious burial at Utskalar and at a subsequent séance Runki expressed his gratitude. He said he had been present at the burial and was able to describe it in great detail.

This wasn't the last that was heard of Runki, as he allegedly stayed in contact with Björnsson and became his main **control**. Over the years he modified his crude ways and even began to help other **discarnate entities** to make contact through Björnsson.

RUSALKA

According to Russian lore, rusalka is the spirit of a maiden who drowned by accident or was murdered by drowning. She haunts the spot where she died. She is not particularly malevolent, and will be allowed to depart in peace if her death is remembered and/or avenged. Rusalki (plural) are also beautiful river nymphs with long green hair that are said to inhabit small islands in southern Russia where, according to lore, they try to help poor hard-working fishermen.

S

SACRED GEOMETRY

The idea that people respond with awe and reverence to certain structures, patterns, designs and objects, either manmade or natural, because they conform to a concept of mathematical harmoney and ratio and by so doing represent the spiritual connection between human and divine. In other words, certain structures and designs are believed to be symbolic of the underlying metaphysical principle of the inseparable relationship of the part to the whole and as such they provide a continuous reminder of humanity's relationship to all things created. Some believe that sacred geometry is the universal language of the subconscious, causing the five senses and the psychic **sixth sense** to respond intuitively to the proportions of certain structures and designs.

Examples of sacred geometry in practice are the Taj Mahal, Leonardo's masterpiece 'The Last Supper', **Stonehenge**, the Pyramids of Egypt and **crop circles**.

SAGE LEAVES

Superstition credits this aromatic spice with the power to enable people to see **ghosts**. In Native American traditions, burning bundles of sage are believed to purify an area or rid it of ghostly influences. In English folklore, a young girl who gathers 12 sage leaves from a garden at midnight on **Halloween** night is said to see a vision of her future husband. In the English county of Lancashire, it is said the same thing will happen if a young woman walks around a churchyard 12 times.

SAI BABA [1926–]

Hindu **avatar** whose alleged miraculous powers have attracted a following in both the East and the West. Sai Baba has been studied by Western psychical researchers and no evidence of **fraud** has been found. He is renowned for his **healing** powers, his ability to materialize objects, **levitation**, **bilocation** and **precognition**.

Sai Baba was born into a low caste family on 23 November 1926, in Southern India. His miraculous powers allegedly began to manifest after he was stung by a black scorpion on 8 March 1940. On 23 May he announced that he was Sathya Sia Baba reborn; the original Sai Baba was a Brahman **fakir** at the turn of the century, who had allegedly produced astonishing miracles. After announcing that he was reborn Sai Baba presented his family with gifts of flowers and sweets, which he seemed to materialize with a wave of his hand.

Although Sai Baba immediately attracted followers he was also criticized and shunned, as avatars traditionally came from high caste families. Despite this prejudice, by the 1970s Sai Baba had a huge following and thousands of people would camp outside his ashram hoping to get a glimpse of him, touch him, receive an **apport** or just listen to him.

Sai Baba's trademark is his ability to produce apports with the wave of his hand; three-quarters of his followers claim to have seen or received one. The apports produced include food and drink, ash, religious statues, jewellery, photographs and stamps bearing his likeness. He is said to fill empty bowls with food and to produce enough to feed hundreds of people at a time. He can also reach into sand and pull out food. All the food produced is fresh and new and if a person does not like a particular apport he has been known to change it to meet their requirements. Sai Baba has explained that his powers came from God and that he produces apports by imagining them first and then transporting them from the superconscious where they already exist to the physical world.

Other phenomena attributed to Sai Baba include the instant changing of colour of his clothes, **psychic surgery**, **telepathy**, **clairvoyance**, levitation and the changing of water into other beverages and gasoline. He has also been known to go into convulsive **trances** lasting several hours; during these trances his body is said to be cold to the touch. The explanation offered by Sai Baba for these trances was that he had been called to help someone in a far distant location and in this distant location he reportedly appeared as if in the flesh.

Sai Baba generally refused to submit to experiments to test his powers but he did allow Erlendur Haraldsson, a psychologist and psychical researcher from the University of Iceland, to investigate his work for a 10-year period from 1973 to 1983. In his research Haraldsson closely observed the materialization of *vibuti*, holy ash, but also came to the conclusion that not all of Sai Baba's precognitive **predictions** were accurate and not all of his cures worked. Despite this a number of prominent Indian scientists believe his powers to be genuine and his followers believe him to be God. Sceptics say that Sai Baba's miracles are performed by sleight of hand, and in recent years the guru has been associated with a great deal of negative publicity including sexual allegations. As to whether Sai Baba is a genuine miracle worker or a fraud the jury is still out, and to this day Sai Baba remains an enigma.

Sai Baba has predicted that he will die in 2020 at the age of 94 and be reborn as Prema Sai Baba.

St Elmo's fire

Ghost lights that typically appear on ships and have been reported by sailors for centuries.

St Elmo's fire is a bright bluish-white glow, appearing like fire in some circumstances, often in double or triple jets, from tall, sharply pointed structures such as masts, spires and chimneys. It can also appear between the tips of cattle horns during a thunderstorm or sharp objects in the middle of a tornado. It is not the same phenomenon as ball lightning, although the two are related.

The phenomenon commonly occurs at the mastheads of ships and makes eerie cracking sounds during thunderstorms at sea. According to **superstition**, if one of the lights should fall to the deck and glow near a particular sailor it is believed this person will soon die. The lights are named after St Elmo, who was the patron saint of Mediterranean sailors. St Elmo died during a storm at sea but before his death he promised the crew that if they were not destined to die like him he would get a message to them. Later, when a glowing light appeared near the mast, the sailors believed it was a message from St Elmo and ever since the appearance of St Elmo's fire is believed to be a sign that the worst of the storm is over.

It seems there is a natural explanation for the phenomenon. Benjamin Franklin correctly observed in 1749 that the lights are electric in nature. What in fact happens is that the light is caused by electrical discharges when the weather begins to clear.

SAINT JOHN'S WORT

Herbaceous shrub of the genus *Hypericum* bearing yellow flowers that is believed to have the power to drive away devils, **demons**, **witches**, imps, **fairies** and **ghosts**.

The ancient Greeks used it in **exorcisms**, as they believed the aroma would drive away the **spirits**. In Christianity the plant was dedicated to St John the Baptist whose feast day is observed on 24 June, a few days after the shrub starts to flower. In the seventeenth century it was used for the exorcism of demons and ghosts and to expose witches and protect against harmful **spells**.

Around midsummer, it is still believed that if Saint John's wort is draped around a child's neck it will protect them from illness for a year. Midsummer, however, isn't the only time this plant is thought to be effective; if gathered on a Friday and worn on the neck it is said to dispel anxiety and drive away all kinds of spirits.

SAKURA, GHOST OF

Famous Japanese ghost story involving the vengeful **ghosts** of farmer Sogoro and his wife.

Seventeenth-century Japan was ruled by feudal lords, many of whom were corrupt. The practice of demanding payment of tax in advance and never repaying the tenants was commonplace. Kotsuke no Suke, the Lord of the Castle of Sakura, was no exception, and when he succeeded his father's estate he imposed additional taxes on an already over-taxed population. The toll on the farmers was great and, finding it impossible to sell their farms because of the high taxation, many fled to other provinces or took to begging in the streets.

Eventually the chiefs of the villages in the province gathered together in a council. Sogoro, the 48-year-old chief of the village of Iwahashi, urged them to go to the capital, Yedo, and petition the Shogun directly.

A petition was duly drawn up. The village chiefs then heard that a high-ranking official, Kuze Yamato, was travelling to the Shogun's palace. The chiefs intercepted him on his journey and handed him the petition. However, the petition was returned to them and they were reprimanded for their audacity. Whereupon Sogoro decided to lie in wait for the Shogun himself to leave the palace and present the petition directly to him.

A few weeks later when the Shogun, Prince Lyemitsu, left his palace, Sogoro tied his petition to a six-foot long bamboo stick and hid himself under a bridge along the route. Boldly, when the Shogun's litter passed over the bridge, he thrust the stick directly into the litter. The Shogun got the petition but Sogoro was arrested and thrown into prison.

Prince Lyemitsu read the petition and forced Kotsuke no Suke to pay back all the money he had extorted from his tenants and to reduce the taxes. Furious and humiliated Kotsuke ordered that Sogoro and his entire family be executed for their conspiracy against him.

As he died, Sogoro cursed Kotsuke. He declared to the watching crowd,

Listen my masters! All you who have come to see this sight. Recollect that I shall pay my thanks to my lord Kotsuke no Suke for this day's work. You shall see it for yourselves, so that it shall be talked about for generations to come. As a sign, when I am dead, my head shall turn and face towards the castle. When you see this doubt not that my words shall come to pass.

True to his words, when he eventually died Sogoro's head turned towards the castle. Frightened councillors acknowledged in public that the execution had been unnec-

essarily cruel and suggested that Sogoro be canonized as St Daimyo. Kotsuke mocked their fear and said that Sogoro had received his just desserts. He then displayed even more cruelty by dismissing, banishing or executing the councillors.

For two years nothing happened, but when Kotsuke's wife was about seven months pregnant ghostly lights began to appear every night in her chamber, accompanied by fiendish laughter and wailing. The ladies-in-waiting were so distressed they petitioned to their lord for help. Kotsuke agreed to stay in his wife's chamber at night. At midnight the ghosts of Sogoro and his wife appeared and grabbed Kotsuke's wife by the hand, saying, 'We have come to meet you. The pains you are suffering are terrible but they are nothing in comparison to those of the hell to which we lead you.' Kotsuke tried to strike the ghosts but they shrieked with laughter and vanished.

Kotsuke tried to have the ghosts exorcised but the **hauntings** grew worse with the ghosts tormenting Kotsuke's wife both day and night. When she eventually died of fear the ghosts turned their attention to Kotsuke and his sons. For two years Kotsuke endured the ordeal. His family urged him to canonize Sogoro and erect a shrine to him as a way to appease the ghost. Kotsuke relented and a shrine was built. Almost immediately the hauntings stopped.

Two years later Kotsuke was in trouble when he fatally wounded a nobleman at a ceremony at the Shogun's castle. He was arrested on charges of treason and thrown into prison. While in prison Kotsuke had a chance to reflect on his misfortunes. He came to the conclusion that he was being punished for his treatment of Sogoro and he pledged that if he and his family were spared ruin he would see to it that the spirit of Sogoro was worshipped with even greater honour.

Soon Kotsuke was pardoned and a few months later, when the Shogun died, he was promoted to the lordship of another castle, Utsunomiya, which had even greater revenues. He kept his promise to elevate the worship of Sogoro as St Daimyo, and the shrine in the saint's honour was continually maintained. People would travel long distances to visit the shrine in the hope of receiving good fortune.

SAMADHI

The highest goal in **yoga meditation**, to attain Samadhi is the final stage on the inner path where absolute unity between mind, body and **spirit** is achieved. This unity leads to self-realization and recognition of the mystic unity of manifestation.

SAMPFORD GHOST

For three years from 1807, the family of Mr John Chave at Sampford Peverell, near Tiverton, Devon was allegedly plagued by a **ghost**. The events were recorded at the time by the Revd Caleb Colton, and were published as *The Narrative of the Sampford Ghost* (1810). Terrible crashes during the day and night, invisible hands attacking the occupants and objects flying around the rooms were the main activities. No explanation has ever been provided, however, the later discovery of secret passageways in the house and the knowledge that smugglers were active at the time suggests the likelihood of **fraud**.

SATAN/SATANISM

Satan, translated from the Hebrew, means 'an enemy'. Considered to be the embodiment of evil in Jewish, Christian and Islamic religions. Satan has many aliases, the Devil, the Prince of Darkness and Beelzebub being among the most common. It is usual not to refer to him directly by name as to utter the sound or name of Satan is thought to draw unwelcome attention. There are those who revere him as a deity, as a source of **black magic**, and rituals are performed to him. The worship of the Devil is known as Satanism.

Unlike many religions and philosophies, Satanism generally focuses upon the spiritual advancement of the self, rather than upon submission to a deity or a set of moral codes. It should be noted also that so-called classic 'Satanism' is not actually known to be practised in the world today. This is the Satanism depicted during the Inquisition with tales of murder, incest and baby-eating.

The emergence of modern Satanism was largely the result of a hoax carried out by French journalist Leo Taxil in the late nineteeth century. In 1884 Taxil published pamphlets detailing a vast Satanic organization, the Palladian order, which was associated with **Freemasonry**. After several years, during which the Catholic Church lent the anti-Palladian crusade its full support, Taxil announed that the whole thing was a **fraud**, concocted to demonstrate how gullible the Catholic Church was. The word 'Satanism' first entered the English language in media accounts of the Palladian affair.

Aleister Crowley's activities gave a major boost to Satanism but the first public Satanic religious organization did not surface until 1966, when Anton LaVey founded the Church of Satan in San Francisco. As much about showmanship as about religion, LaVey's group spawned a number of copycat groups who took Devil worship more literally, and also gave rise to the temple of Set, dedicated to the study of the **left-hand path**.

The 1960s and 70s saw a large-scale campaign to prove that secret conspiracies of Satanists were at work in American society, committing crimes and encouraging sex, violence and revolution. These claims reached a peak of frenzy in the 1980s with dozens of satanic abuse accusations and prosecutions. The 1980s also saw the emergence of Satanism as a small but high profile subculture among American teenagers. Drawing their inspiration from Anton LaVey's *Satanic Bible*, and from other Satan-related ideas in literature, music and popular culture, adolescent Satanists became the focus of a great deal of debate and uproar in the media when a few disturbed teenagers committed crimes in the name of Satanism.

Many contemporary Satanists eschew traditional religious beliefs, attitudes and worship in favour of a more egotistic worldview and practices such as **magic**.

SATURDAY

The last day of the week, representing the end of a cycle which to the superstitious is both lucky and unlucky. For example, some people believe that people born on Saturdays can see **ghosts**. In the lore of Eastern Europe people born on a Saturday are believed to be able to see **vampires**, while in Greek folklore Saturday is believed to be the day for killing vampires in their graves, as it is the only day of the week vampires allegedly sleep in their graves.

SAUCHIE POLTERGEIST

Poltergeist outbreak that occurred in Sauchie, Scotland, in 1960–61. It centred around an 11-year-old girl and is believed to have been caused by intense, repressed emotions on the part of the girl.

Virginia Campbell was the youngest of seven children belonging to James and Annie Campbell. The family was Irish and had been raised in County Donegal, but around 1960 the Campbells decided to move to Scotland. One of their sons, Thomas, lived near Sauchie and worked in the coalmines. In the autumn of 1960 Virginia and her mother went to live with Thomas, his wife, his daughter, Margaret, aged nine, and son Derek, aged six. James Campbell stayed behind in Ireland to dispose of the house and farm.

While her mother went out to work at a boarding house, Virginia was left to live with the family and share a bedroom with Margaret. She was also enrolled in a local primary school. Her teacher found her to be bright and well-mannered but noticed that she had problems mixing with the other children.

The first disturbances began on 22 November 1960, in the Campbell home, when a 'thunking' noise like a bouncing ball was heard in the girls' bedroom. The noise followed the girls around the house and only ceased when Virginia went to sleep. The following day, as well as the knocking a sideboard moved out from the wall and back again. The worried Campbells summoned a local pastor from the Church of Scotland, Revd T W Lund. Revd Lund heard the knocking and also witnessed a large chest rise up and travel about 18 inches. For the next few days the disturbances continued. The family doctor, Dr Nisbet, saw unusual movements, and at school Virginia's teacher witnessed a desk rise off the floor.

On 1 December Dr Nisbet set up a movie camera and recorded a variety of noises while Virginia entered a **trance**. At 11 pm an unsuccessful **exorcism** was performed; knockings and a rasping, sawing noise continued throughout. Following

this Nisbet felt it best to curtail the publicity and announced that Virginia had been cured. Apart from the odd incident here and there, the phenomena gradually began to diminish thereafter.

Mathematician and parapsychologist A R G Owen investigated the case and interviewed the Campbells. He concluded that the Campbells were well-adjusted people and the atmosphere in the house was stable. He declared the phenomena to be paranormal. Geophysical conditions, atmospheric drafts and trickery on the part of Virginia and the other children were ruled out. **Discarnate entities** were also ruled out for none manifested during Virginia's trances and none of the witnesses sensed anything evil. Even Virginia herself did not feel harassed by the phenomena occurring around her.

The conclusion drawn was that Virginia herself was the most likely cause. When the incidents took place she was undergoing a rapid pubescence, which may have generated the energy to create poltergeist forces. These forces may have been triggered by homesickness, shyness or loneliness, or represent a bid for attention or self-consciousness about the physical changes she was going through.

SAWSTON HALL

A sixteenth-century house in Cambridgeshire, England, that is believed to be haunted by the ghosts of Mary Tudor and a **grey lady**.

On the night of 7 July 1553, Mary Tudor, the daughter of Henry VIII of England, was taken in and hidden at Sawston Hall by the occupants, the Huddleston family, when Lady Jane Grey, Henry's grandniece, was declared Queen in Mary's place. On the morning of 8 July, fearing for her life, Mary escaped disguised as a milkmaid. In revenge supporters of Lady Jane burned the house down.

Lady Jane Grey's reign lasted only nine days before Mary Tudor was declared Queen and Lady Jane imprisoned as an impostor and executed. In gratitude for helping her in her hour of need Mary – who later became known as Bloody Mary for her persecution of Protestants – rebuilt Sawston Hall. A portrait of her still hangs in the Great Hall and her ghost is said to have been seen gliding serenely and at great speed through the house. The other ghost associated with Sawston Hall, the lady in grey, is of unknown origin. She is said to knock three times at the door and then float across the room.

SCAPULOMANCY

Method of **divination** that was done by interpreting the cracks and marks on an animal's shoulder blade. The practice was common in Wales, England and Ireland in the twelfth and thirteenth centuries.

The bone used in the divination was typically the right shoulder blade of a slaughtered sheep, as opposed to an animal that had died from disease or been killed by wild animals. To begin with, the shoulder blade must be cleaned of meat and washed in clean water. The diviner then fumigates it with juniper and holds it up with his or her right hand to be reflected in a mirror. Next, he or she invokes the deities, requesting them to give a clear answer. The shoulder blade is then burned in a smokeless fire. During the burning, if the shoulder blade makes a rattling sound it means evil **spirits** are **haunting** the house. Accompanying clucking sounds indicate that they are causing harm and discord in the family. The spine of the shoulder blade falling away very quickly indicates that the above troubles could be dispelled with appropriate rituals. The shoulder blade would then be divided into different areas to enable the diviner to make more detailed predictions.

On the night of the treacherous massacre at Glencoe, Scotland (12 February 1692) it is said that some members of the Macdonald clan were examining the shoulder blade of a sheep that had been prepared to feed the government troops billeted with them. One of those studying the shoulder blade said there would be a great shedding of blood in the glen. Sensing some kind of treason (early next morning the billeted troops would attack the Macdonalds on the command of Sir John Dalrymple, master of Stair) the Macdonalds hastily departed and so escaped the great massacre that would take place.

SCARAB

Ancient Egyptian symbol of rebirth and immortality. The dead were often buried with carvings in the form of a scarab typically in the linen wrappings that bound the body to ensure a safe passage to the underworld. Psychoanalyst **Carl Jung** believed the scarab to be an important **archetype** for rebirth and in his writings cites its appearance in a case study as an example of **synchronicity**.

SCATOMANCY

Divination based on the examination of faeces. James Sanford, in *Agrippa's Of the vanitie and uncertaintie of artes and sciences* (1569), wrote that scatomancy was 'the divinations or Prognostications of Physicians gathered by odours and urines'. The odour of faeces probably played an important part in its interpretation; it was a pointer to age, for example. Consistency also played a part, as did the location of faeces. The faeces were also examined for their contents: seeds, nuts, etc. were all believed to be of significance.

SCEPTIC

A person inclined to discount the alleged reality of the **paranormal** and to challenge parapsychological research methods and conclusions by seeking rational or conventional scientific explanations for anomalous phenomena.

SCHNEIDER BROTHERS

Austrian **physical mediums**, Rudi (1908–1957) and Willi (1903–1971) Schneider were celebrated in their day. Rudi, the younger brother, was studied extensively by psychical researchers in Europe and the United States.

Rudi and Willi's father was a printer in Braunau-am-Inn, Austria, where both were born. One night, when the Schneider family was playing with an **Ouija board**, they discovered that whatever requests were made, such as the movement of objects, they were carried out. Willi was only 14 at the time but it wasn't long before he had developed mediumistic skills with a female **control** called Olga.

News of the phenomena associated with Willi's **séances** spread and came to the attention of **Baron Albert von Schrenck-Notzing**. Schrenck-Notzing was an experienced and respected psychical investigator alert to the potential for trickery. Between December 1921 and July 1922 Willi held 56 séances for Schrenck-Notzing, many of which were witnessed by scientists from a number of different fields. Before each séance the room and Willi were searched. He was also required to wear a skintight outfit covered with luminous pins and buttons so that any movement he made could be detected in the dark. Willi's arms and legs were held by sitters and the objects he was to influence were placed on a table with red light bulbs and separated from him by a wire screen.

Under these tightly controlled conditions Schrenck-Notzing and the other sitters saw objects levitate as well as **materializations** of shapes that resembled human limbs. They also heard **rappings** and felt cold breezes. Among those attending the 1922 sittings were **Harry Price** and an inveterate sceptic, Eric Dingwell. Both Price and Dingwell signed a statement to indicate that what they had witnessed was genuine.

Despite a promising start Willi's career as a medium was short lived. He wanted to be a dentist and the more he concentrated on that the weaker his abilities became. It wasn't long, however, before his younger brother Rudi began to demonstrate similar talents. One night at a séance with Willi at the Schneider home, Willi's control Olga announced that she needed Rudi as his power was stronger than Willi's. Rudi was still a young man at the time and asleep in bed so his parents didn't want to wake him. A few minutes later Rudi, deep in **trance**, opened the door and joined the séance. After that Olga attached herself to Rudi and never communicated through Willi again.

In the spring of 1926 Harry Price brought a reporter from the London *Daily News* to witness phenomena caused by Rudi. The reporter was impressed and Rudi's mediumship began to be widely publicized. Despite this Rudi was accused of **fraud** by a number of sceptics, who implied that Schrenck-Notzing's experi-

mental testing methods were inadequate. Stung by this criticism Schrenck-Notzing arranged for a series of tests to be conducted under a new part-electrical and part-tactile system. Sadly, before the experiments could be carried out, Schrenck-Notzing died.

Price invited Rudi to visit his laboratory for psychical research in London, and in 1929 and 1930 a number of experiments were carried out. These experiments included use of the electrical controls Schrenck-Notzing had planned which included the entire circle of sitters, making it impossible for them to help the phenomena without knowing it. The experiments were highly successful. Cold breezes, movement of objects, **levitations** of the table and materializations of arms and hands all occurred. Price offered £1,000 to any magician who could conjure the same effects under the same conditions. Nobody took up the challenge.

Rudi was also tested at the **Institut Metaphsychique International** in the winter of 1930. This time an infrared beam was shone across the room between Rudi and a table on which were placed the objects he was to move. If the beam was crossed an alarm would go off automatically. The alarm went off many times but Rudi would always be hunched in a chair. Laser experiments to measure the deflection of the beam indicated that something was crossing it and moving the objects on the table but that something was only quasi material.

In 1932 Rudi conducted another series of tests at Price's lab. This time he was distracted by his fiancée, whom he insisted on taking with him. Test results were mixed, suggesting that Rudi's powers were on the wane. Then Price dropped a bombshell into the investigations. He claimed to have found photographic evidence that Rudi had managed to free an arm and move a handkerchief at sittings held in March 1932 at the National Institute for Psychical Research. There were those who believed that Price's vanity and hunger for publicity could have encouraged him to sacrifice his earlier work with Rudi, but whatever the truth of the matter Rudi's reputation was irreversibly damaged.

Rudi married his fiancée and gave up mediumship to become a successful mechanic, eventually owning his own garage.

SCHRENCK-NOTZING, BARON ALBERT VON [1862–1929]

Renowned German psychotherapist and psychical researcher famous for his study of **physical mediumship**, Baron Schrenck-Notzing became known as the 'Ghost Baron'.

Born into a noble family Schrenk-Notzing earned his MD in 1888 in the study of the therapeutic use of **hypnosis** in a Munich hospital. He soon became one of the foremost authorities of his day on hypnosis, sexuality and the criminal mind. His study of hypnosis introduced him to the **psychic** world and in 1892, following his marriage to a wealthy heiress, he was able to give up his medical practice and devote himself entirely to psychical research.

Schrenk-Notzing first confined himself to the study of **telepathy** but after witnessing a series of sittings with **Eusapia Palladino** he started to turn his attention to physical mediumship. He began to travel through Europe to work with different **mediums** – some of whom he exposed as **frauds**. *The Phenomena of Materialisations* (1913) gives a detailed account of Schrenk-Notzing's investigations into physical mediumship, but his work was given the cold shoulder both by the public and fellow researchers alike, who had long since come to the conclusion that physical mediumship was little more than expert conjuring.

Despite this Schrenk-Notzing continued his investigations and went on to conduct the most successful experiments of his career with the **Schneider brothers**. This time elaborate precautions against trickery were taken but when this work too was criticized he developed an electrical system for controlling a medium during **séances**. Sadly Schrenk-Notzing died before he could use this method of electric control in his research, and it was left to others to develop and use the idea.

SCIENTOLOGY

Religious movement started by an American science-fiction writer, L Ron Hubbard, in the mid-twentieth century. Scientology combines elements of psychology, occultism and story telling into a self-help belief system. The main text used is the bestselling *Dianetics*.

Scientology beliefs are structured in a series of levels, with new initiates working their way up by steps to the more advanced strata of **esoteric** knowledge. This is described as the passage up 'the bridge to total freedom', or simply 'the bridge'. The more advanced teachings are kept strictly confidential, and are not revealed to those who are not sufficiently 'spiritually prepared' to learn about them.

The central beliefs of Scientology are that a person is an immortal spiritual being (termed a 'thetan'), who possesses a mind and a body, and is accompanied by a lesser 'genetic entity'; that the thetan has lived through many past lives, stored memories of which can cause problems in the present day; and that a person is basically good, but is 'aberrated' by the memories of past traumas.

Scientology claims to offer an exact methodology to help a person achieve spiritual and ethical education, awareness and improvement, so that he or she may attain a level of spiritual purity as well as greater effectiveness in the physical world. The ultimate goal of Scientology is to 'rehabilitate' the thetan, restoring its superhuman abilities to control 'matter, energy, space and time'.

Scientology is officially represented by the controversial Church of Scientology. The Church presents itself as a non-profit religious organization dedicated to encouraging development of the human spirit. Providing counselling and rehabilitation programmes, the Church offers itself as an alternative to psychiatry, which Scientologists believe to be a barbaric and corrupt profession. Church spokespeople attest that Hubbard's teaching (called 'technology' or 'tech') has freed them from drug and alcohol addictions, depression, learning disabilities, mental disorders and other problems.

Of the many new religious movements to appear during the twentieth century, Scientology has been one of the most controversial almost since its inception. Some investigators have noted similarities in Hubbard's writings to the doctrines of **Aleister Crowley**, though the Church of Scientology denies any such connection. Critics have characterized the Church of Scientology as an unscrupulous commercial organization; it has often been described as a cult that harasses its critics and exploits its members.

Public awareness of Scientology has been promoted by the patronage and testimonials of a number of high-profile celebrities, such as actors John Travolta, Kirstie Alley and Tom Cruise, who aim to spread its goal of spiritual evolution through esoteric testings and great proselytizing efforts. Cruise in particular has made a reputation as an outspoken Scientologist, publicly criticizing actress Brooke Shields on national television in 2005 for her use of anti-depressants in recovering from post-natal depression. Cruise has also publicly attacked psychiatry.

SCOLE EXPERIMENTAL GROUP

Group of sitters in Scole, Norfolk, who practised **physical mediumship** for four years in the mid-1990s. The group believed their purpose was to pioneer a new creative energy as an alternative to **ectoplasm** for **spirit** communication with the material world. The group was investigated by the **Society for Psychical Research** for two years and no evidence of **fraud** was ever found. They did, however, believe they had found evidence of intelligent forces – either **discarnate entities** or originating from the human **psyche** – that may have been able to influence material objects and deliver messages. As soon as the case was published it became controversial.

The Scole group was initiated by Robin and Sandra Foy, both experienced **mediums** and well-known in the **spiritualist** community. In August 1991 they transformed a basement room in their house in Scole for a circle to meet, but it wasn't until 1993 that phenomena developed. Strange noises were heard, splashes of water were felt and dancing lights were seen. A **control** named Manu announced himself, and explained to the sitters that they would be working with new and safer energies made up of a blend of Earth, human and spirit energies. From then on phenomena significantly increased. There were said to be over 40 different types – from **apports**, to **materializations** of walking forms, to **direct voices** to **levitations,** to raps, to dancing lights, and so on.

The spirits encouraged the group to take photographic records of the phenomena produced and often described phenomena before they occurred. One apport that allegedly appeared in 1994 was a pristine copy of the *Daily Mail* newspaper dated 1 April 1944. Visitors were also allowed to witness the phenomena and most testified to the phenomena that occurred.

The first serious investigation of the group was conducted in 1995 by three Society of Psychical Research members: Montague Keen, Arthur Ellison and David Fontana. The spirit team appeared willing to work with the investigators but only if they could first approve procedures set up to protect against fraud.

The investigators were witness to supposed direct voices and music from the other side as well as apports. They also were shown the results of photographic experiments in which the spirits allegedly impressed a series of images on undeveloped and sealed film. The images that appeared ranged from alchemical symbols to poems to the front page of the pre-war *Daily Mirror* newspaper. Despite a willingness for the investigations to continue on the part of the sitters and researchers, the spirits explained that contact had been lost because all the experiments conducted on them had caused 'time space problems relating to an interdimensional doorway'. Allegedly the group's energy vortex had attracted experiments from the future, which were making it difficult for the spirits to make contact.

Not surprisingly the lack of strict protocol surrounding the experiments brought heavy criticism from sceptics, who pointed out that the photographic images could easily have been produced by human hands. The investigators were especially criticized for not allowing infrared equipment for the detection of movement and for agreeing to imperfect protocols. Other criticisms were that luminous hand bands worn by sitters were easy to remove and various phenomena produced, such as music and voices and cold breezes, could easily be done by human agency.

Despite such heavy criticism *The Scole Report* published by the Society for Psychical Research concluded that the sitters had no motive for fraud, as they had received no financial benefit. The investigators were convinced that they had witnessed genuine phenomena even though they acknowledged that they had not been able to achieve 'watertight conditions' to eliminate the potential for fraud.

The Scole group inspired a number of other **home circles** around the world to form and most reported similar phenomena. Enthusiasts believe that this is a sign that the spirits are trying to build an interdimensional web or bridge to the world of the living.

SCOTT, SIR WALTER
[1771–1832]

Scottish writer and poet Sir Walter Scott will long be remembered as the author of *Ivanhoe* and other classics of English literature, but he also wrote a number of ghost stories, including 'The Tapestried Chamber' and 'Wandering Willie's Tale'. Scott's interest in the **paranormal** began after he heard mysterious scratching noises in his home, Abbotsford in Roxburghshire. (Even today, Abbotsford is still widely regarded as haunted because of Scott's stories of **phantom** encounters there.) In his later life, Scott frequently travelled to other reputably haunted locations throughout the

United Kingdom in search of ghosts, many times with his literary peer and close friend, American writer **Washington Irving**.

SCREAMING SKULLS

Ghosts associated with skulls are believed to haunt numerous places, especially in England. Often the skulls seem to wish to continue to live in spirit in a certain house and when they are removed for burial or to a new location they protest with **hauntings** and **poltergeist** phenomena.

Many screaming skulls are those of people who lost their heads through execution or murder. They also often share a wish to be buried within the walls of a house and when their wishes are ignored they allegedly protest with strange noises and unexplained activity. If a house's occupants make the connection between the skull and the haunting and disinter the skull for placement in the house, the hauntings cease. Problems only occur when someone tries to remove the skull from the house. If attempts are made to destroy the skull it is said that the skull will take its revenge by bringing either some type of bad luck, even death, to a relative or by destroying the property.

One famous screaming skull story is that of a skull named Dickie that is believed to haunt Tunstead Farm, near Chapel-en-le-Frith, England. According to lore a girl was murdered in the room where the skull is kept. Another story says that Ned Dixon, an ancestor of the farmhouse's owners, was murdered in the room. Dickie is said to function as a **guardian spirit** of the farm. If strangers approach the farm knockings will be heard. Dickie has also sounded warnings upon the imminent death of a family member. On one occasion Dickie was stolen and taken to nearby Disley. The racket that followed at both Tunstead farm and Disley were allegedly so unbearable that the thieves gladly returned the skull. Similar disturbances were supposedly heard when attempts were made to bury Dickie.

There are a number of other well-known screaming skulls from England, including the Bettiscombe Skull from a house near Lyme Regis, Dorset, the Burton Agnes Skull from North Yorkshire and the Wardley Skull from Wardley Hall near Manchester.

SCRYING

The word scrying means 'seeing', especially seeing into the future. An object or surface is gazed into until **visions** are seen on the surface or in the mind's eye.

Scrying is an ancient form of **divination** that dates back to the early Egyptians and Arabs. The tool of scryers is called a speculum and although this is often thought of as a crystal ball used by gypsies, any reflective surface can in fact be used, for example, polished stones, metals, **crystals** and **mirrors**, ink blots and other dark liquids. An experienced scryer may even be able to use their own polished thumbnail for scrying purposes. The French physician and astrologer **Nostradamus** scryed with a bowl of water set upon a tripod.

Scryers usually have their own unique way of inducing visions. Those who use crystals may focus on points of light. Others enter into a meditative state and allow images to float into their inner awareness. It is believed to be possible to learn the art of scrying with patience and practice. The most important ingredient for success is the ability to relax both body and mind, leaving the mind in a passive, unfocused state. It is said that when **clairvoyance** develops the speculum clouds over with mist and then parts to reveal images.

SEAFORD POLTERGEIST

Poltergeist case characterized by bottles inexplicably popping and spilling their contents that took place in a Seaford Long Island household in 1958. The case involved no communication of any sort, as is sometimes the case with poltergeist disturbances.

The disturbances, which began without warning and ceased equally abruptly five weeks later, affected Mr and Mrs Hermann, their 13-year-old daughter, Lucille and their 12-year-old son, Jimmy. The disturbances began on 6 February, with the inexplicable opening and spilling of bottles in the house when the children were present. On 9 February at 10.15 am, when the

Scrying exercise

One of the easiest ways to make a speculum is to get a small bowl of water and add some drops of black ink. Use a bowl that is plain and unobtrusive and gives you some pleasure to see. If possible reserve this bowl for scrying purposes only.

There is a tradition that scrying powers are at their best when the moon is waxing, preferably when it is nearly full. So you may want to choose that time to begin practising. In any event select a time when you won't be interrupted for at least half an hour.

Complicated ritual isn't considered necessary for successful scrying but the right attitude of mind and the right mood are essential. You should have absolute silence if possible, so that you are not distracted by sounds. You should then do a series of deep breathing exercises to help calm your body and mind.

When you feel ready, light a candle and place it behind you so that it doesn't cause a glare on the surface of your speculum. Set the speculum on a plain dark cloth on a table before you and seat yourself comfortably. The soft indirect light of the candle will help you set the correct mood.

Turn off the lights, close your eyes and relax. Concentrate on your breath. Feel it going in and out rhythmically. If your thoughts wander gently bring them back to focus on your breath and your breath alone. When you are ready open your eyes and look at your speculum with a firm but relaxed gaze. Be prepared to look at it for at least ten minutes.

On your first session you may see nothing at all, but with a little practice you may find that you are looking at the speculum when suddenly the room and everything around you seems to go grey and misty. The speculum stands out, almost luminous. There may also be visual effects such as shimmering lights and flashes. A grey mist will seem to whirl over the surface of the speculum and cloud shapes may appear and fade to reveal images. If this happens try not to get too excited as it will jolt you out of your trance state and the visions will end. Endeavour to stay calm and relaxed throughout. After about ten minutes rouse and shake yourself and put on the lights. Don't blow out the candle yet. Let it burn for a while, then snuff it out gently.

entire family was in the dining room, bottles could be heard popping and spilling in the bedroom, bathroom and kitchen. The Hermanns called the police and when an officer arrived to investigate he also heard the sound of popping. A shampoo bottle that had been recapped had supposedly popped open again.

The case was brought to the attention of parapsychologists **William Roll, J G Pratt** and **J B Rhine**, who spent a total of 10 days investigating the house, the family and the popping. In addition to the bottles household objects such as figurines were thrown about or broken. Some of the disturbances were heard but others were witnessed. Pratt and Roll investigated the matter thoroughly to determine if there was some natural explanation for the bottles popping, but found none. They also eliminated radio waves, floor vibrations and electrical malfunction, down drafts from the chimney, aeroplane noise, plumbing problems and underground water level changes as possible causes.

Jimmy Hermann was immediately suspected as being the **agent** of the disturbances as they tended to happen when he was in the house. The police accused him of trickery but Roll and Pratt believed that **fraud** was unlikely given the fact that a 12-year-old would have found it virtually impossible to create the effects.

On 10 March the disturbances ended as suddenly as they had begun when a bleach bottle in the basement popped for the last time. It's conceivable that Jimmy was an unconscious agent, causing what Roll and Pratt termed 'recurrent spontaneous psychokinesis'.

SÉANCE

A meeting of a group of people who wish to communicate with **spirits** of loved ones or other **supernatural entities**. It is led by a **medium** who acts as a go-between for the group and the spirits.

One of the first references to séance communication dates back to the writings of Porphyry in the third century AD. In 1659 Revd Meric Casaubon wrote *A True and Faithful Relation of What Passed Between Dr Dee and Some Spirits*, but it wasn't until the mid-1800s with the **Fox sisters** and, later, with the rise of **spiritualism** that séances became popular. Early spiritualist séances were dramatic; they would take place in darkened parlours and feature feats of **physical mediumship**, typically produced from behind a **cabinet**, such as **apports**, **materializations**, **rappings** or strange lights. More recently séances have been more informal and tend to involve **mental mediumship**.

General observances are typically adhered to for success. Contrary to popular opinion it is not necessary to sit round a table and join hands in order to conduct a séance – it can take place wherever two or more people gather for such a purpose. However a table is still preferred by many mediums. A circular table with approximately eight sitters is thought to be best. Hands are placed flat on the table with the fingers touching, or sometimes clasped.

As far as sitters are concerned the younger they are the better, as youth is believed to exude more favourable **psychic** attraction. Sitters should also be equally divided by gender. No more than two or three séances should be held weekly and each séance should last no more than two hours. It is considered dangerous to reach out and touch the medium in any way as this could result in an abrupt return to consciousness, potentially resulting in death.

Some mediums consider music, prayers and conversation to be conducive to spirit communication. Sceptics argue that this can provide cover for a multitude of fraudulent noises. Houses and locations steeped in history such as castles and old churches are thought to help set the tone, as can simple furniture, preferably made from wood. Lighting is considered important and although some mediums work in full light most prefer darkness; critics again would claim this helps them to perpetuate **fraud**.

Success rates vary and first time sitters may find themselves disappointed at a séance. Nonetheless the anticipation associated with attending a séance fires the imagination and the nerves. A séance is powerful, dramatic and intense and many believe it can lift the veil between this world and the next so that the living and the dead can temporarily reunite and communicate with one another.

SECOND SIGHT

Term used to describe **psychic** powers; the ability to obtain information about a person, place, event or situation through **ESP** or other **paranormal** means.

Although it has become almost synonymous with ESP there is reason to believe it was originally coined to describe someone with non-ocular perception of energy field manifestations and **auras**.

SEDONA, ARIZONA

Area in central Arizona said to be a psychic vortex or **power spot**. The site is in the red rock country near the town of Sedona and is believed to lie on a **ley line**. The area is sacred to the Yavapai Native Americans who believe deities live in the rocks. There is also a legend that the remains of an advanced civilization lie buried deep beneath the rocks. The site is visited by thousands of people every year. **Paranormal** experiences reported when visiting the site include **visions** of **spirits**, **auras** over the rocks, **past-life recall**, clairvoyant **dreams**, **automatic writing**, **ESP**, physical cures and spiritual transformation.

SEER

Alternative name for a **clairvoyant** or **prophet**.

SELENOMANCY

Ancient practice of **divination** by the appearance of the moon. Patterns on the surface of the moon, the phase of the moon and its visibility through cloud cover are all interpreted in this form of divination.

There are countless moon-related **omens** that have evolved since prehistoric times. The moon has long been used to divine the fate of babies when they are born. For example, there is the belief that if a child is born when the moon is one day old, this person will be blessed with wealth and longevity; if the birth occurs during the moon's waning phase this indicates the child will be unhealthy; if the child is born when the moon is full, he or she will be a very strong individual, but if a child is born in the dark of the moon he or she will need special care and could die young.

In ancient Assyria diviners interpreted the appearance of a ring or halo around the moon as an omen of an impending siege, but if a break appeared in it, it indicated a lucky break. See also **Lunomancy**.

SENSITIVE

Alternative name for a **psychic**.

SETH

See **Roberts, Jane**.

SHADOW

According to **Carl Jung**, the shadow is the hidden or **unconscious** aspect of a person that the conscious self (the ego) has either repressed or ignored. The shadow is mostly composed of those elements of themselves a person finds distasteful, such as taboo urges, resentments and animal instincts. These repressed elements, however, still find a way to be heard by the projection of those qualities on to someone else. In other words, someone else is blamed for a person's own weaknesses. Despite the negative associations of the shadow, acknowledging and assimilating it into the ego is, according to Jung, a sign of a healthy person.

SHAKESPEARE, WILLIAM [1564–1616]

The celebrated Bard, William Shakespeare, was deeply interested in all aspects of the **supernatural**, and **ghosts** in particular. Several of his plays, including *Julius Caesar, The Tempest, A Midsummer's Night Dream* and *Hamlet* all prominently feature **spirits** of the dead, often to the point where ghosts dominate the action in the scenes in which they appear. He, perhaps more than any other dramatist before or since, realized the problems associated with presenting something as etherial as a ghost on stage, as F E Budd has written in *A Survey of the Occult* (1935):

Shakespeare clearly realized that ghosts and witches could not of themselves guarantee the highest imaginative effect. To achieve this, he saw, it was essential to show a sensitive mind reacting to the power of suggestion, and the finer the mind, the richer would be the effect. Moreover, like all great dramatists, he suggests the presence of supernatural forces without necessarily introducing the spectral. The working of fate, the use of tragic irony, and the description of such perturbations of nature as accompanied by the murder of Caesar and Duncan are among the means whereby he endows human action with more than human significance.

Shakespeare combined his own beliefs and experience with a good deal of personal research. He was familiar with many of the classic ghostly tales of Elizabethan England and paid visits to many of these sites in the hope of encountering a ghost himself. His involvement with the supernatural, as well as his great interest in otherworldly phenomena, are subjects that have been explored numerous times in various studies. It could be said that Shakespeare was one of the greatest ghost hunters; not only did he attempt to seek out the truth behind ghostly activity for himself, but through his writings countless others have been inspired to open their eyes to the possibilities and magic of the supernatural.

SHAMAN

A magician-priest-healer-wise person who serves tribal peoples of the Americas, India, Australia, Siberia and Mongolia, as well as in some northern European traditions. In other traditions shamans are also known as **witch doctors** or **medicine men**.

The shaman is a follower of a visionary tradition that reaches back to prehistory and is based on animistic ideas about the world. They are often well versed in herbalism and **spiritual healing** and can enter **altered states of consciousness** to tap into the elemental powers of nature and the **spirit** world for the health and well being of their people. They will typically use rhythmic drumming, dancing, **chanting**, fasting, **drugs** and **vision quests** to induce **trance** states, which allow the shaman's soul to enter the spirit world in order to heal, divine the future, communicate with spirits of the dead and perform other **supernatural** feats.

Shamans also consult **spirit guides** in the form of animal guardians called **totems**. They guide their people to awareness and maturity by helping them to contact their own totem guides, or sometimes through the use of psychogenic or psychedelic substances.

The shaman lives in two worlds: ordinary reality and a non-ordinary reality called the 'shamanic state of consciousness'. Non-ordinary reality is believed to be a unique altered state of consciousness in which the shaman has access to three cosmologies: earth, sky and underworld. The shaman remains lucid throughout his altered state, controls it and recalls afterwards what transpired during it. In this state he has access to information that is closed off during ordinary reality.

This ability to enter the shamanic state at will is essential to a shaman. Techniques for doing so include drumming, chanting, dancing, fasting, sweat baths, staring into flames, visualization and isolating oneself in darkness. In some instances psychedelic **drugs** will be used for this purpose but they are not essential for the shamanic process. The shaman also has the **clairvoyant** skills to see spirits and souls and the mediumistic ability to communicate with them. He is able to take magical flights to the heavens where he serves as an intermediary between the gods and his people; he can also descend to the underworld to the land of the dead. The flights are achieved through **shape-shifting**.

The shaman's primary function is to heal and restore the connectedness of his people to the universe. No distinctions are made between body, mind and spirit: all are seen as part of a great whole. Shamanic healing differs from Western medicine in that it is not so much concerned with extension of life but rather in protecting the soul and preventing it from eternal wandering. The kidnapping of lost souls of the living (see **soul loss**) is believed to be responsible for many kinds of illnesses and only by retrieving the soul can a shaman effect a cure. Other cures are effected by sucking out the disease or illness with the help of spirits.

Dream interpretation is another important function of shamans. They also perform various religious rites, divine the future, control the weather, identify thieves and protect their community against evil spirits.

Shamans can sometimes resort to sleight-of-hand tricks, particularly when it comes to sucking out illnesses or **psychic surgery**. They produce evidence such as stones and pieces of bones, which they say are responsible for the illness, and then palm them and make them magically disappear. Some shamans say that this has nothing to do with the cure and is simply to reassure the patient that a cure has taken place.

Like Western **mediums** shamans can demonstrate their powers at **séances**, which take place in darkened areas such as tents. The séance commences with singing and phenomena include **levitation**, spirit voices, **rapping**, handling of hot coals without injury, speaking in tongues and other **poltergeist** effects. Another similarity with Western mediums is the belief that if a shaman is disturbed during a séance it can jeopardize his life.

Differences also exist between the two. The path to becoming a shaman is long and painful and this is not always the case for a medium. Shamans live outside the everyday life of their people and are regarded as part of another world, which is not the case with mediums. Shamans also tend to be invigorated by séances, whereas mediums are often exhausted by them. And although the spirit helpers contacted during a séance parallel the Western medium's **controls** in that they offer assistance, they exert much more influence on their human agent. The shaman is told by his spirit helpers how to dress, how to live and what to do. If he fails to follow their instructions there is the danger they may become unhappy with him and even kill him.

Shamanism

Term used to refer to the spiritual practices of a **shaman**, a person who can access **altered states of consciousness** through the use of **spirit guides** and through invoking a **trance**-like state using rhythmic drumming, **chanting** or dance. Once in a deep state of trance the shaman is said to be able to access his or her **guardian spirit** known as a **totem**, for healing, guidance and advice.

Shamanism has been described as the 'world's oldest profession'; archaeological evidence suggests shamanic techniques are at least 20,000 years old. Shamans were probably the first healers, priests and **magicians**, who helped people make sense of the world they lived in. Until recently the shamanic tradition was regarded simply as a precursor to modern religion, but today a new breed of urban shaman is attempting to adapt this ancient system to Western life in an effort to regain an understanding of the interconnection of all life.

Shambhala

In Tibetan Buddhism, a mysterious lost land that has existed for all time. It is believed that this mystical land is a hidden paradise of green valleys, high mountains, hot springs and rich vegetation, and those who are able to find it can attain all the **esoteric** wisdom in the universe. The legend of Shambhala was the inspiration for author James Hilton's Shangri-La, the fictional paradise of his novel *Lost Horizons* (1936).

While there is widespread mythic agreement about the existence of Shambhala there is considerably less agreement about where it is and how to get there. The Tibetan Buddhists believe it is located somewhere beyond the peaks of the Himalayan Mountains. Theosophists favour the Gobi dessert. The Chinese think it may be the Kun Lun Mountains. Greek sources favour the Altaic Mountains. Russian legend claims it lies in the Belovodye 'white waters' region; in 1923 an expedition set off across the Kokushi Mountains to find it and never returned.

The fate of the expedition would not have surprised some Buddhists, who believe that Shambhala does not exist on the earthly plane but on another dimension altogether, possibly the **astral plane**; it will return to our existence one day to usher in a new Golden Age. Despite such pointers to an inward Shambhala, rumours of its physical existence still persist.

Shape-shifting

Conscious and deliberate act of transformation from human to animal form through magical or spiritual means. **Shamans**, **witches** and **sorcerers** are believed to use this **supernatural** power to increase their understanding of a situation or to gain the power the chosen animal or bird possess. Types of shape-shifting include the shaman transforming into the tribe's **totem** animal to seek advice and wisdom for his tribe.

SHEEP/GOAT EFFECT

Phenomenon demonstrated in psychical research that demonstrates that people who believe in **psi** tend to score more positively in psi tests and people who do not believe in psi tend to score more negatively. The phenomenon was discovered by American parapsychologist Gertrude Schmeidler, who called it the sheep/goat effect. The sheep are the believers and the goats are the non-believers.

Schmeidler found that sheep are more likely to score hits in psi guessing games and goats are more likely to miss targets and score below chance scores, but the sheep/goat effect only seemed to come into play with strong believers and strong non-believers. Mild believers and mild non-believers tended to score at chance. Schmeidler and other researchers also found that other factors influence **psi** hits and misses. Those subjects who are outgoing, happy and relaxed tend to score above chance and those who are shy, reserved and introverted tend to score below chance.

By the 1970s the sheep/goat effect began to disappear. It has been suggested that this may be because public attitudes about psi have altered significantly since the 1940s. More people are willing to consider the possible existence of psi, and in experiments now they are more likely to be influenced by the attitude of the experimenter.

SHELL HEARING

A branch of conchomancy – an African form of seashell **divination** – shell hearing is believed to be one way of promoting **clairaudience**. In **spiritualism** a **medium** may hold a shell to his or her ear and listen. Through the sounds of the sea that are associated with this, voices may be heard. These, according to **spiritualists**, are voices of the dead who may then be questioned. Some mediums hold one large shell, such as a large conch, to each ear in turn; others hold two shells, one to each ear.

SHIATSU

Japanese holistic massage technique that uses fingertip pressure to stimulate the body's energy pathways. These pathways, called meridians, circulate bioelectric energy (chi or the Japanese term ki) throughout the body along specific channels. It is believed that when ki flow is blocked pain or illness is the result. The practitioner presses down on the meridians with their fingers, thumbs, elbows, knees and feet to free up this bioelectric flow. The therapy, which is a form of **acupressure**, is used for a number of different health conditions and is most often recommended for stress-related conditions, such as depression and anxiety, to produce a feeling of wellbeing and **relaxation**.

SHINS

General term used to refer to malevolent **ghosts** in Chinese tradition. The Chinese have more ghosts than any other people – their tradition lists no fewer than 60 different kinds of shins. Each of these **spirit** types has a specific day for appearing, during a continuously repeated 60-day cycle. To appease these spirits, the Chinese leave small gifts of cakes outside their homes with a letter attached to the 'honourable homeless hosts', begging the ghosts to enjoy the gift, but then depart from the property in peace. These ghosts sometimes initially appear in the form of a mist before gradually assuming a human form, with the head materializing first, then the feet, and finally the body in between. Some sub-forms of shins are also reported to have no chins.

SHINTO

The state religion of Japan, Shinto is known as the Way of the Gods. The religion itself combines ancient nature worship with elements of Buddhism and Confucianism, notably those elements that suggested that the emperor was the divine leader of the nation. Until 1946 it was closely linked with the Japanese monarchy but in that year Emperor Hirohito renounced his status as a living god, effectively disestablishing Shinto from the position it had held since 1868.

Shinto remains a thriving religion in modern Japan with numerous shrines throughout the country. Shinto links living Japanese to their ancestral spirits, ancient gods and the elemental energies of land and nature in a mysterious, shared cosmos where all natural phenomena are considered manifestations of the divine.

SHOJO

A traditional Japanese **ghost** form that haunts the open sea. They are said to have flaming red hair, but intend no harm to humans. They are supposedly addicted to drinking, dancing, and merry-making. Because their favourite drink is saké, some Japanese traditions hold that these **spirits** may be caught by luring them on to land with a jar of the liquor.

SHRIEKING PITS

At Aylmerton in Norfolk, there are a large number of large, circular pits which are thought to have been the remains of a prehistoric settlement. Over the years they have been called the 'Shrieking pits', because a white figure is said to haunt them with the most terrible, agonizing cries. Possible natural explanations for the phenomenon are mist and the cries of birds.

SHROUD OF TURIN

Strip of linen bearing bloodstains and the faded image of the body of a bearded man, which for centuries was believed to be the shroud in which Christ was buried.

The linen measures about 14 feet long and 4 feet wide and has been the subject of controversy and debate and research since it came to light in 1353 in a French church. According to the Vatican the shroud is the most important relic in Christendom; it takes its name from St John's Cathedral in Turin where it has been locked in a silver case since the fifteenth century. In 1988 the Vatican allowed carbon-dating tests on samples of the cloth and, according to the test results, the shroud proved to be a medieval forgery. Despite this, believers maintain that the image was imprinted on to the shroud by some kind of spiritual energy when Jesus rose from the Holy Sepulchre.

SIBYL

A woman who is able to foretell the future. The term comes from ancient Greece where sibyls were prophetesses whose special function was to communicate with the gods on behalf of others. They usually lived in isolated places like caves or rocky precipices.

SIDDHIS

Name ascribed to the alleged **paranormal** powers sometimes associated with the practice of **Yoga**.

SIDGWICK, ELEANOR [1845–1936]

Mathematician and teacher, principal of the first women's college at Cambridge and a prominent member of the **Society for Psychical Research**. She was married to philosopher **Henry Sidgwick**, who shared her interest in psychical research.

Eleanor was born on 11 March 1845 at the Balfour family estate at Wittinghame, East Lothian, Scotland. She was encouraged in her studies by her parents, who supported the education of women, and at the age of 27 she inherited the management of the estate. Like most of the other members of the Balfour family she was interested in psychical phenomena and was part of a group formed in 1874 to investigate **spiritualism**. It was at this group that she met Henry Sidgwick, whom she married in 1876. The couple shared a commitment to women's education as well as an interest in **mediumship**.

From 1892 to 1910 Eleanor served as Principal of Newnham College, Cambridge. Her academic career made her contributions to the Society for Psychical Research even more authoritative and she became actively involved in researching and writing for the Society's journal. In a paper published in the Society's *Proceedings* in 1886, entitled 'Results of a Personal Investigation into the Physical Phenomena of Spiritualism', she came to the conclusion that although work such of that of **Sir William Crookes** with **medium D D Home** supported the possibility of psychic powers, in her personal experience she had encountered a great deal of trickery and **fraud**. Another noteworthy contribution was her discussion of the mediumship of **Leonora Piper** in the *Proceedings* of 1915. In this Eleanor concluded that Piper's **controls** behaved more like secondary personalities than **discarnate entities**, and that some of these secondary personalities may have displayed **ESP**.

In 1901 Sidgwick was elected to the Society's governing council and later became President in 1908 and again in 1932. Throughout her career she exercised a strong influence over the Society. For much of that career she was sceptical about whether there was **survival after death** but in her acceptance speech for her second presidency in 1932, she confessed that her long study of the evidence had finally brought her to a belief in such survival.

SIDGWICK, HENRY [1838–1900]

Cambridge philosopher and founding member and president of the **Society for Psychical Research**.

Henry Sidgwick was born on 31 May 1838 in Skipton, Yorkshire. In 1855 he went to Trinity College, Cambridge to study classics and mathematics. In 1859 he was appointed to a teaching fellowship at Trinity but was unable to commit to being a 'bona fide member of the Church of England' (a requirement for appointment at that time) and resigned in 1869. Despite his religious doubts Trinity created a position for him in moral sciences, and in 1883 Sidgwick was elected Knightsbridge Professor of Moral Philosophy.

Throughout his career Sidgwick was interested and involved in psychical research. As an undergraduate he joined the Cambridge ghost club and in 1860 attended his first **séance**. He later denounced the **medium** at this séance as a **fraud** but this did not dampen his enthusiasm for the psychic world. In 1869 one of Sidgwick's students, **Frederick Myers**, recalled how, on a 'starlight walk' he had asked Sidgwick 'whether he thought that when Tradition, Intuition, Metaphysics had failed to solve the riddle of the Universe, there was a chance that from any actual observable phenomena – ghosts, spirits, whatever they may be – some valid knowledge might be drawn as to the world unseen.' Sidgwick replied that he believed there was a chance, and in 1874 he joined with Myers and two others of his students, Arthur Balfour and **Edmund Gurney**, to begin a series of detailed investigations.

The investigations that followed proved to be disappointing. Either nothing happened or trickery was discovered. The investigations did, however, help Sidgwick become acquainted with Balfour's sister, Eleanor, and the two were married in 1876. Henry and **Eleanor Sidgwick** both shared a passion for psychical research and an interest in the education of women.

Despite discouraging results from his investigations with Myers, Sidgwick was not deterred from accepting an invitation from **Sir William Barrett**, a physicist who conducted a series of experiments on **telepathy**, to serve as the first President of the Society for Psychical Research in 1882. In 1884 Sidgwick proposed the creation of a committee to investigate the mediumistic claims of **Madame Blavatsky**, the cofounder of the Theosophical Society. He played a major role in organizing a census of hallucinations conducted between 1889 and 1894 and took part in investigations of **Eusapia Palladino**, which confirmed his distrust of **physical mediumship**, and **Leonora Piper**, who also failed to impress him.

Sigil

A **symbol**, seal or sign that is used in magic rituals of **witchcraft** and occultism. The symbol is constructed by transforming a set of written words or letters into another word or picture.

Sigils date back to prehistory and may represent complex concepts. In Western magic, sigils are symbols connected to a set of ideas by which **supernatural** powers may be summoned to awareness and controlled. They are used in divinatory and magical practices. The sigil itself does not call forth the power, but it serves as a physical focus through which the practitioner can achieve the desired state of mind.

The **pentacle** is the most powerful sigil used in **Neo-Pagan** witchcraft and by many occultists. Other sigils serve as identifying logos of organizations. Individuals can adopt their personal sigils by selecting a letter from the **runes** or the Theban alphabet. They have personal, secret meaning and are often inscribed on magical tools used in **occult** practices and ceremonies. Sigils also serve as **amulets**, **talismans** or **meditation** tools.

Creating a symbol of intent, a sigil, can be done with or without magical ritual or ceremony. Sigil designs can be derived from geometric shapes, astrological signs or symbols used in **alchemy**. They may be of various signs, such as crosses, associated with different deities. Other sigils are attained through **intuition** and inspiration. Many come through meditation and the practice of **scrying** – when a certain pattern seems to appear upon the object which the individual is gazing at.

Since sigil magic is generally considered Will Magic (see **Magical Will**) the goal of sigil usage is to mobilize the **unconscious** mind towards accomplishing the desires of the conscious mind. It is thought that the sigils a person creates for him or herself in their own individual way are the most potent and can be used to enhance magical working by placing the symbol on

Basic sigil magic

Grab a piece of paper and simply write out a statement of your intent. Be blunt, specific and brief. For example: 'I will pass my driving test next week.'

Write it out in plain English. Now look at the letters of the alphabet. What are they? Symbols. They are just symbols of a statement of intent. So play with them. Rearrange them, move pieces of one letter into another. Leave out repeated letters to make it smaller. They are just lines and curves so make them into some other design. Play with them until they cease to resemble anything remotely associated with your intent.

Once you have your own little symbol you can copy it on to an index card. Now you have a sigil of your own design for your own specific magic. Carry it with you at all times, or place the sigil in your car or on your desk.

How sigil magic works

Sigils (symbols) are our native language. We respond to them daily and filter them and sort them rapidly. The language we speak and think with is an artificial system of order we impose over the natural language of symbols to make sense of them.

When you create your own sigil what you are doing is taking a conscious statement of intent and returning it to a symbolic form. The method involves obscuring the original meaning and that part of the procedure is what makes it so effective. The entire process is geared to remove as much of the conscious focus and inherent conflicts between the conscious and unconscious from the intent. The sigil returns the idea to the realm of the will, and that is where the magic – your magic – begins.

pertinent clothing, packages, letters and so on. In some instances, after creating and meditating on them, sigils are burned or destroyed in some way so that they can pass from the conscious mind into the unconscious mind.

Another way of using sigils is to place them in plain sight and then to forget (in your conscious mind) about them and their original purpose. The idea here is to let your conscious mind's guard down so the message can be seen unhindered by the unconscious mind.

There are many ways to utilize these powerful tools. Occultists believe sigil magic to be one of the most effective forms of magic because the essential part of manifesting magical acts is the ability to communicate conscious intentions to the subconscious mind, and one of the best ways to do this is via symbols, specifically sigils.

SILKY

Female **ghost** who is believed to wear rustling silk clothing and according to lore performs domestic chores in the house after the family have gone to bed. Although silkies can be helpful they are also said to be perverse at times and a house that is left tidy by the owners may be disarrayed. Silkies are particularly found in the borderland between Scotland and England and are said to terrify lazy servants and people who do not do their work. The most famous of these ghosts was the Silky of Black Heddon, who is referred to in William Henderson's *Folk-Lore of the Northern Counties* (1879).

SILVA MIND CONTROL

Jose Silva was born in Texas in 1914. His childhood was poor and he was forced at an early age to work to help support his family. However, by the age of 15 Silva had decided that material gain was not his primary motivation in life. He began a lifelong investigation of the potential of the human mind which moved via **hypnosis** to mind control, and later he developed exercises to raise IQ, improve memory, increase learning speed and even, his followers now claim, stimulate **psychic** powers.

The Silva method of mind control has similarities to **visualization** and **pathworking**, but the non-mystical, down-to-earth way the exercises are presented has appealed to modern audiences. Today the Silva mind control movement has established a good international following.

SILVER

In folklore, silver is believed to be an effective tool for warding off evil. For example, silver bullets are thought to stop **vampires**, **bogies**, giants, **witches**, **spirits** and so on. Silver nails in a coffin are thought to prevent the spirit of the dead escaping and silver is also thought to protect against bewitchment, the **evil eye** and evil spirits. Since ancient times silver has been used in protective **amulets**. Some occultists believe the metal enhances **psychic** ability.

It's likely that silver's power against the **supernatural** has to do with its association with the silvery glow of the Moon, which in folklore has always been linked with magic and mystery and the **Otherworld**.

SILVER BIRCH

Native American spirit **control** of English journalist and **medium** Maurice Barbanell (1902–1981)

Barbanell was born on 3 May 1902 in London. As a young man he was an atheist and sceptical of **spiritualist** claims but this changed when he attended a **home circle** with a **medium** known as Mrs Blaustein and discovered that he had became a medium for a Native American **spirit**.

Barbanell formed his own home circle, which met in secret for several years. At this early stage the name of the spirit communicating through Barbanell was kept confidential.

Barbanell's mediumship remained anonymous for several years until he was persuaded by a member of his circle, Hannen Swaffer, to disseminate the spirit's messages to a wider audience than the home circle. Barbanell eventually agreed to publish them in a spiritualist newspaper called the *Psychic News* on the condition that he remained anonymous. For publication the spirit guide chose the pseudonym Silver Birch.

Throughout his life Barbanell was active in the **Spiritualists National Union** and lectured widely, publishing numerous books and articles. He widely rejected the theory that controls were secondary personalities of a medium and sitters in his circle noticed how different in personality Silver Birch and Barbanell were. For example, Silver Birch believed in **reincarnation** and Barbanell didn't. Barbanell died on 17 July 1981 and the teachings of his control were edited and published posthumously by his wife.

Silver Birch's messages focus on the importance of love, spiritual healing, service to others, the immortality of the soul and the oneness of all life. According to Silver Birch he had been reluctant to leave his own world and return to earth but he had a mission to remind humanity of 'old, old teachings'. He said he had chosen Barbanell because of his scepticism, as it would make him more receptive to the material he wanted to communicate.

SILVER CORD

A silver thread that acts as a connecting link between the physical and the **astral body** that has been reported by some practitioners of **astral projection**. The Bible makes a passing mention of a 'silver cord', severing at the moment of death:

> *Remember him – before the silver cord is*
> *severed,*
> *or the golden bowl is broken;*
> *before the pitcher is shattered at the spring,*
> *or the wheel broken at the well,*
> *and the dust returns to the ground it came*
> *from,*
> *and the spirit returns to God who gave it.*
>
> (*Ecclesiastes 12: 6-7*)

Occultists often take this as a reference to the cord sometimes seen in astral projection.

SITTER GROUP

A group of people who meet on a regular basis in the hope of producing **paranormal** physical phenomena such as **table-tilting** or **rapping**. It is similar to a **home circle** but different in that it is not centred around a **medium**.

The sitter group was first developed by an English psychologist, Kenneth Batcheldor, in the 1960s. Batcheldor believed that **psychic** energy arising out of interpersonal group dynamics rather than any one person was responsible for **psychokinesis**.

According to this concept it would be possible for a group of people to produce phenomena without a medium being present. Batcheldor's theory has been proved by several groups, such as the **Bindelof Society**.

Batcheldor experimented with his own group and believed that for a group to be successful sceptical resistance had to be surmounted and a deep level of acceptance of the possibility of psychokinesis had to be induced. This could even be achieved by trickery because once disbelief was overcome then inhibitions would be freed, opening up the possibility of genuine phenomena.

SIXTH SENSE

Popular alternative term for **extrasensory perception** (**ESP**), as people who possess this ability can often perceive things beyond the powers of their other five senses (sight, hearing, taste, smell and touch).

SKY CLAD

Working magic while naked. Occasionally impractical but preferred way for a **Wiccan witch** to work a **spell** to better channel natural energies and to feel connected to earth, sky and nature without the distraction of clothes. It also suggests a return to purity, innocence, openness and honesty.

SLADE, DR HENRY [1840–1905]

Famous nineteenth-century **slate writing medium** whose slate writing ability impressed scientists, journalists and royalty.

Slade first appeared on the **spiritualist** scene in the 1860s when he began holding **séances** in New York City. After conducting séances for 15 years he received the endorsement of **Madame Blavatsky** and was recommended to study at the University of St Petersburg in Russia. En route to St Petersberg in 1876 he visited London and began holding séances in rooms at Russell Square, impressing sitters by writing on sealed slates, with **levitations** and with materialized hands. Various scientists and psychical researchers met with Slade there and almost all were won over by his abilities.

However, not everyone was so impressed; in September 1876 E Ray Lankester, Professor of Zoology at University College London, attended a séance and discovered a slate with writing on it before it was supposed to appear. He submitted his discovery to *The Times* newspaper and charges were brought against Slade for taking money under false pretences. A controversial court case followed. Spiritualists claimed that the message could have been penned by **spirits** at any time, as spirits followed no timetable, but eventually Slade was convicted and sentenced to three months in prison.

Slade was released on bail pending appeal and when the case was reheard his conviction was overturned on a technicality. In December 1877 Slade submitted to vigorous investigation by Johann Zollner,

Professor of Physics at the University of Leipzig. Zollner was impressed by Slade and his abilities and published his findings in *Transcendental Physics*.

Henry Slade returned to America but his career never fully recovered from the London trial. He was accused of **fraud** on numerous occasions and both his career and his health deteriorated rapidly. He died a penniless alcoholic in a Michigan sanatorium in 1905.

SLATE WRITING

Also known as psychography, slate writing is the appearance of writing on a blank slate, thought to be produced through the intervention of **spirits**.

Slate writing appeared to offer **spiritualists** indisputable proof of spirit presence because **séances** could be held in full light and observers could watch the **medium** at all times. Despite this, **fraud** often occurred.

Slates were commonly used for schoolwork in the nineteenth century. They typically came in single or double frames and could be latched closed. In some cases sitters would bring new, clean slates to the séance, locked and sealed, and be amazed to find that the blank surfaces were covered in writing by spirits.

Typically during a slate writing séance slates would be washed and examined beforehand. A sitter would ask a question and the medium would hold the slate at one end underneath the table top with the fingers of his right hand and keep his thumb above the table. The sitter would hold the other end with one hand and grasp the medium's left hand with his or her other one. Soon scratchy sounds would be heard followed by raps when the spirits were finished. The answer to the question would appear on the slate. In some cases the medium would perform what is known as 'mirror writing'; the medium would write backwards on a slate and then hold it up to a mirror to read.

The most famous slate writer was **Henry Slade** who, despite impressing numerous scientists and psychical researchers, was accused of fraud. Magician **Harry Houdini** later demonstrated that there were two ways of producing slate writing phenomena. The first was to attach a ring or pencil to one of the fingers holding the board to scratch out an answer; the other involved writing the answer beforehand and switching the slates while the sitter's attention was diverted. Slates were very common and most mediums kept a supply of all the types available ready to substitute in any situation. Another method involved writing the answer beforehand and concealing it with a flap covered in silicated gauze or thin slate. Trick slates and manipulation of the hinge mechanism also allowed slate writing mediums to produce writing on the inside of the surface of a locked double slate. Some mediums even employed plants to help make the switch or to read and provide answers. Magnets were also used to move slate writing pencils filled with iron filings, and if mediums needed any more help a number of firms offered trick slates in all shapes and sizes through mail order catalogues.

Sometimes the sitter's question would be sealed in an envelope but once again frauds found a way around this. A tiny wire prong could be inserted into the unsealed part of the envelope, which could pull the message out and replace it with the envelope remaining sealed.

SLEEP PARALYSIS

Sleep paralysis is a condition that occurs in the state just before dropping off to sleep or just before fully awakening from sleep. The condition is characterized by being unable to move or speak. It is often typically associated with a feeling that there is some sort of menacing presence, a feeling that often arouses fear but which is also accompanied by an inability to cry out. The paralysis may last only a few seconds. Sleep paralysis is thought by some to account for alien abduction hallucinations and other **paranormal** or **supernatural** experiences (e.g., **old hag syndrome, incubus** and **succubus** phenomena).

SMITH, HELENE

Pseudonym for Catherine Elise Muller, a late nineteenth-century **medium** from Geneva, Switzerland, who inspired huge controversy over her alleged astral trips to Mars.

Smith's **séances** were characterized by **trances, automatic writing** and speaking in tongues. Once in trance her **control**, Leopold, would speak and write through her. Smith claimed to have been a Hindu princess and Marie Antoinette in previous lives and one of the **spirits** she claimed to channel in her trances was a contemporary of the French queen, the eighteenth-century Italian **sorcerer Cagliostro**. When he appeared witnesses observed that Smith's voice developed a deep bass tone. Leopold, Smith's control, communicated through Smith that he had been transported to Mars and when in trance he took her there. The results of these journeys were crude drawings of the Martian landscape and automatic writing of the Martian language.

In the late 1890s Smith was researched by Theodore Flournoy, a psychology professor from Switzerland and an experienced psychical researcher. Flournoy concluded that Smith had a very active imagination that may have been complemented by **telepathy**. Words used in her so-called Martian language were traced to existing languages and it was suggested that Leopold was a secondary personality.

Flournoy published his conclusions in 1900 in *From India to the Planet Mars*. Instead of decreasing her popularity as might have been expected the book only increased it. Many people sided with Smith and believed that she had in fact visited Mars with the spirits. For the rest of her life she enjoyed comfortable life of fame and wealth.

SMITHFIELD MARKET GHOST

Ghost that allegedly haunted the Smithfield meat market in London in the middle of the seventeenth century. In 1654 a pamphlet called *A True Relation of the Smithfield Ghost*, complete with an illustration, described the ghost as dressed in the gown of a lawyer, with horns on his head, long pointed shoes and a meat cleaver in his hand.

The **spirit** apparently appeared every Saturday night between nine and ten o'clock and pulled joints of meat from the stalls of butchers. Some of the butchers attempted to drive the ghost away but, according to the pamphlet, 'they cannot feel anything but aire'. The description of the ghost wearing a lawyer's gown led to rumours that this was the ghost of a lawyer named Mallet who had died just before the **hauntings** began from eating poisoned meat. Mallet was said to be unsure who had sold him the meat, because after Smithfield he moved on to terrorize the butchers at Whitechapel and Eastcheape. The ghost eventually disappeared and the mystery remains as to whether it was a genuine haunting or a clever prank.

SMOKE GHOSTS

A curious phenomenon not to be confused with **ectoplasm** or 'mist' phenomena, smoke ghosts are said to be **ghost** forms which give the appearance of smoke and are often accompanied by the pungent smell of burning wood. These ghostly columns of smoke are said to move of their own accord while maintaining a disciplined column shape, though it may assume other similar forms, before dissipating in a manner that is alleged to be completely different from smoke drifting in the wind.

Smoke ghosts have been reported in both Europe and the United States for many years. A famous story is that of a girl in the United States who was burned to death during the seventeenth century and her ghostly presence has ever since been recognized by the pungent odour of burning wood. In 1954 a sentry at the Tower of London reported a smoke cloud that moved on its own, changed shape and did not seem to diffuse or drift like ordinary smoke. When the man tried to follow the smoke it disappeared instantly.

SMUDGING

Native North American practice of cleansing an environment with an ancient smoke ritual. Smudging is a form of **geomancy**, a practice that works with the **universal life force** energies of the earth. It involves burning small bundles of herbs and sweet smelling grasses to physically and spiritually cleanse homes and people, replacing **negative energy** with positive. The theory is that during the ritual, as the smoke drifts upwards, it carries all desires and intentions to the Great Spirit in the Native American religion, who will grant them if the sender's intentions are pure.

SMURL HAUNTING

Alleged **haunting** that took place in the home of Jack and Janet Smurl in West Pittston, Pennsylvania from 1985 to 1987. The case attracted widespread interest from the media and even though several **exorcisms** were performed, the **demon** refused to leave. Sceptics believed the case, which was later dramatized in a book and movie, to be a hoax.

In 1973 Jack's parents, John and Mary Smurl, bought the house in West Pittston, which was a duplex built in 1896. They lived in the right half and Jack and Janet and their two daughters, Dawn and Heather, moved into the other half. The Smurl family was a close and loving one and by all accounts they enjoyed living together for the first 18 months. Strange things, however, began to occur after that. In January 1974, a strange stain appeared on a new carpet. Water leaked from pipes after repeated soldering. Scratches appeared on furniture. A television set exploded. Toilets flushed when nobody had used them. Drawers were opened and footsteps were heard. Radios sounded even when unplugged. Strange smells filled the house. Jack felt ghostly caresses. His eldest daughter Dawn allegedly saw figures floating in her bathroom.

In 1985 the annoying disturbances turned into terrifying experiences. The house was often ice cold. Loud and abusive language could be heard and then, in February, a black human-shaped form, about five feet nine inches tall with no face, materialized first to Janet in the kitchen and then to her mother-in-law Mary. According to family reports the haunting increased dramatically after that. Light fixtures fell from the ceiling. Jack levitated. Terrible rapping or scratching noises were heard. The children were tossed out of bed and down the stairs. Bedspreads were shredded and footsteps were heard in the attic. Even the neighbours were not spared, with many of them detecting a presence in their own homes.

In January 1986 Janet contacted psychical researchers from Monroe, Connecticut – Ed and Lorraine Warren. They investigated the house and interviewed the Smurls and the conclusion they came to was that three minor **spirits** and a demon were haunting the house. Without any evidence of family discord the Warrens could only conclude that the demon had lain dormant for centuries but had risen to draw on the emotional energy generated by the girls' move into puberty.

The hauntings again intensified, with the Smurls now reporting assault and rape by a **succubus** and an **incubus**. The Warrens brought in Father Robert F McKenna to perform an exorcism but this only succeeded in infuriating the demon still further. There was little point in the Smurls moving house as by now the demon followed them everywhere, even on family camping trips. Exhausted by the ordeal and disappointed by the repeated refusals of the Catholic Church to help, they decided to appear on television. Remaining anonymous behind a screen the Smurls were interviewed on a local Philadelphia talk show. The demon reacted by levitating Janet and then hurling her against a wall.

In August 1986 the Smurls decided to risk ridicule by going public with the story and granted an interview to the *Sunday Independent* newspaper. As soon as the article appeared their house became a tourist attraction.

Paul Kurtz, chairman of the Committee for the Scientific Investigation of Claims of the Paranormal in Buffalo, New York, offered to put the family up in a hotel for a week, where they could be observed with cameras. The Smurls refused, saying that they believed Kurtz had already made up his mind that the story was a hoax. Kurtz later wrote in an article that the case was not **paranormal** and the Smurls had denied him access because they were afraid of what he might discover. He pointed out a number of discrepancies in the Smurls' story, such as Mrs Smurl saying she had contacted the police when there was no record of her complaints, and suggested natural explanations for the phenomena experienced by the Smurls. These natural explanations included a broken sewer pipe causing foul smells, pranks by the teenagers, delusions and abandoned mine voids in the area creating strange noises. Kurtz also wondered about a possible financial motive as the Smurls had already begun talking to Hollywood producers.

Ed Warren increased doubts more by declining a reporter's requests to stay in the house or to watch alleged recordings of the phenomena. The Warrens meanwhile were planning a mass exorcism with several priests, now that the press coverage had pushed the diocese into action. This time the rituals seemed to have more of an effect and in 1989 the Smurls finally found peace. The movie version of the Smurl haunting, entitled *The Haunted*, was released in 1991.

SNARLY YOW

Terrifying spectral dog with huge paws and a snarling red mouth that allegedly haunts the South Mountain area of Maryland. The Snarly Yow is also called the black dog and is quite similar to the **Black Shuck** of England, although it is not regarded as a **death omen** as is the Black Shuck.

According to lore the dog has appeared for generations, although its origins are not known. It haunts woodland on the mountain east of Hagerstown and when horses were the usual mode of transport it was said to suddenly appear and frighten the horse so that the rider was thrown off. Today the Snarly Yow is said to block the passage of oncoming cars on the National Pike roadway. Sometimes drivers think they have actually hit a dog, but when they stop and get out they see a glimpse of the Snarly Yow with its teeth bared. Then the creature abruptly vanishes.

SOCIETY FOR PSYCHICAL RESEARCH

First major organization established to investigate the **paranormal** scientifically, set up in London in 1882. The Society for Psychical Research (SPR) was formed by a group of individuals whose aim was to discover scientific proof of **spiritualist** phenomena.

The SPR had its origins in the 'Sidgwick group' set up by Trinity College, Cambridge fellows **Henry Sidgwick**, **Frederick Myers** and **Edmund Gurney**, and later included Sidgwick's wife **Eleanor Sidgwick**. Although most of the Sidwick group investigations exposed **fraud** this did not dent the enthusiasm of its members, and when **Sir William Barrett** invited them to join with various spiritualists to form the SPR they readily accepted. Sidgwick was elected the Society's first president.

The Sidgwicks attracted noted scientists and scholars to the Society, including **Sir William Crookes**, **William James** and later **Sigmund Freud** and **Carl Jung**. The first subject areas to be investigated were **telepathy, mesmerism, hypnosis, clairvoyance, apparitions, hauntings** and **physical mediumship**. In 1885 the SPR helped found the **American Society for Psychical Research** in Boston.

In time the SPR turned its attention from **physical mediumship** to other phenomena that might suggest evidence for **ESP** or **survival after death**, such as **mental mediumship**. By 1900 the Society had produced thousands of reports and articles as well as substantial works such as *Phantasms of the Living* (1886), a huge study of apparitions, and *Human Personality and Its Survival of Bodily Death*, a comprehensive study of evidence for survival.

By 1910 most of the key members of the Sidgwick group had died but after death they reportedly communicated through various **mediums**, providing evidence for **cross correspondences**.

The SPR differs from the American society in that for the most part it leaves research to its members, whereas in the ASPR that is left to the staff. Currently it runs a programme of monthly lectures with a variety of invited speakers, held in the Lecture Hall of the Kensington Public Library. Admission is free to SPR members, with an admission fee for non-members. The SPR also runs courses in psychic development and holds an annual conference at different venues around the UK. According to the SPR website:

The principal areas of study of psychical research concern exchanges between minds, or between minds and the environment, which are not dealt with by current, orthodox science. This is a large area, incorporating such topics as extrasensory perception (telepathy, clairvoyance, precognition and retrocognition), psychokinesis (paranormal effects on physical objects, including poltergeist phenomena), near-death and out-of-the-body experiences, apparitions, hauntings, hypnotic regression and paranormal healing. One of the society's aims has been to examine the question of whether or not we survive bodily death, by evaluating the evidence provided by mediumship, apparitions of the dead and reincarnation studies.

The SPR maintains an impressive library and publishes research articles in the Society's *Journal* and *Proceedings*, which, since 1995, have appeared in a magazine called the *Paranormal Review*. Research and information about the society is also available online at www.spr.ac.uk.

SOMNAMBULIST

The term applied to people who perform physical activity while asleep (such as 'sleep-walking'). It also applies to a person in a deep hypnotic trance (see **hypnosis**).

SOOTHSAYER

Alternative name for a **prophet** or **seer**, a person capable of divining and telling the future.

SORCERY, SORCERER

Form of magic that uses **spells**, **charms** and **incantations** to summon up **supernatural** powers or **spirits**, mostly, but not always, for evil purposes or to gain power. It is typically associated with **black magic** and the **left-hand path** and can also include divining the future. Someone who practises sorcery is called a sorcerer if they are male and a sorceress if they are female. In the late Middle Ages the term sorcerer was applied to men of higher learning such as alchemists, **magicians** and physicians, as these were the people most likely to be involved in attempts to foretell the future.

SORTILEGE

Divination by the casting of lots, popular in ancient Rome. It was typically done by casting objects such as stones or dice after they have been mixed together and interpreting how they landed, although drawing straws from a clasped hand was an alternative method. Sortilege has stood the test of time and is still practised today in Western cultures, using straws or dice or taking a card at random from a pack.

SOUL

The soul is believed to be the animating presence within a person and represents the individual's core identity, as distinguished from the physical body. It is thought to live on after death on this plane of existence and, depending on beliefs, lives in **heaven**, **hell** or **purgatory**, is reincarnated or is transformed into another living person, animal, plant or other organic material. If a distinction is made between mind, body and spirit, soul refers to the essence of a person and spirit refers to the life force.

The concept of the soul is difficult to define as it differs according to belief systems. However, in almost all religious traditions, except Buddhism, it is believed to be immortal. In **spiritualism** the soul is conceived of as discarnate and indivisible and each person is normally allocated one. The soul, however, can detach from the body and may leave it during **out-of-body** experiences and **near-death experiences**. It is also the part of a person that is said to travel in the **astral plane**. In some cases **apparitions** are regarded as a reflection of the soul itself.

SOUL LOSS

In traditional societies around the world illness is often explained by a temporary departure of the **soul** from the body. A permanent departure results in death.

In some cultures a person's soul is thought to detach from the body and to wander at night while a person is dreaming. **Shamans** are believed to be able to direct these wanderings, which may in fact be **out-of-body experiences**. This is considered normal and problems only occur when for some reason the soul can't find its way back into the body. Soul loss may be caused by a **ghost** attempting to draw the soul away. It may also be due to **witchcraft** or evil **spirits** or it may result from physical injury to the body. The illnesses caused by soul loss include fainting fits, seizures and comas.

When it leaves the body the soul is believed to head for the land of the dead and the closer it gets to that the weaker the person becomes. It is left to the shaman to search for the soul or fight for the soul if it is being possessed by an evil spirit and bring it back to the body.

SOUL MATE

Romantic belief that every person's **soul** has a counterpart and true happiness and fulfilment can only be found by meeting and joining with that counterpart. In some cases this search may span several **reincarnations**.

The soul-mate tradition is a popular one and so many definitions of soul mate have been put forward that it is difficult to determine its origins. A popular theory is that in a remote time and place a breakage occurred, leaving each soul imperfect and destined to search for its other half. Another theory suggests that a soul mate is not a missing half but another soul with whom one has spent many lives and developed a strong affinity. Such soul mates gravitate towards each other every time they are reincarnated to further develop their relationship and help each other find fulfilment. They are so in tune with each other they can communicate without words. They love each other unconditionally and cannot bear separation. Other theories suggest that soul mates are not necessarily lovers or relatives but certain people with whom we have intimate bonds, or people who come into our lives to teach us important lessons, or people who share a common purpose or ideal.

Some people consult **psychics**, astrologers and so on in an effort to find or attract their soul mate. Opinions differ as to whether soul mates will come together naturally or whether they must earn their affinity. It is generally thought, however, that an obsession with soul mates puts unnecessary pressure on a relationship by creating impossible expectations.

SOULE, MINNIE MESERVE [1867–1936]

American **mental medium** who worked closely with the **American Society for Psychical Research**.

Minnie Soule, as she was later known, was born in Boston on 12 November 1867. She trained to be a teacher and taught in Somerville, Massachusetts, where she met her husband Charles L Soule, whom she married in 1897. As a child she had already begun to have precognitive **dreams** but it was only after her marriage that her mediumship began to develop, when she began **automatic writing** and would receive messages from unknown people who had died many years previously. Her husband took her to meet **spiritualist** friends who immediately recognized her talents.

In the years that followed Soule came to be controlled by several American Indian **spirit guides**. One, called 'White Cloud', was a skilled and talented herbal healer. Another, called 'Sunbeam', claimed to be a 16-year-old Choctaw and when she gave spoken messages she gave them in her native tongue. For the most part Soule was fully aware of the communications but she grew weary of this and asked the **controls** to help her. They obliged by putting her into full **trance** when she spoke.

In 1907 Soule began to work with **James Hyslop** who in that year took over the leadership of the American Society for Psychical Research (ASPR). Her work as a **medium** proved to be impressive and she helped Hyslop with the **Thompson-Gifford case** and in his efforts to treat the multiple personalities of **Doris Fischer**.

Hyslop believed that such cases were actually caused by spirit **possession** and Soule's communications with spirits supported this explanation.

After Hyslop's death Soule began to work for Walter Franklin Prince who succeeded Hyslop at the ASPR. When Prince left to head up the **Boston Society for Psychical Research** in 1925 Soule followed him. During this time she had a series of successful sittings with **John Thomas**, who was trying to contact his dead wife.

Soule died on 28 April 1936. Between 1907 and 1920 Hyslop's work with her was published in the *Proceedings* of the ASPR.

SPACE CLEARING

The practice of clearing clutter from the home and office in order to improve the flow of natural energies through the environment. The aim of space clearing is to create harmony and balance in a person's life by first creating it in personal living spaces. Many believe space clearing to be the first step in applying **feng shui** principles to living and working spaces. It is certainly similar to **geomancy** and other practices that work with the energies of the earth.

Generally there are believed to be three types of clutter: physical, vibrational and internal. Physical clutter relates to the clutter of objects, papers and things that create an untidy environment. Vibrational clutter is those unresolved and negative issues in a person's life, such as unanswered letters, debts and stressful relationships. Dealing with these matters clears the **unconscious** mind and results in more energy. Internal clutter is associated with health and concerns lifestyle choices and habits such as poor diet, lack of exercise and so on. Balancing the internal clutter through positive lifestyle change or energy enhancing treatments like **massage** or **acupuncture** is thought to result in improved health and wellbeing.

Spasmatomancy

Method of **divination** that utilizes convulsive twitching of the limbs, in other word involuntary movements made by the body. For example, in ancient and modern Greece, if the left eyebrow throbs or twitches this can mean an enemy will soon be encountered. If it is the right eyebrow then it will be a friend. Similarly a buzzing in the ear is believed to be a sign that someone will soon be speaking to you – slander and unpleasant words if it is the left ear and good wishes if it is the right. If the left palm itches then money will be paid out. If it is the right palm then money will be coming in. If the sole of the left foot itches then an unsuccessful journey lies ahead, but if the right sole itches the journey will be successful.

Sneezing or hiccupping or choking over food indicates a backbiter at work. The cure is to guess the name of the person. If anyone is interrupted when they are speaking by a sneeze, either his or her own or someone else's, then whatever was being said is regarded as the absolute truth.

Spectre

Word that is generally thought to mean a **ghost** or **apparition** but among ghost hunters it has become employed to describe **hauntings** that eventually prove to be explainable or deliberately fraudulent. The most famous example of this is the 'Spectre of the Brocken' from Germany.

For many years people were fearful of climbing the Brocken Mountains in Germany in case they met an awesome ghostly figure that was said to loom up out of the mist at unwary travellers. The fear was heightened when photographs were produced that supposedly captured a **phantom monk** on film. The photographs were later proved to be fraudulent and in 1818 German scholar Gustave Jordan made several trips to the Brocken and concluded that so-called sightings could easily be explained by a trick of the light caused by the rising and setting sun. Despite this natural explanation the legend of the Spectre of the Brocken still persists in Germany and attracts many tourists to the Harz mountains.

Spells

The following are simple spells for love, luck and psychic power. They can be performed by any responsible, mature adult, as long as intention is pure and due attention is paid to safety. The spells are gathered from various sources and quoted in *The Element Encyclopedia of 5000 Spells* by Judika Illes (HarperElement, 2004), which provides an excellent and comprehensive introduction to the art of successful spellcasting.

Win Your Heart Candle Spell

This spell allegedly enables you to win the heart of the one you desire.

1. Carve your name and that of the desired party nine times each on a pink seven-day candle.
2. Gently warm honey in a bain-marie and then blend in rosewater and powdered orrisroot.
3. Roll the candle in this mixture and burn it.

Dandelion love letter

Blow on a dried dandelion's head and scatter the seeds to the winds. Most people do this for fun; however the dandelion will also provide magical messenger services. Allegedly the seeds will carry loving messages and wishes to the one you love. Focus hard on your desires and blow.

First Star Spell for good luck and fortune

1. Pay attention at twilight, it's easy to miss your opportunity.
2. If you can catch sight of the very first solo star in the sky, gaze at it and make your wish.
3. You may want to incorporate the following rhyme: 'Starlight, star bright, first star I see tonight, I wish I may, I wish I might, have this wish I wish tonight.'
4. If the first star can't be identified, luck isn't with you; save the spell for another night.

Happy Times Powder

Blend the following ingredients together, powdering further if necessary: dried ground strawberry leaves, dried powdered vanilla bean and finely grated orange zest. Sprinkle this powder around the perimeter of your home, behind doors and in all corners for a change of luck and an improvement in fortune.

Problem-solving spell to untie the knots that bind you

1. Write an explicit description of your situation on brown paper.
2. Wrap the paper around some knot grass.
3. Charge the packet with your desire by holding it and focusing on it, and then burn it.

4. Pay attention to your dreams and random words overheard; solutions will appear and you don't want to miss them.

Basil Psychic Power Spell

Create an infused oil of fresh basil leaves. Add the oil to your bath or apply to the body and visualize yourself as regal, commanding and filled with power.

Artemisia Psychic Potion

1. Beginning at the New Moon, soak dried mugwort leaves in a bottle of wine of your choice.

2. Let this steep for seven days, ideally exposing the bottle to nightly moonbeams.
3. Decant the wine straining out the botanicals.
4. Drink small quantities at a time, a glass here and there to increase clairvoyance.

Botanical Psychic Protection

Grow some plants in the garden or indoors in pots. Sit next to them with a clear, meditative mind. Absorb their energy and let inspiration appear unbidden. This is believed to be particularly beneficial when engaged in divination.

SPELL

Procedure usually performed by a **witch**, **wizard** or **magician** that is believed to change a certain situation or outcome. Spells are written or spoken words or intentions (thoughts) believed to have magical power. They are activated by the **invocation** of **spirits**, by **chanting**, by ritual or by the use of magical tools and ingredients. Spells can be positive, for example to improve a person's health or to attract good things into their life, or they can be negative, for example to do harm or to force someone to do something against their will. Whether or not a spell is good or evil depends on the intentions of the spell-caster.

Belief in spells and their use dates back to antiquity. Spells have always been an important part of magical practice. Their methods vary from culture to culture, but all spells function on ritual activity. The spell itself usually consists of words, intentions or **incantations** (sometimes called **charms** or **runes**), which are recited or visualized while a prescribed set of actions (rituals) are performed.

There are various types of spells and their purposes are limitless including **healing**, love, success, money, fertility, longevity, protection against disaster, illness, misfortune and evil, **exorcism** of **ghosts** and spirits, victory in war and over an enemy, truth in **divination**, weather control, accomplishment of **supernatural** feats and so on. A person can cast a spell for himself, or direct it towards another person. A positive spell is called a blessing. A negative spell is usually known as a **hex** or **curse**. Archaic terms for spells include bewitchment and enchantment.

Spells are in some respects similar to **prayer**, in that they both are a means of petitioning something greater than ourselves for a particular desired outcome. They both require a statement of desire and/or ritualized movements or body positions, such as the bowing of the head, the folding or clasping of hands or the shutting of the eyes.

Spells are also closely related to certain methods that employ the power of the mind, such as **visualizations, affirmations** and **positive thinking**. Such methods help the person casting the spell to emphasize his or her mental images so he or she can better identify with these images and form a clear goal in their mind. The person repeats his or her intention to achieve a particular goal and then combines it with the projection of **Magical Will** and the invocation of the aid of the spirits, deities or inner strength.

SPIRIT

A **supernatural** force of nature, **discarnate entity** or the animating essence within our physical bodies; sometimes referred to as **soul** but not precisely the same as the soul. Spirits can also represent places, such as the spirits of lakes, trees, mountains and sacred sites.

Spirit is the divine essence of who we are, an indivisible part of the three aspects of human existence: mind, body and spirit. In many belief systems the spirit survives death and can be contacted by a **medium** on our plane of existence.

Spirits are commonplace in the religions and folklores of the world and come in a multitude of shapes and forms, such as **fairies**, elves, **demons** and **angels**. In some cultures they are also thought to personify characteristics and forces of nature, which are worshiped. They are believed to exist in an invisible realm but can be seen by persons with **clairvoyance**. They are also thought to intervene at times in the affairs of humanity, for better or for worse.

The term is often used to describe all non-physical entities, including **ghosts**, but a spirit is not strictly speaking the same as a ghost even though the distinction between the two is sometimes vague. **Spiritualism** refers to a belief in the immortality of the soul and to communication with spirits of the dead. According to medium **Arthur Ford**, spirit was 'nothing more than the stream of consciousness of a personality with which we are familiar in every human being. This is what survives death not as a spiritual wraith but as an oblong blur.' **Society for Psychical Research** founder **Frederick Myers** suggested in his book *Human Personality and Its Survival After Death* (1903) that the spirit is the unknown part of a man's personality, 'which we discern as operating before or after death in the metetherical environment.'

SPIRIT ATTACHMENT

Form of **possession** in which a **discarnate entity** attaches itself to a human being, much like a parasite. Spirit attachment is similar to possession but is the preferred term in modern times because it does not imply demonic possession. According to therapists who perform **spirit release-ment**, most entities are not evil or demonic but simply confused.

Attachment is thought to occur when a person dies but for some reason, such as unfinished business, emotional ties or lack of awareness of death, his or her spirit cannot leave the earth. The confused spirit attaches itself to a human host at random, although a living person is thought to be more vulnerable if they drink alcohol, use drugs, have suffered a traumatic accident or have had major surgery involving anaesthesia. Being close to a dying person is also believed to make a person more vulnerable, as immediately after death the spirit will be looking for a new host. Some attachments are also believed to be karmic in origin and if the spirit is not released it may remain attached for the lifetime of the host.

Symptoms of spirit attachment include depression, mood swings, multiple person-ality disorder and sudden changes in be-haviour. Symptoms vary according to the degree of attachment; it is thought that when spirit attachment is benign a person may not even know they have attached spirits.

The first medically trained expert to approach mental illness due to spirit attachment was **Carl Wickland** (1861–1945), an American physician who used electric shocks to exorcise unwanted en-tities from the **auras** of his patients. Since the late 1980s reports of spirit attachment have become more common, especially with the development of **past-life therapy**.

SPIRIT GUIDE

A **discarnate entity**, often perceived as the **higher self** or a **spirit** of the dead that serves as a communications bridge, guardian or guide. In **shamanism** the spirit guide is known as a **totem** animal in **spiri-tualism** it is known as the **medium**'s **con-trol**, while in **witchcraft** it is known as a **familiar**.

It is widely held around the world that every person has one or more spirit guides from birth that remain with the person throughout their life. At death these guides assist the soul in crossing over to death. **Psychics** are often very aware of their spirit guides. Some speak to them in **dreams**, see them **clairvoyantly** or receive **clairaudient** messages through **medita-tion** and **visualization**. Children who have **imaginary friends** may be communicating with their guides.

The belief in spirit guides may come from the ancient Greeks who believed in the existence of daemons, intermediary spirits between man and the gods. Dae-mons could be either good or evil. Socrates claimed to be guided by a good daemon throughout his life, but British psychical researcher **Frederick Myers** suggested that Socrates's daemon was most likely his own inner voice. The Church later turned all daemons into evil **demons**, but retained the concept of protector spirits in the form of a guardian **angel**.

SPIRIT LIGHTS

See **Ghost lights, Orbs**.

SPIRIT OBSESSION

See **Possession**.

SPIRIT PHOTOGRAPHY

Photographs allegedly showing a person who is alive complete with the head and shoulders of a deceased relative or a swirling mist hovering above or around them. Most spirit photographs can be explained as flaws in the film or the development of the film and the great majority have been judged as hoaxes.

Like many phenomena associated with **spiritualism**, spirit photography originated in America in the mid-nineteenth century. A man called William Mumler of Boston is credited with having produced the first spirit photographs in 1862 and from this a whole new style of photog-raphy blossomed on both sides of the Atlantic. Individuals would sit for photographers, like **William Hope**, in the hope of seeing the images of dead loved ones (called 'extras') revealed in the print.

Early spirit photographs revealed ghostly faces – sometimes famous faces – floating above or around the person being photographed. In some photographs mists appeared or full **spirit** forms. Almost without exception the spirit figures were introduced on to the photographic plates by double exposure and the liberal use of cotton wool to give a misty effect. Many fraudulent photographs were accepted as real both by the public and by experts such as **Sir Arthur Conan Doyle**.

Spirit photography diminished in popularity when the public learned about the tricks the camera was capable of and most successful fakers were unable to continue beyond 1930. Today spirit photography is very different from the spirit photography of the nineteenth and early twentieth centuries. The camera has become an important tool in **ghost investigation** and sophisticated cameras are used in an effort to record anomalies on film. Cameras are linked to computers and are triggered when a device is activated by possible phenomena. Regular and infrared film is used, as the latter will show invisible sources of heat. Digital cameras are used with caution as prints can easily be manipulated using a computer so most investigators steer clear of these when attempting to take spirit photographs.

When phenomena do show up on film they typically appear as balls or streaks of light or patches of fog and, in some cases, filmy shapes. With the use of high-tech equipment investigators have also captured on film **orbs,** which are invisible to the naked eye but seem to be associated with haunted sites. An explanation that has been offered is that the spirit photograph is created unconsciously by **psychokinesis** on the part of the investigator whose desire to see a ghost somehow imprints itself on the film. The term used to describe this phenomenon is '**thoughtography**', and it was coined in the early 1900s by Tomokichi Fukurai, then president of the Psychical Institute of Japan, who discovered thoughtography in experiments with **mediums**. Later, in the 1960s, Ted Serios of Kansas allegedly created images on a film by staring into a camera lens.

This may explain cases of spirit photography when investigators at haunted sites are intent on seeing a ghost, but it does not explain circumstances when an unusual photograph appears and the person who took it had no interest or desire to see a ghost at all. The famous photograph of the **Brown Lady** of Raynham Hall, which has been declared free of **fraud**, illustrates this point as the **apparition** that was photographed was seen by the photographer's assistant and not the photographer.

The **Ghost Research Society** of Oak Lawn, Illinois houses the most impressive collection of spirit photographs from around the world. According to the Society about 90 per cent of the photographs of alleged spirits or ghosts can be explained naturally by flaws in the film developing process, fog or specks on the camera lens or light reflected from the camera lens. Some people also mistake simulacra for ghosts.

'Simulacra' is the term used to describe shapes that are created by random patterns in vegetation, shadows or other elements in the background of the photograph.

The 10 per cent of spirit photographs that do not seem to have any natural explanations include photographs of blotches of light, fog, streaks and shapes that have no reason for being there. These photographs are considered **paranormal** and for enthusiasts the 'spirit energy' they capture on film provides tantalizing evidence for **survival after death**.

SPIRIT RELEASEMENT

Modern term for the **exorcism** of a **discarnate entity** attached to a person or place. The term is particularly used for exorcisms that are performed without a religious element.

Spirit releasement has become much more common with the growth in popularity of **past-life therapy**. Some past-life therapists say that their clients have **spirit attachments** relating to past lives. Past-life therapist Edith Fiore began releasing entities in the 1970s. In the 1980s Dr William Baldwin began studying releasement and developed techniques now used by many therapists, published in his 1991 book *Spirit Releasement Therapy: A Technique Manual.*

Modern practitioners of spirit releasement work with **spirit guides** who make contact with the spirit **haunting** a site or a person. In many cases it is said that this is an earthbound spirit who has no idea he or she is dead or is bound to the earth because of unfinished business. Practitioners believe that simply finding out the entity's business or story is often enough to persuade the spirit to depart to the next world. Typically the transition to the next world is marked by the appearance of a white light that the spirit moves towards or is guided towards by spirit helpers. Following releasement many clients report feeling much lighter and happier and experience an end to their troubles. The possessing spirits do not return but clients are shown how to protect themselves from future attacks.

See also **Spiritism**.

SPIRITISM

Philosophy associated with **Allan Kardec** that is closely linked with the **Spiritualist** movement of the nineteenth century.

In 1857 a French writer and physician called Hippolyte Leon Denizard Rivail (1804–1869) published *Le Livre des esprits* (Lives of the Spirits) under the pseudonym of Allan Kardec. In this seminal work Kardec outlined his belief that some illnesses, such as epilepsy and multiple personality disorder, have spiritual causes and can be treated through communication with **spirit guides**. He also suggested that these psychic illnesses were not only the result of possessing **spirits** but of unfinished business endured by the individual in past lives.

Kardec's belief in **reincarnation** separated him from many spiritualists of his day who did not hold that belief. He wrote that each time a **soul** is reborn it brings with it remnants of past lives that may blur the reality of the current life. Each rebirth, however traumatic and difficult, is necessary for the soul to improve and perfect itself. Souls will continue to be reborn until they have nothing left to learn.

According to Kardec, a person has three parts: an incarnate soul, a body and a perispirit that is semi-material and unites the body and soul; at death the perispirit helps the soul separate from the body. This process of separation is effortless for spiritually advanced souls but for those who are attached to the material existence it takes longer, and in a case of sudden or violent death the spirit may cling to the body not knowing it is dead. Once the spirit has left the body it returns to the spirit world where, Kardec believed, it reviews its progress and decides which life path to pursue next.

Kardec believed that mental illness was caused by spirits who should have progressed to a higher level devoting their energies to persecution of the living instead. He did not believe, however, that all cases of spirit **possession** were intentional, rather that many spirits were simply confused. **Exorcisms**, he maintained, must be originated by the possessed person him or herself, through **prayer**; they were not possible through the help of outsiders. He strongly believed that 'God helps those who help themselves.'

Spiritism was briefly popular in Europe but its draw soon waned as other interests and crazes took hold. Kardecism, as it became known, did however take hold in Brazil, with its strong association with African spirits and **superstition**. It remains a powerful religious force there today with centres all over the country. It also flourishes in the Philippines.

Kardecist healing involves prayer, counselling, **past-life therapy** through a **medium** guided by spirits and, in some cases, **psychic surgery**. In Brazil Kardecist psychiatric hospitals staffed by trained doctors operate alongside their traditional counterparts and have impressed many non-spiritist physicians with their emphasis on non-material and non-personal gain.

Spiritists do not proselytize or try to convince others to follow their faith. They accept without question the existence of spirits and do not feel the need to seek proof of their existence. Dedicated spiritist mediums insist their talent is God given and refuse to use it for personal gain. They modestly insist that the spirit guides are the true healers. Such humility and selflessness, however, does not characterize every spiritist medium. Little research has been done on spiritist phenomena as it is considered a religion, not a science.

SPIRITUAL BODY

Alternative term for **soul** or **spirit**. See also **Astral body**.

SPIRITUAL EMERGENCE

Term evolved from 'spiritual emergency', which was coined in the 1970s by psychiatrists Stanislav Grof and his wife Christina to describe a range of non-ordinary states of consciousness that can be unsettling because of their sudden onset. From the point of view of psychotherapy such experiences can be described as signs of a mental breakdown, but to the Grofs they are interpreted as indications of spiritual awakening. In 1980, after founding the Spiritual Emergency Network, Christina replaced the word 'emergency' with 'emergence' to emphasize that such experiences need not always be upsetting or traumatic.

Christina Grof drew on her own experience of spiritual awakening, which began shortly after her marriage to Stanislav Grof in the late 1970s. Symptoms of her awakening included feeling overwhelmed with **psychic** energies, emotions and inner experiences. In response to this the Grofs founded the Spiritual Emergence Network to help others 'find their way through unexpected and often unsettling mystical and psychic openings', rather than limit them with traditional psychotherapy.

According to the Grofs spiritual crises last seconds, minutes, hours or weeks and are most likely to occur during times of great physical stress or crisis, such as childbirth, surgery, near death or during sex, during spiritual practices such as **meditation** and during transitional stages of life. In most cases the crisis disrupts the person's ability to function normally. Spiritual emergences are common to humans and need to be integrated into the person's

consciousness, not ignored or suppressed. Integration, which can last several years, leads to spiritual growth. Failure to integrate these experiences can lead to poor mental and physical health.

SPIRITUAL FRONTIERS FELLOWSHIP

Organization founded in 1956 by **medium Arthur Ford** to focus the attention of the Christian Church on the insights and contribution **psychic** phenomena could offer it. The mission statement of the Spiritual Frontiers Fellowship, whose headquarters are in Philadelphia, is to 'sponsor, explore and interpret the growing interest in psychic phenomena and mystical experience within the church, wherever these experiences relate to effective prayer, spiritual healing and personal survival'. A similar organization – the Academy of Religion and Psychical Research, based in Connecticut – is also devoted to an exchange of ideas between religion and psychical research. Despite encouraging signs of an overlap, mainstream Christianity remains disinterested in the psychic world.

SPIRITUAL HEALING

General term used to describe a multitude of methods in which a healer serves as a channel for healing energies to be directed into a patient. This healing energy is believed to stimulate the body's self-healing systems and the healing can be physical, emotional or spiritual. The source of the healing energy depends on individual belief. Some say it is from God, others from the **universal life force**, **spirit guides** and so on.

Although the spiritual healer acts as a channel he or she still needs to have innate healing or **psychic** ability. Healers sometimes touch the person in need of healing to concentrate and focus the energy; at other times they keep their hands just above the body. Sometimes healing takes place from a distance (see **absent healing**).

Spiritual healers do not guarantee a cure but many people who have attended spiritual healing sessions report feelings of tingling or warmth where the energy is directed and a feeling of relaxation afterwards. Because spiritual healing is a **holistic** therapy that aims to treat the whole person it has been found to be particularly beneficial for stress-related conditions and emotional upsets.

SPIRITUAL PLANES

Levels of existence where **discarnate entities** and **spirits** are thought to exist and where there are no boundaries of space, time or tangibility.

See also **Astral planes**.

SPIRITUALISM

Religious and social movement that began in the United States in 1848 and quickly spread to Britain and Europe. Interest peaked in the early twentieth century and then subsided, although today it still remains a vigorous religion around the world, especially in Britain and America. Its appeal originally derived from the evidence it purported to provide of **survival after death**, manifested through **mediums** who allegedly communicated with **spirits** and performed **paranormal** feats.

The official start date of Spiritualism is considered to be 1848, as it was then that the **Fox sisters** of New York became well known for their **rapping** communication with spirits. Public interest in the phenomena of spirit communication had been prepared by **mesmerism** and the writing of **Emanuel Swedenborg**. **Mesmerism** was popular in the United States in the early nineteenth century, with large audiences gathering to hear hypnotized subjects report their experiences of the spirit world and demonstrate **psychic** powers of **telepathy, clairvoyance, automatic writing** and so on. Another key figure was **Andrew Jackson Davis**, who delivered lectures on the fate of the **soul** after death in **trance** state.

Following in the footsteps of the Fox sisters, numerous other mediums sprung up claiming to be able to communicate with the dead. **Séances** were extremely popular. Early séances were mostly rappings but in time they became highly entertaining affairs with huge audiences witnessing incredible paranormal feats such as **levitation**, **apports** and **materializations**. **Fraud** was commonplace but even this did nothing to dampen the public's enthusiasm. Private **home circles** were also conducted and by 1855 Spiritualism claimed 2 million followers on both sides of the Atlantic.

Spiritualists believe that the soul survives death and makes a transition to the spirit world. Communication with these souls is made possible through purposeful contact with the departed – a séance – via a medium. The medium goes into a trance and through his or her psychic ability allegedly establishes a link between this world and the **afterlife**. The spirits then speak through the medium, who is temporarily possessed by this entity. This contact is taken as proof by believers that there is indeed life after death. Traditionally Spiritualism rejected a belief in **reincarnation** although today opinion among spiritualists on the subject of rebirth is divided.

Spiritualism had a difficult relationship with Christianity from the outset. Some Christians rejected it as Satanic and even tried to have it legally banned. Some spiritualists believed in breaking ties with religion while others sought the endorsement of the Church by advocating belief in Christian principles.

Mediums in the early days were typically shunned by their friends and family. Most of the mediums were women and through spiritualism they were able to find freedom from many Victorian restraints, since entranced mediums were thought to be controlled by spirits and not responsible for their actions. This, along with the social equality encouraged by spirit teachings, attracted women involved in the suffragette movement to the spiritualist camp.

When spiritualist phenomena began to be investigated scientifically in the mid- to late nineteenth century it was sincerely hoped that evidence for survival would be found. Unfortunately, scientific proof was and remains inconclusive. What was uncovered, however, was a lot of trickery and gullibility on the part of the mediums and their audiences. Systematic investigations of psychic phenomena began in earnest in 1882 with the formation of the **Society for Psychical Research** in London, followed soon afterwards by the **American Society for Psychical Research**. Sadly scientists who were also keen to explore psychical research tended to see their academic careers suffer because of prejudice from their peers.

The exposure of frauds and the lack of scientific proof for survival after death took its toll on the movement, and by the turn of the twentieth century Spiritualism was on the decline. There was a brief revival during World War I, when the bereaved sought comfort at séances, but it was not significant enough to lift Spiritualism to its former popularity. Despite this, interest in Spiritualism continued quietly on both sides of the Atlantic and in the 1930s psychical research finally moved from the séance into the laboratory, with the work of **J B Rhine**.

Today Spiritualist churches remain active in Britain, the United States, Brazil and other countries. The majority are modelled on protestant churches but without a ministry. The emphasis is on **spiritual healing (prayer, laying on of hands,** energy transfer) and **mental mediumship,** which can include trance messages communicated from spirits to the congregation. Spiritualists believe that their religion has been scientifically proved by the paranormal feats of mediums. This is because, according to believers, Spiritualism offers proof of life after death in a way no other religion can; the living can talk directly to their dearly departed, and, more importantly, learn how best to live to later profit after they themselves pass on.

The largest spiritualist organization in the United States is the **National Spiritualist Association of Churches of the USA** but the largest spiritualist organizations in the world are in the UK: the **Spiritualist Association of Great Britain** and the **Spiritualists National Union**. Until 1951 Spiritualism had no legal status in the UK due to the Witchcraft Act of 1735, which enabled the prosecution of mediums as **witches**, but in 1951 that law was repealed and replaced by a fraudulent mediums' act.

SPIRITUALIST ASSOCIATION OF GREAT BRITAIN

One of the largest spiritualist organizations in the world. The Spiritualist Association of Great Britain was founded in London in 1872 as the Marylebone Spiritualist Association, and its function was to study **psychic** phenomena and **mediumship** and 'to propagate spiritual truth'.

Even though interest in **spiritualism** was steadily growing at the time there was opposition to the group and it had difficulty obtaining halls for meetings and **séances**. In an effort to counteract some of the opposition it changed its name to the Spiritual Evidence Society.

The association managed to survive and by 1960 it had greatly expanded both its membership and its interests. The name was changed again to the Spiritualist Association of Great Britain. Today thousands of visitors are attracted to the society's headquarters in Belgrave Square, London, in particular for its **spiritual healing** services. Describing itself as one of the busiest spiritualist organizations in the world, the society runs events, workshops, classes, demonstrations and meetings. The organization has a prayer room, a library, a chapel and a meeting hall.

According to its website (www.sagb.org.uk), the society's mission statement is as follows:

To offer evidence to the bereaved that man survives the change called death and because he is a spiritual being retains the faculties of individuality, personality and intelligence and can willingly return to those left on earth ties of love and friendship being the motivating force.

To offer spiritual healing to those suffering from disease, whether in mind, body or spirit, in a warm and loving environment.

With both of these objectives in mind, to offer only the best and the highest so that those on both sides of the veil can progress in a truly spiritual sense.

SPIRITUALIST CAMPS

Holiday-camp type settings that offer spiritualist activities, church services, lectures, **home circles** and classes in **mediumship** and **psychic** development. There are 12 such camps in the United States and all are affiliated with and follow the guidelines set by the **National Spiritualist Association of Churches of the USA**. The most famous spiritualist camp is Lily Dale Assembly in New York. Lily Dale was founded way back in 1880 as the Cassadaga Free Lake Association and its current name was chosen in 1906. Lily Dale consists of about 80 acres of land, with a hotel, hundreds of cottages and meeting places, a library, bookstore and post office.

SPIRITUALISTS NATIONAL UNION

Probably one of the largest spiritualist groups in the world, the Spiritualists National Union was founded in Manchester as the Spiritualists National Federation, in an attempt to bring Britain's spiritualists together in one organization.

Spiritualism spread to Britain from the United States in the early 1850s and it soon found followers. The first British spiritualist church was established in 1853 in Yorkshire, and in 1855 the first spiritualist newspaper, the *Yorkshire Spiritualist Telegraph*, was published. By the early 1880s there were numerous spiritualist organizations and churches in all parts of Britain and in 1887 **medium** Emma Hardinge Britten founded a weekly spiritualist journal called *Two Worlds.*

Even though spiritualism had its supporters it became clear that some sort of federation would help unite the churches and societies and assist them to win respect and recognition. In 1890 Britten championed the idea of a federation in her journal and a year later the Spiritualist National Federation was formed.

At first the Federation was only an annual conference; in 1901 it was legally incorporated as a charitable organization. In 1948 it joined with the British Lyceum Union, which had been founded in 1890 for the spiritualist education of children, and in 1970 it launched a Guild of Spiritualist Healers as a branch of the SNU. The guild was formed to establish guidelines for **spiritual healing**.

The SNU adheres to seven principles, which were allegedly given to Britten by the discarnate **spirit** of an early supporter of spiritualism. According to the society's website (www.snu.org.uk) the seven principles of the SNU, which also serve as a philosophy of life, are:

The fatherhood of God.

The brotherhood of man.

The communion of spirits and ministry of **angels.**

The continuous existence of the human **soul.**

Personal responsibility.

Compensation and retribution hereafter for all good or evil done on earth.

The opportunity of eternal progress for every soul.

Membership of the SNU consists of churches and individual members. In 1964 Scottish businessman Arthur Findlay bequeathed his family home, Stansted Hall, to be used as a college for psychic studies. Today Stansted Hall is known as the Arthur Findlay College and it offers courses in psychic development, mediumship and healing.

SPITTING

According to American and British folklore, spitting is believed to protect a person or object against **ghosts** and evil **spirits**. It is said that if a ghost is encountered one must spit on the ground in front of it and say, 'In the name of the Lord, what do you want?' The spittle supposedly protects the individual from harm.

The protective power of saliva dates back to ancient times. Spitting on one's breast was supposed to avert the jealousy of the gods. The Bible records innumerable instances of its superstitious use and its symbolic personification, for example, Jesus healing the blind man by spitting on his eyes. Until quite recently in parts of rural Ireland, a newborn child was spat on by its father; neighbours spat on the child for luck the first day it was brought out, and older women spat on the ground all around it to ward off evil. The origins of the **superstition** are uncertain but it is likely to have originated as a way of instilling humility in those blessed with good fortune, wealth or beauty in case that good fortune invoked the jealousy of the gods.

SPOOK

Generally accepted as an alternative term for **ghost**, the origins of the word may be traced back to American Indian lore and thus regarded as a uniquely American term. In its purest sense, these **spirits** are regarded as benevolent and benign, capable of temporarily taking control of a living body to perform good works. This type of ghost is sometimes said to be able to haunt a person without him or her ever being aware of it, and can absorb themselves into the person at will. Along the Eastern United States, stories can still be discovered in rural areas of men who had achieved little in their lives until a spook took over them, enabling them to achieve wealth and success. The term is also now much used in America and the UK to describe intelligence operatives and government spies.

SPORTS, PSYCHIC PHENOMENA IN

People who push their bodies to the limits often report experiencing a wide range of phenomena, ranging from a heightened state of awareness and psychic experiences such as **clairvoyance** to a feeling of mystical oneness. In most cases the experience improves the performance of the person who is exerting intense physical and mental effort. Athletes describe this experience as being in the 'zone'.

According to a study of several thousand athletes there are at least 60 different sensations that can occur in the zone. At one end of the spectrum are bouts of coordination, energy and the ability to make all the right instinctive moves. At the other end are **out-of-body experiences**, **ESP**, in terms of knowing what the opposition will do next, and the movement of objects (**psychokinesis**). In some cases mystical illumination and a feeling of oneness with all creation may occur.

Athletes who report entering the zone tend to be the best in their fields. Research has shown that during periods of intense concentration there is a decrease in the brain's overall metabolic rate, making it more efficient. It has been suggested that the lower the brain's metabolic rate and the more efficiently it works, the better the sporting performance.

The experience differs according to the sport. For example, football players report feeling that they are bigger and stronger than they are. Runners experience sensations of floating or flying. Baseball or basketball players and golfers report changes in time perception and moments when time seems to stop enabling them to accomplish extraordinary feats of concentration and activity. In solitary sports such as mountaineering and sailing, awareness of ethereal beings is most common. Mountaineers who have climbed the Himalayas report the presence of silent companions or invisible presences who in some cases guide them through dangerous areas.

Transformative, mystical experiences in sports – a sense of oneness with the universe – can be compared to those experienced in **yoga** and **martial art** disciplines. These experiences make superior or peak performances possible. It seems that relaxation, stillness of mind and a letting go that frees the person from concerns about winning or losing allows the sportsperson to be in the moment, and an effortless, superior performance follows where mind and body are as one. Many athletes describe this moment as like being in a **trance**.

In the West cultivating the zone and focusing on right-brain thinking – **intuition** and instinct – instead of left-brain thinking – anxiety, analysis, fear and judgement – is becoming increasingly common. Athletic and sports training now includes Eastern concepts of **meditation, visualization** and **relaxation**. Sports psychologists believe that the same conditions that contribute to peak performance in sports can be applied to almost any area of life.

SPUNKIE

According to lore, spunkies are sad and lonely **ghosts**, the **spirits** of unbaptized children. They are said to be found on both land and sea, wandering in search of someone to provide them with a name. In Scotland, it is said that spunkies sometimes gather together in groups for companionship, while legends from the English West Country state that they can take on the shape of white moths, which flitter about unnoticed by the living. It is thought that these lost spirits are doomed to wander the earth until Judgement Day, but every **Halloween** night they can be found in churches meeting the spirits of those who have recently died.

STAINED GLASS WINDOW EFFECT

Term coined by British journalist and psychic researcher **William Stead** (1849–1912) to describe how psychic perception can be influenced by the subconscious mind. Stead attended numerous **séances** and was able to discover his own ability for **automatic writing**. Drawing on his own experiences he came to the conclusion that the subconscious mind stains and distorts every piece of information that passes through it to the waking self, much as a stained glass window superimposes colours, patterns and shades upon the white light that passes through it.

According to Stead, the stained glass window effect can be seen in psychic perception when information that is received psychically is influenced by the receiver's subconscious attitudes, predispositions and prejudices. Stead believed that all psychically received information is suppressed or altered often without the receiver knowing it is happening.

STANFORD RESEARCH INSTITUTE

In July 1995 the CIA declassified, and approved for release, documents revealing its sponsorship in the 1970s of a programme at Stanford Research Institute in Menlo Park, California to determine whether such phenomena as **remote viewing** 'might have any utility for intelligence collection'. Thus began disclosure to the public of the two-decade-plus involvement of the intelligence community in the investigation of so-called parapsychological or **psi** phenomena.

It appears that throughout this period the CIA had a number of remote viewers operating from Stanford Research Institute and other locations on a contract basis under an umbrella funding agreement known as Project Star Gate. The exact details of the arrangements are somewhat unclear, as expected for a project being run by the intelligence community.

See also **Remote viewing, CIA Star Gate programme**.

Starhawk

See **Witchcraft**.

Staus Poltergeist

Nineteenth-century **poltergeist** named after the village of Staus on the shores of Lake Lucerne, Switzerland.

From 1860 to 1862 members of the Joller family who lived in Staus were allegedly victimized by unexplained activities. The **hauntings** started when a servant girl heard knocks on her bedstead. A short time later Mr Joller's wife and children also heard the raps. Within a few days a close family friend died and the raps were interpreted as a **death omen**. Strange occurrences continued in the months that followed. One of the Jollers' four sons saw

an **apparition** and the servant girl said she saw and heard a sobbing **spirit**. The servant girl was replaced in the hope it would put an end to the haunting but instead the haunting grew worse, with the rapping now accompanied by invisible hands moving objects and locking doors.

The Jollers were forced to seek help for the disturbances and for six days the family left the house for the police to investigate. The police saw or heard no signs of the poltergeist but as soon as the family returned the haunting started up again. Eventually Mr Joller decided to leave his home and put in a tenant, who heard nothing from the poltergeist.

The case remains unsolved but it has been suggested that a member of the Joller household, probably one of the children, was the **agent** for the hauntings (see **psychokinesis**).

Stead, William [1849–1912]

A campaigning journalist who helped outlaw the practice of child prostitution in the 1880s, and a keen supporter of **spiritualism**. He edited his own paper, the monthly *Review of Reviews*. The Christmas 1891 issue of the *Review* was *Real Ghost Stories*. He warned readers to be careful of dabbling in the **supernatural** in case they became exposed to the threat of spirit **possession**. He also put the case for **ghosts** in terms of eye-witness accounts.

As early as 1880 Stead had experienced **premonitions** and by early 1892 he had developed a talent for **automatic writing**. He claimed to receive letters from various persons and his interviews with the dead caused a sensation. Stead's principal **control** was allegedly a woman called Julia Ames, a fellow journalist who had befriended Stead a year before her death. Julia communicated with Stead about a variety of topics and Stead had these communications published as 'Letters from Julia' in the quarterly review of psychic literature called *Borderland* in 1893.

In 1907 Stead's oldest son, Willie, died and this prompted him, under the guidance of Julia, to set an office wherein the bereaved could reach their loved ones on the other side. Almost immediately the office was inundated with applications but lack of funds forced it to close in 1912.

Stead resolutely accepted the concept of the **afterlife** and denied the possibility of **fraud**; however, he did believe that communications from the other side were influenced by the subconscious (see **stained glass window effect**). Throughout his life his premonitions had involved great disasters at sea and on 14 April 1912 Stead was one of 1,600 lives lost on the *Titanic*. This wasn't the last that was heard of Stead, however, as he allegedly appeared to his daughter, his secretary and a number of others three weeks later. They claimed his face looked radiant, he was bursting with joy and called out, 'All I told you is true.' He also allegedly predicted the horrors of World War I through a **medium** called Mrs Tuner and communicated in spirit to **Sir Arthur Conan Doyle**, reassuring him that the work he was doing was 'holy'.

STEINER, RUDOLF [1861–1925]

Austrian mystic and educator who in 1909 founded a movement called Anthroposophy, which is a blend of **Rosicrucian**, **Theosophical** and Christian tradition. Steiner described Anthroposophy as a path for spiritual growth on four levels of human nature: the senses, **imagination**, inspiration and **intuition**.

Steiner experienced **clairvoyant visions** in childhood and at the age of 19 his friend and mentor Felix Korgutski introduced him to an **adept** who gave him his spiritual identity. Steiner called this adept the Master and from the Master he learned his spiritual mission in life, which was to develop a knowledge that synthesized science and religion.

Steiner earned his philosophical doctorate at the University of Rostock in Austria in 1891 and a distinguished teaching career followed. At the age of 40 he felt ready to become a teacher of occultism, suggesting that anyone under 40 was too young for such a challenging task. By this time in his life he had learned a great deal about his own **psychic** abilities and claimed to have learned how to bridge the physical and non-physical realms. He believed that the clues to the secrets of the universe lie inside each one of us. He also claimed to be able to access the **Akashic records**, from which he learned the true history of humanity. He said that at one time mankind had possessed superior **supernatural** qualities but had lost them in a descent to the material plane. At the nadir of human descent Christ had arrived to offer humanity an opportunity to redeem itself.

In the course of his development Steiner allegedly encountered numerous spiritual beings which he called 'Ahrimanic' beings, some of which wanted to encourage humanity's spiritual development while others wanted people to remain mired in materialism. Although he said that anyone could walk the path to higher consciousness he warned that this path required incredible discipline and moral courage.

In 1902 Steiner joined the Theosophical Society, which shared many of his basic tenets of belief, but he grew disillusioned with what he described as the 'triviality and diletantism' he observed there. In 1912 he left the society to form his own Anthroposophical Society as a vehicle to continue his work. That same year he began to design the Goetheanum, a school for **esoteric** research, at Dornach near Basel in Switzerland. The school opened in 1920 but was burned down in 1922. A new building was constructed which now serves as the headquarters for the Anthroposophical Society, which became an international society with Steiner as president in 1923.

During the final decades of his life Steiner travelled across Europe to give thousands of lectures on spiritual sciences, religion, art and education. He published more than 350 titles, most of which are collections of his lectures. His major works outlining his philosophy are *Knowledge of the Higher Worlds and its Attainment* (1923) and *Occult Science: An Outline* (1913).

The Anthroposophical Society has branches all over the world and is strongest in Europe. Steiner's guidelines for **holistic** medicine are still adhered to and his agricultural methods inspired chemical-free gardening and farming. He also developed a system of movement to express the inner meanings of music and words called eurythmy. But Steiner is perhaps best known today for his controversial school theories, which include esoteric spiritual practices and **colour** healing as part of the curriculum.

The Waldorf or Steiner school movement is an approach to the education of children that he developed from his spiritual and scientific research concerning child development. In 1919 Steiner established the first Waldorf School for girls and boys in Stuttgart. With over 600 schools in over 30 countries around the world the Waldorf system, along with the Campbell homes and villages for children with special needs Steiner also founded, is among the most highly regarded (and largest) nonsectarian systems of education in the world. Steiner designed the curriculum of his schools around the theory that children pass through three seven-year stages and that education must take into consideration what is appropriate for 'body, spirit and soul' at each stage.

STIGMATA

Stigmata are the wounds that were, according to the Bible, inflicted on Jesus during his crucifixion. There have been many reports of other individuals who display similar wounds, the causes of which have been subject to considerable debate.

Stigmatics have been measured bleeding as much as a pint of blood a day. Some contend that stigmata are miraculous, others argue they are hoaxes or can be explained medically.

There have been over 500 reported stigmatics who have displayed wounds similar to those supposedly inflicted upon Jesus. The first recorded case of these wounds was in the year 1222, by Stephen Langton of England. St Francis of Assisi also suffered the wounds in La Verna, Italy, in 1224.

Other famous stigmatists include St Catherine of Siena, St John of God and the Blessed Marie of the Incarnation. The most famous stigmatist of the twentieth century was St Pio of Pietrelcina (1887–1968), better known as Padre Pio. Stigmata were more recently experienced by a Brother Roque, a novice in the order of Los Hijos de Los Hijos de La Madre de Dios (The Sons of the Sons of the Mother of God) in Villavicencio, Colombia; Jane Hunt, an English houswife, who began bleeding from her palms in 1985; and a Canadian called Lilian Bernas, who began exhibiting stigmata in 1992.

Stigmata seem to mirror the placement of wounds on the stigmatic's favourite crucifix. Blood at first seems to ooze through the skin but when the skin is wiped no wounds or marks appear. In the later stages blisters and actual wounds may appear that on occasion resemble puncture wounds or give the appearnce of a nail piercing through the skin. In some instances the wounds close up, disappear and then reopen later, typically around the time of religious festivals.

Stigmatics tend to be deeply religious and often follow lengthy contemplations on the crucifixion or deep personal crisis. British researcher Ian Wilson, who conducted a comprehensive study of stigmatics, published as *The Bleeding Mind* (1988), came to the conclusion that bleeding is self-induced by persons undergoing stress. In the experience of stigmata they find refuge from their suffering. He also drew similarities between stigmatics and people with multiple personality disorder, explaining that in both cases an individual is caught up in a flight from reality that provides release and escape. Wilson also proposed that in some cases the mind may cause the bleeding: experiments on people who have been hypnotized show that the body has the ability to bleed on command.

Another theory put forward is that people who fake stigmata suffer from Munchausen Syndrome, characterized by an intense desire for attention. People with Munchausen Syndrome hurt themselves or others or fake an illness hoping to end up in a hospital where they can enjoy attention and care; similarly, people may fake stigmata to get attention and to be recognized as holy.

There is debate over the historical method of crucifixion and whether or not nails were driven through the hands or wrists of the victims. Stigmata appear on the hands of some stigmatists and the wrists of others, and sceptics see this as evidence that the wounds have a human origin rather than a divine one, as divine wounds might be expected to be more consistent.

Stone Age ghost

Possibly the oldest **ghost** on record anywhere in the world is the Stone Age man who is said to gallop on horseback across Cranborne Chase in Dorset. This curious **phantom** is said to be clad in fur skins and riding a shaggy mount without any bridle or stirrups, brandishing what looks like a stone axe in his hand. The ghost has been reported in the vicinity of the Roman road to Old Sarum and the site of the prehistoric camp on the Chase. It has been suggested that he is a warrior who once lived in the camp.

Stonehenge

One of the most famous prehistoric monuments in the world, located on Salisbury Plain in Wiltshire.

Stonehenge was built in stages between 2800 and 1800 BC and appears to have been constructed to mark the sunrise and moonrise of the summer and winter solstices. The remains include a henge and a horseshoe arrangement of standing stones and bluestones weighing up to 26 tons apiece. Some of the stones are topped by lintels, which suggested to the Saxons the name Stonehenge, meaning 'hanging stones'. The construction of Stonehenge represents an incredible feat of engineering for primitive times and numerous legends exist as to how it was accomplished.

The original architects and reasons for building this megalithic stone circle are unknown but since the Roman conquest of Britain it has become known as an important part of **Druid** practice and worship. It is also believed that the site is a repository of **psychic** power. Because of the precise solstice orientation of the stones Stonehenge is thought to have some astronomical significance. It may also have had a religious, social and political function as well. Fifty-six burial pits containing the remains of bones, flints and pottery have been discovered, and it has been suggested that these burial pits, like all burial pits, were associated with entry points to the **Underworld**.

Many of the stones are bluestone from the Preseli Mountains of South Wales, over 135 miles away. This particular site amplifies sound, and if people stand it the centre of the circle even the smallest whisper can be heard. As Stonehenge is also thought by some to be constructed along **ley lines**, it is said that the resonant quality of the stone might also be connected to the theory of **sacred geometry**, where the earth's energy may be tapped for magic and healing.

Dowsers believe the stones are charged with powerful geomagnetic energies, possibly fixed by ancient builders, and there have been reports of light and sound anomalies associated with the stones. However, research conducted in 1987 and 1988 by the Dragon Trust Project, a British organization that studies ancient sites, showed no magnetism registering on the compass or any unusual radiation detected by instruments.

Until 1985 Stonehenge served as a site for **pagan** and **occult** festivities but in that year they were banned due to increasing vandalism by spectators. Today Stone-henge is a designated World Heritage site, but access to it remains limited and tourists can only admire it from afar.

STONE-THROWING DEVIL

Seventeenth-century **poltergeist** case that took place at Great Island, New Hampshire. It was characterized by a mysterious hail of stones that rained down on victims.

According to a pamphlet written by Richard Chamberlain, secretary of the Province of New Hampshire, entitled *Lithobolia, or the Stone-throwing Devil* (1698), the stone-throwing case occurred between May and August 1682. One Sunday night in May at around 10 pm, wealthy landowner George Walton and his family were surprised by a great pounding of stones upon the roof and sides of the house. Walton ran outside and the stones continued to fall, but it was impossible to tell who or what was throwing them.

For four hours the stones rained down, smashing windows and doors, but fortunately no one in the house was harmed. The next day servants reported that items in the house had been rearranged in odd places. The stoning continued for the next two weeks. Sometimes there would be a day of silence only for the attacks to start up again a day or so later. On Monday 28 June the stones fell on members of the household as they ate their supper, breaking the table into small pieces. On another day Walton was injured by what he claimed

was an attack of more than 40 stones; he suffered from his injuries for the rest of his life.

No agent of the stoning was ever seen and no single member of the household seemed to be the focal point of the attacks – all were attacked on one occasion or another, although most of the incidents occurred when Walton was present. A number of individuals, including the governor of West Jersey, signed a statement that they had witnessed some of the stone-throwing attacks.

Chamberlain, who was a guest at the house during this period, was a sceptic about the **supernatural**, but the attacks convinced him that 'there are such things as witches and the effects of witchcraft, or at least the mischievous actions of evil spirits'.

At the time the stone throwing was believed to have been down to **witchcraft** and the suspect in this case was a neighbour of Walton, who was an elderly woman in dispute with him over a piece of land. Walton won his claim to the land and the angry woman was heard to remark that he would 'never quietly enjoy that piece of ground'.

In August 1682 Walton decided to fight witchcraft with witchcraft and, with the help of someone who knew about such things, he tried to cast a **spell** to undo the **curse** and punish his neighbour. This consisted of boiling a pot of urine and crooked pins on the fire but before the urine could boil a stone fell into it and broke the pot.

The hail of stones continued and Walton lodged a complaint with the council in Portsmouth, which summoned him and his neighbour for questioning. The outcome of this council meeting is not recorded although at some point during it the stone throwing stopped.

The case remains unsolved and is likely to remain so given the length of time that has passed. **Fraud** on Walton's part is unlikely as he suffered personal injury but he may have been an unwitting **agent**, even though such agents of **hauntings** are usually adolescents. The only logical explanation is that the angry neighbour or perhaps protestors opposed to Chamberlain's unpopular administration were to blame.

STRING THEORY

The theory that what are perceived as particles are actually vibrations on strings or membranes in a 10- or 11-dimensional space. This theory resolves the incompatibility between general relativity (the principle that gravitational and inertial forces are equivalent) and **quantum theory** and unifies them.

String theory has been developed for several decades, with a goal to become 'the theory of everything', that is, to unify all four fundamental forces – gravity, electromagnetism, and strong and weak nuclear forces. A revolutionary discovery of the theory is that the whole universe should have nine or ten dimensions of space, instead of three (length, width and height).

In an earlier version of string theory, it was assumed that only three dimensions are observed because the other extra dimensions are too small to be seen. However, a few years before 2000, researchers suggested that these extra dimensions could be as large as the ordinary three dimensions. The reason why they cannot be seen is because all matter and electromagnetic waves are confined in a three-dimensional sub-universe, called 'braneworld'.

String theory tries to explain multi-dimensional phenomena beyond Einstein's four dimensions (the three spatial ones, plus time) and because it does this it has been proposed by some physicists as an explanation for so-called **paranormal** phenomena. It attempts to address the mystery of the multi-dimensional nature of reality by hypothesizing the existence of hyperspaces that exist beyond the perceptual boundaries of the physical senses, and by so doing it could potentially validate psychic phenomena. Ultimately, it has been suggested that string theory will be capable of explaining everything there is to explain, including paranormal phenomena, but scientific research has not reached that stage yet and the suggestion remains controversial.

SUBCONSCIOUS

See **Unconscious**.

SUBLIMINAL SELF

An **unconscious** aspect of a person that is thought to perceive sensations, emotions and thoughts below the threshold of the conscious thought. This perception may be of **spirit** beings and other entities on another plane of existence or of taboo impulses not acceptable in society. It is thought that unconscious reactions to such taboo ideas are harnessed in subliminal advertising. In other words, advertisers use images and sound to influence people without them being aware of it.

SUBTLE BODY

Alternative term for the **astral body**.

SUCCUBUS

Female **demon** or **spirit** who is said to disturb the sleep of a man and initiate sexual intercourse with him. Unlike the male equivalent, an **incubus**, whose attentions are typically horrifying to women, in some cases the succubus's attacks are not always unwelcome.

SUMMERS, MONTAGUE [1880–1948]

Celebrated as the world's foremost authority on **occult** matters in the 1920s, Summers was considered to be an expert on many aspects of the **paranormal** including **spirits**, **witchcraft**, **vampires**, werewolves, and **demonology**. British-born Summers achieved notoriety within the field for writing several books on paranormal subjects which have become classics. His numerous works included such titles as *The History of Witchcraft and Demonology* (1926), *The Vampire: His Kith and Kin* (1928) and the first English translation of the fifteenth-century witch-hunter's manual, the *Malleus Maleficarum*.

To the sceptic Summers' research seemed a little naïve and over-trusting of his sources but he was known to have gone to great lengths to gather evidence of **ghosts** and **hauntings**, particularly in the latter part of his life when he was able to explore Europe at leisure with a reputation that allowed him ready access to many allegedly haunted locations.

SUPER ESP

Theory that attempts to explain how **apparitions** of the dead are the result of extraordinary or limitless **ESP** by the living.

The term **super ESP** was coined in the 1950s by American sociologist and psychical researcher **Hornell Hart**, but the concept had already been put forward by the early founders of the **Society for Psychical Research** in the late nineteenth century. In investigating the question of **survival after death** it was suggested by the Society's researchers that some **mediums** could use **telepathy** and **clairvoyance** to gather personal information about the deceased person from the minds of the sitters.

Support for the super ESP theory came in 1925 with the Gordon Davis case. Psychical researcher S G Soal took part in a series of sittings with the medium Blanche Cooper, who contacted a friend of Soal's called Gordon Davis, whom Soal believed had been killed in the War. The information Davis provided was accurate and included personal reminiscences and idiosyncratic speech patterns. Soal was later shocked to discover that Davis was alive and living in London. He theorized that Cooper had telepathically picked up information from either his or Soal's mind. In the 1940s American researcher **Gardner Murphy** suggested that the phenomena of ESP may create pseudo-spirit personalities as well as apparitions of the dead, but researchers have since rejected that idea.

Opponents of super ESP argue that it cannot explain those cases when mediums provide information unknown to the sitters; and if it were possible, mediums should be able to perform extraordinary feats of mind reading, which has not yet been demonstrated in the laboratory. Super ESP also fails to explain **drop in communicators**, unknown entities who show up unexpectedly at a **séance** or sitting, and cases of children who claim past life memories, because such cases involve not just statements of fact but also behaviours consistent with the person talked about. Nor does super ESP successfully explain apparitions of the dead to its critics.

Despite these objections and inconsistencies, super ESP still maintains a number of adherents and it continues to be hotly debated. It is impossible to rule out completely as to date too little is still known about the nature of **psi** and its relationship to human consciousness.

SUPEREGO

According to **Sigmund Freud**, the superego is the higher part of the mind that gives a person a sense of right and wrong, of pride and guilt and of what is acceptable and what is not. It is the opposite of the **id**, which is the unconscious part of a person that only desires gratification of its own needs. The superego tends to make a person act in ways that are acceptable to society by repressing the needs of the id.

An example of this would be the desire to eat another slice of cake when already full. The id would urge a person to gratify their appetite but the superego would impose guilt at the thought of eating something that is unhealthy and unnecessary. The ego, the conscious part of the mind, is in the middle of this battle between the id and the superego, attempting to balance out conflicting desires. This is made easier by the fact that the id and superego tend to operate on an **unconscious** level. If an adult is a reasonably mature person then the id, ego and superego will act in a balanced way, but if not the result is childish, immature behaviour.

SUPERNATURAL

Any experience, occurrence, manifestation or object that is beyond the laws of nature and science and whose understanding may be said to lie with religion, magic or the mystical. The term is often used interchangeably with **paranormal**.

The most popular view of the supernatural contrasts it with the term 'natural', i.e. the assumption that some events occur according to natural laws and others do not, because they are caused by forces external to nature. In essence, the world is seen as operating according to natural law normally until a higher force external to nature, for example God, interferes.

Others deny any distinction between the natural and supernatural. According to this view, because God is sovereign, all events, even seemingly supernatural ones, are directly caused by God not by impersonal powers of any kind. Another view asserts that events that appear to be supernatural occur according to natural laws which we do not yet understand. Some believe the supernatural is a form of magic but others, particularly among the sceptical academic community, believe that all events have natural and only natural causes. They believe that human beings ascribe supernatural attributes to purely natural events in an attempt to cope with fear and ignorance.

SUPERSTITION

Belief in the power of **supernatural** phenomena to direct our lives. For example, the belief that a broken mirror means seven years' bad luck.

Superstitions originated at a time when humanity knew very little about how the universe worked and because of this the borders between daily living, magic, religion and nature were much less defined than they are today. In essence a superstition is a behaviour that is related to a kind of magical thinking, whereby the practitioner believes that the future, or the outcome of certain events, can be influenced by certain specified behaviours. The idea of good or bad luck has given rise to a number of superstitions, such as the belief that it is bad luck to walk under a ladder.

For reasons that are not known superstitious belief can lead to a disregard of reason under what sceptics would say is a false assumption of a divine or **paranormal** form of control over the universe. For instance, a gambler might credit a winning streak in poker to a lucky charm he or she is wearing or to sitting in a certain chair, rather than to skill or to the law of averages. An airline passenger might believe that it is a medal of St Christopher (traditional patron saint of travellers) that keeps him or her safe in the air, rather than the fact that aeroplanes statistically crash very rarely.

SURVIVAL AFTER DEATH

The belief that a spiritual component survives the death of the physical body is associated with all religions, with the exception of Buddhism, which denies the existence of the soul, and is also a tenet of the **animism** characteristic of tribal societies in America, Africa, Asia and Australia. For **spiritualists** belief in the **afterlife** rests not on belief but on evidence provided by the manifestations of **discarnate entities** in **mediumship**, although many psychical researchers believe that such manifestations can be more easily explained by **ESP** between living persons.

Belief in survival after death in one form or another is found all over the world and reaches far back in time. It has been suggested that belief in survival once existed alongside animistic beliefs in **reincarnation** and that these beliefs evolved into those of Hinduism, Buddhism and the Christian idea of resurrection. It could also be said that animistic **soul** beliefs, grounded as they were in **apparitions**, shamanic **trances** and **out-of-body experiences**, have a direct link to **spiritualism**.

Spiritualism reached the peak of its popularity on both sides of the Atlantic at the turn of the twentieth century and this popularity led to attempts to prove the genuineness of its claims. The discovery of trickery and deception among a large number of the **mediums** investigated led to disillusionment and many psychical researchers concluded that spiritualist claims had little substance.

Interests and opinions began to change, however, when the mediumship of **Leono-**ra Piper** was investigated by both the **Society for Psychical Research** and the **American Society for Psychical Research**. Instead of producing physical phenomena such as **levitations** and **materializations**, Piper went into **trance** and seemed to deliver verbal messages from dead people. After Piper other **mental mediums** such as **Eileen Garrett** and **Gladys Leonard** were also responsible for encouraging many psychical researchers to believe in survival after death.

The communications provided by mental mediums were significant because they could be checked for accuracy among written sources and the memories of the living. Establishing the supernatural basis for their insight therefore depended on showing that they could not have obtained their information naturally (or fraudulently), such as by reading the obituaries columns of local papers. Despite this encouraging step, however, it was still possible for mediums to obtain personal information about the deceased from the minds of the living or via ESP.

To make sure ESP wasn't responsible, experiments were done with **proxy sitters**, i.e. stand-ins for the person who wanted to communicate with dead who knew nothing about the dead person. Special attention was also paid to **drop in communicators** and **cross correspondences**, although even in these unique cases it still proved to be impossible to rule out ESP (see **super ESP**). Growing awareness of an inability to prove that ESP was not the case contributed to a decline in psychical research to prove survival in favour of experiments, such as those conducted by **J B Rhine**, to test the limits of ESP.

As far as **physical mediumship** as proof of survival after death was concerned, better evidence was provided by mediums such as **Eusapia Palladino**, who was never found guilty of fraud, and the **Schneider brothers**. Some psychical researchers were convinced that discarnate entities were responsible for physical phenomena such as **table-tilting** and **rapping** but others believed they were still produced by the mediums themselves via **psychokinesis**. The psychokinesis explanation is still popular today among psychical researchers and has also been touted as an explanation for **poltergeist** activity, when objects are thrown around. Poltergeist attacks also tend to concentrate around one person who is regarded as the focus or **agent** causing the action, either consciously or unconsciously.

The evidence for survival provided by out-of-body and **near-death experiences** is inconclusive as it could be argued that they are simply hallucinations. Good evidence for survival can, however, be provided by cases that involve more than one mode of existence. For example, it is hard to imagine how ESP and psychokinesis could explain all of the following: a discarnate entity that communicates through a medium, a poltergeist that moves objects and an apparition that can be seen. Good evidence can also be provided by cases, such as the **Chaffin Will case**, where the spirit seems to have a special purpose such as to convey information unknown to the sitter.

Sceptics point to the numerous examples of so-called communications from the dead that were later proved to be false or to be examples of ESP. For example, in one case the communicator presented as dead by the medium turned out to be alive a few months later. Despite this many researchers, such as **Frederick Myers**, **James Hyslop** and **Hornell Hart**, have argued that survival after death is at least theoretically possible in a fragmentary way.

Spiritualism's popularity in the West has declined, but it does still continue, and the Society for Psychical Research attracts many new members each year. The latest Gallup poll regarding the survival question suggests that as many as two in three people believe in, or hope for, survival after death.

See also **Afterlife, Apparitions, Cross correspondences, Deathbed visions, Mediumship, Near-death experience, Out-of-body experience, Reincarnation**.

SURVIVAL RESEARCH FOUNDATION

Research and educational organization based in Miami, Florida, that is concerned with the question of **survival after death**. The Survival Research Foundation was established in 1971 by authors Frank C Tribber and Susy Smith. The Foundation has investigated and continues to investigate **survival tests, deathbed visions, near-death experiences** and **mediumship**. Awards are offered for those who want to explore new directions in **paranormal** research.

SURVIVAL TESTS

Tests created by people when they are alive with the intention of communicating their solutions through **mediums** after death to provide evidence for **survival after death**. The most popular of these types of tests was the sealed envelope test, which has since been replaced by combination locks and tests encrypted with special codes.

In *The Human Personality and Its Survival of Bodily Death* (1903), psychical researcher **Frederick Myers** described some tests with positive outcomes. In one case study a brother left his sister a sealed envelope and a piece of a brick marked in a special way, telling her he would hide it in a place no one would know. After his death his sister communicated with him through mediums and not only did he allegedly communicate the contents of the sealed letter but he also told her where to look for the brick. The brick was discovered in the place he had indicated.

It has been suggested that sealed letter tests could be interpreted as examples of **clairvoyance** and **telepathy** rather than **spirit** communication. The living person could have read the mind of the deceased person while they were still alive or simply have read the contents of the letter clairvoyantly.

The sealed letter tests eventually proved to be problematic as they could only be opened once. In order to find a way round this, British mathematician and psychical researcher Robert Thouless came up with what he called the 'cipher test'. He invented a code and encoded two messages with the idea that after his death he would commu-nicate not just the message but also the key to the code that would allow the message to be read. This cipher had the advantage that it could be tried any number of times and if the medium provided the solution only after Thouless's death this made it all the more likely that it was received from his spirit.

The cipher test proved to be too complicated for some, prompting psychical researcher Ian Stevenson to introduce the combination lock test. With this, a person would buy a combination lock and set it, committing the solution to memory. As with the cipher test, the idea was that the person would, after death, communicate in spirit a key word that allowed the lock to be opened.

Despite numerous attempts neither the cipher test nor the combination lock proved to be very successful. Psychical researcher **J G Pratt** set a Stevenson combination lock before his death in 1979 but to date no successful communication has been reported from him. Thouless died in 1984 but no successful communications about the code he set have been received either.

SWEDENBORG, EMANUEL [1688–1772]

Swedish scientist, mystic and **medium** who became famous for his otherworldly **visions** and travels to the spiritual planes where he allegedly met the **souls** of the dead.

Swedenborg was born in Stockholm in 1688, trained as a scientist and was noted for his work in the field of astronomy where he developed a theory to explain the creation of the planets. He was also something of a technician and produced plans for an air gun and submarine that were way ahead of his time. But having established his scientific credentials he made one of the greatest U-turns in history by suddenly announcing, in his fifties, that he had become a visionary and a mystic.

Swedenborg revealed that he was in direct communication with **spirit** beings and had frequent visionary experiences, which left him convinced of the mystical truth that all things ultimately were contained within a single godhead. He also demonstrated certain **psychic** powers, such as **clairvoyance** of future events, perhaps via **out-of-body experiences**, including a famous incident in 1759 when he saw a great fire in Stockholm some 300 miles away.

Swedenborg believed he was a divine messenger and his purpose was to disseminate his visions and revelations to others. He quit his job so he could devote himself exclusively to his visions. He experienced **automatic writing** and sometimes his **trances**, which were both spontaneous and self-induced, lasted days. In his other-worldly travels he claimed to have met famous figures from history, including **Plato** and Aristotle.

Many of Swedenborg's peers opposed him and thought that he had gone insane. It wasn't until after his death in 1772 at the age of 84 that a Swedenborg movement began to develop, in London. Along with **mesmerism** Swedenborgism is credited with paving the way for the advance of **spiritualism** in the nineteenth century.

According to Swedenborg God created man to exist in both the physical and spiritual worlds. The spiritual world is an inner vision that most people have lost contact with, and it is this inner world that survives death with its own memory of life intact. The memory influences the soul's fate of **heaven** or **hell**. Swedenborg believed that after death souls go to an earth-like place where they are met by dead loved ones and, after a period of self-judgement, they choose heaven or hell. Swedenborg did not believe Christ's crucifixion saved humankind from its sins and the hell he describes is a hideous place, inhabited by faceless **demons**. Heaven is a copy of earth with angelic souls. In both worlds life is carried on with work, marriage, war, crime, etc. Swedenborg did not believe in **reincarnation** and although souls could advance in the **afterlife** he also believed that heaven and hell were permanent states a soul could not escape from. Spiritualists later adopted many of Swedenborg's views but rejected his concept of hell and divided heaven into seven spheres through which a soul had to pass after death.

The Swedenborg movement became a religion that is still practised today by a select group of followers from all parts of the world. The first churches were established in England in 1778 and in America in 1792. The Swedenborg Society was established in 1810 to spread his message. His most well read text is *On Heaven and Its Wonders and on Hell* (1758), which outlines his theory of life after death.

Symbol

A symbol, in its basic sense, is a representational object or visual image for a concept, object, idea, quality or quantity. It expresses a concept or idea beyond the object or image itself. A symbol can be a material object whose shape or origin is related to the thing it represents: for instance, the cross is the main symbol of Christianity. A symbol can also be an image (icon) or a pattern or **colour**, for example, the **halo** is a conventional symbol of sainthood in Christian imagery and the colour red is often used as a symbol for socialist movements. Symbols can also be immaterial entities like sounds, words and gestures, for example, bowing is a common way to indicate respect. The discipline of semiotics studies symbols and symbol systems in

Some common symbols

There are thousands of symbols that are recognized by most people all over the world, and millions more that are limited to certain regions, religions, societies, etc. Here is just a sample of the best known:

Balance (scale) > justice
Bald eagle > USA
Bat > vampire (Western), luck (Chinese)
Boomerang > Australia
Caduceus > Medical profession
Cheetah > speed
Cherry blossom > Japan
Compass rose > navigation
Crucifix > Christianity
Cupid, heart > love
Dragon > China/Wales
Females > ♀
Flags > the associated countries
Horseshoe > luck
Kangaroo > Australia
Lightbulb > idea
Lightning bolt > electricity, speed
Lotus flower > Hinduism and Buddhism
Males > ♂
Maple leaf > Canada
Mount Fuji > Japan
Panda > China
Penguin > South Pole
Pestle and mortar > Pharmacy
Pink triangle > gay men
Pointed hat and wand > magic
Polar bear > North Pole
Rainbow flag > homosexual people
Red Crescent/Red Cross > First Aid
St Bernard dog > rescue
Shamrock > Ireland
Skull and crossbones > poison, danger
Star and crescent > Islam
Star of David > Judaism
Statue of Liberty > USA
Uncle Sam > USA
Windmills > Netherlands
Yin/yang symbol > Taoism

general; semantics is specifically concerned with the meaning of words.

People respond to symbols both consciously and unconsciously every day. Symbolistic thought dates back to primitive times and in every culture, past and present, symbols play a crucial role both in religion and in society as a whole. Religious and metaphysical writings are known for their use of **esoteric** symbolism, because they are believed to contain secret wisdom accessible only to the initiated. Alchemical writings also made extensive use of symbols for spiritual and chemical processes (which practitioners also saw as symbols of each other). Symbols also play a key part in magical ritual and practice because magic symbols are believed to be the keys to raising within the **magician** the qualities or abilities expressed by the symbols (see **Sigil**).

The interpretation of **dreams** as symbols of one's experiences is a main feature of Freudian psychoanalysis and Jungian analytical psychology, and the understanding of symbols and the integration of them into consciousness is an important part of various psychologies. **Carl Jung** believed that objects and ideas that become symbols are endowed with a great psychological power and can carry empowering messages to the **psyche**. According to Jung symbols are the language of the **unconscious**, but to be effective they must not be interpreted literally as their true meaning must always be beyond the reach of logic and comprehension.

SYNCHRONICITY

The phenomenon of simultaneous events occurring that are related but which have no discernible link to each other. Psychiatrist **Carl Jung**, who coined the phrase, felt the meaningful coincidences that linked seemingly unrelated and unconnected events happened for a reason. He spoke of synchronicity as being an 'acausal connecting principle' (i.e. a pattern of connection that is not explained by causality).

The concept of synchronicity has always been integral to Eastern thought but Jung was largely responsible for developing it in the West. He gave Albert Einstein credit for his inspiration – the two met when Einstein was developing his theory of relativity and it prompted Jung to consider a possible relativity of time as well as space. In his research Jung had encountered numerous synchronicities that he could not explain and which were so meaningful that their occurrence by chance would be highly improbable. As an example Jung quoted an incident that happened to one of his patients, who was describing a **dream** she had about a golden **scarab**. As she spoke Jung heard tapping at the window and when he opened it he found a scarabaeid beetle. His patient was so surprised by the coincidence that she stopped being defensive in therapy and started to consider what this could mean. Jung pointed out that the scarab was an archetypal **symbol** of rebirth and this led to greater maturity in his patient.

Jung also cited a personal example, and the following, from his *Memories, Dreams, Reflections* (1962), sheds light both on the phenomenon itself and how Jung came to think about the relatedness between the inner and outer realms:

I recall one time during the Second World War when I was returning home from Bollingen. I had a book with me, but could not read, for the moment the train started to move I was overpowered by the image of someone drowning. This was a memory of an accident that had happened while I was on military service. During the entire journey I could not rid myself of it. It struck me as uncanny, and I thought, 'What has happened? Can there have been an accident?'

I got out at Erlenbach and walked home, still troubled by this memory. My second daughter's children were in the garden. The family was living with us, having returned to Switzerland from Paris because of the war. The children stood looking rather upset, and when I asked, 'Why, what is the matter?' They told me that Adrian, then the youngest of the boys, had fallen into the water in the boathouse. It is quite deep there and since he could not really swim he had almost drowned. His older brother had fished him out. This had taken place at exactly the time I had been assailed by that memory in the train.

Jung spent many years studying synchronicity in an attempt to discover why it occurred and in the latter part of his life explored **quantum theory** in an effort to explain it. However, he eventually came to accept that the mysterious connection between two seemingly unrelated aspects of mind and matter was that they were two different expressions of the same thing — vibrational energy.

Synchronicity for Jung was an alignment of 'universal forces' with the life experiences of an individual. Jung believed that many experiences perceived as coincidences were not merely due to chance, but instead reflected the creation of an event or circumstance by the coinciding or alignment of such forces. The process of becoming intuitively aware and acting in harmony with these forces is what Jung labelled 'individuation'. Jung said that an individuated person would actually shape events around them through the communication of their **consciousness** with the **collective unconscious**.

Synchronicity has increasingly come to the fore in modern research by psychologists, parapsychologists and scientists on the nature of consciousness. For example, similarities between quantum physics and Eastern thought have been pointed out by Fritjof Capra in *The Tao of Physics* (1984), and in his groundbreaking text *Synchronicity: The Bridge Between Mind and Matter* author F David Peat observes that synchronicity may appear naturally to a mind that is constantly evolving and sensitive to change.

Sceptics argue that the theory of synchronicity is not scientific at all, but an example of magical thinking, but despite this the notion remains popular today and is an important concept in the modern mind/body/spirit canon. Enthusiasts believe that even just being aware of the phenomenon can increase a person's awareness of universal harmonies and correspondences and open him or her up to new ways of thinking, being and living, and to new orders of political, social and spiritual unities. The utopian possibility of a new world order, where due attention is paid to the awesome power and meaning of synchronicity, is explored in James Redfield's surprise bestsellers of the late 1990s, *The Celestine Prophecy* and *The Celestine Vision*.

T

TABLE-TILTING

Spiritualist technique in which **psychokinetic** effects, such as the table vibrating or tilting or turning, sometimes manifest when a group sits around a table with their hands placed lightly on it.

Most table-tipping **séances** are for the purposes of communicating with **spirits** or for **divination**. Typically the sitters are evenly placed around a table, sitting with their fingertips resting lightly on the top edge. One of the members acts as a spokesperson and calls out for a spirit to make contact. Sometimes the table may start to move, shaking and vibrating first. It may rise up on one or two legs or turn, pivoting on one leg. To spell out words, the spokesperson may call out the letters of the alphabet and the table will drop down when the specific letter is reached.

According to the psychical researcher **Nandor Fodor**, table-tilting, tipping or turning is 'the crudest form of communication with the subconscious self or with extraneous intelligences'. Yet tables have been associated with divination and communication with spirits since antiquity. For example, Ammianus Marcellinus (AD 330–395), the author of a history of the Roman Empire, described a table with letters of the alphabet engraved on it, above which a ring was suspended from a thread. The ring would swing to various letters and spell out words.

Table-tilting became extremely popular in the mid-nineteenth century with the rise of **spiritualism**. It originated in America, spread to Europe and arrived in England in 1853. One of the main attractions was that a **medium** was not required; table-tilting was a mediumistic technique that could be done with any group of people in any living room. The phenomenon became so popular that scientists attempted to explain it by showing that the movement was due to the unconscious muscular action of the people with their fingers on the table. In other words, people may have thought they were pressing downwards on the table but they were in fact pressing it in such a way that the table tilted or turned. The force exerted by the people was even given a scientific name, 'ectenic force', but this still did not answer the question as to what or who was directing this force and how tables were sometimes able to give answers that were unknown to those present.

TAI CHI

Chinese **martial art** derived from Kung Fu, which consists of a series of postures linked by slow, graceful movements and accompanied by meditative breathing techniques. The purpose of Tai Chi is to enhance a person's chi or **universal life force** and boost health and wellbeing.

Tai Chi is believed to have originated in the thirteenth century. A Taoist priest, Chang San Feng, adapted the hand techniques of the martial arts he had learned from the Buddhist monks of Shaolin into smoother, softer movements after he had had a visionary dream of a snake and a crane dancing and fighting. His teachings evolved into five main styles, which are still practised today: Yang, Wu, Chen, Woo and Sun. The most commonly practised in the West is Yang style, with its sweeping, open gestures.

Tai Chi is believed to balance out energies in the body to ensure a smooth flow of chi. Studies have indicated that the regular practice of Tai Chi has a number of health benefits, including stress reduction, the lowering of blood pressure and an improved quality of health in people suffering with age-related ailments, such as arthritis.

TALIESIN

Legendary magical bard who is associated with the stories of King Arthur. Taliesin is also believed to have been a historical figure who lived in Wales during the second half of the sixth century. He is believed to have been a **shaman** and a **shape-shifter** in the ancient **Druid** tradition.

Almost as many myths surround Taliesin as the legendary **wizard Merlin**, whom he resembles in some respects. The Welsh legend of Taliesin's birth tells how Gwion Bach, fleeing from Ceridwen's anger after accidentally supping from her Cauldron of Rebirth, changes himself into a hare to get away. Ceridwen changes herself into a greyhound to chase the hare and the shape-shifting continues until Ceridwen changes herself into a black hen, which picks up and eats the grain of wheat into which Gwion Bach had finally transformed himself. After a period of gestation Gwion Bach is reborn as the bard Taliesin.

Taliesin's musical talents were said to be unearthly with the power to charm **fairies** and animals. He allegedly penned the collection of Welsh myths, the *Mabinogion*, while on his travels, and after his death all other bards took the name 'sons of Ceridwen' in his honour.

TALISMAN

Object, drawing or **symbol** that is believed to be a source of **supernatural** or magical power and which then confers its power to those who possess it.

Talismans have been used throughout history to attract good fortune, success, health, virility, love and power and to attempt to control the forces of nature. In the Middle Ages talismans were holy objects and relics prized for their healing powers, and in the Renaissance alchemists sought the talisman of the **philosopher's stone**. As opposed to the passive power of **amulets** – which protect and ward off evil – talismans are believed to be active in seeking out good luck and may even bestow magical powers on the person carrying, using or wearing one.

Horseshoes, four-leaved clovers and lucky stones or coins are talismans, as are magic wands and lamps. Almost any object can be a talisman but generally it is endowed with power through nature (for example, a gem) or supernatural powers (the sword Excalibur) or by creation in a magical ritual (e.g. a **wand**). There are hundreds of rituals in ceremonial magic textbooks for creating talismans for virtually any purpose. Although ancient talismans were often inscribed with magical names or **spells**, today talismans are more often objects charged with the personal power of their creator through **meditation** and/or ritual.

TALKING BOARD

A device similar to the **planchette** that is used for divining answers to questions and talking with **spirits**. Talking boards feature letters of the alphabet and the numerals zero to nine and the words yes and no. The user asks a question, puts their fingers on a pointer and waits for the pointer to spell out the answer. It is thought that the movement of the pointer is directed by **discarnate entities** and spirits of the dead. Sceptics believe the users move the pointer unconsciously without realizing it. The best-known talking board is the **Ouija board**.

TALKING MONGOOSE

Extraordinary animal **ghost** story. In the autumn of 1936 strange noises were reported at an old farmhouse known as Cashens Gap at Dalby in the Isle of Man. The owner of the house, Mr Irving, claimed to have seen a shadow move about the rooms of the farmhouse and then tiny furry feet were spotted through a crack in the ceiling. Most curiously, the creature allegedly began to 'talk' to Mr Irving, identifying itself as Gef, a talking mongoose. The house was investigated by journalists and psychical researchers and none were able to prove that it was a hoax. After the initial flurry of publicity interest in the first recorded instance of a ghostly animal able to communicate with a human began to decline and Gef appeared less frequently. The full story of this remarkable and unusual **haunting** was recorded in great detail by Harry Price and R S Lambert, in *The Haunting of Caspens Gap* (1936).

TANTRA, TANTRIC

School of Hindu and Buddhist thought which attempts to seek enlightenment through ecstatic religious and sexual practices. There is an emphasis on carnal pleasure and intercourse with the aim of awakening **kundalini** energy, the primal **psychic** force that is believed to lie dormant at the base of the spine. This is done by invoking both the female and the male energies of the universe, embodied by the Hindu gods Shiva and Sakti, and delaying orgasm for as long as possible to stimulate the upward movement of kundalini.

Tao

Fundamental mystical principle in the Chinese religion of **Taoism**. Although often translated as 'the Way', the term Tao is a state of being that incorporates three aspects of mystical Chinese thought which have no real English translation: ultimate and unimaginable reality, the **universal life force** and wise order in a person's life which harmonizes with the universal whole. In other words Tao is a state of being, of 'doing but not doing', that accepts that everything is a part of the flow of chi. The Tao is everything and everywhere and it flows unchallenged. It is always changing but never changes. It can be experienced but not defined. It simply is.

Tao Te Ching

Translated as 'The Book of the Way', *Tao Te Ching* is the principal mystical text of **Taoism**, supposedly written by the great Chinese sage Lao Tzu in the sixth century BC. Through a collection of 81 poems it describes the necessary interaction between three things that make up life: *tao*, the way, *te*, power and *ching*, the **universal life force** that flows through all the universe. If a person can balance these three elements life will feel balanced and flow smoothly. This balance can be achieved through techniques such as **meditation**, breath control, dietary change, sexual techniques and alchemical processes, all of which are described in the book.

The main emphasis of the text is on 'the way', which is all about going with the flow and the power of non-action that is a central feature of Taoism. The following quotation from the *Tao Te Ching* sums up Lao Tzu's recipe for a fulfilled and successful life.

There is no need to run outside for better seeing nor to peer from a window. Rather abide at the centre of your being for the more you leave it, the less you learn.

Taoism

Chinese religion that is based on the concept of **Tao**. Taoism is a religion that places great emphasis on non-action, on going with the flow and letting nature take its course. Choosing to do nothing is in itself a choice, and a choice that is thought to balance out the natural energies of **yin** and **yang**. It is believed that the secret to a happy life is a continuous balancing of yin and yang, to achieve harmony in all aspects of life.

The origins of Taoism are thought to date back to the *Tao Te Ching*, supposedly written in the sixth century BC by the sage Lao Tzu. The gentle harmonizing philosophy of the *Tao Te Ching* had great appeal to the Chinese who had grown weary of constant feudal warfare and it quickly became a popular faith. In 440 BC was adopted as a major religion.

The goal of Taoism is positive inaction. This goal is based on Lao Tzu's statement,

'The way to do is to be.' Latter-day followers interpret this as the need to achieve harmony with the **universal life force**, and for those with a more magical turn of mind it is about the exercise of power generated by the fusion of opposites.

The influence of Taoism has spread beyond China and has served as a conceptual basis for many practices of **traditional Chinese medicine**, **acupuncture** and **meditation** and **martial arts** like **Tai Chi**. Taoism, with its emphasis on being, not doing, also appeals to many Westerners exhausted and stressed by the pace of modern life.

Taoist alchemy

System of **Yoga** developed in China in which practitioners believe the individual will not survive physical death unless he or she has prepared, while living, a 'diamond body' as an immortal vehicle for the **spirit**. The diamond body appears to be similar in many respects to the **astral body** of Western occultism, but it is reinforced and strengthened during the **adept**'s lifetime by a mingling of male and female chi or **universal life force** energies. This mingling is typically achieved by intercourse with multiple partners. It is commonly thought that orgasm dissipates the vital supply of chi in men, but that women are blessed with an inexhaustible supply. As a result, in Taoist alchemical intercourse the man suppresses his orgasm while multiple orgasms are encouraged in the woman.

Tarot

Card deck that is used for **divination**, self help, the development of **intuition** and spiritual and **psychic** growth.

The deck of cards known as the tarot is divided into two parts: the Major Arcana and the Minor Arcana. The word 'arcana' is from the Latin word for secret. The Major Arcana consists of 22 cards, each separately titled. These cards depict symbolic figures, such as the Fool, the Magician, the High Priestess and the Empress, elements of nature such as the Star, the Moon and the Sun, and human experiences on the spiritual journey as well as joys, hopes, fears and sorrows. The **symbols** are universal, drawn from legend and from magical belief. Typically the Major Arcana cards are subject to broad interpretations. In essence they are **archetypes** and their sequence from 0 to 21 is believed to represent the soul's journey to awareness, the process of becoming whole or the alchemical process of spiritual transformation. Some have equated the Major Arcana with the 22 letters of the Hebrew alphabet and work them with the **Kabbalah**'s **Tree of Life**.

The Minor Arcana is a combination of four suits; each suit is comprised of cards numbered from one to ten, plus court cards of Page, Knight, Queen and King. The four suits of the Minor Arcana are most commonly known as Cups, Pentacles, Wands and Swords, and it can clearly be seen that the Minor Arcana is the ancestor of our modern playing cards, with their corresponding suits of Hearts, Diamonds, Clubs and Spades. Each suit of the Minor Arcana has a meaning. Traditionally the swords indicate ill fortune or difficulties, the pentacles indicate financial and material success, the cups indicate good fortune and love and the wands indicate enterprise and knowledge.

The actual origins of the tarot are lost in time. There is some evidence to suggest that they originated in the North of India and were brought out of that region by the Romany people. Certainly the Romany were responsible for much of their distribution across Europe, but there is also speculation that the cards originated in China and Northern Italy.

The earliest surviving tarot cards were individually painted on thin sheets of ivory, parchment, silver and gold. A set of tarot cards were painted exclusively for France's Charles VI in 1392 and 17 of these cards survive today in the Bibliotheque Nationale in Paris. With the invention of block printing in Nuremberg in the early part of the fifteenth century tarot cards became more available and more popular. In mid-fifteenth-century England King Edward IV forbade the importation of tarot cards but they were smuggled in by soldiers fighting in France and found their way into the homes of the nobility. By the time of the French Revolution there was a revival of interest in esotericism and use of tarot cards was widespread.

In 1910 English occultist **Arthur Waite** published his interpretation of the tarot with images designed by fellow occultist Pamela Colman Smith. According Waite the tarot cards themselves dated back to the fourteenth century but the images on them were much older. He claimed to have restored the images to their original meaning and when interpreting the cards drew from the Hermetic Kabbalah tradition favoured by the Hermetic Order of the **Golden Dawn**, of which he was a member.

The Rider Waite deck still sets the standard today among tarot packs, even though hundreds of other tarot decks with different designs and themes have since been designed and published. Many of these new designs have broken away from the traditional symbolism and names.

Tarot cards are used in **meditation** and **creative visualization** exercises as a means of spiritual transformation and personal growth.

Some people draw a single card at the start of each day and meditate on it to trigger their imaginative and intuitive powers, but the most common method is to use the cards for divinatory purposes. There is a traditional way of doing this with a variety of different spreads, or layouts.

Typically tarot cards are read by shuffling and then laying out the cards, face down, in various spreads. The cards are then turned over and interpreted. Each position in a spread is thought to have particular significance and each Major and Minor Arcana card laid down has an individual meaning which is influenced by the position it is placed in and whether or not it is upright or reversed. Even though each card has an individual meaning the entire layout must also be considered as a whole. Like the **I Ching** those who use the tarot believe it should not be read for definitive yes or no answers to questions but for a reflection of existing energies and directions concerning a situation. In other words, the tarot is good for helping a person see life from a new perspective.

Sample tarot spread

In Tarot divination, results can be achieved with analysis of just one card, but for more thoroughness combinations of several cards in set patterns are usually used. These patterns are called spreads. There are many, many spreads, although the Celtic Cross is often taught to beginners as their first spread. More experienced practioners will use their own spreads, assigning their own meanings to the relevant positions represented.

The Celtic Cross is one of the best known of spreads and its most common version consists of ten cards, or ten cards plus an optional, eleventh card (the 'significator card'). The significator card represents the person or situation. The enquirer shuffles and cuts the pack with the cards face down while thinking about the question he or she wants an answer to. Then, with the cards still face down, so the person has no idea which cards he or she is going to pick, the first six are picked from the deck; the first card is placed atop the significator card, and the others placed as shown below. The final four of the ten cards are placed in a column to the right.

The cards should be read as they are turned up, which means some will be upright and some will be reversed. Usually the reversed meaning is a negative aspect of the upright meaning, though not always. Some readers believe that it doesn't matter whether the cards are upright or reversed; the full meaning will come out just through the interpretation of the card itself, regardless of how it lies. Many readers will 'feel' the cards by saying what they feel about them, rather than giving the traditional meanings as listed in some books.

Cross Spread

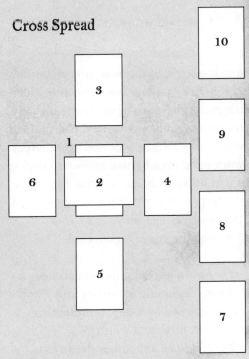

Card 1: The present. Card 2: The immediate challenge facing the enquirer. Card 3: What the enquirer aspires to, what they are capable of achieving. Card 4: The enquirer's deep, basic inner self. Card 5: What is behind the enquirer, i.e. in the

past. **Card 6:** The immediate future (i.e. the next few days or weeks). **Card 7:** Factors or inner feelings affecting the situation. **Card 8:** External influences that will affect the outcome of the question. **Card 9:** Hopes or fears around the situation. **Card 10:** Final outcome in six months or a year ahead. Tarot cards only see the situation with the forces currently at work around the enquirer. With this in mind the final outcome is not truly final and nothing is set in stone; it is within everyone to change positively what is indicated.

An even simpler spread is the three-card spread, which gives a quick answer/overview to a single question/issue. Lay out three cards in a row from left to right. Reading from left to right, the cards represent the past, the present and the future.

Below are some traditional interpretations of the Major Arcana, based on the Rider Waite pack. These are by no means the only set of meanings that exist for the tarot. Different traditions are followed in different countries and even between different decks, and it is universally agreed that by far the best interpretation you can give a tarot card is the one you feel and sense yourself in response to the image on the card.

0 *The Fool:* a jester figure, sometimes shown beginning a journey and accompanied by a dog, representing impulse, birth and youth.

1 *The Magician:* sometimes shown as a juggler or illusionist at a fair, sometimes playing with the symbols of the four suits, representing consciousness, sense of self, control, dexterity.

2 *High Priestess:* shown as a female religious leader, representing women's liberation, wisdom, independence, psychic development.

3 *Empress:* shown as a queen on her throne or as a mother goddess, representing illumination, intelligence, understanding, maternity, creativity.

4 *Emperor:* sometimes shown holding sphere and sceptre, a king on his throne, representing sight, vision, realization, power, strength.

5 *Hierophant or Pope:* sometimes shown as the Pope seated on a throne, religious leader, representing the link between God and man, spiritual discovery, paternal, transcendent, teacher.

6 *Lovers:* shown as two people surrounded by cupids and flowerbeds, representing struggle, beauty, sovereignty, synthesis, union.

7 *Chariot:* sometimes shown as warriors parading triumphant in a chariot or an icon of a hero being paraded around, representing victory, domination of humankind over nature, power, war, self-control.

8   *Strength or Lust:* representing love as a source of strength, endurance, will to survive, strong desires, perseverance.

9   *Hermit:* representing withdrawal, solitude, abandonment of convention via inner conviction, preoccupation with details, often shown as a hermit holding an hourglass.

10 *Wheel of Fortune:* representing karma, reincarnation, consequences of chance happenings, cycles, motifs, optimism, generosity.

11 *Justice:* often shown as 'lady justice' (blindfolded with scale), representing decision, equilibrium.

12 *Hanged Man:* representing sacrifice, violence, transition.

13 *Death:* often shown as a skeleton or as the grim reaper, representing stagnation and routine but also fresh starts, a clean slate, liberation, renewal.

14 *Temperance:* representing enthusiasm, moderation, truthfulness, mixing of opposite ingredients in proper proportion, working together.

15 *The Devil:* representing superficiality, confusion, ignorance, apathy, limitations, frustrations, sexual problems.

16 *The Tower:* representing spiritual awakening, destiny, often shown as 'house of god' or as a ruin.

17 *The Star:* representing meditation, inspiration, hope, immortality, often shown as a woman kneeling on a seashore.

18 *The Moon:* representing illusion, self-deception, confusion, the growth of intuition.

19 *The Sun:* representing enlightenment, clarity, understanding, comprehension, wisdom, happiness, splendour.

20 *Judgement:* often shown as angels blowing trumpets, representing awakening to something new, rebirth.

21 *The World or Universe:* representing completion, reward, perfection, a unity of positive and negative.

TASH

Irish word for a **ghost** that can appear in human or animal form. Ireland has a strong ghost story tradition and gave birth to one of the greatest ghost-story writers of the nineteenth century, Sheridan Le Fanu (1814–73). Irish folklore is particularly rich in legends about **phantom** horses, birds, rabbits and even insects such as butterflies. A large number of these ghosts are believed to be the **spirits** of people who have died a violent death, either having been murdered or having committed suicide, and condemned to haunt the place where they died as a lesson for others. In many parts of Ireland it is considered unwise among the superstitious to mourn a person for too long, 'or else they will be kept from their rest and return as a ghost'.

TASSEOGRAPHY

Divination by means of reading the pattern of tea leaves left in a cup. The art of reading tea leaves for divination was an ancient Chinese practice, which makes sense as tea originated in China. In the mid-1800s it spread to the Western world via nomadic gypsies. Around the turn of the twentieth century tasseography was a popular method of divination in the West, with Gypsy Tea Rooms commonplace in

Reading tea leaves

To read your tea leaves, you must prepare a cup of tea with loose tea leaves. A small, white cup with no designs or patterns on the inside walls is ideal. The tea most often used is China tea but any large leaf variety will do, such as Ceylon or even mint tea. Finer mint tea or coffee grounds can be used but they don't tend to leave such interesting patterns.

Drink your tea, and leave a tiny amount of liquid, as well as some tea leaves, in the bottom of the cup. Holding the cup in your left hand, slowly swirl the contents of the cup around three times clockwise. Try to make sure that the leaves are moved towards the rim of the teacup. Then place the cup upside down on a saucer, holding it there for a few seconds while the fluids drain. When the teacup is placed right side up again, make sure the handle faces towards you and take a look at the patterns made by the tea leaves remaining in the cup.

If you have swirled correctly, the leaves should now be clumped together in several different places on the cup's inside,

including the rim, sides and bottom. These clumps will form the symbols that you will read. You should always begin the interpretation by looking for the simplest symbols first. Several of the leaf clumps may clearly form shapes, letters, or numbers. Letters may refer to the names of friends or relatives, whereas numbers can indicate spans of time, like months or years. With shapes, triangles indicate good karma, squares a need for caution, circles great success and hearts, love (although if combined with a triangle, it could indicate jealousy).

Most of the clumps, however, will form random shapes. With a little staring and a bit of creativity, these shapes can easily be distinguished. Some of their meanings with be traditional and obvious (such as a horseshoe shape indicating luck), but remember, the beauty of tea-leaf reading is that it is entirely up to your creativity. Seeing and interpreting symbols is always best done when that interpretation comes from yourself.

most cities and towns. It is less popular today but still practised.

When a person drinks a cup of tea (or coffee) the leaves or grounds are thought to pick up sympathetic vibrations from that person's **aura**. When the liquid has been drunk the tea leaves remaining at the bottom of the cup form shapes that are said to correspond to that energy. The **symbols** are not always obvious to the naked eye, and imagination must be used by the diviner. It will be found that there may be a suggestion of, say, a bird or a rabbit and this suggestion can trigger the mind into making connections and associations that can then be interpreted. As with so many forms of divination what is actually seen is used as a focal point or trigger for the reader's **intuition**.

similar to mystical enlightenment in that it was likely to have collective and cosmic elements that would help bring people closer to God. The ultimate goal is convergence towards Christ, which he called the 'Omega Point', a place or moment where human consciousness finds ultimate unity.

Teilhard's theories do not advocate living in harmony with the earth, and in his opinion earth's true meaning could only be found in its subordination to humankind. Nevertheless, his theories can be applied to modern ecological concerns on the basis that as we share a connection with all life forms, exploiting the earth is to exploit and destroy an intrinsic part of ourselves.

His theory was an attempt to reconcile Christianity with the advances and discoveries of modern science.

TEILHARD DE CHARDIN, PIERRE [1881–1955]

Theologian, philosopher and palaeontologist whose theories were influential in the development of **New Age** thought. According to Teilhard the universe has a complex **consciousness** with its own evolutionary history. Humanity is psychically connected to all life forms and has the power to become co-creator in the evolutionary processes.

Teilhard believed that humanity was on the verge of a leap of consciousness, 'where it must either lose all belief in the universe or quite resolutely worship it'. This new consciousness, he suggested, would be

TELEKINESIS

The spontaneous movement of objects and people through the air without any physical intervention. These objects are either moved through **paranormal** means, like **levitation** by **spirits** or a **poltergeist**, or by thought or will power alone. If the movement is intentional, it is known as **psychokinesis**. Perhaps the most famous demonstration of deliberate telekinesis occurred in the 1970s when a young Israeli **psychic** called **Uri Geller** came to public attention for his ability to bend spoons and other metal objects using mind power alone.

One theory put forward to explain telekinesis is that the concentration of energy from a person's mind somehow alters the energy structure of the object they are focusing on. When the mind's stream of energy is released, the object reforms itself according to the energy patterns that have been sent. If the person has sent 'bending' the spoon bends, but if he or she sent 'floating' the spoon floats.

An alternative term used for telekinesis is **teleportation**, although the latter tends to imply the paranormal movement or **materialization** of objects across a distance whereas telekinesis tends to refer to the bending, reshaping and vibrating of objects through deliberate use of **psi**.

TELEPATHIC HYPNOSIS

Term coined in the late nineteenth century by psychical researcher **Frederick Myers** to describe a combination of **telepathy** and **hypnosis** in which a person is induced into a hypnotic **trance** by thought projection from a distance.

The ability to hypnotize someone from a distance was first discovered by mesmerists in Europe. In 1881 a Russian surgeon and Professor at the Imperial Academy of St Petersburg recorded an experiment that showed how a person could be acted on from a distance by a hypnotist concentrating his thought. In 1845 another Russian, a hypnotist called Andrey Pashkov, had recorded how he hypnotized a woman who lived 300 miles away. Alleged-ly she obeyed his thought command to fall asleep. In the late 1880s experiments observed and recorded by Myers on French **medium** Leonie B also yielded positive results for telepathic hypnosis, from a distance of about two-thirds of a mile.

From the mid-1920s, Russian scientists began to concentrate more fully on experiments with telepathic hypnosis with the aim of manipulating the behaviour of people from a distance. The experiments were led by L L Vasiliev, who claimed to have successfully hypnotized subjects who were more than 1,700 km away to fall asleep and awake on command.

Today some Russian scientists believe that a person may be telepathically hypnotized from a distance without being aware of it, although they do believe the phenomenon is limited to only a small percentage of susceptible people, around 4 in every 100. It has been suggested that telepathic hypnosis could one day prove to be useful to the military for espionage and warfare.

In 2002 a study conducted by clinical psychologist Susan Simpson, from the Royal Cornhill Hospital in Aberdeen, suggested that telepathic hypnosis (or 'tele-hypnosis') could prove to be more beneficial than face-to-face hypnosis. It is well known that hypnosis can help with treatment of a range of problems from chronic pain to eating disorders, but if a person lives in a remote area it can sometimes be difficult to find a suitably qualified therapist. Based on the results of her pilot study of patients in the Shetland Isles, whom she treated using teleconferencing, Simpson has suggested a possible solution. More than a third actually preferred telepathic hypnosis over face-to-face therapy, and all said they felt much improved and would like further sessions.

TELEPATHY

The mind-to-mind communication of thoughts, feelings and ideas through **psychic** means, especially **ESP**. Telepathy is described in folklore all over the world. In some tribal societies it is accepted as a natural ability everyone possesses but in other societies it is considered an ability that only psychics possess.

The word telepathy derives from the Greek terms *tele* (distant) and *pathe* (feeling) and was coined by psychical researcher **Frederick Myers** in 1882. Research into telepathy began with **mesmerism** in the late eighteenth century when practitioners discovered an apparent ability of some of their subjects to read their minds and carry out unspoken commands. This phenomenon was observed later by psychologists and psychiatrists such as **Sigmund Freud**, **Carl Jung** and **William James**.

When the **Society for Psychical Research** and the **American Society for Psychical Research** were founded in the mid-1880s, telepathy was the first **psychic** phenomenon to be studied scientifically. Early experiments were very simple and involved a person in one room attempting to transmit the thought of a number, image or taste to a person in another room. French physiologist Charles Richet not only observed that telepathy could occur

without hypnotism but also introduced the idea of matching results against mathematical chance. Over the years interest in telepathy grew steadily and mass telepathy experiments were attempted in the United States and Britain.

Studies have shown that when telepathy occurs it frequently happens spontaneously in times of crisis, for example, when one person becomes aware of another person being in danger from a distance. Telepathic information may come in the form of a **dream**, a mental image, through **clairaudience**, through thoughts that pop into the mind or through vague feelings of dread or anxiety. The person who is receiving the information may change their plans or attempt to warn or contact the other person.

It appears that telepathy is closely tied to emotion and it is no coincidence that most receivers tend to be women because women are often (but certainly not always) thought to be more in tune with their emotions and **intuition** than men. It also seems that telepathy has some biological connection as experiments show that the recipient's **brain waves** change to match those of the sender. Telepathy is adversely affected by drugs but positively affected by caffeine. It also improves as a person gets older. Studies on geriatric telepathy seem to indicate that when the physical senses become impaired telepathy becomes stronger.

In the 1930s American parapsychologist **J B Rhine** began a series of experiments using **ESP cards** to test telepathy. He discovered that it was often hard to distinguish between telepathy and **clairvoyance** or **precognition** and concluded that they

Sharpening your telepathic skills

Here's an exercise you can do with a friend to practise and sharpen your telepathic skills.

Agree on a time when you and your friend, in separate locations, both can sit down to meditate for approximately 10 minutes. Use the first five minutes of this time to send and the other five to receive a message, and make sure your times are opposite so that one of you receives when the other sends.

At the agreed-on time begin your meditation. Start with three deep breaths and concentrate on sending a message to your friend. Perceive the message in whatever way you wish but stick to a single representation. When the sending time is up take three deep breaths and shift to receiving mode. Concentrate on opening your mind to the message your friend is sending. When the meditation is finished bring yourself back to physical reality.

Write down everything you can remember about the experience, both the message you were trying to send and the messages you think you received from your friend. Phone or visit each other to compare experiences. How often were you right? How often were you wrong?

Generally speaking if you are more on target than not, you've exceeded the odds of chance. Don't be discouraged if at first results are poor; most people improve with practise.

were different manifestations of the same thing. Rhine also discovered that telepathy is not affected by the degree of distance between senders, and this has been proved correct by later tests.

Over the years numerous theories have been put forward to explain telepathy, but because telepathy, like all psychic phenomena, transcends space and time they are difficult to prove scientifically. Nineteenth-century chemist **Sir William Crookes** believed that telepathy depends on radio-like brain waves. The twentieth-century Russian scientist L L Vasiliev suggested electromagnetic theory. American psycholo-

gist Lawrence LeShan proposed that every person has his or her own reality and that psychics share different realities, which enable them to read the minds of others.

According to twenty-first-century scientists, because **empathy** is intrinsic to human nature we are all naturally telepathic, without being aware of it. Every time we place ourselves in another person's 'mental shoes', and wonder what it must be like to be them, or feel like them, we are using our own mind as a model for theirs and by so doing are 'reading' another person's mind.

TELEPORTATION

Also referred to as **telekinesis**, teleportation is the movement of objects or people across a distance without you yourself moving through the intervening space; it is a form of **psychokinesis**. The term also refers to the passage of solid objects through matter by dematerialization and **materialization**. Also known as the 'apport phenomenon', teleportation has allegedly been studied by the United States and Russian governments for its potential use in times of war and for espionage.

A whole generation of *Star Trek* fans has grown up familiar with the idea of teleportation, when crew members routinely teleported from spaceship to planet using a high technology transporter. This sounds improbable but there are some indications that suggest that teleportation may actually be possible. For example, a remarkable example of teleportation was reported in 1815 at a Prussian prison in Weichselmude when a chained prisoner, called Diderici, simply vanished before the eyes of fellow inmates and warders. He was never seen again.

Teleportation is allegedly accomplished by an **adept** who combines breathing exercises and intense concentration with manipulation of universal energy forces. It was a common occurrence of Victorian **Spiritualism**. The **séance**-room phenomena included apports in which small items such as flowers or jewellery allegedly materialized in thin air. Investigation suggested that these items were not created by **spirits** but somehow taken from other locations and transported to the séance room. Teleportation also appears to be a common phenomenon in reported cases of **poltergeist** activity, where objects move to distant locations or materialize from nowhere.

TEMPORAL DISPLACEMENT

See **Time travel**.

TEMPORAL LOBE ACTIVITY

Electrical activity in the temporal lobes of the brain. Temporal lobe activity is often associated with strange sensations, time distortions and hallucinations. It is sometimes used as an explanation for seemingly **paranormal** experiences such as **apparitions** and alien abduction experiences.

THEOSOPHY

The term 'theosophy' comes from the Greek words *theos* (god) and *sophia* (wisdom) and it is used to refer to a school of mystical thought and belief that arose out of the formation of the Theosophical Society. Theosophy teaches that one can gain knowledge through practise of the **occult** tradition and claims that all religions stem from the same roots of ancient wisdom, and that the study of ancient myths and **symbols** will lead to truth and spiritual awareness.

The primary expression of theosophy is the Theosophical Society, an international, non-sectarian and non-dogmatic organization. Founded in 1875 by **Madame Blavatsky** and others the Society has three stated aims: to form a universal human brotherhood without distinction of race, creed, sex or colour; to encourage studies in comparative religion, philosophy and science; and to investigate the unexplained laws of nature, power and magic. The Society has attracted many prominent intellectuals in its time, including **Aldous Huxley** and **W B Yeats**, who were involved in one of the Society's main activities – translating holy works from Eastern cultures. Much of the credit for the introduction of Indian and Chinese philosophy to the West must be given to theosophists who first translated into English many of the texts still used today in **Yoga**, Buddhism and **New Age** movements.

According to Blavatsky, ancient civilizations such as the Egyptians and Greeks understood **esoteric** wisdom better than we do today. Masters live on through the centuries in various incarnations guarding their knowledge and teaching it to students. Most of the Masters, Blavatsky said, reside in Tibet or India, forming the Brotherhood of Adepts, and it is these Masters who are the real founders of the Theosophical Society.

Blavatsky said that, following the instructions of the Masters on 9 March 1875, she formed the Society with the help of Colonel Henry Steel Olcott, an Ameri-can attorney and federal government official, and others. At first the Society struggled to survive in England but following a visit by Blavatsky and Olcott to India in 1879 it started to gather a following among the British in India, and also attracted high caste Indians.

In 1889 Blavatsky met Annie Besant, an ardent freethinker and feminist activist who had converted to theosophy. Besant became Blavatsky's last major disciple. Following Blavatsky's death in 1891 Besant, a gifted writer and orator who devoted a great deal of her efforts to political and social reform in India, took an active part in running the Theosophical Society. One of the movement's later gurus was Indian-born Jiddu Krishnamurti, who became a popular spiritual leader between the two World Wars and attracted a large following.

Theosophy is a secret doctrine that only reveals its practices and beliefs to the initiated, so it is hard to define exactly. Its motto – current to this day – is the adage 'There is no religion higher than truth'. It remains a curious blend of esoteric Buddhism, Hindu **mysticism**, Lamist doctrines from Tibet and a picture of world history that includes a series of root races stretching back to **Atlantis** and a non-physical period of prehistoric evolution in which the ecosphere gradually solidified into matter.

Today the Theosophical Society's headquarters is based in Adyar, near Madras, but it is a worldwide organization that has lodges and reasonable-sized followings in America, the UK, Europe and other countries. According to the Society's international website (www.ts-adyar.org/):

The Theosophical Society, founded in 1875, is a worldwide body whose primary object is Universal Brotherhood based on the realization that life, and all its diverse forms, human and non-human, is indivisibly One. The Society imposes no belief on its members, who are united by a common search for Truth and desire to learn the meaning and purpose of existence by engaging themselves in study, reflection, purity of life and loving service.

Theosophy is the wisdom underlying all religions when they are stripped of accretions and superstitions. It offers a philosophy which renders life intelligible and demonstrates that justice and love guide the cosmos. Its teachings aid the unfoldment of the latent spiritual nature in the human being, without dependence or fear.

THERAPEUTIC TOUCH

A type of **energy medicine** whereby the therapist moves his or her hands over the patient's 'energy field', allegedly directing the flow of **universal life force** so the patient can heal.

Therapeutic touch was developed by Dora van Gelder Kunz, a **clairvoyant** and **meditation** teacher, and Dolores Krieger, Professor of Nursing at New York University, in the early 1970s. The hands are used to identify and balance out disturbances in the energy field, or **aura**, of patients. It is said that this can help alleviate pain and encourage the healing process.

THIRD EYE

The location of the third eye in the middle of the forehead corresponds to the brow **chakra**; **psychic** energies are believed to be connected to the energy that supposedly emanates from this chakra.

Certain mystical and **esoteric** belief systems postulate that in the far reaches of prehistory, the predecessors of humanity possessed a third eye in the middle of their foreheads which allowed them to see the **spirit** realms directly. According to this theory, as millions of years passed the third eye was used less and less so that it disappeared into the folds of the brain, with the result that spiritual perception was all but lost.

Incredibly there may be a degree of truth in this obscure **occult** doctrine. Scientists have discovered that the pineal gland, a smallish organ buried within the brain at the approximate site of the third eye, has been found to retain a small degree of sensitivity to light, leaving scientists to suggest that it might have been an evolutionary remnant of an organ of sight. Only recently has the actual function of the pineal gland been discovered. It has been found to be one of the triggers in physical growth and the hormonal changes of puberty. It also secretes one of the so-called 'feel good' chemicals known to boost mood, serotonin.

Occultists believe that the pineal gland is unusually active in psychics and can be stimulated by techniques such as **massage**, **acupuncture**, concentration, **meditation** and so on, to produce psychic powers.

THOMAS, JOHN [1874–1940]

Psychologist and teacher from Detroit who was the first person to receive a doctorate in **parapsychology** from a US university.

Thomas's dissertation for Duke University, entitled 'An Evaluative Study of the Mental Content of Certain Trance Phenomena' (published as *Beyond Normal Cognition* in 1937), was a study of communications he supposedly received from his dead wife through a number of **mediums**, in particular **Gladys Osborne Leonard**. His systematic method for assessing material presented by a medium presented a major advance in the analysis of mediumistic communications.

He broke down the communications into categories and evaluated them as verifiable, unverifiable or inconclusive. The verifiable points he then judged as right or wrong. Of a total of 1,908 points from 24 **séances** with Leonard, 89 were judged to be inconclusive and 99 unverifiable, leaving 1,720 verifiable, of which 1,587 were right. Thomas then composed a questionnaire listing points from the records and had this completed by several groups of people as a way of determining to what extent these points were specific to him.

THOMPSON-GIFFORD CASE

Psychical researcher and early founder of the **American Society for Psychical Research**, **James Hyslop** investigated the Thompson-Gifford case and eventually came to the conclusion that it offered proof for the reality of **spirit attachment** or **possession**.

In January 1907 Frederic Thompson, a 39-year-old engraver and part-time artist visited Hyslop. Thompson claimed that he was under the influence of the deceased Robert Swain Gifford, a famous turn-of-the-century landscape painter, and was experiencing unexplained urges to paint trees and rocky coasts that he had never seen before. Thompson had briefly met Gifford one summer but the two men were not friends, or even acquaintances. Thompson moved to New York in 1900 and didn't even know that Gifford had died in January 1905.

By the end of the summer in 1905 Thompson was visualizing pictures he knew Gifford had painted, but he didn't learn about Gifford's death until January 1906, when he saw an exhibition of the works of the 'late R Swain Gifford'. At the exhibition he was struck by the similarities between Gifford's paintings and his own recent work and he allegedly heard a voice saying to him, 'You see what I have done. Go on with the work.'

Thompson continued to paint but his work and health suffered under his compulsion. He believed he was going insane. Hyslop at first suspected some kind of personality disorder but he also organized Thompson to meet with a **medium** called Margaret Gaule on 18 January 1907. Gaule immediately sensed the presence of an artist, even though she had been given no prior information about Thompson. On 16 March Hyslop took Thompson to see celebrated medium **Minnie Meserve Soule**, who gave detailed information about Gifford that was later confirmed by Gifford's widow.

In the summer and autumn of 1907 Thompson travelled to many of Gifford's favourite haunts, recognizing scenes he had felt compelled to paint. By early 1908 Thompson had embraced his compulsion and was selling paintings that critics noticed bore amazing resemblances to Gifford's work.

Hyslop was still not sure whether Thompson's case was about spirit attachment or about a fellow artist incorporating the ideas of another artist in their work, so he decided to try and establish spirit contact with Gifford. During a **séance** on 4 June 1908, Soule began to receive what appeared to be messages from Gifford. The messages revealed how excited he was about his power to return and finish his work through Thompson. Later in the year Hyslop attended another séance with a medium called Mrs Willis Cleaveland and this time the spirit finally identified himself as Gifford through **automatic writing**.

By now Hyslop felt he had all the evidence he needed to establish a genuine case of spirit attachment and although later investigators suspected **fraud**, Hyslop's conclusion has never been completely refuted. Gifford's spirit stopped bothering Thompson after the 1908 séances, and Thompson left his engraving work to make a good living as a full-time artist.

THORNTON HEATH POLTERGEIST

Case involving a house in London that was allegedly haunted by a **poltergeist** in 1938.

The poltergeist activity seemed to centre around Mrs Forbes, a 35-year old woman who was the owner of the house at the time. Psychical researcher **Nandor Fodor** described her case as 'poltergeist psychosis'. By this he meant that Mrs Forbes's **unconscious** mind was responsible for the activities. He believed that the cause was sexual trauma that Mrs Forbes had suffered as a child and which had been repressed.

Almost from the very first day that Fodor investigated the case he suspected that Mrs Forbes might be causing the poltergeist activity by normal means, despite her obvious distress in reaction to the activities and his lack of proof. Fodor insisted that Mrs Forbes be studied at a college where he could keep an eye on her but the strange activities continued even when she was there. Objects from Thornton Heath mysteriously appeared and crashed to the floor, glasses and other objects flew out of Mrs Forbes's hands and choking marks appeared around her neck.

At the same time as Mrs Forbes was being investigated, Fodor also examined her psychological background and discovered that her past clearly showed a history of hysteria and dissociated personality, which included hearing **voices**. He became convinced that Mrs Forbes was a neurotic with a disorganized personality and that she was somehow hiding objects in her clothing. Searches revealed nothing but an

X-ray proved Fodor to be correct. Two small objects seemed to be hidden under Mrs Forbes left breast and they both appeared after she allegedly collapsed.

This event convinced Fodor that Mrs Forbes was fabricating the **hauntings** and taking great delight in fooling her observers. He did, however, believe that the case was important because it suggested a new direction for psychical research – one that attempted to understand the mental patterns that accompany such occurrences, even if these occurrences are fraudulent.

The full story of Thornton Heath did not reach the public until 1945, when Fodor finally published it in the *Journal of Clinical Psychopathology*. The reason for the delay was the criticism that had been directed at him from both the public and psychical researchers for his emphasis on the psychological explanation of the case. Eventually, though, Fodor won recognition for his theory.

THOUGHT FORM

The shapes, patterns or vibrations assumed by thoughts and emotions, which allegedly can be perceived visibly by **clairvoyants** or sensed intuitively by others.

THOUGHTOGRAPHY

Form of **paranormal** photography when images are projected by **psi** onto photographic film.

The term 'thoughtography' was coined by Tomokichi Fukurai, President of the Psychical Institute of Japan, who conducted the first study of it in the early 1900s. Fukurai stumbled on the phenomenon accidentally while testing the **clairvoyance** of a **medium** called Mrs Nagao. He asked her if she could discern three characters he had photographed on an undeveloped film plate. To his surprise Fukurai discovered that the entire surface of the plate had been exposed, not just the characters, and came to the conclusion that the exposure was caused by Nagao's psychic energy. In later experiments Fukurai obtained actual images of film that he called 'thoughtographs'.

In the 1960s research into thoughtography was done under the direction of psychiatrist Ian Stevenson of the University of Virginia and Denver psychiatrist Jule Eisenbud. The research team attracted national attention for its work with **psychic** Ted Serios, who seemed to be able to create images on film simply by staring at a polaroid camera. In 1967 Eisenbud published the results of his work with Serios in his book *The World of Ted Serios*. In it he concluded that the only possible explanation for Serios's thoughtography was **psychokinesis**.

Even though Stevenson and Eisenbud had taken great care to guard against **fraud**, and Serios never admitted to cheating, they were nevertheless charged with fraud. The charges were never proved and

Stevenson and Eisenbud countered by arguing that many of Serios's images were distortions that could not be explained or duplicated with trick camera or other methods of transferring images. For example, on one of Serios's thoughtographs, which has been identified as the Royal Canadian Mounted Police Air Hangar in Ontaro, the word 'Canadian' is mysteriously misspelled 'Cainadain'.

TIBETAN BOOK OF THE DEAD

Also known as the *Bardo Thodol*, the *Tibetan Book of the Dead* is basically a guide to the **afterlife**. Translated, *bardo thodol* means 'liberation by hearing on the after death plane' and aims to be an instruction manual for the **soul** during the state that intervenes between death and the next rebirth. It suggests that following death the soul is faced with the possibility of absorption into the godhead, but for the average soul this possibility is terrifying and so the soul flees through a succession of **dream** worlds in which the environment is unconsciously created by the expectations of the soul. It teaches that awareness, once freed from the body, creates its own reality like that of a dream. This dream projection unfolds in ways both frightening and beautiful. Peaceful and wrathful **visions** appear, and these visions can be overwhelming. Since the awareness is still in shock from no longer being attached to and shielded by a body, it needs guidance and forewarning so that key decisions that lead to enlightenment are made.

The *Tibetan Book of the Dead* teaches how one can attain heavenly realms by recognizing the enlightened realms as opposed to being drawn into the realms of seduction that pull incorporeal awareness into cyclic suffering and rebirth. The unevolved soul pines for the pleasures of the flesh and draws close to the physical world. Sexual fantasies attract it towards couples making love and it is trapped in the womb for another incarnation.

The origins of the *Tibetan Book of the Dead* are unknown. For centuries it was passed down orally and was first put into written form by the legendary Padma Sambhava in the eighth century AD. This Tibetan Buddhist scripture was traditionally read aloud to the dying to help them attain liberation. It guides a person to use the moment of death to recognize the nature of mind and attain liberation.

TIME TRAVEL

Temporal displacement, also known as time travel, has long captured the imagination of people around the world, but is time travel possible? Einstein's theory of relativity proved travelling forward in time was possible and today the possibilities, uncertainties and paradoxes surrounding the concept of time travel continue to lie right at the cutting edge of modern physics.

Humans are in fact always travelling in time – in a linear fashion, from the present to the immediate future. Some theories, most notably special and general relativity, suggest that suitable geometries of space-time, or certain types of motion in space, may allow time travel into the past and future, if these geometries or motions are possible. In physics, the concept of time travel has been used often to examine the consequences of physical theories such as special relativity, general relativity and quantum mechanics. There is no experimental evidence of time travel, and it is not even well understood whether any of the current physical theories permit any kind of time travel, although theories do exist suggesting the possibility of 'folding' time to hop from one point to another.

In contrast to the scientific community, among occultists there is no such controversy or indecision about time travel. Most **psychics** believe it is possible to travel, psychically, to any location in any time period – past past or future – using techniques such as **meditation**, **remote viewing**, **lucid dreaming**, **out-of-body experiences**, **past-life recall**, or sometimes spontaneously in a **dream**, or a 'daydream', or using mind-control exercises. Time travel is also believed to occur in episodes of **precognition**, **retrocognition** and **bilocation**.

TOAD

According to ancient **occult** lore, the toad is believed to be **psychic** and can detect the presence of **ghosts**. Keeping a toad in the house or garden was thought to protect against evil, although in some areas toads are **death omens**. Folklore also holds that toads were once the favoured **familiars** of **witches**.

TOKOLOSH

A semi-human black creature who is supposed to live in rivers and other water courses. The tokolosh is believed to be cruel and revengeful and is sometimes called upon by people to cause trouble for others; a **witch doctor** may be needed to banish him. Most of the time only children can see the tokolosh; and in contrast to its behaviour with adults it shows kindness towards them and it is not unusual for a friendship to develop.

The tokolosh myth is of uncertain origin but well known and feared in most southern African countries. Many people lift their beds high off the ground so that the tokolosh cannot reach them. Some people are afraid to mention its name. The tokolosh can also become invisible and when it vigorously haunts a person or a site there is a strong similarity in many of its actions to that of the European **poltergeist**.

TOTEMS

Spirit guides that appear in animal form, each with symbolic meaning. Totems were also known as power animals and the tribal communities of North America's Pacific Northwest associated themselves with a specific totem they believed represented the spirits of their character and personality – for example the bear is associated with strength, the eagle with nobility and the leopard with speed. When a **shaman** sought wisdom from the community's spirit world, their spirit guide would appear in the form of their selected totem. In some instances a totem was not necessarily an animal – it might be a natural phenomenon, a physical feature or even a hand-made object.

The totem pole custom came from North America where some native peoples would carve their selected totems into logs as protective **amulets** for their villages, and to help channel the qualities of their tribal animals into the hearts and souls of their communities.

TOWER OF LONDON

This historical site, now a major tourist attraction, once served as a prison and execution site and not surprisingly is believed to be haunted by numerous **ghosts** who lost their heads on its scaffold. Many ghosts have been spotted by sentries and members of the public. The ghosts are often headless and include men, women and children, and even a bear that dates back to the Tower's days as a menagerie.

The Bloody Tower was the scene of the infamous disappearance of the two young medieval princes, Edward V and his broth-er the Duke of York, who are thought to have been murdered in 1483 on the command of the Duke of Gloucester, because they stood in the way of him becoming king. According to one report, guards in the late fifteenth century spotted the shadows of two small figures gliding down some stairs. In 1674 workmen found a chest that contained the skeletons of two young children. They were thought to be the remains of the boys and were given a royal burial not long afterwards.

The ghost most frequently seen is that of **Anne Boleyn**, second wife of Henry VIII, whom he beheaded in 1536. She is said to haunt the vicinity of the White Tower, the King's House, Tower Green and the Chapel of St Peter, where her headless body was interred in an arrow case under the floor. In 1864 a sentry is said to have challenged a figure thought to be Anne Boleyn; his bayonet passed straight through her, and he fainted in shock.

Sir Walter Raleigh, executed in 1618 on the orders of King James I, makes an appearance now and again, and has been seen as recently as 1983 by a Yeoman Guard on duty in the Byward Tower. The bungled execution of Lady Salisbury is said to be re-enacted on Tower Green on the anniversary of her death in 1541. The executioner needed several attempts to sever her head and she screamed and struggled between each attempt. Her screams of terror are heard from her ghost about the time of the anniversary of her death.

Lady Jane Grey, the nine-day queen, is also said to appear on the anniversary of her death on 12 February 1554. Other ghostly traditions include the screams of

Guy Fawkes echoing through the Tower, as they did when he was tortured before being hung, drawn and quartered; the ghost of the Duke of Northumberland who was executed in 1553; the ghost of Catherine Howard, another wife executed by Henry VIII; and various other **apparitions** and **spirits** associated with the Tower's bloody history.

TRADITIONAL CHINESE MEDICINE [TCM]

Holistic Chinese philosophy encompassing **yin** and **yang** and the five **elements** of the universe that evolved into a complex system of external examination and diagnosis of health and disease. TCM places a greater emphasis on the prevention of disease than on treating it and in ancient China physicians would only be paid if their patients stayed well, not when they fell ill. TCM dates back 5,000 years and is based on **Taoist** principles surrounding the concept of **universal life force** energy or chi. It has been suggested that TCM is rooted in the practice of **Ayurvedic medicine** and then combined with Taoist philosophy in the fourth century BC.

TCM is based on the ancient Chinese belief that each person is born with a certain amount of chi. This amount is determined by heredity and by the way a person lives their lives. Healthy living can add to chi, but unhealthy lifestyle habits, such as poor diet and lack of exercise, can deplete it. When a person's chi is depleted they die.

The physical body is made up of chi (life energy) jing (vital fluid) and shen (spirit) and to maintain health chi needs to be balanced as this will balance out jing and shen.

Certain factors are believed to block the flow of chi and lead to imbalance or disease:

- *The six excesses – wind, cold, heat, dampness, dryness and phlegm.*
- *The five emotions – joy, anger, sympathy, fear and grief.*
- *Unhealthy eating and drinking habits.*
- *Too little or too much sex.*
- *Too much or too little work or exercise.*

Any of these five factors can block the flow of chi running through the body and can lead to excesses or deficiencies in energy in the different parts/organs of the body.

Four methods of treatment or prevention are used in TCM: herbal medicine, **acupuncture**, regulation of diet and nutrition and exercising the body through active exercises, like the **martial arts**, or passive ones such as **Tai Chi**. TCM practitioners use the philosophy 'to see, to hear, to feel' to diagnose their patients and their four main diagnostic methods are

- *Tongue diagnosis.*
- *Wrist pulse diagnosis.*
- *Palpation of specific acupuncture points on the body.*
- *Specific questioning of the patient's moods, symptoms and past and present lifestyle.*

All this information is then put together and any disease or illness is revealed as a pattern of disease or disharmony in chi. The diagnosis points to the type of long-term or short-term treatment recommended.

The practices of TCM are discussed in detail in two classic texts which are still in use today: *Divine Farmer's Classic of Herbal Medicine*, written in the third century BC, and *Yellow Emperor's Inner Classic*, written in the first century BC. TCM practices were first brought to the West in the seventeenth century by French Jesuit priests and were standardized by Mao Tse-tung during the Chinese Cultural Revolution of the twentieth century.

TCM remains the main healthcare option in China today. In the West it is regarded as **alternative medicine**. TCM practitioners in both the East and the West must go through rigorous medical training. TCM methods are thought to work best for chronic illnesses, such as arthritis or environmental disorders such as stress, hormonal imbalances, obesity and back injury, where permanent changes in lifestyle are often needed to maintain or regain health.

TRANCE

State between sleeping and waking, when a person is half conscious and focusing exclusively on their internal thoughts and **visions** and is unaware of what is going on around them. This **altered state of consciousness** can occur spontaneously or be induced (and self-induced) by **hypnosis**, by **shamans** via sensory deprivation, by a **medium** during a **séance**, by hallucino-

genic **drugs**, by **meditation,** and by rhythmic **chanting**, music and movement.

TRANSCENDENTAL MEDITATION

Type of **meditation**, popular in the United States, Britain and Australia, that was advocated in the 1970s by Indian guru Maharishi Mahesh Yogi, where the meditator concentrates on a particular **mantra** known only to them. The aim of transcendental meditation (TM) is to increase spiritual awareness and find inner peace by achieving transcendental consciousness.

TM is said to bring results more quickly than any other type of meditation, especially **Yoga** and **Zen**. It has been shown to decrease drug use, to increase energy, alertness, concentration, coordination and to ease stress and illness. Physiological changes include lowered blood pressure and increased **brain-wave** activity, and practitioners report overall health improvements. According to the Maharishi, TM is so powerful because it is rooted in traditions that are thousands of years old, for practices that resemble TM can be found in the Hindu Vedas. The knowledge was, however, lost and found many times over the centuries.

After founding the TM movement in the 1970s the Maharishi turned his attention to health and world peace. His work in health is directed to spreading the ancient **Ayurvedic medicine** of India and finding the key to reversing ageing. His world peace programme states that if 7,000 people collectively practise TM the coherence of the brain waves will lead to a reduction in crime, accidents and illness. According to the Maharishi, 7,000 people represent the square root of 1 per cent of the world's population, which is the minimum necessary to cause mass change.

During 1983 and 1984 the Maharishi assembled 7,000 people at the Maharishi International University, now in Fairfield, Iowa, to test this hypothesis. TM researchers claimed that for three weeks after the event the world was a less accident-prone place and disease levels dropped, but critics believe the study was biased towards proving the hypothesis to be true. In 1988 TM meditators claimed responsibility for the peaceful unification of Germany, and in 1990 TM meditators assembled on four continents: TM researchers claimed that international conflict dropped by 44 per cent, although once again critics cast doubt on the conclusions drawn.

TM differs from traditional Eastern teachings in that there is no requirement for withdrawal from daily life in order to achieve enlightenment. Instead the Maharishi insists on the importance of wellbeing in the natural world, but without attachment to it. TM also differs from other forms of meditation in that it does not involve concentration or contemplation, but the use of sacred sound. The Maharishi maintains it can only be taught through personal instruction by a qualified teacher. The student is given a personal mantra and instructed how to use it while meditating twice a day for around 20 minutes. The mantra has no meanings or associations and is not chanted verbally or mentally, rather it is a sound that is thought.

The chief feature of TM is that regular use of the mantra enables the practitioner to reach a higher state of **consciousness**, which the Maharishi describes as pure creative intelligence or pure thought. Thoughts rise from the depths of the mind like tiny seeds rising to the surface, growing in size till they reach the level of conscious awareness. The Maharishi likens the mind to the ocean; its surface is active but its depths are still. TM enables practitioners to experience the origin of thought and thus gain greater access to the state of creative intelligence where the true self lies in a state of restful alertness, where there is no mental activity. This is a fourth state of consciousness, different from waking, sleeping and deep sleep, where boundaries between subject and object disappear and the two become one to find silent joy in seeming emptiness.

Even higher states of consciousness, called the fifth, sixth and seventh states, can be achieved with practice. However, these states can only be achieved when one is permanently and totally free of stress and the aim is to attain absolute awareness of the external world and one's essential unity with all that is. The Maharishi claims that with TM it is possible to reach this enlightenment in around five to ten years, as opposed to decades or a lifetime through Yoga or Zen.

TRANSLIMINALITY

Term introduced by Michael A Thalbourne, Research Fellow at the University of Adelaide in the 1990s, which means literally 'the tendency to cross the threshold into awareness'. According to Thalbourne, persons exhibiting a high degree of transliminality are more likely to believe in, and claim experience of **paranormal** phenomena, as well as to report a more creative personality and be more prone to fantasies, as well as having a history of experience associated with depression and mania. Therefore, transliminality is defined as 'susceptibility to, and awareness of, large volumes of imagery, ideation and emotion – these phenomena being stimulated by subliminal, supraliminal and/or external inputs.'

TRANSLOCATION

See **Teleportation**.

TRANSMIGRATION

Belief similar to **reincarnation** that after death the **soul** can be born again in another physical body. It differs from reincarnation in that this body can be either human or animal.

TRANSPERSONAL PSYCHOLOGY

Controversial school of psychology, still in its infancy, that tries to understand what parts **mysticism**, **peak experiences** and transpersonal experiences play in forming personality and character. In a transpersonal experience the **consciousness** overcomes space and time to identify with other consciousnesses, phenomena or states. Various **paranormal** phenomena, including **telepathy**, **out-of-body experiences**, **clairvoyance**, **precognition** and **time travel**, are regarded as transpersonal experiences.

In the early twentieth century, Italian psychiatrist Roberto Assagioli (1888–1974) developed what he called 'psychosynthesis'; an approach to psychology that focuses on achieving a coming together of various parts of the personality. Once a person's lower self has been psychosynthesized together they can then turn their attention to the 'higher' or 'transpersonal self'. This gives life purpose and meaning, which all people need to feel psychologically healthy.

In transpersonal psychotherapy ego is illusion, something that must be transcended so that the individual can identify with the total self. Body and mind are not separate but sub-systems of each other, and everyone therefore has the capacity for self-healing. Transpersonal psychotherapy includes both Eastern and Western methods of working with the consciousness, including Western methods of **dream** analysis and **imagery** and Eastern **meditation** and **Yoga**.

TREE OF LIFE

Complex **symbol** that is central to the practice and philosophy of **Kabbalah**, the Jewish mystical religion. The Tree of Life incorporates 10 circles, symbolizing 10 different spheres of knowledge (known as *sephiroth*) that a person must achieve to attain wisdom or the 'godhead'. These sephiroth are usually perceived as energies or states on the physical level but also exist as defined places on the **astral plane**. Connecting each of these spheres to one another are 22 pathways, comprised of the letters of the Hebrew alphabet. Each path is a specific astral track to be studied and investigated by the initiated.

Followers of the Kabbalah must work their way up the Tree of Life from the foundation of the tree by study and initiation into the secret knowledge associated with each level, before moving up to the next sphere of wisdom. The base sphere of the Tree is called Malkuth and it signifies the physical aspect of reality, the everyday world we live in. Above Malkuth is the sphere of Yesod, which is associated with **imagination** and the astral plane. To Kabbalists Yesod is the literal foundation on which physical reality rests. As the Kabbalist moves upwards through the spheres of Hod, Netzach, Tiphareth, Geburah, Chesed, Chokmah and Binah more and more subtle aspect of reality are reached, until the final sphere, Kether, is attained, which symbolizes the essential unity of the universe. Combining the 10 spheres and the 22 paths, Kabbalists believe there are 32 ways to reach Kether and the self-development work to get there is known as **pathworking**.

TREE SPIRITS

Trees are believed to be dwelling places for **ghosts** and **spirits** in many parts of the world. In ancient Egypt numerous deities were believed to inhabit trees. In the Old Testament there are numerous references to sacred groves and altars being set up under trees. In Rome tree **omens** were considered important. For instance, the withering of laurels foretold Nero's death. Trees were also sacred to the Celts; in fact they had a whole alphabet based on them.

Throughout Eastern countries there has been a tradition of hanging gifts on sacred trees so that good luck can be enjoyed by the giver. Similarly in England many trees growing alongside sacred wells are decorated with pieces of paper or cloth to attract good fortune. In Northern India many local shrines are built under trees for the propitiation of the resident ghosts. In some cultures trees and their spirits were so highly revered that felling a tree that still had its spirit inside it meant losing your life

In 1981 thousands of people from all over the United States flocked to see an allegedly haunted and crying pecan tree in Gilberton, Alabama. The tree was in the front garden of a home belonging to Mrs Linnie Jenkins, who had reported hearing strange crying sounds coming from the tree. A rumour started that the house was built on the site of an Indian burial site and the noise was the sound of unhappy warrior spirits crying. The media got hold of the story and the crowds descended; Mrs Jenkins began to charge people who wanted to come and listen to the tree. The

Tree spirits

The Celts valued every kind of tree and plant. They would associate trees with a particular character or properties and believed that spirits lived in every one of them. The following is a sample of some of the many superstitions and magical beliefs associated with certain trees:

* **Alder** – The spirit of the alder tree is very protective, and has great knowledge about scrying with the use of water and mirrors. When it leaves the tree, it will often take the form of a raven.

* **Apple** – The apple tree is the home of the unicorn. Traditionally, the unicorn lives beneath the apple tree. The spirit of this tree holds the knowledge of eternal youth and beauty.

* **Ash** – The ash tree has great mysticism and power associated with it. It can teach the magic of poetry and how to weave words into powerful effects. In Norse tradition, it was called the great tree of life. It is a doorway to many dimensions of the fairy realm. Its spirit is strong and holds the knowledge of how events and people are linked together.

* **Cedar** – This tree and its spirit are both protective and healing. This spirit brings calm and balance to emotions and can stimulate inspiring dream activity.

* **Cherry** – The cherry tree is home to the magical phoenix. The spirit of this tree is often fiery in appearance. It has the ability to bring individuals to the threshold of a new awakening.

* **Elder** – The elder tree is sacred to the Druid and Celtic traditions. It was the tree of birth and death, beginning and ending. It teaches how to awaken opportunity to cast out the old and bring in the new. The tree's spirit has knowledge of great magic and can add power to even the slightest of wishes.

* **Hawthorne** – The hawthorne is sacred to the fairies and elves. This tree can stimulate growth and fertility in all areas of your life, making it seem enchanted to others.

* **Oak** – The oak tree is home to a very powerful spirit, which has great strength and endurance. It holds the ancient knowledge of the continuity of life, and just being near it is strengthening to the entire aura field. It is a natural doorway to the fairy realms and their mysteries. Every acorn has its own little fairy and bringing an acorn into your home is a way of inviting more intimate contact with the fairies for brief periods.

* **Pine** – Pine trees found along shorelines are often gathering spots for water spirits and sprites. This tree spirit is healing and balancing, especially to emotions. It is protective against all forms of negativity.

- **Rowan** – Another ancient and magical tree whose spirit understands the mysteries of nature. The wisdom of this spirit is so strong that when linked with, it can help a person invoke spirits, guides and elementals.
- **Sycamore** – The sycamore was sacred to the Egyptians. It can teach humility and how to receive from the universe – be it in the form of assistance, compliments, or any other form. It holds the knowledge of the laws of abundance and supply and how to utilize them to your greatest benefit.
- **Willow** – The willow has a long association with the fairy realm and the spirits and elves that live under it are keepers of the knowledge of herbs. The willow tree can speak audibly to us if we learn to quieten ourselves and listen. The willow tree opens vision, communication and stimulates dream activity. The best time to attune to it and its energies and spirit is at night.

noise died away within the month and no satisfactory explanation was ever put forward. Sceptics believe it was caused by insects or gasses produced from the souring wood in the tree.

TREGEAGLE, JAN

Ghost of a seventeenth-century sinner from Cornwall who, according to lore, was summoned from the grave and now performs, under protest, an eternal and fruitless task. Today the term 'Tregeagle' is assigned to anyone who protests and to children who wail.

It seems that a historical Jan Tregeagle did exist and he wasn't a very pleasant fellow by all accounts. He was an unpopular magistrate who used his position to amass a personal fortune. Rumour has it that he accomplished this by fraud and by selling his **soul** to the devil. Although no proof exists it is also said that he murdered his wife and children. Concerned about his fate in the **afterlife** he was said to have bribed local clergy to have him buried in consecrated land.

According to the legend, several years after his death Tregeagle was summoned from the grave to begin his eternal suffering during a court dispute concerning a loan between two men witnessed by Tregeagle when he was alive. The debtor denied receiving the loan and declared in court that if Tregeagle had witnessed the deal he should declare himself. To the court's amazement and horror Tregeagle appeared to set the record straight. The ghost then told the debtor it would not be easy to return him to his grave.

True to his prediction Tregeagle's ghost followed the debtor everywhere. The debtor asked the clergy for help, who managed to get Tregeagle to Gwenvor Cove and there assigned him the impossible task of making a truss of sand, to be bound with ropes of sand and then carried. According to reports, Tregeagle is still labouring away on the shores of Whitsand Bay, and when a storm destroys his work it is said his howls can be heard throughout the countryside.

TRUMPET

Trumpets made of cardboard and aluminium were once popular in **Spiritualist séances** to amplify the alleged voices of **spirits**, so they could communicate in **direct voice mediumship**. Trumpets were also said to levitate and dance in the air in some séances. The craze seems to have been started by a **medium** called Jonathon Koon in the mid-nineteenth century under the instruction of his **control, John King**, but interest declined along with the decline of interest in **physical mediumship** in the twentieth century.

TSUKUMOGAMI

Spirit in Japanese folklore that closely resembles the **Brownie**. Translated as 'old tool spirits', the tsukumogami inhabit tools and perform household and cleaning chores by themselves at night. If the tools are mistreated or neglected they take revenge by attacking their owners while they are asleep.

TULPA

Tulpa is a Tibetan word used to refer to an entity that, according to Tibetan **occult** beliefs, supposedly attains reality solely by the act of **imagination**. The entity is created entirely within the confines of a person's mind, not drawn out, written down or even verbally described.

If its creator wishes, this 'Tulpa Creation' may become physical reality through intense concentration, **meditation** and **visualization**. However, experts strongly advise that great care be taken to only bring to reality what is helpful to the world, lest its destruction becomes more problematic than its creation.

TURN OF THE SCREW, THE

Classic **ghost** story by Henry James that was published in 1898 and continues to send shivers up the spines of readers to this day. *The Turn of the Screw* tells, with incredible skill and marvellous atmosphere, the story of two small children who are **possessed** by the evil **spirits** of two dead servants.

TURPIN, DICK [1705–1739]

In his lifetime Dick Turpin was one of Britain's most infamous highwaymen and a popular hero as his habit of robbing the rich delighted the poorer folk. His **ghost** is still said to haunt Hounslow Heath and large stretches of highway between London and Scotland.

In contrast to the legendary Robin Hood, Turpin did not give his money to the poor and he was no hero. He committed a number of heinous crimes to increase his wealth. He was finally caught and hanged for his crimes, but the gallant manner of his death impressed the crowd so much that they stole his body and buried it in quicklime to prevent it being sold to anatomists, as was the custom of the day regarding criminals.

Ghost stories about Turpin are connected to his exploits as a highwayman. His cloaked figure astride a spectral black horse has been spotted in so many locations that almost any spectral horseman reported is said to be Dick Turpin. For example, he is said to haunt the A5 between Hinckley and Nuneaton in the Midlands, the A11 between Norwich and London, especially the stretch through Epping Forest, and he has also been spotted by airline staff working at Heathrow Airport in Hounslow, an area once believed to be plagued by highwaymen.

TWAIN, MARK [1835–1910]

One of the most beloved authors in American literature, Twain achieved international acclaim when he penned such classics as *Tom Sawyer* and *The Adventures of Huckleberry Finn*. His interest in the **paranormal** began in his youth when a travelling mesmerist visited his hometown of Hannibal, Missouri, to give a demonstration of hypnotism and 'mind reading'. Later in life Twain noted on several occasions that he had premonitory **dreams** and joked that he was capable of 'mental telegraphy': a term he coined to describe the mental exchange of letters and thoughts with his wife. He also reputedly visited numerous haunted locations and claimed on a few occasions to have spotted an **apparition**.

Twain joined the **Society for Psychical Research** in 1885 and his interest in paranormal research became even deeper following the death of his daughter, Susy, at the age of 24.

TWIGG, ENA [1914–1973]

Famous late-twentieth-century British **medium** who promoted **spiritualism** through radio and television broadcasts. Her high rate of success and her down-to-earth ways prompted thousands of people to seek her advice, either in private **séances** or through letters and phone calls.

Twigg was born in Kent in 1914. From a very early age she claimed to have been aware that she was **psychic**, remembering out-of-body experiences while still a toddler. She also said she often saw **spirits**. Following her marriage at the age of 17 to childhood friend Harry Twigg, Ena's **paranormal** experiences increased. She had **visions** of Harry wherever he was in the world and also communicated with her dead father. Eventually she decided to develop her psychic talents as a **clairvoyant**, healer and **trance** medium for the good of society.

The Twiggs did much to revive the profile of spiritualism. Following the repeal of the 1754 Witchcraft Act in 1951, Ena appeared on television on numerous occasions to promote the **spiritualist** cause. The Twiggs also travelled all over Europe and the United States, gaining many converts with Ena's public clairvoyant performances.

One of her most famous communications began in March 1966 when she sat with Episcopal bishop **James Pike**. The bishop's flat had been plagued with **poltergeist** activity for the previous two weeks and during a séance with Twigg the Bishop's son, James Jr, who had recently died of a pill overdose, came through.

Throughout her career as a medium Twigg taught that spiritualism was about life, not death. She was convinced that death was not the end and that the **spirit** survives deaths, and felt that if people could only believe this they would find their lives and their living much enriched.

TYRELL, GEORGE [1879–1952]

Mathematician, engineer and leading psychical researcher and member of the **Society for Psychical Research**, Tyrell is best known for his studies on **apparitions** and **ESP**. Throughout his research and writing Tyrell's main concern was the relationship between the **unconscious** and ESP. In his book, *Science and Psychical Phenomena* (1938), he suggested that the human personality disintegrated into fragments after death and it was these fragments that **mediums** came in touch with in **séances**. It is for his influential theory of apparitions, however, that Tyrell is best known today. Tyrell believed that apparitions were hallucinations of the **percipient** based on information received via ESP from the **agent**. He suggested that a part of the unconscious, called the 'producer', became aware, via ESP, of the agent's situation and then a 'stage carpenter' produced the apparitional drama using **dreams**, **visions** and impressions.

TYRONE GHOST

The Irish legend of the Tyrone **ghost**, who allegedly appeared to Lady Beresford in 1693, is unique in that that ghost left a memento of his visit by signing his name in a notebook! Prior to his death Lord Tyrone had made a pact with his friend Lady Beresford that whoever would die first would make every effort to return to comfort the others. According to a manuscript written by Lady Elizabeth Cobb, grand-daughter of Lady Beresford, Tyrone did return with news that accurately predicted the future for Lady Beresford. And to prove that he was indeed the ghost of Lord Tyrone he left his easily recognizable signature in her pocket book!

U

UFOs

Unidentified flying objects (UFOs), or 'flying saucers' as they are popularly known, have been the subject of endless debate as to their likelihood and possible source of origin. The existence of **extra-terrestrials**, alien life forms from other planets, continues to be hotly debated even though UFO incidents are currently being researched and investigated by governments all over the world.

One of the most well-known cases occurred in 1947 in Roswell, New Mexico. In this incident an alien spaceship allegedly crashed, and despite evidence that suggests this was a US Army experiment that went wrong many people continue to believe that this explanation is a cover-up for the truth. Another more recent incident occurred in 1980, when a UFO falling to earth was tracked by radar and was witnessed by a large number of people, including three soldiers from the US Air Force. News about the incident was suppressed until 1984. It has never been satisfyingly explained.

Reports of UFO sightings date back to prehistory. For example, an island in the Hunan Province of China contains rock carvings not only of UFOs but also of strange alien beings with them. The carvings have been dated back to 45,000 BC. Reports of UFOs continue to this day with many witnesses and even videotape evidence adding to the belief that perhaps 'we are not alone'.

Those who do not accept that UFOs are sent by aliens from outer space have put forward alternative explanations for the phenomena. Apart from the many cases that can be put down to tricks of the light, strange cloud formations or even natural objects like weather balloons and aircraft, it has also been suggested that people who report seeing a UFO or encountering an alien are suffering from hallucinations they mistake for physical reality. This sounds plausible but does not take into account the incidences when a psychological interpretation does not appear to be enough to explain evidence provided by credible witnesses.

Another explanation put forward is that humanity shares the planet with other alien races. These races are normally invisible but they will make themselves known to certain selected individuals at selected times. Contact has been interpreted as meetings with **fairies** and elves. Yet another explanation suggests that UFOs are actually **spirit** forms, strange **materializations** that have been created from the energy of machinery.

Unconscious

At a simple level, the notion of an unconscious is a useful way to account for aspects of the mind of which we are not directly conscious or aware. In other words the unconscious mind is a storage facility that retains and recalls memories sent there by the **conscious** mind for use at a time when the unconscious perceives action is needed. When this happens the conscious mind often accepts the suggestion and automatically sets it in motion. However, when this simplistic interpretation is examined on a deeper level the topic becomes more complex.

Probably the most detailed and precise theory out of the various notions of 'unconscious mind' – and the one which most people will immediately think of upon hearing the term – is that developed by **Sigmund Freud** and his followers, which lies at the heart of psychoanalysis. Freud's concept was that the unconscious directs the thoughts and feelings of everyone. According to Freud the unconscious mind is the primitive instinctual hangover we all suffer from and which we must overcome in a healthy way in order to become fully and normally developed, i.e. not neurotic or psychotic.

Freud aside, throughout history many different ideas about the unconscious have been advanced. At the present stage, there are still fundamental disagreements within psychology about what the nature of the 'unconscious mind' might be, whereas outside formal psychology a whole world of psychological speculation has grown up in which the 'unconscious mind' is held to have any number of properties and abilities – from the innocent and child-like, to the all-perceiving, mystical and **occult**.

According to psychotherapists the unconscious is not directly accessible to ordinary introspection, but it is capable of being 'tapped' and 'interpreted' by special methods and techniques, such as random association, **dream** analysis and verbal or **Freudian slips**. It is assumed that thoughts, feelings and urges that are repressed are all present in the unconscious mind.

Psychics believe there are three levels of consciousness that play a role in psychic experiences. The conscious, the unconscious and the subconscious, also known as the **universal mind**. These three levels either work with or against each other, and each person must learn to balance the messages from all three levels of awareness. The conscious mind is in charge of reasoning, analysing and making decisions and its focus in on being objective. This isn't always easy as the conscious mind is always receiving input from the unconscious mind, which impairs its ability to remain objective.

Some psychics also believe that the unconscious mind possesses a kind of 'hidden energy' or 'potential' that can realize dreams and thoughts with minimal conscious effort or action from the individual. Some also believe that it has the power to influence and shape a person's destiny. All such claims, however, have so far failed to stand up to scientific scrutiny.

UNDERWOOD, PETER [1923–]

Respected British investigator of the **paranormal** and president of the **Ghost Club Society**.

From an early age Underwood felt drawn to the paranormal. He saw his first **apparition** at the age of nine, when he awoke to see his father (who had died a few hours earlier) before standing at the foot of the bed. Underwood joined the **Society for Psychical Research** in 1947 and in that same year was asked to join the **Ghost**

Club, where he joined forces with **Harry Price** to investigate **Borley Rectory**.

In 1960 Underwood became president of the Ghost Club and 10 years later left his publishing career to research, write and lecture about the paranormal full-time. By now he had become known as 'Britain's number one ghost hunter' and had had witnessed countless **hauntings** as well as **séances** and experiments into **ESP** and other **psychic** phenomena. In 1993 he left the Ghost Club as a result of internal conflict and the following year formed the Ghost Club Society, where he became president and chief investigator.

Throughout his career researching the paranormal Underwood has investigated hundreds of alleged hauntings. His aim has been to establish some kind of middle ground between scepticism and belief. Although he has acknowledged that the majority of hauntings can be explained naturally he believes that there are some types of **ghost** certain people can see. He defines some of the different types of ghosts as follows:

- *Elemental or primitive racial memory manifestations.*
- ***Poltergeists*** *or phenomena activated by intense emotions and trauma such as crisis apparitions.*
- *Historical ghosts associated with old, historic houses.*
- *Mental imprint manifestations, which appear to be a kind of psychic energy imprinted on the atmosphere.*
- *Time-distortion ghosts, which are replays of events from the past.*

- *Ghosts of the living, which may be a projection of a double or* ***doppelgänger***, *as in cases of* **bilocation**.
- *Haunted objects, which are associated with poltergeist phenomena.*

As well as lecturing internationally Underwood is the author of numerous books on the paranormal, ghost hunting and other subjects. His best-known titles include *Into the Occult* (1982), *The Vampire's Bedside Companion* (1975), *The Ghost Hunter's Guide* (1985), *Dictionary of the Supernatural* (1978), *Exorcism* (1990) and *Death in Hollywood* (1993).

UNDERWORLD

In the study of mythology and religion, the underworld is a generic term approximately equivalent to the lay term **afterlife**, referring to any place to which newly dead **souls** go.

UNDINE

The undine is said to be a beautiful, ghostly female **spirit** that wanders stretches of water in many European countries. The **ghosts** are believed to be those of young women who died by drowning, often having committed suicide as a result of a broken love affair. Although they are tragic figures they are said to mean no harm to anyone – except ungrateful lovers.

UNICORN

Mythical creature in folklore. It appears as a white horse with a single horn protruding from its forehead. In many **pagan** religions the unicorn is a divine creature belonging to the moon goddess.

The unicorn is a potent **symbol** of purity and it was thought no one could tame this fierce beast except those with an honest heart. The horn of a unicorn was believed to have magical, purifying and healing qualities.

UNIVERSAL LIFE FORCE/ ENERGY

Universal energy or vital force that is thought to transcend time and space, permeate all things and upon which all things depend for health and life.

Since ancient times the existence of a life force has been universally acknowledged and different cultures and belief systems give it different names, many of which are listed below. Whatever it is called, however, the characteristics of the life force remain the same. In some systems it can be controlled and manipulated for improved health, healing and happiness.

Prana

In Hindu **Yoga**, Prana is a life force associated with breathing that is absorbed into and used by the human body to maintain health and wellbeing. The control of prana plays an important role in Hindu magic and healing, as well as yoga.

Prana is the energy that the **soul** uses. It may be regarded as the soul of force and energy in all forms. It is the principle that causes activity and accompanies life. Prana is in the air, but it is not the air, or even one of its chemical constituents. Prana is taken up by our physical system along with oxygen, yet it is not oxygen. All one can say is that Prana is the One Force, penetrating where the air cannot reach, all pervading, the Spirit of the Breath of Life. In short Prana is believed to be the essence of all life forms and things, including inanimate objects.

While Prana permeates all things it is believed to be more concentrated at the tops of mountains and near running water. It occurs naturally in the atmosphere and is believed to be absorbed into the body by a series of subtle energy centres known as **chakras**.

It is thought that healthy people have plenty of Prana but sick people are depleted in it. It may be transferred by a healthy person to a sick person by the **laying on of hands**. The aim of Hatha Yoga is to direct the flow of Pranic energy to promote health and fitness. Prana is not breath but it is manifested in breath and the control of the flow of breathing (*pranayama*) is central to yoga. *Pranayama* is also thought to control the mind, which in turn controls Prana. During life the mind keeps Prana within the body, but when death occurs both mind and Prana leave the body.

In **Tantric** yoga Prana is used to raise latent **psychic** powers, called **siddhis**. In Hindu magic Prana is the energy source

Prana breathing exercise

According to *Pranayama* experts, Prana comes to us in its freest state in the air we breathe. It is therefore easy to see that it is a comparatively simple thing to keep ourselves charged with Prana, the basic force of all life, when we have learned to breathe correctly.

Do this practice twice a day, for a period of five minutes.

Through both nostrils, breathe in and out to a count of four. Close your right nostril; breathe in through the left nostril to a count of four. Close your left nostril and breathe out, completely, through your right nostril, keeping the left nostril closed to a count of four.

Keeping the left nostril closed, breathe in through the right nostril to a count of four. Close your right nostril and breathe out, completely, through your left nostril, keeping the right nostril closed to a count of four.

As you progress increase the counts for inhalation and exhalation.

---

for all magical feats. Magicians use Prana to energize the will and imagination, which are believed to be the keys to genuine magic.

Qi or Chi

Qi, also known as chi, literally means breath or gas or ether. It was developed as an **esoteric** principle and regarded as the source of health, harmony, creativity and courage by ancient Chinese philosophers, who conceived of it as a dualistic principle that later evolved into the negative/positive polarities of **yin** and **yang**. Yin and yang are said to be in constant ebb and flow and for optimum health they must be in balance. Qi courses through the body in 12 meridians connected to the internal organs. The flow of Qi can be enhanced by the manipulation of points along the meridians (see **acupuncture**).

All living things are believed to be in a constant energy exchange with Qi and if it is depleted illness results. If the exchange ceases death occurs. Qi is received through breath, food and from the environment in general. Unfortunately our ability to absorb it decreases with age.

Control and manipulation of Qi is also part of Chinese **Yoga** and some branches of the **martial arts**. In **Tai Chi,** for example, Qi is controlled through breathing to bring mind and body into balance.

Ki

The Japanese for Qi. The esoteric principle of Qi was introduced into Japan in the Nara period (AD 710–794) and absorbed into

Qi breathing exercise

The Chinese believe it is the disruption of the flow of Qi within the body that causes many diseases, and that re-establishing Qi flows can bring about an upturn in our wellbeing. It is thought that deeper, steady breathing increases the amount of oxygen the body can use to burn out disease, and the amount of chi the body can use, for health and spiritual matters.

A word of caution: be very mindful when performing this yoga breathing exercise and return to normal breathing if you feel light-headed, dizzy or faint. Unless stated all inhalations and exhalations should be through your nostrils – this allows the body greater control over respiration.

Lie down, totally flat, on a comfortable surface. Relax for a second or two. Now breathe in deeply through your nose. Push your belly up while taking the air inside. Stick your chin on your chest and watch your belly rise. When you've taken in as much air as you can hold, stop and hold your breath. Try holding it for 10 or 20 seconds. Breathe out slowly and completely.

You'll probably find this feels strange at first but keep practising. It will take a while to get used to how deep breathing feels. Close your eyes and sense the rhythm of the deep breath you're taking. You will find this relaxing and energizing.

Shinto beliefs about nature. Concepts of Ki began to change with the rise of the Samuri class when Ki became part of the warrior's code of discipline, willpower and courage, when conserving energy and prolonged breathing were considered a matter of life and death. These principles of power breath have carried over into and remained a key part of modern-day martial arts.

Mana

Term used by native Polynesian and Melanesian cultures to describe the energy of the universe, the life force that is inherent in all living things and all matter. It also forms part of their beliefs about the spirit world – that the Mana of someone who has died or the powers of a sacred object can be transmitted to someone else for their magical use. Mana is also thought to flow through the human body in a figure-of-eight pattern and can be manipulated through breathing and **visualization** exercises.

Od

German chemist Baron Karl von Reichenbach (1788–1869) used the term 'Od' to describe a substance that he believed emanated from all things in the universe. According to Reichenbach, Od can be seen and sensed by **clairvoyants**. He also believed it could be affected by breath. Reichenbach's Od theory is important because it was the first attempt by a scientist to put forward a case for the universal life force, by conducting numerous experiments with **sensitives**.

Reichenbach published his research in 1845, but it was rejected by the scientific establishment. One of the first tasks of the **Society for Psychical Research** was to study and later validate many of Reichenbach's conclusions. Despite this Reichenbach and his work continued to be shunned by the scientific community.

Orgone

See **Orgone energy**.

Bioenergy

Eastern European concept of the universal life force which permeates all things and which can be controlled and directed at will. The term was borrowed from **William Reich**, who was probably the first to use it to describe life energy within the body and the universe.

Bioenergy is believed to radiate from human bodies and is strongly associated with psychic phenomena. It is unclear as to whether this force is created within the body or drawn from outside. Eastern European researchers have studied Bioenergy with great interest in the hope that they might be able to store the energy in generators.

UNIVERSAL MIND

Psychics believe there are three levels of consciousness that play a role in psychic experiences: the **conscious,** the **unconscious** and the universal or higher mind, also known as the subconscious.

The universal mind is believed to be the place where spontaneous insights or **intuition** come from. According to psychics it acts as an internal guidance system or a **higher self**, which helps keep a person in line with their life purpose.

UPANISHADS

Esoteric texts of Hindu philosophy, believed to have been written between the eighth and seventh centuries BC, which reflect on the mysteries of death and the oneness of the universe. The Upanishads lay the foundations for **meditation** techniques and ideas later developed in Buddhism and Hinduism. The term 'Upanishad' derives from the Sanskrit words *upa* (near), *ni* (down) and *ṣad* (to sit): thus 'sitting down near' a spiritual teacher to receive instruction.

Due to their mystic nature and intense philosophical bent, which does away with all ritual and completely embraces the principle of oneness, the Upanishads have a universal feel. There are over 100 treatises in the Upanishads, which cover the four stages of **consciousness**: waking, sleeping, dreaming and higher consciousness. To reach the last stage – higher consciousness

– is the goal for all spiritual seekers, as it is only there that one can gain true self-awareness and transcendence over the self. A distinctive quotation that is indicative of the call to self-realization is as follows:

Get up! Wake up! Seek the guidance of an
Illumined teacher and realize the Self.
Sharp like a razor's edge is the path,
The sages say, difficult to traverse.
(*Death instructing Nachiketa in the Katha*
(*Word*) *Upanishad*)

URBAN MYTH

Term used to describe a strange but supposedly real event that happened to a friend of a friend, and so the legend grew. Typically there is some truth to the story but fictional elements are added with the retelling. The central theme or image remains the same but details differ from region to region. With the expansion of the media in the form of books, newspapers, magazines, radio and television reports and the Internet, whole new avenues have been opened for the spread of urban myths. Some **hauntings**, such as the **Phantom hitchhiker** scenario or stories involving a **faceless woman**, are urban myths.

UROMANCY

Also known as urimancy. **Divination** by observation of urine, either by its colour, by its taste, by its flow patterns or the patterns formed when it hits the ground or in a swirling bowl.

The ancient Romans practised uromancy by looking for bubbles in the chamberpot after passing water. If any were present it would mean that one would soon receive a very large sum of money. Uromancy was also used by witch-hunters in the seventeenth century. A common practice was to place iron nails, pins, needles or half horseshoes in a bottle filled with the urine of the accused person, and then stop it up with a cork. If the cork popped out of the bottle of its own accord, it was taken as a sign of guilt.

The use of urine as a therapeutic substance, either by drinking it or bathing skin and wounds in it, is an ancient therapy that dates back to 1500 BC, when the Egyptians used it to cleanse burns. Ayurvedic scriptures dating back to 1000 BC also suggest the use of urine for poultices. Research has shown that urine therapy may not be as disgusting or as unhealthy as one might think. Urea, which is found in urine, is salty and when applied to a wound or sore skin it creates pressure that sucks water out of the area. This has an antiseptic effect on open wounds. The high levels of melatonin in urine also give it a sedative and antiviral effect that may help fight infections. Some people believe it is also a good cosmetic tonic for the skin.

US Capitol Building

Headquarters of the Congress of the United States in Washington, DC, which is said to be haunted by numerous **ghosts**.

The Capitol has been occupied since 1800 and stories about ghosts are as old as the building itself. Just some of the many restless entities *alleged* to haunting the Capitol are detailed below.

The French engineer Pierre Charles L'Enfant was commissioned by President Washington to design the new capital city; his plans included streets that were 100 feet wide, and an avenue 400 feet wide and a mile long. L'Enfant demolished a new manor house because it blocked the view, which led to Washington firing him. Congress refused to pay him for the work that had already been done. Consequently, the **apparition** of Monsieur L'Enfant has been seen pacing the cavernous Capitol halls, still awaiting payment for his bill, now over 200 years overdue.

This ghost is described as a 'sad little man', dressed in eighteenth-century attire, who scurries along the corridors of the Capitol Building with many papers stuffed under his arm, which were probably his city plans. It has been reported that whenever a street change is proposed, his ghost moans and cries as he hurries along the corridors.

The glowing ghost of John Quincy Adams has been seen in the grand hall that was formerly the House of Representatives Chamber, at the exact spot where his desk used to be located. He collapsed at his desk and died in a room off this grand hall before he could give a speech honouring the military leaders responsible for the victory in the Mexican-American War – a conflict that Adams had been against from the outset.

Kentucky Representative William Preston Taulbee is said to remain in the Capitol to continue a feud with the press that did not end when a reporter, Charles Kincaid, shot him on the steps to the House Press Gallery on 28 February 1890. He died of his wounds 11 days later. Stains on the steps leading to the House Press Gallery are said to be bloodstains from Taulbee.

Charles Guiteau, who fatally shot President James Garfield on 2 July 1881, has been seen at a doorway leading to a basement, while the easily recognized ghostly form of General John Alexander has been known to appear at 12.30 am, looking displeased, while listening at the door of the room once used by the Senate Committee on Military and Militia, a committee that he once chaired in the 1890s. He is described as having a long moustache, with dark, piercing eyes, and long black hair.

A ghost of a custodian, who died at work, has been known to help living employees do their job. A mop was seen swishing back and forth over the marble floors, being pushed by this unseen entity.

Finally, a **demon** cat appears and scares late-night workers who have to go to the deep, dark parts of the basement of the Capitol Building. These frightening appearances usually take place before a national tragedy happens and when administrations change. It is first seen as a normal, black cat, which purrs happily as it approaches the unsuspecting human victim in the dimly lit hallway. As this **apparition** comes closer, though, its body swells to the size of a tiger, and the sweet purring turns into a vicious snarl. With its claws extended, this huge cat leaps at the poor person and then vanishes into thin air, leaving the person terrified, but unhurt.

Utukku

Name given by the ancient Assyrians to the **ghost** of evil intentions that lay in wait for unsuspecting travellers and could make anyone it encountered fall ill.

Records suggest that the Assyrians were one of the first people to think about ghosts seriously. They believed that ghosts were the result of leaving bodies unburied or failing to observe the proper rites when a person died. Apart from the Utukku the Assyrians had names for two other malevolent entities that plagued them: the alu and the ekimmu. The alu, a hideous-looking **phantom** that attempted to suffocate its victims, and the ekimmu would appear outside a house to give warning of an impending death. All three spirits made dreadful wailing sounds and to hear their cries was believed to be as ominous as seeing the phantom themselves.

V

Vampire

The undead. A vampire is either the living dead – a resurrected corpse – or the **ghost** of a corpse that leaves its grave at night and enters the world of the living, feeding off them to survive. Some cultures have myths of non-human vampires, such as **demons** or animals like bats, dogs and spiders. Vampires are often described as having a wide variety of additional powers and character traits and are a frequent subject of folklore, cinema and contemporary fiction.

The term 'vampire' entered the English language in 1732 and was handed down by German and French accounts of vampire **superstitions** in Eastern Europe. In the Balkans a vampire cult flourished in the Middle Ages. Vampires were suspected of haunting a graveyard when people reported sightings of **apparitions** of the dead that pestered and bit them, or sat on their chests and suffocated them at night. Vampires were also frequently blamed for wasting diseases that caused death, and for invisible terrors. A search of the graves was made and if a body was found with signs of fresh blood or recent movement it was declared a vampire and was burned or a stake was plunged through the heart. Such measures were universally employed to keep ghosts and vampires from leaving their graves.

Premature burial is a sound natural explanation for corpses that look like they have moved or started to bleed. For example, it is now known that corpses can shift and this may have given the appearance of life when a coffin was opened. It may also make strange noises as air is expelled and blood may still ooze from wounds or orifices.

Despite its early depiction as a revolting, blood sucking and disfigured corpse that roams graveyards at night, over the centuries the vampire has been glamourized, sexualized and popularized by Western ficiton, poetry and film into a fatally attractive and seductive living person who bites people on the neck to drink their blood – a practice popularly described as **vampirism**.

Vampire ghosts

A distinctly different form of the **vampire**, these **spirits** have been recorded in the histories of several European countries, as well as India, where traditions surrounding this spirit type are very prevalent. These spirits are generally regarded as invisible entities that occasionally attack human beings, leaving behind a characteristic bite mark in the flesh.

Vampirism

The practice of drinking blood. In folklore and popular culture the term generally refers to a belief that one can gain **supernatural** powers by drinking human blood. The historical practice of vampirism can generally be considered a more specific and less commonly occurring form of

Vampires in popular culture

Bram Stoker's *Dracula* has been the best-known description of the vampire in popular fiction for the last century. Its portrayal of vampirism as a disease (contagious demonic possession), with its undertones of sex, blood and death, struck a chord in a Victorian England where contagious disease, sexual repression and a preocupation with the afterlife were common.

It was, however, the flamboyant poet Lord Byron who first introduced many common elements of the vampire theme to Western literature in his epic poem the *Giaour* (1813). These include the combination of horror and lust that the vampire feels and the concept of the undead passing its inheritance to the living:

But thou, false Infidel! shalt writhe
Beneath avenging Monkir's scythe;
And from its torment 'scape alone
To wander round lost Eblis' throne;
And fire unquenched, unquenchable,
Around, within, thy heart shall dwell;
Nor ear can hear nor tongue can tell
The tortures of that inward hell!
But first, on earth as vampire sent,
Thy corpse shall from its tomb be rent:
Then ghastly haunt thy native place,
And suck the blood of all thy race;

There from thy daughter, sister, wife,
At midnight drain the stream of life;
Yet loathe the banquet which perforce
Must feed thy livid living corpse:
Thy victims ere they yet expire
Shall know the demon for their sire,
As cursing thee, thou cursing them,
Thy flowers are withered on the stem.

Curiously Byron's own wild life became the model for the protagonist in the first ever vampire novel, *The Vampyre* (1819) by John William Polidori. Polidori's protagonist, Lord Ruthven, resembles modern interpretations of a vampire as an undead being with superior intellect and charm, whereas previously the vampire of folklore had been characterized as an ugly, repellent and revolting creature.

Stoker's classic 1897 depiction of the vampire, however, remains the most well-known today. *Dracula* has all the now familiar themes of sex and wealth, as well as frequent use of Gothic settings and iconography and the vampire's aversion to sunlight and crosses. The book has been the inspiration for numerous authors and film makers. The most recent descendants of the vampire tradition in twenty-first-century literature are the popular Vampire novels written by Anne Rice.

cannibalism. The consumption of another's blood has also been used as a tactic of psychological warfare intended to terrorize the enemy.

VANISHING HITCHHIKER

See **Phantom hitchhiker**.

VEDAS

Four texts, written somewhere between 1800 and 1200 BC, which constitute the beginnings of Indian philosophy and the Hindu canon. Each text covers a different subject and tells the story of the creation of the universe. The four texts are the *Rig Veda*, which discusses religious **consciousness**; the *Sama Veda*, which is a collection of **chants** and **mantras**; the *Yajur-Veda*, which contains rituals and **prayers**; and the *Atharva-Veda*, which consists of **spells** and sacrifices and forms the basis of Indian or **Ayurvedic medicine**.

VEDIC ASTROLOGY

Form of **astrology** practised in Indian culture. Vedic astrology is steeped in the philosophy of the **Vedas**. It differs from Western astrology as it uses fixed star (sidereal) constellations in conjunctions with planets to determine a **horoscope**, as opposed to the tropical system used in the West. It is based on the true celestial position of the constellation and takes into account the precession of the equinoxes; this means that everyone's birth sign moves back a month (Leos become Cancers, etc.). Vedic astrologers believe that the standard sun sign and aspects give a person's general qualities but the fixed constellations supply particular details of character.

Vedic horoscopes indicate a person's spiritual destiny. The Hindu culture believes in **reincarnation** and if a person chooses to follow their spiritual destiny they will be closer to escaping the endless cycle of death and rebirth.

VERSAILLES GHOSTS

The story of two academic English lady tourists who allegedly saw a whole group of **ghosts** in the gardens of the Trianon near Versailles is widely regarded as one of the most famous **hauntings** of the twentieth century.

On 10 August 1901, Eleanor Jourdain, the daughter of a Derbyshire vicar, and Annie Moberly, the daughter of the Bishop of Salisbury, were on their way to looked at the Petit Trianon after walking round the Palace of Versailles. The ladies were keen to visit the Trianon as they knew it had been a little retreat that Louis XVI had created for his queen, Marie Antoinette, as a place for her to relax with her courtiers.

According to later accounts the ladies seemed to get lost for a while. Upon finding the garden and entering it Moberly suddenly felt a strange and rather depressing atmosphere around them. The women saw a couple of men whom they mistook for gardeners, dressed in period costumes of grey-green coats and small three-cornered hats. They asked for directions and were told to continue straight ahead. They saw a bridge and a kiosk and near the kiosk an unpleasant-looking man sat with a slouched hat and cloak. A man with an odd accent ran up behind them and gave them further directions to the house. Near the house, in the English garden in front of the Petit Trianon, Moberly saw a woman wearing a pale green fichu sitting on a seat in the garden. Both women then saw a young man who came out of the house banging the door behind him. He looked amused about something. Puzzled the two women walked on and were soon conscious of another change in atmosphere, back to the normal humidity of an August afternoon.

Later, while discussing their experiences, the two women came to the incredible conclusion that they had stepped back into time to the year 1789 and actually mingled with ladies and gentlemen of the court of Marie Antoinette! Moberly was also convinced that the lady in the gardens was the queen herself, who reputedly liked to sit at that spot. They recalled that though a breeze had been blowing when they started their walk, the air had been 'intensely still' when they arrived at the Petit Trianon and there had been no effects of light or shade. Moberly later said that

she felt as if she was walking in her sleep, 'the heavy dreaminess was oppressive'.

Over the next 10 years Moberly and Jourdain revisited the Petit Trianon several times in an attempt to understand the mystery. On her second visit, on 2 January 1902, Jourdain again encountered the heavy eerie feeling they had experienced before, and thought she saw two labourers dressed in tunics and capes with pointed hoods loading sticks into a cart. When Moberly returned for the second time on 4 July 1904, accompanied by Jourdain, they could not find the route they had taken in 1901 or the bridge and kiosk they had seen. Where the lady on the grass had been seen they found instead an enormous rhododendron bush, many years old, and the door of the house the young man had banged was in fact the ruins of an old chapel.

In 1911 the ladies published their experience in a book, *An Adventure*. Critics from the psychical research community derided them immediately for their amateurish and unreliable research. They had not written down their experiences until November 1901, too long a time for the memory to be certain, and there did not seem to be sufficient grounds to prove a **paranormal** experience. It was suggested that Moberly and Jourdain had seen real persons and things and the details had been altered by tricks of the memory when they decided they had seen ghosts.

Despite widespread criticism *An Adventure* received a lot of publicity and it wasn't long before other people came forward claiming to have had similar experiences at the Trianon. John Crooke from England reported that in July 1908, when he had visited Versailles with his wife and son, he had seen a fair-haired lady in a cream-coloured hat and a white fichu sketching on a piece of paper. The lady paid no attention to Crooke as he passed by her and immediately Crooke believed that she was a ghost as she seemed to grow out of and fade into the scenery. However, critics were quick to point out that Crooke has only come forward with his story after *An Adventure* had been published.

A number of other ghostly reports surfaced from visits to the Trianon. In October 1928 two English women, Ann Lambert and Claire Burrow, also allegedly saw men and women dressed in period costume. In September 1938 Elizabeth Hatton claimed that she saw a man and woman in period peasant dress drawing a wooden trundle cart bearing logs. On 10 October 1949, Jack and Clara Wilkinson allegedly saw a woman in period dress with a parasol. And on 21 May 1955, a London solicitor and his wife claimed to have felt a heavy, oppressive atmosphere as they headed towards the Trianon. They then saw coming towards them an elegant man and a woman in full period costume. Suddenly they noticed that the man and woman had vanished seemingly into thin air – there was nowhere else for them to have gone.

The **Society for Psychical Research** investigated all these reports of ghostly sightings thoroughly. Sceptics were keen to point out that from the standpoint of evidence it was impossible to ascertain later who exactly was in the park and what they might have chosen to wear. Others were more inclined to believe that the hauntings were genuine and a high number of consistencies with the account of Moberly and Jourdain and historical fact were found.

In 1965 an explanation was put forward by Philippe Jullian in his book *Un Prince 1900 – Robert de Montesquiou*. According to Jullian, Montesquiou was in the habit of spending days in the park in period costume at the turn of the century and Moberly and Jourdain had simply witnessed an outdoor party. The matter has, however, not ended and more hauntings have since been reported and investigated by both English and French researchers. It has been suggested that the haunting fits into the pattern of a so-called 'aimless haunting', as the paranormal phenomena reported do not seem to be associated with traumatic or violent events as many hauntings are. Life at Versailles just before the French Revolution was fairly peaceful and it is possible that the area gained great emotional power as its inhabitants may have sensed that an era was drawing to a close. The mystery of Versailles continues.

Vetala

In Indian lore the vetala are not **spirits** of the dead, but spirits that are believed to possess corpses. It lurks in cemeteries, snagging fresh bodies for reanimation. It turns the hands and feet backwards, delighting in the shock value of its appearance. Vetala love to tease the living, but if they feel so inclined they may also guard their villages.

In some respect the vetala resembles the **vampire**, but it is distinct from more traditional vampires in that it can reside by day in the corpses of others, whereas traditional vampires tend to shun the daylight.

VIBRATIONAL HEALING

According to the ancient sages, who understood the workings of the **universal life force**, we are all born with a certain amount of this energy that flows through us. When this energy is flowing smoothly all is well but when it is not every aspect of our life can become out of balance. Understanding and working with this energy is thought to be a big step towards creating happy, fulfilled and healthy lives. Many alternative healers, some of whom are called energy healers, work with this energy. Some see it (a form of **clairvoyance**), others feel it (**clairsentience**). The field of energy is referred to as an **aura** – a vibrating field of energy that pulses around and through the body at all times.

Vibrational healers work with the auric field and focus on repairing, balancing, charging and clearing the energy field on many levels: physical, emotional, mental and spiritual. Whether their healing or **energy balancing** involves the **laying on of hands**, healing touch or faith healing they all involve the idea that the healer and patient are somehow connected on a higher vibrational plane, possibly **psychic**, that

opens an inflow of healing energy to the patient.

VINGOE FIRE

A curious, ghostly phenomenon reported to occur before the death of members of the Vingoe family, who once held the Treville estate in Cornwall, England. The phenomenon is said to appear first as a shimmering light, which gradually takes on the appearance of spurts of flame, gradually growing larger in size. In some cases the flames were reported to be so bright they were said to temporarily blind witnesses. They would also sometimes appear as multiple flames linking together into a ring or circular chain, often accompanied by 'strange and appalling noises'.

VIRGINIA, THE GHOST STATE

Virginia is said to be America's most haunted state, and the town of Fredericksburg in Virginia is thought to be one of the most ghost-ridden places in the United States. The explanation most often offered for this is that many famous people, such as George Washington and James Monroe (President from 1817 to 1825), lived there and haunt the area. The best known of all the **ghosts** is the so-called Lady in White, who is believed to haunt eighteenth-century Chatham Manor. This ghost is said to be the spirit of a young woman who was unlucky in love and who returns every seven years on the anniversary of her death on 21 June. Her next scheduled visit is in 2010.

Fort Monroe, built in 1609, and the longest manned army post in America is also believed to be haunted by a number of ghosts, including those of **Abraham Lincoln**, Edgar Allan Poe and Jefferson Davis, who was president of the confederacy. Virginia cannot claim to be America's most haunted city, however, as that honour goes to New Orleans, which has around 25 regularly reported ghosts, most of which appear in the atmospheric old French quarter.

Vision

A religious **apparition** or a vivid episode of **clairvoyance**.

Visions generally have more clarity than **dreams**, but traditionally fewer psychological connotations. In religion, visions typically comprise of renderings of a future state and/or of a mythical being, and are believed (by followers of the religion) to come from a divine source to inspire or prod the recipient as part of a revelation or an epiphany. Many mystics take the word vision to be synonymous with apparition.

Vision quest

A Native North American ritual where wisdom is sought by provoking a visionary **trance** in order to commune with **spirit guides** for **supernatural** wisdom and power. It is typically undertaken by young men on the brink of manhood and the vision quest is considered to be a powerful force in the maturation process that aims to provide a focus and sense of personal power. Before the quest the seeker is expected to spend a number of days or weeks purifying himself through fasting or sweat baths. Usually the seeker is assisted and guided in preparations by a tribal elder. The seeker then isolates himself in a place of natural power, such as the wilderness or forest, in a small tent he has constructed and will neither eat nor sleep until his task is completed. He will pray for a message from the Great Spirit and a **talisman** to represent the message or **vision** of power conferred, such as a feather, rock or flower. This may be given to the seeker from his spirit guide, who typically will appear in the form of an animal.

Visualization

Technique that uses mental images and **affirmations** to produce positive change within a person. It is thought that the ability to make pictures in the mind can lead to an improved self-image, a greater sense of purpose, better health and can help a person obtain other personal goals.

Visualization

The technique for visualization is simple. First, find a quiet place where you can relax and concentrate. Then construct a detailed mental picture of whatever situation you want to change and/or improve. Then imagine the desired outcome. Think of this outcome as if it were already happening. You may also choose to repeat a positive phrase or affirmation that you will attain your goal. The technique should be repeated for days, weeks, months or years until the goal is achieved.

One simple visualization for general wellbeing and stress-reduction is to first quiet yourself and, after taking some deep breaths, to visualize yourself inhaling golden or white light/energy, and exhaling grey, stale, old energy. The white or golden light represents new, fresh, rejuvenating energy, while the grey energy represents any stress, unhappiness, worries, anger or other negative emotions you may be holding inside you. This visualization is a great way to release the stress and tension of the day and give yourself more energy.

If you have a specific ailment you are trying to relieve yourself of, visualize the same white or golden energy surrounding the area of your body that is in need of healing. Focus on that white or golden light/energy healing and energizing that area of your body. Try to repeat this procedure daily or multiple times daily if you feel compelled to do so. As always, do what feels right for you.

Visualization has formed a part of religious practices for centuries but it only became popular in the West when Shakti Gawain published *Creative Visualisation* in 1977. Gawain's belief that people can use their **imagination** to help them achieve life goals soon spread beyond **esoteric** circles into mainstream culture.

Solid research has shown that visualization works. The scientists aren't sure why but those who study the effect of the mind on health have found visualization to be particularly beneficial in fighting certain diseases. A particular form of visualization, called **guided imagery**, is increasingly being used in psychotherapy and medicine, especially for treating people suffering from stress, anxiety and/or life-threatening illnesses.

VITAL FORCE

Alternative term for **universal life force**.

VITALISM

The theory that vital forces are active in living organisms, and the strength of these vital forces determines health and well-being. Some believers in vitalism equate this element with the **soul**.

Vitalism has a long history in medical philosophy. Most ancient healing practices posited that disease was the result of some imbalance in the vital energies which distinguish living from non-living matter. For example, in Eastern traditions these vital forces were presented as Qi, Prana, etc. (see **universal life force**).

Over the centuries chemical and anatomical discoveries gradually pushed aside the vital force explanation for poor health, as more and more life processes came to be described in purely scientific terms, and explanations for disease focused more and more on the failure of particular organs and processes in the body. Vitalism in medicine did, however, experience a resurgence in the late twentieth century, when attention began to be directed towards preventative medicine and the role played by an individual's state of mind. Modern medical vitalism, as represented by such schools as **homeopathy, acupuncture**, and chiropractics, tends to emphasize this role in both the cause and treatment of diseases.

In terms of the biology of the cell itself, a return to vitalism may be seen in the theory of intelligent design; and the **holistic** idea that life and health are emergent and evolving processes involving mind, body and spirit, which cannot be accurately described simply by understanding any number of chemical processes that occur in the cell.

VOICES, HEARING

See **Clairaudience**.

VOODOO

Magical tradition practised in Haitian and African communities in the Caribbean and Southern United States, which combines Roman Catholic religious traditions with African magical rites. Although Voodoo is specific to Haiti and the Southern US, offshoots and related cults appear all over the world. It is estimated that currently Voodoo has around 50 million followers worldwide.

Voodoo, also known as Voodun, is a product of the slave trade. The African slaves transported to North and South America were forbidden to practise their religion and their masters baptised them as Catholics. As a result Voodoo became a mixture of Catholicism superimposed upon secret native beliefs and rites and some say this is the reason for the ferocious anger at the heart of the religion. Tribal deities took on the form of Catholic saints. **Fetishes** were replaced by Catholic statues, candles and holy relics.

Animal sacrifices, spirit **possession**, **black magic**, sexual magic and shamanic trances are common features of this religion, although some sects do practise **white magic**. Voodoo priests are said to have **supernatural** powers, including the power to raise **zombies** from the dead to do their bidding.

One of the most terrifying and well-known Voodoo magic **spell** is for the voodoo practitioner to make a small doll or puppet in the shape of the person they wish to **curse**. The doll is then tortured and abused with the intention of transferring that pain and harm to the person. It's likely that this voodoo doll is something slaves assimilated from their masters, rather than the other way round, as 'puppet magic' has been practised in European cultures for a long time.

VORTEX

A ghost-hunting term that is applied to photographic anomalies which display a spiral motion, and which is sometimes thought to be indicative of a **spirit** form. The term is also sometimes used to describe a portal between worlds or a site that seemingly draws in energy towards its centre with a spiral motion.

W

Waite, Arthur [1857–1942]

Victorian magician associated with the **Golden Dawn** whose most lasting effect on the **occult** community was to produce the Rider Waite **Tarot** deck, which has since become the most popular tarot card deck in the world.

Born in Brooklyn, America, in 1857, Waite was brought to England by his mother while he was still a baby. Despite living close to poverty Waite had a good education at Roman Catholic schools in London. When he left school he became a clerk and in his spare time he spent long hours in the British Museum reading room studying the occult.

Waite's thinking was heavily influenced by the **spiritualist** movement and by the writings of **Madame Blavatsky**. He entered the Order of the **Golden Dawn** and passed through the grades of the first order, but then resigned due to internal conflicts. A few years later he rejoined and entered the second order, rewriting its body of ceremonial from the viewpoint of Christian **mysticism**. Later his interest turned towards **Freemasonry**, where he attempted to chart a secret tradition underlying various aspects of occultism. He wrote numerous books and poems, which have largely been forgotten mainly due to his scholarly, tedious and at times pompous style. The Rider Waite Tarot deck he produced in collaboration with the artistic talents of Pamela Colman Smith has, however, stood the test of time and remains to this day the most well known and used tarot deck.

Walpurgis Night

Throughout Europe, 30 April is known as *Walpurgis nacht* and it is the night when **ghosts**, **witches** and the **spirits** of darkness are said to be on the loose. The night was named after St Walpurga, who is regarded as the protector of humanity against **black magic**. Walpurga was actually the daughter of the Saxon King Richard who went to Germany over 1,200 years ago. While there she gave her support to the campaign against demonism and her efforts were thought to be so impressive that she was made Abbess of Heidenham. In about the year 777 she was canonized.

Wand

Traditional tool used in magic to help control the energies of a **spell** and send it in the direction that the wand is pointed. In **Wicca** and modern-day **witchcraft**, practitioners use wands to channel energy.

The wand represents the **air** element and is typically made from the wood of living trees. Hazel or elder are considered the best types of wood to use, but willow wands are said to be good for working with the energies of the moon, ash for prosperity spells, oak for strength, apple for binding love spells and rowan for healing and protection spells. If a **crystal** is placed on the top of the wand, it is said to have the effect of intensifying the directional power of the tool. Practitioners usually get a stick from a tree, or even buy wood from a hardware store, and then carve it and add decorations to personalize it; however, one can also purchase ready-made wands.

WATER

One of the four natural **elements** used in **pagan** rituals and magic. In **Wicca** a water **elemental** is one of the four **spirits** that energizes a **spell** and brings its wishes into being. Water is a **symbol** for the female principle – the moon goddess, **intuition**, emotion, love, relationships and the natural cycles of birth, death and rebirth. The magical tool associated with the water element is the cauldron or chalice. Its **colour** is blue and it is associated with the **zodiac** signs of Cancer, Scorpio and Pisces. In Chinese philosophy water represents the deep hidden characteristics of a person. Hearing in general is also associated with this element. Water flows deep and water people tend to be thinkers.

WATSEKA WONDER

Case of spirit **possession** that is considered unusual by parapsychologists because it was for the victim's benefit and not harm. It is also thought to be one of the best cases on record of apparent spirit possession as **reincarnation**.

Mary Roff was a young girl of 18 who lived in Watseka, Illinois, in the nineteenth century. For many years she had suffered fits of depression and self harm. In July 1864, after cutting herself with a knife, she fainted and woke up with **psychic** powers that included **clairvoyance**. This state of heightened reality continued for five days and then Roff died.

Mary Lurancy Vennum, a neighbour but stranger to the Roffs, was three-months old when Roff died. Thirteen years later, in 1877, she appeared to go mad. She experienced **visions** of **angels** and **spirits** of the dead and her physician, Dr E W Stevens, diagnosed **spirit attachment**/obsession when Vennum revealed under **hypnosis** that she felt controlled by evil spirits.

Stevens suggested that one of the spirits might be able to help Vennum control the others and she answered that Mary Roff was willing to do this. On 1 February 1878, the spirit of Roff took possession of Vennum and for the next four months took over Vennum's life for the purposes of healing her. Vennum moved to the Roff home and generally lived as Roff had done 13 years before. She also demonstrated clairvoyant powers and had **out-of-body experiences**. On 21 May, Roff's spirit told her family that Vennum was coming back and said goodbye, before Vennum fell into a **trance**. After a few minutes she became Vennum again and was completely healed, mentally and physically, after supposedly having been protected from evil spirits by Roff's inhabitation.

In 1882 Vennum married a farmer and moved to Rawlings County, Kansas. Over the years Roff's spirit continued to watch over her, taking control from time to time by causing Vennum to go into a trance;

during childbirth, for example, she protected her from pain. Vennum did mention that Roff gave her information clairvoyantly but she never developed her **mediumship** due to her family's disapproval. She died in the late 1940s.

WEIR, THOMAS [1600–1670]

Major Thomas Weir was a respected and influential citizen of Edinburgh but close to his 70th birthday he announced that he and his sister, Jean, had long practised **black magic**, incest and sexual crimes. At first nobody believed that such model citizens could be capable of such evil, but the Weirs insisted they were servants of the devil.

The Weirs were charged with sexual crimes and were brought to trial. Doctors and clergy tried to help but the Weirs remained contemptuous of everyone. They were convicted of adultery, incest, fornication and bestiality and were executed in April 1670. Thomas Weir was strangled and burned and Jean was hanged.

Following their deaths reports soon began to circulate of Thomas Weir's cloaked **ghost** appearing, clutching the magical staff that was said to run before him in the streets to clear the way when he was alive. At Bow House where the Weirs used to live a spectral coach was allegedly seen arriving to drive the Weirs to hell. Because of its reputation for being haunted the house remained empty for a hundred years until the low rent encouraged an eld-

erly couple to move in. The first night they stayed they interpreted a calf staring at them through the window as a **death omen** and left immediately. No one else ever lived there again.

In 1830 the house, in ruins through neglect, was demolished. Its site is unknown but to this day it is said that the Major's staff can still be heard tapping at Grassmarket in Edinburgh.

WELL

According to folklore wells are believed to be entry points for **ghosts** and **spirits** to enter the material world, and if a home or building is built on top of a well it is more likely to be haunted. Covering the well is no solution as it will simply infuriate the spirits and they will clank about looking for another entry point.

The water in wells has a long history of superstitious belief. Water spirits and monsters and other creatures are believed to be the guardians of well waters, hence the custom of propitiating the spirits by throwing in gifts and coins. Water is also believed to have spiritually cleansing properties and evil things cannot cross running water. As a result many wells are also regarded as having healing properties.

WEREWOLF GHOST

The werewolf is believed to be a person who can change into a wolf when the moon is full, feeding on human flesh. The legend of the werewolf comes from the magical tradition of **lycanthropy**, the belief that it is possible through **witchcraft** to transform into the shape of an animal.

There are also a number of stories of werewolf **ghosts**, **spirits** that have returned from the dead as **shape-shifters**. The most famous of these stories concerns England's cruel King John, who was said to have been poisoned and then rose again as a werewolf to terrorize the countryside. A more recent example comes from Flixton in Yorkshire, where it is said that a werewolf ghost haunts the town changing from man into beast and glaring with bloodshot eyes at all those who dare cross its path.

WHALEY HOUSE

Mansion house located in San Diego, California, believed to be haunted by several **ghosts**.

The ghost most often reported is said to be that of Jim Robinson, who was executed in 1852 for attempting to steal a pilot boat in San Diego Harbor. It is thought that Whaley House is built on the site where he was hanged and died a long, lingering death due to an improperly built scaffold.

In 1857, Whaley House was completed after being commissioned by businessman Thomas Whaley and his bride, Anna. After moving in, the Whaleys began to hear heavy footsteps upstairs. It was thought that Robinson's **spirit**, still upset over his death, was making his presence felt.

After the death of the last remaining Whaley family member in 1953 the house was saved from demolition and made into a historic home open to the public. In the 1960s some students staged a play there and once again reports of ghostly footsteps upstairs were made.

Over the years **poltergeist** phenomena as well as **apparitions** of various members of the Whaley household have been reported. **Psychics** who have visited the house say it is home to a whole range of ghostly men, women, children and animals.

WHIRLWIND

According to Native North American lore whirlwinds are the vehicles by which **spirits** of the dead travel and spread their evil about. Various beliefs also exist that whirlwinds can poison or carry off children.

WHITE EAGLE LODGE

Non-denominational Christian Church that was founded by British **spiritualist Grace Cooke** in 1936 according to instructions from her **spirit guide**, White Eagle.

The White Eagle Lodge has an international following. It centres on an eternal spirit composed of the divine energy of the father, the enfolding love of the mother and the Christ light, which is the pure love and light that can be found in every human being. White Eagle's teachings are said to be handed down from the ancient wisdom of the ages. They include the five cosmic laws of **reincarnation, karma**, opportunity, correspondence and equilibrium. Great emphasis is placed on **healing**, which is done via natural remedies, **colours**, scents and music, or via **meditation** or the **laying on of hands**. Followers believe that the **soul** must be healed before any physical cure can take place. The Lodge preaches living in harmony with nature, and the divine laws of love.

WHITE, EDWARD [1873–1946]

American psychical researcher and author who wrote the non-fiction **occult** classic, *The Betty Book*.

On 17 March 1919, during a **séance**, Edward White and his wife, Betty, made contact with the **spirit** world when a whisky glass spelled out the name Betty who, scornful of the whole business, was not participating in the séance. The glass went wild in circles and spelled out that a pencil was needed. The astonished Betty got a pencil and so began almost a year of **automatic writing** in which communicating entities informed Betty that they would be relaying ideas and realities through her.

The Whites named the entities 'the Invisibles' because of their wish to remain anonymous. They said their aim was to encourage humanity to devote more effort to spiritual growth, as there were certain opportunities for spiritual growth on earth that could not be found on the other side.

In the months that followed the Invisibles began to use Betty's vocal cords to communicate instead of automatic writing. Betty did not go into **trance** but remained in a dissociated state. Allegedly, Betty experienced scenes through **clairvoyance** to help get across the point that if spirituality is neglected in this life the result is a pathetic existence in the next. Over and over again the Invisibles stressed the importance of spiritual development while a person is still alive and how it is up to each person to rise up to spirit instead of passively waiting for it to descend. They also stressed how powerful the mind is and how thoughts can magnetize things, people and circumstances.

The sessions lasted for around seven years and in 1937 *The Betty Book* was published. Betty died in 1939, and within half an hour of her death White sensed her invisible presence, an experience he was to have many more times in his life. He organized a séance with **medium** Ruth Finley and received a communication from Betty about the afterworld. In 1940 White published *The Unobstructed Universe*, which was the first full first-person account of life after death since the alleged communications with psychical researcher **Frederick Myers** some 25 years before.

The Betty books proved to be so popular that White went on to write a number of other books concerning the occult. He also served as president of the San Francisco chapter of the **American Society for Psychical Research**.

WHITE HOUSE

Residence and workplace of the president of the United States in Washington DC. The White house is believed to be haunted by numerous **ghosts**.

Construction on the White House began in October 1792 and was completed in 1800 when President John Adams took office. Today the White House is the only private head of state home that is open to the public free of charge, and is one of the most popular tourist attractions in America. It has with six residence levels and 132 rooms, but only two floors are open on the public tour.

The house is said to be haunted by several **spirits**, the most prominent being **Abraham Lincoln**. He was the 16th President of the United States, whose election to office in 1860 incited the secession of the Southern states, leading to the American Civil War (1861–65). He was assassinated by a Southern sympathizer by the name of John Wilkes Booth in April 1865, shortly after beginning his second term in office. Since his death, Abe has been spotted numerous times on and off the White House grounds. His ghostly second-floor footsteps were first reported by the White House staff. He has been spotted putting his boots on in the Lincoln bedroom, and

has been reported to knock on the bedroom door late at night, materializing long enough to spook guests.

The oldest known ghost of the White House is former First Lady Abigail Adams who (along with her husband, John Adams) was the first occupant of the home. The house wasn't quite finished when they moved in so the washing needed to be dried in the East Room of the residence. Frequently, Mrs Adams can be seen carrying spectral laundry towards the East Room and disappearing through the doors.

Other lesser-known spirits are said to reside at the Executive Mansion. A man by the name of David Burns gave the government the land that the White House stands on. It is said that in the Rose Room and the Yellow Oval office, a man's ghostly voice can be heard saying, 'I'm Mr Burns'. It has been rumoured that President Andrew Jackson's ghostly laughing and swearing can still be heard in the Rose Room, a room he liked to sleep in. The attic is said to be haunted by the first president to pass away while in office, William Harrison. And in the basement, on the eve of national tragedies (such as the 1929 Wall Street crash and the assassination of JFK), a ghostly **apparition** of a black cat can be seen prowling around.

The White House grounds are also said to be haunted. In 1809, James Madison became the fourth president of the United States. He and his wife Dolley occupied the residence and she planted a lovely Rose Garden. When Woodrow Wilson took office in 1912, his wife decided that the Rose Garden needed to be replanted. But before one flower was touched Dolley's ghostly apparition appeared to the garden staff and demanded that they leave her precious roses as they were. The gardeners were so terrified that they refused to touch the garden. Today, it continues to bloom just as Dolley planted it around 200 years ago.

WHITE LADIES

Type of **ghost** found in British castles and old houses. They are often the **spirits** of noblewomen who were murdered or died in tragic circumstances. They are also widely known in France, where they are said to be very beautiful and found in the vicinity of bridges. The reason offered for this is that it was once the custom to offer young women as human sacrifices to the spirits of rivers so the spirit would allow people to cross in safety. As in Britain the white ladies have also been reported in castles, where they wander the passages and pathways, sometimes with a cup of poison in their hands.

The White Lady of the Hohenzollerns is a well-known German ghost who is often reported at a number of former royal residences in Germany, including castles at Berlin, Bechin, Neuhaus, Tretzen and Raumleau. The lady is said to be dressed in white, and to wear a widow's band around her head. It is rumoured that she may be the ghost of Princess Bertha, who was cruelly treated by her husband, Baron Steyermark. She died in 1451 but her unhappy spirit cannot bring itself to leave.

WHITE MAGIC

The use of **supernatural** and **psychic** power for healing and promoting what is good; the opposite of **black magic**, which is magic for evil and/or selfish ends.

WICCA

Wicca (Celtic origin: *wicce*, 'wise') is a **Neo-Pagan** religion of nature and goddess worship that has become the dominant force in the **occult** community and the English-speaking world in recent years.

Wicca was originally founded by the British civil servant Gerald Gardner (1884–1964) probably in the 1940s, although it was not openly revealed until 1954. Gardner claimed that it was the original pre-Christian religion of the British Isles, handed down in secret for centuries. Since its founding, various related Wiccan traditions and offshoots have evolved or been created.

Though sometimes used interchangeably, Wicca and **witchcraft** are not the same thing, even though practitioners of both Wicca and witchcraft are often called **witches**. However, not all practitioners of Wicca are witches, and not all witches are practitioners of Wicca. Wicca refers to the religion, and can be a reference to both the initiatory tradition, where initiates are assigned a degree and generally work in groups or covens, and to solitary Wicca, where practitioners self-dedicate themselves to the tradition and generally follow the practice on their own. Both initiates and solitary Wiccans worship the **Goddess**. On the other hand, witchcraft does not require a belief in gods and goddesses and is not a specific spiritual path. The term witchcraft also refers to the use of **black magic** as well as **white magic**; whereas Wiccans only practise white magic.

According to Gardner, Wicca descended from the ancient pre-Christian religion of the British Isles – the worship of a primeval goddess of fertility and a Horned God, which he called the 'Craft of the Wise'. Other covens have made the same claim. According to this view the witchcraft persecutions were Christianity's attempt to stamp out the old religion, but Wiccan covens survived in isolated areas.

Many outside researchers and present-day Wiccans now doubt Gardner's claims of an origin for Wicca, as there is no evidence to support it and all the elements of Wicca were available to him from sources in the occult scene of his day, including the **Druid** movement, the teachings of **Aleister Crowley** and elements of Eastern magic he gathered from his travels to Malaysia. Whatever the origins of Wicca it has established a strong presence in the English-speaking world since Gardner and his followers formed the first known Wiccan coven in the 1940s.

Gardner's public books on the Craft, *Withcraft Today* (1954) and *The Meaning of Witchcraft* (1959), attracted a large following and helped to spark a movement of Wicca as a religion on both sides of the Atlantic. The greatest growth occurred in the 1960s, which saw a proliferation of Gardnerian covens. In the 1980s, along with the rest of the Neo-Pagan scene, Wicca expanded hugely and covens of one sort or another spread throughout America and established themselves in Australia, Canada and several other countries. The introduction of Wicca to America was spearheaded by Raymond and Rosemary Buckland, who were initiated by Gardner prior to moving to the United States.

Other traditions appeared. Some claimed roots as ancient as Gardner's version, and were organized along similar lines. Others were syncretistic, importing aspects of **Kabbalah** or ceremonial magic. In recent years the Wiccan movement has become even more diverse as Wiccan traditions and other forms of modern paganism have blended together more freely; today many groups calling themselves Wiccan have essentialy nothing in common with the movement launched by Gerald Gardner in the early 1950s. In addition to Gardnerian Wicca, some of the many branches of Wicca practised today include:

- *Alexandrian Wicca.*
- *Celtic Wicca.*
- *Dianic or Feminist Wicca.*
- *Eclectic Wicca.*
- *Faery Wicca.*
- *Feri Tradition.*
- *Gnarrains.*
- *Kemetic Wicca.*
- *Kingstone.*
- *Myjestic Order.*
- *Odyssian Wicca.*
- *Seax-Wicca.*
- *Stregheria.*
- *West Country Wicca.*

In an environment that is so diverse, few generalizations can be made about modern Wicca. The following refers essentially to what is sometimes called traditionist Wicca, that is, Wicca that remains close to Gardner's original teachings.

Wicca is a duotheistic religion – it worships two dieties, a God and a Goddess, whose names vary widely in different branches of the movement. The God is typically horned and the Goddess has the three forms of Maiden, Mother and Crone and is associated primarily with the moon. Both are powers of fertility and nature and their mating is the creative source from which all things are born.

Teachings and traditions about the God and Goddess make up the lore of Wicca and are passed on to members though a grade system of three degrees. Each degree is preceded by a course of study that covers a wide range of magical exercises and teachings. An important part of some branches of Wiccan magic is the Great Rite, which is a ritual dramatization of the creation of life – the coupling of the spark of life with life's substance. A traditional and complete Great Rite is the sexual copulation of a man and woman but today this is usually performed symbolically.

Alongside the degree ceremonies and training processes the activities of the coven include seasonal ritual and ceremonies which are ideally performed **sky clad**, that is, naked, although today ceremonial robes are typically worn. Standard equipment for Wiccans includes the athame or black-hilted knife, the **wand** or staff, the cauldron, the **pentacle** and the witch's garter – a length of scarlet cord that is normally worn tied above the left knee when not in use. These correspond to the **elements** of **air, fire, water, earth** and **spirit**, although in some tradition it is just the four elements of air, fire, earth and water.

The elements are thought to symbolize different places, emotions, objects, and natural energies and forces. For instance, **crystals** and stones are objects of the element earth, and seashells are objects of the water element. Each of the elements are commonly assigned a direction and a **colour**. Elemental, directional correspondences and colours may vary between traditions. It has been claimed that the points of the frequently worn pentacle symbolize the five elements.

Those who wish to be initiated into the craft must undertake magical training and in his **Book of Shadows**, Gardner listed the eight ways to raise magical power:

1. **Meditation** or concentration.
2. Chants, **spells** and **invocations.**
3. **Trance** and **astral projection.**
4. Incense, wine and **drugs.**
5. Dancing.
6. Blood control by binding parts of the body with cords.
7. Scouring but not to draw blood.
8. Ritual sex.

Although the Book of Shadows, the **grimoire** that contained the Gardnerian rituals, was supposed to be a secret that could only be obtained from a coven of proper lineage, since the 1970s most of the material covered in the book has been published numerous times.

Today Wiccans join groups called covens or work alone as solitaries. Many beliefs hold that the ideal number of members for a coven is 13. When a coven grows beyond their ideal number of members, they often split (or 'hive') into multiple covens, yet remain together as a group. A grouping of multiple covens is known as a grove.

Wiccan weddings are called **handfastings**. In usual rites the Wiccans assemble inside a magic **circle**, which is drawn out in a ritual manner followed by a cleansing and then a blessing of the space. Prayers to the God and Goddess are said, and spells are sometimes worked. Traditionally, the circle ritual is followed by a meal.

Although modern Wicca has countless characteristics the most distinctive remains that of the *Wiccan Rede*, which is akin to an oath of benign magical intent. The final line sums up the Wiccan philosophy; 'An it harm none, do what ye will.' Others follow the slightly adapted Rede of 'An it harm none, do what ye will; if harm it does, do what ye must.' Either way, the Rede is central to the understanding that it is within personal responsibility, rather than a religious authority, where moral structure resides. The Rede is one of the major differences between Wiccans and other types of witchcraft. Many 'traditional' witches or followers of other craft paths, do not believe in the Rede. The *Wiccan Rede* is taken very seriously by Wiccans, who abjure casting spells to harm others. Magic is to be used to help and heal; harmful magic will bounce back to the perpetrator.

Contrary to what is often thought, Wicca is in fact a very peaceful, harmonious and balanced way of thinking and life which promotes oneness with the divine and all which exists. It is perhaps best summed up by the following quote from one of the largest pagan, wiccan and witchcraft websites, www.wicca.com:

Wicca is a deep appreciation and awe in watching the sunrise or sunset, the forest in the light of a glowing moon, a meadow enchanted by the first light of day. It is the morning dew on the petals of a beautiful flower, the gentle caress of a warm summer breeze upon your skin, or the warmth of the summer sun on your face. Wicca is the fall of colourful autumn leaves, and the softness of winter snow. It is light, and shadow and all that lies in between. It is the song of the birds and other creatures of the wild. It is being in the presence of Mother Earth's nature and being humbled in reverence. When we are in the temple of the Lord and Lady, we are not prone to the arrogance of human technology as they touch our souls. To be a Wiccan Witch is to be a healer, a teacher, a seeker, a giver, and a protector of all things. If this path is yours, may you walk it with honour, light and integrity.

See also **Witchcraft**.

WICKLAND, DR CARL [1861–1945]

Carl A Wickland was born on 14 February 1861 in Liden, Sweden. In 1880 he left Sweden and arrived in St Paul, Minnesota in 1881. He married Anna W Anderson in

1896 and shortly thereafter they moved to Chicago, where Wickland entered Durham Medical College, graduating in 1900.

Dr Wickland became chief psychiatrist at the National Psychopathic Institute of Chicago in 1909, where he remained until 1918. Later the Wicklands moved to Los Angeles, where the doctor founded the National Psychological Institute, a non-profit organization to conduct research in psychology. At the Institute's sanatorium, between six and ten patients at any one time were cared for and brought back to sanity and health.

In 1924 Dr Wickland, in collaboration with Celia and Orlando Goerz and Nelle Watts, his assistants, wrote and published *Thirty Years Among the Dead*, a book that has become a classic in the field of abnormal psychology. In it he warns:

The serious problem of alienation and mental derangement attending ignorant psychic experiments was first brought to my attention by cases of several persons whose seemingly harmless experiences with automatic writing and the Ouija board resulted in such wild insanity that commitment to asylums was necessitated ... Many other disastrous results which followed the use of the supposedly innocent Ouija board came to my notice and my observations led me into research in psychic phenomena for a possible explanation of these strange occurrences.

Wickland found that he was able to cure many of these cases of diagnosed insanity by using an entranced **medium** (his wife), who was taken over by the **spirit** that was obsessing the psychiatric patient. He found

that many of these entities were unaware that they had died; without any knowledge of the **afterlife** they found themselves in a kind of twilight condition. With help from higher intelligences on the other side he was able to persuade them to leave the **aura** of the patient whose light had attracted them.

Thirty Years Among the Dead is a book crammed with thrills, dramatic incidents and poignant emotions. One of its revelations concerns Harry Thaw, the eccentric American millionaire who, for no earthly reason, killed Stanford White, the famous architect of Madison Square Gardens in New York. According to Dr Wickland, Thaw was a psychic **sensitive** 'unquestionably obsessed by avenging spirits who desired retribution for real or fancied injustice done to themselves or kindred'.

Wickland was the first medically trained expert to approach mental illness as being due to **spirit attachment**. He also used electric shocks to exorcise unwanted entities from the auras of his patients. His approach was dismissed as humbug by sceptics and was not taken seriously by the scientific or medical community of his day.

Since the late 1980s claims of spirit attachment have grown more common, especially with the development of **past-life therapy**.

WILD EDRIC

According to an old Shropshire legend, whenever England is threatened with war, the **ghosts** of an Anglo-Saxon fighter, Wild Edric, and his followers ride out from the old lead mine where they dwell to do battle with the enemy. The ghostly soldiers always ride off in the direction from which the opposing forces are coming from. They were last spotted just before the start of the Crimean War in the 1850s.

Edric is said to be dressed in green clothes and cloak with a white feather in his cap, while at his side rides a beautiful woman, also in green, with long blonde hair, known as Lady Godda. According to legend Edric was a real person, the nephew of Edric Strenona, Ealderman of Mercia and it was he who led the men of Shropshire when they rose against William the Conqueror. He was never defeated but eventually made peace with William and settled down with the Lady Godda, whom some say was a **fairy** wife.

WILD HUNT

Spectral nocturnal procession of huntsmen, **ghosts** of the dead, horses and hounds. The huntsmen are said to be **spirits** of the dead and as they fly overhead the spectral dogs often set off the howling of earthly dogs below.

The legend of the Wild Hunt is found all over Northern Europe and has its origins in Norse and Teutonic mythologies, where the god Odin/Woden, in the guise of a huntsman, rides across the sky with a pack of spectral hounds bringing death or disaster to all who watch him pass.

The Wild Hunt has several leaders, both male and female. In British lore the hunt is sometimes led by **Herne the Hunter** or simply the devil. In the lore of Northern Germany it is often led by Holda, goddess of the hearth and motherhood, and in Southern Germany it is led by Bertha or Diana.

WILLARD LIBRARY

Willard Library is largely known for its wonderful collection of art books and research materials but it's also famous for its **ghosts**.

Located at 21 First Avenue in Evansville, Indiana, Willard Library is an impressive Victorian Gothic-style building dating back to 1885. The most-often reported **apparition** is known as The Grey Lady. A former janitor first reported seeing a 'grey lady' in the building's basement in a winter month sometime in the 1930s. The ghost was seen just after 3 am and was clothed in early 1800s-style attire.

The library's basement was almost destroyed by a storm in 1977. After undergoing extensive renovation in 1980, the room was dedicated to Margaret Maier because of her 40-year employment service to the library. Maier had seen the Grey Lady ghost many times herself and during the four-month renovation the Grey Lady allegedly moved into Margaret's home, which she shared with her sister, Ruth. Both sisters saw the ghost on a regular basis during its stay. She would materialize in full at times, at other times marking her presence by turning on the clothes dryer, and sometimes by the overpowering scent of her unmistakable perfume (strange aromas are commonly reported at haunted sites). The ghost returned to the library after the renovations were complete.

After Margaret Maier retired, the **hauntings** slowed but did not stop. To this day, the Children's Room remains a popular haunting spot for residing **spirits** and people continue to report sightings. It is thought by some that children have the ability to communicate with ghosts and maybe that can explain the popularity of this room for the spirits.

WILLINGTON MILL

Haunting of a large house in Willington Mill, England, during the nineteenth century. One of the house's residents, John Procter, a Quaker, kept a diary of the disturbance, which was published in the *Journal* of the **Society of Psychical Research** in 1892.

The disturbances began for the Procters towards the end of 1834 when the nursemaid confessed to being frightened at night by sounds of thumping and pacing coming from an unoccupied room on the second floor. The housemaid left and another was hired, but she too heard noises coming from the room.

Soon the unexplained noises began to occur during the day as well as the night. Witnesses thought a man in heavy boots was roaming about. Curiously if anyone slept in the room or sat up to hear the noises nothing happened, but as soon as they left or went about their business the sounds would return.

As time went on **apparitions** also began to appear; a white lady was seen in a second floor window and later, from the same window, a figure that looked like a priest in a white surplice also was seen. Other noises were heard including moans, cries, voices, whistling and drumming. Objects also began to move. Beds shook and the floor vibrated.

In 1840 there was a brief respite from the haunting, but in May 1841 it began again. As well as noises more apparitions appeared, this time of a monkey and a man opening and shutting the window.

After nearly 13 years of haunting the Procter family left the house. The house was divided into two and occupied by a foreman and chief clerk of a flour mill. These families were disturbed by strange noises and apparitions but not to the same extent as the Procters. In 1867 a firm of millers rented the house and the new tenants suffered greatly.

The Procters eventually put the house up for sale and it remained vacant for some time. During the time it was vacant a **séance** was held when phenomena were produced but no communication with spirits was established. Eventually the mill was closed and turned into a warehouse and the house was divided up. No further disturbances were reported.

WILL-O'-THE-WISP

Perhaps the most popular name in Europe for the mysterious **ghost lights** that are often seen hovering around or near graveyards or over marshy areas. One tradition says the will-o'-the-wisp are the **souls** of dead people appearing as a **death omen** or guarding lost treasure; another claims they are lost souls who cannot enter **heaven** or **hell** and therefore become malignant and do their best to lead those foolish enough to follow them into trouble. Recent research has suggested a natural explanation: the lights are caused by the igniting of gasses escaping from rotting plants or animals.

WILMOT APPARITION

Apparition that occurred on board a steam ship in 1863.

Connecticut manufacturer S R Wilmot set sail from Liverpool, England, to New York on the steamer *City of Limerick* on 3 October 1863. He was accompanied by his sister, Eliza, and shared a stern berth with an Englishman, William Tait.

On the second day of the journey a storm broke out, which lasted nine days. Wilmot, who suffered from seasickness, stayed in his berth most of the time. On the eighth night of the storm Wilmot had a dream about his wife clad in her white nightdress coming to caress him. When he awoke he was surprised to see Tait staring down at him. Tait explained that he had

seen a woman in a white nightdress enter the berth and kiss the sleeping Wilmot. His description matched Wilmot's dream.

The ship reached New York on 22 October and a day later Wilmot went by rail to Watertown, Connecticut where his wife and children were staying. His wife immediately asked him if he had received a visit from her on the night he had had the dream. She told him that on that particular night she had been so worried about his safety during the storm that she couldn't sleep. At about four o'clock in the morning it seemed to her as if she actually went to find her husband on the ship. She described his room accurately and also described how Tait had been watching her. When she awoke the next morning she felt as if she had physically visited her husband.

In 1889 the case was examined by the **Society for Psychical Research**. Tait was deceased but Wilmot and his wife and sister were interviewed at length. The researchers came to the conclusion that the case was unique as it seemed to offer evidence for both collective and reciprocal apparitions. Collective apparitions, in which an apparition is seen by more than one person, are not common, and reciprocal apparitions in which both the **agent** (Mrs Wilmot) and **percipient** (Tait) see one another are even less common. The case is also unusual in that Wilmot saw his wife in a dream and Tait saw her while awake.

Psychic investigators **Edmund Gurney** and **Eleanor Sidgwick** suggested that the most likely explanation was **telepathy** and **clairvoyance**, triggered by Mrs Wilmot's intense desire to know if her husband was safe. Tait in turn had received telepathic vibrations from Wilmot which manifested visually. Another possible explanation, although one that was rejected by the researchers, was that Mrs Wilmot had somehow projected her **doppelgänger/** double out of body. The case remains a mystery.

WINCHESTER MYSTERY HOUSE

Nineteenth-century San Francisco mansion with a bizarre history.

Sarah and William Wirt Winchester, son of the inventor of the Winchester repeating rifle, were married during the American Civil War. Sadly their happiness was short-lived as their first and only child died a month after being born. Fifteen years later William died and Sarah never seemed to recover from her grief. Her behaviour changed and, despite a fortune of about $20 million and a substantial share in the rifle business, she remained a house-bound recluse.

Sarah attempted to contact her husband through **séances**. None were successful until she found a **medium** from Boston called Adam Coons. Coons allegedly made contact with William and gave Sarah a message from him, which warned her that she was under a **curse**. All the **spirits** of the people who had been killed by Winchester rifles had taken their revenge with the death of their child and William, and if Sarah wanted to escape this curse she must make amends to these **souls**.

Sarah followed William's instructions to sell her New Haven house and move to the West, to build a new house for both herself and the **ghosts**. She found an eight-room house in the Santa Clara valley and hired dozens of construction workers to enlarge the house, and domestic workers to take care of it. For the next 38 years, until her death in 1922, building work took place on the house. Gardeners were hired to plant a five-foot high hedge, as she did not want any person not employed by her to see the house.

The builders worked to Sarah's bizarre instructions, which had them destroying work and then redoing it. She kept to a Victorian style but the finished product was an architectural nightmare, with odd-angled rooms, stairways that lead nowhere and doors that opened on to blank walls. In all, the house ended up with 160 rooms and over the years Sarah spent about $5.5 million on the construction of it. She became obsessed with the number 13, and each room had to have 13 windows, 13 lights, 13 closets and so on. The ghosts allegedly wanted no mirrors so none were found in the house. The grounds were just as bizarre as the house itself.

Sarah rarely left the house and not surprisingly her strange behaviour attracted gossip and fanciful stories that probably have little basis in fact. For example it was said that every night at midnight, Sarah would go to her secret chamber, called the blue room, to entertain her ghostly guests by throwing dinner parties.

Sarah died in 1922 at the age of 82. She bequeathed the house to her niece with the instructions that the ghosts continue to be welcomed and cared for, but within six weeks the contents were removed. The house was sold and opened to the public. Today the Winchester mystery house remains a popular tourist attraction. Many visitors claim to have been haunted there by various phenomena, such as **phantom** footsteps, odd sounds and smells, cold spots and windows and doors turning by themselves.

WINDIGO

According to Native American lore, the Windigo is a **spirit** said to haunt the forests of Canada and portions of Minnesota. It is described as extremely tall (some accounts place it at 12 feet high or taller) and white in colour, while other traditions state that a blue star adorns either the forehead or the chest of the spirit. In myth and legend, the Windigo moves with the speed of the wind and is known to eat men and animals alike. Its appearance is considered to be a **death omen. Shamans** consider Windigo sickness to be the most terrifying type of sickness as it can be triggered by the egotistical abuse or loss of control of shamanic powers.

WINDSOR CASTLE

Originally built by William the Conqueror, Windsor Castle in Windsor, England is said to be haunted by four British sovereigns. The **ghost** of King Henry VIII has been reported from time to time in the courtyard, groaning and dragging his ulcerated leg. The ghost of his daughter Elizabeth I allegedly puts in an appearance now and again in the royal library, which is also believed to be a favourite haunt of Charles I and George III.

The ghost of Richard II's forester, **Herne the Hunter,** has also been reported several times over the centuries since he hanged himself from a tree on the castle grounds. A young royal guardsman who committed suicide in 1927 is reportedly seen too.

WITCH DOCTOR

A magical and medical practitioner who uses **spells** and potions to cure the sick and contact **spirit guides** for wisdom and **divination** purposes. The witch doctor can be found in the tribal communities of Africa, South America, the Native North American Indians (where he is known as a **medicine man**) and in parts of Australia and Polynesia.

WITCH OF ENDOR

One of the most well-known tales of the **paranormal** to appear in the Bible, which continues to generate debate to this day. The story of the Endor Witch is told in 1 Samuel 28. King Saul, anxious at the possible outcome of a battle with the Philistines, summons the Witch of Endor to raise the **ghost** of the prophet Samuel to ask his advice. The **spirit** was of little help to Saul and some feel strongly that the entire event might well be an illustration of one of the earliest cases of paranormal **fraud** to have been committed, arguing that the Witch of Endor was little more than a ventriloquist who summoned a spirit using smoke and mirrors.

WITCHCRAFT, WITCH

A belief system of nature and goddess worship, magical practice and folk religion that incorporates numerous other traditions including **divination**, herbalism and **paganism**. A female practitioner is called a witch and a male practitioner is called a warlock. In contrast to **Wicca**, a decidedly **white magic** movement, witchcraft utilizes both white and **black magic**, depending on the choice made by the individual.

Witchcraft is an ancient art that utilizes the powers of nature and the mind to bring about a desired effect. Specific combinations of natural elements draw specific energies. One can tap into these energies by stimulating the senses to induce **altered states of consciousness** that intensify moods and feelings.

The origins of witchcraft are uncertain but there is mention of it as far back as the time of Moses. It is known that magic and **sorcery** were practised in ancient Babylonia, Egypt and throughout the classical world of Greece and Rome. Although black magic was known to exist, witchcraft was not really considered evil until the rise of the Christian Church, which linked witches with the devil. In almost all cultures since witches have been feared as evil and believed to possess **paranormal** powers of invisibility, **shape-shifting**, **clairvoyance** and **astral projection**, all of which they are said to use to harm others. In the fifteenth century witchcraft was declared a heresy and reports were issued outlining the practices of witches, which included devil worship, baby eating, the destruction of crops and murder. Witches were invariably thought to be women, for according to the wisdom of the time women were weak and susceptible to corruption by the devil.

Over 250 years an estimated 200,000 people were executed for witchcraft in the most brutal manner. Most of the executions took place in Europe, especially in Germany. In America the worst case was the Salem witch trials in 1692, in which 141 people were falsely arrested on the basis of accusations by hysterical children; 20 were sentenced to death. Victims of the witch-hunts typically included village wise men and women who had reputed healing or magical powers or psychic powers such as clairvoyance. Victims were often tortured into making confessions.

The advance of science and industry and the growth of urban centres from the eighteenth century onwards contributed to a decline in a belief in witchcraft and to the end of official persecution of witches. Witchcraft remained active, however, in rural areas where folk magic cures were called upon to ensure love, cure sickness and so on. It never quite shook itself of its association with the devil though.

It wasn't until 1951 that witchcraft ceased to be a crime in England. One of the first, if not the first, people to bring witchcraft into the open after the repeal of the Witchcraft Act was Gerald Gardner. Gardner had been initiated into a coven of New Forest witches in 1939, and eventually formed his own coven in 1953, giving birth to the tradition of **Wicca**. In the early years a person could only be initiated into witchcraft by an initiated witch and then advance through degrees of hierarchy in a coven. Today this has changed and the craft is more open; anyone can self-initiate him or herself, and even establish a new tradition. Many witches prefer to practise alone and are known as solitaries.

The witch's year is organized around seasonal festivals and meetings that provide a framework for worship and celebration. They also provide a chance to gather together and concentrate the group's powers to make magic. The practice of witchcraft is ritualistic, involving the use of knives, **wands**, cauldrons and so on, and **spells**, **charms**, **incantations** and potions. Witches gain their magic powers through harnessing the powers of the four natural **elements** of the universe: **air**, **earth**, **fire** and **water**. If witches decided to follow the code of the *Wiccan Rede* of white magic – 'An it harm none, do what ye will' – then they are said to have taken the **right-hand path** of light, healing and inspiration. If instead they use their magic for selfish or evil desires they have taken the **left-hand path** of darkness and black magic.

Only a small proportion of witches practise their religion openly today, due to the dangers of misunderstanding and hostility from a public that still links witchcraft with the devil. Witchcraft is still confused with sorcery, **Satanism** and **Voodoo** and many witches advocate finding another name for their craft. Even though there are some differences between the two, Wicca, with its emphasis on the practice of white magic, remains the most popular alternative name for those who wish to practise witchcraft.

The Spiral Dance: A Rebirth of the Ancient Religion of the Great Goddess by Starhawk, an American witch (b. 1951) is a generally accepted and informative introduction to the craft. It contains specific instructions for **circles**, chants, spells, invocations, creating rituals and in short, everything needed to get started. Other accepted introductory texts include *Drawing Down the Moon: Witches, Druids, Goddess-Worshippers, and Other Pagans in America Today* by Margot Adler and *What Witches Do: The Modern Coven Revealed* by Stewart Farrar.

Your bewitching week

According to witchcraft every day of the week is a magical day. Each day has its own magical correspondences such as deity associations, colours, crystals and herbs, and an awareness of each day's bewitching specialities is one way to bring magic into your life.

Sunday is the day of the sun. It is a day to work for healing as the sun is the life bringer. It is also the planet concerned with the personality, the self. The colour of the sun is gold. This day is full of wonder and all sorts of magical potential for success, wealth, and fame.

Monday is the day of the moon and is more concerned with matters of a psychic nature. The colours of the moon are white or silver. Try sitting under the light of the moon at night to absorb her magic. As the moon is concerned with psychism, Monday is a good time for any sort of meditation or divination, particularly scrying or crystal gazing.

Tuesday is ruled by Mars, the planet associated with fighting and soldiers. Mars is concerned with courage, strength and determination. The colour is red, the metal iron. If you are working a week of magic now is the time to call for the courage to help you achieve your goals.

Wednesday is the day of Mercury, the messenger of the gods, the communicator and bringer of news. However, he is also a joker and a thief so beware of this aspect. His colour is orange or light blue and his metal is quicksilver or mercury. Wednesday is a day of communication, change, cunning, and the arts. Today is a practical day to make travel plans and design talismans for safety or use in all forms of communication.

Thursday is a Jupiter day. Jupiter's colour is a rich, royal blue and the metal is tin. This is the day of the week for prosperity, abundance and good health.

Friday belongs to Venus, both the planet and its namesake the Roman goddess of love. This day of the week is for magical topics such as love, birth, fertility and romance. Colours for today include emerald green, pink and aqua.

Saturday is associated with the planet Saturn. The colour is black and the metal is lead. Today is a good day for protection, banishing negative situations and tidying up loose ends. It is a good day to burn black candles to absorb negativity and to cleanse your mind, replacing draining thoughts and feelings with positive and energetic ones.

Witching Hour

According to **superstition** the hour of midnight on the night of a full moon, when **ghosts, witches, fairies** and other **supernatural** entities visit the earth and are most likely to be seen. The term is often used to mean the hour of midnight in general.

Typically **hauntings** occur between the hours of midnight and 4 am as, according to popular belief, this is the time when **psychic** energies are at their strongest or the veil between the world of the living and the dead is at its thinnest.

Wizard

Term applied to male practitioners of the magical arts or to one who has attained a high level of skill in summoning **spirits** and **supernatural** powers. Alternative titles include warlock, **sorcerer**, **adept**, conjuror, **magi** or **magician**. The term derives from the Middle English term *wis*, or 'wise'.

Woburn Abbey

Woburn Abbey in Bedfordshire, England, was originally a Cistercian abbey but was rebuilt in the mid-eighteenth century. It has been the residence of the dukes of Bedford for over three centuries and is said to be haunted by a number of ghostly forms.

The **ghost** of a monk is said to haunt Woburn. The monk is thought to be the abbot of Woburn who was hanged when he opposed Henry VIII's marriage to **Anne Boleyn**. He has been seen most often in the crypt.

The summerhouse at Woburn Abbey is believed to be haunted by the present Duke's grandmother, who died in her early sixties when the plane she was flying crashed. Her ghost has not been reported but, according to witnesses, an overwhelming feeling of sadness and coldness appears to linger on in the summerhouse.

The most recent **haunting** to allegedly take place at Woburn Abbey is thought to be the ghost of a young man who may have been murdered there. He is never seen but doors are said to open and close for him as he walks through rooms. Witnesses say that a door handle turns and opens, as if a person was coming through. Then a few moments later the door at the other end of the room opens and closes again, as if an invisible figure has walked across the room.

Wood

One of the five **elements** in Chinese philosophy that make up the building blocks of the universe. In **traditional Chinese medicine** wood symbolizes the season of Spring and new beginnings. The colour green, the sound of shouting and the emotion of anger are also associated with this element.

Woodlawn Plantation

Nineteenth-century home located in Virginia that belonged to the nephew of George Washington, Major Lawrence Lewis. It is said to be haunted by numerous **ghosts**.

The stately house was built almost entirely by slave labour. Major Lewis and his wife, Nelly, were its first occupants and took up residence there in 1805. They had eight children there, five of whom died. When Lawrence died in 1839 Nelly moved to Audley, a plantation nearby. The house passed to a succession of owners until the mid-twentieth century when it was acquired and restored by the National Trust for Historic Preservation.

Paranormal phenomena have been reported at the house since the early twentieth century. They include footsteps, slamming doors, noises and whispers. Objects also move about and a ghost, believed to be that of a previous owner, John Mason, who lived there during the American Civil War and who had a wooden leg, is said to thump around.

The Lafayette bedroom is believed to be haunted by a figure that stands by the window when the house is empty. Lorenzo's bedroom (the Lewises' first child was called Lorenzo) is also said to be especially haunted by mysterious noises and doors that open by themselves. In the master bedroom, lights turn on and off mysteriously and animals are said to avoid the central hall where ghostly forms have been reported. The ghost of George Washington is also believed to haunt Woodlawn. He is seen on moonlit nights riding his white horse in the grounds.

Apparitions have been said to appear all over the house but most of the phenomena seems to concentrate on the south side where a **well** was once located. It has been suggested that restless **spirits** are able to return to this world through the well.

Worrall, Ambrose [1899–1972]

British-born **clairvoyant** who became well known for healing with his American wife, **Olga Worrall**.

Worrall was a gifted **psychic** from an early age, claiming that he could see the **spirits** of the dead in his bedroom. As a teenager he discovered that he could project himself out of body to visit others at night. During World War I he began to see impending deaths clairvoyantly; a small thin skeleton would float over someone's head along with a number to indicate the length of the remaining lifespan. Throughout his adulthood Worrall felt compelled to heal. He explained that he felt an invisible force, eight inches in diameter, emerge from his solar plexis and protrude about ten inches in front of him, and that this force literally dragged him towards people in pain and in need of healing.

In 1922 Worrall moved to the United States for a better way of life and began to work as an engineer for the Martin Company. People began to ask him for healing and he was astonished to find that most of those he touched were cured or significantly improved. In 1927 Worrall met Olga. He felt they had known each other before in a previous life and the two were married in June 1928.

In his healing work Worrall never knew what he was going to do, waiting for his **intuition** or the force from his solar plexis to direct him. He believed the healing power originated from the **universal life force**. He called it 'paraelectricity' because he believed it had electrical properties.

From 1929 Worrall began to devote himself more to the healing ministry set up by himself and his wife. Like his wife he was always aware of spirit presences and believed they were instrumental in the healing process, directing healing energy to the patient using him as a channel. One particular entity that manifested to him was a seven-foot tall Native Indian called XYZ. XYZ directed Olga to find a new home in Baltimore, where they established a healing centre.

After his death in 1972 Worrall allegedly began communicating with his wife Olga. He told her that his transition to the other side had been made easier with the help of XYZ. He also told her he would continue to help her in spirit and add to her healing power, and that many doctors, nurses, surgeons and healers were helped in a similar manner by other spirits.

WORRALL, OLGA [1906–1985]

American **clairvoyant** who, along with her husband, **Ambrose Worrall**, became famous as a healer.

Like her husband, Olga's **psychic** powers manifested early. She claimed to be able to see **spirits** of the dead from the age of three and by the age of five could see her own **aura** by looking in the mirror. By the age of 11 she was making precognitive predictions. Her healing ability also manifested early and as a child she found that she could banish headaches simply by placing her hands on people.

Olga met Worrall in 1927 and the two were married the following June. In December 1928 the couple moved to Baltimore in Maryland and lived there for the rest of their lives. Their only children, twin boys, died when they were a month old and their grief prompted them to devote themselves to healing, especially children by setting up a healing room in one of their bedrooms. They refused payment and insisted that their healing be accompanied by traditional medical help.

In 1950 Olga was asked by a Methodist minister, Albert E Day, to establish a spiritual healing clinic with him. The New Life Clinic ran for nine years from Mt Vernon Place Methodist Church before moving to Mt Washington Methodist Church.

Olga's healing often involved communication with spirits of the dead and this came to the attention of parapsychologist **J B Rhine**. She had no medical training but was adept at intuitively knowing what was wrong with a person and how to help them. She believed that **prayer**, love and compassion and the desire to see a person healed were of crucial importance to the healing process. Like many other healers Olga never believed the power came from within herself but from a higher source.

She said gifted healers are like battery chargers that take in the high voltage energy of God and transform it into healing energy that can be used for humans, animals, birds and plants.

Over the years the Worralls did have many spectacular successes, including tumours that shrank in size. Ambrose died in 1972 and almost immediately Olga began communicating with him in spirit. He confirmed to her that healers have an **astral body** that is perfect and healing energy flows through it. He said he would stay near her to help her in her work and when she placed her hands on a patient his hands would be placed on them too. Until her death in 1985 Olga continued to work and heal at the New Life Clinic.

Olga felt strongly that science needed to support **spiritualism** and agreed to numerous scientific experiments designed to see if some kind of energy does indeed flow through healers. During her career as a healer she was tested numerous times by parapsychologists, physicians, physicists and others. Biophysicist Beverly Rubik observed a unique transfer of energy when Worrall prayed or healed, which could energize water, speed the growth of rye grass and create wave patterns in cloud chambers.

In 1979 Olga underwent experiments at the University of California in Berkeley. Tests revealed that there were increases of energy flowing from her hands. They also showed that during healing her **brain waves** were at the delta level, the state of deep sleep – yet she was wide awake.

WORTH, PATIENCE

Famous case of **automatic writing**. Patience Worth was an alleged **spirit** who manifested in 1913 through a St Louis housewife called Pearl Curran.

On 8 July 1913, during a **Ouija board** session, the pointer spelled out a message: 'Many moons ago I lived. Again I come. Patience Worth is my name.'

In the **séances** that followed Patience Worth spoke in archaic dialogue and revealed herself to be an English woman, born in Dorset in 1649. A spinster, she emigrated to the American colonies late in life and was killed in an Indian massacre. Worth then began to dictate a total of a million words over the next five years. Her works, which included poems, plays and six novels, were published and enjoyed great success. Her first novel, *The Sorry Tale*, a 300,000-word epic about the life of Christ took two years to dictate via the Ouija board.

For seven years Curran used the Ouija board and after that she simply recited the words as if they were dictated to her in automatic speech. In 1922, when Curran became pregnant at the age of 39, the relationship between Curran and Worth began to decline, occurring less and less frequently. Curran died in 1937 when public interest in her had declined.

There is considerable debate among researchers as to the real identity of Patience Worth. The novels and writings have been investigated and found to be accurate in historical detail and well constructed, although doubt has been cast over the authenticity of the English used.

The Element Encyclopedia of the Psychic World
781

Some say that even though Curran was uneducated she merely **channelled** material from the depths of her subconscious. Others think that Worth was indeed a **discarnate entity** who, centuries after her death, found a way to express her literary talent.

WRAITH

The **ghost** of a person on the verge of death. According to lore the wraith appears as an exact likeness of its human counterpart, and commonly reveals itself to the friends and family of the person who is about to die. If a person is unfortunate enough to see his or her own wraith, it is regarded as heralding death within a fortnight. The tradition appears to have developed from the ancient belief that a person's **soul** is a precise duplicate of the person's physical form and that it escapes the body when death is imminent. Perhaps the most famous example occurred to the poet Shelley (1792–1822), who supposedly saw his own wraith as he was about to step on a boat which was to take him across the Bay of Spezia in Italy to the town of Livorno and a meeting with his old friend, Leigh Hunt. A storm hit the boat on the return trip and Shelley drowned, fulfilling the tradition of the wraith.

See also **Doppelgänger**.

X

XENOGLOSSY

The sudden ability to speak in an unlearned language or a language that is usually unrecognizable to the speaker. It is not to be confused with **glossolalia** or 'speaking in tongues'.

Xenoglossy is a phenomenon that is associated with **altered states of consciousness**, such as **trance** and sleep and **mediumship**. Often the language spoken can't be identified by the speaker and this has led some people to believe that the person may be speaking in an angelic or otherworldly language.

The term 'xenoglossy' was coined in the late nineteenth century by French physiologist Charles Richet, from the Greek words *xeno* (strange) and *glossia* (tongue). Theories on the origins of xenoglossy range from the **spiritualist** viewpoint of **spirit** communication to the psychologist's view that it comes from a person's subconscious memory, which stores words from foreign languages that are heard in childhood and subsequently forgotten. Sceptics argue that the most likely explanation is **fraud** by the **medium** during **séance** communications.

There are said to be two types of xenoglossy: recitative xenoglossy, when a person speaks in a language but doesn't understand its meaning, and responsive xenoglossy, when a person is able to carry on a conversation in an unlearned language. The former is believed to be more common than the later. One of the most famous cases of recitative xenoglossy is that of a Hindu girl called Swarnlata Mishra. Between the ages of four and six she was able to perform and sing Bengali songs and dances without ever having been exposed to Bengali language or culture. She said that she had been a Bengali woman in a previous life. An early example of responsive xenoglossy was reported in 1862 by a mesmerist called Prince Galitzin, who allegedly mesmerized an uneducated German woman who could not speak French. While in a trance the woman spoke and conversed in fluent French.

From 1955 to 1956 a 37-year-old Philadelphia housewife was hypnotized by her husband in a series of sessions. The personality that the woman subsequently revealed was a male peasant farmer called 'Jensen', who spoke in seventeenth-century colloquial Swedish. The woman claimed to have no knowledge of this language, and under **hypnosis** no subconscious knowledge was discovered.

Another responsive xenoglossy case is that of 'Gretchen', a German-speaking girl, who manifested in 1970 during the hypnotic regression of Doloros Jay from Virginia. 'Gretchen' understood simple English but communicated in imperfect German. She said she was the daughter of a German major, and had lived in the later half of the nineteenth century, dying at the age of 16.

Xenography is the term used to refer to the writing of unlearned languages. As with xenoglossy, some believe it to be a **paranormal** phenomenon while others believe it to be an ability that was learned earlier in life and forgotten.

The significance of cases involving xenoglossy is that, if they are authentic, the **super ESP** hypothesis would be hard pressed to explain them. Is it really possible for a medium to acquire by the sole means of ESP the vocabulary and pronunciation of a foreign language? Parapsychologists simply don't know, but if **ESP** can stretch to this extent then the informational limits of ESP must be virtually boundless.

XENOMANCY

Divination by the chance meeting with or actions of strangers. In Greece to meet a priest is always considered unlucky, but for men so more than women. The luck will be far worse if the priest happens to be riding a donkey. The main action of xenomancy is, however, concerned with the actions of the person met. For example, a raised right hand would be a positive sign while a raised left hand would be unfortunate. Pointing and wild gesticulation and the interaction between two or more strangers would all be significant.

X-RAY VISION

The **paranormal** ability to see into a person's body to diagnose disease and potential problem areas.

More than a hundred years ago, German physicist Wilhelm Röntgen discovered an invisible form of radiation that could be used to make photographs of bones and organs inside a living human body. Many scientists were sceptical at first but over time they were convinced that this was perhaps one of the greatest discoveries in science and medicine.

Natasha Demkina, a teenaged girl from Saransk, Russia, claims to have X-ray-like vision, which lets her see inside human bodies, to make diagnoses that often are more accurate than those of doctors. Natasha says she has been able to see abnormalities down to the cellular level from the age of 10 and her mother says her readings are 100 per cent accurate. Widely recognized in Russia as 'the girl with X-ray eyes', 17-year-old Natasha has convinced a number of patients, doctors and journalists that her powers are genuine. She reached the height of her popularity in 2004, but it began to decline that same year when she agreed to be tested by experts for a Discovery channel film. The experiments yielded disappointing results.

Another teenager with alleged X-ray vision is a 16-year-old called Adam from Vancouver, who claims to be able to use his X-ray vision to heal people. In fact, he's credited with curing rock 'n' roll legend Ronnie Hawkins of terminal pancreatic cancer.

The scientific community has yet to be convinced that X-ray vision is a genuine phenomenon. Sceptics argue that most cases of X-ray vision can be explained by a remarkably simple but effective technique called **cold reading**, which is commonly used by fortune-tellers. Typically, the **psychic** fires questions or makes statements while looking for any that are confirmed or get a reaction.

See also **Medical intuitive**.

Xylomancy

Divination by reading **omens** from the positions of small pieces of dry wood found in one's path, or divination by the casual arrangement of sticks when stacked for burning. Xylomancy is practised extensively in the Slav lands. There the placement of bits of wood is believed to be significant, indicating good or bad fortune lying ahead, further down the path. Large pieces of wood are seen as major obstacles while smaller pieces indicate minor worries. The relationship of various lengths and thicknesses of wood when building a fire possibly originated from the building of pyres for the burning of bodies, and so related to the final destination of the deceased person's **soul**.

Y

YANG

See **Yin/Yang**.

YEATS, WILLIAM BUTLER [1865–1939]

Celebrated Irish poet and playwright whose deep fascination with **mysticism** and **spiritualism** is attested to in his dramatic works such as *The Countess Kathleen* (1892), *The Land of Heart's Desire* (1894), *Cathleen ni Houlihan* (1902), *The King's Threshold* (1904) and *Deirdre* (1907). Yeats was initiated into the Order of the **Golden Dawn** in the summer of 1887, taking the secret name of *Diabolus est Deus Inversus* (The Devil is God Reversed) and later helped write various of the Golden Dawn rituals, drawing on the Egyptian **Book of the Dead**, the visionary works of Blake and various other **esoteric** classics. Yeats was also leader of the movement that expelled **Aleister Crowley** from the Golden Dawn, an action that ultimately led to the Order's fragmentation and gradual decline.

The Golden Dawn was not Yeats's only esoteric interest. He was fascinated by **fairies**, took a critical interest in spiritualism and **Theosophy** and became a member of the London **Ghost Club**, making him arguably one of England's foremost authorities on ritual **magic** and ghostly phenomena. His reputation as a great poet and playwright is without question. His reputation as an occultist and psychical researcher is, however, less well known but it came with numerous investigations of **hauntings** and his association with various other individuals in search of otherworldly phenomena.

YIN/YANG

Chinese **Taoist** belief that the **universal life force** or energy of the universe, known as chi, and everything in it is based on a pair of opposite forces: Yin and Yang. Yin and Yang are complete opposites but they are also interdependent and cannot exist without each other.

The concept of Yin/Yang was first introduced in the second century BC in the **I Ching**, which placed Yin and Yang behind Chi on the existential pyramid of the universe. Below Yin and Yang are the five **elements** of the natural world.

Together Yin and Yang outline the experience of life, which is forever changing. Something is never just Yin or Yang but a combination of the two extremes in different stages of flux. There is always some Yin in Yang and vica versa. Yin is the feminine embodiment of Chi, which represents and symbolizes shadows, earth, night, the moon, dark, cool, calm, passivity, downward motion and moisture. Yang is the masculine component, which represents heaven, day, light, warmth, upward motion, activity, fullness and dryness. The interdependence between the two is symbolized in the taiji or Yin/Yang **symbol**, showing a two-tone circle with a dynamic curve and a contrasting dot that separates Yin from Yang. The line between the two halves is not straight and abrupt, as transitions are never sudden, but gradual like a waving curve. The dot of contrasting colour is there to remind us that there is always some Yin in Yang and some Yang in Yin.

Although everything in the universe is an interdependent combination of Yin and Yang some things will be more one than the other and this holds true for people too. The goal in Chinese philosophy and **traditional Chinese medicine** is always to maintain an equal amount of both, as too much Yin or too much Yang can lead to disease and decay.

YOGA

Yoga is an Indian spiritual philosophy that seeks to join all aspects of a person's body, mind and spirit so that the self can be united with universal consciousness. Its origin is impossible to trace, because it dates back to as far as 3000 BC, when references to it have been found in historic artefacts. Yoga comes in many forms specifically designed to suit different types of people. As a result, some forms of Yoga have gained significant popularity outside India, particularly in the West during the last century where it is best known as a physical discipline.

The word Yoga originates from the Sanskrit word *Yuj* ('to yoke') and is generally translated as 'union' or 'integration'.

According to Yoga experts, the union referred to is that of the individual **soul** (*atma*) with the cosmos, or the Supreme (*Brahma*). The *Yoga Sutras*, which were written sometime between 200 BC and AD 200, refer to the eight limbs or *ashtangas* that make up yogic practice, and if practitioners are able to follow these eight limbs it is thought that they will also develop spiritually and achieve ulitmate bliss or enlightenment.

The eight limbs are: *yama* (moral conduct with groups of people); *niyama* (moral individual conduct); *asana* (physical postures); *pranayama* (breath control); *pratyahara* (sense control); *dharana* (concentration); *dhyana* (**meditation**) and **samadhi** (self-realization). The nine obstacles to yogic practice are also listed in the *Sutras* and these are sickness, laziness, self-doubt, inattention, lack of mental effort, overindulgence, false knowledge, lack of concentration and lack of perseverance.

Yoga has both a philosophical and a practical dimension. The philosophy of yoga deals with the relationship between the individual soul and the cosmos. The practice of yoga, on the other hand, can be any activity that leads or brings the practitioner closer to this mystical union – a state called self-realization. Over thousands of years, special practical yoga techniques have been developed by experts in yoga, who are referred to as Yogis (male) and Yoginis (female).

There are numerous yoga disciplines but the *Sutras* mention four distinctive paths that are the most important: **kundalini**, **mantra**, hatha and raja. Over time all these paths have led to offshoots but hatha yoga,

Schools of Yoga

Westerners tend to think of Yoga largely as a system of gentle, stretching exercises, but there are in fact at least 10 different types of yogas which are recognized as valid paths to the goal of self-realization.

* *Bhakti Yoga* is described as the path of love, devotion and faith. Practitioners believe that love and devotion directed towards God and/or humanity and any living creature is the path to enlightenment.
* *Dhyana Yoga* is the path of contemplation and meditation, a purely mental discipline often involving trance states.
* *Hatha Yoga* emphasizes the development and control of the physical body to such a degree that it no longer interferes in any way with the individual's search for enlightenment. It is the most popular form of yoga in the West by far. One of the most famous positions of Hatha Yoga is the the Lotus Position – a cross-legged sitting posture which originated in meditative practices of Hinduism. The position is said to resemble a lotus flower and to encourage 'proper' breathing and physical stability. Famous depictions of the lotus posture include those of Shiva, the meditating ascetic god of Hinduism, and Buddha. In the lotus position the right foot is placed on the left thigh and the left foot on the right thigh, with the soles of the feet turned up and the spine straight. Hand positions vary but in Hinduism the hands are placed on the knees.
* *Jnana Yoga* is the yoga of knowledge and calls for an understanding of the sacred Vedas of Hinduism.
* *Karma Yoga* is the way of good deeds, usually expressed in helping those in need.
* *Kriya Yoga* is concerned with religious observance and the carrying out of ritual acts.
* *Kundalini Yoga* is concerned with arousing the power of kundalini at the base of the spine so it can climb upwards and illumiate the brain.
* *Laya Yoga* is concerned with the activation of chakras and uses specific mantras to awaken them.
* *Mantra Yoga* is a yoga of sound, using chants and mantras in order to drive the mind towards a higher state.
* *Raja Yoga* charts a system of mental and physical development with the goal of reaching enlightenment.

which focuses on physical routines of the body over the development of the mind, is without doubt the most popular in the West. People of all ages and levels of fitness and experience now practise yoga. Benefits are thought to include stress reduction, **relaxation**, increased flexibility, improved blood and breath circulation, better concentration and overall improvements in self-confidence, health and well-being.

Yoga was first introduced to Western culture when Queen Victoria brought yogis over to Britain to demonstrate yoga postures for her and her guests. It could be said, however, that yoga's growth in the West is due to followers of **theosophy** who, in the late nineteenth and early twentieth centuries translated many of the Hindu Sanskrit texts that outline Yoga philosophies.

Z

ZEN

Buddhist sect that developed in China and Japan and has become the best-known Buddhist sect in the West because of its intelligent, gentle and mystical nature. Zen is the Japanese translation of **meditation** and the way of Zen is the way of meditation that stresses the development of an intuitive wisdom that sees the oneness of all.

Zen can be considered a religion or a philosophy but it is something that can't really be conceptualized and must be experienced. It has been described as a way of life, work and an art form. The role of meditation in pursuing enlightenment is stressed. Enlightenment is the awakening to the true nature of one's being. It is the sole responsibility of the individual to find this enlightenment and it cannot be found through a saviour or faith or in any other way than individual experience.

Zen developed from the teachings of Bodhidharma, an Indian monk with alleged miraculous powers who arrived in China sometime in the sixth century. The true founder of Zen in China is, however, believed to be Hui-neng (637–713), who influenced the adaptation of Buddhism to Chinese thought. It was Hui-neng who described Zen as 'seeing into one's own nature'. After his death Hui-neng was named 'Zen Master of the Great Mirror'. In Zen the **mirror** symbolizes the enlightened mind, the absence of all thought in pure mirror activity, in which the mind clings to no thought. Hui-neng's own experience of enlightenment helped him understand that the mind already possesses enlightenment; it just needs to be realized. Following Hui-neng Zen rose to great prominence in China and two streams of thought emerged concerning it: the Lin-chi sect, which developed the use of paradoxes (*koan*) as a way to enlightenment, and the Ts'ao-tung, which stressed passive, silent meditation as a path to enlightenment.

In Japan Zen ideas arrived during the seventh and eighth centuries but did not fully flourish until the monk Eisai (1141–1215) founded the Rinzai sect of Zen with its Lin-chi emphasis on paradoxes in 1191, and another monk, Dogen (1200–1253), founded the Soto sect with its emphasis on silent meditation. In Japan Zen took on a unique character of its own and has permeated into all parts of Japanese culture. In particular it has influenced the arts and is the basis of the tea ceremony.

In Zen enlightenment (*Satori*) can only be found by turning inwards and meditation is the best way to do this. One of the most basic types of Zen meditation is called *zazen*, which literally means 'sitting meditation'. It is typically done in the lotus position or sitting cross-legged, or even kneeling on a bench, with the eyes open and cast downward and hands resting on the abdomen. Breath counting is used to train the mind to achieve concentration (**Samadhi**). In order to reach this state the mind must empty itself of thoughts, delusions, fantasies (*makyo*) self-doubt, preoccupation with personal problems and physical pain.

The *koan* or paradoxes in Zen are designed to be illogical so that they can achieve a breakthrough in consciousness. Perhaps the best known is 'What is the sound of one hand clapping?' The student may meditate on a paradox for months until an answer comes with sudden illumination.

Satori or enlightenment in Zen is a breakthrough of consciousness and is thought to be the beginning of the Zen experience. *Satori* is the opening of the heart and the **third eye**, seeing things from a new point of view, an awareness of one's own nature and the burning away of material attachments and negativity. Psychiatrist **Carl Jung** interpreted *Satori* as the great liberation of the **unconscious**, the totality of the nature of the **soul**. Satori can occur spontaneously after years of preparation and contemplation but more often than not it occurs during meditation.

Once *Satori* is awakened it is then deepened through further meditation into a state of no-mind or no-thought, which is really seeing beyond the duality of subject–object. The state of no-mind often takes years and lifetimes to achieve but when it does it permeates daily life and manifests in everything a person does. No-mind occurs once a person realizes that nothing and now constitute all there is, that what happens in the present is what life is, not future goals or past dreams, which is why a Zen Buddhist lives by the **mantra** 'be here now, in this moment'.

ZENER CARDS

Card set designed by parapsychologists **J B Rhine** and Karl Zener for use in card-guessing tests of **ESP** abilities. A set of Zener cards consists of 25 cards in total, comprised of five each of a circle, a square, Greek cross, five-pointed star and three wavy lines. Also commonly referred to as **ESP cards**.

ZERO BALANCING

Form of **massage** therapy that concentrates on aligning body energies (chi, prana, etc.) with the body's physical structure. Zero balancing was designed as a scientific technique by Dr Fritz Smith in 1975. He felt there was a need for an **energy balancing** medicine that concentrated on bones and joints, and developed zero balancing after years of study and experimentation. In a typical session the client lies or sits comfortably while the practitioner applies gentle pressure to various places on the trunk, legs, neck and feet. People often report an enhanced sense of wellbeing after a treatment and it can also trigger a cathartic release of emotion.

ZODIAC

The system astrologers use to mark out and name constellations in the sky that the planets move through on a regular basis. The zodiac consists of an organized belt of constellations which, in Western **astrology**, are divided into 12 signs of 30 degrees each, which encompass the stellar constellations symbolized by an animal or mythical person or process, and known as Aries, the Ram; Taurus, the Bull; Gemini, the Twins; Cancer, the Crab; Leo, the Lion; Virgo, the Virgin; Libra, the Balance/Scale; Scorpio, the Scorpion; Sagittarius, the Archer; Capricorn, the Goat; Aquarius, the Water Bearer; and Pisces, the Fish. Each sign acts as an indictor for various personality traits. The correlation between the movements of these constellations is used to interpret future events.

See also **Astrology**, **Horoscope**.

ZOMBIE

In Haitian and West African **Voodoo** traditions, a zombie is a soulless, reanimated corpse resurrected from the dead by a Voodoo priest, known as a 'Bocor', for the purposes of indentured servitude. Etymologists and anthropologists speculate that the term is derived from Nzambi, a West African deity.

A natural explanation may exist for this phenomenon. It has been suggested that the zombie may have been a person who was buried alive and only seemed dead through the administration of a drug containing the poison of various plants and animals and various human remains. The poison puts the victim in a death-like state. Not all those who take the drug survive; those who do remain conscious and witness their own burial and funeral.

After two days the Bocor raises the victim from the tomb and administers a hallucinogenic concoction that awakens the 'zombie', who is now so psychologically traumatized that he or she is willing to answer to a new name and follow the Bocor into a new life, which is usually to work in the fields. Not surprisingly zombification was once described as the African slave's ultimate nightmare, as not even death can release them from never-ending labour.

Voodoo **sorcerers** are said to create zombies by capturing the **souls** of the deceased. If the sorcerer is able to capture the soul he can make a zombie **ghost** who wanders eternally in the **astral plane** at the command of the sorcerer. To prevent this happening relatives of the deceased will often stab corpses in the heart or decapitate them.

ZOOMANCY

Divination by the appearance and/or the behaviours of animals. Also interpreted as predictions made based upon the appearance of imaginary or mythical creatures such as the **unicorn** or salamanders.

Zoomancy can differ from country to country and area to area. Perhaps the best-known example of zoomancy is that of a black cat crossing your path, which is believed to be a warning of bad luck to come. In some areas it only is a bad **omen** if it crosses from right to left. If it crosses from left to right then it signifies the onset of good luck. In other areas this is reversed.

Ailuromancy, divination by the movement of cats, is but one example of zoomancy. There are a tremendous number of signs and omens based on the behaviour of animals. This isn't much of a surprise as animals have always provided people with inspiration and teaching as well as food, clothing and companionship. Animals and divination go together naturally.

Tribal societies have often wanted to ally themselves with the power and strength they can see in animals. Clans and tribes have adopted **totem** animals and the names of places today often recall the tribes and their totems.

From the very beginning, early humans must have watched the way the animals behaved. Survival often depended on being able to 'read' the natural world, not simply for direct indications of food, but also the oddities that might be taken to be signs from the Spirit. Over time some of the ways that animals behaved must have accrued symbolic meanings. In Roman times the art of **augury** – divination by the behaviour of birds – was taken very seriously indeed. If the signs were inauspicious

then the meetings of the Senate the next day would be cancelled.

Many forms of zoomancy still manifest today in **superstitions** concerning the behaviour of animals. For example, bats flying at twilight, a robin flying into the house, seeing a ladybird – are all signs of good luck, whereas bats hitting a building, a frog croaking in the daytime and cattle lying down are all signs that it will rain soon. If a cat washes one ear three times then expect a visitor from the direction in which the cat is looking. If your cat appears around the door, think of a question and call her. If her right paw appears first around the door the answer is yes, if it is the left paw then the answer is no – and so on.

There are countless superstitions associated with animals, and almost as many books detailing them. Two recommended ones are David Pickering's *Dictionary of Superstitions* and *The Encyclopedia of Superstitions* by Christina Hole.

Resources

1. Selected books/ Bibliography

Acorah, Derek *Ghost Hunting* (London: HarperElement, 2005)

Alcock, James E *Parapsychology. Magic or Science?* (Oxford and New York: Pergamon, 1981)

— *Science and Supernature. A Critical Appraisal of Parapsychology* (New York: Prometheus, 1990)

Allison, L W *Leonard and the Soule Experiments* (Boston: Boston Society for Psychical Research, 1929)

Almeder, Robert *Death and Personal Survival: The Evidence for Life After Death* (Boston: Rowman & Littlefield, 1992)

Ashby, R H *The Guidebook for the Study of Psychical Research* (London: Rider, 1972)

Atwater, P M H *Beyond the Light. Near-Death Experiences – The Full Story* (London: Thorsons, 1995)

Auerbach, Lord, *Ghost Hunting: How to Investigate the Paranormal* (Berkeley, Calif.: Ronin Publishing, 2004)

Barrett, William *Death Bed Visions* (reissued Wellingborough: Aquarian Press, 1986)

Barrington, Mary Rose (ed.) *Guide to the Investigation of Apparitions, Hauntings, Poltergeists and Kindred Phenomena* (London: Society for Psychical Research, 1966)

Beard, Paul *Living On. A Study of Altering Consciousness After Death* (London: George Allen & Unwin, 1980)

— *Hidden Man* (Norwich: Pilgrim Books, 1986)

Becker, Carl B *Paranormal Experience and Survival of Death* (New York: State University of New York Press, 1993)

Beloff, John (ed.) *New Directions in Parapsychology* (London: Elek Science, 1974)

— *The Importance of Psychical Research* (London: Society for Psychical Research, 1988)

— *Parapsychology: A Concise History* (London: The Athlone Press, 1993)

Berger, Arthur S *Lives and Letters in American Parapsychology: A Biographical History, 1850–1987* (Jefferson, NC: McFarland, 1988)

Berger, Arthur S and Berger, Joyce *The Encyclopedia of Parapsychology and Psychical Research* (New York: Paragon House, 1991)

Bernstein, M *The Search for Bridey Murphy* (Garden City, NY: Doubleday, 1956)

Besterman, Theodore *Collected Papers on the Paranormal* (New York: Garrett, 1968)

Blackmore, Susan *Beyond the Body. An Investigation of Out-of-the-Body Experiences* (London: Heinemann, 1982)

— *Dying to Live. Near-Death Experiences* (New York: Prometheus Books, 1993)

Blavatsky, Helena *Isis Unveiled* 2 volumes (1877)

— *Secret Doctrine* 2 volumes (1888)

— *The Key to Theosophy* (1889)

— *Voice of the Silence* (1889)

— *Transactions of the Blavatsky Lodge* (1890–91)

Bozzano, E *Animism and Spiritism: A reply to M. Sudre's Introduction à la Métapsychiquer Humaine* (London: Arthur H Stockwell, 1926; first published in French, 1926)

— *Discarnate Influence in Human Life* (London: John Watkins, n.d.)

Bramwell, J M *Hypnotism: Its History, Practice and Theory* (New York: Julian Press, 1957; first published 1903)

Brath, Stanley de *Psychical Research, Science and Religion* (London: Methuen, 1925)

Braude, Stephen E *ESP and Psychokinesis: A Philosophical Influence* (Philadelphia: Temple University Press, 1979; rev. edn Parkland, Fla.: Brown Walker Press, 2002)

— *First Person Plural: Multiple Personality and the Philosophy of Mind* (Lanham, Md: Rowman & Littlefield, 1995)

— *Immortal Remains: The Evidence for Life After Death* (Lanham Md: Rowman & Littlefield, 2003)

Brealey, Gene, with Hunter, Kay *The Two Worlds of Helen Duncan* (London and New York: Regency Press Ltd, 1985)

Brennan, Barbara *Hands of Light: A Guide to Healing Through the Human Energy Field* (London: Bantam, 1993)

Brian, D *The Enchanted Voyager: The Life of J B Rhine* (Englewood Cliffs, NJ: Prentice-Hall, 1982)

Broad, C D *The Mind and its Place in Nature* (London: Routledge & Kegan Paul, 1925)

— *Religion, Philosophy and Psychical Research* (London: Routledge and Kegan Paul, 1953)

— *Personal Identity and Survival.* Myers Memorial Lecture for 1958 (London: Society for Psychical Research, 1958)

— *Lectures on Psychical Research* (London: Routledge & Kegan Paul, 1962)

Broughton, Richard S *Parapsychology: The Controversial Science* (New York: Ballentine, 1991)

Buckland, Raymond *Book of Spirit Communications* (New York: Llewellyn, 2004)

Burt, Cyril *Psychology and Psychical Research.* Myers Memorial Lecture for 1968 (London: Society for Psychical Research, 1968)

— *ESP and Psychology*, edited by Anita Gregory (London: Weidenfeld & Nicolson, 1975)

Byskov, Else *Death is an Illusion: A Logical Explanation Based on Martinus' Worldview* (St Paul, Minn.: Paragon House, 2002)

Carington, Whately *Telepathy: An Outline of its Facts, Theory, and Implications* (London: Meuthen & Co., 1945)

Carpenter, W B *Mesmerism and Spiritualism, &c. Historically and Scientifically Considered* (London: Longmans & Green, 1877)

Carrington, H *Eusapia Palladino and her Phenomena* (London: Werner Laurie, 1909)

— *The Story of Psychic Science* (London: Rider & Co., 1930)

Carroll, Robert Todd *The Skeptic's Dictionary. A Collection of Strange Beliefs, Amusing Deceptions & Dangerous Delusions* (Hoboken, NJ: John Wiley & Sons, 2003)

Choquette, Sonia *Diary of a Psychic: Shattering the Myths* (Carlsbad, Calif.: Hay House, 2003)

Christie-Murray, David *Voices from the Gods: Speaking with Tongues* (London: Routledge & Kegan Paul, 1978)

Cornell, A D *Investigating the Paranormal* (New York: Helix Press, 2002)

Crookall, Robert *The Supreme Adventure. Analyses of Psychic Communications* (London: James Clarke & Co., 1961)

Crookes, William *Researches into the Phenomena of Modern Spiritualism* (Manchester: Two Worlds Publishing Company, 1904)

Crowe, C *The Night-Side of Nature: Or, Ghosts and Ghosts Seers* 2 volumes (London: T Newby, 1848)

Cummins, Geraldine *The Road to Immortality. Being a Description of the After-Life Purporting to be Communicated by the late F W H Myers Through Geraldine Cummins* (London: Ivor Nicholson & Watson, 1932)

— *Beyond Human Personality. Being a Detailed Description of the Future Life Purporting to be Communicated by the late F W H Myers. Containing an Account of the Gradual Development of the Human Personality into Cosmic Personality* (London: Ivor Nicholson & Watson, 1935)

— *Unseen Adventures. An Autobiography Covering Thirty-Four Years of Work in Psychical Research* (London: Rider, 1951)

— *Swan on a Black Sea. A Study in Automatic Writing. The Cummins-Willet Scripts* (London: Routledge & Kegan Paul, 1965)

Dingwall, E J *Some Human Oddities* (New Hyde Park, NY: University Books, 1962)

— *Very Peculiar People* (New Hyde Park, NY: University Books, 1962)

— (ed.) *Abnormal Hypnotic Phenomena: A Survey of Nineteenth-Century Cases* 4 volumes (New York: Barnes & Noble, 1967)

Dingwall, E J, Goldney, K M and Hall, T H *The Haunting of Borley Rectory: A Critical Survey of the Evidence* (London: Gerald Duckworth & Co., 1956)

Douglas, Alfred *Extra-Sensory Powers: A Century of Psychical Research* (London: Gollancz, 1976)

Doyle, Arthur Conan *The Coming of the Fairies* (London, Hodder and Stoughton, 1922)

Driesch, Hans *Psychical Research: The Science of the Super-normal* (London: G Bell & Sons, 1933)

Edge, H L, Morris, R L, Rush, J H and Palmer, J *Foundations of Parapsychology* (London and Boston: Routledge, 1991)

Edwards, Paul *Immortality* (New York: Macmillan, 1985)

Eisenbud, J *The World of Ted Serios. 'Thoughtographic' Studies of an Extraordinary Mind* (London: Cape, 1967)

— *Psi and Psychoanalysis* (New York: Grune and Stratton, 1970)

Ellison, Arthur *The Reality of the Paranormal* (London: Guild Publishing, 1998)

— *Science and the Paranormal. Altered States of Reality* (Edinburgh: Floris Books, 2002)

Fenwick, Peter and Fenwick, Elizabeth *The Truth in the Light. An Investigation of Over 300 Near-Death Experiences* (London: Headline, 1995)

Fielding, Everard *Sittings with Eusapia Palladino & Other Studies* (New Hyde Park, NY: University Books, 1963)

Fielding, Yvette and O'Kieffe, C *Was That a Ghost?* (London: Hodder and Stoughton, forthcoming)

Findlay, Arthur *Where Two Worlds Meet* (London: Psychic Press, 1968)

Flammarion, Camille *The Unknown* (New York and London: Harper Brothers, 1900)

— *Death and Its Mystery: Proofs of the Existence of the Soul* (London: T Fisher Unwin, Ltd, 1909)

— *Death and Its Mystery: Manifestations and Apparitions of the Dead* (London: T Fisher Unwin, Ltd, 1923)

— *Death and Its Mystery: The Soul After Death* (London: T Fisher Unwin, Ltd, 1923)

— *Haunted Houses* (London: T Fisher Unwin, Ltd; New York: D. Appleton and Co., 1924)

Flint, Leslie *Voices in the Dark. My Life as a Medium* (London: Macmillan, 1971)

Flournoy, Theodore *From India to the Planet Mars* (Princeton, NJ: Princeton University Press, 1994; first published 1900)

Fodor, Nandor *These Mysterious People* (London: Rider & Co., 1934)

— *Between Two Worlds* (New York: Parker, 1964)

— *An Encyclopaedia of Psychic Science* (New York: The Citadel Press, 1966; first published 1934)

Fontana, David *Is there an Afterlife? A Comprehensive Overview of the Evidence* (Ropley, Hants.: O Books, 2005)

Fontanay, G de *A Propos d'Eusapia Palladino* (Paris, 1898)

Fortune, Dion *Applied Magic and Aspects of Occultism* (Boston, MA: Weiser, 2000)

— *The Esoteric Philosophy of Love and Marriage* (Boston, MA: Red Wheel/Weiser, 2000)

— *Through the Gates of Death* (Boston, MA: Red Wheel/Weiser, 2000)

— *The Training and Work of an Initiate* (Boston, MA: Weiser, 2000)

— *Psychic Self-Defense* (Boston, MA: Red Wheel/Weiser, 2001)

— *What Is Occultism?* (Boston, MA: Red Wheel/Weiser, 2001)

— *Glastonbury: Avalon of the Heart* (Boston, MA: Red Wheel/Weiser, 2003)

Forwald, H *Mind, Matter and Gravitation.* Parapsychological Monographs No. 11 (New York: Parapsychology Foundation, 1969)

Fournier D'albe, E E *The Life of Sir William Crookes* (London: T Fisher Unwin, 1923)

— *New Light on Immortality* (London: Longmans Green, 1923)

Fryer, C *Geraldine Cummins: An Appreciation* (Norwich: Pilgrim Trust, 1990)

Garrett, Eileen J *My Life as a Search for the Meaning of Mediumship* (London: Rider & Co., 1939)

Gauld, Alan *The Founders of Psychical Research* (London: Routledge & Kegan Paul, 1968)

— *Mediumship and Survival* (London: Heinemann, 1982)

— *A History of Hypnotism* (Cambridge: Cambridge University Press, 1992)

Gauld, Alan, and Cornell, A D *Notes for Investigators of Spontaneous Cases* (London: Society for Psychical Research, 1968)

— *Poltergeists* (London: Routledge & Kegan Paul, 1979)

Geley, Gustave *From the Unconscious to the Conscious* (New York: Harper and Brothers, 1921)

— *Clairvoyance and Materialisation: A Record of Experiments* (London: T Fisher Unwin, 1927; first published in French as *L'ectoplasmie et la clairvoyance*, 1924; reissued New York: Arno Press, 1975)

Grattan-Guiness, Ivor *Psychical Research: A Guide to its History, Principles and Practices. In Celebration of 100 years of the Society for Psychical Research* (Wellingborough: Aquarian Press, 1982)

Grof, Stanislav *Realms of the Human Unconscious. Observations from LSD Research* (London: Souvenir Press, 1979)

Grosso, Michael *Experiencing the Next World Now* (New York: Simon and Schuster, Paraview Pocket Books, 2004)

Guggenheim, Bill and Guggenheim, Judy *Hello from Heaven!* (London: Thorsons, 1995)

Guiley, Rosemary Ellen *Encyclopedia of Mystical and Paranormal Experience* (London: Grange Books, 1993)

— *Encyclopedia of Ghosts and Spirits* (New York: Checkmark, 2000)

Gurney, Edmund, Myers, Frederick and Podmore, Frank *Phantasms of the Living* 2 volumes (London: Trübner & Co., 1886)

Haining, Peter *A Dictionary of Ghosts* (London: Robert Hale, 1999)

Hall, Trevor T *The Search for Harry Price* (London: Gerald Duckworth & Co., 1978)

— *The Enigma of Daniel Home* (New York: Prometheus, 1984)

Hamilton, T Glen *Intention and Survival* (London and New York: Regency Press Ltd, 1942)

Hamilton-Parker, Craig *The Psychic Workbook: Discover and Enhance Your Hidden Psychic Powers* (London and New York: Random House, 1995)

Hansell, C E M *ESP: A Scientific Evaluation* (New York: Charles Scribner's Sons, 1966)

— *ESP and Parapsychology: A Critical Re-Evaluation* (New York: Prometheus, 1980)

— *The Search for Psychic Power. ESP and Parapsychology Revisited* (New York: Prometheus, 1989)

Hardy, A, Harvie, R and Koestler, A *The Challenge of Chance* (London: Hutchinson, 1973)

Harrison, Thomas *Life After Death – Living Proof. A Lifetime's Experiences of Physical Phenomena and Materialisations through the Mediumship of Minnie Harrison* (York: Saturday Night Press, 2004)

Hart, H *The Enigma of Survival: For and Against an Afterlife* (London: Rider, 1959)

— *Toward a New Philosophical Basis for Parapsychological Phenomena* (New York: Parapsychology Foundation, 1965)

Hasted, J B *The Metal-Benders* (London: Routledge & Kegan Paul, 1981)

Heywood, Rosalind *The Sixth Sense: An Inquiry into Extra-Sensory Perception* (London: Chatto & Windus, 1959)

Hodges, David *Do We Survive Death? A Descriptive Bibliography and Discussion on the Evidence Supporting Survival* (Braintree, Essex: Webbs Cottage Press, 2001)

Home, D D *Incidents in My Life* (Microsoft reader e-books, 2002)

Houdini, Harry *A Magician Among the Spirits* (New York: Harper, 1924)

— *Miracle Mongers and their Methods. A Complete Exposé* (New York: Prometheus Books, 1981)

Hyman, Ray *The Elusive Quarry. A Scientific Appraisal of Psychical Research* (New York: Prometheus Books, 1989)

Hyslop, James H *Borderland of Psychical Research* (London: G P Putnam, 1906)

— *Enigmas of Psychical Research* (London: G P Putnam, 1906)

— *Psychical Research and the Resurrection* (London: T Fisher Unwin, 1908)

— *Psychical Research and Survival* (London: G Bells & Sons Ltd., 1914)

— *Life After Death* (New York: E P Dutton & Co., 1918)

— *Contact With the Other World* (New York: Century, 1919)

Illes, Judika *Element Encyclopedia of 5000 Spells* (London: HarperElement, 2004)

Inglis, B *Natural and Supernatural: A History of the Paranormal from Earliest Times to 1914* (London: Hodder & Stoughton, 1977)

— *Science and Parascience: A History of the Paranormal 1914–1939* (London: Hodder & Stoughton, 1984)

— *The Paranormal: An Encyclopedia of Psychic Phenomena* (London: Grafton/Paladin, 1985)

— *The Hidden Power* (London: Jonathan Cape, 1986)

— *Trance: A Natural History of Altered States of Mind* (London: Grafton Books, 1989)

Irwin, H J *An Introduction to Parapsychology* (Jefferson, NC: McFarland, 1989)

James, William *The Varieties of Religious Experience* (London: Longmans, Green and Co., 1929)

Jenkins, E *The Shadow and the Light: A Defence of Daniel Dunglas Home the Medium* (London: Hamish Hamilton, 1982)

Kardec, A *Spiritualist Philosophy: The Spirits' Book* (London: Trübner, 1975)

— *Experimental Spiritism: The Medium's Book, or Guide for Mediums and for Evocations* (London: Trübner, 1976)

Keil, Jurgen (ed.) *Gaither Pratt: A Life for Parapsychology* (Jefferson, NC: McFarland, 1982)

Kelly, E F and Locke, R G *Altered States of Consciousness and Psi: An Historical Survey and Research Prospectus.* Parapsychological Monographs, No. 18 (New York: Parapsychology Foundation, 1981)

Koestler, Arthur *The Roots of Coincidence* (London: Hutchinson & Co., 1972)

Krippner, S (ed.) *Advances in Parapsychological Research* Vol. 5 (Jefferson, NC: McFarland, 1987)

Kübler-Ross, Elizabeth *On Death and Dying* (London: Tavistock Publications, 1969)

— *Questions and Answers on Death and Dying* (New York: Collier Macmillan, 1974)

— *Death, the Final Stage of Growth* (Englewood Cliffs, NJ: Prentice-Hall, 1975)

— *The Wheel of Life. A Memoir of Living and Dying* (New York: Scribner, 1997)

Kurtz, Paul (ed.) *A Skeptic's Handbook of Parapsychology* (New York: Prometheus Books, 1985)

— *The New Skepticism. Inquiry and Reliable Knowledge* (New York: Prometheus Books, 1992)

— *Science and Religion: Are the Compatible?* (Amherst, NY: Prometheus, 2003)

Lawson, David *Your Psychic Potential* (London: Thorsons, 1997)

Leonard, G O *My Life in Two Worlds* (London: Cassell, 1931)

— *Brief Darkness* (London: Cassell, 1942)

Lodge, Oliver *Survival of Man* (London: Methuen, 1909)

— *Raymond or Life After Death* (London: Methuen, 1916)

Lombroso, Cesare *After Death – What?* (Wellingborough: Aquarian Press, 1986)

Lorimer, David *Survival? Body, Mind and the Death in the Light of Psychic Experience* (London: Routledge & Kegan Paul, 1984)

Ludwig, Jan *Philosophy and Parapsychology* (New York: Prometheus Books, 1978)

Marryat, Florence *There is no Death* (Eighth edition; Manchester: Two Worlds, 1925)

McCreery, Charles *Science, Philosophy & ESP* (London: Faber & Faber, 1967)

— *Psychical Phenomena and the Physical World* (London: Hamish Hamilton, 1973)

McDougall, William *Body and Mind: A History and a Defence of Animism* (London: Methuen & Co., 1911)

McKenzie, Andrew *The Unexplained. Some Strange Cases in Psychical Research* (London: Arthur Baker, 1966; New York: Popular Library, 1970)

— *Apparitions and Ghosts. A Modern Study* (London: Arthur Baker; New York: Popular Library, 1971)

— *A Gallery of Ghosts* (London: Arthur Baker; New York: Taplinger, 1973)

— *The Riddle of the Future: A Modern Study of Precognition* (London: Arthur Baker, 1974)

— *Hauntings and Apparitions* (London: Heinemann, 1982)

McKenzie, J H *Spirit Intercourse: Its Theory and Practice* (London: Simpkin, Marshall, Hamilton & Kent, 1916)

McMoneagle, Joseph *Mind Trek. Exploring Consciousness, Time, and Space through Remote Viewing* (Charlottesville, Va: Hampton Roads Publishing Co., 1993)

— *The Ultimate Time Machine. A Remote Viewer's Perception of Time and Predictions for the New Millennium* (Charlottesville, Va: Hampton Roads Publishing Co., 1998)

— *Remote Viewing Secrets. A Handbook* (Charlottesville, Va: Hampton Roads Publishing Co., 2000)

Moody, Raymond *Life After Life* (New York: Mockingbird Books, 1975)

— *Reflections on Life After Life* (London: Corgi Books, 1977)

Moody, Raymond and Perry, Paul *The Light Beyond* (London: Macmillan, 1988)

— *Reunions. Visionary Encounters with Departed Loved Ones* (New York: Villard Books, 1993)

Moore, Garth E *Survival – A Reconsideration.* Myers Memorial Lecture for 1963 (London: Society for Psychical Research, 1963)

Morse, J J *A Brief History of Spirit Photography* (Manchester: Two Worlds, 1909)

Morse, Melvin and Parry, Paul *Closer to the Light. Learning from Children's Near-Death Experiences* (New York: Villard Books, 1990)

— *Transformed by the Light. The Powerful Effect of Near-Death Experience* (New York: Villard Books, 1992)

Moseley, Sydney A *An Amazing Séance and An Exposure* (London and Edinburgh: Sampson Low, Marston & Co., 1919)

Mühl, A M *Automatic Writing: An Approach to the Unconscious* (New York: Helix Press, 1963)

Mumler, W H *Personal Experiences of William H Mumler in Spirit Photography* (Boston: Colby and Rich, 1875)

Murphy, Gardner *The Challenge of Psychical Research* (New York: Harper and Row, 1961)

Murphy, Gardner and Ballou, Robert O *William James on Psychical Research* (London: Chatto & Windus Ltd, 1960)

Myers, Frederick W H *Science and a Future Life* (London: Macmillan, 1901)

— *Human Personality and Its Survival of Bodily Death* 2 volumes (London: Longmans & Green, 1903; reprinted (abridged) Norwich: Pilgrim Books, 1992)

Oesterriech, T Konstantin *Occultism and Modern Science* (London: Methuen & Co., 1920)

Olliver, C W A *The Extension of Consciousness* (London: Rider & Co., 1932)

Oppenheim, J *The Other World: Spiritualism and Psychical Research in England, 1850–1914* (Cambridge: Cambridge University Press, 1985)

Oram, Arthur *The System in Which we Live* (Purley: Talbot Books, 1988)

Osis, K *Death-Bed Observations by Physicians and Nurses* (New York: Parapsychology Foundation, 1961)

Osty, Eugene *Supernormal Faculties in Man* (London: Meuthen & Co., 1923)

Owen, A R G *Can we Explain the Poltergeist?* (New York: Garrett/Helix, 1964)

Owen, I M and Sparrow, M H *Conjuring Up Philip* (New York: Harper & Row, 1977)

Owen, R D *The Debatable Land Between This World and the Next* (London: Trübner, 1871)

Parker, Adrian *Claims of Reincarnation: An Empirical Study of Cases in India* (New Delhi: Harman, 1990)

Pearce-Higgins, J D and Whitby, G Stanley (eds.) *Life, Death & Psychical Research: Studies on Behalf of The Churches' Fellowship for Psychical Research and Spiritual Studies* (London: Rider & Co., 1973)

Pearson, Ronald D *Intelligence Behind the Universe!* (London: The Headquarters Publishing, 1990)

— *Origin of Mind* (Bath: Bathford Publishers, 1992)

— *Quantum Gravitation: The Key to Consciousness* (Bath: Bathford Publishers, 1997)

Penelhum, T *Survival and Disembodied Existence* (London: Routledge & Kegan Paul, 1970)

Pilkington, R (ed.) *Men and Women of Parapsychology: Personal Reflections* (Jefferson, NC: McFarland, 1987)

Piper, A L *The Life and Work of Mrs Piper* (London: Kegan Paul, Trench, Trubner & Co., 1929)

Playfair, Guy Lyon *The Indefinite Boundary: An Investigation into the Relationship between Matter and Spirit* (London: Souvenir Press, 1976)

— *If this Be Magic* (London: Jonathan Cape, 1985)

— *Haunted Pub Guide* (London: Harrap, 1995)

— *Mindforce. Exploring the Mysteries of Everyday Life* (London: Brilliant Books, 1999)

— *Twin Telepathy – the Psychic Connection* (London: Vega, 2002)

Playfair, Guy Lyon and Geller, Uri *The Geller Effect* (London: Jonathan Cape, 1986)

Podmore, Frank *Telepathic Hallucinations* (Halifax: Milner and Co., n.d.)

— *Apparitions and Thought-Transference: An Examination of the Evidence for Telepathy* (London: Walter Scott, 1894)

— *Studies in Psychical Research* (London: Kegan Paul, Trench, Trübner & Co., 1897)

— *Modern Spiritualism: A History and a Criticism* 2 volumes (London: Methuen & Co., 1902)

— *Mesmerism and Christian Science* (London: Meuthen & Co., 1909)

Pratt, J G *Parapsychology: An Insider's View of ESP* (New York: Doubleday & Co., 1964)

Prentice, Margaret *Richard, Spirit and I* (Hertfordshire: Lionheart Press, 1999)

Price, Harry *Fifty Years of Psychical Research: A Critical Survey* (London: Longmans, Green & Co., 1939)

— *Search for Truth: My Life in Psychical Research* (London: Pall Mall, 1942)

— *The Most Haunted House in England* (New York: Time Life Books, 2003)

Prince, W F *The Dissociation of a Personality* (London: Longmans & Green, 1905)

— *Noted Witnesses for Psychic Occurrences* (Boston: Boston Society for Psychical Research, 1928)

— *The Enchanted Boundary: Being a Survey of Negative Reactions to Claims of Psychic Phenomena* (New York: Arno Press, 1975; first published 1930)

Radin, Dean *The Conscious Universe. The Scientific Truth of Psychic Phenomena* (New York: Harper & Row, 1997)

Randall, J L *Parapsychology and the Nature of Life* (London: Souvenir Press, 1975)

— *Tests for Extra Sensory Perception and Psychokinesis* (London: Society for Psychical Research, 1980)

Randi, James *Flim-Flam! Psychics, ESP, Unicorns, and Other Delusions* (New York: Prometheus Books, 1982)

— *The Truth About Uri Geller* (New York: Prometheus Books, 1982)

— *An Encyclopedia of Claims, Frauds, and Hoaxes of the Occult and Supernatural* (New York: St Martin's Press, 1995)

Rao, K Ramakrishna *The Basic Experiments in Parapsychology* (Jefferson, NC: McFarland, 1984)

Ratcliffe, Eric *Unfinished Business: An Account of Research by Sir William Crookes Involving an Unknown Force and the Failure of the Royal Society to Investigate* (Stevenage, Herts: Four Quarters Press, 2005)

Raudive, Konstantin *Breakthrough. Electronic Communication with the Dead May be Possible* (New York: Zebra Books, 1971)

Rhine, J B *Extra-Sensory Perception* (Boston, Boston Society for Psychical Research, 1934)

— *New Frontiers of the Mind: The Story of the Duke Experiments* (New York: Farrar & Rinehart, 1937)

— *The Reach of the Mind* (New York: William Sloane, 1947)

— *Telepathy and Human Personality*. Tenth F W H Myers Memorial Lecture (London: Society for Psychical Research, 1950)

— *New World of the Mind* (New York: William Sloane, 1953)

Rhine, J B and Associates *Parapsychology: From Duke to FRNM* (Durham, NC: Parapsychology Press, 1965)

Rhine, J B and Pratt, J G *Parapsychology: the Frontier Science of the Mind* (Springfield, Ill.: Thomas, 1962)

Rhine, J B, Pratt, J G, Stuart, C E, Smith, B M and Greenwood, J A *Extra-Sensory Perception: After Sixty Years* (New York: Henry Holt & Co., 1940)

Rhine, L E *Hidden Channels of the Mind* (New York: Sloane Association, 1961)

— *ESP in Life and Lab* (New York:
Macmillan, 1967)
— *Psi* (New York: Harper & Row, 1975)
— *The Invisible Picture: A Study of Psychic
Experiences* (Jefferson, NC: McFarland,
1981)
— *Something Hidden* (Jefferson, NC:
McFarland, 1982)
Richards, J T *SORRAT: A History of the
Neihardt Psychokinesis Experiments*
(Metuchen, NJ: Scarecrow Press, 1982)
Richet, Charles *Thirty Years of Psychical
Research* (London: W Collins & Sons,
1923)
— *Our Sixth Sense* (London: W Collins &
Sons, 1927)
Richmond, Z *Evidence of Purpose* (London:
Bell, 1938)
Rickard, Bob and Mitchell, John
Unexplained Phenomena (London: Rough
Guide, 2000)
Ring, Kenneth *Life at Death. A Scientific
Exploration of Near-Death Experience*
(New York: William Morrow, 1980)
— *Heading Toward Omega. In Search of the
Meaning of the Near-Death Experience*
(New York: William Morrow, 1984)
— *The Omega Project. Near-Death
Experience, UFO Encounters and Mind at
Large* (New York: William Morrow,
1992)
Ring, Kenneth and Valarino, Evelyn E
*Lessons from the Light. What we can
Learn from the Near-Death Experience*
(New York: Insight, 1998)
Roberts, Ron and Groome, David
*Parapsychology: The Science of Unusual
Experience* (London: Arnold, 2001)
Rochas, A de *Les Vies successives* (Paris:
Chacornac Frères, 1911)

Rogo, D Scott *The Search for Yesterday: A
Critical Examination of the Evidence for
Reincarnation* (Englewood Cliffs, NJ:
Prentice-Hall, 1985)
— *Life After Death. The Case for Survival of
Bodily Death* (Wellingborough:
Aquarian Press, 1986)
Roll, William G *The Poltergeist* (New York:
New American Library, 1972)
Roll, William G, Morris, R L and
Morris, J D (eds.) *Research in
Parapsychology* (Metuchen, NJ:
Scarecrow Press, 1978)
Roller, Gilbert *A Voice from Beyond* (New
York: Popular Library, 1975)
Roy, Archie *The Archives of the Mind*
(Stansted: SNU Publications, 1996)
Sabom, Michael B *Recollections of Death*
(London: Corgi Books, 1982)
— *Light and Dead. One Doctor's Fascinating
Account of Near-Death Experiences*
(Michigan: Zondervan Grand Rapids,
1998)
Sagan, Carl *The Demon-Haunted World.
Science as a Cradle in the Dark* (New
York and London: Random House,
1995)
Sage, M *Mrs Piper and the Society for
Psychical Research* (London: Brimley
Johnson, 1903)
Sahay, K K N *Reincarnation: Verified Cases
of Rebirth after Death* (Bareilly: N L
Gupta, 1927)
Salter, W H *Trance Mediumship: An
Introductory Study of Mrs Piper and Mrs
Leonard* (London: Society for Psychical
Research, 1950)
— *Zoar. Or the Evidence of Psychical
Research Concerning Survival* (London:
Sidgwick & Jackson, 1961)

Salter, Mrs W H *Ghosts and Apparitions* (London: Bell, 1938)

Saltmarsh, H F *Knowledge and Foreknowledge* (London: Harrison, 1937)

— *Evidence of Personal Survival from Cross-Correspondences* (London: Bell, 1938)

— *Foreknowledge* (London: Bell, 1938)

Schrenck-Notzing, Baron von *Phenomena of Materializations* (London: Kegan, Paul, Trench & Trubner, 1920)

Schwartz, Gary *The Afterlife Experiments: Breakthrough Evidence of Life After Death* (New York: Pocket Books, 2002)

Shermer, Michael *Why People Believe Weird Things. Pseudoscience, Superstition, and Other Confusions of our Time* (New York: W H Freeman and Co., 1997)

Sidgwick, Eleanor Mildred *Henry Sidgwick. A Memoir* (London: Macmillan and Co., 1906)

— *Phantasms of the Living: Cases of Telepathy Printed in the Journal of the Society for Psychical Research During Thirty-five Years* (New Hyde Park, NY: University Books, 1962)

Sinclair, U *Mental Radio* (Springfield, Ill.: Thomas, 1930)

Smythies, J R (ed.) *Science and ESP* (London: Routledge & Kegan Paul, 1967)

Soal, S G *The Experimental Situation in Psychical Research.* Ninth F W H Myers Memorial Lecture (London: Society for Psychical Research, 1947)

Soal, S G and Baterman, F *Modern Experiments in Telepathy* (London: Faber & Faber, 1954)

Soal, S G and Bowden, H T *The Mind Readers: Some Recent Experiments in Telepathy* (New York: Doubleday & Co., 1960)

Society for Psychical Research *Hints on Sitting with Mediums* (London: Society for Psychical Research, 1965)

— *Notes for Investigators of Spontaneous Cases* (London: Society for Psychical Research, 1968)

— *Psychical Research. A Selective Guide to Publications in English* (London: Society for Psychical Research, 1976)

Solomon, Grant and Solomon, Jane *The Scole Experiment* (London: Piatkus, 1999)

Stein, Gordon (ed.) *The Encyclopedia of the Paranormal* (New York: Prometheus Books, 1996)

Stemman, Roy *Spirit Communication. A Comprehensive Guide to the Extraordinary World of Mediums, Psychics and the Afterlife* (London: Piatkus, 2005)

Stevens, E W *The Wateska Wonder* (Chicago: Religio-Philosophical Publishing House, 1887)

Stevenson, I *The Psychiatric Examination* (London: Churchill, 1969)

— *Telepathic Impressions: A Review and Report of Thirty-Five New Cases* (Charlottesville, Va: University of Virginia Press, 1970)

— *Twenty Cases Suggestive of Reincarnation* (rev. ed., Charlottesville, Va: University Press of Virginia, 1974)

— *Xenoglossy: A Review and Report of a Case* (Charlottesville, Va: University Press of Virginia, 1974)

— *Children Who Remember Previous Lives: A Question of Reincarnation* (Charlottesville, Va: University Press of Virginia, 1987)

— *Reincarnation and Biology: A Contribution to the Etiology of Birthmarks and Birth Defects* (Westport, Conn.: Praeger, 1997)

— *Where Biology and Reincarnation Intersect* (Westport, Conn.: Praeger, 1997)

Sudre, Rene *Treatise on Parapsychology* (trans. C Green) (London: George Allen and Unwin, 1960)

Swann, Ingo *Natural ESP* (New York: Bantam Books, 1987)

Tabori, Paul and Phyllis, Raphael *Beyond the Senses: A Report on Psychical Research and Occult Phenomena in the Sixties* (London: Souvenir Press, 1971)

Tanner, A E *Studies in Spiritism* (New York: Appleton, 1910)

Targ, Russell *Miracles of Mind: Exploring Nonlocal Consciousness and Spiritual Healing* (Novata, Calif.: New World Library, 1998)

— *Limitless Mind: A Guide to Remote Viewing* (Novata, Calif.: New World Library, 2004)

Targ, Russell and Haray, Keith *The Mind Race. Understanding and Using Psychic Abilities* (Westminster, Md: Ballantine Books, 1985)

Targ, Russell and Puthoff, Hal *Mind-Reach. Scientists Look at Psychic Ability* (New York: Dell Publishing/Delta Book, 1977)

Tart, Charles *Altered States of Consciousness* (New York: John Wiley & Sons, 1969)

— *States of Consciousness* (New York: Doubleday Anchor, 1972)

— *Learning To Use Extrasensory Perception* (Chicago: The University of Chicago Press, 1976)

— *Psi: Scientific Studies of the Psychic Realm* (New York: E P Dutton & Co., 1977)

— *Body, Mind, Spirit: Exploring the Parapsychology of Spirituality* (Charlottesville, Va: Hampton Roads Publishing Co., 1997)

Thalbourne, Michael *A Glossary of Terms used in Parapsychology* (London: Heinemann, 1982)

Thomas, C Drayton *Some New Evidence for Human Survival* (London: W Collins Sons & Co. Ltd, 1922)

— *Life Beyond Death with Evidence* (London: W Collins Sons & Co Ltd, 1928)

— *Life Beyond Death* (London: W Collins Sons & Co Ltd, 1933)

— *An Amazing Experiment* (London: Lectures Universal, 1936)

Thomas, John F *Case Studies Bearing Upon Survival* (Boston: Boston Society for Psychical Research, 1929)

Thouless, Robert H *Psychical Research Past and Present.* Myers Memorial Lecture for 1952 (London: Society for Psychical Research, 1952)

— *Experimental Psychical Research* (Harmondsworth: Penguin Books, 1963)

— *From Anecdote to Experiment in Psychical Research* (London: Routledge & Kegan Paul, 1972)

Tietza, T R *Margery* (New York: Harper & Row, 1973)

Tischner, Rudolf *Telepathy and Clairvoyance* (London: Kegan, Paul, Trench & Trübner, 1925; first published in German, 1921)

Turner, J (ed.) *Stella C* (London: Souvenir Press, 1973)

Tyrrell, G N M *Grades of Significance* (London: Rider & Co., 1930)

— *Science and Psychical Phenomena* (New York: University Books, 1938)

— *Apparitions* (London: Society for Psychical Research, 1973; first published 1942)

— *The Personality of Man*
(Harmondsworth: Penguin Books, 1946)

Van Over, R and Oteri, L (eds.) *William McDougall, Explorer of the Mind: Studies in Psychical Research* (New York: Garrett/Helix, 1967)

Vasiliev, L L *Mysterious Phenomena of the Human Psyche* (New Hyde Park, NY: University Books, 1965)

Vesme, C de *A History of Experimental Spiritualism* 2 volumes (London: Rider & Co., 1931; first published in French, 1928)

Wallace, Alfred Russel *Miracles and Modern Spiritualism* (New York: Arno Press, 1975; first published 1896)

Walter, Grey *The Neurological Aspects of Hallucinations and Illusionary Experience.* Myers Memorial Lecture for 1963 (London: Society for Psychical Research, 1963)

Warcollier, René *Experiments in Telepathy* (London: Allen and Unwin, 1938)

Warcollier, René, Swann, Ingo and Targ, Russell *Mind to Mind. Studies in Consciousness* (Charlottesville, Va: Hampton Roads Publishing Co., 2001)

Warrick, F W *Experiments in Psychics* (London: Rider & Co, 1939)

West, Donald *Tests for Extra Sensory Perception: An Introductory Guide* (London: Society for Psychical Research, 1953)

— *Psychical Research Today* (London: Gerald Duckworth & Co., 1954)

White, Rhea A and Dale, Laura A *Parapsychology: Sources of Information* (Metuchen, NJ: Scarecrow, 1973)

— *Parapsychology: New Sources of Information* (Metuchen, NJ: Scarecrow, 1990)

Wilson, Colin *Afterlife. An Investigation of the Evidence for Life After Death* (London: Caxton Editions, 1985)

— *Beyond the Occult. Twenty Years' Research into the Paranormal* (London: Bantam Book, 1988)

Wilson, Ian *The After Death Experience* (London: Sidgwick & Jackson, 1987)

Wiseman, Richard *Deception & Self-Deception. Investigating Psychics* (New York: Prometheus Books, 1997)

Wiseman, Richard and Morris, Robert L *Guidelines for Testing Psychic Claimants* (New York: Prometheus Books, 1995)

Wolman, B B *Handbook of Parapsychology* (New York: Van Nostrand Reinhold, 1977)

Wright, Silvia Hart *When Spirits Come Calling. The Open-Minded Skeptic's Guide to After-Death Contacts* (Nevada City: Blue Dolphin Publishing, 2002)

Wyndham, H *Mr Sludge the Medium* (London: Bles, 1937)

Zöllner, J C F *Transcendental Physics* (New York: Arno Press, 1975; first published 1888)

2. Research Facilities

C.I.R.P.
Cognitive Sciences Laboratory
USA
Tel: +1 (323) 549 5025
Fax: +1 (408) 904 6195

Institut Metapsychique International
51, rue de l'Aqueduc
75010, Paris
France
Tel/fax: +33 (0)1 46 07 23 85

**Institut fuer Grenzgebiete der
   Psychologie und Psychohygiene**
Wilhelmstrasse 3a
D-79098 Freiburg i. Br.
Germany
Tel: +49 (0)761 20721 0
Fax: +49 (0)761 20721 99

Institute of Noetic Sciences
101 San Antonio Road
Petaluma, CA 94952
USA
Fax: +1 (707) 781 7420
General Inquiries: +1 (707) 775 3500

**Instituto Latinoamericano de
   Psicologia Paranormal**
Apartado Postal 156
San Juan del Rio, 76800 Queretaro
Mexico

**Instituto de Pesquisas
   Interdisciplinares das Areas
   Fronteiriças da Psicologia**
Rua Vicente Jose de Almeida, 228
Jardim Cupece – Sao Paulo/SP
CEP: 04652-140
Brazil

ISLIS
National Institute of Radiological Sciences
   (NIRS)
9–1, Anagawa-4, Inage-ku, Chiba-shi
   2638555
Japan
Tel: +81 43 206 3066
Fax: +81 43 206 3069

**Koestler Parapsychology Unit
   (University of Edinburgh)**
Department of Psychology
University of Edinburgh
7 George Square
Edinburgh EH8 9JZ
UK
Tel: +44 (0)131 650 3348

Laboratories for Fundamental Research
Tel: +1 (650) 327 2007
Fax: +1 (650) 322 7960

Pacific Neuropsychiatric Institute
Northwest Outpatient Medical Center
10330 Meridian Avenue N. Suite 380
Seattle, WA 98133
USA
Tel: +1 (206) 527 6289
Fax: +1 (206) 526 2335
http://www.pni.org/

Perrott-Warrick Research Unit
University of Hertfordshire
College Lane, Hatfield,
Herts AL10 9AB
UK
Tel: +44 (0)1707 284800
Fax: +44 (0)1707 284870

**Princeton Engineering Anomalies
   Research (PEAR)**
C-131, Engineering Quadrangle
Princeton University
Princeton, NJ 08544
USA
Tel: +1 (609) 258 5950

**Rhine Research Center (Institute for
   Parapsychology)**
2741 Campus Walk Avenue, Building 500
Durham, NC 27705
USA
Tel: +1 (919) 688 8241
Fax: +1 (919) 683 4338

3. Online Parapsychology Journals

**Frontier Perspectives (CFS,
   Philadelphia, USA)**
http://www.temple.edu/CFS/index.html

**International Journal of
   Parapsychology (PF, New York, USA)**
http://parapsychology.org/dynamic/
   050100.html

**Japanese Journal of Parapsychology
   (JSPP, Tokyo, Japan)**
http://wwwsoc.nii.ac.jp/jspp2/issue_e.ht
   m

**La Revue de Parapsychologie
   (1971–1989) (GERP, St Denis,
   France) (in French)**
http://gerp.free.fr/REVUEP.htm

Luce ed Ombra (Bologna, Italy)
http://www2.comune.bologna.it/bologna
   /fbibbdb/leo.htm

**Metapsichica, the Italian Journal of
   Parapsychology (AISM, Milan, Italy)
   (in Italian)**
http://www.metapsichica.it/pubblicazioni.
   htm

Psychological Bulletin (PB)
http://www.apa.org/journals/bul/

**Quaderni di Parapsicologia (CSP,
   Bologna, Italy)**
http://digilander.libero.it/cspbologna/
   csp-new1/QP/QP.htm

**Revue Française de Parapsychologie
   (GEEPP, Toulouse, France) (in
   French)**
http://geepp.or3p.free.fr/geepp-or3p/
   or3p/rfp.htm

**Revue Métapsychique (IMI, Paris,
   France) (in French)**
http://geepp.or3p.free.fr/geepp-or3p/
   abreges/index.htm

**The electronic Journal for Anomalous
   Phenomena (eJAP@psy.uva.nl)**
http://www.fmg.uva.nl/psychologie/
   PsychologieActueel.cfm

**The European Journal of
   Parapsychology (EJP) (KPU,
   Edinburgh, UK)**
http://ejp.org.uk/

The Journal of ISLIS (International
Society of Life Information Science)
(Chiba-shi, Japan)
http://wwwsoc.nii.ac.jp/islis/journal.htm

The Journal of Paraphysics (J. E.
Beichler and S. Stansfield)
http://members.aol.com/jebco1st/
Paraphysics/issue7.htm

The Journal of Parapsychology (JP)
(Fairhaven, Vt, USA)
http://www.rhine.org/

The Journal of Scientific Exploration
(JSE) (SSE, Stanford, USA)
http://www.scientificexploration.org/

The Journal of the Society for
Psychical Research (SPR, London,
UK)
http://www.spr.ac.uk/index.php3?
page=journal

The Journal of the American Society
for Psychical Research (ASPR, New
Bern, NC, USA)
http://www.aspr.com/jaspr.htm

Zeitschrift für Parapsychologie und
Grenzgebiete der Psychologie
(APGP, Freiburg, Germany) (in
German)
http://www.psychologie.uni-freiburg.de/
einrichtungen/Grenzgebiete/
zfpgdp.html

4. Parapsychology/Psychic World Organizations/ Research Institutes/ Societies

American Association for Parapsychology
Box 225, Canoga Park, CA 91305
USA
Tel: +1 (818) 883 0887
http://www.parapsychologydegrees.com/
Offers complete course in Parapsychology

American Society for Psychical Research, Inc.
5 West 73rd Street
New York, New York 10023
USA
Tel: +1 (212) 799 5050
Fax: +1 (212) 496 2497
http://www.aspr.com/who.htm

Anomalous Cognition Group
Department of Psychology
University of Amsterdam
Holland

Antioch University
13274 Fiji Way
Marina Del Ray, Los Angeles
CA 90192
USA
Tel: +1 (310) 578 1080
Offers Psi-related course work or degree programmes

Association for Research and Enlightenment
PO Box 595
Virginia Beach, VA 23541-0595
USA
Tel: +1 (804) 428 3588
www.are-cayce.com
Offers Psi-related course work or degree programmes

Association for the Study of Dreams
PO Box 1600
Vienna, VA 22183
USA
Tel: +1 (703) 242 0062
www.ASDreams.org

Association for Transpersonal Psychology
PO Box 50187
Palo Alto
CA 94303
USA
Tel: +1 (650) 424 8764
www.atpweb.org

Atlantic University
215 67th Street
Virginia Beach, VA 23451
USA
Tel: (toll free) 1 800 428 1512
www.atlanticuniv.edu
Offers Masters Degree in Transpersonal Psychology

Australian Institute of Parapsychological Research
PO Box 445
Lane Cove, NSW 2066
Australia

Boundary Institute
18488 Prospect Road, Suite 14
Saratoga, CA 95070
USA
Tel: +1 (408) 996 7184
www.boundaryinstitute.org
Investigation of anomalous phenomena relating to consciousness

California Institute for Human Science
609 South Vulcan Avenue, Suite 201
Encinitas, CA 92024
USA
Tel +1 (619) 634 1771
Offers Psi-related course work or degree programmes

California Institute for Integral Studies
[Course:] Intuition, Parapsychology and Consciousness
1453 Mission St
San Francisco, CA 94103
USA
Tel: +1 (415) 575 6100
Offers Psi-related course work or degree programmes

Centro Italiano di Parapsicologia
Via Poggio de Mari, 16
80129 Napoli
Italy

Centre for Frontier Sciences
Temple University, Ritter Hall (003-00),
  Room 478
1301 Cecil B. Moore Ave. (13th &
  Montgomery Streets)
Philadelphia, PA 19122
USA
Tel: +1 (215) 204 8487
Fax: +1 (215) 204 5553

Central Premonitions Online Registry
(http://mainportals.com/precog.shtml)

College of Psychic Studies
16 Queensberry Place
London SW7 2EB
UK
Tel: +44 (0)20 7589 3292
http://www.collegeofpsychicstudies.co.uk/
  index.html
Offers psychic development classes

Esalen Institute
Highway 1
Big Sur
CA 93920
USA
Tel: +1 (408) 667 3000
www.Esalen.org
Exploration of human potential

**Exceptional Human Experience
  Network**
Rhea White
414 Rockledge Road
New Bern
NC 28562
USA
Tel: +1 (919) 636 8734
www.ehe.org

Foundation for Mind Being Research
FMBR
PO Box 449
Los Altos
CA 94023-0449
USA
http://www.fmbr.org/
Global awareness/mind change

Fondation Odier de Psychophysique
Route de la Capite 77
1223 Cologny (Genève)
Switzerland

Franklin Pierce College
PO Box 60, College Road
Rindge, New Hampshire 03461-0060
USA
Tel: +1(603) 899 4100
*Offers Psi-related course work or degree
  programmes*

Global Consciousness Project
http://noosphere.princeton.edu/index.ht
  ml

Greenwich University
103 Kapliolani Street
Jilo
HI 96720
USA
Tel: +1 (808) 935 9934
www.greenwich.edu
*Offers Psi-related course work or degree
  programmes*

Inner Vision Extended Remote Viewing Training
Inner Vision
1836 Pinchot Street
Las Vegas, NV 89115
USA
Offers Psi-related course work or degree programmes

Institut Metapsychique International
51, rue de l'Aqueduc
75010, Paris
France
Tel/fax: +33 (0)1 46 07 23 85
http://www.metapsychique.org/

International Science of Life Foundation
ISLIS Head Office
c/o International Research Institute (IRI)
40A, KK Buildg., 1108-2, Sonno, Inage,
Chiba 263-0051
Japan
Tel: +81 43 255 5481?
Fax: +81 43 255 5482?
http://wwwsoc.nii.ac.jp/islis/en/islis.htm

Institute for Parapsychology
Rhine Research Center
PO Box 6847
College Station
Durham, NC 27708-6847
USA
Tel: +1 (919) 688 8241
www.rhine.org
Offers Psi-related course work or degree programmes

Institute of Noetic Sciences
101 San Antonio Road
Petaluma, CA 94952
USA
Tel: +1 (707) 775 3500
www.noetic.org
Research on psychic themes

Institute for Transpersonal Psychology
744 San Antonio Rd.,
Palo Alto, CA 94303
USA
Tel: +1 (415) 493 4430
www.itp.edu
Psi-related course work or degree programmes

Instituto de Psicologia Paranormal
Asociacion Ibero-Americana de Parapsicologia
Salta 2015 (1137) Capital Federal
Buenos Aires
Argentina

Instituto de Parapsicologia
Zabala 1930
1712 Castelar
Prov. De Buenos Aires
Argentina

International Society for the Study of Subtle Energies and Energy Medicine
11005 Ralston Road
Arvada, CO 80004
USA
Tel: +1 (303) 425 4625
www.issseem.org

Japanese Society for Parapsychology
29-24-204, Sakuragaoka-cho, Shibuya-ku,
Tokyo-to 150-0031
Japan
http://wwwsoc.nii.ac.jp/jspp2/jspp_e.htm

John F. Kennedy University (JFK)
12 Altarinda Road
Orinda, CA 94563
USA
Tel: +1 (510) 254 0200
Psi-related course work or degree programmes

Koestler Parapsychology Unit
PPLS, University of Edinburgh
7 George Square
Edinburgh EH8 9JZ
UK
Tel: +44 (0)131 650 3348
Fax: +44 (0)131 650 3369
Psi-related course work or degree programmes

Kripalu Center for Yoga and Health
PO Box 793
Lenox, MA 01240
USA
Tel: +1 (413) 448 3400
www.kripalu.org

National Guild of Hypnotists
PO Box 308
Merrimack
NH 03054
USA
Tel: +1 (603) 429 9438
www.ngh.net

Omega Institute for Holistic Studies
260 Lake Drive
Rhinebeck
NY 12572-3212
USA
www.eomega.org

Parapsychology, Chair of
Univ. of Utrecht, Postbus 80125
3508 TC Utrecht
Holland

Parapsychology Institute
Springweg 7
3511 VH Utrecht
Holland

Parapsychology Foundation
228 East 71st Street
New York NY 10021
USA
Tel: +1 (212) 628 1550
www.parapsychology.org

Parapsychological Association, Inc.
2474-342 Walnut St
Cary, NC 27511
USA
http://www.parapsych.org

**Parapsychological Study Centre of
Bologna**
CSP c/o Dr Piero Cassoli
Via Valeriani 39
40134 Bologna
Italy
Tel: +39 (0)51 614 31 04
Fax: +39 (0)51 614 31 04
http://digilander.libero.it/cspbologna/
csp-new1/English/english.htm

Rhine Research Center
Institute for Parapsycology
2741 Campus Walk Avenue
Building 500
Durham, NC 27705
USA
http://www.rhine.org/index.shtml

Rosebridge Graduate School
1040 Oak Grove Road, Suite 103
Concord, CA 94518
USA
Tel: +1 (510) 689 0560
*Psi-related course work or degree programmes
of Integrative Psychology*

Saybrook Institute
450 Pacific 3rd Floor
San Francisco, CA 94133
USA
Tel: +1 (415) 433 9200 or 1-800 825 4480
*Offers Psi-related course work or degree
programmes*

Society for Psychical Research
49 Marloes Road
Kensington
London W8 6LA
UK
Tel: +44 (0)20 7937 8984
http://moebius.psy.ed.ac.uk/~spr/

**Society for Scientific Exploration
(without limits)**
Department of Astronomy, PO Box 3818
Charlottesville, VA 22903-0818
USA
Tel: +1 (434) 924 7494
http://www.scientificexploration.org/
index.html

Touching Spirit Center
16 South Street
PO Box 337
Litchfield CT 06759
USA
Tel: +1 (860) 567 0600
www.touchingspirit.org
*Offers training in intuitive development and
healing*

West Georgia College
Department of Psychology
Carrolton, GA 30118
USA
Tel: +1 (404) 836 6510
*Offers Psi-related course work or degree
programmes*

5. Spiritualist Organizations

USA

Lily Dale Assembly (school)
5 Melrose Park
Lily Dale, NY 14752
Tel: +1 (716) 595 8721
www.lilydale.org

Morris Pratt Institute (school)
11811 Watertown Plank Road
Milwaukee
WI 53226-3342
Tel: +1 (414) 774 2994
www.morrispratt.org

National Spiritualist Alliance
Lake Pleasant
Montague
Franklin County, MA
http://www.thenationalspiritualallianceinc
    .org/

**National Spiritualist Association of
    Churches in the USA**
General Offices
PO Box 217
Lily Dale, NY 14752
Tel: +1 (716) 595 2000
http://www.nsac.org/contacts/index.htm

UK

The Spiritualists National Union
Redwoods
Stansted Hall
Stansted Mountfitchett
Essex, CM24 8UD
Tel: 0845 4580 768
http://www.snu.org.uk/home02.htm

Arthur Finlay College
Stansted Hall
Stansted Mountfitchett
Essex, CM24 8UD
Tel: +44 (0)1279 813636
E-mail: afc@snu.org.uk

**The Spiritualist Association of Great
    Britain**
33 Belgrave Square
London, SW1X 8QB
Tel: +44 (0)20 7235 3351
http://www.sagb.org.uk/

6. Exploring the Psychic World Online

www.Akashicuniversity.com
Online learning community focusing on
    intuition, astrology and spirituality

www.beliefnet.com
Information on all aspects of spirituality

www.parapsychology.org/
www.PsiResearch.org
Parapsychology FAQ

www.Interluderetreat.com
Meditations and thoughts for the week

www.intuition.org
Website devoted to the development of
    inner intuitive resources

www.SoulfulLiving.com
Soul study

www.spiritualityhealth.com
Spirituality and holistic health

www.dreamgate.com
www.dreamtree.com
Websites for people interested in dreams
    and dreaming

http://www.blavatskyarchives.com/
Online information on the teachings of
    Madame Blavatsky

http://www.theparasychologist.com/
Exposing the facts about ghost
    investigation so you can decide

http://www.parascience.org.uk/
Para.Science was established to conduct
    serious study, research and investigation
    into all types of paranormal phenomena

http://www.psychicworld.net/
An informative and interactive site dealing
    with the paranormal in an enlightening
    and entertaining way

http://www.paraworld.info/
Website devoted to parapsychology and
    psychic development

www.haunt.net
How to deal with hauntings

http://www.allspiritual.com/index.php3
Gateway to spirituality online

http://www.topsitelists.com/bestsites/
    mystic/topsites.html
Online resource for psychics and mediums

www.OfSpirit.com
Energy healing, spirits and angels

www.snu.org.uk
Information about spiritualism

www.astrology.com
Astrology on the web

www.spiritweb.com
Information about chakras

www.dowsers.com
American Society of Dowsers

www.tarotsociety.org
International Society of Tarot

www.lightofthesoul.net
Links to mediums

www.theseance.com
Information about séances

http://istina.rin.ru/eng/para/
    gadanie.html
http://www.serenapowers.com/
Informative websites that explain and
    explore numerous methods of
    divination and also offer fortune-telling
    services online

www.ufomind.com
Well organized paranormal website

www.spirit.web.org
www.spiritonline.org
www.newagecom
Explore the psychic world

7. Popular Magazines

USA

Body and Soul
42 Pleasant Street
Watertown MA 02472
www.bodyandsoulmag.com

Fate Magazine
PO Box 460
Lakeville MN 55044
www.fatemag.com

Magical Blend Magazine
PO Box 600
Chico CA 95927
www.magicalblend.com

New York Spirit Magazine
107 Sterling Place
Brooklyn NY 11217
www.nyspirit.com

Earthwise Spirituality
Blessed Bee Inc
PO Box 641
Point Arena CA 95468
www.pangaia.com

Shaman's Drum
PO Box 270
Williams OR 97544

Whole Life Times
PO Box 1187
Malibu CA 90265
www.wholelifetimes.com

Intuition Magazine
275 Brannan Street
San Francisco CA 94107
www.intuitionmagazine.com

UK

Fate and Fortune
H Bauer Publishing
24–28 Oval Road
London NW1 7DT

Fortean Times
Box 2409
London NW5 4NP
www.forteantimes.com

Kindred Spirit
Sandwell Barns
Harberton, Totnes
Devon TQ9 7LJ
http://www.kindredspirit.co.uk/

Prediction
IPC Country and Leisure, Focus House
Dingwell Avenue
Croydon CR9 2TA
http://www.predictionmagazine.com

Spirit and Destiny
Academic House
24–28 Oval Road
London NW1 7DT
E-mail: spirit.destiny@bauer.co.uk

8. QUOTATIONS

'I have always strenuously supported the right of every man to his own opinion, however different that opinion might be to mine. He who denies to another this right, makes a slave of himself to his present opinion, because he precludes himself the right of changing it.'

(Thomas Paine)

'The intuitive mind is a sacred gift and the rational mind is a faithful servant ...We have created a society that honors the servant and has forgotten the gift.'

(Albert Einstein)

'The spiritual life does not remove us from the world, but it leads us deeper into it.'

(Henri Nouwen)

'Whatever you can do, or dream you can do, begin it, boldness has genius, power and magic in it.'

(Goethe)

'Life is not a problem to be solved, but a mystery to be lived.'

(Thomas Merton)

'The deeper I listen, the more wondrous life becomes.'

(Anon.)

'Let us remember that within us there is a palace of immense significance.'

(St Teresa of Avila)

'It is only when we realize that life is taking us nowhere that it begins to have meaning.'

(P D Ospensky)

'The only way to find the limits of the possible is by going beyond them to the impossible.'

(Arthur C Clarke)

'The universe is filled with magical things patiently waiting for us to Awaken.'

(Anon.)

'Great spirits have always encountered violent opposition from mediocre minds.'

(Albert Einstein)

'What we are today comes from our thoughts of yesterday, and our present thoughts build our life of tomorrow: our life is the creation of our mind.'

(Buddha)

'We cannot discover new oceans until we have the courage to loose sight of the shore.'

(Anon.)

'Where there is an open mind, there will always be a frontier.'

(Dorothea Brande)

'When I let go of what I am, I become what I might be.'

(Lao Tzu)

'What lies behind us and what lies before us are small matters compared to what lies within us.'

(Ralph Waldo Emerson)

'There are only two ways to live a life. One is as though nothing is a miracle. The other is as though everything is a miracle.'

(Albert Einstein)

'Knowledge of any kind ... brings about a change in awareness from where it is possible to create new realities.'

(Deepak Chopra)

'Just because a man lacks the use of his eyes doesn't mean he lacks vision.'

(Stevie Wonder)

'In dreams and in love there are no impossibilities.'

(Anon.)

'Unity consciousness is a state of enlightenment where we pierce the mask of illusion which creates separation and fragmentation. Behind the appearance of separation is one unified field of wholeness. Here the seer and the scenery are one.'

(Deepak Chopra)

'What is essential is invisible to the eyes.'

(Antoine de Saint-Exupéry)

'When one realizes one is asleep, one is already half awake.'

(Anon.)

'Yesterday is but today's memory, and Tomorrow is today's dream.'

(Kahlil Gibran)

'Surrender is faith that the power of love can accomplish anything ... even when you cannot foresee the outcome.'

(Deepak Chopra)

'The greatest discovery of my generation is that man can alter his life simply by altering his attitude of mind.'

(William James)

'The world we are experiencing today is the result of our collective consciousness, and if we want a new world, each of us must start taking responsibility for helping create it.'

(Rosemary Fillmore Rhea)

'The authentic self is the soul made visible.'

(Sarah Ban Breathnach)

'The ultimate value of life depends upon awareness and the power of contemplation rather than upon mere survival.'

(Aristotle)

'Insight occurs when, and to the degree that, one knows oneself.'

(Andrew Schneider)

'Everything that irritates us about others can lead us to an understanding about ourselves.'

(Carl Jung)

'Divinity is the true self of man.'

(Kahlil Gibran)

'Destiny is not a matter of chance, it is a matter of choice. It is not a thing to be waited for, it is a thing to be achieved.'

(William Jennings Bryan)

'The man who can see all creatures in himself and himself in all creatures, knows no sorrow.'

(Eesha Upanishad)

'Everyone and everything around you is your teacher.'

(Ken Keys Jr)

'Go confidently in the direction of your dreams and live the life you imagined! As you simplify your life, the laws of the universe will be simpler; solitude will not be solitude, poverty will not be poverty, nor weakness weakness.'

(Henry David Thoreau)

'Every moment of your life is infinitely creative and the universe is endlessly bountiful … Just put forth a clear enough request and everything your heart desires must come to you.'

(S Gawain)

'The real voyage of discovery consists not in seeking new landscapes, but in having new eyes.'

(Marcel Proust)

'Each today, well-lived, makes yesterday a dream of happiness and each tomorrow a vision of hope. Look, therefore, to this one day, for it and it alone is life.'

(Sanskrit poem)

'You must live in the present, launch yourself on every wave, find your eternity in each moment.'

(Henry David Thoreau)

'Remain open. There is something bigger than you know going on here.'

(Ivanla Van Zant)

'Our deepest fear is not that we are inadequate. Our deepest fear is that we are powerful beyond belief.'

(Nelson Mandela)

'Watch your thoughts, for they become words … Choose your words, for they become actions … Understand your actions, for they become habits … Study your habits, for they become your character … Develop your character, for it becomes your destiny.'

(Anon.)

'I never came upon any of my discoveries through the process of rational thinking.'

(Albert Einstein)

'Know the Truth and the Truth will set you free.'

(Jesus Christ)

'To see things in a seed, that is genius.'

(Lao Tzu)

'A coincidence is when God performs a miracle, and decides to remain anonymous.'

(Anon.)

'Life is 10 percent of what happens to you, and 90 percent of how you respond to it.'

(Anon.)

'Everything seeks its source.'

(A universal principle)

'A closed mind is a dying mind.'

(Edna Ferber)

'We make a living by what we get, but we make a life by what we give.'

(Winston Churchill)

'Vision: the art of seeing things invisible.'

(Jonathan Swift)

'The secret to health in both mind and body, is not to mourn for the past, nor worry about the future ... But to live in the present moment wisely and earnestly.'

(Buddha)

'If you can dream it, you can do it.'

(Walt Disney)

'Yesterday is history ... Tomorrow is a mystery ... Today is a gift, that is why it is called the Present.'

(Anon.)

'All the darkness of the world cannot put out the light of one small candle.'

(Anon.)

'When it is dark enough, you can see the stars.'

(Charles A. Beard)

'We must be the "change" we wish to see.'

(Mahatma Gandhi)

'You must do the thing you think you cannot do.'

(Eleanor Roosevelt)

'In order to disprove the fact that all crows are black, it is enough to find one white crow.'

(William James)

'If you hear a voice within you saying, "You are not a painter", then by all means paint ... and that voice will be silenced.'

(Vincent Van Gogh)

'A single grateful thought raised to heaven, is the most perfect prayer.'

(G E Lessing)

'Perhaps it would be a good idea, fantastic as it sounds, to muffle every telephone and halt all activity for one hour some day to give people a chance to ponder for a few moments on what it is all about, why they are living, and what they really want.'

(James Truslow Adams)

'A human being is a part of the whole, called by us "Universe," a part limited in time and space. He experiences himself, his thoughts and feelings as something separated from the rest — a kind of optical delusion of his consciousness. This delusion is a kind of prison for us, restricting us to our personal desires and to affection for a few persons nearest to us. Our task must be to free ourselves from this prison by widening our circle of compassion to embrace all living creatures and the whole of nature in its beauty. Nobody is able to achieve this completely, but the striving for such achievement is in itself a part of the liberation and a foundation for inner security.'

(Albert Einstein)

'If you are not shocked by quantum physics, then you do not understand it.'

(Ernest Schroedinger)

'Life is not measured by the number of breaths we take, but by the moments that take our breath away.'

(Anon.)

'We still do not know one-ten thousandth of one percent of what nature has revealed to us.'

(Albert Einstein)

Index

Angels of Mons 64
anima mundi 13
animal
  divination 799–800
  hauntings 24, 701
  psi **23–4**
  superstitions 800
  totem 720, 800
animal magnetism *see*
  mesmerism
animism **24–5**, 209
  and reincarnation 24,
  604–5
Ankou **25**
Anne, Queen 280
Anson, Jay 21
Anthony of Padua, St 70
Anthroposophical Society
  681
Anthroposophy 680
Antietam **25–6**, 111
Apache people 249
apantomancy **26**
apparition **26–9**
  Encyclopaedia Britannica
  379
  familial **206**
  hag **277**
  Hart's theory 283
  Marian **426–7**
  studies 63, 132–3, 611
  Tyrell's theory 731
  Wilmot **772–3**
  see also ghost
applied psi **29–30**, 609
apport **30**, 329
  Charlton House teacup
  109
  Guppy 269
  Sai Baba 30, 624
  see also teleportation
Arabian tradition
  Afrit **10**
  alchemy 16
  scrying 637
arcana 354
archangels **30**
archetypes **30–1**, 120, 233,
  346, 431
  cellular memory 102
  scarab 631, 694
  tarot 703
Arguelles, Jose 282
Aristotle 16, 463, 520, 545,
  551, 582, 692
arithmancy **31**
Arnaud, F L 152
aromatherapy **31–2**, 194,
  434
arrival cases **32–3**
art, psychic **33**
Artemidorus 168
Arthur, King 50–1, 252,
  258, 446, 700

Arundel Castle **33–4**
Ash Manor ghost **34–5**, 220
Asimov, Isaac 123
asport **36**
Assagioli, Roberto **725**
Association for Research
  and Enlightenment
  100–1
Association of Past Life
  Research and Therapy
  (APRT) 528
Assyrians
  channelling 106
  evil eye 196
  iron amulets 335
  moon divination 641
  omens 500
  phantom armies 536
  utukku **744**
astral body (subtle body)
  36–7, 162, 195, 393,
  412, 781
  dream travels 171
  ectoplasm 181
  silver cord 509, 652
astral doorways **37**
astral plane 36, **37–8**,
  195–6, 336, 393, 661,
  726
  and psychic attack 569,
  571
astral plane inhabitants
  devas 155
  Eck masters 180
  hidden masters 294
  illuminati 318
  intelligence 330
  People of the Rainbow
  330
  zombies 799
astral projection/astral
  travel **38**, 393
  Eckankar **180–1**
  to Mars 655
  using tattwas 37
  see also out-of-body
  experience
astrology **38–43**, 291, 450
  Vedic **749**
  see also horoscope; zodiac
*Athenodorus, The Haunting
  of* **43–4**
Atlantis **44–5**, 190, 249,
  714
atmosphere **45–6**
Attention Deficit Disorder
  (ADD) 324
Attention Deficit
  Hyperactivity Disorder
  (ADHD) 324
Aubrey, John **46**, 534
augury **46**, 160, 800
Augustine, St 168, 409
aumakua **47**

aura **47–8**, 77, 709, 715
  colours 122
  halo 278
  Indigo Children 322–3
  Kirlian photography
  364–5
  medical intuition 78, 437,
  438
  strengthening 572
  thought form attack 473
  trapped spirits 154, 769
  vibrational healing 751
  see also astral body; etheric
  body
auric sight 47, 117, 278,
  640
Australia 590
Australian aboriginals 171
Austria 86, 259
automatic painting *see* art,
  psychic
automatic writing **48–9**,
  179, 316, 355
  Bond 80, 568
  Moses 459
  from Myers 519, 548
  Roberts 613
  Stead 680
  White 763
  Worth 781–2
automatism **50**
  Ouija board 507
Avalon **50–1**, 252
avatar **51** *see also* Sai Baba
Avebury **52**
axinomancy **52**
Ayurvedic medicine **52–3**,
  195, 322, 552, 585, 723,
  749
Aztecs viii, 39, 377

ba **57**
Babbitt, Edwin 122
Babcock, Joseph P 425
Babylonians 98, 488, 775
  aeromancy 8
  astrology 39
  capnomancy 98
  channelling 106
  evil eye 196
  haruspicy 283
  iron amulets 335
  magic and sorcery 775
  numerology 489
  omens 500
  oneiromancy 501
Bach, Edward 218
Bach Remedies 217–18
Bachelor's Grove Cemetery
  57–8, 248, 541
Bacon, Francis 48
Bacon, Roger 16
Baggally, M W 518
bakechochin **58**

balance **58–9**
Baldwin, William 669
Balfour, Arthur James 519,
  648
Balfour, Francis M 519
Balinovski, Eduardo 398
Ballechin House **59–60**
Baltimore poltergeist **60–2**,
  220
banshee **62**, 296, 391
Barbanell, Maurice 651–2
Barker, J A 559
Barksdale, William 241
Barlow, Fred 574
Barrett, William Fletcher
  63, 149, 462, 523, 649,
  659
Barrington, Mary Rose 344
Barron, James 151
Barry, Clive 235
Bartlett, John 568
Batcheldor, Kenneth 652–3
Batten, Mabel 390
Battle Abbey **63**
battlefield hauntings **63–4**
  see also Alamo; Antietam;
  Chickamauga;
  Gettysburg; phantom
  armies
Bealings House bell ringer
  64–5
beans **65**
Beardie, Earl 250–1
Beethoven 50, 328
behavioural medicine **65–6**
Beldoff, John 189
Belk, William 305
Bell Witch **66–8**
Benedict XIV, Pope 523
Benedictsson, Einar 295
Bennett, Ernest 219
Bennett, William 215
Benson, Herbert 439
Bentham, Jeremy **68**
Béraud, Marthe 181, 237,
  435–6, 564
Beresford, Lady 731–2
Berger, Hans 72
Bermuda Triangle **68–9**
Bernard of Clairvaux, St
  366
Berne, Eric 294
Bernstein, Morey 527
Berry Pomeroy Castle **69**
Bertha 770
Besant, Annie 714
Betty Book, The 763
bhut **69**
Bible 163, 168, 196, 381,
  652, 676
  Witch of Endor **775**
  see also New Testament;
  Old Testament
bibliomancy **70**

causinomancy **100**
Cayce, Edgar ix, 12, 13, 45,
    100–1, 112, 356–7,
    438, 507, 564
Cele, Clara Germana 394
celestial light **102**
cellular memory **102**
Celtic Spirituality 515
Celtic tradition
    Ankou **25**
    Arawn 74
    Avalon **50–1**, 252
    channelling 106
    cloud reading 118
    fairies 204
    Halloween 278
    handfasting 280
    hippomancy 295
    horse soul-carriers 301
    sacred trees 726
    see also Druids, Druidry
Central America 196
Central Europe 78
cerebral anoxia **102**
ceremonial magic 239, 291,
    421–2, 478, 602
Ceridwen 700
Cernunnos 293
ceromancy **102**
Cezanne, Paul 615
Chaffin will case **102–4**,
    169, 690
chair test 130
Chaitanya 51
chakras 77, **104–6**, 136,
    195, 273, 278, 370,
    392–3, 603, 738
    kundalini meditation 372
    see also third eye
Chaldeans 169, 529
Chambercombe Manor 264
Chamberlain, Richard 684
Chambers' *Cyclopaedia* 464,
    610
Chang Sang-fen 432, 699
channelling **106–7**
    A Course in Miracles 5
    music composition 50
    Seth 613–15
chanting **107–8** *see also*
    mantra
chaos theory **108**
charismatic **109**
Charles I 182, 229, 280,
    471, 774
Charles II 34, 174, 361
Charles VI of France 704
Charles VII of France
    342–3
Charles IX of France 487
Charlton House **109**
charms 6, **110**, 196
    see also amulet; talisman
Chase, Salmon P 399

Chase Vault **110–11**
Chave, John 627
Cheltenham haunting *see*
    Morton case
Chester Beatty Papyrus 167
Chevreul, Michel 316
chi *see* Qi/Chi; universal life
    force
Chiaia, Ercole 516–17
Chiang-shih **111**
Chichester, Arthur 326
Chickamauga **111–12**
Chihuacohuatl 377
children **112**
    ghost sickness 249
    invisible friends **334**
    mini Geller **452**
    past-life recall 526–7, 605
    spunkie ghosts 678
China
    alchemy 15
    astrology 40
    channelling 106
    Chiang-shih **111**
    communication with the
        dead 507
    dowsing 163
    dragon paths 398
    dream precognition 169
    elements 211, 449, 722,
        778
    exorcism 197
    Feng Shui practice 207
    Freemasonry banned 226
    ghosts 242
    graphology 259
    grateful dead 259–61
    Hunan Province carvings
        735
    jade 340
    mah-jong 425
    martial arts 431–2
    massage 434
    music 463
    names 471
    out-of-body experience
        509
    palmistry 520
    peach amulets 22
    phallomancy 535
    podomancy 552
    qi 739
    qi gong 585
    reading bones **80–1**
    scrying 135
    shins **646**
    Taoist alchemy 703
    tasseography 708
    Zen 797
    see also I Ching; Taoism;
        traditional Chinese
        medicine
Chopra, Deepak 585
Chou, Duke of 315

Christianity, Christian
    Church 22, 77, 253,
        479, 482
    afterlife 10
    archangels 30
    chanting 108
    cross symbol 693
    death obsession 148
    denial of magic 421
    divination condemned 160
    divine guidance 106
    dolphins 161
    exorcism 197
    faith healing 286–7
    fish symbol 316
    forced conversion 74
    and ghosts 27
    and Glastonbury 252
    glossolalia 253–4
    Gnosticism 254
    guardian angels 267
    hell 289
    Last Judgment 381
    levitating saints 394
    meditation 439
    neo-pagan rejection 479
    necromancy condemned
        477
    oracles banned 502
    pagan deities demonized
        78, 153
    pagan persecution 619
    and possession 555
    and the psychic 672
    resurrection 689
    Saint John's Wort 625
    Satan 627
    and spiritualism 673
    Virgin Mary cult 256
    witchcraft persecution
        766, 775
Church Fathers 168
Church of All Worlds
    (CAW) 480
Church of Scientology 634
Churchill, Winston 226
Churchward, James 388,
    461–2
churel **112**
CIA
    psi research 678–9
    STAR GATE Programme
        113, 607, 679
cipher test 691
circle **113**
    fairy ring **205**
Circle Sanctuary 480
City of Limerick 772
clairaudience 23, **114–15**,
    645
    medical intuition 437
    mental mediumship 442,
        445
clairfragrance **115**

clairgustus **115**
clairsentience 45, **115–16**,
    186, 273, 359, 579
    medical intuition 437
    mental mediumship 442,
        445
clairvoyance 101, **115–17**,
    242, 248, 281, 506, 637
    and apparitions 102, 772–3
    chakra diagnosis 105–6
    and haunting 247
    medical intuitives 437
    and mediumistic
        communication 117,
        131, 519–20, 687, 691
    mental mediumship 442,
        445
    testing 194
    see also auric sight;
        precognition;
        retrocognition
clairvoyant dreams 341–2,
    426
clairvoyant reality 236, 287
Clark, James Langton 98
Clark, Willliam C 175
Cleaveland, Mrs Willis 717
cledonomancy **118**
Clement V, Pope 367
Clement XIV, Pope 70
Clemm, Virginia 182
Clemons, Albert Adsit 277
cloud busting 118
cloud reading **118**
Coates, Nancy 420
Cock Lane ghost **118–19**
Cocke, J R 548
Cockeram, Henry 478
Coe, Myrne Reid 212
coincidence *see*
    synchronicity
cold reading **119**
    and X-ray vision 786
Cold War 113, 606, 607
Coleridge, Samuel Taylor
    169
collective unconscious 42,
    102, **119–20**, 153, 168,
    193, 543, 695
College of Psychic Studies
    120, 235, 459, 589
Colley, Thomas 300
colour divination **121–2**
colours 121, **122–3**
Colton, Caleb 627
Columbus, Christopher 68
Coly, Eileen 525
Coly, Lisette 525
combination lock test 691
Committee for the
    Investigation of Claims
    of the Paranormal **123**
cone of power 108
Confucianism 646

gyromancy **274**
halomancy **279**
haruspicy **283**
hippomancy **295**
hydromancy **306–7**
I Ching **315–16**
icthyomancy **316**
Internet 331
kephalonomancy **357**
knissomancy **368**
kumalak **370**
labiomancy **377**
lampadomancy **378**
lecanomancy **384–5**
lithomancy **401**
logomancy **406–7**
lunomancy **412**
macromancy **419**
mah-jong tiles 425
mazomancy **437**
meconomancy **437**
metagnomy **448–9**
metopomancy **450**
micromancy **451–2**
mirror gazing 453
moleosophy **454–6**
myomancy **465**
by numbers 490
oculomancy **498**
odontomancy **499**
ololygmancy **500**
oneiromancy **501–2**
ophidiomancy **502**
orinthomancy **505**
ovomancy **512**
palmistry **520–2**
phallomancy **535**
phyllomancy **545**
physiognomancy **545–6**
podomancy **552**
pyromancy **581**
reading bones **80–1**
rhapsodomancy **610**
scapulomancy **630**
scatomancy **631**
scrying **637**
selenomancy **641**
shell hearing **645**
sortilege **660**
spasmatomancy **663**
table 507, 699
tarot 705–6
tasseography **708–9**
by trance visions 448
uromancy **742**
xenomancy **786**
xylomancy **787**
zoomancy **799–800**
Dixon, Jeanne 160–1, 564
Dogen 797
dolphins **161–2**
domovik **162**
Don Pedro, Captain 496, 497
Donne, John 209

Donnelly, Ignatius 44
doors **162**
doppelgänger/double
    162–3, 509
    see also arrival cases;
    bilocation; fetch; ka
doshas 53
Dossey, Larry 6
Douglas, Janet 250
Dowding, Lord Hugh **163**
dowsing 50, **163–5**, 316,
    396
    Geller 238–9
    ley lines 165, 396
    map **428–9**
    medical 596
    power spots 556
    use of pendulum 531
Doyle, Arthur Conan 75,
    128, 130, **165–6**, 215,
    221, 297, 303, 362, 431,
    433, 668, 680
Dragon Project Trust 444,
    556, 683
Dragsholm Castle **166–7**
Drake, Francis 537
Drayton Thomas, Charles
    391
Drbal, Karl 581
dreamcatcher **167**
dreams **167–71**
    and archetypes 31
    Chaffin will case 102–3
    of death 169, 400, 413,
    501
    displacement 159
    Dragon Project Trust
    project 444
    and ESP 193, 234
    expression of the id 316
    false awakening **206**
    ghosts in 242, 248
    of horses 301–2
    incubation **322**, 501
    interpretation 97, 167–8,
    170, 227, 643, 694
    journals 171
    Jung's 347
    Maimonedes experiments
    234, **426**, 524
    oneiromancy **501–2**
    precognitive 159, 169,
    473, 501–2, 558
    of snakes 502
    telepathic 169–70, 426
    two types 392
    see also lucid dreaming;
    nightmares/terrors
dreamtime 171
drop in communicator
    171–2, 687
    Runolfur Runolfsson 172,
    619–20
drugs **172**, 306, 643

Druids, Druidry **172–3**, 396
    capnomancy 98
    cloud reading 118
    revival 173, 479
    scrying 135
    Stonehenge 683
    tree worship 84
drummer of Cortachy **173**
drummer of Tedworth **174**,
    251
Drummond, Lillias 229
Drury Lane Theatre **174**
Dudley Town, Connecticut
    174–5
Duke, Carolyn 89
Duke University
    Parapsychology
    Laboratory 84, 283,
    417, 462, 506, 523, 554,
    557, 574, 610, 611, 612,
    615
Dunne, J W 559
Dunninger, Joseph 303
duppy **175**
Du Pre, Mr 210
dybbuk **175**, 199

Ear of Dionysius **179**
earth **179–80**
earth lights **180**
earthquake effect **180**
Eastern Europe
    bioenergy concept 741
    psi investigation 525
    psychotronics 579
Eastern European folklore
    broom 87
    kikimora **359**
    Saturday births 628
    vampire superstitions 747
Eckankar **180–1**
eco-paganism 515
ectoplasm 130, 158, **181**,
    279, 435, 436
    pseudopod **564**
    voice box 215–16
Edenhall luck 411–12
Edgar Allan Poe House
    182
Edgehill, battle of **182**
Edison, Thomas 183, 215,
    328
Edmund, St 539
Edward II 367
Edward IV 704
Edward VI 280
Edwards, Francis 589
Edwards, Frederick 84, 417
EEG (electroencephalo-
    graphy) **183**
Eglinton, William 250
ego 227, 346, 566, 641, 688
Egypt, ancient viii
    afterlife 11

alchemy 15–16
astrology 39
aura 47
ba **57**
burial rites 90
candles 97
channelling 106
Chester Beatty Papyrus
    167–8
death obsession 148
dowsing 163
dream precognition 169
evil eye 196
Eye of Horus 22, 199
halo 278
hermeticism roots 289–91
hydrotherapy 307
hypnosis 308
illuminati 317
incubation 501
iron amulets 335
jade 340
ka 162, **353**, 509
khu **358**
Kore 533
lampadomancy 378
magic and sorcery 775
maze 436
mystery cults 466
names 471
palmistry 520
pathworkings 529
scarab 631
scrying 637
snake dreams 502
spirit-releasing images
    268
tree spirits 726
urine therapy 742
Egyptian Book of the Dead
    11, 57, **81**, 580
Einstein, Albert 165, 328,
    329, 448, 452, 478, 586,
    694, 719
Eisai 797
Eisenbud, Jule 718–19
ekimmu 744
El Greco 186
electrokinesis **183**
electronic coin flipper
    575–6
electronic voice phenomena
    (EVP) **183–5**, 248, 329,
    599–600
    Bachelor's Grove
    Cemetery 58
element **185**
    and alchemy 16
    Chinese system 211, 449,
    722, 778
    and Feng Shui 207
    Hindu system 13, 185, 195
    in Wicca 767
    in witchcraft 776

spiritual healing;
traditional Chinese
medicine
holistic massage 322, 434
Holotropic Breathwork 86
Holy Trinity Church, York
265, 539
Home, Daniel Dunglas 88,
180, 186, **296–9**, 395,
436, 441, 459, 523, 525,
575, 599, 648
home circle **296**, 636
homeopathy **299–300**
Homer **300**
Homerton, Charles 234
Hong Kong 207
Hook, Sidney 123
Hope, William 130, **300–1**,
562, 668
Hopkins, Robert Thurston
301
Horned God 481, 766, 767
horoscope 39–40, 152, **301**
Vedic 749
horse **301–2**
hot reading **302**
Hotel Del Coronado **302**
Houdini, Harry 129, 145,
181, 221, 299, **303**,
599, 654
Howard, Catherine 280, 722
Howard, Thomas 589–90
Hubbard, L Ron 633
Hudson, Henry 446
Huff, Mari 58
Hughlings, John 467
Hui-ning 797
Hull House **303–4**
Huna **304–5**
hunch **305**
Hunt, Leigh 782
Hurkos, Peter **305–6**
Hurle, Henry 173
Hutchins, Imogen 458
Huxley, Aldous **306**, 714
Huxley, Julian 244, **306**
hydromancy **306–7**
hydrotherapy **307**
Hyman, Ray 123, 316
hypnagogic state **307**
hypnosis 227, 272, **307–10**,
447, 633
and past lives 527, 528
telepathic 448, **709–10**
hypnotherapy **310**
Hyslop, James Hervey
212–13, **310–11**, 548,
556, 662, 690, 716–17

I Ching 81, 160, 207,
315–16, 482, 791
Iamblichus 481
icthyomancy **316**
id 227, **316**, 688

ideomotor effect **316**
pendulum 531–3
ignis fatuus **317**
ikiryoh **317**
Iktomi 167
illuminati **317–18**, 618
imagery **318–19**
healing power 66
hypnagogic state 307
see also guided imagery
imagination **319–20**
and self-image 129
incantation 321
incorruptibility **321–2**
incubation **322**, 501
incubus **322**, 430, 657
India
animistic soul beliefs 604
aura 47
Ayurvedic medicine **52–3**
churel **112**
crossroad
superstitions 132
fakir **205–6**
fire walking 211
hydrotherapy 307
iron as protection 335
Masters 714
palmistry 520
phallomancy 535
tree spirits 726
utukku **744**
vampire ghosts 747
Vedic astrology **749**
Indian head massage **322**
Indian Religious Freedom
Act (1978) 74
Indigo Children **322–4**
indirect voice mediumship
324
Indonesia 266
Indridason, Indridi **324–5**
Ingham, Eunice 602
initiation **325–6**
fraternal lodges 404–5
Inner Child 326
Inner Light, Society of 224,
326
inner voice/inner guide
114–15, **326–7**
innocence ghost 327
inspiration **328**
Institut Metapsychique
International 237, 273,
329, 506, 524, 632
instrumental
transcommunication
(ITC) **329–30**
intelligence **330**
intelligent design 755
International General
Assembly of
Spiritualists 220, 221

International Network for
Instrumental
Transcommunicaton
(INIT) 330
International Spiritualist
Federation (ISF) **331**
Internet **331**
intuition **332**, 333–4
deductive psychic **151–2**
goal-focused **255**
and lucid dreaming 410
medical **437–8**
and right brain 85
random psychic **598**
see also applied psi; gut
feeling; hunch
invisibility **332–4**
invisible assailants **334**,
339
invisible friends/invisibles
334–5, 339
Invisibles 763
invocation 196, **335**, 422
Ireland
Celtic Spirituality 515
Celtic survival 173
scapulomancy 630
Irish folklore
banshee 62
crossroad protection 132
fairies 132, 204
fairy horses 357
fetch 209
jack-o'-lantern legend 340
puca 580
spitting protection 676
tash **707**
iron 22, **335**
Irving, Washington **336**,
636
Irwin, H Carmichael 595
Islam/ Muslim
Afrit 10
angels 22
apports 30
chanting 108
divine guidance 106
exorcism 197
ghoul **249**
hell 289
prophecy 564
Satan 627
self-levitation 394
Isle of Man 342

Jabuticabal poltergeist **339**
Jack in Irons **339**
jack-o'-lantern **340**
see also ignis fatuus
Jackson, Andrew 66, 67
Jacolliot, Louis 394
Jacques de Molay 367
jade 137, **340**
James I 721

James, Henry 341, 460
Turn of the Screw, The **729**
James, William 20, **341–2**,
443, 466, 548–9, 615,
659, 711
Japan
aroma systems 32
bakechochin **58**
buruburu **90**
Feng Shui 207
gashadokuro **237**
ghost of Sakura **625–7**
ikiryoh **317**
Ki 739–40
kitsune **365–6**
konakijijii **369**
kubikajiri **370**
martial arts 432
mononoke **456**
Mujina 203
ninja-assassin-mystics 334
nurikabe **491**
rainbow soul bridge 86
Reiki rediscovered 603
shiatsu **645–6**
Shinto **646**
shojo **646**
tsukumogami **729**
Zen 797
Japhet, Celina 355
Jay, Dolores 785
'Jeanne Dixon effect' 161
Jenkins, Linnie 726
Jimmy Squarefoot **342**
Joad, C E M **342**
Joan of Arc 114, 318,
342–3, 564
John, King 762
John, St 161, 239, 564
Johnson, Samuel **343**
John the Baptist, St 625
Johnston, Ernest 595
Joller family 679
Jonas, Hans 254
Jones, Eryl Mai 501
Jones family 60–2
Jordan, Gustave 663
Joseph (Hebrew patriarch)
384–5
Joseph of Arimathea 252,
258
JOTT (just one of those
things) **344**
Jourdain, Eleanor 749–50
journals, parapsychology
344–5
Judaism
angels 22
archangels 30
divine guidance 106
dybbuk **175**
exorcism 197
hell 289
Last Judgment 381

Madison, James 764
magi **420**
magic **421–3**
   candle 97
   chanting in 108
   elementals in 185
   Eye of Horus 199
   gypsy **274**
   Huna **304–5**
   illuminati 318
   imagery in 319
   incantation in 321
   jade in 340
   and Kabbalah 354
   mandrake in 426
   mantra in 428
   Maori **428**
   and metaphysics 449
   mirrors in 453
   moon 457
   periwinkle and 534
   quartz in 588
   ritual **612–13**
   self-transformation 423
   sigil 650
   symbols in 694
   see also black magic;
      Enochian magic;
      mentalism; sorcery;
      white magic
magical personality **423–4**
Magical Will 421, **424**, 479,
   554, 557
magician **424**
   invisibility 332–4
   see also Houdini, Harry;
      Levi, Eliphas; Marriott,
      William
magick **424**
Maginot, Adele 118
magnetic energy fields 398,
   424–5
magnetic healing/therapy
   425
Maharishi Mahesh Yogi
   723–4
mah-jong **425**
Maier, Margaret 770–1
Maimonedes experiments
   234, **426**, 524
Malaysia 207, 766
Malcolm II 251
Maltwood, Katherine 253
Mana 304, 740
mandalas **426**, 427
mandrake **426–7**
manes **428**
Manson, Charles 305
mantra **428**, 429
   Om **500**
   transcendental meditation
      723, 724
many-worlds theory 586
Mao Tse-tung 723

Maori tradition
   magic **428**
   rainbow soul bridge 86
map dowsing **428–9**, 531
mara 277, **429–30**
marchers of the night **430**
Marcus Varro 464
Marfa Lights 180, **430**
Marian apparitions **430–1**
Marie Antoinette 749, 750
Marquis, Pat 199
Marriott, William **431**
Marryat, Frederick 87–8
Marsh, George 539
Marshall, Mary 279
Marshall, Miss 561
martial arts 319, **431–2**
Mary Celeste **432–3**, 540
Mary I (Bloody Mary) 434,
   539, 630
Mary, Queen of Scots 261,
   292, 589
Mary, Virgin 149, 408, 599
   Marian apparitions **430–1**
Mary Worth/Bloody Mary
   433–4
Maslow, Abraham 467, 529
Mason, John 779
massage 194, **434–5**
   zero balancing **798**
materialization **435–6**
   Béraud 237, 435–6
   Cook/Katie King 125–6,
      270, 362–3, 435
   fraud 126, 273–4, 436
   Guppy 269–70, 435
   Guzyk 237, 273
   Kluski plasters 237
Mathers, Moina 224
Mathers, Samuel Liddell
   MacGregor 256, 257
Matlock, James 526
Mayans 282
maze **436**
mazomancy **437**
meconomancy **437**
medical intuition/intuitive
   78, **437–8**
medicine man **438**, 473 *see
   also* shaman; witch
   doctor
meditation **439**, 440
   biofeedback and 72
   brain waves in 18, 85
   grounding **267**
   and healing 597
   Holotropic Breath Work
      85–6
   imagery use 319
   kundalini 372
   labyrinth use 377
   magical aids 422
   mandala use 426
   occult 445

under pyramid 581
   samadhi **627**
   Zen 797
medium/mediumship
   439–43
   cryptomnesia **134–6**
   drop in communicator
      171–2
   fraud *see* fraud
   and ghost investigation
      247
   shaman compared 643
   and super ESP 687
   see also control; direct
      voice mediumship;
      indirect voice
      mediumship; mental
      mediumship; physical
      mediumship;
      spiritualism
mediums *see* names of
   mediums
Meek, George 184
megaliths 239, 395, **444**
   see also Avebury;
      Stonehenge
Melampus 456
Melanesia 740
Melmoth, William 43
menehune **444–5**
mental illness
   and mediumship 442–3
   and past life experience
      528
   and spirit
      attachment/possession
      89–90, 154, 197,
      212–13, 555–6, 662,
      667, 670, 769
mental mediumship/
   phenomena 442, **445**,
   639
   fraud 442
   psychical research into
      443
   survival after death
      evidence 442, 689
mental plane/body/energy
   445
mentalism **445–6**
meridians 6, 7, 136, 645
Merlin 50, 224, 318, 424,
   446
mermaids **446–7**
Mesmer, Franz Anton 47,
   308, 318, 335, 425,
   447–8, 523
mesmerism 438, 441,
   447–8, 673, 711
Mesopotamia 135, 501
Messing, Wolf Grigorievich
   448
metagnomy **448–9**
metal **449**, 577

metal bending **449**
   mini Geller **452**
   Geller 238, 449, 549, 709
   PK party **549**
metaphysics 449
meteors **449–50**
metopomancy **450**
Mexico
   Day of the Dead 148
   evil eye 196
   La Llorona **377–8**
Meyer, Jean 329
Miami poltergeist **450–1**
Michell, John 398
Michon, Abbé 259
micro PK **451**
micromancy **451**
Milbanke, Anne 91
Miller, Hugh 205
Milward, Jessie 7, 8
mind reading *see* telepathy
mini Geller **452**
Min-Min lights 590
miracle **452**
mirror **452–4**
   Halloween ritual 434, 454
   mirror gazing 453
   as otherworld portal 576
   stagnant chi remedy 207
   in Zen 797
Mishlove, Jeffrey 29
Mishra, Swarnlata 785
Moberly, Annie 749–50
moleosophy **454–6**
Mompesson, John 174
mononoke **456**
Monroe, James 752
Monroe, Marilyn **456**
Monroe, Robert A 510–11
Montgomery, Ruth 221
Moody, Raymond 474, 475,
   576
moon **456–8**
   moon-infused waters 457
   and silver 651
   see also lunomancy;
      selenomancy
Moore, Edward 64–5
Mordred 51
Morgan, Kate 302
Moriarty, Theodore 224
Morton case **458–9**
Moses, William Stainton
   134, 243, **459–60**, 464
Moses ben Shemtob de
   Leon 353
Mount, The **460–1**
Mountbatten, Earl 244
movement of objects *see*
   psychokinesis
moving coffins **461**
Mozart 226, 328
Mu 388, **461–2**
Muhammad 564

Goddess worship 256, 515
Grail in 258
Herne the Hunter 293
handfasting **280–1**
moon symbol 457
persecution 619
unicorn in 738
see also Druidry; neo-
paganism; shamanism;
Wicca; witchcraft
Pagan Federation 480
Pagan Way 480
Pagenstecher, Gustav 577
Palatine light **515–16**
Palladino, Eusapia 362, 407,
442, 464, **516–18**, 564,
633, 649, 690
Palm Sunday case **518–20**
Palmer, Annie 616
palmistry **520–2**
Paracelsus 16, 319, 438
paranormal **522**
classes of phenomena 542
dreams and 169–71
orbs 503
statistical procedure 443
Parapsychological
Association **522–3**, 525
Parapsychological Society
616
parapsychology **523–5**
Edinburgh chair 369
first US degree 417, 716
and Jung/Freud split 346
metal bending
controversy 449
and Ouija board 507
see also applied psi; psi
testing; psychical
research
Parapsychology Foundation
236, 506, **525**
parapsychology journals
344–5
Parapsychology Laboratory
see Duke University
Parapsychology
Laboratory
Paris, Jacques 381–2
Parker Brothers 507
parsley **526**
Parsons, Mr 118–19
Pashkov, Andrey 710
past-life dreams 170–1
past-life nightmares 484
past-life recall 308, **526–8**
cryptomnesia 134
and karma 357
past-life therapy **528–9**
depossession 154
spirit releasement 669
past lives *see* reincarnation
pathworking 354, **529**, 530,
726

Patrick, St 252
Paul, Philip 244
Paul, St 253
Pauls, Ted 60–2, 220
Pavlia, Robert 579
Pawley, Percival 203
Pawleys Island, Faceless
Gray Man **203**
peak experience 467,
529–30
Pearlin Jean **530–1**
Peat, F David 695
Pedder, John 585
pendulum **531–3**
dactylomancy **143**
radiesthesia 596
see also dowsing; map
dowsing
Penfield, Wilder 467
Penn, Sibell 280
pentacle/pentagram **533**,
649
People of the Rainbow 330
percipient **533**, 611
Perelandra 211
perfume ghosts **533–4**
periwinkle **534**
Perks, Thomas **534**
Persia
magi **420**
mirror origins 453
mystery cults 466
necromancy 477
podomancy 552
'persona theory' 283
Peru 395
Peter, St 340
Peterhouse College **534–5**
phallomancy **535**
phantasm **535**
phantasmagoria **536**
phantom **536**
phantom armies **536**
Edgehill 182
phantom bells **536–7**
phantom birds **537**
phantom cats
Lang family death omen
379
US Capitol building 743–4
White House 764
phantom coach **537**
Littlecote death omen 403
Ocean-born Mary 497
phantom dogs
Black Shuck **75**
Bosun 75
Lemp Mansion 387
Littlecote House 403
Old Shuck **499–500**
Snarly Yow **658**
phantom funeral train 400
phantom heads **538**
phantom hitchhiker **538**

phantom horse *see* nuggle
phantom monks and nuns
539
Borley Rectory 82, 83
Brocken Mountain 663
Newstead Abbey 91
Woburn Abbey 778
phantom rabbits 109
phantom ships **539–40**
Flying Dutchman **218–19**
Mary Celeste **432–3**
Palatine light **515–16**
phantom travellers **540–1**
phantom vehicles **541–2**
Bachelor's Grove
Cemetery 57
phasmophobia **542**
phenomena **542**
Philadelphia Experiment
542–3
Philip **543**
Philip IV of France 367
Philippines 572
philosopher's stone 15, 16,
258, **543–4**
Philoxenus 179
phone calls from the dead
544–5
Photius 401
phyllomancy **545**
physical mediumship 442,
545
fraud 341, 442, 443,
517–18, 633
psychical research 443, 633
survival after death
evidence 690
see also apport; asport;
levitation;
materialization;
rapping; table tilting
physiognomancy **545–6**
Pickens County Courthouse
546
picture test **546**
Pike, Bishop James 221,
546–7, 731
pineal gland 715
Pio, Padre 70–1, 682
Piper, Leonora 341, 391,
406, 442, 443, 462, 464,
547–9, 552, 648, 649,
689
Pius VI, Pope 95
PK *see* psychokinesis
PK party **549**
planchette **549–50** *see also*
Ouija board
Planck, Max 586
planetary consciousness
550
plants **550–1**
Plato 44, 191, 509, **551**,
582, 692

Pliny the Elder 456, 509
Pliny the Younger ix, 43
Plotinus 481
Plutarch 162, 505
Podmore, Frank 132, 270,
299, 518, 524, **551–2**
podomancy **552**
Poe, Edgar Allan 147, 169,
182, 222, 753
poetry *see* rhapsodomancy
polarity therapy 435, **552–3**
police psychics *see* psychic
criminology
Polidori, John William 748
poltergeist 284, **553–4**
agent **12**
Amherst Haunting **20–1**
Baltimore **60–2**, 220
Bell Witch **66–8**
Borley Rectory **82–3**
Calvados Castle **95–6**
Cock Lane **118–19**
Cottage City **127–8**
Dagg **143–4**
drummer of Tedworth
174
Enfield **188–9**
Epworth Rectory **191–2**
focal person **219**
Glamis Castle 251
Grottendieck stone-
thrower **266**
Helpidius attack 289
Hofdi **295**
Jabuticabal **339**
and levitation **394–5**
Miami **450–1**
nurikabe **491**
Oakland **495**
and odour 499
Philip (artificial
poltergeist) 543
and (recurrent
spontaneous)
psychokinesis 21, 191,
220, 451, 495, 553–4,
601, 611, 615, 616, 639,
690
Rosenheim **617**
Sauchie **628–9**
Seaford **637–9**
Staus **679**
stone-throwing devil
684–5
studies 219, 381, 557, 574
Thornton Heath **717–18**
Polynesia 86, 211, 740
Pomeroy family 69
Pomona 278
Poole, Elizabeth 279
Porphyry 481, 639
'portal' theory 285
positive thinking **554**, 555,
558, 565

Jung's belief 348
liberation from 108, 271, 484
MacLaine's belief 482
neo-pagan belief 480
and past-life recall 526, 604
and past-life therapy 528
possession as 760–1
Rosicrucians and 618
and soul mate 661
and spiritism 355, 356, 670
spiritualist beliefs 221, 673
relativity theory 452, 478, 685, 694, 719
relaxation **605–6**
aromatherapy 31
and biofeedback 72
brain waves in 85, 605
and fire walking 212
and healing 66, 287
and hypnotherapy 310
and psi 605
REM sleep 167
remote influencing 576
remote viewing 113, **606–7**
Repo, Don 214
Rescue Remedy 218
residual haunting **608**
Resurrection Mary **608**
retrocognition 63, 101, 117, **609**
see also Dieppe Raid case; Versailles ghosts
revenant **609–10**
Reyes de Zierold, Maria 577
rhapsodomancy **610**
Rhine, J B 24, 84, 118, 192–3, 194, 283, 344, 417, 451, 462, 506, 523, 524, 554, 557, 559, 575, **610–11**, 615, 639, 674, 689, 711, 780, 798
Rhine, Louis B 193
Rhine, Louisa Ella Weckesser 610, **611**
Rhine Research Centre **611–12**
Riccardo, Martin V 248
Rice, H H 615
Richard II 134, 293
Richet, Charles 118, 165, 181, 436, 711, 785
Richmond, Cora 441
Richter, Sigmund 618
Rider Waite tarot deck 704, 759
right-hand path 385–6, **612**, 776
Ring, Kenneth 474
Ritalin 324
ritual magic **612–13**

Rivail, Hippolyte Leon Denizard *see* Kardec, Allan
Roberts, Jane 107, **613–15**
Robertson, E G 536
Robertson, Morgan 561
Robinson, Jim 762
Roff, Mary 760–1
Roll, William 450–1, 554, 557, 574, 601, **615–16**, 639
Romains, Jules 199
Roman mythology 203–4
Romany people
dukkerin 224
gypsy magic **274**
Tarot 704
Rome, ancient viii
alectromancy 17
augury 46, 800
aura 47
bean rituals 65
breath ritual 85
candles 97
channelling 106
cledonomancy 118
crow superstitions 600
dream interpretation 501
dream precognition 169
Druidism banned 173
garlic amulets 22
graphology 259
haruspicy 283
Lares **380**
laurel trees 144
lemure **387**
magic and sorcery 775
manes **428**
meteor beliefs 449–50
mirror origins 453
nature spirits 473
necromancy 477
orinthomancy 505
ovomancy 512
parsley 526
poltergeists 553
Pomona festival 278
pyromancy 581
rhapsodomancy 610
sibyls 502
sortilege 660
table divination 507, 699
tree omens 726
uromancy 742
Röntgen, Wilhelm 786
Rose Hall **616**
Rosenheim poltergeist **617**
Rosenkreutz, Christian 617
Rosicrucians 13, 257, 293, 317, 367, 421, 496, **617–18**
Roswell incident 198, 735
Roy family 496–7
Rubik, Beverly 781

Rudolph, Kurt 254
Rugg, Peter 540–1
runes **618–19**
running water **619**
Runolfur Runolfsson case 172, **619–20**
rusalka **620**
Russell, Peter 550
Russia/ Soviet Union 448
dowsing experiments 165
eyeless vision research 199–200
psychokinetic research 575
psychotronics 113, 525
remote viewing projects 607
telepathic hypnosis research 710
Russian folklore
domovik **162**
rainbow 'Gate to Heaven' 86
rusalka **620**

sabbats 481
Sabom, Dr 476
sacred geometry **623**
sage leaves **623**
Sai Baba 30, 36, **623–4**
St Elmo's fire **624–5**
St Germain, Comte de 367
St James Sag Church, Chicago 539
Saint John's Wort **625**
Sakura, ghost of **625–7**
Salem Witch Trial 286, 775
Salisbury, Lady 721
salt 17, 110, 279
Salter, W H 390
Saltmarsh, Henry 443
samadhi 422, **627**, 797
Sambhava, Padma 719
Samhain 278
Sampford ghost **627**
Samuel 775
Sanford, James 631
Sartre, Jean-Paul 289
Satan/Satanism 385, **627–8**
Satori 798
Saturday **628**
Sauchie poltergeist **628–9**
Saul, King 477, 775
Sawston Hall **629–30**
Saxons 335, 619, 683
Scandinavian folklore 429
scapulomancy **630**
scarab 340, **631**, 694
scatomancy **631**
sceptic **631**
schizophrenia 442–3
Schmeidler, Gertrude 605, 645

Schmidt, Helmut 575–6
Schneider brothers 329, 562, 563, **631–3**, 690
Rudi 506, 575, 632–3
Willi 631–2
Schreiber, Klaus 329–30
Schrenck-Notzing, Albert von 181, 562–3, 631–2, **633**
Schroeder, Lyn 364
Schucman, Helen 5
Scientology **633–4**
Sclater, Philip 388
Scole experimental group **634–6**
Scot, Reginald 234
Scotland
Celtic Spirituality 515
Celtic survival 173
Glencoe massacre 630
Scott, Walter 336, **636**
Scottish folklore
banshee 62
brownie **88**
departure of the fairies 205
ghost seers 248
kelpie **357**
raven superstitions 600
'spirits of the living' 32
spunkie 678
screaming skulls **636–7**
scrying 99, 135, 498, **637**, 638, 649
Dee and Kelley 152
Nostradamus 487
Seaford poltergeist 554, 557, 615, **637–9**
sealed envelope test 691
séance **639–40**
home sitting **296**
popularity 225, 673
proxy sitting **564**
psychic cold 569
psychometry 577
shamanic 643
see also medium/ mediumship
second sight **640**
Sedona, Arizona **640**
seer **640**
selenomancy **641**
Semkina, Natasha 786
sensitive **641**
sephiroth 354, 726
Serios, Ted 669, 718–19
serotonin 715
Seth 107, 613–15
Seton, Alexander 229
Severus of Ravenna, St 70
Seymour, Jane 79, 280, 402
shadow 346, 566, **641**
Shakespeare, William 152, 168, 251, 381, **641–2**

Voodoo queens *see* Glapion, Marie Laveau; Laveau, Marie
vortex **756**

Waite, Arthur 704, **759**
Waldorf schools 681
Wales
  Celtic Spirituality 515
  scapulomancy 630
  Taliesin **700**
  see also Welsh folklore
Wallace, Alfred Russel 269
Walpole, Robert 87
Walpurga, St 759
Walpurgis Night **759**
Walton, George 684
Wambach, Helen 527–8
wand **759–60**
  and air element 13, 759
  crystal 136, 759
  fire association 211
Ward, Woodrow 579
Warren, Ed and Lorraine 657, 658
Washington, George 23, 226, 420, 743, 752, 779
Washington family 537
Watchers 79–80
water 161, **760**
  hydromancy **306–7**
  hydrotherapy **307**
  running 619
  well 761
Watkins, Alfred 395–6
Watseka wonder **760–1**
Watts, Nelle 769
wave-particle duality 586
Weatherby, Lionel A 534
Weir, Thomas **761**
Weishaupt, Adam 317
Weisner, W P 565
well **761**
Wells, H G 385
Wells family 418
Welsh folklore
  bwca 88
  corpse candles 127
  crossroad spirits 132
  crow superstitions 600
  fairies 204
  periwinkle 534
Wen, King 335
Wenzel, Martin 329
werewolf *see* lycanthropy
werewolf ghost **762**
Wesley, Samuel 598
Wesley family 191–2
West Africa
  ancestor worship 22
  juju 265
  zombie 799
West Indian tradition
  duppy **175**

Westcott, William Wynn 256–7
Whaley House **762**
Wharton, Duke of 412
Wharton, Edith 460–1
whirlwind **762**
White, Betty 763
White, Edward **763–4**
White, Stanford 769
White Eagle Lodge 126, **762–3**
White House 401, **764–5**
White Ladies 58, 69, 166, 280, 482, **765**
white magic 321, 421, **765**
  pentagram 533
  right-hand path 612
  Wicca 766
Whiteman, J H M 510
Wicca **765–8**
  apple pentagram 533
  elementals 13, 185, 760
  Gardner and 134, 480, 765, 766, 776
  Herne the Hunter 293
  sabbats 481
  Samhain 278
  sky clad 481, **653**, 767
  wand 759
  witchcraft compared 765–6
Wiccan Rede 768, 776
Wickland, Anna 154
Wickland, Carl 154, 197, 666, **768–9**
Wild Edric **770**
Wild Hunt **770**
Wilhelm, Richard 315
Wilkinson, Jack and Clara 751
Willard Library **770–1**
Willett, Winifred 179, 519
William the Conqueror 8, 63, 770, 774
Willington Mill **771**
will-o'-the-wisp **772**
Wilmot apparition **772–3**
Wilson, Colin 294
Wilson, Ian 682
Wilson, Mary *see* Ocean-born Mary
Wilson, Nancy 418
Wilson, Robert Anton 318
Wilson, Woodrow 764
Winchester, Sarah 773–4
Winchester mystery house **773–4**
Windigo **774**
Windsor, Anna 48
Windsor Castle **774**
Winter, William 465
witch doctor 502, 720, **774**
  see also medicine man; shaman

witch lights 317
Witch of Endor 477, **775**
witchcraft, witch **775–7**
  accusations 339, 684
  Book of Shadows **81**
  broom **87**
  cone of power 108
  devil's mark 156
  familiar **206**
  as fertility religion 391
  Fortune and 223
  Goddess worship 256
  horse susceptibility 301
  imagery in 319
  and iron 335
  Leek **385**
  low magic 421
  magical weekdays 777
  mara role 430
  and the moon 457–8
  persecution 250, 286, 367, 433, 766, 775
  sigil 649
  wand 759
  water test 307
  Wicca compared 765–6
Witchcraft Act (1735) 674
  repealed (1951) 480, 731, 776
witching hour **778**
wizard 292, 446, **778**
Woburn Abbey 240, **778**
Wolsey, Thomas 280
wood **778**
Woodlawn Plantation **779**
Woods, Sidney George 216
Woodstock, Percy 143
World Trade Center attack (9/11) 488
  precognitive dreams 169, 502
World War I 109, 221, 224, 235, 389, 779
  Angels of Mons 64
  book tests 82
  gremlins 263–4
  phantom army stories 536
  predictions of 80, 680
  Spiritualist revival 674
World War II 68, 109, 293, 331, 540, 588, 589
  battlefield hauntings 64
  Dieppe Raid case **157**
  gremlins 263
  Padre Pio's bilocation 70
  Pendulum Institute 531
  phantom army stories 536
  predictions 302, 448
  swastika 619
Worrall, Ambrose **779–80**
Worrall, Olga 779, **780–1**
Worth, Patience 507–9, **781–2**
wraith **782**

Wren, Christopher 226, 280
Wright, Elsie 128
Wright, Machaelle Small 211

Xavier, Chico 339
xenoglossy 253, **785–6**
xenography 785
xenomancy **786**
X-ray vision 117, **786**
xylomancy **787**
XYZ 780

Yang *see* Yin/Yang
Yeats, William Butler 62, 257, 714, **791**
Yin/Yang 315, 386, 702, 722, 739, **791–2**
  and Feng Shui 206–7
Yoga **792–4**
  akasha 13
  breathing exercise 86
  and clairaudience 114
  conscious dreaming 409–10
  and imagery 319
  koshas **369–70**
  left and right-hand tantra 385
  meditation 439, 500
  nirvana 484
  prana 738
  schools of 793
  siddhis 647, 738
  see also kundalini; Taoist alchemy
Yogananda, Paramahansa 321–2

zazen 439, 797
Zen **797–8**
Zener, Karl 194
Zener cards 798
zero balancing 435, **798**
zodiac 301, **798–9**
  ages of 11
  air signs 13
  earth signs 179–80
  and facial spots/moles 450
  fire signs 211
  at Glastonbury 253
  and palm lines 520
  and personality traits 40–1
  water signs 760
Zohar 353
Zollner, Johann 653–4
zombie 365, 477, 756, **799**
'zone' 677
zoomancy **799–800**
Zugan, Eleanor 563
Zulus 11
Zuni people 355

The Element Encyclopedia of the Psychic World